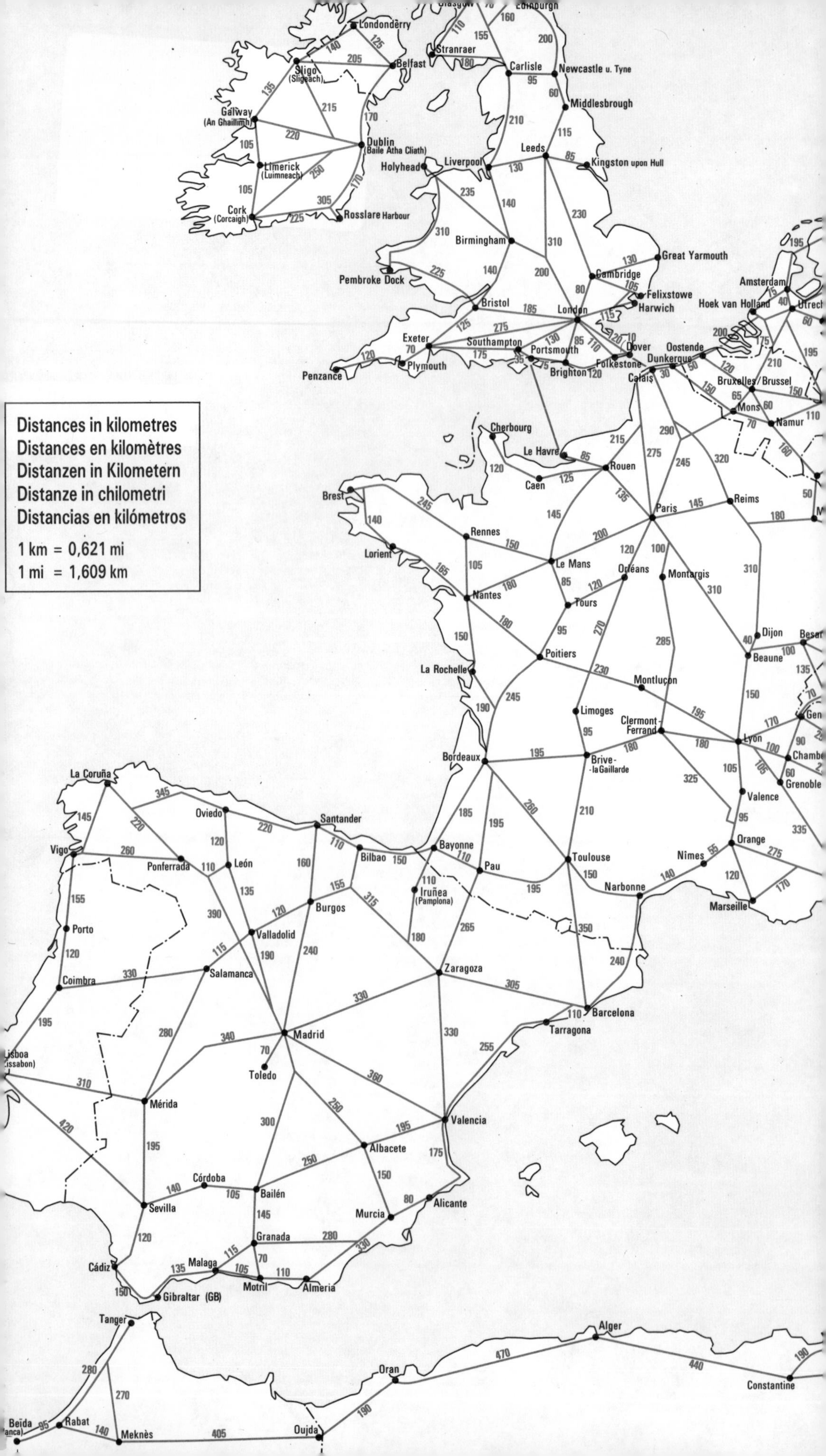

Distances in kilometres
Distances en kilomètres
Distanzen in Kilometern
Distanze in chilometri
Distancias en kilómetros

1 km = 0,621 mi
1 mi = 1,609 km

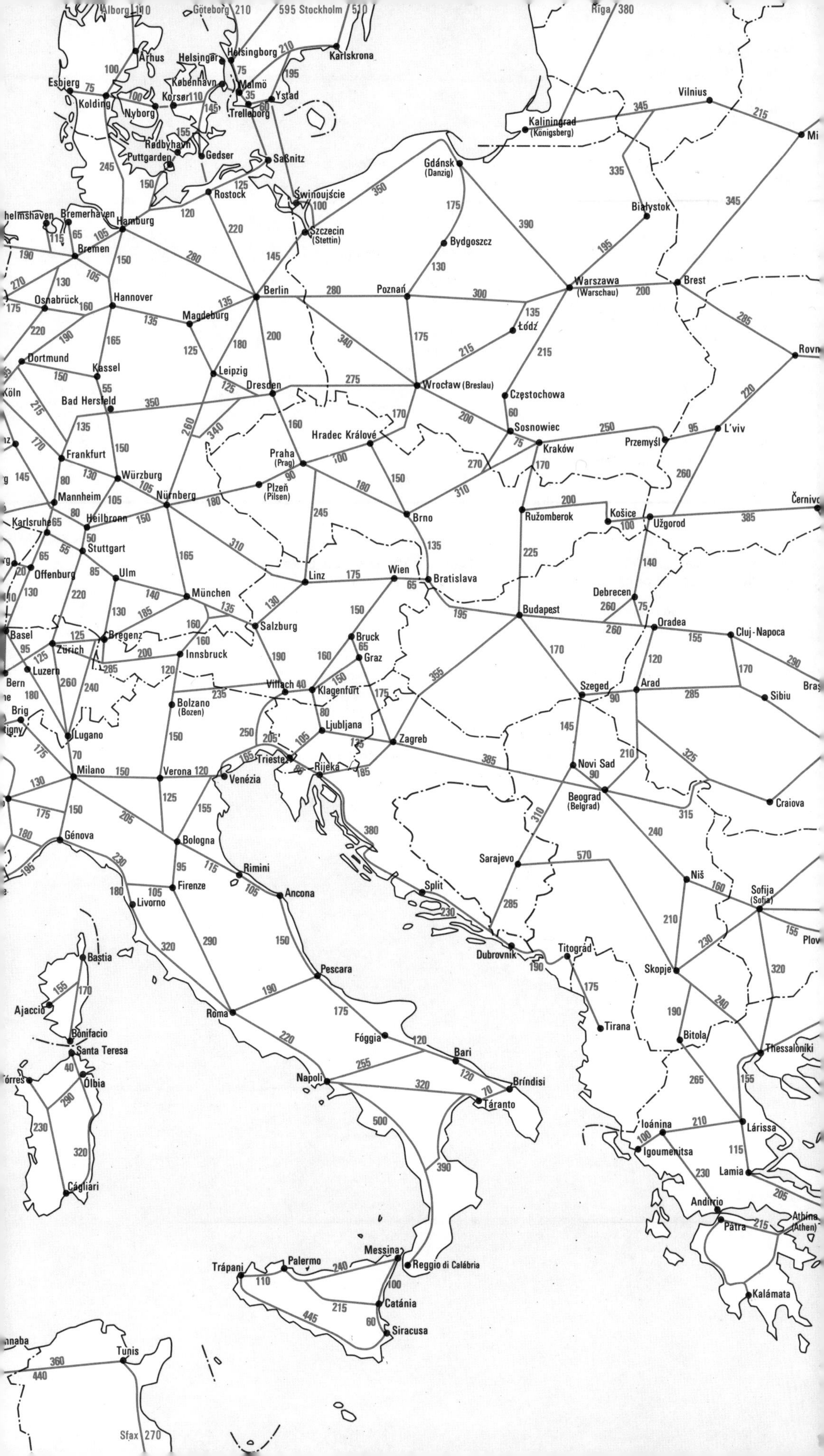

Ålborg 110
Göteborg 210
595 Stockholm 510
Riga 380
Århus
Helsingør
Helsingborg
Karlskrona
København
Malmö
Ystad
Esbjerg
Kolding
Korsør
Nyborg
Trelleborg
Vilnius
Kaliningrad
(Königsberg)
Mi
Rødbyhavn
Puttgarden
Gedser
Saßnitz
Gdánsk
(Danzig)
Rostock
Świnoujście
Białystok
helmshaven
Bremerhaven
Hamburg
Szczecin
(Stettin)
Bydgoszcz
Bremen
Berlin
Poznań
Warszawa
(Warschau)
Brest
Osnabrück
Hannover
Magdeburg
Łódź
Dortmund
Kassel
Leipzig
Dresden
Wrocław (Breslau)
Częstochowa
Rovn
Köln
Bad Hersfeld
Sosnowiec
L'viv
Hradec Králové
Kraków
Przemyśl
Frankfurt
Praha
(Prag)
Würzburg
Plzeň
(Pilsen)
Mannheim
Nürnberg
Brno
Ružomberok
Košice
Užgorod
Černiv
Karlsruhe
Heilbronn
Stuttgart
Offenburg
Ulm
Linz
Wien
Bratislava
München
Debrecen
Budapest
Basel
Bregenz
Salzburg
Oradea
Cluj-Napoca
Zürich
Innsbruck
Bruck
Graz
Luzern
Bern
Villach
Klagenfurt
Szeged
Arad
Sibiu
Bras
Brig
Bolzano
(Bozen)
Ljubljana
Zagreb
Lugano
Trieste
Rijeka
Novi Sad
Milano
Verona
Venézia
Beograd
(Belgrad)
Craiova
Génova
Bologna
Sarajevo
Rimini
Niš
Firenze
Ancona
Split
Sofija
(Sofia)
Livorno
Plov
Bastia
Pescara
Dubrovnik
Titograd
Skopje
Ajaccio
Roma
Tirana
Bonifacio
Fóggia
Bitola
Santa Teresa
Bari
Thessaloniki
Olbia
Napoli
Bríndisi
Tórres
Táranto
Ioánina
Lárissa
Igoumenitsa
Lamia
Cágliari
Andírrio
Pátra
Athína
(Athen)
Messina
Reggio di Calábria
Trápani
Palermo
Catánia
Siracusa
Kalámata
nnaba
Tunis
Sfax 270

Note on Spellings
Note sur l'Orthographe
Bemerkungen zur Schreibweise
Note riguardando l'Ortografia
Notas sobre Ortografía

Spellings of place names in this atlas are in accordance with the national language. Alphabetical listings will therefore need to be used with care. Eg: Wien (Vienna); København (Copenhagen).

Dans cet atlas, les lieux sont épelés selon la langue du pays. Donc la liste alphabétique devra être lue attentivement. Ex: Wien (Vienne); København (Copenhague).

In diesem Atlas hält sich die Schreibweise der Ortsnamen an die jewellige Landensprache. Das alphabetische Verzeichnis bedarf deshalb besonderer Aufmerksamkeit bei dessen Gebrauch.

In questo atlante, i nomi delle località sono elencati conformemente all'ortografia della lingua del paese. Perciò, l'elenco deve essere usato con massima cura. Esempio: Wien (Vienna); København (Cobenhaghen).

La ortografía de los nombres propios de los lugares citados en este atlas está de acuerdo con el lengua nacional. Por lo tanto, la lista alfabética deberá ser usada con cuidado. Ejemplo: Wien (Viena); København (Copenhage).

Details regarding driving in Europe may be found in the RAC European Motoring Guide, or contact the tourist office of the country concerned.

Published by RAC Publishing Limited, RAC House, South Croydon CR2 6XW

© RAC Enterprises Limited 1992
Cartography © Recta Foldex
Printed in Germany

A catalogue record for this book is available from the British Library

ISBN 0 86211 216 8

RAC

MOTORING ATLAS ROUTIER

EUROPE

Contents

Road Maps

Legend 1:1,000,000   1
Legend 1:2,750,000   2
Key to maps   3
Road maps   4

City Approach Maps

Legend   2
Key to maps   3
City approach maps   4

Index of Place Names

Table des Matières

Cartes Routières

Légende 1:1,000,000   1
Légende 1:2,750,000   2
Tableau d'assemblage   3
Cartes routières   4

Plans de Villes Synoptiques

Légende   2
Index des cartes   3
Plans de villes synoptiques   4

Localités Citées

Indice

Carte Stradali

Leggenda 1:1,000,000   1
Leggenda 1:2,750,000   2
Indice delle carte   3
Carte stradali   4

Piante di Città Sinottiche

Leggenda   2
Indice delle piante   3
Piante di città sinottiche   4

Località Citate

Inhaltsverzeichnis

Strassenkarten

Zeichenerklärung 1:1,000,000   1
Zeichenerklärung 1:2,750,000   2
Bauanleitung   3
Strassenkarten   4

Stadtübersichtspläne

Zeichenerklärung   2
Index   3
Stadtübersichtspläne   4

Ortsverzeichnis

Contenido

Mapas de Carreteras

Signos convencionales 1:1,000,000   1
Signos convencionales 1:2,750,000   2
Clave de mapas   3
Mapas de carreteras   4

Planos de Ciudades Sinópticos

Signos convencionales   2
Indice de planos   3
Planos de ciudades sinópticos   4

Localidades Citadas

Legend Légende Zeichenerklärung Leggenda Signos Convencionales

1 : 1,000,000

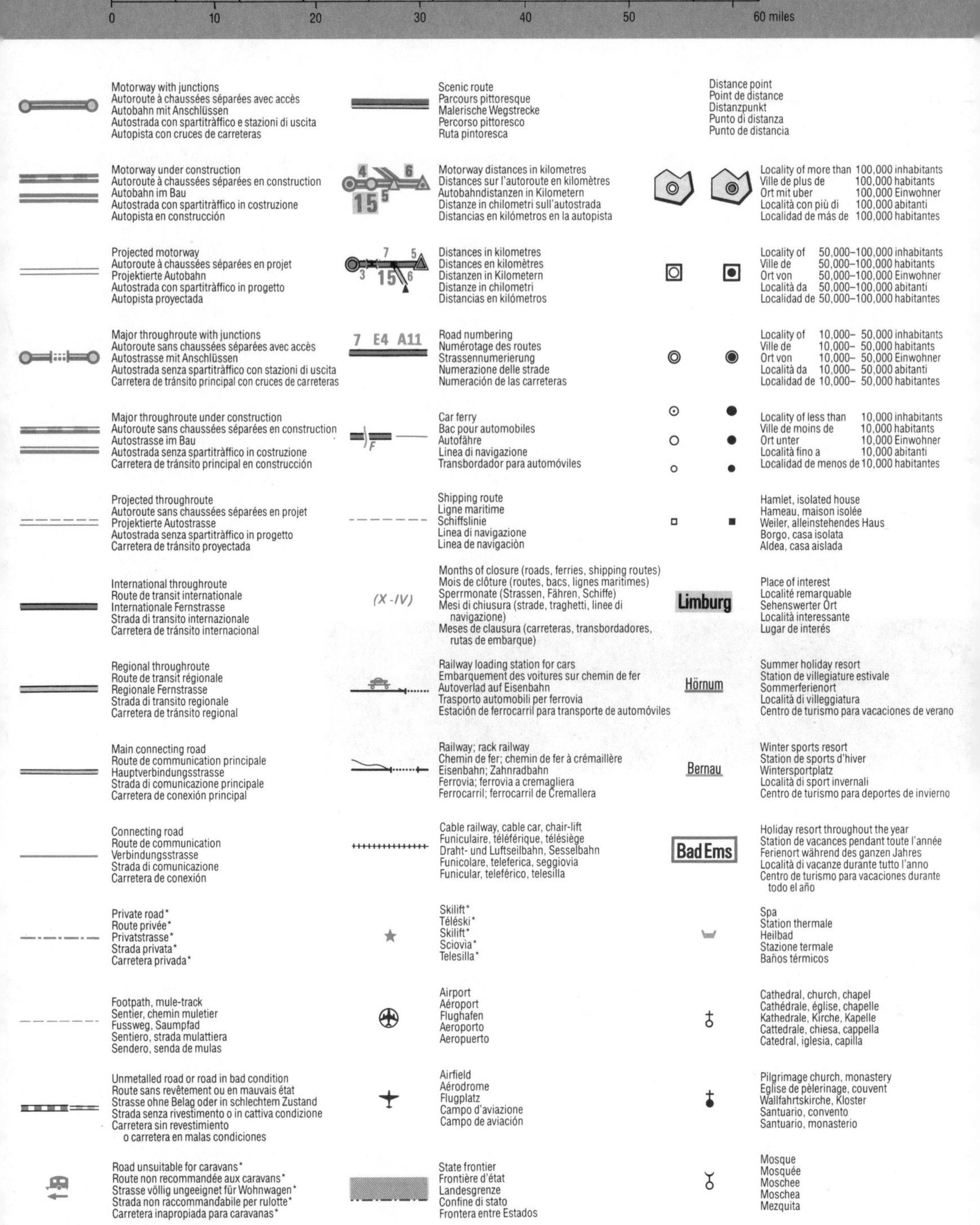

Motorway with junctions
Autoroute à chaussées séparées avec accès
Autobahn mit Anschlüssen
Autostrada con spartitràffico e stazioni di uscita
Autopista con cruces de carreteras

Motorway under construction
Autoroute à chaussées séparées en construction
Autobahn im Bau
Autostrada con spartitràffico in costruzione
Autopista en construcción

Projected motorway
Autoroute à chaussées séparées en projet
Projektierte Autobahn
Autostrada con spartitràffico in progetto
Autopista proyectada

Major throughroute with junctions
Autoroute sans chaussées séparées avec accès
Autostrasse mit Anschlüssen
Autostrada senza spartitràffico con stazioni di uscita
Carretera de tránsito principal con cruces de carreteras

Major throughroute under construction
Autoroute sans chaussées séparées en construction
Autostrasse im Bau
Autostrada senza spartitràffico in costruzione
Carretera de tránsito principal en construcción

Projected throughroute
Autoroute sans chaussées séparées en projet
Projektierte Autostrasse
Autostrada senza spartitràffico in progetto
Carretera de tránsito proyectada

International throughroute
Route de transit internationale
Internationale Fernstrasse
Strada di transito internazionale
Carretera de tránsito internacional

Regional throughroute
Route de transit régionale
Regionale Fernstrasse
Strada di transito regionale
Carretera de tránsito regional

Main connecting road
Route de communication principale
Hauptverbindungsstrasse
Strada di comunicazione principale
Carretera de conexión principal

Connecting road
Route de communication
Verbindungsstrasse
Strada di comunicazione
Carretera de conexión

Private road*
Route privée*
Privatstrasse*
Strada privata*
Carretera privada*

Footpath, mule-track
Sentier, chemin muletier
Fussweg, Saumpfad
Sentiero, strada mulattiera
Sendero, senda de mulas

Unmetalled road or road in bad condition
Route sans revêtement ou en mauvais état
Strasse ohne Belag oder in schlechtem Zustand
Strada senza rivestimento o in cattiva condizione
Carretera sin revestimiento
   o carretera en malas condiciones

Road unsuitable for caravans*
Route non recommandée aux caravans*
Strasse völlig ungeeignet für Wohnwagen*
Strada non raccommandabile per rulotte*
Carretera inapropiada para caravanas*

24%
Road with steep gradient (more than 15%)
Route à forte montée (plus de 15%)
Strasse mit starker Steigung (über 15%)
Strada con forte salita (oltre il 15%)
Carretera con pendiente empinada (más de 15%)

Road with traffic restrictions
Route à trafic limité
Strasse mit Verkehrsbeschränkung
Strada con limitazione di tràffico
Carretera con limitaciones para el tráfico

Toll road
Route à péage
Strasse mit Gebuhr
Strada a pedaggio
Carretera con peaje

Scenic route
Parcours pittoresque
Malerische Wegstrecke
Percorso pittoresco
Ruta pintoresca

Motorway distances in kilometres
Distances sur l'autoroute en kilomètres
Autobahndistanzen in Kilometern
Distanze in chilometri sull'autostrada
Distancias en kilómetros en la autopista

Distances in kilometres
Distances en kilomètres
Distanzen in Kilometern
Distanze in chilometri
Distancias en kilómetros

7 E4 A11
Road numbering
Numérotage des routes
Strassennumerierung
Numerazione delle strade
Numeración de las carreteras

Car ferry
Bac pour automobiles
Autofähre
Linea di navigazione
Transbordador para automóviles

Shipping route
Ligne maritime
Schiffslinie
Linea di navigazione
Linea de navigación

Months of closure (roads, ferries, shipping routes)
Mois de clôture (routes, bacs, lignes maritimes)
(X -IV) Sperrmonate (Strassen, Fähren, Schiffe)
Mesi di chiusura (strade, traghetti, linee di navigazione)
Meses de clausura (carreteras, transbordadores, rutas de embarque)

Railway loading station for cars
Embarquement des voitures sur chemin de fer
Autoverlad auf Eisenbahn
Trasporto automobili per ferrovia
Estación de ferrocarril para transporte de automóviles

Railway; rack railway
Chemin de fer; chemin de fer à crémaillère
Eisenbahn; Zahnradbahn
Ferrovia; ferrovia a cremagliera
Ferrocarril; ferrocarril de Cremallera

Cable railway, cable car, chair-lift
Funiculaire, téléférique, télésiège
Draht- und Luftseilbahn, Sesselbahn
Funicolare, teleferica, seggiovia
Funicular, teleférico, telesilla

Skilift*
Téléski*
Skilift*
Sciovia*
Telesilla*

Airport
Aéroport
Flughafen
Aeroporto
Aeropuerto

Airfield
Aérodrome
Flugplatz
Campo d'aviazione
Campo de aviación

State frontier
Frontière d'état
Landesgrenze
Confine di stato
Frontera entre Estados

Regional boundary
Frontière régionale
Regionalgrenze
Confine regionale
Límite regional

Nature reserve
Réserve naturelle
Naturschutzgebiet
Parco nazionale
Reserva natural

Restricted area
Zone interdite
Sperrzone
Zona proibita
Area restringida

Distance point
Point de distance
Distanzpunkt
Punto di distanza
Punto de distancia

Locality of more than 100,000 inhabitants
Ville de plus de   100,000 habitants
Ort mit uber   100,000 Einwohner
Località con più di 100,000 abitanti
Localidad de más de 100,000 habitantes

Locality of   50,000–100,000 inhabitants
Ville de   50,000–100,000 habitants
Ort von   50,000–100,000 Einwohner
Località da   50,000–100,000 abitanti
Localidad de   50,000–100,000 habitantes

Locality of   10,000– 50,000 inhabitants
Ville de   10,000– 50,000 habitants
Ort von   10,000– 50,000 Einwohner
Località da   10,000– 50,000 abitanti
Localidad de 10,000– 50,000 habitantes

Locality of less than   10,000 inhabitants
Ville de moins de   10,000 habitants
Ort unter   10,000 Einwohner
Località fino a   10,000 abitanti
Localidad de menos de 10,000 habitantes

Hamlet, isolated house
Hameau, maison isolée
Weiler, alleinstehendes Haus
Borgo, casa isolata
Aldea, casa aislada

Limburg
Place of interest
Localité remarquable
Sehenswerter Ort
Località interessante
Lugar de interés

Hörnum
Summer holiday resort
Station de villegiature estivale
Sommerferienort
Località di villeggiatura
Centro de turismo para vacaciones de verano

Bernau
Winter sports resort
Station de sports d'hiver
Wintersportplatz
Località di sport invernali
Centro de turismo para deportes de invierno

Bad Ems
Holiday resort throughout the year
Station de vacances pendant toute l'année
Ferienort während des ganzen Jahres
Località di vacanze durante tutto l'anno
Centro de turismo para vacaciones durante todo el año

Spa
Station thermale
Heilbad
Stazione termale
Baños térmicos

Cathedral, church, chapel
Cathédrale, église, chapelle
Kathedrale, Kirche, Kapelle
Cattedrale, chiesa, cappella
Catedral, iglesia, capilla

Pilgrimage church, monastery
Eglise de pèlerinage, couvent
Wallfahrtskirche, Kloster
Santuario, convento
Santuario, monasterio

Mosque
Mosquée
Moschee
Moschea
Mezquita

Parochial village*
Village paroissial*
Kirchort*
Villaggio parrocchiale*
Aldea parroquial*

Castle   Palace, mansion
Château   Palais, villa
Schloss, Burg   Palast, Villa
Castello   Palazzo, villa
Castillo   Palacio, mansión

Prehistoric monument
Monument de culture préhistorique
Vorgeschichtliches Kulturdenkmal
Monumento di civiltà preistorica
Monumento prehistórico

1 : 1,000,000

∴ Ancient monument / Monument antique / Antikes Baudenkmal / Antichità / Monumento antiguo	**★** Viewpoint / Point de vue / Aussichtspunkt / Punto panoramico / Punto panorámico	**⚓ ⋔** Isolated hotel; Motel / Hôtel isolé; Môtel / Alleinstehendes Hotel; Motel / Albergo isolato; Motel / Hotel aislado, motel
L Mediaeval ruin / Ruine du moyen age / Mittelalter Ruine / Rovine medioevo / Ruina medieval	**⚲** Lighthouse / Phare / Leuchtturm / Faro / Faro	**⊤** Beach / Plage / Strandbad / Spiaggia / Playa
⚑ ⊥ Monument; Tower / Monument; Tour / Denkmal; Turm / Monumento; Torre / Monumento; Torre	**⚒** Windmill / Moulin à vent / Windmühle / Mulino a vento / Molino de viento	**▲** Campsite open throughout the year / Camping permanent / Ganzjähriger Campingplatz / Campeggio aperto tutto l'anno / Camping abierto durante todo el año
M Museum / Musée / Museum / Museo / Museo	**Δ** Lapp settlement / Camp de lappons / Lappenlager / Accampamento lappone / Pueblo lapón	**▲** Seasonal campsite / Camping saisonnier / Saisoncampingplatz / Campaggio stagionale / Camping estacional
∩ Cave, grotto / Caverne, grotte / Höhle, Grotte / Caverna, grotta / Caverna, gruta	**⌂** Holiday camp* / Village de vacances* / Feriendorf* / Villaggio di vacanze* / Campamento de vacaciones*	**⊖** Frontier crossing, open day and night / Passage frontalier, ouvert jour et nuit / Grenzübergang, durchgehend offen / Passaggio di frontiera, aperto giorno e notte / Cruce de fronteras abierto día y noche
★ Other places of interest / Autres curiosités / Andere Sehenswurdigkeiten / Altre curiosita / Otros lugares de interés		

* These symbols refer only to Great Britain and the Scandinavian countries
Les signes correspondants n'apparaissent que pour la Grande Bretagne et les pays nordiques
Entsprechende Signaturen kommen nur in Grossbritannien und in den nordischen Ländern vor
I corrispondenti simboli appaiono solamente in Gran Bretagna e nei paesi nordici
Estos símbolos se refieren solo a Gran Bretaña y los países escandinavos

1 : 2,750,000

| 0 | 25 | 50 | 75 | 100 | 125 | 150 km |
| 0 | | 25 | | 50 | 75 | 100 miles |

Motorway with junctions / Autoroute à chaussées séparées avec accès / Autobahn mit Anschlussen / Autostrada con spartitràffico e stazioni di uscita / Autopista con cruces de carreteras	Motorway distances in kilometres / Distances sur l'autoroute en kilomètres / Autobahndistanzen in Kilometern / Distanze in chilometri sull'autostrada / Distancias en kilómetros en la autopista	10 22 12
Motorway under construction / Autoroute à chaussées séparées en construction / Autobahn im Bau / Autostrada con spartitràffico in costruzione / Autopista en construcción	Distances in kilometres / Distances en kilomètres / Distanzen in Kilometern / Distanze in chilometri / Distancias en kilómetros	10 22 12
Major throughroute with junctions / Autoroute sans chaussées séparées avec accès / Autostrasse mit Anschlussen / Autostrada senza spartitràffico con stazioni di uscita / Carretera de tránsito principal con cruce de carreteras	Numbering of European main roads / Numérotage des routes d'Europe / Europastrassen-Numerierung / Numerazione della rete stradale europea / Numeración de las principales carreteras Europeas	E107
International throughroute / Route de transit internationale / Internationale Fernstrasse / Strada di transito internazionale / Carretera de tránsito internacional	Distance point / Point de distance / Distanzpunkt / Punto di distanza / Punto de distancia	
Regional throughroute / Route de transit régionale / Regionale Fernstrasse / Strada di transito regionale / Carretera de tránsito regional	Locality of more than 500,000 inhabitants / Ville de plus de 500,000 habitants / Ort mit uber 500,000 Einwohner / Località con più di 500,000 abitanti / Localidad de más de 500,000 habitantes	⬠ ⬠
Main connecting road / Route de communication principale / Hauptverbindungsstrasse / Strada di comunicazione principale / Carretera de conexión principal	Locality of 100,000–500,000 inhabitants / Ville de 100,000–500,000 habitants / Ort von 100,000–500,000 Einwohner / Località da 100,000–500,000 abitanti / Localidad de 100,000–500,000 habitantes	▢ ▣
Connecting road / Route de communication / Verbindungsstrasse / Strada di comunicazione / Carretera de conexión	Locality of 50,000–100,000 inhabitants / Ville de 50,000–100,000 habitants / Ort von 50,000–100,000 Einwohner / Località da 50,000–100,000 abitanti / Localidad de 50,000–100,000 habitantes	◎ ◉
Railway / Chemin de fer / Eisenbahn / Ferrovia / Ferrocarril	Locality of 10,000–50,000 inhabitants / Ville de 10,000–50,000 habitants / Ort von 10,000–50,000 Einwohner / Località da 10,000–50,000 abitanti / Localidad de 10,000–50,000 habitantes	⊙ ●
Car ferry / Bac pour automobiles / Autofähre / Linea di navigazione / Transbordador de automóviles	Locality of less than 10,000 inhabitants / Ville de moins de 10,000 habitants / Ort unter 10,000 Einwohner / Località fino a 10,000 abitanti / Localidad de menos de 10,000 habitantes	○ ●

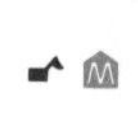

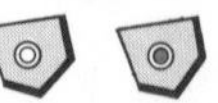

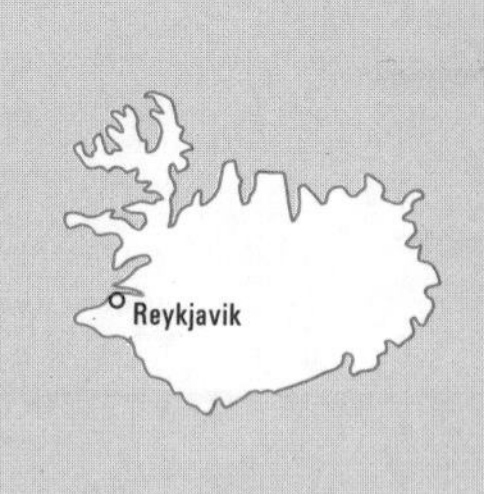

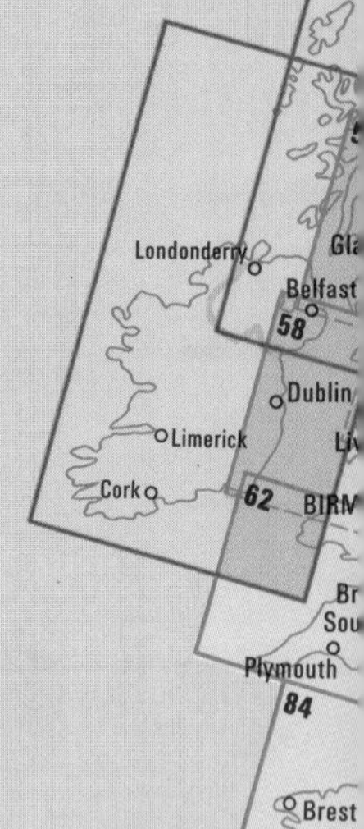

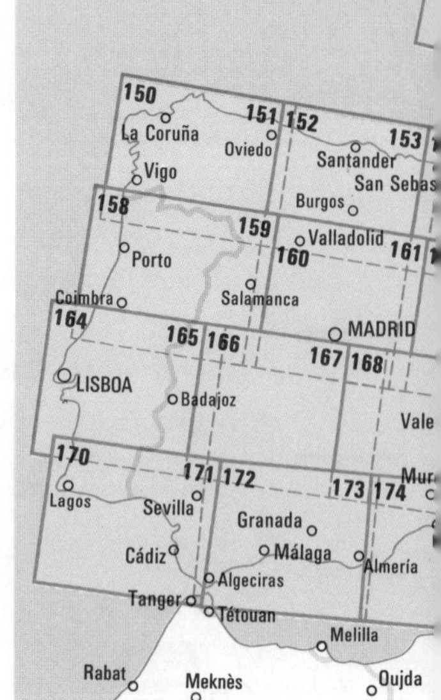

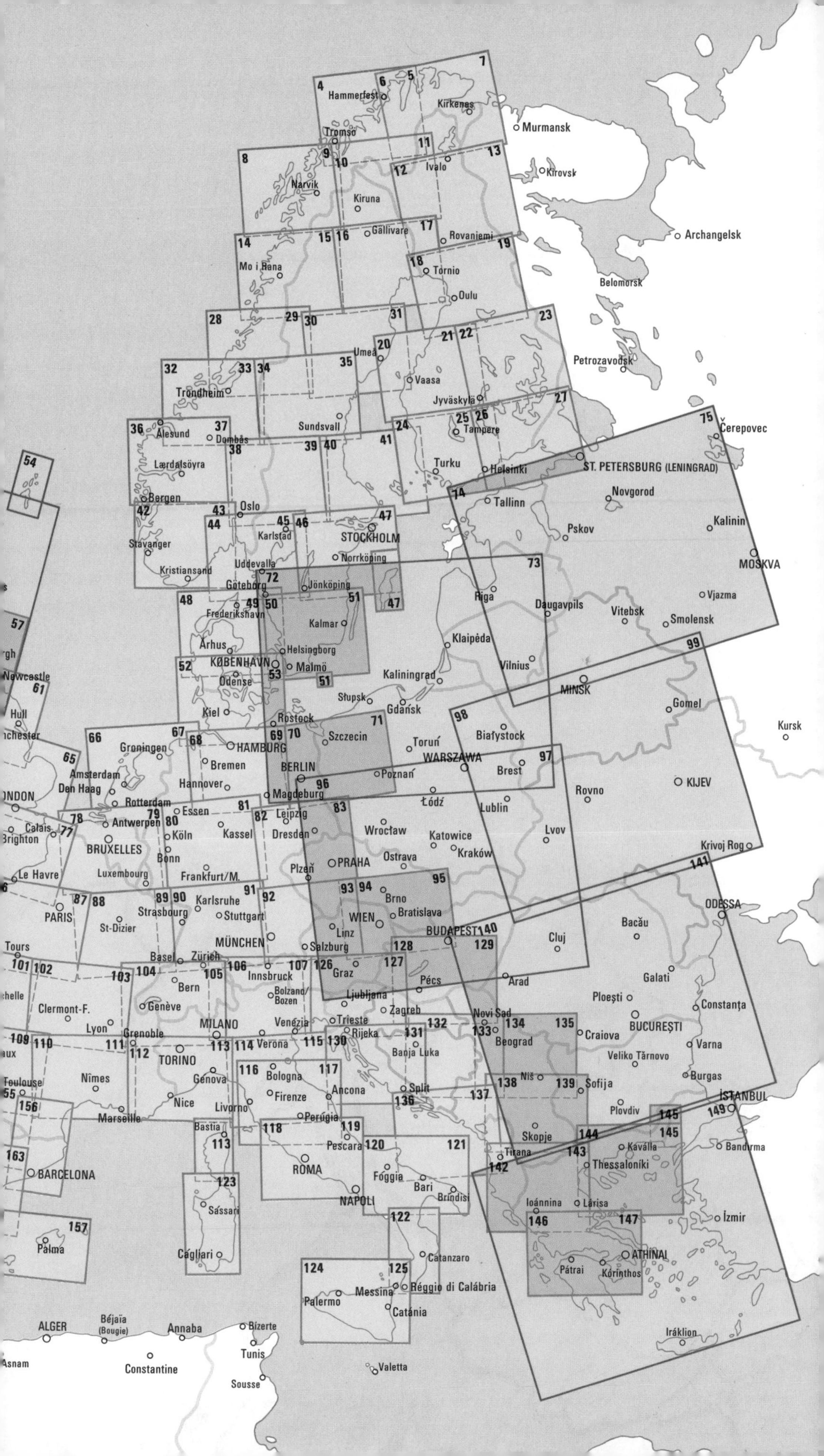

4
Hammerfest
6
5
7
Kirkenes
Murmansk
Tromsø
9
10
11
13
8
Narvik
12
Ivalo
Kirovsk
Kiruna
14
15
16
Gällivare
17
Rovaniemi
19
Archangelsk
Mo i Rana
18
Tornio
Oulu
Belomorsk
28
29
30
31
23
20
Umeå
21
22
Petrozavodsk
32
33
34
35
Trondheim
Vaasa
Jyväskylä
25
26
27
36
Ålesund
37
Dombås
Sundsvall
24
Tampere
75
Čerepovec
38
39
40
41
54
Lærdalsöyra
Turku
Helsinki
ST. PETERSBURG (LENINGRAD)
Bergen
74
Tallinn
Novgorod
42
43
Oslo
44
45
Karlstad
46
47
STOCKHOLM
Pskov
Kalinin
Stavanger
Norrköping
MOSKVA
Kristiansand
Uddevalla
73
Göteborg
72
Jönköping
Riga
48
49
50
Frederikshavn
51
47
Daugavpils
Vjazma
57
Vitebsk
Smolensk
Kalmar
Århus
Klaipėda
Helsingborg
KØBENHAVN
Malmö
Vilnius
Newcastle
52
53
Odense
51
99
61
Kaliningrad
MINSK
Słupsk
Gdańsk
Gomel
Hull
Kiel
Rostock
71
98
66
67
68
69
70
Groningen
HAMBURG
Szczecin
Białystock
Kursk
65
Amsterdam
Bremen
Toruń
WARSZAWA
Brest
97
Den Haag
Hannover
BERLIN
Poznań
96
KIJEV
Rotterdam
Magdeburg
Łódź
Rovno
78
79
80
81
82
Leipzig
83
Essen
Lublin
77
Calais
Antwerpen
Köln
Kassel
Dresden
Wrocław
Katowice
Lvov
Brighton
BRUXELLES
Bonn
Kraków
Krivoj Rog
Le Havre
Luxembourg
Frankfurt/M.
Plzeň
PRAHA
Ostrava
141
87
88
89
90
Karlsruhe
91
92
93
94
95
Brno
ODESSA
PARIS
St-Dizier
Strasbourg
Stuttgart
WIEN
Bratislava
Bacău
Tours
MÜNCHEN
Linz
BUDAPEST
140
Cluj
Basel
Zürich
Salzburg
128
129
101
102
103
104
105
106
107
126
127
Innsbruck
Graz
Arad
Galati
Bern
Bolzano/Bozen
Pécs
Clermont-F.
Genève
Ljubljana
Ploești
Constanța
MILANO
Venezia
Trieste
Zagreb
Novi Sad
Lyon
Grenoble
Rijeka
131
132
134
135
BUCUREȘTI
109
110
111
112
113
114
115
130
133
Beograd
Craiova
TORINO
Verona
Banja Luka
Varna
Veliko Tărnovo
Nîmes
Toulouse
Genova
116
Bologna
117
138
Niš
139
Sofija
Burgas
55
156
Nice
Ancona
Split
ISTANBUL
Firenze
136
137
Plovdiv
149
Marseille
Livorno
Perúgia
145
Bastia
118
119
144
Skopje
145
163
113
Pescara
120
121
Tirana
Bandırma
143
Kavála
142
BARCELONA
ROMA
Foggia
Thessaloníki
123
Bari
Brindisi
NAPOLI
Ioánnina
Lárisa
Sássari
122
146
147
İzmir
157
Palma
Catanzaro
ATHINAI
Cágliari
Pátrai
Kórinthos
124
125
Palermo
Messina
Réggio di Calábria
Catánia
ALGER
Béjaïa (Bougie)
Annaba
Bizerte
Iráklion
Tunis
Constantine
Valetta
Sousse

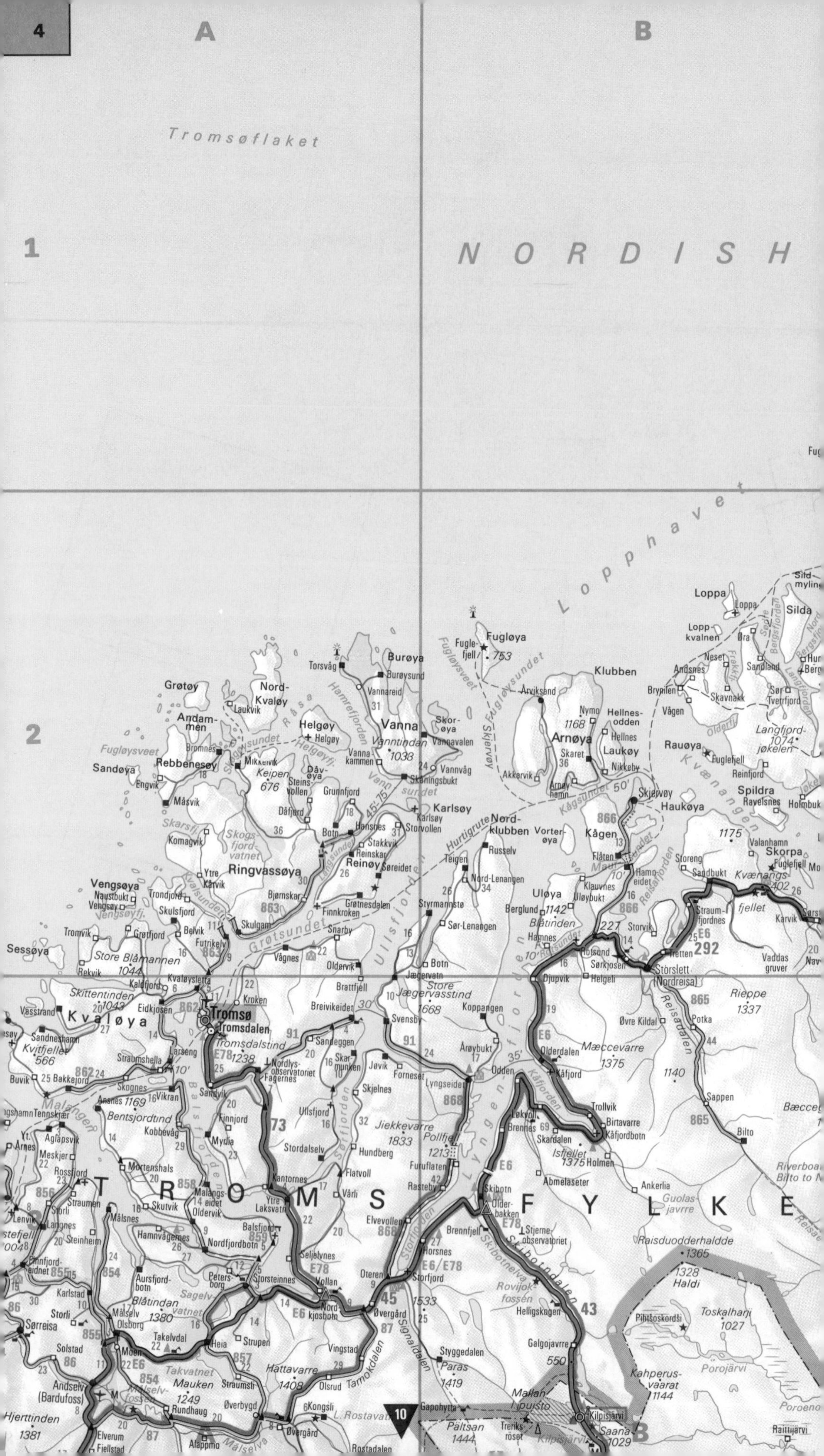
A
B
1
2
Tromsøflaket
NORDISH
Lopphavet
Loppa
Silda
Fugløya
Fugle-fjell
753
Burøya
Torsvåg
Burøysund
Vannareid
Vanna
Vanntindan
1038
Skorøya
Vannavalen
Vannvåg
Skåningsbukt
Karlsøy
Nord-Kvaløy
Grøtøy
Laukvik
Andammen
Helgøy
Rebbenesøy
Bromnes
Mikkelvik
Keipen
676
Dåvøya
Sandøya
Engvik
Måsvik
Fugløysveet
Ringvassøya
Komagvik
Skogsfjordvatnet
Ytre Kårvik
Reinøy
Stakkvik
Reinskar
Søreidet
Bjørnskar
Grøtnesdalen
Finnkroken
Vengsøya
Vengsøy
Trondjord
Skulsfjord
Skulgam
Grøtsundet
Tromvik
Grøtfjord
Belvik
Futrikelv
Sessøya
Store Blåmannen
1044
Rekvik
Kvaløysletta
Kaldfjord
Skittentinden
1043
Vasstrand
Kvaløya
Eidkjosen
Tromsø
Tromsdalen
Tromsdalstind
1238
Kroken
Sandnesharn
Kvitfjellet
566
Straumshella
Larseng
Buvik
Bakkejord
Skognes
Vikran
Malangen
Ansnes
1169
Bentsjordtind
Sandvik
Finnjord
Mydla
Kobbevåg
Tennskjær
Aglapsvik
Meskjer
Rossfjord
Mortenshals
Straumen
Storli
Lenvik
Langnes
Steinheim
Finnfjordeidet
Målsnes
Skutvik
Malangseidet
Oldervik
Hamnvågernes
Nordfjordbotn
Balsfjord
Balsfjorden
Kantornes
Ytre Laksvatn
Seljelvnes
Storsteinnes
Peters-borg
Aursfjordbotn
Karlstad
Storli
Sørreisa
Målselv
Olsborg
Blåtindan
1380
Takelvdal
Heia
Strupen
Moen
Solstad
Andselv (Bardufoss)
Takvatnet
Mauken
1249
Målselvfossen
Straumsli
Rundhaug
Øverbygd
Hjerttinden
1381
Elverum
Fjellstad
Alappmo
Målselva
Vollan
Nordkjosbotn
Øvergård
Vingstad
Hattavarre
1408
Olsrud
Tamokdalen
Kongsli
L. Rostavatn
Øvergård
Rostadalen
Nordlys-observatoriet
Fagernes
Sandeggen
Skarmunken
Jøvik
Skjelnes
Ullsfjord
Stordalselv
Sørfjorden
Hundberg
Flatvoll
Vårli
Elvevollen
Brattfjell
Breivikeidet
Vågnes
Oldervik
Snarby
Ullsfjorden
Svensby
Forneset
Jægervatn
Store Jægervasstind
1668
Botn
Koppangen
Årøybukt
Odden
Lyngseidet
Jiekkevarre
1833
Pollfjell
1213
Furuflaten
Rasteby
Lyngenfjorden
Storfjorden
Brennfjell
Horsnes
Storfjord
Oteren
Signaldalen
Styggedalen
Paras
1419
Gapohytta
Påltsan
1444
Treriksrøset
Kilpisjärvi
Saana
1029
Mallan
Skibotn
Olderbakken
Stjerne-observatoriet
Skibotnelva
Skibotndalen
Rovijokfossen
Helligskogen
Galgojavrre
550
Nord-klubben
Russelv
Teigen
Nord-Lenangen
Styrmannstø
Sør-Lenangen
Hurtigruten
Skjervøy
Fuglesundet
Årviksand
Arnøya
Nymo
1168
Skaret
Akkarvik
Arnøyhamn
Laukøy
Hellnes-odden
Hellnes
Nikkeby
Klubben
Kågsundet
Kågen
Vorterøya
Flåten
Maursundet
Hamneidet
Uløya
Klauvnes
Uløybukt
Berglund
1142
Blåtinden
Hamnes
Rotsund
Sørkjosen
Helgeli
Djupvik
Storvik
Straumfjordnes
Storslett (Nordreisa)
Tretten
Reisafjorden
Reisadalen
Rieppe
1337
Øvre Kildal
Potka
Mæccevarre
1375
Olderdalen
Kåfjord
Kåfjorden
Trollvik
Birtavarre
Kåfjordbotn
Løkvoll
Brennes
Skardalen
Isfjellet
1375
Holmen
Abmelaseter
Ankerlia
Guolasjavrre
Sappen
Bilto
1140
Raisduodderhaldde
1365
1328 Haldi
Pihtsoskordši
Toskalharji
1027
Kahperusvaarat
1144
Porojärvi
Raittijärvi
Loppkvalnen
Øra
Andsnes
Neset
Sandland
Brynilen
Skavnakk
Vågen
Sør-Tverrfjord
Langfjordjøkelen
1074
Rauøya
Fuglefjell
Reinfjord
Kvænangen
Spildra
Ravelsnes
Holmbukt
Haukøya
Valanhamn
Skorpa
Storeng
Sandbukt
Kvænangsfjellet
402
1175
Karvik
Vaddas gruver
Riverboat Bilto to
TROMS FYLKE
E6
E8
E78
E6/E78
91
862
863
866
868
865
292
855
856
857
858
859
854
86
87
45
43
73
10

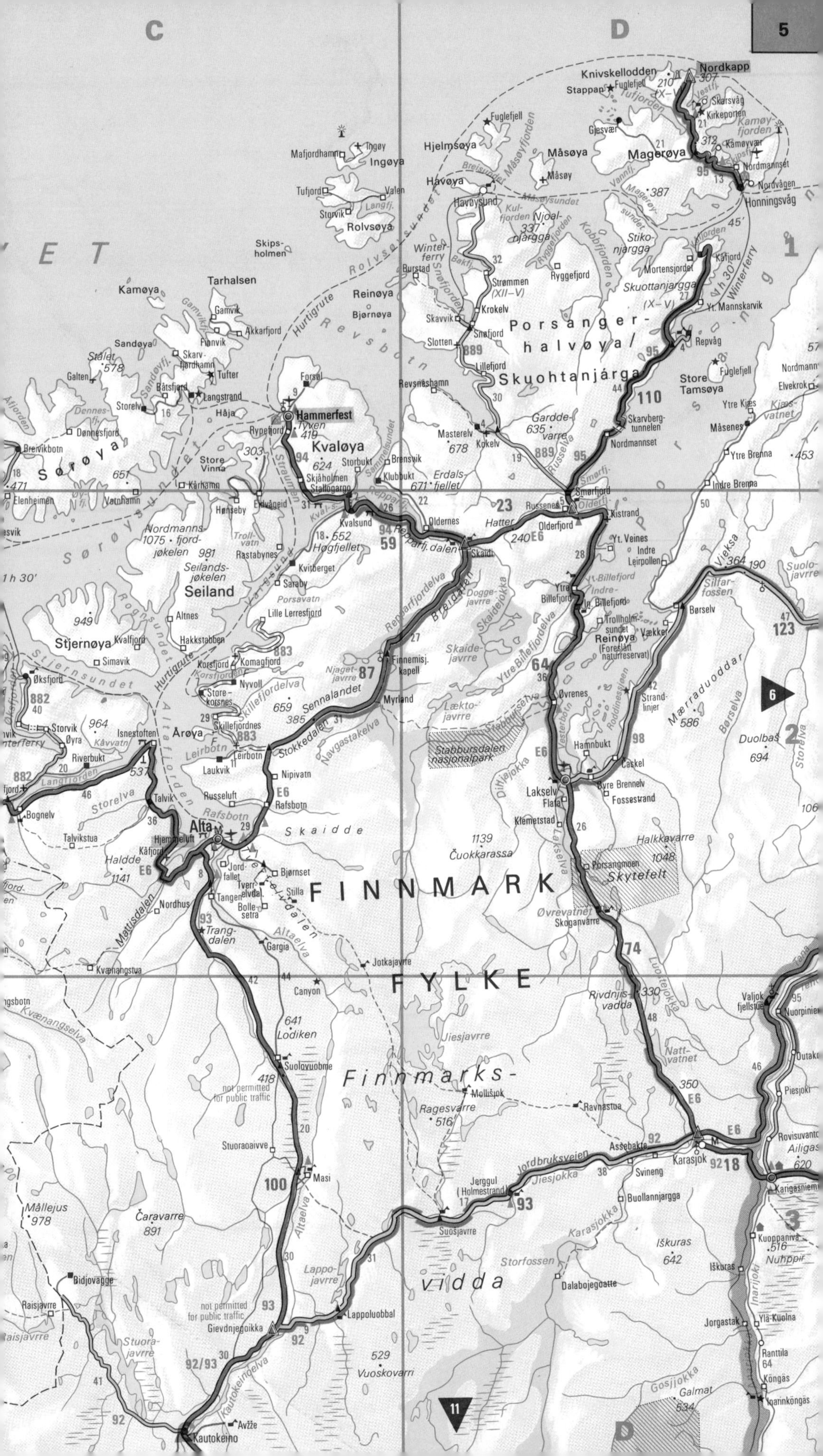
C
D
Nordkapp
Knivskjellodden
Stappan
Fuglefjell
Magerøya
Gjesvær
Skarsvåg
Kirkeporten
Kamøyvær
Nordmannset
Nordvågen
Honningsvåg
Måsøya
Måsøy
Hjelmsøya
Havøya
Havøysund
Ingøya
Mafjordhamn
Tufjord
Valen
Storvik
Rolvsøya
Skipsholmen
Tarhalsen
Kamøya
Gamvik
Akkarfjord
Sandøya
Finnvik
Stålet
578
Galten
Tufter
Båtsfjord
Langstrand
Storelv
Håja
Dønnesfjord
Breivikbotn
Sørøya
Hammerfest
Tyven
419
Kvaløya
Forsøl
Rypefjord
Reinøya
Bjørnøya
Revsbotn
Hurtigrute
Burstad
Skavvik
Snøfjord
Slotten
Lillefjord
Krokelv
Strømmen
Kokelv
Masterelv
678
Revsneshamn
Porsangerhalvøya / Skuohtanjárga
Kåfjord
Mortensjordet
Repvåg
Store Tamsøya
Fuglefjell
Skarvbergtunnelen
Nordmannset
Garddevarre
635
Smørfjord
Russenes
Olderfjord
Kistrand
Ytre Brenna
Indre Brenna
Måsenes
Ytre Kjæs
Seiland
Seilandsjøkelen
Nordmannsfjordjøkelen
1075
981
Hønseby
Kårhamn
Vatnhamn
Elenheimen
Kvalsund
Oldernes
Hatter
Skaidi
Høgfjellet
552
Kvitberget
Rastabynes
Saraby
Porsavatn
Lille Lerresfjord
Stjernøya
Kvalfjord
Simavik
Hakkstabben
Altnes
Øksfjord
Korsfjord
Komagfjord
Nyvoll
Storekorsnes
Skillefjordnes
Årøya
Leirbotn
Laukvik
Russeluft
Rafsbotn
Nipivatn
Finnemisj. kapell
Myrland
Sennalandet
Stokkedalen
Skaidejavrre
Læktojavrre
Stabbursdalen nasjonalpark
Ytre Billefjord
Indre Billefjord
Trollholmsundet
Reinøya
Børselv
Vækker
Silfarfossen
Vieksa
Øvrenes
Strandlinjer
Mærraduoddar
586
Hamnbukt
Caskel
Lakselv
Flata
Klemetstad
Øvre Brennelv
Fossestrand
Duolbaš
694
Halkkavarre
1048
Porsangmoen Skytefelt
Øvrevatnet
Skoganvarre
Alta
Hjemmeluft
Kåfjord
Talvik
Talvikstua
Bognelv
Storvik
Øyra
Isnestoften
Riverbukt
Langfjorden
Haldde
1141
Jordfallet
Tverrelvdal
Bjørnset
Stilla
Bollesetra
Tangen
Nordhus
Trangdalen
Gargia
Kvænangstua
Mattisdalen
Altafjorden
Skaidde
FINNMARK
FYLKE
Čuokkarassa
1139
Jotkajavrre
Canyon
Lodiken
641
Suolovuobme
418
not permitted for public traffic
Finnmarksvidda
Mollišjok
Ragesvarre
516
Ravnastua
Jiesjavrre
Rivdnjisvadda
330
Nattvatnet
Stuoraoaivve
Masi
Mållejus
978
Čaravarre
891
Assebakte
Karasjok
Svineng
Jerggul (Holmestrand)
Jordbruksveien
Suosjavrre
Buollannjargga
Iškuras
642
Storfossen
Dalabojegoatte
Lappojavrre
Lappoluobbal
Bidjovagge
Raisjavrre
Gievdnjegoikka
Stuorajavrre
529
Vuoskovarri
Kautokeino
Avžže
Galmat
534
Valjok fjellstue
Nuorpiniemi
Outakoski
Piesjoki
Rovisuvanto
Ailigas
620
Karigasniemi
Kuoppaniva
516
Nuhppir
Iškuras
Jorgastak
Ylä-Kuolna
Ranttila
Köngäs
Inarinköngäs
Inarijoki
Winterferry
E6
6
11
1
2
3

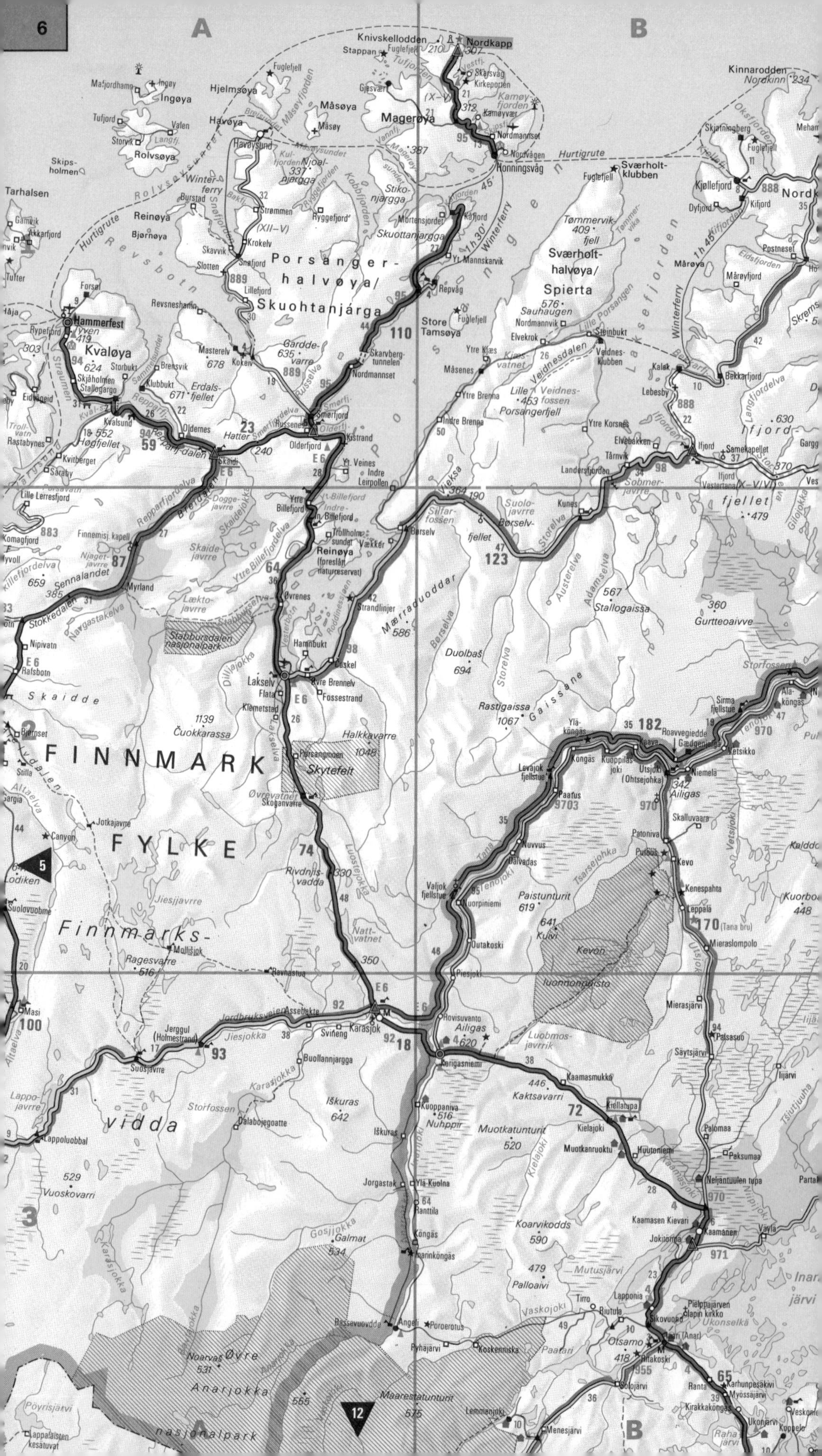
A
B
Knivskellodden
Nordkapp
307
Stappan
Fuglefjell
Gjesvær
Skarsvåg
Kirkeporten
Kamøyvær
Magerøya
Nordmannset
Nordvågen
Honningsvåg
Hurtigrute
Kinnarodden
Nordkinn
234
Ingøy
Ingøya
Hjelmsøya
Måsøya
Måsøy
Havøya
Havøysund
Rolvsøya
Skipsholmen
Tarhalsen
Hurtigrute
Reinøya
Bjørnøya
Revsbotn
Winterferry
Strømmen
Krokelv
Skavvik
Slotten
Snefjord
Ryggefjord
Porsanger-
halvøya/
Skuohtanjárga
Kåfjord
Repvåg
Store
Tamsøya
Sværholt-
klubben
Tømmervik-
409
fjell
Sværholt-
halvøya/
Spierta
576
Sauhaugen
Nordmannvik
Elvekrok
Steinbukt
Veidnes-
klubben
Laksefjorden
Kjøllefjord
Dyfjord
Kifjord
Mårøya
Måroyfjord
Bekkarfjord
Kalak
Lebesby
Ifjord
Forsøl
Hammerfest
Tyven
419
Kvaløya
624
Skjåholmen
Stallogargo
Kvalsund
Høgfjellet
Revsneshamn
Masterelv
Kokelv
Klubbukt
Brensvik
678
Erdals-
fjellet
Gardde-
635
varre
Skarsvåg
Skarvberg-
tunnelen
Nordmannset
Russenes
Smørfjord
Olderfjord
Kistrand
Repparfjord-dalen
Skaidi
Ytre Brenna
Indre Brenna
Måsenes
Lille
453
Porsangerfjell
Veidnes-
fossen
Ytre Korsnes
Elvebakken
Tårnvik
Landersfjorden
Sobmer-
javrre
Ifjord-
fjellet
Lille Lerresfjord
Komagfjord
Finnemisj. kapell
Breidalen
Skaide-
javrre
Sennalandet
Myrland
Stokkedalen
Ytre Billefjordelva
Ytre
Billefjord
Indre
Billefjord
Trollholm-
sundet
Vækker
Reinøya
(fredslått
naturreservat)
Børselv
Børselv-
fjellet
Silfar-
fossen
Øvrenes
Strandlinjer
Mærraduoddar
586
Stabbursdalen
nasjonalpark
Nipivatn
Rafsbotn
Skaidde
Hamnbukt
Lakselv
Flata
Klemetstad
Øvre Brennelv
Fossestrand
Duolbaš
694
Stallogaissa
567
360
Gurtteoaivve
Rastigaissa
1067
Gaissane
1139
Čuokkarassa
FINNMARK
FYLKE
Halkkavarre
1048
Porsangmoen
Skytefelt
Øvrevatnet
Skoganvarre
Ylä-
köngäs
Roavvegiedde
Kongäs
Kuoppilas-
joki
Utsjoki
(Ohtsejohka)
Levajok
fjellstue
Paatus
Niemelä
Ailigas
342
Skalluvaara
Patoniva
Nuvvus
Dalvadas
Kevo
Kenespahta
Leppälä
Tana bru
Sirma
fjellstue
Jotkajavrre
Canyon
Lodiken
Suolovuobme
Rivdnjis-
vadda
330
Valjok
fjellstue
Nuorpiniemi
Paistunturit
619
641
Kuivi
Kevon
luonnonpuisto
Mieraslompolo
Finnmarks-
vidda
Mollišjok
Ragesvarre
516
Ravnastua
Natt-
vatnet
350
Outakoski
Piesjoki
Mierasjärvi
Masi
Jerggul
(Holmestrand)
Jordbruksveien
Assebakte
Karasjok
Sviñeng
Rovisuvanto
Ailigas
620
Karigasniemi
Luobmos-
javrrik
Kaamasmukka
Palsasuo
Säytsjärvi
Suosjavrre
Jiesjokka
Buollannjargga
Karasjokka
Lappo-
javrre
vidda
Storfossen
Dalabojegoatte
Iškuras
642
Kuoppaniva
516
Nuhppir
446
Kaktsavarri
Muotkatunturit
520
Kielajoki
Kiellatupa
Muotkanruoktu
Huutoniemi
Palomaa
Paksumaa
Neljäntuulen tupa
Lappoluobbal
529
Vuoskovarri
Jorgastak
Ylä-Kuolna
Ranttila
Köngäs
Karigasniemi
Gosjokka
Galmat
534
Koarvikodds
590
479
Palloaivi
Mutusjärvi
Kaamasen Kievari
Kaamanen
Jokitorma
Väylä
Tirro
Riutula
Lapponia
Pielppajärven
Erämaan kirkko
Sikovuono
Bassevuovdde
Angeli
Poroerotus
Pyhäjärvi
Koskenniska
Paatari
Otsamo
418
Inari (Anar)
Rahakoski
Noarvas
531
Øvre
Anarjokka
nasjonalpark
565
Maarestatunturit
575
Lemmenjoki
Menesjärvi
Solojärvi
Ranta
Karhunpesäkivi
Myössäjärvi
Kirakkakongäs
Ukonjärvi
Veskoniemi
Koppelo
Pöyrisjärvi
Lappalaisten
kesätuvat
Inarijärvi
Ukonselkä
5
12

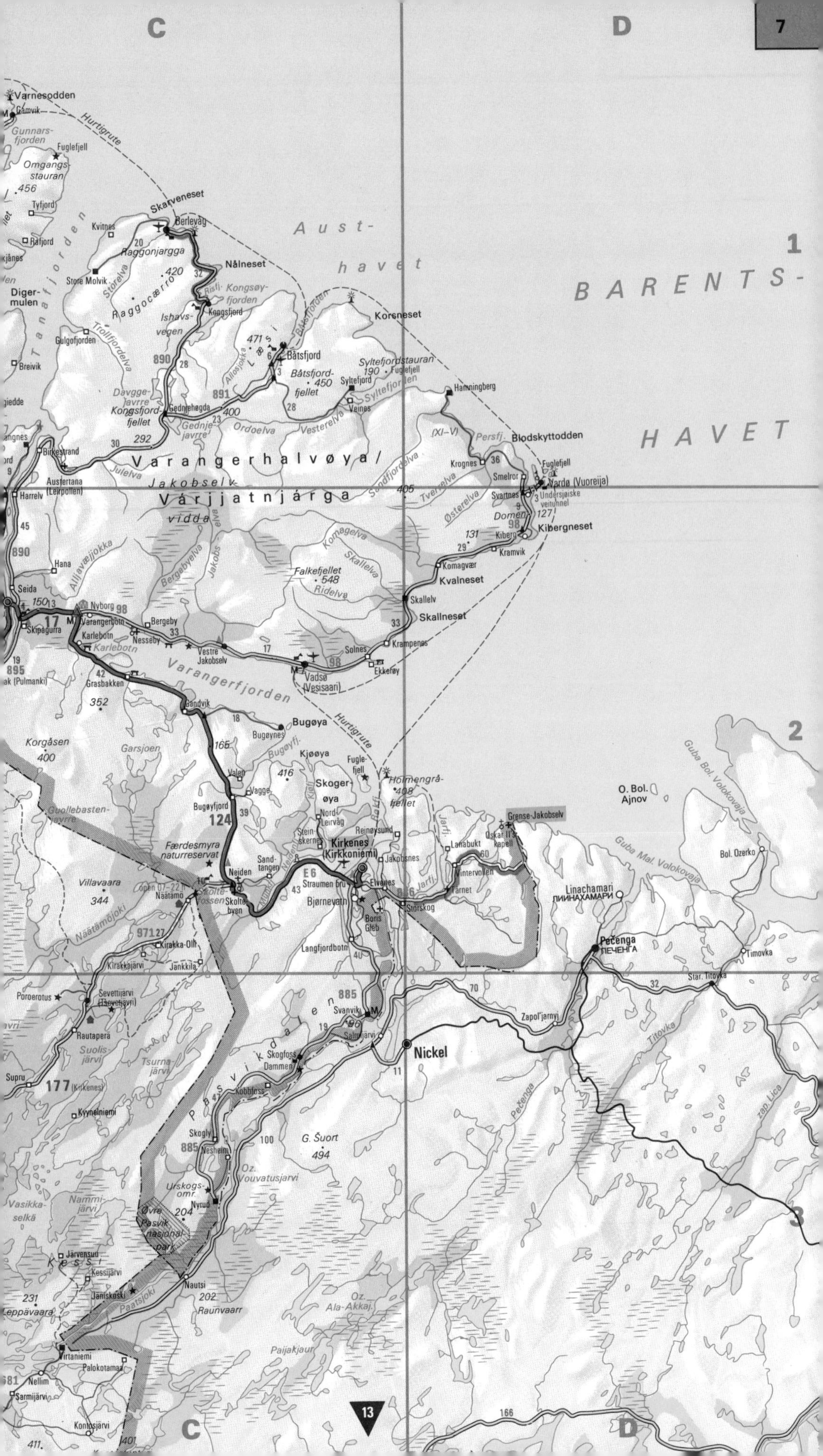
C
D
1
2
3
BARENTS-
HAVET
Austhavet
Varnesodden
Gamvik
Hurtigrute
Skarveneset
Berlevåg
Nålneset
Kongsfjord
Båtsfjord
Korsneset
Syltefjordstauran
Syltefjord
Hamningberg
Blodskyttodden
Vardø (Vuoreija)
Kibergneset
Varangerhalvøya/
Várjjatnjárga
Falkefjellet
548
Kvalneset
Skallelv
Skallneset
Vadsø
(Vesisaari)
Ekkerøy
Krampenes
Nyborg
Varangerbotn
Nesseby
Vestre
Jakobselv
Varangerfjorden
Bugøya
Bugøynes
Kjøøya
Skogerøya
Kirkenes
(Kirkkoniemi)
Bjørnevatn
Elvenes
Storskog
Grense-Jakobselv
Oskar II's kapell
Neiden
Færdesmyra
naturreservat
Näätämö
Sevettijärvi
(Čevetjávri)
Svanvik
Nickel
Pečenga
ПЕЧЕНГА
Linachamari
ЛИНАХАМАРИ
Zapol'jarnyj
Star. Titovka
Timovka
O. Bol.
Ajnov
Bol. Ozerko
Guba Bol. Volokovaja
Guba Mal. Volokovaja
Pasvikdalen
Skogfoss
Dammen
Nesheim
Nyrud
Øvre
Pasvik
nasjonal-
park
Nautsi
Raunvaarr
Virtaniemi
Nellim
Kontosjärvi
E6
13

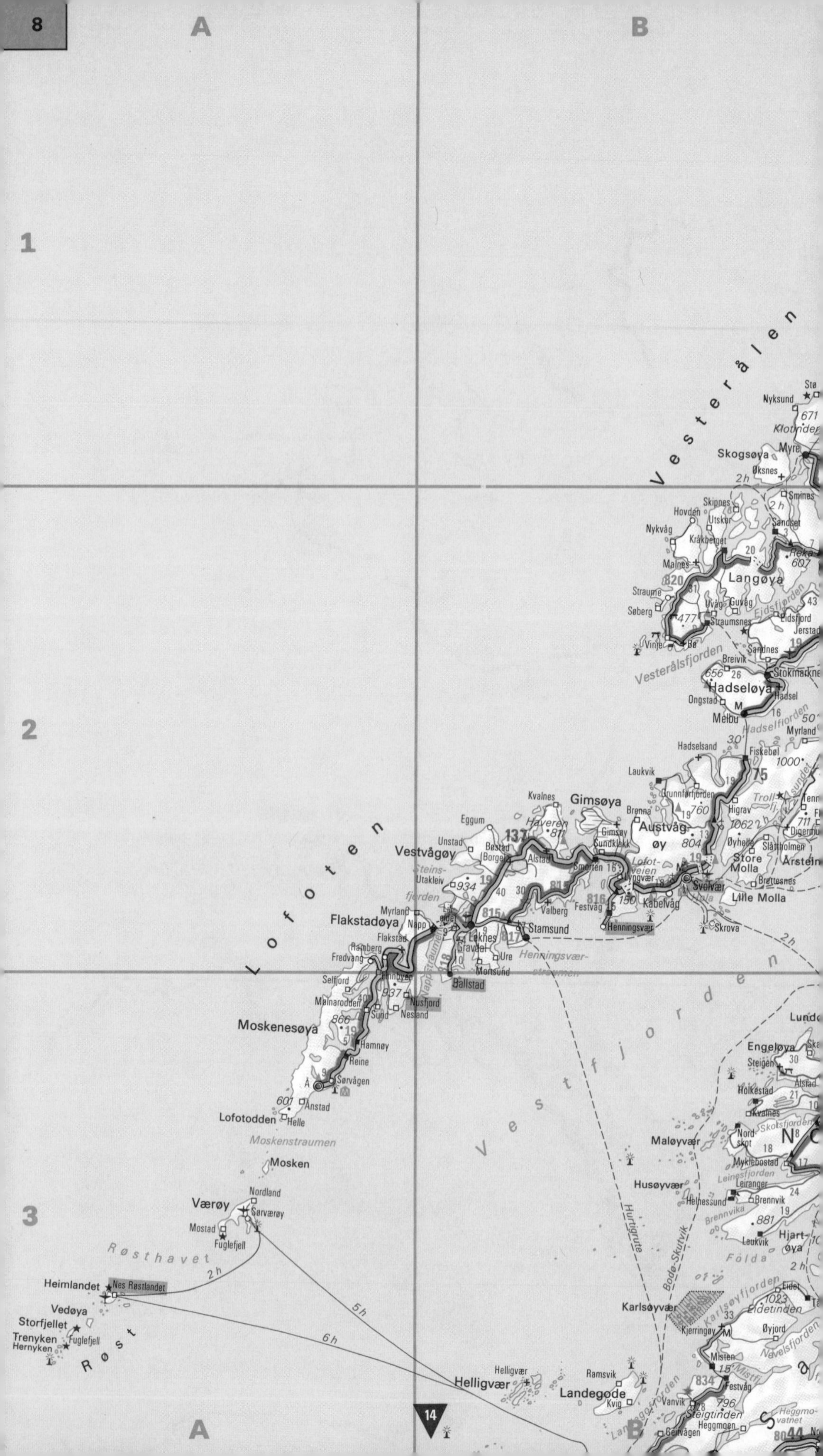

A
B
1
2
3
Vesterålen
Lofoten
Vestfjorden
Langøya
Hadseløya
Austvågøy
Vestvågøy
Flakstadøya
Moskenesøya
Gimsøya
Skogsøya
Nyksund
Stø
Myre
Øksnes
Sandset
Malnes
Straume
Søberg
Vinje
Bø
Straumsnes
Eidsfjord
Sortland
Stokmarknes
Melbu
Hadsel
Laukvik
Kvalnes
Eggum
Unstad
Alstad
Svolvær
Kabelvåg
Henningsvær
Skrova
Stamsund
Leknes
Ballstad
Ramberg
Fredvang
Reine
Hamnøy
Sørvågen
Å
Nusfjord
Lofotodden
Helle
Anstad
Moskenstraumen
Mosken
Værøy
Sørværøy
Mostad
Fuglefjell
Røsthavet
Heimlandet
Nes Røstlandet
Vedøya
Storfjellet
Trenyken
Hernyken
Røst
Helligvær
Landegode
Kvig
Ramsvik
Karlsøyvær
Maløyvær
Husøyvær
Engeløya
Steigen
Hjartøya
Leinesfjorden
Fólda
Kjerringøy
Misten
Festvåg
Steigtinden
Vanvik
Heggmoen
Geitvågen
Hurtigrute
Bodø-Skutvik
Eidetinden
Lille Molla
Store Molla
2h
5h
6h
14

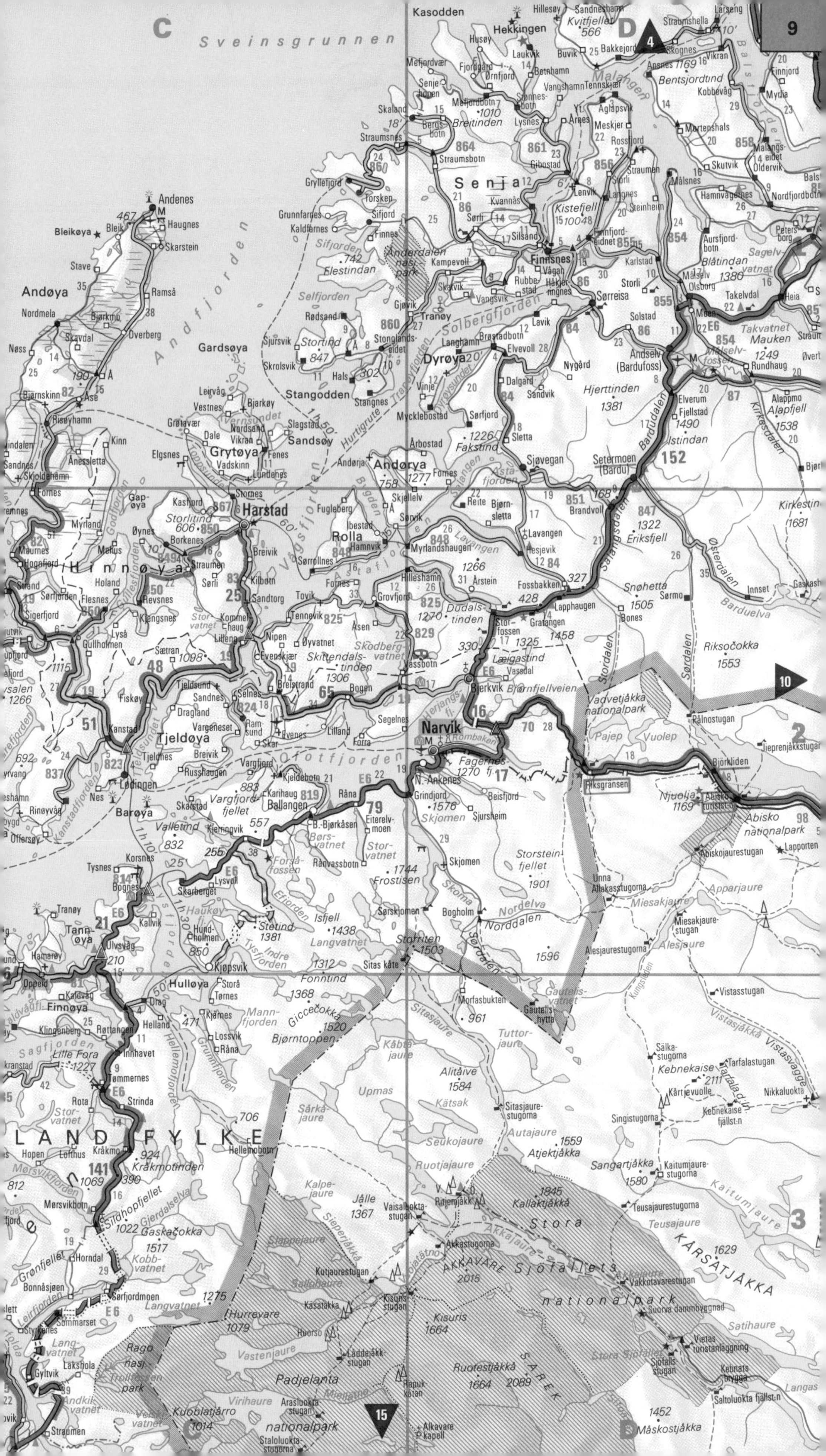
C
D
Sveinsgrunnen
4
10
15
2
3
Kasodden
Hekkingen
Hillesøy
Sandneshamn
Kvitfjellet
566
Larseng
Straumshella
Husøy
Laukvik
Bakkejord
Skognes
Vikran
Buvik
Mefjordvær
Fjordgård
Ørnfjord
Bøtnhamn
Malangen
Ansnes
1169
Bentsjordtind
Finnjord
Senjehopen
Vangshamn
Tennskjær
Kobbevåg
Mydla
Skaland
Mefjordbotn
1010
Breitinden
Stønnesbotn
Lysnes
Årnes
Aglapsvik
Bergsbotn
Meskjer
Mortenshals
Straumsnes
Straumsbotn
861
Gibostad
Rossfjord
Malangseidet
Oldervik
Senja
Straumen
Skutvik
Gryllefjord
Lenvik
Målsnes
Torsken
Kvannås
Kistefjell
1004
Langnes
Hamnvågnes
Andenes
Grunnfarnes
Sifjord
Steinheim
Nordfjordbotn
Haugnes
Kaldfarnes
Finnes
Sørli
Silsand
Finnfjordeidet
Aursfjordbotn
Bleikøya
Bleik
Skarstein
Sifjorden
Ånderdalen nasjonalpark
Kampevoll
Finnsnes
Karlstad
Blåtindan
1380
Stave
742
Elestindan
Vågan
Rubbestad
Håkjerringnes
Storli
Målselv
Olsborg
Sagelvvatnet
Andøya
Ramså
Skatvik
Vangsvik
Sørreisa
Takelvdal
Heia
Selfjorden
Gjøvik
Solbergfjorden
Solstad
Møen
Nordmela
Bjørkmo
Tranøy
Brøstadbotn
Lavik
Takvatnet
Dverberg
Rødsand
Langhamn
Elvevoll
Andselv (Bardufoss)
Mauken
Skavdal
860
Stongelandseidet
Nygård
1249
Nøss
Andfjorden
Gardsøya
Sjursvik
Stortind
847
Dyrøya
Rundhaug
Øvertå
Skrolsvik
302
Hals
Dalgard
Hjerttinden
1381
Elverum
Alappmo
Alapfjell
1538
Bjørnskinn
Stangodden
Vinje
Sandvik
Fjellstad
1490
Åse
Leirvåg
Stangnes
Mycklebostad
Bardudalen
Istindan
Kirkesdalen
Risøyhamn
Vestnes
Bjarkøy
Hurtigrute
Sørfjord
Grøtavær
Kvernsundet
Nordsand
Slagstad
Sandsøy
1226
Fakstind
Sletta
Kinn
Dale
Vikran
Grytøya
Fenes
Årbostad
Sjøvegan
Setermoen (Bardu)
Elgsnes
Vadskinn
Andørja
Andørya
Fornes
Åstafjorden
Ånessletta
Lundenes
758
1277
Kirkestind
1681
Skjoldehamn
Toppsundet
Stornes
Salangen
Reite
Bjørnsletta
Brandvoll
Fornes
Gapøya
Kasfjord
Harstad
Fugleberg
Skjellelv
1322
Eriksfjell
Myrland
Storlitind
606
Ibestad
Sørvik
Vågsfjorden
Lavangen
Godfjorden
Øynes
Borkenes
Rolla
Hamnvik
Myrlandshaugen
Hesjevik
Østerdalen
Maurnes
Mehus
Hinnøya
Straumen
Breivik
Sørrollnes
1266
Hognfjord
Holand
Sørli
Kilbotn
Fornes
Hilleshamn
Årstein
Fossbakken
Snøhetta
1505
Innset
Gaskashytta
Strand
Sørfjorden
Flesnes
Revsnes
Sandtorg
Tovik
Grovfjord
Dudalstinden
428
Lapphaugen
Bones
Sørmo
Barduelva
Sigerfjord
Kjengsnes
Kommelhaug
Tennevik
Åsen
1270
Storfossen
Gratangen
1458
Storvatnet
Lysa
Gullholmen
Lilleng
Nipen
Øyvatnet
Skodbergvatnet
1325
Riksočokka
1553
1115
Sætran
1098
Evenskjær
Skittendalstinden
1306
Vassbotn
330
Læigastind
Vassdal
Sordalen
Sørdalen
Tjeldsund
Fiskøy
Sandnes
Selnes
Brelstrand
Bogen
Bjerkvik
Bjørnfjellveien
Vadvetjåkka nationalpark
1266
Dragland
Ramsund
Segelnes
Herjangsfjorden
Narvik
Rombaken
Pålnostugan
Kanstad
Vargeneset
Evenes
Lilland
Forra
Fagernesfjell
1270
Pajep
Vuolep
Jieprenjåkkstugan
Tjeldøya
Breivik
Skar
Ofotfjorden
Riksgränsen
Björkliden
692
Tjelnes
Vargfjord
Kjeldebotn
N. Ankenes
Njuolja
1169
Abisko turistst.
Lødingen
Russhaugen
883
Karihaug
Ballangen
Råna
Grindjord
Beisfjord
Abisko nationalpark
Nes
Barøya
Vargfjordfjellet
Skarstad
1576
Sjursheim
Rinøyvåg
Valletind
832
557
Kjerringvik
B.-Bjørkåsen
Eiterelvmoen
Skjomen
Abiskojaurestugan
Lapporten
Offersøy
Børsvatnet
Storvatnet
Storsteinfjellet
1901
Kanstadfjorden
Korsnes
255
Forsåfossen
Rånvassbotn
1744
Frostisen
Unna Allakasstugorna
Apparjaure
Tysnes
Bognes
Skarberget
Lysvoll
Nordelva
Miesakjaure
Tysfjorden
Haukøyfjell
Efjorden
Isfjell
Sørskjomen
Bogholm
Norddalen
Miesakjaurestugan
Tranøy
Tannøya
Kallvik
Stetind
1381
1438
Hundholmen
850
Langvatnet
Storriten
1503
1596
Alesjaurestugorna
Alesjaure
Ulvsvåg
210
Indre Tysfjorden
Kjøpsvik
1312
Fonntind
Sitas kåte
Hamarøy
Oppeid
Hulløya
Storå
Tørnes
1368
Morfasbukten
Gautelisvatnet
Kungsleden
Vistasstugan
Karlsøy
Drag
Kjærnes
Mannfjorden
Giccecokka
1520
961
Gautelishytta
Finnøya
Klingenberg
Røttangen
Helland
471
Lossvik
Råna
Bjørntoppen
Sitasjaure
Tuttorjaure
Vistasjåkka
Vistasvagge
Sagfjorden
Lille Fora
1227
Innhavet
Grunnfjorden
Hellemofjorden
Kåbtåjaure
Sälkastugorna
Tarfalastugan
Kebnekaise
2111
Tarfaladalen
Tømmernes
Upmas
Alitåive
1584
Kårtjevuolle
Nikkaluokta
Rota
Strinda
Kätsak
Kebnekaise fjällst:n
Storvatnet
706
Sårkajaure
Sitasjaurestugorna
Singistugorna
Autajaure
1559
Atjekjåkka
LAND FYLKE
Hopen
Lofthus
Kråkmo
Hellemobotn
Seukojaure
924
Kråkmotinden
Ruotjajaure
Sangartjåkka
1580
Kaitumjaurestugorna
812
Mørsvikfjorden
1069
390
1845
Kallaktjåkka
Kaitumjaure
Mørsvikbotn
Kalpejaure
Jålle
1367
Vaisaluoktastugan
Ritjemjåkk
Stora
Teusajaurestugorna
Sildhopfjellet
Gjerdalselva
1022
Gaskačokka
Siepperjåkka
Teusajaure
Kårsatjåkka
1517
Akkajaure
Akkastugorna
1629
Horndal
Kobbvatnet
Slappejaure
Akkavare
Sjöfallets
Grønfjellet
Kutjaurestugan
2015
Vakkotavarestugan
Bonnåsjøen
Sørfjordmoen
nationalpark
1275
Kisuris stugan
Suorva dammbyggnad
Leirfjorden
Langvatnet
Hurrevare
1079
Kisuris
1664
Satihaure
Sommarset
Kasatåkka
Sarek
Styrkenes
Rago nasjonalpark
Vastenjaure
Huorso
Låddejåkkstugan
Stora Sjöfallet
Vietas turistanläggning
Langvatnet
Sjöfallsstugan
Lakshola
Trollfossen
Padjelanta
Rapukkåtan
Ruotestjåkkå
1664
2089
Kebnats brygga
Gyltvik
Andkilvatnet
Virihaure
Araslouktastugan
Saltoluokta fjällst:n
Langas
Kuoblatjårro
1014
1452
Måskostjåkka
Straumen
nationalpark
Alkavare kapell
Staloluoktastugorna

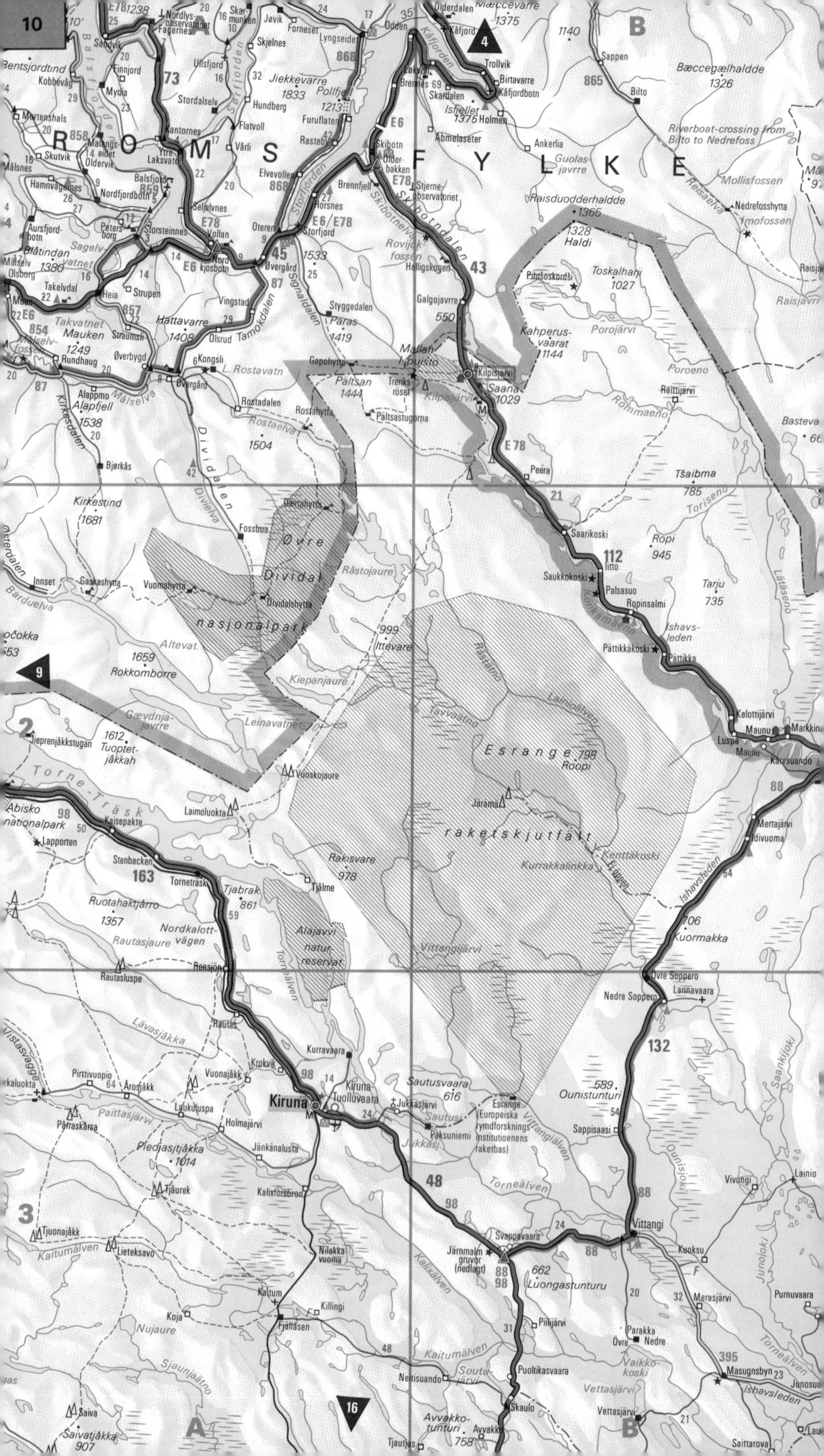
R O M S F Y L K E
Kiruna
Sandvik
Nordlys-observatoriet
Fagernes
Skarmunken
Jøvik
Forneset
Lyngseidet
Odden
Olderdalen
Mæccevarre 1375
Kåfjord
Trollvik
Birtavarre
Kåfjordbotn
Skardalen
Isfjellet 1375
Holmen
Jiekkevarre 1833
Pollfjell 1213
Skibotn
Olderbakken
Sappen
Bilto
Bæccegælhaldde 1326
Riverboat-crossing from Bilto to Nedrefoss
Mollisfossen
Nedrefosshytta
Imofossen
Raisduodderhaldde 1365
1328 Haldi
Toskalharji 1027
Kahperusvaarat 1144
Kilpisjärvi
Saana 1029
Treriksrøset
Pältsan 1444
Galgojavrre
Helligskogen
Storfjord
Nordkjosbotn
Vollan
Storsteinnes
Balsfjord
Tromsdalen
Hattavarre 1408
Mauken 1249
Rundhaug
Øverbygd
Kongsli
L. Rostavatn
Rostadalen
Dividalen
Fossbua
Øvre Dividal nasjonalpark
Dividalshytta
Vuomahytta
Gaskashytta
Innset
Barduelva
Altevat.
Rokkomborre 1659
Kiepanjaure
Råstojaure
Ittevare 999
Esrange 798 Roopi
Järämä
raketskjutfält
Kenttäkoski
Kurrakkalinkka
Saarikoski
Iitto
Saukkokoski
Palsasuo
Ropinsalmi
Ishavsleden
Pättikkäkoski
Pättikkä
Kelottijärvi
Maunu
Markkina
Luspa
Karesuando
Mertajärvi
Idivuoma
Kuormakka 706
Övre Soppero
Nedre Soppero
Lannavaara
Tuoptetjåkkah 1612
Torne-Träsk
Abisko nationalpark
Lapporten
Kaisepakte
Stenbacken
Tornetrask
Tjabrak 861
Ruotahaktjårro 1357
Nordkalottvägen
Rautasjaure
Alajavvi naturreservat
Rakisvare 978
Tjålme
Rensjön
Rautas
Kurravaara
Krokvik
Vuonajåkk
Sautusvaara 616
Kiruna-Tuolluvaara
Jukkasjärvi
Esrange (Europeiska rymdforskningsinstitutionens raketbas)
Paksuniemi
Ounistunturi 589
Sappisaasi
Vittangi
Svappavaara
Järnmalmgruvor (nedlagt)
Luongastunturu 662
Kalixforsbron
Nilakkavuoma
Kaitum
Killingi
Fjällåsen
Koja
Nujaure
Piedjasjtjåkka 1014
Tjaurek
Tjuonajåkk
Lieteksavo
Kaitumälven
Holmajärvi
Laukuluspa
Årosjåkk
Pirttivuopio
Paittasjärvi
Pålnoviken
Kuoksu
Merasjärvi
Parakka
Övre
Nedre
Masugnsbyn
Vettasjärvi
Puoltikasvaara
Nertisuando
Skaulo
Avvakkotunturi 758
Tjautjas
Saivatjåkka 907
Saiva
Torneälven
Kalixälven
Vittangiälven
Junosuando
Saittarova
Lainio
Vivungi
Purnuvaara

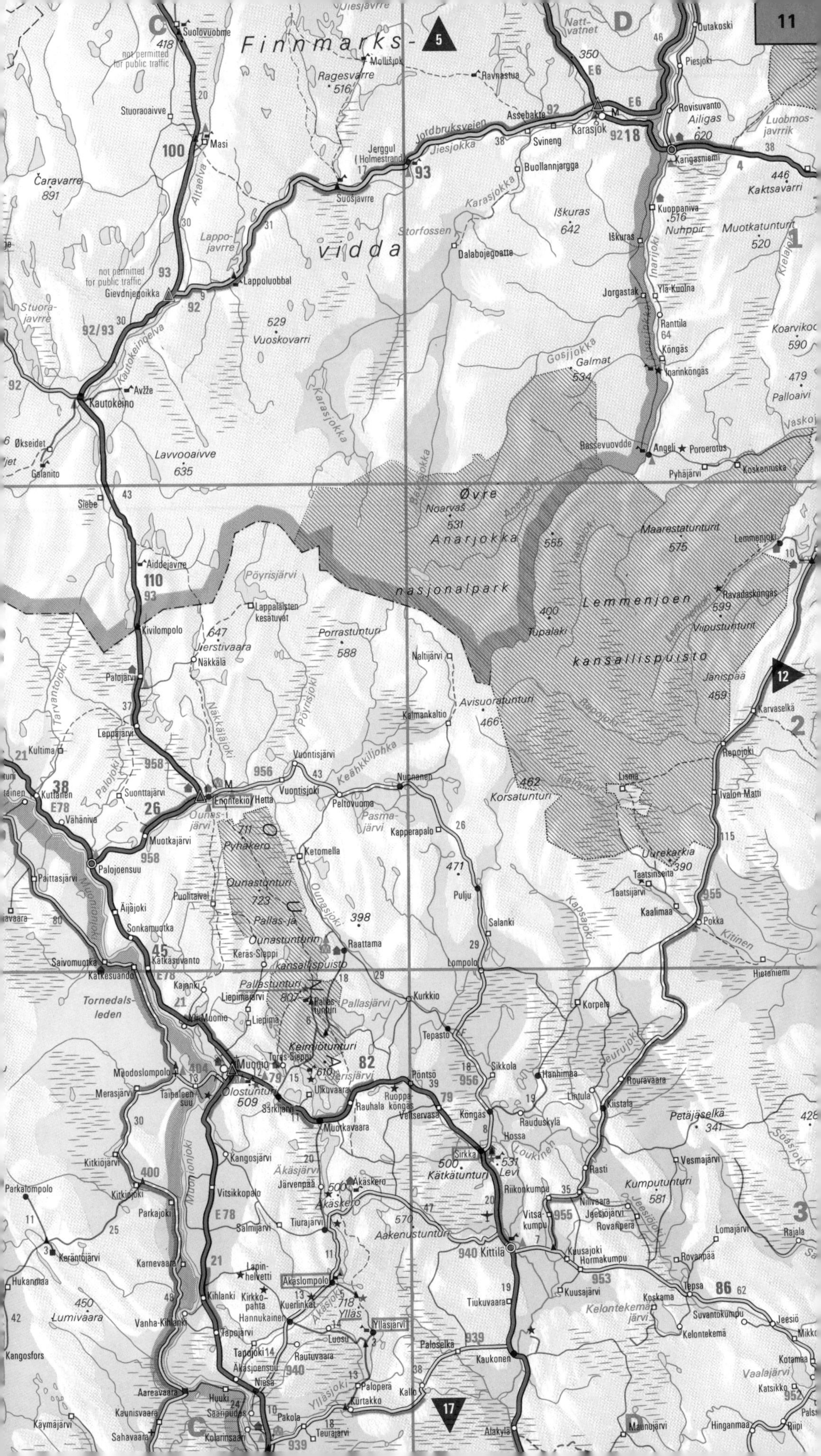
Finnmarks-
vidda
5
Suolovuobme
not permitted for public traffic
Mollišjok
Ragesvarre
516
Ravnastua
Stuoraoaivve
Masi
Čaravarre
891
Altaelva
Lappojavrre
Gievdnjegoikka
Lappoluobbal
Stuorajavrre
Kautokeinoelva
Kautokeino
Avžže
Vuoskovarri
529
Lavvooaivve
635
Øksejdet
Galanito
Jerggul (Holmestrand)
Jotdbruksveien
Jiesjokka
Suosjavrre
Storfossen
Karasjokka
Dalabojegoatte
Assebakte
Svineng
Karasjok
Buollanjargga
Iškuras
642
E6
Nattvatnet
Outakoski
Piesjoki
Rovisuvanto
Ailigas
620
Luobmosjavrrik
Karigasniemi
446
Kaktsavarri
Kuoppaniva
516
Nuhppir
Muotkatunturit
520
Iškuras
Jorgastak
Ylä-Kuolna
Inarijoki
Ranttila
Köngäs
Koarvikoddat
590
Gosjjokka
Galmat
534
Inarinköngäs
479
Palloaivi
Vaskojoki
Bassevuovdde
Angeli
Poroerotus
Pyhäjärvi
Koskenniska
Siebe
Aiddejavre
Pöyrisjärvi
Lappalaisten kesätuvat
Kivilompolo
647
Jierstivaara
Näkkälä
Porrastunturi
588
Øvre Anarjokka nasjonalpark
Noarvaš
531
555
Maarestatunturit
575
Lemmenjoki
Lemmenjoen kansallispuisto
Ravadaskongäs
599
Viipustunturit
400
Tupalaki
Jänispää
459
12
Karvaselkä
Naltijärvi
Avisuoratunturi
466
Kalmankaltio
Repojoki
Palojärvi
Tarvantojoki
Leppajärvi
Kultima
Palojoki
Suonttajärvi
Kuttanen
Vähäniva
Enontekiö/Hetta
Ounasjärvi
Vuontisjärvi
Vuontisjoki
Keahkkiljohka
Nunnanen
Peltovuoma
Pasmajärvi
Kapperapalo
462
Korsatunturi
Lisma
Ivalon Matti
Muotkajärvi
Palojoensuu
711
Pyhäkero
Ketomella
471
Pulju
Uurekarkia
390
Taatsinseita
Taatsijärvi
Kaalimaa
Pokka
Kitinen
Paittasjärvi
Muonionjoki
Äijäjoki
Puolitaival
Ounastunturi
723
Pallas-ja Ounastunturin kansallispuisto
Ounasjoki
398
Salanki
Sonkamuotka
Raattama
Saivomuotka
Katkesuando
Katkasuvanto
Keräs-Sieppi
Lompolo
Hietaniemi
Tornedalsleden
Kajanki
Liepimäjärvi
Pallastunturi
807
Pallasjärvi
Kurkkio
Korpela
Ylimuonio
Liepimä
Keimiötunturi
Tepasto
Torassieppi
Jerisjärvi
Sikkola
Hanhimaa
Muonio
Muodoslompolo
Merasjärvi
Taipaleensuu
Olostunturi
509
Särkijärvi
Ulkuvaara
Ruoppakongäs
Pöntsö
Venservasa
Köngäs
Rauhala
Lintula
Kiistala
Rouravaara
Petäjäselkä
341
Muotkavaara
Hossa
Rauduskylä
Sirkka
500
Kätkätunturi
531
Levi
Rasti
Vesmajärvi
Kangosjärvi
Kitkiöjärvi
Äkäsjärvi
Järvenpää
Äkäskero
500
Kumputunturi
581
Parkalompolo
Kitkiöjoki
Vitsikkopalo
570
Aakenustunturi
Riikonkumpu
Nilivaara
Jeesiöjärvi
Rovanperä
Vitsakumpu
Lomajärvi
Rajala
Parkajoki
Salmijärvi
Tiurajärvi
Kittilä
Kuusajoki
Hormakumpu
Rovanpää
Kerantojärvi
Karnevaara
Lapinhelvetti
Äkäslompolo
Kuusajärvi
Tepsa
Hukanmaa
Kihlanki
Kirkkopahta
Kuerlinkatu
718
Ylläs
Tiukuvaara
Koskama
Kelontekemäjärvi
Suvantokumpu
Jeesiö
450
Lumivaara
Vanha-Kihlanki
Hannukainen
Luosu
Ylläsjärvi
Kelontekemä
Mikko
Tapojärvi
Tapojoki
Rautuvaara
Paloselka
Kaukonen
Kotamaa
Kangosfors
Äkäsjoensuu
Niesa
Ylläsjoki
Paloperä
Vaalajärvi
Aareavaara
Huuki
Kaunisvaara
Saaripudas
Pakola
Kurtakko
Kallo
17
Katsikko
Käymäjärvi
Sahavaara
Kolarinsaari
Teurajärvi
Alakylä
Maunujärvi
Hinganmaa
Riipi
Palsi

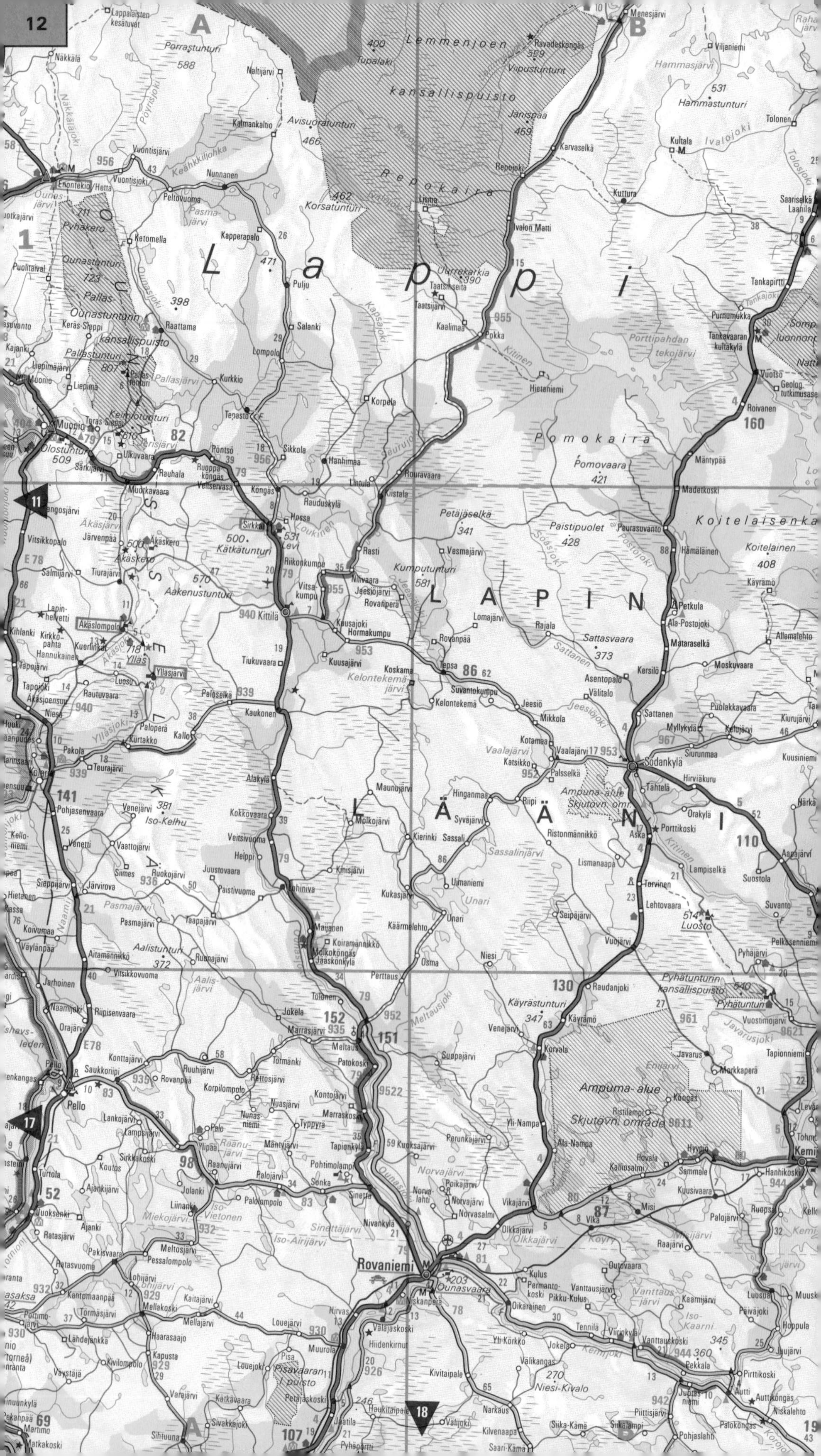
A
B
Lappi
LAPIN
LÄÄNI
Lemmenjoen kansallispuisto
Repokaira
Pomokaira
Koitelaisenka
Pallas-Ounastunturin kansallispuisto
Pyhätunturin kansallispuisto
Pisavaaran l. puisto
Ampuma-alue Skjutovn. omr.
Ampuma-alue Skjutovn. område
Porttipahdan tekojärvi
Enontekiö/Hetta
Muonio
Kittilä
Levi
Sodankylä
Luosto
Rovaniemi
Ounasvaara
Pello
Kemi
Ylläs
Äkäslompolo
Yllästunturi
Pallastunturi
Kätkätunturi
Aakenustunturi
Kumputunturi
Sattasvaara
Käyrästunturi
Pomovaara
Petäjäselkä
Paistipuolet
Koitelainen
Hammastunturi
Porrastunturi
Avisuoratunturi
Korsatunturi
Ounastunturi
Pyhäkero
Olostunturi
Aalistunturi
Iso-Kelhu
Kittinen
Kemijoki
Ounasjoki
Ivalojoki
Unari
Vaalajärvi
Sassalinjärvi
Olkkajärvi
Norvajärvi
Sinettäjärvi
Iso-Vietonen
Miekojärvi
Pasmajärvi
Aalisjärvi
Pallasjärvi
Kelontekemäjärvi
Vanttausjärvi
Iso-Kaarni
Niesi-Kivalo
11
17
18
E 78
E78

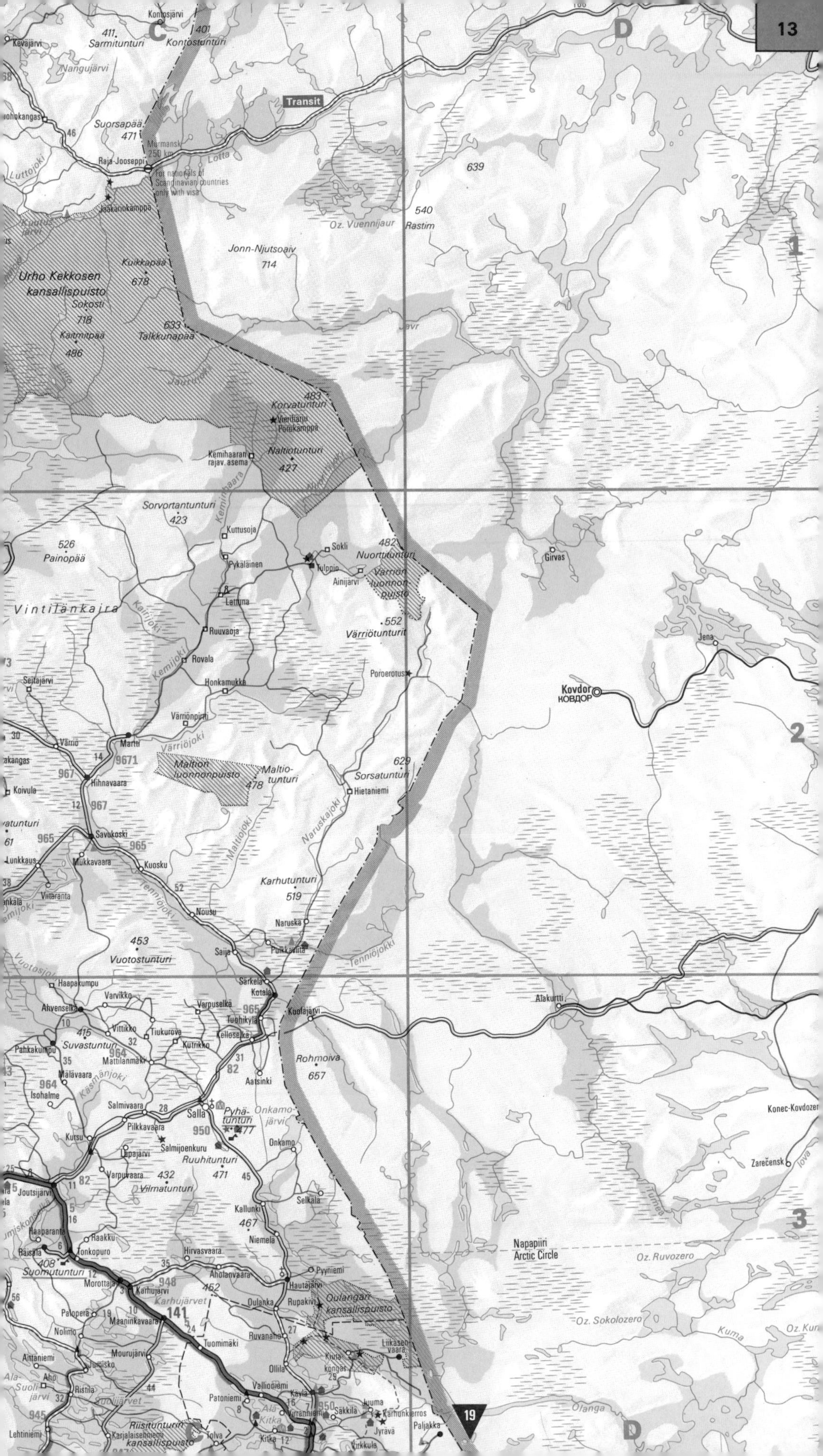
13
C
D
Kontosjärvi
401
Kontostunturi
Keväjärvi
411
Sarmitunturi
Nangujärvi
Transit
Suorsapää
471
Murmansk
250 km
Lotta
Raja-Jooseppi
For nationals of
Scandinavian countries
only with visa
Luttojoki
Jääkäriokämppä
639
540
Rastim
Oz. Vuennijaur
Jonn-Njutsoaiv
714
1
Kuikkapää
678
Urho Kekkosen
kansallispuisto
Sokosti
718
Kaitmitpää
486
633
Talkkunapää
Javr
483
Korvatunturi
Vierihaarju
Porokämppä
Kemihaaran
rajav. asema
Naltiotunturi
427
Sorvortantunturi
423
Kemihaara
Kuttusoja
526
Painopää
Pykäläinen
Sokli
Tulppio
482
Nuorttitunturi
Ainijärvi
Värriön
luonnon-
puisto
Girvas
Vintilänkaira
Kairijoki
Lattuna
552
Värriötunturit
Ruuvaoja
Jena
Rovala
Kemijoki
Honkamukka
Poroerotus
Kovdor
КОВДОР
Seitajärvi
Värriönpirtti
2
Värriö
Martti
Värriöjoki
14
9671
Maltion
luonnonpuisto
478
Maltio-
tunturi
629
Sorsatunturi
967
Hihnavaara
Hietaniemi
Koivula
12
967
965
Savukoski
965
Naruskajoki
Maltiojoki
Lunkkaus
Mukkavaara
Kuosku
Vitteranta
52
Tenniöjoki
Karhutunturi
519
Nousu
Naruska
453
Vuotostunturi
Saija
Pulkkaviita
Tenniöjokki
Haapakumpu
Särkelä
Kotala
Varvikko
Ahvenselkä
Varpuselkä
965
Tuohikylä
Kuolajärvi
Alakurtti
10
Vittikko
Tiukurova
Kelleselkä
415
Suvastunturi
32
964
Kutrikko
Pahkakumpu
35
Mattilanmäki
31
Rohmoiva
657
82
Mälävaara
Käsmänjoki
Aatsinki
964
Isohalme
Salmivaara
28
Salla
Pyhä-
tunturi
Onkamo-
järvi
477
Konec-Kovdozer
950
Pilkkavaara
Salmijoenkuru
Kursu
Onkamo
Lapajärvi
Ruuhitunturi
471
Zarečensk
Iova
432
Varpuvaara
Vilmatunturi
45
11
82
Joutsijärvi
Selkälä
Tumcha
Kallunki
5
467
3
16
Haaparanta
Niemelä
Napapiiri
Arctic Circle
Raakku
Räisälä
6
Tonkopuro
Hirvasvaara
408
Suomutunturi
35
Oz. Ruvozero
12
Pyyniemi
948
Aholanvaara
Morottaja
Karhujärvi
452
Hautajärvi
56
Karhujärvet
Oulanka
Rupakivi
Oulangan
kansallispuisto
10
141
Palopera
19
Maaninkavaara
24
Oz. Sokolozero
Oz. Kur
Kuma
Nolimo
Tuomimäki
Ruvanaho
27
Liikasen-
vaara
Aittaniemi
Mourujärvi
Kiutaköngäs
Jamisko
Ollila
29
Ala-
Aho
Suoli
järvi
Ristilä
44
Vallioniemi
Suolijärvet
Käylä
Juuma
32
Patoniemi
16
950
945
Alä
Kitka
Virranniemi
Säkkilä
Karhunkierros
Olanga
19
Riisitunturin
kansallispuisto
Paljakka
Lehtiniemi
Karjalaisenniemi
Tolva
Kitka
12
Jyrävä
Virkkula
C
D

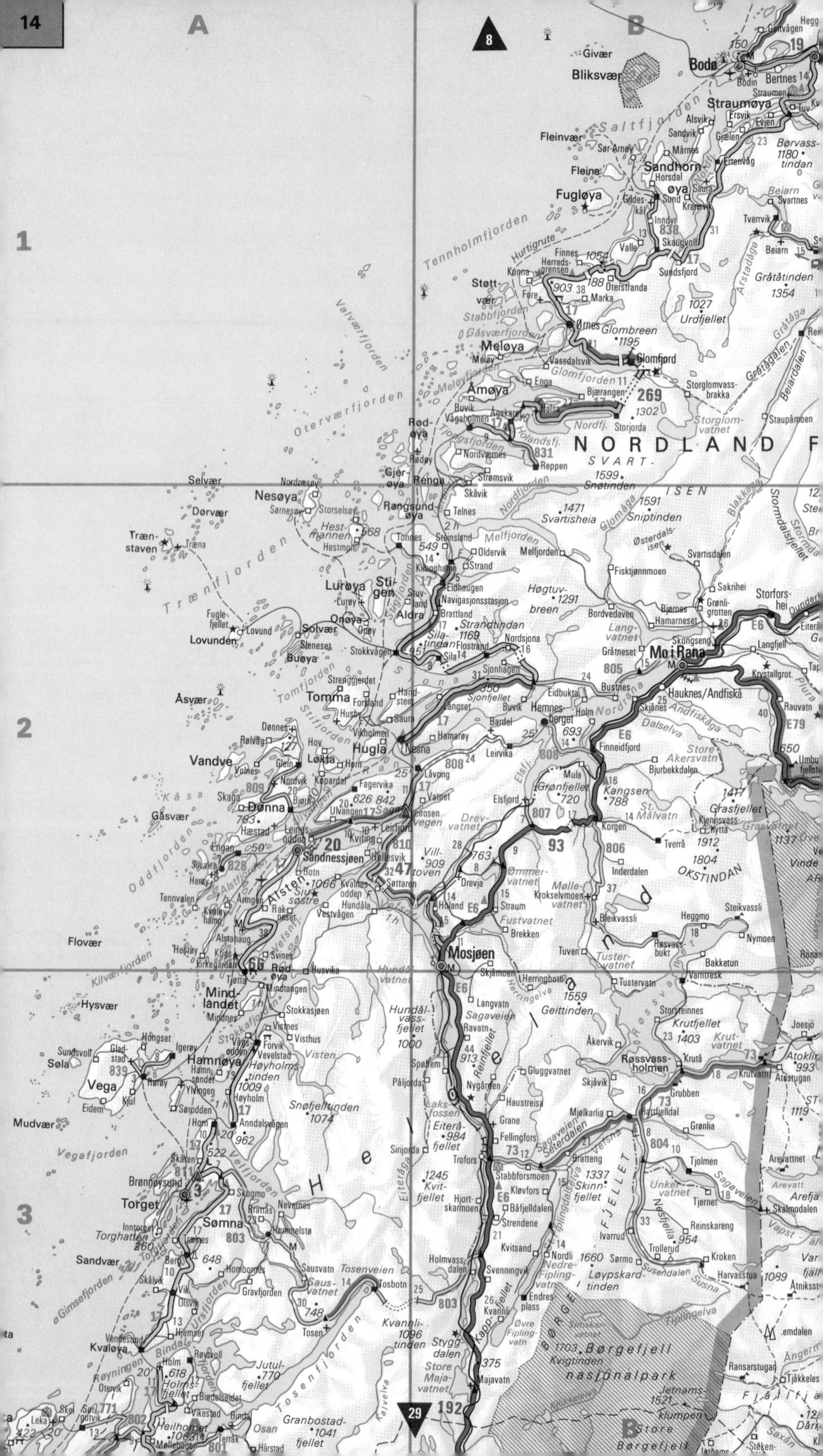
A
B
8
1
2
3
29
Givær
Bliksvær
Bodø
Bodin
Bertnes
Straumøya
Saltfjorden
Fleinvær
Sør-Arnøy
Fleina
Sandhornøya
Fugløya
Gildeskål
Inndyr
Kransvik
Tennholmfjorden
Hurtigrute
Finnes
Støttvær
Stabbfjorden
Gåsværfjorden
Ørnes
Glombreen
1195
Meløya
Glomfjord
Vassdalsvik
Valværfjorden
Oterværfjorden
Meløyfjorden
Åmøya
Enga
Bjærangen
Halsa
Storglomvassbrakka
Rødøya
Rødøy
Reppen
NORDLAND
SVARTISEN
1599
Snøtinden
Gjerøya
Selvær
Nesøya
Dørvær
Træna
Trænstaven
Rangsundøya
Hestmannen
Tonnes
Melfjorden
Lurøya
Stigen
Trænfjorden
Lovunden
Solvær
Onøya
Aldra
Svartisheia
1591
Sniptinden
Storforshei
Strandtindan
1169
Høgtuvbreen
1291
Mo i Rana
Sjona
Åsvær
Tomma
Hemnesberget
Hauknes/Andfiskå
Krystallgrot.
Dønnes
Vandve
Løkta
Hugla
Nesna
Kåsa
Dønna
Gåsvær
Sandnessjøen
Alsten
Sju søstre
1066
Oddfjorden
Flovær
Mosjøen
Korgen
Kangsen
788
Grønfjellet
720
Okstindan
1804
1912
Røsvassbukt
Tustervatnet
Røssvatnet
Mindlandet
Hysvær
Kilværfjorden
Sundsvoll
Søla
Vega
Hamnøya
Høyholmstinden
1009
Snøfjelltinden
1074
Mudvær
Vegafjorden
Hundålvassfjellet
1000
Geittinden
1559
Røssvassholmen
Krutfjellet
1403
Atoklimp
993
Hattfjelldal
Brønnøysund
Torget
Sømna
Velfjorden
Torghatten
260
Sandvær
Gimsefjorden
Kvaløya
Bindal
Holmsfjellet
618
Jutulfjellet
770
Tosenfjorden
Tosen
Kvannlitinden
1096
Stygg-dalen
Store Majavatnet
Majavatn
Børgefjell
Kvigtinden
1703
Børgefjell nasjonalpark
Jetnamsklumpen
1521
Leka
Heilhornet
1063
Granbostadfjellet
1041
Kvitfjellet
1245
Eiteråfjellet
984
Skinnfjellet
1337
Løypskardtinden
1660
Reinskareng
954
Heilan
Helgeland

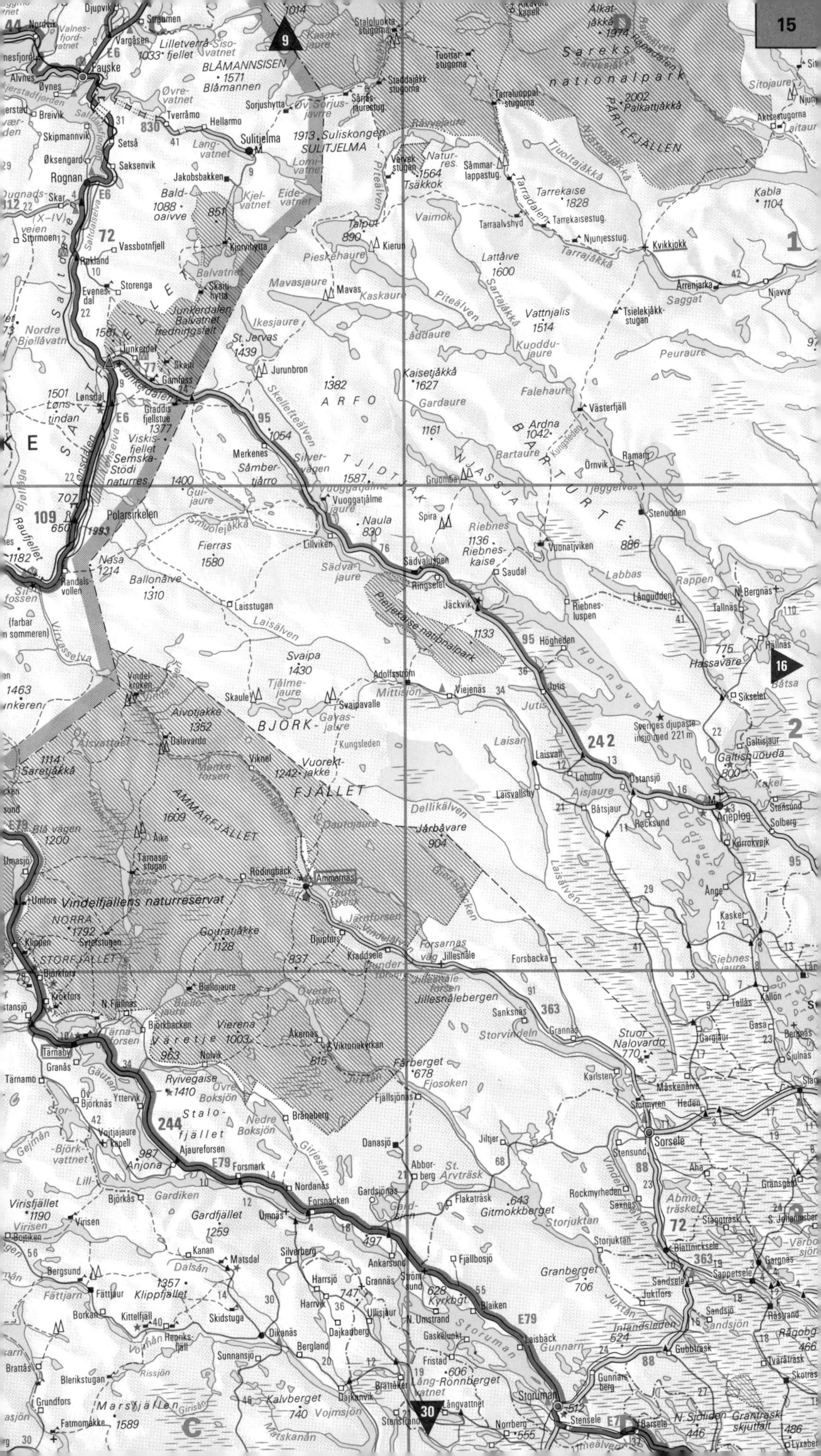
Djupvik
Straumen
Nordvik
Valnesfjordvatnet
Vargåsen
Lilletverrå-vatnet
Siso-vatnet
Fauske
E6
1033 fjellet
BLÅMANNSISEN
1571 Blåmannen
Alvnes
Øynes
Øvre-vatnet
Breivik
Tverråmo
Hellarmo
Sulitjelma
Skipmannvik
Setså
Langvatnet
Øksengard
Saksenvik
Rognan
Jakobsbakken
Bald-1088 oaivve
Kjelvatnet
Eidevatnet
Skar
Saltdalselva
Storjord
Stormoen
72
Vassbotnfjell
Kjorvihytta
Røkland
Storenga
Evenesdal
Balvatnet
Skaitihytta
Junkerdalen-Balvatnet fredningsfelt
Nordre Bjøllåvatn
Junkerdal
Skaiti
Gamfoss
1501 Lønstindan
Lønsdal
Graddis fjellstue
1377
Viskisfjellet
Semska-Stødi naturres.
Lønsdalen
Polarsirkelen
109
Raufjellet 1182
Randalsvollen
Nasa 1214
Ballonaive 1310
Laisstugan
Laisälven
Virvasselva
(farbar sommeren)
1463
Vindelkroken
Aivotjakke 1352
Dalavardo
1114 Saretjåkkå
Övre Alsvattnet
Blå vägen 1200
E79
1609
AMMARFJÄLLET
Aike
Tärnasjöstugan
Umasjö
Umfors
Vindelfjällens naturreservat
NORRA 1792
Syterstugan
Klippen
STORFJÄLLET
Björkfors
Krokfors
N. Fjällnäs
Björkbacken
Tärnaforsen
Tärnaby
Granås
Tärnamo
Öv. Björknäs
Yttervik
Ryivegaise 1410
Övre Boksjön
Stalo-fjället
244
Voitjajaure kapell
Björkvattnet
987 Anjona
Ajaureforsen
Forsmark
Nordanås
Nedre Boksjön
Brånaberg
Gardiken
Björkås
Virisfjället 1190
Virisen
Gardfjället 1259
Umnäs
Forsnacken
Kanan
Matsdal
Dalsån
Bergsund
Fättjaur
1357 Klippfjället
Borkan
Kittelfjäll
Henriksfjäll
Skidstuga
Dikanäs
Sunnansjö
Bergland
Brattås
Blerikstugan
Rissjön
Marsfjällen
1589
Grundfors
Fatmomakke
Kalvberget 740
Vojmsjön
Dajkanvik
Matskanån
30
Staloluokta stugorna
Kasakjaure
Tuottar stugorna
Staddajåkk stugorna
Sorjushytta
Särjåsjaurestug.
Rävvejaure
1913 Suliskongen
SULITJELMA
Lomivatnet
Varvek stugan
Naturres.
1564 Tsåkkok
Piteälven
Talput 890
Kierun
Pieskehaure
Vaimok
Mavasjaure
Mavas
Kaskaure
Ikesjaure
St. Jervas 1439
Jurunbron
1382
ARFO
Skellefteälven
Merkenes
Såmbertjårro
Silvervägen
TJIDTJAK
1587
Vuoggatjålme
Vuoggatjålmejaure
Naula 830
Lillviken
Fierras 1580
Sädvajaure
Sädvaluspen
Ringselet
Pieljekaise nationalpark
Svaipa 1430
Tjålmejaure
Skaule
Svaipavalle
Gavasjaure
Adolfsström
Mittisjön
Viejenäs
BJÖRK-
FJÄLLET
Viknel
Vuorektjakke 1242
Kungsleden
Dautojaure
Rödingbäck
Ammarnäs
Gautsträsk
Järnforsen
Vindelälven
Djupfors
Kraddsele
Gouratjåkke 1128
837
Biellojaure
Överstjuktan
Vierena 1003
Våretje
963
Nolvik
Åkernäs
Viktoriakyrkan
815
Färberget 678
Fjosoken
Fjällsjönäs
Juktån
Girjesån
Danasjö
Abborberg
St. Arvträsk
Gardsjönäs
Gardsjön
Silverberg
Harrsjö
Grannäs
Harrvik
Ullisjaur
Dajkanberg
Strömsund
628 Kyrkbgt.
N. Umstrand
Gaskeluokt
Fristad
606 Lång-Rönnberget
Långvattnet
Brattåker
Stensträsk
Storuman
Alkatjåkkå
Sareks nationalpark
1974 Rapadalen
Tarraluoppal-stugorna
2002 Palkattjåkkå
PÄRTEFJÄLLEN
Sitojaure
Aktsestugorna
Laitaure
Tjuoltajåkkå
Njåtsosjåkkå
Såmmarlappastug.
Tarrekaise 1828
Tarradalen
Tarraalvshyd
Tarrekaisestug.
Njunjesstug.
Kvikkjokk
Kabla 1104
Tarrajåkkå
Lattaive 1600
Årrenjarka
Njavve
Saggat
Tsielekjåkk-stugan
Sartajåkkå
Vattnjalis 1514
Kuoddujaure
Läddaure
Peuraure
Kaisetjåkkå 1627
Gardaure
Falehaure
Västerfjäll
Ardna 1042
BARTURTE
1161
NJASSJA
Bartaure
Kungsleden
Örnvik
Ramanj
Gruomba
Tjeggelvas
Stenudden
Spira
Riebnes 1136
Riebneskaise
Vuonatjviken
886
Saudal
Labbas
Rappen
Jäckvik
Riebnesluspen
Långudden
N. Bergnäs
Tallnäs
1133
95
Högheden
Hornavan
Hassavare 775
Hällnäs
Båtsa
Jutis
Sikselet
Sveriges djupaste insjö med 221 m
Galtisjaur
Galtisbuouda 800
Laisan
Laisvall
242
Loholm
Östansjö
Aisjaure
Laisvallsby
Båtsjaur
Arjeplog
Stensund
Solberg
Racksund
Uddjaure
Kurrokvejk
Dellikälven
Jårbåvare 904
Laisälven
Gierttsbäcken
Ånge
Kasker
Forsarnas väg
Jillesnäle
Forsbacka
Siebnesjaure
Jillesnåleforsen
Jillesnålebergen
Tallås
Kallön
Sanksnäs
363
Grannäs
Storvindeln
Stuor Nalovardo 770
Gargjaur
Gasa
Bergnäs
Sjulnäs
Karlsten
Måskenåive
Stormyren
Heden
Sorsele
Stensund
Jiltjer
88
Aha
Gransgård
Rockmyrheden
Saxnäs
Abmoträsket
Staggträsk
S. Johannisber
Flakaträsk
643 Gitmokkberget
Storjuktan
Storjuktan
Blattnicksele
Fjällbosjö
Granberget 706
Sandsele
Sappetsele
Gargnäs
Juktfors
Sandsjö
Sandsjön
Råstrand
Blaiken
E79
Laisbäck
Gunnarn
Inlandsleden 524
Gubbträsk
Rågobg 466
Tväråträsk
Gunnarsberg
Skotträsk
512
Stensele
Norrberg 555
Barsele
N. Sjöliden 446
Granträsk skjutfält
486
Lyxaberg
16
1
2

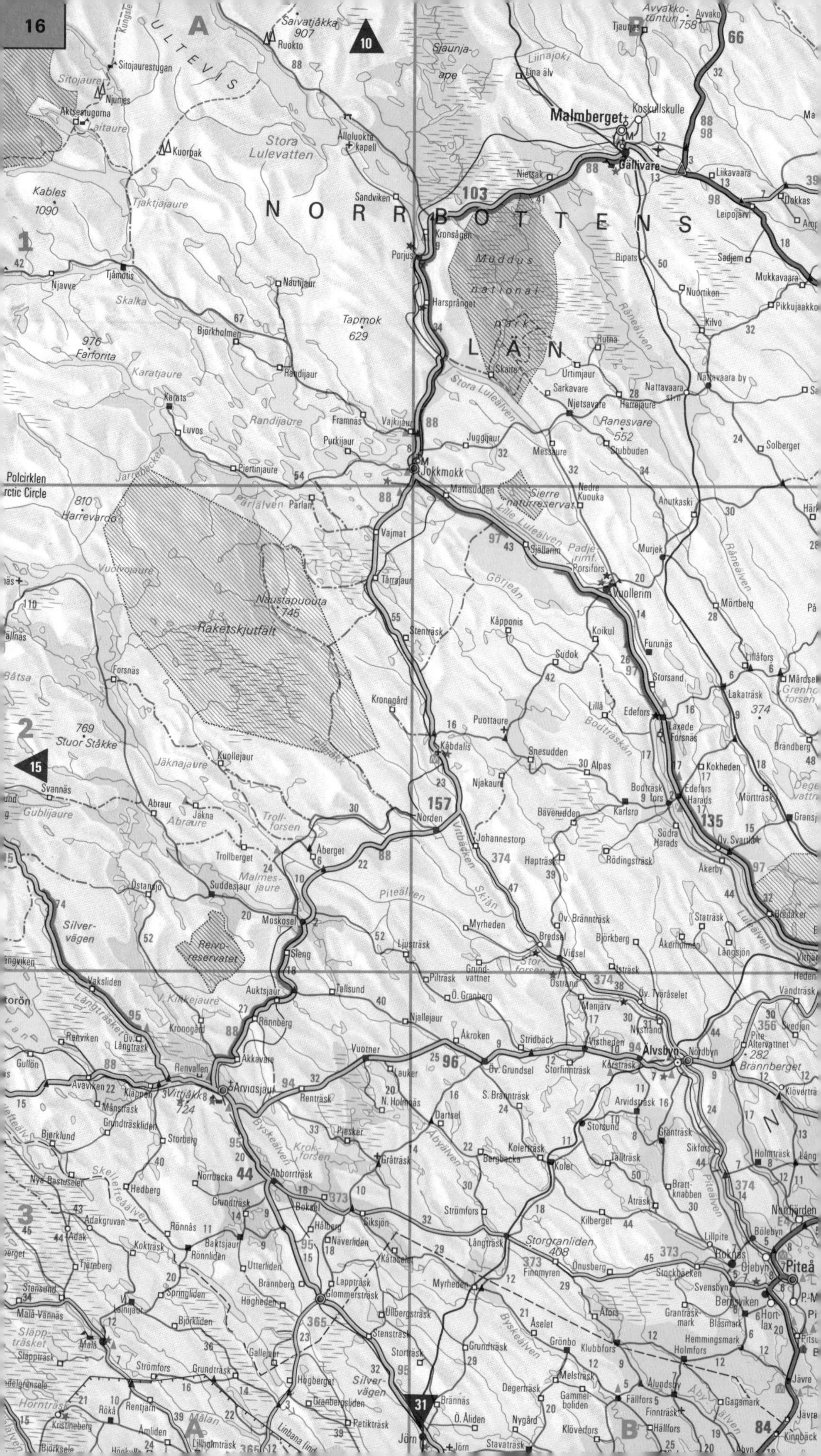
16
A
ULTEVIS
Saivatjåkka
907
Ruokto
10
Sjaunja-
ape
Avvakko-
tunturi
758
Avvakko
Tjautjas
B
66
Liinajoki
Lina älv
Malmberget
Koskullskulle
Gällivare
Liikavaara
Dokkas
Leipojärvi
Sadjem
Mukkavaara
Pikkujaakko
Nuortikon
Kilvo
Ripats
Sitojaure
Sitojaurestugan
Njunjes
Aktsestugorna
Laitaure
Kuorpak
Stora
Lulevatten
Alloluokta
kapell
Sandviken
Kables
1090
Tjaktjajaure
NORRBOTTENS
LÄN
Nietsak
Kronsågen
Porjus
Muddus
national
park
Harsprånget
Tapmok
629
Skaite
Stora Luleälven
Urtimjaur
Rutna
Råneälven
Sarkavare
Njetsavare
Harrejaure
Nattavaara
Nattavaara by
Ranesvare
552
Stubbuden
Messaure
Juggijaur
Solberget
Njavve
Tjåmotis
Skalka
Nautijaur
Björkholmen
Randijaur
976
Farforita
Karatjaure
Karats
Luvos
Randijaure
Framnäs
Vajkijaur
Purkijaur
Piertinjaure
Jokkmokk
Polcirklen
Arctic Circle
810
Harrevardo
Parlälven
Parlan
Mattisudden
Sierre
naturreservat
Nedre
Kuouka
Anutkaski
Vajmat
Lilla Luleälven
Sjöllanim
Padje-
rimf.
Porsifors
Murjek
Vuollerim
Tårrajaur
Görjeån
Vuolvojaure
Naustapuouta
745
Raketskjutfält
Mörtberg
Stenträsk
Kåpponis
Koikul
Furunäs
Sudok
Storsand
Lilläfors
Mårdsel
Forsnäs
Båtsa
Kronogård
Lillå
Edefors
Laxede
Forsnäs
374
Puottaure
Bodträskån
Brändberg
769
Stuor Ståkke
Kåbdalis
Snesudden
Alpas
Kokheden
15
Jäknajaure
Kuollejaur
Njakaure
Svannäs
Gublijaure
Abraur
Jäkna
Abraure
Trollforsen
Norden
157
Bäverudden
Karlsro
Bodträsk
fors
Edefors
Harads
Mörtträsk
135
Gransjö
Johannestorp
Södra
Harads
Öv. Svartlå
Trollberget
Åberget
Hapträsk
Rödingsträsk
Åkerby
Östansjö
Suddesjaur
Malmesjaure
Piteälven
Skiän
Öv. Brännträsk
Staträsk
Bredåker
Silvervägen
Moskosel
Myrheden
Bredsel
Björkberg
Åkerholmen
Långsjön
Reivo-
reservatet
Sleng
Ljusträsk
Vidsel
Storforsen
Vitträsk
Vaksliden
Piltträsk
Grundvattnet
Östrand
Istrask
Heden
Vändträsk
Auktsjaur
Tallsund
Ö. Granberg
Manjärv
Öv. Tväråselet
V. Kikkejaure
Långträsket
Kronogård
Rönnberg
Njallejaur
Nystrand
Svedjan
Pite-
Altervattnet
282
Renviken
Öv. Långträsk
Åkroken
Stridbäck
Vistheden
Älvsbyn
Nordbyn
Gullön
Renvallen
Akkavare
Vuotner
Lauker
Öv. Grundsel
Storfinnträsk
Korsträsk
Brännberget
Avaviken
Klappen
Vittjåkk
724
Arvidsjaur
Renträsk
N. Holmnäs
S. Brännträsk
Arvidsträsk
Klöverträsk
Månsträsk
Grundträskliden
Dartsel
Storsund
Björklund
Storberg
Byskeälven
Krokforsen
Pjesker
Åbyälven
Granträsk
Sikfors
Holmträsk
Gråträsk
Bergbacka
Kolerträsk
Koler
Tallträsk
Skellefteälven
Nya Bastuselet
Hedberg
Norrbacka
Abborrträsk
Grundträsk
Brattknabben
Norrfjärden
Boksel
Siksjön
Strömfors
Åträsk
Adakgruvan
Adak
Rönnås
Hålberg
Näverliden
Långträsk
Storgranliden
408
Kilberget
Lillpite
Bölebyn
Kokträsk
Baktsjaur
Rönnliden
Utterliden
Kåtaselet
Finnmyren
Önusberg
Stockbäcken
Rokna
Öjebyn
Piteå
Tjernberg
Brännberg
Lappträsk
Glommersträsk
Myrheden
Svensbyn
Bergsviken
Hortlax
Stensund
Malå-Vännäs
Lainijaur
Springliden
Högheden
Ullbergsträsk
Åfors
Granträsk-
mark
Blåsmark
Slappträsket
Björkliden
Stenstrask
Åselet
Hemmingsmark
Malå
Grundträsk
Grönbo
Klubbfors
Holmfors
Slappträsk
Strömfors
Gallejaur
Storträsk
Melsträsk
Jävre
Högberget
Silvervägen
Degerträsk
Gammelboliden
Alunsdby
Fällfors
Finnträsk
Gagsmark
Horntråsk
Röka
Rentjarn
Mälån
Granbergsliden
31
Brännäs
Kristineberg
Amliden
Petikträsk
Ö. Åliden
Nygård
Klöverfors
Hällfors
Åbyälven
Javre
Kinnbäck
84
Björksele
Lillholmträsk
Linbana
Jörn
Stavaträsk
Abyn

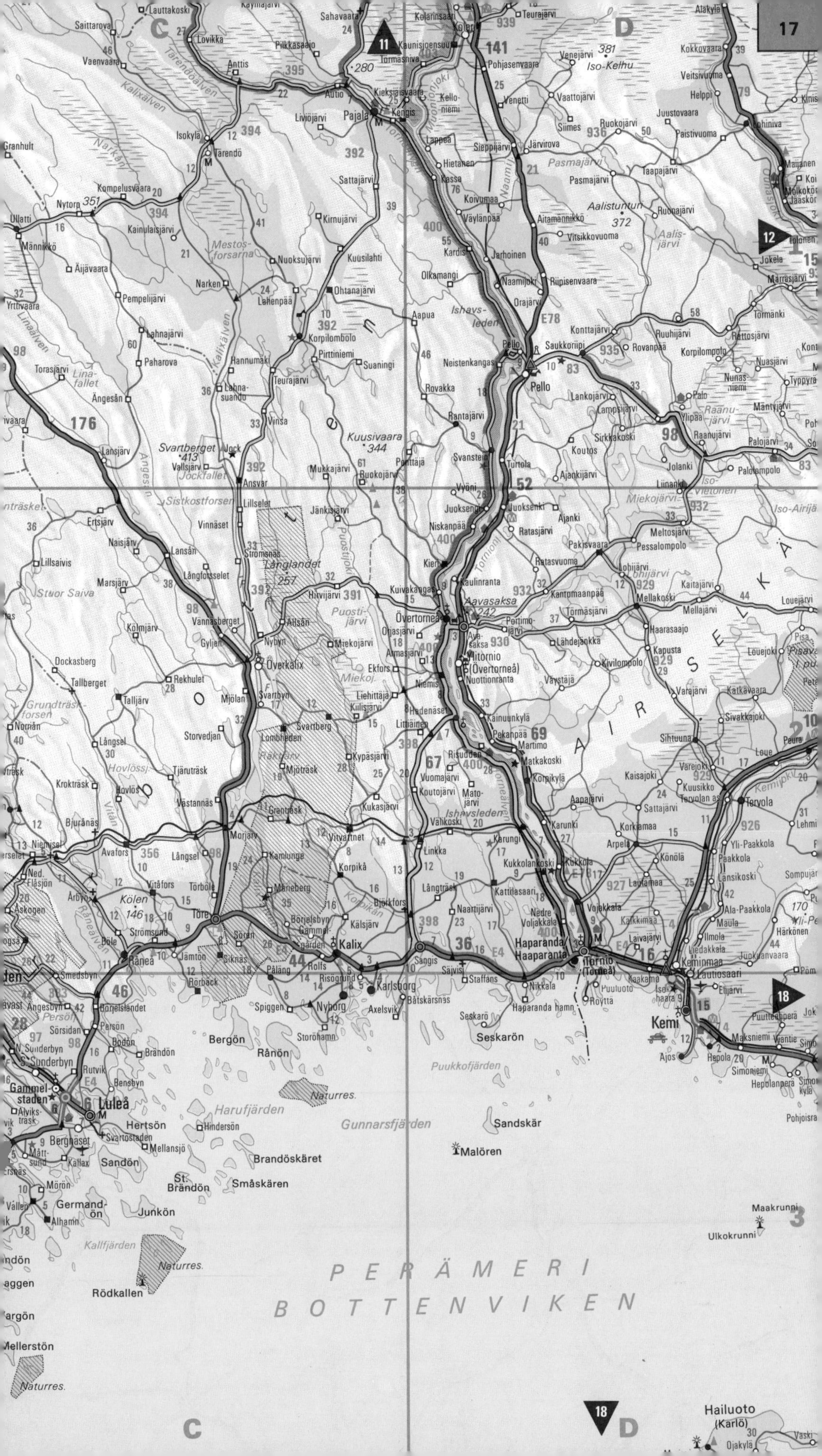
17
C
D
11
12
18
18
C
D
Lauttakoski
Saittarova
Lovikka
Pilkkasaajo
Sahavaara
Kolarinsaari
Kolari
Teurajärvi
Alakylä
Vaenvaara
Anttis
Kaunisjoensuu
Tormasniva
280
Pohjasenvaara
Venejärvi
381
Iso-Kelhu
Kokkovaara
Tärendöälven
Kalixälven
Autio
Kieksisjaisvaara
Kengis
Pajala
Kello-niemi
Venetti
Vaattojärvi
Veitsivuoma
Helppi
Kinisjärvi
Liviöjärvi
Siimes
Ruokojärvi
Juustovaara
Lohiniva
Granhult
Narkån
Isokylä
Tärendö
Lappea
Sieppijärvi
Järvirova
Paistivuoma
Hietanen
Pasmajärvi
Taapajärvi
Maijanen
Molkokönkäs
Jääskö
Kompelusvaara
Nytorp
351
Sattajärvi
Kassa
Koivumaa
Väylänpää
Aalistunturi
372
Ruonajärvi
Ullatti
Männikkö
Kainulaisjärvi
Kirnujärvi
Aitamännikkö
Vitsikkovuoma
Aalis-järvi
Mestos-forsarna
Kardis
Jarhoinen
Tolonen
Äijävaara
Nuoksujärvi
Kuusilahti
Jokela
Narken
Olkamangi
Naamijoki
Riipisenvaara
Marrasjärvi
Yrttivaara
Pempelijärvi
Lahenpää
Ohtanajärvi
Orajärvi
Linaälven
Ishavs-leden
Aapua
E78
Tormänki
Lahnajärvi
Korpilombolo
Konttajärvi
Ruuhijärvi
Rattosjärvi
Saukkoriipi
Rovanpää
Korpilompolo
Paharova
Kalixälven
Pirttiniemi
Suaningi
Neistenkangas
Pello
Nuasjärvi
Nunas-niemi
Typpyrä
Torasjärvi
Lina-fallet
Hannumaki
Teurajärvi
Lankojärvi
Lampsijärvi
Palo
Raanu-järvi
Mäntyjärvi
Ängesån
Lahna-suando
Rovakka
Ylipää
Raanujärvi
Vinsa
Rantajärvi
Sirkkakoski
Palojärvi
Kuusivaara
344
Lansjärv
Svartberget
413
Jock
Vallsjärv
Jockfallet
Angesån
Ansvar
Mukkajärvi
Ruokojärvi
Penttäjä
Svanstein
Turtola
Koutos
Ajankijärvi
Jolanki
Paloiompolo
Liinanki
Iso-Vietonen
Miekojärvi
Sistkostforsen
Lillselet
Vyöni
Juoksenki
Ajanki
Iso-Airijärvi
Ertsjärv
Vinnäset
Jänkisjärvi
Puostijoki
Niskanpää
Ratasjärvi
Meltosjärvi
Naisjärv
Strömsnäs
Pakisvaara
Pessalompolo
Lillsaivis
Långlandet
257
Kieri
Ratasvuoma
Lohijärvi
Lånsån
Långfotsselet
Tornionjoki
Kaulinranta
Marsjärv
Kuivakangas
Kantomaanpää
Mellakoski
Kaitajärvi
Stuor Saiva
Hirvijärvi
Aavasaksa
242
Louejärvi
Vännäsberget
Puosti-järvi
Övertorneå
Portimo-järvi
Törmäsjärvi
Mellajärvi
Allsån
Orjasjärvi
Ava-saksa
Haarasaajo
Kölmjärv
Gyljen
Nybyn
Miekojärvi
Ylitornio
(Övertorneå)
Lähdejänkkä
Kapusta
Louejoki
Pisavaara
Dockasberg
Överkalix
Armasjärvi
Nuottionranta
Kivilompolo
Tallberget
Rekhulet
Ekfors
Miekoj.
Väystäjä
Niemis
Varajärvi
Katkävaara
Talljärv
Mjölan
Svartbyn
Liehittäjä
Hedenäset
Kainuunkylä
Grundträsk-forsen
Kiilisjärvi
Sivakkajoki
Norrån
Svartberg
Littiäinen
Pekanpää
Martimo
Storvedjan
Lombheden
Sihtuuna
Peura
Långsel
Risudden
Loue
Hovlössj.
Kypäsjärvi
Matkakoski
Tjäruträsk
Rakträsk
Mjöträsk
Vuomajärvi
Korpikylä
Krokträsk
Hovlös
Koutojärvi
Mato-järvi
Kaisajoki
Varejoki
Kuusikko
Tervolan as
Tervola
Västannäs
Kukasjärvi
Grenträsk
Ishavsleden
Aapajärvi
Sattajärvi
Bjurånäs
Vitån
Välikoski
Karunki
Korkiamaa
Lehmi
Niemisel
Avafors
Långsel
Morjärv
Vitvattnet
Karungi
Arpela
Yli-Paakkola
Kamlunge
Linkka
Paakkola
Ned. Flåsjön
Vitåfors
Korpikå
Kukkolankoski
Kukkola
Könölä
Länsikoski
Sompujärvi
Arbyn
Töreboda
Långträsk
Kattilasaari
Lautamaa
Kölen
146
Maneberg
Björkfors
Ala-Paakkola
Åskogen
Råneälven
Strömsund
Töre
Börjelsbyn
Naartijärvi
Nedre Voljakkala
Voljakkala
Kalkkimaa
Maula
Härkönen
Gammel-gården
Kälsjärv
Kalix
Ilmola
Laivajärvi
Liedakkala
Bole
Sören
Haparanda/
Haaparanta
Tornio
(Torneå)
Keminmaa
Jyvänvaara
Råneå
Jämtön
Siknäs
Rolfs
Sangis
Säjvis
Lautiosaari
Smedsbyn
Rörbäck
Påläng
Risögrund
Karlsborg
Staffans
Nikkala
Kaakamo
Puuluoto
Iso-haara
Eliljärvi
Ängesbyn
Börjelslandet
Spiggen
Nyborg
Båtskärsnäs
Haparanda hamn
Röyttä
Kemi
Sörsidan
Person
Axelsvik
Seskarö
Puuttehpera
Bodön
Bergön
Storöhamn
Seskarön
Maksniemi
N. Sunderbyn
Brändön
Rånön
Ajos
Hepola
S. Sunderbyn
Rutvik
Puukkofjärden
Simoniemi
Gammel-staden
Bensbyn
Naturres.
Hepolanperä
Luleå
Harufjärden
Alviks-träsk
Hertsön
Hindersön
Gunnarsfjärden
Sandskär
Pohjoisranta
Bergnäset
Svartöstaden
Mellansjö
Måt-sund
Kallax
Sandön
Brandöskäret
Malören
St. Brändön
Småskären
Mörön
Germand-ön
Vallen
Alhamn
Junkön
Maakrunni
Ulkokrunni
Kallfjärden
Naturres.
Rödkallen
PERÄMERI
BOTTENVIKEN
Mellerstön
Naturres.
Hailuoto
(Karlö)
Ojakylä
Vaski

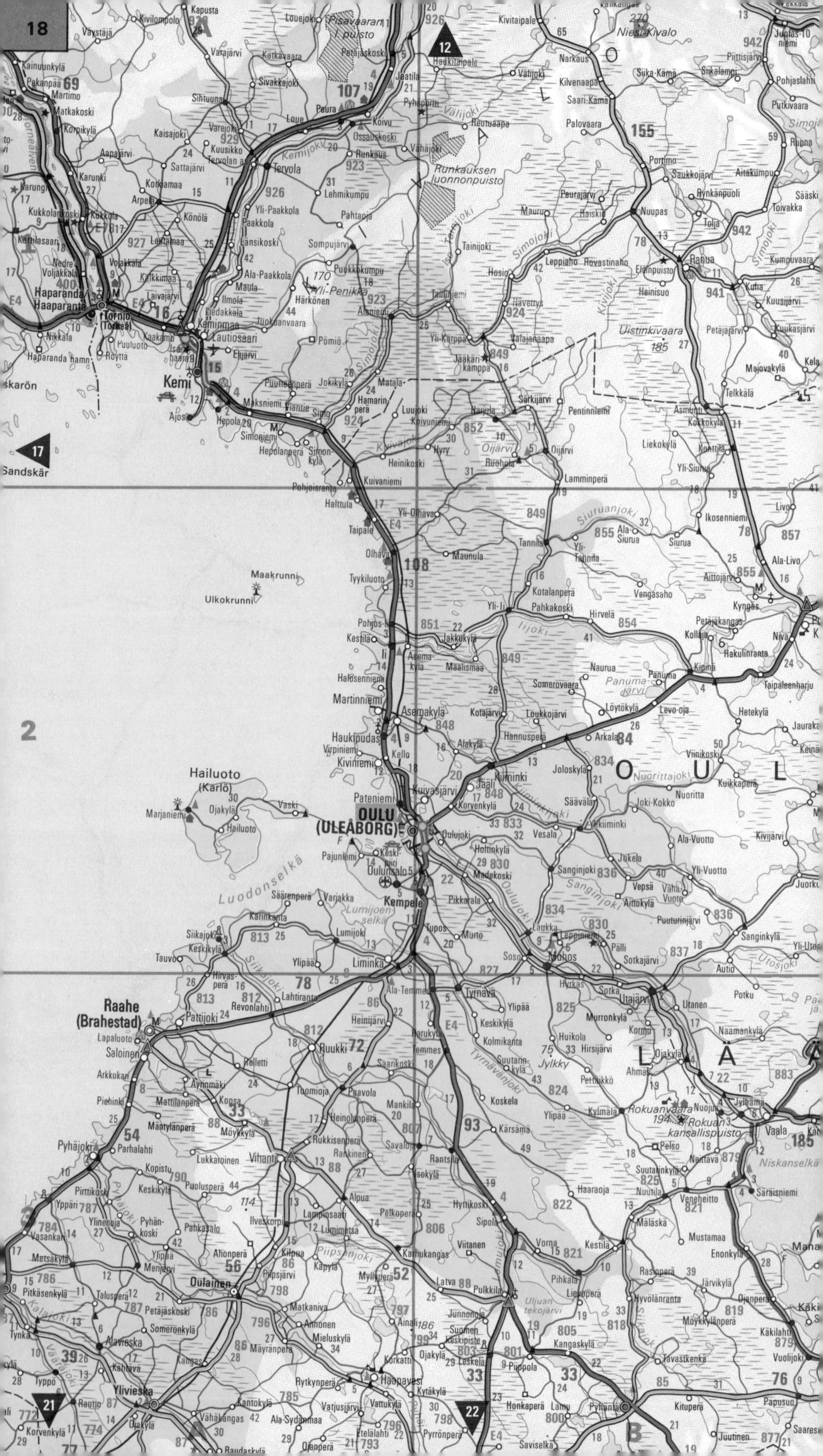
12
17
21
22
2
Väystäjä
Kivilompolo
Kapusta
Louejoki
Pisavaaran l. puisto
Petäjäskoski
Jaatila
Haukitaipale
Kivitaipale
Niesi-Kivalo
Narkaus
Vähäjoki
Kilvenaapa
Saari-Kämä
Palovaara
Siika-Kämä
Siikalampi
Juntas-niemi
Piittisjärvi
Pohjaslahti
Putkivaara
Rupina
Kainuunkylä
Pakanpää
Martimo
Matkakoski
Korpikylä
Varajärvi
Kätkävaara
Sivakkajoki
Sihtuuna
Varejoki
Kaisajoki
Kuusikko
Tervolan as.
Tervola
Peura
Koivu
Ossauskoski
Runkaus
Reutuaapa
Pyhäportti
Välijoki
Runkauksen luonnonpuisto
Kemijoki
Aapajärvi
Karunki
Sattajärvi
Korkiamaa
Arpela
Könölä
Lehmikumpu
Yli-Paakkola
Paakkola
Länsikoski
Pahtaoja
Sompujärvi
Tainijoki
Portimo
Saukkojärvi
Aitakumpu
Rynkänpuoli
Toivakka
Peurajärvi
Raiskio
Mauru
Nuupas
Tolja
Kukkolankoski
Kukkola
Kattilasaari
Nedre Voljakkala
Voljakkala
Laitamaa
Kalkkimaa
Ala-Paakkola
Puukkokumpu
Yli-Penikka
Härkönen
Ilmola
Eteläkylä
Laivajärvi
Leppiaho
Rovastinaho
Simojoki
Hosio
Eläinpuisto
Ranua
Heinisuo
Kumpuvaara
Kuha
Kuusijärvi
Haparanda
Haaparanta
Tornio (Torneå)
Nikkala
Puuluoto
Röyttä
Haparanda hamn
Keminmaa
Lautiosaari
Eljärvi
Juokuanvaara
Pömiö
Alaniemi
Taininiemi
Yli-Karppa
Jääkäri-kamppa
Haverys
Valajanaapa
Uistinkivaara
Petäjäjärvi
Kuukasjärvi
Majovakylä
Telkkälä
Asmunti
Kemi
Ajos
Maksniemi
Viantie
Simo
Puutteenperä
Jokikylä
Matala
Hamarinperä
Luujoki
Koivuniemi
Narkula
Sarkijärvi
Pentinniemi
Kotkokylä
Liekokylä
Konttila
Yli-Siurua
Hepola
Simoniemi
Hepolanperä
Simonkylä
Heinikoski
Hyry
Kuivajoki
Oijärvi
Ruohola
Lamminperä
Sandskär
Pohjoisranta
Kuivaniemi
Halttula
Taipale
Yli-Olhava
Olhava
Maunula
Tannila
Yli-Tannila
Siuruanjoki
Ala-Siurua
Siurua
Ikosenniemi
Livo
Ala-Livo
Aittojärvi
Kyngäs
Vengasaho
Kotalanperä
Pahkakoski
Hirvelä
Yli-Ii
Maakrunni
Ulkokrunni
Tyykiluoto
Pohjois-Ii
Kestilä
Ii
Jakkukylä
Asemakylä
Maalismaa
Iijoki
Petäjäkangas
Kollaja
Hakulinranta
Niva
Kipinä
Taipaleenharju
Halosenniemi
Martinniemi
Asemakylä
Kotajärvi
Loukkojärvi
Naurua
Panuma
Panumajärvi
Somerovaara
Löytökylä
Levo-oja
Hetekylä
Haukipudas
Virpiniemi
Kiviniemi
Kello
Alakylä
Hannusperä
Arkala
Joloskylä
Viinikoski
Kuikkaperä
Nuoritta
Nuorittajoki
OULU
Hailuoto (Karlö)
Marjaniemi
Ojakylä
Hailuoto
Vaski
Pateniemi
Kuivasjärvi
Jääli
Kiiminki
Korvenkylä
Säävälä
Ylikiiminki
Joki-Kokko
OULU (ULEÅBORG)
Oulujoki
Vesala
Ala-Vuotto
Kivijärvi
Pajuniemi
Keskipiiri
Oulunsalo
Kempele
Holtinkylä
Madekoski
Sanginjoki
Jukela
Yli-Vuotto
Vepsä
Vähä Vuoto
Aittokylä
Luodonselkä
Säärenperä
Varjakka
Lumijoenselkä
Pikkarala
Puuturinjärvi
Siikajoki
Karinkanta
Lumijoki
Tupos
Murto
Laukka
Leppiniemi
Pälli
Sanginkylä
Keskikylä
Ylipää
Liminka
Soso
Muhos
Sotkajärvi
Autio
Tauvo
Hirvasperä
Lahtiranta
Revonlahti
Ala-Temmes
Tyrnävä
Hyrkäs
Sotka
Utajärvi
Utanen
Potku
Raahe (Brahestad)
Pattijoki
Lapaluoto
Saloinen
Heinijärvi
Ruukki
Harukylä
Temmes
Keskikylä
Kolmikanta
Murronkylä
Huikola
Hirsijärvi
Kormu
Ojakylä
Naamankylä
Arkkukari
Relletti
Ayrinmäki
Saarikoski
Suutarinkylä
Jylkky
Pettäikkö
Ahmas
Piehinki
Mattilanperä
Toumioja
Paavola
Mankila
Tyrnävänjoki
Koskela
Kylmälä
Rokuanvaara
Rokuan kansallispuisto
Nuojua
Jylhämä
Vaala
Mäntylänperä
Kopsa
Möykkylä
Heinolanperä
Rukkisenperä
Kärsämä
Ylipää
Pelso
Neittävä
Niskanselkä
Pyhäjoki
Parhalahti
Lukkaroinen
Vihanti
Rankinen
Savaloja
Rantsila
Suutarinkylä
Nuutila
Veneheitto
Säräisniemi
Pirttikoski
Kopistu
Keskikylä
Puolusperä
Ilveskorpi
Alpua
Isokylä
Hyttikoski
Haaraoja
Mäläskä
Yppäri
Ylinenoja
Pyhänkoski
Lampinsaari
Lumimetsä
Pelkoperä
Sipola
Vasankari
Pahkasalo
Metsäkylä
Ylipää
Merijärvi
Ahonperä
Kilpua
Kapylä
Karhukangas
Viitanen
Vorna
Kestilä
Mustamaa
Enonkylä
Pitkäsenkylä
Talusperä
Oulainen
Piipsjärvi
Myllyperä
Piipsanjoki
Latva
Pulkkila
Pihkala
Lievoperä
Rasinperä
Järvikylä
Petäjäskoski
Somerokylä
Matkaniva
Annonen
Mieluskylä
Ainali
Junnonoja
Suomenkeskipiste
Leskelä
Piippola
Uljuan tekojärvi
Hyvölänranta
Kangaskylä
Ojanperä
Möykkylänperä
Käkilahti
Vuolijoki
Tynkä
Alavieska
Kahtava
Kangas
Mäyränperä
Korkatti
Ojakylä
Tavastkenkä
Typpö
Ylivieska
Rautio
Kantokylä
Rytkynperä
Haapavesi
Kytäkylä
Vattukylä
Vatjusjärvi
Pyhäntä
Kitupera
Papusuo
Honkaperä
Lamu
Korvenkylä
Vähäkangas
Ojakylä
Ala-Sydänmaa
Etelälahti
Pyrrönperä
Saviselkä
Juutinen
Ojanperä
Baudaskylä

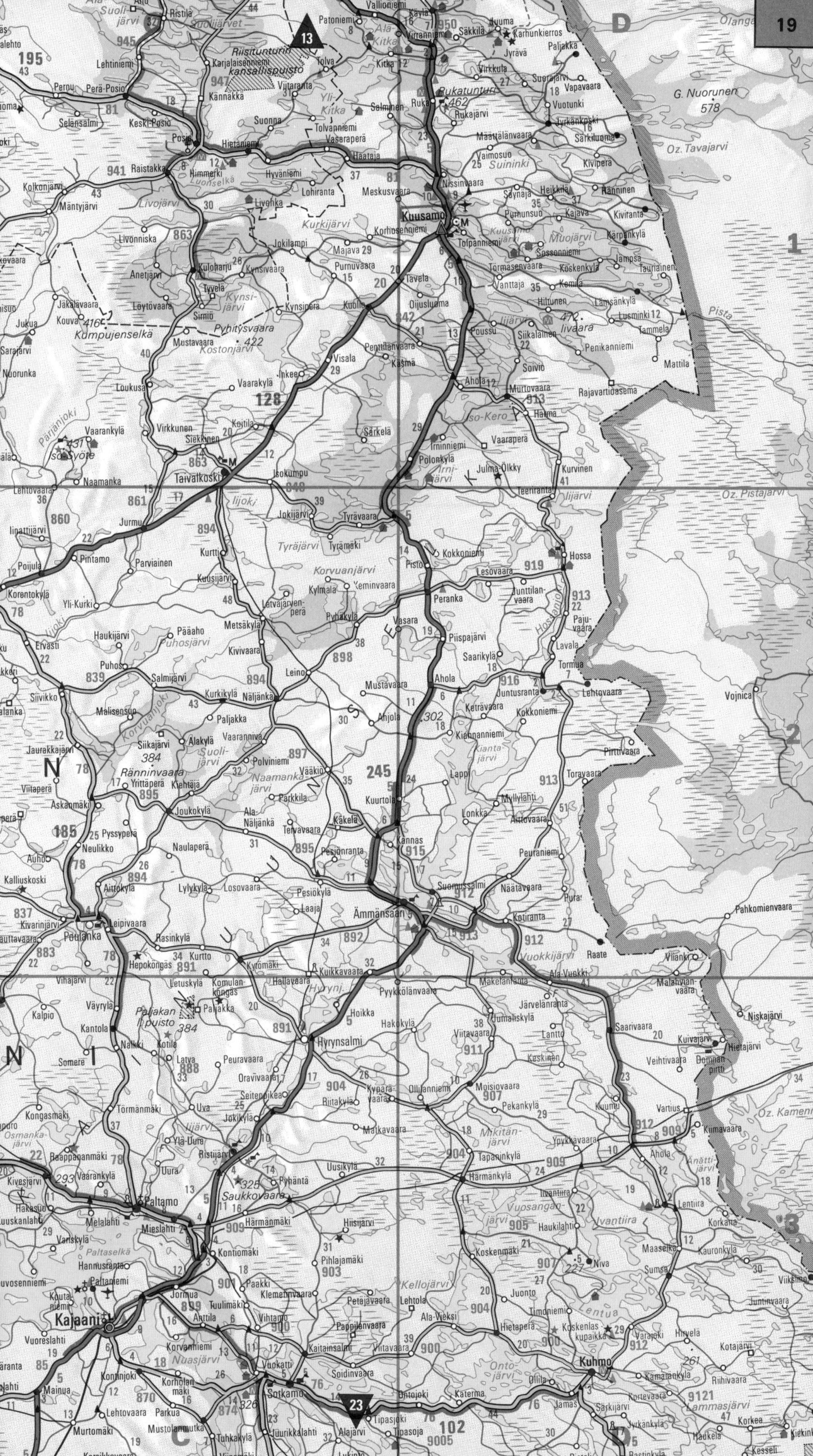
Suolijärvi
Ristilä
Suolijärvet
Vallioniemi
Käylä
Patoniemi
Ala-Kitka
Virranniemi
Säkkilä
Juuma
Karhunkierros
Jyrävä
Paljakka
Olanga
Lehtiniemi
Riisitunturin kansallispuisto
Karjalaisenniemi
Tolva
Kitka
Virkkula
Suorajärvi
Vapavaara
Perä-Posio
Kännäkkä
Vijtaranta
Yli-Kitka
Rukatunturi
462
Ruka
Vuotunki
G. Nuorunen
578
Selänsalmi
Keski-Posio
Suonna
Salminen
Rukajärvi
Jyrkänkoski
Tolvanniemi
Vasaraperä
Särkiluoma
Posio
Hietaniemi
Määttälänvaara
Oz. Tavajärvi
Raistakka
Himmerki
Luonselkä
Hyvänniemi
Haataja
Vaimosuo
Suininki
Kivipera
Kolkonjärvi
Lohiranta
Meskusvaara
Nissinvaara
Säynäjä
Heikkilä
Hänninen
Mäntyjärvi
Livojärvi
Livonka
Kuusamo
Purhunsuo
Kajava
Kivitanta
Kurkijärvi
Korhosenniemi
Kuusamojärvi
Muojärvi
Kärpänkylä
Livonniska
Jokilampi
Majava
Tolpanniemi
Sossonniemi
Kulohariu
Kynsivaara
Purnuvaara
Tavela
Törmäsenvaara
Koskenkylä
Jämpsä
Tauriainen
Anetjärvi
Tyvelä
Kynsijärvi
Vanttaja
Komila
Jäkälävaara
Löytövaara
Kynsiperä
Kuolio
Oijusluoma
Hiltunen
Lämsänkylä
Jukua
Kouva
Kumpujenselkä
Simiö
Pyhitysvaara
422
Iijärvi
472
Iivaara
Lusminki
Tammela
Pista
Mustavaara
Kostonjärvi
Poussu
Siikalainen
Penttilänvaara
Penikanniemi
Mattila
Sarajärvi
Nuorunka
Visala
Inkee
Käsmä
Soivio
Vaarakylä
Loukusa
Aholа
Murtovaara
Rajavartioasema
Harma
Iso-Kero
Pärjänjoki
Vaarankylä
Virkkunen
Koitila
Siekkinen
Särkelä
Irninniemi
Vaaraperä
431
Iso-Syöte
Taivalkoski
Isokumpu
Polonkylä
Irnijärvi
Julma-Ölkky
Kurvinen
Naamanka
Lehtovaara
Jurmu
Iijoki
Jokijärvi
Tyrävaara
Teeriranta
Oz. Pistajärvi
Iinattijärvi
Tyräjärvi
Tyrämäki
Pisto
Kokkoniemi
Hossa
Poijula
Pintamo
Parviainen
Kurtti
Korvuanjärvi
Keminvaara
Kusijärvi
Kylmälä
Lesovaara
Peranka
Korentokylä
Latvajärvenperä
Junttilanvaara
Pajuvaara
Yli-Kurki
Metsäkylä
Pyhäkylä
Vasara
Pääaho
Puhosjärvi
Haukijärvi
Piispajärvi
Lavala
Hossanjoki
Ervasti
Kivivaara
Saarikylä
Tormua
Puhos
Salmijärvi
Leino
Ahola
Juntusranta
Lehtovaara
Vojnica
Siivikko
Malisensuo
Kurkikylä
Näljänkä
Mustavaara
Keträvaara
Kokkoniemi
Korvuanjoki
Paljakka
Anjola
302
Kiannanniemi
Siikajärvi
Alakylä
Suolijärvi
Vaaranniva
Kiantajärvi
Pirttivaara
Jaurakkajärvi
Polviniemi
384
Ränninvaara
Vääkiö
Lappi
Toravaara
Yrittäperä
Kiehtäjä
Naamankajärvi
Myllylahti
Viitaperä
Askanmäki
Joukokylä
Parkkila
Kuurtola
Lonkka
Aittovaara
Ala-Näljänkä
Pyssyperä
Tervavaara
Käkelä
Kannas
Neulikko
Naulaperä
Pesionranta
Peuraniemi
Auho
Kalliuskoski
Aittokylä
Lylykylä
Losovaara
Pesiökylä
Suomussalmi
Näätävaara
Puras
Pahkomienvaara
Kivarinjärvi
Leipivaara
Laaja
Ämmänsaari
Kotiranta
Poulanka
Rasinkylä
Hepokongäs
Kurtto
Kytömäki
Vuokkijärvi
Raate
Vlianki
Vihajärvi
Letuskylä
Komulankongäs
Hallavaara
Kuikkavaara
Hyrynj.
Pyykkölänvaara
Mäkelänranta
Ala-Vuokki
Malahvianvaara
Kalpio
Väyrylä
Paljakan l. puisto
Paljakka
Hoikka
Hakokylä
Järvelänranta
Jumaliskylä
Niskajärvi
Kantola
Nalkki
Kotila
Hyrynsalmi
Viitavaara
Saarivaara
Lantto
Kuivajärvi
Hietajärvi
Somere
Latva
Peuravaara
Keskinen
Veihtivaara
Domnan pirtti
Oravivaara
Seitenoikea
Kyparävaara
Ollijanniemi
Moisiovaara
Pekankylä
Uva
Riitakylä
Vartius
Oz. Kamenn
Törmänmäki
Jokikylä
Kongasmäki
Osmankajärvi
Iijärvi
Ylä-Uura
Matkavaara
Mikitänjärvi
Yöykkävaara
Kuumu
Kuivavaara
Kumavaara
Raappananmäki
Ristijärvi
Tapaninkylä
Ahola
Änättijärvi
Kivesjärvi
293
Vaarankylä
Uura
Uusikylä
Härmänkylä
325
Pyhäntä
Saukkovaara
Lentiira
Hakasuo
Paltamo
Ilvantiira
Kuuskanlahti
Melalahti
Mieslahti
Härmänmäki
Haukilahti
Ivantiira
Vupsanganjärvi
Korkana
Varisklyä
Paltaselkä
Hiisijärvi
Koskenmäki
Niva
227
Maaselkä
Kauronkylä
Hannusranta
Kontiomäki
Pihlajamäki
Sumsa
Viiksimo
Leuvosenniemi
Paltaniemi
Paakki
Klemetinvaara
Kellojärvi
Juonto
Kouta
Jormua
Tuulimäki
Petäjävaara
Lehtola
Timoniemi
Juntinvaara
Kajaani
Anttila
Vihtamo
Ala-Vieksi
Lentua
Vuoreslahti
Korvanniemi
Pappilanvaara
Hietaperä
Koskenlaskupaikka
Varajoki
Hirvelä
Nuasjärvi
Kaitainsalmi
Viitavaara
Kotajärvi
Kontinjoki
Korholanmäki
Vuokatti
Soidinvaara
Ontojärvi
Ollila
Kuhmo
261
Mainua
Sotkamo
326
Kamarankylä
Riihivaara
Lehtovaara
Parkua
Ontojoki
Katerma
Kortevaara
Lammasjärvi
Murtomäki
Mustolanmutka
Tipasjoki
Jamas
Särkijärvi
Korkea
Tuhkakylä
Juurikkalahti
Alajärvi
Tipasoja
Jyrkänkylä
Haukela
Kieksi
Kesseli
Karsikkovaara
Lykinto
Bastinkylä
D
N
N
I
A
C
E
S
U
K
Y
1
2
3

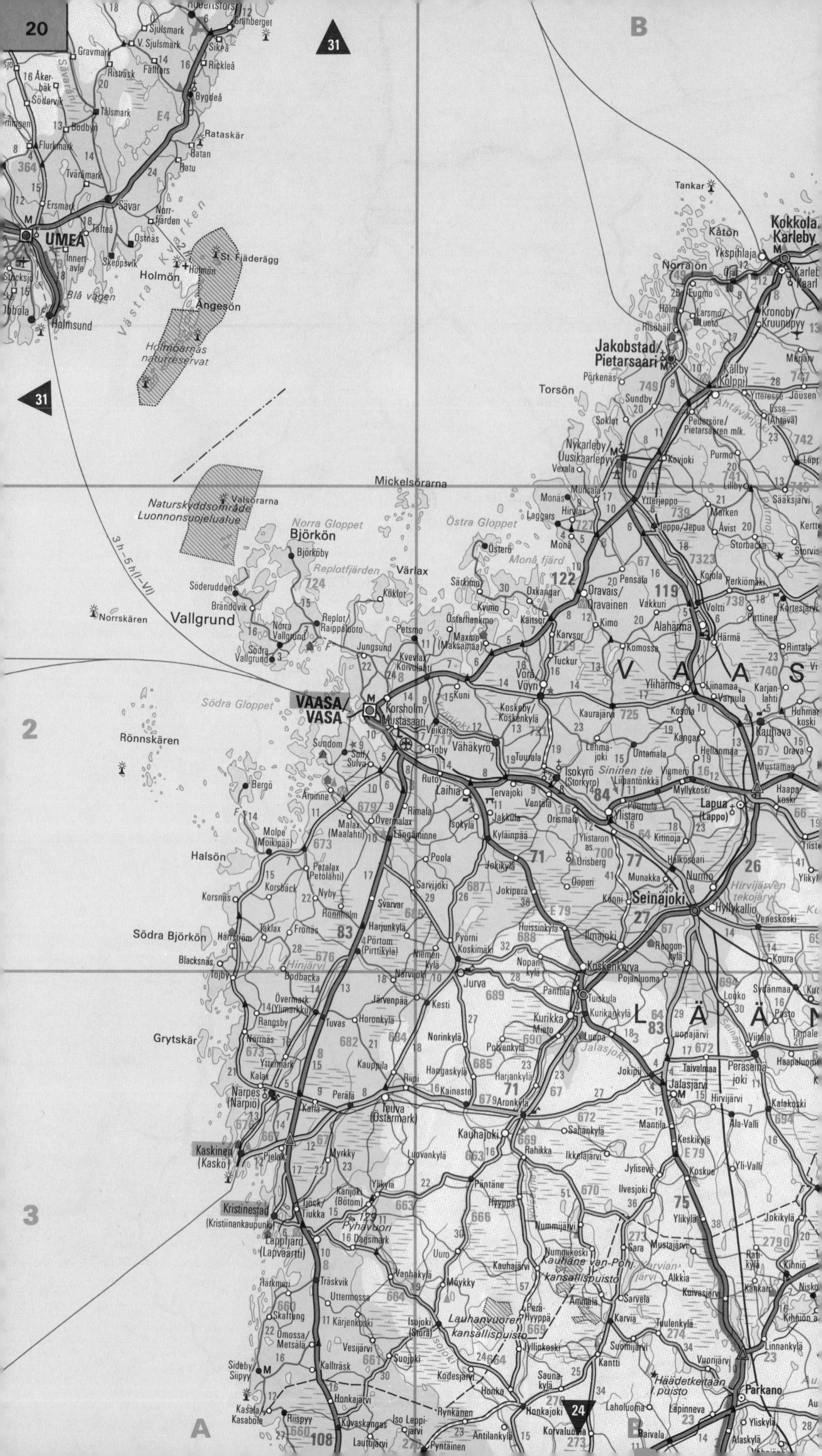
31
B
Sjulsmark
Granberget
V. Sjulsmark
Gravmark
Sikeå
Risträsk
Fällfors
Rickleå
Åkerbäk
Södervik
Bygdeå
Tålsmark
Bodbyn
E4
Rataskär
Flurkmark
Ratan
Ratu
364
Tvärålmark
Ersmark
Sävar
Norrfjärden
Täfteå
UMEÅ
Ostnäs
Innertavle
Skeppsvik
St. Fjäderägg
Holmön
Holmön
Stöcksjö
Blå vägen
Västra Kvarken
Ängesön
Obbola
Holmsund
Holmöarnas naturreservat
31
Tankar
Kokkola/
Karleby
Kåtön
Ykspihlaja
Norra ön
749
Eugmo
Larsmo/
Luoto
Kronoby/
Kruunupyy
Risöhäll
Jakobstad/
Pietarsaari
Märjärv
Pörkenäs
Kållby
(Kolppi)
747
Torsön
749
Jousen
Sundby
Ytteresse
Esse
(Ähtävä)
Soklot
Ähtävänjoki
Pedersöre/
Pietarsaaren mlk.
742
Nykarleby/
Uusikaarlepyy
Kovjoki
Purmo
Vexala
741
Lillby
Mickelsörarna
Munsala
Monäs
Ytterjeppo
Sääksjärvi
Hirvlax
739
Naturskyddsområde
Luonnonsuojelualue
Valsörarna
Laggars
727
Jeppo/Jepua
Marken
Ävist
Norra Gloppet
Östra Gloppet
Björkön
Monå
Storbacka
Björköby
Östero
7323
Monå fjärd
Replotfjärden
Värlax
67
724
Pensala
Kojola
Perkiömäki
Söderudden
Särkimo
122
119
Oxkangar
Oravais/
Oravainen
Köklot
Vakkuri
Voltti
738
Kortesjärvi
Brändövik
Kvimo
Replot/
Raippaluoto
Pirttinen
Vallgrund
Österhankmo
Kaitsor
Kimo
Alahärmä
Norrskären
Norra Vallgrund
Maxmo
(Maksamaa)
Karvsor
729
Härmä
Petsmo
Komossa
Rintala
Södra
Vallgrund
Jungsund
Tuckur
Kvevlax/
Koivulahti
V A A S
740
Vörå/
Vöyri
Ylihärmä
Liinamaa
Varpula
Karjanlahti
Södra Gloppet
VAASA/
VASA
Kuni
Korsholm/
Mustasaari
Koskeby/
Koskenkylä
Kaurajärvi
725
Kosola
Humnarkoski
2
Veikars
Kyrönjoki
Kauhava
Rönnskären
Sundom
717
Vähäkyrö
731
Lehmäjoki
Kangas
Toby
Untamala
Hellanmaa
Orava
Solf/
Sulva
Tuurala
Isokyrö
(Storkyrö)
Sininen tie
Vimero
Mustamaa
Ruto
Liipantönkkä
Myllykoski
Haapakoski
Bergö
Laihia
Tervajoki
84
Lapua
(Lappo)
Äminne
Ventälä
Pouttula
66
Jakkula
Orismala
Ylistaro
Malax
(Maalahti)
679
Rimala
Övermalax
Isokylä
Kitinoja
Långåminne
Kyläinpää
Ylistaron as.
Molpe
(Moikipää)
673
71
700
77
Halsön
Poola
Jokikylä
Orisberg
Halkosaari
Nurmo
26
Petalax
(Petolahti)
Munakka
Sarvijoki
687
Ooperi
Hirvijärven tekojärvi
Korsbäck
Jokiperä
Korsnäs
Nyby
Könni
Seinäjoki
Hyllykallio
Svarvar
E 79
27
Ronnholm
685
Veneskoski
Taklax
Fronäs
83
Harjunkylä
Huissinkylä
688
Ilmajoki
Södra Björkön
Härstrom
Pyörni
Koskimäki
Rengonkylä
Pörtom
(Pirttikylä)
Niemenkylä
Nopankylä
Koskenkorva
Blacksnäs
Hinjärvi
676
Koura
Töjby
Bodbacka
Närvijoki
Jurva
Pojanluoma
Panttila
Tuiskula
694
Sydänmaa
Övermark
(Ylimarkku)
Järvenpää
Kesti
689
Louko
Rangsby
Kurikka
Kurikankylä
L Ä Ä N
Mieto
Pasto
Grytskär
Tuvas
Horonkylä
64
83
Norrnäs
682
684
Norinkylä
690
Luopa
Luopajärvi
Viitala
673
Polvenkylä
Jalasjoki
672
Ytermark
Kauppila
Hangaskylä
685
Harjankylä
Jokipii
Peräseinäjoki
Kalax
Taivalmaa
71
Riipi
Kainasto
Jalasjärvi
Närpes
(Närpiö)
Perälä
679
Aronkylä
Hirvijärvi
Kaila
Teuva
(Östermark)
Kalakoski
672
Mantila
Ala-Valli
Sahankylä
694
Kaskinen
(Kaskö)
Pjelax
Myrkky
669
Keskikylä
Kauhajoki
Rahikka
Ikkelajärvi
E 79
Luovankylä
663
Jylisevä
Koskue
Yli-Valli
Karijoki
(Bötom)
Ylikylä
Päntäne
670
Ilvesjoki
3
Tjöck/
Tiukka
Hyyppä
75
Kristinestad
(Kristiinankaupunki)
Pyhävuori
663
666
Ylikylä
Jokikylä
Nummijärvi
Lappfjärd
(Lapvaartti)
Dagsmark
273
Sara
Mustajärvi
2790
Nummikoski
Kauhaneva-Pohjankangas
kansallispuisto
Karvianjärvi
Uuro
Ratikylä
Kihniö
Kauhajärvi
Alkkia
Träskvik
Vanhakylä
Härkmeri
Möykky
Kankari
Kuivasjärvi
Uttermossa
664
Sarvela
Ammälä
Perähyyppä
Kärjenkoski
Lauhanvuoren
kansallispuisto
669
Skaftung
Karvia
Tuulenkylä
Isojoki
(Stora)
274
Omossa/
Metsälä
Vesijärvi
Jyllinkoski
Suomijärvi
Linnankylä
661
Suojoki
Kantti
Vuorijärvi
23
Sideby/
Siipyy
Kallträsk
Kodesjärvi
Saunakylä
Häädetkeitaan
l. puisto
Honkajärvi
Honko
Parkano
Kasala/
Kasaböle
Rynkänen
Honkajoki
Laholuoma
Lapinneva
24
A
B
Riispyy
1660
108
Kuivaskangas
Iso Leppijärvi
Lauttijärvi
Antilankylä
Korvaluoma
273
Raivala
Yliskylä
Alaskylä
Pyntäinen

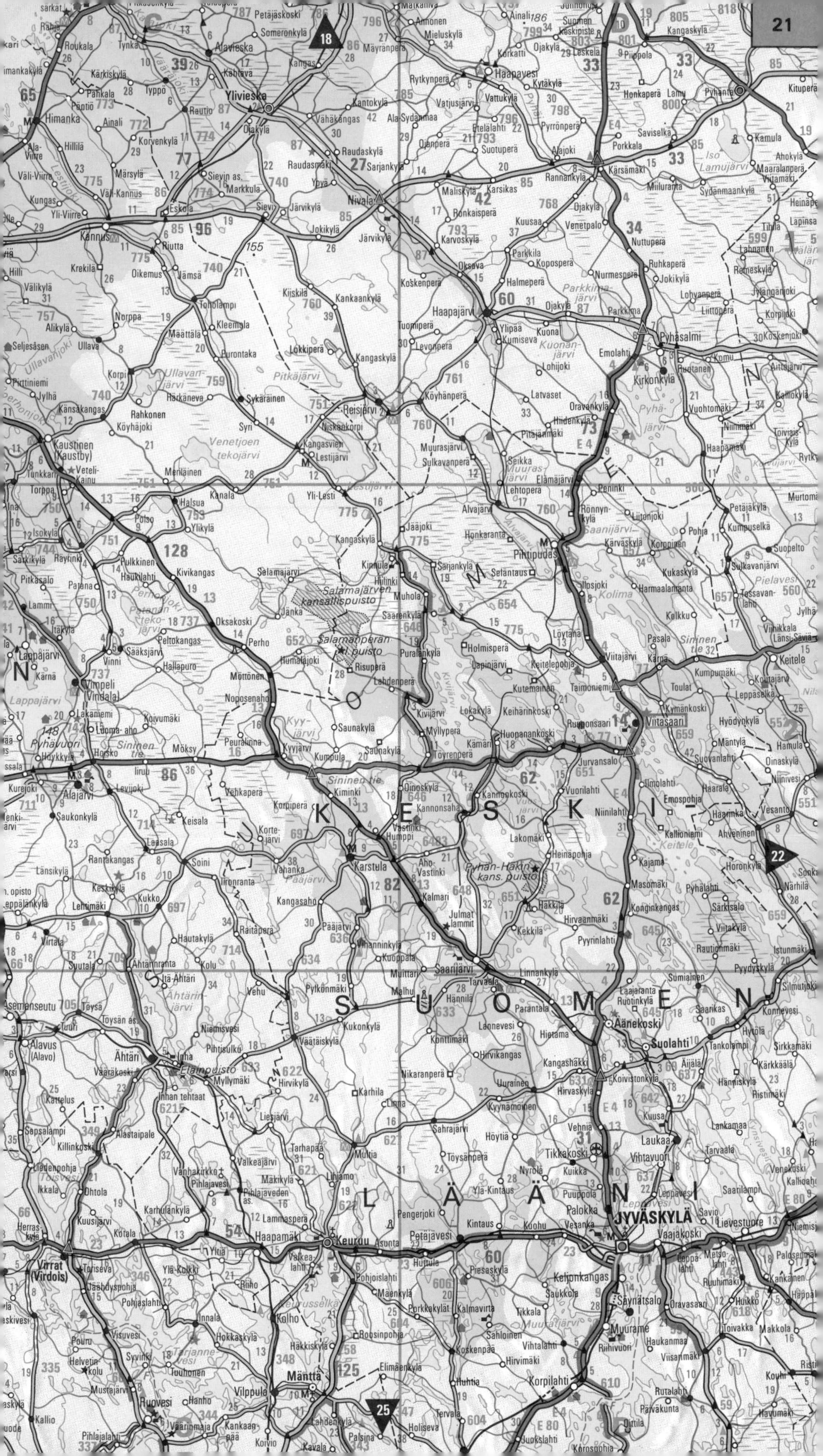

18
22
25
Ylivieska
Alavieska
Himanka
Kannus
Sievi
Nivala
Haapavesi
Kärsämäki
Pyhäntä
Haapajärvi
Reisjärvi
Pyhäsalmi
Kirkonkylä
Kaustinen
(Kaustby)
Veteli
Ullava
Halsua
Perho
Lestijärvi
Pihtipudas
Kinnula
Kivijärvi
Viitasaari
Keitele
Vimpeli
(Vindala)
Lappajärvi
Alajärvi
Kyyjärvi
Karstula
Saarijärvi
Kannonkoski
Soini
Ähtäri
Alavus
(Alavo)
Töysä
Äänekoski
Suolahti
Laukaa
Tikkakoski
Multia
Keuruu
Haapamäki
Petäjävesi
JYVÄSKYLÄ
Vaajakoski
Säynätsalo
Muurame
Korpilahti
Mänttä
Vilppula
Ruovesi
Virrat
(Virdois)
Salamajärven kansallispuisto
Pyhä-Häkin kans. puisto
Sininen tie
KESKI-SUOMEN LÄÄNI

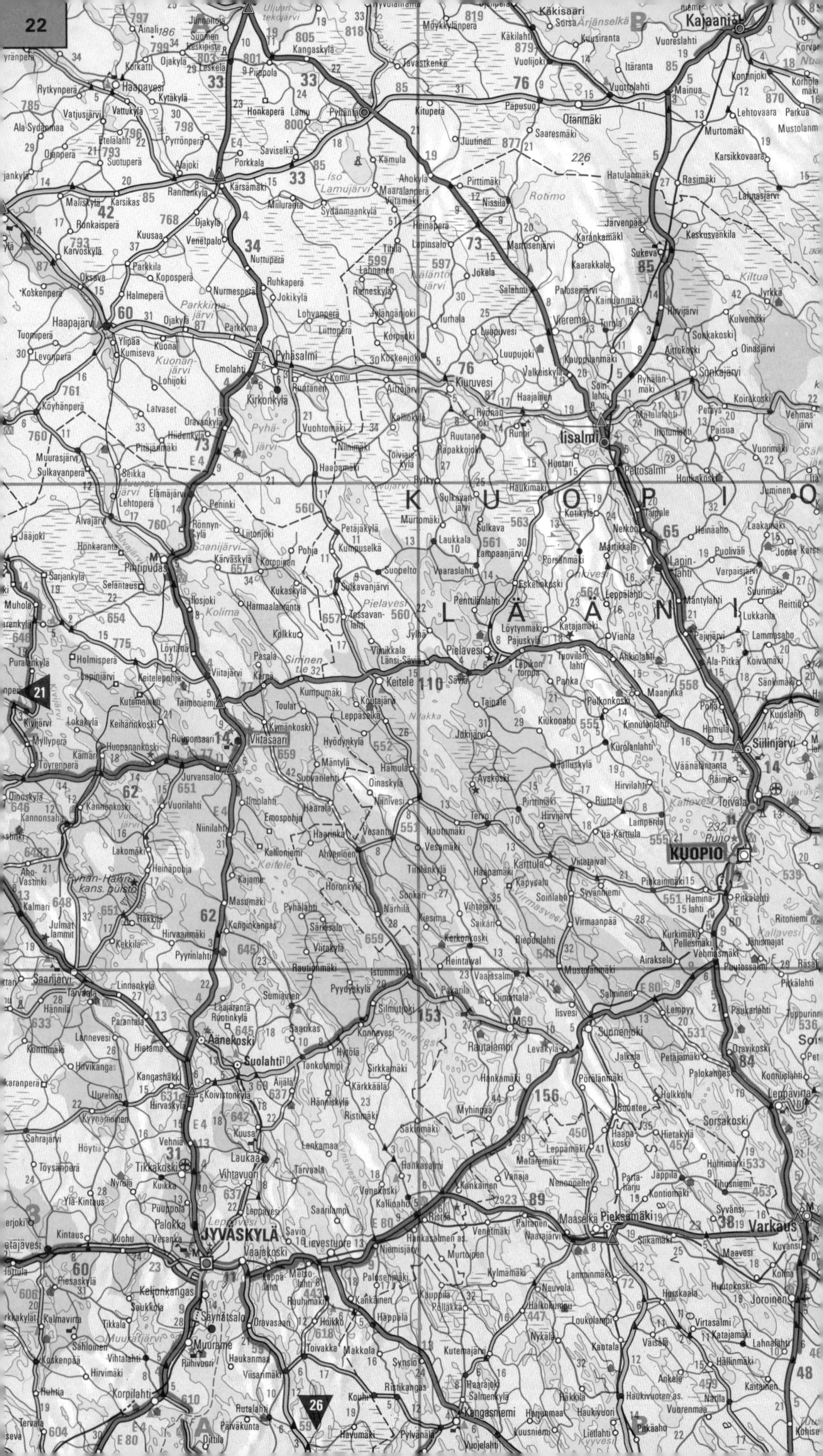
KUOPION LÄÄNI
Kajaani
Käkisaari
Sorsa
Ärjänselkä
Kuusiranta
Vuoreslahti
Vuolijoki
Käkilahti
Itäranta
Vuottolahti
Mainua
Kontinjoki
Otanmäki
Papusuo
Saaresmäki
Murtomäki
Lehtovaara
Parkua
Mustolanmäki
Karsikkovaara
Hatulanmäki
Rasimäki
Lahnasjärvi
Rotimo
Järvenpää
Keskusvaara
Sukeva
Kiltua
Jyrkkä
Hirvijärvi
Kulvemäki
Sonkakoski
Oinasjärvi
Sonkajärvi
Ryhälänmäki
Koirakoski
Vehmasjärvi
Paisua
Vuorimäki
Juminen
Iisalmi
Peltosalmi
Runni
Haukimäki
Kotikylä
Nerkoo
Lapinlahti
Heinäaho
Laakamäki
Puoliväli
Varpaisjärvi
Suurimäki
Reittiö
Mäntylahti
Lukkarila
Lammasaho
Pajujärvi
Ala-Pitkä
Koivumäki
Sänkimäki
Polvijärvi
Kuuslahti
Hamula
Siilinjärvi
Väänälänranta
Räimä
Toivala
Kallavesi
Puijo
KUOPIO
Pitkälahti
Ritoniemi
Janismajat
Vehmasmäki
Puutossalmi
Räsälä
Pitkälahti
Paukarlahti
Tuppurinmäki
Oravikoski
Konnuslahti
Leppävirta
Sorsakoski
Huutomäki
Tihusniemi
Syvänsi
Varkaus
Kuvansi
Maavesi
Kolma
Joroinen
Huutokoski
Virtasalmi
Katajamäki
Lahnalahti
Hällinmäki
Kaitainen
Kohisevä
Haapavesi
Ainali
Suomen keskipiste
Junnonoja
Uljuan tekojärvi
Möykkylänperä
Leskelä
Piippola
Kangaskylä
Tavastkenkä
Korkatti
Ojakylä
Rytkynperä
Kytäkylä
Vattukylä
Vatjusjärvi
Ala-Sydänmaa
Pyrrönperä
Etelälahti
Ojanperä
Suotuperä
Honkaperä
Lamu
Pyhäntä
Kitupera
Juutinen
Saviselkä
Porkkala
Alajoki
Kärsämäki
Kamula
Iso Lamujärvi
Ahokylä
Pirttimäki
Nissilä
Rannankylä
Maliskylä
Karsikas
Miiluranta
Maaralanperä
Viitamäki
Sydänmaankylä
Ronkaisperä
Ojakylä
Kuusaa
Venetpalo
Karvoskylä
Heinäperä
Lapinsalo
Marttisenjärvi
Karankamäki
Tihilä
Nuttuperä
Parkkila
Koposperä
Lahnanen
Näläntöjärvi
Jokela
Kaarakkala
Oksava
Koskenperä
Halmeperä
Nurmesperä
Ruhkaperä
Jokikylä
Rameskylä
Salahmi
Palosenjärvi
Kainuunmäki
Haapajärvi
Parkkimajärvi
Lohvanperä
Jylänganjoki
Turhala
Vieremä
Turkia
Tuomiperä
Ylipää
Kumiseva
Kuona
Kuonanjärvi
Parkkima
Liittoperä
Korpijoki
Luupuvesi
Aittokoski
Levonperä
Pyhäsalmi
Koskenjoki
Luupujoki
Kauppilanmäki
Emolahti
Komu
Kiuruvesi
Valkeiskylä
Lohijoki
Kirkonkylä
Ruotanen
Aittojärvi
Haajainen
Köyhänperä
Latvaset
Oravankylä
Pyhäjärvi
Kalliokylä
Ryönänjoki
Vuohtomäki
Niinimäki
Ruutana
Hiidenkylä
Rapakkojoki
Pitäjänmäki
Toiviaiskylä
Murasjärvi
Sulkavanperä
Seikka
Haapamäki
Huotari
Rytky
Elämäjärvi
Karvujärvi
Lehtoperä
Peninki
Sulkavanjärvi
Sulkava
Alvajärvi
Murtomäki
Rönnynkylä
Liitonjoki
Petäjäkylä
Laukkala
Lampaanjärvi
Jääjoki
Saanijärvi
Kumpuselkä
Pörsänmäki
Martikkala
Honkaranta
Pihtipudas
Kärväskylä
Korppinen
Pohja
Suopelto
Vaaraslahti
Eskelinkoski
Onkivesi
Sarjankylä
Selantaus
Sulkavanjärvi
Leppälahti
Ilosjoki
Kukaskylä
Pielavesi
Penttilänlahti
Muhola
Kolima
Harmaalanranta
Tessavanlahti
Jylhä
Löytynmäki
Pajuskylä
Katajamäki
Vianta
Kalkku
Löytänä
Vinnikkala
Länsi-Sävia
Tuovilanlahti
Ahkiolahti
Puralankylä
Holmispera
Pasala
Sininen tie
Keitele
Sävia
Lepikon torppa
Lapinjärvi
Keiteleponja
Viitajärvi
Kärnä
Panka
Maaninka
Kutemainen
Taimoniemi
Kumpumäki
Koutajärvi
Tainale
Pulkonkoski
Kinnulanlahti
Kivijärvi
Lokakylä
Keiharinkoski
Toulat
Leppäselkä
Nilakka
Jokijärvi
Kiukooaho
Myllyperä
Huopanankoski
Ruuponsaari
Viitasaari
Kymönkoski
Hyödynkylä
Kurolanlahti
Kämäri
Töyrenperä
Jurvansalo
Mäntylä
Hamula
Talluskylä
Hirvilahti
Suovanlahti
Oinaskylä
Äyskoski
Oinoskylä
Kannonkoski
Vuorilahti
Ilmolahti
Niinivesi
Pirttimäki
Riuttala
Kannonsaha
Emospohja
Haarala
Hirvijärvi
Lamperila
Niinilahti
Tervo
Itä-Karttula
Haarinka
Vesanto
Hautomäki
Lakomäki
Kalloniemi
Ahveninen
Vesamäki
Karttula
Viitataival
Pirkkainmäki
Aho-Vastinki
Heinäpohja
Keitele
Tiililänkylä
Haapamäki
Kapysalo
Syvänniemi
Hamina-lahti
Pyhän-Häkin kans. puisto
Kajamo
Horonkylä
Sonkari
Soinlahti
Kalmari
Masomäki
Pyhälahti
Närhilä
Vihtajärvi
Virmasvesi
Kurkimäki
Pellesmäki
Julmat lammit
Häkkilä
Hirvaanmäki
Konginkangas
Särkisalo
Kiesimä
Saikari
Virmaanpää
Kekkilä
Pyyrinlahti
Viitakylä
Kerkonkoski
Riepponlahti
Airaksela
Heintaival
Saarijärvi
Rautionmäki
Istunmäki
Vaajasalmi
Mustolanmäki
Tarvaala
Linnankylä
Pyydyskylä
Pakarila
Liimattala
Hännilä
Laajaranta
Ruotinkylä
Sumiainen
Silmutjoki
Salminen
Lempyy
Parantala
Saarikas
Konnevesi
Iisvesi
Suonenjoki
Lannevesi
Hietama
Äänekoski
Konnevesi
Rautalampi
Levä kylä
Jalkala
Petäjämäki
Palokangas
Konttimäki
Suolahti
Hytölä
Hirvikangas
Tankolampi
Sirkkamäki
Hankamäki
Pörölänmäki
Kangashäkki
Aijälä
Kärkkäälä
Hulkkola
Karanperä
Koivistonkylä
Hänniskylä
Myhinpää
Suontee
Uurainen
Hirvaskylä
Ristimäki
Haapakoski
Hietakylä
Kyynämöinen
Kuusa
Sakinmäki
Leppämäki
Sahrajärvi
Höytiä
Vehniä
Laukaa
Lenkamaa
Matarmäki
Huhtimäki
Töysänperä
Tikkakoski
Vihtavuori
Tarvaala
Hankasalmi
Kankainen
Vanaja
Nenonpelto
Partaharju
Jäppilä
Kontiomäki
Nyrölä
Kuikka
Venekoski
Kalliolahti
Ylä-Kintaus
Puuppola
Leppävesi
Saarilampi
Ristiina
Venetmäki
Paltanen
Maaselkä
Pieksämäki
Palokka
Leppävesi
Savio
Lievestuore
Niemisjärvi
Hankasalmen as.
Naarajärvi
Siikamäki
Kintaus
Kuohu
JYVÄSKYLÄ
Vesanka
Vaajakoski
Murtoinen
Petäjävesi
Piesaskylä
Leppälahti
Metsolahti
Palosenmäki
Kylmämäki
Lamminmäki
Hurskaala
Kelionkangas
Ruuhimäki
Kankainen
Kauppila
Pöllakka
Neuvola
Saukkola
Säynätsalo
Häppälä
Halkokumpu
Kalmaviiria
Tikkala
Oravasaari
Hoikko
Loukolampi
Muuratjärvi
Sahloinen
Muurame
Toivakka
Makkola
Synsiö
Kutemajärvi
Nykälä
Kantala
Väisälä
Koskenpää
Vihtalahti
Riihivuori
Haukanmaa
Hirvimäki
Viisanmäki
Ristikangas
Haarajoki
Kangasniemi
Ankele
Huhtia
Korpilahti
Kouhi
Hakkila
Haukivuoren as.
Vuorenmaa
Näsilä
Rutalahti
Haukivuori
Pitkäaho
Päiväkunta
Havumäki
Pylvänälä
Kuusniemi
Lietlahti
Seva
Oittila
Vuojalahti
Kyyvesi
E 4
E 80
A
B
21
26

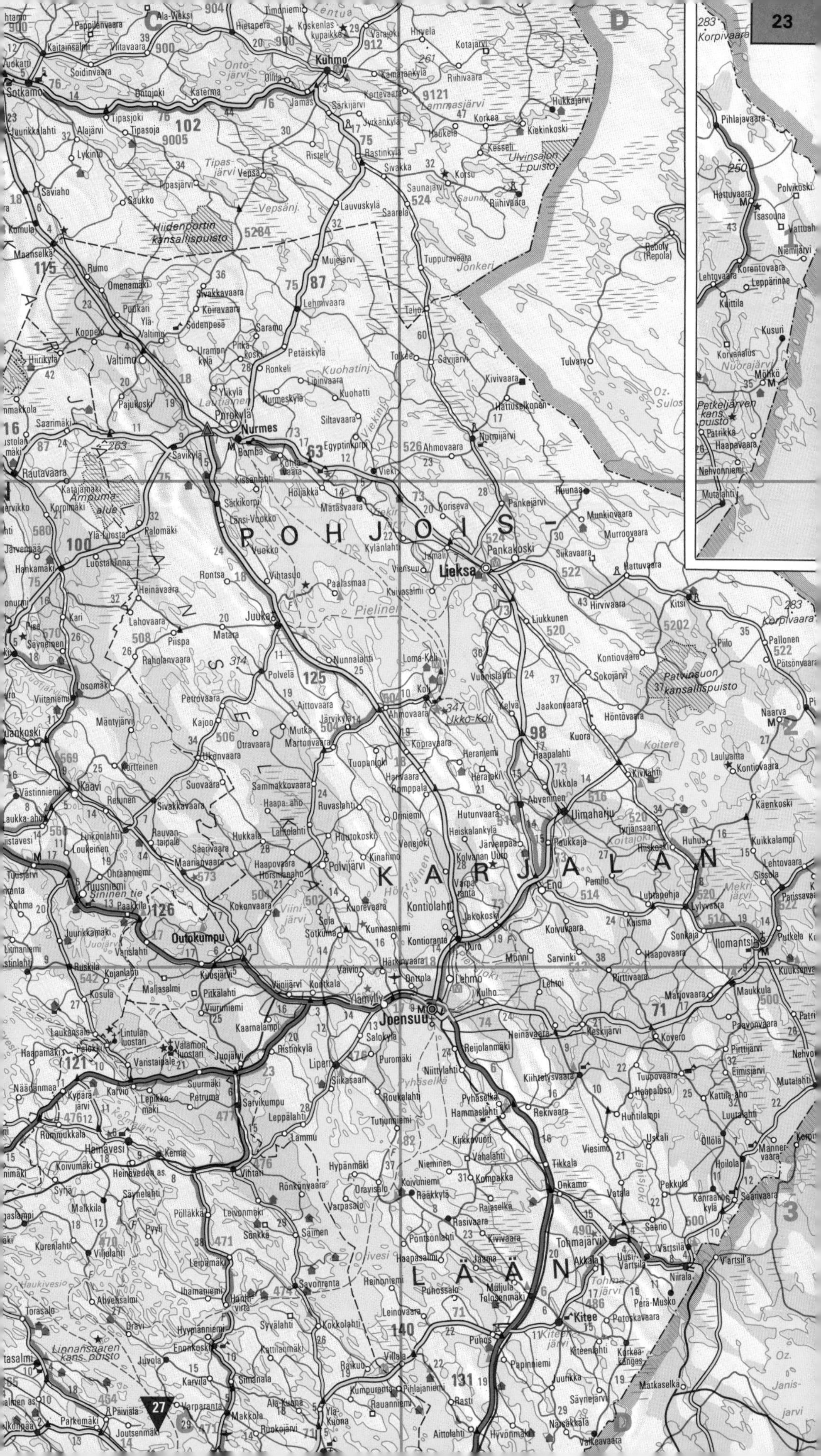

C
D
Korpivaara
Ala-Vieksi
Timoniemi
Lentua
Pappilanvaara
Hietaperä
Koskenlas kupaikka
Varajoki
Hyvelä
Kotajärvi
Kaitainsalmi
Viitavaara
Kuhmo
Soidinvaara
Ontojärvi
Ollila
Kamarankylä
Riihivaara
Sotkamo
Ontojoki
Katerma
Jamas
Kortevaara
Lammasjärvi
Hukkajärvi
Tipasjoki
Särkijärvi
Jyrkänkylä
Korkea
Kiekinkoski
Juurikkalahti
Alajärvi
Tipasoja
Haukelä
Kesseli
Ulvinsalon luonnonpuisto
Lykinto
Risteli
Rastinkylä
Tipasjärvi
Vepsä
Sivakka
Korsu
Saunajärvi
Saviaho
Saukko
Vepsänj.
Lauvuskylä
Saarela
Riihivaara
Hiidenportin kansallispuisto
Kontiolahti
Maanselkä
Mujejärvi
Tuppuravaara
Jonkeri
Rumo
Omenamäki
Sivakkavaara
Lehmivaara
Koiravaara
Taljo
Puukari
Ylä-Valtimo
Sudenpesä
Saramo
Koppelo
Pitkäkoski
Uramonkylä
Petäiskylä
Tolkee
Savijärvi
Tulvary
Hiirikylä
Valtimo
Ronkeli
Kuohatinj.
Lipinvaara
Kuohatti
Kivivaara
Pajukoski
Ylikylä
Nurmeskylä
Hattuselkonen
Lautiainen
Siltavaara
Porokylä
Nurmes
Egyptinkorpi
Vieki
Ahmovaara
Nurmijärvi
Saarimäki
Bomba
Savikylä
Rautavaara
Kohtavaara
Kissanlahti
Höljäkkä
Matasvaara
Koriseva
Pankejärvi
Ruunaa
Katajamäki
Ampuma-alue
Korpimäki
Särkikorpi
Lansi-Vuokko
Munkinvaara
Ylä-Luosta
Palomäki
POHJOIS-
Kylänlahti
Jamali
Murroovaara
Hankamäki
Luostanlinna
Vuokko
Pankakoski
Siikavaara
Hattuvaara
Rontsa
Vihtasuo
Paalasmaa
Viensuu
Lieksa
Heinävaara
Kuivasalmi
Pielinen
Hirvivaara
Kitsi
Kari
Lahovaara
Juuka
Liukkunen
Korpivaara
Piispa
Matara
Pallonen
Säyneinen
Raholanvaara
Nunnalahti
Loma-Koli
Kontiovaara
Sokojärvi
Patvinsuon kansallispuisto
Losomäki
Polvela
Koli
Vuonislahti
Pötsönvaara
Viitaniemi
Petrovaara
Aittovaara
Ukko-Koli
Kelvä
Jaakonvaara
Kajoo
Järvikylä
Ahmovaara
Höntövaara
Naarva
Mäntyjärvi
Otravaara
Mutka
Martonvaara
Kopravaara
Kuora
Ukonvaara
Tuopanjoki
Heraniemi
Haapalahti
Koitere
Laulualtta
Kontiovaara
Kortteinen
Herajoki
Kivilahti
Kaavi
Suovaara
Sammakkovaara
Harivaara
Romppala
Ukkola
Relunen
Sivakkavaara
Haapa-aho
Ruvaslahti
Orinniemi
Ahvenmes
Uimaharju
Käenkoski
Hutunvaara
Tyrjänsaari
Rauvantaipale
Koitajoki
Luikonlahti
Hukkala
Lattolahti
Heiskalankylä
Huhus
Kuikkalampi
Loukeinen
Saarivaara
Hautokoski
Venejoki
Järvenpää
Paukkaja
Hiiskoski
Lehtovaara
Maarianvaara
Haapovaara
Kinahmo
Kolvanan Uuro
Polvijärvi
Tuusniemi
Ohtaanniemi
Horsmanaho
Höytiäinen
KARJALAN
Sissola
Sininen tie
Varparanta
Eno
Pamilo
Mekrijärvi
Parissavaara
Paakkila
Kokonvaara
Viinijärvi
Kuorevaara
Luhtapohja
Lylyvaara
Juurikkamäki
Sola
Kontiolahti
Jakokoski
Koivuvaara
Kuisma
Outokumpu
Juojärvi
Kunnasniemi
Sotkuma
Kontioranta
Uuro
Sonkaja
Ilomantsi
Varislahti
Putkela
Härkinvaara
Mönni
Sarvinki
Haapovaara
Ruskila
Kojanlahti
Kuusjärvi
Vaivio
Onttola
Pielisjoki
Lehtoi
Pirttivaara
Kuuksenvaara
Kosula
Maljasalmi
Pitkälahti
Viinijärvi
Kontkala
Ylämylly
Lehmo
Kulho
Marjovaara
Maukkula
Viurunniemi
Joensuu
Patrikka
Laukansalo
Lintulan luostari
Kaarnalampi
Salokylä
Heinävaara
Keskijärvi
Paavonvaara
Valamon luostari
Ristinkylä
Reijolanmäki
Kovero
Pirttijärvi
Haapamäki
Palokki
Varistaipale
Juojärvi
Liperi
Puromäki
Niittylahti
Eimisjärvi
Näädänmaa
Karvio
Suurmäki
Siikasaari
Pyhäselkä
Kiihtelysvaara
Tuupovaara
Mutalahti
Kyparajärvi
Lepikkomäki
Petruma
Sarvikumpu
Roukalahti
Pyhäselkä
Hammaslahti
Rekivaara
Haapaloso
Kattila-aho
Leppälahti
Tutjunniemi
Huhtilampi
Luutalahti
Rummukkala
Heinävesi
Kerma
Lammu
Kirkkovuori
Vahalahti
Viesimo
Uskali
Öllölä
Männervaara
Koivumäki
Heinäveden as.
Vihtari
Hypänmäki
Nieminen
Kompakka
Tikkala
Hoilola
Syrjä
Rönkönvaara
Koivuniemi
Oravisalo
Rääkkylä
Onkamo
Pekkula
Kenraalinkylä
Saarivaara
Säynelahti
Varpasalo
Rajaselkä
Vatala
Malkkila
Pöllökkä
Leivonmäki
Sonkka
Saimen
Rasivaara
Saario
Korenlahti
Pyyli
Viljolahti
Orivesi
Pontsonlahti
Kivivaara
Tohmajärvi
Värtsilä
Leipämäki
Haapasalmi
Jaama
Uusi-Värtsilä
V'artsil'a
Haukivesi
Ihamaniemi
Savonranta
Heinoniemi
LÄÄNI
Akkala
Niirala
Ahvensalmi
Hanhivirta
Puhossalo
Möljula
Tolosenmäki
Tohmajärvi
Torasalo
Oravi
Hyypänniemi
Syvälahti
Kokkolahti
Leinovaara
Kitee
Perä-Musko
Potoskavaara
Linnansaaren kans. puisto
Enonkoski
Kattilanmäki
Villala
Puhos
Kiteenjärvi
Kiteenlahti
Korkeakangas
Juvola
Raikuu
Papinniemi
Oz. Janisjarvi
Karvila
Simanala
Kumpuranta
Pihlajaniemi
Juurikka
Matkaselkä
Päivisla
Varparanta
Ala-Kuona
Ylä-Kuona
Rauanniemi
Rasti
Säynejärvi
Parkumäki
Makkola
Joutsenmäki
Ruokojärvi
Aittolahti
Hyvönmäki
Närsäkkälä
Valkeavaara
Pihlajavaara
Polvikoski
Hattuvaara
Tsasouna
Vattuvaara
Niemijärvi
Korentovaara
Leppärinne
Lehtovaara
Kuittila
Kusuri
Korvanalus
Nuorajärvi
Möhkö
Petkeljärven kans. puisto
Patrikka
Haapavaara
Nehvonniemi
Mutalahti
Reboly (Repola)
Oz. Sulos

A B

1

2

3

41

20

TURUN JA PORIN LÄÄNI

Kasala
Kasaböle
Riispyy
Kuvaskangas
Iso Leppijärvi
Lauttijärvi
Rynkänen
Pyntäinen
Antinlankylä
Ala-Honkajoki
Honkajoki
Laholuoma
Lapinneva
Korvaluoma
Pohjan kangas
Raivala
Yliskylä
Alaskylä
Vahojärvi
Sydänmaa
Kovelahti
Jämijärven as.
Jämijärvi
Mansoniemi
Riitiala
Tevaniemi
Merikarvia
Alakylä
Tuorila
Siikainen
Otamo
Samminmaja
Venesjärvi
Niinisalo
Kankaanpää
Köörtilä
Etelämaa
Leväsjoki
Isojärvi
Veneskoski
Honkakoski
Pohjansaha
Pirttijärvi
Tuunajärvi
Vihtilajärvi
Kuninkaanlähde
Hämeenkangas
Kilvakkala
Ikaalinen
Kyrösjärvi
Saukonpera
Lunalahti
Villakkala
Osara
Ahlainen
Pomarkku (Påmark)
Saunajoki
Harjakoski
Vehuvarpe
Niemenkylä
Kyröskoski
Hämeenkyrö (Tavastkyro)
Lampaluoto
Lamppi
Lassila
Haunia
Riiho
Sävi
Vesajärvi
Reposaari
Kellahti
Noormarkku (Norrmark)
Rudanmaa
Lavia
Karhijärvi
Tupale
Kintus
Mäntyluoto
Pihlava
Yyteri
Kyläsaari
Söörmarkku
Harjakangas
Mustajoki
Riuttala
Suodenniemi
Haukijärvi
Kuuminainen
Ruosniemi
Harjunpää
Palus
Saarijärvi
Kuorsumaa
Putaja
Mouhijärvi
Jumesniemi
Säppi
PORI (BJÖRNEBORG)
Kullaa
Siuro
Ulvila (Ulvsby)
Sääksjärvi
Tervahauta
Kiikoinen
Hanjaa
Suoniemi
Viasvesi
Lankoori
Vanhakylä
Levanpelto
Rautu
Karkku
Niemi
Friitala
Häyhtjonmaa
Myllymaa
Ellivuori
Sarkola
Luvia
Nakkila
Korkeaoja
Heinoo
Hormisto
Pirkkala-Vinnare
Lievikoski
Vammala
Lemlahti
Peränkylä
Harjavalta
Kauvatsa
Kiikka
Stormi
Rämsö
Kuivalahti
Saarenmaa
Äetsä
Roismala
Irjanne
Peipohja
Tulkkila
Kolkya
Olkiluoto
Ilavainen
Panelia
Kokemäki (Kumo)
Lauhankylä
Sammaljoki
Eurajoki
Kiukainen
Raijala
Rekikoski
Illo
Halkivaha
Lapijoki
Sydänmaa
Huittinen-Lauttakylä
Rauma (Raumo)
Uotila
Lutta
Naarjoki
Ehtamo
Eura
Lähteenkylä
Vanttila
Oriniemi
Lappi
Kauttua
Köyliö
Yttilä
Naatula
Punkalaidun
Unaja
Vasarainen
Mestilä
Säkylä
Vuorenmaa
Rutava
Huhtamo
Jalasjoki
Tursa
Rihtniemi
Vermuntila
Kodisjoki
Kodiksami
Mannila
Vampula
Alamenjoki
Kanteemaa
Reila
Ihode
Korpi
Sieravuori
Pyhäjoki
Kojonperä
Pitkäluoto
Polttila
Hinnerjoki
Honkilahti
Koskenkylä
Alastaro
Köylionkylä
Metsämaa
Venäjä
Pyhämaa
Pyharanta
Otajärvi
Suontaka
Soukainen
Virttaa
Kammela
Untamala
Lellainen
Kolvaa
Heinjoki
Tourula
Onkijoki
Tuorlahti
Mauramaa
Laitila
Katinhäntä
Vaskijärven l.puisto
Kalmakoski
Haaronen
Korpi
Lyökki
Vohdensaari
Kalanti
Laajoki
Kaijalankylä
Yläne
Loimaan kunta
Ypäjän as.
Minkiö
Musopora
Uusikaupunki (Nystad)
Kovero
Oripää
Loimaa
Ypäjä
Jokioinen
Putsaari
Haydo
Nästi
Karjala
Kalela
Niitynpää
Pöytyä
Pappinen
Mellilä
Kuusjoki
Isokari
Lahti
Sairinen
Vehmalainen
Mynäjoki
Karhunoja
Isoperä
Varanpää
Mattinen
Vehmaa
Vinkkilä
Kivikylä
Tarvainen
Takkula
Saksala
Riihikoski
Kyrö
Karinainen
Seljänkulma
Pitkäjärvi
Merimotelli
Lokalahti
Puotila
Tortinmäki
Valpperi
Kaurissalo
Helsinki
Rauttua
Mietoinen
Mynämäki
Nousiainen
Auran as.
Koski
Pyöli
Iso-Rahi
Vehanen
Louhisaari
Askainen
Vahto
Nummi
Aura
Tilkainen
Tarvasjoki
Tapala
Kerkola
Kustavi
Taivassalo (Tövsala)
Lemu
Masku
Paattinen
Rusko
Liedon as.
Pokkola
Marttila
Vättilä
Raatala
Kanunki
Jurmo
Osnäs
Etelä-Vartsala
Laupunen
Hakkenpää
Ohensaari
Mäentaka
Livonsaari
Raisio (Reso)
Maaria
Suksela
Lieto
Tammisilta
Kaleva
Vaskio
Kuusjoki
Fiskö
Åva
Iniöfjärden
Velkua
Merimasku
Teersalo
Kultaranta
Naantali (Nådendal)
Littoinen
Paimio (Pemar)
Korsö
Brändö
Iniö
Iskola
TURKU ÅBO
Kaarina
Piikkiö (Pikis)
Hajala
Mäly
Ittula
Perttelii
Inkere
Velkuanmaa
Poikko
Ruissalo
Empo
Kuusiston linna
Aakoinen
Halikko
Salo
Enklinge
Björkö
Keistiö
Rymättylä
Kakskerta
Pöylä
Muurla
Torsholma
Lappo
Pakinainen
Röölä
Kirjala
Harvaluoto
Joensuu
Varsala
Uskela
Kokkila
Kaukola
Kumlinge
Mossala
Alakylä
Sydmo
Lielax
Sauvo (Sagu)
Ruskola
Angelniemi
Pohjankylä
Tuohittu
Houtsala
Pargas/Parainen
Ovidja
Karuna
Ristniemi
Kirjakkala
Rajalahti
Kila
Kiila
Teijo
Perniön as.
Ylikulma
Skiftet
Airisto
Houtskär (Houtskari)
Lillmälö
Nagu/Nauvo
Våno
Eknäs
Mjösund
Tjuda
Mathildedal
Perniö (Bjärnå)
Strömma
Galtby
Stor-landet
Granvik
Attu
Korpo/Korppoo
Väcklax
Simonby
Nordvik
Vreta
Kimito/Kemiö
Ylönkylä
Latterla
Koski
Aijala
Kappelskär–Naantali 8 h, Norrt.–Turku 8 h 45
Korpoström
Kirjais
Hästö
Kalkkala
Husö
Björkboda
Särkisalo/Finby
Forby
Svenskby
Dragsfjärd
Kulla
Västanfjärd
Söderlångvik
Dalsbruk (Taalintehdas)
Malarby
Tenala/Tenhola
Bromary
Prästkulla
Kökar
Hellsö
Karlby
Aspö
Nötö
Högsåra
Padva
Pargas
Gullkrona fjärd
Kasnäs
Östanberg
Skärgårdshavets nationalpark
Saaristomeren kansallispuisto
Jurmofjärden
Jurmo
Rosala
Hitis/Hiittinen
Hanko/Hangö
Hangö västra fjärd
Hangon läntinen selkä
Lappohja/Lappvik
Täktom
Tvärminne
Utö
Jussarö naturpark
Jussarön luonnonpuisto

A B

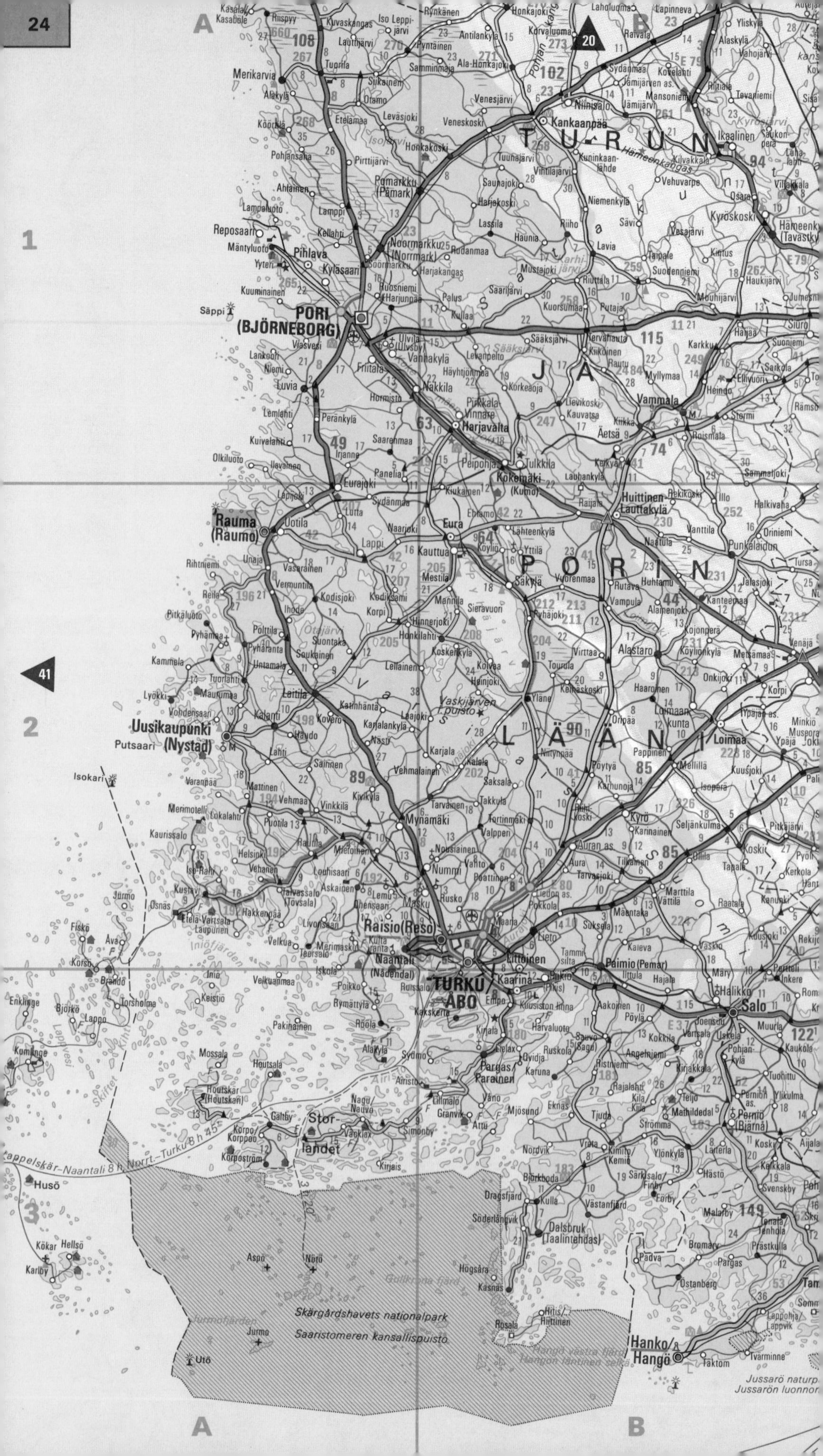

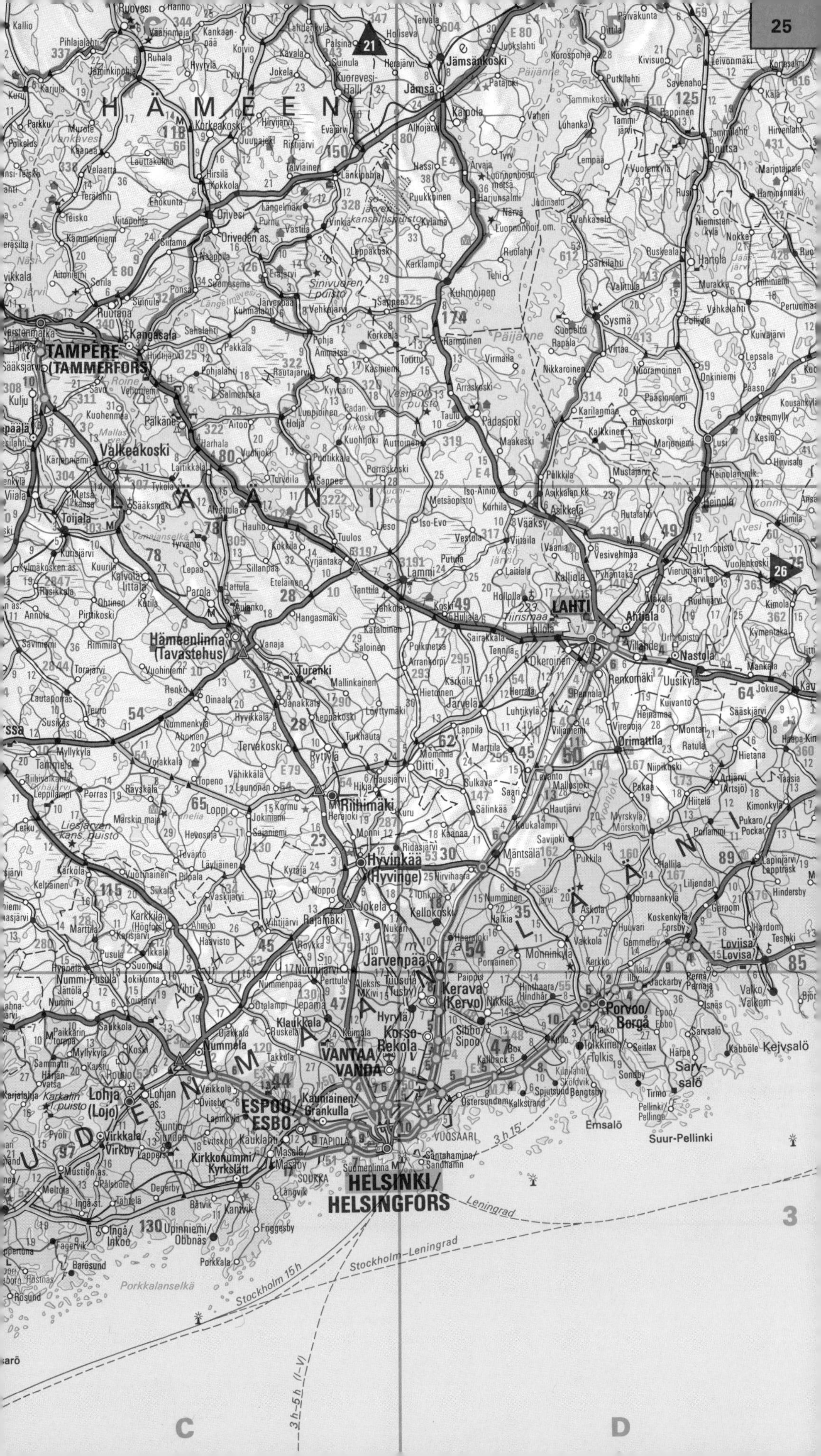
HÄMEEN
LÄÄNI
UUDENMAAN
LÄÄNI
TAMPERE (TAMMERFORS)
LAHTI
HELSINKI/
HELSINGFORS
ESPOO/
ESBO
VANTAA
VANDA
Hämeenlinna
(Tavastehus)
Hyvinkää
(Hyvinge)
Riihimäki
Valkeakoski
Toijala
Kangasala
Orivesi
Jämsä
Jämsänkoski
Kuhmoinen
Padasjoki
Sysmä
Hartola
Joutsa
Heinola
Asikkala
Vääksy
Lammi
Orimattila
Mäntsälä
Järvenpää
Kerava
(Kervo)
Porvoo/
Borgå
Loviisa
Lovisa
Lohja
(Lojo)
Karkkila
(Högfors)
Nummela
Kauniainen/
Grankulla
Kirkkonummi/
Kyrkslätt
Sipoo
Sibbo
Korso
Rekola
Tuusula
(Tusby)
Nastola
Päijänne
Suur-Pellinki
Porkkalanselkä
Stockholm–Leningrad
Stockholm 15h
Leningrad
21
26
C
D
3

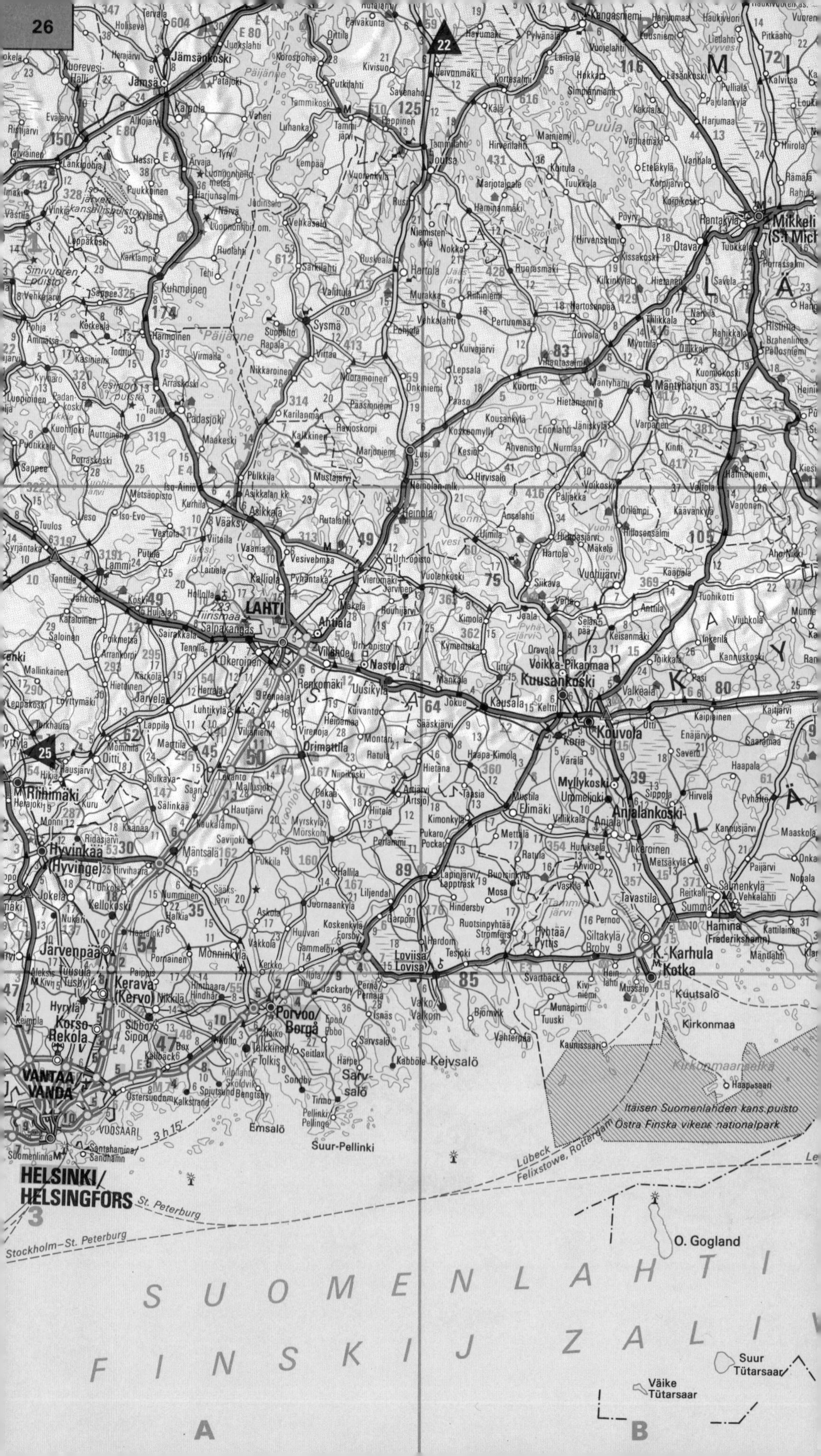

Jämsänkoski
Jämsä
Kuorevesi-Halli
Kaipola
Päijänne
Sysmä
Joutsa
Hartola
Heinola
Heinolan mlk
Mikkeli (S:t Mich
Kangasniemi
Puula
Pertunmaa
Mäntyharjun as.
Ristiina
Kuhmoinen
Padasjoki
Vääksy
Asikkala
Lahti
Ahtiala
Villähde
Nastola
Kausala
Kuusankoski
Voikka-Pikanmaa
Kouvola
Valkeala
Myllykoski
Anjalankoski
Elimäki
Orimattila
Lammi
Riihimäki
Hyvinkää (Hyvinge)
Mäntsälä
Järvenpää
Kerava (Kervo)
Tuusula (Tusby)
Korso-Rekola
Vantaa/Vanda
Helsinki/Helsingfors
Porvoo/Borgå
Loviisa/Lovisa
Pyhtää/Pyttis
K. Karhula
Kotka
Hamina (Fredrikshamn)
Kirkonmaa
Kirkonmaanselkä
Itäisen Suomenlahden kans.puisto
Östra Finska vikens nationalpark
Emsalö
Suur-Pellinki
Kejvsalö
Lübeck
Felixstowe, Rotterdam
St. Peterburg
Stockholm–St. Peterburg
3 h 15'
O. Gogland
SUOMENLAHTI
FINSKIJ ZALIV
Suur Tütarsaar
Väike Tütarsaar
M I K K E L I
P Ä I J Ä T - H Ä M E
K Y M I
A
B

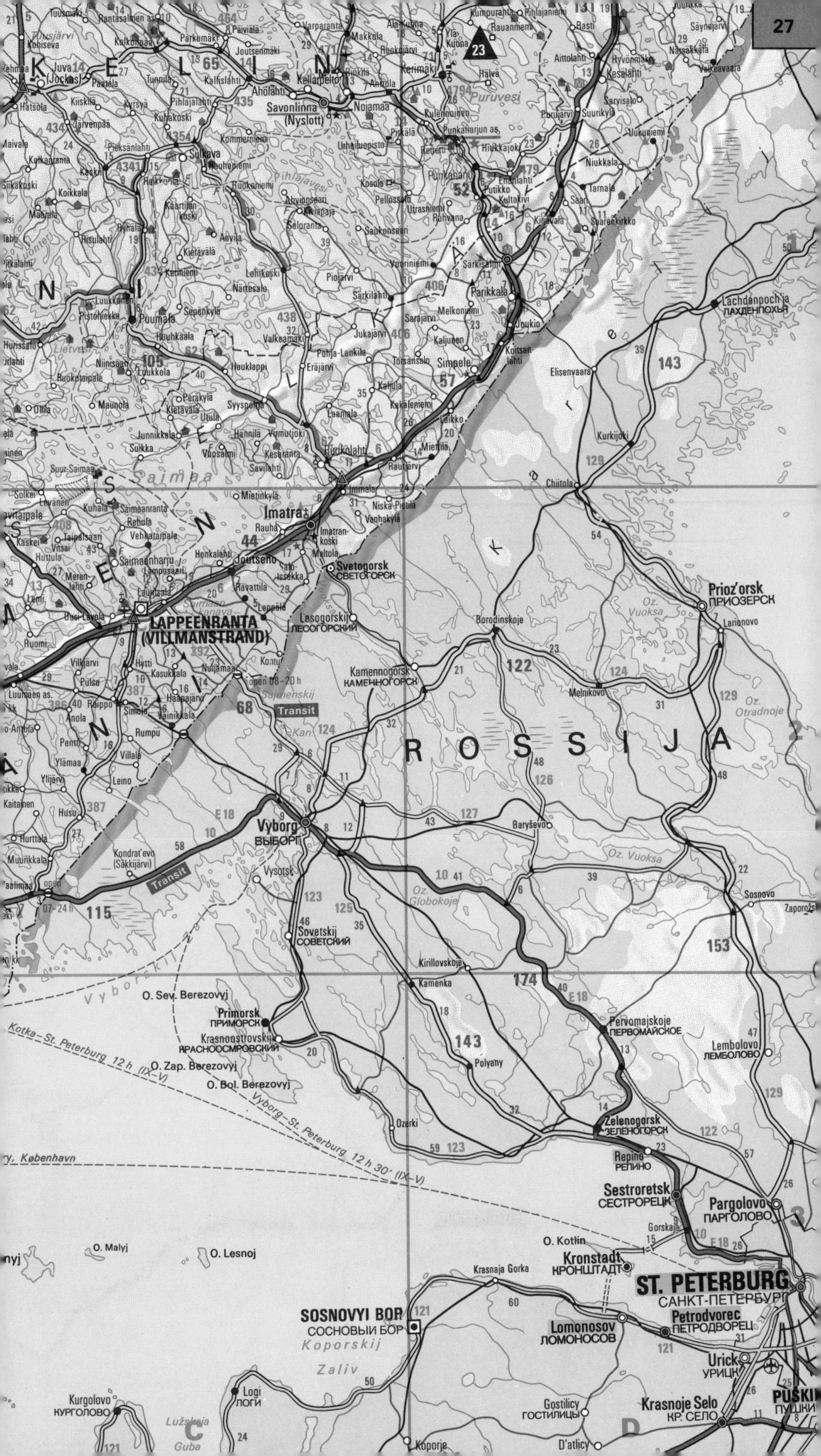

Savonlinna
(Nyslott)
Imatra
Svetogorsk
СВЕТОГОРСК
LAPPEENRANTA
(VILLMANSTRAND)
Lesogorskij
ЛЕСОГОРСКИЙ
Kamennogorsk
КАМЕННОГОРСК
Prioz'orsk
ПРИОЗЕРСК
Lachdenpoch'ja
ЛАХДЕНПОХЬЯ
ROSSIJA
Vyborg
ВЫБОРГ
Sovetskij
СОВЕТСКИЙ
Primorsk
ПРИМОРСК
Krasnoostrovskij
КРАСНООСТРОВСКИЙ
Pervomajskoje
ПЕРВОМАЙСКОЕ
Lembolovo
ЛЕМБОЛОВО
Zelenogorsk
ЗЕЛЕНОГОРСК
Repino
РЕПИНО
Sestroretsk
СЕСТРОРЕЦК
Pargolovo
ПАРГОЛОВО
Kronstadt
КРОНШТАДТ
ST. PETERBURG
САНКТ-ПЕТЕРБУРГ
SOSNOVYI BOR
СОСНОВЫЙ БОР
Lomonosov
ЛОМОНОСОВ
Petrodvorec
ПЕТРОДВОРЕЦ
Urick
УРИЦК
Krasnoje Selo
КР. СЕЛО
Gostilicy
ГОСТИЛИЦЫ
Logi
ЛОГИ
Kurgolovo
КУРГОЛОВО
Koporskij
Zaliv
Kotka–St. Peterburg 12 h (IX–V)
Vyborg–St. Peterburg 12 h 30' (IX–V)
Transit

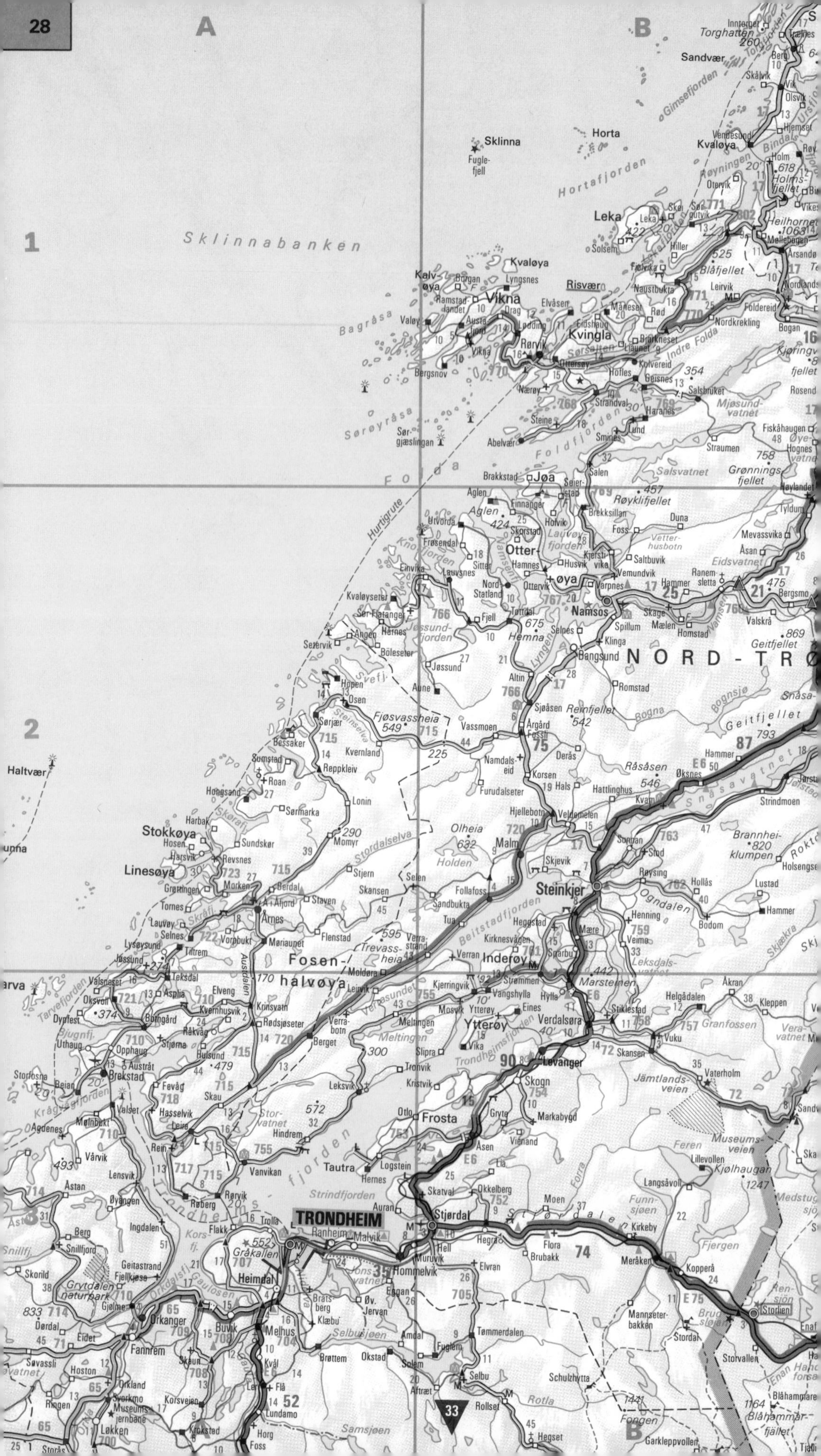
A
B
1
2
Torghatten
260
Sandvær
Gimsefjorden
Sklinna
Fugle-
fjell
Horta
Hortafjorden
Kvaløya
Sklinnabanken
Leka
Heilhornet
1063
Bindalsfjord
Kvaløya
Kalv-
øya
Vikna
Risvær
Bagråsa
Rørvik
Kvingla
Indre Folda
Nærøy
Sørøyråsa
Sør-
gjæslingan
Abelvær
Foldfjorden
Folda
Salsvatnet
Grønningsfjellet
Jøa
Røyklifjellet
Hurtigrute
Aglen
Otter-
øya
Namsos
Eidsvatnet
NORD-TR
Geitfjellet
Bangsund
Jøssundfjorden
Hemna
Fjøsvassheia
549
Reinfjellet
Bogna
Snåsa-
Geitfjellet
793
Råsåsen
546
Snåsavatnet
Haltvær
Stokkøya
Linesøya
Stordalselva
Olheia
632
Malm
Holden
Brannhei-
klumpen
820
Steinkjer
Ogndalen
Beitstadfjorden
Fosen-
halvøya
Trevassheia
595
Inderøy
Marsteinen
442
Verdalsøra
Ytterøy
Levanger
Trondheimsfjorden
Jämtlandsveien
Brekstad
Frosta
Museumsveien
Kjølhaugan
1247
Tautra
Strindfjorden
TRONDHEIM
Stjørdal
Stjørdalen
Kirkeby
Meråker
Heimdal
Gråkallen
552
Orkanger
Melhus
Selbusjøen
Storlien
Grytdalen naturpark
Selbu
Rotla
Løkken
Samsjøen
Blåhammar-
fjället
1164
33
E6
E75

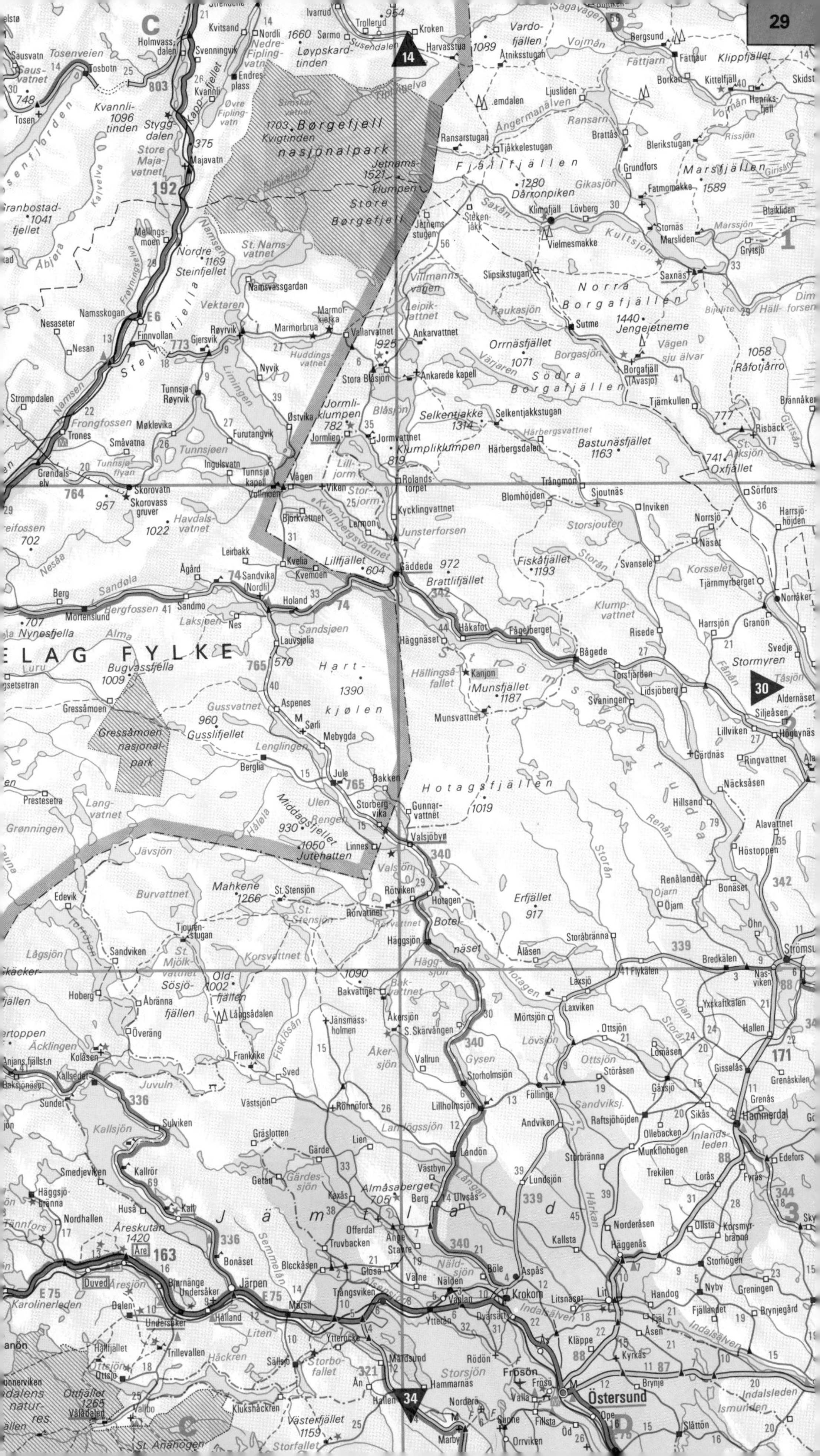

C
D
Sausvatn
Tosenveien
Saus-vatnet
Tosbotn
Tosen
748
Kvannli-tinden
1096
Stygg-dalen
Store Maja-vatnet
Majavatn
Granbostad-fjellet
1041
Åbjøra
Kalvelva
Holmvass-dalen
Kvitsand
Nordli
Svenningvik
Kappfjellet
Endres-plass
Kvannli
Øvre Fipling-vatn
Nedre-Fipling-vatn
Ivarrud
Trollerud
954
1660
Sørmo
Løypskard-tinden
Susendalen
Kroken
Harvasstua
14
1703
Børgefjell
Kvigtinden
nasjonalpark
Jetnams-klumpen
1521
Store Børgefjell
Sagavägen
Bergsund
Vardo-fjällen
1089
Vojmån
Åtnikksstugan
Fättjarn
Fättjaur
Klippfjället
Borkan
Kittelfjäll
Henriks-fjäll
Skidst
Ljusliden
Ångermanälven
Ransarn
Brattås
Blerikstugan
Rissjön
Ransarstugan
Tjäkkelestugan
Fjällfjällen
Grundfors
Marsfjällen
1589
1280
Dårronpiken
Gikasjön
Fatmomakke
Klimpfjäll
Lövberg
Saxån
Stekenjåkk
Jetnems-stugen
Vielmesmakke
Kultsjön
Stornäs
Marsliden
Blaikliden
Grytsjö
Mellings-moen
Nordre Steinfjellet
1169
St. Nams-vatnet
Namsvassgardan
Frøyningselva
Vektaren
Namsskogan
Nesaseter
Nesan
Finnvollan
Gjersvik
Røyrvik
Marmorbrua
Marmor-kjelka
Vallarvatnet
Huddings-vatnet
Steinfjella
Strompdalen
Namsen
Nyvik
Limingen
Tunnsjø-Røyrvik
Frongfossen
Møklevika
Trones
Småvatna
Furutangvik
Tunnsjøen
Tunnsjø-flyan
Ingulsvatn
Tunnsjø kapell
Vollmoen
Vågen
Viken
Grøndals-elv
Skorovatn
Skorovass gruver
764
957
Havdals-vatnet
1022
702
Stora Blåsjön
Jormli-klumpen
782
Jormlien
Blåsjön
Jormvattnet
Klumpliklumpen
819
Lill-jorm
Stor-jorm
Rolands-torpet
Kycklingvattnet
Junsterforsen
Lemon
Bjorkvattnet
Kvarnbergsvattnet
Villmanns-vågen
Leipik-vattnet
Ankarvattnet
1925
Ankarede kapell
Slipsikstugan
Raukasjön
Orrnäsfjället
1071
Värjaren
Södra Borgafjällen
Norra Borgafjällen
Sutme
1440
Jengejetneme
Borgasjön
Borgafjäll (Avasjo)
Vägen sju älvar
1058
Råfotjårro
Saxnäs
Selkentjakke
1314
Selkentjakkstugan
Härbergsvattnet
Härbergsdalen
Bastunäsfjället
1163
Tjärnkullen
777
Risbäck
St. Arksjön
741
Oxfjället
Brännåker
Tångmon
Blomhöjden
Sjoutnäs
Storsjouten
Inviken
Sörfors
Norrsjö
Näset
Harrsjö-höjden
Fiskåfjället
1193
Storån
Svansele
Korsselet
Tjärnmyrberget
Klump-vattnet
Risede
Norråker
Harrsjön
Granön
Svedje
Stormyren
Fånån
Täsjön
30
Aldernäset
Leirbakk
Ågård
Sandvika (Nordli)
Kvelia
Kvemoen
Lillfjället
604
Gäddede
972
Brattlifjället
Sandøla
Berg
Mortenslund
Bergfossen
Sandmo
Holand
Laksjøen
Nes
707
Nynesfjella
Alma
Sandsjøen
Lauvsjølia
Häggnäset
Håkafot
Fågelberget
Bågede
Torsfjärden
Lidsjöberg
Ström
Hällingså-fallet
Kanjon
Munsfjället
1187
Svaningen
Bugvassfjella
1009
Hart-kjølen
1390
570
Gussvatnet
Aspenes
Sørli
Mebygda
960
Gusslifjellet
Gressåmoen
Gressåmoen nasjonal-park
Lenglingen
Berglia
Jule
Bakken
Munsvattnet
Siljeåsen
Lillviken
Höglunäs
Gärdnäs
Ringvattnet
Näcksåsen
Hotagsfjällen
1019
Hillsand
Prestesetra
Lang-vatnet
Grønningen
Ulen
Rengen
Middagsfjellet
930
1050
Jutehatten
Storberg-vika
Gunnar-vattnet
Valsjöbyn
Linnes
Valsjön
Renån
Alavattnet
Höstoppen
Jävsjön
Edevik
Burvattnet
Mahkene
1266
St. Stensjön
Rötviken
Hotagen
Rörvattnet
Erfjället
917
Renålandet
Öjarn
Bonäset
Botel-näset
Häggsjön
Storåbränna
Ålåsen
Öhn
Strömsund
Tjouren-stugan
Sandviken
Lågsjön
St. Mjölk-vattnet
Old-fjällen
1002
Sösjö-fjällen
Korsvattnet
1090
Bakvattnet
Laxsjö
Flykälen
Bredkälen
Nas-viken
Hoberg
Åbränna
Långsådalen
Överäng
Laxviken
Yxskaftkälen
Hallen
Ansjön
Jänsmäss-holmen
Åkersjön
S. Skärvången
Mörtsjön
Lövsjön
Ottsjön
Lomåsen
Fisklösån
Vallrun
Gysen
Storholmsjön
Storåsen
Gisselås
Änjans fjällstn
Kolåsen
Kallsedet
Bakisjönäset
Sundet
Frankrike
Sved
Juvuln
Föllinge
Gåxsjö
Sandviksj.
Raftsjöhöjden
Sikås
Grenås
Hammerdal
Grenåskilen
Västsjön
Rönnöfors
Lillholmsjön
Andviken
Ollebacken
Inlands-leden
Edefors
Sulviken
Kallsjön
Gräslotten
Lien
Landögssjön
Landön
Munkflohögen
Storbränna
Smedjeviken
Kallrör
Gärde
Getan
Gärdes-sjön
Västbyn
Lundsjön
Trekilen
Lorås
Fyrås
Häggsjö-bränna
Huså
Kall
Almåsaberget
705
Kaxås
Berg
Ulvsås
Jämtland
Hårkan
Nordhallen
Tännfors
Åreskutan
1420
Åre
Offerdal
Änge
Stavre
Truvbacken
Kallsta
Norderåsen
Ollsta
Korsmyr-bränna
Häggenås
Storhögen
Duved
Åresjön
Bonäset
Björnänge
Undersåker
Järpen
Semmelån
Bleckåsen
Glösa
Välne
Nälden
Näldsjön
Böle
Aspås
Krokom
Litsnäset
Lit
Handog
Nyby
Greningen
Karolinerleden
Dalen
Undersåker
Hålland
Mörsil
Trångsviken
Vaplan
Ytterån
Dvärsätt
Indalsälven
Fjällandet
Brynjegård
Fjäl
Åsen
Hallfjället
Trillevallen
Liten
Häckren
Ytteråcke
Sällsjö
Storbo-fallet
Mattsund
Rödön
Kläppe
Kyrkås
Ottsjön
Ottsjö
Ottfjället
1265
Vålådalen
Vallbo
Klukshåckren
Ån
Hallen
Hammarnäs
Storsjön
Frösön
Frösö
Valla
Östersund
Brynje
Indalsleden
Ismunden
Västerfjället
1159
Norderö
Marby
Sunne
Fillsta
Orrviken
Öd
Ope
Slåttön
Storfallet
St. Anahögen
E6
E75
34

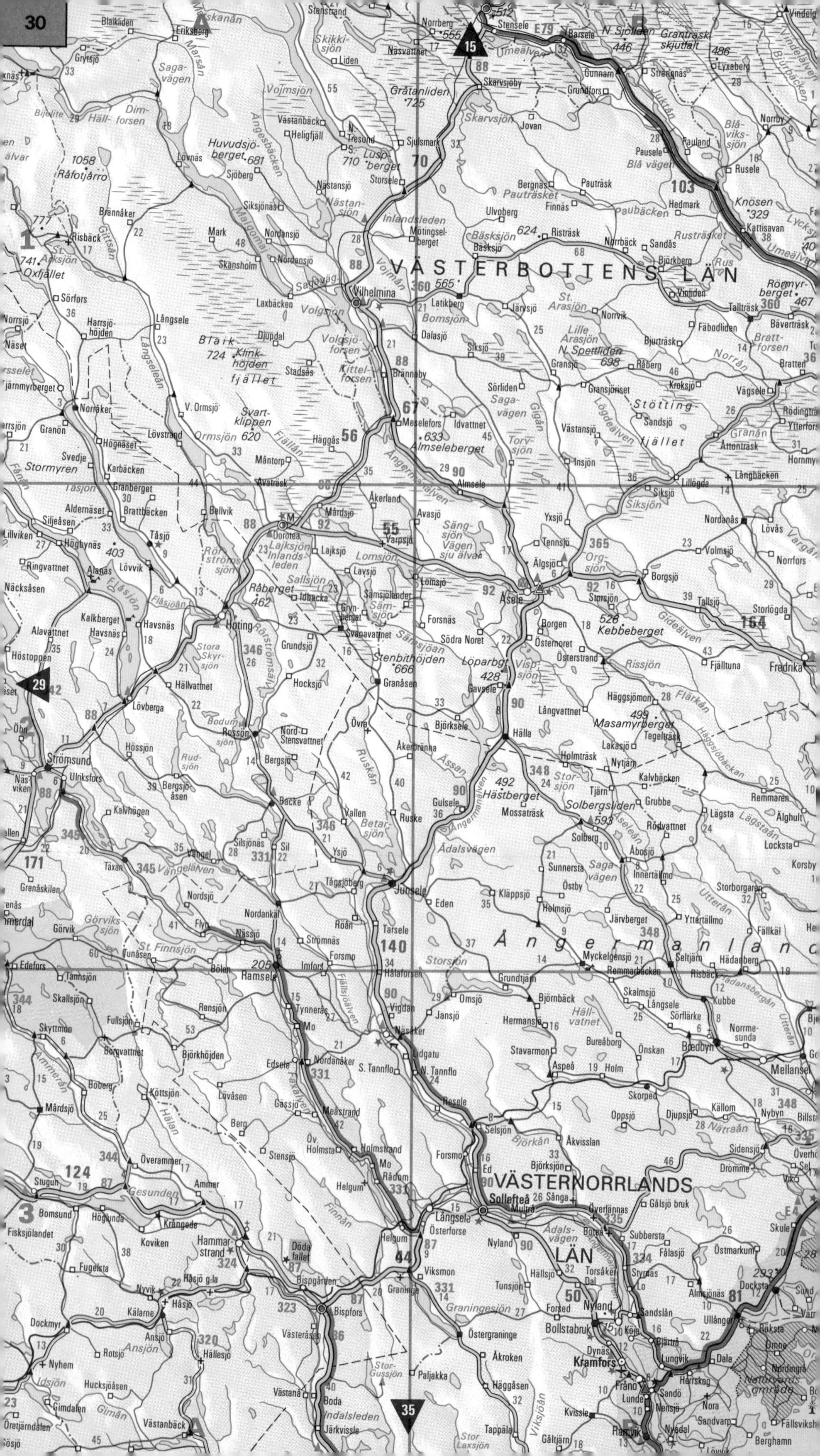
VÄSTERBOTTENS LÄN
VÄSTERNORRLANDS
LÄN
Ångermanland
Vilhelmina
Dorotea
Åsele
Hoting
Strömsund
Junsele
Ramsele
Sollefteå
Kramfors
Bollstabruk
Nyland
Långsele
Helgum
Bispgården
Bispfors
Hammarstrand
Fredrika
Bredbyn
Mellansel
Stensele
Storsele
Saxnäs
Ångermanälven
Umeälven
Fjällsjöälven
Faxälven
Indalsleden
Inlandsleden
Sagavägen
Ådalsvägen
Blå vägen
Malgomaj
Volgsjön
Kultsjön
Flåsjön
Gesunden
Graningesjön
Stor Gussjön
Döda fallet
Naturvårdsområde
Stöttingfjället
Blaikfjället
Klinkhöjden
Almseleberget
Kebbeberget
Hästberget
Masamyrberget
Stenbithöjden
Råberget
Gråtanliden
Luspberget
Huvudsjöberget
Råfotjärro
Oxfjället
Knösen
Rörmyrberget
Granträsk skjutfält
E79
E4
15
29
35
1
2
3
88
90
92
103
140
164
171
323
331
345
346
348
360
365

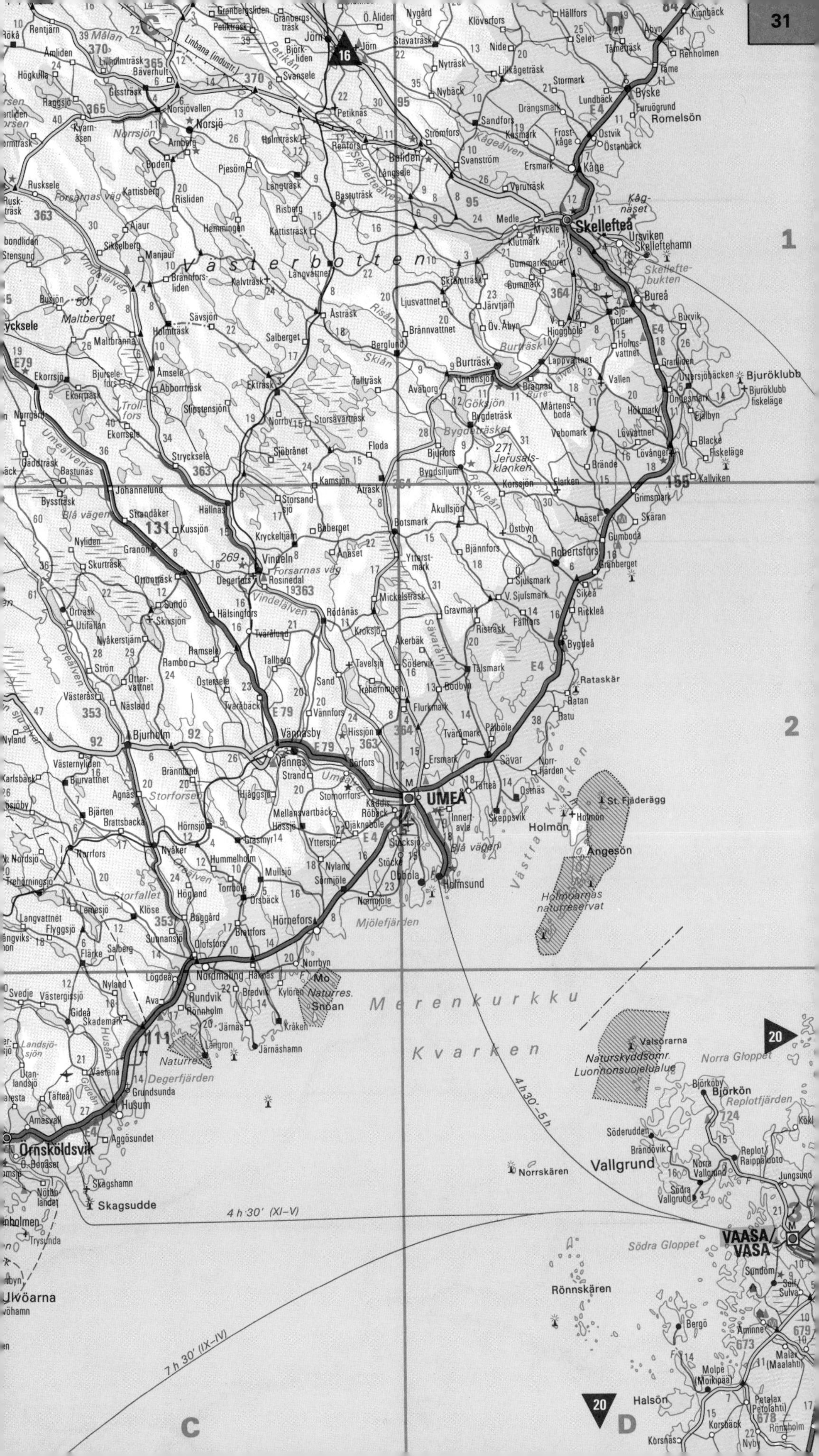
C
D
1
2
Västerbotten
Skellefteå
Skelleftehamn
Ursviken
Kåge
Byske
Bureå
Burträsk
Boliden
Norsjö
Jörn
Bjuröklubb
Lövånger
Robertsfors
Vindeln
Vännäs
Vännäsby
UMEÅ
Holmsund
Obbola
Sävar
Hörnefors
Nordmaling
Bjurholm
Husum
Örnsköldsvik
Holmön
Ängesön
Holmöarnas naturreservat
Västra Kvarken
Merenkurkku
Kvarken
Naturskyddsomr.
Luonnonsuojelualue
Valsörarna
Norrskären
Rönnskären
Vallgrund
Björkön
Replot
Raippaluoto
VAASA/
VASA
Sundom
Solf/
Sulva
Malax
(Maalahti)
Molpe
(Moikipää)
Petalax
(Petolahti)
Korsnäs
Halsön
Bergö
Norra Gloppet
Södra Gloppet
Replotfjärden
Skagsudde
Ulvöarna
4 h 30' (XI–V)
4 h 30'–5 h
7 h 30' (IX–IV)
Umeälven
Vindelälven
Skellefteälven
Kågeälven
Öreälven
Mjölefjärden
Degerfjärden
Blå vägen
Forsarnas väg
Linbana (industr.)
E4
E79
20

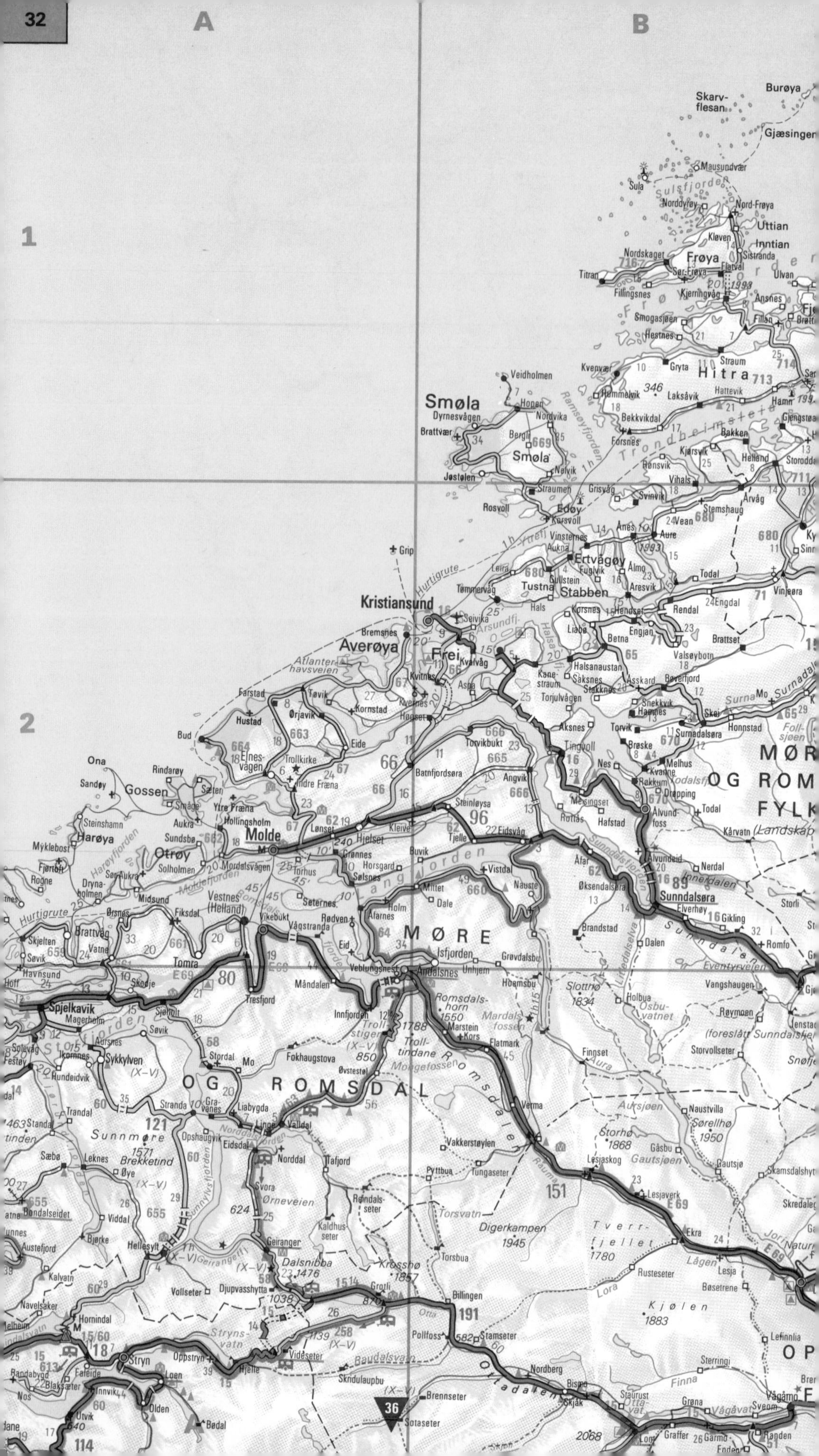
A
B
1
2
Burøya
Skarv-
flesan
Gjæsingen
Mausundvær
Sula
Sulsfjorden
Norddyrøy
Nord-Frøya
Uttian
Kløven
Inntian
Sistranda
Nordskaget
Frøya
Flatval
Titran
Sør-Frøya
Ulvan
Fillingsnes
Kjerringvåg
Frøyfjorden
Ansnes
Smogasjøen
Fillan
Hestnes
Kvenvær
Gryta
Straum
Hitra
Veidholmen
Smøla
Hopen
Dyrnesvågen
Nordvika
Hummelvik
Laksåvik
Hattevik
Hamn
Brattvær
Bergli
Bekkvikdal
Ramsøyfjorden
Forsnes
Bakken
Gjengstøa
Smøla
Trondheimsleia
Kjørsvik
Hellend
Rønsvik
Vihals
Nålvik
Jøstølen
Straumen
Grisvåg
Svinvik
Arvåg
Stemshaug
Rosvoll
Edøy
Korsvoll
Vean
Ånes
Aure
Vinsternes
Aukna
Grip
Ertvågøy
Fuglvik
Ålmo
Leira
Gullstein
Todal
Tømmervåg
Tustna
Stabben
Aresvik
Hurtigrute
Kristiansund
Hals
Korsnes
Hendset
Rendal
Engdal
Vinjeøra
Seivika
Arsundfj.
Bremsnes
Averøya
Liabø
Engjan
Brattset
Betna
Valsøybotn
Frei
Kvalvåg
Atlanter-
havsveien
Halsanaustan
Kvitnes
Kane-
straum
Saksnes
Stakknes
Asskard
Bøverfjord
Aspa
Farstad
Tøvik
Kornstad
Kvernes
Torjulvågen
Snekkvik
Hamnes
Skei
Surna
Surnadal
Mo
Hustad
Ørjavik
Høgset
Honnstad
Bud
Eide
Torvikbukt
Aksnes
Torvik
Surnadalsøra
Tingvoll
Brøske
Elnes-
vågen
Trollkirke
Ona
Rindarøy
Indre Fræna
Batnfjordsøra
Angvik
Nes
Melhus
Kvanne
Todalsfj.
MØRE
OG ROMSDAL
FYLKE
Sandøy
Gossen
Sæter
Smågø
Rokkum
Drøpping
Aukra
Ytre Fræna
Hollingsholm
Steinløysa
Mesingset
Rottås
Hafstad
Ålvund-
foss
Todal
Steinshamn
Harøya
Sundsbø
Molde
Lønset
Hjelset
Kleive
Tjelle
Eidsvåg
Kårvatn (Landskap
Myklebost
Otrøy
Harøyfjorden
Grønnes
Buvik
Sunndalsfjorden
Ålvundeid
Fjørtoft
Solholmen
Mordalsvågen
Torhus
Horsgard
Langfjorden
Vistdal
Åfar
Nerdal
Rogne
Sør-Aukra
Sølsnes
Nauste
Øksendalsøra
Innerdalen
Dryna-
holmen
Moldefjorden
Mittet
Dale
Sunndalsøra
Midsund
Vestnes
(Helland)
Seternes
Elverhøy
Storli
Hurtigrute
Ørsnes
Fiksdal
Rødven
Holm
Afarnes
Gikling
Brattvåg
Vikebukt
Vågstranda
MØRE
Brandstad
Dalen
Sunndalen
Romfo
Skjelten
Vatne
Tomra
Eid
Isfjorden
Grøvdalsbu
Eventyrvegen
Søvik
Veblungsnes
Åndalsnes
Unhjem
Vangshaugen
Havnsund
Skodje
Måndalen
Hoemsbu
Slottho
1834
Holbua
Osbu-
vatnet
Spjelkavik
Tresfjord
Innfjorden
Romsdals-
horn
1550
Mardals-
fossen
Røymoen
Magerholm
Sjøholt
Trollstigen
(X–V)
1788
Marstein
Kors
(foreslått Sunndalsfj.)
Solevåg
Festøy
Aursnes
Søvik
Troll-
tindane
Flatmark
Finnset
Aura
Storvollseter
Snøfj.
Ikornnes
Sykkylven
Stordal
Mo
Fokhaugstova
850
Mongefossen
Hundeidvik
OG
ROMSDAL
Øvstestøl
Romsdalen
Trandal
Stranda
Gra-
vanes
Liabygda
Aursjøen
Naustvilla
Sørellhø
1950
Standal-
tinden
Sunnmøre
Opshaugvik
Linge
Valldal
Verma
Storhø
1868
Sæbø
Leknes
1571
Brekketind
Eidsdal
Norddal
Tafjord
Vakkerstøylen
Gåsbu
Gautsjøen
Gautsjø
Skamsdalshytt
Øye
Pyttbua
Tungaseter
Lesjaskog
Skredalen
Bondalseidet
Svora
Ørneveien
Røndals-
seter
Lesjaverk
Viddal
Kaldhus-
seter
Torsvatn
Digerkampen
1945
Tverr-
fjellet
1780
Ekra
Austefjord
Bjørke
Hellesylt
Geirangerfj.
Geiranger
Torsbua
Lågen
Lesja
Kalvatn
Dalsnibba
1476
Krosshø
1857
Rusteseter
Bøsetrene
Vollseter
Djupvasshytta
Grotli
Billingen
Lora
Navelsaker
Hornindal
Kjølen
1883
Strynsvatn
Otta
Pollfoss
Stamseter
Lefinnlia
Stryn
Oppstryn
Videseter
Baudalsvatn
Sterringi
Randabygd
Faleide
Loen
Hjelle
Skridulaupbu
Nordberg
Finna
Blaksæter
Innvik
Brennseter
Bismo
Ottadalen
Skjåk
Vågåmo
Nos
Utvik
Olden
Sotaseter
Grøna
Vågåvatn
Sveøm
Bødal
2068
Lom
Graffer
Garmo
Randen
36

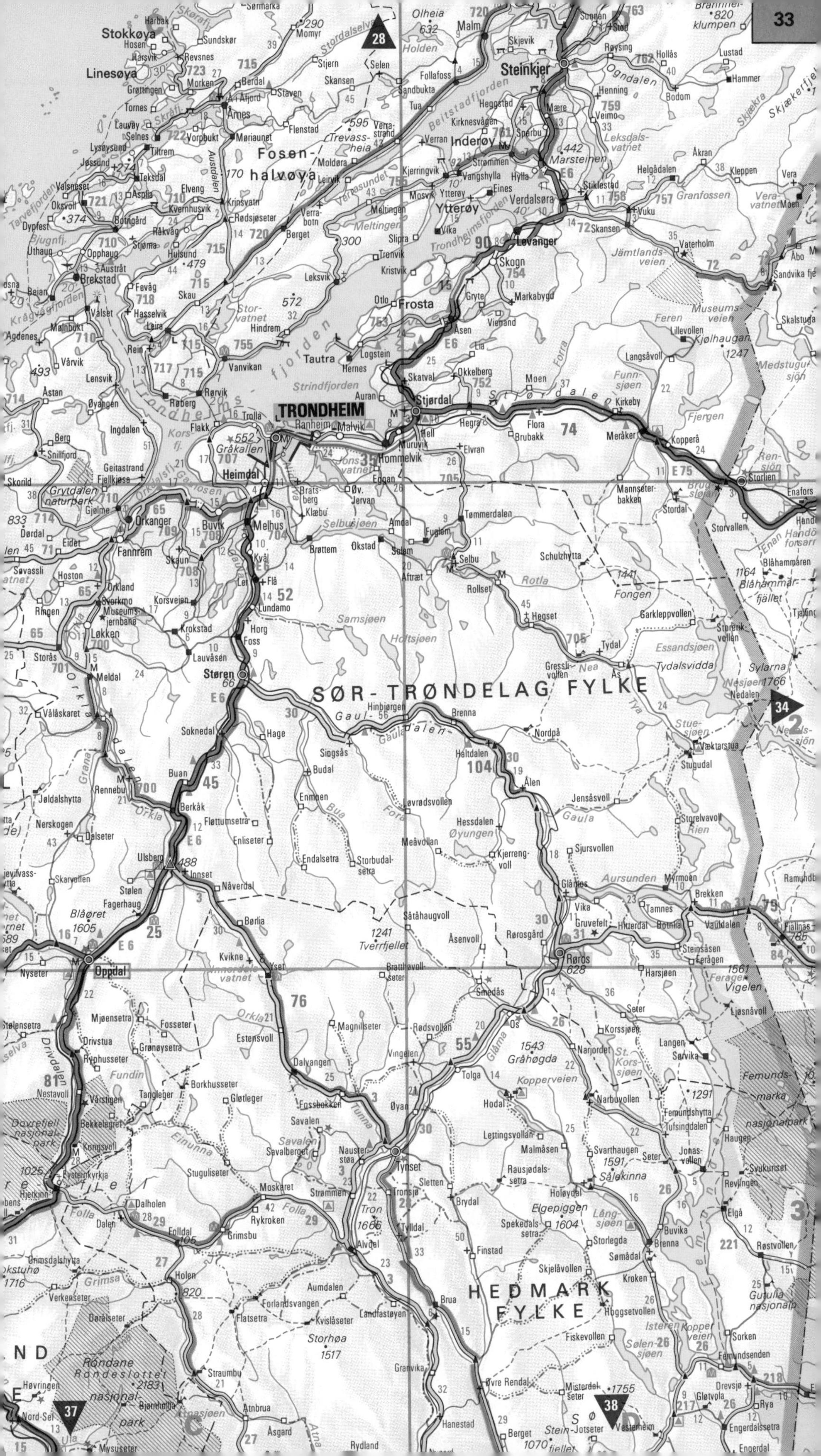
28
34
37
38
Stokkøya
Linesøya
Fosen-
halvøya
Brekstad
Steinkjer
Inderøy
Ytterøy
Verdalsøra
Levanger
Skogn
Frosta
Tautra
Stjørdal
TRONDHEIM
Ranheim
Malvik
Hommelvik
Heimdal
Orkanger
Fannrem
Buvik
Melhus
Selbu
Støren
Løkken
Meldal
Berkåk
Oppdal
Røros
Os
Tolga
Tynset
Alvdal
Folldal
Kongsvoll
Meråker
Storlien
SØR-TRØNDELAG FYLKE
HEDMARK
FYLKE
Trondheimsfjorden
Beitstadfjorden
Strindfjorden
Selbusjøen
Aursunden
Femundsmarka
nasjonalpark
Rondane
nasjonalpark
Gutulia
nasjonalp.
Dovrefjell
nasjonalpark
E6
E75

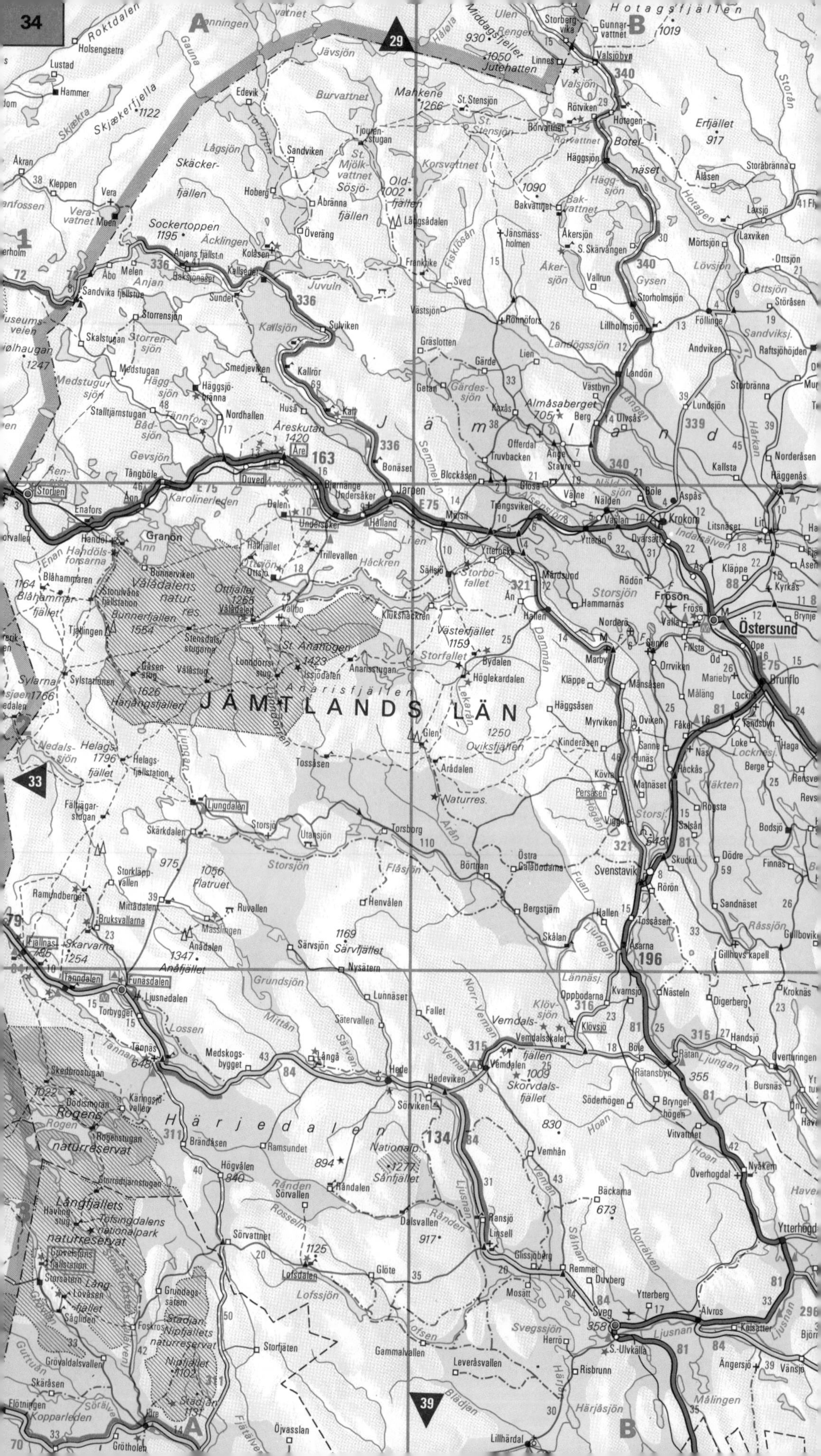
A
B
29
33
39
1
3
Roktdalen
Holsengsetra
Lustad
Hammer
Skjækerfjella
1122
Åkran
Kleppen
Vera
Veravatnet
Moen
Gauna
Jävsjön
Edevik
Burvattnet
Mahkene
1266
St. Stensjön
Hotagsfjällen
1019
Gunnarvattnet
Storbergvika
Linnes
Valsjöbyn
Valsjön
Middagsfjället
930
1050
Jutehatten
Rötviken
Hotagen
Börvattnet
Botelnäset
Erfjället
917
Tjouren-stugan
Sandviken
Lågsjön
Skäckerfjällen
Hoberg
St. Mjölkvattnet
Sösjöfjällen
Old-fjällen
1002
Åbränna
Överäng
Lägg sådalen
Häggsjön
1090
Bakvattnet
Åkersjön
S. Skärvången
Jänsmässholmen
Åsen
Storåbränna
Hotagen
Laxsjö
Laxviken
Mörtsjön
Lövsjön
Ottsjön
Sockertoppen
1195
Äcklingen
Anjans fjällst.n
Kolåsen
Kallsedet
Baksjönäset
Åbo
Melen
Anjan
336
72
Sandvika fjällstue
Sunnet
Juvuln
Frankrike
Sved
Vallrun
Gysen
340
Storholmsjön
Lillholmsjön
Föllinge
Ottsjön
Storåsen
Sandviksj.
Raftsjöhöjden
Andviken
Västsjön
Rönnöfors
Landögssjön
Storrensjön
Skalstugan
Kallsjön
Sulviken
Gräslotten
Lien
Gärde
Getan
Gärdessjön
Landön
Västbyn
Almåsaberget
705
Kaxås
Berg
Ulvsås
Lundsjön
Storbränna
Medstugan
Medstugusjön
Smedjeviken
Kallrör
Häggsjöbränna
Stalltjärnstugan
Tännfors
Nordhallen
Bådsjön
Huså
Kall
Åreskutan
1420
Åre
163
Gevsjön
Jämtland
Offerdal
Änge
Stavre
Truvbacken
Kallsta
Norderåsen
Häggenås
339
Tångböle
Storlien
Duved
Enafors
Ånn
Karolinerleden
Bonäset
Järpen
Björnänge
Undersåker
Blockåsen
Glösa
Välne
Nälden
Aspås
Bjölsta
E75
Mörsil
Trångsviken
Alsensjön
Vaplan
Krokom
Litsnäset
Handöl
Granön
Enan
Handölsforsarna
Dalen
Hälland
Liten
Ytterån
Dvärsätt
Indalsälven
Hallfjället
Trillevallen
Ottsjön
Sällsjö
Storbofallet
Ytteröcke
Mårdsund
Rödön
Kläppe
Blåhammaren
1164
Blåhammarfjället
Bunnerviken
Vålådalens naturres.
Ottfjället
1265
Storulvåns fjällstation
Bunnerfjällen
1554
Vålådalen
Vallbo
Håckren
Klukshackren
321
Ån
Storsjön
Hammarnäs
Frösön
Frösö
Östersund
Kyrkås
Brynje
Tjallingen
Stensdalsstugorna
Gåsenstug.
St. Anahögen
1423
Västerfjället
1159
Storfallet
Bydalen
Höglekardalen
Hallen
Dammån
Norderö
Marby
Valla
Sunne
Fillsta
Orrviken
Öd
Marieby
Ope
Brunflo
Sylarna
1766
Sylstationen
Vålåstug.
Lunndörrsstug.
Issjödalen
Anarisstugan
Anarisfjällen
Lunndörren
1626
Harjångsfjällen
JÄMTLANDS LÄN
Kläppe
Månsåsen
Mälang
Lockne
Häggsåsen
Myrviken
Oviken
Fåker
Tandsbyn
Helags
1796
Helagsfjället
Helagsfjällstation
Nedalssjön
Ljungan
Glen
1250
Oviksfjällen
Kinderåsen
Sanne
Funäs
Näs
Loke
Locknesj.
Haga
Tossåsen
Arådalen
Kövra
Persåsen
Matnäset
Häckås
Näkten
Berge
Fältjägarstugan
Ljungdalen
Naturres.
Storsj.
Rogsta
Skärkdalen
Storsjö
Utansjö
Torsborg
110
Vigge
Salsån
548
Bodsjö
Arån
Hogån
Storklappvallen
975
1056
Flatruet
Storsjön
Flåsjön
Börtnan
Östra Galabodarna
Svenstavik
Skucku
Dödre
Finnäs
Ramundberget
Mittådalen
Ruvallen
Henvålen
Bergstjärn
Röron
Sandnäset
Fuan
Bruksvallarna
Skarvarna
1254
Måsslingen
Anådalen
1347
Anåfjället
Särvsjön
1169
Särvfjället
Hallen
Tossåsen
Råssjön
Gillhovs kapell
Skålan
Asarna
196
Fjällnäs
785
84
Tänndalen
Funäsdalen
Ljusnedalen
Torbygget
Grundsjön
Nysätern
Lunnäset
Lännäsj.
Oppbodarna
Kvarnsjö
Nästeln
Digerberg
Kroknäs
Lossen
Mittån
Sätervallen
Särvan
Fallet
Norr-Veman
Klövsjö
Vemdalsfjällen
316
315
Handsjö
Tännäs
648
Tännan
Medskogsbygget
Långå
Hede
Sör-Veman
Vemdalsskalet
Vemdalen
1009
Skorvdalsfjället
Böle
Rätan
Ljungan
355
Överturingen
Bursnäs
Skedbrostugan
1022
Dödismoran
Rogen
Rogens naturreservat
Rogenstugan
Käringsjövallen
Härjedalen
311
Hedeviken
Sörviken
134
Nationalp.
1277
Sånfjället
830
Söderhögen
Bryngelhögen
Vitvattnet
Hoan
Brändåsen
Ramsundet
894
Vemhån
Högvålen
840
Rånden
Sörvallen
Råndalen
Bäckarna
673
Överhogdal
Nyåkern
Storrödtjärnstugan
Långfjällets naturreservat
Havlingstug.
Töfsingdalens nationalpark
Rosseln
Dalsvallen
917
Ransjö
Linsell
Ljusnan
Sålnan
Norrälven
Ytterhogdal
Grövelsjöns fjällstation
Sörvattnet
1125
20
Glissjöberg
Remmet
Duvberg
Storsätern
Långfjället
Lovåsen
Sågliden
Lofsdalen
Glöte
Lofssjön
Mosätt
Ytterberg
Älvros
Kolsätter
Grundagssätern
Stadjan-Nipfjällets naturreservat
Foskros
Lofsen
Svegssjön
Sveg
358
S. Ulvkälla
Herrö
Ljusnan
Ängersjö
Vänsjö
Grövelsjön
Storfjäten
Gammalvallen
Leveråsvallen
Risbrunn
Grövaldalsvallen
Nipfjället
1102
Skäråsen
Stadjan
1131
Härjån
Härjåsjön
Målingen
Flötningen
Kopparleden
Idre
Grötholen
Fjätälven
Öjvasslan
Blådjan
Lillhärdal

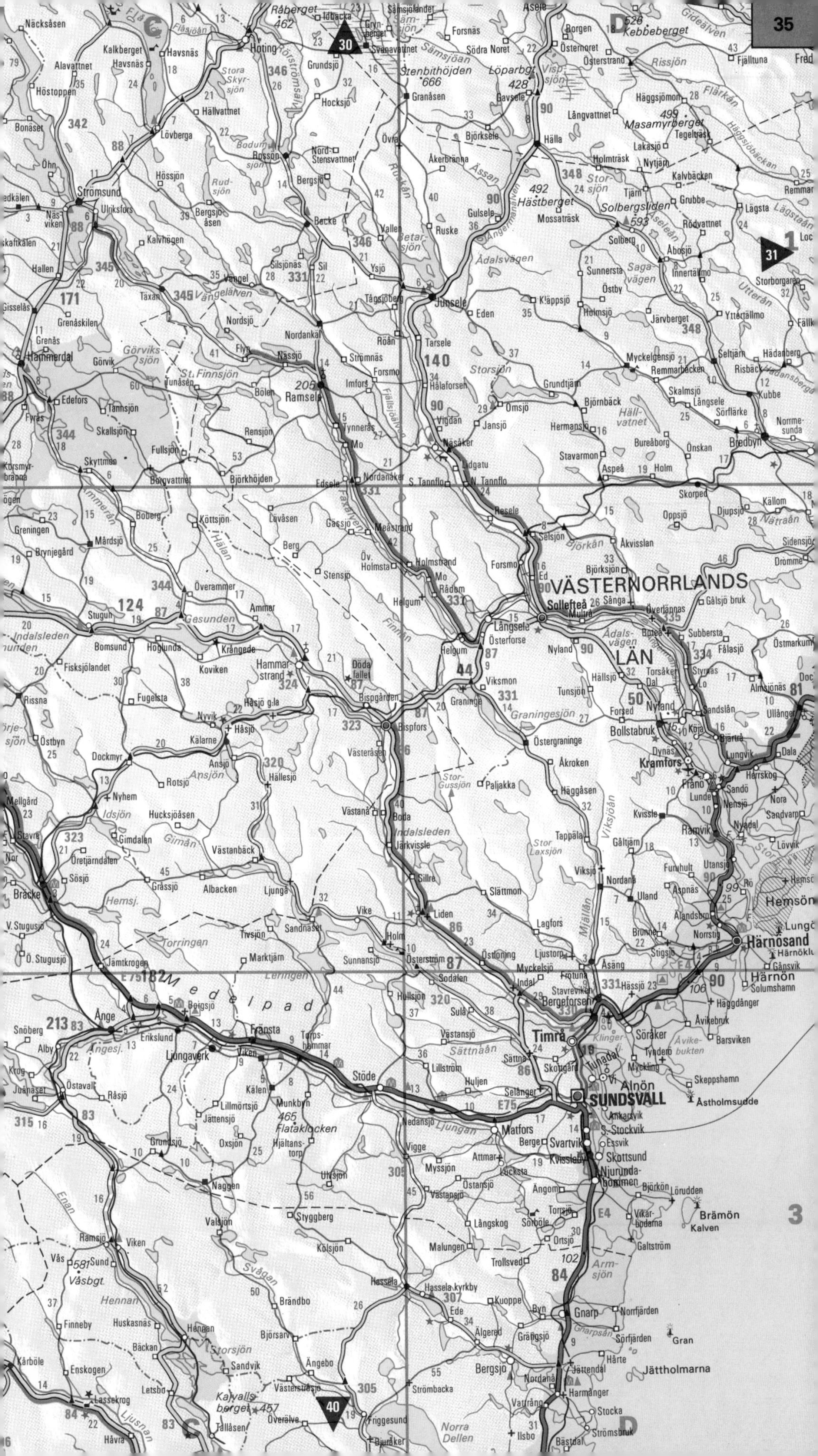
Näcksåsen
Råberget
462
Idbacka
Sämsjölandet
Åsele
Borgen
526
Kebbeberget
Gideälven
Fjälltuna
Hoting
Kalkberget
Havsnäs
Alavattnet
30
Svanavattnet
Forsnäs
Södra Noret
Österstrand
Rissjön
Höstoppen
Grundsjö
Stenbithöjden
666
Löparbgt
428
Gavsele
Hocksjö
Granåsen
Hällvattnet
Långvattnet
Häggsjömon
499
Masamyrberget
Tegelträsk
Bonäset
342
Lövberga
Björksele
Hälla
Lakasjö
Bodum
Rossön
Nord-Stensvattnet
Åkerbränna
Holmträsk
Nytjärn
Kalvbäcken
Öhn
Hössjön
Strömsund
Bergsjö
348
Tjärn
Grubbe
Lägsta
Remmar
492
Hästberget
Solbergsliden
593
Gulsele
Mossaträsk
Ulriksfors
Bergsjöåsen
Becke
Ruske
Vallen
Kalvhögen
Solberg
Åbosjö
Rödvattnet
31
Hallen
345
Silsjönäs
Sil
Ysjö
Ådalsvägen
Sunnersta
Innertällmo
Storborgaren
Vängel
Junsele
Östby
171
Täxan
Vängelälven
Tågsjöberg
Eden
Kläppsjö
Holmsjö
Järvberget
Ytterällmo
Fällk
Gisselås
Grenåskilen
Nordsjö
Grenås
Nordankäl
Tarsele
Hammerdal
Görvik
Görviksjön
Flyn
Nässjö
Strömnäs
Röån
140
Storsjön
Myckelgensjö
Remmarbäcken
Seltjärn
Hädanberg
Risbäck
St. Finnsjön
Tunåsen
Bölen
Forsmo
205
Ramsele
Imfors
Hålaforsen
Grundtjärn
Skalmsjö
Långsele
Kubbe
Edefors
Tannsjön
Omsjö
Björnbäck
Sörflärke
Fyrås
344
Skallsjön
Rensjön
Tynnerås
Mo
Vigdan
Jansjö
Hermansjö
Hällvatnet
Norrmesunda
Bureåborg
Önskan
Bredbyn
Fullsjön
Skyttmon
Näsåker
Stavarmon
Lidgatu
Aspeå
Holm
Borgvattnet
Björkhöjden
Edsele
Nordanåker
S. Tannflo
N. Tannflo
Korsmyrbränna
Skorped
Källom
Boberg
Köttsjön
Lövåsen
Gässjö
Meåstrand
Resele
Oppsjö
Djupsjö
Nätraån
Greningen
Mårdsjö
Berg
Selsjön
Björkån
Åkvisslan
Brynjegård
Stensjö
Öv. Holmsta
Holmstrand
Forsmo
Björksjön
Sidensjö
Drömme
Mo
Rådom
VÄSTERNORRLANDS
LÄN
344
Överammer
Sollefteå
Mulltrå
Sånga
Överlännas
Gälsjö bruk
124
Stugun
Gesunden
Ammer
Helgum
Långsele
Österforse
Subbersta
Östmarkum
Indalsleden
Bomsund
Höglunda
Krångede
Hammarstrand
Döda fallet
Helgum
Nyland
Torsåker
Dal
Styrnäs
Fålasjö
Fisksjölandet
Koviken
324
Bispgården
Viksmon
Graningesjön
Hällsjö
Tunsjön
Almsjönäs
Lo
Ullånger
Rissna
Fugelsta
Håsjö g:la
Graninge
331
Forsed
Nyland
Bollstabruk
Sandslån
Köja
Bjärtrå
Nyvik
Håsjö
Bispfors
Östergraninge
Östbyn
Kälarne
323
Västeråsen
Dynäs
Kramfors
Lungvik
Dala
Dockmyr
Ansjö
Ansjön
Hällesjö
Åkroken
Frånö
Herrskog
Sandö
Rotsjö
Stor-Gussjön
Paljakka
Häggåsen
Lunde
Nensjö
Nora
Mellgård
Nyhem
Idsjön
Hucksjöåsen
Västanå
Boda
Kvissle
Nyadal
Sandvarp
Stavre
323
Gimdalen
Gimån
Västanbäck
Indalsleden
Järkvissle
Tappåla
Stor Laxsjön
Viksjöån
Ramvik
Gåltjärn
Lövvik
Nor
Öretjärndalen
Utansjö
Sösjö
Grässjö
Albacken
Ljungå
Sillre
Slättmon
Viksjö
Nordanå
Funhult
Uland
Aspnäs
Hemsö
Hemsön
Bräcke
Hemsj.
Vike
Liden
Ålandsbro
Norrstig
V. Stugusjö
Tivsjön
Sandnäset
Torringen
Holm
Lagfors
Brunne
Stigsjö
Lungö
Härnösand
Ö. Stugusjö
Jämtkrogen
Marktjärn
Sunnansjö
Österström
Östloning
Ljustorp
Åsang
Härnökl
Gånsvik
182
Medelpad
Sodalen
Myckelsjö
Indal
Fröttuna
Hässjö
Härnön
Solumshamn
Hullsjön
Stavreviken
Bergeforsen
Häggdånger
Ånge
213
Borgsjö
Sulå
Åvikebruk
Snöberg
Erikslund
Fränsta
Torpshammar
Västansjö
Timrå
Klingerfjärden
Söråker
Barsviken
Åvikebukten
Alby
Angesj.
Ljungaverk
Viken
Sättnaån
Sättna
Skottgård
Tunadal
Tynderö
Krog
Juanäset
Östavall
Råsjö
Stöde
Lillström
Huljen
Myckling
Skeppshamn
Kälen
Munkbyn
Selånger
Vi
Alnön
SUNDSVALL
Åstholmsudde
315
83
Lillmörtsjö
Jättensjö
465
Flataklocken
Nedansjö
Ljungan
Matfors
Ankarsvik
S. Stockvik
Essvik
Grundsjö
Oxsjön
Hjältanstorp
Vigge
Berge
Svartvik
Skottsund
Attmar
Lucksta
Kvissleby
Njurundabommen
Naggen
Ulvsjön
Myssjön
Östansjö
Ängom
Björkön
Lörudden
Enan
Västansjö
Brämön
Kalven
Vikarbodarna
Valsjön
Styggberg
Långskog
Sörböle
Torrsjö
Ortsjö
Ramsjö
Viken
Kölsjön
Malungen
Galtström
Vås
581
Sund
Våsbgt.
Trollsved
102
Armsjön
84
Hennan
Svågan
Hassela
Hassela kyrkby
307
Brändbo
Kuoppe
Gnarp
Norrfjärden
Byn
Finneby
Huskasnäs
Ede
Henaan
Gnarpsån
Sörfjärden
Gran
Bäckan
Björsarv
Älgered
Grängsjö
Hårte
Storsjön
Kårböle
Enskogen
Sandvik
Ängebo
Bergsjö
Jättendal
Jättholmarna
Letsbo
Strömbacka
Nordanå
Harmånger
Lassekrog
Kajvallsberget
457
305
Västerstudsjö
40
Överälva
Vattrång
Stocka
Ljusnan
Tallåsen
Friggesund
Norra Dellen
Ilsbo
Strömsbruk
Håvra
Bjuråker
Bästdal

1

2

Ålesund
Spjelkavik
Godøy
Langevåg
Sula
Sykkylven
Hareid
Hareidlandet
Ulsteinvik
Fosnavåg
Gurskøy
Moldtustranda
Ørsta
Volda
Kolåstinden
Standa
Sunnmøre
Brekketind
Øye
Geiranger
Djupvasshytta
Norddal
Eidsdal
Hellesylt
Loen
Stryn
Olden
Oppstryn
Briksdal

Stadlandet
Selje
Åheim
Vågsøy
Måløy
Bremanger
Bremangerlandet
Frøya
Kalvåg
Florø
Skorpa
Nordfjordeid
Nordfjord
Hornindalsvatn
Lodalskåpa
Jostedalsbreen
Jostedal

Svelgen
Ålfotbreen
Blånibba
Storfjorden
Førde
Skei
Byrkjelo
Bygstad
Dale
Viksdalen
Sunnfjord
Gaupne
Luster
Veitastrondsvatnet

Værlandet
Atløy
Askvoll
Guddal
Høyanger
SOGN OG FJORDANE
Fjærland
Fjærlandsfjorden
Sogndal
Sogndalsfjøra
Kaupanger
Urnes

Sula
Yt. Sula
Husøy
Rutledal
Gulen
Ytre Oppedal
Lavik
Vadheim
Balestrand
Leikanger
Hermansverk
Vangsnes
Sognefjord
Viksøyri
Hopperstad
Fresvik
Fresvikbreen
Aurland
Flåm
Gudvangen
Nærøydalen
Myrdal
Voss
Vossevangen
(Voss)
Mjølfjell
Uppsete

Sande
Mjømna
Byrknes
Masfjorden
Modalen
Eksingedal
Eidsfjorden
Nordhordland
Lindås
Osterøya
Dale
Evanger
Bulken
Granvin
Ulvik
Bruravik
Brimnes
Hardanger

Radøy
Askøy
BERGEN
Osterøy
Vaksdal
Samnanger
Kvanndal
Djønno
Ålvik
Øystese
Norheimsund
HORDALAND
Hardangerfjorden
Eidfjord
(Øv. Eidfjord)
Vøringfossen
Fossli
Maurset

Store Sotra
Telavåg
Fana
Fusa
Jondal
Strandebarm
Ullensvang
Lofthus
Kinsarvik
Aga
Hardanger

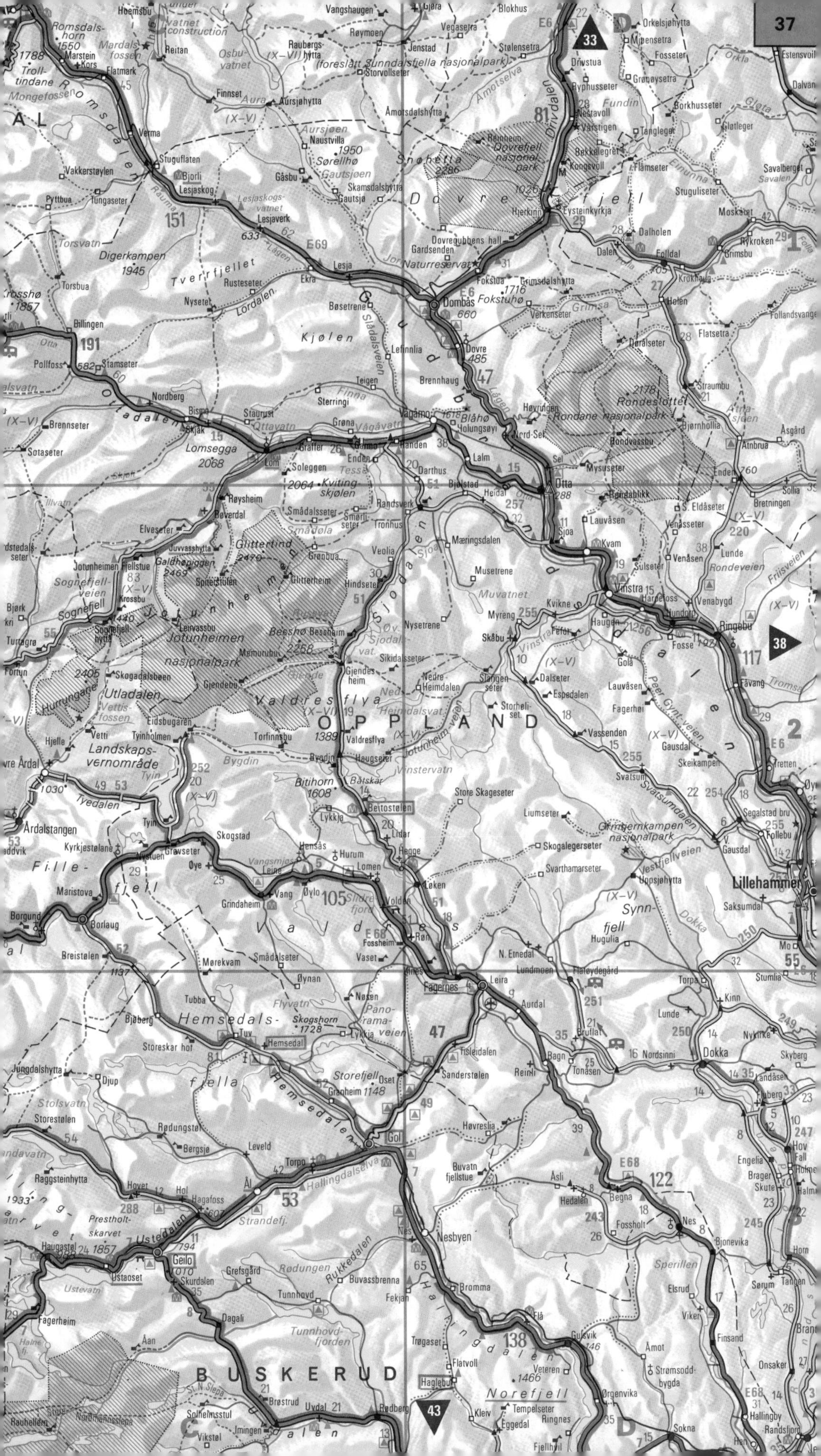
33
38
43
OPPLAND
BUSKERUD
Romsdalshorn 1550
Trolltindane
Mongefossen
Romsdalen
Marstein
Flatmark
Verma
Stuguflaten
Bjorli
Lesjaskog
Lesjaverk
Vakkerstøylen
Pyttbua
Tungaseter
Digerkampen 1945
Tverrfjellet
Torsbua
Krosshø 1857
Billingen
Pollfoss
Stamseter
Ottadalen
Nordberg
Bismo
Skjåk
Brennseter
Søtaseter
Lom
Lomsegga 2068
Staurust
Ottavatn
Grøna
Vågåvatn
Garmo
Vågåmo
Lesja
Ekra
Rusteseter
Nyseter
Lordalen
Bøsetrene
Kjølen
Sjodalsveien
Lefinnlia
Teigen
Sterringi
Dombås 660
Dovre 485
Brennhaug
Blåhø
Holungsøyi
Lalm
Otta 288
Sel
Nord-Sel
Hjerkinn
Eysteinkyrkja
Dovre fjell
Dovrefjell nasjonalpark
Snøhetta 2286
Dovregubbens hall
Gardsenden
Naturreservat
Fokstua
Grimsdalshytta
Fokstuhø
Drivdalen
Drivstua
Ryphusseter
Nestavoll
Vårstigen
Kongsvoll
Reinheim
Orkelsjøhytta
Fosseter
Grønøysetra
Borkhusseter
Tangleget
Flåmseter
Stuguliseter
Savalberget
Moskaret
Dalholen
Dalen
Folldal
Rykkroken
Grimsbu
Krokhaug
Holen
Follandsvangen
Flatsetra
Døralseter
Straumbu
Rondeslottet 2178
Rondane nasjonalpark
Høvringen
Rondvassbu
Bjørnhollia
Atnbrua
Åsgård
Mysuseter
Enden 760
Sollia
Bretningen
S. Eldåseter
Venåsseter
Rondeveien
Frisvegen
Lunde
Kvam
Sjoa
Sulseter
Venåsen
Vinstra
Harpefoss
Hundorp
Venabygd
Ringebu
Fåvang
Kvikne
Myreng
Skåbu
Haugen
Fefor
Gola
Fosse
Dalseter
Espedalen
Lauvåsen
Fagerhøi
Peer Gynt-veien
Vassenden
Gausdal
Skeikampen
Svatsum
Svatsumdalen
Gudbrandsdalen
Tretten
Segalstad bru
Follebu
Gausdal
Lillehammer
Saksumdal
Mo
Stumlia
Dokka
Torpa
Kinn
Lunde
Nykirke
Skyberg
Landåsen
Fluberg
Hov
Fall
Engelia
Brager
Skute
Bjonevika
Sørum
Tangen
Onsaker
Hallingby
Randsfjord
Finsand
Viker
Sperillen
Elsrud
Nes
Begna
Fossholt
Hedalen
Åsli
Buvatn fjellstue
Høvreslia
Sanderstølen
Reinli
Bagn
Tonåsen
Nordsinni
Bruflat
Aurdal
Leira
Fagernes
Lundmoen
Flatøydegård
N. Etnedal
Hugulia
Synnfjell
Uppsjøhytta
Vestfjellveien
Skogalegerseter
Svarthamarseter
Liumseter
Gråtjernkampen nasjonalpark
Store Skageseter
Heidal
Bjølstad
Darthus
Randsverk
Tronhus
Mæringsdalen
Musetrene
Muvatnet
Nysetrene
Sikkilsdalseter
Nedre Heimdalen
Heimdalsvat.
Slangen seter
Storhøliset.
Jotunheimveien
Vinstervatn
Valdresflya
Haugseter
Bygdin
Båtskar
Beitostølen
Lykkja
Lidar
Hegge
Hurum
Lomen
Løken
Volden
Slidrefjord
Vang
Øylo
Grindaheim
Valdres
Røn
Fossheim
Vaset
Smådalseter
Øynan
Nøsen
Panoramaveien
Flyvatn
Skogshorn 1728
Mørekvam
Tubba
Hemsedalsfjella
Hemsedal
Tuv
Storeskar hof
Bjøberg
Hemsedalen
Storefjell
Oset
Granheim 1148
Gol
Leveld
Torpo
Ål
Hallingdalselva
Bergsjø
Rødungstøl
Jungdalshytta
Djup
Stolsvatn
Storestølen
Raggsteinhytta
Hovet
Hol
Hagafoss
Strandefj.
Prestholtskarvet
Haugastøl
Ustedalen
Geilo
Ustaoset
Ustevatn
Skurdalen
Grefsgård
Rødungen
Rukkedalen
Buvassbrenna
Tunnhovd
Tunnhovdfjorden
Dagali
Fagerheim
Åan
Nesbyen
Bromma
Fekjan
Hallingdalen
Flå
Trøgaset
Flatvoll
Haglebu
Norefjell
Tempelseter
Eggedal
Ringnes
Kleiv
Veteren
Gulsvik
Ørgenvika
Sokna
Åmot
Strømsoddbygda
Uvdal
Brøstrud
Rødberg
Solheimsstul
Imingen
Vikstøl
Nordmannsslepa
Rauhellern
Jotunheimen
Jotunheimen nasjonalpark
Glittertind 2470
Galdhøpiggen 2469
Spiterstulen
Glitterheim
Juvvasshytta
Jotunheimen Fjellstue
Røysheim
Bøverdal
Elveseter
Sognefjellveien
Sognefjell
Krossbu
Leirvassbu
Sognefjellhytta
Memurubu
Besshø
Besseggen
Gjendesheim
Gjendebu
Skogadalsbøen
Hurrungane 2405
Utladalen
Vettisfossen
Eidsbugarden
Tyinholmen
Torfinnsbu
Vetti
Hjelle
Landskapsvernområde
Årdal
Tyin
Tyedalen
Årdalstangen
Kyrkjestølane
Filefjell
Nystuen
Grøvseter
Skogstad
Øye
Maristova
Borlaug
Borgund
Breistølen
Bitihorn 1608
Kviting-skjølen
Soleggen
Smådalsseter
Smørli seter
Veolia
Grønbua
Hindseter
Sjodalen
Tessa
Turtagrø
Fortun
Bjørk
E6
E68
E69

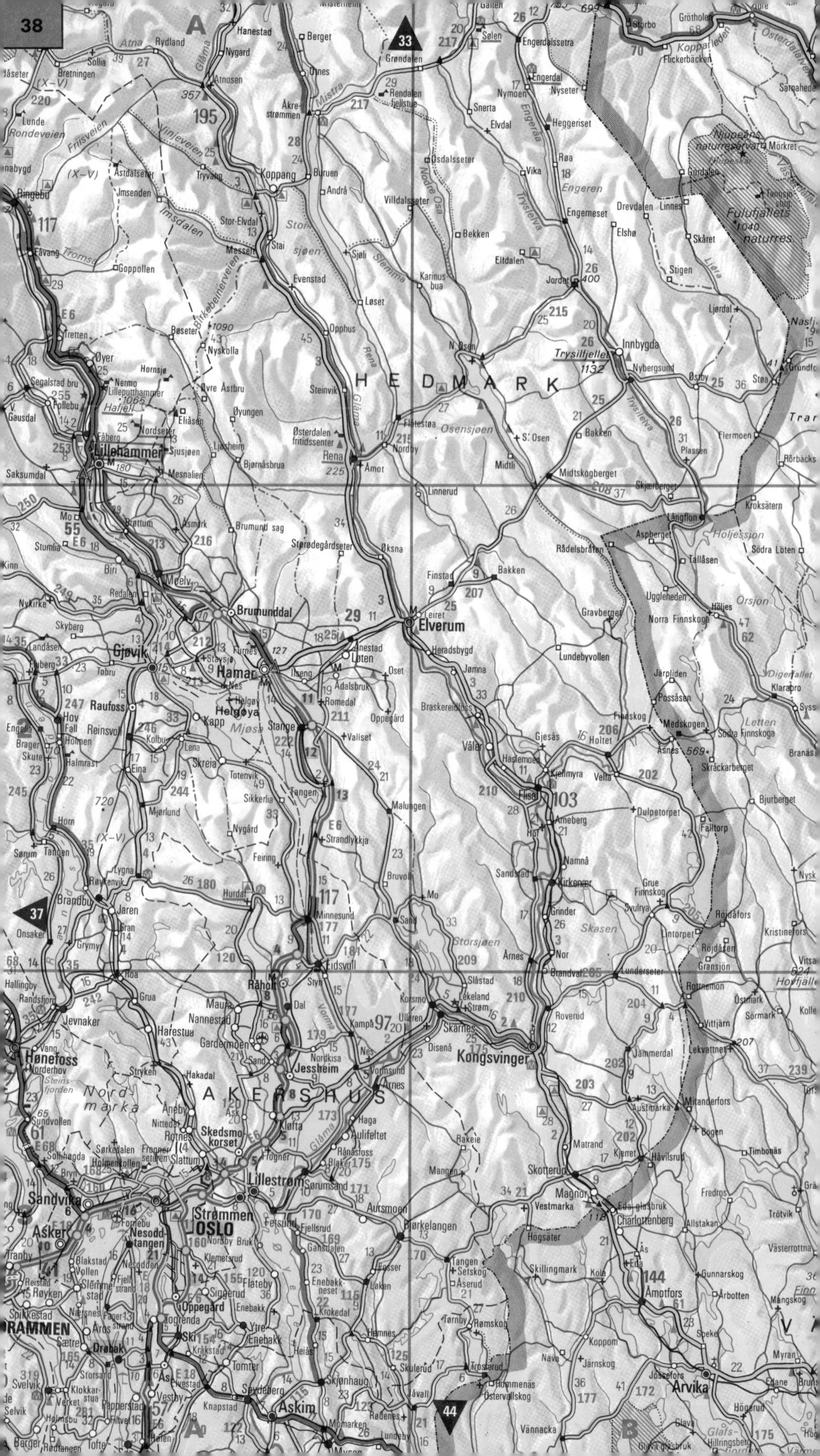
33
37
44
HEDMARK
AKERSHUS
Hanestad
Rydland
Sollia
Bretningen
Lunde
Rondeveien
Friisveien
Atnosen
Nygard
Berget
Grøndalen
Ønnes
Rendalen fjellstue
Åkrestrømmen
Mistra
Engerdalssetra
Engerdal
Nyseter
Nymoen
Snerta
Elvdal
Heggeriset
Røa
Vika
Engeren
Engerneset
Storbo
Grötholen
Kopparleden
Flickerbäcken
Särnahede
Österdalälven
Mörkret
Gördalen
Drevdalen
Linnes
Elshø
Skåret
Fulufjällets naturres.
Stigen
Ljørdal
Ljøra
Innbygda
Trysilfjellet
1132
Nybergsund
Østby
Støa
Grundfor
Bakken
Flermoen
Plassen
Midtskogberget
Skjærberget
Långflon
Kroksätern
Holjessjön
Södra Löten
Aspberget
Rådelsbråten
Tallåsen
Uggleheden
Höljes
Orsjön
Norra Finnskoga
Gravberget
Lundebyvollen
Järpliden
Possåsen
Digerfallet
Klarabro
Letten
Medskogen
Södra Finnskoga
Skråckarberget
Bjurberget
Dulpetorpet
Falltorp
Grue Finnskog
Svulrya
Röjdåfors
Kristinefors
Lintorpet
Röjdåsen
Gransjön
Lunderseter
Rottnemon
Östmark
Sörmark
Vittjärn
Lekvattnet
Hoffjället
Mitandersfors
Bogen
Timbonäs
Håvilsrud
Fredros
Trötvik
Eda glasbruk
Charlottenberg
Allstakan
Västerrottna
Gunnarskog
Åmotfors
Årbotten
Mangskog
Speke
Arvika
Myran
Edane
Högerud
Glava
Glava glasbruk
Hillringsberg
Josefors
Koppom
Järnskog
Näva
Vännacka
Skillingmark
Kola
Högsäter
Vestmarka
Magnor
Skotterud
Matrand
Kjerret
Austmarka
Jammerdal
Roverud
Brandval
Nor
Årnes
Skasen
Grinder
Kirkenær
Namnå
Sandstad
Arneberg
Flisa
Kjellmyra
Haslemoen
Gjesås
Holtet
Velta
Finnskog
Våler
Braskereidfoss
Jømna
Heradsbygd
Elverum
Leiret
Finstad
Bakken
Øksna
Linnerud
Rena
Åmot
Nordby
Flatestøa
Osensjøen
S. Osen
Midtli
N. Osen
Østerdalen fritidssenter
Steinvik
Opphus
Løset
Evenstad
Sjøli
Slemma
Karinusbua
Eltdalen
Bekken
Villdalsseter
Østdalsseter
Nordre Osa
Trysilelva
Koppang
Buruen
Andrå
Stor-Elvdal
Stai
Messelt
Storsjøen
Tryvang
Åstdalseter
Imsenden
Imsdalen
Vinjeveien
Goppollen
Ringebu
Fåvang
Tromsa
Tretten
Øyer
Segalstad bru
Follebu
Gausdal
Hafjell
Nermo
Lillehammer
Fåberg
Nordseter
Sjusjøen
Mesnalien
Eliåsen
Hornsjø
Nyskolla
Bøseter
Øvre Åstbru
Øyungen
Ljøsheim
Bjørnåsbrua
Birkebeinerveien
Saksumdal
Brøttum
Åsmark
Brumund sag
Størødegårdseter
Stumlia
Biri
Moelv
Redalen
Nykirke
Skyberg
Brumunddal
Landåsen
Gjøvik
Hamar
Furnes
Stavsjø
Nes
Helgøya
Ilseng
Løten
Ånestad
Oset
Ådalsbruk
Romedal
Oppegård
Stange
Vallset
Kapp
Mjøsa
Raufoss
Hov
Holmen
Reinsvoll
Kolbu
Lena
Skreia
Totenvik
Sikkerlia
Eina
Mjørlund
Nygård
Tangen
Strandlykkja
Malungen
Bruvoll
Mo
Sand
Storsjøen
Sørum
Lygna
Røykenvik
Brandbu
Jaren
Gran
Grymyr
Hurdal
Feiring
Minnesund
Eidsvoll
Onsaker
Hallingby
Randsfjord
Jevnaker
Roa
Grua
Harestua
Maura
Nannestad
Råholt
Dal
Styri
Vorma
Kampå
Ullern
Korsmo
Slåstad
Lekeland
Strøm
Skarnes
Disenå
Kongsvinger
Hønefoss
Vang
Norderhov
Steinsfjorden
Nordmarka
Stryken
Hakadal
Gardermoen
Nordkisa
Jessheim
Nes
Vormsund
Årnes
Haga
Aulifeltet
Rånåsfoss
Blaker
Sørumsand
Kløfta
Skedsmokorset
Frogner
Lillestrøm
Glåma
Rakeie
Mangen
Aurtsmoen
Bjørkelangen
Fetsund
Fjellsrud
Gansdalen
Enebakkneset
Krokedal
Lauken
Fosser
Tangen
Setskog
Åserud
Rømskog
Tørnby
Trosterud
Rømmenås
Østervallskog
Hemnes
Heiås
Skulerud
Jåvall
Askim
Skjønhaug
Mysen
Momarken
Rødenes
Lundeby
Sundvollen
Sollihøgda
Bryn
Sørkedalen
Frognerseteren
Holmenkollen
Slattum
Sandvika
Asker
Strømmen
OSLO
Nesoddtangen
Fornebu
Norbybruk
Klemetsrud
Flateby
Siggerud
Oppegård
Enebakk
Ytre Enebakk
Tograna
Ski
Kråkstad
Tomter
Ås
Vestby
Spydeberg
Knapstad
Drøbak
Røyken
Spikkestad
DRAMMEN
Sætre
Svelvik
Klokkarstua
Verket
Storsand
Pepperstad
Hvitsten
Hølen
Selvik
Berger
Tofte
Hurum
Blakstad
Vollen
Slemmestad
Nærsnes
Åros
Fjellstrand
Tranby

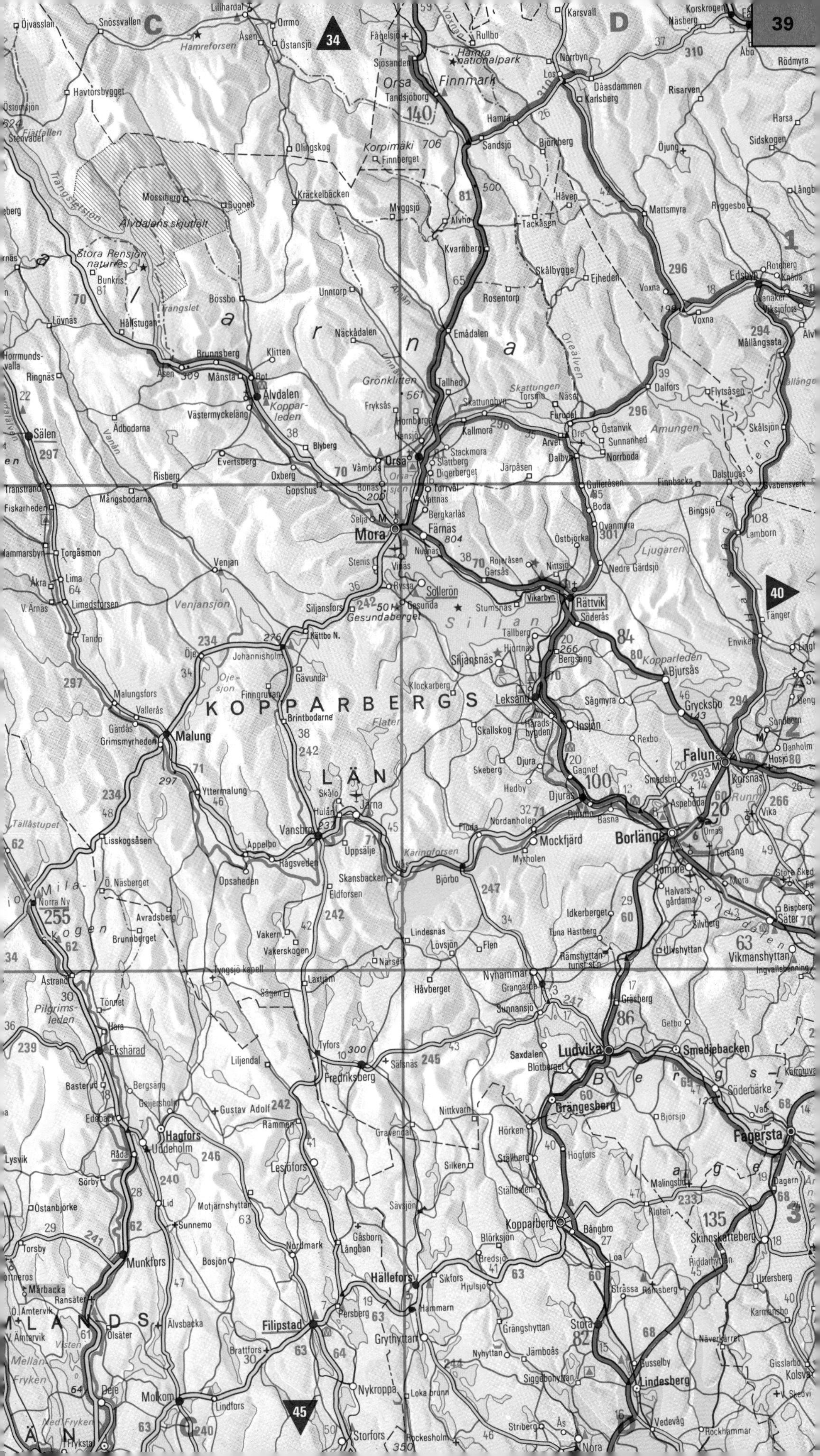
C
D
34
40
45
Öjvasslan
Snössvallen
Lillhärdal
Orrmo
Åsen
Östansjö
Hamreforsen
Fågelsjö
Rullbo
Hamra nationalpark
Sjösanden
Orsa Finnmark
Tandsjöborg
Karsvall
Näsberg
Korskrogen
Åbo
Rödmyra
Norrbyn
Los
Dåasdammen
Karlsberg
Risarven
Havtorsbygget
Östomsjön
Fjätfallen
Stenvadet
Olingskog
Korpimäki
Finnberget
Hamra
Sandsjö
Björkberg
Öjung
Harsa
Sidskogen
Trängslet
Trängsletsjön
Mossiberg
Sugnet
Älvdalens skjutfält
Kräckelbäcken
Myggsjö
Alvho
Håven
Tackåsen
Mattsmyra
Ryggesbo
Långbo
Stora Rensjön naturres.
Bunkris
Kvarnberg
Skålbygge
Ejheden
Voxna
Edsbyn
Roteberg
Knåda
Ovanåker
Viksjöfors
Bössbo
Unntorp
Rosentorp
Lövnäs
Hällstugan
Näckådalen
Emådalen
Mållångssta
Horrmundsvalla
Ringnäs
Brunnsberg
Klitten
Åsen
Månsta
Rot
Älvdalen
Kopparleden
Grönklitten
Tallhed
Skattungen
Skattungbyn
Torsmo
Näset
Dalfors
Flytsåsen
Ädbodarna
Västermyckeläng
Fryksås
Hornberga
Kallmora
Furudal
Östanvik
Sunnanhed
Amungen
Skålsjön
Sälen
Vanån
Blyberg
Hansjö
Stackmora
Arvet
Ore
Dalby
Norrboda
Risberg
Evertsberg
Oxberg
Våmhus
Orsa
Slättberg
Digerberget
Järpåsen
Dalstugan
Svabensverk
Transtrand
Gopshus
Bonäs
Orsasjön
Forrväl
Vattnäs
Gulleråsen
Finnbacka
Fiskarheden
Mångsbodarna
Boda
Bingsjö
Selja
Mora
Färnäs
Bergkarlås
Ovanmyra
Lamborn
Hammarsbyn
Torgåsmon
Nusnäs
Östbjörka
Ljugaren
Venjan
Stenis
Vinäs
Rojeråsen
Garsås
Nittsjö
Nedre Gärdsjö
Åkra
Lima
Rysssa
Sollerön
Limedsforsen
Venjansjön
Siljansfors
Gesunda
Gesundaberget
Stumsnäs
Vikarbyn
Rättvik
Tänger
V. Ärnäs
Söderås
Siljan
Tando
Öje
Johannisholm
Kättbo N.
Tällberg
Hjortnäs
Bergsäng
Kopparleden
Enviken
Siljansnäs
Bjursås
Gävunda
Ojesjön
Finngruvan
Klockarberg
Leksand
Sågmyra
Grycksbo
Malungsfors
Vallerås
KOPPARBERGS
LÄN
Gärdås
Grimsmyrheden
Malung
Brintbodarne
Flaten
Skallskog
Hårads-bygden
Insjön
Rexbo
Sundborn
Falun
Danholm
Hosjö
Skeberg
Djura
Gagnef
Smedsbo
Korsnäs
Yttermalung
Skålo
Järna
Hedby
Djurås
Aspeboda
Runn
Vika
Tällåstupet
Lisskogsåsen
Hulån
Vansbro
Nordanholen
Floda
Djurmo
Bäsna
Mockfjärd
Borlänge
Ornäs
Torsång
Äppelbo
Rågsveden
Uppsälje
Kåringforsen
Näs
Björbo
Myrholen
Romme
Stora Skedvi
Mora
Halvarsgårdarna
Dalälven
Bispberg
Säter
Ö. Näsberget
Opsaheden
Skansbacken
Eldforsen
Mila-skogen
Norra Ny
Avradsberg
Brunnberget
Vakern
Vakerskogen
Lindesnäs
Lövsjön
Flen
Idkerberget
Tuna Hästberg
Silvberg
Ulvshyttan
Vikmanshyttan
Ingvallsbenning
Rämshyttan turist stn
Åstrand
Tyngsjö kapell
Narsen
Laxtjärn
Nyhammar
Grangärde
Håvberget
Tönnet
Pilgrimsleden
Sågen
Sunnansjö
Gräsberg
Getbo
Hara
Ekshärad
Tyfors
Liljendal
Saxdalen
Blötberget
Ludvika
Smedjebacken
Säfsnäs
Fredriksberg
Basterud
Bergsäng
Gustav Adolf
Rämmen
Nittkvarn
Grängesberg
Bergslagen
Söderbärke
Karrbo
Edebäck
Geijersholm
Hagfors
Uddeholm
Gravendal
Hörken
Bjorsjö
Fagersta
Lysvik
Råda
Lesjöfors
Silken
Ställberg
Högfors
Malingsbo
Dagarn
Sörby
Lid
Motjärnshyttan
Ställdalen
Kloten
Skinnskatteberg
Östanbjörke
Sunnemo
Sävsjön
Kopparberg
Bångbro
Gåsborn
Långban
Nordmark
Blörksjön
Torsby
Munkfors
Bosjön
Bredsjö
Löa
Riddarhyttan
Uttersberg
Mårbacka
Ransäter
Hällefors
Sikfors
Hjulsjö
Strässa
Ramsberg
Ö. Amtervik
Persberg
Hammarn
Karmansbo
V. Amtervik
Olsäter
Älvsbacka
Filipstad
Grythyttan
Grängshyttan
Stora
Näverkärret
Visten
Mellan-Fryken
Brattfors
Nyhyttan
Järnboås
Gusselby
Gisslarbo
Kolsva
Deje
Siggebohyttan
Lindesberg
V. Skedvi
Molkom
Lindfors
Nykroppa
Loka brunn
Vedevåg
Ned Fryken
Frykstad
Storfors
Rockesholm
Striberg
Ås
Nora
Rockhammar
VÄRMLANDS LÄN

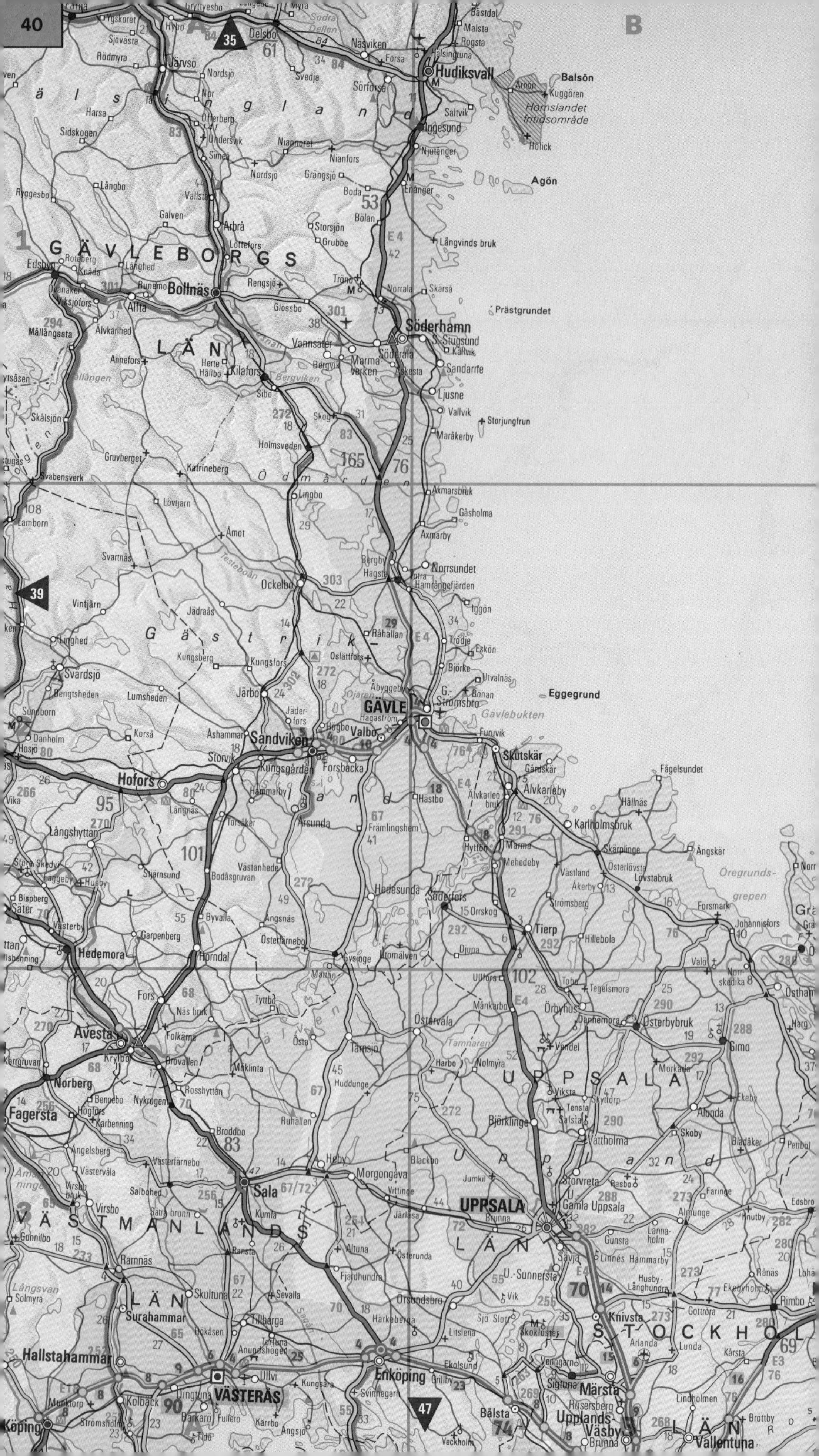
B
Hudiksvall
Balsön
Kuggören
Hornslandet fritidsområde
Hölick
Agön
Iggesund
Njutånger
Enånger
Långvinds bruk
Delsbo
Järvsö
Forsa
Näsviken
Bästdal
Malsta
Rogsta
Hälsingtuna
Saltvik
Sörforsa
Hälsingland
Nordsjö
Harsa
Sidskogen
Undersvik
Simeå
Nianfors
Gnarp
Grängsjö
Boda
Bölan
Långbo
Ryggesbo
Vallsta
Galven
Arbrå
Storsjön
Grubbe
Lottefors
GÄVLEBORGS
LÄN
Edsbyn
Rotaberg
Knåda
Långhed
Runemo
Bollnäs
Rengsjö
Trönö
Norrala
Skärså
Alfta
Viksjöfors
Ovanåker
Glossbo
Söderhamn
Prästgrundet
Mållångssta
Alvkarlhed
Vannsäter
Stugsund
Kalkvik
Sandarne
Annefors
Herte
Hällbo
Kilafors
Bergvik
Marmaverken
Söderala
Askesta
Ljusne
Vallvik
Storjungfrun
Skålsjön
Sibo
Bergviken
Skog
Holmsveden
Maråkerby
Gruvberget
Katrineberg
Ödmården
Svabensverk
Lingbo
Axmarsbruk
Gåsholma
Lamborn
Lövtjärn
Åmot
Axmarby
Svartnäs
Testeboån
Bergby
Hagsta
Norrsundet
Totra
Hamrångefjärden
Ockelbo
Iggön
Vintjärn
Jädraås
Gästrikland
Råhällan
Trödje
Eskön
Linghed
Kungsberg
Kungsfors
Oslättfors
Björke
Svärdsjö
Utvalnäs
Bönan
Bengtsheden
Lumsheden
Järbo
Åbyggeby
Eggegrund
GÄVLE
Strömsbro
Gävlebukten
Sundborn
Hagaström
Jäderfors
Danholm
Korså
Åshammar
Sandviken
Högbo
Valbo
Furuvik
Hosjö
Storvik
Kungsgården
Forsbacka
Skutskär
Gårdskär
Fågelsundet
Hofors
Hästbo
Älvkarleby
Älvkarleö bruk
Vika
Långnäs
Hammarby
Torsåker
Årsunda
Karlholmsbruk
Hållnäs
Främlingshem
Långshyttan
Hytton
Marma
Skärplinge
Ängskär
Stora Skedvi
Mehedeby
Östervlövsta
Lövstabruk
Öregrundsgrepen
Husby
Västanhede
Bodåsgruvan
Västland
Åkerby
Bispberg
Stjärnsund
Hedesunda
Söderfors
Strömsberg
Forsmark
Säter
Orrskog
Johannisfors
Västerby
Byvalla
Ängsnäs
Tierp
Hillebola
Garpenberg
Österfärnebo
Djuna
Hedemora
Horndal
Gysinge
Ulfors
Valö
Norrskedika
Östhammar
Mattön
Tobo
Tegelsmora
Fors
Näs bruk
Tyttbo
Månkarbo
Örbyhus
Dannemora
Österbybruk
Harg
Avesta
Östervala
Gimo
Krylbo
Folkärna
Östa
Tärnsjö
Tämnaren
Vendel
Brovallen
Möklinta
Harbo
Nolmyra
Norberg
Rosshyttan
Huddunge
UPPSALA
Morkarla
Bennebo
Nykroppa
Viksta
Skyttorp
Ekeby
Fagersta
Hogfors
Karbenning
Ruhällen
Tensta
Salsta
Alunda
Björklinge
Vattholma
Skoby
Broddbo
Bladåker
Ängelsberg
Västerfärnebo
Heby
Blackbo
Uppland
Västervåla
Morgongåva
Jumkil
Storvreta
Rasbo
Faringe
Virsbo
Salbohed
Sala
Vittinge
Järlåsa
UPPSALA
Brunna
Gamla Uppsala
Almunge
Knutby
Edsbro
VÄSTMANLANDS
LÄN
Sätra brunn
Kumla
Lännaholm
Gunnilbo
Ransta
Altuna
Österunda
Sävja
Gunsta
Linnés Hammarby
Ramnäs
Fjärdhundra
U. Sunnersta
Husby-Långhundra
Rånäs
Lohärad
Solmyra
Skultuna
Sevalla
Örsundsbro
Vik
Ekebyholm
Rimbo
Surahammar
Tillberga
Harkeberga
Knivsta
Gottröra
Hökåsen
Tortuna
Anundshögen
Litslena
Sjö
Slottsskogen
Skokloster
STOCKHOLMS
Arlanda
Lunda
Kårsta
Hallstahammar
VÄSTERÅS
Ullvi
Dingtuna
Enköping
Ekolsund
Grillby
Venngarn
Sigtuna
Märsta
Kungsåra
Svinnegarn
Kolbäck
Barkarö
Fullerö
Kärrbo
Rosersberg
Lindholmen
Munktorp
Strömsholm
Köping
Ängsjö
Bålsta
Upplands Väsby
Brunna
Vallentuna
Brottby
Tidö
Veckholm
35
39
47

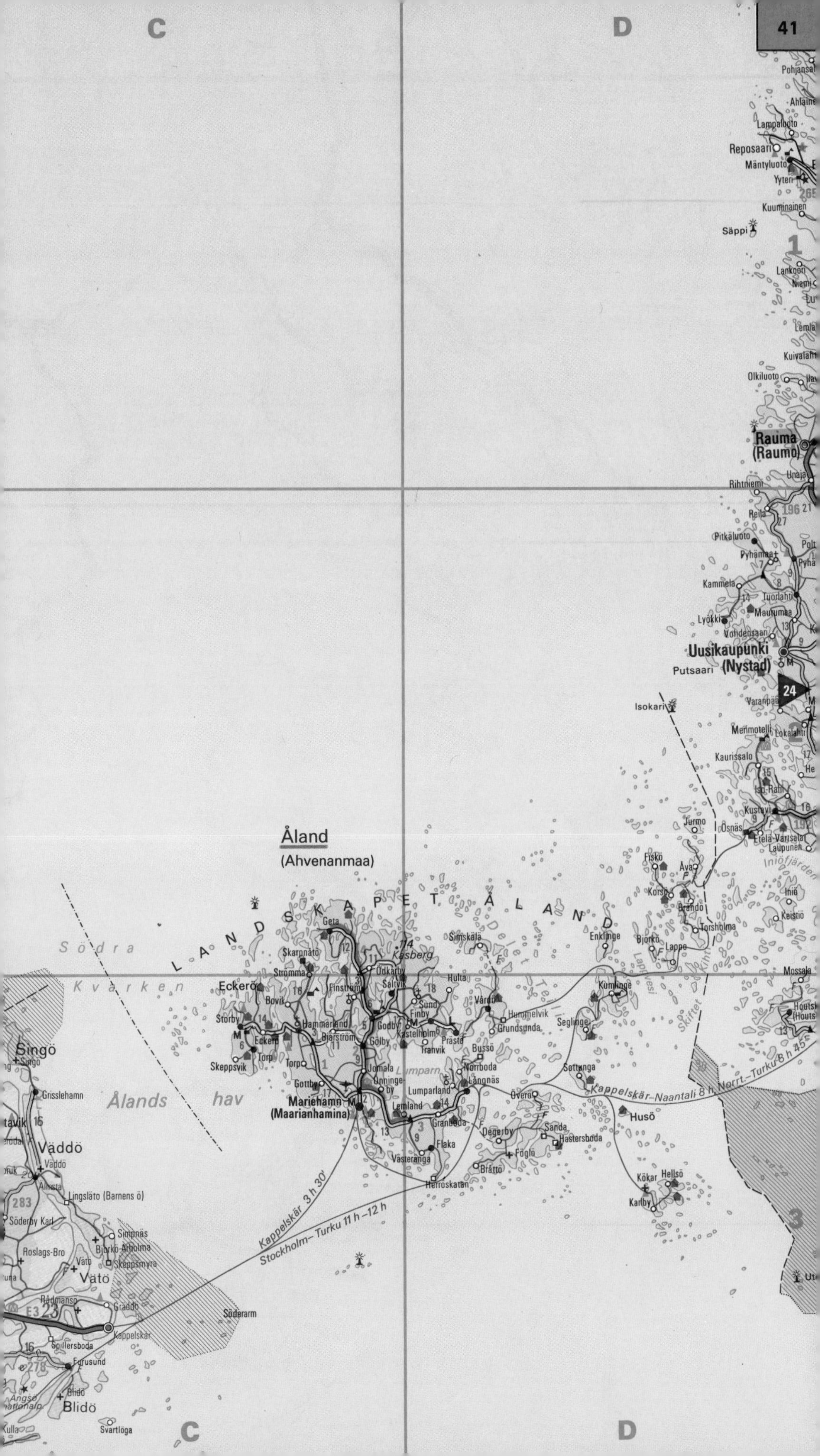
C
D
Pohjansa
Ahlaine
Lampaluoto
Reposaari
Mäntyluoto
Yyteri
Kuuminainen
Säppi
1
Lankoori
Niemi
Lemla
Kuivalahti
Olkiluoto
Rauma
(Raumo)
Unaja
Rihtniemi
Reila
Pitkäluoto
Pyhämaa
Kammela
Tuorlahti
Lyökki
Maunumaa
Vohdensaari
Uusikaupunki
(Nystad)
Putsaari
24
Isokari
Varanpää
Merimotelli
Lokalahti
2
Kaurissalo
Iso-Rahi
Kustavi
Jurmo
Osnäs
Etelä-Vartsala
Laupunen
Iniöfjärden
Fiskö
Åva
Korsö
Brändö
Iniö
Keistiö
Torsholma
Åland
(Ahvenanmaa)
L A N D S K A P E T Å L A N D
Geta
Kasberg
Simskälä
Enklinge
Björkö
Lappo
Södra
Kvarken
Skarpnäto
Strömma
Odkarby
Saltvik
Hulta
Eckerö
Finström
Sund
Vårdö
Hummelvik
Kumlinge
Mossala
Bovik
Finby
Grundsunda
Seglinge
Storby
Hammarland
Godby
Kastelholm
Präst
Eckerö
Bjärström
Gölby
Tranvik
Bussö
Torp
Skeppsvik
Torp
Jomala
Lumparn
Norrboda
Sottunga
Singö
Gottby
Önningeby
Lumparland
Långnäs
Grisslehamn
Ålands
hav
Mariehamn
(Maarianhamina)
Lemland
Överö
Kappelskär–Naantali 8 h
Norrt.–Turku 8 h 45
Husö
Väddö
Granboda
Degerby
Sanda
Hastersboda
Flaka
Föglö
Västeränga
Brätto
Herröskatan
Kökar
Hellsö
Karlby
Almsta
Lingslätö (Barnens ö)
283
Söderby Karl
Kappelskär 3 h 30'
Stockholm– Turku 11 h–12 h
3
Simpnäs
Björkö-Arholma
Roslags-Bro
Vätö
Skeppsmyra
Vätö
Rådmansö
Gräddö
E3 23
Söderarm
Kappelskär
Spillersboda
Furusund
Blidö
Blidö
Svartlöga
C
D

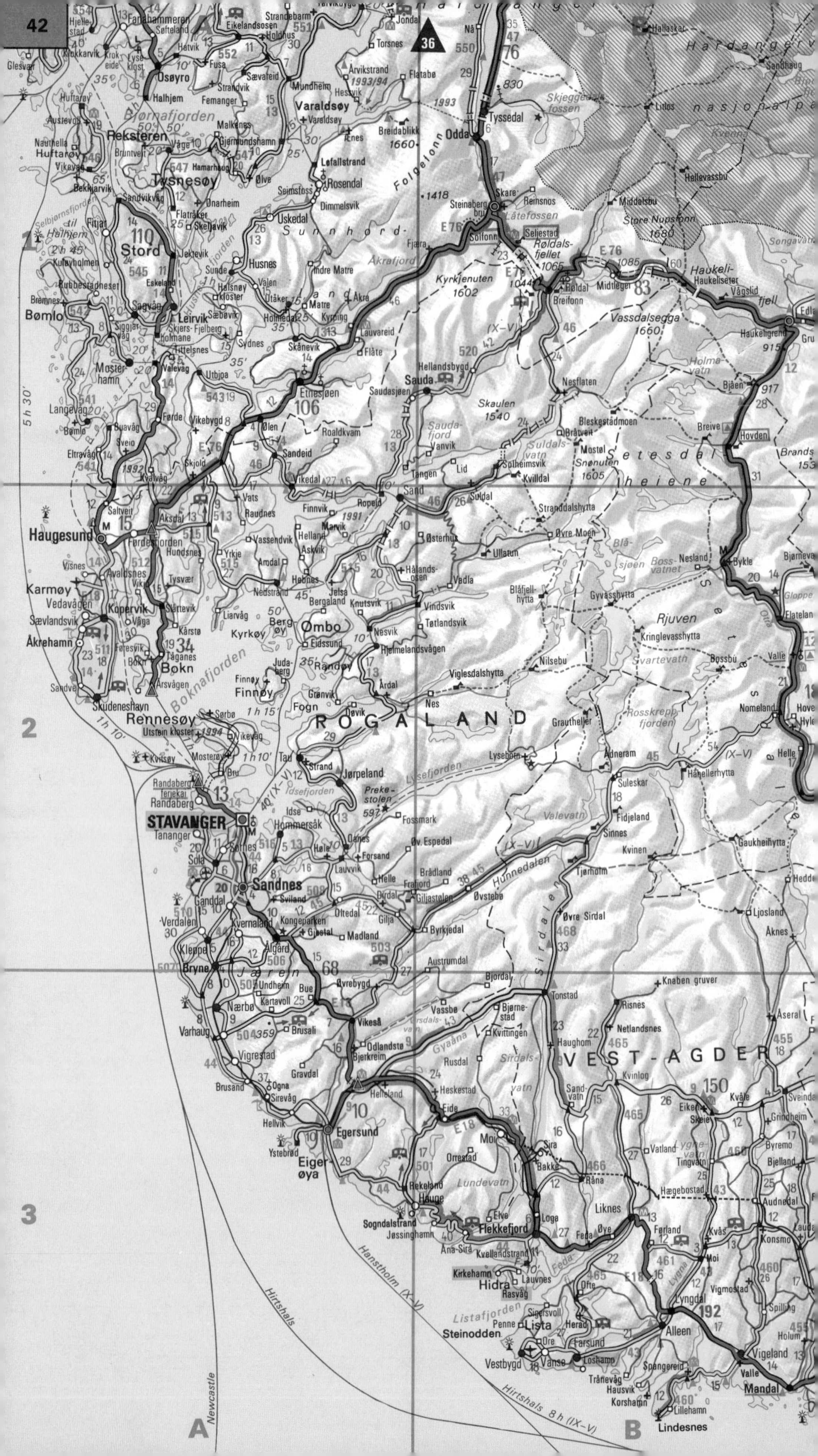

Fanahammeren
Søfteland
Strandebarm
Eikelandsosen
Holdhus
Jondal
Torsnes
Nå
Hallaskar
Hardanger
Sandhaug
nasjonalpark
Glesvær
Krokeide
Lysekloster
Osøyro
Fusa
Hatvik
Årvikstrand
Flatabø
Mundheim
Hesvik
Varaldsøy
Halhjem
Strandvik
Femanger
Huftarøy
Austevoll
Bjørnafjorden
Malkenes
Gjermundshamn
Enes
Breidablikk
1660
Odda
Tyssedal
Skjeggedalsfossen
Litlos
Reksteren
Nauthella
Huftarøy
Vikevåg
Bekkjarvik
Bruntveit
Våge
Tysnesøy
Hamarhaug
Ølve
Løfallstrand
Rosendal
Folgefonna
Seimsfoss
Dimmelsvik
1418
Skare
Reinsnos
Steinaberg bru
Låtefossen
Hellevassbu
Middalsbu
Store Nupsfonn
1680
Sandvikvåg
Ønarheim
Flatråker
Skeljavik
Uskedal
Sunnhordland
Fjæra
Solfonn
Seljestad
Røldalsfjellet
1065
Songavatn
Selbjørnsfjorden
Halhjem
Fitjar
Stord
Jektevik
Husnes
Kulavholmen
Rubbestadneset
Bremnes
Bømlo
Eskeland
Sagvåg
Leirvik
Sunde
Halsnøy kloster
Valen
Uttåker
Indre Matre
Åkrafjord
Åkra
Matre
Kyrkjenuten
1602
Røldal
Breifonn
Midtlæger
Haukeli
Haukeliseter
Vågslid
fjell
1085
Skjersholmane
Holmane
Sæbøvik
Sydnes
Holmedal
Kyrping
Lauvareid
Vassdalsegga
1660
Haukeligrend
915
Mosterhamn
Tittelsnes
Valevåg
Utbjoa
Skånevik
Flåte
Hellandsbygd
Sauda
Holmavatn
Langevåg
Etnesjøen
Saudasjøen
Nesflaten
Bjåen
917
Bømlo
Buavåg
Sveio
Førde
Vikebygd
Ølen
Roaldkvam
Skaulen
1540
Saudafjord
Bleskestadmoen
Bråtveit
Mostøl
Snønuten
1605
Breive
Hovden
Eltravåg
Skjold
Sandeid
Vanvik
Suldalsvatn
Setesdalsheiene
Brandsfjell
Kvalvåg
Vikedal
Sand
Tangen
Lid
Solheimsvik
Kvilldal
Haugesund
Saltveit
Aksdal
Vats
Raudnes
Finnvik
Ropeid
1991
Suldal
Stranddalshytta
Førdesfjorden
Hundsnes
Vassendvik
Helland
Marvik
Askvik
Østerhus
Øvre Moen
Ullatun
Blåsjøen
Bossvatnet
Nesland
Bykle
Bjørnevatn
Visnes
Karmøy
Vedavågen
Avaldsnes
Vikje
Tysvær
Yrkje
Amdal
Hebnes
Jelsa
Hålandsosen
Vadla
Blåfjellhytta
Gyvasshytta
Gloppe
Flatelan
Sævlandsvik
Åkrehamn
Kopervik
Våga
Førresvik
Stølevik
Kårstø
Nedstrand
Liarvåg
Kyrkøy
Bergøy
Bergaland
Knutsvik
Ombo
Vindsvik
Tøtlandsvik
Nesvik
Hjelmelandsvågen
Rjuven
Kringlevasshytta
Svartevatn
Bossbu
Valle
Sandve
Skudeneshavn
Bokn
Tåganes
Arsvågen
Boknafjorden
Eidssund
Randøy
Judaberg
Finnøy
Årdal
Viglesdalshytta
Nilsebu
Nes
Grønvik
Fogn
Døvik
ROGALAND
Grautheller
Rosskreppfjorden
Nomeland
Hovet
Rennesøy
Sørbø
Utstein kloster
Vikevåg
Mosterøy
Bru
Kvitsøy
Randaberg ferjekai
Randaberg
Tau
Strand
Jørpeland
Lysefjorden
Lysebotn
Ådneram
Suleskar
Håhellerhytta
Helle
STAVANGER
Tananger
Idsefjorden
Preikestolen
597
Idse
Hommersåk
Fossmark
Valevatn
Fidjeland
Sinnes
Kvinen
Gaukheihytta
Sola
Sømes
Høle
Oanes
Forsand
Øv. Espedal
Lauvvik
Helle
Frafjord
Brådland
Hunnedalen
Tjørholm
Sandnes
Sviland
Ganddal
Verdalen
Kvernaland
Kongeparken
Gjesdal
Dirdal
Gilja
Giljastølen
Øvstebø
Øvre Sirdal
Ljosland
Hedde
Oltedal
Madland
Byrkjedal
Åknes
Klepp
Ålgård
Bryne
Jæren
Austrumdal
Sirdalen
Undheim
Bue
Øvrebygd
Bjordal
Knaben gruver
Nærbø
Kartavoll
Vikeså
Tonstad
Risnes
Varhaug
Brusali
359
Vassbø
Bjørnestad
Kvittingen
Netlandsnes
Åseral
Odlandstø
Bjerkreim
Haughom
VEST-AGDER
Vigrestad
Gyaåna
Rusdal
Sirdalsvatn
Gravdal
Kvinlog
Brusand
Ogna
Sirevåg
Helleland
Heskestad
Sandvatn
Eiken
Skeie
Kvåle
Sveindal
Hellvik
Egersund
Eide
Grindheim
Ystebrød
Eigerøya
Moi
Orrestad
Sira
Bakke
Vatland
Tingvatn
Byremo
Bjelland
Lundevatn
Råna
Hægebostad
Audnedal
Rekeland
Hauge
Sogndalstrand
Jøssinghamn
Elve
Flekkefjord
Loga
Liknes
Øye
Feda
Førland
Kvås
Konsmo
Åna-Sira
Kvellandstrand
Moi
Kirkehamn
Hidra
Lauvnes
Rasvåg
Ofte
Lygna
Vigmostad
Listafjorden
Sigersvoll
Lista
Penne
Herad
Lyngdal
Spilling
Steinodden
Farsund
Alleen
Holum
Vestbygd
Vanse
Loshamn
Vigeland
Trånevåg
Hausvik
Spangereid
Valle
Mandal
Korshamn
Lillehamn
Lindesnes
Hanstholm (X–V)
Hirtshals
Hirtshals 8 h (IX–V)
Newcastle
A
B
1
2
3

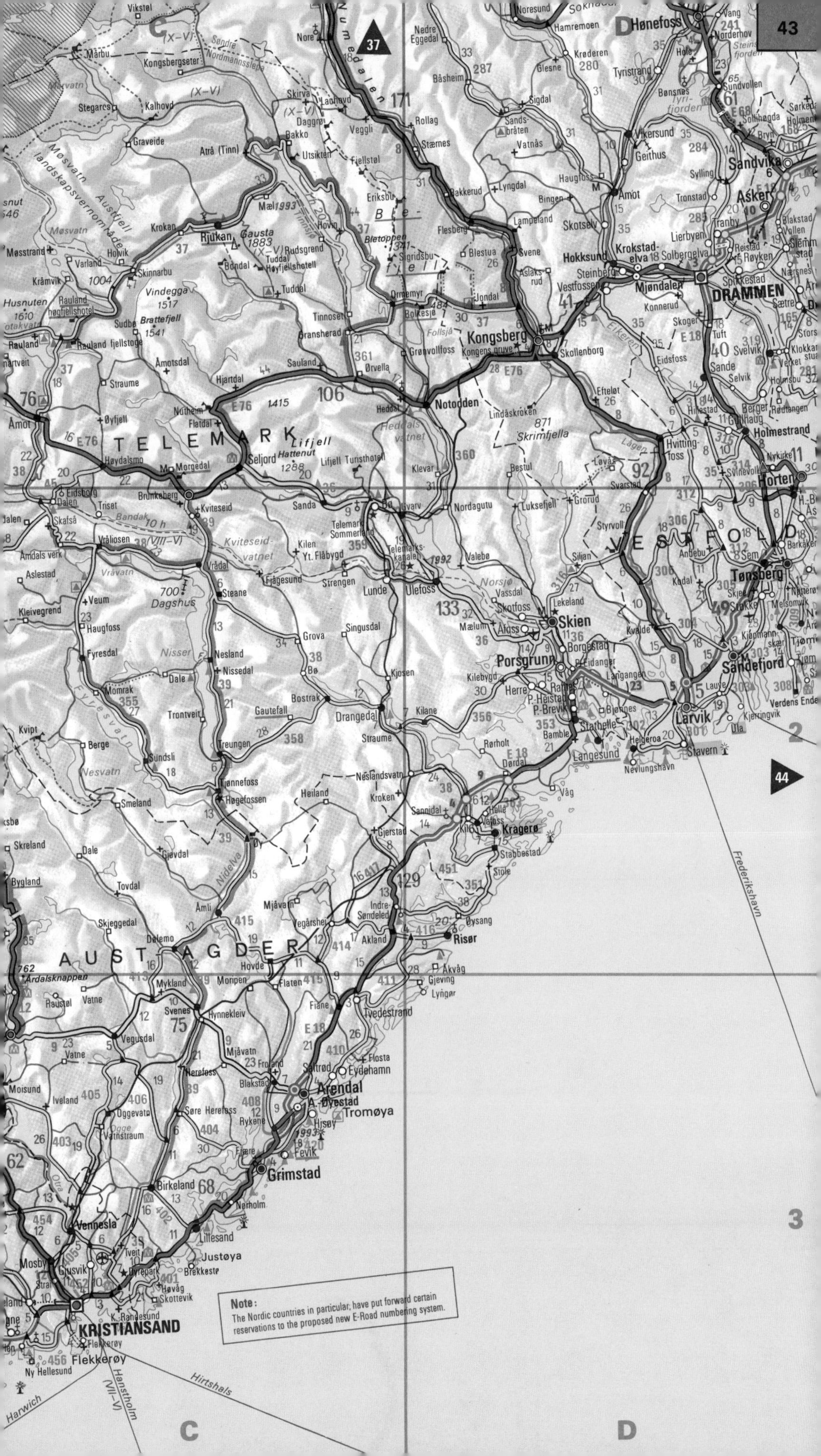
C
D
TELEMARK
VESTFOLD
AUST AGDER
Hønefoss
Drammen
Sandvika
Asker
Kongsberg
Notodden
Rjukan
Gausta
1883
Seljord
Lifjell
Skien
Porsgrunn
Tønsberg
Horten
Sandefjord
Larvik
Stavern
Langesund
Kragerø
Risør
Tvedestrand
Arendal
Grimstad
Lillesand
Kristiansand
Flekkerøy
Ny Hellesund
Vennesla
Evje
Åmli
Treungen
Nissedal
Fyresdal
Dalen
Kviteseid
Vrådal
Bø
Ulefoss
Lunde
Drangedal
Tromøya
Hirtshals
Hanstholm
Harwich
Frederikshavn
37
44
2
3
Note:
The Nordic countries in particular, have put forward certain reservations to the proposed new E-Road numbering system.

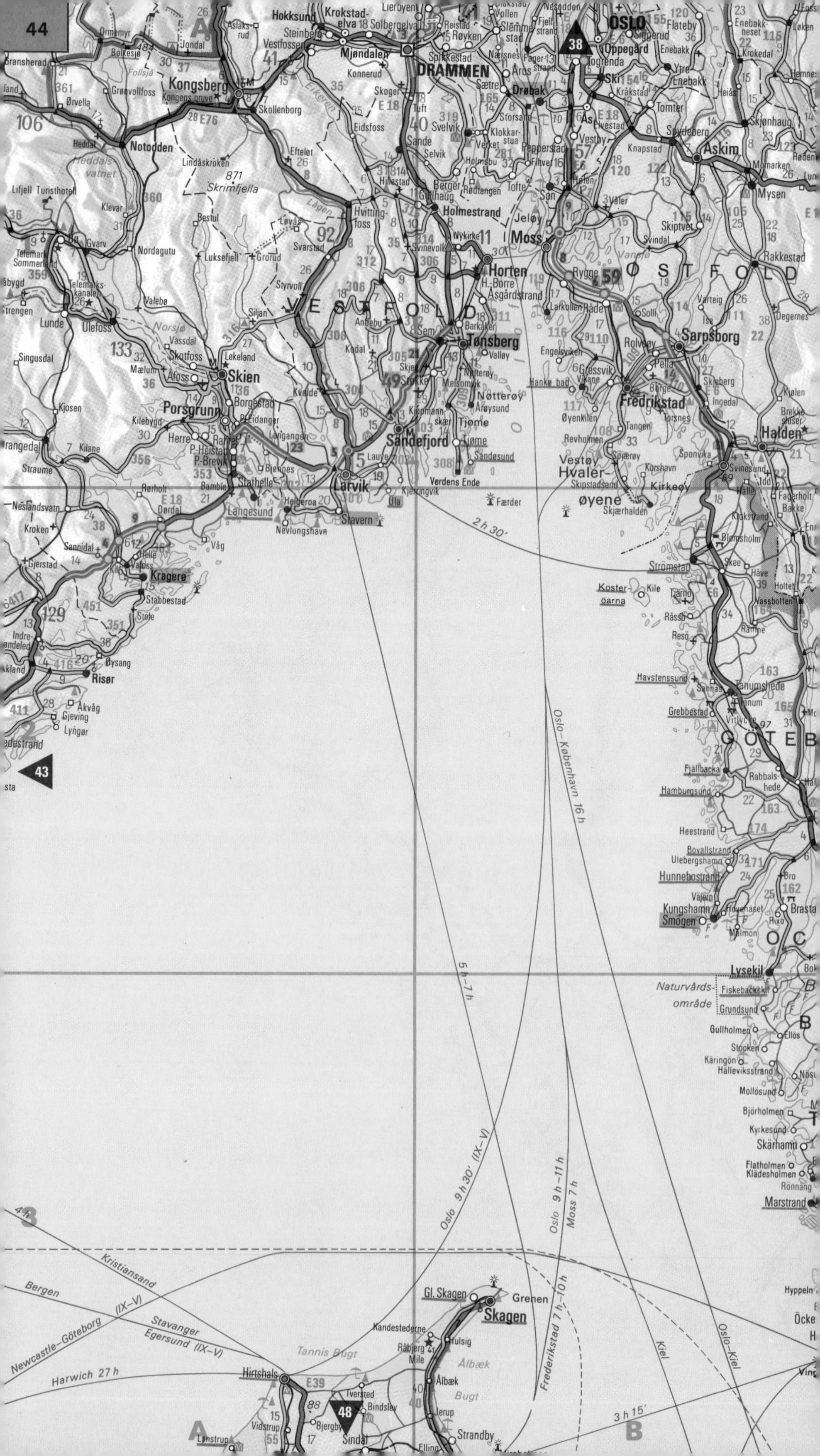
44
Hokksund
Krokstad-elva
Solbergelva
Steinberg
Vestfossen
Mjøndalen
DRAMMEN
OSLO
Oppegård
Flateby
Enebakk
Ytre Enebakk
Kongsberg
Kongens gruve
Skollenborg
Notodden
Heddal
Heddalsvatnet
Lifjell Turisthotell
Skrimfjella
871
Sande
Selvik
Svelvik
Drøbak
Ås
Vestby
Pepperstad
Askim
Mysen
Spydeberg
Holmestrand
Hvittingfoss
Horten
Moss
Jeløy
Rygge
Råde
ØSTFOLD
VESTFOLD
Tønsberg
Nøtterøy
Tjøme
Sandefjord
Larvik
Stavern
Verdens Ende
Færder
Sarpsborg
Fredrikstad
Halden
Hvaler-øyene
Skien
Porsgrunn
Bø
Ulefoss
Lunde
Langesund
Kragerø
Risør
Lyngør
Strömstad
Kosteröarna
Tanumshede
Grebbestad
Fjällbacka
Hamburgsund
Kungshamn
Smögen
Lysekil
Naturvårds-område
Marstrand
Skärhamn
Mollösund
Skagen
Gl. Skagen
Grenen
Hirtshals
Ålbæk
Ålbæk Bugt
Tannis Bugt
Sindal
Strandby
Harwich 27 h
Newcastle–Göteborg (IX–V)
Bergen
Kristiansand
Stavanger
Egersund (IX–V)
Oslo 9 h 30′ (IX–V)
5 h–7 h
Oslo 9 h–11 h
Moss 7 h
Frederikstad 7 h–10 h
Oslo–København 16 h
Oslo–Kiel
Kiel
2 h 30′
3 h 15′
4 h
38
43
48
A
B

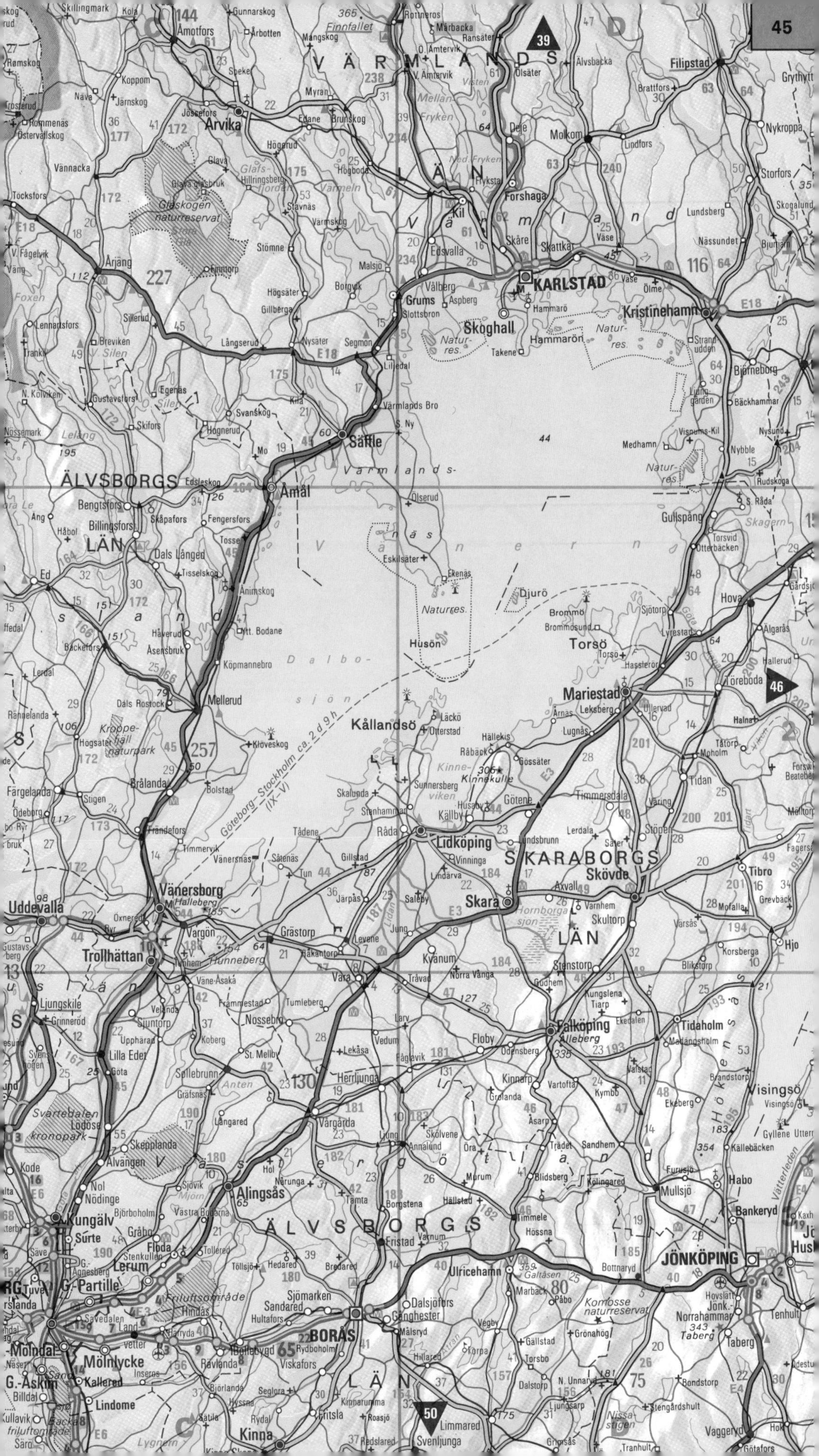
VÄRMLANDS
LÄN
Värmland
Vänern
ÄLVSBORGS
LÄN
Dalsland
SKARABORGS
LÄN
ÄLVSBORGS
LÄN
Skillingmark
Kola
Åmotfors
Gunnarskog
Årbotten
Finnfallet
Rottneros
Mårbacka
Ransäter
Mangskog
Ö. Ämtervik
V. Ämtervik
Älvsbacka
Olsäter
Filipstad
Grythyttan
Brattfors
Rømskog
Koppom
Näva
Järnskog
Speke
Myran
Brunskog
Edane
Mellan-Fryken
Deje
Molkom
Lindfors
Nykroppa
Hommenäs
Östervallskog
Jössefors
Arvika
Högerud
Ned. Fryken
Fryksta
Forshaga
Storfors
Skogalund
Glava
Glafsfjorden
Hillringsberg
Glava glasbruk
Hogboda
Värmeln
Kil
Vännacka
Tocksfors
Glaskogen naturreservat
Stavnäs
Värmskog
Lundsberg
Nässundet
Bjurtjärn
Edsvalla
Skåre
Skattkärr
Väse
V. Fågelvik
Stömne
Malsjö
Årjäng
Fintorp
Borgvik
Vålberg
KARLSTAD
Ölme
Grums
Aspberg
Hammarö
Foxen
Högsäter
Gillberga
Slottsbron
Kristinehamn
Skoghall
Hammarön
Natur-res.
Lennartsfors
Sillerud
Strand udden
Breviken
Långserud
Nysäter
Segmon
Takene
Trankil
V. Silen
Liljedal
Björneberg
N. Kolviken
Gustavsfors
Egenäs
Silen
Kila
Värmlands Bro
Ljunggården
Bäckhammar
Skifors
Svanskog
S. Ny
Nössemark
Lelång
Hognerud
Säffle
Medhamn
Visnums-Kil
Nysund
Mo
Nybble
Värmlands-näs
Rudskoga
Bengtsfors
Edsleskog
Åmål
Ölserud
S. Råda
Ång
Billingsfors
Skåpafors
Fengersfors
Gullspång
Håbol
Tösse
Skagern
Torsvid
Otterbäcken
Dals Långed
Eskilsäter
Ed
Tisselskog
Ekenäs
Djurö
Ånimskog
Naturres.
Brommö
Sjötorp
Hova
Gårdsjö
Brommösund
Håverud
Ütt. Bodane
Lyrestad
Älgarås
Torsö
Åsensbruk
Husön
Backefors
Hasslerör
Hallerud
Dalbo-sjön
Köpmannebro
Töreboda
Lerdal
Mariestad
Mellerud
Dals Rostock
Ullervad
Kållandsö
Läckö
Leksberg
Ottersta
Årnäs
Halna
Rännelanda
Kroppefjäll naturpark
Lugnås
Hällekis
Tåtorp
Högsäter
Kloveskog
Råbäck
Gössäter
Moholm
Göteborg–Stockholm ca. 2 d 9 h
Kinnekulle
Kinne-viken
Sunnersberg
Skalunda
Tidan
Forshem
Beateberg
Fargelanda
Brålanda
Bolstad
Husaby
Götene
Timmersdala
Stigen
Stenhammar
Källby
Väring
Mölltorp
Ödeborg
Tådene
Råda
Lidköping
Lundsbrunn
Lerdala
Säter
Stöpen
Frändefors
Timmervik
Vinninga
Fagersta
Vänersnäs
Sätenäs
Gillstad
Skövde
Tibro
Tun
Lindärva
Axvall
Grevbäck
Vänersborg
Halleberg
Järpås
Saleby
Skara
Varnhem
Uddevalla
Öxnered
Hornborgasjön
Skultorp
Mofalla
Varsås
Vargön
Grästorp
Jung
Hjo
Korsberga
Trollhättan
Hunneberg
Håkantorp
Levene
Kvänum
Stenstorp
Blikstorp
Väne-Åsaka
Vara
Tråvad
Norra Vånga
Gudhem
Kungslena
Tiarp
Ljungskile
Frammestad
Tumleberg
Grinneröd
Velanda
Sjuntorp
Nossebro
Larv
Falköping
Ekedalen
Tidaholm
Alleberg
Uppeharad
Koberg
Vedum
Floby
Odensberg
Mattängsholm
Lilla Edet
St. Mellby
Lekåsa
Fåglavik
Valstad
Hökensås
Göta
Sollebrunn
Anten
Herrljunga
Kinnarp
Vartofta
Brandstorp
Visingsö
Grätsnäs
Kymbo
Ekeberg
Svartedalen kronopark
Lödöse
Vårgårda
Grolanda
Åsarp
Gyllene Uttern
Långared
Skölvene
Skepplanda
Kode
Alvängen
Ljung
Annalund
Öra
Trädet
Sandhem
Källebäcken
Hol
Furusjö
Nol
Nödinge
Sjövik
Mjörn
Alingsås
Nårunga
Tämta
Mörum
Blidsberg
Kölingared
Habo
Mullsjö
Kungälv
Björboholm
Västra Bodarna
Borgstena
Hällstad
Timmele
Bankeryd
Surte
Gråbo
Hössna
Säve
Floda
Tollered
Fristad
Varnum
G.-Agnesberg
Stenkullen
Lerum
Töllsjö
Hedared
Bredared
Ulricehamn
Galtåsen
Bottnaryd
JÖNKÖPING
Tuve
G.-Partille
Friluftsområde
Hindås
Sjömarken
Dalsjöfors
Marbäck
Påbo
Komosse naturreservat
Hovslätt
Jönk.-Norrahammar
Tenhult
Sävedalen
Land
Sandared
Hultafors
Gånghester
Målsryd
Taberg
Mölndal
Härryda
Vetter
Bollebygd
Rydboholm
BORÅS
Vegby
Grönahög
Gällstad
Mölnlycke
Rävlanda
Viskafors
Hillared
Korpa
Torsbo
G.-Askim
Inseros
Kållered
Björlanda
Seglora
N. Unnaryd
Bondstorp
Billdal
Lindome
Hyssna
Kinnarumma
Dalstorp
Ljungsarp
Stengårdshult
Kullavik
Säro
Backa friluftsområde
Sätila
Rydal
Fritsla
Roasjö
Limmared
Nissastigen
Lygnern
Kinna
Redslared
Svenljunga
Grimsås
Tranhult
Vaggeryd
Götafors
Vätterleden
E18
E3
E6
E4
39
46
50

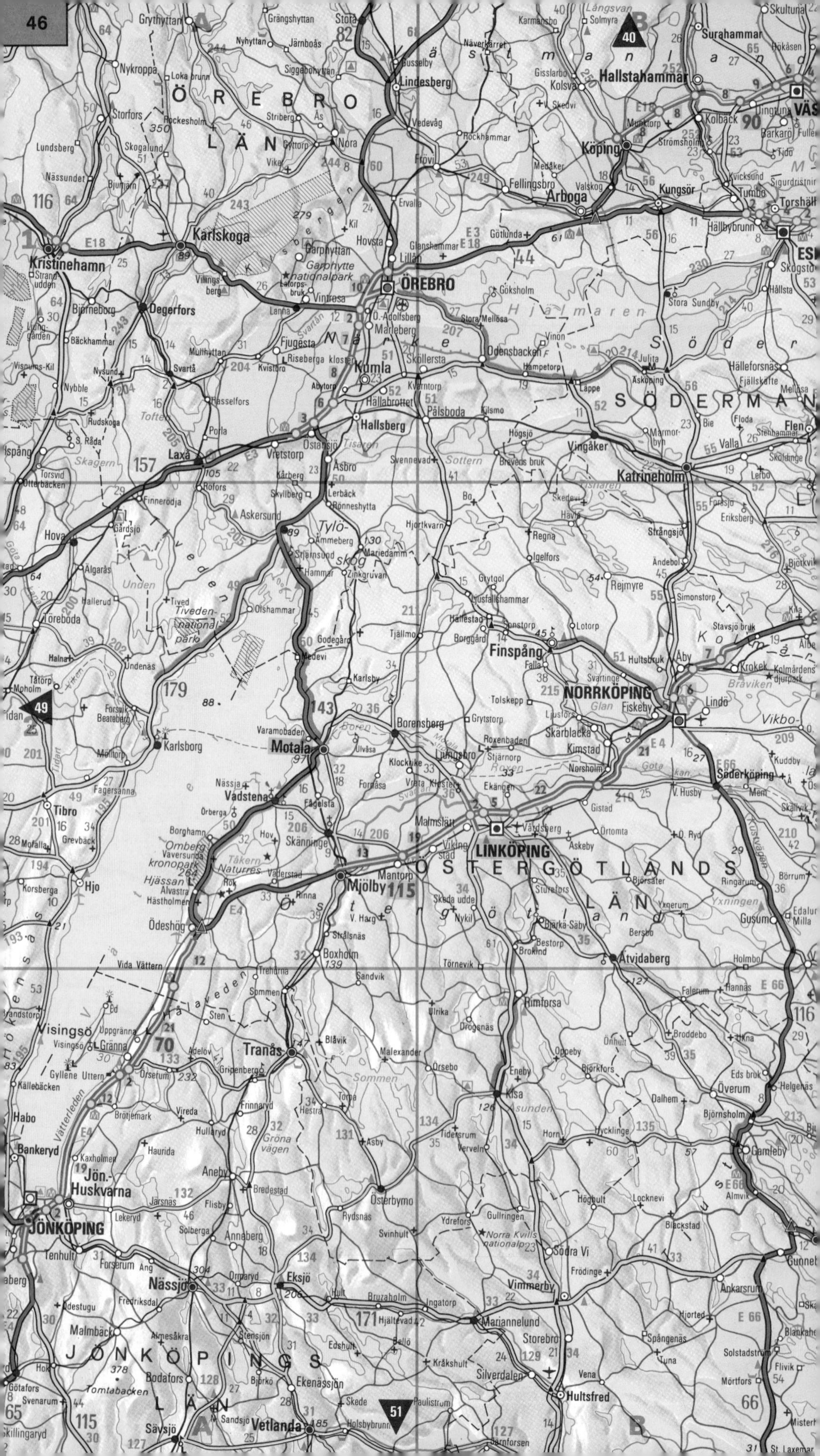

ÖREBRO
LÄN
SÖDERMAN
ÖSTERGÖTLANDS
LÄN
JÖNKÖPINGS
LÄN
Hjälmaren
Närke
Östergötland
Kolmården
Tylöskog
Tiveden
Grythyttan
Grängshyttan
Stora
Karmansbo
Solmyra
Långsvan
Skultuna
Surahammar
Hökåsen
Nyhyttan
Järnboås
Näverkärret
Hallstahammar
Nykroppa
Loka brunn
Siggebohyttan
Gusselby
Lindesberg
Gisslarbo
Kolsva
Västerås
Storfors
Rockesholm
Striberg
Ås
Vedevåg
V. Skedvi
Munktorp
Kolbäck
Dingtuna
Lundsberg
Skogalund
Gyttorp
Nora
Rockhammar
Köping
Strömsholm
Barkarö
Tidö
Nässundet
Bjurtjärn
Vikt
Frövi
Medåker
Kvicksund
Sigurdsristnin
Fellingsbro
Valskog
Kungsör
Tumbo
Torshälla
Karlskoga
Kil
Ervalla
Arboga
Hällbybrunn
Eskilstuna
Kristinehamn
Garphyttan
Hovsta
Götlunda
Glanshammar
Garphyttans nationalpark
Lillån
ÖREBRO
Skogstorp
Strand-udden
Villingsberg
Laxå
Latorpsbruk
Vintrosa
Göksholm
Stora Sundby
Hällsta
Björneborg
Degerfors
Lanna
Ö.-Adolfsberg
Marieberg
Stora Mellösa
Bäckhammar
Fjugesta
Vinön
Odensbacken
Hampetorp
Julita
Hälleforsnäs
Visnums-Kil
Mullhyttan
Riseberga kloster
Kvistbro
Skållersta
Kumla
Åsköping
Fjällskäfte
Nysund
Svartå
Abytorp
Kvarntorp
Läppe
Mellösa
Nybble
Hasselfors
Hällabrottet
Pålsboda
Kilsmo
Toften
Rudskoga
Hallsberg
Bie
Floda
Flen
Porla
Östansjö
Högsjö
Vingåker
Marmorbyn
S. Råda
Vretstorp
Tisaren
Svennevad
Sottern
Brevens bruk
Valla
Stenhammar
Väspång
Skagern
Åsbro
Katrineholm
Sköldinge
Torsvid
Otterbacken
Rofors
Kårberg
Lerbäck
Lerbo
Finnerödja
Skyllberg
Rönneshytta
Bo
Skedevi
Forssjö
Askersund
Åsarna
Eriksberg
Hova
Gårdsjö
Hjortkvarn
Strångsjö
Ammeberg
Mariedamm
Regna
Stjärnsund
Zinkgruvan
Hammar
Igelfors
Ändebol
Älgarås
Unden
Rejmyre
Grytgol
Hallerud
Tived
Tiveden nationalpark
Olshammar
Hällestad
Lusfallshammar
Simonstorp
Töreboda
Sonstorp
Lotorp
Stavsjö bruk
Tjällmo
Borggård
Godegård
Finspång
Hultsbruk
Åby
Krokek
Kolmårdens djurpark
Halna
Medevi
Falla
Svärtinge
Undenäs
Karlsby
Bråviken
Tåtorp
Moholm
NORRKÖPING
Lindö
Glan
Fiskeby
Tolskepp
Forsvik
Beateberg
Borensberg
Grytstorp
Ljusfors
Vikbolandet
Varamobaden
Skärblacka
Karlsborg
Boren
Roxenbaden
Motala
Kimstad
Ulvåsa
Stjärnorp
Klockrike
Ljungsbro
Söderköping
Mölltorp
Kuddby
Fagersanna
Norsholm
Roxen
Göta kanal
Nässja
Vadstena
Fornåsa
Vreta Kloster
Ekängen
Tibro
Gistad
V. Husby
Mem
Skällvik
Fågelsta
Örberga
Malmslätt
Värdsberg
Ö. Ryd
Örtomta
Borghamn
Hov
Skänninge
Grevbäck
LINKÖPING
Askeby
Viking-stad
Mofalla
Omberg
Vaversunda
Tåkern
kronopark
Naturres
Väderstad
Mantorp
Björsäter
Ringarum
Börrum
Korsberga
Hjo
Hjässan
Alvastra
Rök
Mjölby
Stureforn
Sturefors
Hästholmen
Rinna
Skeda udde
Nykil
Yxnerum
Yxningen
Gusum
Edalun
Ödeshög
V. Harg
Bjärka-Säby
Bersbo
Stråisnäs
Bestorp
Brokind
Boxholm
Åtvidaberg
Vida Vättern
Törnevik
Holmbo
Trehörna
Sandvik
Falerum
Hannäs
Brandstorp
Ed
Sommen
Rimforsa
Visingsö
Uppgränna
Sten
Ulrika
Drögsnäs
Gränna
Adelöv
Blåvik
Önhult
Broddebo
Ukna
Tranås
Malexander
Gyllene Uttern
Gripenberg
Örsebo
Oppeby
Björkfors
Eds bruk
Helgenäs
Källebäcken
Orserum
Eneby
Kisa
Åsunden
Överum
Vätterleden
Frinnaryd
Torpa
Dalhem
Björnsholm
Hestra
Habo
Brötjemark
Vireda
Gröna vägen
Tidersrum
Hycklinge
Hullaryd
Asby
Horn
Bankeryd
Haurida
Kaxholmen
Verveln
Gamleby
Jön.-Huskvarna
Aneby
Bredestad
Österbymo
Högbult
Locknevi
Almvik
JÖNKÖPING
Järsnäs
Flisby
Ydrefors
Gullringen
Lekeryd
Rydsnäs
Svinhult
Norra Kvills nationalpark
Blackstad
Solberga
Annaberg
Södra Vi
Tenhult
Forserum
Ång
Gunnebo
Frödinge
Ormaryd
Eksjö
Vimmerby
Ankarsrum
Nässjö
Ödestugu
Fredriksdal
Hult
Bruzaholm
Ingatorp
Hjorted
Hjältevad
Mariannelund
Malmbäck
Almesåkra
Stensjön
Storebro
Spångenäs
Edshult
Bellö
Blankaholm
Tuna
Solstadström
Kråkshult
Silverdalen
Flivik
Hok
Bodafors
Björkö
Ekenässjön
Vena
Mörtfors
Götafors
Tomtabacken
Hultsfred
Svenarum
Skede
Paulistrom
Sandsjö
Vetlanda
Holsbybrunn
Sävsjö
Skillingaryd
Järnforsen
Misterhult
St. Laxemar
Kustvägen
Hålaveden

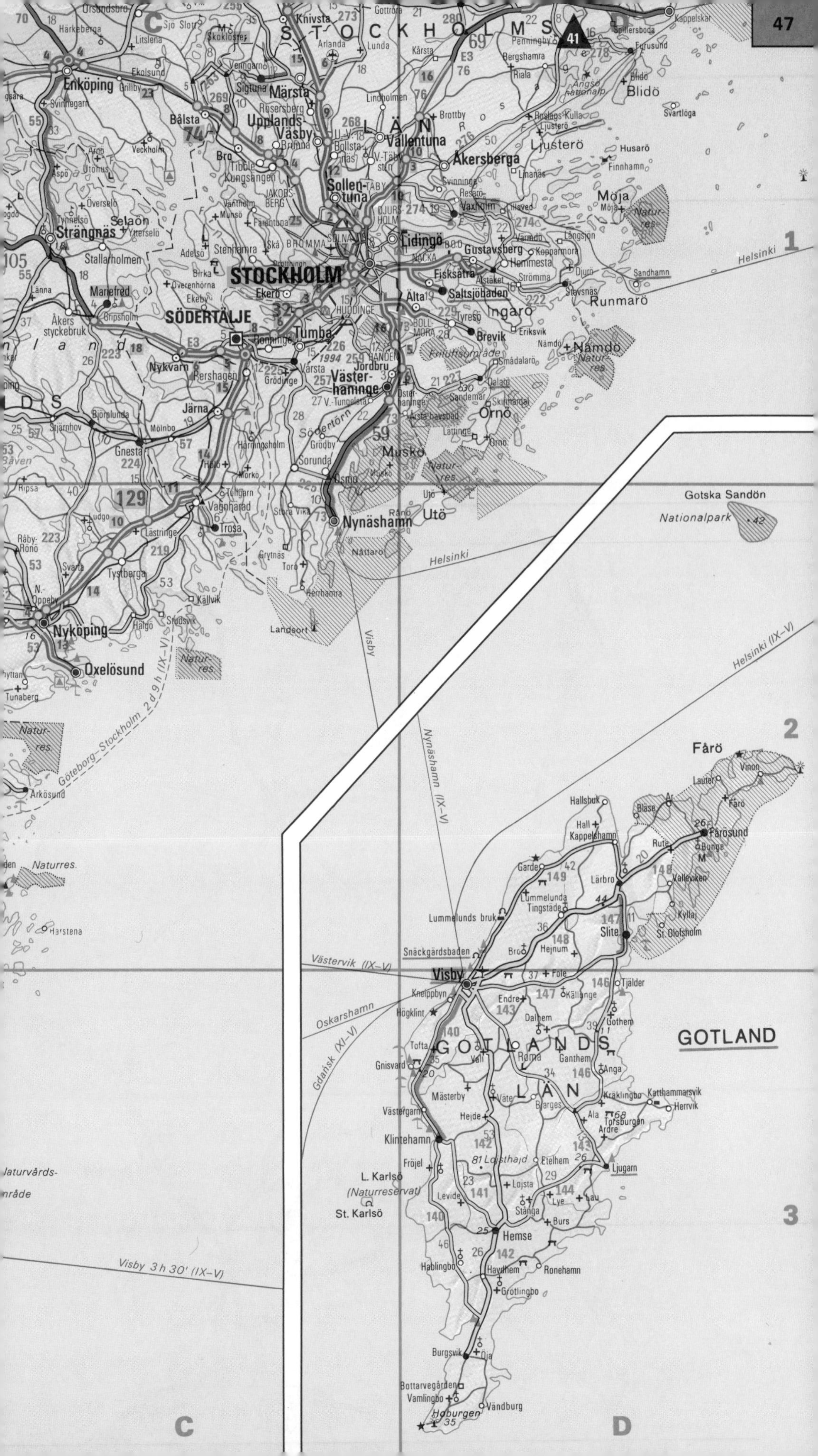

STOCKHOLM
SÖDERTÄLJE
STOCKHOLMS LÄN
Enköping
Strängnäs
Märsta
Upplands-Väsby
Vallentuna
Åkersberga
Sollentuna
Lidingö
Gustavsberg
Saltsjöbaden
Tumba
Västerhaninge
Nynäshamn
Nyköping
Oxelösund
Trosa
Gnesta
Järna
Ljusterö
Blidö
Möja
Runmarö
Nämdö
Ornö
Utö
Muskö
Gotska Sandön
Nationalpark
Helsinki
Visby
Nynäshamn (IX–V)
Västervik (IX–V)
Oskarshamn
Gdańsk (XI–V)
Göteborg–Stockholm 2 d 9 h (IX–V)
Visby 3 h 30' (IX–V)
Helsinki (IX–V)
GOTLAND
GOTLANDS LÄN
Fårö
Fårösund
Slite
Visby
Klintehamn
Hemse
Ljugarn
Burgsvik
Hoburgen
L. Karlsö
(Naturreservat)
St. Karlsö
Natur-res.
Naturres.
C
D
1
2
3

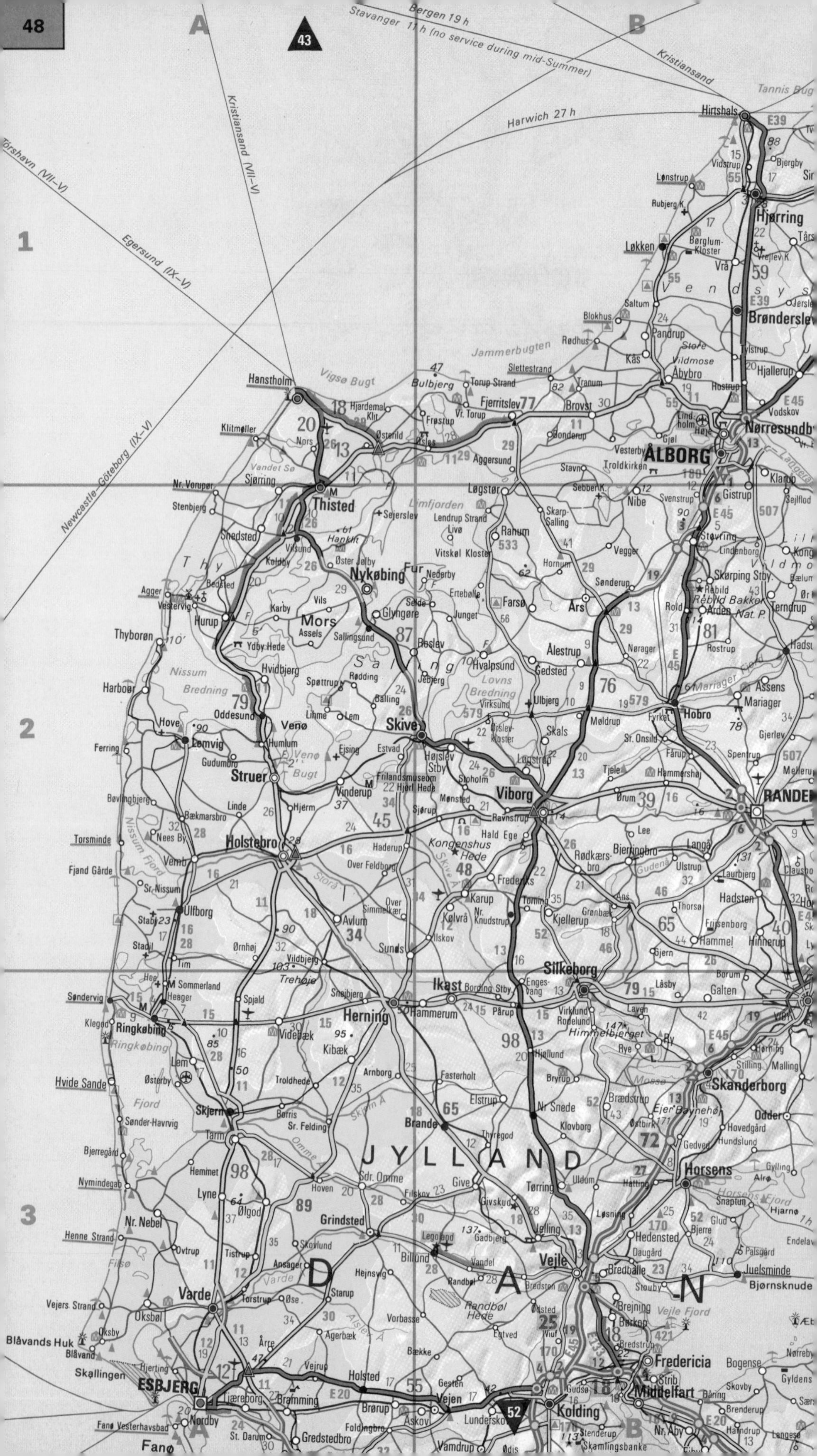
43
Bergen 19 h
Stavanger 11 h (no service during mid-Summer)
Kristiansand
Harwich 27 h
Kristiansand (VII–V)
Tórshavn (VII–V)
Egersund (IX–V)
Newcastle–Göteborg (IX–V)
Tannis Bugt
Hirtshals
E39
Bjergby
Vidstrup
Lønstrup
Rubjerg K.
Hjørring
Børglum-Kloster
Løkken
Vrå
Vejlev K.
V e n d s y s
Saltum
Brønderslev
Blokhus
Pandrup
Rødhus
Jammerbugten
Store Vildmose
Kås
Tylstrup
Hjallerup
Slettestrand
Tranum
Åbybro
Hostrup
Vodskov
Vigsø Bugt
Bulbjerg
Torup Strand
Hanstholm
Hjardemål Klit
Fjerritslev
Brovst
Vr. Torup
Frøstup
Lindholm
Høje
Nørresundby
Klitmøller
Nors
Østerild
Øsløs
Bonderup
Gjøl
Vesterby
ÅLBORG
Aggersund
Vandet Sø
Stavn
Troldkirken
Nr. Vorupør
Sjørring
Thisted
Løgstør
Sebber K.
Klarup
Stenbjerg
Limfjorden
Nibe
Svenstrup
Gistrup
Sejerslev
Lendrup Strand
Skarp-Salling
Sejlflod
Livø
Ranum
Støvring
Snedsted
Hanklit
Vitsund
Vitskøl Kloster
Vegger
Lindenborg
T h y
Koldby
Øster Jølby
Hornum
Nykøbing
Fur
Nederby
Sønderup
Skørping Stby.
Rebild
Rebild Bakker Nat. P.
Agger
Bedsted
Vils
Selde
Ertebølle
Farsø
Års
Vestervig
Hurup
Karby
Mors
Glyngøre
Junget
Rold
Arden
Terndrup
Thyborøn
Assels
Sallingsund
Ydby Hede
Roslev
Ålestrup
Nørager
Rostrup
Hadsund
Nissum Bredning
S a l l i n g
Hvalpsund
Harboøre
Hvidbjerg
Spøttrup
Rødding
Jebjerg
Lovns Bredning
Gedsted
Mariager Fjord
Assens
Mariager
Oddesund
Balling
Virksund
Ulbjerg
Hobro
Fyrkat
Lihme
Lem
Hove
Venø
Lemvig
Skive
Ørslev-Kloster
Skals
Møldrup
Gjerlev
Ferring
Humlum
Ejsing
Estvad
Højslev Stby
Sr. Onsild
Fårup
Spentrup
Gudumbro
Venø Bugt
Løgstrup
Tjele
Hammershøj
Struer
Frilandsmuseum Hjerl Hede
Stoholm
Viborg
Vinderup
Mønsted
Ørum
Randers
Bøvlingbjerg
Linde
Hjerm
Sjørup
Ravnstrup
Bækmarsbro
Hald Ege
Lee
Torsminde
Nees By
Kongenshus Hede
Rødkærsbro
Bjerringbro
Langå
Holstebro
Haderup
Nissum Fjord
Vemb
Over Feldborg
Gudenå
Ulstrup
Fjand Gårde
Storå
Fredenks
Laurbjerg
Sr. Nissum
Over Simmelkær
Karup
Hadsten
Ulfborg
Kølvrå
Nr. Knudstrup
Tørring
Kjellerup
Grønbæk
Thorsø
Stabi
Avlum
Frijsenborg
Stadil
Ørnhøj
Sunds
Ilskov
Hammel
Hinnerup
Tim
Vildbjerg
Trehøje
Gjern
Silkeborg
Engesvang
Borum
Lasby
Hee
Sommerland
Heager
Søndervig
Snejbjerg
Ikast
Bording Stby.
Galten
Ringkøbing
Herning
Hammerum
Pårup
Virklund
Rodelund
Laven
Klegod
Videbæk
Himmelbjerget
Ry
Rye
Kibæk
Lem
Fasterholt
Hjøllund
Stilling
Malling
Østerby
Arnborg
Bryrup
Skanderborg
Hvide Sande
Troldhede
Elstrup
Mossø
Ejer Bavnehøj
Odder
Fjord
Skjern
Borris
Brande
Nr. Snede
Brædstrup
Sønder-Havrvig
Sr. Felding
Skjern Å
Østbirk
Tarm
Thyregod
Klovborg
Hovedgård
Hundslund
Bjerregård
Omme
J Y L L A N D
Gedved
Hemmet
Horsens
Gylling
Nymindegab
Sdr. Omme
Uldum
Hatting
Alrø
Hoven
Filskov
Give
Tørring
Lyne
Snaptun
Horsens Fjord
Hjarnø
Ølgod
Givskud
Nr. Nebel
Grindsted
Løsning
Glud
Bjerre
Henne Strand
Skovlund
Gadbjerg
Jelling
Hedensted
Endelave
Ovtrup
Tistrup
Legoland
Palsgård
Ansager
Billund
Vandel
Daugård
Filsø
Varde
D
Hejnsvig
Randbøl
Vejle
Bredballe
A
Juelsminde
Bredsten
Stouby
N
Bjørnsknude
Starup
Vejers Strand
Torstrup
Øse
Randbøl Hede
Ødsted
Brejning
Vejle Fjord
Oksbøl
Vorbasse
Børkop
Oksby
Ansager
Alslev Å
Egtved
Viuf
Æ
Blåvands Huk
Blåvand
Agerbæk
Bække
Bredstrup
Fredericia
Nørreby
Årre
Vejrup
Hjerting
Holsted
Gesten
Strib
Bogense
Skallingen
Gyldens
ESBJERG
Tjæreborg
Bramming
Vejen
Gudsø
Middelfart
Skovby
Kolding
Båring
Særs
Fanø Vesterhavsbad
Nordby
Brørup
Askov
Lunderskov
52
Brenderup
Foldingbro
Fanø
St. Darum
Gredstedbro
Vamdrup
Ødis
Stenderup
Skamlingsbanke
Nr. Åby
Hindrup
Langesø
E20
E45
A
B
1
2
3

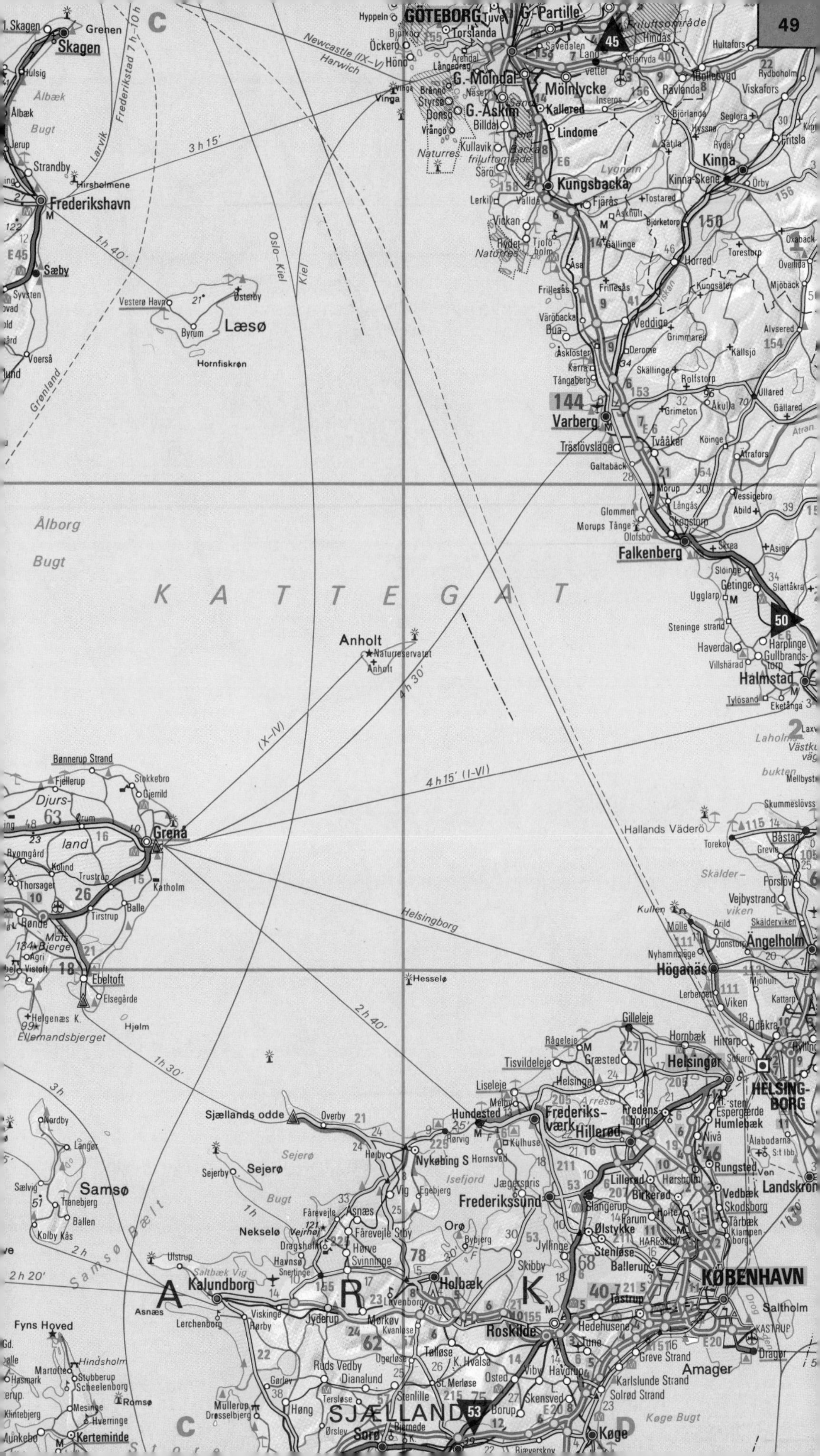

Skagen
Grenen
Hulsig
Ålbæk
Ålbæk Bugt
Jerup
Strandby
Hirsholmene
Frederikshavn
Sæby
Syvsten
Voerså
Frederikstad 7 h–10 h
Larvik
Grønland
3 h 15′
1 h 40′
Vesterø Havn
Østerby
Byrum
Læsø
Hornfiskrøn
Newcastle (IX–V)
Harwich
Oslo–Kiel
Kiel
Vinga
Hyppeln
GÖTEBORG
Tuve
G.-Partille
Torslanda
Öckerö
Hönö
Arendal
Långedrag
G.-Mölndal
Brännö
Styrsö
Donsö
Vrångö
G.-Askim
Billdal
Kullavik
Särö
Naturres.
friluftområde
Savedalen
Landvetter
Härryda
Friluftsområde
Hindås
Mölnlycke
Kållered
Lindome
Råvlanda
Bollebygd
Hultafors
Rydboholm
Viskafors
Seglora
Fritsla
Kinna
Kinna-Skene
Örby
Kungsbacka
Lerkil
Vallda
Fjärås
Tostared
Åskhult
Björketorp
Vickan
Rydet
Tjolöholm
Gällinge
Åsa
Frillesås
Torestorp
Horred
Öxabäck
Överlida
Mjöbäck
Kungsäter
Värö backa
Bua
Veddige
Grimmared
Viskan
Alvsered
Åskloster
Derome
Källsjö
Kärra
Tångaberg
Skällinge
Rolfstorp
Ullared
Gällared
Varberg
Grimeton
Åkulla
Träslövsläge
Tvååker
Köinge
Ätrafors
Galtabäck
Atran
Morup
Vessigebro
Långås
Abild
Glommen
Morups Tånge
Olofsbo
Skogstorp
Falkenberg
Skrea
Asige
Slöinge
Getinge
Slättåkra
Ugglarp
Steninge strand
Haverdal
Harplinge
Villshärad
Gullbrandstorp
Halmstad
Tylösand
Eketånga
Laholmsbukten
Mellbystrand
Ålborg Bugt
KATTEGAT
Anholt
Naturreservatet
4 h 30′
(X–IV)
4 h 15′ (I–VI)
Bønnerup Strand
Fjellerup
Stokkebro
Gjerrild
Djurs-land
Ørum
Grenå
Ryomgård
Kolind
Trustrup
Katholm
Thorsager
Tirstrup
Balle
Rønde
Mols Bjerge
Agri
Vistoft
Ebeltoft
Elsegårde
Helgenæs K.
Ellemandsbjerget
Hjelm
Helsingborg
Hallands Väderö
Torekov
Skummeslövs
Båstad
Grevie
Skälder–viken
Förslöv
Vejbystrand
Kullen
Mölle
Arild
Skälderviken
Jonstorp
Ängelholm
Nyhamnsläge
Höganäs
Mjöhult
Lerberget
Viken
Kattarp
Ödåkra
Hittarp
Hesselø
2 h 40′
1 h 30′
3 h
Gilleleje
Rågeleje
Hornbæk
Græsted
Tisvildeleje
Helsingør
Helsinge
Liseleje
HELSINGBORG
Arresø
Frederiksværk
Fredensborg
Espergærde
Humlebæk
Hundested
Nivå
Sjællands odde
Overby
Nykøbing S
Hornsved
Rørvig
Højby
Kulhuse
Hillerød
Rungsted
Sejerø
Sejerby
Sejerø Bugt
Isefjord
Jægerspris
Lillerød
Hørsholm
Vedbæk
Landskrona
Nordby
Langør
Samsø
Sælvig
Tranebjerg
Ballen
Kolby Kås
Nekselø
Vejrhøj
Fårevejle
Asnæs
Vig
Egebjerg
Frederikssund
Birkerød
Skodsborg
Tårbæk
Klampenborg
Dragsholm
Fårevejle Stby
Hørve
Svinninge
Orø
Bybjerg
Slangerup
Farum
Ølstykke
Stenløse
Ballerup
Jyllinge
Skibby
Holbæk
Samsø Bælt
Ulstrup
Saltbæk Vig
Kalundborg
Asnæs
Lerchenborg
Viskinge
Rørby
Jyderup
Løvenborg
Mørkøv
Kvanløse
Roskilde
Hedehusene
Tåstrup
KØBENHAVN
Saltholm
Kastrup
Dragør
Amager
Fyns Hoved
Hindsholm
Martofte
Stubberup
Scheelenborg
Romsø
Mesinge
Hverringe
Kerteminde
Mullerup
Drosselbjerg
Høng
Gørlev
Ruds Vedby
Dianalund
Tølløse
K. Hvalsø
Osted
Viby
Havdrup
Greve Strand
Karlslunde Strand
Solrød Strand
Skensved
Sorø
Bjernede
Stenlille
SJÆLLAND
Borup
Køge
Køge Bugt
Tuno
Ugerløse

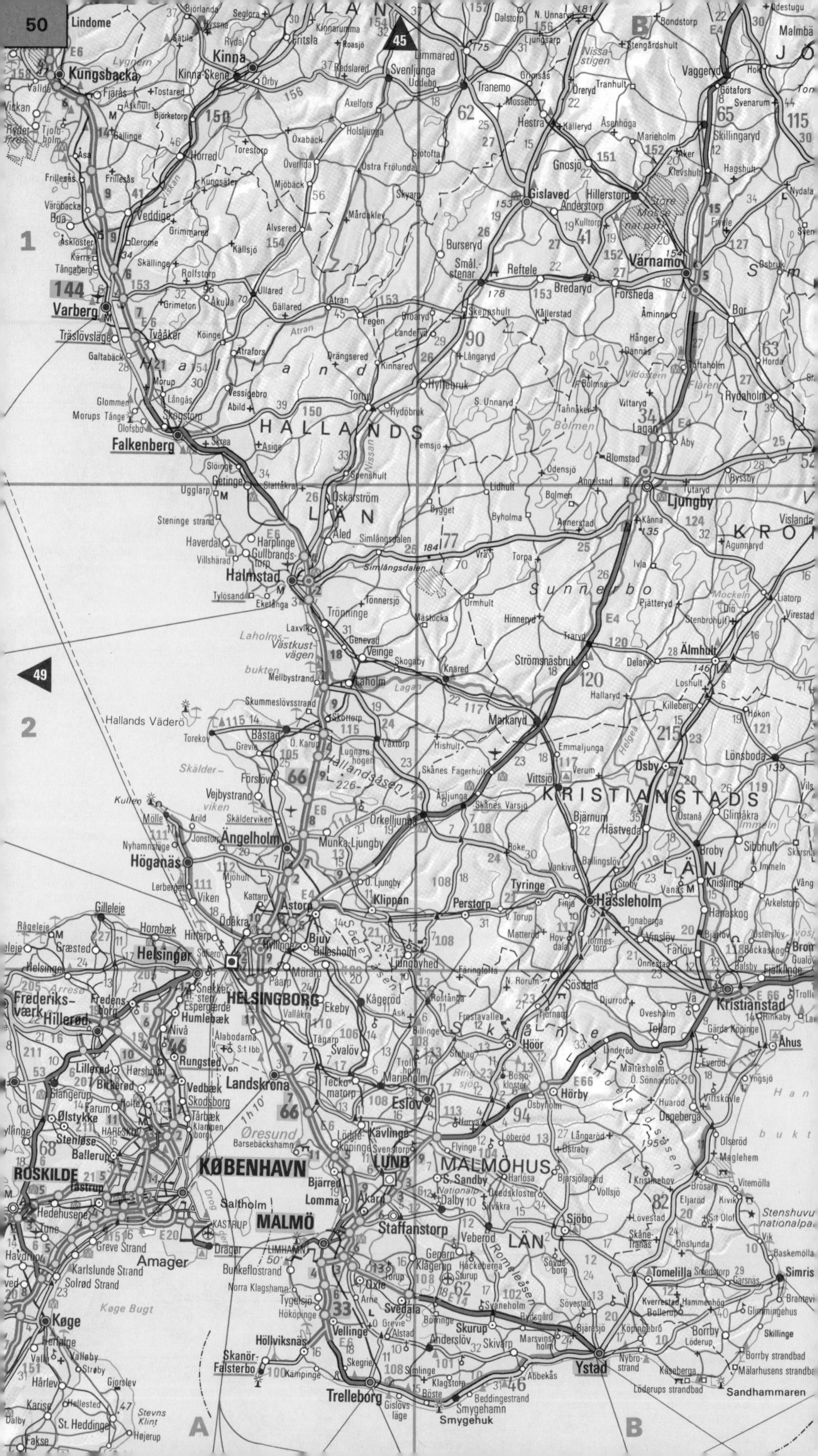
Lindome
Kungsbacka
Kinna
Svenljunga
Tranemo
Vaggeryd
Gislaved
Anderstorp
Hillerstorp
Värnamo
Store Mosse nat.park
Varberg
Träslövsläge
Tvååker
Falkenberg
Halland
HALLANDS LÄN
Halmstad
Tylösand
Laholm
Laholmsbukten
Västkustvägen
Ljungby
Lagan
Sunnerbo
Bolmen
Älmhult
Markaryd
Hallands Väderö
Torekov
Båstad
Hallandsåsen
Skälderviken
Kullen
Ängelholm
Höganäs
Åstorp
Klippan
Perstorp
Hässleholm
Osby
KRISTIANSTADS LÄN
Kristianstad
Åhus
Gilleleje
Helsingør
HELSINGBORG
Landskrona
Hillerød
Frederiksværk
Rungsted
Øresund
KØBENHAVN
ROSKILDE
Saltholm
Kastrup
Dragør
Amager
MALMÖ
LUND
Eslöv
Kävlinge
Höör
Hörby
MALMÖHUS LÄN
Sjöbo
Staffanstorp
Svedala
Skurup
Tomelilla
Simrishamn
Stenshuvud nationalpark
Ystad
Trelleborg
Smygehuk
Skanör-Falsterbo
Køge
Køge Bugt
Stevns Klint
St. Heddinge
Hanöbukten
Romeleåsen
Linderödsåsen
Söderåsen

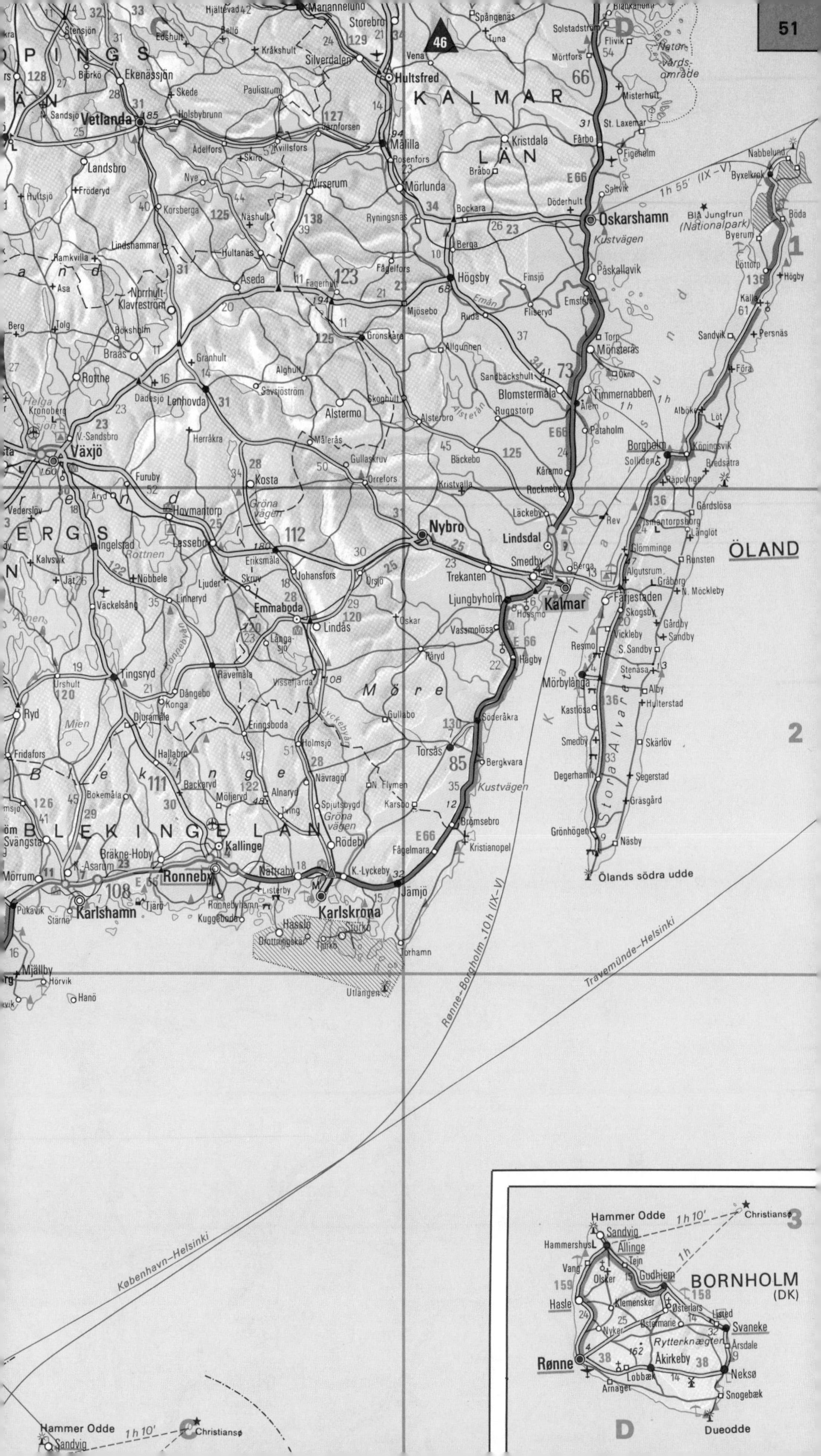
KALMAR LÄN
BLEKINGE LÄN
ÖLAND
BORNHOLM (DK)
Vetlanda
Ekenässjön
Hultsfred
Mörlunda
Oskarshamn
Kristdala
Högsby
Växjö
Lenhovda
Åseda
Alstermo
Nybro
Kosta
Orrefors
Lessebo
Hovmantorp
Ingelstad
Emmaboda
Lindås
Kalmar
Smedby
Lindsdal
Ljungbyholm
Mönsterås
Påskallavik
Timmernabben
Borgholm
Färjestaden
Mörbylånga
Torsås
Bergkvara
Söderåkra
Tingsryd
Ryd
Ronneby
Kallinge
Karlskrona
Karlshamn
Jämjö
Rödeby
Nättraby
Mörrum
Mjällby
Hanö
Utlängen
Ölands södra udde
Byxelkrok
Böda
Blå Jungfrun (Nationalpark)
Kustvägen
Gröna vägen
Möre
Stora Alvaret
Kalmarsund
Hammer Odde
Sandvig
Allinge
Gudhjem
Hasle
Rønne
Åkirkeby
Nexø
Svaneke
Dueodde
Christiansø
Rønne–Borgholm 10 h (IX–V)
Travemünde–Helsinki
København–Helsinki
1 h 55′ (IX–V)
1 h 10′
1 h

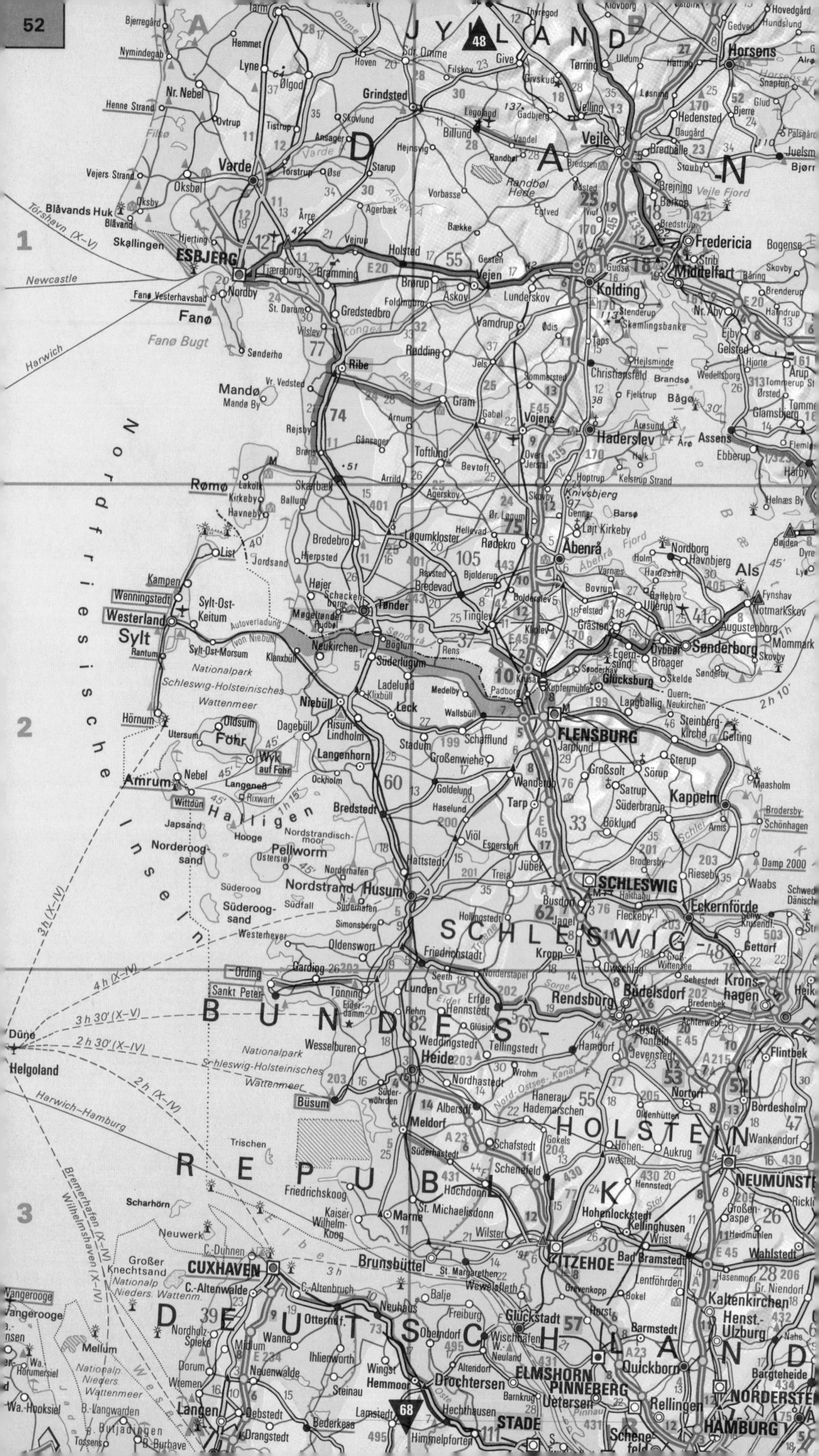
JYLLAND
DANMARK
SCHLESWIG-HOLSTEIN
BUNDESREPUBLIK DEUTSCHLAND
Nordfriesische Inseln
Halligen
Bjerregård
Hemmet
Nymindegab
Lyne
Ølgod
Nr. Nebel
Henne Strand
Ovtrup
Tistrup
Varde
Vejers Strand
Oksbøl
Blåvands Huk
Blåvand
Hjerting
Skallingen
ESBJERG
Newcastle
Harwich
Fanø
Fanø Vesterhavsbad
Nordby
Fanø Bugt
Sønderho
Mandø
Mandø By
Sdr. Omme
Hoven
Grindsted
Skovlund
Ansager
Starup
Agerbæk
Årre
Vejrup
Bramming
Tjæreborg
Gredstedbro
Ribe
Vr. Vedsted
Rejsby
Brøns
Skærbæk
Rømø
Lakolk
Kirkeby
Havneby
List
Jordsand
Kampen
Wenningstedt
Westerland
Sylt
Sylt-Ost-Keitum
Sylt-Ost-Morsum
Rantum
Hörnum
Nationalpark
Schleswig-Holsteinisches
Wattenmeer
Föhr
Oldsum
Utersum
Wyk auf Föhr
Amrum
Nebel
Wittdün
Langeneß
Hooge
Japsand
Norderoog-sand
Pellworm
Nordstrand
Süderoog
Süderoog-sand
Westerhever
Husum
Niebüll
Dagebüll
Risum-Lindholm
Langenhorn
Bredstedt
Leck
Neukirchen
Süderlügum
Tønder
Højer
Møgeltønder
Bredebro
Løgumkloster
Give
Thyregod
Horsens
Hovedgård
Gedved
Tørring
Uldum
Hatting
Filskov
Billund
Legoland
Gadbjerg
Givskud
Jelling
Vejle
Bredballe
Randbøl
Randbøl Hede
Vorbasse
Bække
Egtved
Holsted
Gesten
Vejen
Brørup
Askov
Lunderskov
Kolding
Fredericia
Middelfart
Strib
Bogense
Vejle Fjord
Børkop
Brejning
Juelsminde
Bjørn
Hedensted
Snaptun
Glud
Bjerre
Palsgård
Foldingbro
Vamdrup
Rødding
Gram
Jels
Christiansfeld
Hejlsminde
Sommersted
Vojens
Haderslev
Årøsund
Årø
Assens
Ebberup
Nr. Aby
Ejby
Gelsted
Hjorte
Årup
Tommerup St
Ørsted
Glamsbjerg
Haarby
Helnæs By
Toftlund
Bevtoft
Arnum
Gånsager
Arrild
Agerskov
Ballum
Hellevad
Ør. Løgum
Rødekro
Åbenrå
Åbenrå Fjord
Løjt Kirkeby
Knivsbjerg
Genner
Barsø
Hoptrup
Kelstrup Strand
Nordborg
Havnbjerg
Holm
Als
Fynshav
Notmarkskov
Augustenborg
Mommark
Sønderborg
Dybbøl
Broager
Gråsten
Egernsund
Kliplev
Bolderslev
Tinglev
Bredevad
Bjolderup
Rens
Padborg
Kruså
Kupfermühle
Glücksburg
Skelde
Sønderby
Quern
Neukirchen
Langballig
FLENSBURG
Jarplund
Steinbergkirche
Gelting
Maasholm
Sterup
Sörup
Großsolt
Satrup
Süderbrarup
Kappeln
Arnis
Schlei
Brodersby-Schönhagen
Damp 2000
Rieseby
Waabs
SCHLESWIG
Eckernförde
Gettorf
Kronshagen
Wanderup
Tarp
Jübek
Böklund
Treia
Viöl
Hattstedt
Medelby
Wallsbüll
Schafflund
Großenwiehe
Stadum
Goldelund
Haselund
Klixbüll
Ladelund
Esperstoft
Busdorf
Jagel
Kropp
Owschlag
Rendsburg
Büdelsdorf
Friedrichstadt
Tönning
Garding
Ording
Sankt Peter
Oldenswort
Simonsberg
Lunden
Erfde
Hennstedt
Seeth
Eider-damm
Wesselburen
Heide
Weddingstedt
Tellingstedt
Büsum
Meldorf
Albersdorf
Hamdorf
Hanerau Hademarschen
Nortorf
Bordesholm
Flintbek
Wankendorf
Aukrug
Hohenwestedt
Schafstedt
Schenefeld
Marne
Friedrichskoog
Kaiser-Wilhelm-Koog
Trischen
Scharhörn
Neuwerk
CUXHAVEN
C.-Duhnen
C.-Altenwalde
C.-Altenbruch
Brunsbüttel
St. Margarethen
Wewelsfleth
Wilster
ITZEHOE
Kellinghausen
Hohenlockstedt
Wrist
Bad Bramstedt
NEUMÜNSTER
Kaltenkirchen
Henstedt-Ulzburg
Barmstedt
Glückstadt
Wischhafen
Freiburg
Balje
Neuhaus
Otterndorf
Wanna
Nordholz
Spieka
Midlum
Ihlienworth
Neuenwalde
Dorum
Wremen
Langen
Debstedt
Bederkesa
Wingst
Hemmoor
Drochtersen
Steinau
ELMSHORN
PINNEBERG
Uetersen
Quickborn
Rellingen
HAMBURG
STADE
Himmelpforten
Hechthausen
Dingstedt
Butjadingen
Tossens
Burhave
Wangerooge
Mellum
Helgoland
Düne
Harwich-Hamburg
Bremerhaven (X-IV)
Wilhelmshaven (X-IV)
Elbe
Weser
Großer Knechtsand
Nationalp. Nieders. Wattenm.
Bargteheide
Norderstedt
Nahe
Wahlstedt
Nord-Ostsee-Kanal
Eider
Sorge
Treene
48
68

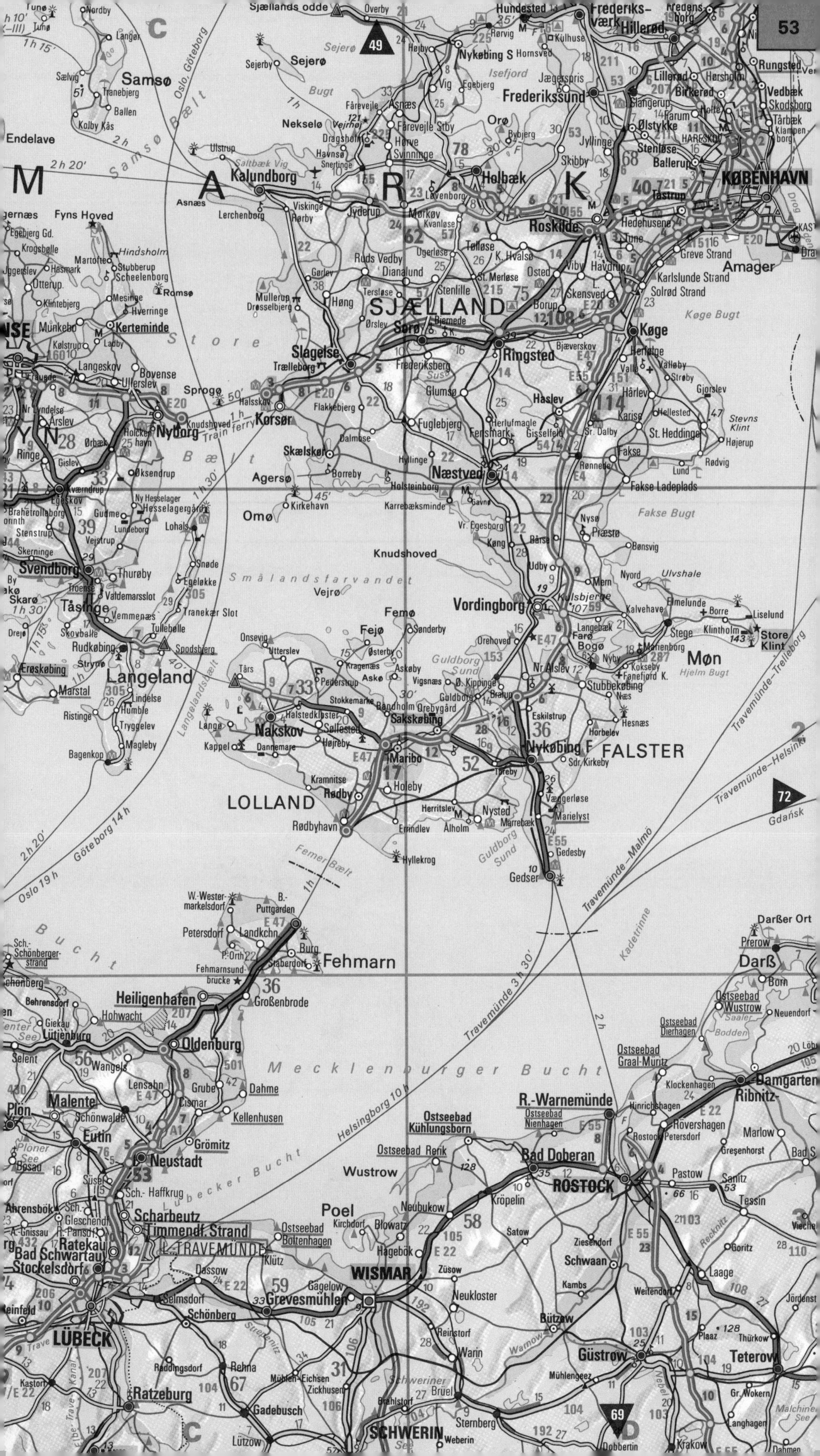
Samsø
Endelave
Samsø Bælt
Oslo, Göteborg
Sjællands odde
Sejerø
Sejerø Bugt
Nekselø
Hundested
Frederiksværk
Hillerød
Rungsted
Nykøbing S
Isefjord
Frederikssund
Lillerød
Birkerød
Vedbæk
Skodsborg
Kalundborg
Holbæk
Roskilde
KØBENHAVN
Tåstrup
Amager
Fyns Hoved
Hindsholm
Kerteminde
SJÆLLAND
Køge
Køge Bugt
Slagelse
Sorø
Ringsted
Korsør
Nyborg
Store Bælt
Train ferry
Haslev
Stevns Klint
Skælskør
Næstved
Fakse
Fakse Ladeplads
Fakse Bugt
Agersø
Omø
Svendborg
Smålandsfarvandet
Knudshoved
Vejrø
Femø
Fejø
Vordingborg
Stege
Møn
Store Klint
Langeland
Rudkøbing
Marstal
Ærøskøbing
Nakskov
Maribo
Sakskøbing
Nykøbing F
FALSTER
LOLLAND
Rødby
Rødbyhavn
Gedser
Femer Bælt
Fehmarn
Puttgarden
Burg
Heiligenhafen
Oldenburg
Mecklenburger Bucht
Lübecker Bucht
Travemünde–Malmö
Travemünde–Trelleborg
Travemünde–Helsinki
Gdańsk
Helsingborg 10 h
Oslo 19 h
Göteborg 14 h
Darßer Ort
Darß
Prerow
Ostseebad Wustrow
Ostseebad Dierhagen
Ostseebad Graal-Müritz
Ribnitz-Damgarten
R.-Warnemünde
Ostseebad Kühlungsborn
Ostseebad Rerik
Bad Doberan
ROSTOCK
Wustrow
Poel
WISMAR
Grevesmühlen
Güstrow
Teterow
Bützow
Plön
Malente
Eutin
Neustadt
Grömitz
Kellenhusen
Dahme
Lütjenburg
Scharbeutz
Timmendf. Strand
L.-TRAVEMÜNDE
Bad Schwartau
Stockelsdorf
Ratekau
LÜBECK
Ratzeburg
Gadebusch
Rehna
SCHWERIN
Schweriner See
Sternberg
Bruel
Warin
Neukloster

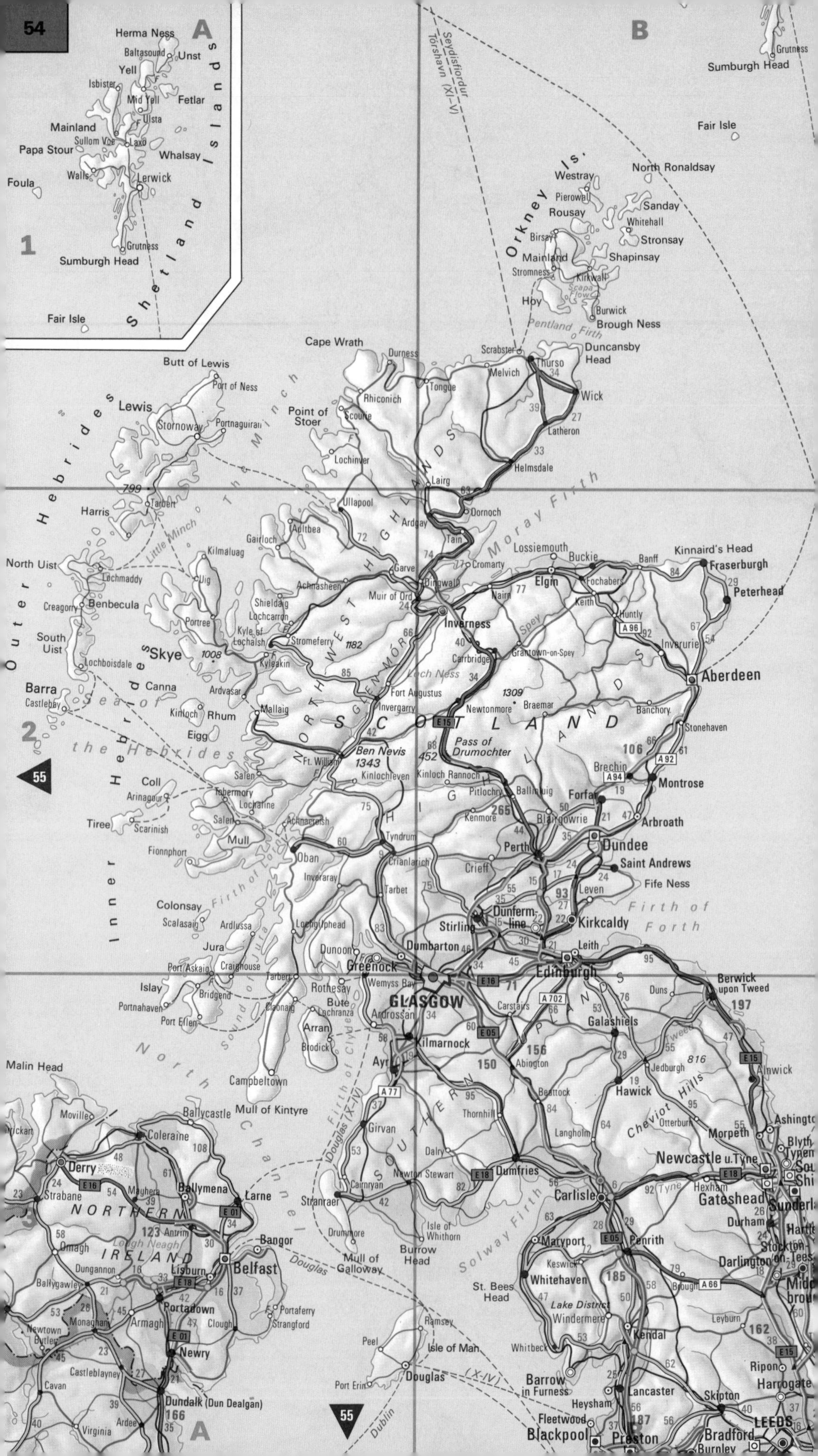
A
B
1
2
Herma Ness
Baltasound
Unst
Yell
Fetlar
Mainland
Papa Stour
Whalsay
Foula
Lerwick
Sumburgh Head
Fair Isle
Shetland Islands
Orkney Is.
North Ronaldsay
Westray
Sanday
Rousay
Stronsay
Shapinsay
Kirkwall
Stromness
Hoy
Pentland Firth
Thurso
Wick
Cape Wrath
Butt of Lewis
Lewis
Stornoway
Harris
Outer Hebrides
Skye
Barra
Inner Hebrides
Mull
Oban
Fort William
Ben Nevis 1343
Inverness
Moray Firth
Aberdeen
Dundee
Perth
Stirling
Edinburgh
GLASGOW
Firth of Forth
SCOTLAND
NORTH WEST HIGHLANDS
HIGHLANDS
SOUTHERN UPLANDS
Islay
Jura
Arran
Kilmarnock
Ayr
Dumfries
Carlisle
Newcastle u.Tyne
Berwick upon Tweed
Cheviot Hills
NORTHERN IRELAND
Derry
Belfast
Coleraine
Ballymena
Newry
Isle of Man
Douglas
Lake District
Kendal
Lancaster
Blackpool
Preston
LEEDS
Bradford
Harrogate
Darlington
Durham
55

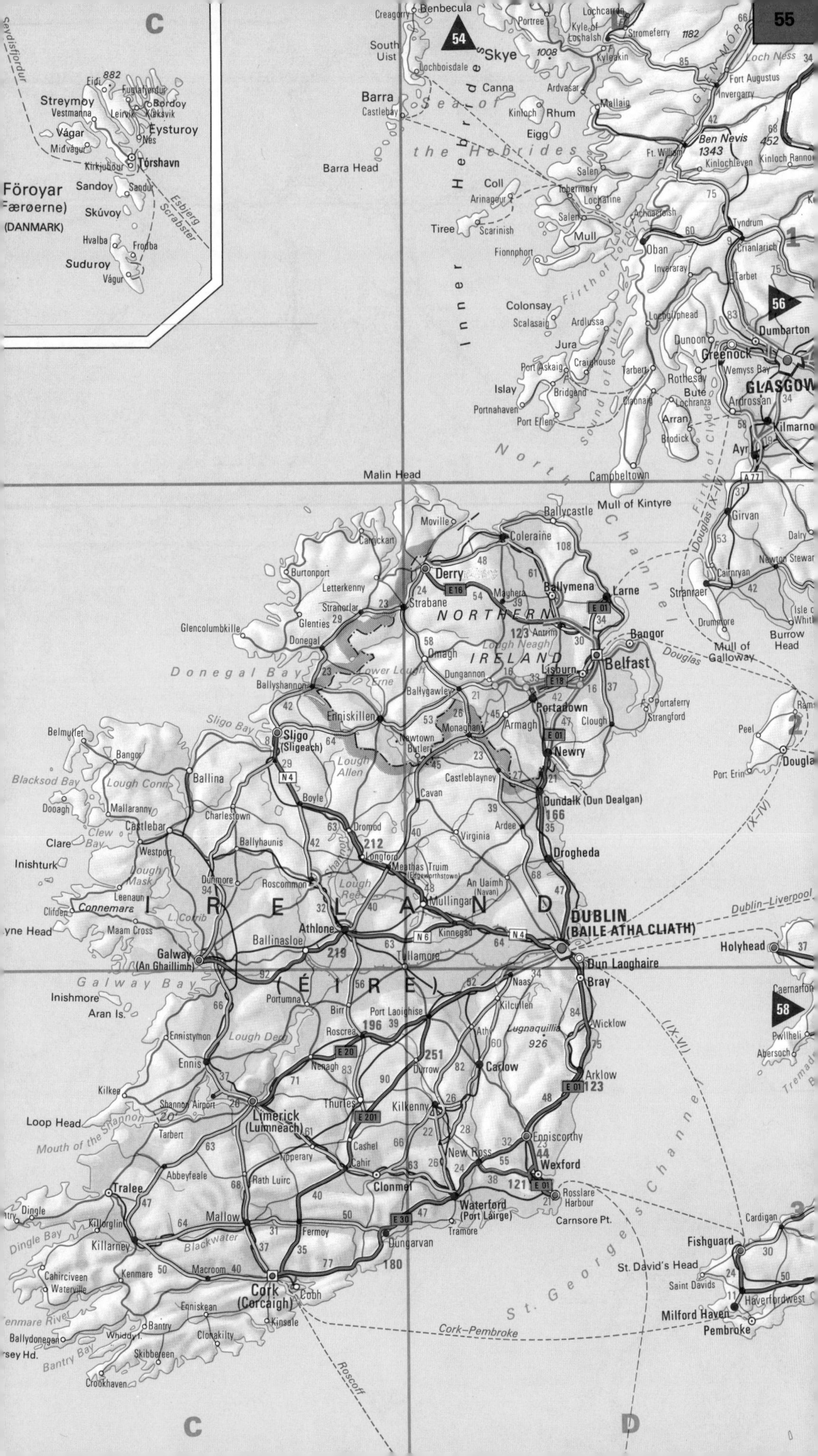
Föroyar
(Færøerne)
(DANMARK)
Streymoy
Eysturoy
Vágar
Tórshavn
Sandoy
Skúvoy
Suduroy
Skye
Barra
South Uist
Benbecula
Canna
Rhum
Eigg
Coll
Tiree
Mull
Oban
Colonsay
Jura
Islay
Arran
Inner Hebrides
Sea of the Hebrides
Ben Nevis
1343
Fort Augustus
Loch Ness
Glen Mór
Dumbarton
Greenock
GLASGOW
Kilmarnock
Ayr
Girvan
Stranraer
Mull of Galloway
Campbeltown
Mull of Kintyre
North Channel
Malin Head
Derry
Coleraine
Ballymena
Larne
Bangor
Belfast
Lisburn
Portadown
Armagh
Newry
Enniskillen
Omagh
Strabane
Letterkenny
Donegal
NORTHERN IRELAND
Lough Neagh
Donegal Bay
Sligo
(Sligeach)
Sligo Bay
Ballina
Castlebar
Westport
Clew Bay
Lough Allen
Cavan
Dundalk (Dun Dealgan)
Drogheda
Longford
Mullingar
Athlone
DUBLIN
(BAILE ATHA CLIATH)
Dun Laoghaire
Bray
Wicklow
Lugnaquillia
926
Arklow
IRELAND
(ÉIRE)
Galway
(An Ghaillimh)
Galway Bay
Aran Is.
Inishmore
Connemara
Ennis
Limerick
(Lumneach)
Shannon Airport
Loop Head
Mouth of the Shannon
Tralee
Killarney
Dingle Bay
Mallow
Cork
(Corcaigh)
Cobh
Kinsale
Bantry Bay
Waterford
(Port Lairge)
Wexford
Rosslare Harbour
Carnsore Pt.
Kilkenny
Carlow
Clonmel
Dungarvan
St. Georges Channel
Cork–Pembroke
Roscoff
Dublin–Liverpool
Holyhead
Fishguard
Pembroke
Milford Haven
Haverfordwest
St. David's Head
Cardigan
Douglas
Peel
Port Erin
54
56
58
C
D

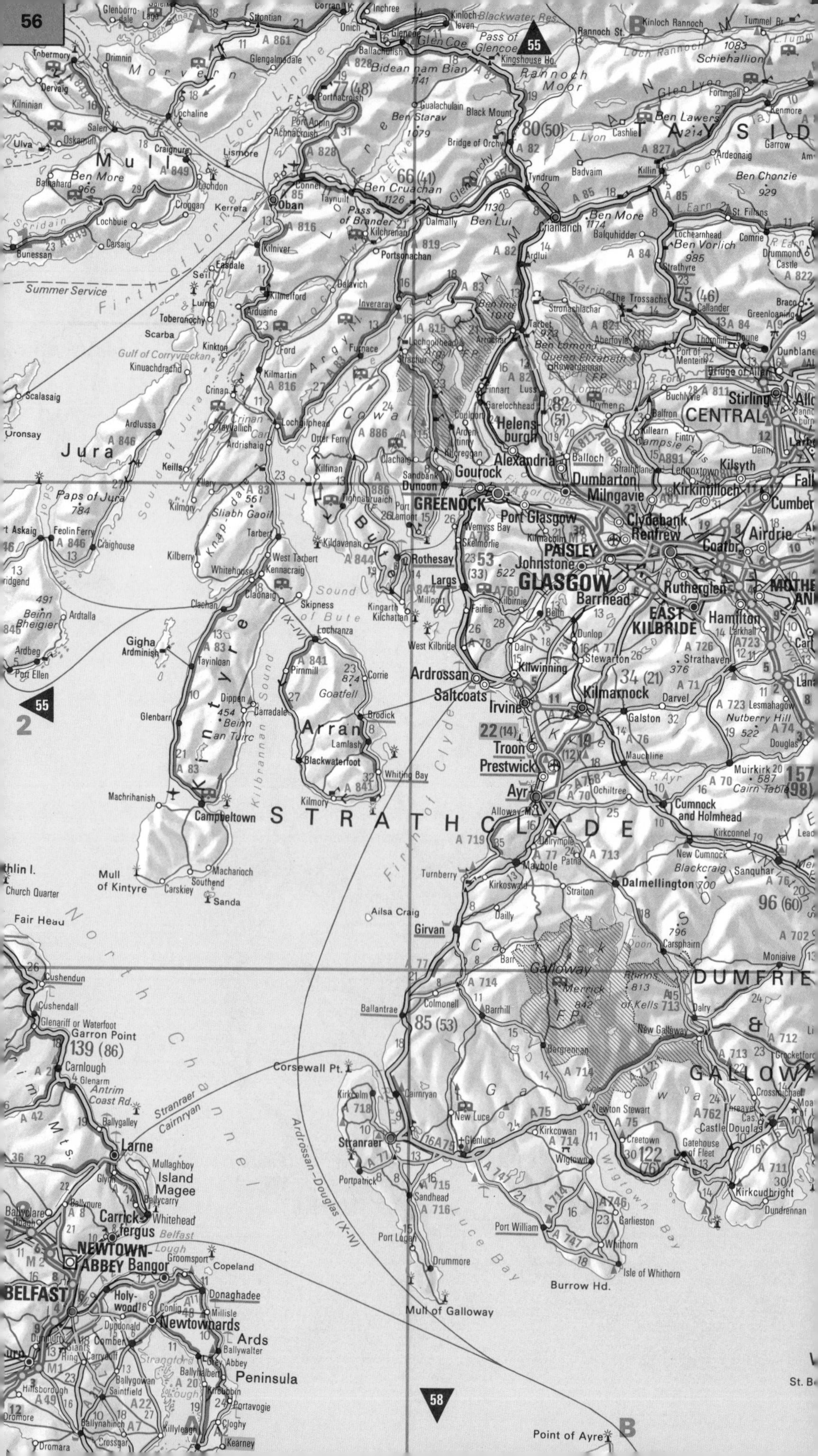

55
Mull
Jura
Arran
Bute
Kintyre
STRATHCLYDE
CENTRAL
TAYSIDE
DUMFRIES & GALLOWAY
Tobermory
Dervaig
Salen
Craignure
Lochaline
Strontian
Glencoe
Ballachulish
Pass of Glencoe
Kingshouse Ho.
Rannoch Moor
Rannoch St.
Kinloch Rannoch
Schiehallion
Loch Rannoch
Glen Lyon
Fortingall
Kenmore
Ben Lawers
Killin
Bunessan
Lochbuie
Ben More
Oban
Connel
Taynuilt
Pass of Brander
Ben Cruachan
Dalmally
Ben Lui
Tyndrum
Crianlarich
Balquhidder
Lochearnhead
St. Fillans
Comrie
Ben Vorlich
Strathyre
Callander
The Trossachs
Aberfoyle
Dunblane
Stirling
Bridge of Allan
Inveraray
Arrochar
Tarbet
Ben Lomond
Queen Elizabeth F.P.
Easdale
Kilmelford
Summer Service
Firth of Lorne
Gulf of Corryvreckan
Scarba
Kilmartin
Crinan
Lochgilphead
Ardrishaig
Cowal
Dunoon
Gourock
Greenock
Helensburgh
Alexandria
Balloch
Dumbarton
Milngavie
Clydebank
Renfrew
Paisley
Glasgow
Johnstone
Barrhead
Rutherglen
East Kilbride
Hamilton
Airdrie
Coatbridge
Kirkintilloch
Kilsyth
Rothesay
Largs
Millport
Tarbert
Kennacraig
West Tarbert
Tayinloan
Gigha
Port Ellen
Ardbeg
Paps of Jura
Craighouse
Feolin Ferry
Lochranza
Brodick
Goatfell
Lamlash
Blackwaterfoot
Whiting Bay
Kilmory
Campbeltown
Machrihanish
Mull of Kintyre
Carradale
Saltcoats
Ardrossan
Irvine
Kilwinning
Kilmarnock
Troon
Prestwick
Ayr
Maybole
Cumnock and Holmhead
Dalmellington
Girvan
Ailsa Craig
Turnberry
Ballantrae
Barrhill
Newton Stewart
Galloway F.P.
Merrick
Castle Douglas
Kirkcudbright
Gatehouse of Fleet
Creetown
Wigtown
Whithorn
Isle of Whithorn
Port William
Glenluce
Stranraer
Cairnryan
Portpatrick
Corsewall Pt.
Drummore
Mull of Galloway
Luce Bay
Burrow Hd.
North Channel
Stranraer Cairnryan
Ardrossan–Douglas (X–V)
Fair Head
Cushendun
Cushendall
Glenariff or Waterfoot
Garron Point
Carnlough
Antrim Coast Rd.
Larne
Island Magee
Whitehead
Carrickfergus
Belfast Lough
Newtownabbey
Bangor
Belfast
Holywood
Donaghadee
Newtownards
Ards Peninsula
Point of Ayre
58

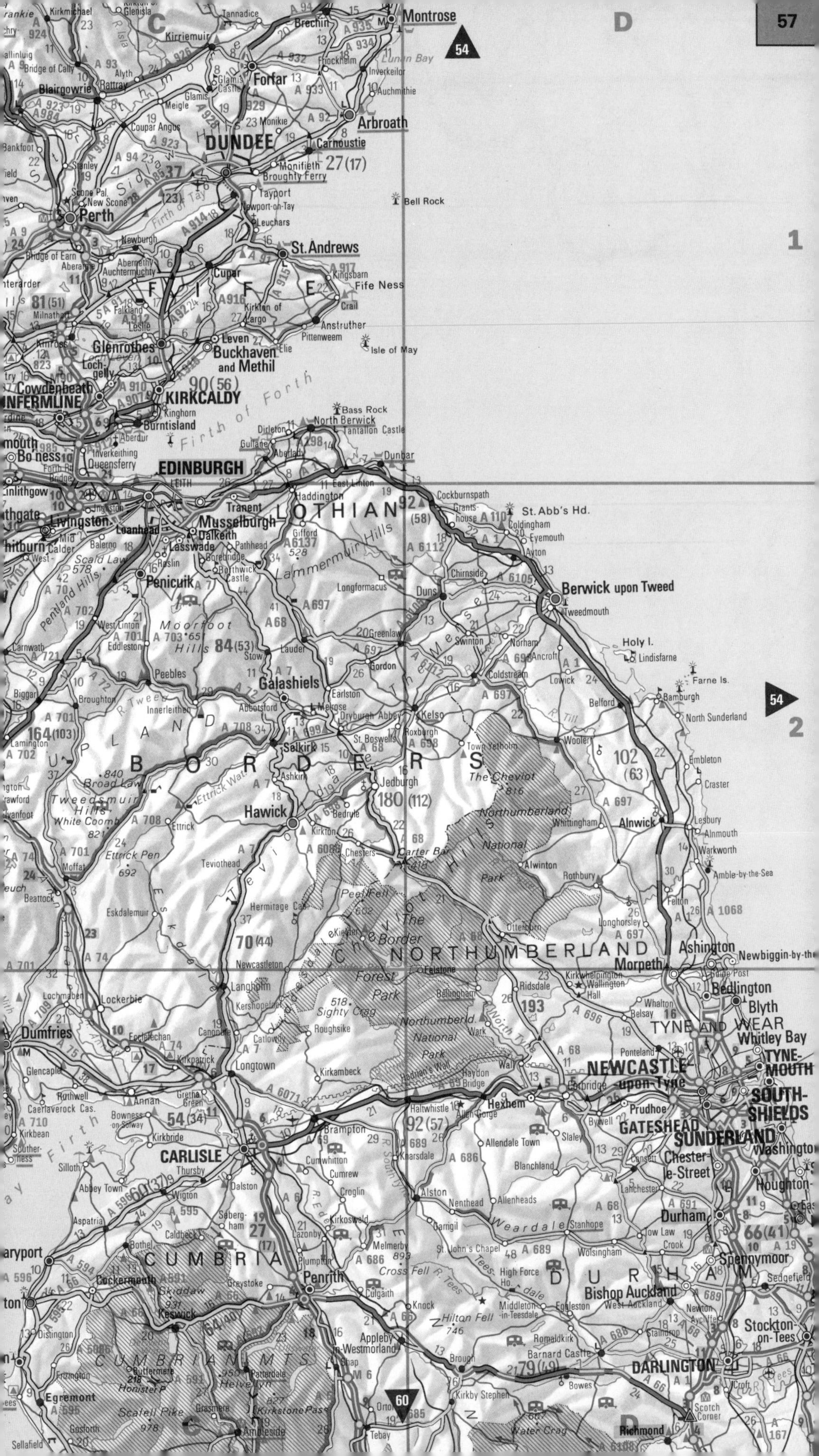

C
D
54
1
2
54
60
Montrose
Brechin
Kirriemuir
Tannadice
Kirkmichael
Blairgowrie
Bridge of Cally
Alyth
Rattray
Meigle
Glamis
Forfar
Friockheim
Inverkeilor
Lunan Bay
Auchmithie
Arbroath
Carnoustie
Monikie
Coupar Angus
DUNDEE
Monifieth
Broughty Ferry
27 (17)
Bankfoot
Stanley
Sidlaw Hills
Scone Pal.
New Scone
Perth
Firth of Tay
Tayport
Newport-on-Tay
Leuchars
Bell Rock
Newburgh
Bridge of Earn
Aberargie
Abernethy
Auchtermuchty
Cupar
St. Andrews
Kingsbarn
Fife Ness
Crail
F I F E
Kirkton of Largo
Anstruther
Pittenweem
Isle of May
Elie
Milnathort
Kinross
Falkland
Leslie
Glenrothes
Leven
Buckhaven and Methil
Loch Leven
Lochgelly
81 (51)
90 (56)
Cowdenbeath
KIRKCALDY
Kinghorn
Burntisland
Aberdour
Firth of Forth
Inverkeithing
Queensferry
Forth Rd Bridge
Bo'ness
Linlithgow
Bass Rock
North Berwick
Tantallon Castle
Dirleton
Gullane
Aberlady
Dunbar
EDINBURGH
LEITH
East Linton
Haddington
Cockburnspath
Grantshouse
St. Abb's Hd.
Coldingham
Eyemouth
Ayton
Tranent
Musselburgh
Dalkeith
Loanhead
Lasswade
LOTHIAN
Livingston
Mid Calder
Balerno
Pathhead
Gifford
Lammermuir Hills
Roslin
Gorebridge
Borthwick Castle
Scald Law 578
Pentland Hills
Penicuik
Longformacus
Duns
Chirnside
Berwick upon Tweed
Tweedmouth
Holy I.
Lindisfarne
Farne Is.
Bamburgh
North Sunderland
Carnwath
West Linton
Eddleston
Moorfoot Hills
84 (53)
Stow
Lauder
Greenlaw
Gordon
Swinton
Norham
Ancroft
Lowick
Coldstream
Belford
Biggar
Broughton
Peebles
Innerleithen
Galashiels
Earlston
Abbotsford
Melrose
Dryburgh Abbey
Kelso
Roxburgh
St. Boswells
Selkirk
Town Yetholm
Wooler
102 (63)
Embleton
Craster
Lamington
164 (103)
U P L A N D
B O R D E R S
Broad Law 840
Tweedsmuir Hills
White Coomb 821
Ettrick Water
Ashkirk
Jedburgh
180 (112)
The Cheviot 816
Hawick
Ettrick
Bedrule
Northumberland National Park
Whittingham
Alnwick
Lesbury
Alnmouth
Warkworth
Amble-by-the-Sea
Kirkton
Chesters
Carter Bar 418
Alwinton
Rothbury
Moffat
Ettrick Pen 692
Teviothead
Beattock
Eskdalemuir
Peel Fell 602
Hermitage Cas.
The Border Forest Park
Kielder
Otterburn
Longhorsley
Felton
Ashington
Newbiggin-by-the
Morpeth
NORTHUMBERLAND
70 (44)
Newcastleton
Falstone
Bedlington
Blyth
Lochmaben
Lockerbie
Langholm
Kershopefoot
Ridsdale
Kirkwhelpington
Wallington Hall
Whalton
Belsay
Bellingham
Sighty Crag 518
193
TYNE AND WEAR
Whitley Bay
Dumfries
Ecclefechan
Canonbie
Catlowdy
Roughsike
Northumberld. National Park
Wark
Ponteland
TYNEMOUTH
Glencaple
Kirkpatrick
Longtown
Kirkambeck
Hadrian's Wall
Haydon Bridge
Wall
Corbridge
NEWCASTLE upon Tyne
SOUTH SHIELDS
Caerlaverock Cas.
Ruthwell
Annan
Gretna Green
Hexham
Prudhoe
Kirkbean
Bowness-on-Solway
54 (34)
Brampton
Haltwhistle
Allen Gorge
92 (57)
Bywell
GATESHEAD
SUNDERLAND
Washington
Southerness
Kirkbride
Slaley
Chester-le-Street
Silloth
CARLISLE
Thursby
Cumwhitton
Cumrew
Knarsdale
Allendale Town
Blanchland
Consett
Houghton
Abbey Town
60 (37)
Wigton
Dalston
Croglin
Alston
Nenthead
Allenheads
Lanchester
Durham
Aspatria
Sebergham
Caldbeck
Kirkoswald
Garrigil
Weardale
Stanhope
Tow Law
66 (41)
Bothel
27 (17)
Lazonby
Melmerby 893
St. John's Chapel
Wolsingham
Crook
Spennymoor
Maryport
C U M B R I A
Plumpton
Cross Fell
High Force Ho.
Teesdale
D U R H A M
Sedgefield
Cockermouth
Skiddaw 931
Greystoke
Penrith
Culgaith
Bishop Auckland
West Auckland
Workington
Keswick
64 (40)
Knock
Hilton Fell 746
Middleton-in-Teesdale
Eggleston
Newton Aycliffe
Stockton-on-Tees
Distington
Appleby-in-Westmorland
Romaldkirk
Staindrop
CUMBRIAN MTS
Frizington
Buttermere
Honister P.
Helvellyn 950
Patterdale
Shap
Brough
Barnard Castle
79 (49)
DARLINGTON
Egremont
Scafell Pike 978
Kirkstone Pass
Grasmere
Orton
Kirkby Stephen
Bowes
Croft
Scotch Corner
Gosforth
Ambleside
Tebay
Water Crag
Richmond
Sellafield

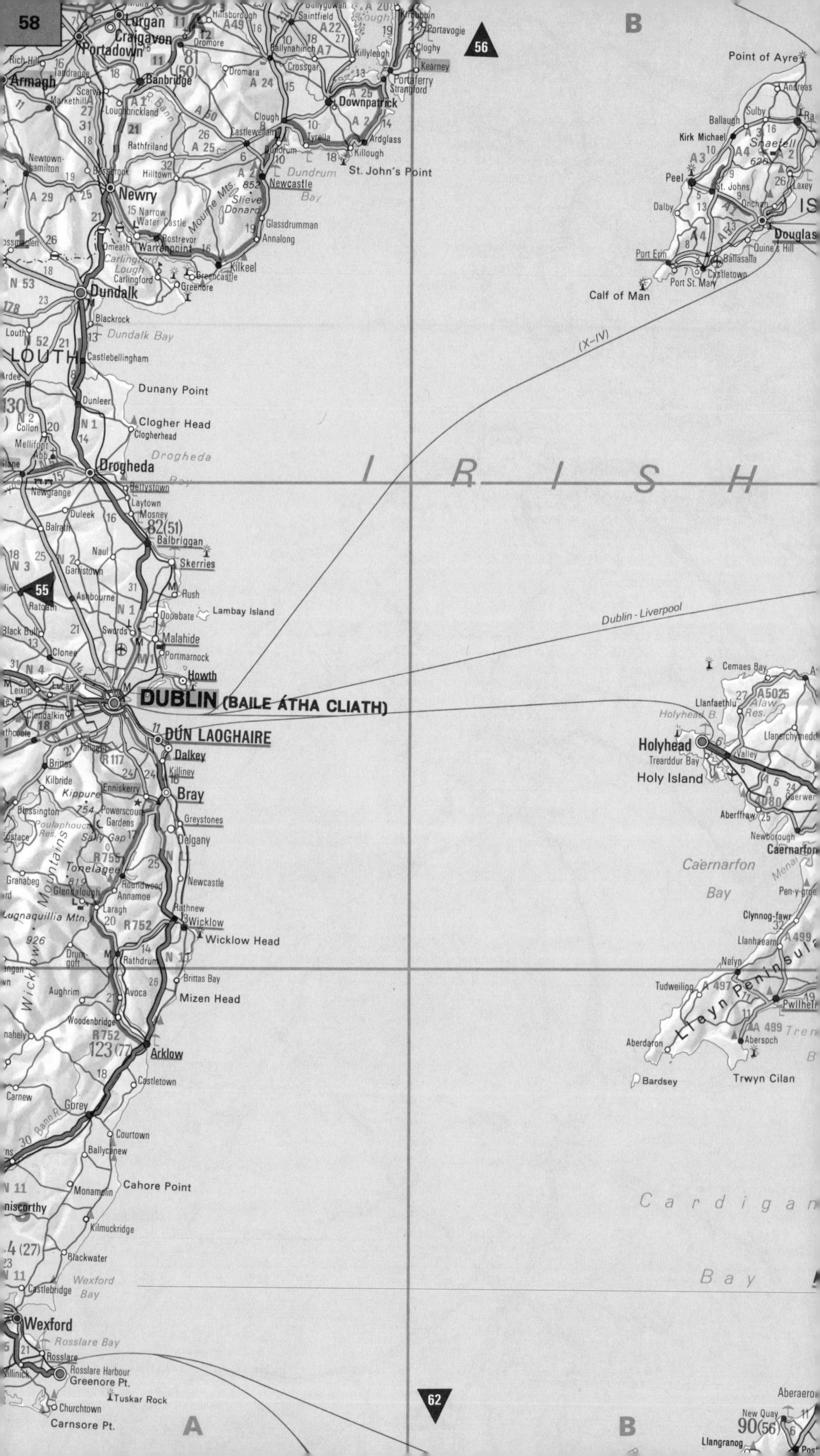

58
B
56
Lurgan
Craigavon
Portadown
Hillsborough
Saintfield
Dromore
Ballynahinch
Killyleagh
Portavogie
Cloghy
Kearney
Portaferry
Strangford
Armagh
Banbridge
Dromara
Crossgar
Downpatrick
Loughbrickland
Clough
Castlewellan
Tyrella
Ardglass
Killough
Dundrum
Rathfriland
Hilltown
Newry
Dundrum Bay
St. John's Point
Newcastle
Mourne Mts.
Slieve Donard
Narrow Water Castle
Rostrevor
Warrenpoint
Glassdrummond
Annalong
Omeath
Carlingford Lough
Carlingford
Kilkeel
Greencastle
Greenore
Dundalk
Blackrock
Dundalk Bay
LOUTH
Castlebellingham
Dunany Point
Dunleer
Clogher Head
Clogherhead
Collon
Mellifont Abbey
Drogheda
Drogheda Bay
Newgrange
Bettystown
Laytown
Mosney
Duleek
Balrath
Naul
Balbriggan
Skerries
Garristown
Rush
Ashbourne
Donabate
Lambay Island
Ratoath
Swords
Malahide
Portmarnock
Howth
Clonee
Lucan
Leixlip
DUBLIN (BAILE ÁTHA CLIATH)
Clondalkin
DÚN LAOGHAIRE
Dalkey
Killiney
Brittas
Kilbride
Enniskerry
Bray
Kippure
Powerscourt Gardens
Blessington
Poulaphouca Res.
Sally Gap
Greystones
Delgany
Tonelagee
Roundwood
Annamoe
Newcastle
Glendalough
Laragh
Rathnew
Wicklow
Wicklow Head
Lugnaquillia Mtn.
Wicklow Mountains
Drumgoff
Rathdrum
Brittas Bay
Aughrim
Avoca
Mizen Head
Woodenbridge
Arklow
Castletown
Carnew
Gorey
Courtown
Ballycanew
Cahore Point
Monamolin
Enniscorthy
Kilmuckridge
Blackwater
Wexford Bay
Castlebridge
Wexford
Rosslare Bay
Rosslare
Rosslare Harbour
Greenore Pt.
Tuskar Rock
Churchtown
Carnsore Pt.
A
62
B
Point of Ayre
Andreas
Ballaugh
Sulby
Kirk Michael
Snaefell
Peel
St. Johns
Laxey
Dalby
Onchan
Douglas
Quine's Hill
Port Erin
Ballasalla
Castletown
Port St. Mary
Calf of Man
(X-IV)
IRISH
Dublin - Liverpool
Cemaes Bay
Llanfaethlu
Alaw Res.
Holyhead B.
Holyhead
Trearddur Bay
Holy Island
Valley
Gaerwen
Aberffraw
Newborough
Caernarfon
Caernarfon Bay
Pen-y-groes
Clynnog-fawr
Llanhaearn
Nefyn
Tudweiliog
Lleyn Peninsula
Pwllheli
Aberdaron
Abersoch
Trwyn Cilan
Bardsey
Cardigan Bay
Aberaeron
New Quay
Llangranog

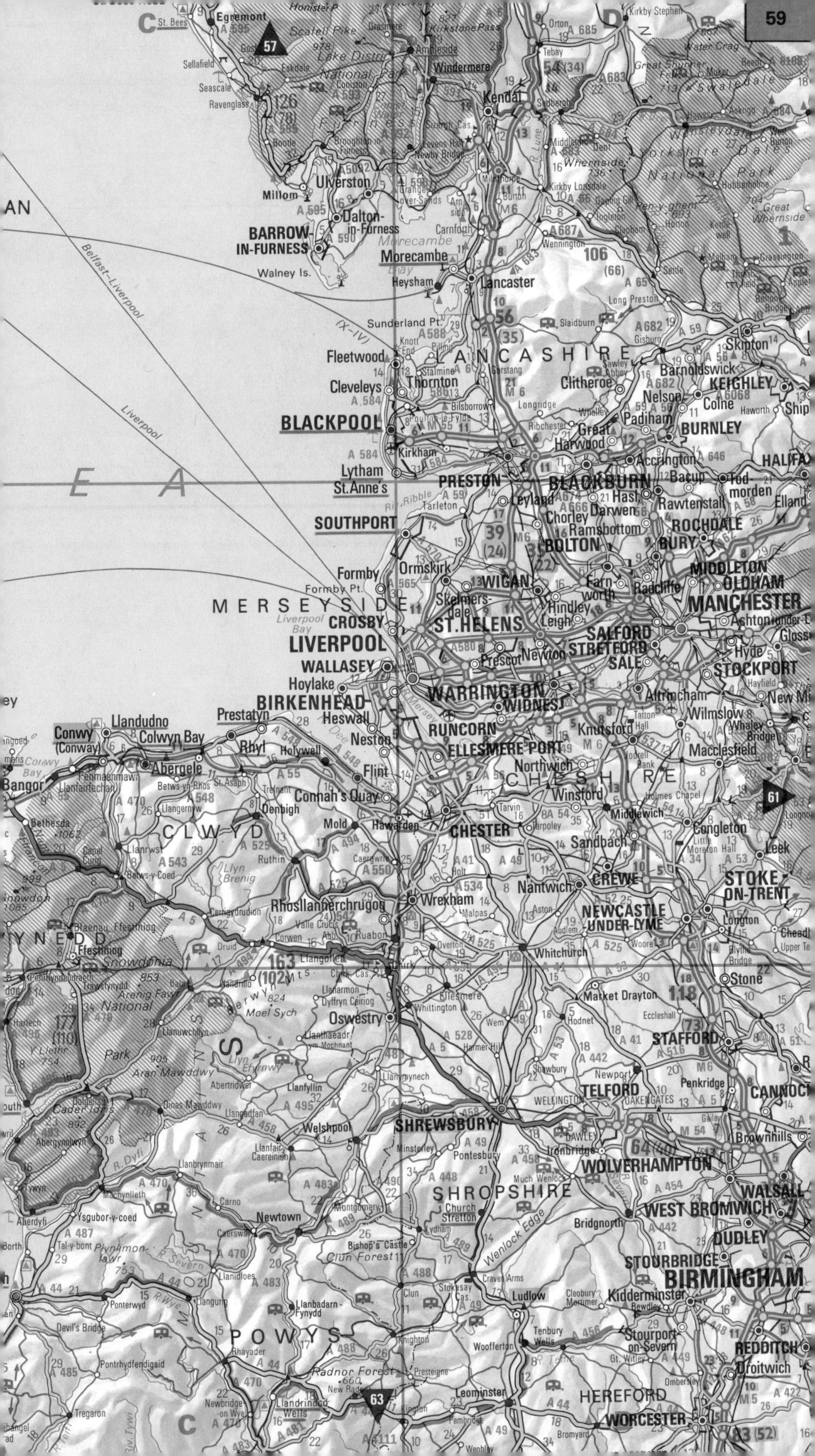

St. Bees
Egremont
Sellafield
Seascale
Ravenglass
Eskdale
Scafell Pike
Lake District
National Park
Coniston
Grasmere
Ambleside
Kirkstone Pass
Windermere
Kendal
Tebay
Orton
Kirkby Stephen
Sedbergh
Dent
Whernside
Kirkby Lonsdale
Ingleton
Settle
Horton
Pen-y-ghent
Hawes
Wensleydale
Yorkshire Dales
National Park
Great Whernside
Grassington
Malham
Swaledale
Great Shunner Fell
Muker
Water Crag
Bootle
Broughton-in-Furness
Newby Bridge
Levens Hall
Sizergh Cas.
Ulverston
Millom
Dalton-in-Furness
BARROW-IN-FURNESS
Walney Is.
Grange-over-Sands
Arnside
Milnthorpe
Burton
Carnforth
Morecambe
Morecambe Bay
Heysham
Lancaster
Wennington
Clapham
Long Preston
Slaidburn
Gisburn
Skipton
Belfast–Liverpool
Liverpool
Sunderland Pt.
Knott End
Pilling
Fleetwood
Thornton
Stalmine
Cleveleys
Garstang
LANCASHIRE
Clitheroe
Sawley Abbey
Barnoldswick
Nelson
Colne
KEIGHLEY
Haworth
BLACKPOOL
Bilsborrow
Poulton-le-Fylde
Longridge
Ribchester
Whalley
Padiham
BURNLEY
Great Harwood
Accrington
Kirkham
Lytham
St. Anne's
PRESTON
BLACKBURN
Bacup
Todmorden
HALIFAX
Leyland
Tarleton
Riv. Ribble
Chorley
Darwen
Haslingden
Rawtenstall
Elland
SOUTHPORT
Ramsbottom
ROCHDALE
BOLTON
BURY
Formby
Formby Pt.
Ormskirk
WIGAN
Farnworth
Radcliffe
MIDDLETON
OLDHAM
MERSEYSIDE
Skelmersdale
Hindley
Leigh
MANCHESTER
Liverpool Bay
CROSBY
ST. HELENS
SALFORD
Ashton-under-Lyne
LIVERPOOL
Prescot
Newton
STRETFORD
SALE
Hyde
STOCKPORT
WALLASEY
Hoylake
WARRINGTON
WIDNES
Altrincham
Wilmslow
BIRKENHEAD
Heswall
Prestatyn
Llandudno
Conwy (Conway)
Colwyn Bay
Rhyl
Holywell
Neston
RUNCORN
ELLESMERE PORT
Knutsford
Tatton Hall
Whaley Bridge
Macclesfield
Penmaenmawr
Llanfairfechan
Abergele
St. Asaph
Flint
Northwich
CHESHIRE
Bangor
Bethesda
Betws-yn-Rhos
Llangernyw
Denbigh
Connah's Quay
Hawarden
Tarvin
Tarporley
Winsford
Middlewich
Holmes Chapel
Congleton
Leek
CLWYD
Mold
CHESTER
Sandbach
Llanrwst
Capel Curig
Ruthin
Llyn Brenig
Caergwrle
Holt
Nantwich
CREWE
STOKE-ON-TRENT
Snowdon
Betws-y-Coed
Wrexham
Malpas
Aston
NEWCASTLE-UNDER-LYME
Longton
Cerrigydrudion
Rhosllannerchrugog
Blaenau Ffestiniog
Ffestiniog
Snowdonia
Valle Crucis Abb.
Ruabon
Druid
Corwen
Llangollen
Overton
Audlem
Woore
Whitchurch
Blythe Bridge
Penrhyndeudraeth
Trawsfynydd
Arenig Fawr
Bala
Llandrillo
Berwyn Mts.
Chirk
Chirk Cas.
Ellesmere
Market Drayton
Stone
National Park
Llanarmon Dyffryn Ceiriog
Moel Sych
Whittington
Oswestry
Wem
Hodnet
Eccleshall
Harlech
Llanuwchllyn
Llanthaeadr-ym-Mochnant
STAFFORD
Y Llethr
Park
Aran Mawddwy
Lake Vyrnwy
Harmer Hill
Shawbury
Abertridwr
Llanymynech
Newport
Penkridge
Llanfyllin
TELFORD
WELLINGTON
OAKENGATES
CANNOCK
Dolgellau
Dinas Mawddwy
Cader Idris
Llangadfan
Welshpool
SHREWSBURY
Abergynolwyn
Llanfair Caereinion
Minsterley
Pontesbury
DAWLEY
Ironbridge
Brownhills
R. Dyfi
Llanbrynmair
WOLVERHAMPTON
Tywyn
Machynlleth
Carno
Much Wenlock
SHROPSHIRE
WALSALL
Aberdyfi
Ysgubor-y-coed
Newtown
Montgomery
Church Stretton
WEST BROMWICH
Caersws
Lydham
Bridgnorth
DUDLEY
Tal-y-bont
Plynlimon-fawr
Bishop's Castle
Clun Forest
Wenlock Edge
R. Severn
Llanidloes
STOURBRIDGE
BIRMINGHAM
Craven Arms
Clun
Stokesay Cas.
Ludlow
Cleobury Mortimer
Kidderminster
Bewdley
Ponterwyd
Llangurig
Llanbadarn-Fynydd
R. Wye
Devil's Bridge
POWYS
Knighton
Tenbury Wells
Wooferton
Stourport-on-Severn
REDDITCH
Gt. Witley
Droitwich
Rhayader
Pontrhydfendigaid
Radnor Forest
Presteigne
R. Teme
Ombersley
New Radnor
Leominster
HEREFORD
Newbridge-on-Wye
Llandrindod Wells
Kington
Pembridge
WORCESTER
Tregaron
Bromyard
Weobley
R. Tywi
M 6
M 55
M 54
M 5
A 59
A 65
A 55
A 548
A 5
A 49
A 41

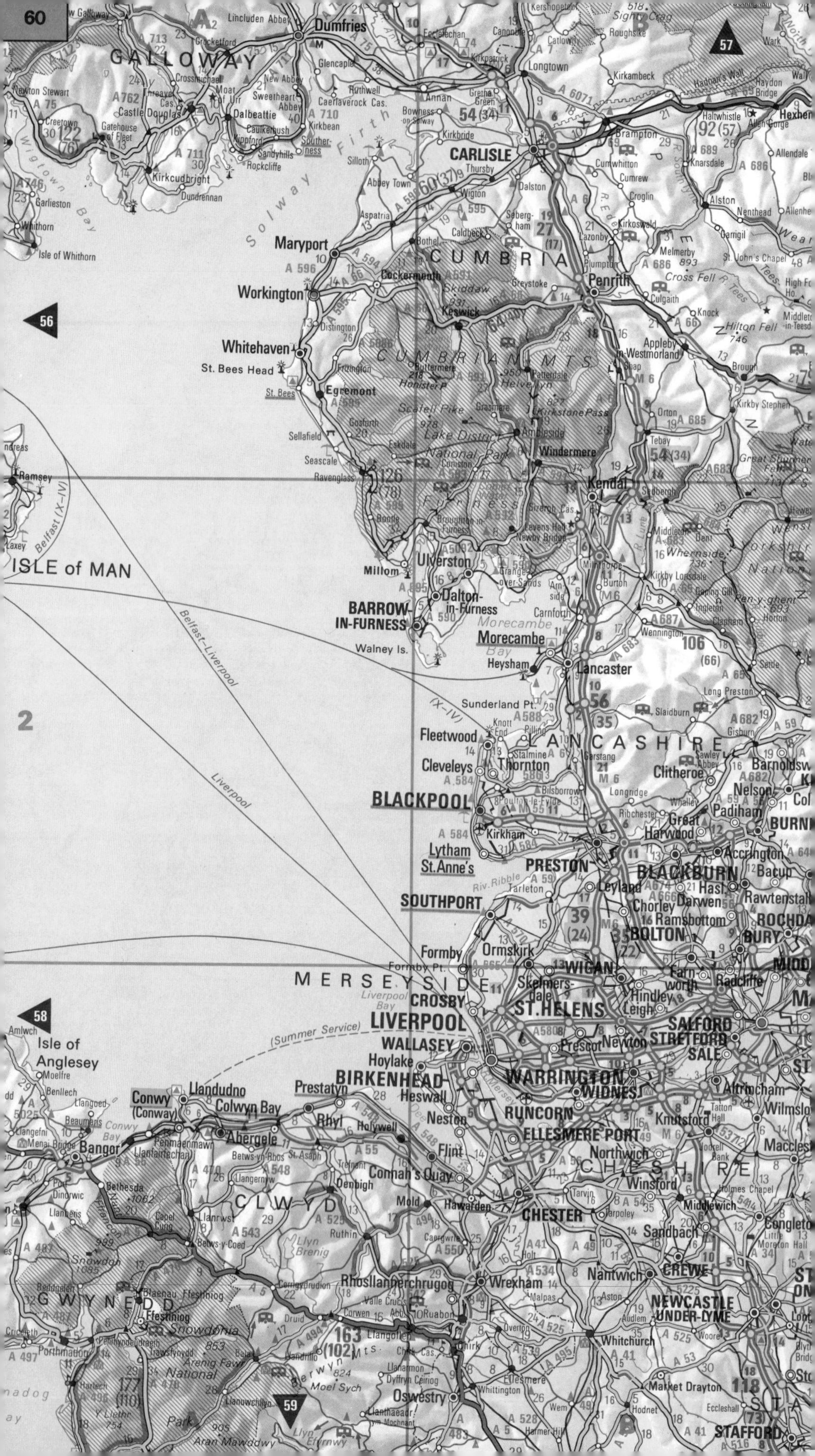
GALLOWAY
Dumfries
Newton Stewart
Castle Douglas
Dalbeattie
Kirkcudbright
Gatehouse of Fleet
Creetown
Garlieston
Whithorn
Isle of Whithorn
Wigtown Bay
Solway Firth
Annan
Gretna Green
Longtown
Brampton
Haltwhistle
Hexham
CARLISLE
Wigton
Silloth
Maryport
Workington
Cockermouth
CUMBRIA
Penrith
Keswick
Skiddaw
Whitehaven
St. Bees Head
St. Bees
Egremont
CUMBRIAN MTS
Buttermere
Honister P.
Patterdale
Helvellyn
Scafell Pike
Lake District National Park
Grasmere
Ambleside
Kirkstone Pass
Windermere
Coniston
Sellafield
Seascale
Ravenglass
Bootle
Broughton in Furness
Kendal
Sedbergh
Alston
Cross Fell
Appleby in-Westmorland
Shap
Kirkby Stephen
Tebay
Orton
Hilton Fell
Brough
Ramsey
ISLE of MAN
Millom
Ulverston
Dalton-in-Furness
BARROW-IN-FURNESS
Walney Is.
Grange-over-Sands
Morecambe Bay
Morecambe
Heysham
Lancaster
Carnforth
Kirkby Lonsdale
Whernside
Pen-y-ghent
Settle
Slaidburn
Belfast-Liverpool
Liverpool
Sunderland Pt.
Fleetwood
Cleveleys
Thornton
LANCASHIRE
Garstang
Clitheroe
BLACKPOOL
Kirkham
Lytham St. Anne's
PRESTON
BLACKBURN
Leyland
Chorley
Darwen
Ramsbottom
SOUTHPORT
BOLTON
BURY
Formby
Formby Pt.
Ormskirk
WIGAN
MERSEYSIDE
Skelmersdale
ST.HELENS
Farnworth
Radcliffe
CROSBY
LIVERPOOL
Liverpool Bay
(Summer Service)
WALLASEY
Hoylake
BIRKENHEAD
Heswall
WARRINGTON
WIDNES
RUNCORN
ELLESMERE PORT
SALFORD
STRETFORD
SALE
Altrincham
Knutsford
Northwich
CHESHIRE
Winsford
Middlewich
Sandbach
Congleton
CREWE
Nantwich
NEWCASTLE UNDER-LYME
Market Drayton
STAFFORD
Isle of Anglesey
Amlwch
Moelfre
Benllech
Llangefni
Bangor
Llandudno
Conwy (Conway)
Colwyn Bay
Abergele
Prestatyn
Rhyl
Holywell
Flint
Connah's Quay
Neston
St. Asaph
Denbigh
Mold
Hawarden
CHESTER
CLWYD
Llanberis
Bethesda
Betws-y-Coed
Llanrwst
Ruthin
Llyn Brenig
Snowdon
GWYNEDD
Blaenau Ffestiniog
Ffestiniog
Snowdonia National Park
Criccieth
Porthmadog
Harlech
Bala
Corwen
Llangollen
Ruabon
Wrexham
Chirk
Oswestry
Ellesmere
Whitchurch
Whittington
Berwyn Mts.
Moel Sych
Aran Mawddwy
Llyn Efyrnwy
Hodnet
Eccleshall
56
57
58
59
2

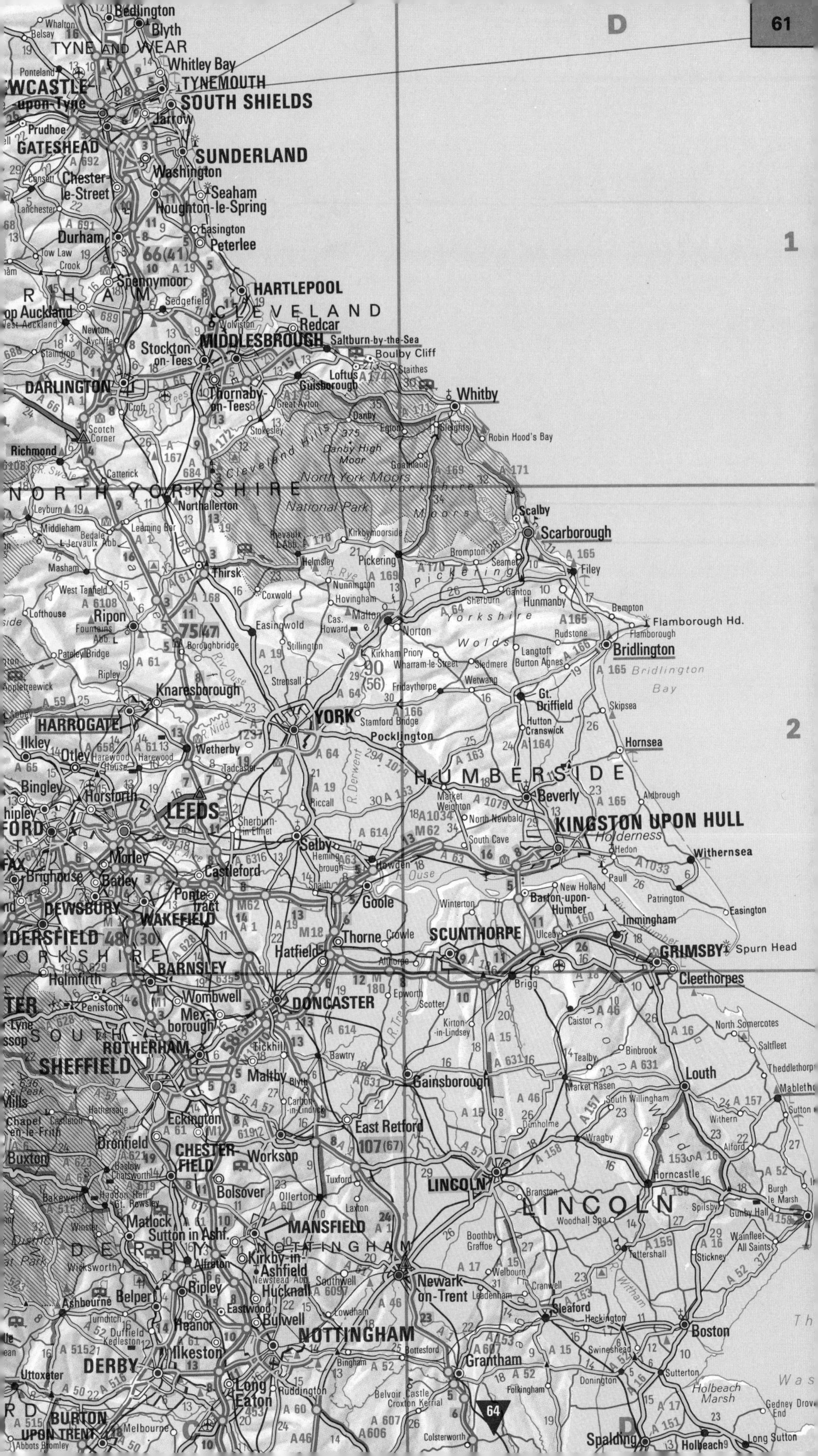
D
1
2
Bedlington
Blyth
Whalton
Belsay
TYNE AND WEAR
Whitley Bay
Ponteland
TYNEMOUTH
SOUTH SHIELDS
-upon-Tyne
Jarrow
Prudhoe
GATESHEAD
SUNDERLAND
Washington
Chester-le-Street
Seaham
Houghton-le-Spring
Lanchester
Durham
Easington
Peterlee
Tow Law
Crook
Spennymoor
HARTLEPOOL
Sedgefield
CLEVELAND
West Auckland
Newton Aycliffe
Redcar
MIDDLESBROUGH
Saltburn-by-the-Sea
Boulby Cliff
Stockton-on-Tees
Staindrop
Loftus
Staithes
Guisborough
DARLINGTON
Thornaby-on-Tees
Great Ayton
Whitby
Croft
Danby
Egton
Sleights
Scotch Corner
Stokesley
Robin Hood's Bay
Richmond
Cleveland Hills
Danby High Moor
Catterick
North York Moors
Goathland
NORTH YORKSHIRE
Northallerton
Yorkshire Moors
National Park
Scalby
Scarborough
Leyburn
Middleham
Bedale
Jervaulx Abb.
Leeming Bar
Rievaulx Abb.
Kirkbymoorside
Masham
Thirsk
Helmsley
Pickering
Brompton
Seamer
Filey
R. Rye
Nunnington
Vale of Pickering
West Tanfield
Coxwold
Hovingham
Ganton
Hunmanby
Sherburn
Ripon
Lofthouse
Cas. Howard
Malton
Yorkshire Wolds
Bempton
Flamborough Hd.
Flamborough
Rudstone
Fountains Abb.
Easingwold
Norton
Boroughbridge
Stillington
Bridlington
Pateley Bridge
Kirkham Priory
Wharram-le-Street
Sledmere
Langtoft
Burton Agnes
Ripley
Riv. Ouse
Strensall
Bridlington Bay
Fridaythorpe
Wetwang
Appletreewick
Knaresborough
Gt. Driffield
YORK
Stamford Bridge
HARROGATE
Skipsea
Hutton Cranswick
Pocklington
Ilkley
Otley
Harewood
Harewood House
Wetherby
R. Nidd
Hornsea
HUMBERSIDE
Bingley
Tadcaster
R. Derwent
Horsforth
Market Weighton
Beverly
Aldbrough
Riccall
North Newbald
LEEDS
KINGSTON UPON HULL
Sherburn-in-Elmet
Holderness
Selby
South Cave
Hedon
Withernsea
Morley
Castleford
Hemingbrough
Howden
Batley
Brighouse
Paull
Pontefract
Goole
New Holland
R. Ouse
DEWSBURY
Patrington
Barton-upon-Humber
Winterton
WAKEFIELD
Easington
Immingham
Thorne
Crowle
SCUNTHORPE
Ulceby
Spurn Head
Hatfield
GRIMSBY
BARNSLEY
Holmfirth
Althorpe
Cleethorpes
Brigg
Wombwell
Epworth
DONCASTER
Penistone
Mexborough
Scotter
Caistor
ROTHERHAM
Kirton-in-Lindsey
North Somercotes
Tickhill
Saltfleet
SHEFFIELD
Bawtry
Binbrook
Tealby
Theddlethorpe
Maltby
Gainsborough
Louth
Market Rasen
Hathersage
Blyth
Carlton-in-Lindrick
South Willingham
Mablethorpe
Castleton
Chapel-en-le-Frith
Eckington
Withern
Sutton
Bronfield
East Retford
Dunholme
Wragby
Alford
CHESTERFIELD
Worksop
Buxton
Baslow
Chatsworth
Horncastle
Bakewell
Haddon Hall
Bolsover
Tuxford
LINCOLN
Burgh le Marsh
Spilsby
Gunby Hall
Gt. Rowsley
Ollerton
Branston
Laxton
Woodhall Spa
Winster
Matlock
Sutton in Ashf.
MANSFIELD
Wainfleet All Saints
Boothby Graffoe
Tattershall
Stickney
DERBY
NOTTINGHAM
Wirksworth
Alfreton
Kirkby-in-Ashfield
Newstead Abb.
Southwell
Welbourn
Newark-on-Trent
Cranwell
Leadenham
Ashbourne
Belper
Ripley
Hucknall
R. Witham
Eastwood
Lowdham
Sleaford
Heanor
Bulwell
Heckington
Boston
Turnditch
Duffield
Kedleston
Ilkeston
Swineshead
Bottesford
Grantham
Bingham
Sutterton
Donington
Uttoxeter
Folkingham
Long Eaton
Ruddington
Belvoir Castle
Croxton Kerrial
Holbeach Marsh
Gedney Drove End
Wash
BURTON UPON TRENT
Melbourne
64
Colsterworth
Spalding
Holbeach
Long Sutton
Abbots Bromley

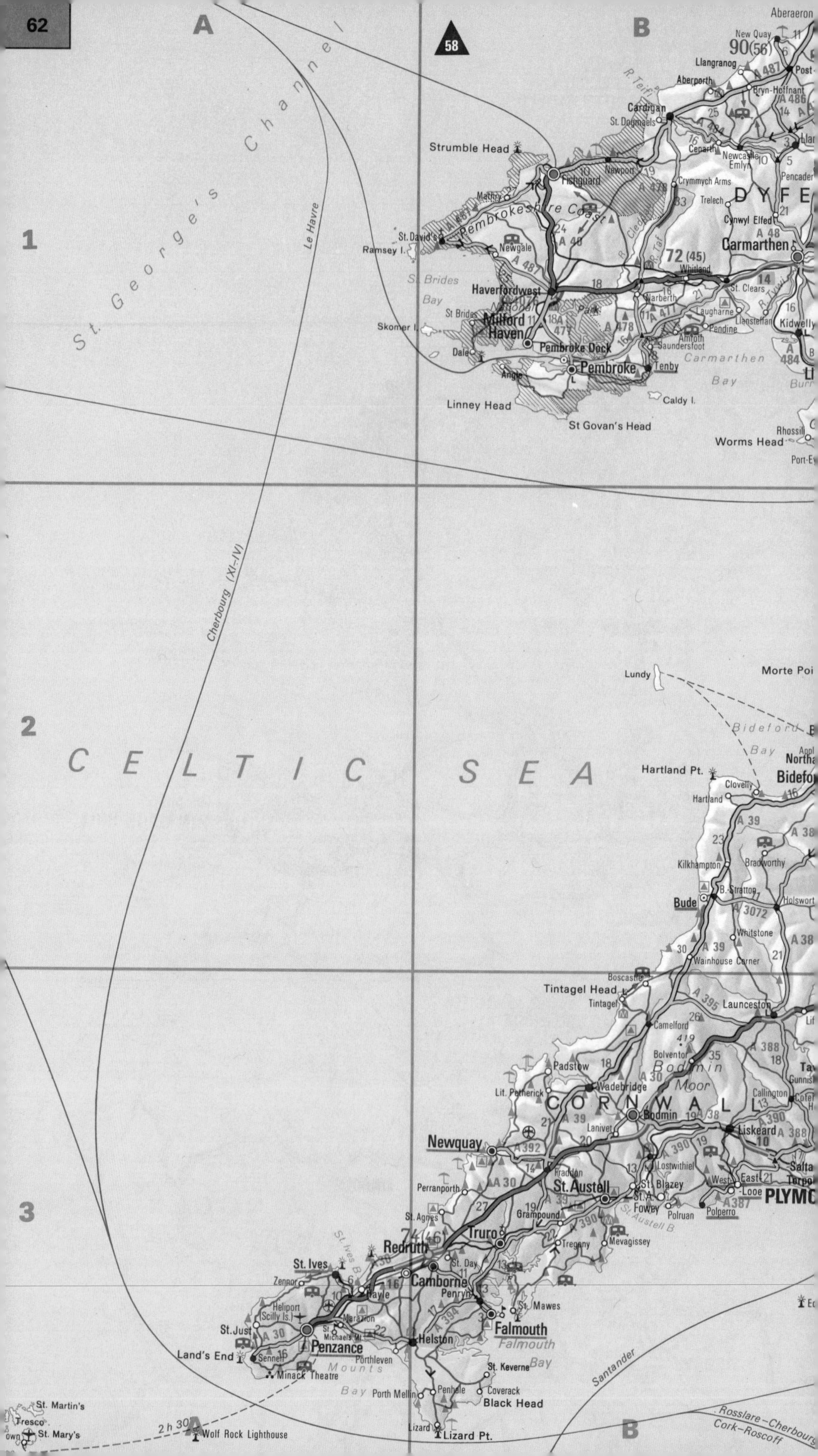
A
B
58
1
2
3
St. George's Channel
CELTIC SEA
Le Havre
Cherbourg (XI.-IV)
Aberaeron
New Quay
Llangranog
Aberporth
Cardigan
St. Dogmaels
Cenarth
Newcastle Emlyn
Strumble Head
Fishguard
Newport
Crymmych Arms
Mathry
Pembrokeshire Coast
DYFED
Trelech
Cynwyl Elfed
St. David's
Ramsey I.
Newgale
Carmarthen
Whitland
St. Brides Bay
Haverfordwest
St. Clears
Kidwelly
Narberth
Laugharne
Llansteffan
St Brides
Milford Haven
Skomer I.
Amroth
Pendine
Saundersfoot
Dale
Pembroke Dock
Pembroke
Tenby
Carmarthen Bay
Angle
Linney Head
Caldy I.
St Govan's Head
Rhossili
Worms Head
Port-Ey
Lundy
Morte Poi
Bideford Bay
Hartland Pt.
Bidefo
Clovelly
Hartland
Kilkhampton
Bradworthy
B. Stratton
Bude
Holswort
Whitstone
Wainhouse Corner
Boscastle
Tintagel Head
Tintagel
Launceston
Camelford
Bolventor
Bodmin Moor
Padstow
Wadebridge
Lit. Petherick
CORNWALL
Callington
Bodmin
Lanivet
Liskeard
Newquay
Lostwithiel
Fraddon
St. Blazey
Perranporth
St. Austell
Fowey
Polruan
Polperro
West Looe
East Looe
PLYMO
St. Agnes
Grampound
St. Austell B.
Truro
Tregony
Mevagissey
Redruth
St. Ives
St. Ives B.
St. Day
Camborne
Zennor
Hayle
Penryn
St. Mawes
Heliport (Scilly Is.)
Marazion
St. Michaels Mt.
St. Just
Penzance
Helston
Falmouth
Falmouth Bay
Land's End
Sennen
Porthleven
Minack Theatre
Mounts Bay
St. Keverne
Porth Mellin
Penhale
Coverack
Black Head
Santander
St. Martin's
Tresco
St. Mary's
2 h 30
Wolf Rock Lighthouse
Lizard
Lizard Pt.
Rosslare–Cherbourg
Cork–Roscoff

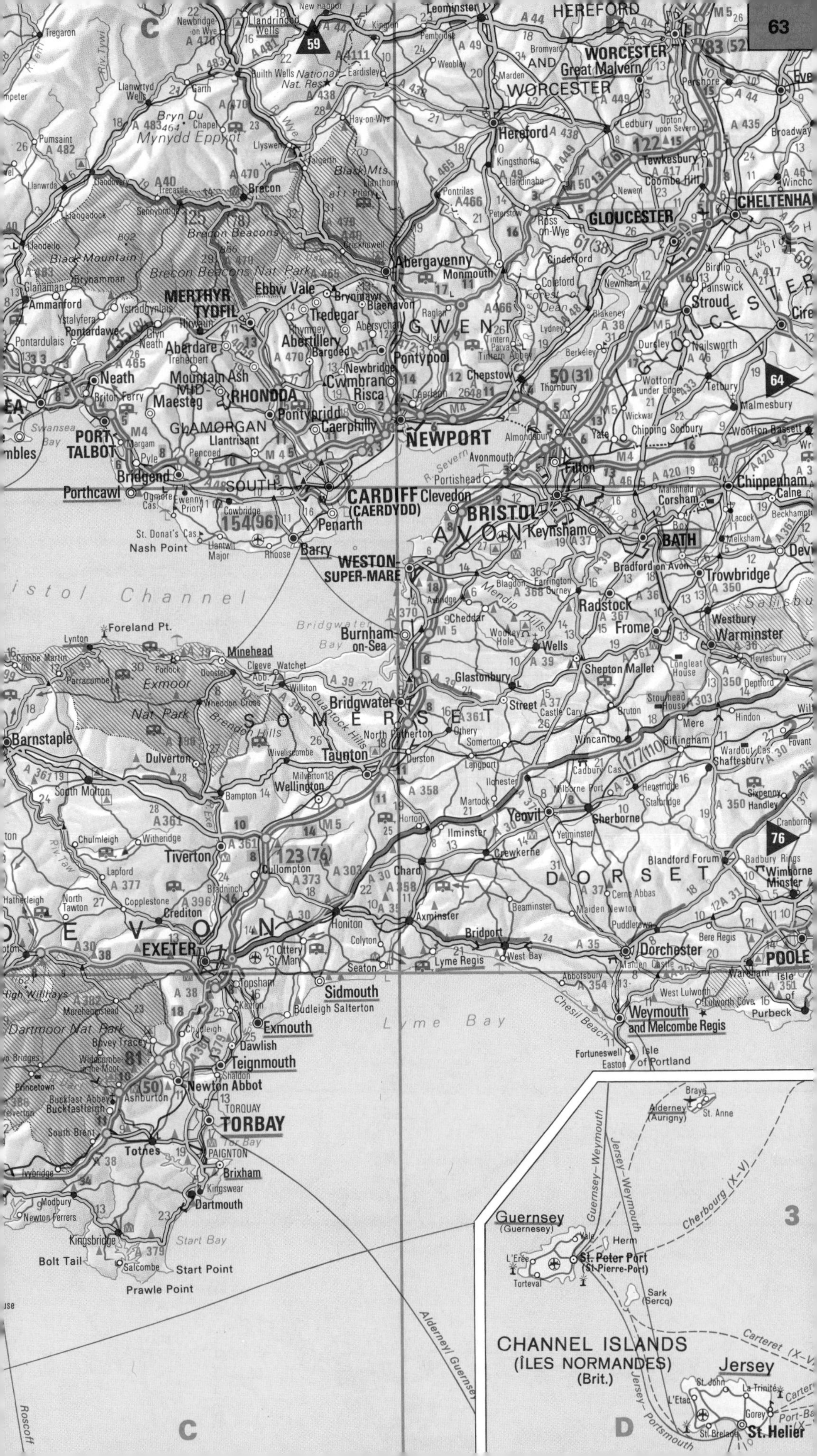

HEREFORD AND WORCESTER
WORCESTER
Great Malvern
Leominster
Hereford
Ledbury
Tewkesbury
Pershore
Evesham
CHELTENHAM
GLOUCESTER
Ross on-Wye
Monmouth
Abergavenny
Brecon
Brecon Beacons
Brecon Beacons Nat. Park
Black Mountain
Black Mts.
Mynydd Eppynt
Builth Wells
Llandrindod Wells
Llandovery
Tregaron
Ammanford
MERTHYR TYDFIL
Ebbw Vale
Tredegar
Abertillery
Aberdare
Neath
Pontardawe
Mountain Ash
RHONDDA
MID-GLAMORGAN
Maesteg
Pontypridd
Caerphilly
Pontypool
Cwmbran
Risca
GWENT
Chepstow
NEWPORT
PORT TALBOT
Bridgend
Porthcawl
SOUTH GLAMORGAN
CARDIFF (CAERDYDD)
Penarth
Barry
Nash Point
Bristol Channel
Clevedon
Portishead
Avonmouth
BRISTOL
AVON
Keynsham
BATH
Chippenham
Stroud
GLOUCESTER
Cirencester
Malmesbury
Tetbury
Thornbury
Yate
Filton
Trowbridge
Bradford on Avon
WESTON-SUPER-MARE
Burnham-on-Sea
Bridgwater Bay
Cheddar
Mendip Hills
Wells
Radstock
Frome
Warminster
Westbury
Shepton Mallet
Glastonbury
Street
Bridgwater
Quantock Hills
SOMERSET
Taunton
Wellington
Minehead
Exmoor Nat. Park
Brendon Hills
Foreland Pt.
Lynton
Barnstaple
South Molton
Dulverton
Wincanton
Gillingham
Shaftesbury
Yeovil
Sherborne
Ilminster
Crewkerne
Chard
DORSET
Blandford Forum
Wimborne Minster
POOLE
Dorchester
Bridport
Lyme Regis
Axminster
Honiton
Sidmouth
Exmouth
Lyme Bay
Weymouth and Melcombe Regis
Chesil Beach
Isle of Portland
Isle of Purbeck
Tiverton
Cullompton
Crediton
EXETER
DEVON
Dartmoor Nat. Park
Teignmouth
Dawlish
Newton Abbot
TORBAY
Totnes
Brixham
Dartmouth
Kingsbridge
Salcombe
Bolt Tail
Start Point
Prawle Point
Start Bay
Ivybridge
Alderney/Guernsey
Roscoff
Guernsey (Guernesey)
St. Peter Port (St-Pierre-Port)
Herm
Sark (Sercq)
Alderney (Aurigny)
Braye
St. Anne
Jersey–Weymouth
Guernsey–Weymouth
Cherbourg (X–V)
Carteret (X–V)
Jersey–Portsmouth
CHANNEL ISLANDS
(ÎLES NORMANDES)
(Brit.)
Jersey
St. Helier
Gorey
St. Brelade
59
64
76
C
D
3

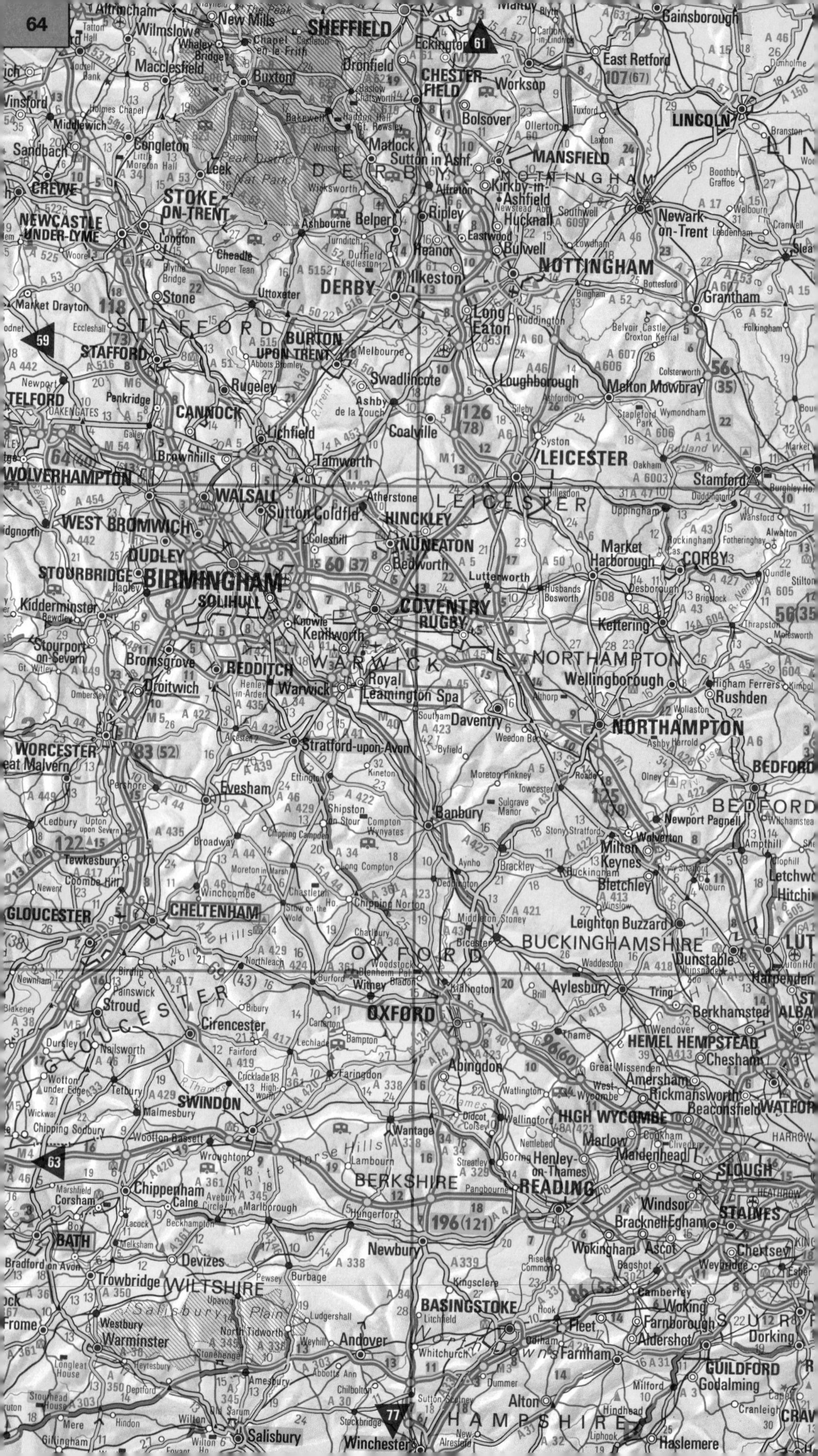
SHEFFIELD
CHESTERFIELD
LINCOLN
MANSFIELD
DERBY
NOTTINGHAM
STOKE-ON-TRENT
NEWCASTLE UNDER-LYME
CREWE
STAFFORD
LEICESTER
WOLVERHAMPTON
WALSALL
WEST BROMWICH
BIRMINGHAM
SOLIHULL
COVENTRY
RUGBY
NORTHAMPTON
BEDFORD
WORCESTER
GLOUCESTER
CHELTENHAM
OXFORD
SWINDON
READING
BATH
BASINGSTOKE
SLOUGH
HIGH WYCOMBE
GUILDFORD
Salisbury
Winchester

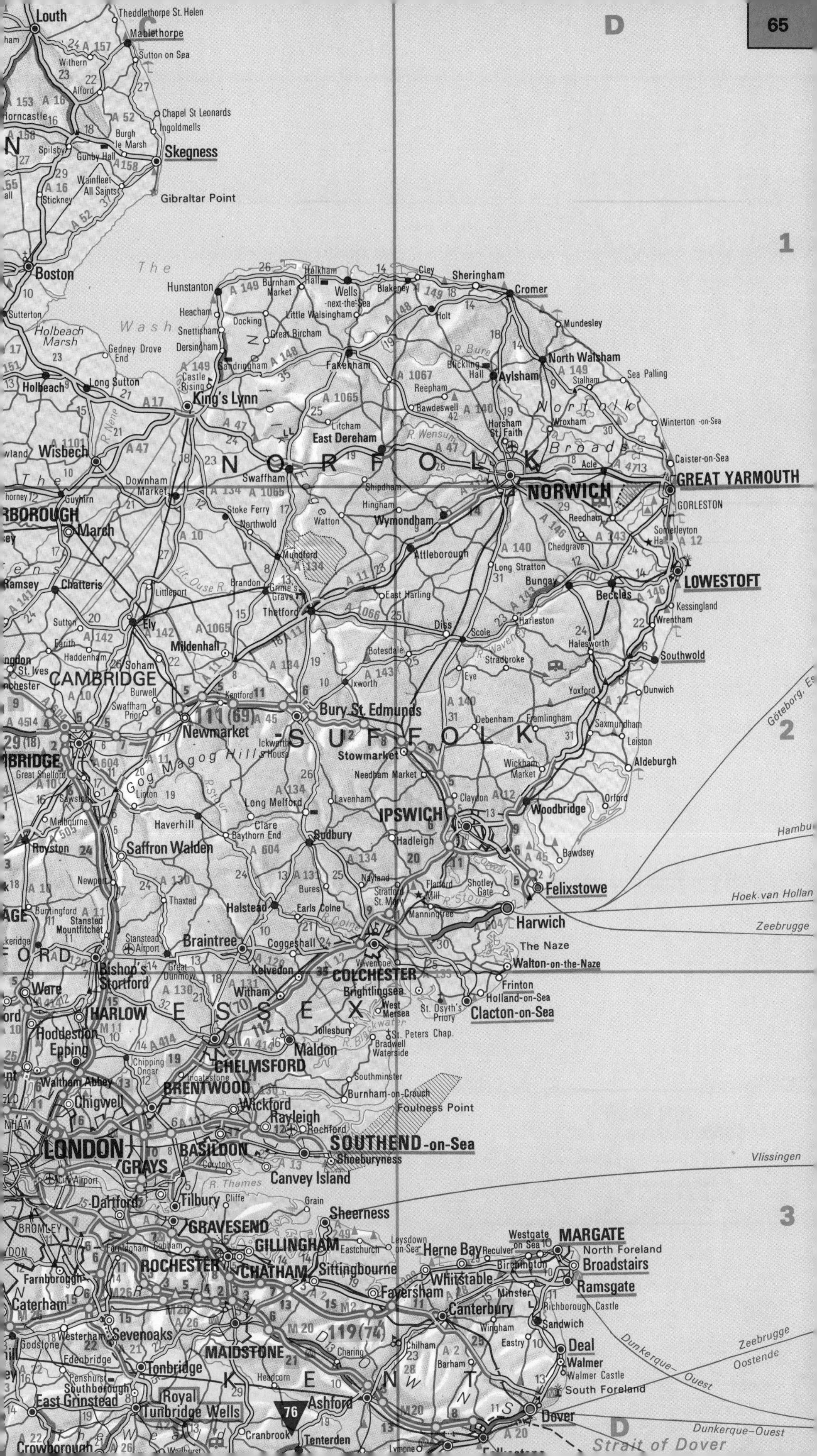
C
D
1
2
3
Louth
Theddlethorpe St. Helen
Mablethorpe
Sutton on Sea
Withern
Alford
Chapel St Leonards
Ingoldmells
Horncastle
Burgh le Marsh
Spilsby
Gunby Hall
Skegness
Wainfleet All Saints
Stickney
Gibraltar Point
Boston
Sutterton
The Wash
Holbeach Marsh
Gedney Drove End
Holbeach
Long Sutton
Hunstanton
Heacham
Snettisham
Dersingham
Sandringham
Castle Rising
King's Lynn
Docking
Burnham Market
Holkham Hall
Wells -next-the-Sea
Blakeney
Cley
Sheringham
Cromer
Little Walsingham
Great Bircham
Holt
Mundesley
Fakenham
Blickling Hall
Aylsham
North Walsham
Stalham
Sea Palling
Reepham
Bawdeswell
Horsham St. Faith
Wroxham
Winterton -on-Sea
Norfolk Broads
Caister-on-Sea
Acle
GREAT YARMOUTH
GORLESTON
Litcham
East Dereham
NORFOLK
Wisbech
Swaffham
Downham Market
Shipdham
Hingham
Wymondham
Watton
NORWICH
Reedham
Somerleyton Hall
Chedgrave
March
Stoke Ferry
Northwold
Mundford
Attleborough
Long Stratton
Bungay
Beccles
LOWESTOFT
Kessingland
Wrentham
Chatteris
Ramsey
Littleport
Brandon
Grime's Graves
Thetford
East Harling
Lit. Ouse R.
Sutton
Ely
Mildenhall
Diss
Scole
Harleston
Halesworth
Southwold
Earith
Haddenham
Soham
Botesdale
Stradbroke
Eye
St. Ives
CAMBRIDGE
Burwell
Kentford
Ixworth
Yoxford
Dunwich
Swaffham Prior
Newmarket
Bury St. Edmunds
Debenham
Framlingham
Saxmundham
Leiston
SUFFOLK
Ickworth House
Stowmarket
Needham Market
Wickham Market
Aldeburgh
Great Shelford
Gog Magog Hills
Sawston
Linton
Long Melford
Lavenham
Claydon
IPSWICH
Woodbridge
Orford
Melbourne
Haverhill
Clare
Baythorn End
Sudbury
Hadleigh
Bawdsey
Royston
Saffron Walden
Newport
Thaxted
Nayland
Bures
Stratford St. Mary
Flatford Mill
Shotley Gate
Felixstowe
Halstead
Earls Colne
Manningtree
Harwich
Buntingford
Stansted Mountfitchet
Stansted Airport
Braintree
Coggeshall
The Naze
Walton-on-the-Naze
Bishop's Stortford
Great Dunmow
Kelvedon
Wivenhoe
COLCHESTER
Frinton
Holland-on-Sea
Ware
HARLOW
Witham
Brightlingsea
West Mersea
St. Osyth's Priory
Clacton-on-Sea
ESSEX
Tollesbury
St. Peters Chap.
Bradwell Waterside
Hoddesdon
Epping
Chipping Ongar
CHELMSFORD
Maldon
Ingatestone
Southminster
Waltham Abbey
Chigwell
BRENTWOOD
Burnham-on-Crouch
Foulness Point
Wickford
Rayleigh
Rochford
LONDON
BASILDON
SOUTHEND-on-Sea
GRAYS
Corringham
Shoeburyness
City Airport
R. Thames
Canvey Island
Dartford
Tilbury
Cliffe
Grain
Sheerness
BROMLEY
GRAVESEND
Leysdown -on-Sea
Westgate on Sea
MARGATE
North Foreland
Farningham
Cobham
GILLINGHAM
Eastchurch
Herne Bay
Reculver
Birchington
Broadstairs
ROCHESTER
CHATHAM
Sittingbourne
Whitstable
Ramsgate
Farnborough
Faversham
Minster
Richborough Castle
Caterham
Canterbury
Sandwich
Sevenoaks
Westerham
Wingham
Deal
Godstone
MAIDSTONE
Chilham
Eastry
Walmer
Edenbridge
Charing
Barham
Walmer Castle
Tonbridge
Penshurst
Headcorn
South Foreland
Southborough
KENT
East Grinstead
Royal Tunbridge Wells
Ashford
Dover
Cranbrook
Tenterden
Lympne
Crowborough
The Weald
Strait of Dover
Göteborg, Es
Hamburg
Hoek van Hollan
Zeebrugge
Vlissingen
Zeebrugge
Oostende
Dunkerque-Ouest
Dunkerque-Ouest
76
111 (69)
119 (74)

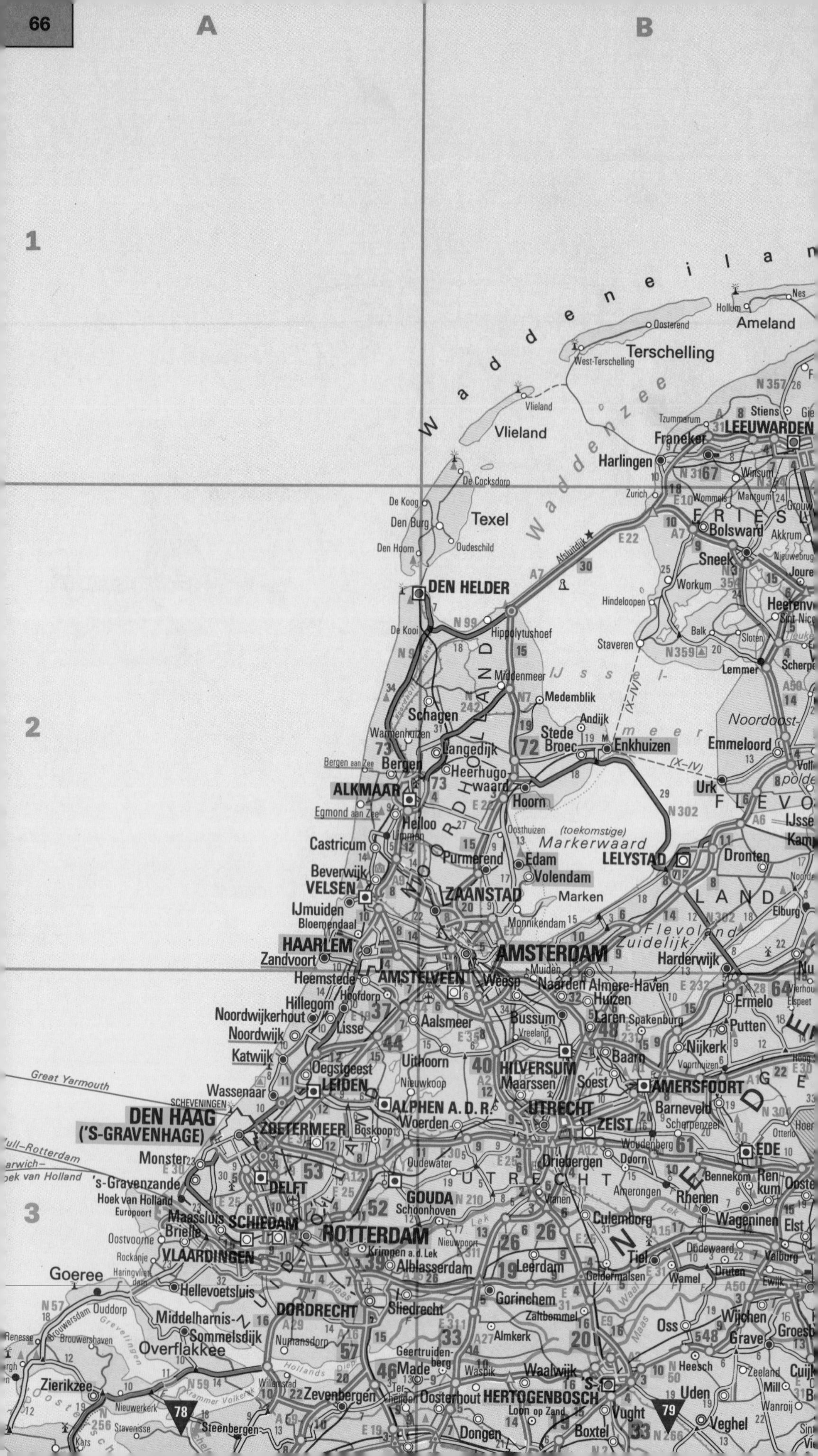
A
B
1
2
3
Waddeneilanden
Waddenzee
Ameland
Hollum
Nes
Terschelling
Oosterend
West-Terschelling
Vlieland
Texel
De Cocksdorp
De Koog
Den Burg
Den Hoorn
Oudeschild
DEN HELDER
De Kooi
Hippolytushoef
Afsluitdijk
Harlingen
Franeker
LEEUWARDEN
Stiens
Tzummarum
Winsum
Zurich
Wommels
Mantgum
Bolsward
Akkrum
Sneek
Workum
Joure
Heerenveen
Hindeloopen
Staveren
Balk
Sloten
Lemmer
FRIESLAND
IJsselmeer
Noordoost-polder
Emmeloord
Urk
Schagen
Middenmeer
Medemblik
Andijk
Stede Broec
Enkhuizen
Warmenhuizen
Langedijk
Bergen aan Zee
Bergen
Heerhugowaard
ALKMAAR
Egmond aan Zee
Heiloo
Hoorn
NOORD-HOLLAND
Castricum
Limmen
Purmerend
Edam
Volendam
Oosthuizen
(toekomstige)
Markerwaard
LELYSTAD
Dronten
Beverwijk
VELSEN
IJmuiden
ZAANSTAD
Marken
Monnikendam
FLEVOLAND
Flevoland
Zuidelijk-
Elburg
Harderwijk
Bloemendaal
HAARLEM
Zandvoort
AMSTERDAM
Heemstede
AMSTELVEEN
Weesp
Muiden
Naarden
Almere-Haven
Huizen
Ermelo
Hoofddorp
Hillegom
Noordwijkerhout
Noordwijk
Lisse
Aalsmeer
Bussum
Laren
Spakenburg
Putten
Vreeland
Nijkerk
Katwijk
Oegstgeest
Uithoorn
HILVERSUM
Baarn
Great Yarmouth
Wassenaar
LEIDEN
Nieuwkoop
Maarssen
Soest
AMERSFOORT
SCHEVENINGEN
DEN HAAG
('S-GRAVENHAGE)
ZOETERMEER
ALPHEN A. D. R.
Woerden
Boskoop
UTRECHT
ZEIST
Barneveld
Scherpenzeel
Woudenberg
EDE
Hull–Rotterdam
Harwich–Hoek van Holland
Monster
's-Gravenzande
Hoek van Holland
Europoort
DELFT
Oudewater
GOUDA
Schoonhoven
Driebergen
Doorn
Amerongen
Rhenen
Bennekom
Renkum
Wageningen
UTRECHT
Vianen
Culemborg
Lek
Maassluis
SCHIEDAM
Brielle
Oostvoorne
Rockanje
VLAARDINGEN
ROTTERDAM
Krimpen a.d. Lek
Alblasserdam
Nieuwpoort
Leerdam
Tiel
Dodewaard
Goeree
Hellevoetsluis
Geldermalsen
Wamel
Druten
Gorinchem
Zaltbommel
Sliedrecht
DORDRECHT
ZUID-HOLLAND
Middelharnis
Sommelsdijk
Overflakkee
Numansdorp
Oss
Wijchen
Grave
Brouwershaven
Renesse
Zierikzee
Almkerk
Geertruidenberg
Made
Waspik
Waalwijk
Heesch
Zeeland
Mill
Willemstad
Zevenbergen
Terheijden
Oosterhout
HERTOGENBOSCH
Uden
Nieuwerkerk
Loon op Zand
Vught
Veghel
Wanroij
Steenbergen
Stavenisse
Kats
Dongen
Boxtel
Maas
Waal
Hollands Diep
Grevelingen
Oosterschelde
Krammer Volkerak
78
79

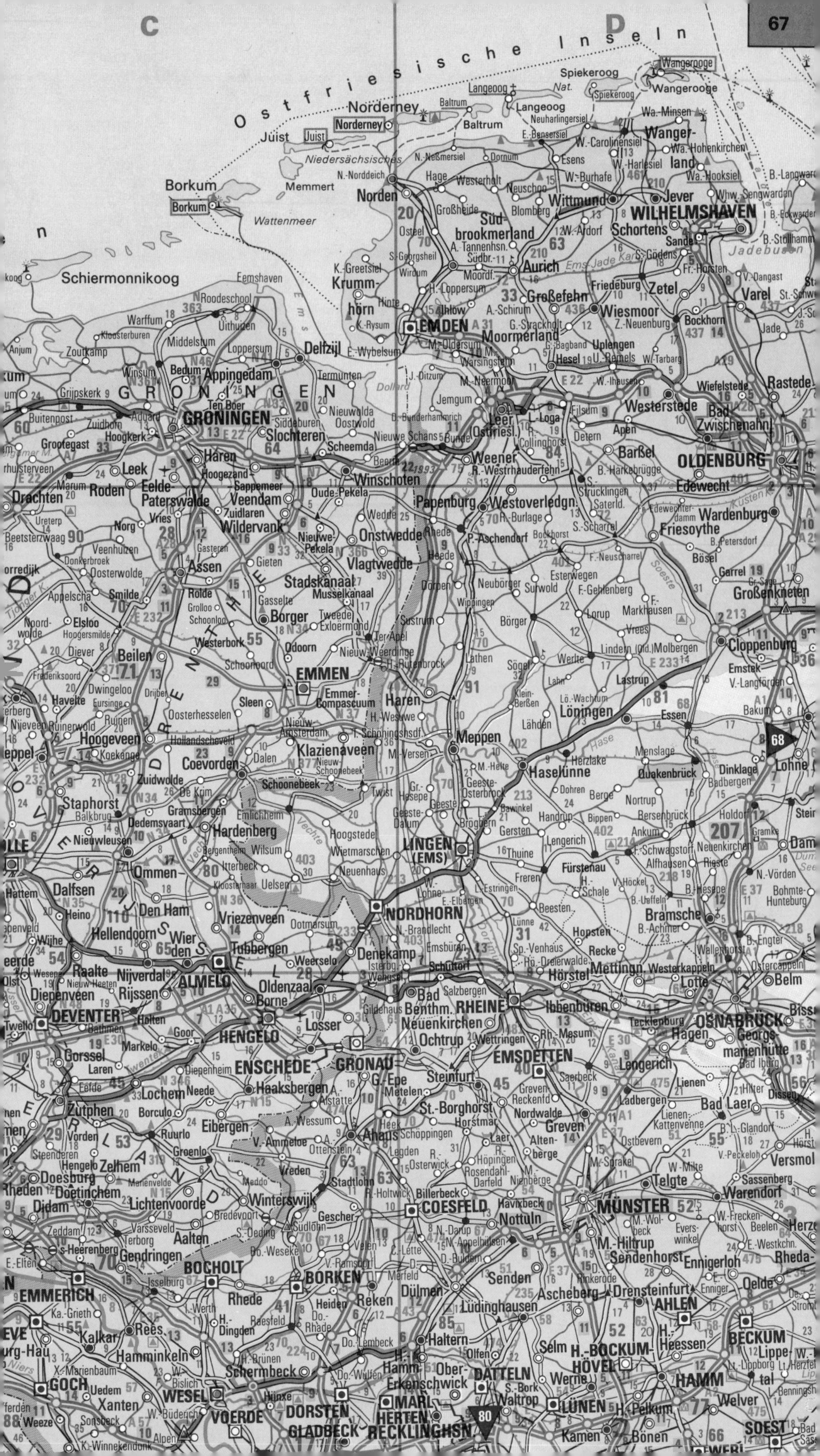

67
C
D
Ostfriesische Inseln
Wangerooge
Spiekeroog
Langeoog
Baltrum
Norderney
Juist
Borkum
Memmert
Niedersächsisches
Wattenmeer
Schiermonnikoog
Norden
Wittmund
Jever
WILHELMSHAVEN
Schortens
Südbrookmerland
Aurich
Großefehn
Wiesmoor
Friedeburg
Zetel
Varel
Krummhörn
EMDEN
Moormerland
Uplengen
Hesel
Westerstede
Bad Zwischenahn
Rastede
OLDENBURG
Edewecht
Wardenburg
Friesoythe
Leer (Ostfriesl.)
Weener
Papenburg
Westoverledgn.
Barßel
Delfzijl
Appingedam
GRONINGEN
Slochteren
Haren
Leek
Roden
Winschoten
Drachten
Veendam
Wildervank
Assen
Stadskanaal
Onstwedde
Vlagtwedde
Borger
EMMEN
Beilen
Hoogeveen
Coevorden
Klazienaveen
Meppen
Haselünne
Löningen
Cloppenburg
Großenkneten
Lohne
Dinklage
Quakenbrück
Sögel
Börger
Lathen
Haren
Hardenberg
Ommen
LINGEN (EMS)
NORDHORN
Fürstenau
Bramsche
Staphorst
Dalfsen
Den Ham
Vriezenveen
Tubbergen
ALMELO
Nijverdal
Rijssen
Raalte
Hellendoorn
Oldenzaal
Borne
HENGELO
ENSCHEDE
Losser
GRONAU
Bad Bentheim
RHEINE
Ibbenbüren
Hörstel
Mettingen
OSNABRÜCK
EMSDETTEN
Lengerich
DEVENTER
Zutphen
Lochem
Haaksbergen
Eibergen
Ahaus
Steinfurt
Ochtrup
Greven
Warendorf
Telgte
MÜNSTER
Doetinchem
Winterswijk
Lichtenvoorde
Aalten
COESFELD
Nottuln
Senden
BOCHOLT
BORKEN
Dülmen
Lüdinghausen
Ahlen
BECKUM
EMMERICH
Rees
Kalkar
Haltern
Hamminkeln
WESEL
Schermbeck
DORSTEN
MARL
HERTEN
RECKLINGHSN.
GLADBECK
VOERDE
DATTELN
Waltrop
LÜNEN
Werne
HAMM
Welver
SOEST
GOCH
Xanten
68
80

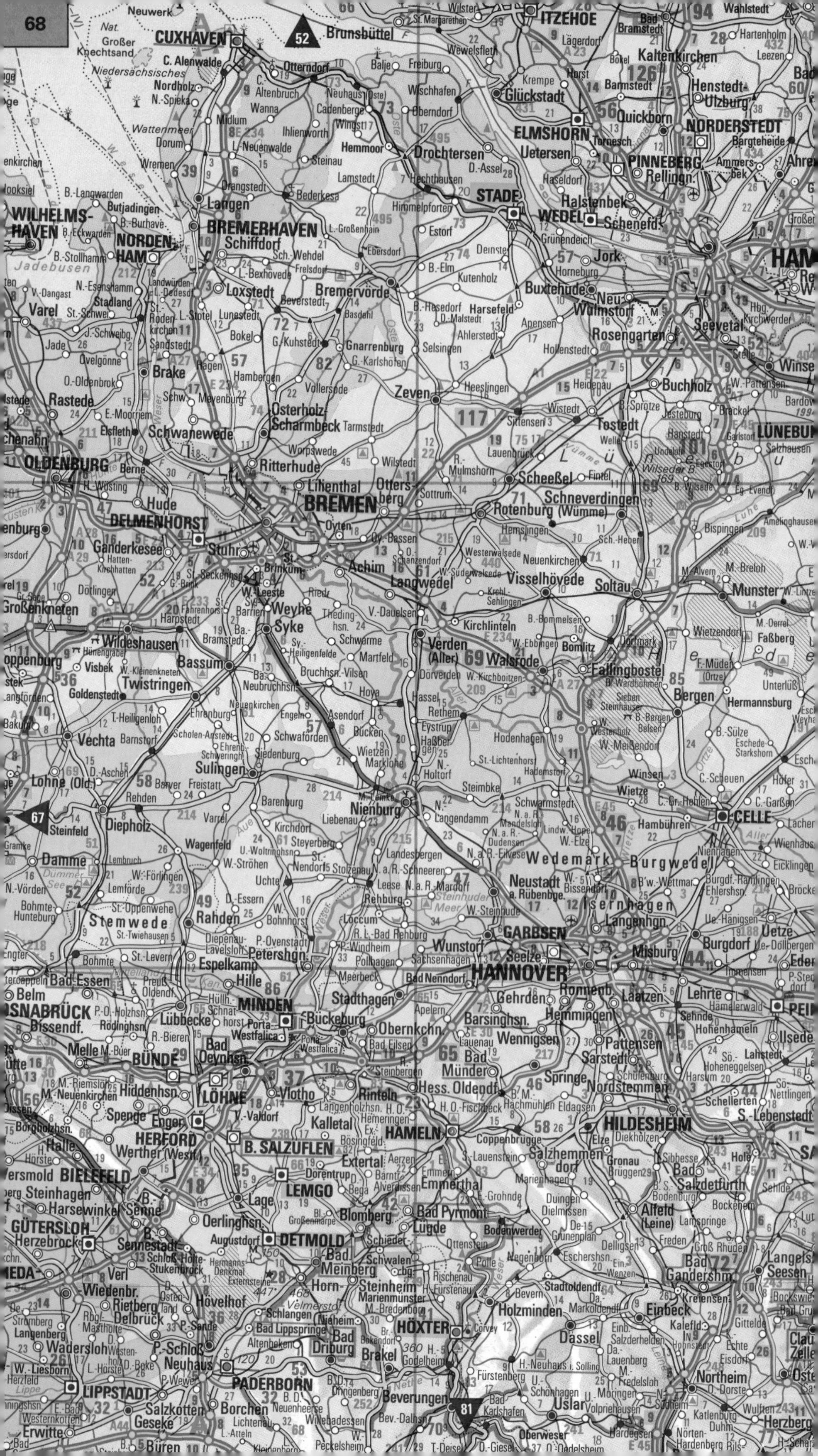

CUXHAVEN
Brunsbüttel
ITZEHOE
Bad Bramstedt
Kaltenkirchen
Henstedt-Ulzburg
NORDERSTEDT
Quickborn
Glückstadt
ELMSHORN
Uetersen
PINNEBERG
Rellingen
WEDEL
Schenefeld
Halstenbek
STADE
Drochtersen
Otterndorf
Neuhaus (Oste)
Cadenberge
Hemmoor
Wischhafen
Freiburg
Langen
BREMERHAVEN
Schiffdorf
WILHELMSHAVEN
NORDENHAM
Jadebusen
Varel
Loxstedt
Bremervörde
Buxtehude
Jork
Neu Wulmstorf
Rosengarten
Seevetal
Buchholz
Winsen
Tostedt
Zeven
Brake
Rastede
Elsfleth
Schwanewede
Osterholz-Scharmbeck
Ritterhude
Lilienthal
Ottersberg
BREMEN
OLDENBURG
Hude
DELMENHORST
Ganderkesee
Stuhr
Achim
Langwedel
Rotenburg (Wümme)
Scheeßel
Schneverdingen
Visselhövede
Soltau
Munster
Lüneburger Heide
Großenkneten
Wildeshausen
Harpstedt
Weyhe
Syke
Bassum
Twistringen
Verden (Aller)
Walsrode
Fallingbostel
Bergen
Vechta
Lohne (Old.)
Diepholz
Sulingen
Nienburg
Celle
Wedemark
Burgwedel
Neustadt a. Rübenbge.
Isernhagen
Langenhagen
GARBSEN
Seelze
HANNOVER
Wunstorf
Burgdorf
Lehrte
Laatzen
Misburg
Damme
Stemwede
Rahden
Espelkamp
Petershagen
Hille
MINDEN
Bückeburg
Stadthagen
Bad Nenndorf
Gehrden
Ronnenberg
Hemmingen
Pattensen
Sarstedt
Barsinghausen
Wennigsen
OSNABRÜCK
Bad Essen
Lübbecke
Bünde
Melle
Bad Oeynhausen
Löhne
Porta Westfalica
Vlotho
Rinteln
Hess. Oldendorf
Bad Münder
Springe
Nordstemmen
HILDESHEIM
HAMELN
HERFORD
B. SALZUFLEN
LEMGO
BIELEFELD
Lage
Blomberg
Bad Pyrmont
Lügde
Emmerthal
Alfeld (Leine)
Bad Salzdetfurth
GÜTERSLOH
DETMOLD
Bad Meinberg
Horn
Steinheim
HÖXTER
Holzminden
Einbeck
Bad Gandersheim
Seesen
PADERBORN
LIPPSTADT
Salzkotten
Bad Driburg
Brakel
Beverungen
Uslar
Northeim
Dassel
Geseke
Büren
Erwitte

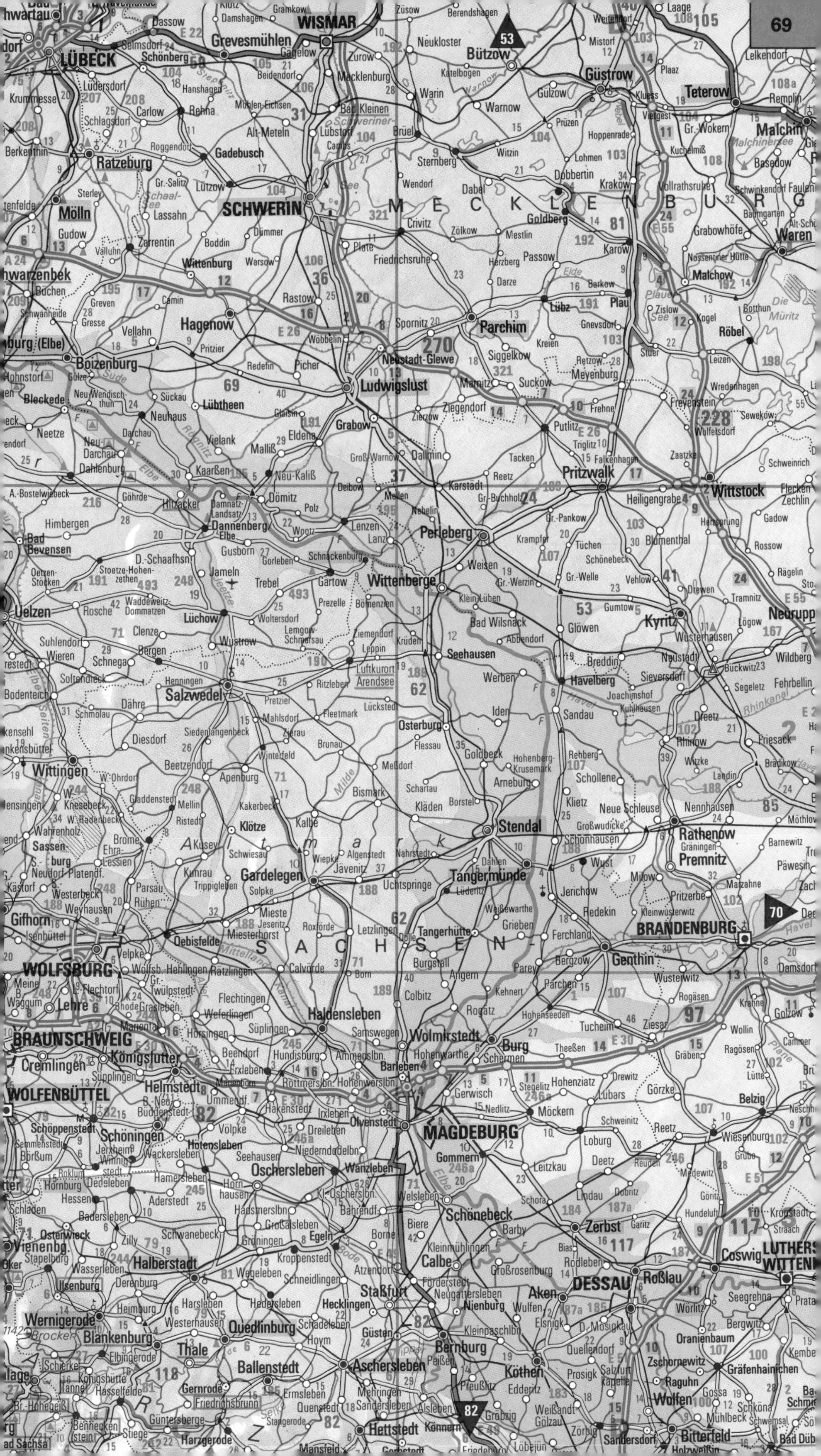

WISMAR
Lübeck
Grevesmühlen
Schönberg
Rehna
Gadebusch
Ratzeburg
Mölln
SCHWERIN
Bützow
Güstrow
Teterow
Malchin
Laage
Krakow
Goldberg
Sternberg
Crivitz
Warin
Brüel
Bad Kleinen
M E C K L E N B U R G
Waren
Malchow
Plau
Lübz
Parchim
Röbel
Hagenow
Wittenburg
Zarrentin
Boizenburg
Lübtheen
Ludwigslust
Neustadt-Glewe
Grabow
Meyenburg
Putlitz
Pritzwalk
Wittstock
Perleberg
Wittenberge
Dömitz
Lenzen
Dannenberg
Hitzacker
Lüchow
Uelzen
Bad Bevensen
Salzwedel
Seehausen
Havelberg
Kyritz
Neuruppin
Wittingen
Gifhorn
WOLFSBURG
BRAUNSCHWEIG
Königslutter
WOLFENBÜTTEL
Helmstedt
Schöningen
Klötze
Gardelegen
Osterburg
Stendal
Tangermünde
Rathenow
Premnitz
BRANDENBURG
Genthin
Burg
Haldensleben
Wolmirstedt
Oebisfelde
A l t m a r k
S A C H S E N -
MAGDEBURG
Oschersleben
Halberstadt
Wernigerode
Blankenburg
Quedlinburg
Thale
Ballenstedt
Aschersleben
Staßfurt
Schönebeck
Calbe
Bernburg
Köthen
Zerbst
DESSAU
Roßlau
Coswig
Belzig
Wolfen
Bitterfeld
Hettstedt
Harzgerode
Sandersdorf
Aken
Burg
Elbe
Havel
Müritz

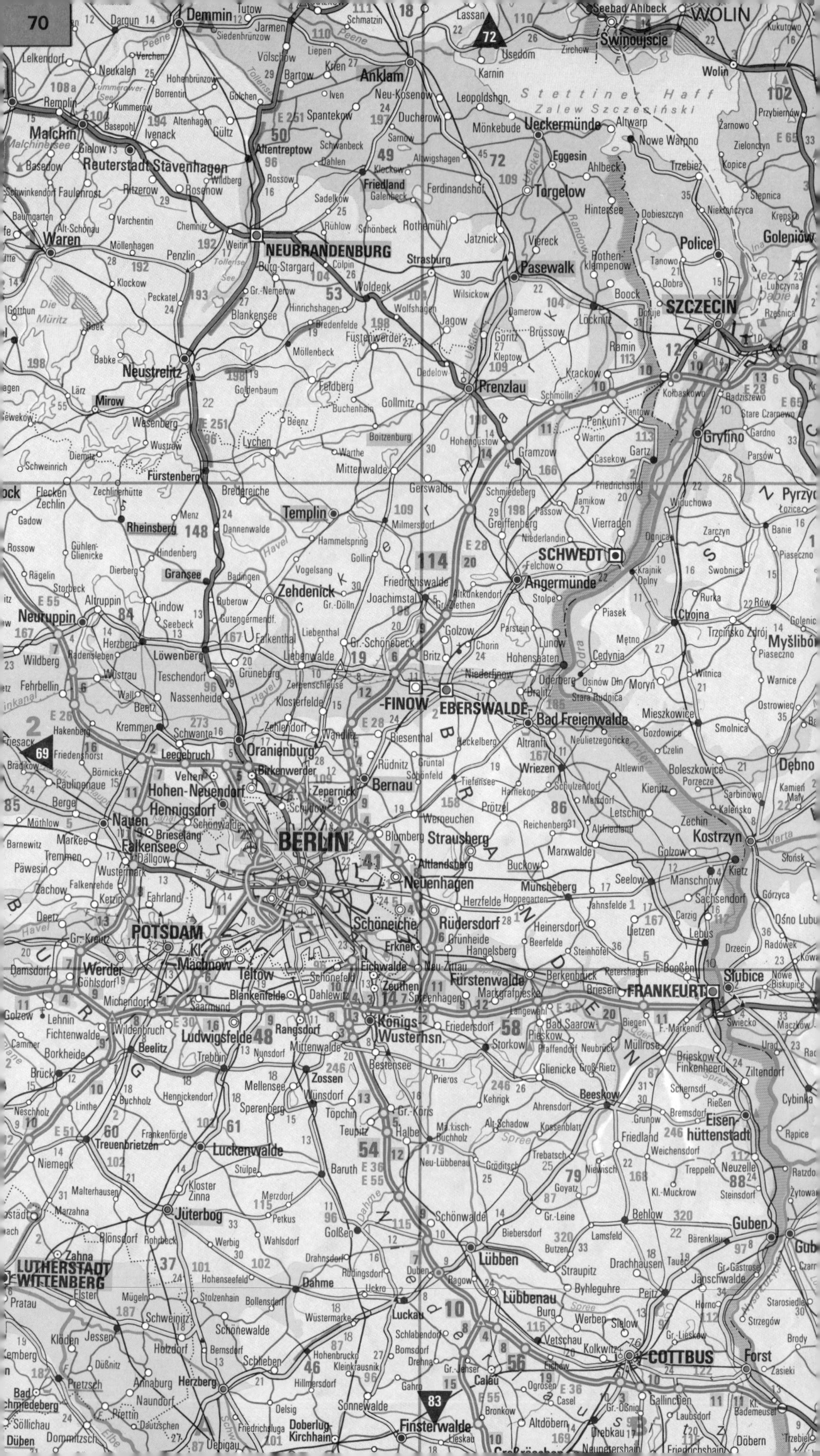

70
72
69
83
Demmin
Dargun
Jarmen
Anklam
Lassan
Usedom
Seebad Ahlbeck
Swinoujscie
WOLIN
Wolin
Stettiner Haff
Zalew Szczeciński
Ueckermünde
Eggesin
Torgelow
Altwarp
Nowe Warpno
Malchin
Reuterstadt Stavenhagen
Altentreptow
Friedland
Ferdinandshof
Waren
NEUBRANDENBURG
Burg-Stargard
Strasburg
Pasewalk
Police
Goleniów
Woldegk
Löcknitz
SZCZECIN
Neustrelitz
Mirow
Prenzlau
Feldberg
Gryfino
Lychen
Fürstenberg
Templin
Gerswalde
Schwedt
Angermünde
Rheinsberg
Gransee
Zehdenick
Joachimsthal
Neuruppin
Löwenberg
Chojna
Myślibórz
Oderberg
Cedynia
Oranienburg
FINOW
EBERSWALDE
Bad Freienwalde
Wriezen
Dębno
Hohen Neuendorf
Hennigsdorf
Bernau
Nauen
Falkensee
BERLIN
Strausberg
Kostrzyn
POTSDAM
Neuenhagen
Rüdersdorf
Müncheberg
Seelow
Werder
Teltow
Kl. Machnow
Fürstenwalde
FRANKFURT
Słubice
Ludwigsfelde
Königs Wusterhsn.
Beelitz
Zossen
Storkow
Bad Saarow-Pieskow
Beeskow
Eisenhüttenstadt
Treuenbrietzen
Luckenwalde
Jüterbog
Lübben
Lübbenau
Guben
LUTHERSTADT WITTENBERG
Dahme
Luckau
COTTBUS
Forst
Herzberg
Doberlug-Kirchhain
Finsterwalde
Calau
Spree
Havel
Oder
Odra
Peene
Die Müritz

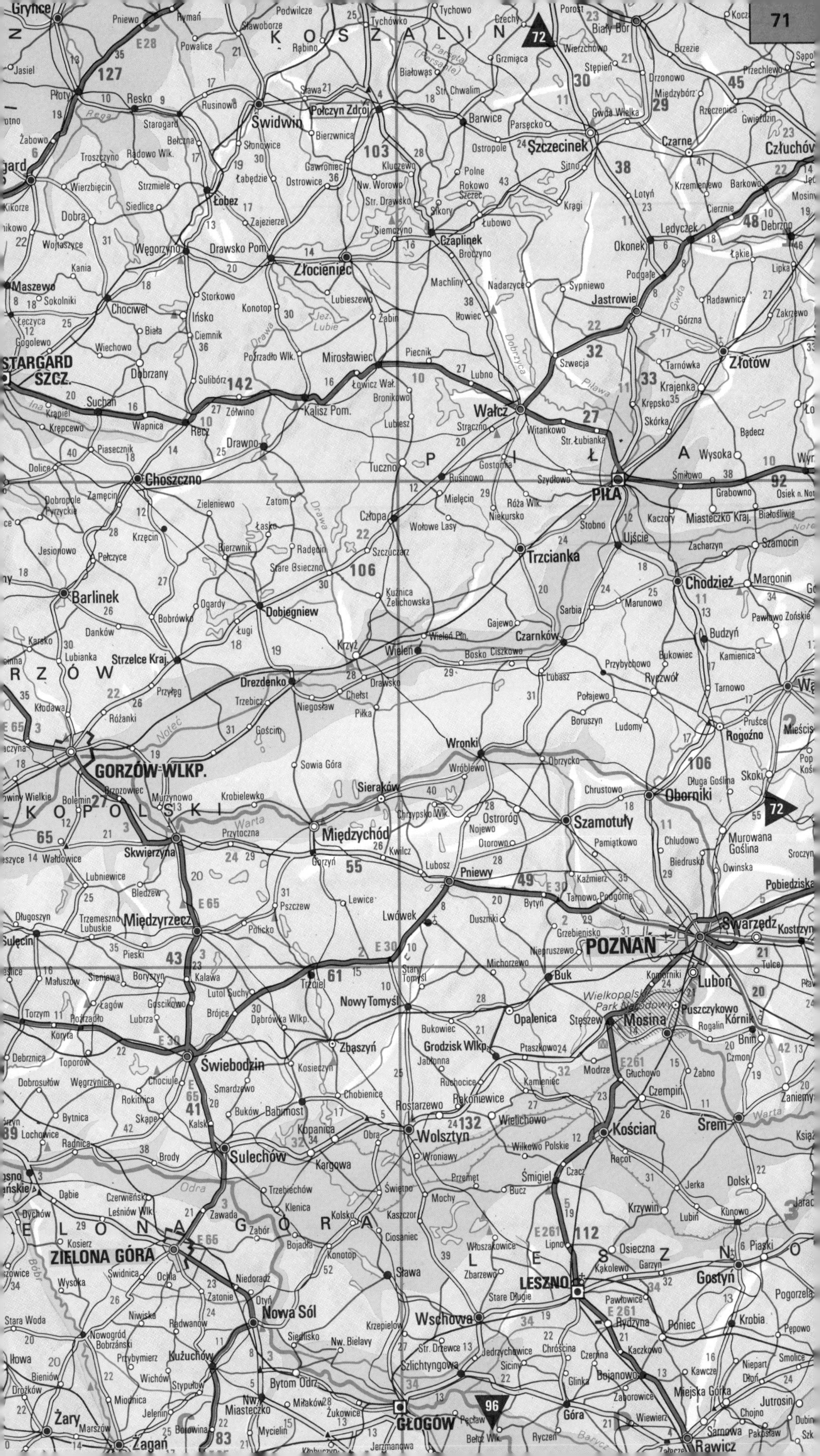

KOSZALIN
PIŁA
GORZÓW
WIELKOPOLSKI
ZIELONA GÓRA
LESZNO
Gryfice
Pniewo
Rymań
Podwilcze
Sławoborze
Tychowo
Tychówko
Czechy
Porost
Biały Bór
Jasiel
Płoty
Resko
Rusinowo
Powalice
Rąbino
Białowąs
Grzmiąca
Wierzchowo
Stępień
Drzonowo
Brzezie
Przechlewo
Sąpolno
Świdwin
Sława
Połczyn Zdrój
Str. Chwalim
Barwice
Parsęcko
Gwda Wielka
Międzybórz
Rzeczenica
Gwieździn
Starogard
Bełczna
Słonowice
Bierzwnica
Szczecinek
Czarne
Człuchów
Żabowo
Troszczyno
Radowo Wlk.
Gawroniec
Kluczewo
Ostropole
Polne
Sitno
Rokowo
Szczec
Łabędzie
Ostrowice
Nw. Worowo
Str. Drawsko
Sikory
Krągi
Lotyń
Kremienewo
Barkowo
Wierzbięcin
Strzmiele
Łobez
Siedlice
Zajezierze
Łubowo
Cierznie
Debrzno
Kikorze
Dobra
Wojtaszyce
Węgorzyno
Drawsko Pom.
Siemczyno
Czaplinek
Broczyno
Okonek
Lędyczek
Łąkie
Lipka
Mosiny
Złocieniec
Kania
Maszewo
Sokolniki
Chociwel
Storkowo
Ińsko
Konotop
Lubieszewo
Machliny
Nadarzyce
Sypniewo
Podgaje
Radawnica
Zakrzewo
Jastrowie
Łowiec
Żabin
Jez. Lubie
Drawa
Dobrzyca
Gwda
Łęczyca
Gogolewo
Biała
Ciemnik
Wiechowo
Połrzadło Wlk.
Mirosławiec
Piecnik
Lubno
Szwecja
Górzna
Tarnówka
Złotów
STARGARD SZCZ.
Dobrzany
Sulibórz
Łowicz Wał.
Bronikowo
Wałcz
Piława
Krajenka
Krępsko
Skórka
Suchań
Wapnica
Żółwino
Kalisz Pom.
Lubiesz
Strączno
Witankowo
Str. Łubianka
Krąpiel
Krępcewo
Recz
Drawno
Piasecznik
Choszczno
Dolice
Tuczno
Gostomia
Szydłowo
Wysoka
Bądecz
Śmiłowo
Grabowno
Osiek n. Not.
Rusinowo
Mielęcin
Róża Wlk.
Niekursko
Dobropole Pyrzyckie
Zamęcin
Zieleniewo
Zatom
Człopa
Wołowe Lasy
Stobno
Ujście
Kaczory
Miasteczko Kraj.
Białośliwie
Noteć
Krzęcin
Łasko
Radęcin
Bierzwnik
Szczuczarz
Trzcianka
Zacharzyn
Szamocin
Jesionowo
Pełczyce
Stare Osieczno
Chodzież
Margonin
Barlinek
Ogardy
Dobiegniew
Kuźnica Żelichowska
Sarbia
Marunowo
Pawłowo Żońskie
Bobrówko
Danków
Ługi
Gajewo
Czarnków
Budzyń
Karsko
Lubianka
Strzelce Kraj.
Krzyż
Wieleń
Wieleń Płn.
Bosko
Ciszkowo
Przybychowo
Bukowiec
Kamienica
Ryczywół
Drezdenko
Drawsko
Chełst
Lubasz
Połajewo
Tarnowo
Kłodawa
Różanki
Przyłęg
Trzebicz
Niegosław
Piłka
Boruszyn
Ludomy
Rogoźno
Pruśce
Mieścisko
Gościm
Wronki
Obrzycko
Skoki
GORZÓW WLKP.
Sowia Góra
Wróblewo
Brzozowiec
Murzynowo
Krobielewko
Sieraków
Chrzypsko Wlk.
Chrustowo
Oborniki
Długa Goślina
Bolemin
Przytoczna
Warta
Ostroróg
Nojewo
Szamotuły
Murowana Goślina
Skwierzyna
Międzychód
Kwilcz
Otorowo
Pamiątkowo
Chludowo
Sroczyn
Wałdowice
Gorzyń
Lubosz
Pniewy
Kaźmierz
Biedrusko
Owinska
Lubniewice
Bledzew
Pszczew
Lewice
Bytyń
Tarnowo Podgórne
Pobiedziska
Długoszyn
Trzemeszno Lubuskie
Międzyrzecz
Policko
Lwówek
Duszniki
Grzebienisko
Swarzędz
Kostrzyn
Sulęcin
Pieski
Nowy Tomyśl
Stary Tomyśl
Michorzewo
Niepruszewo
POZNAŃ
Małuszów
Sieniawa
Boryszyn
Kalawa
Trzciel
Buk
Komorniki
Luboń
Tulce
Łagów
Goscikowo
Lutol Suchy
Torzym
Pożrzadło
Brójce
Dąbrówka Wlk.
Opalenica
Stęszew
Wielkopolski Park Narodowy
Mosina
Puszczykowo
Kórnik
Rogalin
Bnin
Koryta
Lubrza
Zbąszyń
Bukowiec
Grodzisk Wlkp.
Ptaszkowo
Czmoń
Debrznica
Toporów
Świebodzin
Kosieczyn
Jabłonna
Modrze
Głuchowo
Żabno
Dobrosułów
Węgrzynice
Chociule
Smardzewo
Chobienice
Ruchocice
Kamieniec
Czempiń
Rokitnica
Buków
Babimost
Rostarzewo
Rakoniewice
Wielichowo
Zaniemyśl
Bytnica
Skąpe
Kalsk
Kopanica
Obra
Wolsztyn
Kościan
Śrem
Lochowice
Radnica
Brody
Sulechów
Kargowa
Wroniawy
Wilkowo Polskie
Racot
Książ
Trzebiechów
Świętno
Przemęt
Śmigiel
Czacz
Jerka
Dolsk
Dąbie
Czerwieńsk
Leśniów Wlk.
Klenica
Mochy
Bucz
Krzywiń
Lubiń
Kunowo
Dychów
Zawada
Kolsko
Kaszczor
Odra
Kosierz
Zabór
Bojadła
Ciosaniec
Lipno
Osieczna
Piaski
Włoszakowice
Zbarzewo
Kąkolewo
Garzyn
Gostyń
Swidnica
Ochla
Konotop
Sława
Niedoradz
Zatonie
Stare Długie
LESZNO
Pawłowice
Pogorzela
Wysoka
Otyń
Nowa Sól
Wschowa
Rydzyna
Poniec
Krobia
Stara Woda
Niwiska
Radwanów
Siedlisko
Nw. Bielawy
Krzepielów
Str. Drzewce
Jędrzychowice
Chróścina
Czernina
Kaczkowo
Pępowo
Nowogród Bobrzański
Kożuchów
Smolice
Iłowa
Przybymierz
Wichów
Szlichtyngowa
Sicin
Glinka
Bojanowo
Kawcze
Niepart
Dłoń
Bieniów
Stypułów
Bytom Odrz.
Zaborowice
Miejska Górka
Drożków
Miodnica
Nw. Miasteczko
Miłaków
Żukowice
GŁOGÓW
Pęcław
Góra
Wiewierz
Jutrosin
Chojno
Żary
Marszów
Jelenin
Borowina
Żagań
Mycielin
Jerzmanowa
Bełcz Wlk.
Ryczeń
Barycz
Sarnowa
Pakosław
Rawicz
Zaborze
Kłobuczyn

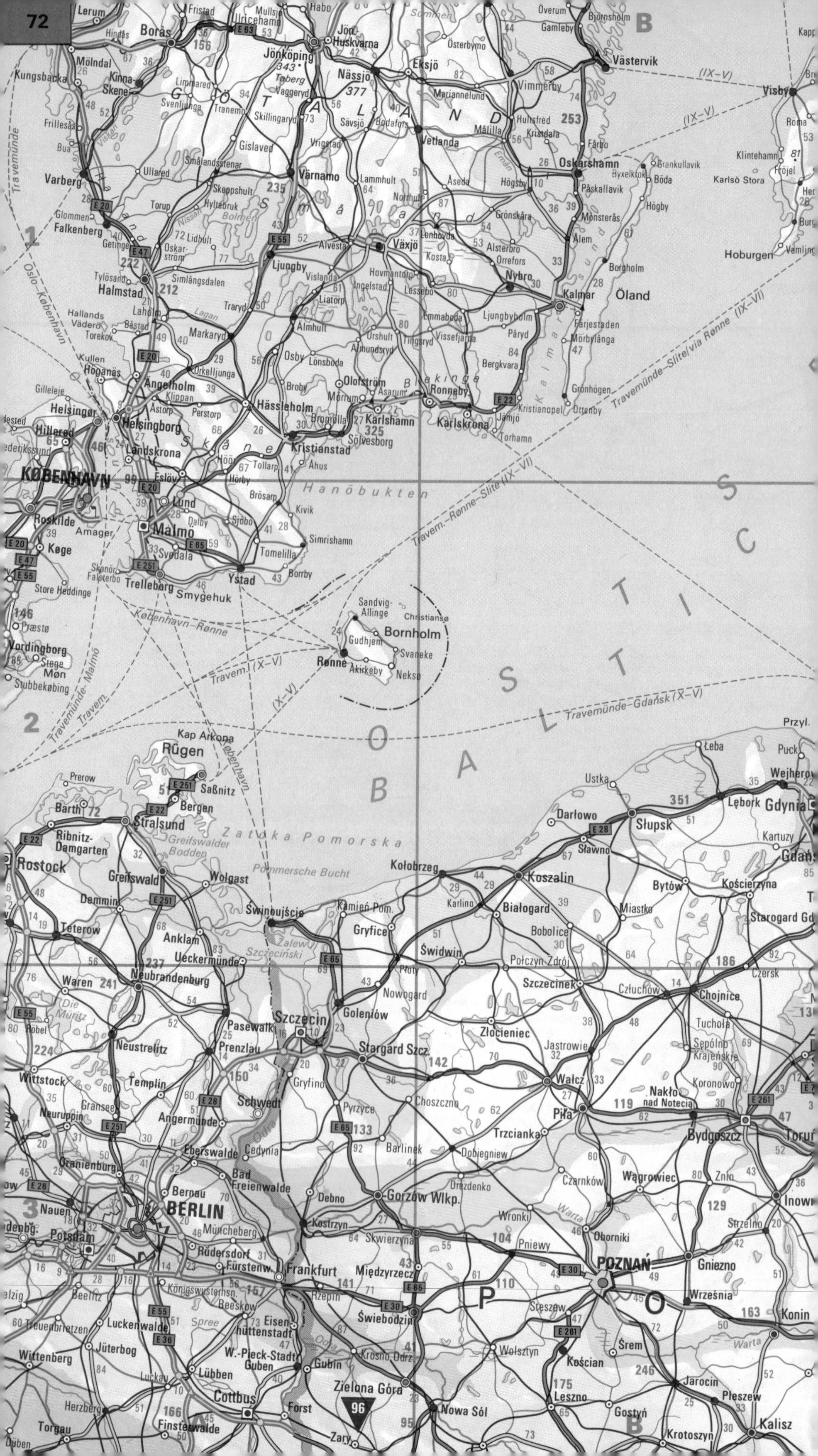

B
Lerum
Borås
Ulricehamn
Habo
Jönköping
Huskvarna
Överum
Gamleby
Björnsholm
Västervik
Mölndal
Kinna-Skene
Kungsbacka
Nässjö
Eksjö
Vimmerby
Visby
Taberg
Vaggeryd
Mariannelund
Limmared
Svenljunga
Tranemo
Skillingaryd
Sävsjö
Bodafors
Hultsfred
Kristdala
Frillesås
Vetlanda
Målilla
Bua
Gislaved
Fårbo
Varberg
Ullared
Smålandsstenar
Värnamo
Lammhult
Åseda
Högsby
Oskarshamn
Påskallavik
Byxelkrok
Böda
Klintehamn
Fröjel
Karlsö Stora
Skeppshult
Hyltebruk
Torup
Norrhult
Lenhovda
Grönskåra
Mönsterås
Ålem
Högby
Glommen
Falkenberg
Getinge
Lidhult
Oskarström
Nissan
Bolmen
Ljungby
Alvesta
Växjö
Kosta
Alsterbro
Orrefors
Nybro
Borgholm
Hoburgen
Vamlingbo
Tylösand
Halmstad
Simlångsdalen
Vislanda
Hovmantorp
Ingelstad
Lessebo
Kalmar
Öland
Laholm
Hallands Väderö
Båstad
Torekov
Lagan
Traryd
Liatorp
Älmhult
Emmaboda
Ljungbyholm
Färjestaden
Mörbylånga
Påryd
Markaryd
Urshult
Almundsryd
Tingsryd
Vissefjärda
Bergkvara
Kullen
Höganäs
Örkelljunga
Osby
Lönsboda
Olofström
Blekinge
Ronneby
Gilleleje
Helsingør
Hillerød
Helsingborg
Ängelholm
Klippan
Åstorp
Perstorp
Hässleholm
Broby
Mörrum
Asarum
Karlshamn
Bromölla
Sölvesborg
Kristianstad
Karlskrona
Kristianopel
Ottenby
Grönhögen
Jämjö
Torhamn
Travemünde–Slite/via Rønne (IX–VI)
Landskrona
Höör
Tollarp
Åhus
Hörby
Eslöv
KØBENHAVN
Lund
Hanöbukten
Brösarp
Kivik
Roskilde
Amager
Malmö
Dalby
Sjöbo
Simrishamn
Køge
Svedala
Tomelilla
Skanör
Falsterbo
Trelleborg
Ystad
Borrby
Store Heddinge
Smygehuk
Sandvig-Allinge
Christiansø
Bornholm
Gudhjem
Rønne
Svaneke
Akirkeby
Nexø
Præstø
Vordingborg
Stege
Møn
Stubbekøbing
København–Rønne
Travem. (X–V)
Travem.–Rønne–Slite (IX–VI)
Travemünde–Gdańsk (X–V)
Oslo–København
Travemünde–Malmö
Travemünde
BALTIC
Kap Arkona
Rügen
Saßnitz
Bergen
Prerow
Barth
Stralsund
Ribnitz-Damgarten
Greifswalder Bodden
Zatoka Pomorska
Pommersche Bucht
Rostock
Greifswald
Wolgast
Demmin
Teterow
Anklam
Ueckermünde
Świnoujście
Kamień Pom.
Gryfice
Kołobrzeg
Karlino
Koszalin
Białogard
Sławno
Darłowo
Ustka
Słupsk
Łeba
Lębork
Gdynia
Wejherowo
Puck
Kartuzy
Bytów
Miastko
Kościerzyna
Starogard Gd.
Bobolice
Połczyn Zdrój
Świdwin
Szczecinek
Człuchów
Chojnice
Czersk
Tuchola
Sępólno Krajeńskie
Koronowo
Nakło nad Notecią
Bydgoszcz
Toruń
Jastrowie
Wałcz
Piła
Złocieniec
Neubrandenburg
Waren
Müritz
Pasewalk
Szczecin
Goleniów
Nowogard
Płoty
Stargard Szcz.
Zalew Szczeciński
Neustrelitz
Prenzlau
Wittstock
Templin
Gryfino
Pyrzyce
Choszczno
Trzcianka
Neuruppin
Gransee
Schwedt
Angermünde
Oranienburg
Eberswalde
Cedynia
Barlinek
Dobiegniew
Czarnków
Wągrowiec
Żnin
Inowrocław
Nauen
Bernau
Bad Freienwalde
BERLIN
Debno
Gorzów Wlkp.
Drezdenko
Wronki
Warta
Oborniki
Potsdam
Müncheberg
Rüdersdorf
Fürstenwalde
Kostrzyn
Skwierzyna
Pniewy
Strzelno
Gniezno
POZNAŃ
Frankfurt
Międzyrzecz
Beelitz
Königswusterhausen
Beeskow
Rzepin
Świebodzin
Września
Konin
Treuenbrietzen
Luckenwalde
Spree
Eisenhüttenstadt
Odra
Stęszew
Śrem
Jüterbog
W.-Pieck-Stadt Guben
Gubin
Krosno Odrz.
Wolsztyn
Kościan
Wittenberg
Lübben
Luckau
Cottbus
Zielona Góra
Leszno
Jarocin
Pleszew
Herzberg
Forst
Nowa Sól
Gostyń
Torgau
Finsterwalde
Żary
Krotoszyn
Kalisz
96
P
O

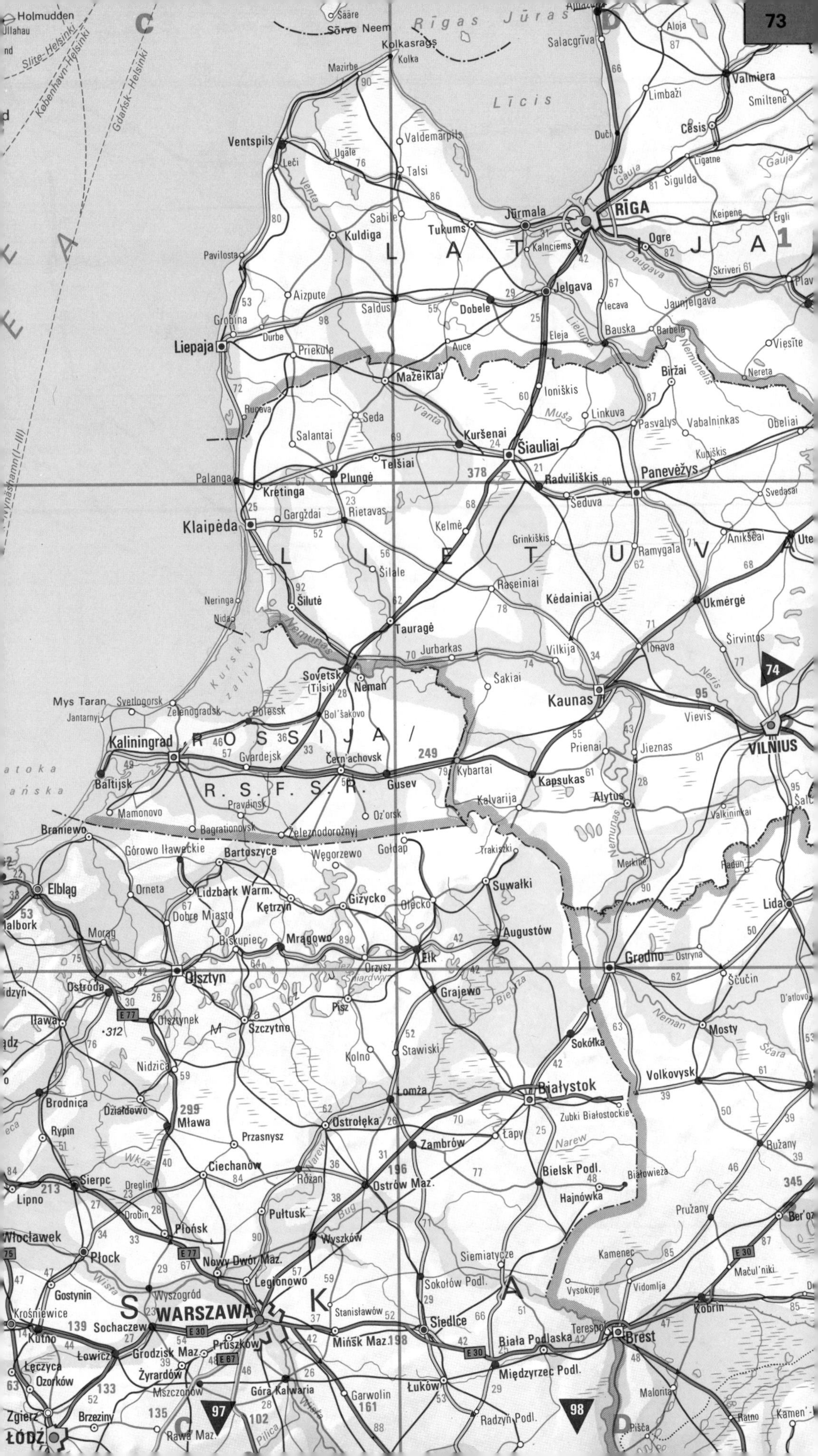
Holmudden
Ullahau
Slite-Helsinki
København-Helsinki
Gdańsk-Helsinki
C
D
Sääre
Sõrve Neem
Rīgas Jūras
Līcis
Ainaži
Salacgrīva
Aloja
Valmiera
Smiltene
Limbaži
Cēsis
Duči
Ligatne
Sigulda
Gauja
Kolkasrags
Kolka
Mazirbe
Valdemārpils
Talsi
Ventspils
Ugāle
Leči
Venta
Sabile
Kuldiga
Tukums
Jūrmala
RĪGA
Keipene
Ērgli
Ogre
Kalnciems
LATVIJA
Daugava
Skriveri
Plav
Pavilosta
Jelgava
Aizpute
Saldus
Dobele
Iecava
Jaunjelgava
Grobina
Liepaja
Durbe
Priekule
Auce
Eleja
Lielupe
Bauska
Barbele
Viesīte
Nereta
Mažeikiai
Ioniškis
Biržai
Nemunelis
Rucava
Seda
Linkuva
Muša
Pasvalys
Vabalninkas
Obeliai
Salantai
Kuršenai
Šiauliai
Kupiškis
Telšiai
Plungė
Radviliškis
Panevėžys
Palanga
Kretinga
Šeduva
Svedasai
Klaipėda
Gargždai
Rietavas
Kelmė
Grinkiškis
Anykščiai
Ute
LIETUVA
Ramygala
Šilale
Raseiniai
Kėdainiai
Ukmergė
Neringa
Nida
Šilutė
Tauragė
Nemunas
Kurskij zaliv
Jurbarkas
Vilkija
Širvintos
Jonava
Neris
Sovetsk (Tilsit)
Neman
Šakiai
Kaunas
Vievis
74
Mys Taran
Svetlogorsk
Zelenogradsk
Polessk
Jantarnyj
Bol'šakovo
Kaliningrad
ROSSIJA / R.S.F.S.R.
Gvardejsk
Černachovsk
Prienai
Jieznas
VILNIUS
Baltijsk
Gusev
Kybartai
Kapsukas
Alytus
Pravdinsk
Kalvarija
Mamonovo
Oz'orsk
Valkininkai
Šalč
Braniewo
Bagrationovsk
Železnodorožnyj
Trakiszki
Merkinė
Radun'
Górowo Iławeckie
Bartoszyce
Węgorzewo
Gołdap
Elbląg
Orneta
Lidzbark Warm.
Kętrzyn
Giżycko
Olecko
Suwałki
Lida
Malbork
Dobre Miasto
Morąg
Biskupiec
Mrągowo
Ełk
Augustów
Grodno
Ostryna
Olsztyn
Orzysz
Śniardwy
Grajewo
Biebrza
Ščučin
Ostróda
E 77
Olsztynek
Szczytno
Pisz
Neman
Mosty
D'atlovo
Iława
Sokółka
Ščara
Stawiski
Kolno
Nidzica
Łomża
Białystok
Volkovysk
Brodnica
Działdowo
Mława
Ostrołęka
Zubki Białostockie
Rypin
Przasnysz
Łapy
Zambrów
Narew
Ružany
Wkra
Ciechanów
Różan
Bielsk Podl.
Sierpc
Dreglin
Ostrów Maz.
Białowieża
Lipno
Hajnówka
Drobin
Pułtusk
Bug
Pružany
Ber'oz
Włocławek
Płońsk
Wyszków
Płock
E 77
Nowy Dwór Maz.
Siemiatycze
Kamenec
E 30
Mačul'niki
Legionowo
Gostynin
Wisła
Wyszogród
Sokołów Podl.
Vysokoje
Vidomlja
Krośniewice
Kobrin
WARSZAWA
Stanisławów
POLSKA
Sochaczew
Siedlce
Kutno
Terespol
Brest
Łowicz
Pruszków
Grodzisk Maz.
Mińsk Maz.
Biała Podlaska
E 30
E 67
Łęczyca
Żyrardów
Międzyrzec Podl.
Ozorków
Mszczonów
Góra Kalwaria
Łuków
Malorita
Garwolin
97
98
Zgierz
Brzeziny
Radzyń Podl.
Ratno
Kamen'
ŁÓDŹ
Rawa Maz.
Pilica
Pišča

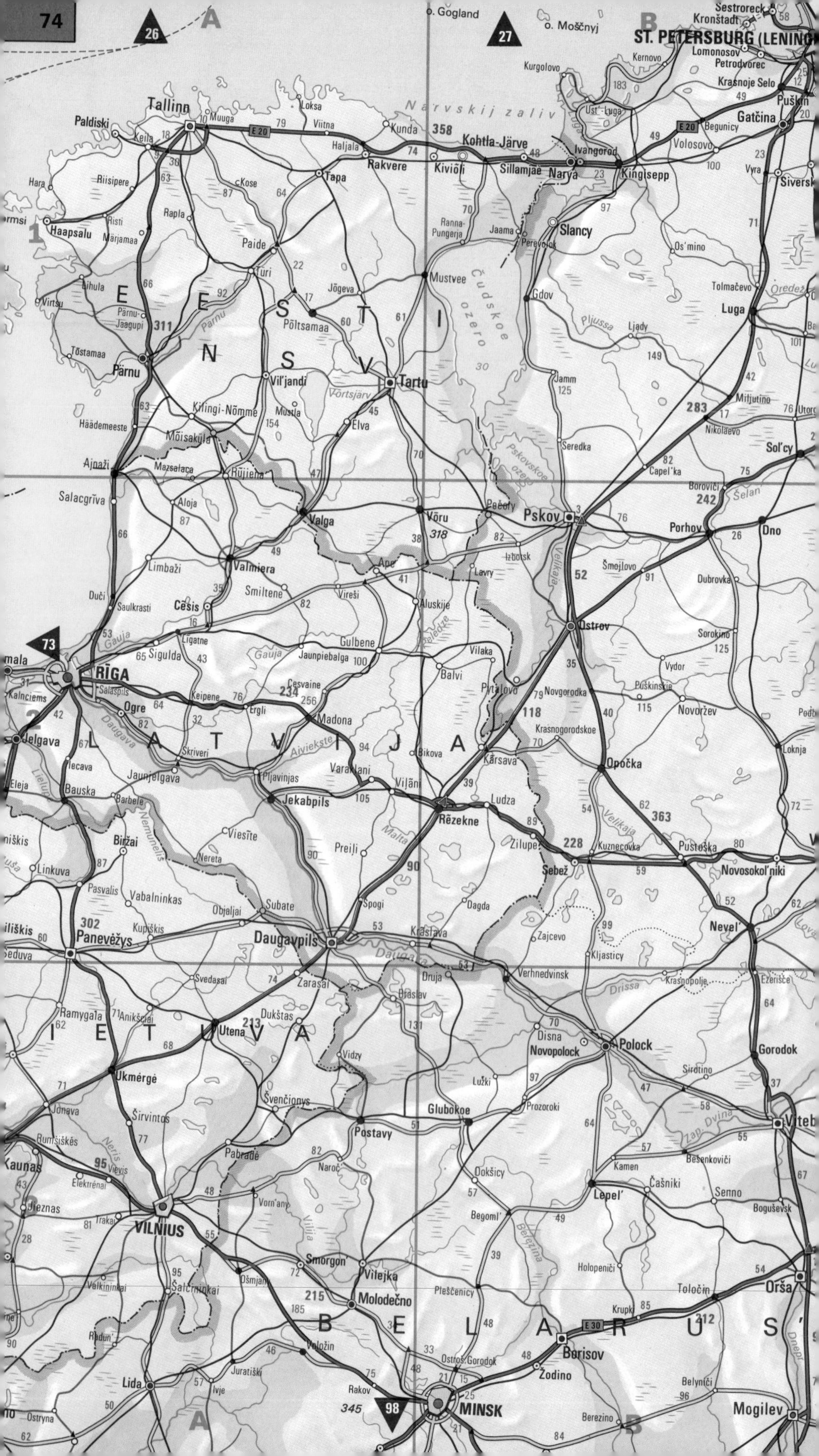

26
27
73
98
A
B
1
2
o. Gogland
o. Moščnyj
ST. PETERSBURG (LENING
Sestroreck
Kronštadt
Lomonosov
Petrodvorec
Krasnoje Selo
Puškin
Gatčina
Kingisepp
Ivangorod
Narva
Kohtla-Järve
Sillamjae
Kiviõli
Rakvere
Kunda
Haljala
Tapa
Loksa
Tallinn
Muuga
Paldiski
Keila
Haapsalu
Riisipere
Rapla
Kose
Paide
Türi
Märjamaa
Risti
Hara
Lihula
Virtsu
Pärnu-Jaagupi
Tõstamaa
Pärnu
Viljandi
Põltsamaa
Jõgeva
Mustvee
Tartu
Elva
Võrtsjärv
Mustla
Kilingi-Nõmme
Häädemeeste
Mõisaküla
Ajnaži
Mazsalaca
Rūjiena
Salacgrīva
Aloja
Valga
Võru
Pečory
Pskov
Izborsk
Lavry
Ape
Valmiera
Limbaži
Smiltene
Cēsis
Saulkrasti
Duči
Vireši
Aluskije
RĪGA
Sigulda
Līgatne
Jaunpiebalga
Gulbene
Vilaka
Balvi
Pytalovo
Salaspils
Ogre
Keipene
Ergli
Cesvaine
Madona
Jelgava
Kalnciems
Skriveri
Jaunjelgava
Pļaviņas
Jekabpils
Varaklani
Viļāni
Bikova
Kārsava
Rēzekne
Ludza
Zilupe
Sebež
Iecava
Bauska
Eleja
Barbele
Biržai
Viesīte
Nereta
Preiļi
Linkuva
Pasvalis
Vabalninkas
Objaljai
Subate
Spogi
Dagda
Panevėžys
Kupiškis
Daugavpils
Krāslava
Zajcevo
Kljasticy
Seduva
Svedasai
Zarasai
Druja
Braslav
Verhnedvinsk
Ramygala
Anikščiai
Utena
Dukštas
Disna
Novopolock
Polock
Ukmergė
Vidzy
Lužki
Prozoroki
Jonava
Širvintos
Švenčionys
Glubokoe
Postavy
Rumšiškės
Kaunas
Vievis
Elektrėnai
Pabradė
Naroč
Dokšicy
Kamen
Lepel'
Čašniki
Senno
Vorn'any
Begoml'
Trakai
VILNIUS
Smorgon'
Vilejka
Molodečno
Pleščenicy
Holopeniči
Valkininkai
Šalčininkai
Ošmjany
Radun'
Voložin
Juratiški
Ivje
Lida
Ostryna
Rakov
Ostrošk. Gorodok
MINSK
Borisov
Žodino
Krupki
Toločin
Orša
Belyniči
Mogilev
Berezino
Vitebsk
Gorodok
Sirotino
Bešenkoviči
Bogušesk
Ezerišče
Krasnopolje
Nevel'
Novosokol'niki
Pustoška
Kuznecovka
Opočka
Krasnogorodskoe
Novgorodka
Ostrov
Šmojlovo
Dubrovka
Sorokino
Vydor
Puškinskie
Novoržev
Loknja
Porhov
Dno
Borovići
Sol'cy
Capel'ka
Seredka
Jamm
Gdov
Ljady
Luga
Tolmačevo
Miljutino
Nikolaevo
Utorg
Os'mino
Slancy
Perevolok
Jaama
Ranna-Pungerja
Volosovo
Begunicy
Kernovo
Kurgolovo
Ust'-Luga
Vyra
Siversk
Narvskij zaliv
Čudskoe ozero
Pskovskoe ozero
Pljussa
Oredež
Šelan
Velikaja
Gauja
Daugava
Aiviekste
Lielupe
Nemunelis
Malta
Drissa
Zap. Dvina
Neris
Vilija
Berezina
Dnepr
Pärnu
Rēzekne
E 20
E 30
EESTI
LATVIJA
LIETUVA
BELARUS'

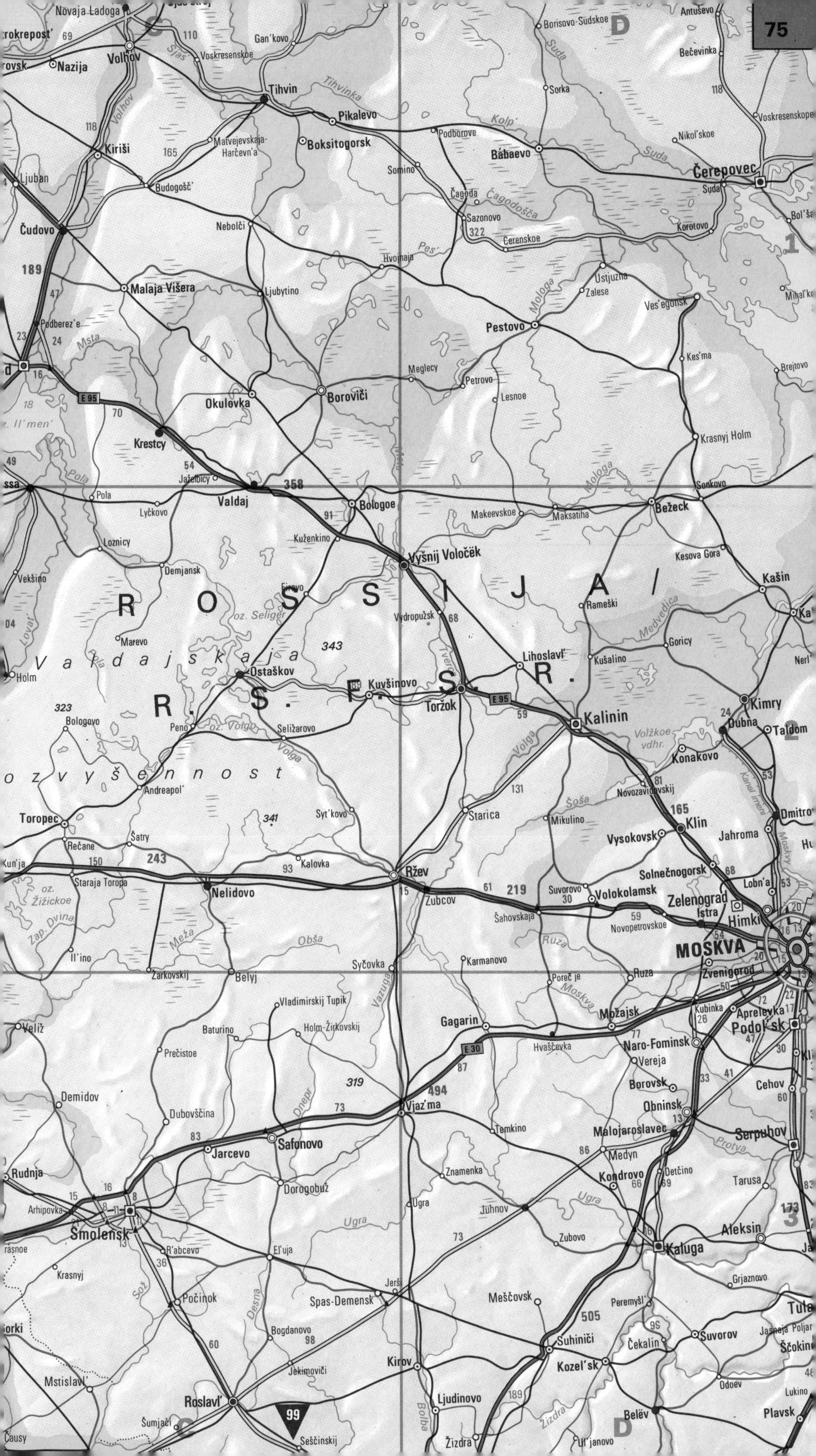
Novaja Ladoga
Volhov
Nazija
Gan'kovo
Voskresenskoe
Tihvin
Tihvinka
Pikalevo
Boksitogorsk
Kiriši
Matvejevskaja-Harčevn'a
Budogošč'
Ljuban
Čudovo
Nebolči
Malaja Višera
Ljubytino
Podberez'e
Msta
Okulovka
Boroviči
Krestcy
Valdaj
Jažel'bicy
Pola
Lyčkovo
Loznicy
Demjansk
Vekšino
Holm
Marevo
Ostaškov
Peno
Seližarovo
Andreapol'
Toropec
Rečane
Šatry
Staraja Toropa
Nelidovo
Il'ino
Žarkovskij
Belyj
Veliž
Demidov
Rudnja
Arhipovka
Smolensk
Krasnyj
Počinok
Mstislavl'
Roslavl'
Šumjači
Seščinskij
Jekimoviči
Bogdanovo
Spas-Demensk
Jerši
El'nja
R'abcevo
Dorogobuž
Jarcevo
Safonovo
Dubovščina
Baturino
Pričistoe
Holm-Žirkovskij
Vladimirskij Tupik
Syčovka
Vjaz'ma
Gagarin
Znamenka
Ugra
Juhnov
Temkino
Kirov
Ljudinovo
Žizdra
Kozel'sk
Suhiniči
Meščovsk
Kaluga
Zubovo
Kondrovo
Medyn
Maloярoslavec
Obninsk
Borovsk
Vereja
Naro-Fominsk
Hvaščevka
Možajsk
Ruza
Zvenigorod
Kubinka
Aprelevka
Podol'sk
Serpuhov
Tarusa
Aleksin
Grjaznovo
Tula
Suvorov
Čekalin
Peremyšl'
Odoev
Belëv
Ul'janovo
Plavsk
Lukino
Ščokino
Jasnaja Poljana
Detčino
Cehov
Moskva
Himki
Istra
Zelenograd
Solnečnogorsk
Lobn'a
Novopetrovskoe
Volokolamsk
Šahovskaja
Suvorovo
Karmanovo
Zubcov
Ržev
Kalovka
Syt'kovo
Starica
Mikulino
Vysokovsk
Klin
Jahroma
Dmitrov
Novozavidovskij
Konakovo
Kalinin
Lihoslavl'
Kušalino
Goricy
Kimry
Dubna
Taldom
Rameški
Kašin
Kesova Gora
Bežeck
Sonkovo
Maksatiha
Makeevskoe
Bologoe
Kuženkino
Vyšnij Voloček
Vydropužsk
Kuvšinovo
Toržok
Lesnoe
Petrovo
Meglecy
Pestovo
Zalese
Ustjužna
Ves'egonsk
Kes'ma
Brejtovo
Krasnyj Holm
Hvojnaja
Sazonovo
Čagoda
Somino
Podborove
Babaevo
Borisovo-Sudskoe
Sorka
Čerepovec
Suda
Korotovo
Čerenskoe
Nikol'skoe
Voskresenskoe
Bečevinka
Antuševo
ROSSIJA / R. S. F. S. R.
Valdajskaja vozvyšennost
oz. Seliger
oz. Il'men'
Volga
Mologa
Medvedica
Volžkoe vdhr.
Kanal imeni Moskvy
Moskva
Oka
Ugra
Dnepr
Desna
Obša
Meža
Zap. Dvina
oz. Žižickoe
Lovat'
Protva
E 95
E 30
99

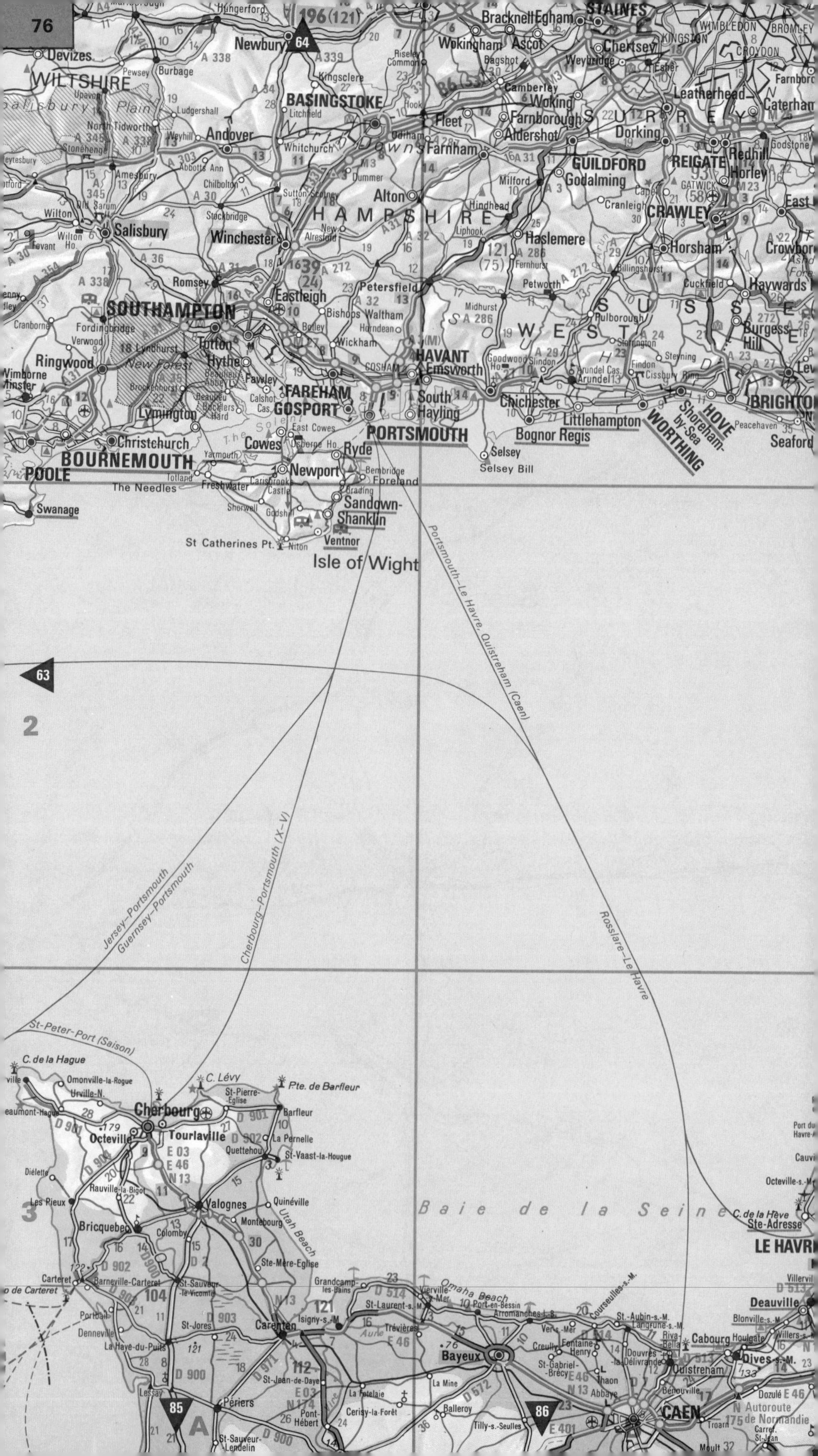

Devizes
WILTSHIRE
Salisbury Plain
Hungerford
Newbury
64
196 (121)
BASINGSTOKE
Kingsclere
Andover
Ludgershall
North Tidworth
Stonehenge
Amesbury
Whitchurch
Salisbury
Wilton
Winchester
Stockbridge
Romsey
Eastleigh
SOUTHAMPTON
Fordingbridge
Ringwood
New Forest
Lyndhurst
Totton
Hythe
Fawley
Lymington
Christchurch
BOURNEMOUTH
POOLE
Swanage
The Needles
Yarmouth
Cowes
Newport
Ryde
Sandown-Shanklin
Ventnor
St Catherines Pt.
Isle of Wight
FAREHAM
GOSPORT
PORTSMOUTH
HAVANT
Emsworth
South Hayling
Chichester
Bognor Regis
Selsey
Selsey Bill
Littlehampton
WORTHING
Shoreham-by-Sea
HOVE
BRIGHTON
Seaford
Peacehaven
Arundel
Petersfield
Bishops Waltham
Wickham
Alton
HAMPSHIRE
Farnham
Fleet
Aldershot
Farnborough
Camberley
Woking
Wokingham
Ascot
Bracknell
Egham
STAINES
Chertsey
Weybridge
GUILDFORD
Godalming
Haslemere
Dorking
REIGATE
Redhill
Horley
CRAWLEY
Horsham
Leatherhead
Caterham
WIMBLEDON
CROYDON
SURREY
WEST SUSSEX
Petworth
Pulborough
Cuckfield
Haywards Heath
Burgess Hill
Midhurst
63
2
Portsmouth–Le Havre, Ouistreham (Caen)
Jersey–Portsmouth
Guernsey–Portsmouth
Cherbourg–Portsmouth (X–V)
Rosslare–Le Havre
St-Peter-Port (Saison)
C. de la Hague
C. Lévy
Pte. de Barfleur
Cherbourg
Octeville
Tourlaville
Barfleur
St-Vaast-la-Hougue
Valognes
Les Pieux
3
Bricquebec
Baie de la Seine
Utah Beach
Omaha Beach
Ste-Mère-Eglise
Carteret
Barneville-Carteret
St-Sauveur-le-Vicomte
Carentan
Isigny-s.-M.
Grandcamp-les-Bains
Bayeux
Port-en-Bessin
Arromanches-l.-B.
Courseulles-s.-M.
Ouistreham
Cabourg
Houlgate
Dives-s.-M.
Deauville
CAEN
LE HAVRE
Ste-Adresse
C. de la Hève
Périers
Lessay
La Haye-du-Puits
85
86
Autoroute de Normandie
A

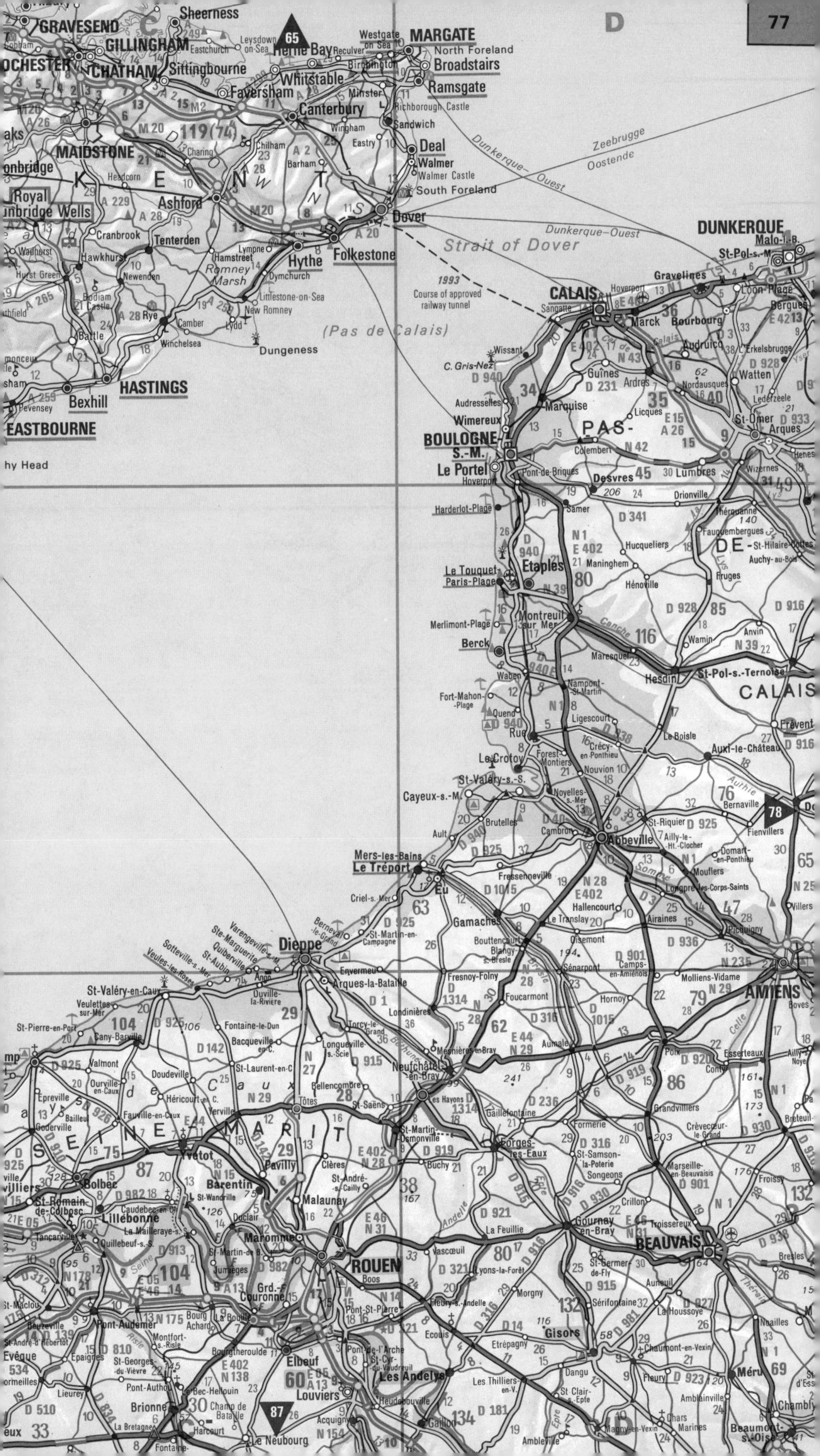
Sheerness
GRAVESEND
GILLINGHAM
ROCHESTER
CHATHAM
Sittingbourne
Leysdown on-Sea
Eastchurch
Herne Bay
Reculver
Westgate on Sea
MARGATE
North Foreland
Broadstairs
Birchington
Ramsgate
Minster
Richborough Castle
Whitstable
Faversham
Canterbury
Sandwich
Wingham
Eastry
Deal
Walmer
Walmer Castle
South Foreland
Chilham
Charing
Barham
MAIDSTONE
Tonbridge
Headcorn
KENT
DOWNS
Royal Tunbridge Wells
Ashford
Dover
Cranbrook
Tenterden
Hamstreet
Lympne
Hythe
Folkestone
Wadhurst
Hawkhurst
Newenden
Romney Marsh
Dymchurch
Hurst Green
Bodiam Castle
Rye
Littlestone-on-Sea
New Romney
Camber
Lydd
Battle
Winchelsea
Dungeness
HASTINGS
Bexhill
Pevensey
EASTBOURNE
Zeebrugge
Oostende
Dunkerque–Ouest
Strait of Dover
1993
Course of approved railway tunnel
(Pas de Calais)
DUNKERQUE
Malo-l.-B.
St-Pol-s.-M.
Gravelines
Hoverport
CALAIS
Sangatte
Marck
Bourbourg
Loon-Plage
Bergues
Audruicq
Wissant
C. Gris-Nez
Guînes
Ardres
Nordausques
Watten
Marquise
Licques
Audresselles
Wimereux
BOULOGNE S.-M.
Le Portel
PAS-
Colembert
St-Omer
Arques
Pont-de-Briques
Desvres
Lumbres
Wizernes
Samer
Drionville
Harderlot-Plage
Thérouanne
Fauquembergues
Hucqueliers
DE-
St-Hilaire-Cottes
Auchy-au-Bois
Le Touquet-Paris-Plage
Etaples
Maninghem
Hénoville
Fruges
Montreuil sur Mer
Merlimont-Plage
Berck
Anvin
Wamin
Maresquel
Hesdin
St-Pol-s.-Ternoise
CALAIS
Waben
Nampont-St-Martin
Fort-Mahon-Plage
Quend
Ligescourt
Rue
Frévent
Le Boisle
Le Crotoy
Forest-Montiers
Crécy-en-Ponthieu
Auxi-le-Château
Nouvion
St-Valéry-s.-S.
Cayeux-s.-M.
Noyelles-s.-Mer
Bernaville
Brutelles
St-Riquier
Ailly-le-Ht.-Clocher
Fienvillers
Ault
Cambron
Abbeville
Mers-les-Bains
Le Tréport
Eu
Domart-en-Ponthieu
Moufliers
Fressenneville
Criel-s.-Mer
Longpré-les-Corps-Saints
Hallencourt
Villers
Gamaches
Le Translay
Airaines
Picquigny
Berneval-le-Grand
St-Martin-en-Campagne
Bouttencourt
Blangy-s.-Bresle
Oisemont
Dieppe
Varengeville-s.-M.
Ste-Marguerite
Quiberville
St-Aubin
Sotteville-s.-Mer
Veules-les-Roses
Sénarpont
Camps-en-Amiénois
Molliens-Vidame
AMIENS
Envermeu
Arques-la-Bataille
Fresnoy-Folny
St-Valéry-en-Caux
Ango
Ouville-la-Rivière
Foucarmont
Hornoy
Boves
Veulettes-sur-Mer
Londinières
St-Pierre-en-Port
Cany-Barville
Fontaine-le-Dun
Bacqueville-en-C.
Torcy-le-Grand
Longueville-s.-Scie
Mesnières-en-Bray
Aumale
Poix
Esserteaux
Ailly-s.-Noye
Fécamp
Valmont
Doudeville
St-Laurent-en-C
Neufchâtel-en-Bray
Conty
Ourville-en-Caux
Caux
Bellencombre
Epreville
Héricourt-en-C.
Yerville
Tôtes
St-Saëns
Les Hayons
Gaillefontaine
Grandvilliers
Breteuil
Bailleul
Fauville-en-Caux
Goderville
SEINE-MARITIME
St-Martin-Osmonville
Formerie
Crèvecoeur-le-Grand
Yvetot
Pavilly
Clères
Buchy
Forges-les-Eaux
St-Samson-la-Poterie
Bolbec
Barentin
St-André-s.-Cailly
Songeons
Marseille-en-Beauvaisis
Froissy
Lillebonne
St-Romain-de-Colbosc
Caudebec-en-C.
St-Wandrille
Malaunay
Crillon
Tancarville
La Mailleraye-s.-S.
Duclair
Maromme
La Feuillie
Gournay-en-Bray
Troissereux
Quillebeuf-s.-S.
Seine
St-Martin-de-B.
Jumièges
ROUEN
Vascoeuil
BEAUVAIS
Boos
Lyons-la-Forêt
St-Germer-de-Fly
Auneuil
Bresles
St-Maclou
Couronne
Grd.-
Morgny
Sérifontaine
La Houssoye
Beuzeville
Pont-Audemer
Bourg Achard
La Bouille
Pont-St-Pierre
Fleury-s.-Andelle
St-André-d'Hébertot
Montfort-s.-Risle
Bourgtheroulde
Elbeuf
Pont-de-l'Arche
St-Cyr-du-Vaudreuil
Ecouis
Etrépagny
Gisors
Chaumont-en-Vexin
Noailles
Evêque
Epaignes
St-Georges-du-Vièvre
Louviers
Les Andelys
Dangu
Méru
Cormeilles
Lieurey
Pont-Authou
Le Bec-Hellouin
Les Thilliers-en-V.
St Clair-s.-Epte
Fleury
Amblainville
St-d'Esserent
Brionne
Champ de Bataille
Heudebouville
Chambly
La Bretagne
Harcourt
Le Neubourg
Acquigny
Gaillon
Amblerville
Magny-en-Vexin
Chars
Marines
Beaumont-s.-Oise
Fontaine-

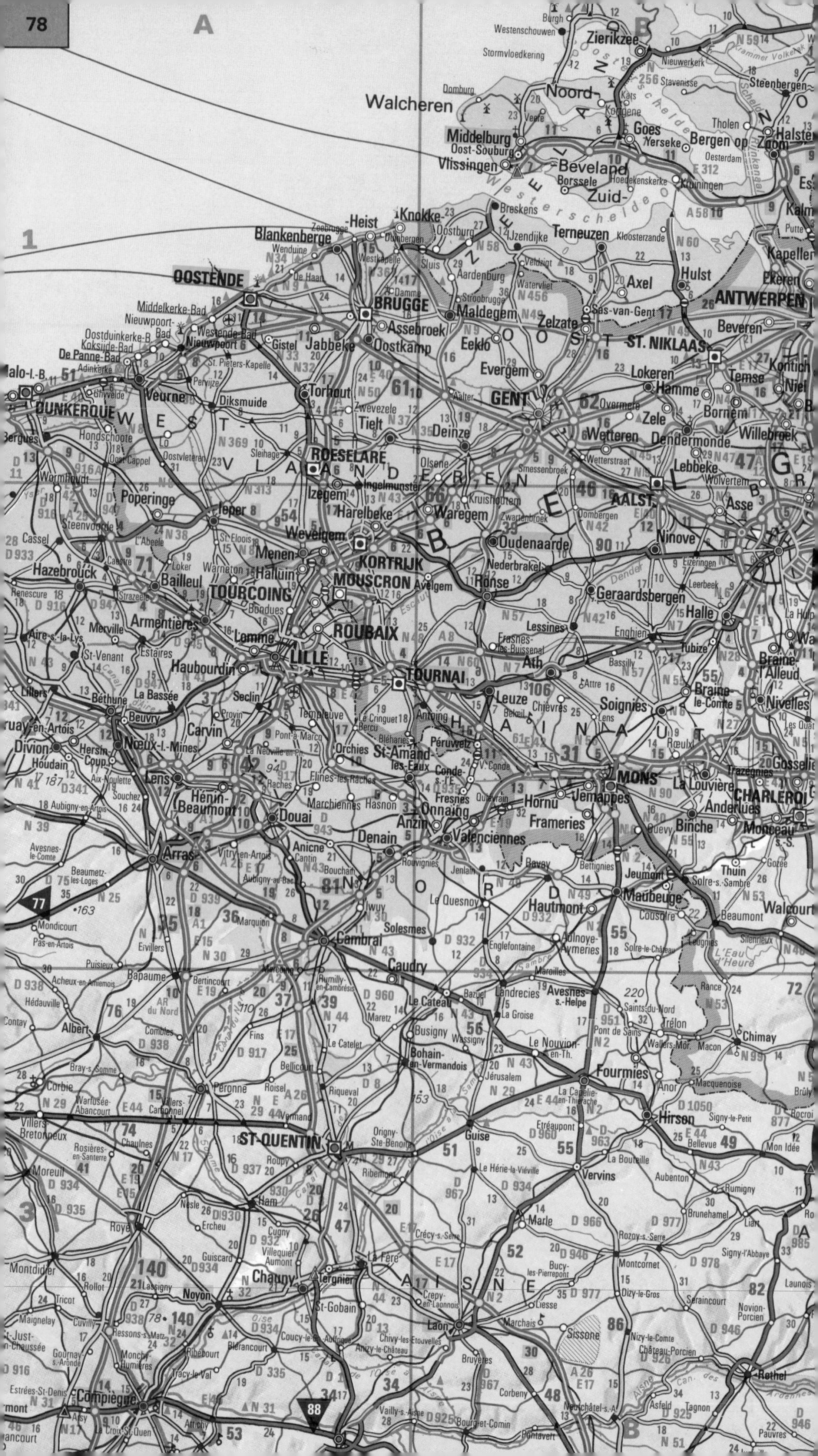

A
B
1
Walcheren
Westenschouwen
Burgh
Zierikzee
Stormvloedkering
Nieuwerkerk
Stavenisse
Steenbergen
Noord-
Beveland
Zuid-
Domburg
Veere
Kats
Kortgene
Goes
Yerseke
Tholen
Bergen op Zoom
Halsteren
Middelburg
Oost-Souburg
Vlissingen
Borssele
Hoedekenskerke
Kruiningen
Osterdam
Westerschelde
Oosterschelde
Breskens
Knokke-Heist
Zeebrugge
Blankenberge
Wenduine
Oostburg
IJzendijke
Terneuzen
Kloosterzande
Putte
Kapellen
Ekeren
Dumbergen
Westkapelle
Sluis
Aardenburg
Veldzicht
Watervliet
Axel
Hulst
OOSTENDE
De Haan
Damme
BRUGGE
Stroobrugge
Maldegem
Sas-van-Gent
Zelzate
ANTWERPEN
Middelkerke-Bad
Nieuwpoort-Bad
Westende-Bad
Nieuwpoort
Oostduinkerke-B
Koksijde-Bad
De Panne-Bad
Adinkerke
Gistel
Jabbeke
Assebroek
Oostkamp
Eeklo
Evergem
ST. NIKLAAS
Beveren
Kontich
Temse
Lokeren
Hamme
St. Pieters-Kapelle
Pervijze
Torhout
Zwevezele
Tielt
Aalter
GENT
Overmere
Zele
Bornem
Niel
Willebroek
Malo-l.-B.
DUNKERQUE
Ghyvelde
Veurne
Diksmuide
Bergues
Hondschoote
WEST-VLAANDEREN
OOST-VLAANDEREN
Deinze
Wetteren
Dendermonde
Oost-Cappel
Oostvleteren
Sleihage
ROESELARE
Olsene
Smessenbroek
Wetterstraat
Lebbeke
Wolvertem
Wormhoudt
Ingelmunster
Izegem
Kruishoutem
Zwartenbroek
AALST
Asse
Poperinge
Ieper
Harelbeke
Waregem
Dombergen
Ninove
Steenvoorde
St. Eloois
L'Abeele
Wevelgem
Menen
KORTRIJK
Oudenaarde
Cassel
Caëstre
Loker
Warneton
Halluin
Nederbrakel
Eizeringen
Dender
Hazebrouck
Bailleul
TOURCOING
MOUSCRON
Avelgem
Ronse
Geraardsbergen
Leerbeek
Renescure
Strazeele
Bondues
Escaut
Halle
Armentières
Merville
Aire-s.-la-Lys
Lomme
ROUBAIX
Lessines
Fresnes-les-Buissenal
Enghien
La Hulpe
St-Venant
Estaires
LILLE
Ath
Bassilly
Tubize
Braine-l'Alleud
Hauboudin
TOURNAI
Attre
Lillers
Béthune
La Bassée
Seclin
Leuze
Beloeil
Chièvres
Soignies
Braine-le-Comte
Nivelles
Beuvry
Provin
Templeuve
Le Cringuet
Bercu
Antoing
Lens
Les Quat
Bruay-en-Artois
Carvin
Pont-à-Marcq
Blèharies
Péruwelz
HAINAUT
Roeulx
Divion
Hersin-Coup.
Noeux-l.-Mines
La Neuville-en-Ph.
Orchies
St-Amand-les-Eaux
V. Condé
Houdain
Aix-Noulette
Flines-les-Raches
Raches
Condé-s.-l'E.
MONS
Trazegnies
Gosselies
Souchez
Hénin-Beaumont
Fresnes
Quiévrain
Hornu
Jemappes
La Louvière
CHARLEROI
Aubigny-en-Artois
Marchiennes
Hasnon
Onnaing
Anzin
Frameries
Anderlues
Binche
Douai
Valenciennes
Quévy
Monceau-s.-S.
Avesnes-le-Comte
Arras
Vitry-en-Artois
Anicne
Cantin
Denain
Rouvignies
Jenlain
Bavay
Bettignies
Jeumont
Thuin
Gozée
Beaumetz-les-Loges
Aubigny-au-Bac
Bouchain
Solre-s.-Sambre
77
NORD
Le Quesnoy
Hautmont
Maubeuge
Beaumont
Walcourt
Mondicourt
Marquion
Iwuy
Cousolre
Pas-en-Artois
Ervillers
Solesmes
Cambrai
Aulnoye-Aymeries
Solre-le-Château
Leugnies
Silenrieux
Englefontaine
L'Eau d'Heure
Caudry
Puisieux
Bapaume
Bertincourt
Marcoing
Rumilly-en-Cambrésis
Maroilles
Acheux-en-Amienois
Hédauville
AR du Nord
Bazuel
Le Cateau
Landrecies
Avesnes-s.-Helpe
Rance
Maretz
La Groise
Saints-du-Nord
Trélon
Contay
Albert
Combles
Busigny
Wassigny
Le Nouvion-en-Th.
Pont de Sains
Wallers-Mor.
Macon
Chimay
Fins
Le Catelet
Bohain-en-Vermandois
Bray-s.-Somme
Bellicourt
Jérusalem
Fourmies
Corbie
Péronne
Roisel
Riqueval
Anor
Macquenoise
Warfusée-Abancourt
Villers-Carbonnel
La Capelle-en-Thiérache
Brûly
Villers-Bretonneux
Vermand
Hirson
Signy-le-Petit
Rocroi
Rosières-en-Santerre
Chaulnes
ST-QUENTIN
Orignu-Ste-Benoite
Guise
Étréaupont
Bellevue
Mon Idée
Moreuil
Roupy
Ribemont
Le Hérie-la-Viéville
Vervins
La Bouteille
Aubenton
Rumigny
Nesle
Ham
Ercheu
Cugny
Marle
Brunehamel
Liart
Roye
Villequier-Aumont
Crécy-s.-Serre
Rozoy-s.-Serre
Montdidier
Guiscard
La Fère
Bucy-les-Pierrepont
Montcornet
Signy-l'Abbaye
Chauny
Tergnier
AISNE
Launois
Tricot
Rollot
Lassigny
Noyon
Crepy-en-Laonnois
Dizy-le-Gros
Seraincourt
Novion-Porcien
Maignelay
Cuvilly
St-Gobain
Liesse
Laon
Marchais
Sissonne
St-Just-en-Chaussée
Ressons-s.-Matz
Coucy-le-Ch.-Auffrique
Chivy-les-Etouvelles
Anizy-le-Château
Nizy-le-Comte
Château-Porcien
Gournay-s.-Aronde
Monchy-Humières
Ribécourt
Blérancourt
Bruyères
Rethel
Tracy-le-Val
Corbeny
Estrées-St-Denis
Compiègne
88
Vailly-s.-Aisne
Bourg-et-Comin
Neufchâtel-s.-A.
Asfeld
Tagnon
Pauvres
Arsy
La Croix-St-Ouen
Attichy
Pontavert

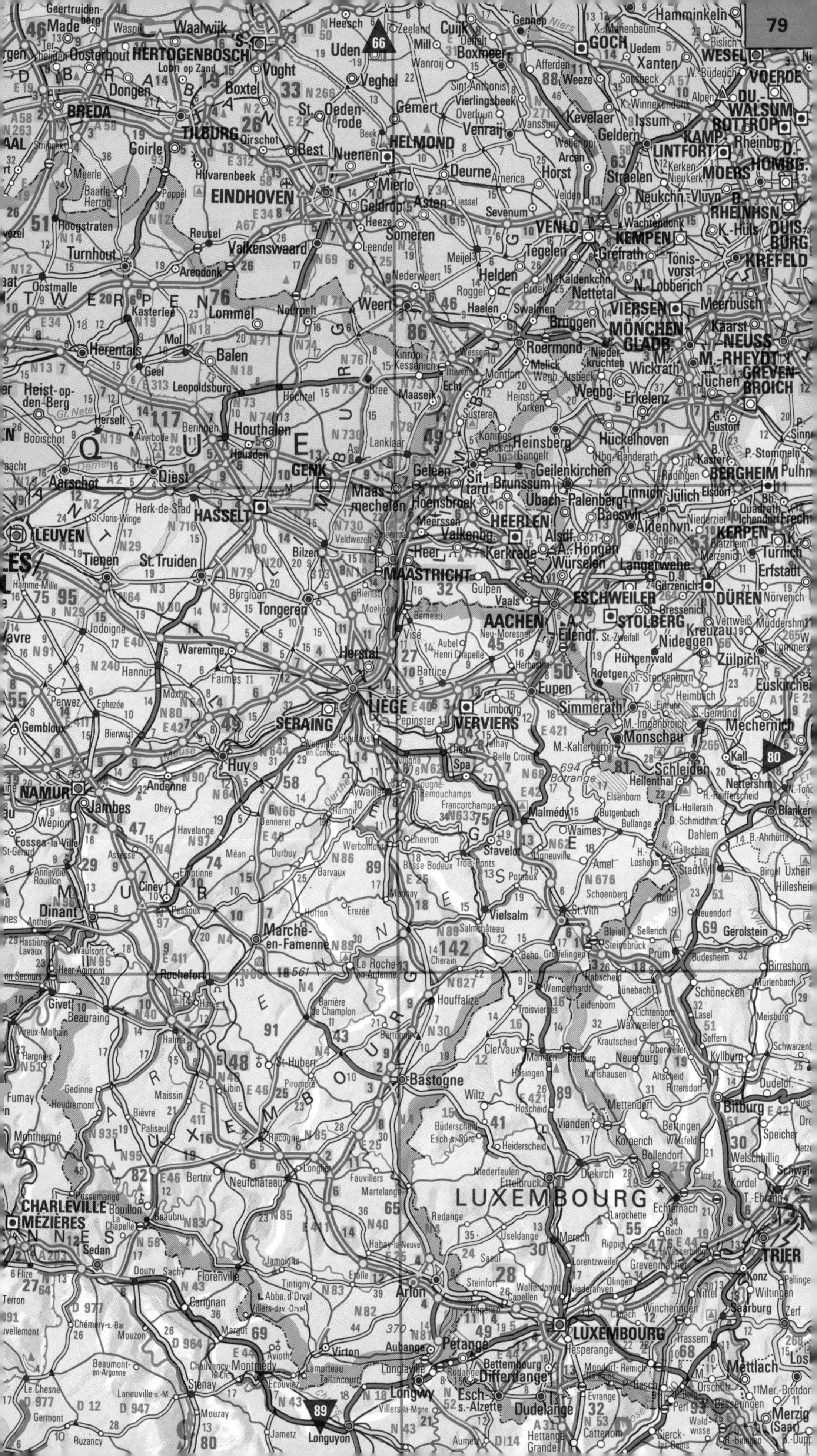

79
Made
Waalwijk
'S-HERTOGENBOSCH
Oosterhout
Vught
Heesch
Uden
Cuijk
Boxmeer
Gennep
GOCH
Uedem
Xanten
Hamminkeln
WESEL
VOERDE
Dongen
Boxtel
Veghel
Gemert
BREDA
TILBURG
Oirschot
St. Oedenrode
HELMOND
Venray
Kevelaer
Geldern
Issum
KAMP-LINTFORT
MOERS
BOTTROP
Goirle
Best
Nuenen
Deurne
Horst
Straelen
Hilvarenbeek
EINDHOVEN
Mierlo
Geldrop
Asten
Sevenum
VENLO
KEMPEN
Neukchn.-Vluyn
Hoogstraten
Reusel
Valkenswaard
Heeze
Someren
Tegelen
Grefrath
KREFELD
Turnhout
Arendonk
Leende
Meijel
Helden
Nettetal
N.-Lobberich
Tönisvorst
Oostmalle
Kasterlee
Lommel
Neerpelt
Weert
Roggel
Haelen
Swalmen
Brüggen
VIERSEN
Meerbusch
MÖNCHEN-GLADB.
Kaarst
NEUSS
Herentals
Mol
Balen
Roermond
M.-RHEYDT
Wickrath
GREVENBROICH
Geel
Leopoldsburg
Hechtel
Bree
Maaseik
Echt
Montfort
Wegbg.
Erkelenz
Jüchen
Heist-op-den-Berg
Herselt
Beringen
Houthalen
Susteren
Heinsberg
Hückelhoven
Booischot
Heusden
Lankaar
Gangelt
Geilenkirchen
BERGHEIM
Aarschot
Diest
GENK
Geleen
Sittard
Brunssum
Linnich
Jülich
Herk-de-Stad
HASSELT
Maasmechelen
Hoensbroek
Übach-Palenberg
Baesweiler
LEUVEN
HEERLEN
Alsdf.
Aldenhvn.
KERPEN
Tienen
St. Truiden
Bilzen
Valkenbg.
Kerkrade
Würselen
Langerwehe
Türnich
Erfstadt
MAASTRICHT
Gulpen
Vaals
ESCHWEILER
DÜREN
Borgloon
Tongeren
AACHEN
STOLBERG
Jodoigne
Waremme
Visé
Herstal
Nideggen
Kreuzau
Wavre
Hannut
Battice
Eupen
Zülpich
LIÈGE
VERVIERS
Simmerath
Euskirchen
Perwez
SERAING
Limbourg
Mechernich
Gembloux
Huy
Spa
Monschau
Kall
NAMUR
Andenne
Schleiden
Jambes
Malmédy
Hellenthal
Nettersheim
Stavelot
Dinant
Ciney
Vielsalm
St. Vith
Gerolstein
Marche-en-Famenne
Prüm
Givet
Rochefort
La Roche-en-Ardenne
Houffalize
Bastogne
Clervaux
Bitburg
St-Hubert
Wiltz
Vianden
Libin
Diekirch
Ettelbruck
Echternach
LUXEMBOURG
Neufchâteau
Bouillon
CHARLEVILLE MÉZIÈRES
Sedan
Mersch
TRIER
Florenville
Arlon
Konz
Saarburg
Carignan
Pétange
LUXEMBOURG
Virton
Differdange
Esch-s.-Alzette
Dudelange
Mettlach
Stenay
Longwy
Longuyon
Merzig (Saar)
66
80
89

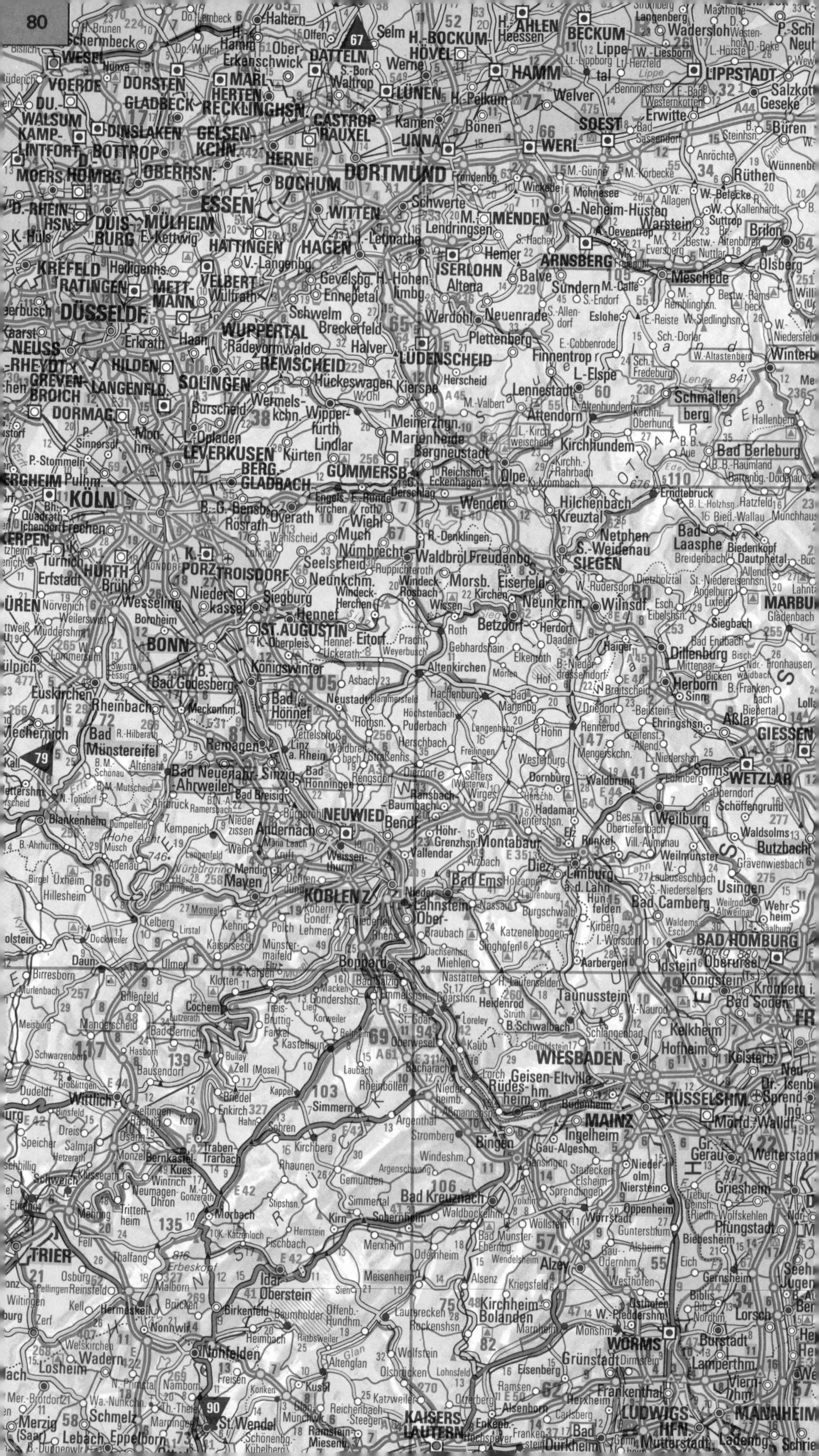

Haltern
Selm
H.-BOCKUM-HÖVEL
H.-AHLEN
BECKUM
Wadersloh
WESEL
VOERDE
DORSTEN
MARL
HERTEN
RECKLINGHSN.
DATTELN
Waltrop
LÜNEN
HAMM
LIPPSTADT
GLADBECK
CASTROP-RAUXEL
Kamen
Bönen
Welver
SOEST
Erwitte
Geseke
Salzkotten
DU.-WALSUM
DINSLAKEN
BOTTROP
GELSEN-KCHN.
HERNE
DORTMUND
UNNA
WERL
Büren
KAMP-LINTFORT
MOERS
OBERHSN.
BOCHUM
Fröndenbg.
Rüthen
ESSEN
WITTEN
Schwerte
MENDEN
A.-Neheim-Hüsten
Warstein
Brilon
DUISBURG
MÜLHEIM
HATTINGEN
HAGEN
ISERLOHN
ARNSBERG
Olsberg
KREFELD
RATINGEN
VELBERT
METTMANN
Altena
Balve
Sundern
Meschede
DÜSSELDF.
Schwelm
Ennepetal
Werdohl
Neuenrade
Eslohe
NEUSS
Erkrath
Haan
WUPPERTAL
Radevormwald
Halver
Plettenberg
LÜDENSCHEID
RHEYDT
HILDEN
SOLINGEN
REMSCHEID
Hückeswagen
Kierspe
Finnentrop
L.-Elspe
Winterberg
GREVEN-BROICH
LANGENFLD.
Wermelskchn.
Wipperfürth
Lennestadt
Schmallenberg
DORMAG.
Burscheid
Meinerzhgn.
Marienheide
Attendorn
LEVERKUSEN
Kürten
Lindlar
GUMMERSB.
Bergneustadt
Kirchhundem
Bad Berleburg
BERG.-GLADBACH
Olpe
KÖLN
Overath
Wiehl
Wenden
Hilchenbach
Erndtebrück
Frechen
Rösrath
Much
Kreuztal
Netphen
Bad Laasphe
Biedenkopf
HÜRTH
K.-PORZ
TROISDORF
Nümbrecht
Waldbröl
Freudenbg.
SIEGEN
Erfstadt
Brühl
Seelscheid
Neunkchm.
Eiserfeld
Wesseling
Niederkassel
Siegburg
Hennef
Morsb.
Neunkchn.
Wilnsdf.
MARBURG
ST. AUGUSTIN
Eitorf
Betzdorf
BONN
Königswinter
Altenkirchen
Dillenburg
Bad Godesberg
Herborn
Euskirchen
Rheinbach
Bad Hönnef
Neustadt
Hachenburg
Aßlar
GIESSEN
Mechernich
Bad Münstereifel
Remagen
Linz a. Rhein
Puderbach
Rennerod
WETZLAR
Bad Neuenahr-Ahrweiler
Sinzig
Bad Breisig
Westerburg
Dornburg
Solms
Blankenheim
Andernach
NEUWIED
Bendf.
Hadamar
Weilburg
Montabaur
Limburg a. d. Lahn
Butzbach
Adenau
Mayen
KOBLENZ
Vallendar
Bad Ems
Diez
Usingen
Lahnstein
Nassau
Bad Camberg
BAD HOMBURG
Boppard
Idstein
Oberursel
Daun
Ulmen
Königstein
Cochem
Taunusstein
Bad Soden
Wittlich
Zell (Mosel)
Kastellaun
WIESBADEN
Hofheim
Simmern
Bacharach
Rüdesheim
Geisen-Eltville
RÜSSELSHM.
MAINZ
Ingelheim
Bingen
Traben-Trarbach
Bernkastel-Kues
Kirchberg
Gau-Algeshm.
Groß-Gerau
Griesheim
Bad Kreuznach
Oppenheim
Pfungstadt
TRIER
Morbach
Alzey
Idar-Oberstein
Birkenfeld
Kirchheim-Bolanden
Lorsch
Hermeskeil
WORMS
Bürstadt
Wadern
Nohfelden
Grünstadt
Lampertheim
Losheim
Kusel
Frankenthal
Viernheim
Merzig (Saar)
Schmelz
Lebach
Eppelborn
St. Wendel
KAISERSLAUTERN
LUDWIGSHFN.
MANNHEIM
Hohe Acht
Nürburgring
Erbeskopf
ROTHAAR-GEB.
SAUERLAND
WESTERWALD
TAUNUS
HUNSRÜCK
EIFEL
67
79
90

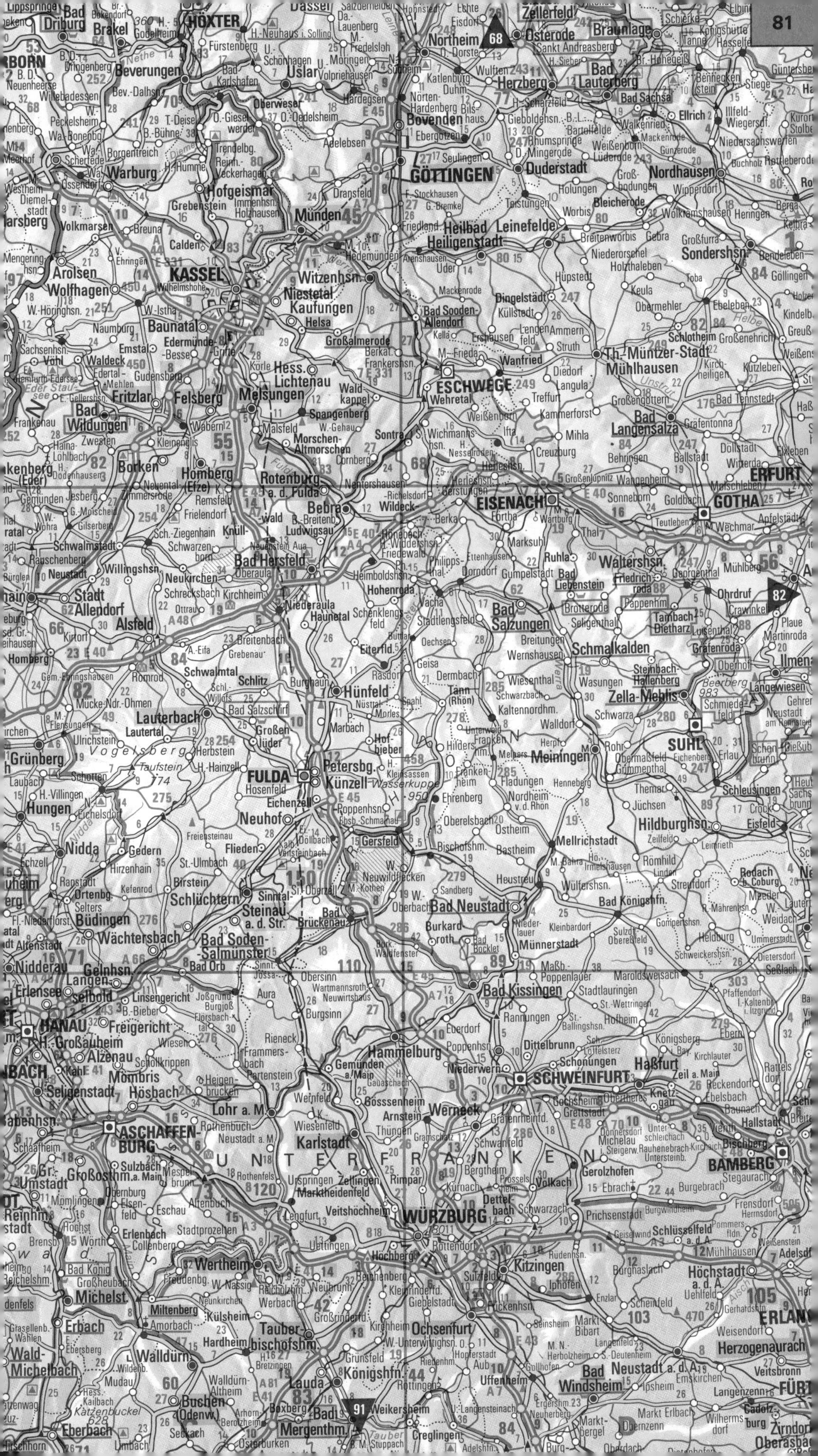
Höxter
Bad Driburg
Brakel
Beverungen
Northeim
Osterode
Zellerfeld
Braunlage
Uslar
Herzberg
Bad Lauterberg
Bad Sachsa
Bovenden
Warburg
Hofgeismar
Göttingen
Duderstadt
Nordhausen
Münden
Heilbad Heiligenstadt
Leinefelde
Sondershsn.
Kassel
Arolsen
Wolfhagen
Witzenhsn.
Niestetal
Kaufungen
Baunatal
Bad Sooden-Allendorf
Dingelstädt
Großalmerode
Hess. Lichtenau
Eschwege
Wanfried
Th.-Müntzer-Stadt Mühlhausen
Fritzlar
Felsberg
Melsungen
Bad Wildungen
Spangenberg
Bad Langensalza
Sontra
Borken
Homberg (Efze)
Rotenburg a. d. Fulda
Bebra
Eisenach
Erfurt
Gotha
Schwalmstadt
Bad Hersfeld
Waltershsn.
Stadt Allendorf
Alsfeld
Bad Salzungen
Schmalkalden
Zella-Mehlis
Hünfeld
Lauterbach
Schlitz
Suhl
Meiningen
Grünberg
Fulda
Künzell
Hungen
Neuhof
Hildburghsn.
Nidda
Gersfeld
Mellrichstadt
Schlüchtern
Steinau a. d. Str.
Büdingen
Wächtersbach
Bad Neustadt
Bad Brückenau
Bad Soden-Salmünster
Gelnhsn.
Bad Kissingen
Hanau
Freigericht
Alzenau
Hammelburg
Schweinfurt
Haßfurt
Seligenstadt
Aschaffenburg
Lohr a. M.
Werneck
Karlstadt
Bamberg
Unterfranken
Würzburg
Kitzingen
Wertheim
Michelst.
Höchstadt a. d. A.
Erbach
Miltenberg
Ochsenfurt
Tauberbischofshm.
Herzogenaurach
Walldürn
Königshfn.
Lauda
Bad Windsheim
Neustadt a. d. A.
Buchen (Odenw.)
Bad Mergenthm.
Eberbach

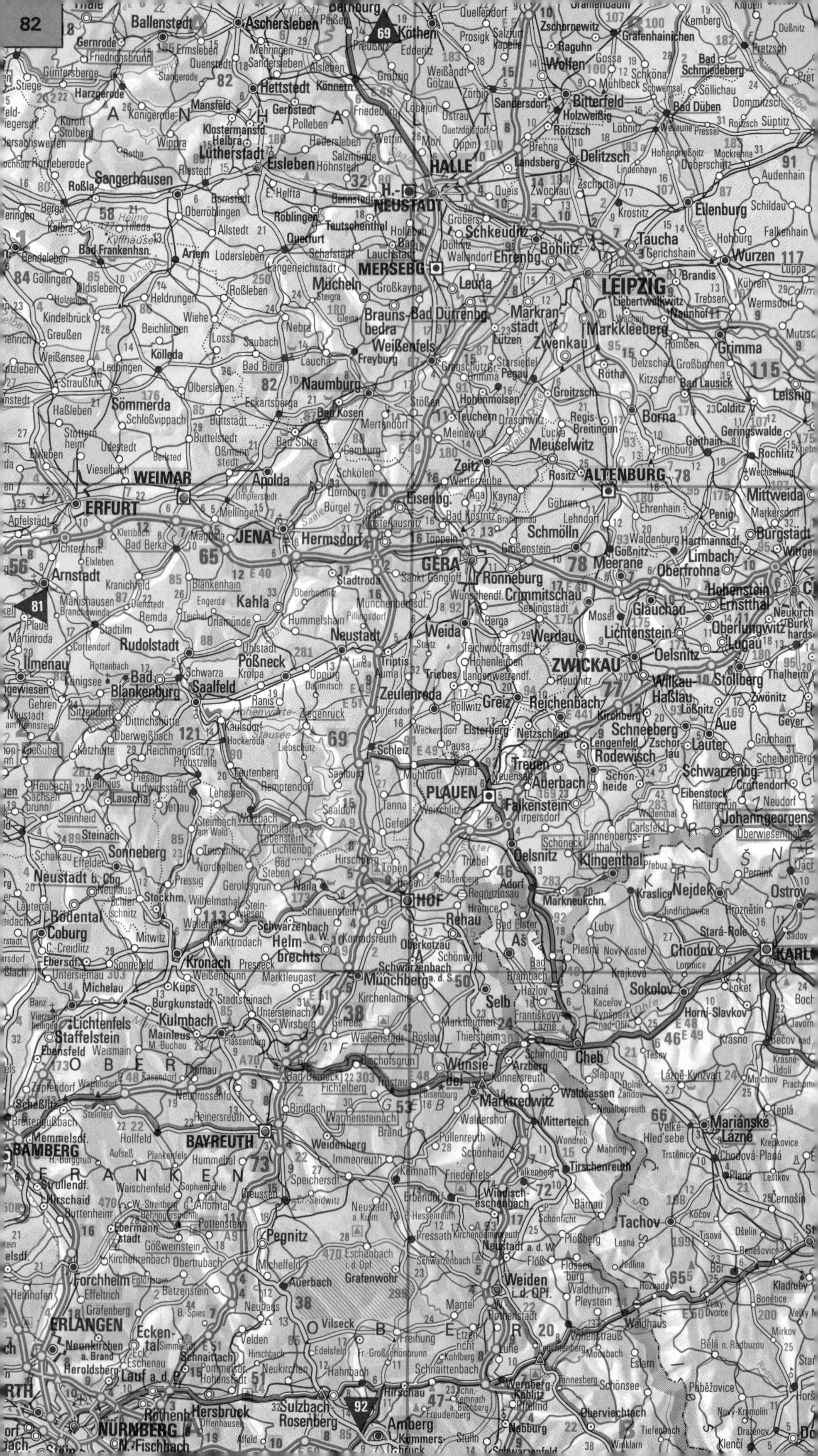

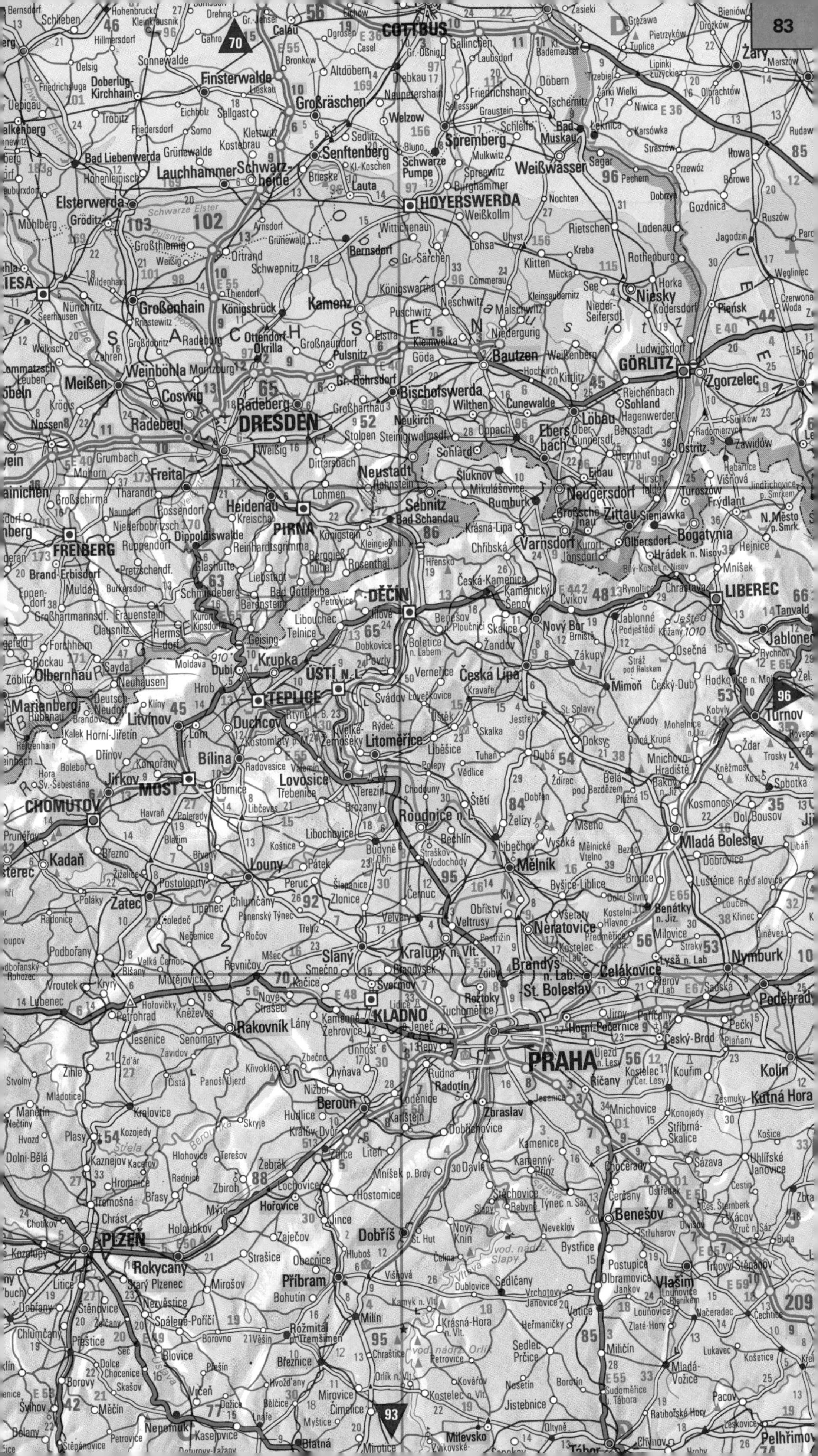
Cottbus
Finsterwalde
Doberlug-Kirchhain
Großräschen
Senftenberg
Spremberg
Weißwasser
Bad Muskau
Bad Liebenwerda
Lauchhammer
Schwarzheide
Elsterwerda
Hoyerswerda
Niesky
Großenhain
Königsbrück
Kamenz
Bautzen
Görlitz
Zgorzelec
Meißen
Weinböhla
Coswig
Radeberg
Dresden
Radebeul
Bischofswerda
Löbau
Freital
Heidenau
Pirna
Neustadt
Sebnitz
Bad Schandau
Neugersdorf
Zittau
Freiberg
Dippoldiswalde
Děčín
Varnsdorf
Liberec
Bogatynia
Ústí n. L.
Teplice
Krupka
Litvínov
Most
Chomutov
Jirkov
Bílina
Duchcov
Lovosice
Litoměřice
Česká Lípa
Mladá Boleslav
Turnov
Kadaň
Žatec
Louny
Roudnice n. L.
Mělník
Neratovice
Slaný
Kralupy n. Vlt.
Kladno
Brandýs n. Lab.-St. Boleslav
Čelákovice
Nymburk
Poděbrady
Rakovník
Praha
Kolín
Kutná Hora
Beroun
Plzeň
Rokycany
Příbram
Dobříš
Benešov
Vlašim
Nepomuk
Blatná
Milevsko
Tábor
Pelhřimov
Žary
Żary
Sprotte
Polen
Sachsen
Oberlausitz

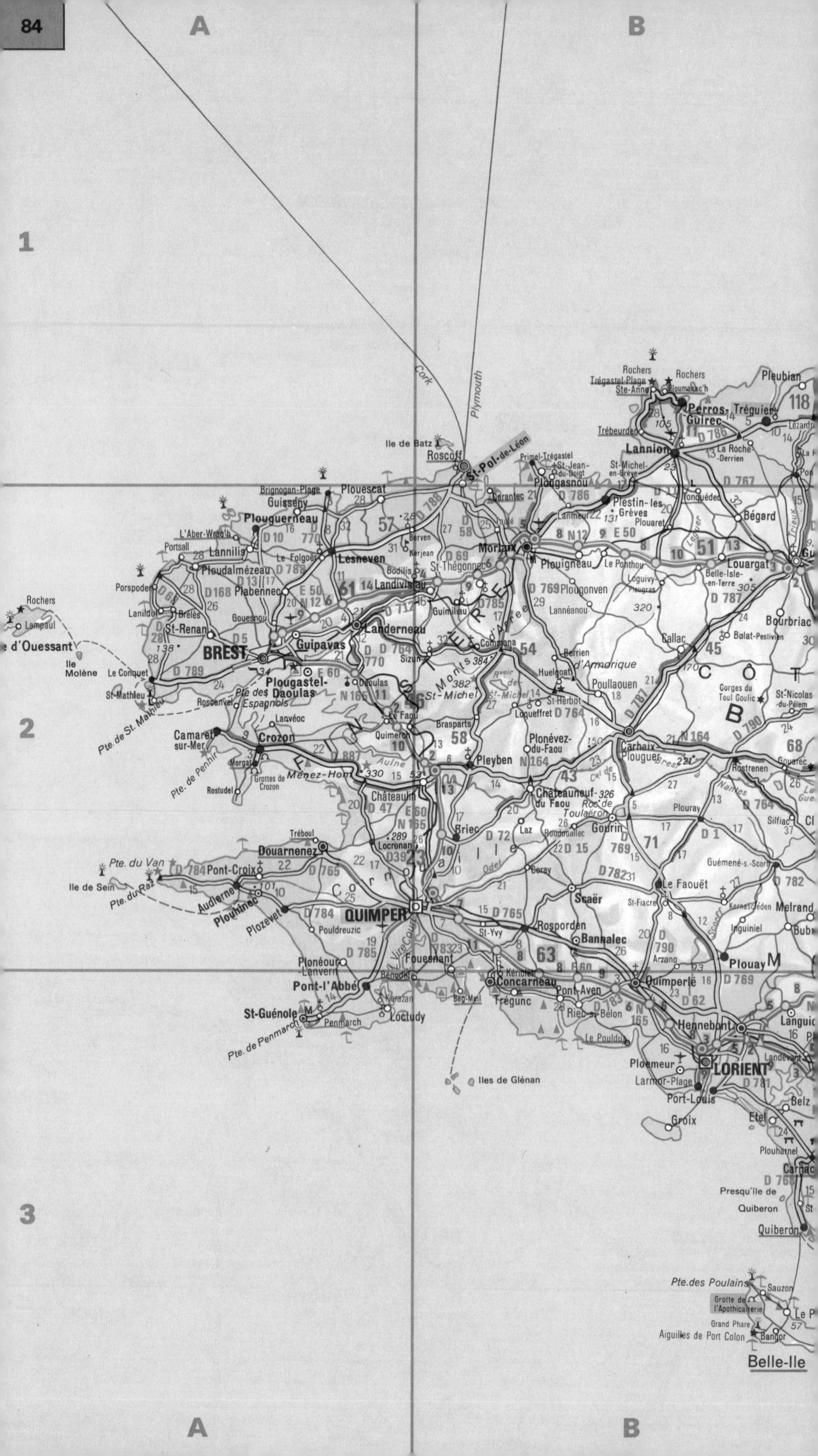
A
B
1
2
3
Cork
Plymouth
Ile de Batz
Roscoff
St-Pol-de-Léon
Lannion
Perros-Guirec
Tréguier
Pleubian
Trégastel Plage
Ste-Anne
Ploumanac'h
Trébeurden
Primel-Trégastel
St-Jean-du-Doigt
Plougasnou
St-Michel-en-Grève
Plestin-les-Grèves
Plouaret
Tonquédec
Bégard
Carantec
Brignogan-Plage
Plouescat
Guissény
Plouguerneau
L'Aber-Wrac'h
Portsall
Lannilis
Ploudalmézeau
Lesneven
Le Folgoët
Berven
Kerjean
Bodilis
Landivisiau
St-Thégonnec
Morlaix
Plouigneau
Le Ponthou
Louargat
Belle-Isle-en-Terre
Loguivy-Plougras
Plougonven
Lannéanou
Bourbriac
Bulat-Pestivien
Callac
Porspoder
Plabennec
Rochers
Lampaul
d'Ouessant
Ile Molène
Lanildut
Brélès
St-Renan
Gouesnou
BREST
Guipavas
Landerneau
Guimiliau
Commana
Sizun
Le Conquet
St-Mathieu
Pte. de St. Mathieu
Plougastel-Daoulas
Daoulas
Pte des Espagnols
Roscanvel
Lanvéoc
Le Faou
Monts d'Arrée
St-Michel
Huelgoat
Berrien
d'Armorique
Poullaouen
St-Herbot
Loqueffret
Brasparts
Camaret-sur-Mer
Crozon
Morgat
Pte. de Penhir
Grottes de Crozon
Rostudel
Quimerch
Ménez-Hom
Aulne
Pleyben
Plonévez-du-Faou
Carhaix-Plouguer
Gorges du Toul Goulic
St-Nicolas-du-Pélem
Rostrenen
Gouarec
Châteaulin
Châteauneuf-du-Faou
Roc de Toullaëron
Gourin
Plouray
Silfiac
Tréboul
Douarnenez
Locronan
Briec
Laz
Roudouallec
Coray
Le Faouët
Guémené-s.-Scorff
Pte. du Van
Ile de Sein
Pte. du Raz
Pont-Croix
Audierne
Plouhinec
Plozévet
QUIMPER
Pouldreuzic
Scaër
St-Fiacre
Kernascléden
Melrand
Inguiniel
Rosporden
Bannalec
St-Yvy
Arzano
Plouay
Plonéour-Lanvern
Fouesnant
Bénodet
Pont-l'Abbé
Concarneau
Kériolet
Pont-Aven
Quimperlé
St-Guénolé
Kerazan
Loctudy
Beg-Meil
Trégunc
Riec-s-Bélon
Penmarch
Pte. de Penmarch
Le Pouldu
Hennebont
Languidic
Landévant
Iles de Glénan
Ploemeur
LORIENT
Larmor-Plage
Port-Louis
Belz
Groix
Etel
Plouharnel
Carnac
Presqu'ile de Quiberon
Quiberon
Pte.des Poulains
Sauzon
Grotte de l'Apothicairerie
Grand Phare
Aiguilles de Port Colon
Bangor
Belle-Ile
A
B

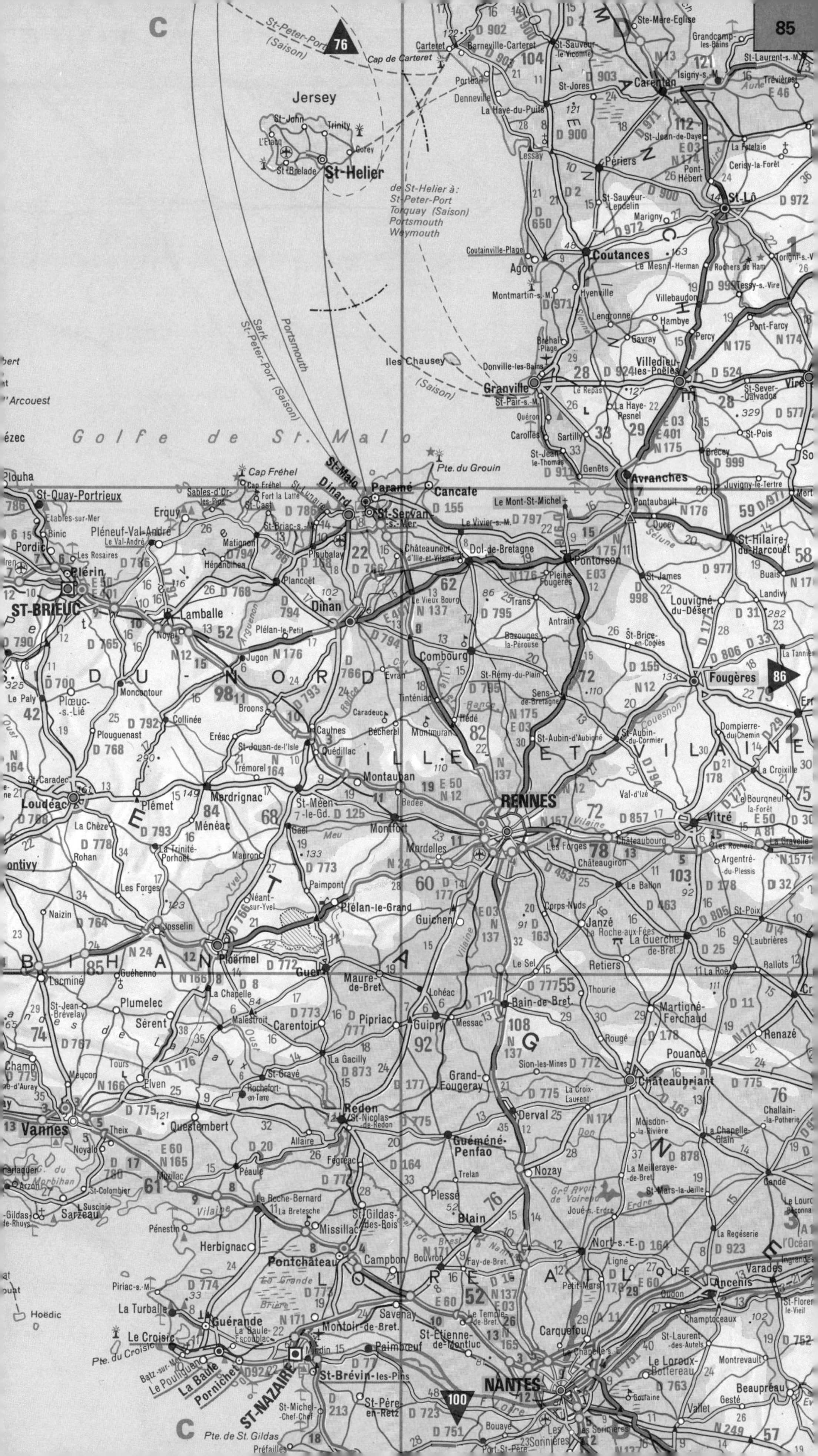

76
St-Peter-Port (Saison)
Cap de Carteret
Jersey
St-John
Trinity
L'Etacq
Gorey
St-Brelade
St-Helier
de St-Helier à:
St-Peter-Port
Torquay (Saison)
Portsmouth
Weymouth
Sark
St-Peter-Port (Saison)
Portsmouth
Iles Chausey
(Saison)
Golfe de St. Malo
Ste-Mère-Eglise
Grandcamp-les-Bains
St-Laurent-s.-M.
Trévières
Carteret
Barneville-Carteret
St-Sauveur-le-Vicomte
Portbail
Denneville
La Haye-du-Puits
St-Jores
Carentan
Isigny-s.-M.
St-Jean-de-Daye
La Fotelaie
Cerisy-la-Forêt
Lessay
Périers
Pont-Hébert
St-Lô
St-Sauveur-Lendelin
Marigny
Coutainville-Plage
Agon
Coutances
Le Mesnil-Herman
Rochers de Ham
Torigni-s.-Vire
Montmartin-s.-M.
Hyenville
Villebaudon
Tessy-s.-Vire
Lengronne
Hambye
Percy
Gavray
Pont-Farcy
Bréhal-Plage
Donville-les-Bains
Villedieu-les-Poêles
Granville
St-Pair-s.-M.
Le Repas
St-Sever-Calvados
Vire
Quéron
La Haye-Pesnel
Carolles
Sartilly
St-Pois
St-Jean-le-Thomas
Genêts
Brécey
Avranches
Juvigny-le-Tertre
Pte. du Grouin
Cap Fréhel
St-Malo
Dinard
Paramé
Cancale
Le Mont-St-Michel
Pontaubault
St-Servan-s.-Mer
Le Vivier-s.-M.
Quesy
Sélune
St-Hilaire-du-Harcouët
Plouha
St-Quay-Portrieux
Sables-d'Or-les-Pins
Fort la Latte
St-Cast
Erquy
Etables-sur-Mer
Binic
Pléneuf-Val-André
Le Val-André
St-Briac-s.-M.
Matignon
Pordic
Les Rosaires
Hénanbihen
Ploubalay
Châteauneuf-d'Ille-et-Vilaine
Dol-de-Bretagne
Pontorson
St James
Buais
Plérin
Plancoët
Pleine-Fougères
Landivy
ST-BRIEUC
Lamballe
Dinan
Le Vieux Bourg
Trans
Louvigné-du-Désert
Noyal
Plélan-le-Petit
Bazouges-la-Pérouse
Antrain
St-Brice-en-Coglès
Jugon
Evran
Combourg
St-Rémy-du-Plain
Fougères
86
Moncontour
Le Paly
Plœuc-s.-Lié
Broons
Tinténiac
Sens-de-Bretagne
Collinée
Plouguenast
Eréac
Caradeuc
Bécherel
Montmuran
Hédé
St-Aubin-d'Aubigné
St-Aubin-du-Cormier
Couesnon
Dompierre-du-Chemin
St-Jouan-de-l'Isle
Caulnes
Quédillac
Trémorel
Montauban
St-Caradec
Loudéac
Plémet
Merdrignac
St-Méen-le-Gd.
Bedée
RENNES
Val-d'Izé
La Croixille
Le Bourgneuf-la-Forêt
Vitré
La Chèze
Ménéac
Gaël
Meu
Montfort
Mordelles
Vilaine
Châteaubourg
Les Forges
Les Rochers
La Gravelle
Rohan
La Trinité-Porhoët
Mauron
Paimpont
Châteaugiron
Argentré-du-Plessis
Pontivy
Les Forges
Yvel
Néant-sur-Yvel
Plélan-le-Grand
Le Ballon
St-Poix
Naizin
Josselin
Guichen
Corps-Nuds
Janzé
La Roche-aux-Fées
La Guerche-de-Bret.
Laubrières
Ploërmel
Le Sel
Retiers
Ballots
Locminé
Guéhenno
Guer
Maure-de-Bret.
Lohéac
Thourie
La Roë
La Chapelle
Bain-de-Bret.
Martigné-Ferchaud
St-Jean-Brévelay
Plumelec
Malestroit
Carentoir
Pipriac
Guipry
Messac
Renazé
Sérent
Oust
Rougé
Pouancé
Tours
La Gacilly
Sion-les-Mines
Meucon
Elven
St-Gravé
Grand-Fougeray
Châteaubriant
Rochefort-en-Terre
Derval
La Croix-Laurent
Challain-la-Potherie
Vannes
Theix
Questembert
Redon
St-Nicolas-de-Redon
Noyalo
Allaire
Guémené-Penfao
Moisdon-la-Rivière
La Chapelle-Glain
Golfe du Morbihan
Péaule
Fégréac
Trelan
Nozay
La Meilleraye-de-Bret.
Arzon
St-Colombier
Muzillac
Candé
Sarzeau
St-Gildas-de-Rhuys
La Roche-Bernard
La Bretesche
Plessé
Grd Réservoir de Vioreau
St-Mars-la-Jaille
St-Gildas-des-Bois
Missillac
Blain
Joué-s.-Erdre
Erdre
Pénestin
Herbignac
La Regéserie
Pontchâteau
Campbon
Bouvron
Fay-de-Bret.
Nort-s.-E.
Ligné
Varades
Ancenis
Piriac-s.-M.
La Grande Brière
Petit-Mars
Oudon
Hoëdic
La Turballe
Savenay
Le Temple-de-Bret.
Guérande
Montoir-de-Bret.
Carquefou
Champtoceaux
St-Florent-le-Vieil
Le Croisic
Pte. du Croisic
La Baule-Escoublac
St-Etienne-de-Montluc
St-Laurent-des-Autels
Batz-sur-Mer
Le Pouliguen
La Baule
Pornichet
ST-NAZAIRE
Mindin
Paimbœuf
St-Brévin-les-Pins
La Chapelle-s.-E.
Le Loroux-Bottereau
Montrevault
NANTES
Loire
100
St-Michel-Chef-Chef
St-Père-en-Retz
Bouaye
Goulaine
Vallet
Geste
Beaupréau
Pte. de St. Gildas
Préfailles
Port-St-Père
Les Sorinières
C
D

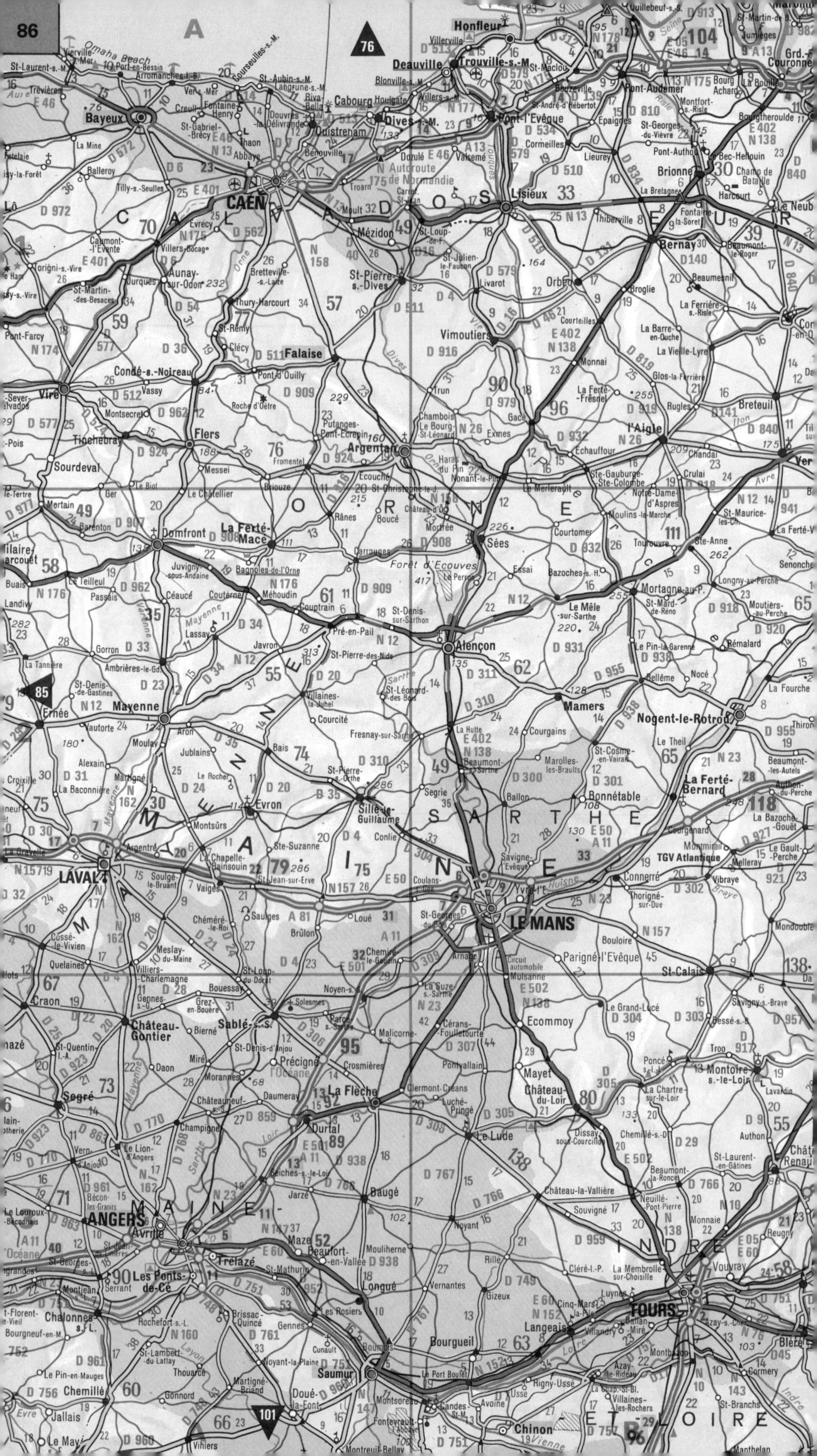

86
76
85
101
Honfleur
Deauville
Trouville-s.-M.
Cabourg
Houlgate
Dives-s.-M.
Ouistreham
Bayeux
Omaha Beach
Arromanches-l.-B.
Courseulles-s.-M.
CAEN
Lisieux
Pont-l'Évêque
Pont-Audemer
Brionne
Bernay
Autoroute de Normandie
C A L V A D O S
E U R
Mézidon
St-Pierre-s.-Dives
Livarot
Orbec
Vimoutiers
Falaise
Thury-Harcourt
Villers-Bocage
Aunay-sur-Odon
Vire
Condé-s.-Noireau
Flers
Tinchebray
Sourdeval
Mortain
Domfront
La Ferté-Macé
Argentan
Gacé
l'Aigle
Breteuil
O R N E
Sées
Alençon
Mortagne-au-P.
Bellême
Mamers
Nogent-le-Rotrou
Forêt d'Écouves
Pré-en-Pail
Bagnoles-de-l'Orne
Mayenne
Ernée
Laval
Évron
Sillé-le-Guillaume
M A Y E N N E
S A R T H E
LE MANS
La Ferté-Bernard
Connerré
St-Calais
Ecommoy
Château-du-Loir
Sablé-s.-S.
Château-Gontier
Craon
Segré
La Flèche
Le Lude
Durtal
Baugé
ANGERS
Les Ponts-de-Cé
Trélazé
M A I N E - E T - L O I R E
Saumur
Chinon
Bourgueil
Langeais
TOURS
I N D R E - E T - L O I R E
Montoire-s.-le-Loir
Chemillé
Doué-la-Font.
Fontevraud-l'Abbaye

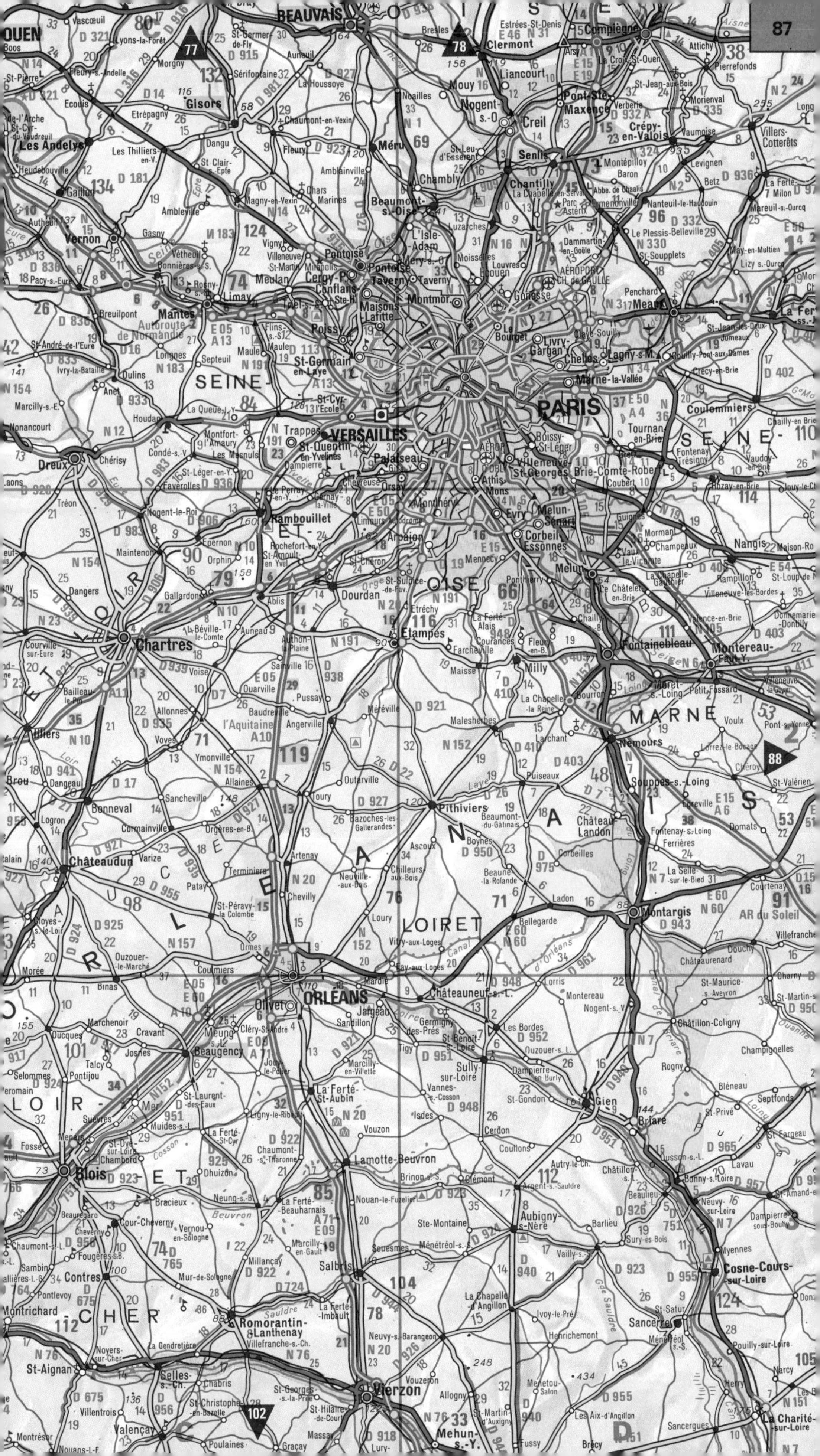

87
BEAUVAIS
Clermont
Compiègne
Gisors
Les Andelys
Vernon
Mantes
Creil
Senlis
Chantilly
Crépy-en-Valois
Villers-Cotterêts
Méru
Beaumont-s.-Oise
L'Isle-Adam
Pontoise
Cergy-P.
Meulan
Limay
Poissy
St-Germain-en-Laye
Maisons-Laffitte
Montmor.
Gonesse
Le Bourget
Livry-Gargan
Chelles
Lagny-s-M.
Meaux
Marne-la-Vallée
PARIS
Coulommiers
VERSAILLES
Trappes
St-Quentin-en-Yvelines
Palaiseau
Orsay
Villeneuve-St-Georges
Brie-Comte-Robert
Rambouillet
Montlhéry
Arpajon
Evry
Corbeil-Essonnes
Melun
Nangis
Dreux
Chartres
Dourdan
Etampes
Milly
Fontainebleau
Montereau-Faut-Y.
Nemours
Pithiviers
Châteaudun
Bonneval
Montargis
ORLÉANS
Olivet
Beaugency
Blois
Châteauneuf-s.-L.
Sully-sur-Loire
Gien
Briare
La Ferté-St-Aubin
Lamotte-Beuvron
Romorantin-Lanthenay
Salbris
Vierzon
Aubigny-s.-Nère
Cosne-Cours-sur-Loire
Sancerre
La Charité-sur-Loire
St-Aignan
SEINE-
ET-
OISE
SEINE-
MARNE
LOIRET
LOIR-
ET-
CHER

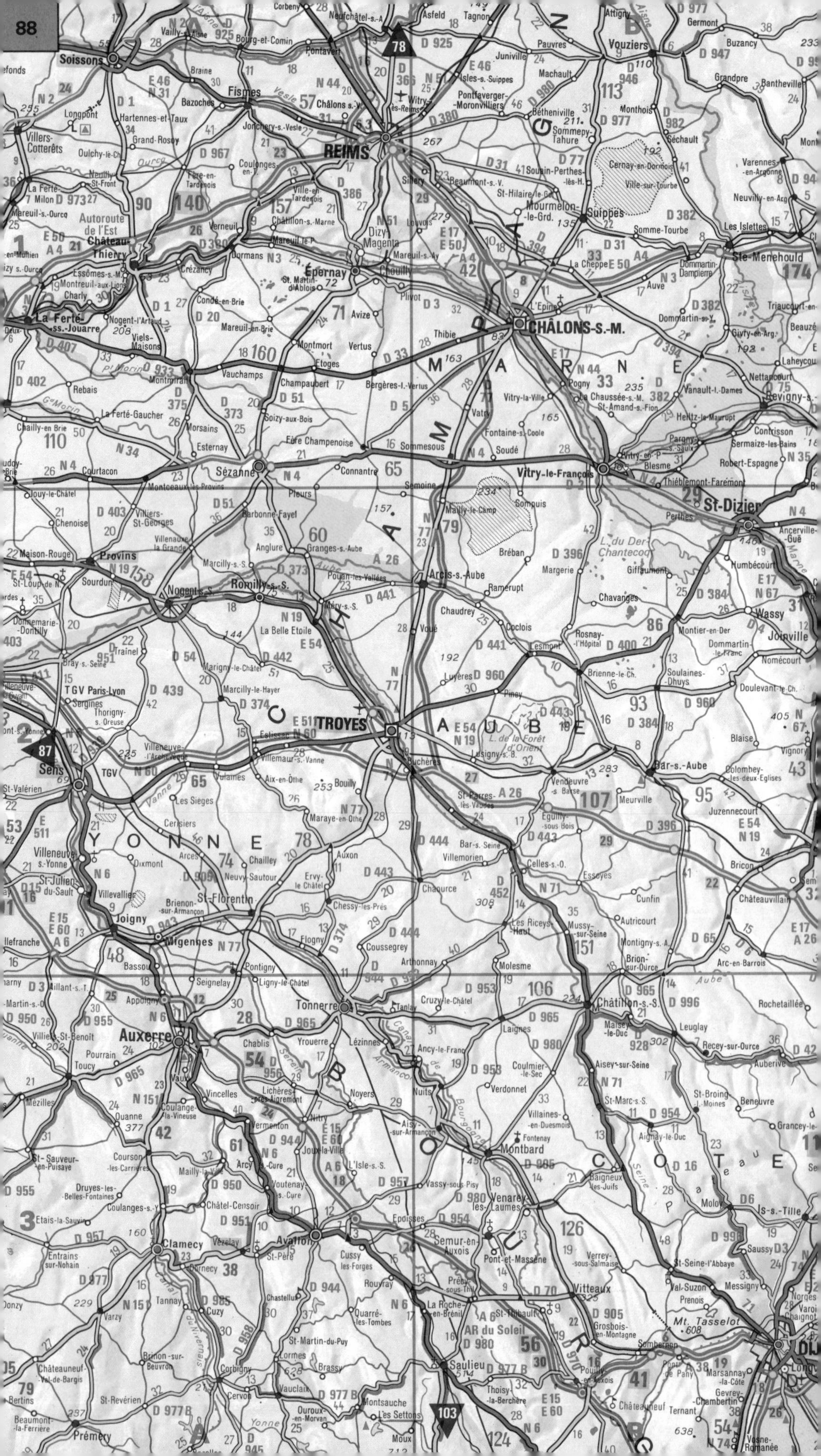
Soissons
Vailly-s.-Aisne
Bourg-et-Comin
Corbeny
Neufchâtel-s.-A.
Asfeld
Tagnon
Attigny
Vouziers
Germont
Buzancy
Pontavert
Pauvres
Juniville
Grandpre
Braine
Fismes
Bazoches
Isles-s.-Suippes
Machault
Monthois
Châlons-s.-V.
Witry-lès-Reims
Pontfaverger-Moronvilliers
Bétheniville
Séchault
Longpont
Hartennes-et-Taux
Jonchery-s.-Vesle
Sommepy-Tahure
Villers-Cotterêts
Grand-Rozoy
REIMS
Oulchy-le-Ch.
Coulonges-en-T.
Cernay-en-Dormois
Ville-sur-Tourbe
Varennes-en-Argonne
Neuilly-St-Front
Fère-en-Tardenois
Sillery
Beaumont-s.-V.
Souain-Perthes-lès-H.
La Ferté-Milon
Ville-en-Tardenois
St-Hilaire-le-G.
Mourmelon-le-Grd.
Suippes
Neuvilly-en-Arg.
Mareuil-s.-Ourcq
Autoroute de l'Est
Châtillon-s.-Marne
Louvois
Dizy-Magenta
Somme-Tourbe
Les Islettes
Château-Thierry
Verneuil
Dormans
Mareuil-le-P.
Mareuil-s.-Ay
La Cheppe
Ste-Menehould
Essômes-s.-M.
Crézancy
Épernay
Chouilly
Dommartin-Dampierre
Montreuil-aux-Lions
St-Martin-d'Ablois
Auve
Charly
Condé-en-Brie
Avize
Plivot
L'Épine
Triaucourt-en-
La Ferté-ss.-Jouarre
Nogent-l'Artaud
Mareuil-en-Brie
CHÂLONS-S.-M.
Dommartin-s.-Y.
Beauzé
Viels-Maisons
Montmort
Vertus
Thibie
Givry-en-Arg.
Étoges
Laheycourt
Montmirail
Vauchamps
Champaubert
Bergères-l.-Vertus
MARNE
Pogny
La Chaussée-s.-M.
St-Amand-s.-Fion
Vanault-l.-Dames
Nettancourt
Revigny-s.-
Rebais
Soizy-aux-Bois
Vitry-la-Ville
Vatry
La Ferté-Gaucher
Fère Champenoise
Fontaine-s.-Coole
Heiltz-le-Maurupt
Contrisson
Chailly-en Brie
Morsains
Sommesous
Soudé
Pargny-s.-Saulx
Sermaize-les-Bains
Esternay
Vitry-le-François
Vitry-en-P.
Blesme
Robert-Espagne
Courtacon
Sézanne
Connantre
Thiéblemont-Farémont
Montceaux-les-Provins
Pleurs
Semoine
Jouy-le-Châtel
Barbonne-Fayel
Mailly-le-Camp
Sompuis
Perthes
St-Dizier
Chenoise
Villiers-St-Georges
Ancerville-Gué
Villenauxe-la-Grande
Anglure
Granges-s.-Aube
L. du Der-Chantecoq
Maison-Rouge
Provins
Bréban
Margerie
Humbécourt
St-Loup-de-N.
Sourdun
Marcilly-s.-S.
Arcis-s.-Aube
Giffaumont
Nogent-s.-S.
Romilly-s.-S.
Pouan-les-Vallées
Ramerupt
Chavanges
Méry-s.-S.
Wassy
Donnemarie-Dontilly
Chaudrey
Coclois
Montier-en-Der
Joinville
La Belle Etoile
Voué
Lesmont
Rosnay-l'Hôpital
Dommartin-le-Franc
Traînel
Bray-s.-Seine
Marigny-le-Châtel
Brienne-le-Ch.
Soulaines-Dhuys
Nomécourt
Luyères
Marcilly-le-Hayer
Piney
Doulevant-le-Ch.
TGV Paris-Lyon
Sergines
Thorigny-s.-Oreuse
TROYES
AUBE
L. de la Forêt d'Orient
Lusigny-s.-B.
Blaise
Estissac
Villeneuve-l'Archevêque
Villemaur-s.-Vanne
Buchères
Bar-s.-Aube
Vignory
Sens
Vulaines
Aix-en-Othe
Vendeuvre-s.-Barse
Colombey-les-deux-Eglises
St-Valérien
Bouilly
Les Sieges
St-Parres-lès-Vaudes
Meurville
Juzennecourt
Maraye-en-Othe
Eguilly-sous-Bois
Cerisiers
YONNE
Villeneuve-s.-Yonne
Dixmont
Arces
Chailley
Auxon
Bar-s.-Seine
Villemorien
Celles-s.-O.
Bricon
St-Julien-du-Sault
Neuvy-Sautour
Ervy-le-Châtel
Chaource
Essoyes
Villevallier
Brienon-sur-Armançon
St-Florentin
Chessy-les-Prés
Cunfin
Châteauvillain
Joigny
Les Riceys-Haut
Mussy-sur-Seine
Autricourt
Migennes
Flogny
Coussegrey
Montigny-s.-A.
Arc-en-Barrois
Bassou
Pontigny
Arthonnay
Molesme
Brion-sur-Ource
Seignelay
Ligny-le-Châtel
Cruzy-le-Châtel
Appoigny
Tonnerre
Tanlay
Laignes
Châtillon-s.-S.
Rochetaillée
Villiers-St-Benoît
Auxerre
Chablis
Yrouerre
Lézinnes
Maisey-le-Duc
Leuglay
Recey-sur-Ource
Pourrain
Toucy
Ancy-le-Franc
Coulmier-le-Sec
Aisey-sur-Seine
Auberive
Vaux
Vincelles
Lichères-près-Aigremont
Noyers
Nuits
Verdonnet
Mézilles
Coulange-la-Vineuse
St-Marc-s.-S.
St-Broing-l.-Moines
Beneuvre
Ouanne
Vermenton
Nitry
Aisy-sur-Armançon
Villaines-en-Duesmois
Fontenay
Aignay-le-Duc
Grancey-le-
St-Sauveur-en-Puisaye
Courson-les-Carrières
Arcy-s.-Cure
Joux-la-Ville
Montbard
CÔTE
Mailly-la-Ville
Voutenay-s.-Cure
L'Isle-s.-S.
Vassy-sous-Pisy
Baigneux-les-Juifs
Druyes-les-Belles-Fontaines
Châtel-Censoir
Venarey-les-Laumes
Molov
Is-s.-Tille
Coulanges-s.-Y.
Epoisses
Etais-la-Sauvin
Avallon
Semur-en-Auxois
Pont-et-Massène
Verrey-sous-Salmaise
Saussy
Entrains-sur-Nohain
Clamecy
Vézelay
St-Père
Cussy-les-Forges
St-Seine-l'Abbaye
Cornecy
Rouvray
Précy-sous-Thil
Vitteaux
Val-Suzon
Messigny
Tannay
Chastellux
Quarré-les-Tombes
La Roche-en-Brénil
St-Thibault
Prenois
Cuzy
Grosbois-en-Montagne
Mt. Tasselot
Varzy
St-Martin-du-Puy
AR du Soleil
Sombernon
Pont-de Pany
Brinon-sur-Beuvron
Lormes
Brassy
Saulieu
Pouilly-en-Auxois
Marsannay-la-Côte
Châteauneuf-Val-de-Bargis
Corbigny
Vauclaix
Thoisy-la-Berchère
Châteauneuf
Gevrey-Chambertin
Bertins
St-Révérien
Cervon
Montsauche
Les Settons
Ternant
Beaumont-la-Ferrière
Prémery
Ouroux-en-Morvan
Moux
Vosne-Romanée

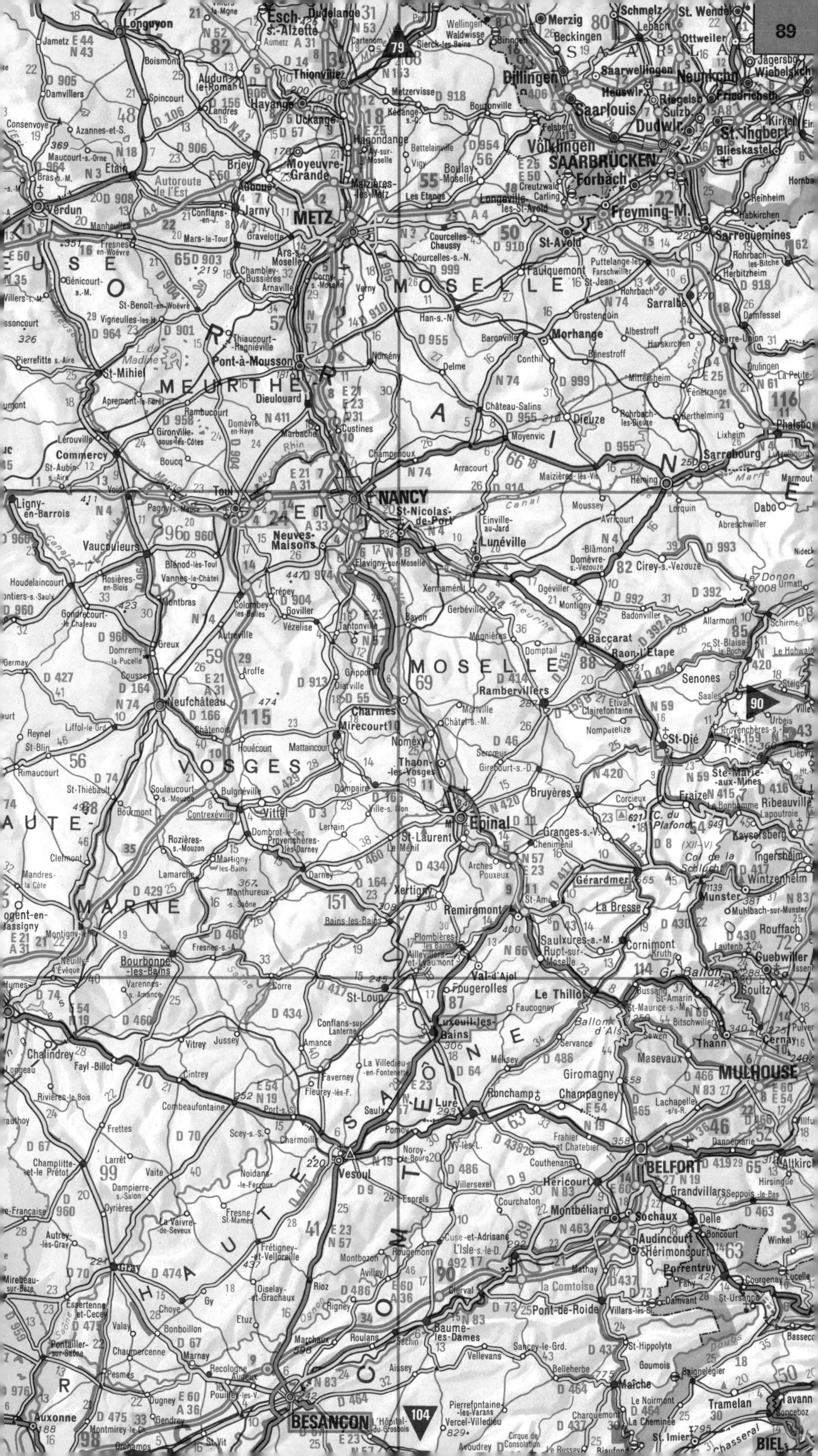

Longuyon
Esch-s.-Alzette
Dudelange
Merzig
Beckingen
Schmelz
St. Wendel
Lebach
Ottweiler
Dillingen
Saarlouis
Saarwellingen
Neunkchn
Friedrichsth.
Dudwlr.
St. Ingbert
Blieskastel
Völklingen
SAARBRÜCKEN
Forbach
Freyming-M.
Sarreguemines
Thionville
Hayange
Uckange
Hagondange
Moyeuvre-Grande
Maizières-lès-Metz
Briey
Jarny
METZ
Boulay-Moselle
Longeville-lès-St-Avold
St-Avold
Faulquemont
Sarralbe
Verdun
Etain
Damvillers
Spincourt
Audun-le-Roman
Mars-la-Tour
Gravelotte
Ars-s.-Moselle
Conflans-en-J.
Autoroute de l'Est
MOSELLE
Morhange
Château-Salins
Dieuze
Sarrebourg
Phalsbourg
St-Mihiel
Commercy
Pont-à-Mousson
Dieulouard
Thiaucourt-Regniéville
Toul
NANCY
St-Nicolas-de-Port
Lunéville
Baccarat
Raon-l'Etape
Cirey-s.-Vezouze
Blâmont
Ligny-en-Barrois
Vaucouleurs
Neuves-Maisons
Gondrecourt-le Château
Colombey-les-Belles
Vézelise
Bayon
Rambervillers
Senones
St-Dié
Neufchâteau
Châtenois
Mirecourt
Charmes
Thaon-les-Vosges
Epinal
Bruyères
Gérardmer
Ste-Marie-aux-Mines
Ribeauvillé
Kaysersberg
Munster
Wintzenheim
Vittel
Contrexéville
Bulgnéville
Remiremont
Plombières-les-Bains
La Bresse
Cornimont
Le Thillot
Guebwiller
Thann
Cernay
MULHOUSE
VOSGES
MEURTHE-ET-MOSELLE
LORRAINE
MEUSE
HAUTE-MARNE
HAUTE-SAÔNE
FRANCHE-COMTÉ
Bourbonne-les-Bains
Luxeuil-les-Bains
St-Loup
Fougerolles
Val-d'Ajol
Lure
Ronchamp
Champagney
Giromagny
Masevaux
BELFORT
Héricourt
Montbéliard
Sochaux
Audincourt
Delle
Porrentruy
Altkirch
Chalindrey
Fayl-Billot
Jussey
Combeaufontaine
Port-s.-S.
Vesoul
Villersexel
Champlitte-et-le Prétot
Gray
Rioz
Baume-les-Dames
Clerval
Pont-de-Roide
L'Isle-s.-le-D.
St-Hippolyte
Maîche
Saignelégier
Tramelan
BESANÇON
Marnay
Pesmes
Auxonne
Vercel-Villedieu
St. Imier
BIEL

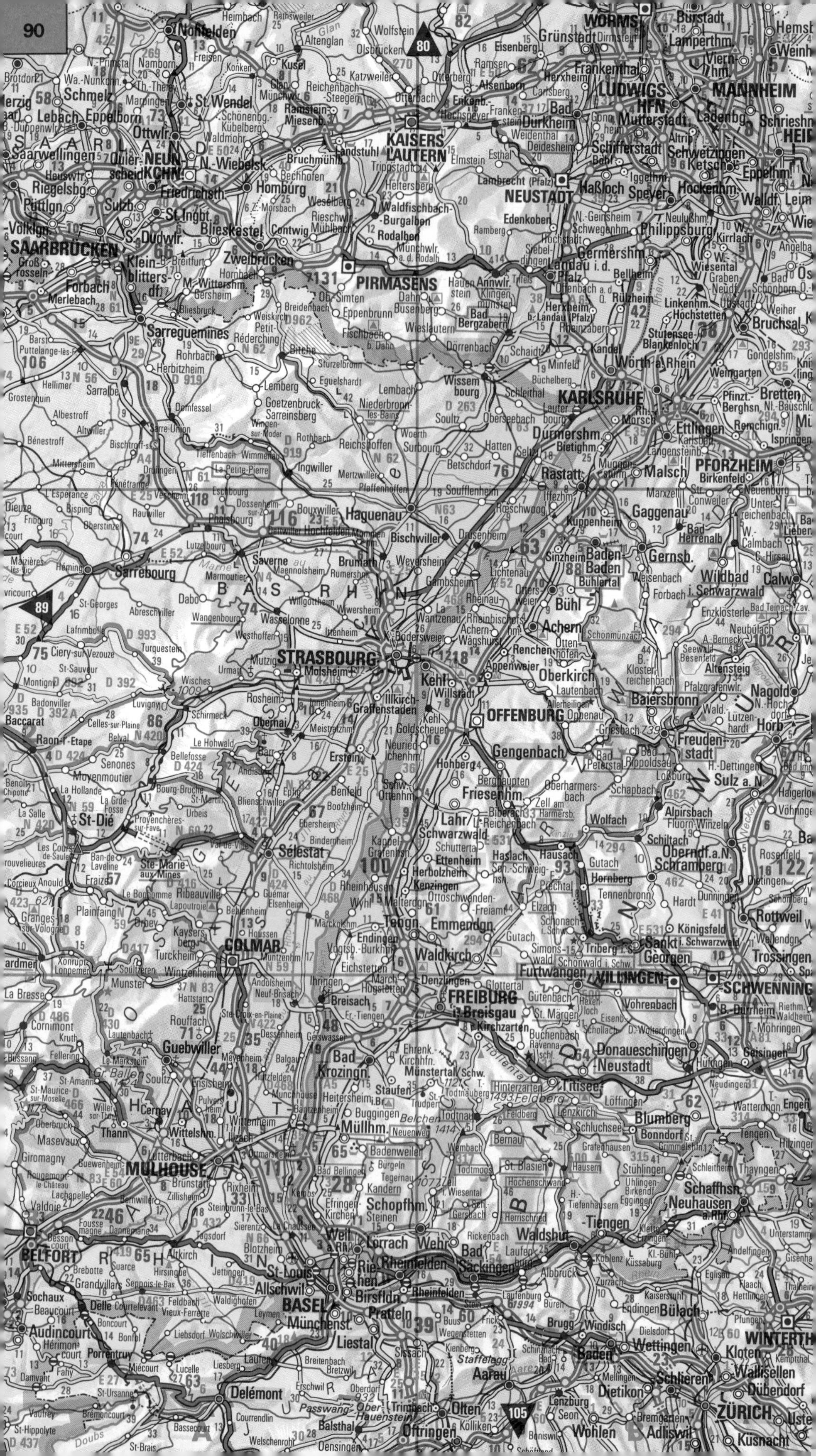
Worms
Grünstadt
Frankenthal
Ludwigshafen
Mannheim
Bad Dürkheim
Mutterstadt
Schifferstadt
Schwetzingen
Speyer
Hockenhm.
Kaiserslautern
Neustadt
Haßloch
Philippsburg
Germershm.
Landau i. d. Pfalz
Pirmasens
Zweibrücken
Homburg
Saarbrücken
St. Wendel
Neunkchn.
St. Ingbt.
Blieskastel
Forbach
Merlebach
Sarreguemines
Bitche
Bruchsal
Karlsruhe
Ettlingen
Pforzheim
Rastatt
Gaggenau
Baden-Baden
Bühl
Achern
Wörth a. Rhein
Wissembourg
Haguenau
Saverne
Sarrebourg
Phalsbourg
Strasbourg
Molsheim
Kehl
Offenburg
Oberkirch
Gengenbach
Freudenstadt
Nagold
Horb
Calw
Wildbad i. Schwarzwald
Lahr/Schwarzwald
Sélestat
Colmar
St-Dié
Ste-Marie-aux-Mines
Emmendgn.
Waldkirch
Freiburg i. Breisgau
Breisach
Guebwiller
Mulhouse
Belfort
Montbéliard
Donaueschingen
Villingen
Schwenningen
Rottweil
Titisee-Neustadt
Furtwangen
Triberg
Sankt Georgen
Müllhm.
Lörrach
Weil a. Rhein
Rheinfelden
Säckingen
Waldshut-Tiengen
Schaffhsn.
Neuhausen a. Rhf.
Basel
Liestal
Delémont
Porrentruy
Olten
Aarau
Baden
Wettingen
Zürich
Winterthur
Kloten
Dietikon
Schlieren
Bülach
BAS-RHIN
SAARLAND
89
80
105

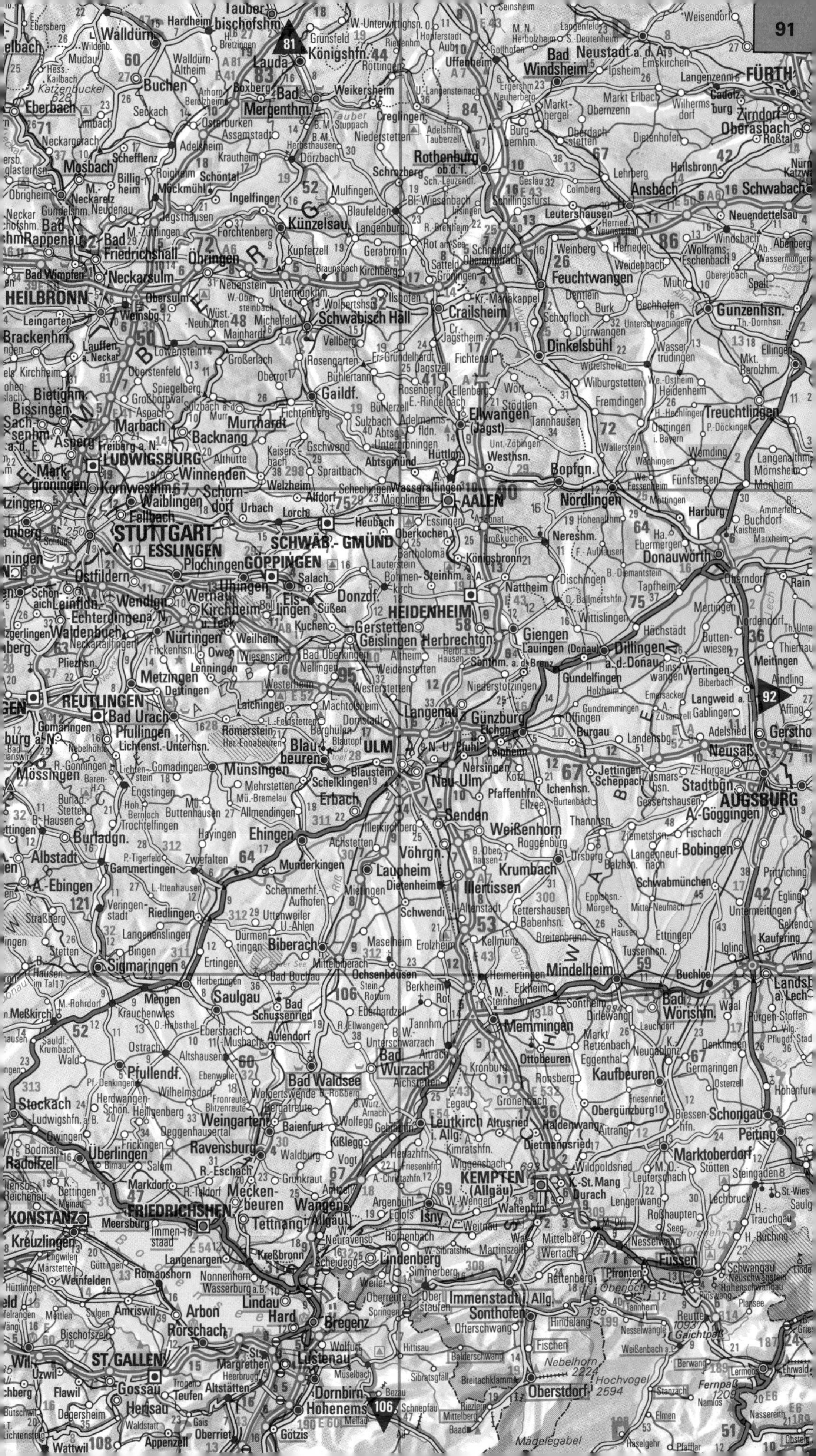
Walldürn
Hardheim
Tauberbischofshm.
Lauda
Königshfn.
Grünsfeld
Uffenheim
Aub
Bad Windsheim
Neustadt a. d. A.
Weisendorf
Fürth
Buchen
Eberbach
Bad Mergenthm.
Weikersheim
Creglingen
Rothenburg ob d. T.
Markt Erlbach
Cadolzburg
Zirndorf
Oberasbach
Roßtal
Mosbach
Schefflenz
Adelsheim
Osterburken
Schöntal
Möckmühl
Dörzbach
Schrozberg
Schillingsfürst
Ansbach
Heilsbronn
Schwabach
Bad Rappenau
Bad Friedrichshall
Neckarsulm
Öhringen
Künzelsau
Langenburg
Kirchberg
Leutershausen
Neuendettelsau
Windsbach
Wolframs-Eschenbach
Abenberg
Bad Wimpfen
Heilbronn
Weinsbg.
Neuenstein
Schwäbisch Hall
Crailsheim
Feuchtwangen
Dinkelsbühl
Gunzenhsn.
Spalt
Brackenhm.
Lauffen a. Neckar
Löwenstein
Murrhardt
Gaildf.
Ellwangen (Jagst)
Wassertrüdingen
Ellingen
Bietighm.-Bissingen
Marbach
Backnang
Treuchtlingen
Oettingen i. Bayern
Ludwigsburg
Winnenden
Schorndorf
Welzheim
Aalen
Bopfgn.
Nördlingen
Wemding
Monheim
Kornwesthm.
Waiblingen
Fellbach
Stuttgart
Esslingen
Plochingen
Göppingen
Schwäb.-Gmünd
Lorch
Heubach
Oberkochen
Neresheim
Harburg
Donauwörth
Ostfildern
Uhingen
Eislingen
Süßen
Donzdf.
Heidenheim
Nattheim
Dischingen
Rain
Leinfldn.-Echterdingen
Wendlgn.
Kirchheim u. Teck
Nürtingen
Waldenbuch
Gerstetten
Geislingen
Herbrechtgn.
Giengen
Lauingen (Donau)
Dillingen a. d. Donau
Höchstädt
Metzingen
Reutlingen
Bad Urach
Pfullingen
Langenau
Günzburg
Leipheim
Wertingen
Meitingen
Gersthofen
Neusäß
Augsburg
Blaubeuren
Ulm
Neu-Ulm
Senden
Münsingen
Mössingen
Ehingen
Erbach
Laupheim
Weißenhorn
Krumbach
Jettingen-Scheppach
Burgau
Bobingen
Schwabmünchen
Burladgn.
Albstadt
A.-Ebingen
Gammertingen
Riedlingen
Munderkingen
Illertissen
Biberach
Babenhsn.
Mindelheim
Buchloe
Landsberg a. Lech
Sigmaringen
Mengen
Saulgau
Bad Buchau
Ochsenhausen
Memmingen
Bad Wörishfn.
Meßkirch
Pfullendf.
Bad Schussenried
Aulendorf
Bad Wurzach
Ottobeuren
Kaufbeuren
Bad Waldsee
Stockach
Weingarten
Ravensburg
Leutkirch i. Allg.
Obergünzburg
Schongau
Peiting
Überlingen
Radolfzell
Marktoberdorf
Konstanz
Friedrichshfn.
Meckenbeuren
Tettnang
Wangen i. Allgäu
Isny
Kempten (Allgäu)
Durach
Kreuzlingen
Meersburg
Kreßbronn
Lindenberg
Füssen
Schwangau
Lindau
Bregenz
Immenstadt i. Allg.
Sonthofen
Pfronten
Reutte
Arbon
Rorschach
St. Gallen
Gossau
Herisau
Lustenau
Dornbirn
Hohenems
Oberstdorf
Nebelhorn 2224
Hochvogel 2594
Fernpaß 1209
Gaichtpaß 1093
Mädelegabel
Götzis
Appenzell
Wattwil
Oberriet

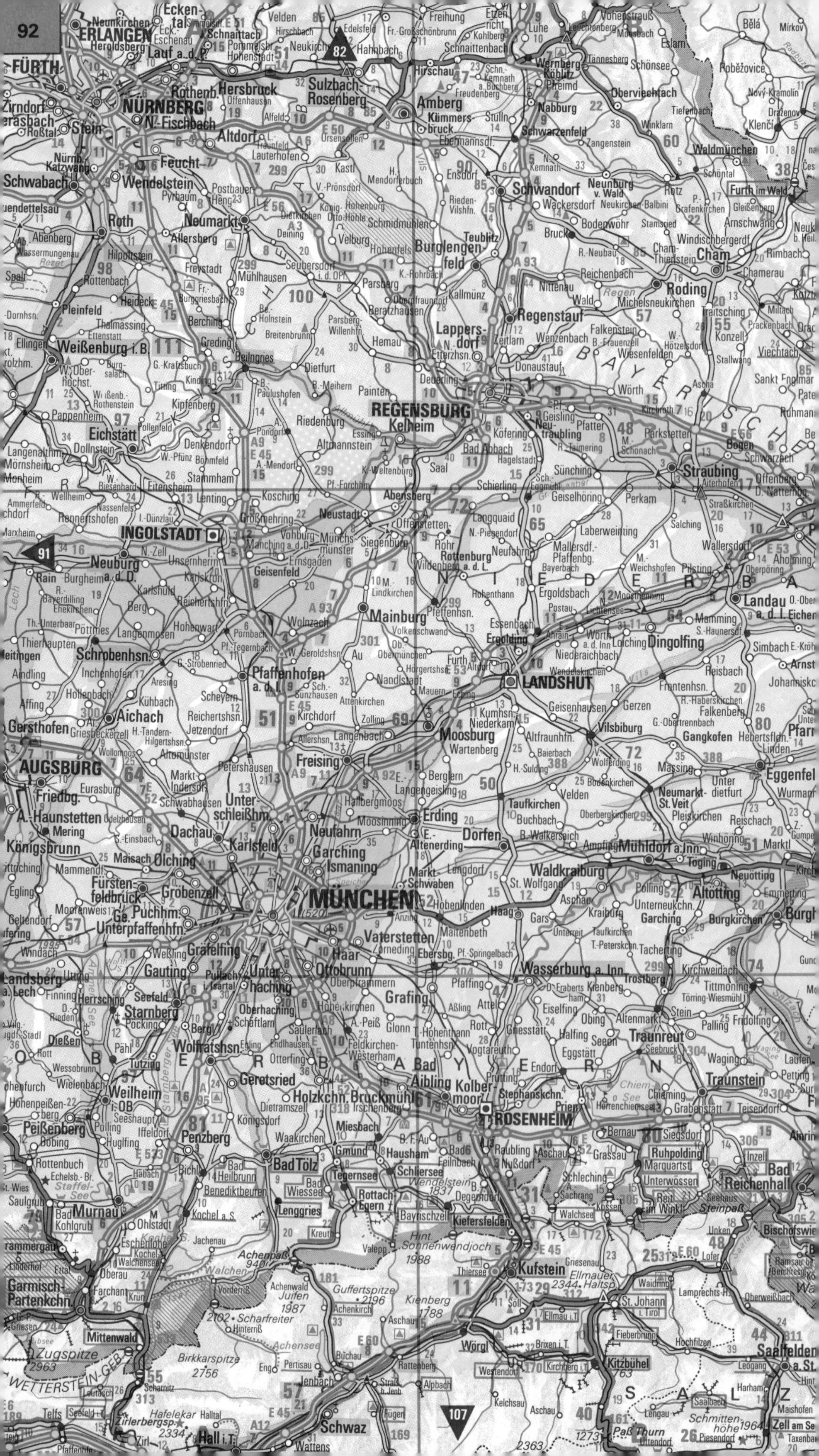

ERLANGEN
FÜRTH
NÜRNBERG
Zirndorf
Stein
Schwabach
Roth
Feucht
Wendelstein
Altdorf
Lauf a. d. P.
Hersbruck
Sulzbach-Rosenberg
Amberg
Hirschau
Nabburg
Schwarzenfeld
Schwandorf
Neunburg v. Wald
Waldmünchen
Furth im Wald
Cham
Roding
Neumarkt
Burglengenfeld
Teublitz
Regenstauf
Lappersdorf
Beilngries
Dietfurt
Hemau
Parsberg
Greding
Weißenburg i. B.
Eichstätt
Kipfenberg
Riedenburg
Kelheim
REGENSBURG
Neutraubling
Wörth
Straubing
Bogen
Viechtach
INGOLSTADT
Neuburg a. d. D.
Neustadt
Abensberg
Mainburg
Rottenburg
Landau a. d. I.
Dingolfing
Ergolding
LANDSHUT
Vilsbiburg
Pfaffenhofen a. d. I.
Schrobenhausen
Aichach
Gersthofen
AUGSBURG
Friedberg.
Königsbrunn
Freising
Moosburg
Erding
Dorfen
Neumarkt-St. Veit
Eggenfelden
Mühldorf a. Inn
Waldkraiburg
Altötting
Burghausen
Dachau
Unterschleißheim
Karlsfeld
Neufahrn
Garching
Ismaning
Olching
Fürstenfeldbruck
Gröbenzell
Germering
Puchheim
Unterpfaffenhofen
MÜNCHEN
Haar
Vaterstetten
Ottobrunn
Unterhaching
Gräfelfing
Gauting
Pullach i. Isartal
Starnberg
Landsberg a. Lech
Grafing
Ebersberg
Wasserburg a. Inn
Trostberg
Traunreut
Traunstein
Wolfratshausen
Geretsried
Penzberg
Weilheim i. OB
Peißenberg
Holzkirchen
Bruckmühl
Bad Aibling
Kolbermoor
ROSENHEIM
Prien
Bad Tölz
Miesbach
Tegernsee
Schliersee
Lenggries
Murnau
Garmisch-Partenkirchen
Mittenwald
Kiefersfelden
Kufstein
Wörgl
Kitzbühel
St. Johann i. Tirol
Saalfelden a. St.
Bad Reichenhall
Ruhpolding
Reit im Winkl
Jenbach
Schwaz
Hall i. T.
Zugspitze 2963
Achensee
Chiemsee
Ammersee
Starnberger See
Altmühl
Regen
B A Y E R I S C H E
N I E D E R B A Y E R N
O B E R B A Y E R N
82
91
107

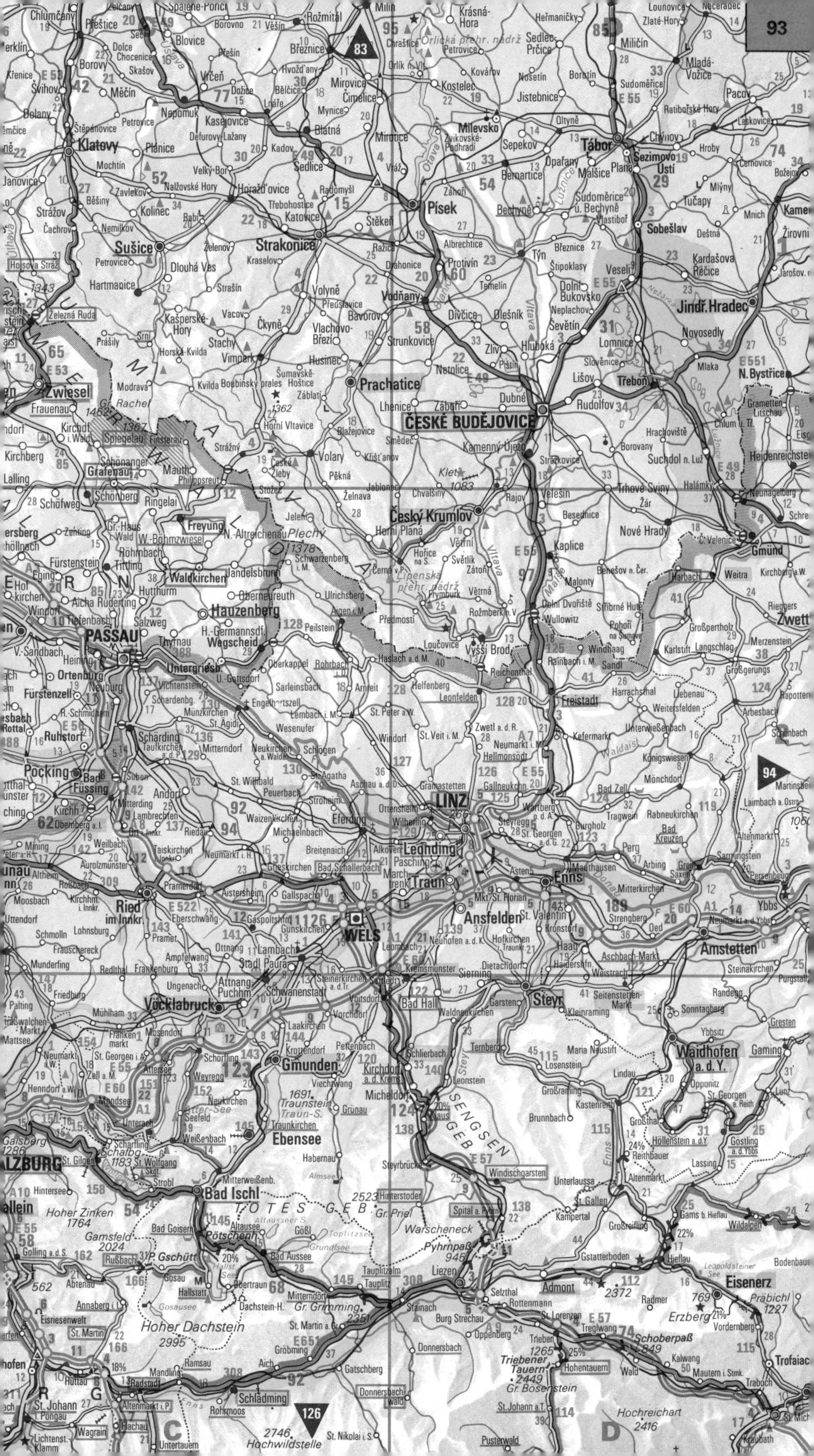

Chlumčany
Přeštice
Blovice
Rožmitál
Milín
Krásná-Hora
Heřmaničky
Lounovice
Neveklov
Miličín
Mladá-Vožice
83
Březnice
Chraštice
Orlická přehr. nádrž
Petrovice
Sedlec-Prčice
Borovy
Dolce
Chocenice
Skašov
Přešín
Vrčeň
Hvožďany
Mirovice
Čimelice
Kovářov
Nosetín
Borotín
Kostelec
Jistebnice
Sudoměřice
Pacov
Švihov
Měčín
Dožice
Nepomuk
Kasejovice
Lnáře
Bělčice
Mynice
Milevsko
Oltyně
Ratibořské Hory
Leskovice
Dolany
Štěpánovice
Petrovice
Defurovy Lažany
Blatná
Mirotice
Zvíkovské Podhradí
Sepekov
Tábor
Chýnov
Klatovy
Plánice
Kadov
Sedlice
Vráž
Bernartice
Opařany
Malšice
Sezimovo Ústí
Planá
Hroby
Černovice
Božejov
Mochtín
Velký Bor
Horažďovice
Radomyšl
Zahoří
Mlýny
Janovice
Nalžovské Hory
Zavlekov
Třebohostice
Katovice
Písek
Sudoměřice u. Bechyně
Vlastiboř
Tučapy
Strážov
Běšiny
Kolinec
Rabí
Strakonice
Štěkeň
Bechyně
Sobešlav
Mnich
Čachrov
Nemilkov
Albrechtice
Březnice
Deštná
Žirovnice
Sušice
Želenov
Ražice
Protivín
Týn
Kardašova Řečice
Petrovice
Kraselov
Drahonice
Štipoklasy
Jarošov
Hojsova Stráž
Dlouhá Ves
Volyně
Temelín
Veselí
Hartmanice
Strašín
Předslavice
Vodňany
Dolní Bukovsko
Jindř. Hradec
Železná Ruda
Kašperské-Hory
Vacov
Bavorov
Dívčice
Olešník
Neplachov
Ševětín
Čkyně
Vlachovo-Březí
Strunkovice
Lomnice
Novosedly
Prášily
Srní
Stachy
Hluboká
Zliv
Horská-Kvilda
Vimperk
Husinec
Netolice
Slověnice
Lišov
Mlaka
N. Bystřice
Zwiesel
Modrava
Kvilda
Boubínský prales
Šumavské-Hoštice
Záblatí
Prachatice
Pišín
Třeboň
Frauenau
Rachel
1362
Lhenice
Zábořı
Dubné
Rudolfov
Gramatten
Litschau
Kirchdf. i. Wald
Spiegelau
Finsterau
Horní Vltavice
Blažejovice
ČESKÉ BUDĚJOVICE
Hrachoviště
Chlum u. Tř.
Smědeč
Kamenný Újezd
Borovany
Heidenreichstein
Kirchberg
Schönanger
Mauth
Strážný
Volary
Křišťanov
Klet
1083
Strážkovice
Suchdol n. Luž.
Lalling
Grafenau
Philippsreut
České Žleby
Pěkná
Jablonec
Chvalšiny
Rájov
Velešín
Trhové Sviny
Halámky
Schönberg
Ringelai
Stožec
Želnava
Český Krumlov
Besednice
Žár
Neunagelberg
Schöfweg
Freyung
Jelení
Horní Planá
Vyšší Brod
Nové Hrady
Č. Velenice
Gmünd
N.-Altreichenau
Plechý
1378
Hořice na Š.
Větřní
Kaplice
Gr.-Haus Wald
W.-Böhmzwiesel
Röhrnbach
Tittling
Schwarzenberg i. M.
Černá v. P.
Světlík
Zátoň
Fürstenstein
Waldkirchen
Jandelsbrunn
Lipenská přehr. nádrž
Frymburk
Malonty
Benešov n. Čer.
Harbach
Weitra
Kirchberg a. W.
Eging
Hutthurm
Oberneureuth
Ulrichsberg
Větrná
Dolní Dvořiště
Hofkirchen
Aicha
Ruderting
Hauzenberg
Aigen i. M.
Předmostí
Rožmberk n. V.
Stříbrné Hutě
Rieggers
Zwettl
Windorf
Tiefenbach
Salzweg
Peilstein
Wullowitz
Pohoří na Šumavě
Großpertholz
PASSAU
H.-Germannsdf.
Wegscheid
Loučovice
Windhaag
Karlstift
Langschlag
Merzenstein
V.-Sandbach
Thyrnau
Oberkappel
Rohrbach
Haslach a. d. M.
Rainbach i. M.
Sandl
Heining
Ortenburg
Neuburg
Untergriesb.
U.-Gottsdorf
Sarleinsbach
Arnreit
Helfenberg
Reichenthal
Großgerungs
Fürstenzell
Vichtenstein
Engelhartszell
Lembach i. M.
Leonfelden
Freistadt
Harrachsthal
Liebenau
Rapottenstein
R.-Schmidham
Schardenbg.
Münzkirchen
St. Peter a. W.
Weitersfelden
Arbesbach
Rottal
Ruhstorf
Schärding
St. Ägidi
Wesenufer
Zwettl a. d. R.
Unterweißenbach
Taufkirchen a. d. P.
Mitterndorf
Neukirchen a. Walde
Schlögen
Windorf
St. Veit i. M.
Neumarkt i. M.
Kefermarkt
Schönbach
Pocking
Bad Füssing
Hellmonsödt
Waldaist
Königswiesen
Sobon
St. Willibald
St. Agatha
Aschau a. d. D.
Mönchdorf
94
Andorf
Peuerbach
Gramastetten
Gallneukchn.
Bad Zell
Martinsberg
Mitterding
Lambrechten
Stroheim
Ottensheim
LINZ
Wartberg o. d. A.
Tragwein
Rabneukirchen
Laimbach a. Ostrong
Obernberg a. I.
Ort i. Innkr.
Riedau
Waizenkirchen
Eferding
Wilhering
Steyregg
St. Georgen a. d. G.
Burgholz
Bad Kreuzen
Weilbach
Michaelnbach
Altenmarkt
Mining
Taiskirchen
Neumarkt i. H.
Breitenaich
Alkoven
Leonding
Perg
Arbing
Grein
Sarmingstein
Aurolzmünster
Grieskirchen
Bad Schallerbach
Pasching
Mauthausen
Saxen
Persenbeug
Altheim
Roßbach
Ried im Innkr.
Pramerdorf
Aistersheim
Gallspach
Marchtrenk
Traun
Asten
Enns
Mitterkirchen
Moosbach
Kirchhm. i. Innkr.
Gaspoltshfn.
Gunskirchen
WELS
Mkt. St. Florian
Ansfelden
St. Valentin
Strengberg
Oed
Ybbs
Neumarkt a. d. Ybbs
Uttendorf
Eberschwang
Kronstorf
Schmolln
Lohnsburg
Pramet
Lambach
Leombach
Neuhofen a. d. K.
Hofkirchen i. Traunkr.
Haag
Amstetten
Frauschereck
Ottnang
Ampflwang
Stadl Paura
Haidershfn.
Aschbach-Markt
Munderfing
Redlthal
Frankenburg
Kremsmünster
Sierning
Dietachdorf
Weistrach
Steinakirchen
Steinerkirchen a. d. Tr.
Sattledt
Ungenach
Attnang-Puchhm.
Schwanenstadt
Bad Hall
Garsten
Steyr
Seitenstetten-Markt
Randegg
Friedburg
Palting
Mühlham
Vöcklabruck
Voitsdorf
Vorchdorf
Waldneukirchen
Kleinraming
Sonntagberg
Gresten
Straßwalchen
Mattsee
Frankenmarkt
Mösendorf
Laakirchen
Pettenbach
Ternberg
Maria Neustift
Ybbsitz
Waidhofen a. d. Y.
Gaming
Neumarkt a. W.
St. Georgen i. A.
Schörfling
Krottendorf
Gmunden
Schlierbach
Losenstein
Lindau
Zell a. M.
Attersee
Weyregg
Kirchdorf a. d. Krems
Viechtwang
Leonstein
Opponitz
Lunz
Henndorf a. W.
Mondsee
Neukirchen
Micheldorf
Großraming
St. Georgen a. Reith
Unterach
Seefeld
Traunstein
1691
Traun-S.
Grünau
Klaus
Kastenreith
Brunnbach
Großhollenstein
Traunkirchen
SENGSEN GEB.
Gaisberg
1286
Scharfling
Weißenbach
Ebensee
Höllenstein a. d. Y.
Göstling a. d. Ybbs
Reithbauer
SALZBURG
St. Gilgen
Schafbg.
1183
St. Wolfgang
Habernau
Steyrbrücke
Windischgarsten
Lassing
Strobl
Almsee
Hintersee
Mitterweißenb.
Bad Ischl
Hinterstoder
Unterlaussa
Altenmarkt
Hallein
Hoher Zinken
1764
TOTES GEB.
2523
Gr. Priel
Spital a. Pyhrn
St. Gallen
Kampertal
Gams b. Hieflau
Wildalpen
Bad Goisern
Altaussee
Gößl
Toplitzsee
Warscheneck
Gamsfeld
2024
Pötschenh.
Grundlsee
Großreifling
Pyhrnpaß
945
Hieflau
Bodenbauer
Golling a. d. S.
Rußbach
P. Gschütt
Hallst. See
Bad Aussee
Tauplitzalm
Gstatterboden
Leopoldsteiner See
Eisenerz
Abtenau
Gosau
Hallstatt
Obertraun
Tauplitz
Liezen
Admont
2372
Radmer
769
Präbichl
1227
Annaberg i. L.
Gosausee
Dachstein-H.
Mitterndorf
Gr. Grimming
2351
Stainach
Selzthal
Rottenmann
Erzberg
Vordernberg
Eisriesenwelt
St. Martin
Hoher Dachstein
2995
St. Martin a. Gr.
Burg Strechau
Oppenberg
St. Lorenzen
Treglwang
Schoberpaß
849
Gröbming
Donnersbach
Trieben
Kalwang
Trofaiach
Werfen
Hüttau
Ramsau
Mandling
Aich
Triebener Tauern
1274
Hohentauern
Wald
Mautern i. Stmk.
Radstadt
Schladming
Gatschberg
2449
Gr. Bösenstein
Traboch
St. Johann i. Pongau
Altenmarkt i. P.
Donnersbach wald
St. Johann a. T.
Hochreichart
2416
St. Michael
Lichtenst.-Klamm
Wagrain
Flachau
Rohrmoos
126
2746
Hochwildstelle
St. Nikolai i. S.
Untertauern
Pusterwald
Kraubath
C
D

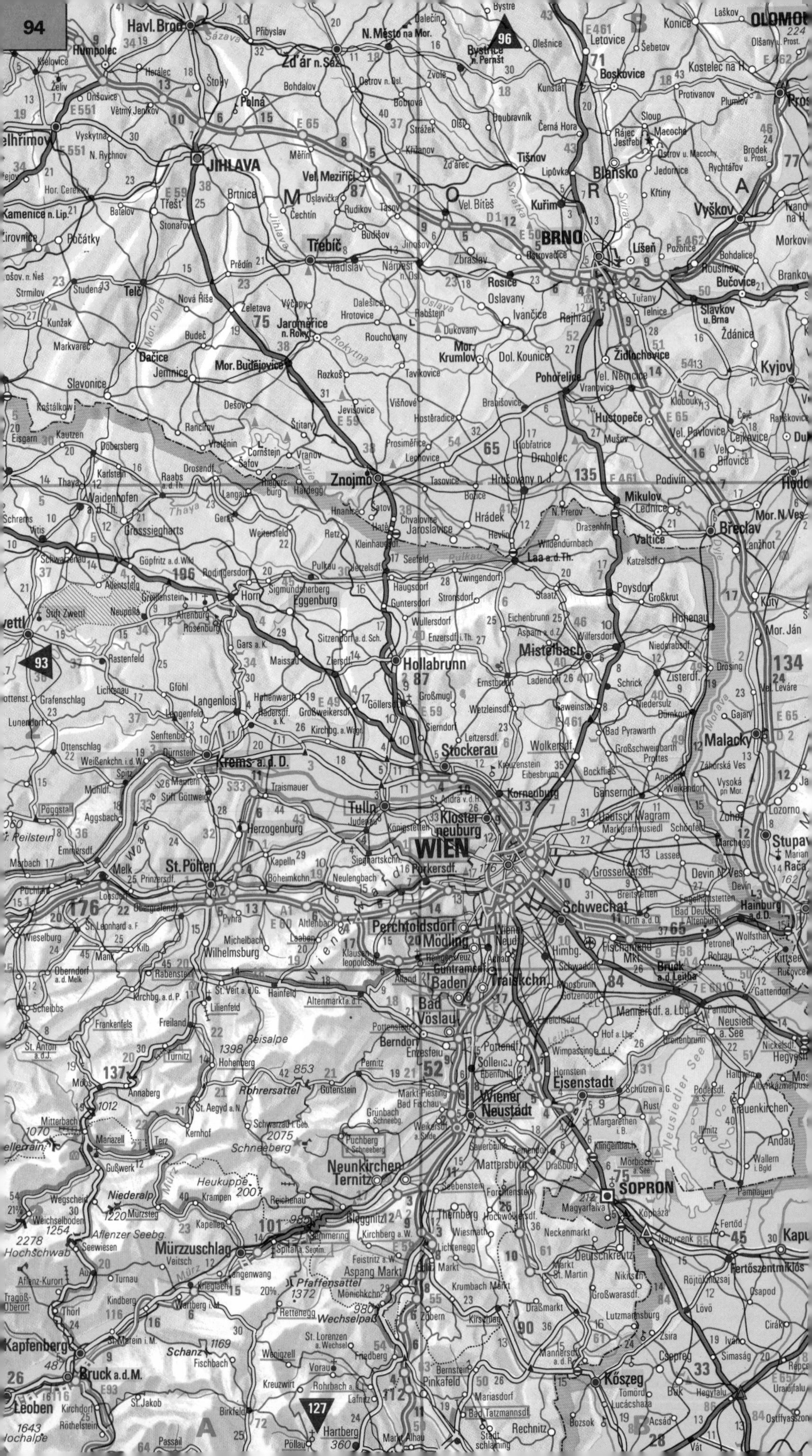
Havl. Brod
Přibyslav
N. Město na Mor.
Bystrice n. Pernšt
Olešnice
Letovice
Konice
Laškov
OLOMOUC
Humpolec
Žďár n. Sáz.
Boskovice
Kostelec na H.
Křelovice
Herálec
Štoky
Polná
Bohdalov
Ostrov n. Osl.
Bobrová
Zvole
Kunštát
Protivanov
Plumlov
Želiv
Onšovice
Větrný Jeníkov
Stražek
Olší
Doubravník
Černá Hora
Sloup
Rájec Jestřebí
Macocha
Pelhřimov
Vyskytná
Měřín
Křižanov
Ždárec
Tišnov
Lipůvka
Blansko
Ostrov u. Macochy
Jedomice
Brodek u. Prost.
Rychtářov
N. Rychnov
JIHLAVA
Vel. Meziříčí
Brtnice
Oslavička
Rudíkov
Tasov
Vel. Bíteš
Kuřim
Křtiny
Vyškov
Hor. Cerekev
Třešť
Čechtín
Kamenice n. Lip.
Batelov
Stonařov
Budišov
BRNO
Líšeň
Pozořice
Žirovnice
Počátky
Třebíč
Jinošov
Bohdalice
Rousínov
Bučovice
Předín
Vladislav
Náměšť n. Osl.
Zbraslav
Rosice
Ostrovačice
Telč
Studená
Strmilov
Oslavany
Ivančice
Rajhrad
Tuřany
Telnice
Slavkov u. Brna
Želetava
Nová Říše
Výčapy
Dalešice
Hrotovice
Rabštejn
Dukovany
Kunžak
Jaroměřice n. Rokyt.
Rouchovany
Mor. Krumlov
Dol. Kounice
Židlochovice
Ždánice
Markvarec
Budeč
Dačice
Mor. Budějovice
Rozkoš
Tavíkovice
Pohořelice
Vel. Němčice
Kyjov
Slavonice
Jemnice
Vranovice
Klobouky
Koštálkov
Dešov
Jevišovice
Višňové
Branišovice
Hustopeče
Čejč
Rancířov
Štitary
Hostěradice
Vel. Pavlovice
Čejkovice
Eisgarn
Kautzen
Dobersberg
Vratěnín
Cornštejn
Vranov
Prosiměřice
Litobratřice
Mušov
Velké Bílovice
Šafov
Lechovice
Drnholec
Karlstein
Raabs a. d. Th.
Drosendf.
Znojmo
Hrušovany n. J.
Podivín
Hodonín
Thaya
Waidhofen a. d. Th.
Langau
Riegersburg
Hardegg
Tasovice
Bozice
Mikulov
Lednice
Schrems
Vitis
Grosssiegharts
Gerás
Hnanice
Šatov
Chvalovice
Hrádek
N. Přerov
Valtice
Mor. N. Ves
Weitersfeld
Retz
Hatě
Jaroslavice
Hevlín
Drasenhfn.
Břeclav
Lanžhot
Schwarzenau
Kleinhaugsdf.
Wildendürnbach
Göpfritz a. d. Wild
Rodingersdorf
Pulkau
Zellerndf.
Seefeld
Laa a. d. Th.
Katzelsdf.
Allentsteig
Sigmundsherberg
Eggenburg
Haugsdorf
Zwingendorf
Staatz
Poysdorf
Großkrut
Kúty
Stift Zwettl
Neupölla
Greillenstein
Horn
Guntersdorf
Stronsdorf
Zwettl
Altenburg
Rosenburg
Wullersdorf
Eichenbrunn
Asparn a. d. Z.
Wilfersdorf
Hohenau
Mor. Ján
Gars a. K.
Sitzendorf a. d. Sch.
Enzersdf. i. Th.
Mistelbach
Niederabsdf.
Rastenfeld
Maissau
Ziersdf.
Hollabrunn
Ernstbrunn
Ladendorf
Schrick
Zisterdf.
Drösing
Vel. Leváre
Lichtenau
Gföhl
Langenlois
Hohenwarth
Großmugl
Wetzleinsdf.
Niedersulz
Dürnkrut
Grafenschlag
Hadersdf. a. K.
Großweikersdf.
Göllersdf.
Gaweinstal
Gajary
Lunendorf
Lengenfeld
Kirchbg. a. Wagr.
Sierndorf
Leitzersdf.
Bad Pyrawarth
Malacky
Ottenschlag
Senftenbg.
Wolkersdf.
Großschweinbarth
Prottes
Weißenkchn. i. d. W.
Spitz
Dürnstein
Krems a. d. D.
Stockerau
Kreuzenstein
Eibesbrunn
Bockfließ
Záhorská Ves
Mühldf.
Mautern
Stift Göttweig
Traismauer
Tulln
St. Andrä v. d. H.
Korneuburg
Gänserndf.
Weikendorf
Vysoká pri Mor.
Pöggstall
Aggsbach
Judenau
Königstetten
Klosterneuburg
Deutsch Wagram
Markgrafneusiedl
Schönfeld
Zohor
Lozorno
Herzogenburg
WIEN
Stupava
Reilstein
Emmersdf.
Kapelln
Siegharskchn.
Purkersdf.
Lassee
Marchegg
Marianka
Marbach
Melk
St. Pölten
Prinzersdf.
Böheimkchn.
Neulengbach
Grossenzersdf.
Devin N. Ves
Rača
Pöchlarn
Loosdorf
Obergrafendf.
Breitstetten
Engelhartstetten
Schwechat
Orth a. d. D.
Bad Deutsch Altenburg
Hainburg a. d. D.
Wieselburg
St. Leonhard a. F.
Pyhra
Altlenbach
Laaben
Perchtoldsdorf
Mödling
Wiener Neudorf
Himbg.
Fischamend Mkt.
Petronell
Rohrau
Wolfsthal
Kittsee
Mank
Kilb
Michelbach
Wilhelmsburg
Klausen-leopoldsdf.
Heiligenkreuz
Guntramsdf.
Schwadorf
Bruck a. d. Leitha
Oberndorf a. d. Melk
Rabenstein
Alland
Baden
Traiskchn.
Moosbrunn
Gotzendorf
Gattendorf
Scheibbs
Kirchbg. a. d. P.
St. Veit a. d. G.
Lilienfeld
Hainfeld
Altenmarkt a. d. T.
Bad Vöslau
Mannersdf. a. Lbg.
Parndorf
Neusiedl a. See
Frankenfels
Freiland
Pottenstein
Berndorf
Ebreichsdorf
Hof a. Lbg.
Nickelsdf.
Hegyeshalom
Reisalpe
St. Anton a. d. J.
Türnitz
Hohenberg
Enzesfeld
Pottendf.
Wimpassing a. d. L.
Breitenbrunn
Mönchhof
Mos
Pernitz
Sollenau
Ebenfurth
Hornstein
Halbturn
Albertkázmérpuszta
Annaberg
Rohrersattel
Gutenstein
Markt Piesting
Bad Fischau
Eisenstadt
Schützen a. G.
Podersdf. a. S.
Mitterbach
St. Aegyd a. N.
Schwarzau i. Geb.
Grünbach a. Schneebg.
Wiener Neustadt
Rust
Frauenkirchen
Weikersdf. a. Stde.
St. Margarethen i. B.
Illmitz
Mariazell
Terz
Kernhof
Schneeberg
Puchberg a. Schneebg.
Sauerbrunn
Zemendorf
Klingenbach
Neusiedler See
Andau
Gußwerk
Heukuppe
Neunkirchen
Ternitz
Mattersburg
Draßburg
Mörbisch a. See
Wallern i. Bgld
Niederalp
Mürzsteg
Krampen
Reichenau
Seebenstein
Forchtenstein
SOPRON
Pamhagen
Weichselboden
Gloggnitz
Thernberg
Hochwolkersdf.
Magyarfalva
Kópháza
Aflenzer Seebg.
Kapellen
Semmering
Kirchberg a. W.
Wiesmath
Neckenmarkt
Nagycenk
Fertőd
Kapuvár
Hochschwab
Seewiesen
Mürzzuschlag
Veitsch
Spital a. Semm.
Lichtenegg
Deutschkreutz
Fertőszentmiklós
Aflenz-Kurort
Turnau
Langenwang
Feistritz a. W.
Aspang Markt
Markt St. Martin
Nikitsch
Röjtökmuzsaj
Tragöß-Oberort
Krieglach
Pfaffensattel
Mönichkchn.
Krumbach Markt
Großwarasdf.
Csapod
Kindberg
Thörl
Wartberg i. M.
Retteneg
Wechselpaß
Zöbern
Draßmarkt
Lutzmannsburg
Lövő
Kirchschlag
Kapfenberg
St. Marein i. M.
Schanz
Fischbach
St. Lorenzen a. Wechsel
Friedberg
Zsira
Iván
Cirák
Wenigzell
Mannersdorf a. d. R.
Csepreg
Simaság
Répcelak
Bruck a. d. M.
Vorau
Bernstein
Pinkafeld
Kőszeg
Bük
Leoben
Kirchdorf
Röthelstein
St. Jakob
Kreuzwirt
Rohrbach a. d. L.
Lafnitz
Mariasdorf
Tömörd
Lucácsháza
Hegyfalu
Uraiújfalu
Hochalpe
Birkfeld
Hartberg
Bad Tatzmannsdf.
Rechnitz
Bozsok
Acsád
Ostffyasszonyfa
Passail
Pöllau
Markt Allhau
Stadt Schlaining
Vát
Bystré

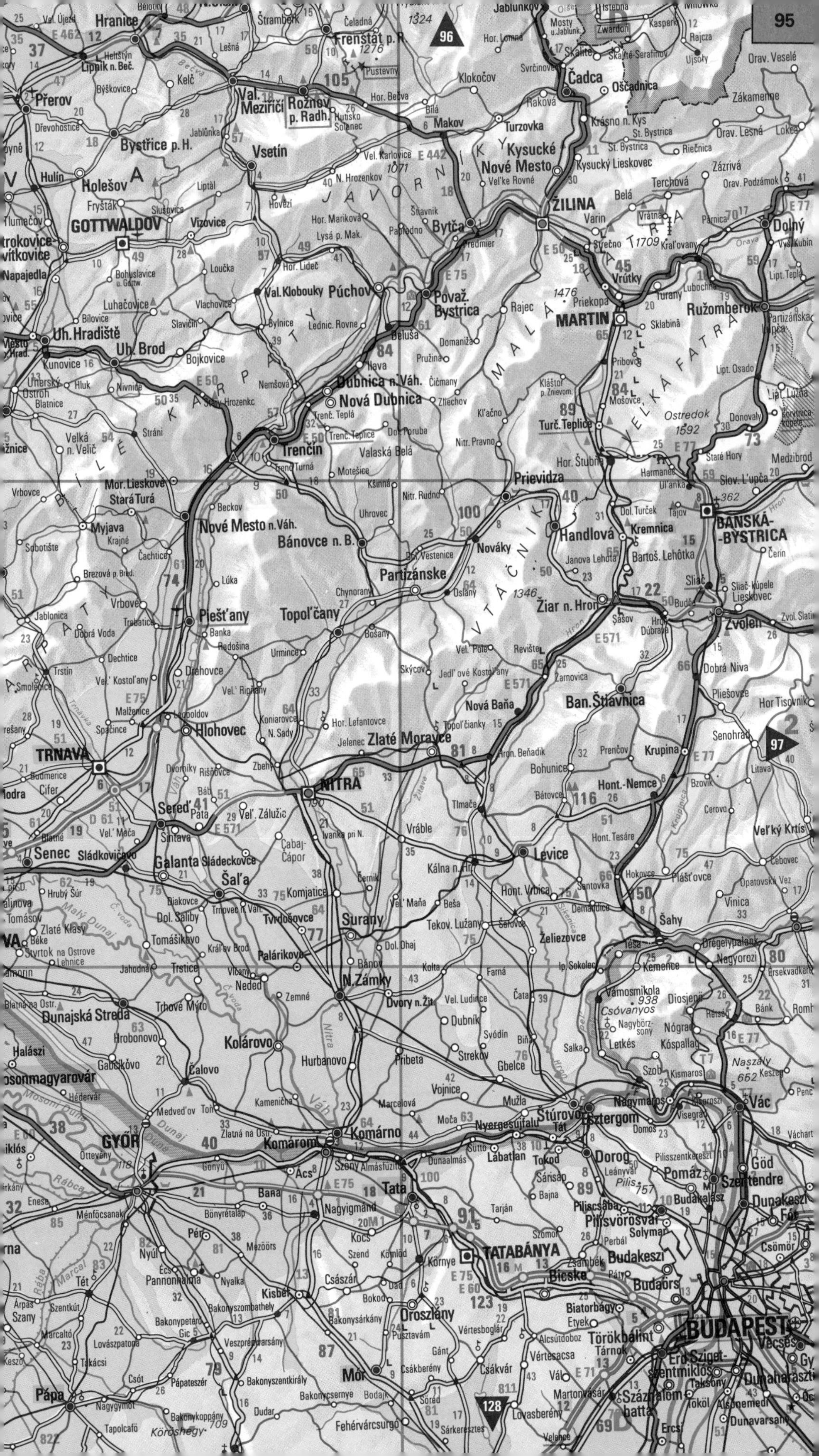

Hranice
Lipník n. Beč.
Přerov
Bystřice p. H.
Val. Meziříčí
Rožnov p. Radh.
Frenštát p. R.
Štramberk
Čeladná
Pustevny
Jablunkov
Mosty u.Jablunk.
Zwardoń
Čadca
Oščadnica
Vsetín
Holešov
Hulín
GOTTWALDOV
Vizovice
Napajedla
Luhačovice
Uh. Hradiště
Uh. Brod
Kunovice
Bojkovice
Val. Klobouky
Púchov
Považ. Bystrica
Makov
Turzovka
Kysucké Nové Mesto
ŽILINA
Bytča
Krásno n. Kys.
Terchová
Vrútky
MARTIN
Ružomberok
Dolný Kubín
JAVORNÍKY
MALÁ FATRA
VEĽKÁ FATRA
BIELE KARPATY
Dubnica n. Váh.
Nová Dubnica
Trenčín
Ilava
Rajec
Prievidza
Handlová
Turč. Teplice
Kremnica
BANSKÁ-BYSTRICA
Nové Mesto n. Váh.
Bánovce n. B.
Partizánske
Nováky
Myjava
Stará Turá
Piešťany
Topoľčany
Žiar n. Hron
Zvolen
Sliač
Hlohovec
TRNAVA
Zlaté Moravce
Nová Baňa
Ban. Štiavnica
Krupina
NITRA
Sereď
Galanta
Senec
Šaľa
Levice
Šahy
Vráble
Surany
N. Zámky
Dunajská Streda
Kolárovo
Komárno
Komárom
Štúrovo
Esztergom
GYŐR
Tata
TATABÁNYA
Dorog
Szentendre
Vác
BUDAPEST
Budaörs
Budakeszi
Érd
Pápa
Kisbér
Oroszlány
Mór
Pannonhalma
Bicske
Dunakeszi
Mosonmagyaróvár

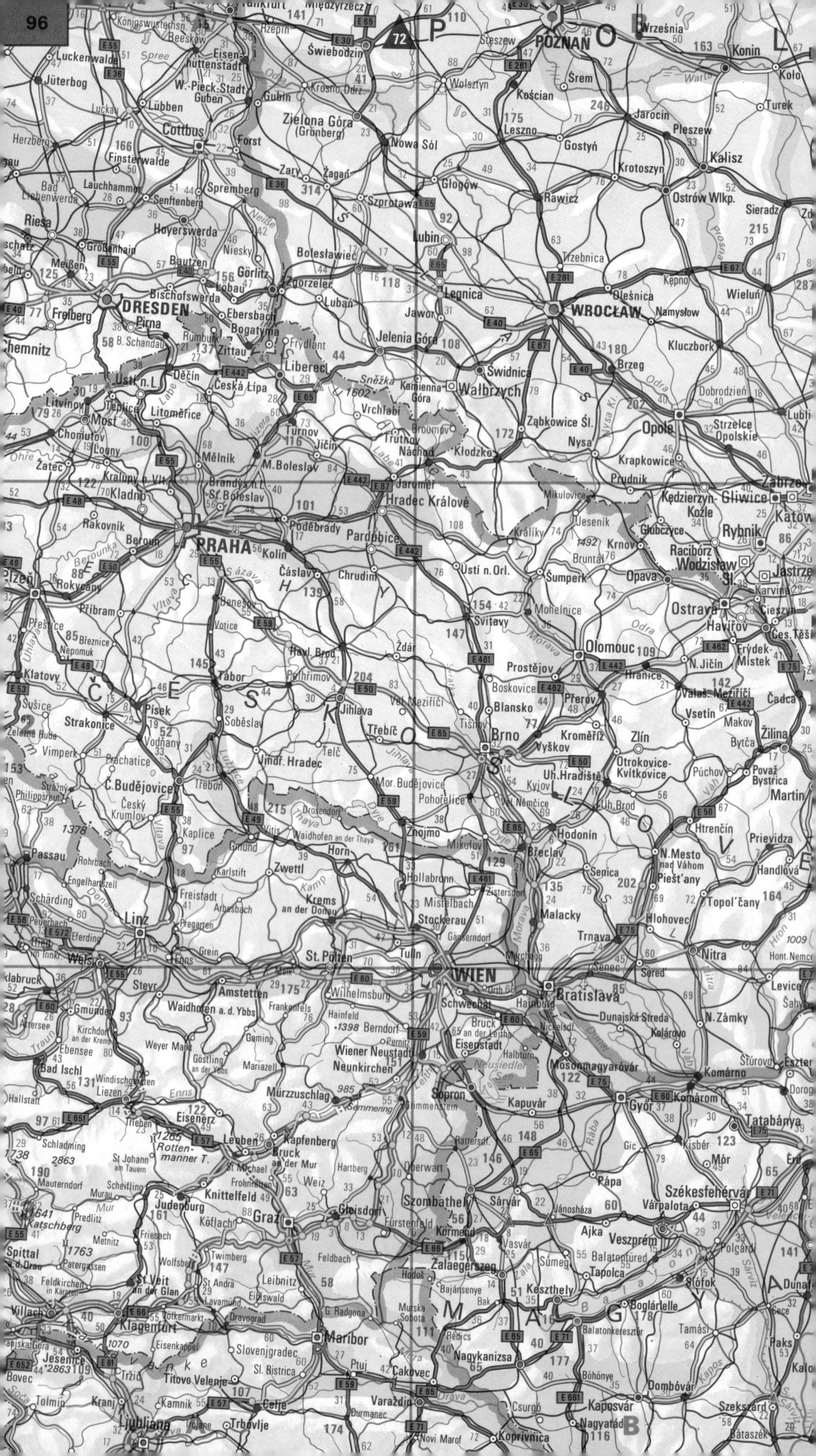
Frankfurt
Międzyrzecz
Königswusterhsn.
Rzepin
Beeskow
Świebodzin
Steszew
POZNAŃ
Września
Konin
Luckenwalde
Eisenhüttenstadt
Jüterbog
W.-Pieck-Stadt
Guben
Krosno Odrz.
Wolsztyn
Śrem
Kościan
Koło
Lübben
Gubin
Zielona Góra
(Grünberg)
Leszno
Jarocin
Turek
Herzberg
Cottbus
Forst
Nowa Sól
Gostyń
Pleszew
Finsterwalde
Kalisz
Żary
Żagań
Głogów
Krotoszyn
Bad Liebenwerda
Lauchhammer
Spremberg
Senftenberg
Szprotawa
Rawicz
Ostrów Wlkp.
Sieradz
Riesa
Hoyerswerda
Lubin
Großenhain
Niesky
Bolesławiec
Trzebnica
Meißen
Bautzen
Görlitz
Kępno
Wieluń
Löbau
Zgorzelec
Legnica
Oleśnica
Bischofswerda
Lubań
DRESDEN
Ebersbach
WROCŁAW
Namysłów
Freiberg
Pirna
Bogatynia
Jawor
Chemnitz
B. Schandau
Rumburk
Zittau
Frýdlant
Jelenia Góra
Kluczbork
Brzeg
Ústí n.L.
Děčín
Liberec
Świdnica
Česká Lípa
Sněžka
Kamienna Góra
Wałbrzych
Litvínov
Teplice
Most
Litoměřice
Vrchlabí
Chomutov
Turnov
Trutnov
Broumov
Ząbkowice Śl.
Opole
Dobrodzień
Strzelce Opolskie
Louny
Mělník
Jičín
Náchod
Kłodzko
Nysa
Krapkowice
Žatec
M.Boleslav
Kralupy n. Vlt.
Brandýs n.L.
St.Boleslav
Jaroměř
Prudnik
Zabrze
Kladno
Hradec Králové
Mikulovice
Kędzierzyn-Koźle
Gliwice
Rakovník
Poděbrady
Pardubice
Jeseník
Głubczyce
Rybnik
Katow
Beroun
PRAHA
Kolín
Králíky
Krnov
Racibórz
Wodzisław Śl.
Jastrzę
Plzeň
Rokycany
Čáslav
Chrudim
Ústí n. Orl.
Bruntál
Šumperk
Opava
Karviná
Příbram
Benešov
Svitavy
Mohelnice
Ostrava
Havířov
Cieszyn
Přeštice
Votice
Český Těšín
Březnice
Nepomuk
Havl. Brod
Žďár
Olomouc
Frýdek-Místek
Klatovy
Tábor
Pelhřimov
Prostějov
Hranice
N. Jičín
Boskovice
Přerov
Valaš. Meziříčí
Čadca
Sušice
Písek
Jihlava
Vel. Meziříčí
Blansko
Vsetín
Strakonice
Soběslav
Třebíč
Tišnov
Kroměříž
Zlín
Makov
Žilina
Vodňany
Brno
Bytča
Vimperk
Prachatice
Telč
Vyškov
Otrokovice-Kvítkovice
Púchov
Považ Bystrica
Jindř. Hradec
Uh.Hradiště
Martin
Č.Budějovice
Třeboň
Mor. Budějovice
Kyjov
Český Krumlov
Pohořelice
Vel. Němčice
Uh.Brod
Kaplice
Vitis
Waidhofen an der Thaya
Znojmo
Hodonín
Htrenčín
Prievidza
Passau
Gmünd
Horn
Mikulov
Břeclav
N.Mesto nad Váhom
Handlová
Karlstift
Zwettl
Hollabrunn
Senica
Piešt'any
Engelhartszell
Schärding
Freistadt
Krems an der Donau
Mistelbach
Zistersdorf
Topoľčany
Arbesbach
Malacky
Hlohovec
Peuerbach
Eferding
Linz
Stockerau
Gänserndorf
Trnava
Nitra
Ried im Innkr.
Pregarten
St. Pölten
Tulln
Marchegg
Senec
Sereď
Wels
Grein
Enns
Melk
WIEN
Orth
Bratislava
Levice
Šahy
Stevr
Amstetten
Wilhelmsburg
Schwechat
Hainburg
Gmunden
Waidhofen a. d. Ybbs
Frankenfels
Hainfeld
Berndorf
Bruck an der Leitha
Nickelsdf.
Dunajská Streda
N. Zámky
Kolárovo
Attersee
Kirchdorf an der Krems
Weyer Markt
Gaming
Pernitz
Eisenstadt
Halbturn
Ebensee
Göstling an der Ybbs
Mariazell
Wiener Neustadt
Neunkirchen
Neusiedler See
Mosonmagyaróvár
Štúrovo
Esztergom
Bad Ischl
Windischgarsten
Liezen
Komárno
Hallstatt
Mürzzuschlag
Semmering
Sopron
Kapuvár
Győr
Komárom
Dorog
Trieben
Eisenerz
Semmerstein
Tatabánya
Schladming
Rottenmanner T.
Leoben
Kapfenberg
Bruck an der Mur
Rattersdf.
Kisbér
St Johann am Tauern
St Michael
Hartberg
Oberwart
Gic
Mór
Mauterndorf
Scheifling
Murau
Fohnleiten
Weiz
Pápa
Székesfehérvár
Predlitz
Knittelfeld
Judenburg
Szombathely
Sárvár
Jánosháza
Várpalota
Katschberg
Köflach
Graz
Gleisdorf
Fürstenfeld
Ajka
Veszprém
Körmend
Vasvár
Polgárdi
Spittal a.d.Drau
Metnitz
Friesach
Wolfsberg
Twimberg
Patergassen
Feldbach
Zalaegerszeg
Sümeg
Balatonfüred
Tapolca
Feldkirchen in Kärnten
St Veit an der Glan
St Andrä
Leibnitz
Hodoš
Bajánsenye
Keszthely
Siófok
Dunaf
Lavamünd
Eibiswald
Villach
Klagenfurt
Völkermarkt
Dravograd
G. Radgona
Murska Sobota
Bak
Boglárlelle
Cece
Kranjska Gora
Jesenice
Eisenkappel
Maribor
Rédics
Balatonkeresztúr
Tamási
Paks
Tržič
Slovenjgradec
Nagykanizsa
Kalo
Bovec
Titovo Velenje
Sl. Bistrica
Ptuj
Čakovec
Böhönye
Dombóvár
Tolmin
Kranj
Kamnik
Celje
Varaždin
Csurgó
Kaposvár
Szekszárd
Ljubljana
Trbovlje
Đurmanec
Novi Marof
Koprivnica
Nagyatád
Bátaszék
Spree
Oder
Warta
Neiße
Prosna
Odra
Nysa Kł.
Labe
Ohře
Vltava
Berounka
Sázava
Jizera
Morava
Lužnice
Thaya
Dyje
Jihlava
Svratka
Kamp
Donau
Traun
Enns
Mur
Leitha
Dunaj
Váh
Nitra
Hron
Rába
Zala
Sárvíz
Kapos
Drava
Soča
Balaton
P O L
S L
Č E S K O S L O V
Y
M A G Y A
B
1602
1492
1378
1009
1398
985
1265
2863
1738
1641
1763
1070
E 30
E 65
E 261
E 36
E 55
E 40
E 67
E 442
E 48
E 49
E 50
E 53
E 59
E 461
E 462
E 75
E 56
E 572
E 60
E 80
E 651
E 57
E 66
E 71
E 61
E 652
E 661
72

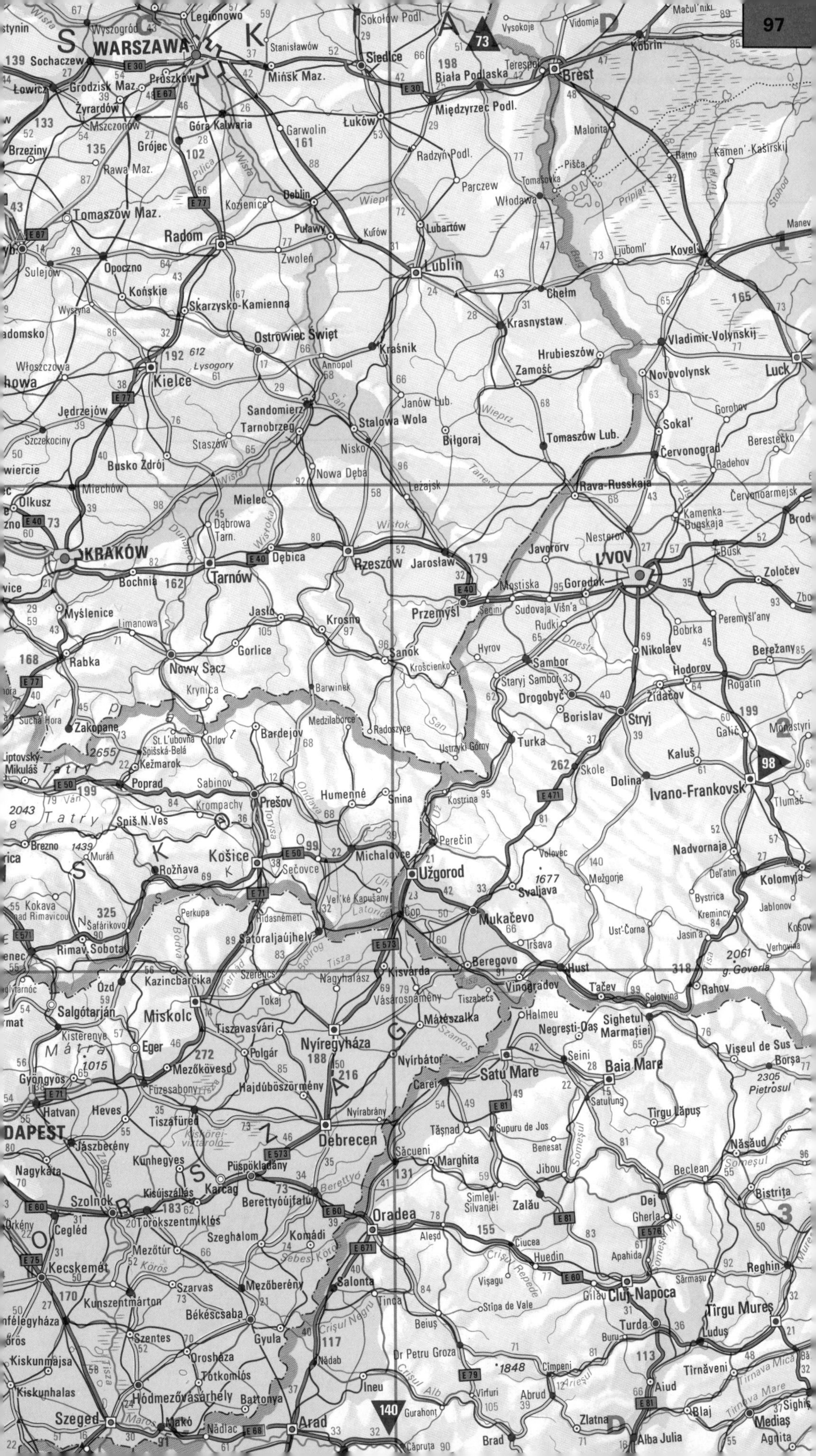

WARSZAWA
Legionowo
Wyszogród
Sochaczew
Łowicz
Grodzisk Maz.
Pruszków
Żyrardów
Mszczonów
Grójec
Góra Kalwaria
Brzeziny
Rawa Maz.
Mińsk Maz.
Stanisławów
Sokołów Podl.
Siedlce
Garwolin
Łuków
Biała Podlaska
Międzyrzec Podl.
Radzyń Podl.
Parczew
Terespol
Brest
Kobrin
Malorita
Vysokoje
Vidomja
Mačul'niki
Ratno
Kamen'-Kaširskij
Pišča
Tomašovka
Włodawa
Pripjat'
Stohod
Manev
Tomaszów Maz.
Kozienice
Dęblin
Puławy
Kurów
Lubartów
Radom
Zwoleń
Lublin
Opoczno
Sulejów
Końskie
Skarżysko-Kamienna
Chełm
Ljuboml'
Kovel'
Krasnystaw
Vladimir-Volynskij
Luck
Ostrowiec Świet
Kraśnik
Annopol
Hrubieszów
Novovolynsk
Zamość
Kielce
Lysogory
Włoszczowa
Jędrzejów
Sandomierz
Tarnobrzeg
Janów Lub.
Stalowa Wola
Biłgoraj
Tomaszów Lub.
Sokal'
Gorohov
Berestečko
Červonograd
Radehov
Szczekociny
Staszów
Nisko
Nowa Dęba
Busko Zdrój
Miechów
Olkusz
Mielec
Dąbrowa Tarn.
Leżajsk
Rava-Russkaja
Červonoarmejsk
Kamenka-Bugskaja
Nesterov
Brody
KRAKÓW
Bochnia
Tarnów
Dębica
Rzeszów
Jarosław
Javorov
L'VOV
Busk
Zoločev
Mostiska
Gorodok
Przemyśl
Sudovaja Višn'a
Myślenice
Limanowa
Jasło
Krosno
Rudki
Peremyšl'any
Bobrka
Gorlice
Sanok
Hyrov
Nikolaev
Berežany
Rabka
Nowy Sącz
Krościenko
Sambor
Staryj Sambor
Hodorov
Rogatin
Krynica
Barwinek
Drogobyč
Židačov
Borislav
Stryj
Zakopane
Sucha Hora
Bardejov
Medzilaborce
Radoszyce
Ustrzyki Górny
Turka
Galič
Monastyri
St. L'ubovňa
Orlov
Spišská-Belá
Kežmarok
Liptovský-Mikuláš
Tatry
Skole
Kaluš
Dolina
Ivano-Frankovsk
Poprad
Sabinov
Humenné
Snina
Kostrina
Tlumač
Krompachy
Prešov
Spiš.N.Ves
Perečin
Brezno
Murán
Košice
Rožňava
Sečovce
Michalovce
Užgorod
Volovec
Nadvornaja
Del'atin
Kolomyja
Mežgorje
Svaljava
Kokava
Rimavicou
Šafárikovo
Perkupa
Hidasnémeti
Veľké Kapušany
Čop
Mukačevo
Bystrica
Kremincy
Jablonov
Ust'-Čorna
Jasin'a
Kosov
Rimav. Sobota
Sátoraljaújhely
Iršava
Verhovina
g. Goverla
Ózd
Kazincbarcika
Szerencs
Nagyhalász
Kisvárda
Beregovo
Hust
Tačev
Rahov
Solotvina
Vinogradov
Salgótarján
Miskolc
Tokaj
Vásárosnamény
Tiszabecs
Halmeu
Negrești-Oaș
Sighetul Marmației
Vișeul de Sus
Borșa
Tiszavasvári
Nyíregyháza
Mátészalka
Kisterenye
Eger
Mátra
Polgár
Nyírbátor
Seini
Baia Mare
Pietrosul
Gyöngyös
Mezőkövesd
Hajdúböszörmény
Carei
Satu Mare
Hatvan
Heves
Füzesabony
Tiszafüred
Kiskörei-víztároló
Nyírábrány
Debrecen
Tășnad
Supuru de Jos
Benesat
Satulung
Tîrgu Lăpuș
Năsăud
BUDAPEST
Jászberény
Nagykáta
Kunhegyes
Püspökladány
Săcueni
Marghita
Jibou
Someșul
Beclean
Bistrița
Szolnok
Kisújszállás
Karcag
Berettyóújfalu
Simleul-Silvaniei
Zalău
Dej
Gherla
Cegléd
Törökszentmiklós
Oradea
Szeghalom
Komádi
Aleșd
Ciucea
Huedin
Apahida
Reghin
Kecskemét
Mezőtúr
Körös
Sebes-Körös
Salonta
Crișul Repede
Vișagu
Cluj-Napoca
Sărmașu
Szarvas
Mezőberény
Kunszentmárton
Békéscsaba
Tinca
Stîna de Vale
Gilău
Turda
Tîrgu Mureș
Kiskunfélegyháza
Szentes
Gyula
Crișul Negru
Beiuș
Buru
Luduș
Kiskunmajsa
Orosháza
Nădab
Dr Petru Groza
Cîmpeni
Arieșul
Aiud
Tîrnăveni
Tîrnava Mică
Tîrnava Mare
Tótkomlós
Kiskunhalas
Hódmezővásárhely
Battonya
Ineu
Crișul Alb
Vîrfuri
Abrud
Blaj
Sighiș
Szeged
Maros
Makó
Nădlac
Arad
Gurahont
Zlatna
Mediaș
Căprușa
Brad
Alba Julia
Agnita

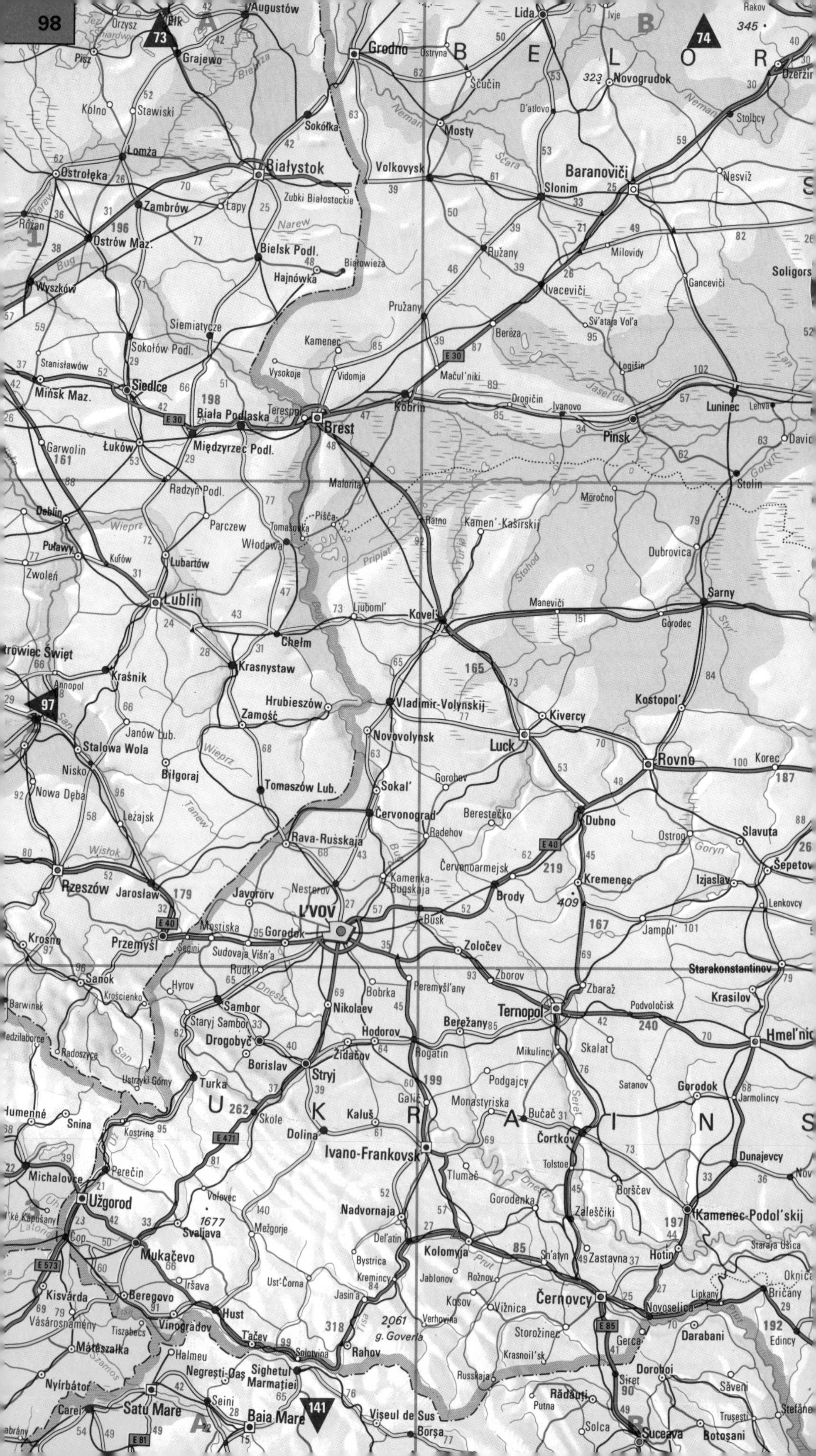
73
74
97
141
B E L O R
U K R A I N
Augustów
Ełk
Orzysz
Pisz
Grajewo
Kolno
Stawiski
Łomża
Ostrołęka
Różan
Zambrów
Łapy
Ostrów Maz.
Wyszków
Białystok
Zubki Białostockie
Bielsk Podl.
Hajnówka
Białowieża
Sokółka
Grodno
Ostryna
Lida
Ivje
Rakov
Novogrudok
Dzeržinsk
Ščučin
Mosty
D'atlovo
Stolbcy
Volkovysk
Baranoviči
Slonim
Nesviž
Ružany
Milovidy
Soligorsk
Ivaceviči
Ganceviči
Pružany
Sv'ataja Vol'a
Bereza
Logišin
Siemiatycze
Sokołów Podl.
Stanisławów
Mińsk Maz.
Siedlce
Kamenec
Vysokoje
Vidomja
Mačul'niki
Drogičin
Ivanovo
Kobrin
Luninec
Lenva
Pinsk
David-Gorodok
Stolin
Terespol
Biała Podlaska
Brest
Garwolin
Łuków
Międzyrzec Podl.
Radzyń Podl.
Malorita
Moročno
Dęblin
Parczew
Tomašovka
Pišča
Ratno
Kamen'-Kaširskij
Puławy
Włodawa
Dubrovica
Kurów
Lubartów
Zwoleń
Lublin
Ljuboml'
Kovel'
Manevići
Sarny
Gorodec
Chełm
Krasnystaw
Ostrowiec Święt.
Kraśnik
Annopol
Hrubieszów
Vladimir-Volynskij
Kivercy
Kostopol'
Zamość
Janów Lub.
Novovolynsk
Luck
Stalowa Wola
Nisko
Biłgoraj
Rovno
Korec
Nowa Dęba
Tomaszów Lub.
Sokal'
Gorohov
Dubno
Leżajsk
Červonograd
Berestečko
Radehov
Ostrog
Slavuta
Rava-Russkaja
Šepetovka
Rzeszów
Jarosław
Červonoarmejsk
Kremenec
Izjaslav
Javorov
Nesterov
Kamenka-Bugskaja
Brody
Lenkovcy
L'VOV
Busk
Jampol'
Krosno
Przemyśl
Mostiska
Gorodok
Segini
Sudovaja Višn'a
Zoločev
Starakonstantinov
Sanok
Rudki
Zborov
Zbaraž
Hyrov
Krościenko
Bobrka
Peremyšl'any
Krasilov
Barwinek
Sambor
Nikolaev
Ternopol
Podvoločisk
Staryj Sambor
Hodorov
Berežany
Medzilaborce
Drogobyč
Hmel'nickij
Radoszyce
Židačov
Rogatin
Mikulincy
Skalat
Borislav
Stryj
Ustrzyki Górny
Turka
Podgajcy
Satanov
Gorodok
Jarmolincy
Humenné
Galič
Monastyriska
Snina
Skole
Kaluš
Bučač
Dolina
Kostrina
Čortkov
Michalovce
Perečin
Ivano-Frankovsk
Tlumač
Tolstoe
Dunajevcy
Užgorod
Volovec
Borščev
Veľké Kapušany
Gorodenka
Čop
Nadvornaja
Mežgorje
Svaljava
Zaleščiki
Kamenec-Podol'skij
Mukačevo
Del'atin
Kolomyja
Sn'atyn
Zastavna
Hotin
Staraja Ušica
Bystrica
Kremincy
Jablonov
Rožnov
Iršava
Ust'-Čorna
Kisvárda
Beregovo
Jasin'a
Kosov
Vižnica
Černovcy
Lipkany
Novoselica
Okniča
Bričany
Hust
Vásárosnamény
Vinogradov
Tiszabecs
Verhovina
Storožinec
Gerca
Darabani
Edincy
Mátészalka
Tačev
Solotvina
Rahov
g. Goverla
Krasnoil'sk
Halmeu
Negrești-Oaș
Sighetul Marmației
Russkaja
Doroboi
Săveni
Nyírbátor
Satu Mare
Seini
Rădăuți
Siret
Putna
Trușești
Ștefănești
Carei
Baia Mare
Vișeul de Sus
Borșa
Solca
Suceava
Botoșani
Nyírbátor
Narew
Bug
Biebrza
Neman
Ščara
Jasel'da
Pripjat'
Stohod
Turija
Goryn'
Styr'
Wieprz
Tanew
Wisłok
San
Dnestr
Seret
Prut
Tisa
Latorica
Uh
Szamos
E 30
E 40
E 471
E 573
E 81
E 85
345
323
409
1677
2061

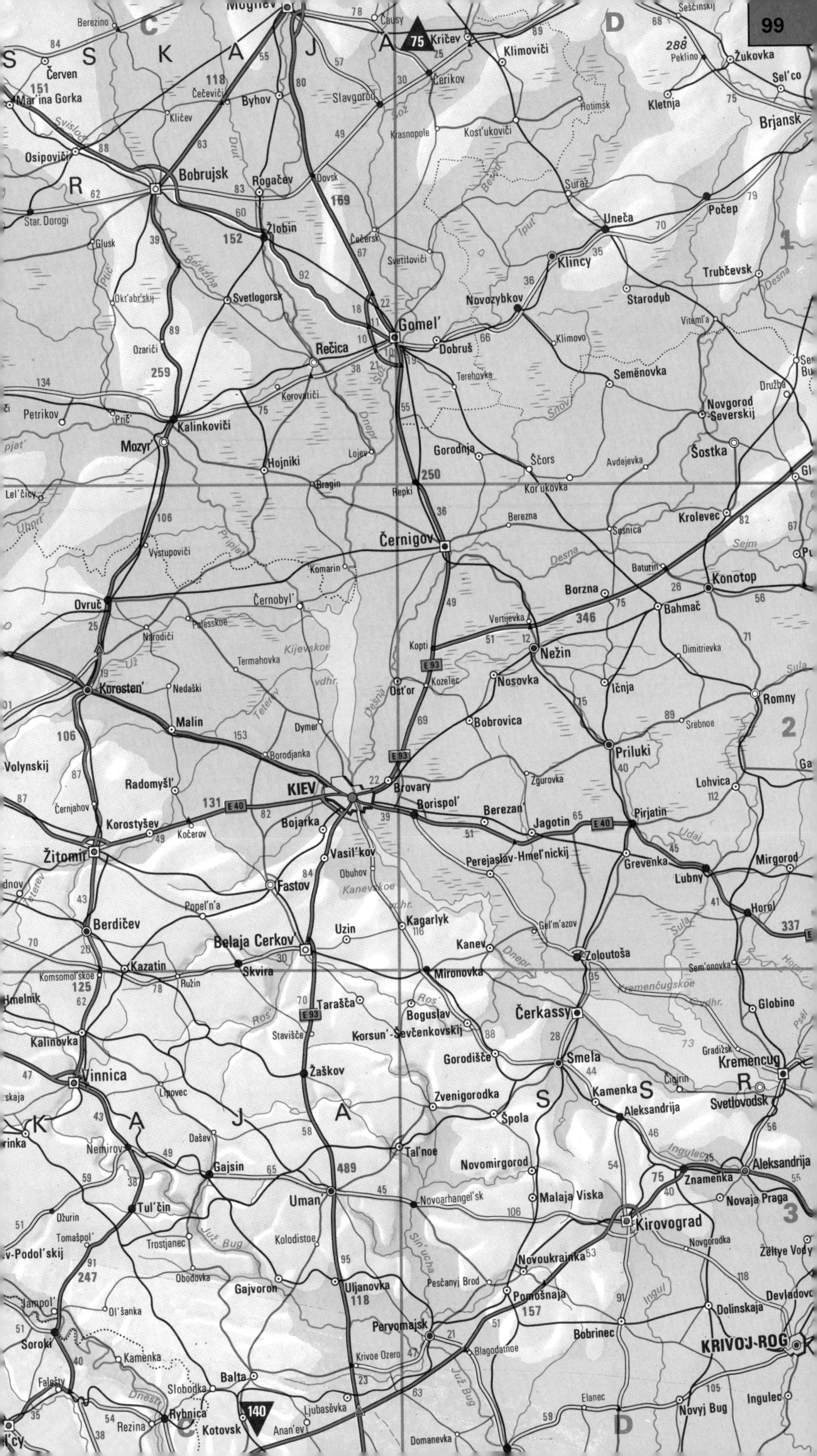

Mogilev
Berezino
Čausy
Kričev
Klimoviči
Sešćinskij
Peklino
Žukovka
Sel'co
Červen
Mar'ina Gorka
Čečeviči
Byhov
Slavgorod
Čerikov
Kletnja
Hotimsk
Brjansk
Ključev
Krasnopole
Kosťukoviči
Osipoviči
Bobrujsk
Rogačev
Dovsk
Suraž
Počep
Star. Dorogi
Žlobin
Čečersk
Unecha
Uneča
Glusk
Svetiloviči
Klincy
Trubčevsk
Svetlogorsk
Novozybkov
Starodub
Okt'abr'skij
Gomel'
Dobruš
Vitemľa
Ozariči
Rečica
Klimovo
Semënovka
Terehovka
Korovatiči
Petrikov
Prič
Kalinkoviči
Novgorod Severskij
Mozyr'
Lojev
Gorodnja
Ščors
Avdejevka
Šostka
Hojniki
Bragin
Repki
Korukovka
Lel'čicy
Berezna
Krolevec
Sosnica
Černigov
Výstupoviči
Komarin
Baturin
Konotop
Borzna
Ovruč
Černobyl'
Bahmač
Vertijevka
Narodiči
Polesskoe
Kopti
Nežin
Dimitrievka
Termahovka
Kijevskoe vdhr.
Korosten'
Nedaški
Ost'or
Kozelec
Nosovka
Ičnja
Romny
Malin
Dymer
Bobrovica
Srebnoe
Priluki
Volynskij
Borodjanka
Radomyšl'
Zgurovka
Lohvica
KIEV
Brovary
Černjahov
Borispol'
Berezan'
Pirjatin
Korostyšev
Kočerov
Bojarka
Jagotin
Žitomir
Vasil'kov
Perejaslav-Hmel'nickij
Grevenka
Lubny
Mirgorod
Obuhov
Fastov
Kanevskoe vdhr.
Horol
Popeľ'n'a
Berdičev
Kagarlyk
Gel'm'azov
Uzin
Belaja Cerkov'
Kanev
Zoloutoša
Kazatin
Skvira
Komsomol'skoe
Ružin
Mironovka
Sem'onovka
Kremenčugskoe vdhr.
Hmelnik
Taraščа
Boguslav
Čerkassy
Globino
Stavišče
Korsun'-Ševčenkovskij
Kalinovka
Gorodišče
Smela
Gradižsk
Kremenčug
Vinnica
Lipovec
Zvenigorodka
Kamenka
Čigirin
Svetlovodsk
Žaškov
Aleksandrija
Špola
Dašev
Nemirov
Tal'noe
Gajsin
Novomirgorod
Znamenka
Novaja Praga
Uman'
Malaja Viska
Tul'čin
Novoarhangel'sk
Kirovograd
Džurin
Tomašpol'
Trostjanec
Kolodistoe
Novgorodka
Žëltye Vody
Novoukrainka
Obodovka
Gajvoron
Uljanovka
Pesčanyj Brod
Pomošnaja
Devladovo
Dolinskaja
Jampol'
Ol'šanka
Pervomajsk
Soroki
Bobrinec
KRIVOJ ROG
Blagodatnoe
Kamenka
Krivoe Ozero
Balta
Slobodka
Falešty
Rybnica
Rezina
Kotovsk
Ljubaševka
Anan'ev
Elanec
Novyj Bug
Ingulec
Domanevka
Svisloč
Druť
Berezina
Ptič
Pripjat'
Ubort'
Už
Teterev
Desna
Dnepr
Sož
Besed'
Iput'
Snov
Sejm
Sula
Udaj
Ros'
Južnyj Bug
Juž. Bug
Sin'ucha
Ingul
Ingulec
Psël
Dnestr
C
D
S
K
A
J
R
1
2
3
E 40
E 93

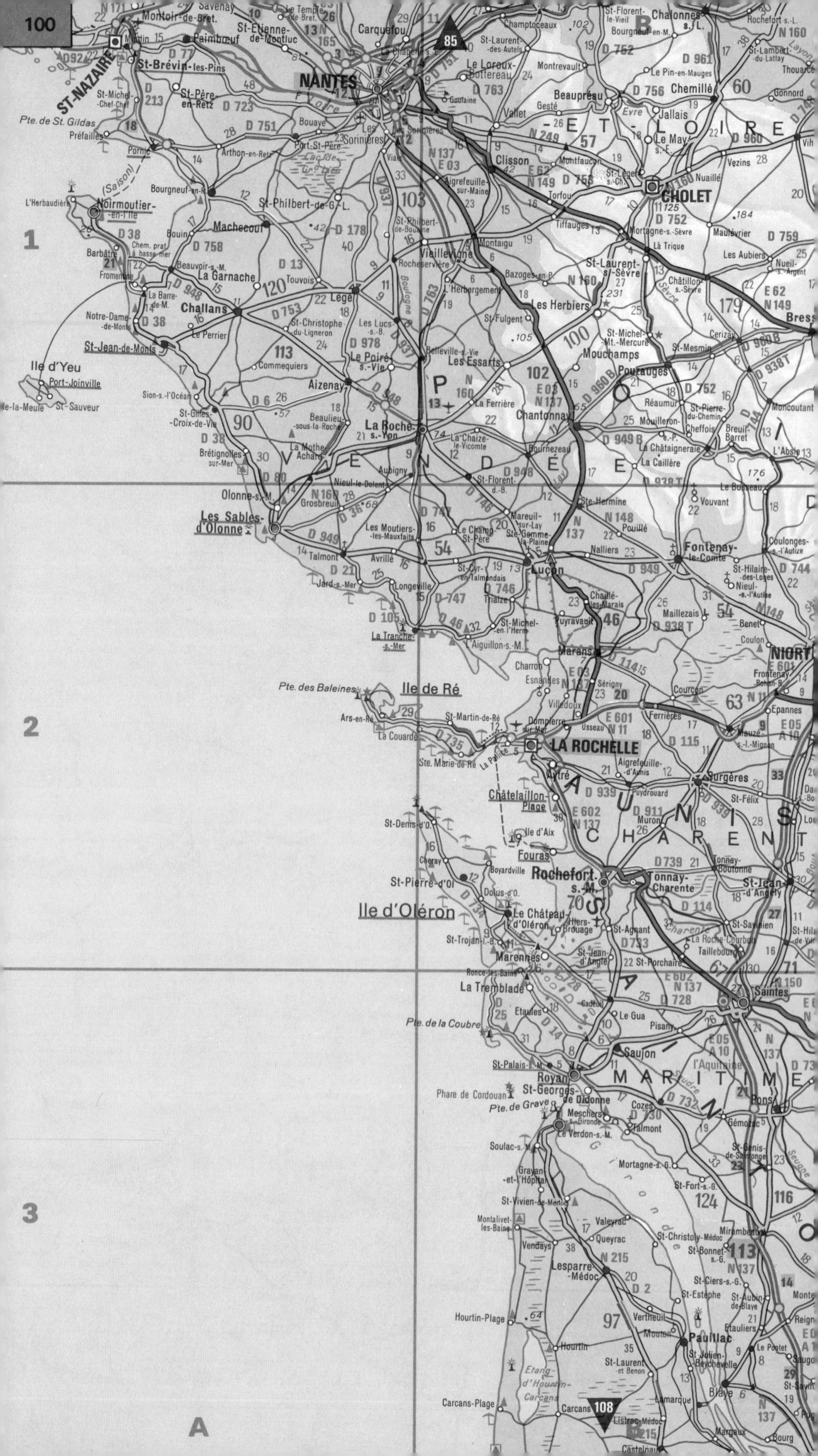

ST-NAZAIRE
Montoir-de-Bret.
Savenay
Le Temple-de-Bret.
St-Etienne-de-Montluc
Carquefou
Paimbœuf
St-Brévin-les-Pins
NANTES
St-Michel-Chef-Chef
St-Père-en-Retz
Pte. de St. Gildas
Préfailles
Pornic
Bouaye
Port-St-Père
Lac de Grand-Lieu
Les Sorinières
Arthon-en-Retz
Bourgneuf-en-R.
St-Philbert-de-G.-L.
L'Herbaudière
Noirmoutier-en-l'Ile
Machecoul
Barbâtre
Bouin
Fromentine
Beauvoir-s.-M.
La Garnache
Challans
Touvois
Legé
La Barre-de-M.
Notre-Dame-de-Monts
St-Christophe-du-Ligneron
Le Perrier
St-Jean-de-Monts
Ile d'Yeu
Port-Joinville
St-Sauveur
Commequiers
Aizenay
Sion-s.-l'Océan
St-Gilles-Croix-de-Vie
Brétignolles-sur-Mer
La Roche-s.-Yon
La Mothe-Achard
Beaulieu-sous-la-Roche
Aubigny
Nieul-le-Dolent
Olonne-s.-M.
Les Sables-d'Olonne
Grosbreuil
Talmont
Avrillé
Jard-s.-Mer
Longeville
Les Moutiers-les-Mauxfaits
La Tranche-s.-Mer
L'Aiguillon-s.-M.
Champtoceaux
St-Laurent-des-Autels
Le Loroux-Bottereau
Vallet
Clisson
Aigrefeuille-sur-Maine
Montaigu
Vieillevigne
Rocheservière
L'Herbergement
Les Lucs-s.-B.
Le Poiré-s.-Vie
Belleville-s.-Vie
Les Essarts
La Ferrière
La Chaize-le-Vicomte
St-Florent-d.-B.
Mareuil-sur-Lay
Ste-Gemme-la-Plaine
Luçon
St-Cyr-en-Talmondais
Triaize
St-Michel-en-l'Herm
Chalonnes-s.-L.
St-Florent-le-Vieil
Bourgneuf-en-M.
Montrevault
Le Pin-en-Mauges
Chemillé
Beaupréau
Gesté
Jallais
Le May-s.-E.
MAINE-ET-LOIRE
Montfaucon
St-Léger-s.-Ch.
Torfou
CHOLET
Tiffauges
Mortagne-s.-Sèvre
La Trique
Maulévrier
Les Aubiers
Nueil-s.-Argent
St-Laurent-s/-Sèvre
Châtillon-s.-Sèvre
Bazoges-en-P.
Les Herbiers
St-Fulgent
St-Michel-Mt.-Mercure
Mouchamps
Pouzauges
St-Mesmin
Cerizay
Réaumur
St-Pierre-du-Chemin
Chantonnay
Mouilleron-Cheffois
Breuil-Barret
Bournezeau
La Châtaigneraie
La Caillère
Moncoutant
L'Absie
VENDÉE
Ste-Hermine
Vouvant
Pouillé
Nalliers
Fontenay-le-Comte
Coulonges-s.-l'Autize
St-Hilaire-des-Loges
Nieul-s.-l'Autise
Chaillé-les-Marais
Maillezais
Puyravault
Benet
Coulon
NIORT
Marans
Charron
Esnandes
Sérigny
Courçon
Frontenay-Rohan-R.
Pte. des Baleines
Ile de Ré
Ars-en-Ré
La Couarde
St-Martin-de-Ré
Ste. Marie-de-Ré
Villedoux
Dompierre-sur-Mer
Usseau
Ferrières
Mauzé-s.-l.-Mignon
Epannes
LA ROCHELLE
La Pallice
Aigrefeuille-d'Aunis
Aytré
Surgères
Puydrouard
St-Félix
Châtelaillon-Plage
AUNIS
Muron
Ile d'Aix
Fouras
St-Denis-d'O.
Chéray
Boyardville
St-Pierre-d'Ol
Rochefort-s.-M.
Tonnay-Charente
Tonnay-Boutonne
St-Jean-d'Angély
Dolus-d'O.
Ile d'Oléron
Le Château-d'Oléron
Hiers-Brouage
St-Agnant
St-Savinien
St-Trojan-l.-B.
St-Jean-d'Angle
St-Porchaire
La Roche-Courbon
Taillebourg
Marennes
Ronce-les-Bains
La Tremblade
Cadeuil
Saintes
CHARENTE-MARITIME
Etaules
Le Gua
Pisany
Pte. de la Coubre
Saujon
St-Palais-s.-M.
Royan
St-Georges-de-Didonne
Phare de Cordouan
Pte. de Grave
Meschers-s.-Gironde
Cozes
Talmont
Le Verdon-s.-M.
Gémozac
Pons
Soulac-s.-M.
Gironde
St-Genis-de-Saintonge
Mortagne-s.-G.
Grayan-et-l'Hôpital
St-Fort-s.-G.
St-Vivien-de-Médoc
Montalivet-les-Bains
Valeyrac
Vendays
Queyrac
St-Christoly-Médoc
Mirambeau
St-Bonnet-s.-G.
Lesparre-Médoc
St-Ciers-s.-G.
St-Estèphe
St-Aubin-de-Blaye
Hourtin-Plage
Vertheuil
Mouton
Pauillac
Etauliers
Hourtin
St-Laurent-et Benon
St-Julien-Beychevelle
Le Pontet
Etang d'Hourtin-Carcans
Blaye
Carcans-Plage
Carcans
Lamarque
Listrac-Médoc
Margaux
Bourg
Castelnau

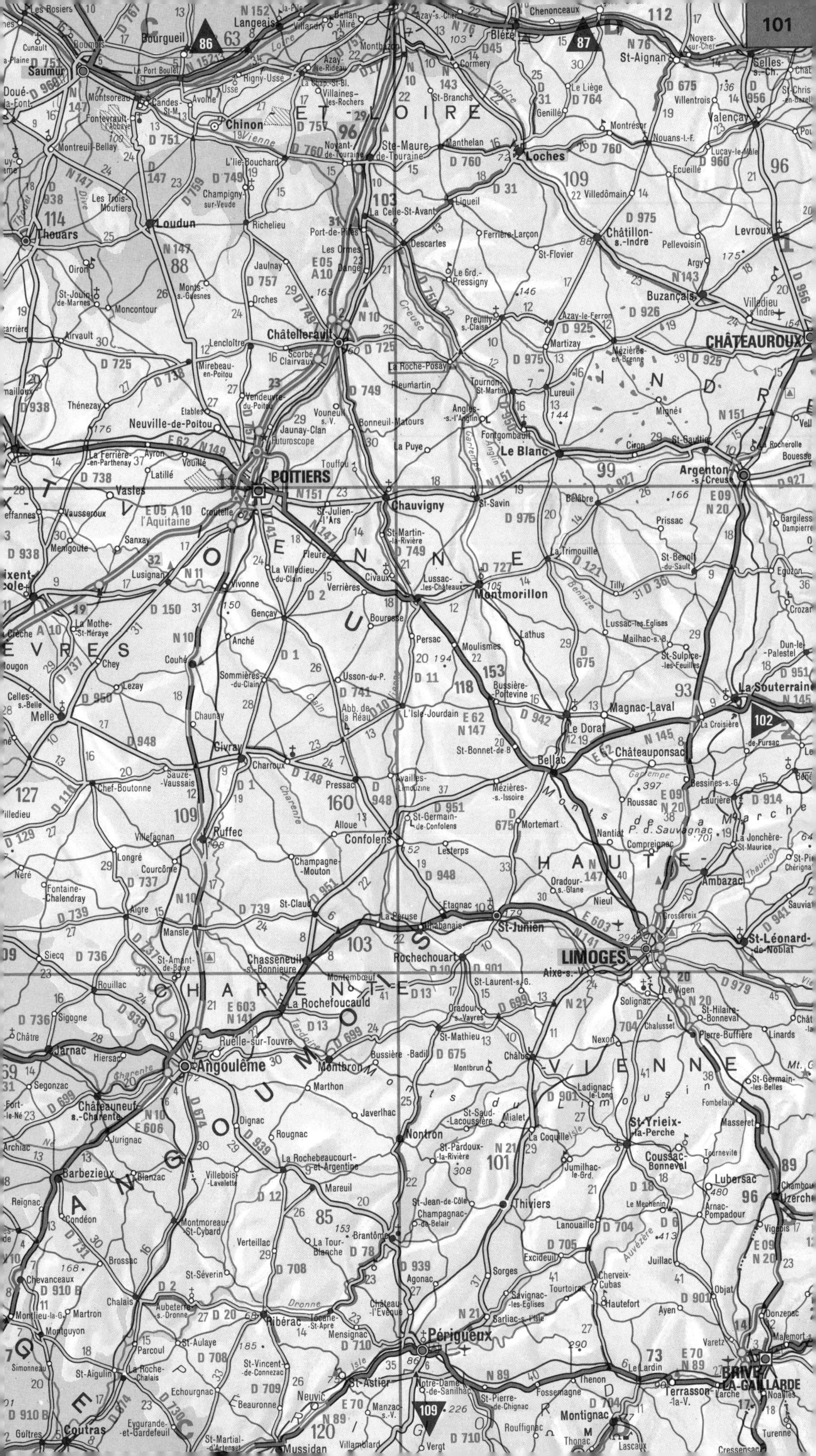
Saumur
Bourgueil
Langeais
Chenonceaux
Bléré
St-Aignan
Selles-s.-Ch.
Chinon
Loudun
Thouars
Montsoreau
Fontevrault-l'Abbaye
Montreuil-Bellay
L'Ile-Bouchard
Ste-Maure-de-Touraine
Loches
Manthelan
Montrésor
Nouans-l.-F.
Valençay
Ligueil
Châtillon-s.-Indre
Levroux
Buzançais
Richelieu
Descartes
Port-de-Piles
Dangé
Châtellerault
Lencloître
Mirebeau-en-Poitou
Preuilly-s.-Claise
Mézières-en-Brenne
CHÂTEAUROUX
La Roche-Posay
Pleumartin
Tournon-St-Martin
Neuville-de-Poitou
Futuroscope
Vouneuil-s.-V.
Bonneuil-Matours
Angles-s.-l'Anglin
Fontgombault
Le Blanc
St-Gaultier
Argenton-s.-Creuse
POITIERS
Chauvigny
St-Savin
Bélâbre
La Trimouille
Lussac-les-Châteaux
Montmorillon
St-Benoît-du-Sault
Lusignan
Vivonne
Gençay
Couhé
Melle
Civray
Charroux
L'Isle-Jourdain
Le Dorat
Magnac-Laval
La Souterraine
Bellac
Châteauponsac
Bessines-s.-G.
Ruffec
Confolens
Chef-Boutonne
St-Junien
Ambazac
LIMOGES
St-Léonard-de-Noblat
Rochechouart
Chasseneuil-s.-Bonnieure
La Rochefoucauld
Jarnac
Angoulême
Montbron
Châlus
Châteauneuf-s.-Charente
Nontron
St-Yrieix-la-Perche
Uzerche
Barbezieux
Thiviers
Brantôme
Lubersac
Montmoreau-St-Cybard
Chalais
Aubeterre-s.-Dronne
Ribérac
Périgueux
St-Astier
Neuvic
Montignac
Terrasson-la-V.
BRIVE-LA-GAILLARDE
Coutras
Mussidan
VIENNE
HAUTE-VIENNE
CHARENTE
ANGOUMOIS
INDRE
INDRE-ET-LOIRE
DEUX-SÈVRES
LIMOUSIN
Monts de la Marche
Monts du Limousin

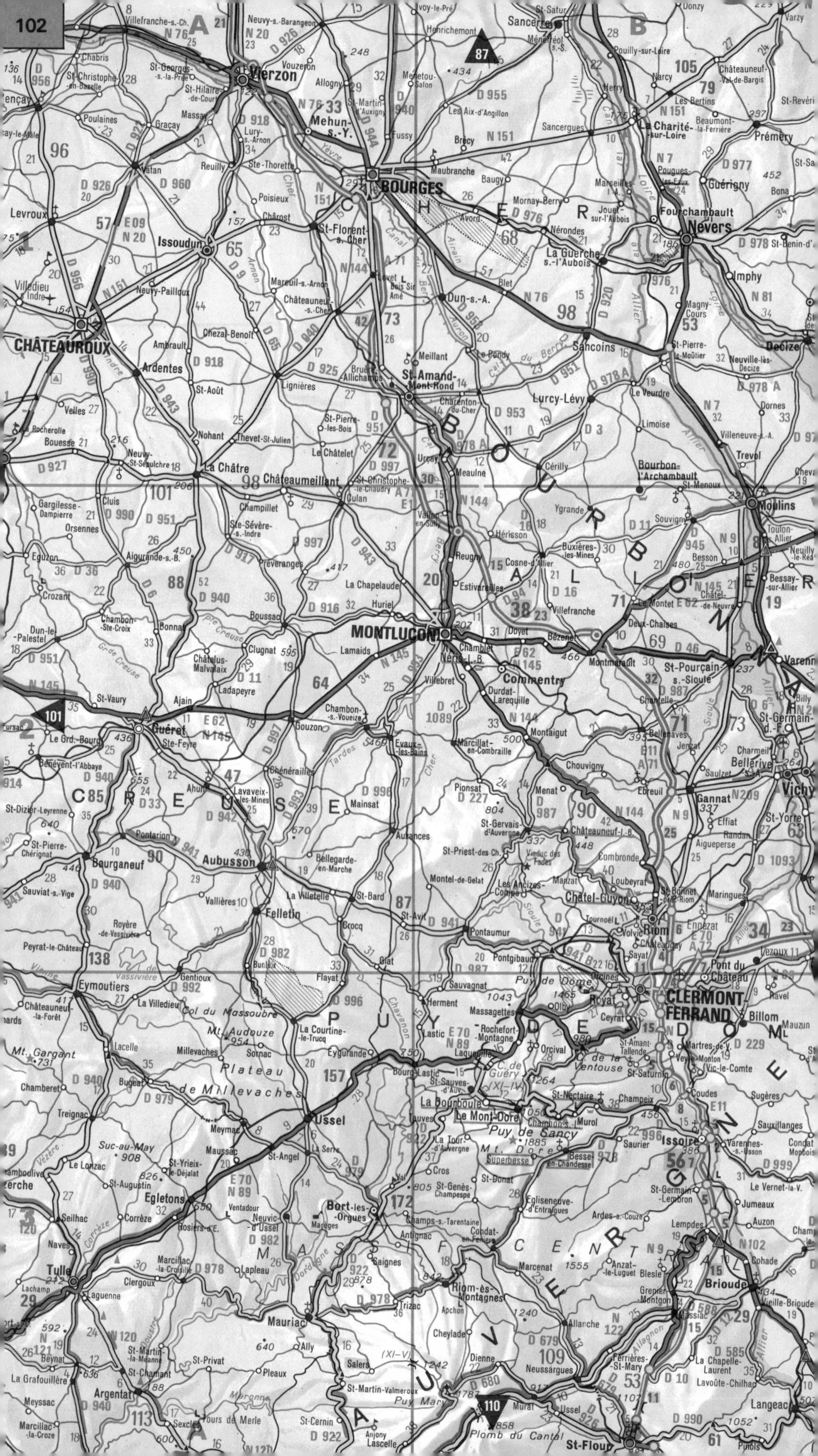
Vierzon
BOURGES
Sancerre
La Charité-sur-Loire
Nevers
Fourchambault
Mehun-s.-Y.
Henrichemont
Châteauneuf-Val-de-Bargis
Prémery
Guérigny
Issoudun
CHÂTEAUROUX
Levroux
Vatan
Reuilly
Gracay
Chârost
St-Florent-s. Cher
Dun-s.-A.
La Guerche s.-l'Aubois
Sancoins
Imphy
Decize
St-Pierre-le-Moûtier
Ardentes
Lignières
St-Amand-Mont-Rond
Châteaumeillant
La Châtre
Lurcy-Lévy
Cérilly
Bourbon-l'Archambault
Moulins
Souvigny
Ygrande
Hérisson
Cosne-d'Allier
MONTLUÇON
Néris-l.-B.
Commentry
Montmarault
St-Pourçain-s.-Sioule
Varennes
Vallon-en-Sully
Culan
Boussac
Huriel
Aigurande-s.-B.
Eguzon
Crozant
Dun-le-Palestel
Guéret
Ajain
Gouzon
Chambon-s.-Voueize
Evaux-les-Bains
Chénérailles
Aubusson
Felletin
Bourganeuf
Eymoutiers
Gannat
Vichy
Bellerive
St-Yorre
Aigueperse
Riom
Châtel-Guyon
Menat
St-Gervais-d'Auvergne
Pontaumur
Pontgibaud
CLERMONT-FERRAND
Royat
Billom
Puy de Dôme
Rochefort-Montagne
La Bourboule
Le Mont-Dore
Puy de Sancy
Besse-en-Chandesse
St-Nectaire
Murol
Issoire
Brioude
Ussel
Meymac
Egletons
Tulle
Bort-les-Orgues
Mauriac
Riom-ès-Montagnes
Argentat
Allanche
Murat
Neussargues
St-Flour
Salers
Puy Mary
Plomb du Cantal
Langeac
Plateau de Millevaches
BOURBONNAIS
CREUSE
PUY DE DÔME
MASSIF CENTRAL
AUVERGNE

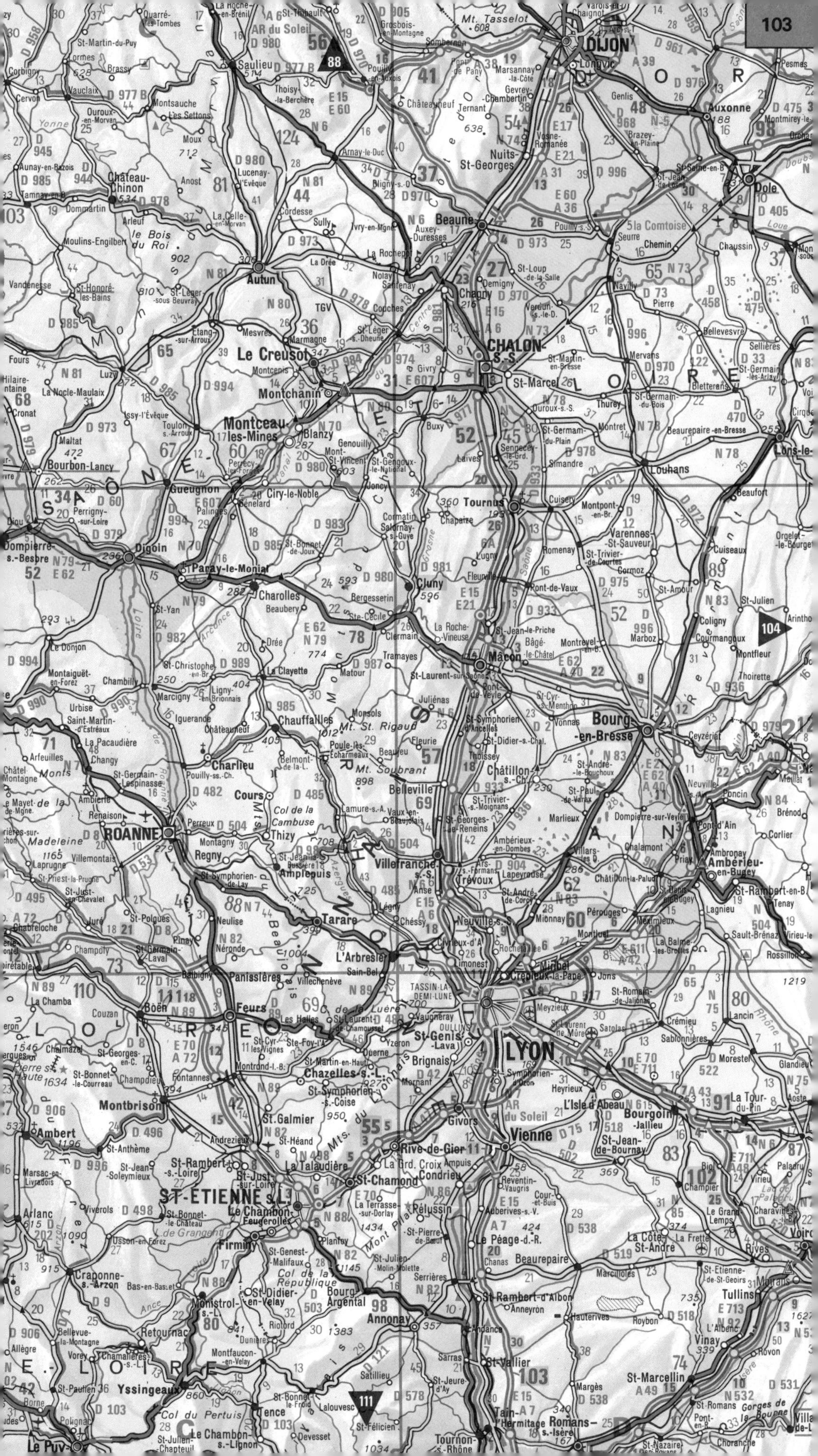
DIJON
Longvic
Genlis
Auxonne
Dole
Pesmes
Saulieu
Quarré-les-Tombes
St-Martin-du-Puy
Lormes
Corbigny
Vauclaix
Montsauche
Les Settons
Ouroux-en-Morvan
Moux
Château-Chinon
Aunay-en-Bazois
Tamnay-en-B.
Dommartin
Arleuf
le Bois du Roi
Moulins-Engilbert
Vandenesse
St-Honoré-les-Bains
St-Léger-sous-Beuvray
Autun
Lucenay-l'Évêque
Anost
La Celle-en-Morvan
Thoisy-la-Berchère
Pouilly-en-Auxois
Sombernon
Grosbois-en-Montagne
Mt. Tasselot
Marsannay-la-Côte
Gevrey-Chambertin
Châteauneuf
Arnay-le-Duc
Bligny-s.-O.
Vosne-Romanée
Nuits-St-Georges
Beaune
Auxey-Duresses
Sully
Ivry-en-Mgne
La Rochepot
Nolay
Santenay
Chagny
Couches
St-Léger-s.-Dheune
Le Creusot
Montcenis
Montchanin
Marmagne
Mesvres
Étang-sur-Arroux
Givry
CHALON-S.-S.
St-Marcel
Seurre
Chemin
Chaussin
Pierre
Verdun-s.-le-D.
St-Loup-de-la-Salle
Demigny
Bellevesvre
Sellières
Mervans
Bletterans
St-Germain-du-Bois
Thurey
Montret
Louhans
Beaurepaire-en-Bresse
Lons-le-S.
Beaufort
Cuiseaux
Luzy
La Nocle-Maulaix
Issy-l'Évêque
Toulon-s.-Arroux
Montceau-les-Mines
Blanzy
Genouilly
Mont-St-Vincent
St-Gengoux-le-National
Buxy
Sennecey-le-Grd.
Simandre
Laives
Tournus
Cuisery
Montpont-en-Br.
Varennes-St-Sauveur
Bourbon-Lancy
Gueugnon
Perrecy-les-Forges
Ciry-le-Noble
Génelard
Palinges
Perrigny-sur-Loire
Digoin
Paray-le-Monial
Charolles
Dompierre-s.-Besbre
Cormatin
Chapaize
Salornay-s.-Guye
Lugny
Romenay
St-Trivier-de-Courtes
Cormoz
St-Amour
Cluny
Fleurville
Pont-de-Vaux
Bergesserin
Ste-Cécile
St-Julien
Coligny
Courmangoux
Montfleur
Thoirette
Arinthod
Orgelet-le-Bourget
St-Yan
Le Donjon
Beaubery
La Roche-Vineuse
Clermain
Tramayes
Mâcon
St-Jean-le-Priche
Bâgé-le-Châtel
Montrevel-en-B.
Marboz
St-Christophe-en-Br.
Montaiguët-en-Forez
Chambilly
Marcigny
La Clayette
Matour
St-Laurent-sur-Saône
Pont-de-Veyle
St-Cyr-s.-Menthon
Vonnas
Bourg-en-Bresse
Ceyzériat
Ligny-en-Brionnais
Urbise
Saint-Martin-d'Estréaux
La Pacaudière
Iguerande
Châteauneuf
Chauffailles
Monsols
Mt. St. Rigaud
Juliénas
St-Symphorien-d'Ancelles
St-Didier-s.-Chal.
Thoissey
Fleurie
Beaujeu
Changy
Arfeuilles
Charlieu
Pouilly-s.-Ch.
Belmont-de-la-L.
Poule-les-Écharmeaux
Mt. Soubrant
Châtillon-s.-Ch.
St-André-le-Bouchoux
St-Paul-de-Varax
Neuville-s.-Ain
Poncin
St-Germain-Lespinasse
Ambierle
Cours
Belleville
St-Trivier-s.-Moignans
Marlieux
Dompierre-sur-Veyle
Pont-d'Ain
Brénod
Corlier
Renaison
ROANNE
Perreux
Montagny
Col de la Cambuse
Thizy
Lamure-s.-A.
Vaux-en-Beaujolais
St-Georges-de-Reneins
Ambérieux-en-Dombes
Villars-les-D.
Chalamont
Priay
Ambronay
Ambérieu-en-Bugey
Madeleine
Villemontais
Lapругne
Regny
Amplepuis
Villefranche-s.-S.
Ars-s.-Formans
Trévoux
Lapeyrouse
St-André-de-Corcy
Châtillon-la-Palud
St-Denis-en-Bugey
St-Rambert-en-B.
Tenay
St-Priest-la-Prugne
St-Just-en-Chevalet
St-Symphorien-de-Lay
Anse
Légny
Chessy
Mionnay
Pérouges
Meximieux
Lagnieu
Sault-Brénaz
Virieu-le-
Juré
St-Polgues
Neulise
Tarare
Néronde
Pinay
Champoly
St-Germain-Laval
L'Arbresle
Sain-Bel
Civrieux-d'A.
Limonest
Neuville-s.-S.
Rochetaillée
Miribel
Montluel
La Balme-les-Grottes
Rossillon
Balbigny
Panissières
Villechenève
Crépieux-la-Pape
Jons
Meyzieux
St-Romain-de-Jalionas
La Chamba
Couzan
Boën
Feurs
Les Halles
St-Laurent-de-Chamousset
Vaugneray
TASSIN-LA-DEMI-LUNE
OULLINS
St-Genis-Laval
LYON
St-Laurent-de-Mûre
Satolas
Crémieu
Lancin
Chalmazel
St-Georges-en-C.
St-Cyr-les-Vignes
Ste-Foy-l'A.
Yzeron
Duerne
St-Martin-en-Haut
Chazelles-s.-L.
Brignais
St-Symphorien-d'Ozon
Heyrieux
Sablonnières
Morestel
Glandieu
Pierre s. Haute
St-Bonnet-le-Courreau
Champdieu
Montrond-l.-B.
Fontannes
Mornant
L'Isle-d'Abeau
Bourgoin-Jallieu
La Tour-du-Pin
Aoste
Montbrison
St-Symphorien-s.-Coise
St-Galmier
Givors
Vienne
St-Jean-de-Bournay
Ambert
St-Anthème
Andrezieux
St-Héand
Mts. du Lyonnais
Rive-de-Gier
Marsac-en-Livradois
St-Jean-Soleymieux
St-Rambert-s.-Loire
St-Just-sur-Loire
La Talaudière
St-Chamond
La Grd. Croix
Ampuis
Condrieu
Reventin-Vaugris
Biol
Virieu
Paladru
ST-ÉTIENNE
Le Chambon-Feugerolles
La Terrasse-sur-Dorlay
Pélussin
Cour-et-Buis
Champier
Le Grand-Lemps
Charavines
Arlanc
Viverols
St-Bonnet-le-Château
Usson-en-Forez
Firminy
Planfoy
St-Genest-Malifaux
Mont Pilat
St-Pierre-de-Bœuf
Auberives-s.-V.
Le Péage-d.-R.
La Côte-St-André
La Frette
Rives
Voiron
Craponne-s.-Arzon
Bas-en-Basset
Col de la République
St-Julien-Molin-Molette
Serrières
Chanas
Beaurepaire
Marcilloles
St-Étienne-de-St-Geoirs
Tullins
Moirans
Monistrol-s.-L.
St-Didier-en-Velay
Riotord
Bourg-Argental
Annonay
St-Rambert-d'Albon
Anneyron
Hauterives
Roybon
L'Albenc
Vinay
Bellevue-la-Montagne
Allègre
Vorey
Chamalières-s.-L.
Retournac
Dunières
Montfaucon-en-Velay
Andance
Sarras
St-Vallier
St-Jeure-d'Ay
Margès
St-Marcellin
Rovon
St-Paulien
Yssingeaux
Satillieu
St-Bonnet-le-Froid
Lalouvesc
St-Romans
Gorges de la Bourne
Borne
Polignac
Le Puy
Col du Pertuis
St-Julien-Chapteuil
Le Chambon-s.-Lignon
Tence
Devesset
St-Félicien
Tournon-s.-Rhône
Tain-l'Hermitage
Romans-s.-Isère
St-Nazaire
Pont-en-R.
Choranche
CÔTE-D'OR
SAÔNE-ET-LOIRE
LOIRE
AIN
RHÔNE
HTE-LOIRE
JURA
Mts. du Beaujolais
Monts du Forez
Monts du Mâconnais
Monts du Charolais
88
104
111

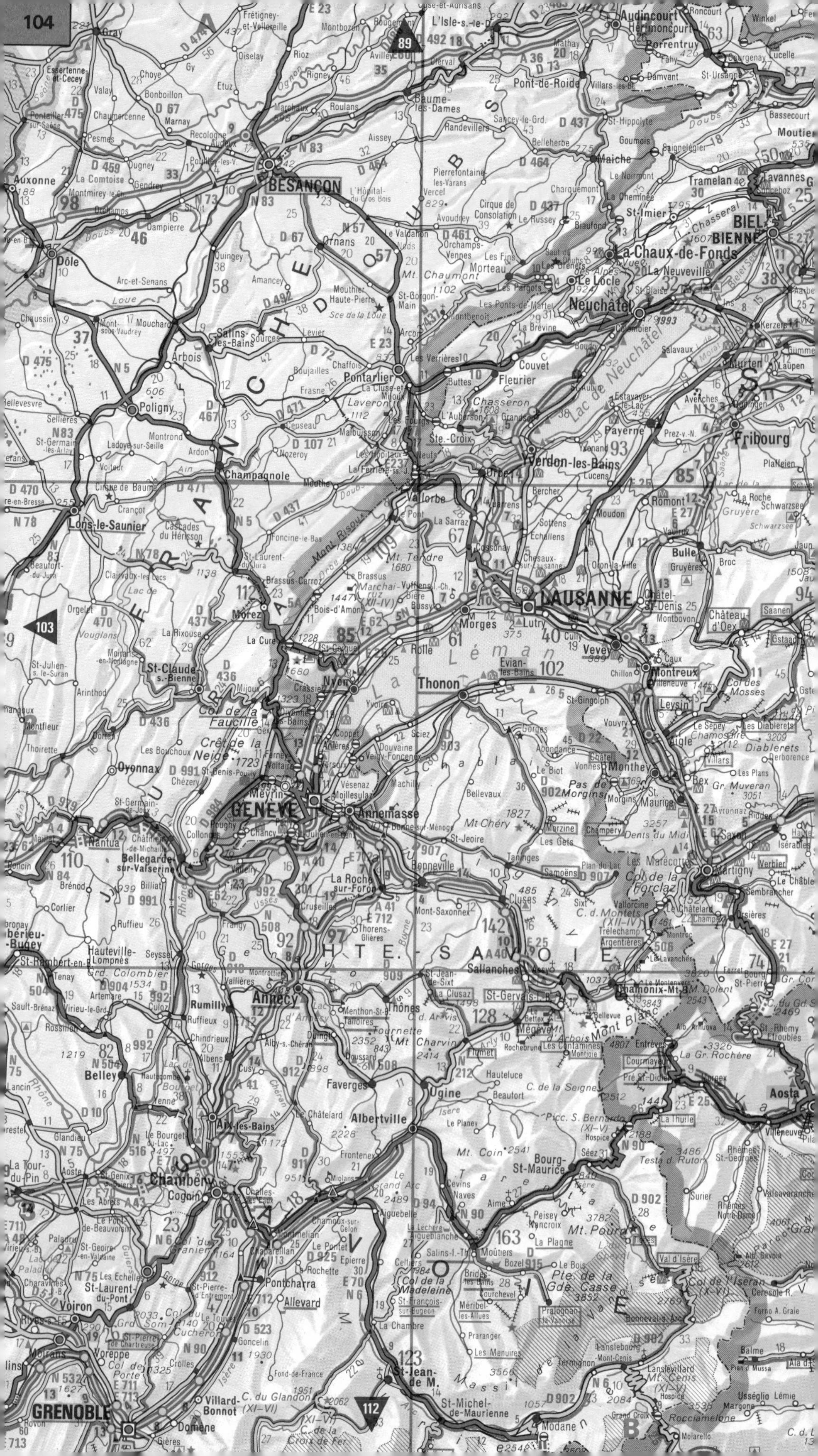
Gray
Fretigney-et-Velloreille
Montbozon
L'Isle-s.-le-D.
Audincourt
Hérimoncourt
Porrentruy
St-Ursanne
Delémont
89
Essertenne-et-Cecey
Pontailler-sur-Saône
Choye
Gy
Oiselay
Rioz
Rigney
Clerval
Pont-de-Roide
Baume-les-Dames
Marnay
Pesmes
Recologne
Audeux
Roulans
Sancey-le-Grd.
St-Hippolyte
Goumois
Saignelégier
Tramelan
Tavannes
Auxonne
La Comtoise
Montmirey-le-Ch.
BESANÇON
Pierrefontaine-les-Varans
Maiche
Le Noirmont
Orchamps
Dampierre
L'Hôpital-du-Gros Bois
Vercel
Cirque de Consolation
Le Russey
Charquemont
St-Imier
Chasseral
BIEL
BIENNE
Dôle
Quingey
Ornans
Le Valdahon
Orchamps-Vennes
Morteau
La-Chaux-de-Fonds
Le Locle
La Neuveville
Arc-et-Senans
Amancey
Mouthier Haute-Pierre
Mt. Chaumont
Neuchâtel
St-Gorgon-Main
Sce de la Loue
Montbenoît
La Brévine
Chaussin
Mont-sous-Vaudrey
Mouchard
Salins-les-Bains
Levier
Arçon
Kerzers
Arbois
Boujailles
Chaffois
Pontarlier
Les Verrières
Buttes
Couvet
Fleurier
Lac de Neuchâtel
Murten
Laupen
Poligny
Frasne
La Cluse-et-Mijoux
Chasseron
Avenches
Estavayer-le-Lac
Bellevesvre
Sellières
Montrond
Les Fourgs
L'Auberson
Grandson
Payerne
Fribourg
St-Germain-les-Arlay
Ardon
Nozeroy
Ste.-Croix
Yverdon-les-Bains
Voiteur
Champagnole
Mouthe
Les Hôpitaux-Neufs
Orbe
Lucens
Romont
Cirque de Baume
Vallorbe
Lons-le-Saunier
Crançot
Cascades du Hérisson
La Sarraz
Moudon
Schwarzsee
Gruyère
Foncine-le-Bas
Mont Risoux
Mt. Tendre
Cossonay
Bulle
Gruyères
Beaufort-du-Jura
Clairvaux-les-Lacs
St-Laurent-du-Jura
Brassus-Carroz
Le Brassus
Oron-la-Ville
Châtel-St-Denis
LAUSANNE
Orgelet
Bois-d'Amont
Morges
Lutry
Vevey
Château-d'Oex
Saanen
Gstaad
103
Morez
La Rixouse
La Cure
Rolle
Lac Léman
Cully
Montbovon
St-Julien-s.-le-Suran
St-Claude-s.-Bienne
Nyon
Thonon
Evian-les-Bains
Montreux
Chillon
Col des Mosses
Arinthod
Mijoux
Crassier
Yvoire
St-Gingolph
Villeneuve
Leysin
Montfleur
Col de la Faucille
Divonne-les-Bains
Gex
Coppet
Douvaine
Sciez
Gorges
Abondance
Vouvry
Aigle
Les Diablerets
Diablerets
Thoirette
Crêt de la Neige
Les Bouchoux
Ferney-Voltaire
Versoix
Chablais
Châtel
Monthey
Bex
Villars
Oyonnax
St-Genis-Pouilly
Chézery
Meyrin
GENÈVE
Machilly
Bellevaux
Le Biot
Pas de Morgins
Morgins
St.-Maurice
Gr. Muveran
St-Germain-de-Joux
Annemasse
Mt Chéry
Morzine
Champéry
Dents du Midi
Nantua
Châtillon-de-Michaille
Collonges
Chancy
St-Julien-en-Genevois
Bonne-sur-Ménoge
St-Jeoire
Les Gets
Saxon
Bellegarde-sur-Valserine
Bonneville
Taninges
Samoëns
Plan-du-Lac
Les Marécottes
Martigny
Le Châble
Brénod
La Roche-sur-Foron
Col de la Forclaz
Billiat
Cluses
Sixt
Vallorcine
Sembrancher
Corlier
Cruseilles
Mont-Saxonnex
C. d. Montets
Orsières
Ruffieu
Frangy
Thorens-Glières
Trélechamp
Argentières
Ambérieu-en-Bugey
Hauteville-Lompnès
Seyssel
HTE.-SAVOIE
St-Rambert-en-B.
Tenay
Grd. Colombier
Vallières
Sallanches
Bourg-St-Pierre
Artemare
Virieu-le-Grd.
Rumilly
Annecy
Thônes
La Clusaz
St-Gervais-l.-B.
Chamonix-Mt-B.
Mt. Dolent
Sault-Brénaz
Rossillon
Ruffieux
Chindrieux
Menthon-St-B.
Talloires
Tournette
Mt Charvin
Mégève
Mont Blanc
Col du Gd St-Bernard
St.-Rhémy
Etroubles
Belley
Albens
Alby-s.-Chéran
Duingt
Rochebrune
Les Contamines-Montjoie
Entrèves
Courmayeur
La Gr. Rochère
Lancin
Cusy
Doussard
Flumet
Hauteluce
Pré St-Didier
Aosta
Lac du Bourget
Faverges
Ugine
C. de la Seigne
Aix-les-Bains
Le Châtelard
Albertville
Beaufort
Picc. S. Bernardo
La Thuile
Villeneuve
Glandieu
Le Bourget-du-Lac
Le Planey
Hospice
Mt. Coin
Séez
Testa d. Rutor
Rhêmes-St-Georges
La Tour-du-Pin
Aoste
St-Genix-s.-G.
Chambéry
Frontenex
Bourg-St-Maurice
Les Abrets
Cognin
Challes-les-Eaux
Miolans
Grand Arc
Cevins
Naves
Aime
Surier
Valsavarenche
Le Pont-de-Beauvoisin
Col du Granier
Aiguebelle
Chamoux-sur-Gelon
Montmélian
Le Lechère
Aigueblanche
Peisey Nancroix
Mt. Pourri
Rhêmes Notre Dame
St-Geoire-en-Valdaine
Chapareillan
Le Pontet
Epierre
Salins-l.-Th.
Moûtiers
La Plagne
Val d'Isère
Paladru
Les Echelles
St-Laurent-du-Pont
St-Pierre-d'Entremont
Pontcharra
Allevard
Cellier
Col de la Madeleine
Brides-les-Bains
Bozel
Courchevel
Pte. de la Gde. Casse
Col de l'Iseran
Ceresole R.
Charavines
Voiron
Grd Som
Cucheron
Le Touvet
Goncelin
St-François-sur-Bugeon
Méribel-les-Allues
Pralognan-la-Vanoise
Bonneval-s.-Arc
Forno A. Graie
Rives
St-Pierre-de-Chartreuse
Voreppe
Col de Porte
Crolles
La Chambre
Praranger
Les Menuires
Lanslebourg-Mont-Cenis
Balme
Moirans
Fond-de-France
Termignon
Lanslevillard
Mt. Cenis
Ala di S.
Pian d. Mussa
St-Jean-de M.
Massif de la Vanoise
Usséglio
Lémie
Margone
GRENOBLE
Villard-Bonnot
C. du Glandon
112
St-Michel-de-Maurienne
Modane
Rocciamelone
Grand Croix
Voiron
Domène
Gières
C. de la Croix de Fer
Molaretto
C. d. L.

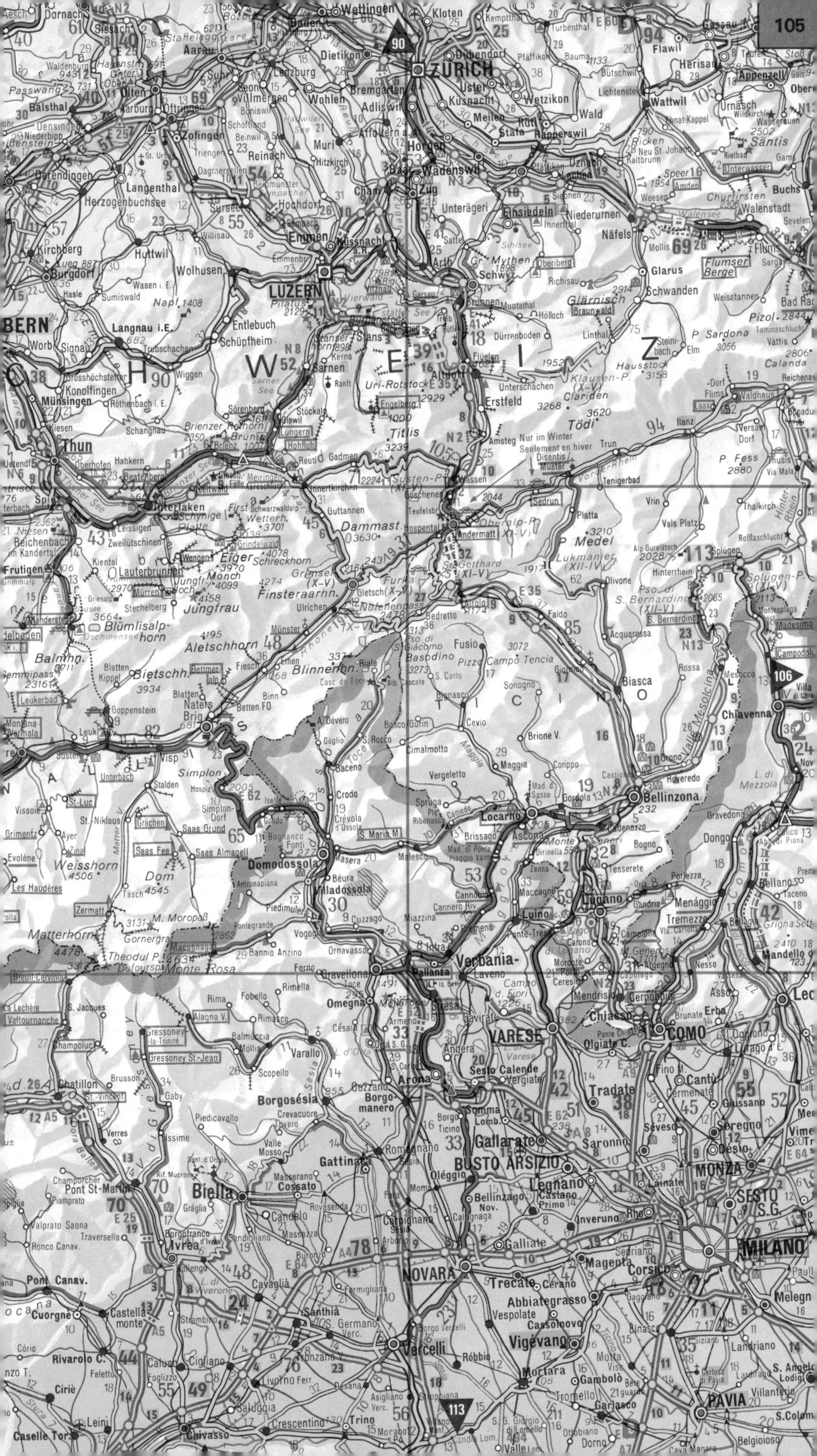
90
106
113
ZÜRICH
LUZERN
BERN
MILANO
S C H W E I Z
Baden
Wettingen
Kloten
Aarau
Olten
Zofingen
Lenzburg
Dietikon
Bremgarten
Wohlen
Uster
Küsnacht
Meilen
Stäfa
Wetzikon
Wald
Rapperswil
Horgen
Wädenswil
Zug
Cham
Baar
Langenthal
Herzogenbuchsee
Burgdorf
Kirchberg
Huttwil
Wolhusen
Emmen
Küssnacht a.R.
Sursee
Hochdorf
Einsiedeln
Schwyz
Glarus
Näfels
Schwanden
Walenstadt
Flums
Wattwil
Herisau
Appenzell
Säntis
Flawil
Gossau
Buchs
Lachen
Niederurnen
Langnau i.E.
Entlebuch
Schüpfheim
Sarnen
Stans
Altdorf
Flüelen
Erstfeld
Amsteg
Wassen
Göschenen
Andermatt
Hospental
Münsingen
Konolfingen
Thun
Spiez
Interlaken
Brienz
Meiringen
Innertkirchen
Grindelwald
Wengen
Lauterbrunnen
Mürren
Eiger
Mönch
Jungfrau
Schreckhorn
Finsteraarhn.
Aletschhorn
Titlis
Tödi
Clariden
Dammast.
Frutigen
Reichenbach
Kandersteg
Leukerbad
Leuk
Visp
Brig
Naters
Fiesch
Gletsch
Ulrichen
Simplon
Zermatt
Saas Fee
Saas Grund
Matterhorn
Monte Rosa
Weisshorn
Dom
St. Gotthard
Airolo
Faido
Biasca
Bellinzona
Locarno
Ascona
Lugano
Chiasso
Mendrisio
Como
Luino
Verbania-Pallanza
Domodossola
Villadossola
Omegna
Stresa
Arona
Varese
Sesto Calende
Gallarate
Busto Arsizio
Legnano
Saronno
Tradate
Cantù
Seregno
Monza
Sesto S.G.
Rho
Magenta
Abbiategrasso
Vigévano
Mortara
Pavia
Novara
Vercelli
Biella
Ivrea
Borgosésia
Varallo
Gattinara
Cossato
Santhià
Chivasso
Trino
Cuorgnè
Rivarolo C.
Ciriè
Caselle Tor.
Châtillon
Pont St-Martin
Chiavenna
Menággio
Bellano
Lecco
Mandello
Erba
Splügen
Ilanz
Disentis
Flims
Chur
Sargans
Vättis
Oberalp-P.
Susten-P.
Furka
Grimsel
Nufenenpass
Lukmanier
S. Bernardino
Klausen-P.
Splügen-P.
Sedrun
Olivone
Thalkirch
Mesocco
Roveredo
Gravedona
Dongo
Tremezzo
Ornavasso
Gravellona
Borgomanero
Romagnano
Crevacuore
Candelo
Cavaglià
Galliate
Trecate
Corsico
Binasco
Garlasco
Gambolò
Motta
Vespolate
Mortara
Cassolnovo
Landriano
S. Angelo Lodigiano
Melegnano
Villanterio
S. Colombano

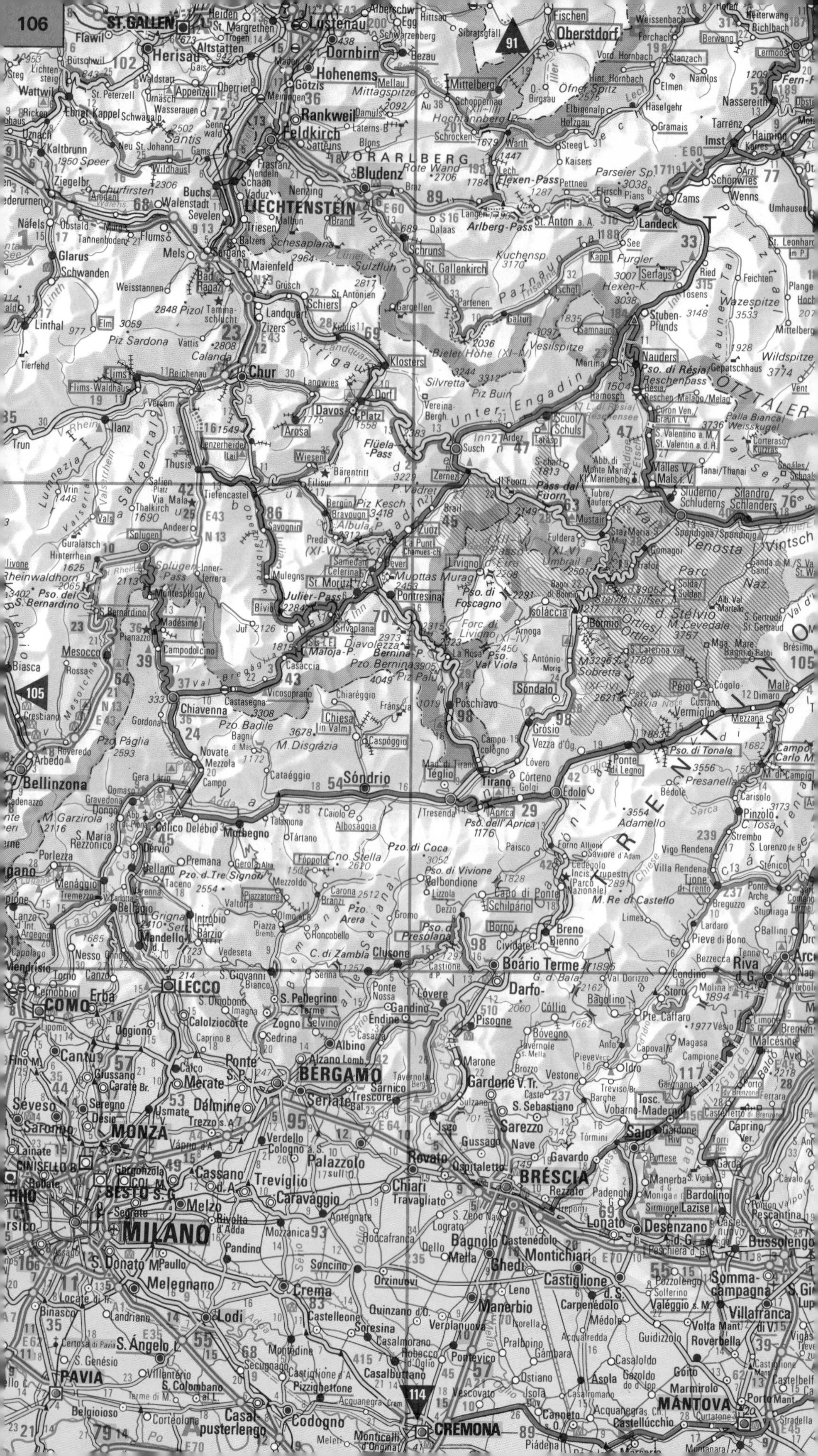
St. Gallen
Lustenau
Oberstdorf
Fischen
Herisau
Dornbirn
Hohenems
Götzis
Altstätten
Appenzell
Wattwil
Rankweil
Feldkirch
Säntis
Mittelberg
Warth
Lech
Vorarlberg
Bludenz
Liechtenstein
Vaduz
Schaan
Buchs
Walenstadt
Flums
Sargans
Bad Ragaz
Glarus
Schwanden
Näfels
Linthal
Maienfeld
Landquart
Schiers
Chur
Flims
Klosters
Davos
Arosa
Thusis
Ilanz
Lenzerheide
Schruns
St. Gallenkirch
St. Anton a. A.
Arlberg-Pass
Flexen-Pass
Landeck
Imst
Zams
Ischgl
Galtür
Samnaun
Nauders
Pso. di Résia
Reschenpass
Silvretta
Piz Buin
Unter-Engadin
Scuol/Schuls
Zernez
Susch
Flüela-Pass
Pass dal Fuorn
Mals i. V.
Schluderns
Schlanders
Vinschgau
Val Venosta
Ötztaler
Paznaun Tal
Julier-Pass
St. Moritz
Samedan
Pontresina
Silvaplana
Maloja-P.
Bernina-P.
Pzo. Bernina
Livigno
Bormio
Stelvio
Ortler
M. Cevedale
Poschiavo
Tirano
Sóndrio
Splügen
Splügen-Pass
San Bernardino
Pso. del S. Bernardino
Mesocco
Chiavenna
Madésimo
Campodolcino
Biasca
Bellinzona
Arbedo
Morbegno
Colico
Dongo
Gravedona
Menággio
Bellagio
Lecco
Como
Erba
Cantù
Seregno
Desio
Monza
Milano
Sesto S. G.
Rho
Cinisello B.
Lainate
Saronno
Seveso
Merate
Dàlmine
Bergamo
Seriate
Treviglio
Caravaggio
Melzo
Gorgonzola
Cassano d'A.
Melegnano
S. Donato M.
Lodi
Crema
S. Angelo L.
Pavia
Codogno
Casalpusterlengo
Cremona
Chiari
Rovato
Palazzolo
Sàrnico
Lóvere
Clusone
Darfo-Boário Terme
Breno
Edolo
Ponte di Legno
Pso. di Tonale
Aprica
Pso. dell' Aprica
Adamello
Trentino
Pinzolo
Tione di Trento
Riva d. G.
Malcesine
Salò
Gardone V. T.
Brescia
Desenzano d. G.
Lonato
Montichiari
Castiglione d. S.
Manerbio
Ghedi
Orzinuovi
Soncino
Villafranca di V.
Bussolengo
Sommacampagna
Mantova
Valéggio s. M.
Peschiera d. G.
Lazise
Bardolino
Male
Dimaro
Vermiglio
Lago di Garda
Lago d'Iseo
Lago di Como

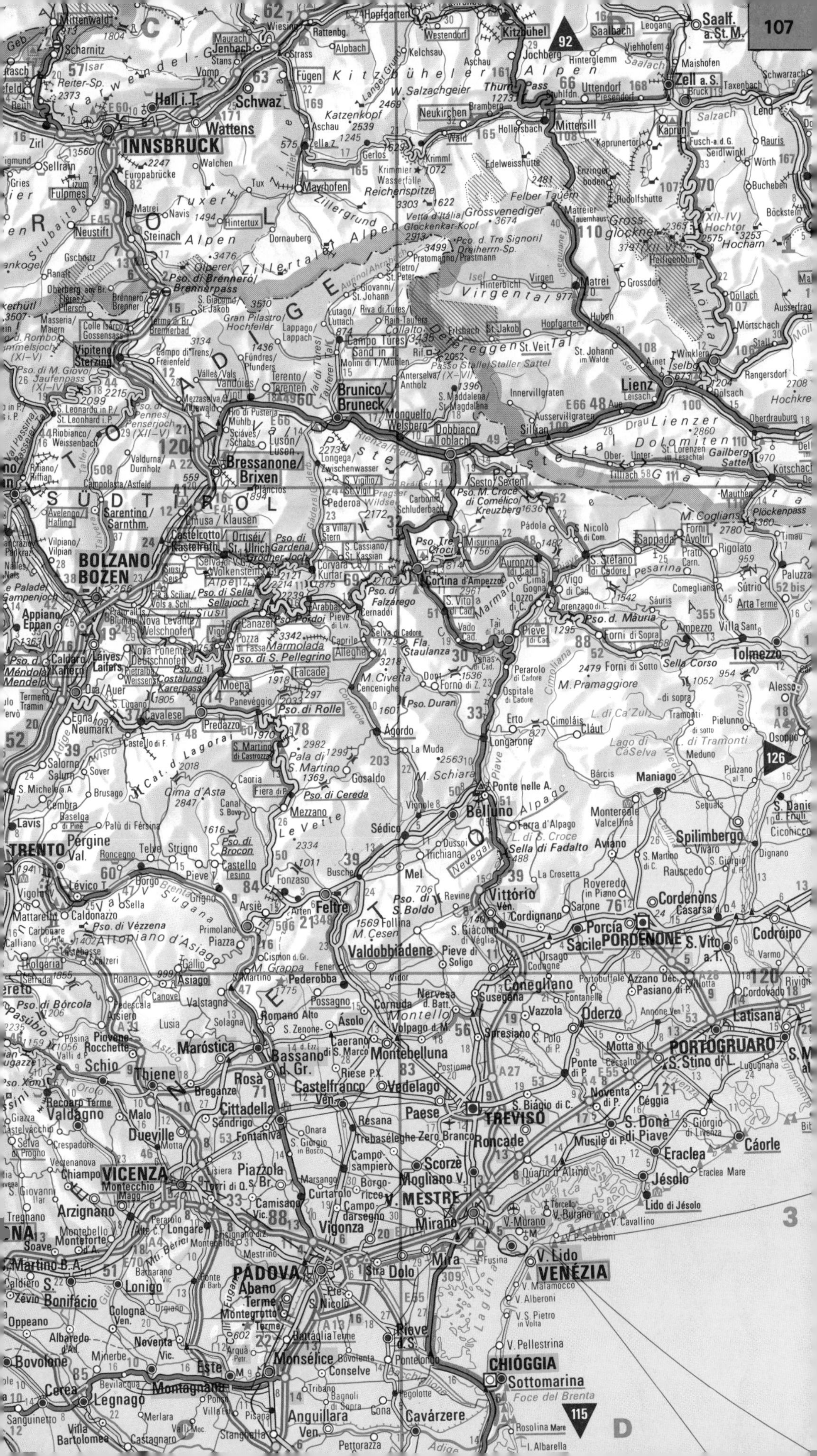

Mittenwald
Scharnitz
Karwendel-G.
Jenbach
Stans
Vomp
Hall i.T.
Schwaz
Wattens
INNSBRUCK
Zirl
Sellrain
Europabrücke
Fulpmes
Neustift
Matrei
Navis
Steinach
Tuxer Alpen
Hintertux
Mayrhofen
Zillertal
Zillertaler Alpen
Fügen
Kitzbüheler Alpen
Hopfgarten
Wiesing
Rattenbg.
Alpbach
Westendorf
Kitzbühel
Kelchsau
Aschau
Jochberg
Thurn Pass
Gerlos
Krimml
Krimmler Wasserfälle
Reichenspitze
Neukirchen
Bramberg
Hollersbach
Mittersill
Wald
Saalf. a.St.M.
Saalbach
Leogang
Viehhofen
Hinterglemm
Maishofen
Zell a.S.
Bruck
Taxenbach
Schwarzach
Lend
Uttendorf
Piesendorf
Kaprun
Fusch a.d.G.
Rauris
Seidlwinkl
Wörth
Bucheben
Böckstein
Edelweisshütte
Enzingerboden
Rudolfshütte
Felber Tauern
Grossvenediger
Grossglockner
Hochtor
Hocharn
Heiligenblut
Dreiherrn-Sp.
Prastmann
Matrei i.O.
Virgen
Virgental
Hinterbichl
Grossdorf
Dollach
Mölltal
Huben
Hopfgarten
St. Jakob
Defereggen
St. Veit
Staller Sattel
St. Johann im Walde
Ainet
Iselsberg
Winklern
Mörtschach
Ausserfrag
Stall
Rangersdorf
Lienz
Leisach
Dölsach
Oberdrauburg
Hochkre
Innervillgraten
Ausservillgraten
Sillian
Lienzer Dolomiten
Pustertal
Ober-Tilliach
Unter-Tilliach
St. Lorenzen im Lesachtal
Gailberg Sattel
Kötschach
Mauthen
Plöckenpass
Gailtal
Brennero/Brenner
Pso. di Brennero/Brennerpass
Olperer
Colle Isarco/Gossensass
Vipiteno/Sterzing
Campo di Trens/Freienfeld
Pso. di M. Giovo/Jaufenpass
Pso. di Pennes/Penserjoch
St. Leonhard i.P.
Riobianco/Weissenbach
Valdurna/Durnholz
Sarentino/Sarnthm.
Avelengo/Hafling
Vilpiano/Vilpian
BOLZANO
BOZEN
Appiano/Eppan
Caldaro/Kaltern
Pso. d. Méndola/Mendelp.
Termeno/Tramin
Ora/Auer
Egna/Neumarkt
Laives/Leifers
Nova Ponente/Deutschnofen
Nova Levante/Welschnofen
Pso. di Costalunga/Karerpass
Cavalese
Predazzo
Moena
Bressanone/Brixen
Plancios
Chiusa/Klausen
Castelrotto/Kastelruth
Ortisei/St. Ulrich
Selva/Wolkenstein
Pso. di Gardena/Grödner Joch
Pso. di Sella/Sellajoch
Alpe di Siusi
Canazei
Pso. Pordoi
Marmolada
Pso. di S. Pellegrino
Falcade
Pso. di Rolle
S. Martino di Castrozza
Pala di S. Martino
Fiera di P.
Pso. di Cereda
Corvara/Kurfar
Arabba
La Villa/Stern
S. Cassiano/St. Kassian
Pso. di Falzarego
Cortina d'Ampezzo
Pso. Tre Croci
Misurina
Dobbiaco/Toblach
Monguelfo/Welsberg
Brunico/Bruneck
Campo Tures/Sand in T.
Val di Tures
Valle Aurina/Ahrntal
Anterselva/Antholz
Sesto/Sexten
Pso. M. Croce di Comélico/Kreuzberg
Auronzo di Cad.
S. Stefano di Cadore
Sappada
Forni Avoltri
M. Coglians
Rigolato
Paluzza
Sútrio
Arta Terme
Comeglians
Ampezzo
Villa Sant.
Tolmezzo
Forni di Sopra
Forni di Sotto
Pso. d. Máuria
Sella Corso
Sáuris
Lorenzago di C.
Lozzo di C.
Pieve di Cad.
Vigo di Cad.
S. Vito di Cad.
Vodo Cad.
Marmarole
Fla. Staulanza
M. Civetta
Alleghe
Caprile
Selva di Cadore
Cencenighe
Ágordo
Pso. Duran
Forno di Z.
Longarone
Erto
Cimoláis
Cláut
M. Pramaggiore
Ospitale di Cadore
Perarolo di Cadore
Lago di CáSelva
Tramonti di sopra
Tramonti di sotto
Meduno
Osoppo
Alesso
Pielunno
Maniago
Bárcis
Pinzano al T.
Sequals
Spilimbergo
Montereale Valcellina
S. Daniele d. Friuli
Ciconicco
Dignano
Vivaro
Aviano
Rauscedo
S. Giorgio d. R.
Cordenòns
Casarsa d.D.
Codróipo
PORDENONE
Porcía
Sacile
S. Vito a.T.
Varmo
Roveredo in Piano
Sarone
Cordignano
Vittório Vén.
Sella di Fadalto
Farra d'Alpago
Alpago
Belluno
Ponte nelle A.
Nevegal
Trichiana
Mel
Sédico
Pso. di S. Boldo
Revine
Follina
Valdobbiádene
Pieve di Soligo
Conegliano
Susegana
Vazzola
Oderzo
Motta di L.
Portobuffolè
Azzano Dec.
Pasiano di P.
Cordovado
Latisana
PORTOGRUARO
S. Stino di L.
Lugugnana
Ceggia
S. Donà di Piave
S. Giorgio di Livenza
Cáorle
Eraclea
Eraclea Mare
Jésolo
Lido di Jésolo
Musile di P.
Noventa di P.
Cessalto
Ponte di P.
Spresiano
Roncade
TREVISO
Quarto d'Altino
S. Biágio di C.
Paese
Zero Branco
Trebaséleghe
Scorzè
Mogliano V.
V. MESTRE
Mirano
Mira
Dolo
Stra
V. Burano
V. Torcello
V. Murano
V. Cavallino
V. Lido
VENÉZIA
V. Malamocco
V. Alberoni
V. S. Pietro in Volta
V. Pellestrina
CHIÓGGIA
Sottomarina
Foce del Brenta
Rosolina Mare
I. Albarella
Piove d.S.
Pontelongo
Cavárzere
Conselve
Bovolenta
Battáglia Terme
Monsélice
Este
Montagnana
Anguillara Ven.
Legnago
Cerea
Bovolone
Sanguinetto
Villa Bartolomea
Castagnaro
PÁDOVA
Abano Terme
Montegrotto Terme
Vigonza
Camposampiero
Castelfranco Ven.
Vedelago
Montebelluna
Cornuda
Ásolo
Nervesa d. Batt.
Bassano d. Gr.
Rosà
Cittadella
Fontaniva
Piazzola s. Br.
Camisano Vic.
VICENZA
Montecchio Magg.
Arzignano
Chiampo
Valdagno
Recoaro Terme
Schio
Thiene
Marostica
Breganze
Sandrigo
Dueville
Malo
Lonigo
Noventa Vic.
Soave
S. Bonifácio
Caldiero
Zevio
Oppeano
Albaredo d'Adige
Montebello Vic.
Montecchia
Longare
Barbarano Vic.
Piovene Rocchette
Arsiero
Asiago
Gállio
Altopiano d'Asiago
Pso. di Vézzena
Lavarone
Folgaria
Caldonazzo
Lévico T.
Pergine Val.
TRENTO
Lavis
Cembra
Sover
Borgo
Valsugana
Grigno
Primolano
Arsiè
Feltre
Fonzaso
Pso. di Brocon
Castello Tesino
Strigno
Pieve T.
Telve
Roncegno
Lago di Caldonazzo
Pso. di Bórcola
Pasúbio
Valstagna
Pederobba
Possagno
Romano Alto
M. Grappa
Cat. d. Lagorai
Cima d'Asta
Salorno
Salurn
S. Michele a.A.
Mezzano
Sover
Brusago
Canal S. Bovo
Caoria
Le Vette
Gosaldo
M. Schiara
La Muda
Vignole
Busche
TRENTINO
SÜDTIROL
ALTO ADIGE
VENETO
TIROL
Salzach
Saalach
Isel
Drau
Piave
Adige
Brenta
Livenza
Laguna
3
C
D
62
92
115
126

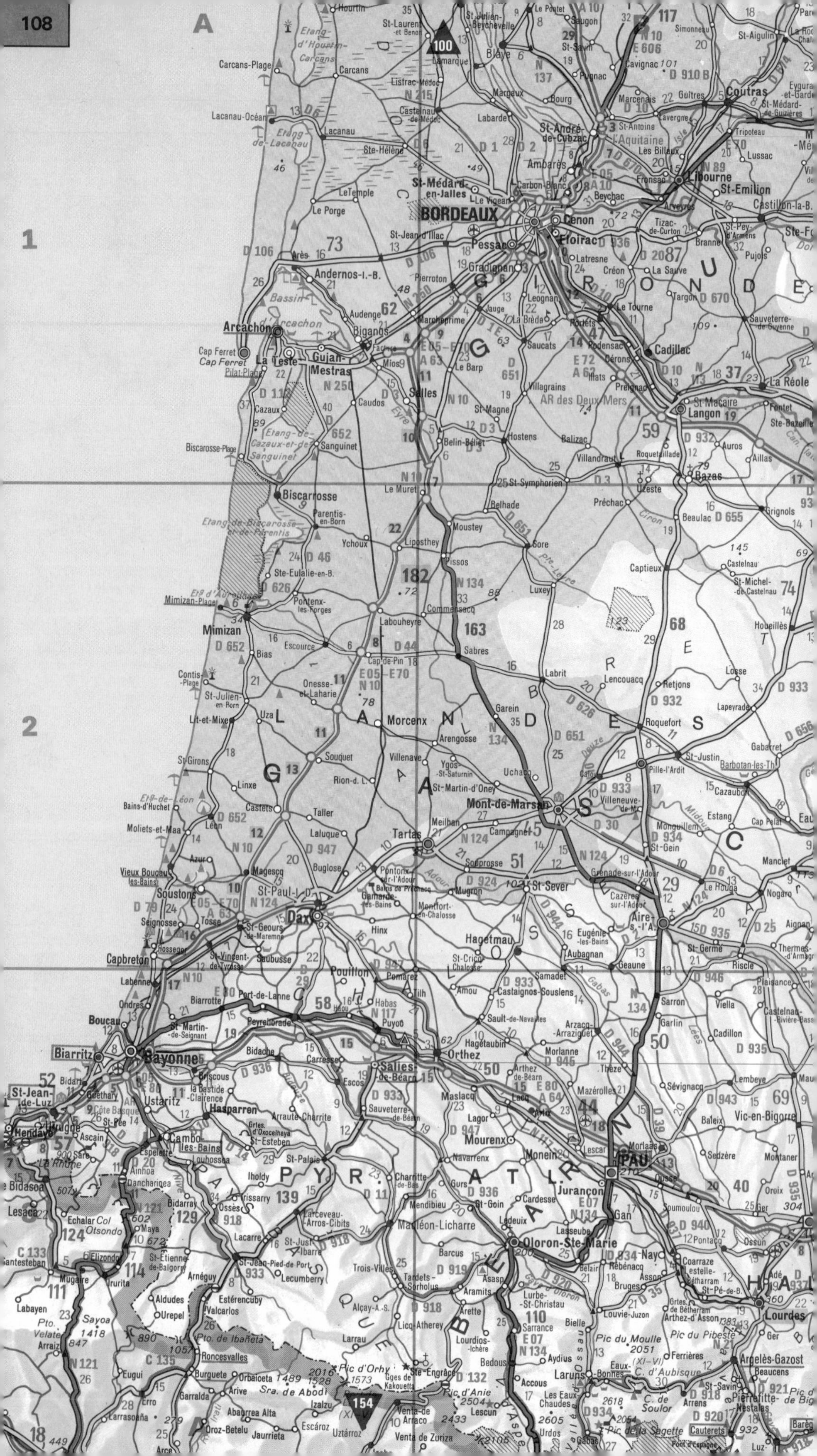
A
1
2
BORDEAUX
Arcachon
Bassin d'Arcachon
Cap Ferret
La Teste
Gujan-Mestras
Lacanau-Océan
Lacanau
Carcans-Plage
Carcans
Hourtin
St-Médard-en-Jalles
Blaye
Libourne
St-Emilion
Coutras
Cenon
Floirac
Pessac
Gradignan
Mérignac
Andernos-l.-B.
Biganos
Salles
Belin-Béliet
Cadillac
Langon
La Réole
Bazas
Biscarrosse
Parentis-en-Born
Mimizan
Mimizan-Plage
Labouheyre
Pissos
Sabres
Morcenx
Mont-de-Marsan
Roquefort
Villeneuve-de-M.
Tartas
Dax
St-Sever
Hagetmau
Aire-s.-l'A.
Soustons
Vieux Boucau-les-Bains
Hossegor
Capbreton
Labenne
Boucau
Biarritz
Bayonne
St-Jean-de-Luz
Hendaye
Ustaritz
Hasparren
Cambo-les-Bains
Peyrehorade
Orthez
Salies-de-Béarn
Sauveterre-de-Béarn
Mourenx
Lacq
Artix
PAU
Jurançon
Oloron-Ste-Marie
Mauléon-Licharre
St-Jean-Pied-de-Port
St-Palais
Nay
Lourdes
Argelès-Gazost
Cauterets
Laruns
Eaux-Bonnes
Roncesvalles
Elizondo
Pic d'Orhy
Pic d'Anie
Pic du Midi d'Ossau
Col d'Aubisque
G I R O N D E
L A N D E S
L A N D E S
G A S C O G N E
P Y R É N É E S - A T L A N T I Q U E S
B É A R N
P A Y S B A S Q U E
N 10
N 134
N 124
N 117
A 63
A 64
E 05 - E 70
E 80
100
154

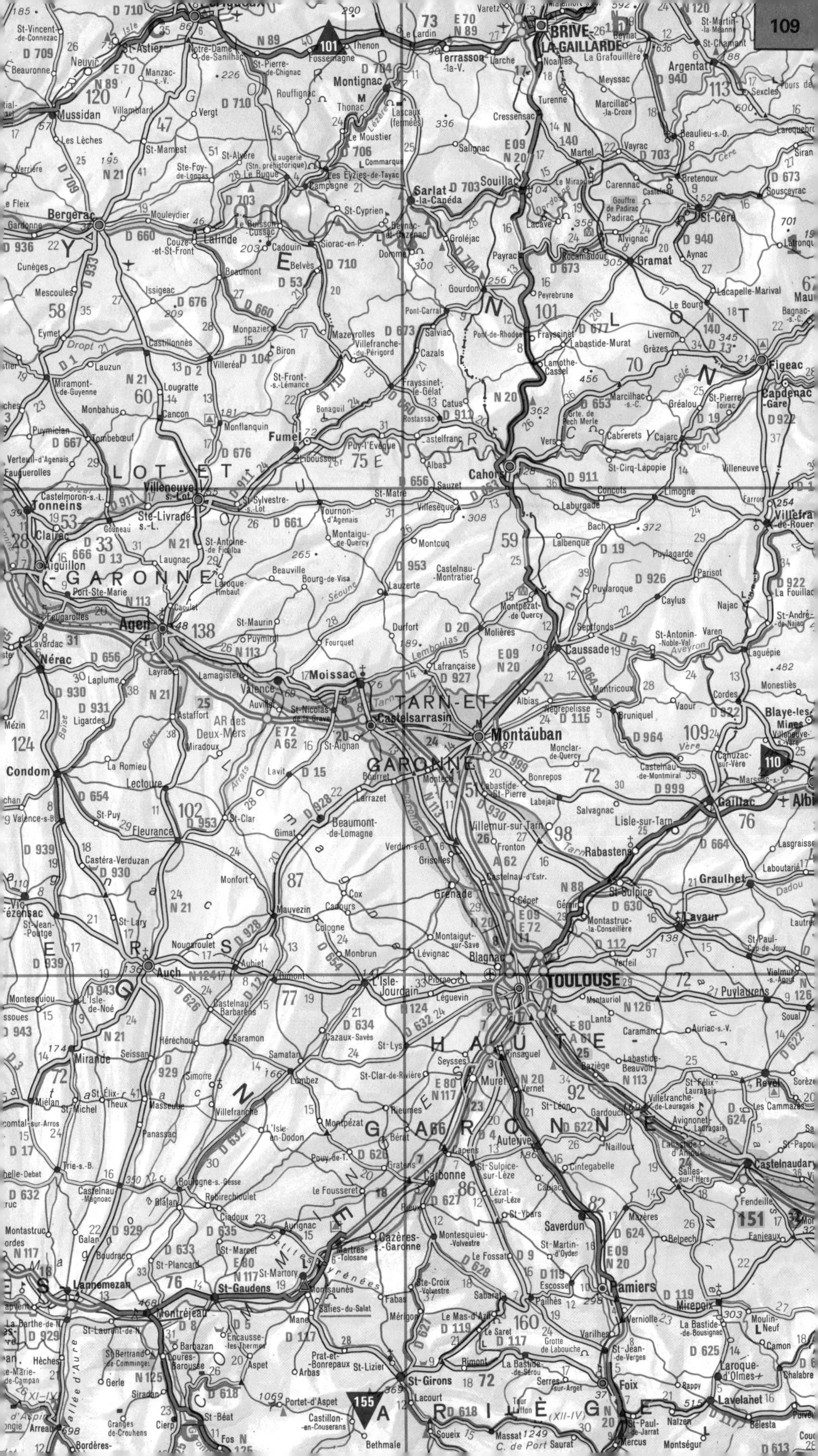
BRIVE-LA-GAILLARDE
Terrasson-la-V.
Montignac
Lascaux (fermée)
Le Moustier
Les Eyzies-de-Tayac
Sarlat-la-Canéda
Souillac
Martel
Turenne
Meyssac
Argentat
Beaulieu-s.-D.
Bretenoux
St-Céré
Gramat
Rocamadour
Padirac
Gouffre de Padirac
Gourdon
Figeac
Capdenac-Gare
Cahors
St-Cirq-Lapopie
Cajarc
Grte. de Pech Merle
Labastide-Murat
Mussidan
Neuvic
St-Astier
Bergerac
Lalinde
Le Buisson-Cussac
Cadouin
Belvès
Siorac-en-P.
St-Cyprien
Beynac-et-Cazenac
Domme
Eymet
Issigeac
Beaumont
Monpazier
Villeréal
Castillonnès
Lauzun
Miramont-de-Guyenne
Monflanquin
Fumel
Puy-l'Évêque
Villefranche-du-Périgord
Biron
Villeneuve-s.-Lot
Ste-Livrade-s.-L.
Tonneins
Clairac
Aiguillon
Port-Ste-Marie
Agen
Nérac
Lavardac
LOT-ET-GARONNE
Tournon-d'Agenais
Montaigu-de-Quercy
Montcuq
Lauzerte
Bourg-de-Visa
Castelnau-Montratier
Montpezat-de-Quercy
Caussade
Molières
Moissac
Valence
Auvillar
Castelsarrasin
TARN-ET-GARONNE
Montauban
Nègrepelisse
Bruniquel
St-Antonin-Noble-Val
Caylus
Najac
Villefranche-de-Rouergue
Laguépie
Cordes
Gaillac
Albi
Lisle-sur-Tarn
Rabastens
Graulhet
Lavaur
St-Sulpice
Villemur-sur-Tarn
Fronton
Grenade
Blagnac
TOULOUSE
Puylaurens
Revel
Castelnaudary
Villefranche-de-Lauragais
Muret
Seysses
Auterive
Carbonne
Rieumes
Samatan
Lombez
L'Isle-Jourdain
Mauvezin
Auch
Fleurance
Lectoure
Condom
Mirande
Vic-Fezensac
Beaumont-de-Lomagne
Verdun-s-G.
Castelnau-Magnoac
Trie-s.-B.
Boulogne-s.-Gesse
Lannemezan
Montréjeau
St-Gaudens
St-Bertrand-de-Comminges
Aspet
St-Girons
St-Lizier
Salies-du-Salat
Cazères-s.-Garonne
Le Fousseret
Montesquieu-Volvestre
Le Mas-d'Azil
Saverdun
Pamiers
Mirepoix
Foix
Lavelanet
Tarascon-s.-A.
Massat
Castillon-en-Couserans
Bagnères-de-Luchon
St-Béat
HAUTE-GARONNE
ARIÈGE
GERS
LOT
DORDOGNE
101
110
155

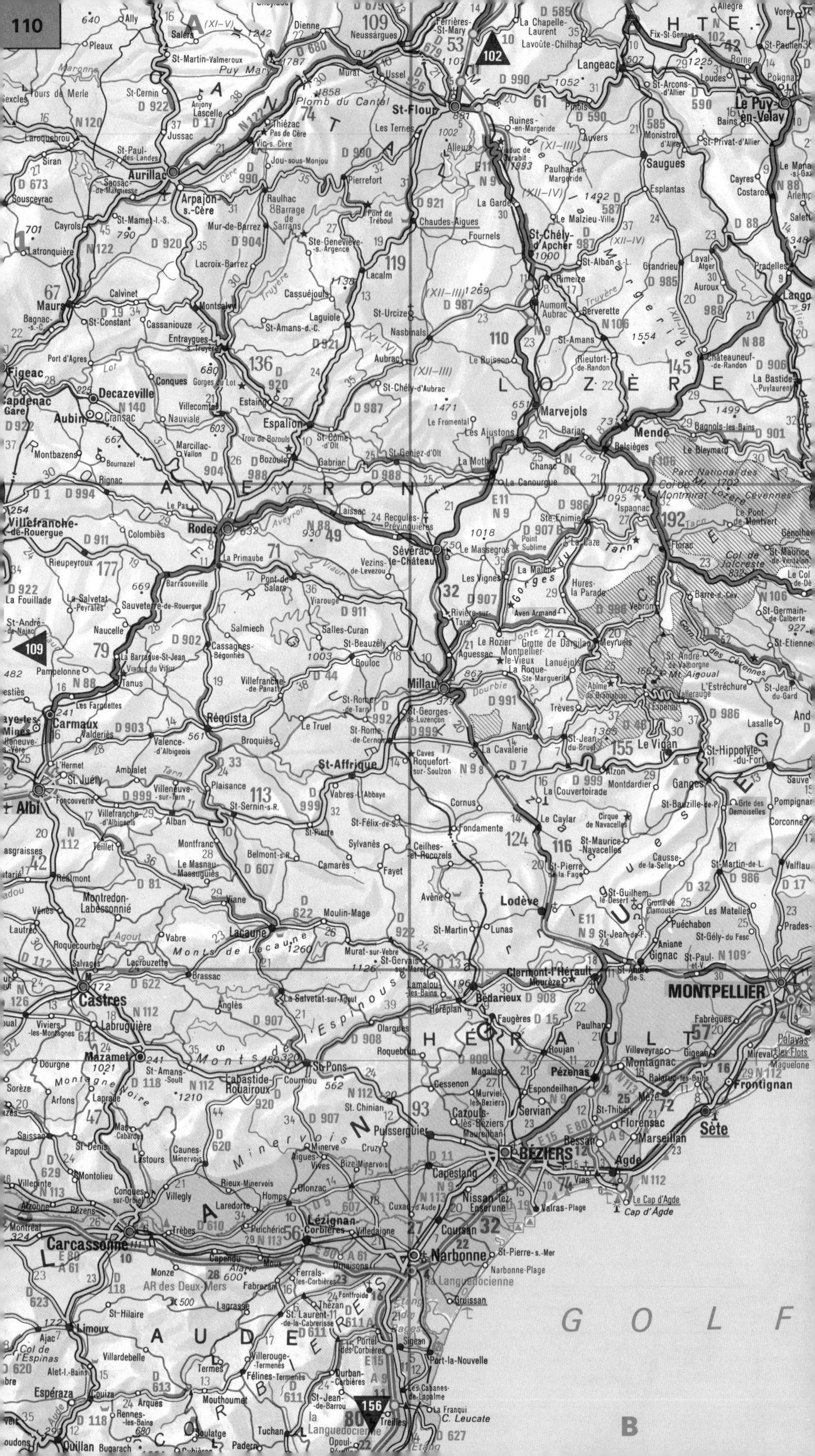
Salers
St-Martin-Valmeroux
Puy Mary
Pleaux
Tours de Merle
St-Cernin
Anjony
Lascelle
Thiézac
Pas de Cère
Vic-s.-Cère
Jussac
Laroquebrou
Siran
St-Paul-des-Landes
Aurillac
Sansac-de-Marmiesse
Arpajon-s.-Cère
Sousceyrac
St-Mamet-l.-S.
Cayrols
Latronquière
Mur-de-Barrez
Lacroix-Barrez
Maurs
Calvinet
Bagnac-s.-C.
St-Constant
Cassaniouze
Montsalvy
Entraygues-s.-Truyère
Port d'Agres
Figeac
Capdenac Gare
Conques
Gorges du Lot
Decazeville
Aubin
Cransac
Villecomtal
Nauviale
Estaing
Espalion
Trou de Bozouls
Bozouls
Marcillac-Vallon
Montbazens
Bournazel
Rignac
Villefranche-de-Rouergue
Colombiès
Rodez
Le Pas
La Primaube
Rieupeyroux
Baraqueville
La Fouillade
La Salvetat-Peyralès
Sauveterre-de-Rouergue
St-André-de-Najac
Naucelle
La Barraque-St-Jean
Viaduc du Viaur
Tanus
Pampelonne
Les Farguettes
Carmaux
Valderiès
Albi
St-Juéry
L'Hermet
Ambialet
Foncouverte
Villefranche-d'Albigeois
Teillet
Réalmont
Montredon-Labessonnié
Vènes
Lautrec
Roquecourbe
Salvagès
Castres
Viviers-les-Montagnes
Labruguière
Mazamet
Dourgne
St-Amans-Soult
Montagne Noire
Sorèze
Arfons
Laprade
Saissac
Papoul
St-Denis
Lastours
Villepinte
Montolieu
Alzonne
Conques-sur-Orbiel
Villegly
Pézens
Carcassonne
Trèbes
Montréal
Capendu
Monze
AR des Deux-Mers
Limoux
Ajac
Col de l'Espinas
Villardebelle
Alet-l.-Bains
Espéraza
Couiza
Arques
Rennes-les-Bains
Quillan
Bugarach
Soulatge
Tuchan
Paderne
A U D E
C O R B I È R E S
Dienne
Neussargues
Murat
Plomb du Cantal
Ussel
St-Flour
Les Ternes
Jou-sous-Monjou
Pierrefort
Raulhac
Barrage de Sarrans
Pont de Tréboul
Ste-Geneviève-s.-Argence
Chaudes-Aigues
Lacalm
Cassuéjouls
Laguiole
St-Amans-d.-C.
St-Urcize
Nasbinals
Aubrac
St-Chély-d'Aubrac
St-Côme-d'Olt
Gabriac
St-Geniez-d'Olt
A V E Y R O N
Laissac
Recoules-Prévinquières
Sévérac-le-Château
Vezins-de-Levezou
Pont-de-Salars
Viarouge
Salmiech
Salles-Curan
Cassagnes-Bégonhès
St-Beauzély
Bouloc
Villefranche-de-Panat
Réquista
Le Truel
St-Rome-de-Tarn
Millau
St-Georges-de-Luzençon
St-Rome-de-Cernon
Broquiès
Valence-d'Albigeois
Villeneuve-sur-Tarn
Plaisance
St-Affrique
Roquefort-sur-Soulzon
Vabres-l'Abbaye
St-Sernin-s.-R.
Alban
St-Pierre
St-Félix-de-S.
Montfranc
Le Masnau-Massuguiès
Belmont-s.-R.
Camarès
Sylvanès
Fayet
Ceilhes-et-Rocozels
Viane
Vabre
Lacaune
Monts de Lacaune
Moulin-Mage
Murat-sur-Vèbre
St-Gervais-sur-Mare
Lacrouzette
Brassac
La Salvetat-sur-Agout
Anglès
Monts de l'Espinouse
Lamalou-les-Bains
Hérépian
Olargues
Labastide-Rouairoux
Courniou
St-Pons
Roquebrun
St. Chinian
Minerve
Caunes-Minervois
Rieux-Minervois
Laredorte
Homps
Olonzac
Puichéric
Lézignan-Corbières
Villedaigne
Moux
Fabrezan
Ferrals-les-Corbières
Ornaisons
Lagrasse
St. Laurent-de-la-Cabrerisse
Fontfroide
Thézan
Villerouge-Termenès
Termes
Félines-Termenès
Mouthoumet
Durban-Corbières
Portel-des-Corbières
St-Jean-de-Barrou
Opoul-Périllos
Ferrières-St-Mary
La Chapelle-Laurent
Lavoûte-Chilhac
Langeac
Fix-St-Geneys
Allègre
Vorey
St-Paulien
Polignac
Loudes
Borne
St-Arcons-d'Allier
Le Puy-en-Velay
Bains
St-Privat-d'Allier
Monistrol-d'Allier
Saugues
Pinols
Ruines-en-Margeride
Viaduc de Garabit
Alleuze
Auvers
Paulhac-en-Margeride
Esplantas
Cayres
Costaros
Le Malzieu-Ville
La Garde
Fournels
St-Chély-d'Apcher
St-Alban-s.-L.
Grandrieu
Laval-Atger
Auroux
Pradelles
Langogne
Rimeize
Aumont-Aubrac
Serverette
St-Amans
Le Buisson
Rieutort-de-Randon
Châteauneuf-de-Randon
La Bastide-Puylaurent
L O Z È R E
Marvejols
Barjac
Mende
Balsièges
Le Bleymard
Bagnols-les-Bains
Le Fromental
Les Ajustons
La Mothe
Chanac
La Canourgue
Parc National des Cévennes
Col de Montmirat
Mt. Lozère
Ispagnac
Le Pont-de-Montvert
Génolhac
Ste-Enimie
Le Massegros
Point Sublime
La Caze
Florac
Col de Jalcreste
St-Maurice-de-Ventalon
Le Col de Dé
Les Vignes
La Malène
Gorges du Tarn
Hures-la Parade
Barre-d.-Cév.
Aven Armand
Vebron
Rivière-sur-Tarn
Le Rozier
Grotte de Dargilan
Meyrueis
Aguessac
Montpellier-le-Vieux
La Roque-Ste-Marguerite
Lanuéjols
St-Germain-de-Calberte
St-Etienne
St-André-de-Valborgne
Mt. Aigoual
Abîme de Bramabiau
L'Espérou
Valleraugue
L'Estréchure
St-Jean-du-Gard
Trèves
Nant
St-Jean-du-Bruel
Le Vigan
La Cavalerie
Alzon
Montdardier
Lasalle
St-Hippolyte-du-Fort
Ganges
La Couvertoirade
St-Bauzille-de-P.
Grte des Demoiselles
Pompignan
Corconne
Cornus
Le Caylar
Cirque de Navacelles
Fondamente
St-Maurice-Navacelles
St-Pierre-de-la-Fage
Causse-de-la-Selle
St-Martin-de-L.
Valflaunès
Avène
Lodève
St-Guilhem-le-Désert
Grotte de Clamouse
Les Matelles
Prades-le-Lez
St-Martin
Lunas
St-Jean-de-F.
Puéchabon
St-Gély-du Fesc
Aniane
Gignac
St-Paul-et-V.
Clermont-l'Hérault
Mourèze
St-André-de-S.
MONTPELLIER
Bédarieux
Faugères
Paulhan
H É R A U L T
Fabrègues
Palavas
Villeveyrac
Gigean
Mireval
Les Flots
Maguelone
Roujan
Magalas
Pézenas
Montagnac
Balaruc-les-Bains
Frontignan
Cessenon
Murviel-lès-Béziers
Espondeilhan
Servian
St-Thibéry
Mèze
Sète
Cazouls-lès-Béziers
Maureilhan
Puisserguier
Cruzy
Florensac
Marseillan
Bessan
Béziers
Agde
Vias
Le Cap d'Agde
Cap d'Agde
Aigues-Vives
Bize-Minervois
Capestang
Nissan-lez-Enserune
Valras-Plage
Cuxac-d'Aude
Coursan
Narbonne
St-Pierre-s.-Mer
Narbonne-Plage
Gruissan
Sigean
Port-la-Nouvelle
Les Cabanes-de-Lapalme
La Franqui
C. Leucate
Treilles
Languedocienne
G O L F
B

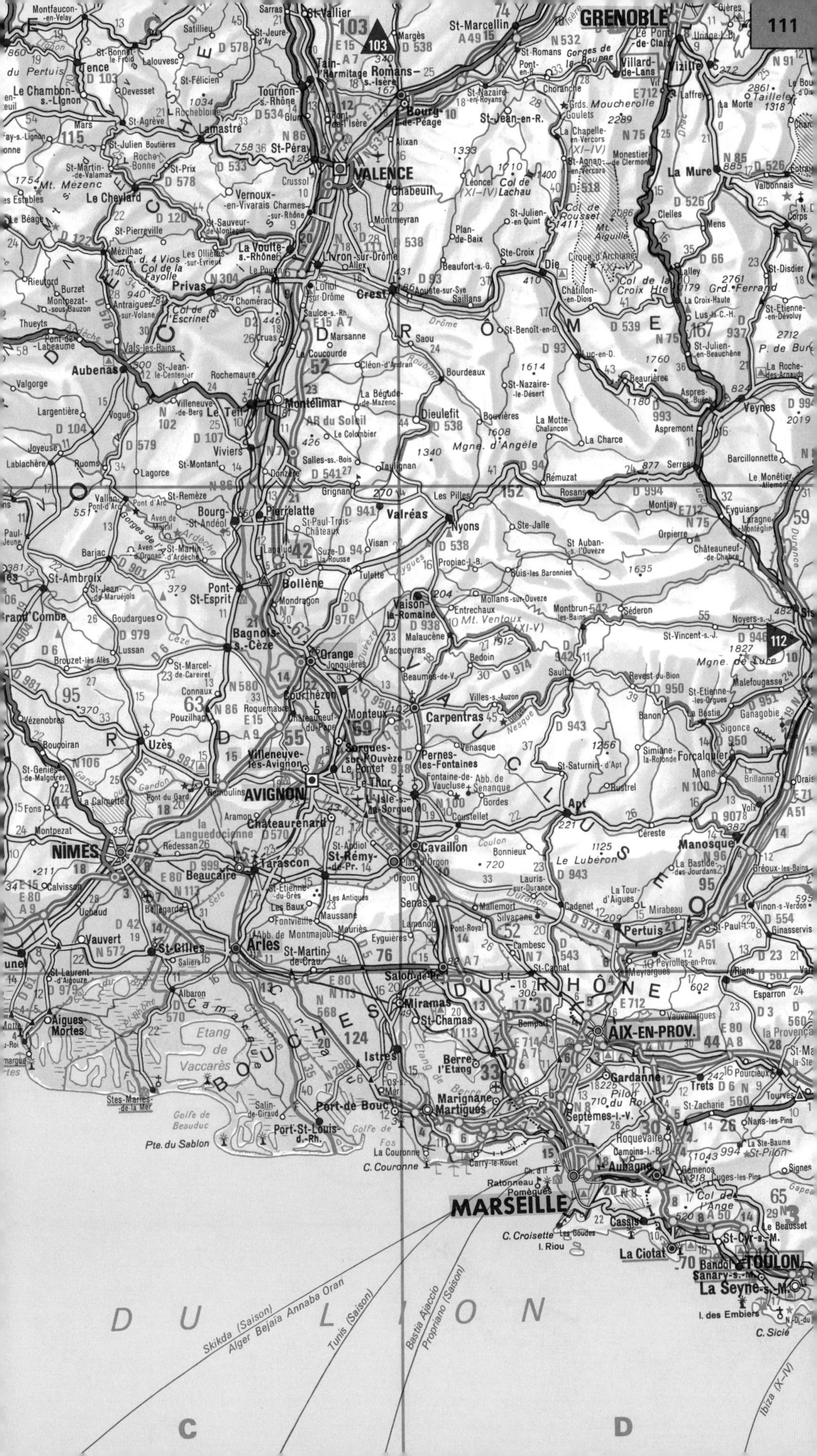
GRENOBLE
Montfaucon-en-Velay
Tence
Le Chambon-s.-Lignon
St-Agrève
Lamastre
Le Cheylard
Mt. Mézenc
St-Vallier
Tain-l'Hermitage
Tournon-s.-Rhône
Romans-s.-Isère
Bourg-de-Péage
St-Péray
VALENCE
Chabeuil
St-Marcellin
St-Romans
Pont-en-R.
Villard-de-Lans
Vizille
St-Nazaire-en-Royans
St-Jean-en-R.
Grds. Moucherolle
La Chapelle-en-Vercors
St-Agnan-en-Vercors
Monestier-de-Clermont
La Mure
Col de Lachau
Col de Rousset
Mt. Aiguille
Crussol
Vernoux-en-Vivarais
Charmes-sur-Rhône
St-Sauveur-de-Montagut
La Voulte-s.-Rhône
Livron-sur-Drôme
Allex
Privas
Le Pouzin
Loriol-sur-Drôme
Crest
Saillans
Die
Châtillon-en-Diois
Col de la Croix Hte
Clelles
Mens
Corps
St-Disdier
Grd. Ferrand
Lus-la-C.-H.
Col de l'Escrinet
Vals-les-Bains
Aubenas
Montélimar
Dieulefit
Bourdeaux
Saou
Marsanne
Cléon-d'Andran
La Bégude-de-Mazenc
Le Teil
Viviers
Villeneuve-de-Berg
Largentière
Joyeuse
Ruoms
Vallon-Pont-d'Arc
Gorges de l'Ardèche
Bourg-St-Andéol
Pierrelatte
St-Paul-Trois-Châteaux
Grignan
Valréas
Nyons
Rémuzat
Rosans
Serres
Aspres-s.-Buëch
Veynes
Laragne-Montéglin
Orpierre
Châteauneuf-de-Chabre
Barcillonnette
Le Monêtier-Allemont
Eyguians
Buis-les-Baronnies
Ste-Jalle
St-Auban-s.-l'Ouvèze
Montbrun-les-Bains
Séderon
Noyers-s.-J.
St-Vincent-s.-J.
Mgne. de Lure
Bollène
Pont-St-Esprit
St-Ambroix
Barjac
Bagnols-s.-Cèze
Mondragon
Vaison-la-Romaine
Malaucène
Mt. Ventoux
Orange
Jonquières
Courthézon
Carpentras
Sault
Banon
Forcalquier
Mane
Manosque
Uzès
Pont du Gard
Remoulins
Villeneuve-lès-Avignon
AVIGNON
Sorgues
Châteauneuf-du-Pape
Pernes-les-Fontaines
Fontaine-de-Vaucluse
Gordes
Apt
Le Lubéron
Cavaillon
Châteaurenard
St-Rémy-de-Pr.
Tarascon
Beaucaire
NÎMES
Arles
St-Gilles
Vauvert
Aigues-Mortes
Stes-Maries-de-la-Mer
Etang de Vaccarès
Camargue
Salon-de-Pr.
Miramas
St-Chamas
Istres
Berre l'Etang
Martigues
Marignane
Port-de-Bouc
Port-St-Louis-d.-Rh.
Golfe de Fos
Pertuis
Cadenet
Lambesc
AIX-EN-PROV.
Gardanne
Trets
St-Maximin-la-Ste-Baume
Aubagne
MARSEILLE
Cassis
La Ciotat
Bandol
Sanary-s.-M.
TOULON
La Seyne-s.-M.
C. Sicié
C. Couronne
C. Croisette
BOUCHES-DU-RHÔNE
VAUCLUSE
DRÔME
ARDÈCHE
DU LION
Skikda (Saison)
Alger Bejaïa Annaba Oran
Tunis (Saison)
Bastia Ajaccio
Propriano (Saison)
Ibiza (X-IV)
103
112
C
D

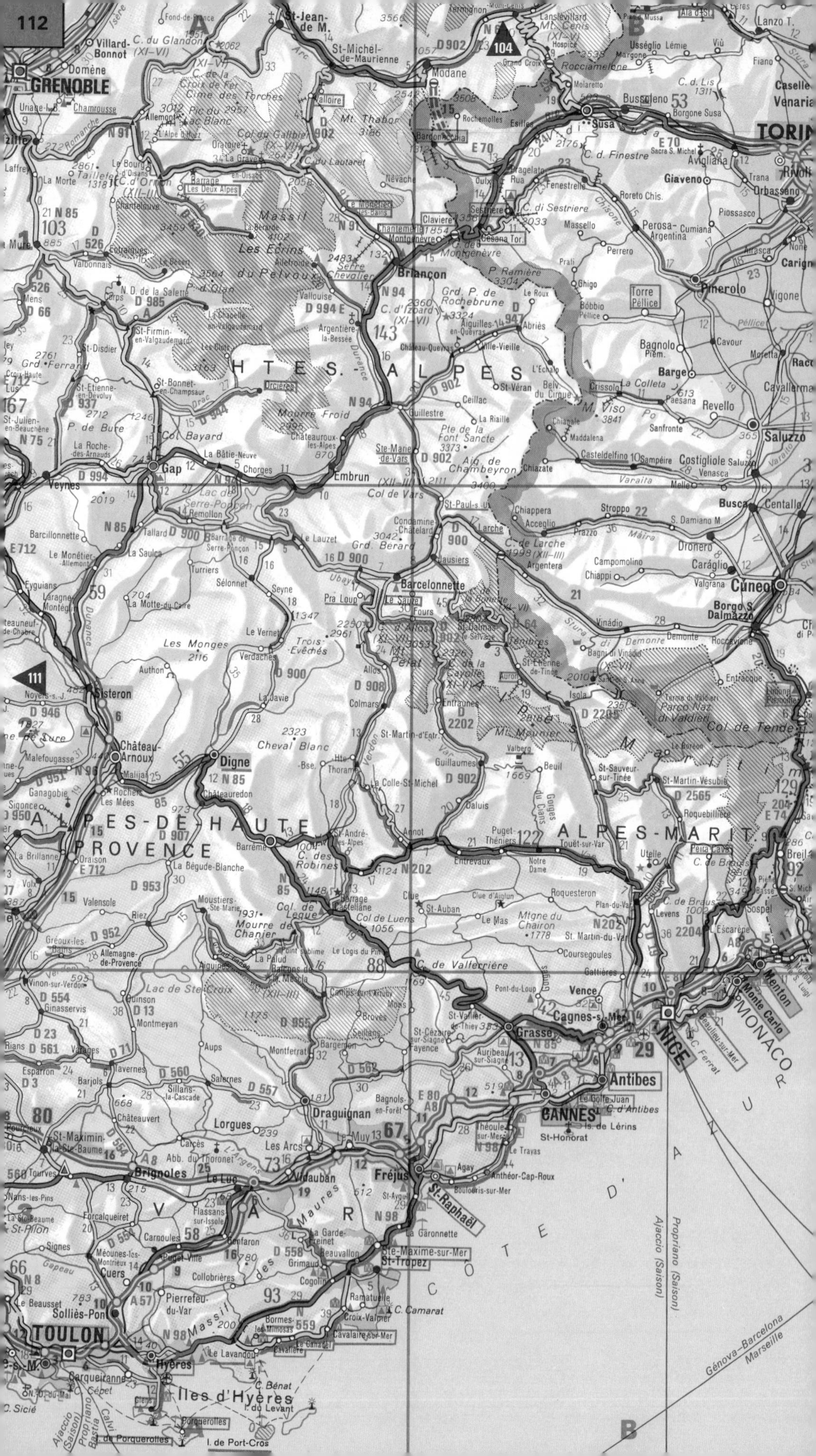

GRENOBLE
Villard-Bonnot
Domène
Chamrousse
C. du Glandon
St-Jean-de M.
St-Michel-de-Maurienne
Modane
Lanslevillard
Mt. Cenis
Ala di Stura
Lanzo T.
Usséglio
Margone
Rocciamelone
Caselle
Venaria
TORINO
Susa
Bussoleno
Borgone Susa
Avigliana
Giaveno
Rivoli
Orbassano
Trana
Piossasco
Cumiana
Pinerolo
Vigone
Bardonecchia
Rochemolles
Esilles
C. d. Finestre
Sacra S. Michel
Fenestrelle
Roreto Chis.
Perosa-Argentina
Pragelato
Oulx
Sestriere
C. di Sestriere
Cesana Tor.
Claviere
Montgenèvre
Massello
Perrero
Prali
Ghigo
Bòbbio Pellice
Torre Pellice
Bagnolo Piem.
Barge
Cavour
Moretta
Cavallermaggiore
Paesana
Revello
Saluzzo
Sanfronte
Crissolo
M. Viso
La Colletta
Costigliole Saluzzo
Venasca
Sampéire
Casteldelfino
Chiazale
Maddalena
Chianale
Melle
Busca
Centallo
Stroppo
S. Damiano M
Dronero
Caráglio
Cuneo
Valgrana
Campomolino
Chiappi
Borgo S. Dalmazzo
Vinádio
Demonte
Roccavione
Entracque
Parco Naz. di Valdieri
Terme di Valdieri
Col de Tende
Limone Piemonte
Chiappera
Acceglio
Prazzo
Argentera
C. de Larche
Larche
Allemont
Pic du Lac Blanc
L'Alpe d'Huez
Col du Galibier
La Grave
Oratoire
Valloire
Mt. Thabor
C. du Lautaret
Névache
Le Monêtier-les-Bains
Chantemerle
Briançon
Serre Chevalier
Ailefroide
Massif des Écrins
Les Écrins
du Pelvoux
La Bérarde
Les Deux Alpes
Le Bourg-d'Oisans
C. d'Ornon
Chantelouve
Uriage-L.B.
Vizille
Laffrey
La Morte
La Mure
Valbonnais
Entraigues
Le Désert
Mens
N. D. de la Salette
Corps
St-Firmin-en-Valgaudemard
La Chapelle-en-Valgaudemard
Les Clots
St-Disdier
Grd. Ferrand
Croix-Haute
St-Bonnet-en-Champsaur
St-Étienne-en-Dévoluy
P. de Bure
Orcières
St-Julien-en-Beauchêne
La Roche-des-Arnauds
Col Bayard
Gap
Veynes
La Bâtie-Neuve
Chorges
Vallouise
Argentière-la-Bessée
C. d'Izoard
Grd. P. de Rochebrune
Aiguilles-en-Queyras
Château-Queyras
Ville-Vieille
Abriès
Le Roux
L'Échalp
St-Véran
Belv. du Cirque
Ceillac
La Riaille
Pte de la Font Sancte
Aig. de Chambeyron
Guillestre
HTES. ALPES
Mourre Froid
Châteauroux-les-Alpes
Ste-Marie-de-Vars
Col de Vars
Embrun
St-Paul-s.-U.
Lac de Serre-Ponçon
Remollon
Barrage de Serre-Ponçon
Tallard
La Saulce
Barcillonnette
Le Monêtier-Allemont
Eyguians
Laragne-Montéglin
Le Lauzet
Grd. Bérard
Condamine-Châtelard
Jausiers
Barcelonnette
Pra Loup
Le Sauze
Fours
Turriers
Sélonnet
Seyne
La Motte-du-Caire
Le Vernet
Les Monges
Trois-Évêchés
Authon
Verdaches
Col d'Allos
Mt. Pelat
Allos
Colmars
St-Dalmas-le-Selvage
C. de la Cayolle
Ténibres
St-Étienne-de-Tinée
Auron
Isola
Entraunes
Mt. Mounier
Bagni di Vinádio
Le Boréon
Sisteron
Noyers-s.-J.
Châteauneuf-de-Chabre
Château-Arnoux
Malijai
Malefougasse
Ganagobie
Les Mées
Sigonce
Digne
Châteauredon
La Javie
Cheval Blanc
Thorame-Bse.
Thorame-Hte
St-Martin-d'Entr.
La Colle-St-Michel
Guillaumes
Valberg
Beuil
Gorges du Cians
Daluis
Puget-Théniers
St-Sauveur-sur-Tinée
St-Martin-Vésubie
Roquebillière
Breil
Sospel
ALPES-DE-HAUTE PROVENCE
ALPES-MARIT.
Barrême
St-André-les-Alpes
C. des Robines
Annot
Entrevaux
Touët-sur-Var
Notre Dame
Utelle
Peïra-Cava
C. de Braus
La Brillanne
Oraison
La Bégude-Blanche
Volx
Valensole
Riez
Moustiers-Ste-Marie
Mourre de Chanier
Col de Leque
Barrage Castellane
Castellane
Col de Luens
Clue
St-Auban
Clue d'Aiglun
Le Mas
Roquesteron
Plan-du-Var
Mtgne du Chairon
St. Martin-du-Var
Levens
L'Escarène
Gréoux-les-Bains
Allemagne-de-Provence
La Palud
Point Sublime
Aiguines
Balcons de la Mescla
Le Logis du Pin
C. de Valferrière
Coursegoules
Gattières
Vence
Cagnes-s.-Mer
NICE
Menton
Monte Carlo
MONACO
Beaulieu-sur-Mer
C. Ferrat
Vinon-sur-Verdon
Lac de Ste Croix
Quinson
Ginasservis
Montmeyan
Comps-sur-Artuby
Mons
Brovès
St-Vallier-de-Thiey
Grasse
St-Cézaire-sur-Siagne
Fayence
Seillans
Bargemon
Montferrat
Aups
Auribeau-sur-Siagne
Antibes
Rians
Varages
Tavernes
Esparron
Barjols
Sillans-la-Cascade
Salernes
Châteauvert
Lorgues
Draguignan
Bagnols-en-Forêt
Le Golfe-Juan
C. d'Antibes
CANNES
Is. de Lérins
St-Honorat
Théoule-sur-Mer
Le Trayas
St-Maximin-la-Ste-Baume
Pourcieux
Tourves
Brignoles
Abb. du Thoronet
Carcès
Les Arcs
Le Muy
Fréjus
St-Raphaël
Agay
Anthéor-Cap-Roux
Boulouris-sur-Mer
Le Luc
Vidauban
Nans-les-Pins
Forcalqueiret
Flassans-sur-Issole
Massif des Maures
St-Pilon
Signes
Méounes-lès-Montrieux
Carnoules
Puget-Ville
Gonfaron
La Garde-Freinet
Grimaud
Beauvallon
Ste-Maxime-sur-Mer
St-Tropez
La Garonnette
Cuers
Collobrières
Cogolin
Ramatuelle
C. Camarat
Le Beausset
Solliès-Pont
Pierrefeu-du-Var
Croix-Valmer
Bormes-les-Mimosas
Cavalaire-sur-Mer
Le Canadel
Cavalière
Le Lavandou
TOULON
Hyères
Carqueiranne
C. Bénat
Îles d'Hyères
I. du Levant
I. de Port-Cros
Porquerolles
I. de Porquerolles
C. Sicié
CÔTE D'AZUR
VAR
Ajaccio (Saison)
Propriano (Saison)
Génova-Barcelona
Marseille
Calvi
Bastia
104
111

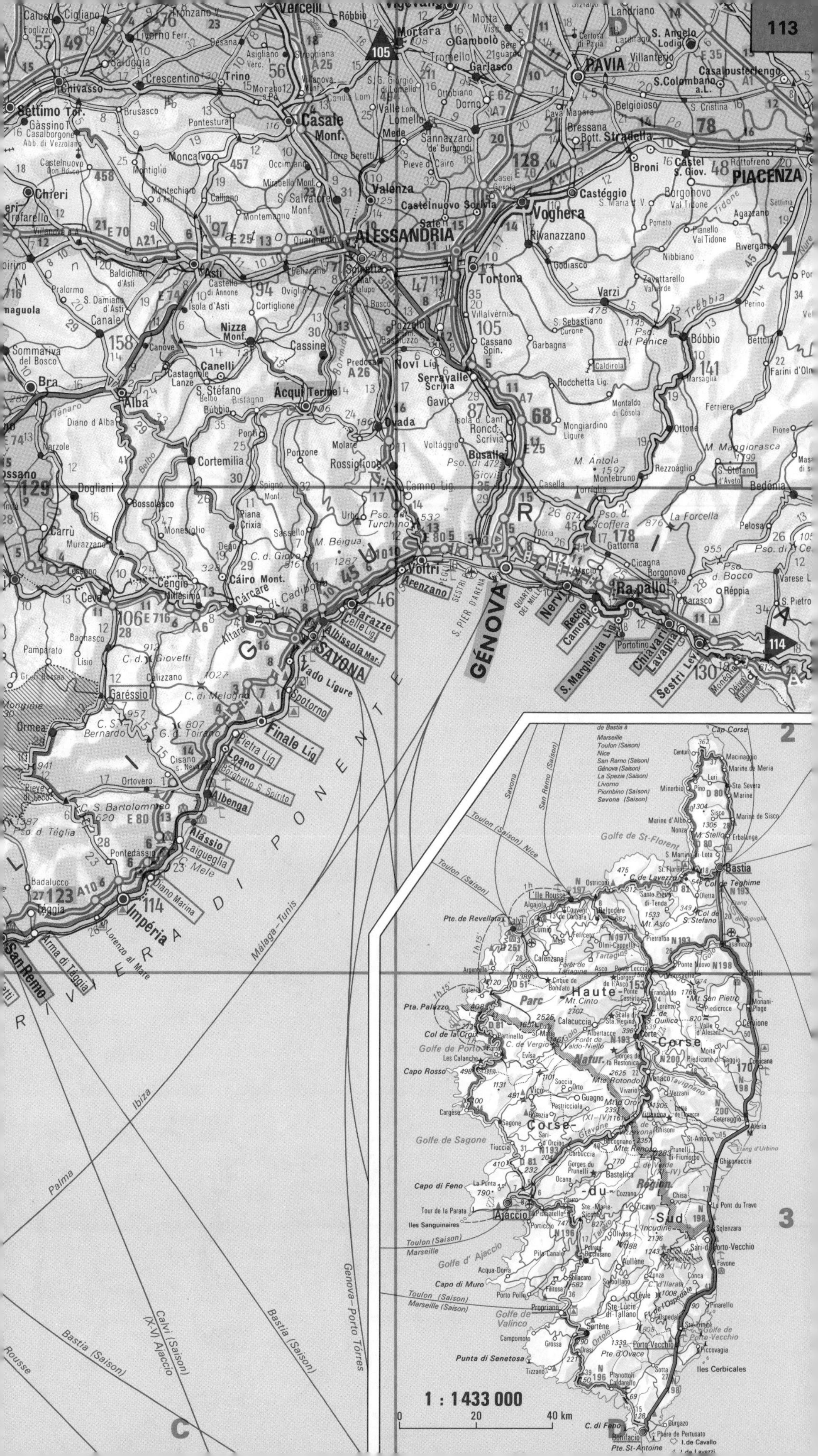
Vercelli
Mortara
Vigevano
Landriano
S. Angelo Lodig.
PAVIA
Villanterio
Casalpusterlengo
S.Colombano a.L.
Chivasso
Crescentino
Trino
Settimo Tor.
Casale Monf.
Valle Lom.
Lomello
Garlasco
Gambolò
Tromello
Belgioioso
Bressana
Stradella
Broni
Castel S. Giov.
PIACENZA
Moncalvo
Valenza
Chieri
Casteggio
Voghera
ALESSANDRIA
Castelnuovo Scrivia
Asti
Tortona
Varzi
Nizza Monf.
Canelli
Cassine
Novi Lig.
Serravalle Scrivia
Bóbbio
Bra
Alba
Ácqui Terme
Ovada
Gavi
Cortemilia
Rossiglione
Busalla
Dogliani
Ottone
M. Ántola 1597
Pso. d. Scoffera
Bedónia
Carrù
Ceva
Cengio
Cáiro Mont.
Cárcare
Voltri
Arenzano
Varazze
Celle Lig.
Albissola Mar.
SAVONA
Vado Ligure
Spotorno
Finale Líg.
Pietra Lig.
Loano
Borghetto S. Spirito
Albenga
Alássio
Laigueglia
Diano Marina
Impéria
San Remo
Arma di Tággia
GÉNOVA
Nervi
Recco
Camogli
S. Margherita Lig.
Portofino
Rapallo
Chiavari
Lavagna
Sestri Lev.
Garéssio
Ormea
C. di Melogno
C. S. Bernardo
Pso. d. Téglia
Taggia
RIVIERA DI PONENTE
LIGURIA
Cap Corse
Bastia
St. Florent
Golfe de St-Florent
Calvi
L'Ile Rousse
Corte
Haute-Corse
Corse-du-Sud
Parc Natur. Région.
Mt. Cinto 2707
Mte Rotondo 2625
Mte d'Oro
Mte Renoso
Ajaccio
Golfe d'Ajaccio
Golfe de Sagone
Golfe de Porto
Golfe de Valinco
Propriano
Sartène
Porto-Vecchio
Bonifacio
Solenzara
Ghisonaccia
Aléria
Cervione
Sagone
Cargèse
Capo Rosso
Capo di Feno
Capo di Muro
Punta di Senetosa
Iles Sanguinaires
Iles Cerbicales
C. di Feno
Pte. St-Antoine
Toulon (Saison)
Marseille
Málaga–Tunis
Genova–Porto Tórres
Bastia (Saison)
Calvi (Saison) (X-V) Ajaccio
Ibiza
Palma
1 : 1 433 000
0 20 40 km
105
114
C
D
2
3

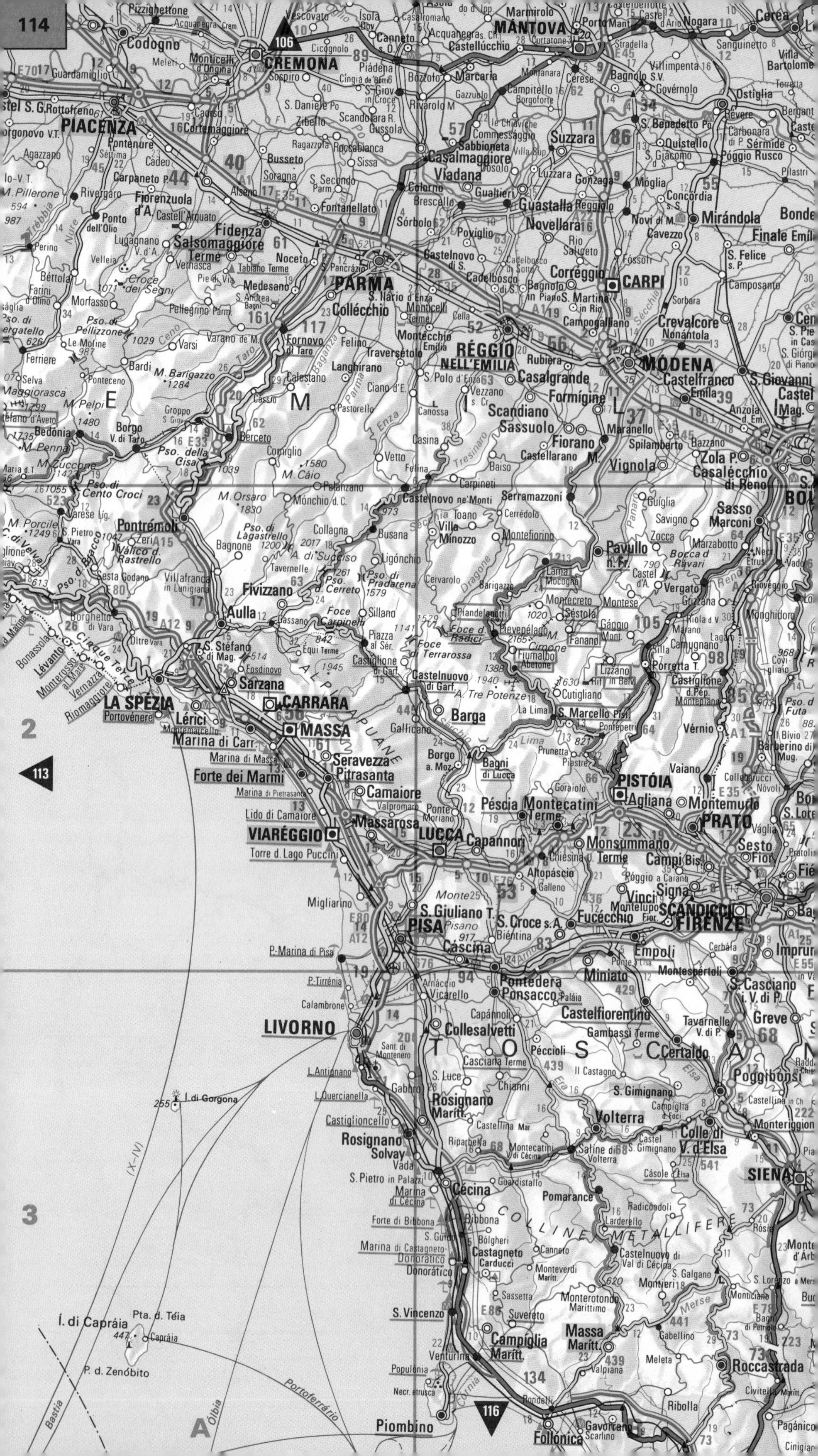
106
113
116
2
3
CREMONA
MÀNTOVA
PIACENZA
Pizzighettone
Codogno
Guardamiglio
Rottofreno
Monticelli d'Ongina
Caorso
Cortemaggiore
Pontenure
Cadeo
Carpaneto P.
Fiorenzuola d'A.
Castell'Arquato
Alseno
Busseto
Soragna
Fidenza
Salsomaggiore Terme
Medesano
Noceto
Fontanellato
Colorno
Sòrbolo
PARMA
Collécchio
Fornovo di Taro
Felino
Langhirano
Traversétolo
Montecchio Emilia
RÉGGIO NELL'EMILIA
Casalmaggiore
Viadana
Sabbioneta
Suzzara
Gonzaga
Luzzara
Guastalla
Gualtieri
Brescello
Novellara
Correggio
CARPI
Rubiera
Casalgrande
Scandiano
Sassuolo
Formìgine
Fiorano
Maranello
Castellarano
MÒDENA
Castelfranco Emilia
Nonàntola
Crevalcore
S. Giovanni
Mirándola
Concordia
Moglia
Novi di M.
Cavezzo
Finale Emilia
S. Felice s. P.
Camposanto
Vignola
Spilamberto
Zola P.
Casaléchio di Reno
Bazzano
Sasso Marconi
Pavullo n. Fr.
Serramazzoni
Castelnovo ne' Monti
Villa Minozzo
Montefiorino
Vergato
Porretta T.
Gàggio Mont.
Fanano
Sèstola
Pievepélago
M. Cimone
Abetone
Castiglione d. Pep.
Vèrnio
Barberino di Mug.
Vaiano
PISTÓIA
Agliana
Montemurlo
PRATO
Sesto Fior.
Campi Bis.
Signa
SCANDICCI
FIRENZE
Empoli
Vinci
Fucécchio
Monsummano Terme
Montecatini Terme
Péscia
Capannori
Altopàscio
LUCCA
Barga
Bagni di Lucca
Castelnuovo di Garf.
Borgo a Moz.
Gallicano
Piazza al Sér.
Fivizzano
Aulla
Pontrémoli
Villafranca in Lunigiana
Sarzana
S. Stéfano di Mag.
LA SPÉZIA
Portovénere
Lérici
CARRARA
MASSA
Marina di Carr.
Marina di Massa
Seravezza
Pitrasanta
Forte dei Marmi
Camaiore
Marina di Pietrasanta
Lido di Camaiore
Massarosa
VIARÉGGIO
Torre d. Lago Puccini
Migliarino
PISA
S. Giuliano T.
Càscina
S. Croce s. A.
P. Marina di Pisa
P. Tirrénia
Calambrone
Pontedera
Ponsacco
Miniato
Castelfiorentino
Montespértoli
S. Casciano i. V. di P.
Greve
Tavarnelle V. di P.
Certaldo
Poggibonsi
S. Gimignano
Colle di V. d'Elsa
Monteriggioni
SIENA
LIVORNO
Collesalvetti
Sant. di Montenero
L. Antignano
L. Quercianella
Castiglioncello
Rosignano Maritt.
Rosignano Solvay
Vada
S. Pietro in Palazzi
Marina di Cécina
Cécina
Volterra
Saline di Volterra
Pomarance
Larderello
Castelnuovo di Val di Cécina
Forte di Bibbona
Bibbona
Bólgheri
Marina di Castagneto-Donoratico
Castagneto Carducci
Donorático
S. Vincenzo
Suvereto
Campíglia Maritt.
Massa Maritt.
Monterotondo Marittimo
Venturina
Populónia
Piombino
Follónica
Roccastrada
I. di Gorgona
Í. di Capráia
Capráia
P. d. Zenóbito
Pta. d. Téia
Bastia
Ólbia
Portoferráio
Cinque Terre
Levanto
Monterosso al Mare
Vernazza
Riomaggiore
Bedónia
Borgo V. di Taro
Berceto
Pso. della Cisa
Bardi
Varsi
M. Orsaro
Pso. di Cento Croci
Pso. di Lagastrello
Pso. d. Cerreto
Foce d. Radici
Foce di Terrarossa
Alpi Apuane
Colline Metallifere
E M I L
T O S C A N

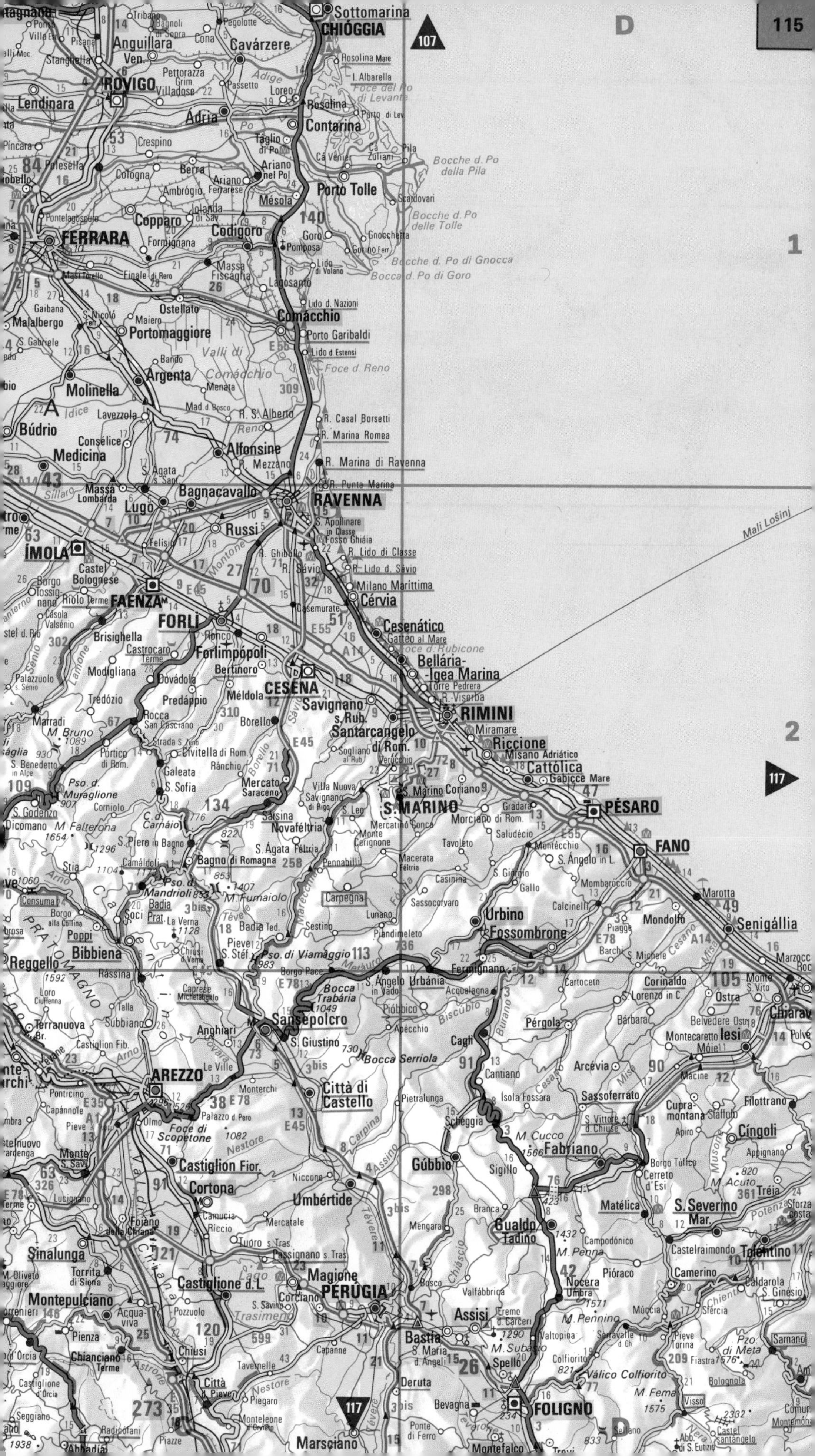
D
107
Sottomarina
CHIÓGGIA
ROVIGO
Anguillara Ven.
Cavárzere
Lendinara
Ádria
Contarina
Rosolina
Porto Tolle
Bocche d. Po della Pila
Bocche d. Po delle Tolle
Bocche d. Po di Gnocca
Bocca d. Po di Goro
1
FERRARA
Copparo
Codigoro
Mésola
Pomposa
Comácchio
Porto Garibaldi
Lido d. Estensi
Foce d. Reno
Valli di Comácchio
Portomaggiore
Argenta
Molinella
Búdrio
Medicina
Alfonsine
R. Casal Borsetti
R. Marina Romea
R. Marina di Ravenna
R. Punta Marina
RAVENNA
Bagnacavallo
Lugo
Russi
ÍMOLA
FAENZA
FORLÌ
Cérvia
Milano Maríttima
Cesenático
Bellária-Igea Marina
Mali Lošinj
CESENA
Forlimpópoli
RIMINI
Riccione
Cattólica
Gabicce Mare
PÉSARO
FANO
2
117
S. MARINO
Santarcangelo di Rom.
Savignano s. Rub.
Urbino
Fossombrone
Senigállia
Mondolfo
Marotta
Novafeltria
Pennabilli
Carpegna
Bagno di Romagna
Marradi
Brisighella
Modigliana
Pso. d. Muraglione
M. Falterona
Bibbiena
Poppi
Reggello
Sansepolcro
Città di Castello
AREZZO
Castiglion Fior.
Cortona
Umbértide
Gúbbio
Cagli
Fabriano
Iesi
Chiaravalle
Ostra
Cíngoli
S. Severino Mar.
Tolentino
Camerino
Matélica
Gualdo Tadino
Nocera Umbra
Assisi
PERÚGIA
Bastia
Spello
FOLIGNO
Magione
Castiglione d.L.
Lago Trasimeno
Chiusi
Chianciano Terme
Montepulciano
Sinalunga
Città d. Pieve
Marsciano
Deruta
Bevagna
Montefalco
Sarnano
D
117

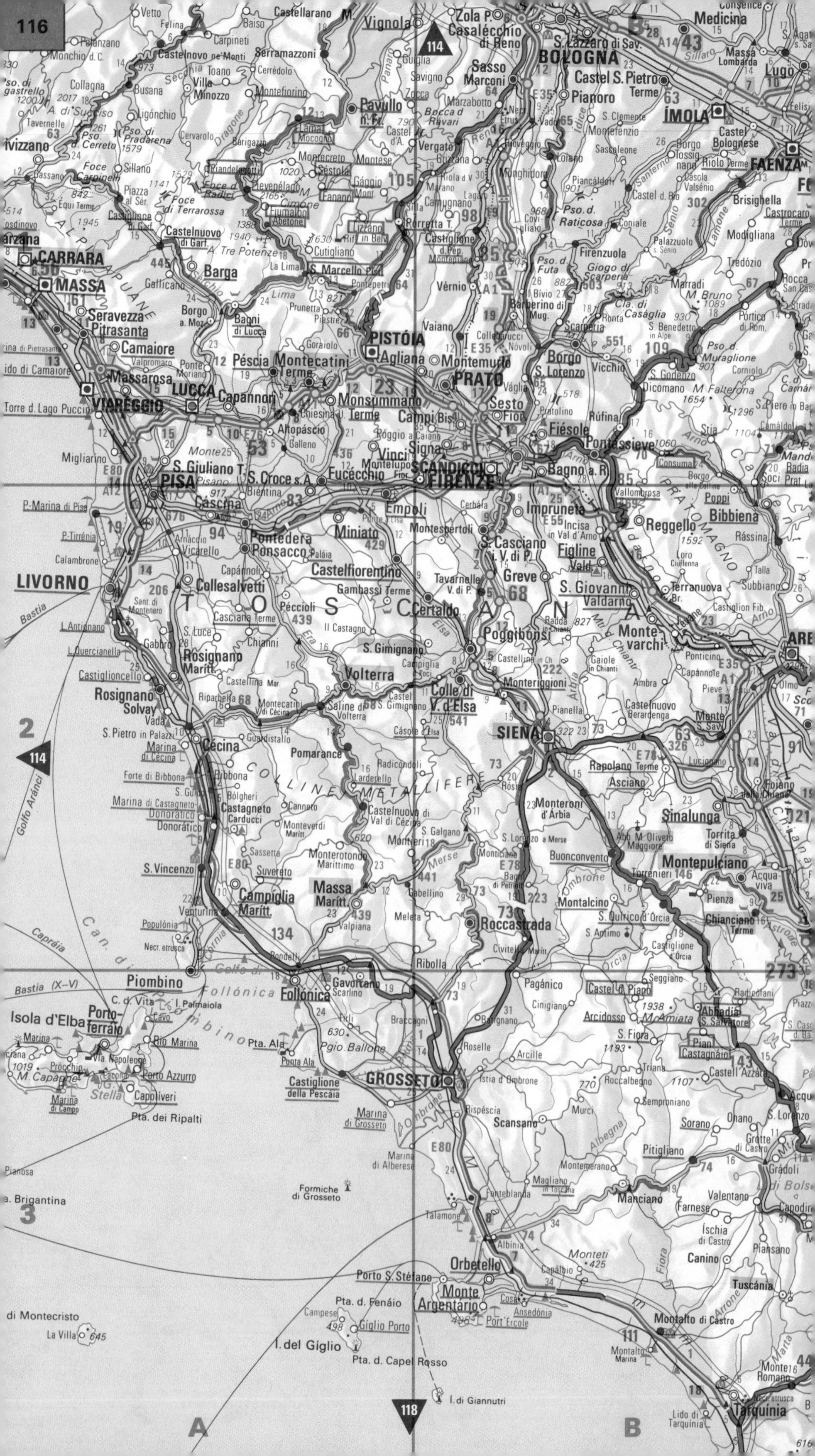
114
BOLOGNA
Casaléccchio di Reno
Zola P.
Vignola
Castellarano
S. Lazzaro di Sav.
Medicina
Castel S. Pietro Terme
ÍMOLA
Lugo
FAENZA
Sasso Marconi
Pianoro
Pavullo n. Fr.
Castelnovo ne' Monti
Brisighella
Modigliana
Porretta T.
Vergato
Firenzuola
Marradi
Castelnuovo di Garf.
Barga
CARRARA
MASSA
Seravezza
Pitrasanta
Camaiore
Massarosa
VIARÉGGIO
LUCCA
Capannori
Péscia
Montecatini Terme
PISTÓIA
Agliana
Montemurlo
PRATO
Sesto Fior.
Monsummano Terme
Vinci
Signa
SCANDICCI
FIRENZE
Fiésole
Pontassieve
Bagno a R.
Borgo S. Lorenzo
Dicomano
Stia
Poppi
Bibbiena
Migliarino
S. Giuliano T.
PISA
S. Croce s. A.
Fucécchio
Empoli
Cascina
Pontedera
Ponsacco
Miniato
Castelfiorentino
Impruneta
Reggello
S. Casciano i. V. di P.
Figline Vald.
Greve
S. Giovanni Valdarno
Montevarchi
LIVORNO
Collesalvetti
T O S C A N A
Certaldo
Poggibonsi
S. Gimignano
Volterra
Colle di V. d'Elsa
Monteriggioni
Castellina in Ch.
Rosignano Maritt.
Rosignano Solvay
Castiglioncello
Cécina
SIENA
Asciano
Sinalunga
Montepulciano
Chianciano Terme
Pienza
Pomarance
Larderello
C O L L I N E   M E T A L L Í F E R E
Castagneto Carducci
Donorático
S. Vincenzo
Campiglia Maritt.
Massa Maritt.
Roccastrada
Buonconvento
Montalcino
S. Quirico d'Orcia
Abbadia S. Salvatore
Piombino
Follónica
Golfo di Follónica
Isola d'Elba
Portoferraio
Rio Marina
Porto Azzurro
Capolíveri
M. Capanne
Pta. dei Ripalti
Castiglione della Pescaia
GROSSETO
Marina di Grosseto
Scansano
Pitigliano
Sorano
Manciano
Orbetello
Porto S. Stéfano
Monte Argentario
Port'Ercole
Ansedónia
I. del Gíglio
Gíglio Porto
di Montecristo
Pianosa
Formiche di Grosseto
I. di Giannutri
Montalto di Castro
Tarquínia
Tuscánia
Canino
Capalbio
Arcidosso
M. Amiata
Castel d. Piano
Bastia
Golfo Aránci
Can. di Piombino
Caprária
2
114
3
A
B
118

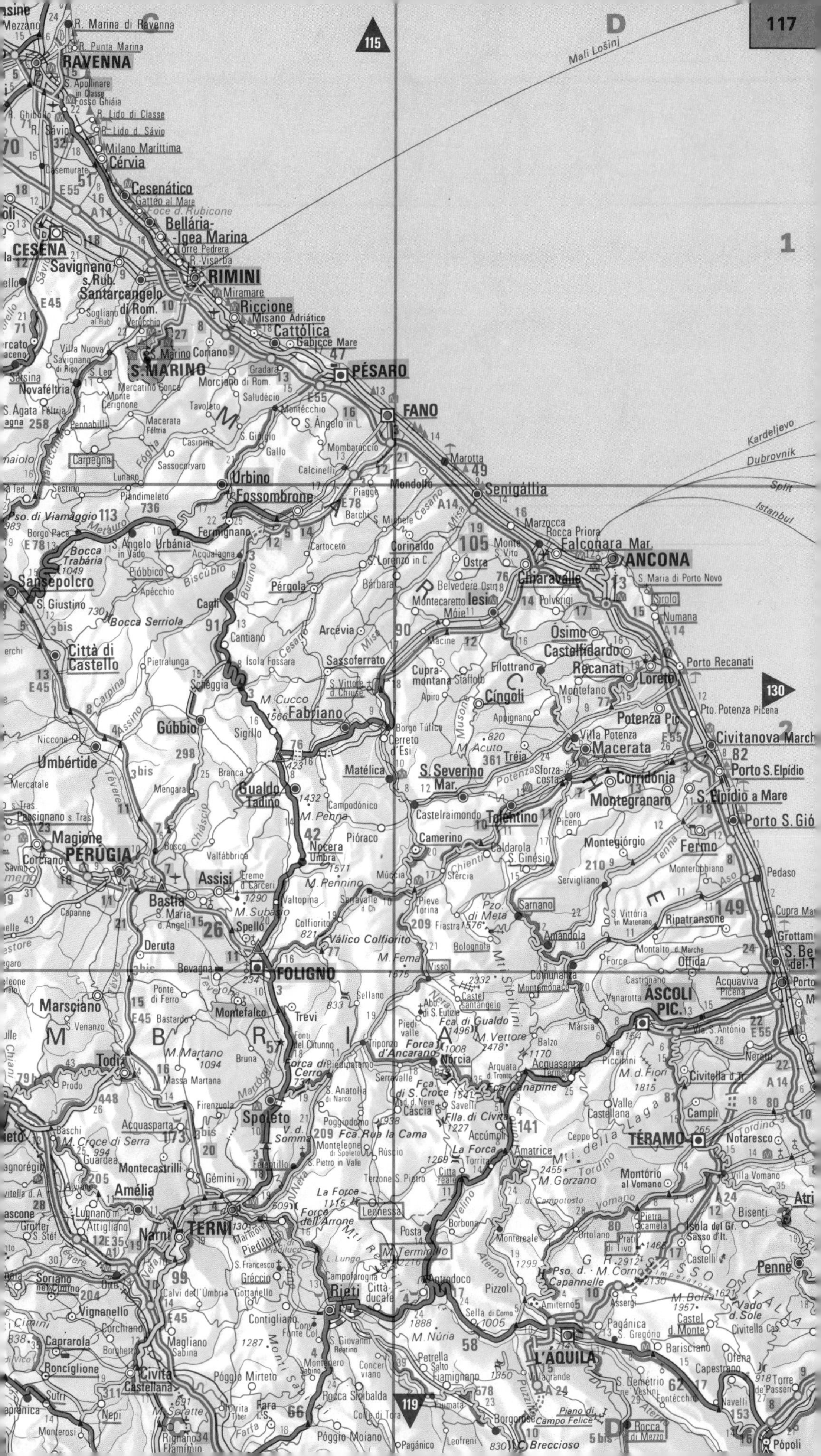

C
D
115
1
2
130
119
Mali Lošinj
Kardeljevo
Dubrovnik
Split
Istanbul
R. Marina di Ravenna
R. Punta Marina
RAVENNA
S. Apollinare in Classe
Fosso Ghiáia
R. Lido di Classe
R. Lido d. Sávio
Milano Maríttima
Cérvia
Cesenático
Gatteo al Mare
Foce d. Rubicone
Bellária-Igea Marina
Torre Pedrera
R. Viserba
CESENA
Savignano s. Rub.
Santarcangelo di Rom.
RIMINI
Miramare
Riccione
Misano Adriático
Cattólica
Gabicce Mare
PÉSARO
FANO
Marotta
Senigállia
Marzocca
Rocca Priora
Falconara Mar.
ANCONA
S. Maria di Porto Novo
Sirolo
Numana
Ósimo
Castelfidardo
Recanati
Loreto
Porto Recanati
Pto. Potenza Picena
Potenza Pic.
Civitanova March
Porto S. Elpídio
S. Elpídio a Mare
Porto S. Gió
Fermo
Pedaso
Cupra Ma
Grottam
S. Be del T
Porto
ASCOLI PIC.
S. MARINO
Coriano
Novafeltria
S. Ágata Feltria
Pennabilli
Carpegna
Urbino
Fossombrone
Fermignano
Urbánia
S. Angelo in Vado
Piobbico
Apécchio
Cagli
Sansepolcro
S. Giustino
Bocca Trabária
Bocca Serriola
Città di Castello
Pérgola
Arcévia
Sassoferrato
Fabriano
Jesi
Chiaravalle
Cíngoli
Macerata
Corridónia
Montegranaro
Tolentino
Camerino
S. Severino Mar.
Matélica
Gúbbio
Gualdo Tadino
Nocera Umbra
Umbértide
Magione
PERÚGIA
Assisi
Bastia
Spello
FOLIGNO
Montefalco
Trevi
Spoleto
Todi
Marsciano
Deruta
Bevagna
Norcia
Cascia
Amatrice
TÉRAMO
Campli
Civitella d. Tr.
Notaresco
Atri
Penne
Amélia
Narni
TERNI
Rieti
Cittàducale
Antrodoco
L'ÁQUILA
Assergi
Pagánica
Civita Castellana
Caprarola
Ronciglione
Vignanello
Póggio Mirteto
Leonessa
M. Terminillo
Visso
Sarnano
Amandola
Offida
Ripatransone
Montalto d. Marche
Mti. Sibillini
Mti. della Laga
GRAN SASSO D'ITALIA
Monti Sabini
Pópoli

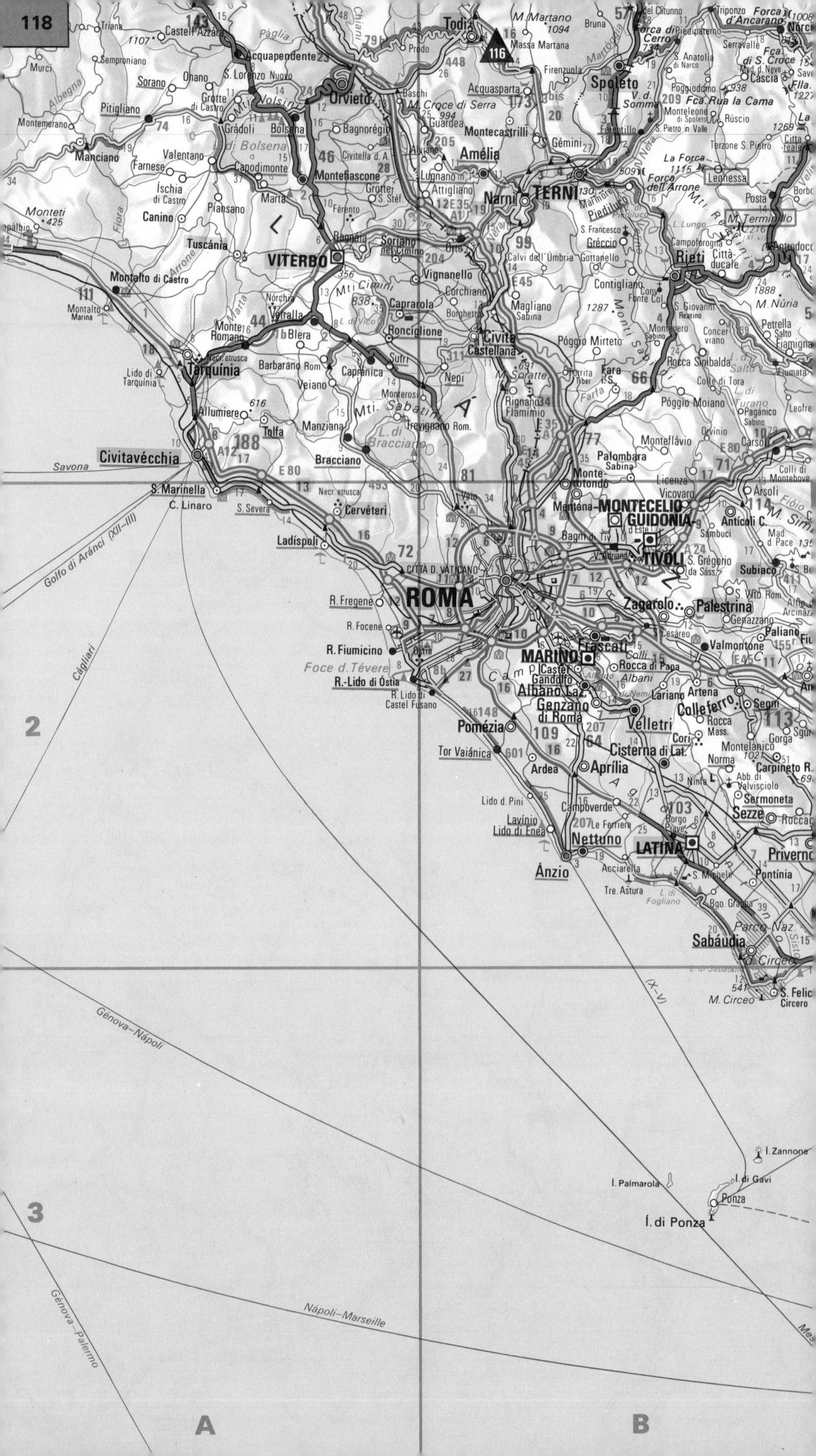

Triana
Castell Azzara
Semproniano
Acquapendente
S. Lorenzo Nuovo
Murci
Sorano
Onano
Pitigliano
Grotte di Castro
Gràdoli
Bolsena
Montemerano
Manciano
Valentano
Farnese
Capodimonte
Ìschia di Castro
Marta
Montefiascone
Piansano
Canino
Tuscània
VITERBO
Montalto di Castro
Montalto Marina
Monte Romano
Vetralla
Nòrchia
Blera
Tarquìnia
Lido di Tarquìnia
Necr. etrusca
Barbarano Rom.
Capranica
Sutri
Veiano
Allumiere
Tolfa
Manziana
Bracciano
L. di Bracciano
Mti. Sabatini
Trevignano Rom.
Civitavècchia
Savona
S. Marinella
C. Linaro
S. Severa
Cervéteri
Ladíspoli
Golfo di Aránci (XII–III)
Cágliari
Orvieto
Todi
M. Martano
Massa Martana
Prodo
Baschi
M. Croce di Serra
Guardea
Bagnorégio
Civitella d. A.
Alviano
Lugnano in T.
Attigliano
Grotte S. Stef.
Férento
Bagnaia
Soriano nel Cimino
Vignanello
Mti. Cimini
Caprarola
L. di Vico
Ronciglione
Corchiano
Borghetto
Nepi
Civita Castellana
Acquasparta
Montecastrilli
Amélia
Narni
TERNI
Gémini
Firenzuola
Spoleto
Ferentillo
Magliano Sabina
Calvi dell'Úmbria
Gottanello
Otricoli
M. Soratte
Rignano Flaminio
Monterosi
Póggio Mirteto
Fara
Torrita Tiber
Greccio
Contigliano
Rieti
Cittàducale
Antrodoco
Marmore
Piediluco
L. di Piediluco
S. Francesco
Leonessa
M. Terminillo
La Forca
Forca dell'Arrone
Monti Sabini
Montenero Sabino
Concerviano
Rocca Sinibalda
Petrella Salto
Fiamignano
L. di Salto
Colle di Tora
L. di Turano
Póggio Moiano
Pagánico Sabino
Monteflávio
Orvinio
Carsoli
Palombara Sabina
Monterotondo
Mentana
MONTECELIO
GUIDONIA
TIVOLI
Licenza
Vicovaro
Àrsoli
Ánticoli C.
Sambuci
S. Grégorio da Sáss.
Subiaco
Bagni di Tivoli
V. Adriana
Veio
CITTÀ D. VATICANO
ROMA
R. Fregene
R. Focene
R. Fiumicino
Ostia
Foce d. Tévere
R.-Lido di Óstia
R. Lido di Castel Fusano
Pomézia
Tor Vaiánica
Ardea
Aprília
Frascati
MARINO
Castel Gandolfo
Albano Laz.
Genzano di Roma
Colli Albani
Rocca di Papa
Velletri
Lariano
Artena
Zagarolo
Palestrina
Genazzano
Valmontone
Colleferro
Segni
Rocca Mass.
Cori
Cisterna di Lat.
Norma
Ninfa
Sermoneta
Sezze
Priverno
Campoverde
Le Ferriere
Lido d. Pini
Lavínio Lido di Enea
Nettuno
Ánzio
LATINA
Borgo Piave
Acciarella
Tre. Astura
S. Michele
Bgo. Grappa
Pontínia
Sabáudia
Parco Naz.
M. Circeo
S. Felice Circeo
I. Zannone
I. Palmarola
I. di Gavi
Ponza
Í. di Ponza
Génova–Nápoli
Nápoli–Marseille
Génova–Palermo
(X–V)
2
3
A
B

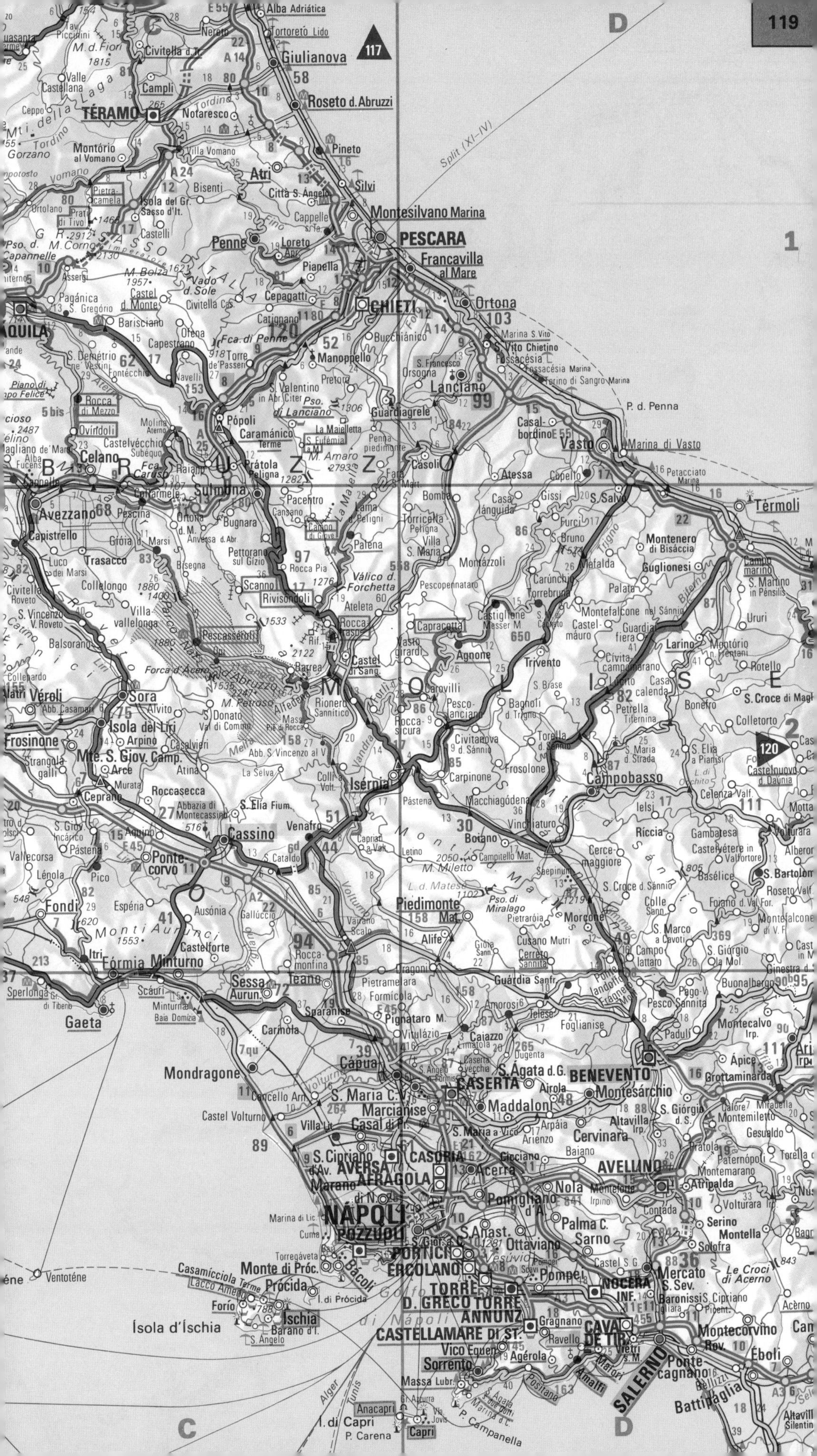

C
D
117
120
1
2
Alba Adriática
Tortoreto Lido
Giulianova
Roseto d. Abruzzi
Téramo
Notaresco
Pineto
Atri
Silvi
Città S. Angelo
Montesilvano Marina
Pescara
Francavilla al Mare
Chieti
Ortona
S. Vito Chietino
Fossacésia
Lanciano
Vasto
Marina di Vasto
Tèrmoli
Penne
Loreto Apr.
Pianella
Cepagatti
Manoppello
Guardiagrele
Caramánico Terme
Pópoli
Sulmona
L'Aquila
Avezzano
Celano
Pescina
Scanno
Pescasséroli
Castel di Sangro
Agnone
Isérnia
Campobasso
Cassino
Sora
Isola del Liri
Frosinone
Véroli
Fondi
Gaeta
Fórmia
Minturno
Sessa Aurun.
Teano
Cápua
Caserta
Benevento
Montesárchio
Avellino
Aversa
Afragola
Casoria
Nápoli
Pozzuoli
Pórtici
Ercolano
Torre d. Greco
Torre Annunz.
Castellammare di St.
Sorrento
Pompei
Nocera Inf.
Cava de Tir.
Salerno
Amalfi
Positano
Ischia
Prócida
Ísola d'Ischia
I. di Capri
Capri
Anacapri
Eboli
Battipáglia
Montecorvino Rov.
Piedimonte Mat.
Alife
Mondragone
Castel Volturno
Nola
Sarno
Ottaviano
Maddaloni
Marcianise
S. Maria C. V.
Pescara
Monti Aurunci
Golfo di Nápoli
Vesúvio
A B R U Z Z O
M O L I S E
Split (XI–IV)

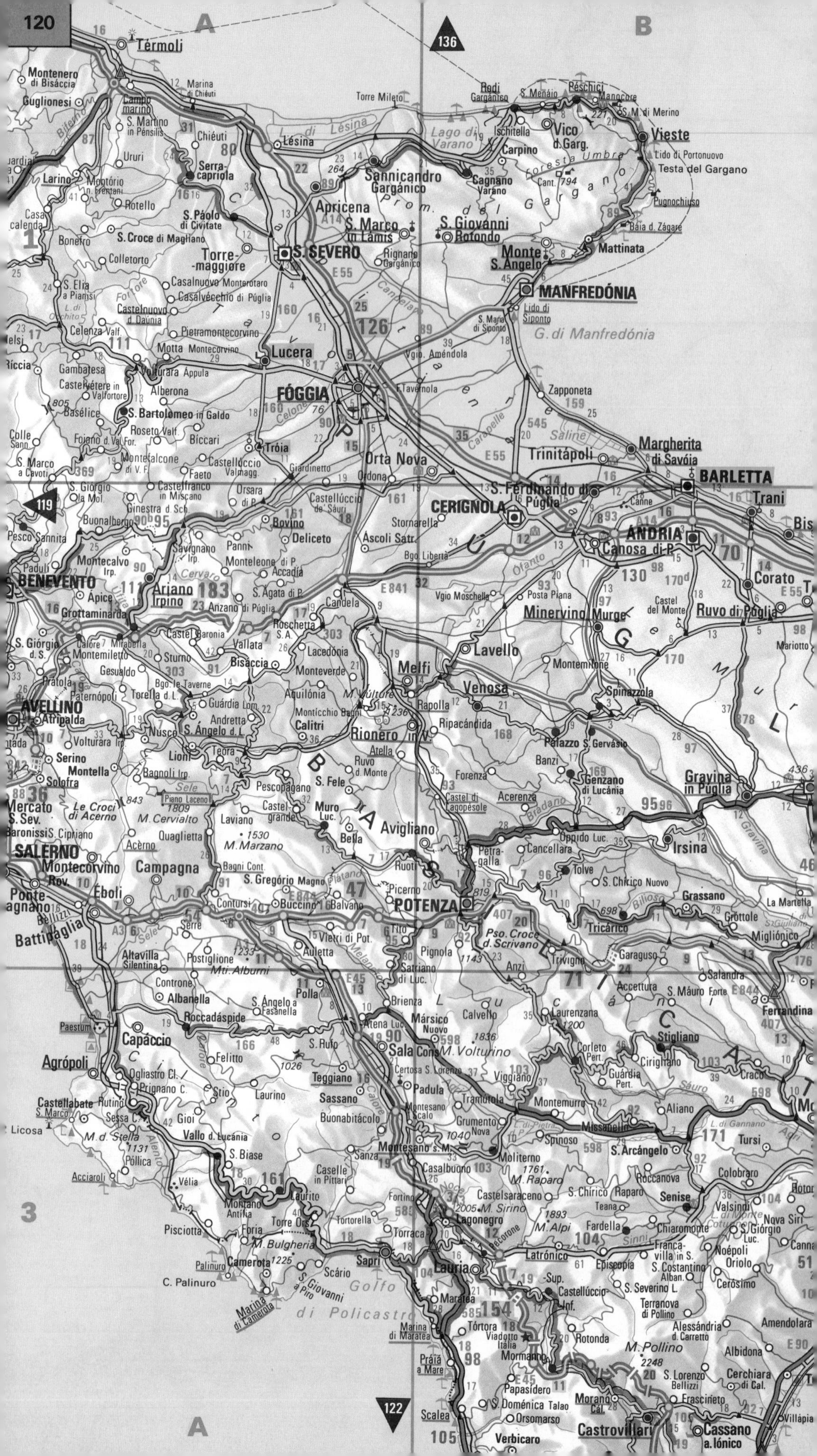

Térmoli
Vieste
S. SEVERO
MANFREDÓNIA
FÓGGIA
Lucera
CERIGNOLA
BARLETTA
ÁNDRIA
Trani
Corato
BENEVENTO
AVELLINO
SALERNO
Éboli
Battipaglia
POTENZA
Melfi
Venosa
Gravina in Puglia
Irsina
Agrópoli
Lauria
Castrovillari
Golfo di Policastro
G. di Manfredónia
136
119
122

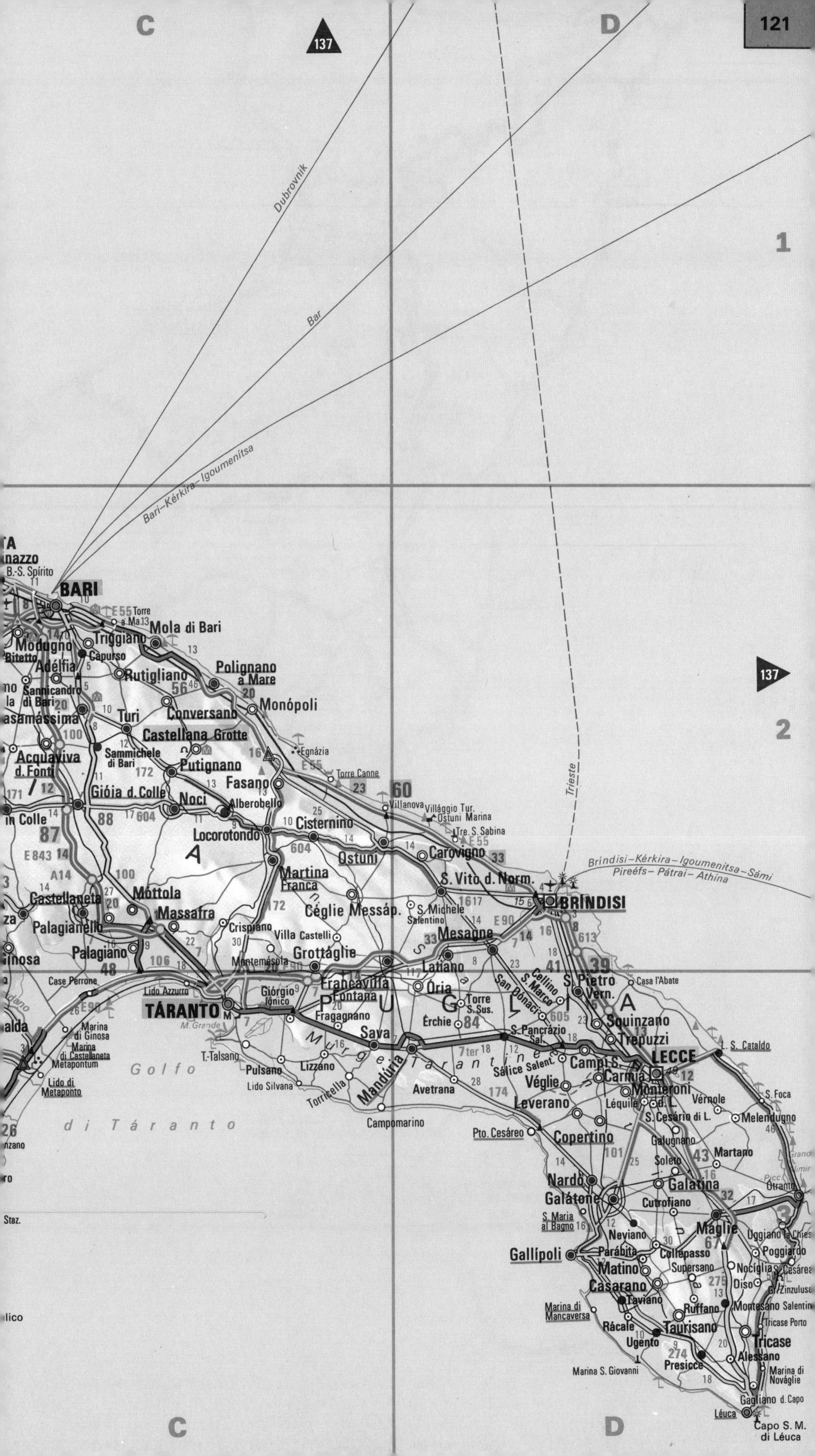
C
D
137
Dubrovnik
Bar
Bari–Kérkira–Igoumenítsa
1
2
Trieste
Bríndisi–Kérkira–Igoumenitsa–Sámi
Pireéfs–Pátrai–Athína
BARI
B.-S. Spírito
Torre a Ma.
Mola di Bari
Modugno
Triggiano
Bitetto
Capurso
Adélfia
Rutigliano
Polignano a Mare
Sannicandro di Bari
Monópoli
Conversano
Turi
Castellana Grotte
Sammichele di Bari
Egnázia
Acquaviva d. Fonti
Putignano
Torre Canne
Fasano
Gióia d. Colle
Noci
Alberobello
Villanova
Villággio Tur. Ostuni Marina
Tre. S. Sabina
Cisternino
Locorotondo
Ostuni
Carovigno
Martina Franca
S. Vito d. Norm.
BRÍNDISI
Castellaneta
Móttola
Céglie Messáp.
S. Michele Salentino
Palagianello
Massafra
Crispiano
Villa Castelli
Mesagne
Palagiano
Grottáglie
Latiano
Montemésola
Ginosa
Case Perrone
Lido Azzurro
Francavilla Fontana
Cellino S. Marco
S. Pietro Vern.
Casa l'Abate
TÁRANTO
M. Grande
Giórgio Iónico
Ória
Torre S. Sus.
San Dónaci
Squinzano
Marina di Ginosa
Fragagnano
Érchie
Marina di Castellaneta
Metapontum
Sava
S. Pancrázio Sal.
Trepuzzi
L. S. Cataldo
T.-Talsano
LECCE
Lido di Metaponto
Pulsano
Lizzano
Manduria
Sálice Salent.
Campi S.
Carmiano
Lido Silvana
Torricella
Avetrana
Véglie
Monteroni d. L.
Vérnole
S. Foca
Leverano
Léquile
S. Cesário di L.
Melendugno
Golfo di Táranto
Campomarino
Pto. Cesáreo
Copertino
Galugnano
Martano
Soleto
Nardò
Galatina
Otranto
Galátone
Cutrofiano
S. Maria al Bagno
Neviano
Maglie
Uggiano la Chiesa
Gallípoli
Parábita
Collepasso
Poggiardo
Matino
Supersano
Nocíglia
Casarano
Diso
Taviano
Ruffano
Montesano Salentino
Marina di Mancaversa
Tricase Porto
Rácale
Taurisano
Tricase
Ugento
Presicce
Alessano
Marina S. Giovanni
Marina di Novàglie
Gagliano d. Capo
Léuca
Capo S. M. di Léuca
P U G L I A
M u r g e   T a r a n t i n e
E 55
E 90
E 843
A 14

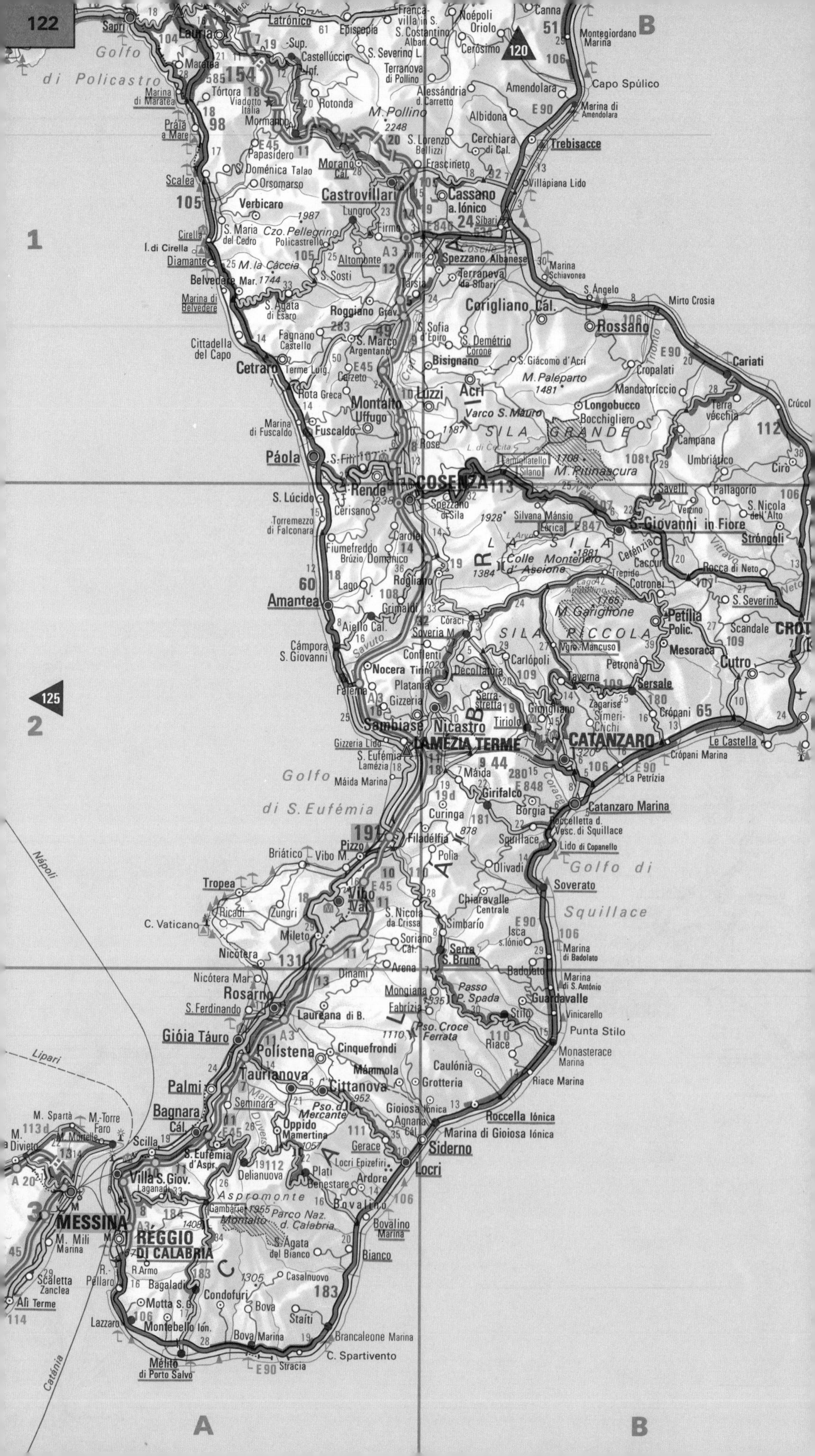
B
120
1
125
2
3
A
B
Golfo
di Policastro
Sapri
Lauria
Latrónico
Episcopia
Francavilla in S.
S. Costantino Alban.
Noépoli
Oriolo
Canna
Montegiordano Marina
Cerósimo
Maratea
Castelluccio Sup.
Castelluccio Inf.
S. Severino L.
Terranova di Pollino
Capo Spúlico
Marina di Maratea
Tórtora
Viadotto Itália
Rotonda
Alessándria d. Carretto
Amendolara
Marina di Amendolara
Albidona
Práia a Mare
Mormanno
M. Pollino
2248
S. Lorenzo Bellizzi
Cerchiara di Cal.
Trebisacce
Papasidero
S. Doménica Talao
Morano Cal.
Frascineto
Villápiana Lido
Scalea
Orsomarso
Castrovillari
Cassano a. Iónico
Sibari
Verbicaro
Lungro
Firmo
1987
S. Maria del Cedro
Czo. Pellegrino
Policastrello
Cirella
I. di Cirella
Diamante
M. la Cáccia
Altomonte
Terme
Spezzano Albanese
Coscile
Marina Schiavonea
Belvedere Mar.
1744
S. Sosti
Terranova da Sìbari
Tarsia
S. Ángelo
Mirto Crosia
Marina di Belvedere
S. Ágata di Esaro
Roggiano Grav.
Corigliano Cal.
Rossano
Fagnano Castello
S. Sofia d'Epiro
S. Marco Argentano
S. Demétrio Corone
Cittadella del Capo
Cetraro
Terme Luig.
Bisignano
S. Giácomo d'Acri
M. Paleparto
1481
Cropalati
Cariati
Cerzeto
Rota Greca
Montalto Uffugo
Luzzi
Acri
Mandatoríccio
Longobucco
Terra vecchia
Crúcol
Marina di Fuscaldo
Fuscaldo
Varco S. Mauro
SILA GRANDE
Bocchigliero
Campana
Páola
S. Fili
Rose
L. di Cécita
Camigliatello Silano
1708
M. Pitinascura
Umbriático
Cirò
Rende
COSENZA
Savelli
Pallagorio
S. Lúcido
Cerisano
Spezzano d. Sila
1928
Silvana Mánsio
Lorica
S. Giovanni in Fiore
Verzino
S. Nicola dell'Alto
Torremezzo di Falconara
LA SILA
Strongoli
Fiumefreddo Brúzio
Domanico
Carolei
1881
Ceténzia
Caccuri
Rocca di Neto
Colle Montenero d' Ascione
1384
Trepido
Cotronei
Rogliano
Lago
Amantea
Grimaldi
Lago Ampollino
1765
M. Gariglione
S. Severina
Petília Polic.
Scandale
Aiello Cal.
Cóczęsto
Soveria M.
SILA PICCOLA
Vgro. Mancuso
Mesoraca
Cámpora S. Giovanni
Savuto
Conflenti
Carlópoli
Petronà
Cutro
Nocera Tirin.
Decollatura
Taverna
Sersale
Falerna
Platania
Serra stretta
Zagarise
Gizzeria
Gimigliano
Simeri-Crichi
Cropani
Sambiase
Nicastro
Tiriolo
Gizzeria Lido
LAMÉZIA TERME
CATANZARO
Le Castella
S. Eufémia Lamézia
Máida
Cropani Marina
Golfo
Máida Marina
Girifalco
Coráce
La Petrízia
di S. Eufémia
Curinga
Borgia
Catanzaro Marina
Roccelletta d. Vesc. di Squillace
Filadélfia
878
Squillace
Lido di Copanello
Briático
Vibo M.
Pizzo
Polia
Olivadi
Golfo di
Tropea
Vibo Val.
Chiaravalle Centrale
Soverato
Squillace
Ricadi
Zungri
S. Nicola da Crissa
Simbarío
Isca s. Iónio
C. Vaticano
Mileto
Soriano Cal.
Serra S. Bruno
Marina di Badolato
Nicótera
Arena
Badolato
Nicótera Mar.
Dinami
Marina di S. António
Rosarno
Mongiana
Passo P. Spada
Guardavalle
S. Ferdinando
Laureana di B.
Fabrízia
1335
Stilo
Vinicarello
Gióia Táuro
Pso. Croce Ferrata
1110
Punta Stilo
Lipari
Políst ena
Cinquefrondi
Riace
Monasterace Marina
Mámmola
Caulónia
Palmi
Taurianova
Cittanova
Grotteria
Riace Marina
Seminara
Pso. d. Mercante
952
Bagnara Cál.
Gioiosa Iónica
Roccella Iónica
M. Spartà
M. Torre Faro
Oppido Mamertina
Agnana Cál.
M. Divieto
Scilla
Gerace
Marina di Gioiosa Iónica
Siderno
S. Eufémia d'Aspr.
Locri Epizefiri
Locri
Villa S. Giov.
Delianuova
Platì
Ardore
Benestare
Laganadi
Aspromonte
Bovalino
MESSINA
Gambárie
1955
Parco Naz. d. Calabria
Bovalino Marina
REGGIO DI CALABRIA
Montalto
S. Ágata del Bianco
M. Milì Marina
Bianco
R. Armo
Casalnuovo
Scaletta Zanclea
R. Pellaro
Bagaladi
1305
Alì Terme
Condofuri
Motta S. G.
Bova
Staíti
Lazzaro
Montebello Ion.
Bova Marina
Brancaleone Marina
C. Spartivento
Mélito di Porto Salvo
Stracia
Catánia
Nápoli
A3
E45
E90
E846
E847
E848

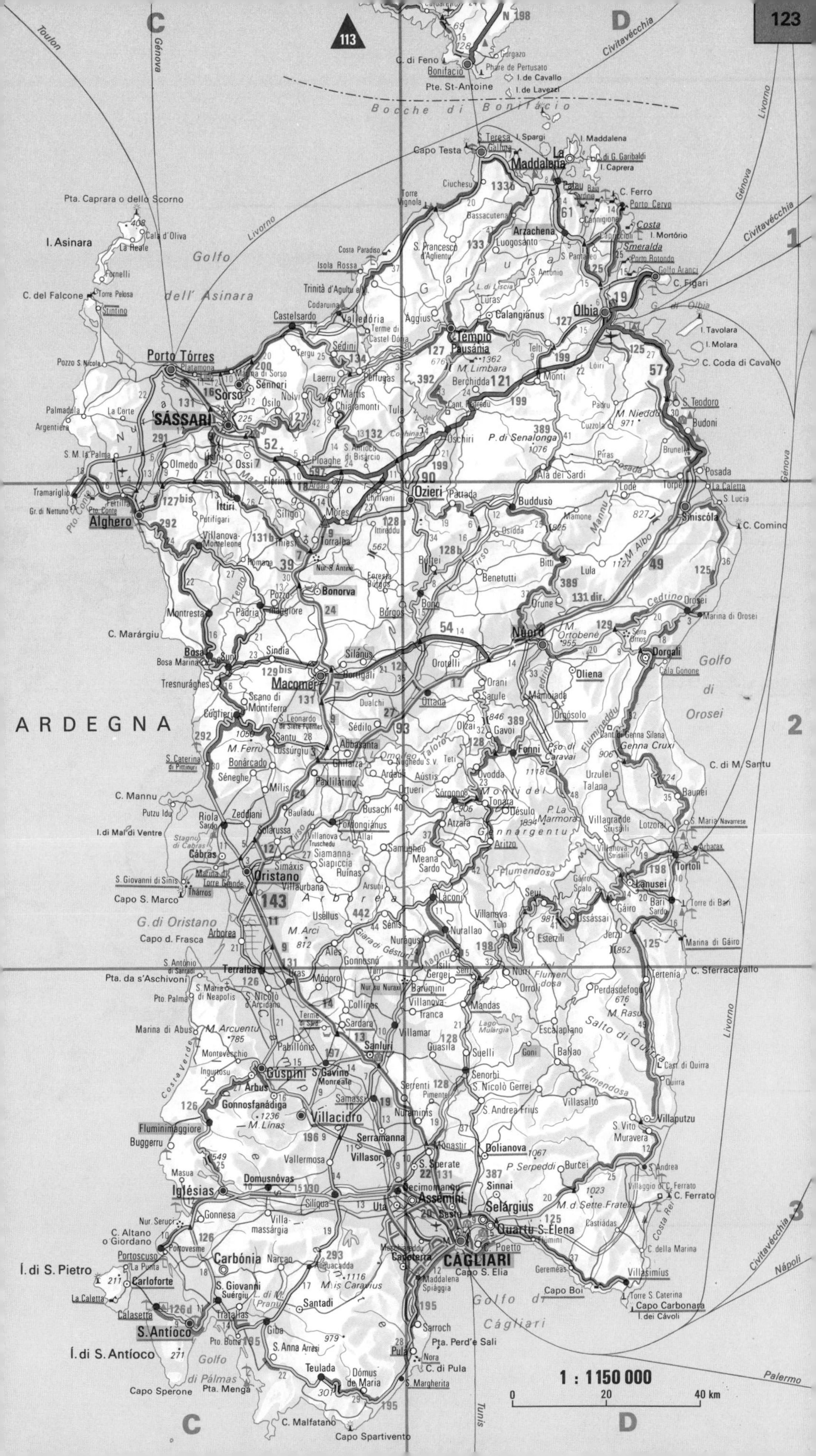

C
D
113
Toulon
Génova
Civitavécchia
Livorno
N 198
C. di Feno
Bonifacio
Phare de Pertusato
I. de Cavallo
I. de Lavezzi
Pte. St-Antoine
Bocche di Bonifacio
S. Teresa Gallura
I. Spargi
I. Maddalena
Capo Testa
La Maddalena
C. di G. Garibaldi
I. Caprera
Torre Vignola
Ciuchesu
Palau
C. Ferro
Porto Cervo
Bassacutena
Arzachena
Cannigione
Costa Smeralda
I. Mortório
Pta. Caprara o dello Scorno
I. Asinara
Cala d'Oliva
La Reale
Golfo dell' Asinara
Fornelli
C. del Falcone
Torre Pelosa
Stintino
Costa Paradiso
Isola Rossa
S. Francesco d'Aglientu
Luogosanto
Gallura
S. Pantaleo
Porto Rotondo
Golfo Aranci
C. Figari
Trinità d'Agultu
Codaruina
Castelsardo
Valledória
Aggius
L. di Liscia
Luras
Calangianus
Ólbia
G. di Olbia
I. Tavolara
I. Molara
Terme di Castel Doria
Sédini
Tempio Pausánia
M. Limbara
Telti
Porto Tórres
Platamona
Marina di Sorso
Sénnori
Sorso
Tergu
Laerru
Perfugas
Berchidda
Monti
Lóiri
C. Coda di Cavallo
Pozzo S. Nicola
Nulvi
Mártis
Chiaramonti
Tula
Cant. Ogreddu
Padru
M. Nieddu
S. Teodoro
Budoni
Palmadula
Argentiera
La Corte
SÁSSARI
Ósilo
Oschiri
P. di Senalonga
Cuzzola
S. M. la Palma
Usini
Ossi
Ploaghe
S. Antioco di Bisarcio
Alà dei Sardi
Píras
Brunella
Posada
Olmedo
Florinas
Ardara
Ozieri
Pattada
Lode
Torpè
La Caletta
S. Lucia
Tramariglio
Gr. di Nettuno
Fertilia
Pto. Conte
Alghero
Ittiri
Putifigari
Chilivani
Mores
Ittireddu
Buddusò
Mamone
Siniscóla
C. Comino
Villanova Monteleone
Romana
Torralba
Nur. S. Antine
Bultei
Osidda
Benetutti
Bitti
Lula
M. Albo
Bonorva
Foresta Burgos
Búrgos
Bono
Orune
Pozzomaggiore
Pádria
Montresta
C. Marárgiu
Bosa
Bosa Marina
Suni
Sindia
Silánus
Bortigali
Orotelli
Núoro
M. Ortobene
Orosei
Marina di Orosei
Cedrino
Serra Orrios
Dorgali
Cala Gonone
Golfo di Orosei
Tresnurághes
Macomer
Scano di Montiferro
Cúglieri
Oliena
Orani
Sarule
Mamoiada
Orgósolo
ARDEGNA
S. Leonardo de Siete Fuentes
Santu Lussúrgiu
Dualchi
Ottana
Sédilo
Olzai
Gavoi
Abbasanta
Ghilarza
M. Ferru
S. Caterina di Pittinuri
Bonárcado
Séneghe
Omodeo
Fonni
Pso. di Caravai
Cant. di Genna Silana
Genna Cruxi
C. di M. Santu
Ardauli
Aústis
Teti
Ovodda
Urzulei
Talana
Baunei
C. Mannu
Putzu Idu
Riola Sardo
Zeddiani
Milis
Paulilátino
Busachi
Ortueri
Sórgono
Tonara
Désulo
P. La Marmora
Villagrande Strisáili
Lotzorai
S. Maria Navarrese
I. di Mal di Ventre
Stagno di Cabras
Cábras
Solarussa
Bauladu
Fordongianus
Villanova Truschedu
Allai
Samugheo
Atzara
Meana Sardo
Aritzo
Gennargentu
Villanova Strisáili
Arbatax
Tortolì
S. Giovanni di Sinis
Marina di Torre Grande
Siamanna
Siapiccia
Simáxis
Oristano
Ruinas
Villaurbana
Flumendosa
Lanusei
Capo S. Marco
Thárros
Arsuni
Arborea
Seui
Gáiro Scalo
Gáiro
Bari Sardo
Torre di Bari
G. di Oristano
Usellus
Láconi
Villanova Tulo
Ussássai
Jerzu
Capo d. Frasca
M. Arci
Sénis
Nurallao
Esterzili
Marina di Gáiro
Giara di Gésturi
Nuragus
Ales
Gonnosnó
Isili
S. Antonio di Santadi
Pta. da s'Aschivoni
Terralba
Uras
Mógoro
Gergei
Serri
Nurri
Orroli
Flumendosa
Tertenia
C. Sferracavallo
S. Maria di Neapolis
S. Nicolò d'Arcidano
Pto. Palma
Nur su Nuraxi
Barúmini
Villanova-franca
Perdasdefogu
Collinas
Mandas
Marina di Abus
M. Arcuentu
Terme di Sardara
Sardara
Lago Mulargia
Escalaplano
Salto di Quirra
M. Rasu
Montevecchio
Pabillonis
Sanluri
Villamar
Guasila
Suelli
Goni
Ballao
Costa Verde
Ingurtosu
Guspini
S. Gavino Monreale
Senorbì
S. Nicolò Gerrei
Cast. di Quirra
Quirra
Arbus
Serrenti
Pimentel
Gonnosfanádiga
M. Linas
Villacidro
Samassi
Nuraminis
S. Andrea Frius
Villasalto
Fluminimaggiore
Villaputzu
S. Vito
Muravera
Buggerru
Serramanna
Monastir
Dolianova
Villasor
Vallermosa
S. Sperate
P. Serpeddi
Burcei
S. Andrea
Masua
Domusnóvas
Decimomannu
Sinnai
Villaggio di C. Ferrato
C. Ferrato
Iglésias
Assémini
Siliqua
Sestu
Selárgius
M. d. Sette Fratelli
Nur. Seruci
Gonnesa
Villamassárgia
Uta
Quartu S. Elena
Flumini
Castiádas
Costa Rei
C. Altano o Giordano
Portovesme
Portoscuso
La Punta
Carbónia
Narcao
Macchiareddu
Capoterra
CÁGLIARI
C. Poetto
Capo S. Elia
C. della Marina
Í. di S. Pietro
Carloforte
S. Giovanni Suérgiu
Acquacadda
M. is Caravius
Maddalena Spiaggia
Gereméas
Villasimíus
La Caletta
Calasetta
Tratalias
Santadi
L. di M. Pranu
Golfo di Cágliari
Capo Boi
Torre S. Caterina
Capo Carbonara
I. dei Cávoli
S. Antíoco
Giba
Sarroch
Pta. Perd'e Sali
Pto. Botte
S. Anna Arresi
Pula
Nora
C. di Pula
Í. di S. Antíoco
Golfo di Pálmas
Teulada
Dómus de María
S. Margherita
Capo Sperone
Pta. Menga
C. Malfatano
Capo Spartivento
Tunis
Nápoli
Palermo
1 : 1150 000
0
20
40 km
1
2
3

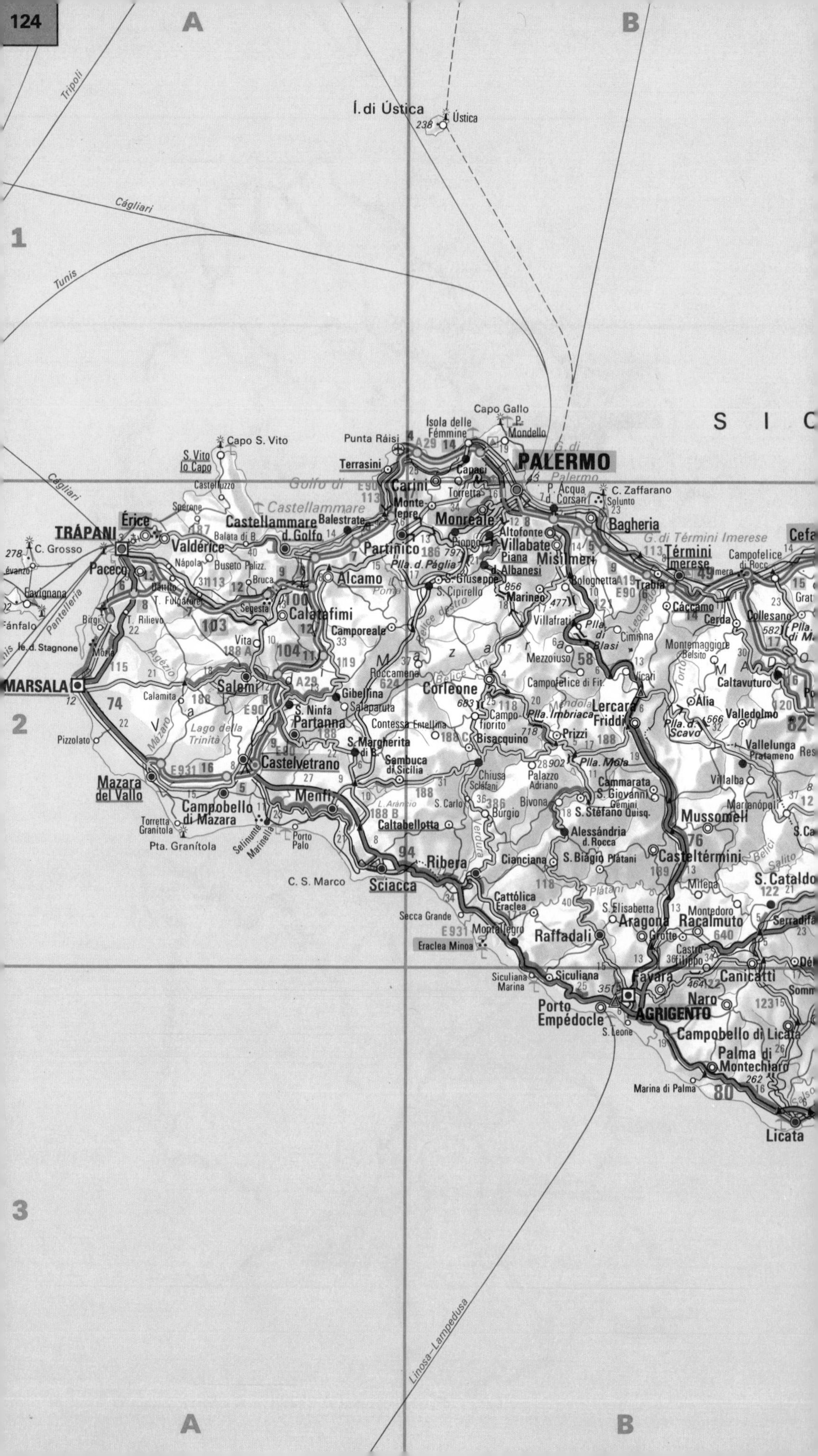
A
B
1
2
3
Tripoli
Cágliari
Tunis
Í. di Ústica
Ústica
238
Capo Gallo
Ísola delle Fémmine
P. Mondello
Punta Ráisi
Terrasini
PALERMO
G. di Palermo
S I C
Capo S. Vito
S. Vito lo Capo
Castelluzzo
Golfo di Castellammare
Sperone
Érice
TRÁPANI
C. Grosso
Favignana
Fánfalo
Valdérice
Paceco
Castellammare d. Golfo
Balestrate
Carini
Capaci
Torretta
Monte Iepre
Monreale
P. Acqua d. Corsari
C. Zaffarano
Solunto
Bagheria
G. di Términi Imerese
Términi Imerese
Campofelice di Rocc.
Cefa
Altofonte
Villabate
Piana d. Albanesi
Misilmeri
Bologhetta
Trabia
Partinico
Plla. d. Páglia
Pioppo
Alcamo
S. Giuseppe
S. Cipirello
Marineo
Buseto Palizz.
Nápola
Balata di B.
Bruca
Segesta
T. Fulgatore
Dattilo
T. Rilievo
Birgi
Calatafimi
Camporeale
Villafrati
Plla. di Blasi
Cimınna
Cáccamo
Cerda
Collesano
Montemaggiore Belsito
Caltavuturo
Pantelleria
Is. d. Stagnone
Mozia
MARSALA
Vita
Salemi
Calamita
Agézio
Gibellina
Roccamena
Corleone
Mezzoiuso
Campofelice di Fit.
Vicari
Lercara Friddi
Alia
Valledolmo
Lago della Trinità
S. Ninfa
Partanna
Salaparuta
Contessa Entellina
Campo fiorito
Plla. Imbriaca
Prizzi
Bisacquino
Plla. d. Scavo
Vallelunga Pratameno
Pizzolato
Mazaro
Castelvetrano
S. Margherita di B.
Sambuca di Sicilia
Chiusa Sclàfani
Palazzo Adriano
Plla. Mola
Villalba
Mazara del Vallo
Campobello di Mazara
Torretta Granítola
Pta. Granítola
Selinunte
Marinella
Porto Palo
Menfi
L. Arancio
Caltabellotta
S. Carlo
Burgio
Bivona
Cammarata
S. Giovanni Gemini
S. Stéfano Quisq.
Alessándria d. Rocca
Mussomeli
Marianópoli
Casteltérmini
Ribera
Cianciana
S. Biagio Plátani
Milena
S. Cataldo
C. S. Marco
Sciacca
Cattólica Eraclea
S. Elisabetta
Secca Grande
Montallegro
Raffadali
Aragona
Montedoro
Racalmuto
Grotte
Serradifa
Eraclea Minoa
Castrofilippo
Siculiana Marina
Siculiana
Favara
Canicattì
Porto Empédocle
AGRIGENTO
Naro
S. Leone
Campobello di Licata
Palma di Montechiaro
Marina di Palma
Licata
Linosa–Lampedusa
A
B

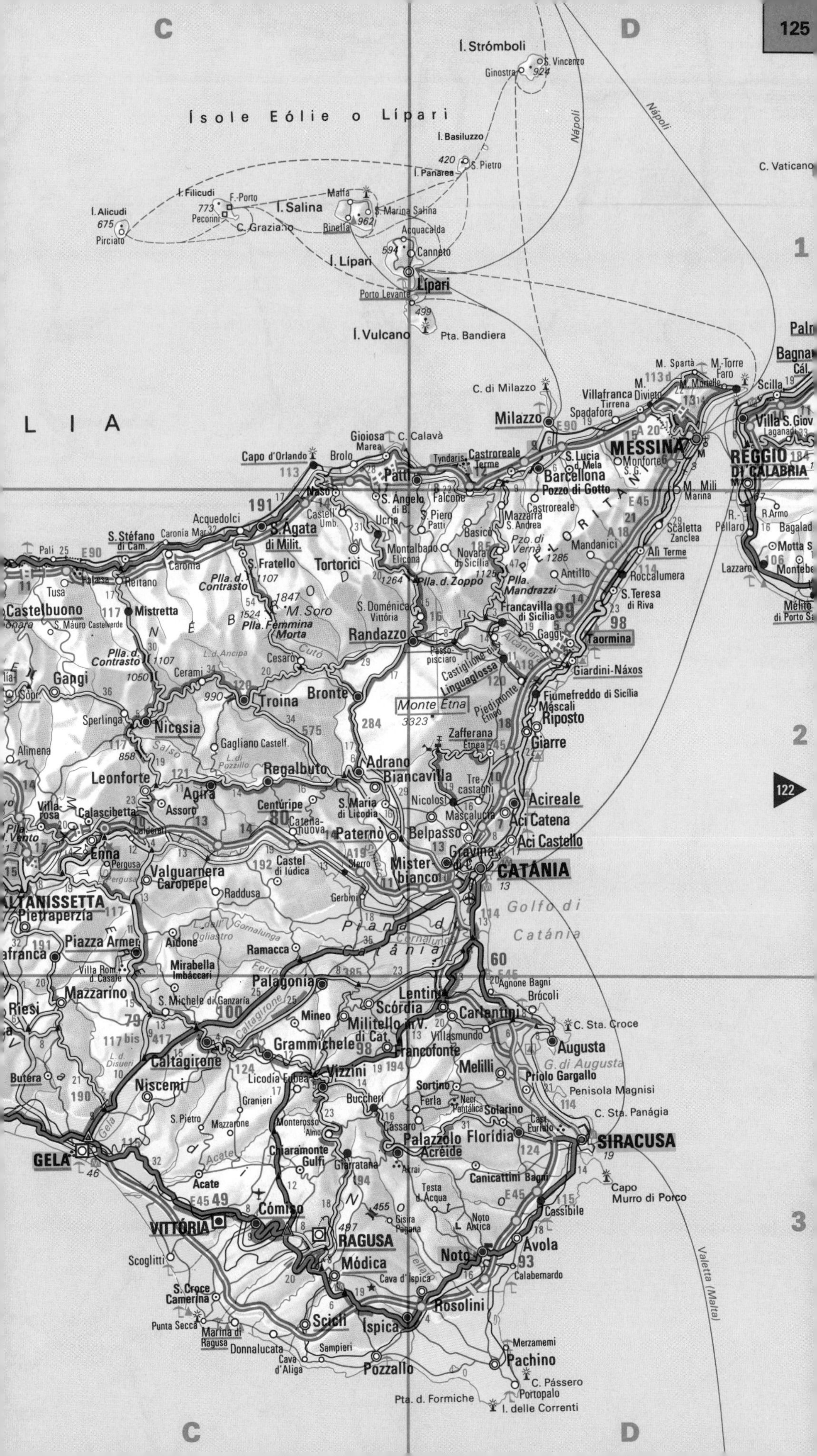
C
D
Í. Strómboli
S. Vincenzo
Ginostra
924
Ísole Eólie o Lípari
Nápoli
Í. Basiluzzo
420
S. Pietro
Í. Panarea
C. Vaticano
Í. Filicudi
F.-Porto
773
Pecorini
Malfa
Í. Salina
S. Marina Salina
962
Rinella
Í. Alicudi
675
Pirciato
C. Graziano
Acquacalda
594
Canneto
1
Í. Lípari
Lípari
Porto Levante
499
Í. Vulcano
Pta. Bandiera
M. Spartà
M.-Torre Faro
Bagnara Cál.
Scilla
C. di Milazzo
Villafranca Tirrena
Spadafora
Milazzo
E90
L I A
Gioiosa Marea
C. Calavà
Capo d'Orlando
Brolo
Patti
Tyndaris
Castroreale Terme
S. Lucia d. Mela
Barcellona Pozzo di Gotto
MESSINA
Monforte S. G.
Villa S. Giov
REGGIO DI CALABRIA
M. Mili Marina
E45
Castroreale
Naso
S. Ángelo di B.
Falcone
Acquedolci
191
S. Ágata di Milit.
Castell' Umb.
Ucria
S. Piero Patti
Basicò
Mazzarrà S. Andrea
Scaletta Zanclea
R. Pellaro
Bagalad
S. Stéfano di Cam.
Caronía Mar.
Pzo. di Vernà
Mandanici
Alì Terme
Motta S
Pali
Caronía
Montalbano Elicona
Novara di Sicilia
1285
Antillo
Roccalumera
Lazzaro
Montebe
Tusa
Reitano
S. Fratello
Tortorici
Plla. d. Zoppo
Plla. Mandrazzi
S. Teresa di Riva
Mélito di Porto Sa
Castelbuono
117
Mistretta
Plla. d. Contrasto
M. Soro
1847
S. Doménica Vittória
Francavilla di Sicília
89
98
S. Máuro Castelverde
Plla. Femmina Morta
Randazzo
Gaggi
Taormina
Plla. d. Contrasto
L. d. Ancipa
Cesarò
Passo-pisciaro
Castiglione di S.
Linguaglossa
Giardini-Náxos
Gangi
Cerami
Bronte
Monte Etna
3323
Fiumefreddo di Sicília
Máscali
Riposto
Troina
Sperlinga
Nicosia
Salso
575
284
Zafferana Etnea
Giarre
2
Alimena
Gagliano Castelf.
L. di Pozzillo
Adrano
Biancavilla
Leonforte
Regalbuto
121
Agira
Tre-castagni
Acireale
122
Villa-rosa
Calascibetta
Assoro
Centúripe
S. Maria di Licodia
Nicolosi
Mascalucia
Aci Catena
80
Catena-nuova
Paternò
Belpasso
Enna
Pergusa
Aci Castello
Valguarnera Caropepe
Castel di Iúdica
Mister-bianco
Gravina di C.
CATÁNIA
Raddusa
Gerbini
Golfo di Catánia
CALTANISSETTA
Pietraperzía
117
Piana di Catánia
Aidone
Piazza Armerina
Ramacca
Villa Rom. d. Casale
Mirabella Imbáccari
60
Palagonía
Agnone Bagni
Mazzarino
Lentini
Brúcoli
Riesi
S. Michele di Ganzaría
Scórdia
Carlentini
Mineo
Militello in V. di Cat.
C. Sta. Croce
Villasmundo
Caltagirone
Grammichele
Francofonte
Augusta
G. di Augusta
Butera
Niscemi
Licodía Eubea
Vizzini
Melilli
Priolo Gargallo
Penisola Magnisi
Granieri
Sortino
Ferla
Buccheri
Necr. Pantálica
Solarino
C. Sta. Panágia
S. Pietro
Mazzarrone
Monterosso Almo
Cássaro
Palazzolo Acréide
Florídia
SIRACUSA
GELA
Chiaramonte Gulfi
Giarratana
Akrai
Acate
Canicattini Bagni
Capo Murro di Porco
Testa d. Acqua
Cómiso
Noto Antica
Cassíbile
3
VITTÓRIA
Gisira Pagana
RAGUSA
Noto
Ávola
Scoglitti
Módica
Cava d'Íspica
Calabernardo
Valetta (Malta)
S. Croce Camerina
Rosolini
Punta Secca
Marina di Ragusa
Scicli
Íspica
Donnalucata
Sampieri
Merzamemi
Cava d'Aliga
Pozzallo
Pachino
C. Pássero
Portopalo
Pta. d. Formiche
I. delle Correnti

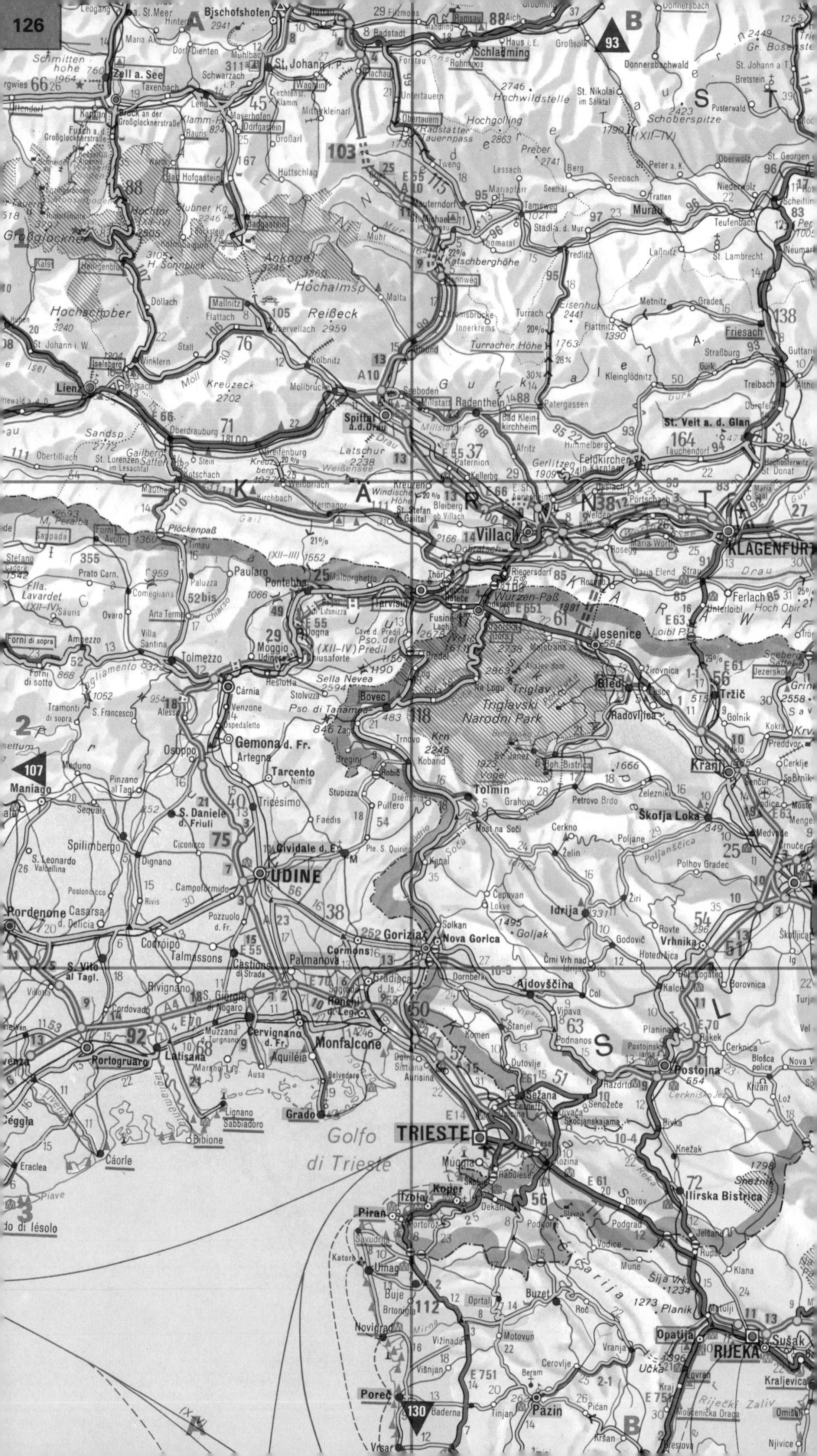
93
Bischofshofen
St. Johann i. P.
Radstadt
Schladming
Zell a. See
Bruck an der Großglocknerstraße
Schwarzach i. P.
Dorfgastein
Bad Hofgastein
Badgastein
Großglockner
Heiligenblut
Hochalmsp
Reißeck
Mallnitz
Obervellach
Kolbnitz
Gmünd
Spittal a. d. Drau
Millstatt
Radenthein
Bad Kleinkirchheim
Mauterndorf
St. Michael im Lungau
Tamsweg
Murau
Katschberghöhe
Obertauern
Radstätter Tauernpass
Hochgolling
Schoberspitze
Turracher Höhe
Friesach
St. Veit a. d. Glan
Feldkirchen in Kärnten
Lienz
Oberdrauburg
Kötschach
Hermagor
Weißensee
Villach
KLAGENFURT
Velden
Pörtschach
Maria Wörth
Ferlach
Wurzen-Paß
Loibl P.
Plöckenpaß
Tolmezzo
Pontebba
Malborghetto
Tarvisio
Moggio Udinese
Chiusaforte
Sella Nevea
Predil
Bovec
Kobarid
Tolmin
Triglav
Triglavski Narodni Park
Kranjska Gora
Jesenice
Bled
Radovljica
Tržič
Kranj
Škofja Loka
Idrija
Vrhnika
Gemona d. Fr.
Tarcento
Tricésimo
S. Daniele d. Friuli
Spilimbergo
Maniago
107
Cividale d. F.
UDINE
Pordenone
Casarsa d. Delicia
Codróipo
Palmanova
Cormons
Gorizia
Nova Gorica
Ajdovščina
Postojna
Monfalcone
Cervignano d. Fr.
Aquiléia
Latisana
Portogruaro
Grado
Lignano Sabbiadoro
Bibione
Cáorle
Golfo di Trieste
TRIESTE
Sežana
Koper
Izola
Piran
Umag
Novigrad
Poreč
130
Buje
Motovun
Pazin
Buzet
Ilirska Bistrica
Snežnik
Opatija
RIJEKA
Sušak
Učka
Kraljevica

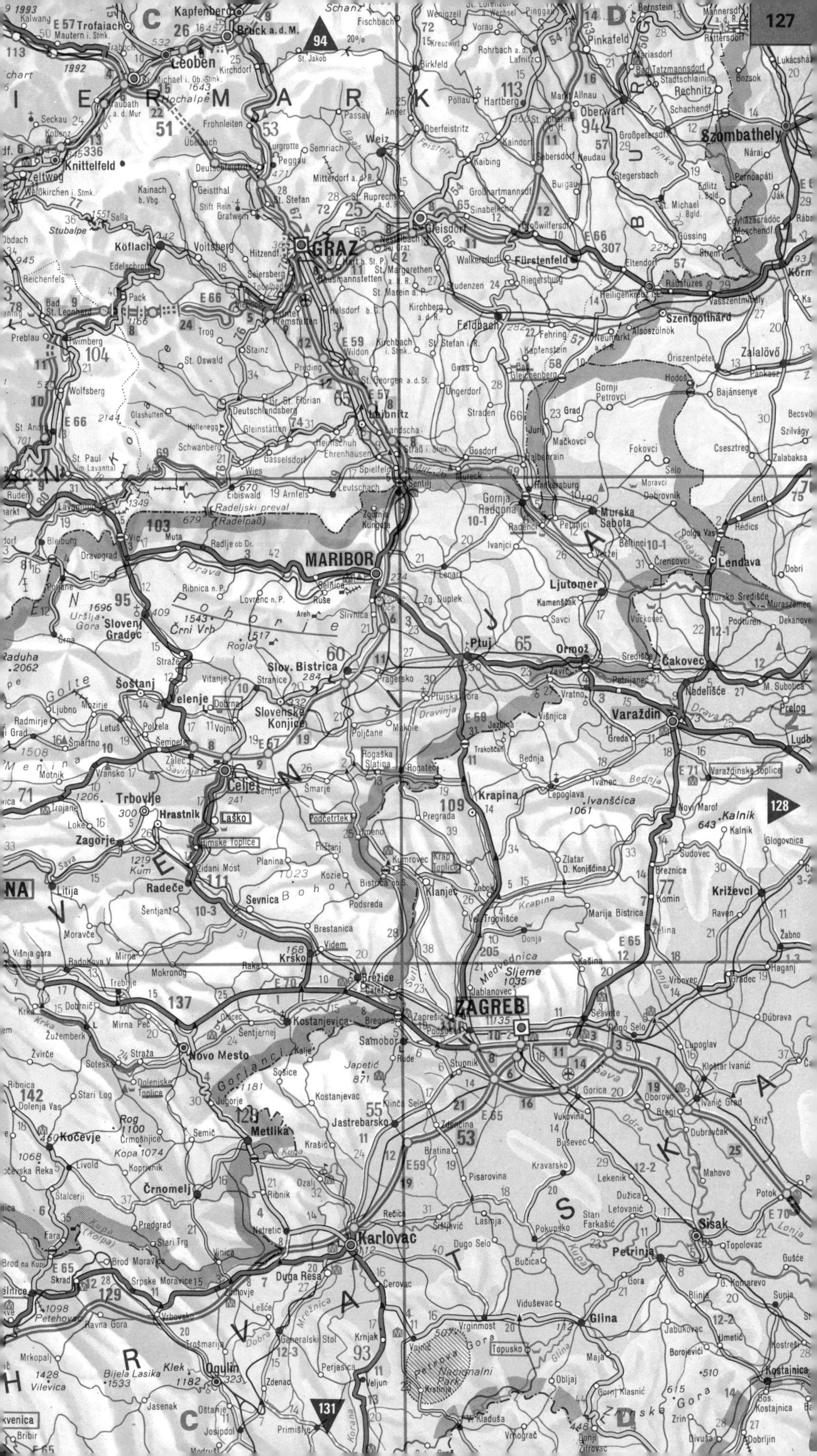
Kapfenberg
Bruck a. d. M.
Trofaiach
Leoben
St. Michael i. Ob.-Stmk.
Knittelfeld
Zeltweg
Weißkirchen i. Stmk.
Stubalpe
Frohnleiten
Übelbach
Deutschfeistritz
Peggau
Semriach
Passail
Weiz
Birkfeld
Vorau
Pinkafeld
Bernstein
Rohrbach a. d. L.
Lafnitz
Pöllau
Hartberg
Markt Allnau
Oberwart
Rechnitz
Szombathely
Großpetersdorf
Stegersbach
Güssing
Gleisdorf
Fürstenfeld
Heiligenkreuz i. L.
Szentgotthárd
Köflach
Voitsberg
Graz
Hausmannstätten
Kalsdorf b. G.
Feldbach
Kirchbach i. Stmk.
Wildon
Leibnitz
Bad Gleichenberg
Straden
Mureck
Spielfeld
Leutschach
Arnfels
Deutschlandsberg
Stainz
Schwanberg
Wies
Eibiswald
Wolfsberg
St. Andrä
St. Paul im Lavanttal
Bad St. Leonhard
Twimberg
Preblau
Radeljski preval (Radelpaß)
Maribor
Ruše
Slivnica
Lenart
Gornja Radgona
Radenci
Murska Sobota
Beltinci
Lendava
Ljutomer
Ptuj
Ormož
Čakovec
Varaždin
Slov. Bistrica
Pragersko
Rogla
Pohorje
Dravograd
Muta
Radlje ob Dr.
Slovenj Gradec
Velenje
Šoštanj
Slovenske Konjice
Celje
Žalec
Laško
Hrastnik
Trbovlje
Zagorje
Litija
Radeče
Sevnica
Krško
Brežice
Rogaška Slatina
Rogatec
Krapina
Lepoglava
Ivanec
Ivanščica
Novi Marof
Kalnik
Križevci
Zlatar
Zabok
Klanjec
Kumrovec
Pregrada
Marija Bistrica
Donja Stubica
Medvednica
Sljeme 1035
Zagreb
Zaprešić
Samobor
Sesvete
Dugo Selo
Vrbovec
Velika Gorica
Ivanić Grad
Novo Mesto
Kostanjevica
Trebnje
Metlika
Črnomelj
Kočevje
Jastrebarsko
Karlovac
Duga Resa
Ogulin
Sisak
Petrinja
Glina
Topusko
Petrova Gora
Nacionalni Park
Kostajnica
Bos. Kostajnica
Dvor
Slunj
Velika Kladuša
Kupa
Drava
Mur
Sava
Lonja
94
128
131
S T E I E R M A R K
B U R G E N L A N D
S L O V E N I J A
H R V A T S K A

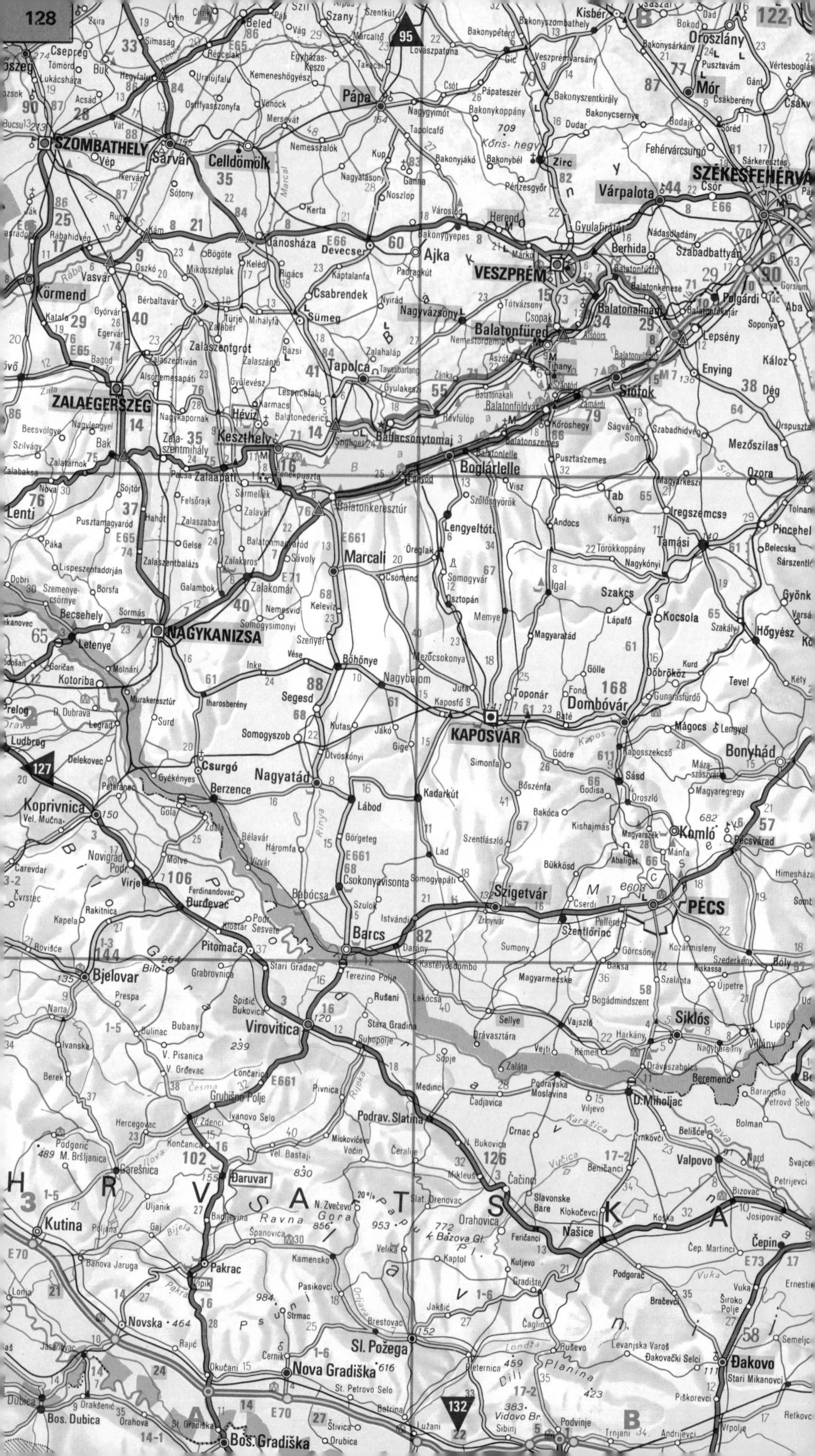
95
122
127
132
Kisbér
Oroszlány
Mór
Pápa
Bakonypéterd
Bakonyszombathely
Veszprémvarsány
Bakonyszentkirály
Bakonycsernye
Pápateszér
Bakonykoppány
Nagygyimót
Tapolcafő
Kőris-hegy
Zirc
Dudar
Bakonybél
Bakonyjákó
Pénzesgyőr
Várpalota
SZÉKESFEHÉRVÁR
Csór
Fehérvárcsurgó
Sárkeresztes
Bodajk
Csákberény
Söréd
Gánt
Pusztavám
Bakonysárkány
Bokod
Dad
Szany
Szentkút
Marcaltő
Lovászpatona
Gic
Csót
Vág
Egyházaskeszó
Takácsi
Kemeneshőgyész
Beled
Iván
Cirák
Zsira
Csepreg
Simaság
Répcelak
Uraiújfalu
Hegyfalu
Ostffyasszonyfa
Vönöck
Mersevát
Nemesszalók
Kup
Ganna
Nagyalásony
Noszlop
Kerta
Városlőd
Herend
Márkó
Bakonygyepes
Gyulafirátót
Berhida
Nádasdladány
Szabadbattyán
Bucsu
Vát
SZOMBATHELY
Vép
Sárvár
Celldömölk
Ikervár
Sótony
Bük
Tömörd
Lukácsháza
Acsád
Ják
Rábahidvég
Rum
Kám
Bögöte
Jánosháza
Devecser
Ajka
Padragkút
Káptalanfa
Rigács
Keléd
Mikosszéplak
Oszkó
Vasvár
Körmend
Bérbaltavár
Csabrendek
Nyirád
Sümeg
Nagyvázsony
VESZPRÉM
Tótvázsony
Csopak
Balatonfüred
Balatonalmádi
Balatonfűzfő
Balatonkenese
Balatonakarattya
Polgárdi
Balatonfőkajár
Lepsény
Enying
Soponya
Káloz
Dég
Aba
Tác
Gorsium
Katafa
Győrvár
Egervár
Türje
Zalabér
Mihályfa
Zalaszentgrót
Zalaszentiván
Zalaszántó
Bazsi
Tapolca
Zalahaláp
Tavasbarlang
Gyulakeszi
Nemesvámos
Aszófő
Tihany
Zánka
Balatonakali
Szántód
Siófok
Zamárdi
Balatonföldvár
Bagod
Alsónemesapáti
Gyülevész
Lesencefalu
Karmacs
Hévíz
Balatonederics
Szigliget
Badacsonytomaj
Révfülöp
Kőröshegy
Ságvár
Som
Szabadhidvég
Mezőszilas
Ózora
ZALAEGERSZEG
Beesvölgye
Nagylengyel
Bak
Szilvágy
Nagykapornak
Zalaszentmihály
Keszthely
Balatonszemes
Balatonlelle
Boglárlelle
Pusztaszemes
Zalabaksa
Zalatárnok
Nova
Pacsa
Zalaapáti
Fenékpuszta
Fonyód
Visz
Magyarkeszi
Lenti
Sójtör
Felsőrajk
Hahót
Sármellék
Zalavár
Balatonkeresztúr
Szőlősgyörök
Lengyeltóti
Tab
Kánya
Iregszemcse
Tolnanémedi
Pusztamagyaród
Zalaszabar
Pincehely
Páka
Gelse
Balatonmagyaród
Sávoly
Marcali
Öreglak
Andocs
Törökkoppány
Nagykónyi
Tamási
Belecska
Sárszentlőrinc
Lispeszentadorján
Zalaszentbalázs
Zalakaros
Csömend
Somogyvár
Igal
Szakcs
Kocsola
Gyönk
Dobri
Szemenye-csörnye
Borsfa
Galambok
Zalakomár
Kelevíz
Osztopán
Memye
Lápafő
Szakály
Hőgyész
Becsehely
Sormás
Nemesvid
Somogysimonyi
Letenye
NAGYKANIZSA
Szenyér
Magyaratád
Kanovec
Goričan
Molnári
Vése
Inke
Böhönye
Mezőcsokonya
Gölle
Kurd
Dőbrököz
Kotoriba
Nagybajom
Juta
Toponár
Fonó
Dombóvár
Tevel
Kéty
Prelog
Murakeresztúr
Iharosberény
Segesd
Kaposfő
KAPOSVÁR
Baté
Gunarasfürdő
D. Dubrava
Legrad
Surd
Kutas
Jákó
Gige
Mágocs
Lengyel
Drava
Ludbreg
Somogyszob
Otvöskónyi
Simonfa
Gödre
Kaposszekcső
Bonyhád
Delekovec
Csurgó
Sásd
Mázaszászvár
Magyaregregy
Peteranec
Gyékényes
Berzence
Nagyatád
Lábod
Kadarkút
Bőszénfa
Godisa
Oroszló
Koprivnica
Vel. Mučna
Gola
Zdala
Bakóca
Kishajmás
Komló
Pécsvárad
Bélavár
Háromfa
Görgeteg
Magyarszék
Novigrad Podr.
Molve
Vízvár
Ladó
Szentlászló
Abaliget
Mánfa
Carevdar
Virje
Ferdinandovac
Đurđevac
Babócsa
Csokonyavisonta
Somogyapáti
Bükkösd
Čvrstec
Szigetvár
Cserdi
Himesháza
Rakitnica
Kapela
Podr. Sesvete
Kloštar
Szulok
Istvándi
Zrinyivár
Pellérd
PÉCS
Szentlőrinc
Roviśće
Pitomača
Barcs
Darány
Sumony
Görcsöny
Kozármisleny
Bóly
Bjelovar
Bilo
Grabrovnica
Stari Gradac
Terezino Polje
Kastélyosdombó
Magyarmecske
Baksa
Szalánta
Szederkény
Kiskassa
Újpetre
Prespa
Špišić Bukovica
Rušani
Lakócsa
Bogádmindszent
Siklós
Narta
Virovitica
Stara Gradina
Sellye
Vajszló
Harkány
Nagyharsány
Villány
Lippó
Bulinac
Bubany
Suhopolje
Drávasztára
Vejti
Kémes
Ivanska
V. Pisanica
V. Grđevac
Lončarica
Zaláta
Drávaszabolcs
Beremend
Berek
Česma
Grubišno Polje
Pivnica
Rijeka
Medinci
Podravska Moslavina
Viljevo
D. Miholjac
Baranjsko Petrovo Selo
Hercegovac
V. Zdenci
Ivanovo Selo
Podrav. Slatina
Čadjavica
Bolman
Podgorić
M. Bršljanica
Končanica
Mikovićevo
Voćin
Vel. Bastaji
Čeralije
N. Bukovica
Crnac
Karašica
Crnkovci
Belišće
Garešnica
Đaruvar
Mikleuš
Vučica
Benićanci
Valpovo
Nard
Švajcer
Petrijevci
H R V A T S K A
Uljanik
Badljevina
N. Zvečevo
Ravna Gora
Slat. Drenovac
Čačinci
Slavonske Bare
Klokočevci
Bizovac
Josipovac
Kutina
Poljana
Gaj
Bijela
Španovica
Papuk
Bazova Gl.
Orahovica
Feričanci
Našice
Koška
Čepin
E70
Banova Jaruga
Pakrac
Lipik
Kamensko
Velika
Kaptol
Kutjevo
Čep. Martinci
E73
Lonja
Pasikovci
Gradište
Podgorač
Vuka
Ernestinovo
Psunj
Orljava
Jakšić
Bračevci
Široko Polje
Novska
Rajić
Strmac
Brestovac
Sl. Požega
Čaglin
Levanjska Varoš
Đakovački Selci
Semeljci
Jasenovac
Cernik
Nova Gradiška
Pleternica
Londža
Dilj Planina
Ruševo
Đakovo
Stari Mikanovci
Dubica
Okučani
St. Petrovo Selo
Piškorevci
Bos. Dubica
Drakšenić
Orahova
Batrina
Lužani
Vidovo Br.
Podvinje
Retkovci
Sl. Gradiška
Bos. Gradiška
Štivica
Orubica
Sibinj
Trnjani
Andrijevci
Vrpolje
A
B

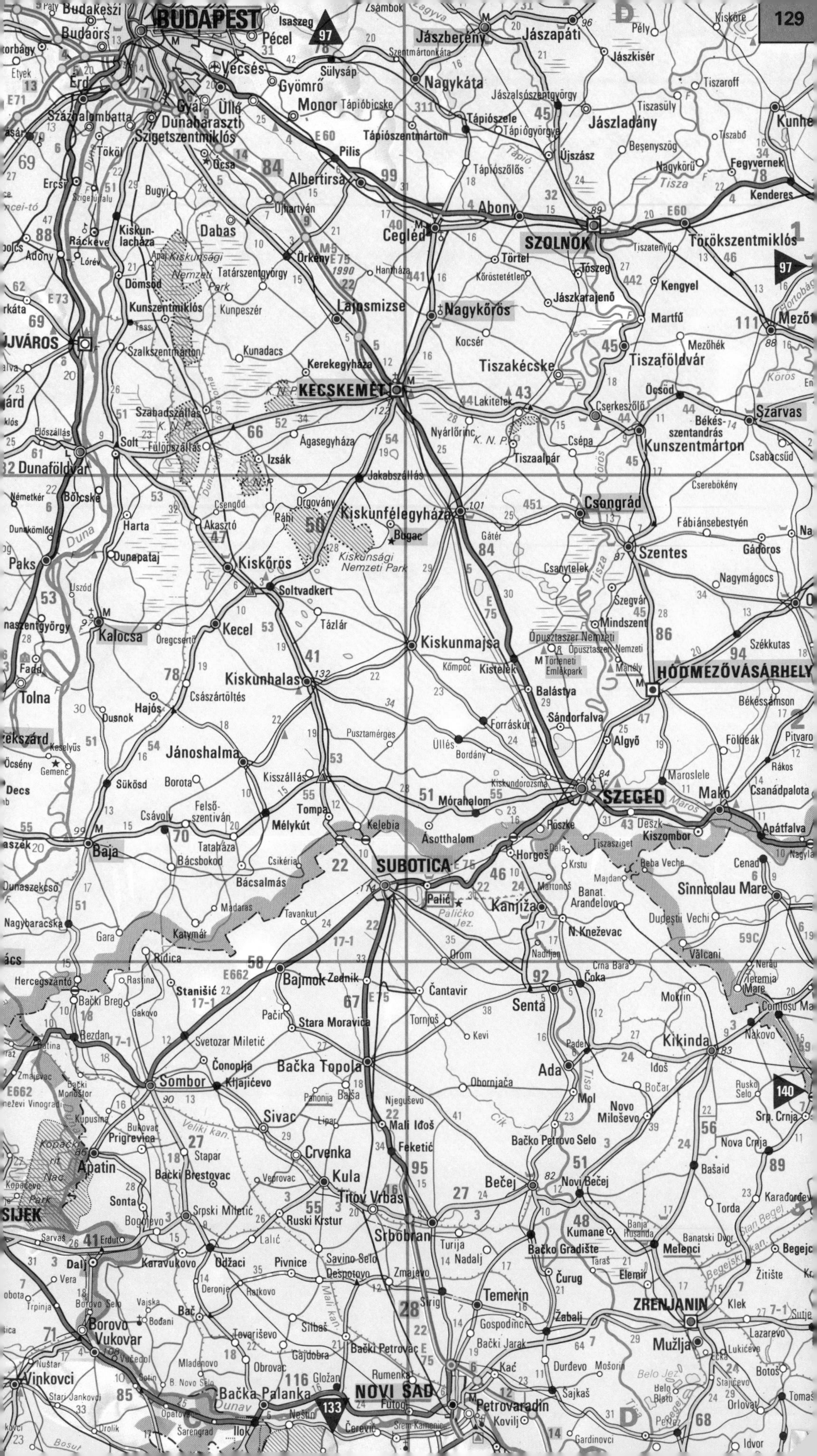
BUDAPEST
Kecskemét
Szolnok
Szeged
Subotica
Novi Sad
Zrenjanin
Hódmezővásárhely
Kiskunfélegyháza
Kiskunhalas
Baja
Sombor
Cegléd
Nagykőrös
Csongrád
Szentes
Kikinda
Senta
Kalocsa
Kiskőrös
Vukovar
Vinkovci
Bačka Palanka
Bačka Topola
Mako
Dunaföldvár

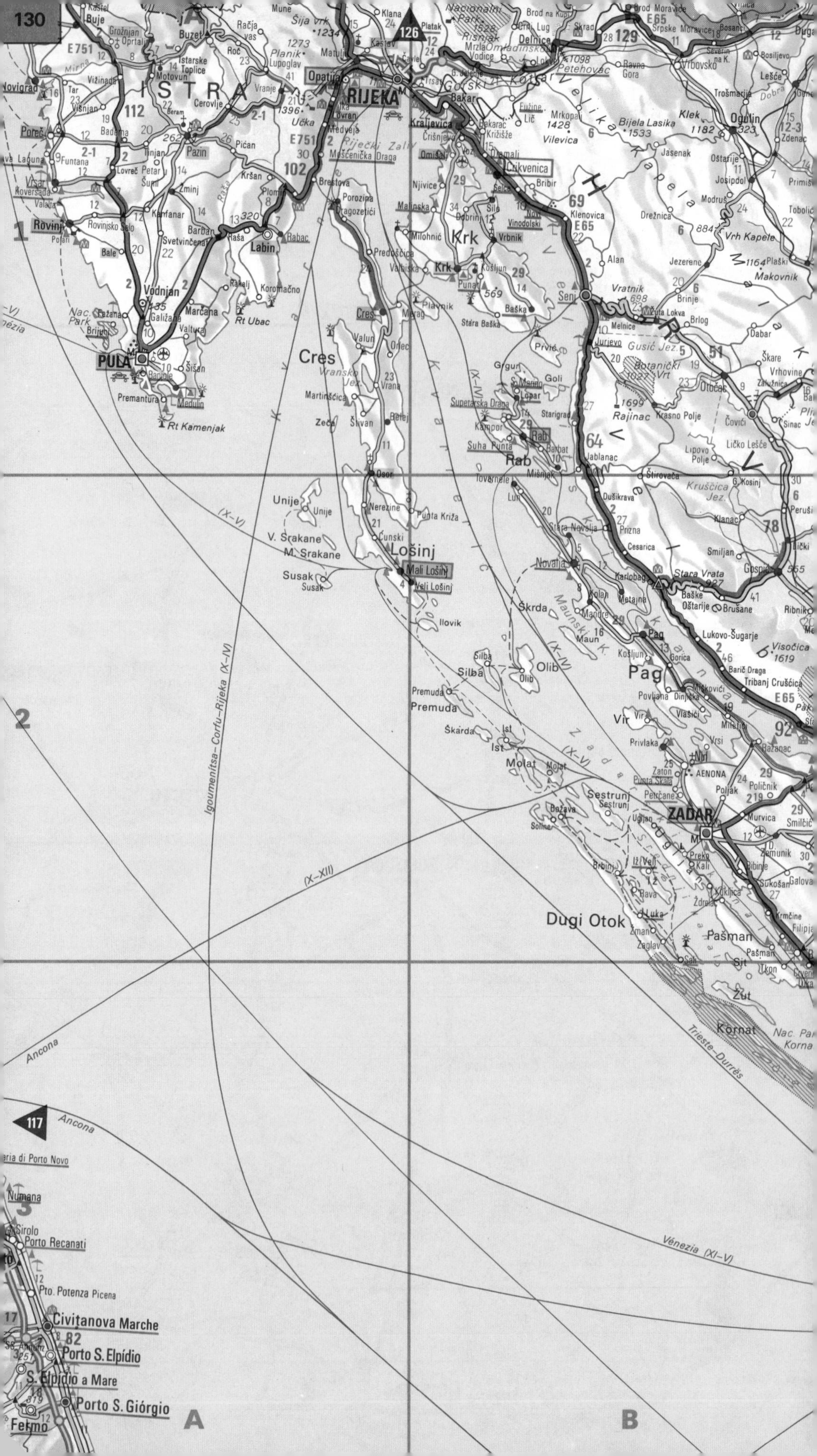

Buje
Grožnjan
Oprtalj
Buzet
Račja vas
Roč
Istarske Toplice
Motovun
Mune
Šija vrk
Klana
Kastav
Matulji
Platak
Nacionalni Park
Risnjak
Brod na Kupi
Crni Lug
Skrad
Delnice
Mrzla Vodice
Lokve
Brod Moravice
Srpske Moravice
Bosanci
Severin na K.
Vrbovsko
Bosiljevo
Lešće
E751
E65
ISTRA
Novigrad
Tar
Višnjan
Vižinada
Poreč
Baderna
Funtana
Laguna
Vrsar
Koversada
Valalta
Rovinj
Rovinjsko Selo
Pofari
Bale
Tinjan
Lovreč
Petar
Šumi
Žminj
Kanfanar
Cerovlje
Beram
Pazin
Pićan
Kršan
Plomin
Svetvinčenat
Barban
Raša
Labin
Rabac
Vodnjan
Galižana
Fažana
Nac. Park
Brijuni
Marčana
Valtura
Rakalj
Koromačno
Rt Ubac
PULA
Banjole
Šišan
Premantura
Medulin
Rt Kamenjak
Vranje
Lupoglav
Planik
Učka
Lovran
Medveja
Opatija
RIJEKA
Mošćenička Draga
Brestova
Rječki Zaliv
Bakar
Kraljevica
Bakarac
Križišće
Čavle
Trsat
Gorski
Kotar
Petehovac
Ravna Gora
Fužine
Lič
Mrkopalj
Vilevica
Bijela Lasika
Klek
Ogulin
Jasenak
Oštarije
Josipdol
Trošmarija
Zdenac
Primišlje
Tobolić
Modruš
Drežnica
Vrh Kapele
Plaški
Makovnik
Jezerane
Brinje
Križpolje
Vratnik
Žuta Lokva
Brlog
Dabar
Šćare
Vrhovine
Otočac
Čovići
Sinac
Ličko Lešće
Lipovo Polje
Štirovača
Kruščica Jez.
G. Kosinj
Klanac
Perušić
Smiljan
Lički
Gospić
Ribnik
Visočica
Lukovo-Šugarje
Baške Oštarije
Brušane
Stara Vrata
Karlobag
Cesarica
Prizna
Dušikrava
Jablanac
Rajinac
Krasno Polje
Botanički Vrt
Gusić Jez.
Jurjevo
Melnice
Senj
Alan
Klenovica
Novi Vinodolski
Bribir
Crikvenica
Dramalj
Selce
Čišnjeva
Omišalj
Njivice
Malinska
Dobrinj
Šilo
Vrbnik
Milohnić
Krk
Punat
Košljun
Baška
Stara Baška
Plavnik
Porozina
Dragozetići
Predošćica
Valbiska
Cres
Merag
Valun
Orlec
Vransko Jez.
Vrana
Martinšćica
Zeča
Belej
Osor
Nerezine
Punta Križa
Čunski
Lošinj
Mali Lošinj
Veli Lošinj
Ilovik
Unije
V. Srakane
M. Srakane
Susak
Prvić
Grgur
Goli
S. Marino
Lopar
Supetarska Draga
Kampor
Starigrad
Rab
Barbat
Suha Punta
Mišnjak
Tovarnele
Lun
Stara Novalja
Novalja
Kolan
Metajna
Mandre
Škrda
Maun
Maunski K.
Pag
Košljun
Gorica
Povljana
Dinjiška
Miškovići
Vlašići
Baric Draga
Tribanj Krušćica
Vir
Privlaka
Nin
AENONA
Zaton
Punta Skala
Petrčane
Poljak
Poličnik
Bažanac
Vrsi
Smilčić
ZADAR
Murvica
Zemunik
Silba
Olib
Premuda
Škarda
Ist
Molat
Sestrunj
Božava
Soline
Ugljan
Preko
Kali
Bibinje
Sukošan
Galovac
Brbinj
Iž Veli
Rava
Luka
Kukljica
Ždrelac
Dugi Otok
Zman
Zaglav
Sali
Pašman
Sit
Tkon
Ćrvena
Žut
Kornat
Nac. Park Kornati
Krmčine
Filipjakov
Trieste-Durrës
Igoumenitsa-Corfu-Rijeka (X-IV)
(X-V)
(X-IV)
(X-XII)
Ancona
Venezia (XI-V)
Numana
Sirolo
Porto Recanati
Pto. Potenza Picena
Civitanova Marche
Porto S. Elpídio
S. Elpídio a Mare
Porto S. Giórgio
Fermo
A
B

126
129
117

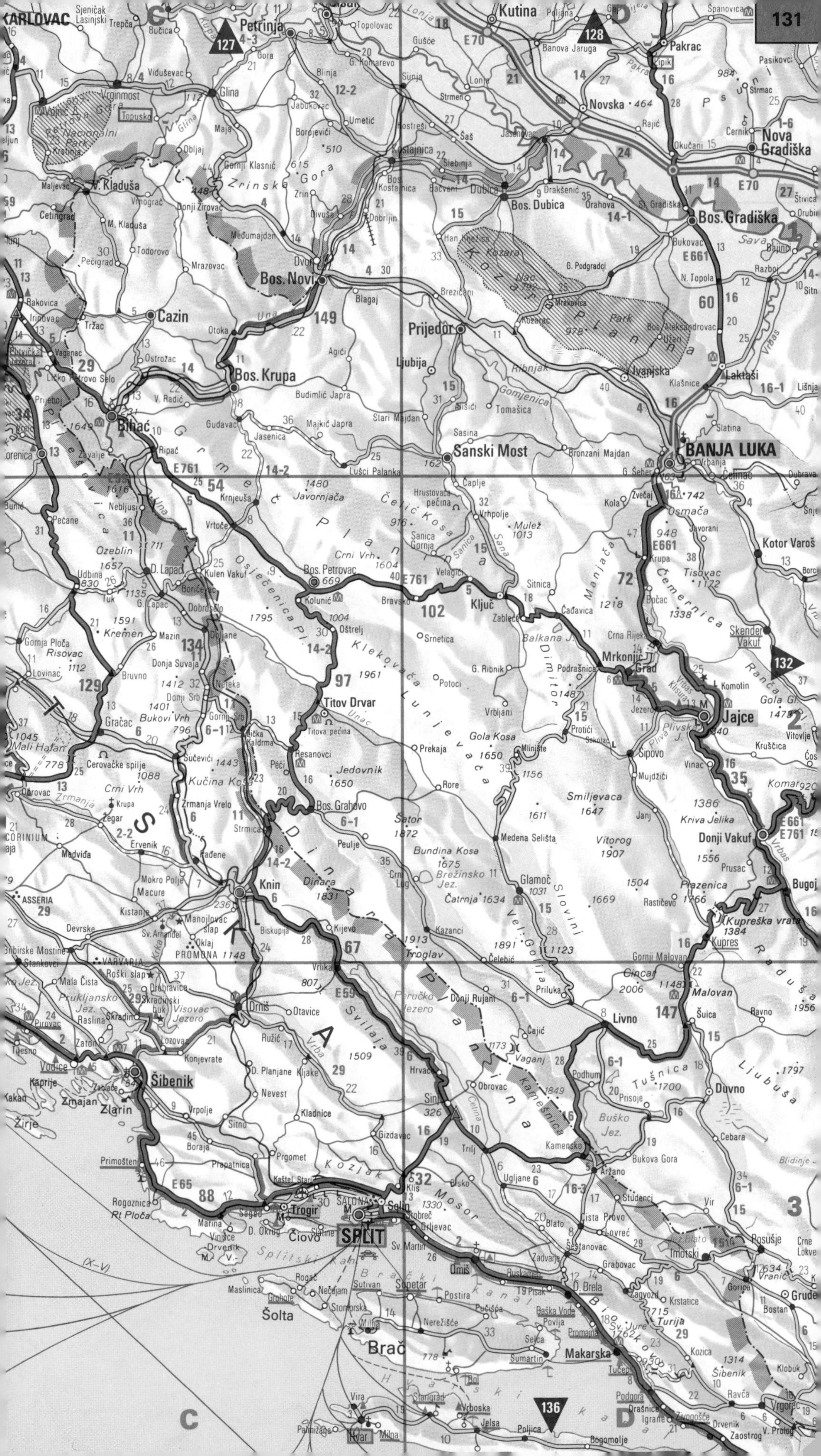
Karlovac
Petrinja
Kutina
Pakrac
Glina
Vrginmost
Topusko
Novska
Nova Gradiška
Jasenovac
Kostajnica
Bos. Dubica
Bos. Gradiška
V. Kladuša
Bos. Novi
Cazin
Bos. Krupa
Prijedor
Ljubija
Bihać
Sanski Most
Banja Luka
Bos. Petrovac
Ključ
Kotor Varoš
Titov Drvar
Mrkonjić Grad
Jajce
Udbina
Gračac
Bos. Grahovo
Šipovo
Donji Vakuf
Bugojno
Knin
Glamoč
Kupres
Drniš
Vrlika
Livno
Šibenik
Sinj
Duvno
Trogir
Split
Solin
Omiš
Imotski
Posušje
Grude
Makarska
Brač
Šolta
Hvar
Vrgorac
Zrinska Gora
Kozara Nac. Park
Grmeč Planina
Klekovača
Dinara
Svilaja
Kamešnica
Mosor
Biokovo
Kupreška vrata
Plitvička Jezera
E70
E661
E761
E59
E65
127
128
132
136

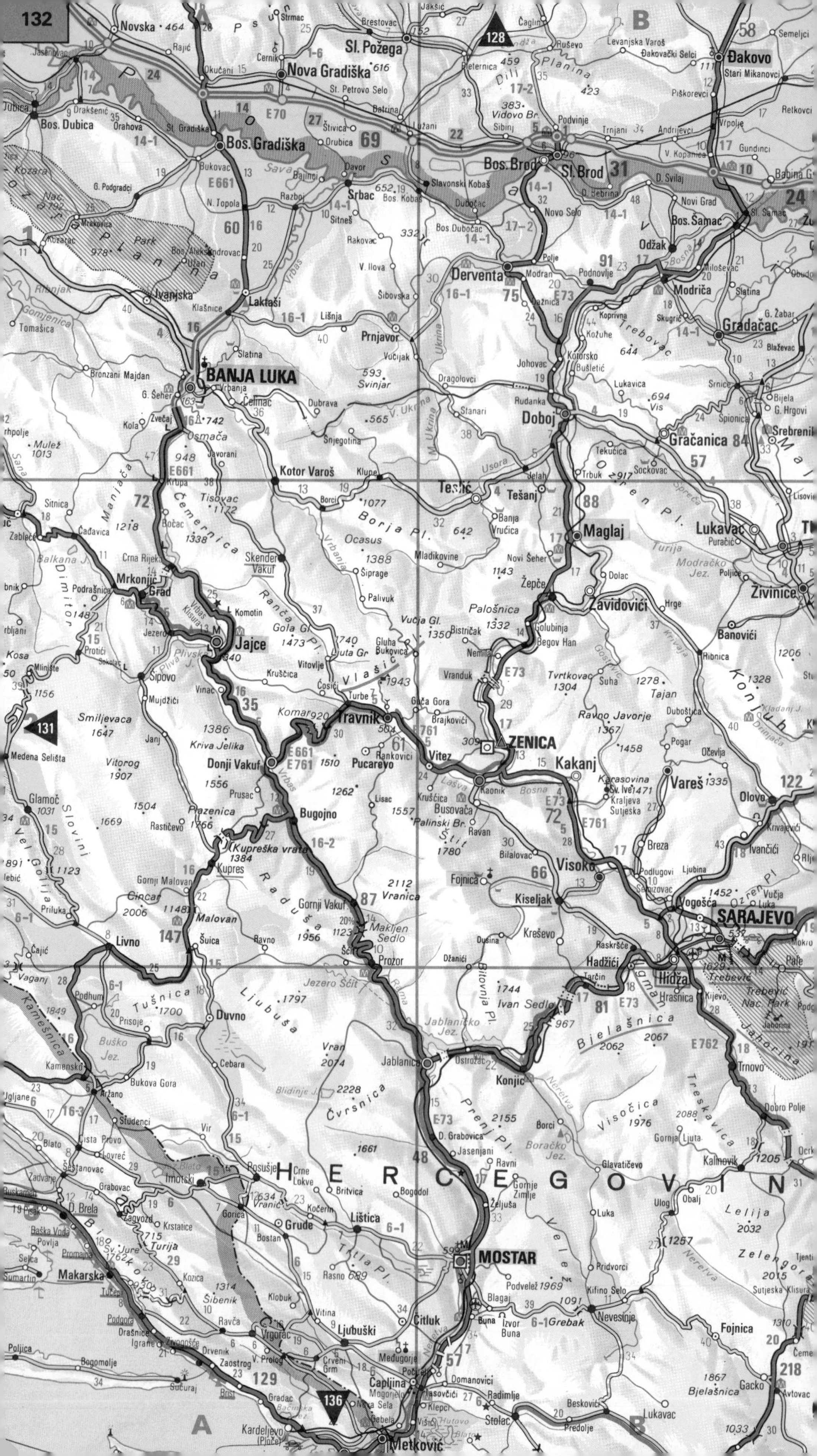
128
131
136
Novska
Jasenovac
Bos. Dubica
Dubica
Okučani
Nova Gradiška
Sl. Požega
Brestovac
Čaglin
Pleternica
Levanjska Varoš
Đakovački Selci
Đakovo
Stari Mikanovci
Piškorevci
Retkovci
Vrpolje
Andrijevci
Trnjani
Podvinje
Vidovo Br.
Dilj Planina
Bos. Gradiška
St. Gradiška
Štivica
Orubica
Davor
Bos. Brod
Sl. Brod
Slavonski Kobaš
Bos. Kobaš
Srbac
Gundinci
V. Kopanica
Babina Greda
D. Svilaj
D. Bebrina
Novi Grad
Bos. Šamac
Sl. Šamac
Odžak
Miloševac
Modriča
Obudovac
Slatina
Gradačac
G. Žabar
Blaževac
Sava
Kozara
Nac. Park
G. Podgradci
Mrakovica
Kozarac
Bukovac
N. Topola
Razboj
Sitneš
Rakovac
V. Ilova
Bos. Dubočac
Dubočac
Novo Selo
Derventa
Modran
Polje
Podnovlje
Dažnica
Bos. Aleksandrovac
Ivanjska
Laktaši
Klašnice
Šibovska
Lišnja
Prnjavor
Vučijak
Svinjar
Kotorsko
Koprivna
Kožuhe
Trebovac
Skugrić
Johovac
Bušletić
Lukavica
Vis
Srnice
Bijela
G. Hrgovi
Spionica
Srebrenik
Slatina
BANJA LUKA
Bronzani Majdan
G. Šeher
Vrbanja
Čelinac
Dubrava
Dragolovci
Rudanka
Doboj
Stanari
Gračanica
Tomašica
Gomjenica
Rinjak
Kola
Zvečaj
Osmača
Javorani
Snjegotina
Kotor Varoš
Klupe
Teslić
Tešanj
Jelah
Tekućica
Trbuk
Sočkovac
Ozren Pl.
Mulež
Krupa
Manjača
Tisovac
Borci
Borja Pl.
Ocasus
Banja Vrućica
Maglaj
Lukavac
Puračić
Modračko Jez.
Sitnica
Zableće
Čađavica
Crna Rijeka
Čemernica
Bočac
Skender Vakuf
Šiprage
Mladikovine
Novi Šeher
Žepče
Dolac
Zavidovići
Hrge
Živinice
Poljice
Balkana J.
Dimitor
Mrkonjić Grad
Podrašnica
Komotin
Gola Gl.
Rančaa Pl.
Palivuk
Vučja Gl.
Bistričak
Palošnica
Golubinja
Begov Han
Banovići
Protići
Jezero
Jajce
Pliva
Plivsko J.
Šipovo
Liuta Gr.
Gluha Bukovica
Vitovlje
Kruščica
Nemila
Vranduk
Tvrtkovac
Suha
Tajan
Ribnica
Konjuh
Kosa
Mlinište
Vinac
Čosići
Turbe
Vlašić
Gača Gora
Brajkovići
Dubostica
Mujdžići
Smiljevaca
Komar
Travnik
Vitez
ZENICA
Ravno Javorje
Pogar
Očevlja
Kladanj
Medena Selišta
Janj
Kriva Jelika
Donji Vakuf
Rankovici
Pucarevo
Kakanj
Karasovina
Sv. Ive
Vareš
Kraljeva Sutjeska
Olovo
Vitorog
Prusac
Lisac
Kruščica
Busovača
Kaonik
Lašva
Bosna
Glamoč
Slovinj
Plazenica
Rastičevo
Bugojno
Palinski Br.
Ravan
Štit
Bilalovac
Breza
Krivajevići
Ivančići
Kupreška vrata
Kupres
Radusa
Fojnica
Visoko
Podlugovi
Ljubina
Semizovac
Golija
Gornji Malovan
Vranica
Kiseljak
Vogošća
Ozren Pl.
Vučja
Cincar
Malovan
Priluka
Gornji Vakuf
Kreševo
SARAJEVO
Livno
Šuica
Ravno
Makljen Sedlo
Prozor
Dusina
Džanići
Raskršće
Hadžići
Ilidža
Trebević
Mokro
Pale
Čajić
Vagani
Jezero Ščit
Bitovnja Pl.
Tarčin
Igman
Hrasnica
Kijevo
Nac. Park
Podhum
Tušnica
Ljubuša
Ivan Sedlo
Jahorina
Kamešnica
Prisoje
Duvno
Jablaničko Jez.
Bjelašnica
Buško Jez.
Vran
Jablanica
Ostrožac
Konjic
Trnovo
Kamensko
Cebara
Bukova Gora
Blidinje J.
Čvrsnica
Prenj Pl.
Neretva
Visočica
Treskavica
Aržano
Ugljane
Studenci
Vir
D. Grabovica
Borci
Boračko Jez.
Gornja Ljuta
Dobro Polje
Blato
Cista Provo
Lovreć
Jasenjani
Ravni
Glavatičevo
Kalinovik
Šestanovac
Zadvarje
Grabovac
Imotski
Posušje
HERCEGOVINA
Crne Lokve
Britvica
Bogodol
Gornje Zimlje
Željuša
Ulog
Obalj
Lelija
Brela
D. Brela
Pisak
Zagvozd
Krstatice
Gorica
Vranić
Kočerin
Grude
Lištica
Luka
Baška Voda
Povlja
Promajna
Sv. Jure
Biokovo
Turija
Bostan
Trtla Pl.
Velež
Zelengora
Selca
Sumartin
Makarska
Tučepi
Kozica
Šibenik
Rasno
MOSTAR
Podvelež
Pridvorci
Kifino Selo
Sutjeska Klisura
Tjentište
Podgora
Drašnice
Igrane
Živogošće
Ravča
Vrgorac
Klobuk
Vitina
Ljubuški
Čitluk
Blagaj
Buna
Izvor Buna
Grebak
Nevesinje
Fojnica
Poljica
Bogomolje
Drvenik
Zaostrog
Sućuraj
Brist
V. Prolog
Crveni Grm
Međugorje
Počitelj
Čapljina
Domanovići
Radimlje
Bjelašnica
Gacko
Avtovac
Gradac
Bačinska Jez.
Mogorjelo
Hasovčići
Klepci
Nova Sela
Gabela
Višići
Hutovo Blato
Stolac
Beskovići
Predolje
Lukavac
Ploče
Kardeljevo
Metković

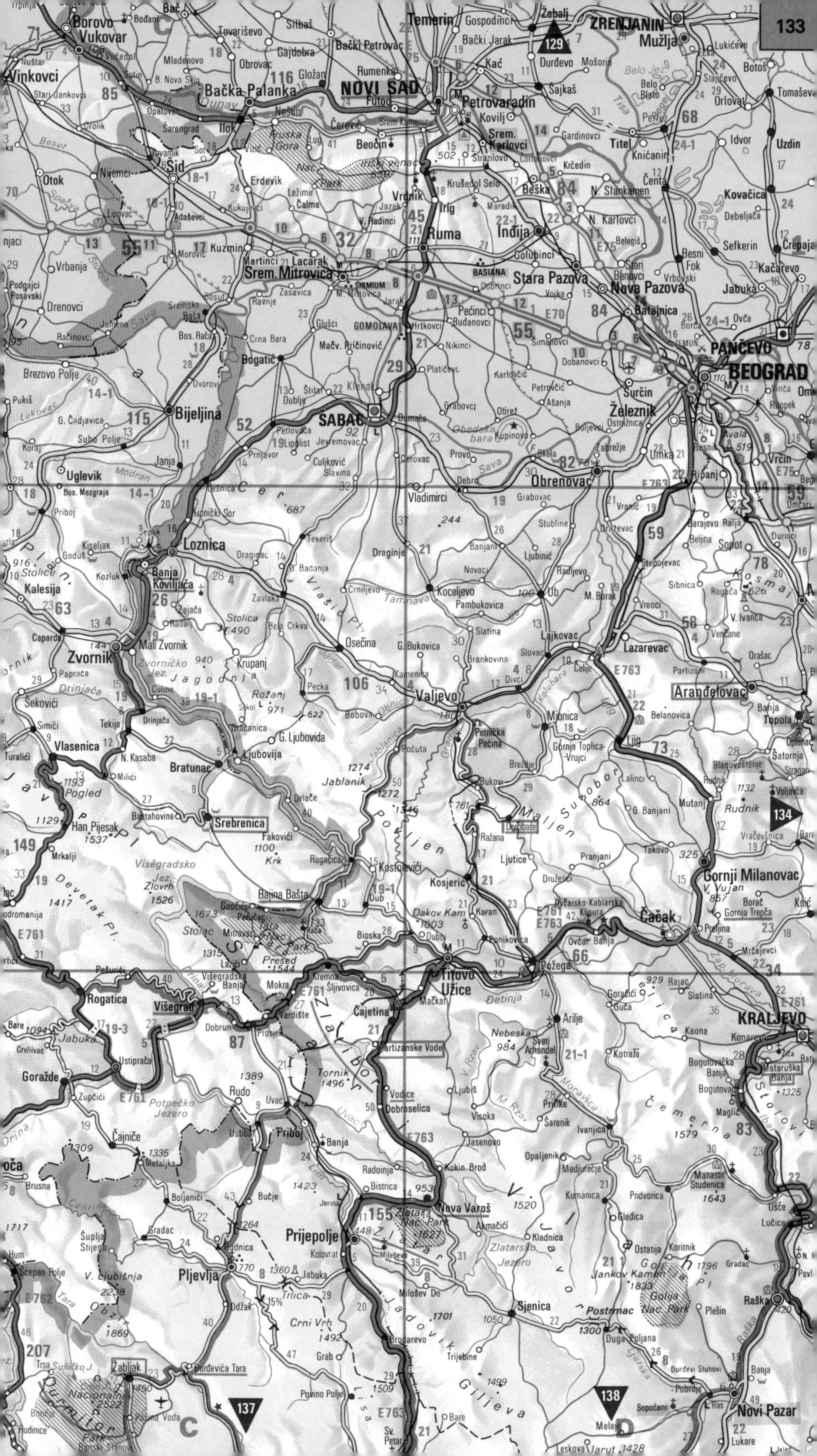

Borovo
Vukovar
Vinkovci
Bač
Tovariševo
Silbaš
Bački Petrovac
Temerin
Gospodinci
Žabalj
ZRENJANIN
Mužlja
129
Bačka Palanka
NOVI SAD
Petrovaradin
Futog
Kać
Đurđevo
Šajkaš
Ilok
Šid
Otok
Nijemci
Erdevik
Beočin
Čerević
Fruška Gora
Nac. Park
Iriški venac
Srem. Karlovci
Titel
Knićanin
Čenta
Kovačica
Uzdin
Vrdnik
Irig
Krušedol Selo
Beška
N. Slankamen
Ruma
Inđija
Kuzmin
Martinci
Lačarak
Srem. Mitrovica
SIRMIUM
BASIANA
Stara Pazova
Nova Pazova
Golubinci
Batajnica
Crepaja
Sefkerin
Jabuka
Kačarevo
Pećinci
Budanovci
Šimanovci
Dobanovci
GOMOLAVA
Hrtkovci
Mačv. Pričinović
Bogatić
Bijeljina
PANČEVO
BEOGRAD
ZEMUN
Surčin
Železnik
Brezovo Polje
ŠABAC
Obedska bara
Kupinovo
Obrenovac
Umka
Ripanj
Avala
Vrčin
Ugljevik
Janja
Loznica
Banja Koviljača
Cer
Vladimirci
Grabovac
Kiseljak
Kalesija
Zvornik
Mali Zvornik
Krupanj
Koceljevo
Ub
Lajkovac
Lazarevac
Stepojevac
Barajevo
Ralja
Sopot
Kosmaj
Osečina
Valjevo
Divci
Mionica
Aranđelovac
Topola
Vlasenica
Bratunac
Ljubovija
Srebrenica
Jablanik
Povlen
Maljen
Suvobor
Divčibare
Lig
Rudnik
Han Pijesak
Rogačica
Bajina Bašta
Kosjerić
Gornji Milanovac
Čačak
Ovčar Banja
Požega
Tara Nac. Park
Titovo Užice
Rogatica
Višegrad
Čajetina
Zlatibor
Arilje
KRALJEVO
Goražde
Ustiprača
Rudo
Priboj
Tornik
Nova Varoš
Zlatar Nac. Park
Ivanjica
Golija Nac. Park
Prijepolje
Pljevlja
Sjenica
Raška
Novi Pazar
Žabljak
Durmitor Nacionalni Park
Đurđevića Tara
137
138
134
C
D

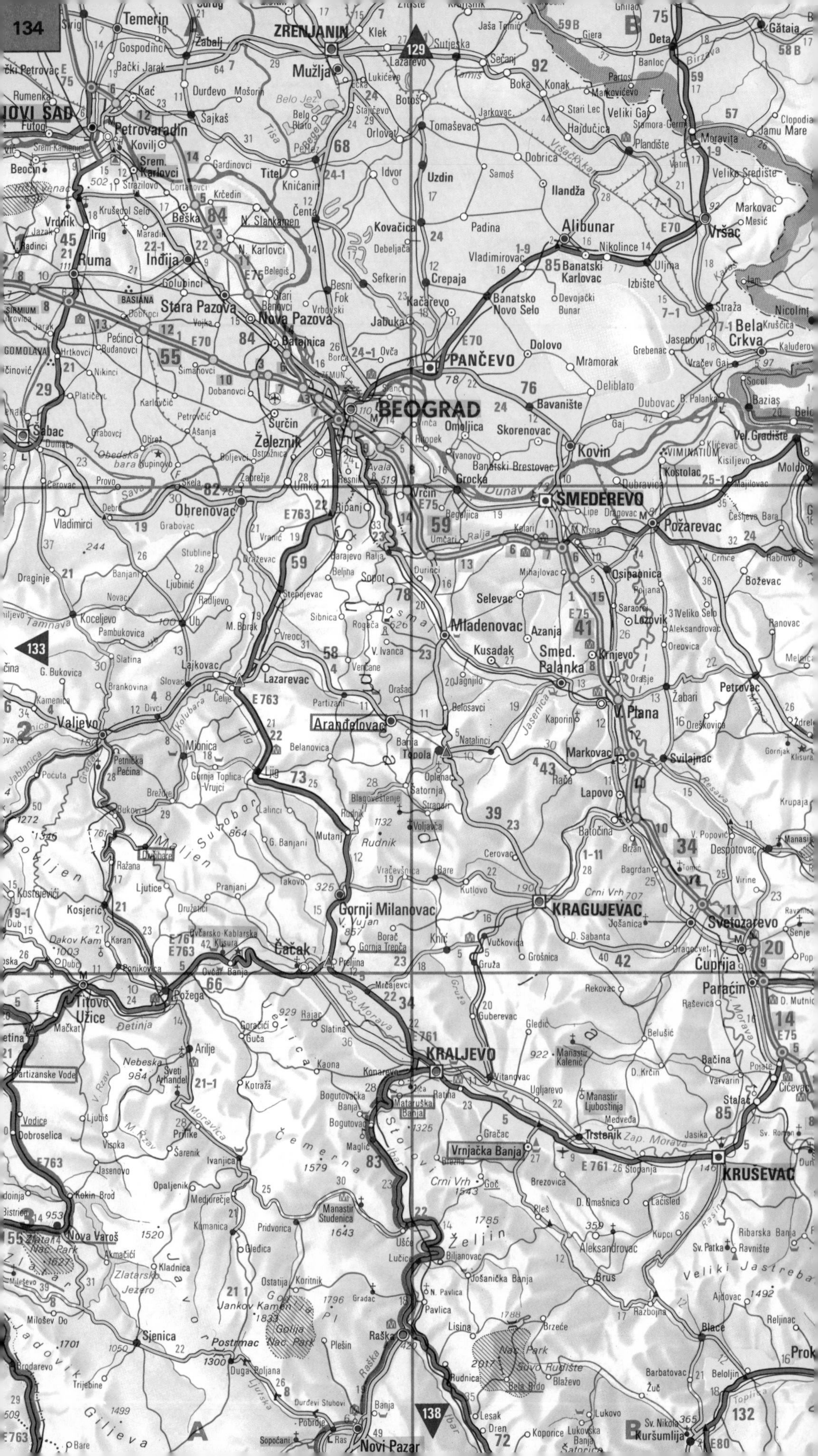
Temerin
Zrenjanin
Klek
Jaša Tomić
Sutjeska
Sečanj
Lazarevo
Mužlja
Gospodinci
Žabalj
Bački Jarak
Bački Petrovac
Kać
Đurđevo
Mošorin
Rumenka
Novi Sad
Futog
Petrovaradin
Šajkaš
Belo Blato
Botoš
Stajićevo
Orlovat
Tomaševac
Jarkovac
Boka
Konak
Markovićevo
Stari Lec
Veliki Gaj
Hajdučica
Plandište
Deta
Banloc
Birzava
Gătaia
Clopodia
Jamu Mare
Moravita
Veliko Središte
Beočin
Srem. Karlovci
Kovilj
Gardinovci
Titel
Knićanin
Perlez
Idvor
Uzdin
Samoš
Dobrica
Ilandža
Markovac
Mesić
Vršac
Čenta
Vrdnik
Krušedol Selo
Beška
Krčedin
N. Slankamen
Irig
Kovačica
Padina
Alibunar
Nikolince
Uljma
Izbište
Jazak
Radinci
Maradik
Ruma
Inđija
N. Karlovci
Debeljača
Vladimirovac
Banatski Karlovac
Crepaja
Sefkerin
Besni Fok
Belegiš
Golubinci
Basiana
Sirmium
Stara Pazova
Stari Banovci
Nova Pazova
Vrbovski
Kačarevo
Jabuka
Banatsko Novo Selo
Devojački Bunar
Straža
Nicolint
Bela Crkva
Kruščica
Kaluđerovo
Dobrinci
Vojka
Jarak
Pećinci
Batajnica
Gomolava
Hrtkovci
Budanovci
Šimanovci
Borča
Ovča
Pančevo
Dolovo
Mramorak
Grebenac
Jasenovo
Vračev Gaj
Nikinci
Dobanovci
Zemun
Platičevo
Karlovčić
Beograd
Deliblato
Dubovac
B. Palanka
Socol
Baziaş
Omoljica
Bavanište
Šabac
Grabovci
Petrovčić
Ašanja
Surčin
Železnik
Vinča
Ritopek
Skorenovac
Gaj
Klićevac
Vel. Gradište
Dumača
Obedska bara
Kupinovo
Boljevci
Ostružnica
Ivanovo
Kovin
Viminatium
Kisiljevo
Moldova
Provo
Zabrežje
Umka
Avala
Resnik
Banatski Brestovac
Kostolac
Grocka
Dunav
Smederevo
Dubravica
Majilovac
Obrenovac
Vrčin
Ripanj
Begaljica
Lipe
Drugovac
Požarevac
Češljeva Bara
Vladimirci
Grabovac
Vranić
Umčari
Ralja
Kolari
Krsna
Barajevo
Đurinci
Stubline
Draževac
Mihajlovac
Osipaonica
Rabrovo
Božević
Draginje
Banjani
Ljubinić
Beljina
Sopot
Radljevo
Stepojevac
Selevac
Koceljevo
Pambukovica
Ub
M. Borak
Sibnica
Rogača
Kosmaj
Vreoci
Mladenovac
Azanja
Saraorci
Lozovik
Veliko Selo
Aleksandrovac
Ranovac
Slatina
Lajkovac
Lazarevac
V. Ivanica
Vencane
Kusadak
Smed. Palanka
Krnjevo
Oreovica
G. Bukovica
Brankovina
Slovac
Čelije
Orašac
Jagnjilo
Orašje
Žabari
Petrovac
Valjevo
Divci
Kolubara
Partizani
Aranđelovac
Belosavci
Kaporin
V. Plana
Oreškovica
Ždrelo
Jablanica
Petnička Pećina
Mionica
Belanovica
Banja
Topola
Natalinci
Markovac
Svilajnac
Gornjak
Klisura
Pocuta
Gornja Toplica
Vrujci
Ljig
Oplanac
Šatornja
Rača
Lapovo
Resava
Bukovi
Brežđe
Blagoveštenje
Rudnik
Voljavča
Stragari
Krupaja
Povlen
Maljen
Suvobor
Lalinci
Mutanj
G. Banjani
Batočina
Brzan
V. Popović
Despotovac
Manasija
Divčibare
Ražana
Ljutice
Pranjani
Takovo
Vračevšnica
Cerovac
Bare
Bagrdan
Kostojevići
Kosjerić
Družetići
Gornji Milanovac
Kutlovo
Kragujevac
Crni Vrh
Svetozarevo
Virine
Senje
Dub
Dakov Kam
Karan
Ovčarsko-Kablarska Klisura
V. Vujan
Borač
Gornja Trepča
Knić
Vučkovica
Jošanica
D. Sabanta
Dragocvet
Ćuprija
Dubci
Ponikovica
Čačak
Preljina
Ovčar Banja
Gruža
Grošnica
Paraćin
Titovo Užice
Požega
Mrčajevci
Rekovac
Raševica
D. Mutnica
Mačkat
Đetinja
Goračići
Rajac
Slatina
Zap. Morava
Guberevac
Gledić
Gučа
Arilje
Kraljevo
Manastir Kalenić
Belušić
Bačina
Pojate
Ćićevac
Partizanske Vode
Nebeska
Sveti Arhanđel
Kaona
Konarevo
Žiča
Ratina
Vitanovac
Ugljarevo
D. Krčin
Varvarin
Kotraža
Bogutovačka Banja
Mataruška Banja
Manastir Ljubostinja
Medveđa
Stalać
Vodice
Dobroselica
Ljubiš
Moravica
Prilike
Šarenik
Bogutovac
Čemerna
Maglič
Stolovi
Gračac
Vrnjačka Banja
Trstenik
Jasika
Kruševac
Sv. Roman
Visoka
Jasenovo
Ivanjica
Brezna
Crni Vrh
Goč
Brezovica
Stopanja
Opaljenik
Kokin Brod
Međurečje
Manastir Studenica
D. Omašnica
Lacisled
Nova Varoš
Kumanica
Pridvorica
Željin
Pleš
Kupci
Ribarska Banja
Zlatar
Nac. Park
Akmačići
Kladnica
Gledica
Ušće
Lučice
Biljanovac
Aleksandrovac
Sv. Patka
Ravnište
Zlatarsko Jezero
Javor
Ostatija
Koritnik
Jošanička Banja
Brus
Veliki Jastrebac
Milešovo
Jankov Kamen
Golija
Gradac
N. Pavlica
Pavlica
Ajdovac
Miloševo Do
Sjenica
Postinac
Plešin
Raška
Lisina
Brzeće
Razbojna
Blace
Reljinac
Prokuplje
Jadovnik
Brodarevo
Duga Poljana
Golija Nac. Park
Nac. Park
Suvo Rudište
Blaževo
Rudnica
Bela Brdo
Barbatovac
Žuč
Beloljin
Toplica
Trijebine
Ljudska
Đurđevi Stubovi
Banja
Lukovo
Sv. Nikola
Kuršumlija
Giljeva
Bare
Sopoćani
Pobrđe
Ras
Novi Pazar
Lesak
Dren
Koporice
Lukovska Banja
Šatorica
Ibar
Tisa
Tamiš
Sava
Tamnava
Kolubara
Rasina
Morava
Jasenica
Gruža

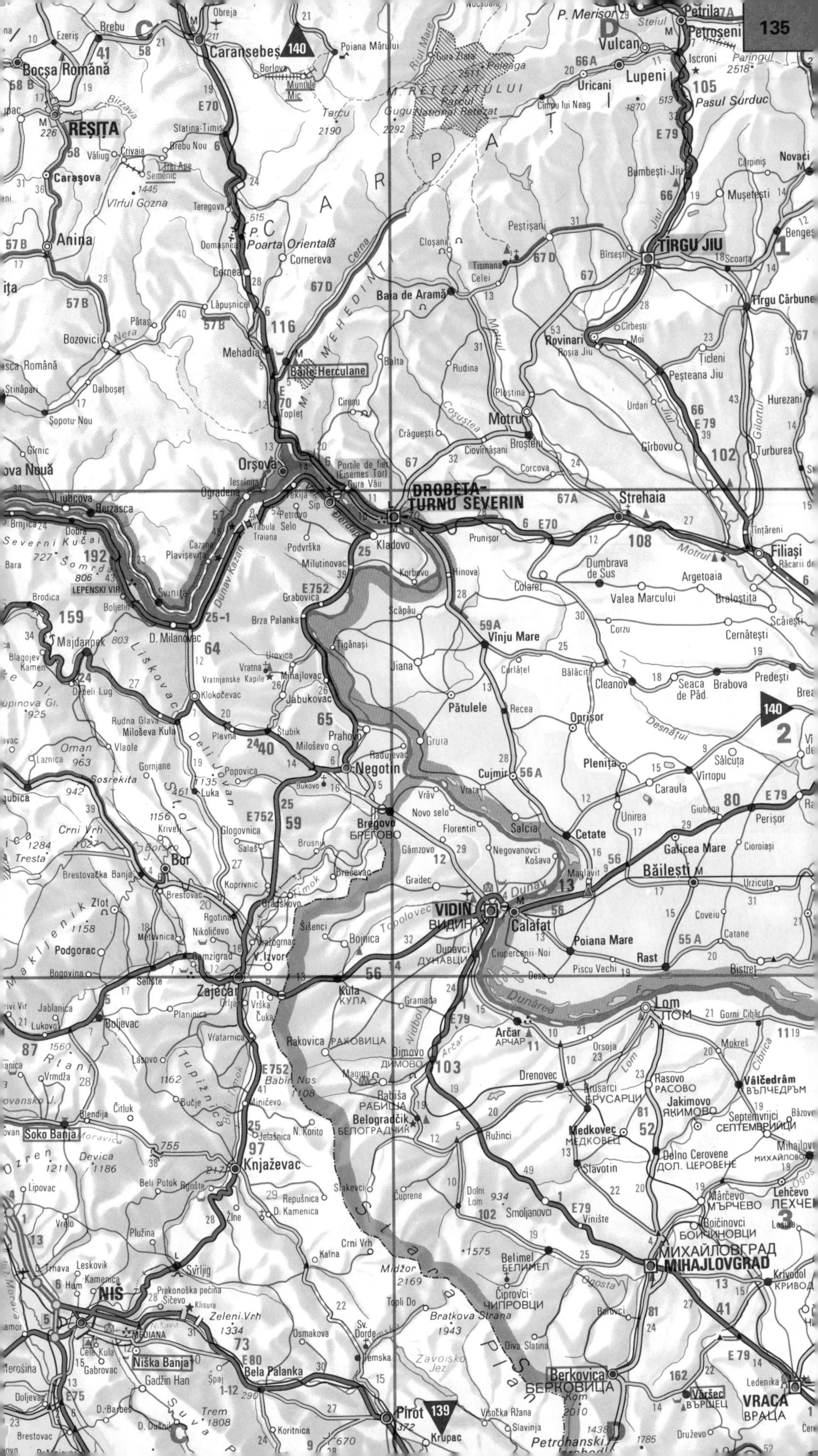

Caransebeş
140
Poiana Mărului
Reşiţa
Bocşa Română
Petrila
Petroşeni
Vulcan
Lupeni
Uricani
Parcul Naţional Retezat
M. Retezatului
Pasul Surduc
Carpaţi
Caraşova
Anina
Vîrful Gozna
Poarta Orientală
Cornereva
Tîrgu Jiu
Baia de Aramă
Tismana
Novaci
Bumbeşti-Jiu
Tîrgu Cărbuneşti
Rovinari
Mehadia
Băile Herculane
Bozovici
Orşova
Motru
Porţile de fier (Eisernes Tor)
Drobeta-Turnu Severin
Strehaia
Filiaşi
Kladovo
Majdanpek
D. Milanovac
Lepenski Vir
Negotin
Vînju Mare
Cujmir
Pleniţa
Cetate
Băileşti
Calafat
Vidin
ВИДИН
Bregovo
БРЕГОВО
Bor
Zaječar
Kula
КУЛА
Lom
ЛОМ
Dunărea
Belogradčik
БЕЛОГРАДЧИК
Vălčedrăm
ВЪЛЧЕДРЪМ
Knjaževac
Soko Banja
Mihajlovgrad
МИХАЙЛОВГРАД
Niš
Niška Banja
Bela Palanka
Pirot
139
Berkovica
БЕРКОВИЦА
Vraca
ВРАЦА
Stara Planina
Midžor 2169
E70
E79
E752
E80
E75

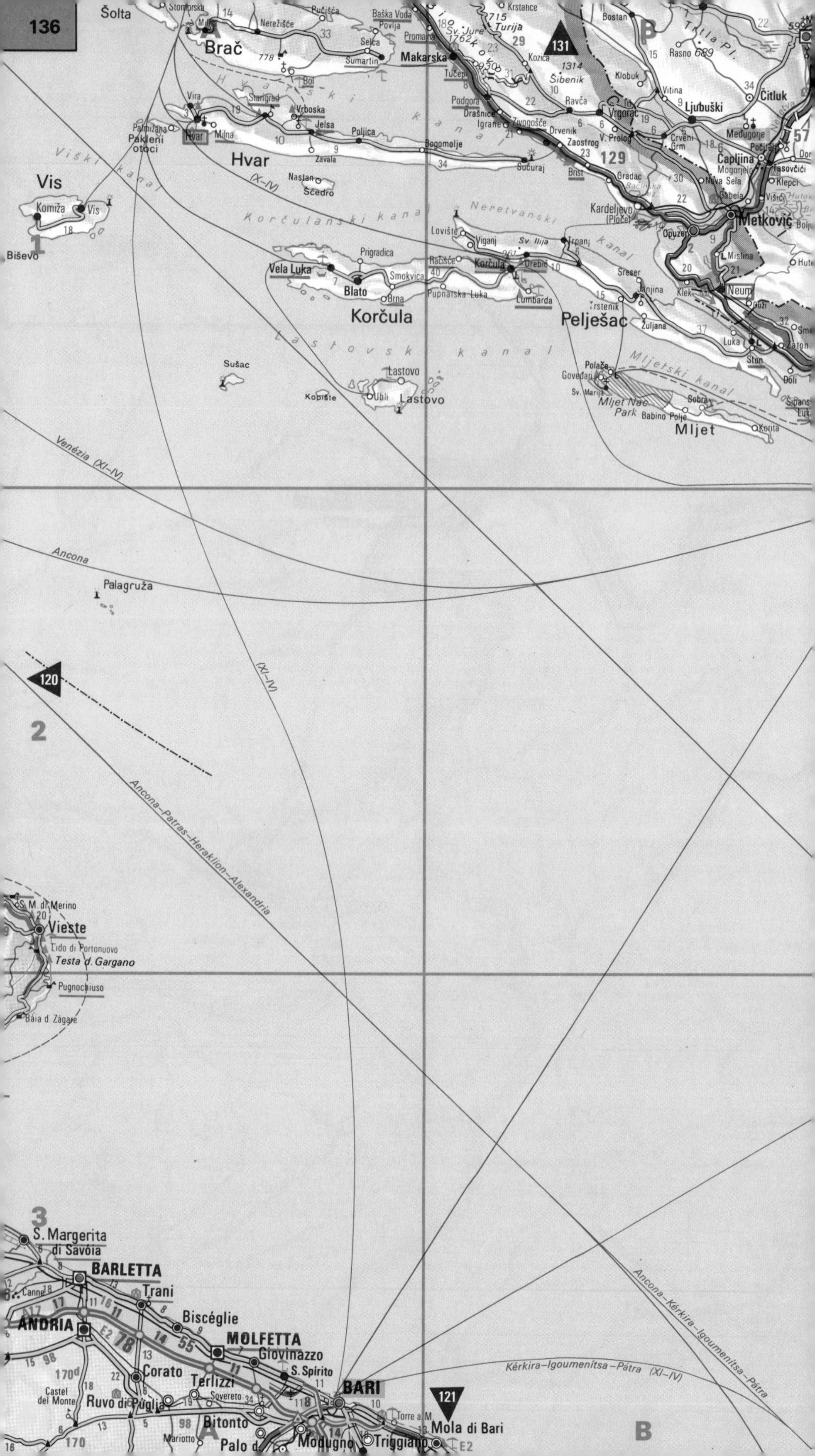

Šolta
Brač
Makarska
Hvar
Vis
Komiža
Biševo
Korčula
Vela Luka
Blato
Lastovo
Sušac
Pelješac
Mljet
Metković
Ljubuški
Čitluk
Čapljina
Neum
Ston
Viški kanal
Korčulanski kanal
Lastovski kanal
Neretvanski kanal
Mljetski kanal
Venézia (XI–IV)
Ancona
Palagruža
Ancona–Patras–Heraklion–Alexandria
Vieste
Testa d. Gargano
S. Margerita di Savòia
BARLETTA
Trani
ANDRIA
Biscéglie
MOLFETTA
Giovinazzo
Corato
Terlizzi
Ruvo di Púglia
Bitonto
BARI
Mola di Bari
Ancona–Kérkira–Igoumenítsa–Pátra
Kérkira–Igoumenítsa–Pátra (XI–IV)
131
120
121
129

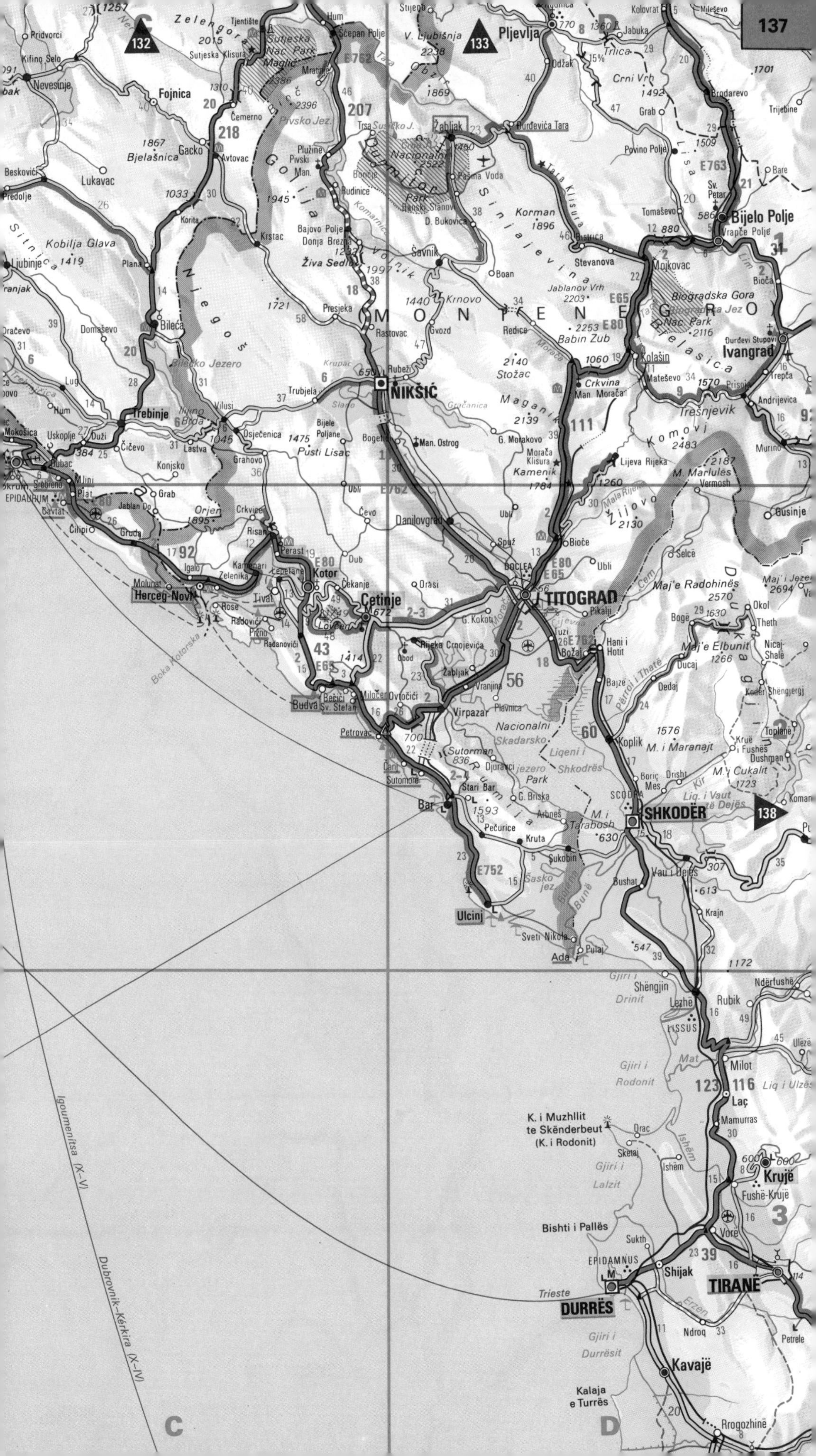

132
133
138
Zelengora
Tjentište
Hum
Šćepan Polje
Sutjeska Nac. Park
Maglić
Sutjeska Klisura
Pridvorci
Kifino Selo
Nevesinje
Fojnica
Gacko
Čemerno
Avtovac
Bjelašnica
Lukavac
Beskovići
Predolje
Korita
Krstac
Golija
Pivsko Jez.
Pluzine
Pivski Man.
Rudinice
Bajovo Polje
Donja Brezna
Živa Sedlo
Kobilja Glava
Ljubinje
Plana
Bileća
Bilećko Jezero
Njegoš
Domaševo
Dračevo
Lug
Hum
Trebinje
Vilusi
Ilijino Brdo
Osječenica
Uskoplje
Duži
Čičevo
Lastva
Grahovo
Konjsko
Mokošica
Dubrovnik
Gruž
Mlini
Srebreno
Plat
Cavtat
Čilipi
Gruda
Epidaurum
Jablan Do
Grab
Orjen
Crkvice
Risan
Perast
Igalo
Zelenika
Kamenari
Molunat
Herceg-Novi
Rose
Tivat
Lepetane
Kotor
Radovići
Prčno
Radanovići
Budva
Bečići
Sv. Stefan
Miločer
Petrovac
Čanj
Sutomore
Bar
Stari Bar
Sutorman
Rumija
Pečurice
Kruta
Ulcinj
Šasko jez.
Sveti Nikola
Ada
Pulaj
Cetinje
Lovćen
Čekanje
Rijeka Crnojevića
Obod
Žabljak
Vranjina
Virpazar
Plavnica
Nacionalni Skadarsko jezero Park
Liqeni i Shkodrës
Djuravci
G. Briska
Arbneš
M. i Tarabosh
Šukobin
Bushat
Vau i Dejës
Krajn
Shkodër
Scodra
Koplik
Bajzë
Hani i Hotit
Bozaj
Tuzi
Titograd
Doclea
Pikalji
Ubli
Spuž
Bioče
Danilovgrad
Čevo
Dub
Orasi
G. Kokoti
Nikšić
Trubjela
Bogetići
Man. Ostrog
Bijele Poljane
Pusti Lisac
Presjeka
Rastovac
Rubeži
Krupac
Gvozd
Krnovo
Šavnik
Durmitor Nacionalni Park
Žabljak
Pašina Voda
Bosača
Boan
Sinjajevina
Korman
Jablanov Vrh
Redice
Babin Zub
Stožac
Maganik
G. Morakovo
Morača Klisura
Kamenik
Crkvina
Man. Morača
Kolašin
Mateševo
Lijeva Rijeka
Komovi
Montenegro
Biogradska Gora Nac. Park
Biogradsko Jez.
Bjelasica
Mojkovac
Stevanova
Bistrica
Tara Klisura
Đurđevića Tara
Pljevlja
Odžak
Trlica
Crni Vrh
Jabuka
Kolovrat
Mileševo
Grab
Povino Polje
Brodarevo
Trijebine
Lisa
Bare
Sv. Petar
Tomaševo
Bijelo Polje
Vrapče Polje
Bioča
Đurđevi Stupovi
Ivangrad
Trepča
Prisoja
Andrijevica
Trešnjevik
Murino
M. Marlulës
Vermosh
Gusinje
Žijovo
Selcë
Maj'e Radohinës
Bogë
Theth
Okol
Maj'e Elbunit
Nicaj-Shale
Dukagjin
Ducaj
Dedaj
Kodër Shëngjergj
M. i Maranajt
Krüe i Fushës
Dushman
Toplanë
M. i Cukalit
Boriç Mes
Drisht
Liq. i Vaut të Dejës
Koman
Shëngjin
Gjiri i Drinit
Lezhë
Lissus
Rubik
Ndërfushë
Ulëz
Mat
Milot
Liq. i Ulzës
Gjiri i Rodonit
Laç
Mamurras
K. i Muzhllit te Skënderbeut (K. i Rodonit)
Drac
Sketaj
Ishëm
Gjiri i Lalzit
Krujë
Fushë-Krujë
Bishti i Pallës
Sukth
Vorë
Epidamnus
Shijak
Tiranë
Durrës
Trieste
Erzen
Ndroq
Petrele
Gjiri i Durrësit
Kavajë
Kalaja e Turrës
Rrogozhinë
Boka Kotorska
Igoumenitsa (X–V)
Dubrovnik–Kérkira (X–IV)
E762
E80
E65
E752
E763
C
D

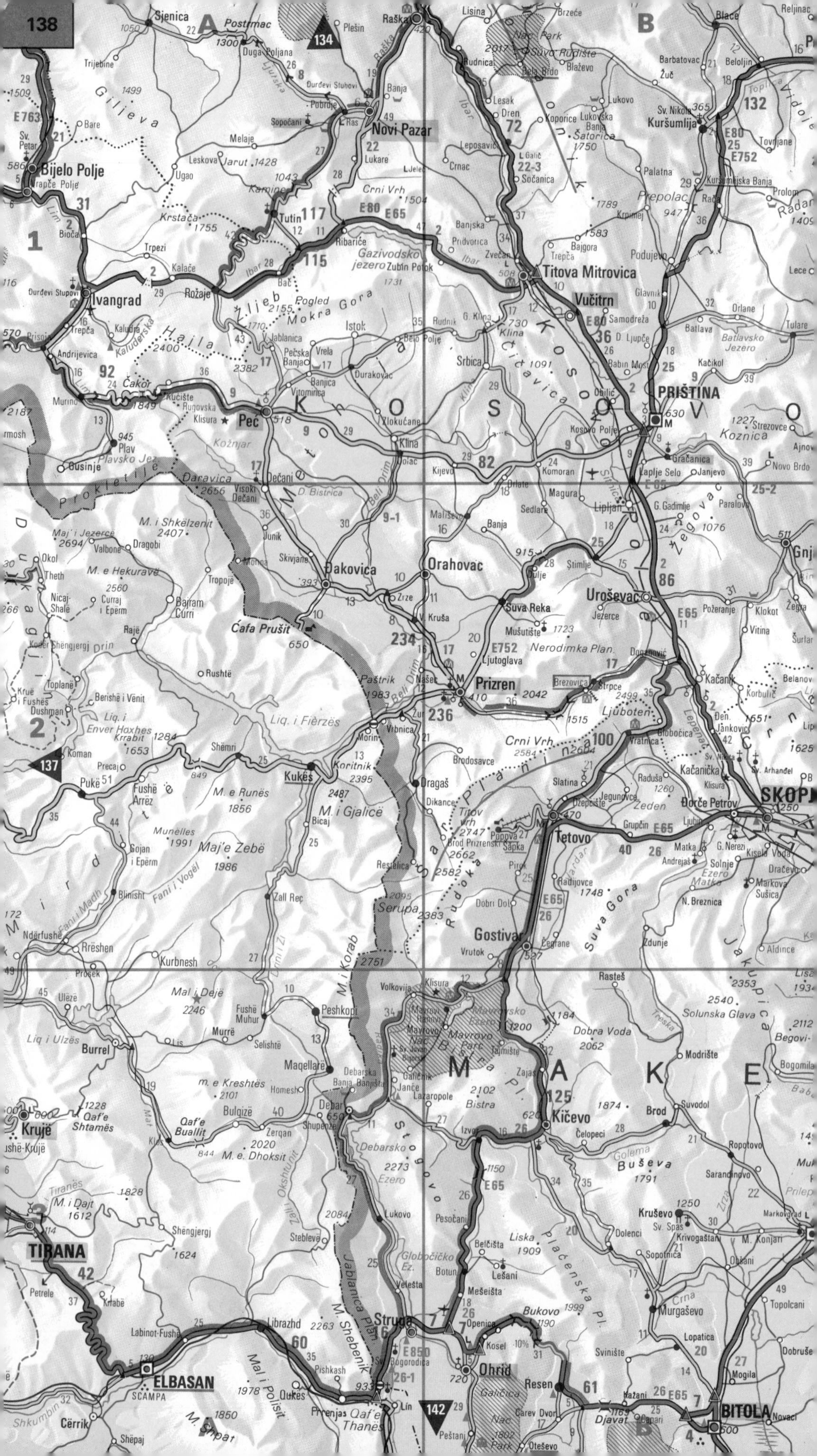

A
B
134
1
2
Sjenica
Postrmac
Duga Poljana
Trijebine
Bare
Sv. Petar
E763
Bijelo Polje
Rapče Polje
Lim
Bioča
Gilјeva
Melaje
Ugao
Leskova
Jarut
Kamine
Tutin
Krstača
Trpezi
Kalače
Rožaje
Đurđevi Stupovi
Ivangrad
Trepča
Kaludra
Kaluđerska
Prisoja
Andrijevica
Hajla
Žljeb
Pogled
Mokra Gora
V. Jablanica
Čakor
Kućište
Rugovska Klisura
Murino
Plav
Plavsko Jez.
Gusinje
Kožnjar
Prokletije
Daravica
Peć
Dečani
Visoki Dečani
Raška
Plešin
Đurđevi Stubovi
Pobrđe
Sopoćani
Ras
Banja
Novi Pazar
Lukare
Crni Vrh
Ribariće
Gazivodsko jezero
Zubin Potok
Bač
Istok
Pečska Banja
Vrela
Banjica
Vitomirica
Durakovac
Belo Polje
Rudnik
G. Klina
Klina
Srbica
Zlokućane
Metohija
Kosovo
Lisina
Brzeće
Nac. Park
Suvo Rudište
Rudnica
Bela Brdo
Blaževo
Lesak
Dren
Koporice
Leposavić
Crnac
L. Galič
Sočanica
Ibar
Banjska
Pridvorica
Zvečan
Titova Mitrovica
Vučitrn
Samodreža
Kopaonik
Blace
Reljinac
Barbatovac
Žuč
Beloljin
Toplica
Vidoje
Lukovo
Lukovska Banja
Šatorica
Sv. Nikola
Kuršumlija
E80
E752
Tovrljane
Palatna
Kuršumlijska Banja
Prolom
Prepolac
Rača
Radan
Krpimej
Bajgora
Trepča
Podujevo
Lece
Glavnik
Orlane
Batlava
Batlavsko Jezero
Tulare
D. Ljupče
Babin Most
Kačikol
Obilić
Priština
Kosovo Polje
Gračanica
Laplje Selo
Janjevo
Koznica
Strezovce
Ajnovce
Novo Brdo
Čičavica
Kijevo
Komoran
Orlate
Magura
Sedlare
Lipljan
G. Gadimlje
Žegovac
Paralovo
Gnjilane
D. Bistrica
Beli Drim
Malisevo
Banja
Junik
Skivjane
Morina
Đakovica
Orahovac
Dulje
Štimlje
Uroševac
Suva Reka
Zrze
V. Kruša
Mušutište
Nerodimka Plan.
Jezerce
Požeranje
Klokot
Vitina
Žegra
Šurlane
Ljutoglava
Prizren
Našec
Brezovica
Štrpce
Doganović
Kačanik
Korbulić
Belanovce
Ljuboten
Đen. Janković
Globočica
Vratnica
Lepenac
Sv. Nikita
Sv. Arhanđel
Kačanička Klisura
Crna Gora
M. i Shkëlzenit
Maj' i Jezerce
Valbone
Dragobi
Okol
Theth
M. e Hekuravë
Nicaj-Shalë
Curraj i Epërm
Bajram Curri
Tropojë
Rajë
Ćafa Prušit
Koder Shëngjergj
Drin
Rushtë
Toplanë
Berishë i Vënit
Kruë i Fushës
Dushman
Liq. i Enver Hoxhes
Krrabit
Liq. i Fierzës
Paštrik
Vrbnica
Žur
Morin
Koritnik
Dragaš
Brodosavce
Crni Vrh
Šar Planina
Slatina
Raduša
Jegunovce
Žeden
Đorče Petrov
Skopje
Koman
Precaj
Pukë
Shëmri
Kukës
Fushë Arrëz
M. e Runës
M. i Gjalicë
Bicaj
Dikance
Titov vrh
Popova Šapka
Brod Prizrenski
Tetovo
Grupčin
Ljubin
Matka
Andrejaš
G. Nerezi
Solnje
Kisela Voda
Dračevo
Markova Sušica
Munëlles
Maj'e Zebë
Gojan i Epërm
Restelica
Pirok
Radijovce
Vardar
Matko Ezero
N. Breznica
Mirditë
Blinisht
Fani i Vogël
Fani i Madh
Zall Reç
Serupa
Rudoka
Dobri Dol
Gostivar
Čegrane
Suva Gora
Zdunje
Aldince
Ndërfushë
Rrëshen
Kurbnesh
Vrutok
Jakupica
M. i Korab
Klisura
Volkovija
Mavrovi Hanovi
Mavrovo
Mavrovsko Ezero
Mavrovo Nac. Park
Rasteš
Dobra Voda
Solunska Glava
Begovi-
Prosek
Ulëzë
Mal i Dejë
Fushë Muhur
Peshkopi
Liq i Ulzës
Burrel
Lis
Murrë
Selishtë
Maqellarë
Bistra
Tajmište
Zajas
Modrište
Bogomila
Sv. Jovan Bigorski
Galičnik
Janče
Lazaropole
Debarska Banja
Banjište
Debar
Homesh
m. e Kreshtës
Makedonija
Qaf'e Shtamës
Krujë
Fushë-Krujë
Qaf'e Buallit
Bulqizë
Zerqan
M. e. Dhoksit
Shupenzë
Debarsko Ezero
Stogovo
Izvor
Kičevo
Čelopeci
Brod
Suvodol
Golema
Buševa
Ropotovo
Sarandinovo
Prilep
Klos
Mat
Tiranës
M. i Dajt
Tirana
Shëngjergj
Zall i Okshtunit
Stebleve
Lukovo
Pesočani
E65
Liska
Plačenska Pl.
Kruševo
Sv. Spas
Krivogaštani
M. Konjari
Markovgrad
Dolenci
Sopotnica
Obšani
Petrele
Krrabë
Labinot-Fushë
Librazhd
Mal i Polisit
Jablanica Plan.
M. Shebenik
Globočičko Ez.
Veleštа
Botun
Belčišta
Lešani
Mešeišta
Bukovo
Murgaševo
Crna
Topolcani
Struga
Bogorodica
E850
Oktisi
Openica
Kosel
Ohrid
Resen
Evla
Lopatica
Dobruše
Elbasan
Scampa
Pishkash
Qukës
Prrenjas
Qaf'e Thanës
Lin
142
Galičica Nac. Park
Carev Dvor
Djavat
Kažani
Capari
Mogila
Bitola
Novaci
Shkumbin
Cërrik
Shëpaj
M. Shpat
Peštani
Oteševo

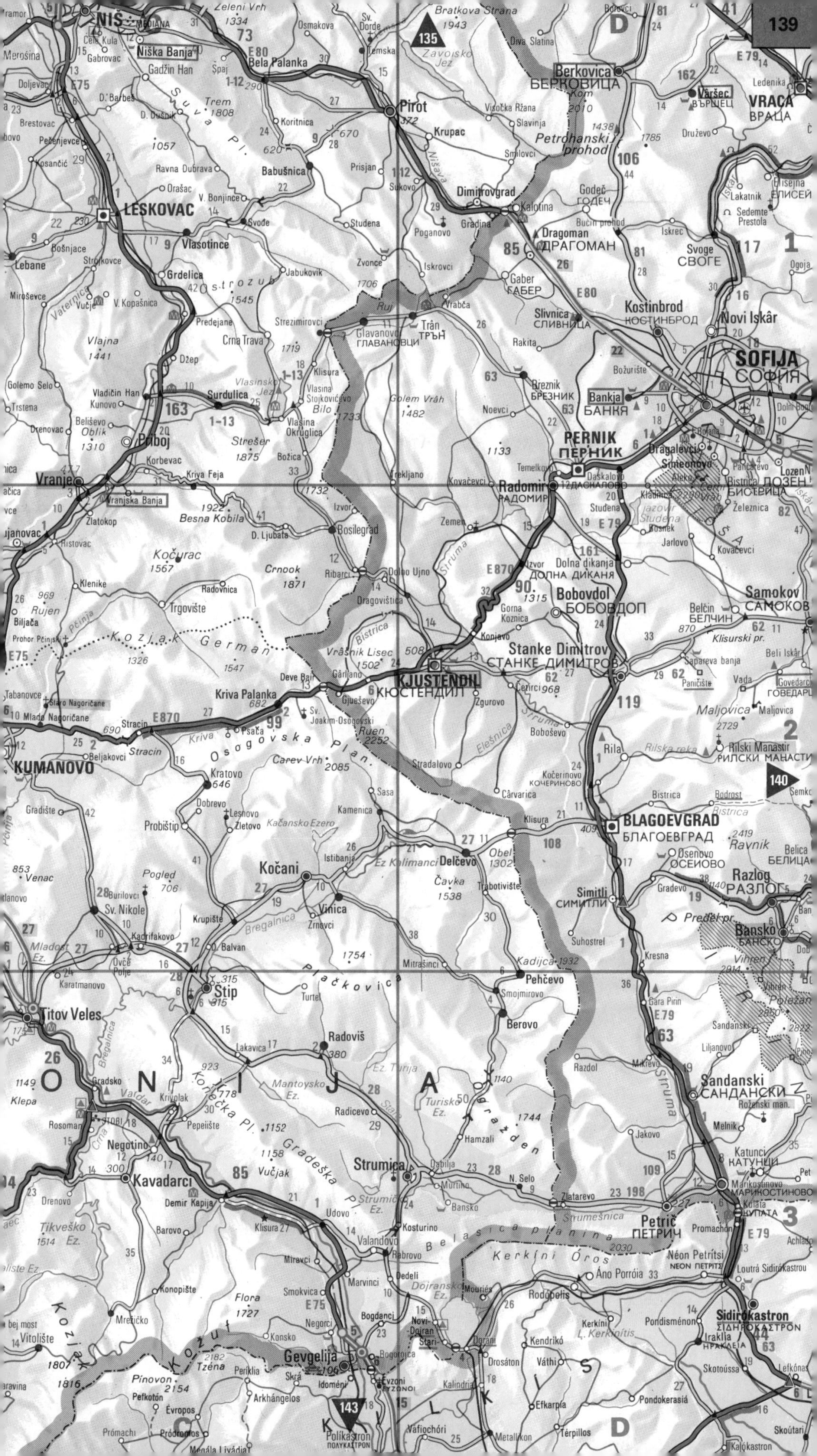

Niš
Niška Banja
Bela Palanka
Pirot
Berkovica
БЕРКОВИЦА
Vršec
ВЪРШЕЦ
VRACA
ВРАЦА
Leskovac
Vlasotince
Dimitrovgrad
Kalotina
Dragoman
ДРАГОМАН
Svoge
СВОГЕ
Grdelica
Gaber
ГАБЕР
Slivnica
СЛИВНИЦА
Kostinbrod
КОСТИНБРОД
Novi Iskâr
SOFIJA
СОФИЯ
Trân
ТРЪН
Glavanovci
ГЛАВАНОВЦИ
Crna Trava
Surdulica
Vladičin Han
Brèznik
БРЕЗНИК
Bankja
БАНКЯ
Priboj
PERNIK
ПЕРНИК
Vranje
Vranjska Banja
Radomir
РАДОМИР
Bosilegrad
Dolna dikanja
ДОЛНА ДИКАНЯ
Bobovdol
БОБОВДОЛ
Samokov
САМОКОВ
Trgovište
Stanke Dimitrov
СТАНКЕ ДИМИТРОВ
KJUSTENDIL
КЮСТЕНДИЛ
Kriva Palanka
Osogovska Plan.
Rilski Manastir
РИЛСКИ МАНАСТИ
KUMANOVO
Kratovo
Probištip
BLAGOEVGRAD
БЛАГОЕВГРАД
Kočani
Delčevo
Simitli
СИМИТЛИ
Razlog
РАЗЛОГ
Sv. Nikole
Vinica
Bansko
БАНСКО
Štip
Pehčevo
Berovo
Titov Veles
Radoviš
Sandanski
САНДАНСКИ
Negotino
Kavadarci
Strumica
Petrič
ПЕТРИЧ
Kulata
КУЛАТА
Belasica planina
Kerkíni Óros
Gevgelija
Sidirókastron
ΣΙΔΗΡΟΚΑΣΤΡΟΝ
Polikastron
ΠΟΛΥΚΑΣΤΡΟΝ
135
140
143

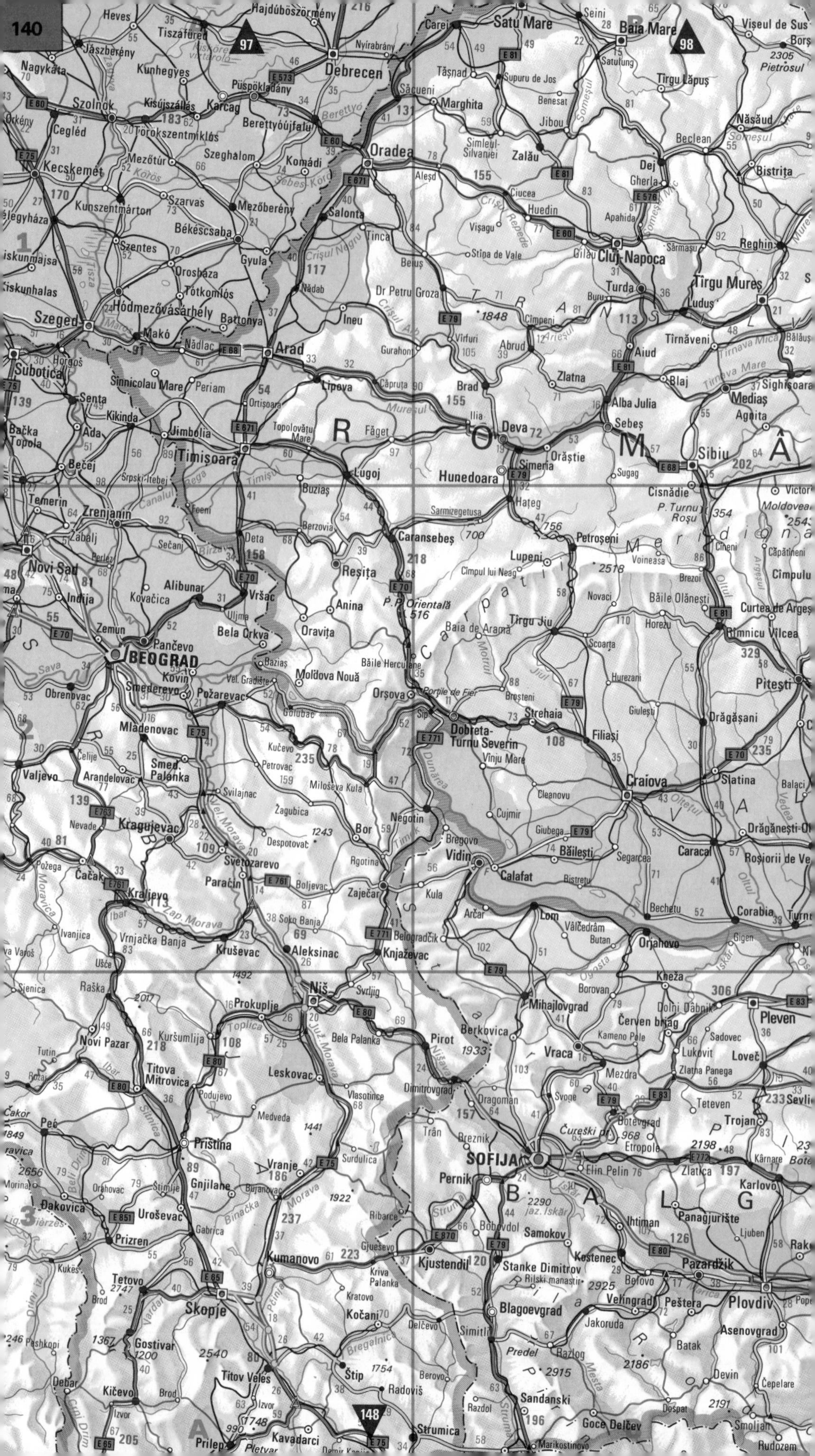
97
98
148
Heves
Hajdúböszörmény
Tiszafüred
Jászberény
Nagykáta
Kunhegyes
Debrecen
Nyírábrány
Püspökladány
Karcag
Kisújszállás
Szolnok
Cegléd
Törökszentmiklós
Berettyóújfalu
Komádi
Szeghalom
Mezőtúr
Kecskemét
Kunszentmárton
Szarvas
Mezőberény
Békéscsaba
Szentes
Gyula
Orosháza
Tótkomlós
Hódmezővásárhely
Battonya
Szeged
Makó
Nădlac
Arad
Subotica
Senta
Kikinda
Ada
Bačka Topola
Bečej
Jimbolia
Timişoara
Sinnicolau Mare
Periam
Lipova
Făget
Lugoj
Buziaş
Temerin
Zrenjanin
Žabalj
Novi Sad
Indija
Alibunar
Kovačica
Vršac
Deta
Reşiţa
Caransebeş
Anina
Oraviţa
Bela Crkva
Zemun
Pančevo
BEOGRAD
Kovin
Smederevo
Požarevac
Obrenovac
Mladenovac
Valjevo
Arandelovac
Smed. Palanka
Kragujevac
Svetozarevo
Paraćin
Čačak
Kraljevo
Kruševac
Aleksinac
Vrnjačka Banja
Niš
Prokuplje
Leskovac
Pirot
Dimitrovgrad
Novi Pazar
Titova Mitrovica
Priština
Peć
Gnjilane
Uroševac
Vranje
Đakovica
Prizren
Tetovo
Skopje
Gostivar
Kičevo
Titov Veles
Prilep
Kavadarci
Kumanovo
Štip
Kočani
Radoviš
Strumica
Carei
Satu Mare
Seini
Baia Mare
Vişeul de Sus
Borşa
Tăşnad
Marghita
Săcueni
Oradea
Salonta
Tinca
Beiuş
Dr Petru Groza
Ineu
Zalău
Jibou
Şimleul-Silvaniei
Aleşd
Huedin
Dej
Gherla
Beclean
Năsăud
Bistriţa
Cluj-Napoca
Turda
Tîrgu Mureş
Reghin
Cîmpeni
Abrud
Zlatna
Aiud
Alba Julia
Blaj
Tîrnăveni
Mediaş
Sighişoara
Sebeş
Sibiu
Agnita
Deva
Brad
Orăştie
Hunedoara
Simeria
Haţeg
Petroşeni
Lupeni
Tîrgu Jiu
Orşova
Dobreta-Turnu Severin
Strehaia
Filiaşi
Craiova
Caracal
Slatina
Drăgăşani
Rîmnicu Vîlcea
Piteşti
Corabia
Calafat
Vidin
Negotin
Zaječar
Bor
Knjaževac
Lom
Orjahovo
Mihajlovgrad
Berkovica
Vraca
Mezdra
Pleven
Loveč
Trojan
Teteven
Botevgrad
SOFIJA
Pernik
Samokov
Kjustendil
Blagoevgrad
Pazardžik
Plovdiv
Asenovgrad
Karlovo
Panagjurište
Ihtiman
Kostenec
Velingrad
Sandanski
Goce Delčev
Smoljan
R
O
M
Â
B
A
L
G

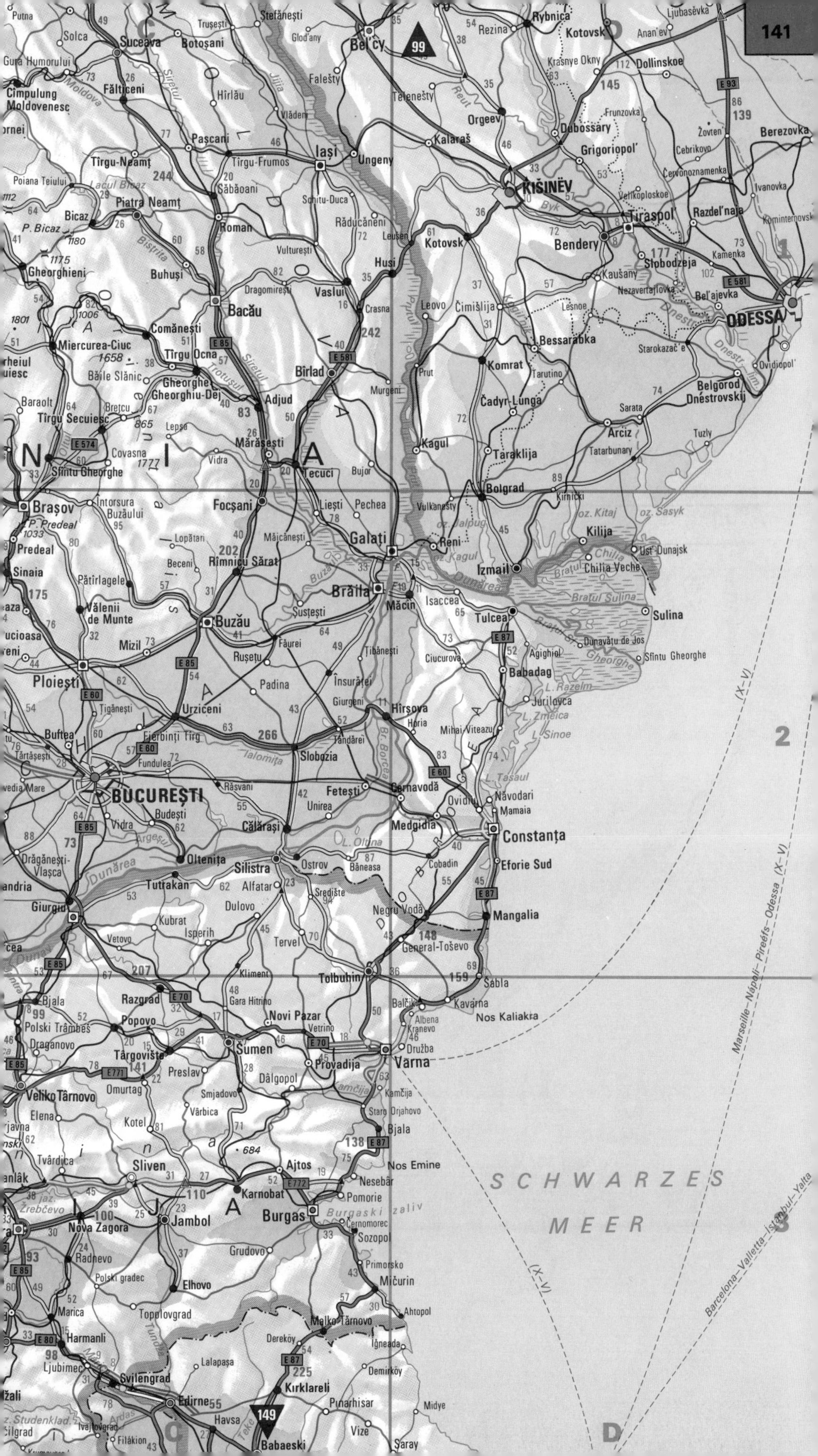
Suceava
Botoşani
Bel'cy
Rybnica
Kotovsk
Rezina
Fălticeni
Cîmpulung Moldovenesc
Orgeev
Dubossary
Grigoriopol'
Paşcani
Iaşi
Ungeny
Tîrgu-Neamţ
Tîrgu-Frumos
KIŠINËV
Piatra Neamţ
Bicaz
Roman
Tiraspol'
Bendery
Kotovsk
Huşi
Vaslui
Gheorghieni
Buhuşi
Bacău
Slobodzeja
ODESSA
Comăneşti
Miercurea-Ciuc
Tîrgu Ocna
Bîrlad
Komrat
Bessarabka
Gheorghe Gheorghiu-Dej
Adjud
Čadyr-Lunga
Belgorod Dnéstrovskij
Tîrgu Secuiesc
Mărăşeşti
Kagul
Arciz
Sfîntu Gheorghe
Tecuci
Taraklija
Bolgrad
Braşov
Focşani
Galaţi
Reni
Kilija
Izmail
Predeal
Sinaia
Rîmnicu Sărat
Brăila
Măcin
Tulcea
Sulina
Vălenii de Munte
Buzău
Babadag
Ploieşti
Urziceni
Slobozia
Hîrşova
Cernavodă
BUCUREŞTI
Feteşti
Constanţa
Călăraşi
Medgidia
Eforie Sud
Olteniţa
Silistra
Tutrakan
Mangalia
Giurgiu
Negru Vodă
General-Toševo
Tolbuhin
Razgrad
Novi Pazar
Popovo
Šumen
Provadija
Varna
Târgovište
Veliko Târnovo
Bjala
Sliven
Ajtos
Karnobat
Burgas
Nova Zagora
Jambol
Sozopol
Mičurin
Elhovo
Harmanli
Svilengrad
Edirne
Kırklareli
Babaeski
SCHWARZES MEER
Marseille–Nápoli–Pireéfs–Odessa (X–V)
Barcelona–Valletta–İstanbul–Yalta
E 85
E 581
E 60
E 87
E 70
E 80
E 772
E 771
E 574
E 93
99
149

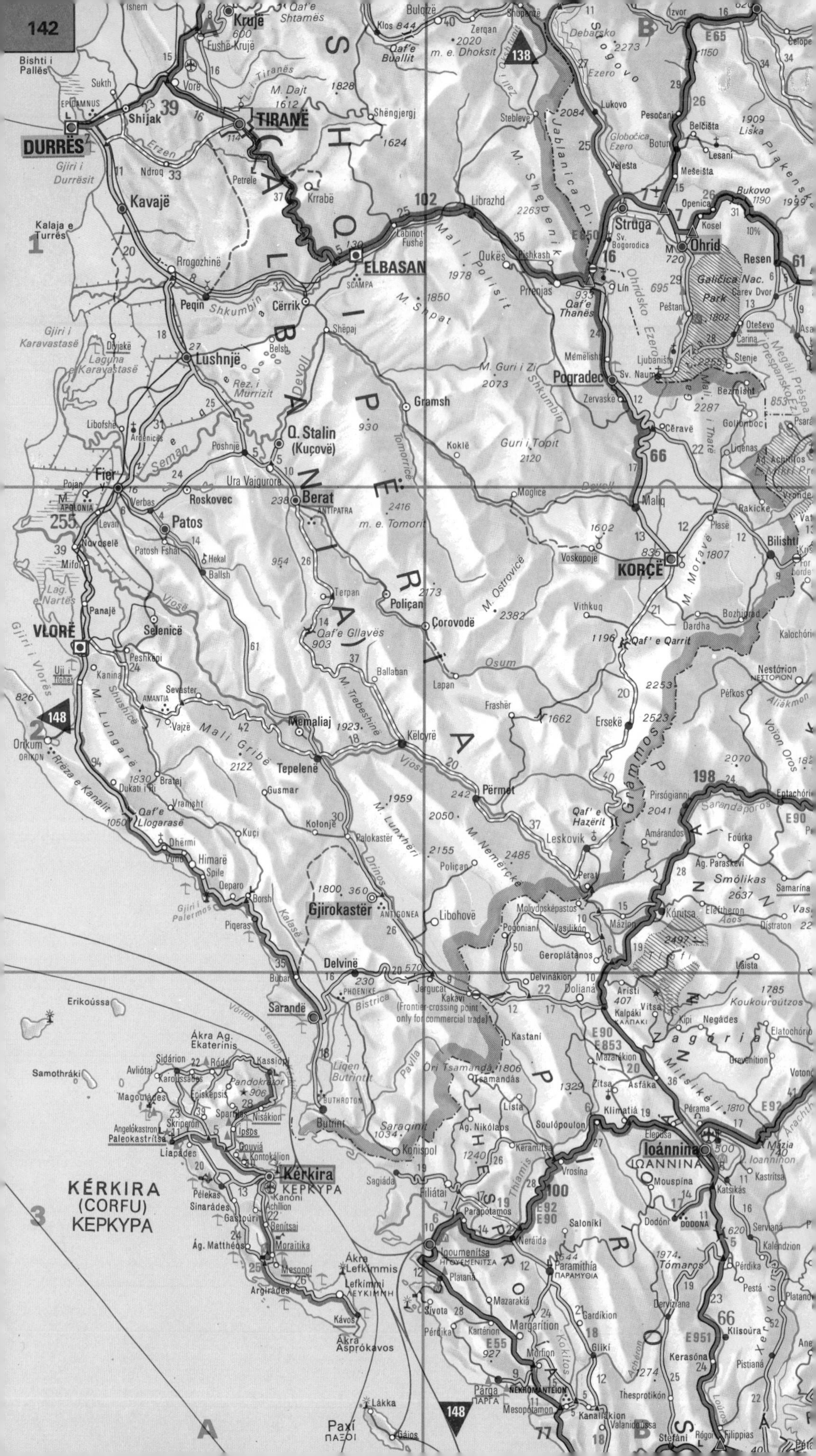

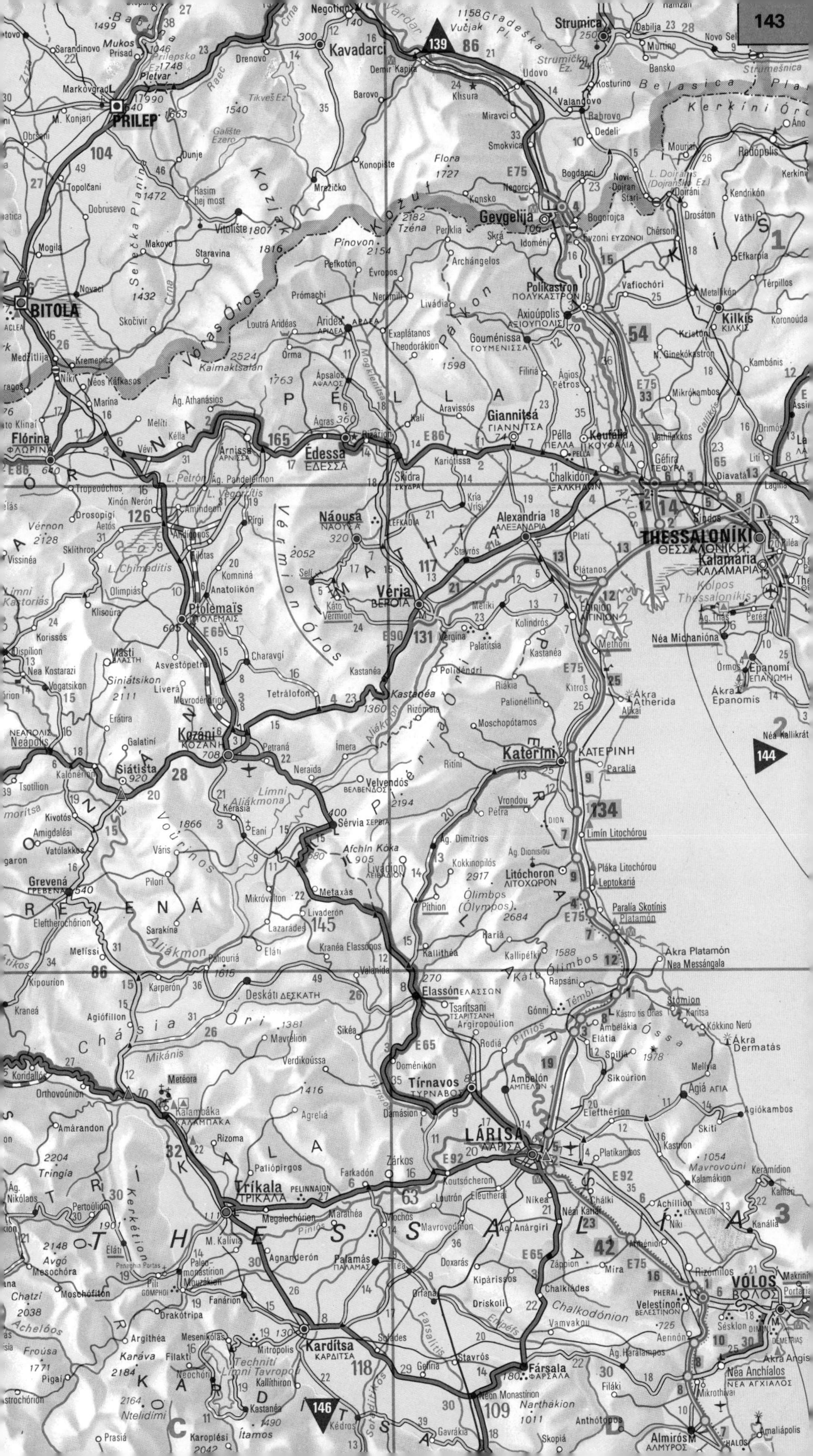
Negotino
Kavadarci
Demir Kapija
Strumica
Dabilja
Novo Selo
Murtino
Bansko
Strumičko Ez.
Udovo
Kosturino
Belasica Planina
Kerkíni Óros
Valandovo
Rabrovo
Dedeli
Miravci
Smokvica
Klisura
Vučjak
Gradeška Pl.
Prilep
Mukos
Prisad
Sarandinovo
Pletvar
Markovgrad
M. Konjari
Obršani
Topolčani
Dobrusevo
Mogila
Novaci
Bitola
Skočivir
Kremenica
Medžitlija
Niki
Néos Káfkasos
Marína
Flórina
ΦΛΩΡΙΝΑ
Meliti
Vévi
Kella
Drenovo
Raec
Tikveš Ez.
Galište Ezero
Barovo
Konopište
Mrežičko
Dunje
Rasim bej most
Vitolište
Makovo
Staravina
Kozjak
Selečka Planina
Voras Óros
Kaimaktsalán
Kožuf
Tzéna
Pínovon
Flora
Gevgelija
Negorci
Konsko
Bogdanci
Novi-Dojran
Stari-
L. Doirani (Dojranško Ez.)
Doiráni
Mouriaí
Rodópolis
Kerkíni
Kendrikón
Váthi
Drosáton
Bogorojca
Evzoni ΕΥΖΩΝΟΙ
Idoméni
Skrá
Perikleia
Archángelos
Chérson
Efkarpía
Térpillos
Polikastron ΠΟΛΥΚΑΣΤΡΟΝ
Axioúpolis ΑΞΙΟΥΠΟΛΙΣ
Vafiochóri
Metallikón
Kilkís ΚΙΛΚΙΣ
Koronoúda
Kristóni
N. Ginekókastron
Kambánis
Goumenissa ΓΟΥΜΕΝΙΣΣΑ
Filiriá
Ágios Pétros
Mikrókambos
Pefkotón
Évropos
Prómachi
Livádia
Aridéa ΑΡΙΔΕΑ
Loutrá Aridéas
Exaplátanos
Theodorákion
Órma
Ápsalos ΑΨΑΛΟΣ
Ágras
Kalí
Aravissós
Giannitsá ΓΙΑΝΝΙΤΣΑ
Pélla ΠΕΛΛΑ
Koufália ΚΟΥΦΑΛΙΑ
Vathilakkos
Géfira ΓΕΦΥΡΑ
Diavatá
Liti
Lagina
PÉLLA
Edessa ΕΔΕΣΣΑ
Arnissa ΑΡΝΙΣΣΑ
Ág. Athanásios
Ág. Pandeleimon
L. Petrón
L. Vegorritis
Skídra ΣΚΥΔΡΑ
Kariótissa
Kría Vrísi
Chalkidón ΧΑΛΚΗΔΩΝ
Thessaloníki ΘΕΣΣΑΛΟΝΙΚΗ
Kalamaria ΚΑΛΑΜΑΡΙΑ
Síndos
Kolpos Thessalonikis
Tropeouchos
Xinón Nerón
Drosopigí
Aetós
Vérnon
Amindeon
Anargyroi
Fílotas
Pírgi
Komniná
Anatolikón
Náousa ΝΑΟΥΣΑ
Lefkadia
Alexandria ΑΛΕΞΑΝΔΡΙΑ
Platí
Plátanos
Sklíthron
L. Chimaditis
Olimpiás
Vissinéa
Limni Kastorias
Ptolemaïs ΠΤΟΛΕΜΑΪΣ
Klisoura
Korissós
Dispílion
Vlásti ΒΛΑΣΤΗ
Nea Kostarazi
Vogatsikon
Siniátsikon
Asvestópetra
Charavgí
Liverá
Mavrodéndrion
Vérmion Óros
Seli
Káto Vermion
Véria ΒΕΡΟΙΑ
Stavrós
Meliki
Egínion ΑΙΓΙΝΙΟΝ
Methóni
Néa Michanióna
Peréa
Ág. Triás
Epanomí ΕΠΑΝΟΜΗ
Ákra Epanomis
Vergina
Palatítsia
Kolindrós
Kastanéa
Kítros
Ákra Atherida
Alikai
Polidéndri
Riákia
Palionéllini
Moschopótamos
Tetrálofon
Kastanéa
Rizómata
Katerini ΚΑΤΕΡΙΝΗ
Paralía
Erátira
Neapolis ΝΕΑΠΟΛΙΣ
Galatini
Kozáni ΚΟΖΑΝΗ
Petraná
Imera
Neraïda
Velvendós ΒΕΛΒΕΝΔΟΣ
Ritini
Siátista
Kalonérion
Tsotílion
Límni Aliákmona
Kerasiá
Eaní
Sérvia ΣΕΡΒΙΑ
Vrondou
Pétra
Dion
Ág. Dimítrios
Limín Litochórou
Kivotós
Amigdaléai
Vatólakkos
Vourinos
Váris
Afchin Kóka
Livádion ΛΙΒΑΔΙΟΝ
Kokkinopilós
Ág. Dionisíou
Litóchoron ΛΙΤΟΧΩΡΟΝ
Pláka Litochórou
Leptokariá
Grevená ΓΡΕΒΕΝΑ
Pilori
Mikrovalton
Metaxás
Pithion
Ólimbos (Ólympos)
Paralía Skotínis
Platamón
Eleftherochórion
Sarakína
Livaderón
Lazarádes
Kranéa Elassónos
Kallithéa
Rapsáni
Ákra Platamón
Nea Messángala
Melíssi
Aliákmon
Paliouriá
Eláti
Valanida
Elassón ΕΛΑΣΣΩΝ
Tsaritsani ΤΣΑΡΙΤΣΑΝΗ
Argiropoúlion
Gónni
Témbi
Kástro tis Orias
Ambelákia
Stómion
Karitsa
Kókkino Neró
Kipourion
Kraneá
Agiófillon
Karperón
Deskáti ΔΕΣΚΑΤΗ
Chásia Óri
Mavrélion
Sikéa
Rodiá
Elátia
Spilia
Óssa
Ákra Dermatás
Koridallós
Orthovoúnion
Mikánis
Meteora
Kalambáka ΚΑΛΑΜΠΑΚΑ
Verdikoússa
Doménikon
Tírnavos ΤΥΡΝΑΒΟΣ
Ambelón ΑΜΠΕΛΩΝ
Sikoúrion
Melívia
Agiá ΑΓΙΑ
Agiókambos
Amárandon
Agreliá
Damásion
Eleftherion
Skiti
Rizoma
Lárisa ΛΑΡΙΣΑ
Platikambos
Kastrion
Mavrovoúni
Keramídion
Tringia
Paliópirgos
Zárkos
Farkadón
Koutsócheron
Eleutheraí
Kalamákion
Kamári
Ág. Nikólaos
Pertoúlion
Tríkala ΤΡΙΚΑΛΑ
Pelinnaion
Megalochórion
Marathéa
Vlochós
Loutrón
Chálki
Achillion
Kerkineon
Níki
Kanália
Kerkétion
Nikea
Néai Kariai
Eláti
Avgó
M. Kalívia
Piniós
Mavrovoúnion
Ág. Anárgiri
Arménion
Mesochóra
Panagia Portas
Paleo-monastirion
Agnanderón
Palamás ΠΑΛΑΜΑΣ
Itéa
Doxarás
Kipárissos
Záppion
Míra
Rizómilos
Vólos ΒΟΛΟΣ
Makrinítsa
Portariá
Chatzí
Moschofiton
Gomphoi
Mouzákion
Fanárion
Orfaná
Driskoli
Chalkiádes
Chalkodónion
Pherai
Velestínon ΒΕΛΕΣΤΙΝΟΝ
Drakótripa
Enipéfs
Vamvakou
Sésklon
Dimini
Demetrias
Achelóos
Argithéa
Mesenikólas
Mitrópolis
Karditsa ΚΑΡΔΙΤΣΑ
Sofádes
Farsalitis
Aerinón
Ág. Haralampos
Ákra Angistri
Néa Anchíalos ΝΕΑ ΑΓΧΙΑΛΟΣ
Froúsa
Karáva
Filakti
Techniti Limni Tavropou
Neochóri
Kallíthiron
Stavrós
Gefíria
Fársala ΦΑΡΣΑΛΑ
Filáki
Mikrothívai
Pigaí
Kastanéa
Neon Monastirion
Narthákion
Anthótopos
Ntelidimi
Ítamos
Kédros
Gavrákia
Skopiá
Almirós ΑΛΜΥΡΟΣ
Halos
Amaliápolis
Prasiá
Karoplési
Strochórion
139
144
146

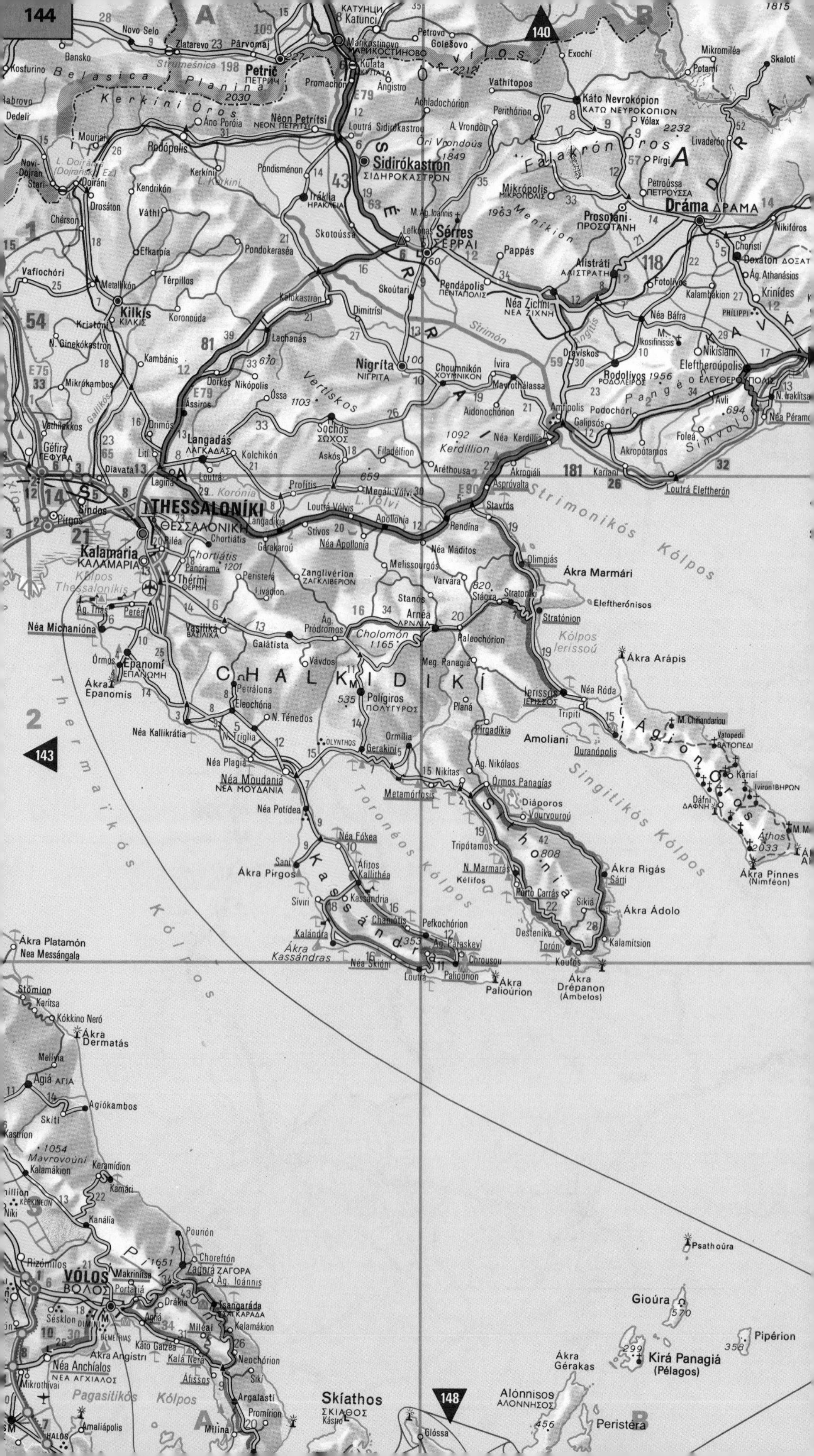

144
140
143
148
Novo Selo
Zlatarevo
Pârvomaj
Bansko
Petrič
ПЕТРИЧ
Kosturino
Belasica
Planina
Kerkíni Óros
Strumešnica
Katunci
КАТУНЦИ
Marikostinovo
МАРИКОСТИНОВО
Kulata
КУЛАТА
Petrovo
Goleševo
Promachón
Ángistro
Achladochórion
Vathítopos
Exochí
Mikromiléa
Potamí
Skalotí
Káto Nevrokópion
ΚΑΤΩ ΝΕΥΡΟΚΟΠΙΟΝ
Vólax
Falakrón Óros
Livaderón
Pírgi
Petroússa
ΠΕΤΡΟΥΣΣΑ
Dráma
ΔΡΑΜΑ
Prosotáni
ΠΡΟΣΟΤΑΝΗ
Mikrópolis
ΜΙΚΡΟΠΟΛΙΣ
Menikion
Perithórion
A. Vrondoú
Óri Vrondoús
Néon Petrítsi
ΝΕΟΝ ΠΕΤΡΙΤΣΙ
Loutrá Sidirókastrou
Sidirókastron
ΣΙΔΗΡΟΚΑΣΤΡΟΝ
Áno Poróia
Rodópolis
Mouriés
Novi-Dojran
Stari-Dojran
Dojráni
L. Doiráni
Kerkíni
L. Kerkíni
Pondisménon
Iráklia
ΗΡΑΚΛΕΙΑ
M. Ag. Ioánnis
Sérres
ΣΕΡΡΑΙ
Lefkónas
Skotoússa
Pondokeraséa
Kendrikón
Drosáton
Chérson
Váthi
Efkarpía
Térpillos
Vafiochóri
Metallikón
Kilkís
ΚΙΛΚΙΣ
Kristóni
Koronoúda
N. Ginekókastron
Kambánis
Mikrókambos
Vathílakkos
Géfira
ΓΕΦΥΡΑ
Kalókastron
Skoútari
Dimitrísi
Pappás
Pendápolis
ΠΕΝΤΑΠΟΛΙΣ
Néa Zichni
ΝΕΑ ΖΙΧΝΗ
Mistráti
ΑΛΙΣΤΡΑΤΗ
Nikifóros
Choristí
Doxáton
ΔΟΞΑΤΟΝ
Ág. Athanásios
Fotolívos
Kalambákion
Krinídes
PHILIPPI
Néa Báfra
M. Ikosifinissis
Nikisiani
Eleftheroúpolis
ΕΛΕΥΘΕΡΟΥΠΟΛΙΣ
N. Iraklítsa
Néa Péramos
Dravískos
Rodolívos
ΡΟΔΟΛΕΙΒΟΣ
Pangéo
Avli
Podochóri
Galipsós
Amfípolis
Foleá
Símvolo
Akropótamos
Kariani
Loutrá Eleftherón
Strimón
Lachanás
Nigríta
ΝΙΓΡΙΤΑ
Choumnikón
ΧΟΥΜΝΙΚΟΝ
Ívira
Mavrothálassa
Aidonochórion
Vertískos
Dorkás
Nikópolis
Óssa
Ássiros
Sochós
ΣΟΧΟΣ
Néa Kerdíllia
Kerdíllion
Langadás
ΛΑΓΚΑΔΑΣ
Kolchikón
Askós
Filadélfion
Aréthousa
Akrogiáli
Asprovalta
Lití
Drimós
Diavatá
Lagina
Loutrá
Profítis
Megáli Vólvi
L. Korónia
L. Vólvi
THESSALONÍKI
ΘΕΣΣΑΛΟΝΙΚΗ
Sindos
Pírgos
Langadíkia
Loutrá Vólvis
Apollonía
Rendína
Stavrós
Strimonikós Kólpos
Kalamaria
ΚΑΛΑΜΑΡΙΑ
Piléa
Chortiátis
Gerakaroú
Stívos
Néa Apollonía
Néa Máditos
Panórama
Thérmi
ΘΕΡΜΗ
Peristerá
Zanglivérion
ΖΑΓΚΛΙΒΕΡΙΟΝ
Melissourgós
Varvára
Olimpiás
Ákra Marmári
Kólpos Thessaloníkis
Livádion
Stanós
Stágira
Stratoniki
Stratónion
Eleftherónisos
Ág. Triás
Peréa
Néa Michanióna
Vasiliká
ΒΑΣΙΛΙΚΑ
Galátista
Ág. Pródromos
Cholomón
Arnéa
ΑΡΝΑΙΑ
Paleochórion
Kólpos Ierissoú
Ákra Arápis
Órmos
Epanomí
ΕΠΑΝΟΜΗ
Ákra Epanomís
Vávdos
Meg. Panagiá
CHALKIDIKÍ
Petrálona
Eleochória
Polígiros
ΠΟΛΥΓΥΡΟΣ
Planá
Ierissós
ΙΕΡΙΣΣΟΣ
Néa Róda
Tripití
M. Chiliandariou
Vatopédi
ΒΑΤΟΠΕΔΙ
Néa Kallikrátia
N. Ténedos
N. Tríglia
OLYNTHOS
Ormília
Gerakiní
Pirgadíkia
Amoliani
Ouranópolis
Ágion Óros
Kariaí
Iviron
ΙΒΗΡΩΝ
Dáfni
ΔΑΦΝΗ
Néa Plagiá
Néa Moudaniá
ΝΕΑ ΜΟΥΔΑΝΙΑ
Nikitas
Ág. Nikólaos
Órmos Panagías
Metamórfosis
Diáporos
Vourvouroú
Singitikós Kólpos
Néa Potídea
Thermaïkós Kólpos
Toronéos Kólpos
Néa Fókea
Tripótamos
Sithonía
Áthos
Ákra Pinnes
(Nimféon)
Sani
Ákra Pirgos
Áfitos
Kallithéa
Kassándra
N. Marmarás
Kélifos
Ákra Rigás
Sárti
Síviri
Kassándria
Chaniótis
Porto Carrás
Sikiá
Ákra Ádolo
Pefkochórion
Destenika
Torón
Kalamítsion
Kalándra
Ákra Kassándras
Ag. Paraskeví
Néa Skióni
Loutrá
Chrousou
Paliourion
Ákra Paliourion
Koufós
Ákra Drépanon
(Ámbelos)
Ákra Platamón
Nea Messángala
Stómion
Karítsa
Kókkino Neró
Ákra Dermatás
Melívia
Agiá
ΑΓΙΑ
Agiókambos
Skití
Kastrion
Mavrovoúni
Kalamákion
Keramídion
Kamári
Kanália
Pourión
Choreftón
Zagorá
ΖΑΓΟΡΑ
Ág. Ioánnis
Rizómilos
VÓLOS
ΒΟΛΟΣ
Makrinítsa
Portariá
Drákia
Tsangaráda
ΤΣΑΓΚΑΡΑΔΑ
Sésklon
DIMINI
DEMETRIAS
Agriá
Miléai
Kalamákion
Káto Gatzéa
Kalá Nerá
Neochórion
Ákra Angistri
Néa Anchíalos
ΝΕΑ ΑΓΧΙΑΛΟΣ
Mikrothívai
Áfissos
Sikí
Pagasitikós Kólpos
Argalastí
Promírion
Amaliápolis
HALOS
Milína
Skíathos
ΣΚΙΑΘΟΣ
Kástro
Glóssa
Alónnisos
ΑΛΟΝΝΗΣΟΣ
Ákra Gérakas
Peristéra
Psathoúra
Gioúra
Kirá Panagiá
(Pélagos)
Pipérion

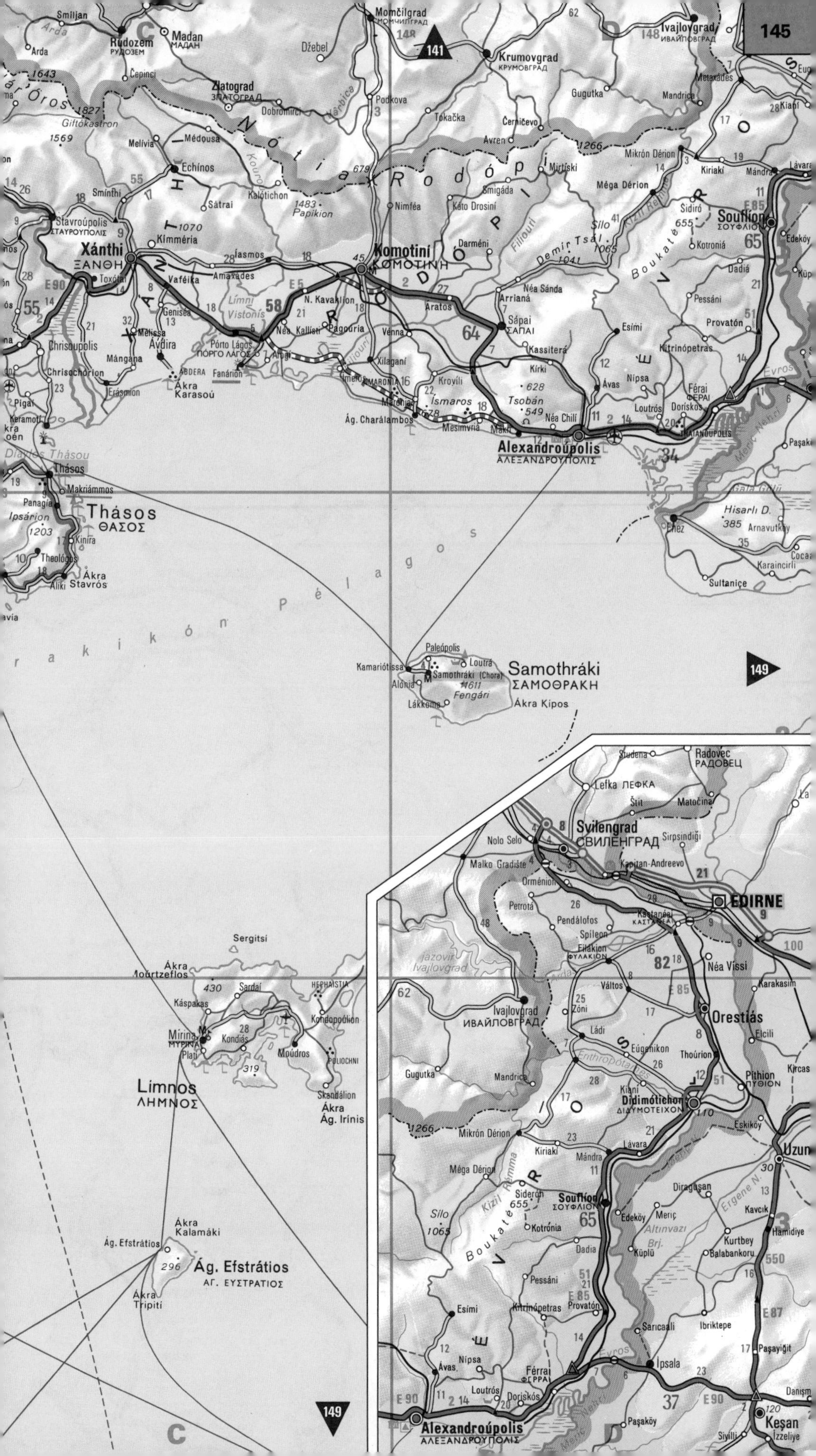
Momčilgrad
МОМЧИЛГРАД
141
Krumovgrad
КРУМОВГРАД
Ivajlovgrad
ИВАЙЛОВГРАД
Smiljan
Arda
Rudozem
РУДОЗЕМ
Madan
МАДАН
Džebel
Zlatograd
ЗЛАТОГРАД
Podkova
Tokačka
Gugutka
Mandrica
Metaxádes
Giftókastron
Mélivia
Médousa
Echínos
Sátrai
Kalótichon
Nótia Rodópi
Papíkion
Nimféa
Káto Drosiní
Smigáda
Mirtíski
Mikrón Dérion
Kiriakí
Mándra
Méga Dérion
Sidiró
Soufli
ΣΟΥΦΛΙ
Kotroniá
Dadiá
Stavroúpolis
ΣΤΑΥΡΟΥΠΟΛΙΣ
Xánthi
ΞΑΝΘΗ
Kimméria
Íasmos
Komotiní
ΚΟΜΟΤΙΝΗ
Darméni
Demir Tsál
Boukatevo
Toxótai
Amaxades
Vaféika
Genisea
N. Kavaklion
Néa Kallísti
Pagouría
Aratos
Arriana
Néa Sánda
Sápai
ΣΑΠΑΙ
Pessáni
Provatón
Esími
Kitrinópetras
Kassiterá
Kírki
Ávas
Nipsa
Férai
ΦΕΡΑΙ
Chrisoúpolis
Mélissa
Ávdira
Pórto Lágos
ΠΟΡΤΟ ΛΑΓΟΣ
Fanárion
Arogí
Vénna
Xilaganí
Maróneia
Ímeros
Kroviíi
Ísmaros
Tsobán
Loutrós
Doriskós
Chrisochórion
Mángana
Erásmion
ABDERA
Ákra Karasoú
Ág. Charálambos
Mesimvría
Makrí
Néa Chilí
Alexandroúpolis
ΑΛΕΞΑΝΔΡΟΥΠΟΛΙΣ
Evros
Pigaí
Keramotí
Diaulos Thásou
Thásos
Makriámmos
Panagía
Ipsárion
Thásos
ΘΑΣΟΣ
Kínira
Theológos
Alikí
Ákra Stavrós
Hisarlı D.
Arnavutköy
Enez
Karaincirli
Sultaniçe
Thrakikón Pélagos
Paleópolis
Kamariótissa
Loutrá
Samothráki (Chora)
Fengári
Alónia
Lákkoma
Samothráki
ΣΑΜΟΘΡΑΚΗ
Ákra Kípos
149
Studena
Radovec
РАДОВЕЦ
Lefka ΛΕΦΚΑ
Štit
Matočina
Svilengrad
СВИЛЕНГРАД
Nolo Selo
Malko Gradište
Sirpsindiği
Kapitan-Andreevo
Orménion
Petrotá
Pendálofos
Spíleon
Kastanéai
EDIRNE
Filákion
ΦΥΛΑΚΙΟΝ
Néa Víssi
Jazovir Ivajlovgrad
Ivajlovgrad
ИВАЙЛОВГРАД
Váltos
Zóni
Karakasim
Orestiás
Ládi
Eúgenikon
Thoúrion
Elcili
Gugutka
Mandrica
Kiani
Pithion
ΠΥΘΙΟΝ
Didimótichon
ΔΙΔΥΜΟΤΕΙΧΟΝ
Kircas
Eskiköy
Mikrón Dérion
Kiriakí
Mándra
Lávara
Uzun
Méga Dérion
Siderón
Souflíon
ΣΟΥΦΛΙΟΝ
Diragasan
Edeköy
Meriç
Kavcık
Hamidiye
Kotrónia
Dadia
Küplü
Kurtbey
Balabankoru
Pessáni
Esími
Kitrinópetras
Provatón
Sarıcaali
Ibriktepe
Ávas
Nípsa
Férrai
ΦΕΡΡΑΙ
İpsala
Paşayiğit
Loutrós
Doriskós
Alexandroúpolis
ΑΛΕΞΑΝΔΡΟΥΠΟΛΙΣ
Paşaköy
Keşan
İzzeliye
Sergitsí
Ákra Moúrtzeflos
Sardaí
Káspakas
HEPHAISTIA
Kondopoúlion
Mírina
ΜΥΡΙΝΑ
Kondiás
Moúdros
POLIOCHNI
Platí
Límnos
ΛΗΜΝΟΣ
Skandálion
Ákra Ág. Irínis
Ákra Kalamáki
Ág. Efstrátios
Ág. Efstrátios
ΑΓ. ΕΥΣΤΡΑΤΙΟΣ
Ákra Tripití
149

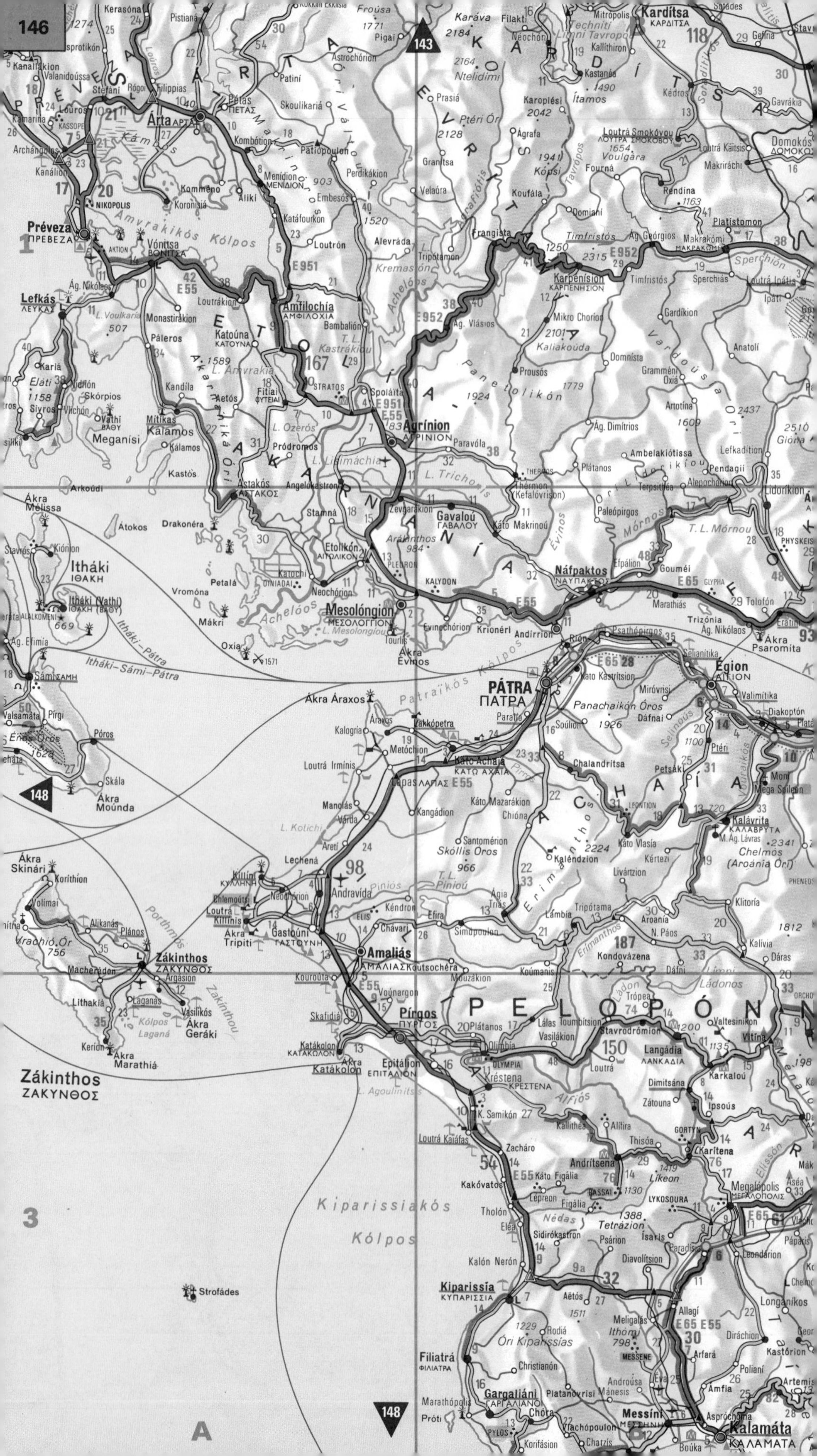
143
Kardítsa
ΚΑΡΔΙΤΣΑ
Árta ΑΡΤΑ
Préveza
ΠΡΕΒΕΖΑ
NIKOPOLIS
Amvrakikós Kólpos
Vónitsa
ΒΟΝΙΤΣΑ
Lefkás
ΛΕΥΚΑΣ
Amfilochía
ΑΜΦΙΛΟΧΙΑ
Katoúna
ΚΑΤΟΥΝΑ
Karpenísion
ΚΑΡΠΕΝΗΣΙΟΝ
Agrínion
ΑΓΡΙΝΙΟΝ
Meganísi
Kalamos
Astakós
ΑΣΤΑΚΟΣ
Gavaloú
ΓΑΒΑΛΟΥ
Itháki
ΙΘΑΚΗ
Ithákí (Vathí)
Etolikón
ΑΙΤΩΛΙΚΟΝ
Mesolóngion
ΜΕΣΟΛΟΓΓΙΟΝ
Náfpaktos
ΝΑΥΠΑΚΤΟΣ
Lidoríkion
Sámi ΣΑΜΗ
Ithákí–Pátra
Ithákí–Sámi–Pátra
Patraïkós Kólpos
PÁTRA
ΠΑΤΡΑ
Égion
ΑΙΓΙΟΝ
Panachaikón Óros
Káto Achaïa
ΚΑΤΩ ΑΧΑΙΑ
Kalávrita
ΚΑΛΑΒΡΥΤΑ
148
Zákinthos
ΖΑΚΥΝΘΟΣ
Kilíni
ΚΥΛΛΗΝΗ
Andravída
Gastoúni
ΓΑΣΤΟΥΝΗ
Amaliás
ΑΜΑΛΙΑΣ
Pírgos
ΠΥΡΓΟΣ
Olimbía
OLYMPIA
Langádia
ΛΑΝΚΑΔΙΑ
Vitína
Kréstena
ΚΡΕΣΤΕΝΑ
Katákolon
ΚΑΤΑΚΟΛΟΝ
Epitálion
ΕΠΙΤΑΛΙΟΝ
Andrítsena
Karítena
Megalópolis
ΜΕΓΑΛΟΠΟΛΙΣ
Kiparissiakós Kólpos
Kiparissía
ΚΥΠΑΡΙΣΣΙΑ
Filiatrá
ΦΙΛΙΑΤΡΑ
Gargaliáni
ΓΑΡΓΑΛΙΑΝΟΙ
Messíni
ΜΕΣΣΗΝΗ
Kalamáta
ΚΑΛΑΜΑΤΑ
Strofádes
P E L O P Ó N
A C H A Í A
E T O L
A K A R N A N Í A
E V R I T A N Í A
Zákinthos
ΖΑΚΥΝΘΟΣ
1
3
A
148

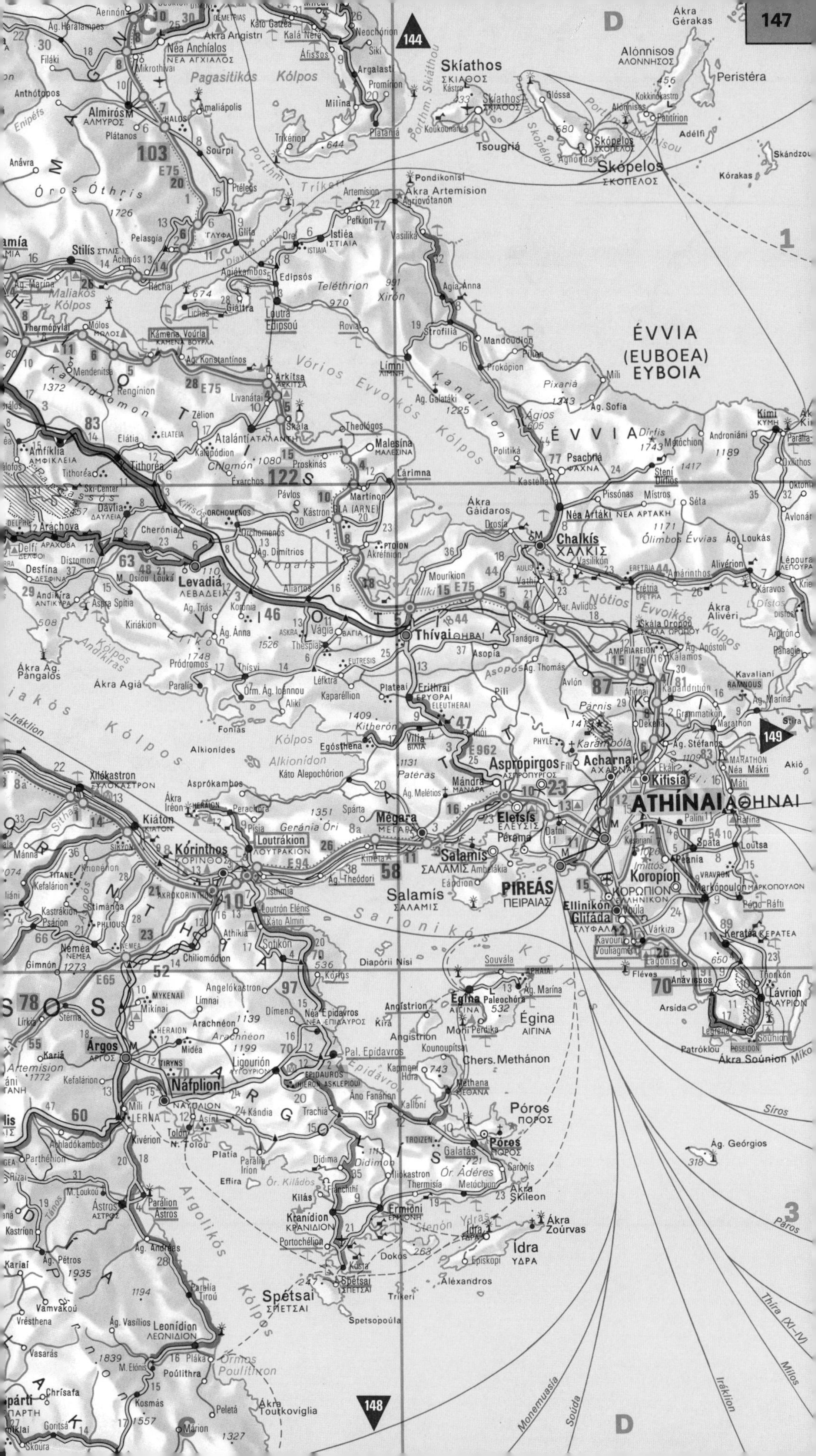
144
148
149
D
C
1
3
Pagasitikós Kólpos
Néa Anchíalos
ΝΕΑ ΑΓΧΙΑΛΟΣ
Almirós
ΑΛΜΥΡΟΣ
Óros Óthris
Skíathos
ΣΚΙΑΘΟΣ
Alónnisos
ΑΛΟΝΝΗΣΟΣ
Peristéra
Skópelos
ΣΚΟΠΕΛΟΣ
Tsougriá
Ákra Artemísion
Istiéa
ΙΣΤΙΑΙΑ
Stilís
Maliakós Kólpos
Thermópylai
Kámena Voúrla
ΚΑΜΕΝΑ ΒΟΥΡΛΑ
Loutrá Edipsoú
Edipsós
Límni
ΛΙΜΝΗ
Vórios Evvoikós Kólpos
ÉVVIA
(EUBOEA)
ΕΥΒΟΙΑ
É V V I A
Kími
ΚΥΜΗ
Psachná
ΨΑΧΝΑ
Chalkís
ΧΑΛΚΙΣ
Néa Artáki
ΝΕΑ ΑΡΤΑΚΗ
Erétria
ΕΡΕΤΡΙΑ
Nótios Evvoikós Kólpos
Atalánti
ΑΤΑΛΑΝΤΗ
Arkítsa
Malesína
ΜΑΛΕΣΙΝΑ
Lárimna
Delfí
ΔΕΛΦΟΙ
Aráchova
ΑΡΑΧΟΒΑ
Levadiá
ΛΕΒΑΔΕΙΑ
Thívai
ΘΗΒΑΙ
Orchomenós
Kopaís
Tanágra
Ákra Agiá
Alkionídes
Kólpos Alkionídon
Xilókastron
ΞΥΛΟΚΑΣΤΡΟΝ
Kiáton
ΚΙΑΤΟΝ
Kórinthos
ΚΟΡΙΝΘΟΣ
Loutrákion
ΛΟΥΤΡΑΚΙΟΝ
Mégara
ΜΕΓΑΡΑ
Elefsís
ΕΛΕΥΣΙΣ
Salamís
ΣΑΛΑΜΙΣ
Asprópirgos
ΑΣΠΡΟΠΥΡΓΟΣ
Acharnaí
ΑΧΑΡΝΑΙ
Kifisiá
ATHÍNAI
ΑΘΗΝΑΙ
PIREÁS
ΠΕΙΡΑΙΑΣ
Ellinikón
Glifáda
ΓΛΥΦΑΔΑ
Koropíon
ΚΟΡΩΠΙΟΝ
Markópoulon
ΜΑΡΚΟΠΟΥΛΟΝ
Rafína
Marathon
Keratéa
ΚΕΡΑΤΕΑ
Lávrion
ΛΑΥΡΙΟΝ
Ákra Soúnion
Saronikós Kólpos
Égina
ΑΙΓΙΝΑ
Chers. Methánon
Póros
ΠΟΡΟΣ
Nemea
ΝΕΜΕΑ
Árgos
ΑΡΓΟΣ
Náfplion
ΝΑΥΠΛΙΟΝ
Néa Epídavros
Ligourión
Argolís
Argolikós Kólpos
Ermióni
ΕΡΜΙΟΝΗ
Kranídion
ΚΡΑΝΙΔΙΟΝ
Ídra
ΥΔΡΑ
Spétsai
ΣΠΕΤΣΑΙ
Ástros
ΑΣΤΡΟΣ
Leonídion
ΛΕΩΝΙΔΙΟΝ
Ág. Geórgios
Síros
Páros
Thíra (XI–IV)
Mílos
Iráklion
Soúda
Monemvasía

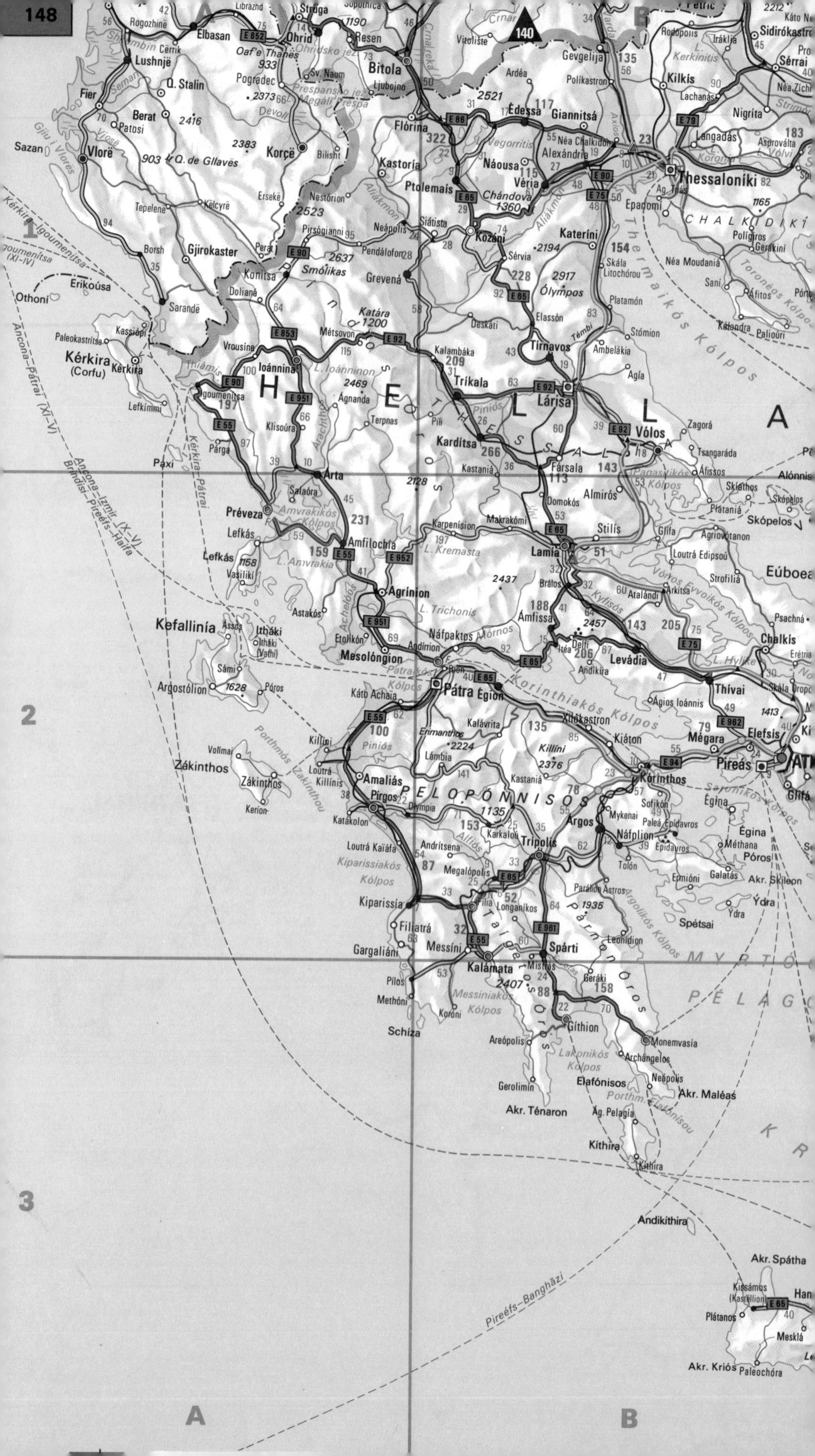

Elbasan
Ohrid
Resen
Bitola
Lushnjë
Fier
Berat
Q. Stalin
Pogradec
Korçë
Vlorë
Sazan
Tepelenë
Gjirokaster
Sarandë
Konitsa
Kérkira
(Corfu)
Paxi
Ioánnina
Igoumenitsa
Párga
Préveza
Arta
Lefkás
Kefallinía
Argostólion
Itháki
Zákinthos
Flórina
Kastoria
Ptolemaís
Kozáni
Grevená
Édessa
Giannitsá
Náousa
Véria
Thessaloníki
Kilkís
Sérrai
Katerini
Olympos
Tírnavos
Lárisa
Tríkala
Kardítsa
Vólos
Lamía
Agrínion
Mesolóngion
Pátra
Égion
Amfíssa
Delfí
Levádia
Thívai
Chalkís
Mégara
Elefsís
Pireás
Kórinthos
Argos
Náfplion
Trípolis
Pírgos
Olympia
Kalamáta
Spárti
Kiparissía
Monemvasía
Gíthion
Kíthira
Andikíthira
Akr. Maléas
Akr. Ténaron
Akr. Spátha
Kissámos
Paleochóra
E L L A
H
PELOPÓNNISOS
CHALKIDIKÍ
Thermaïkós Kólpos
Korinthiakós Kólpos
Pireéfs–Banghāzi
Ancona–Pátrai (XI–V)
Brindisi–Pireéfs–Haifa
A
B
1
2
3

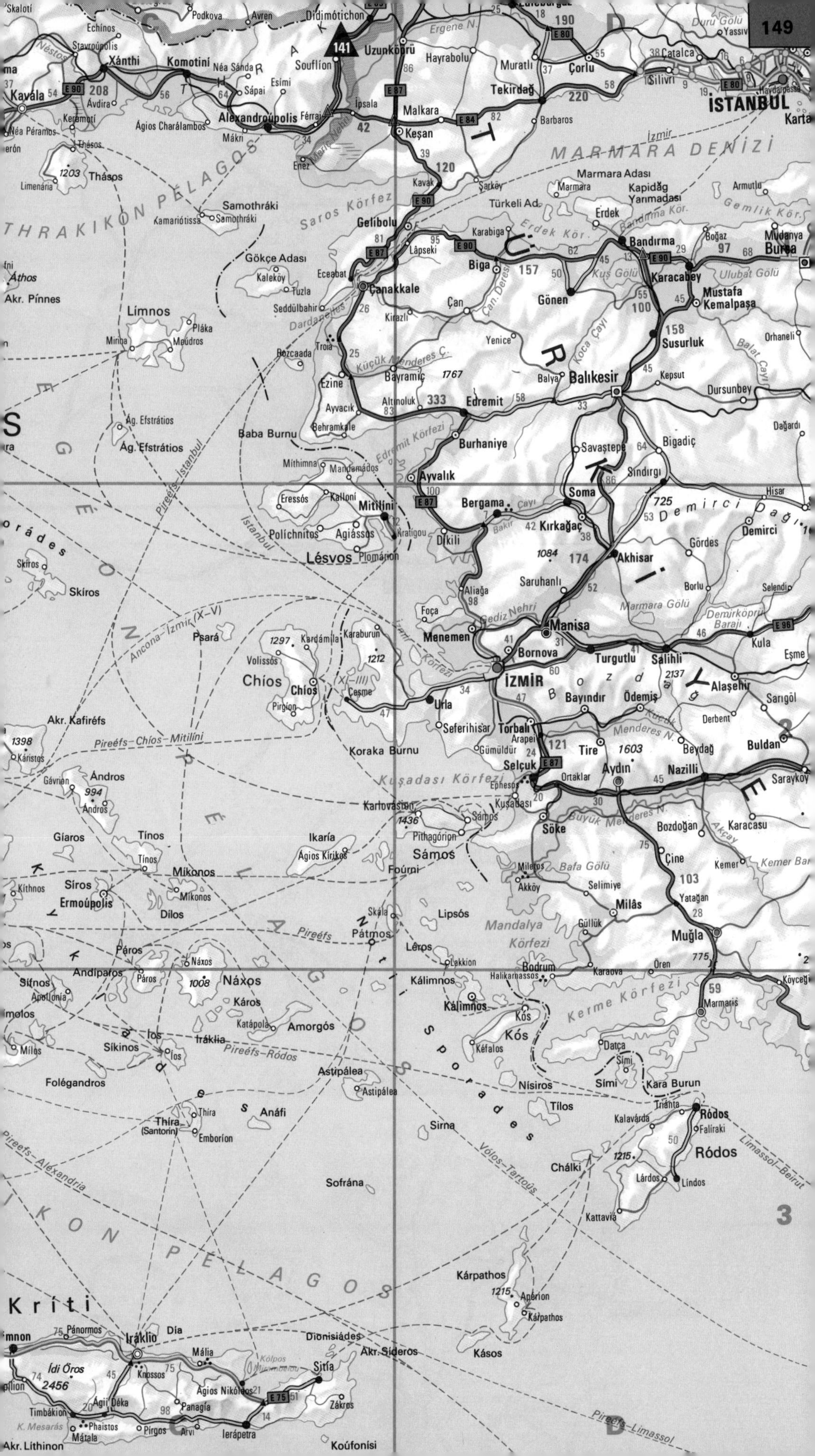
İSTANBUL
MARMARA DENİZİ
Tekirdağ
Çorlu
Çatalca
Silivri
Edirne
Uzunköprü
Keşan
Gelibolu
Çanakkale
Biga
Bandırma
Karacabey
Bursa
Mustafa Kemalpaşa
Susurluk
Balıkesir
Edremit
Ayvalık
Bergama
Soma
Akhisar
Manisa
İZMİR
Turgutlu
Salihli
Alaşehir
Ödemiş
Tire
Selçuk
Kuşadası
Aydın
Nazilli
Söke
Milâs
Muğla
Bodrum
Marmaris
Xánthi
Komotiní
Alexandroúpolis
Kavála
Thásos
Samothráki
Límnos
Lésvos
Mitilíni
Chíos
Psará
Skíros
Ándros
Tínos
Míkonos
Síros
Ermoúpolis
Náxos
Páros
Amorgós
Íos
Thíra
Sámos
Ikaría
Pátmos
Léros
Kálimnos
Kós
Sími
Tílos
Ródos
Kárpathos
Kásos
Kríti
Iráklio
Sitía
Ierápetra
THRAKIKON PÉLAGOS
AIGAION PÉLAGOS
KRITIKON PÉLAGOS
Sporades
Kiklades
Saros Körfezi
Edremit Körfezi
İzmir Körfezi
Kuşadası Körfezi
Kerme Körfezi
Pireéfs–İstanbul
Pireéfs–Chíos–Mitilíni
Pireéfs–Ródos
Pireéfs–Alexándria
Pireéfs–Limassol
Limassol–Beirut
Vólos–Tartoûs
Ancona–İzmir (X–V)

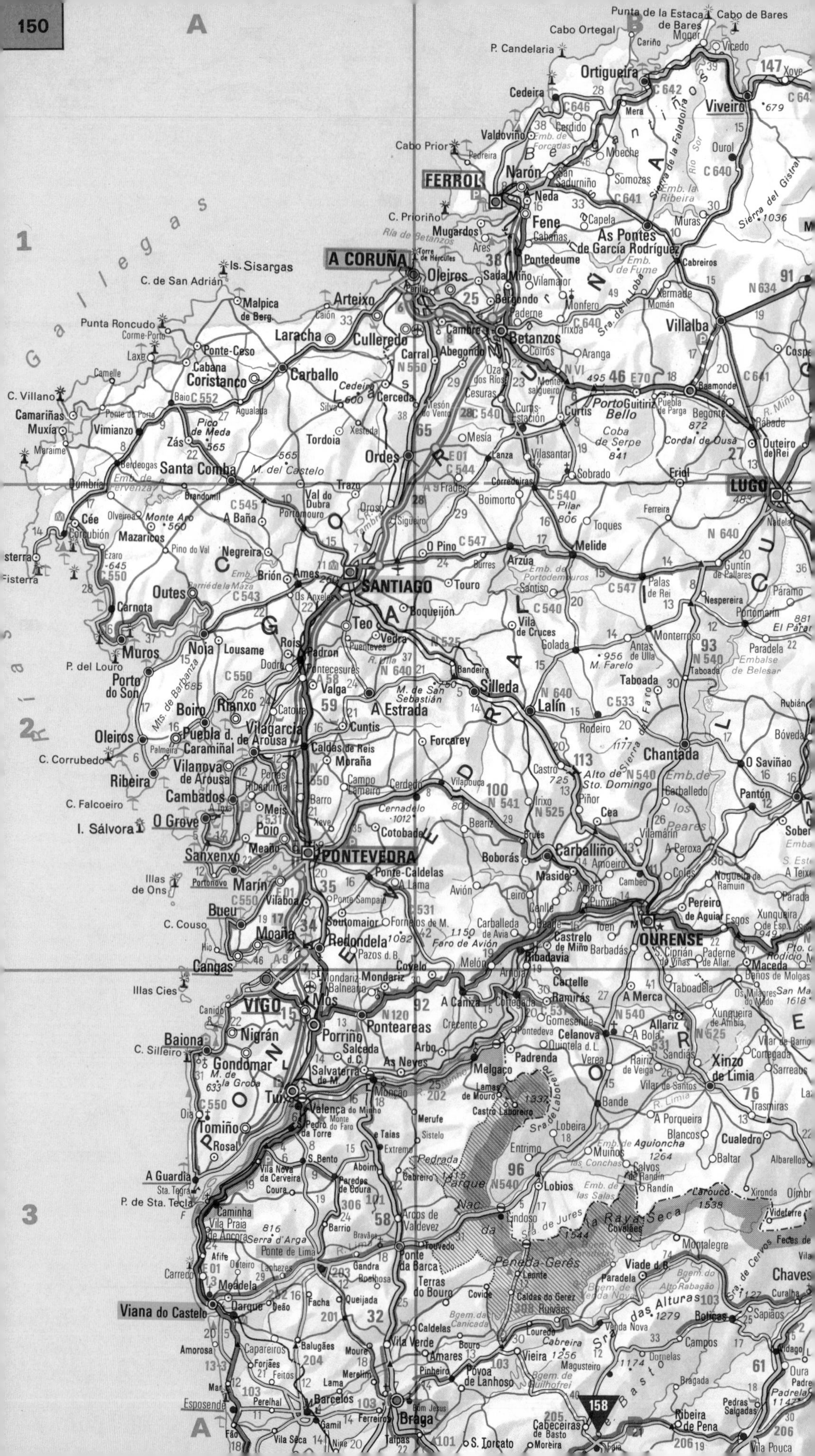

A
B
1
2
3
Rías Gallegas
Punta de la Estaca
Cabo de Bares
Cabo Ortegal
P. Candelaria
Cariño
Vicedo
147
Xove
Ortigueira
Cedeira
Viveiro
Valdoviño
Cerdido
Cabo Prior
Moeche
Ourol
Sierra de la Faladoira
Sierra del Gistral
FERROL
Narón
Neda
San Sadurniño
Somozas
Fene
Capela
Muras
C. Prioriño
Mugardos
As Pontes de García Rodríguez
A CORUÑA
Oleiros
Pontedeume
Cabreiros
Is. Sisargas
C. de San Adrián
Malpica de Berg.
Arteixo
Sada
Miño
Bergondo
Xermade
Monfero
N 634
Punta Roncudo
Corme-Porto
Laracha
Culleredo
Cambre
Betanzos
Villalba
Laxe
Ponte-Ceso
Cabana
Coristanco
Carballo
Carral
Abegondo
Coirós
Aranga
Cospeito
Camelle
N 550
Oza dos Ríos
N VI
E 70
Baamonde
C. Villano
Camariñas
Muxía
Vimianzo
Baio
C 552
Pico de Meda
Zás
Cerceda
Cesuras
Curtis
Guitiriz
Begonte
Rábade
Tordoia
Mesón do Vento
Mesía
Porto Bello
Coba de Serpe
Cordal de Ousá
Outeiro de Rei
Santa Comba
M. del Castelo
Ordes
Lanza
Vilasantar
Sobrado
Friol
Dumbría
Frades
LUGO
Cée
Corcubión
Val do Dubra
Trazo
Boimorto
Monte Aro
A Baña
Mazaricos
Sigüeiro
Pilar
Toques
Fisterra
Ezaro
Pino do Val
Negreira
O Pino
Melide
N 640
Carnota
Brión
Ames
SANTIAGO
Arzúa
Touro
Guntín de Pallares
Outes
Boqueijón
Palas de Rei
Páramo
Muros
Noia
Lousame
Teo
Vedra
Vila de Cruces
Golada
Portomarín
P. del Louro
Padrón
Antas de Ulla
Monterroso
Paradela
Porto do Son
Pontecesures
Valga
N 525
M. Farelo
Taboada
Embalse de Belesar
Mts. de Barbanza
Boiro
Rianxo
Catoira
A Estrada
Silleda
Lalín
Rodeiro
Rubián
Oleiros
Puebla d. Caramiñal
Vilagarcía de Arousa
Cuntis
Forcarey
Chantada
Bóveda
C. Corrubedo
Ribeira
Vilanova de Arousa
Caldas de Reis
Moraña
Alto de Sto. Domingo
O Saviñao
C. Falcoeiro
Cambados
Campo Lameiro
Cerdedo
Castro
Irixo
Piñor
Carballedo
Pantón
I. Sálvora
O Grove
Meis
Poio
Cotobade
Cea
Sanxenxo
PONTEVEDRA
Boborás
Carballiño
A Peroxa
Illas de Ons
Marín
Ponte-Caldelas
Maside
Amoeiro
Bueu
Vilaboa
Avión
Pereiro de Aguiar
C. Couso
Moaña
Soutomaior
Redondela
Carballeda de Avia
Faro de Avión
Castrelo de Miño
OURENSE
Esgos
Xunqueira de Esp.
Cangas
Ribadavia
Barbadás
Maceda
Illas Cíes
VIGO
Mos
Mondariz
Cartelle
Ramirás
A Merca
Baños de Molgas
Nigrán
Porriño
Ponteareas
A Cañiza
Crecente
Gomesende
Celanova
Allariz
Baiona
C. Silleiro
Gondomar
Salceda d. C.
Arbo
As Neves
Padrenda
Melgaço
Xunqueira de Ambía
Vilar de Barrio
Tui
Salvaterra de M.
Monção
Sandiás
Xinzo de Limia
Sarreaus
Oia
Tomiño
Valença do Minho
Bande
Trasmiras
Rosal
Merufe
Castro Laboreiro
Lobeira
A Porqueira
Cualedro
A Guardia
Vila Nova de Cerveira
Paredes de Coura
Entrimo
Muiños
Calvos de Randín
Baltar
P. de Sta. Tecla
Caminha
Vila Praia de Ancora
Arcos de Valdevez
Lobios
Parque Nac. da Peneda-Gerês
Sierra de la Raya Seca
Serra d'Arga
Ponte de Lima
Ponte da Barca
Montalegre
Chaves
Carreço
Meadela
Viana do Castelo
Darque
Terras do Bouro
Caldas do Gerez
Ruivães
Viade d.B.
Paradela
Serra das Alturas
Boticas
Vila Verde
Amares
Vieira
Cabreira
Campos
Póvoa de Lanhoso
Esposende
Barcelos
Braga
Bom Jesus
Cabeceiras de Basto
Ribeira de Pena
Pedras Salgadas
Vila Seca
S. Torcato
158

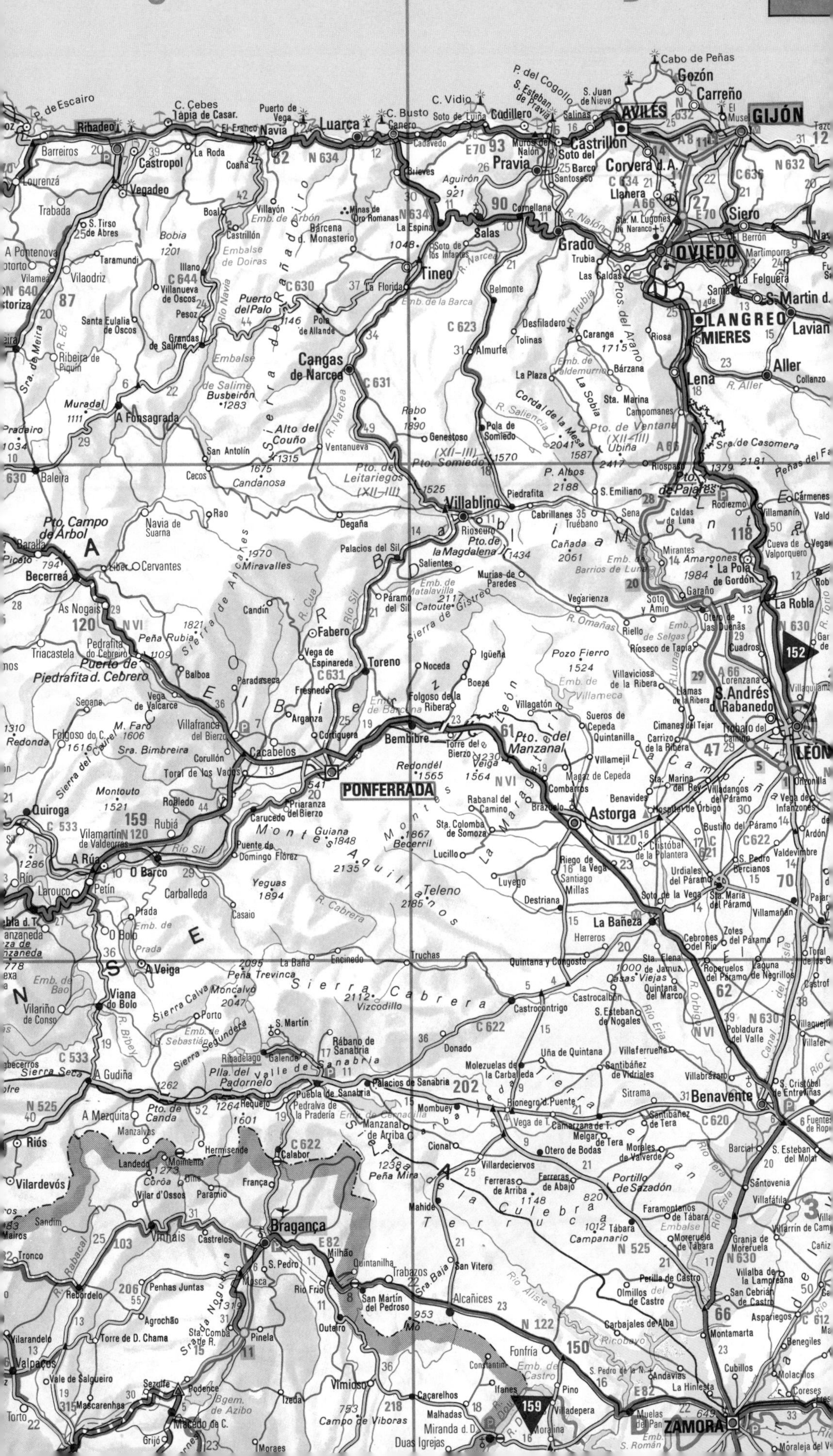
C
D
Cabo de Peñas
Gozón
Carreño
GIJÓN
AVILÉS
Castrillón
Corvera d.A.
Llanera
Pravia
Cudillero
C. Vidio
C. Busto
Luarca
Navia
Tapia de Casar.
C. Cebes
P. de Escairo
Ribadeo
Castropol
Vegadeo
Barreiros
Lourenzá
Trabada
S. Tirso de Abres
Taramundi
Vilaodriz
A Pontenova
Boal
Villayón
Coaña
La Roda
El Franco
Canero
Cadavedo
Soto de Luiña
Brieves
Minas de Oro Romanas
Bárcena d. Monasterio
La Espina
Salas
Cornellana
Grado
Trubia
Las Caldas
OVIEDO
Siero
Sta. M. Lugones de Naranco
El Berrón
Martimporra
La Felguera
Sama de L.
S. Martín d.
LANGREO
MIERES
Lavian
Aller
Collanzo
Lena
R. Aller
Riosa
Caranga
Bárzana
La Plaza
Tolinas
Desfiladero
Belmonte
Almurfe
Tineo
La Florida
Pola de Allande
Puerto del Palo
Cangas de Narcea
Sierra de Rañadoiro
Genestoso
Rabo
Pola de Somiedo
Ventanueva
Alto del Couño
Pto. Somiedo
Pto. de Leitariegos
Villablino
Piedrafita
Cabrillanes
Truébano
S. Emiliano
Sena
Caldas de Luna
Rodiezmo
Villamanín
Cueva de Valporquero
Pto. de Pajares
Riospaso
Ubiña
Pto. de Ventana
Cordal de la Mesa
La Sobia
Sta. Marina
Campomanes
Sra. de Casomera
Peñas del Fa
Cármenes
Mirantes
Amargones
La Pola de Gordón
Barrios de Luna
Garaño
Soto y Amío
La Robla
Otero de las Dueñas
Cuadros
Lorenzana
S. Andrés d. Rabanedo
LEÓN
Trobajo del Camino
Villadangos del Páramo
Hospital de Órbigo
Astorga
Benavides
Bustillo del Páramo
Valdevimbre
La Bañeza
Soto de la Vega
Villamañán
Laguna de Negrillos
Pobladura del Valle
Benavente
Santibáñez de Tera
Villabrázaro
Villalpando
Santovenia
Villafáfila
Granja de Moreruela
Tábara
Faramontanos de Tábara
Moreruela de Tábara
Campanario
Perilla de Castro
Olmillos de Castro
Carbajales de Alba
Montamarta
Andavias
La Hiniesta
ZAMORA
Muelas del Pan
Alcañices
Trabazos
San Vitero
Mahide
Ferreras de Arriba
Ferreras de Abajo
Sierra de la Culebra
Portillo de Sazadón
Villardeciervos
Otero de Bodas
Camarzana de T.
Vega de T.
Mombuey
Manzanal de Arriba
Cional
Peña Mira
Palacios de Sanabria
Puebla de Sanabria
Requejo
Pedralva de la Pradería
Galende
Ribadelago
Rábano de Sanabria
S. Martín
Pto. de Padornelo
Sierra Segundera
Sierra Cabrera
Peña Trevinca
Vizcodillo
Castrocontrigo
Castrocalbón
S. Esteban de Nogales
Uña de Quintana
Villaferrueña
Santibáñez de Vidriales
Molezuelas de la Carballeda
Rionegro d. Puente
Sitrama
Donado
Truchas
Quintana y Congosto
Destriana
Luyego
Lucillo
Teleno
Montes Aquilianos
Sta. Colomba de Somoza
Rabanal del Camino
Pto. del Manzanal
Bembibre
Torre del Bierzo
Folgoso de la Ribera
Noceda
Igüeña
Boeza
Toreno
Fabero
Vega de Espinareda
Cubillos del Sil
Cacabelos
Villafranca del Bierzo
PONFERRADA
Priaranza del Bierzo
Carucedo
O Barco
A Rúa
Petín
Larouco
Quiroga
Rubiá
Sierra del Caurel
Pedrafita do Cebreiro
Puerto de Piedrafita d. Cebrero
Triacastela
Becerreá
As Nogais
Pto. Campo de Árbol
Cervantes
Navia de Suarna
Degaña
Rao
Candanosa
San Antolín
A Fonsagrada
Baleira
Muradal
Busbeirón
Embalse de Salime
Grandas de Salime
Pesoz
Santa Eulalia de Oscos
Villanueva de Oscos
Ribeira de Piquín
Sra. de Meira
Castrillón
Illano
Embalse de Doiras
Bobia
Viana do Bolo
A Veiga
A Gudiña
A Mezquita
Pto. de Canda
Hermisende
Calabor
Bragança
Vinhais
Rebordelo
Penhas Juntas
Agrochão
Torre de D. Chama
Valpaços
Vale de Salgueiro
Mascarenhas
Macedo de C.
Podence
Izeda
Pinela
S. Pedro
Milhão
Quintanilha
Rio Frio
Outeiro
San Martín del Pedroso
Vimioso
Caçarelhos
Campo de Víboras
Malhadas
Miranda d. D.
Duas Igrejas
Constantim
Ifanes
Fonfría
Pino
Villadepera
Moralina
Vilardevós
Ríos
Vilariño de Conso
Sandim
Tronco
Mairos
Landedo
Moimenta
Paramio
França
Vilar d'Ossos
Vilarandelo
Torto
Sezulfe
Grijó
Moraes

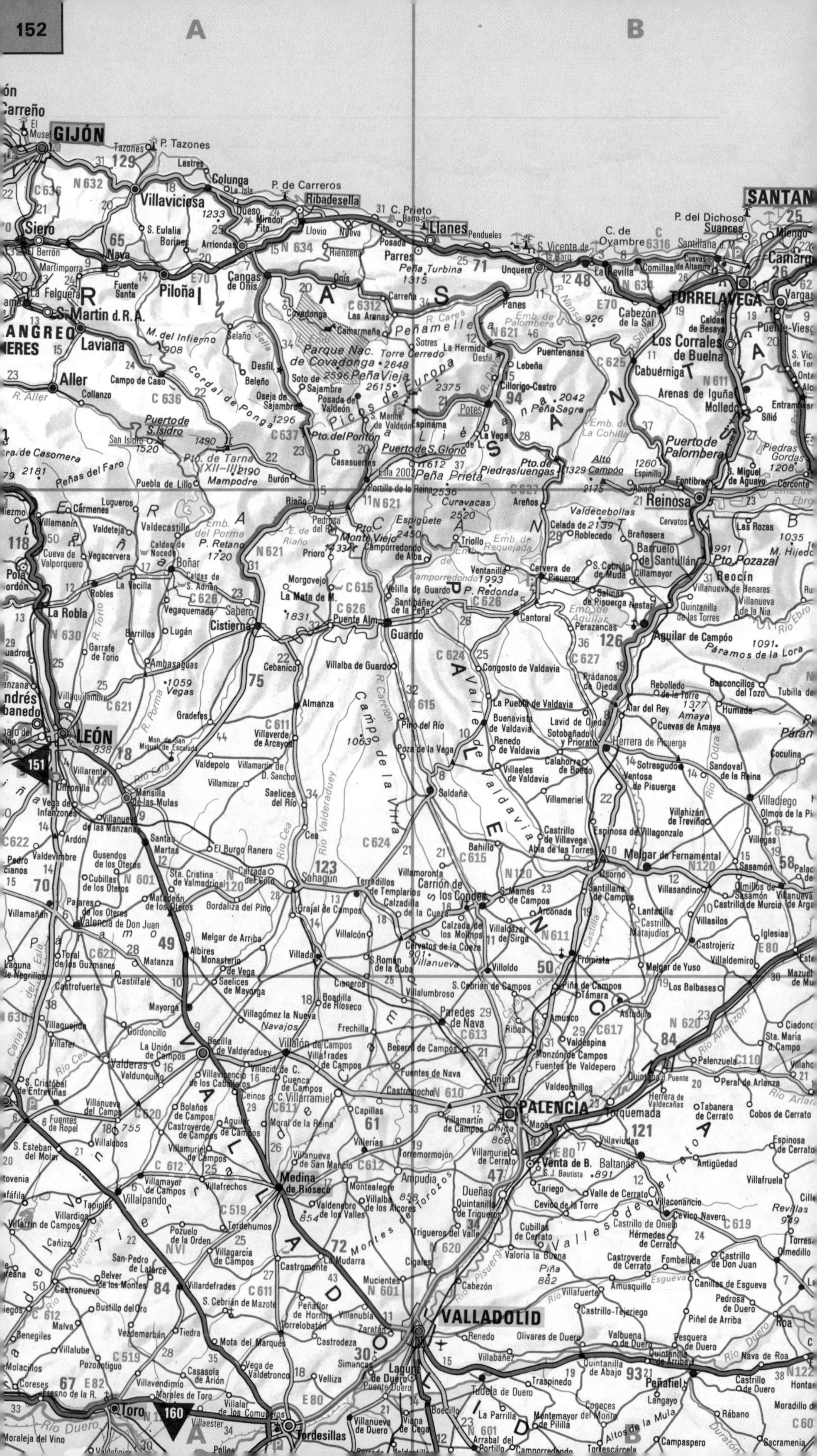

A
B
Carreño
El Musel
GIJÓN
Tazones
P. Tazones
129
Lastres
Colunga
La Isla
P. de Carreros
Ribadesella
Villaviciosa
Mirador Fito
C. Prieto
Llanes
Pendueles
P. del Dichoso
Suances
SANTAN
Siero
El Berrón
S. Eulalia
Borines
Arriondas
Llovio
Nueva
Posada
Parres
Peña Turbina
1315
71
Unquera
S. Vicente de la Barq.
C. de Oyambre
La Revilla
Comillas
Santillana d. M.
Cuevas de Altamira
TORRELAVEGA
Nava
Martimporra
Fuente Santa
Piloña
Cangas de Onís
Onís
Covadonga
Carreña
Las Arenas
Panes
Cabezón de la Sal
Caldas de Besaya
Vargas
La Felguera
S. Martín d. R. A.
LANGREO
Laviana
M. del Infierno
908
Selaño
Parque Nac. de Covadonga
Camarmeña
Peñamellera
Sotres
Torre Cerredo
2648
Peña Vieja
2596
2615
Picos de Europa
2375
La Hermida
Desfil.
Lebeña
Puentenansa
Emb. de Palombera
Los Corrales de Buelna
Cabuérniga
Arenas de Iguña
Molledo
Aller
Collanzo
R. Aller
Campo de Caso
Cordal de Ponga
Beleño
Oseja de Sajambre
Soto de Sajambre
Posada de Valdeón
Cillorigo-Castro
Peña Sagra
2042
Potes
Espinama
S. Marina de Valdeón
Emb. de La Cohilla
Puerto de Palombera
Entrambasaguas
Puerto de S. Isidro
San Isidro
1520
1490
Pto. de Tarna
Pto. del Pontón
Puerto de S. Glorio
La Vega
Pto. de Piedrasluengas
Alto Campóo
Espinilla
1260
Piedras Gordas
1208
S. Miguel de Aguayo
Casasuertes
Peña Prieta
Esla
Mampodre
Burón
Puebla de Lillo
Peñas del Faro
Portilla de la Reina
Curavacas
2520
Areños
Fontibre
Abiada
Reinosa
Corconte
Riaño
Lugueros
Cármenes
Villamanín
Valdeteja
Valdecastillo
Emb. del Porma
P. Retano
1720
Pedrosa del Rey
Pto. Monte Viejo
Espigüete
2450
Triollo
Emb. de Requejada
Celada de Roblecedo
Valdecebollas
Brañosera
Barruelo de Santullán
Cervatos
Las Rozas
M. Hijedo
Pto. Pozazal
Pola de Gordón
Cueva de Valporquero
Vegacervera
Boñar
Caldas de Nocedo
Prioro
Camporredondo de Alba
Ventanilla
1993
Cervera de Pisuerga
S. Cebrián de Muda
Cillamayor
Reocín
La Robla
Robles
La Vecilla
Morgovejo
La Mata de M.
Velilla de Guardo
Santibáñez de la Peña
P. Redonda
Salinas de Pisuerga
Nestar
Villanueva de Henares
Villanueva de la Nia
Quintanilla de las Torres
Vegaquemada
Sabero
Cistierna
Puente Alm.
Guardo
Cantoral
Emb. de Aguilar
Perazancas
Aguilar de Campóo
126
Páramos de la Lora
Barrillos
Lugán
Garrafe de Torío
Ambasaguas
Cebanico
Villalba de Guardo
Congosto de Valdavia
Prádanos de Ojeda
Rebolledo de la Torre
Basconcillos del Tozo
Tubilla del
Vegas
1059
75
Villaquilambre
Gradefes
Almanza
La Puebla de Valdavia
Buenavista de Valdavia
Alar del Rey
Amaya
1377
Humada
Cuevas de Amaya
Lavid de Ojeda
Sotobañado y Priorato
LEÓN
838
18
Mon. de San Miguel de Escalada
Villaverde de Arcayos
Pino del Río
Renedo de Valdavia
Herrera de Pisuerga
Coculina
151
Villarente
Valdepolo
Villamartín de D. Sancho
Poza de la Vega
Calahorra de Boedo
Villaeles de Valdavia
Sotresgudo
Sandoval de la Reina
Onzonilla
Mansilla de las Mulas
Villamizar
Saelices del Río
Saldaña
Ventosa de Pisuerga
Villadiego
Vega de Infanzones
Villanueva de las Manzanas
Villameriel
Villahizán de Treviño
Olmos de la Pi
Ardón
Campo de la Vírgen
Castrillo de Villavega
Abia de las Torres
Espinosa de Villagonzalo
Villegas
Valdevimbre
Gusendos de los Oteros
Santas Martas
El Burgo Ranero
Cea
Bahillo
Melgar de Fernamental
Sasamón
Sta. Cristina de Valmadrigal
Calzada del Coto
Sahagún
123
Terradillos de Templarios
Villamoronta
Carrión de los Condes
Osorno
Villasandino
Olmillos de Sasamón
Cubillas de los Oteros
Matadeón de los Oteros
Gordaliza del Pino
Grajal de Campos
Calzadilla de la Cueza
S. Mamés de Campos
Arconada
Santillana de Campos
Lantadilla
Castrillo Matajudíos
Castrillo de Arga
Villamañán
Pajares de los Oteros
Valencia de Don Juan
Melgar de Arriba
Villalcón
Calzada de los Molinos
Villalcázar de Sirga
Villasilos
Iglesias
Toral de los Guzmanes
49
Albires
Cervatos de la Cueza
Castrojeriz
Villaldemiro
Laguna de Negrillos
Matanza
Monasterio de Vega
Villada
S. Román de la Cuba
Villanueva
Villoldo
50
Frómista
Melgar de Yuso
Castrofuerte
Castilfalé
Saelices de Mayorga
Cisneros
Villalumbroso
S. Cebrián de Campos
Piña de Campos
Támara
Los Balbases
Mazuelo de Mu
Mayorga
Boadilla de Rioseco
Paredes de Nava
Amusco
Astudillo
Villaquejida
Villagómez la Nueva
Navajos
Frechilla
Ribas
Valdespina
N 620
Ciadoncha
Villafer
Gordoncillo
La Unión de Campos
Becilla de Valderaduey
Villalón de Campos
Villafrades de Campos
Becerril de Campos
84
Sta. María d. Campo
Valderas
Valdunquillo
Villavicencio de los Caballeros
Villacid de C.
Cuenca de Campos
Fuentes de Nava
Monzón de Campos
Fuentes de Valdepero
Palenzuela
S. Cristóbal de Entreviñas
Ceinos de C.
Villarramiel
Castromocho
Grijota
Valdeolmillos
Quintana d. Puente
Peral de Arlanza
Villanueva del Campo
Bolaños de Campos
Moral de la Reina
Capillas
61
PALENCIA
Torquemada
Herrera de Valdecañas
Tabanera de Cerrato
Cobos de Cerrato
Fuentes de Ropel
755
Castroverde de Campos
Aguilar de Campos
Villamartín de Campos
Magaz
121
Espinosa de Cerrato
S. Esteban del Molar
Villalobos
Villamuriel de Campos
Villerías
Torremormojón
Villamuriel de Cerrato
Villaviudas
Antigüedad
Villafruela
Villamayor de Campos
Villafrechós
Villanueva de San Mancio
Ampudia
47
Venta de B.
Baltanás
S. J. Bautista
891
Tapioles
Villalpando
Medina de Rioseco
Montealegre
Villalba de los Alcores
858
Dueñas
Tariego
Valle de Cerrato
Villaconancio
Villardiga
Villarrín de Campos
Valdenebro de los Valles
854
Quintanilla de Trigueros
Cevico de la Torre
Cevico Navero
Revillas
949
Cañizo
Pozuelo de la Orden
Tordehumos
Montes de Torozos
Trigueros del Valle
Cubillas de Cerrato
Valles de Cerrato
Castrillo de Onielo
Hérmedes de Cerrato
Torresandino
Olmedillo
San Pedro de Latarce
Villagarcía de Campos
72
La Mudarra
Cigales
Valoria la Buena
Piña
882
Castroverde de Cerrato
Fombellida
Castrillo de Don Juan
Belver de los Montes
84
Villardefrades
Castromonte
Mucientes
Cabezón
Río Villafuerte
Amusquillo
Canillas de Esgueva
Pedrosa de Duero
Castronuevo
S. Cebrián de Mazote
Peñaflor de Hornija
Villanubla
Castrillo-Tejeriego
Piñel de Arriba
Bustillo del Oro
Torrelobatón
Zaratán
VALLADOLID
Roa
Malva
Vezdemarbán
Tiedra
Mota del Marqués
Castrodeza
Renedo
Olivares de Duero
Valbuena de Duero
Pesquera de Duero
Benegiles
Villalube
Pozoantiguo
Casasola de Arión
Vega de Valdetronco
Simancas
30
Villabáñez
Quintanilla de Arriba
Nava de Roa
Molacillos
Coreses
67
Fresno de la R.
Villavendimio
Morales de Toro
Velliza
Laguna de Duero
Puente Duero
Quintanilla de Abajo
93
Traspinedo
Peñafiel
Castrillo de Duero
Toro
160
Villalar de los Comuneros
Villaester
Tordesillas
Villanueva de Duero
Viana de Cega
Boecillo
Tudela de Duero
La Parrilla
Montemayor del Monte
Cogeces del Monte
Langayo
Altos de la Mula
Rábano
Moraleja del Vino
Río Duero
Pollos
Arrabal del Portillo
Camporredondo
Torrescárcela
Campaspero
Sacramenia
Moradillo de

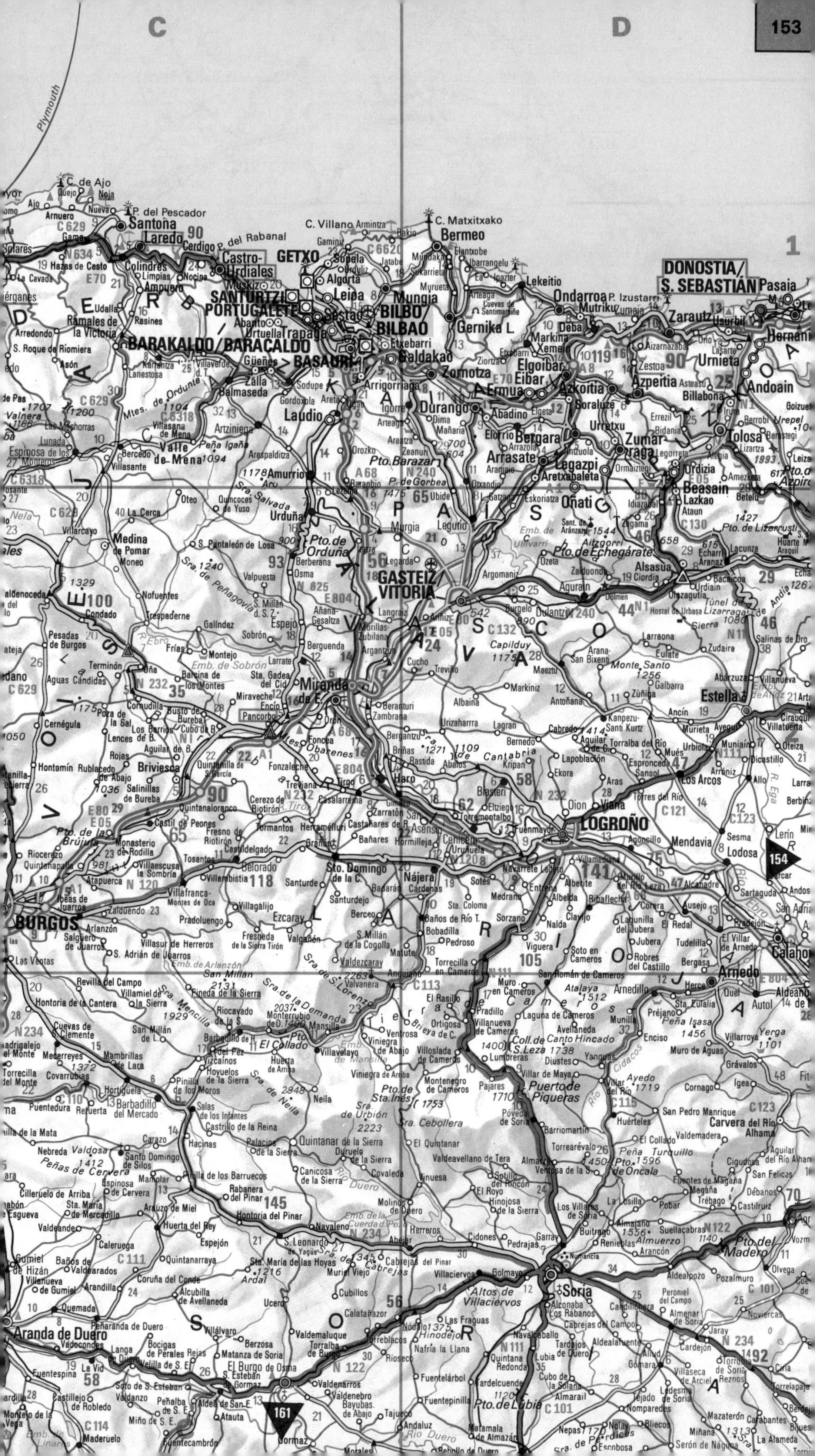
C
D
1
Plymouth
C. de Ajo
Noja
Santoña
P. del Pescador
Laredo
Castro-Urdiales
C. Villano
Armintza
C. Matxitxako
Bermeo
GETXO
Sopela
Algorta
Leioa
Mungia
SANTURTZI
PORTUGALETE
BILBO/
BILBAO
BARAKALDO/BARACALDO
BASAURI
Galdakao
Gernika
Lekeitio
Ondarroa
P. Izustarri
DONOSTIA/
S. SEBASTIÁN
Pasaia
Zarautz
Usurbil
Hernani
Zumaia
Mutriku
Deba
Markina
Zestoa
Azpeitia
Urnieta
Andoain
Zornotza
Ermua
Eibar
Elgoibar
Azkoitia
Durango
Abadino
Bergara
Arrasate
Legazpi
Aretxabaleta
Oñati
Zumarraga
Urretxu
Tolosa
Ordizia
Beasain
Lazkao
Amurrio
Laudio
Balmaseda
Valle de Mena
Orduña
Urduña
Pto. Barazar
Pto. de Orduña
Murgia
Legutio
GASTEIZ/
VITORIA
Alsasua
Altsasu
Agurain
Pto. de Echegárate
Medina de Pomar
Villarcayo
Espinosa de los Monteros
Trespaderne
Espejo
Miranda de E.
Pancorbo
Briviesca
Oña
Frías
Haro
Sto. Domingo de la C.
Nájera
LOGROÑO
Viana
Los Arcos
Estella
Mendavia
Lodosa
Lerín
Calahorra
Arnedo
Ezcaray
Belorado
BURGOS
Sra. de la Demanda
San Millán de la Cogolla
Pto. de Piqueras
Soria
Aranda de Duero
Burgo de Osma
Sra. Cebollera
Sra. de Urbión
Salas de los Infantes
Covarrubias
Lerma
Hontoria del Pinar
San Leonardo de Yagüe
Navaleno
Almazán
Golmayo
Sierra de Cameros
Pto. de Oncala
Agreda
Pto. del Madero
Olvega
154
161

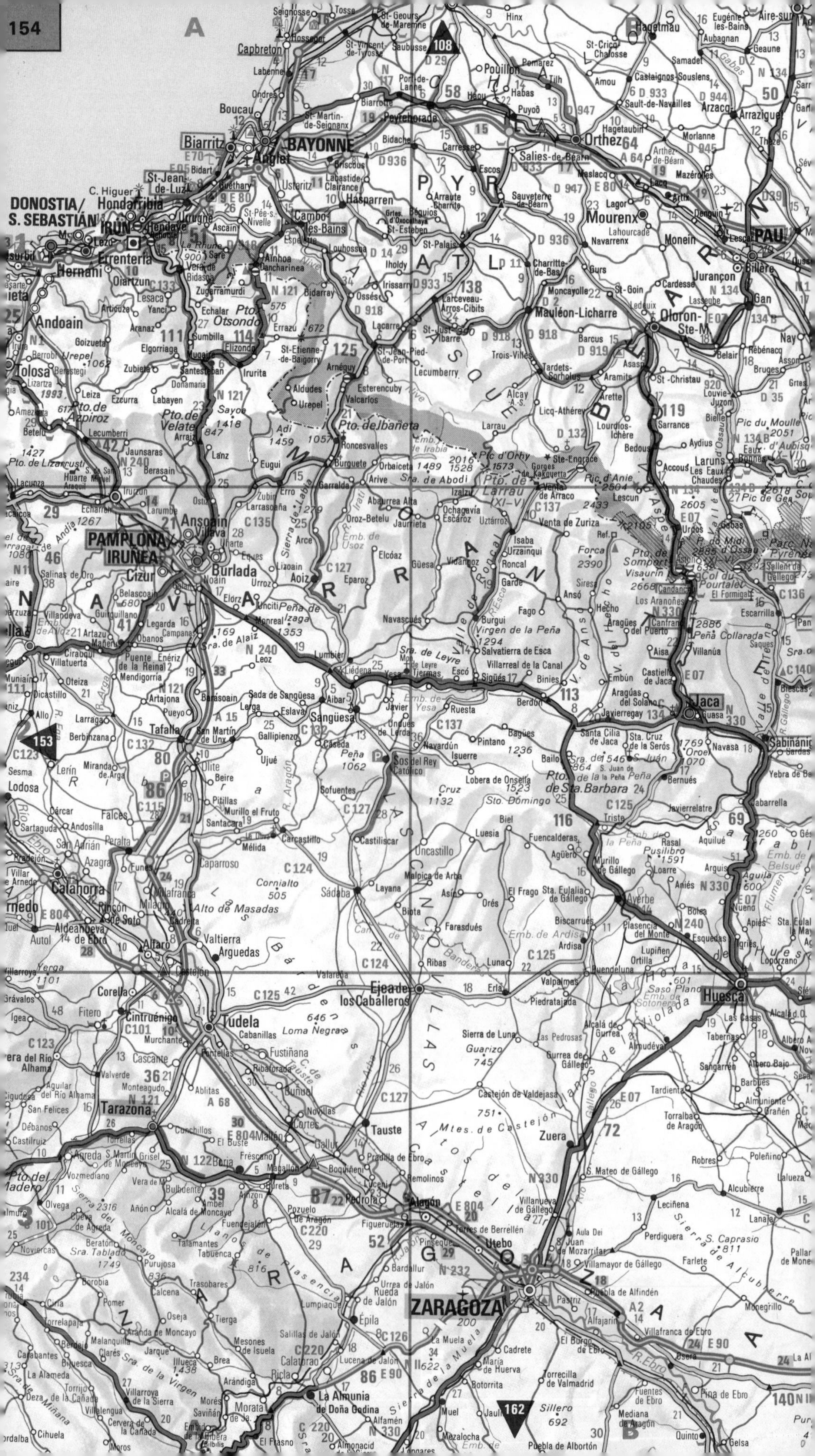

A

Seignosse · Tosse
St-Geours-de-Maremne · Hinx · Eugénie-les-Bains · Aire-sur
St-Vincent-de-Tyrosse · Gaubisse · Pomarez · Samadet · Hagetmau · Aubagnan · Arzacq-Arraziguet
Capbreton · Port-de-Lanne · Pouillon · Amou · Castaignos-Souslens · N 134 · Sarr
Boucau · Ondres · Habas · Puyôo · Sault-de-Navailles · Morlanne · 50
Anglet · Bidache · Carresse · Salies-de-Béarn · Orthez 64 · Arthez-de-Béarn · Thèze · Sév

DONOSTIA / S. SEBASTIÁN
BIARRITZ · BAYONNE
St-Jean-de-Luz · Bidart · Ustaritz · Hasparren · Sauveterre-de-Béarn · Mourenx · PAU
IRUN · Hendaye · Cambo-les-Bains · St-Palais · Mauléon-Licharre · Oloron-Ste-M
Hernani · Oiartzun · Ainhoa · Dancharinea · Iholdy · Irissarry · Charritte-de-Bas · Gurs · Juran-çon · Gan

Andoain · Lesaka · Zugarramurdi · St-Etienne-de-Baigorry · St-Jean-Pied-de-Port · Mauléon · Oloron · Laruns
Tolosa · Elizondo · Arnéguy · Lecumberry · Trois-Villes · Aramits · Eaux-Chaudes
Pto. de Velate · Roncesvalles · Orbaiceta · Pic d'Orhy · Ste-Engrâce · Pic d'Anie · Eaux-Bonnes

PAMPLONA / IRUÑEA · Burlada · Aoiz · Ochagavía · Isaba · Roncal · Ansó · Hecho · Jaca
Cizur · Monreal · Lumbier · Navascués · Burgui · Virgen de la Peña · Aragüés del Puerto · Canfranc
Tafalla · Sangüesa · Sos del Rey Católico · Sigüés · Embún · Jaca · Sabiñánigo

Olite · Caparroso · Uncastillo · Agüero · Murillo de Gállego · Ayerbe · Huesca
Calahorra · Arguedas · Ejea de los Caballeros · Sádaba · Luna · Almudévar · Loporzano

Corella · Cintruénigo · Tudela · Tauste · Zuera · Huesca
Tarazona · Cortes · Pedrola · Alagón · Utebo · Villamayor de Gállego

ZARAGOZA
La Almunia de Doña Godina · Épila · Cadrete · Fuentes de Ebro · Quinto
Calatorao · Ricla · Morata · Botorrita · María de Huerva · Mediana de Aragón

B

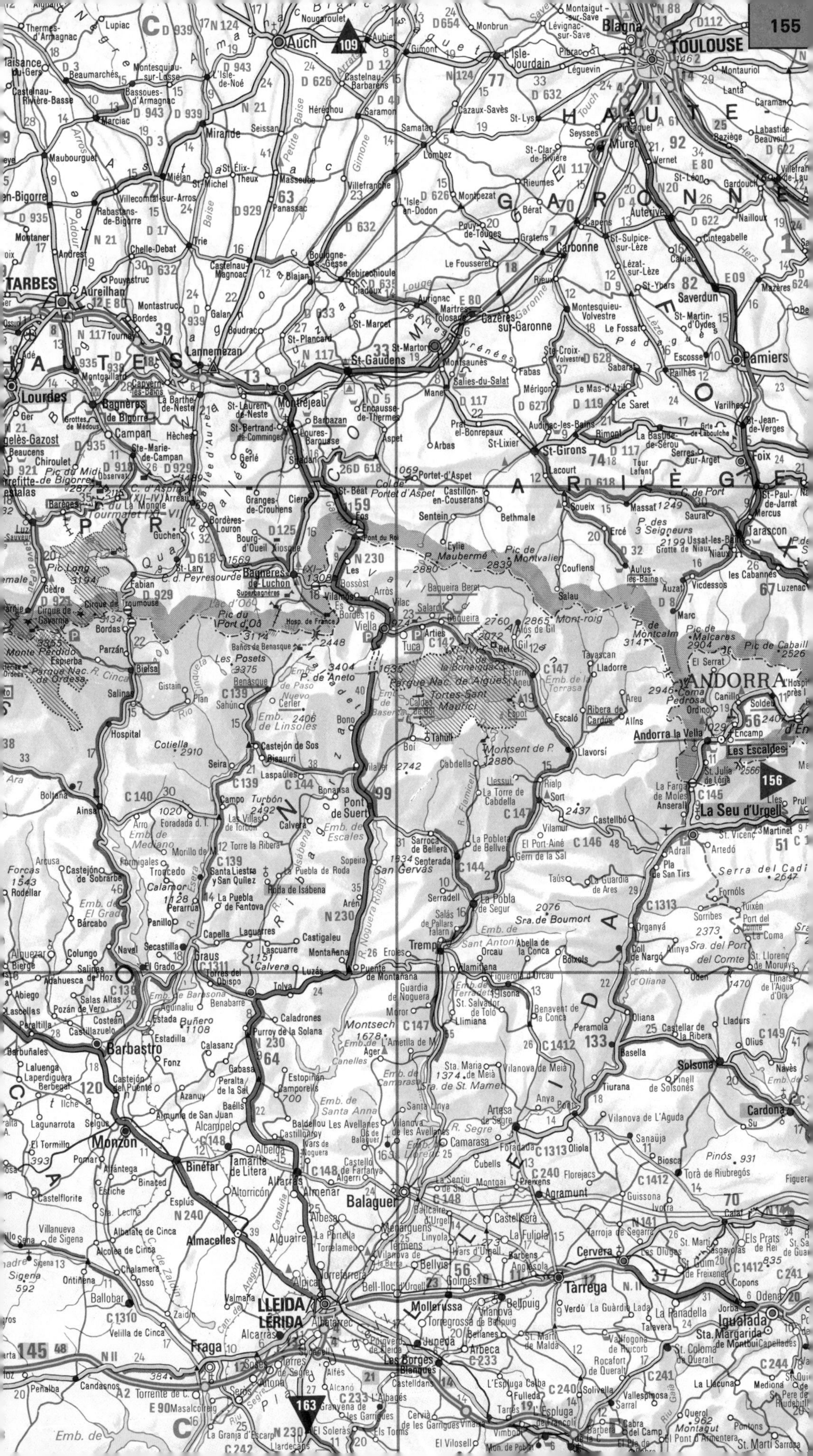
Auch
Blagnac
TOULOUSE
L'Isle-Jourdain
Mirande
Marciac
Maubourguet
Miélan
Trie
TARBES
Aureilhan
Lourdes
Bagnères de Bigorre
Lannemezan
Montréjeau
St-Gaudens
St-Martory
Cazères sur-Garonne
Carbonne
Muret
Auterive
Saverdun
Pamiers
St-Girons
Foix
Tarascon
Bagnères de-Luchon
Viella
ANDORRA
Andorra la Vella
Les Escaldes
La Seu d'Urgell
Pont de Suert
Tremp
Graus
Barbastro
Monzon
Binéfar
Balaguer
Solsona
Cardona
Agramunt
Cervera
Tàrrega
Igualada
Mollerussa
LLEIDA LÉRIDA
Fraga
Almacelles
Les Borges Blanques
HAUTE-GARONNE
ARIÈGE
HAUTES-PYRÉNÉES
LLEIDA
Pic de Montcalm
Pic de Montvalier
P. de Aneto
Parque Nac. de Aigües Tortes-Sant Maurici
Parque Nac. R. Cinca de Ordesa
Monte Perdido
Serra del Cadi
109
156
163

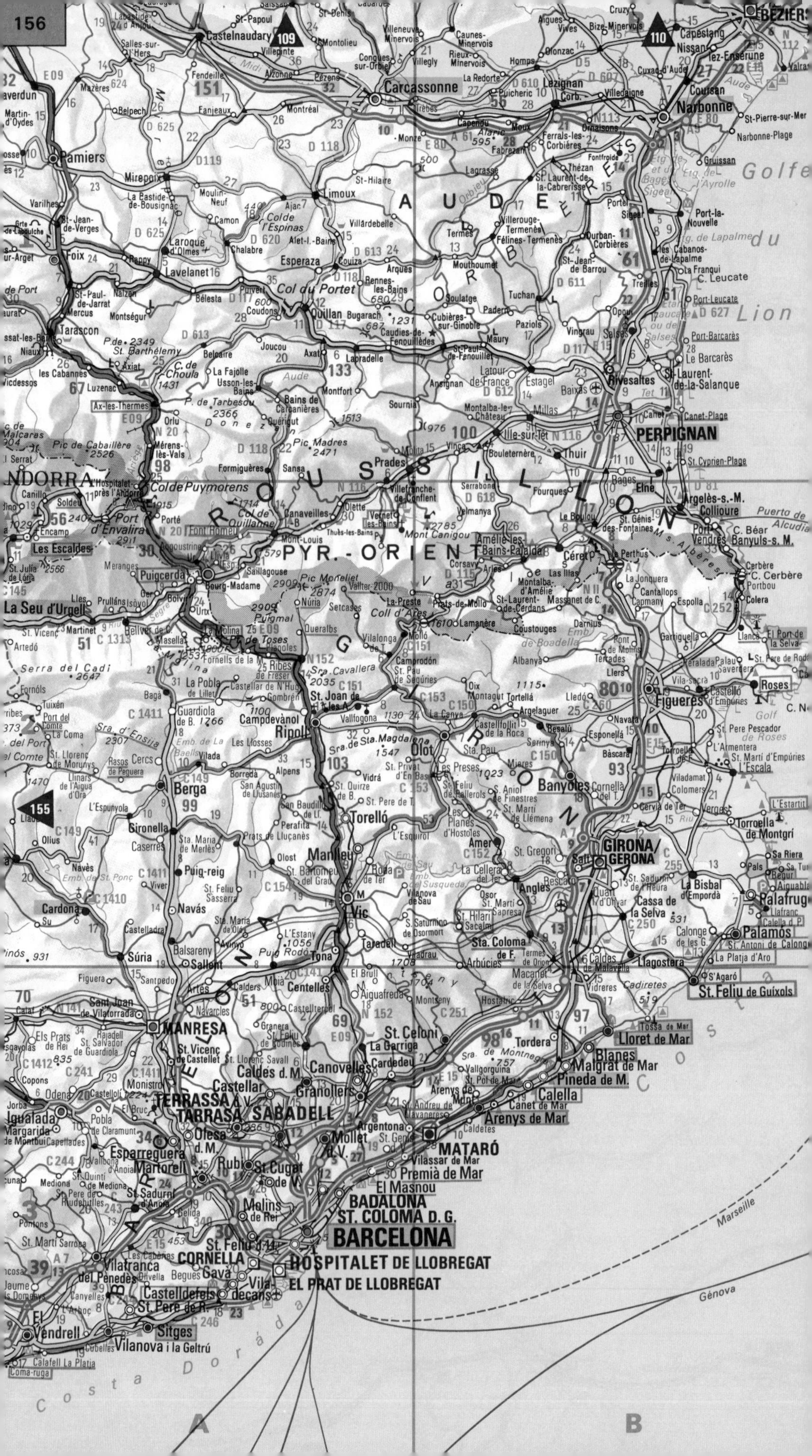
109
110
155
Castelnaudary
Carcassonne
Lézignan
Narbonne
Béziers
Capestang
Nissan
Coursan
Pamiers
Mirepoix
Limoux
Foix
Lavelanet
Quillan
Tarascon
Ax-les-Thermes
AUDE
CORBIÈRES
Golfe du Lion
Rivesaltes
PERPIGNAN
St. Cyprien-Plage
Elne
Argelès-s.-M.
Collioure
Port Vendres
Banyuls-s. M.
Cerbère
Portbou
Le Barcarès
Canet-Plage
Ille-sur-Têt
Thuir
Prades
Céret
Amélie-les-Bains-Palalda
ROUSSILLON
PYR.-ORIENT.
ANDORRA
Les Escaldes
Puigcerdà
Bourg-Madame
La Seu d'Urgell
Col de Puymorens
Mont Canigou
Figueres
Roses
Golf de Roses
L'Escala
GIRONA/GERONA
GIRONA
Banyoles
Olot
Ripoll
Camprodón
Berga
Vic
Manlleu
Torelló
Cardona
Súria
MANRESA
Palafrugell
Palamós
St. Feliu de Guíxols
Lloret de Mar
Tossa de Mar
Blanes
Malgrat de Mar
Pineda de M.
Calella
Arenys de Mar
MATARÓ
Premià de Mar
El Masnou
BADALONA
ST. COLOMA D. G.
BARCELONA
HOSPITALET DE LLOBREGAT
EL PRAT DE LLOBREGAT
CORNELLA
TERRASSA / TARRASA
SABADELL
Granollers
Mollet
St. Cugat
Rubí
Martorell
Igualada
Vilafranca del Penedès
Castelldefels
Sitges
Vilanova i la Geltrú
El Vendrell
Costa Dorada
Costa Brava
Marseille
Génova
A
B

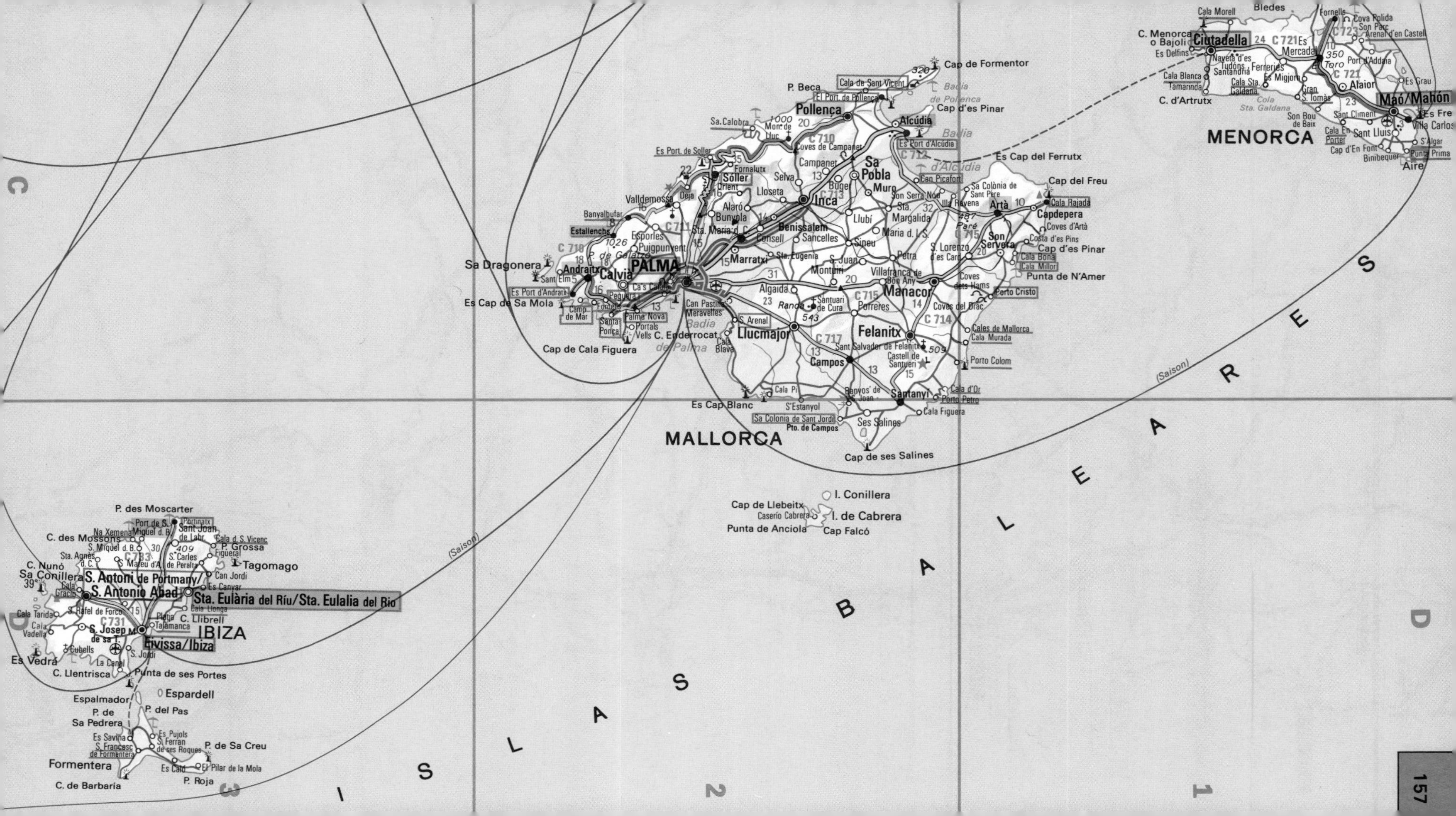
ISLAS BALEARES
MALLORCA
MENORCA
IBIZA
PALMA
Ciutadella
Maó/Mahón
Alaior
Es Mercadal
Ferreries
Es Migjorn Gran
Sant Lluís
Sant Climent
Fornells
C. d'Artrutx
C. Menorca o Bajolí
Cala Morell
Bledes
Sa Dragonera
Andratx
Calvià
Estallenchs
Banyalbufar
Valldemossa
Deià
Sóller
Es Port. de Sóller
Sa Calobra
Pollença
El Port. de Pollença
Cala de Sant Vicent
P. Beca
Cap de Formentor
Cap d'es Pinar
Alcúdia
Es Port d'Alcúdia
Badia d'Alcúdia
Es Cap del Ferrutx
Cap del Freu
Cala Rajada
Capdepera
Artà
Son Servera
Cap d'es Pinar
Punta de N'Amer
Porto Cristo
Manacor
Felanitx
Porto Colom
Santanyí
Cala Figuera
Cap de ses Salines
Ses Salines
Campos
Llucmajor
S. Arenal
Es Cap Blanc
Inca
Sa Pobla
Muro
Binissalem
Sineu
Petra
Algaida
Randa
Marratxí
Bunyola
Alaró
Lloseta
Selva
Campanet
Esporles
Puigpunyent
Es Port d'Andratx
Es Cap de Sa Mola
Cap de Cala Figuera
Palma Nova
Badia de Palma
I. Conillera
I. de Cabrera
Cap de Llebeitx
Punta de Anciola
Cap Falcó
P. des Moscarter
C. des Mossons
C. Nunó
Sa Conillera
S. Antoni de Portmany/S. Antonio Abad
Sta. Eulària del Riu/Sta. Eulalia del Río
Eivissa/Ibiza
Tagomago
P. Grossa
Es Vedrà
C. Llentrisca
Punta de ses Portes
Espardell
Espalmador
P. del Pas
P. de Sa Pedrera
P. de Sa Creu
Formentera
C. de Barbaría
P. Roja
Es Pujols
El Pilar de la Mola
(Saison)
C 710
C 711
C 712
C 713
C 714
C 715
C 717
C 719
C 721
C 731
C 733
C

Viana do Castelo — Braga — Guimarães — Vila Real — Chaves — Verín

Barcelos — Póvoa de Varzim — Vila do Conde — Porto — Vila Nova de Gaia

Amarante — Lamego — Régua — Moimenta da Beira — Sernancelhe

Espinho — S. João da Madeira — Ovar — Oliveira de Azeméis — Aveiro — Águeda — Viseu — Mangualde — Guarda — Celorico da Beira

Ílhavo — Mira — Cantanhede — Coimbra — Seia — Covilhã — Fundão

Figueira da Foz — Pombal — Lousã — Góis — Pampilhosa — Castelo Branco

Leiria — Batalha — Fátima — Sertã — Proença a Nova — Vila Velha de Ródão

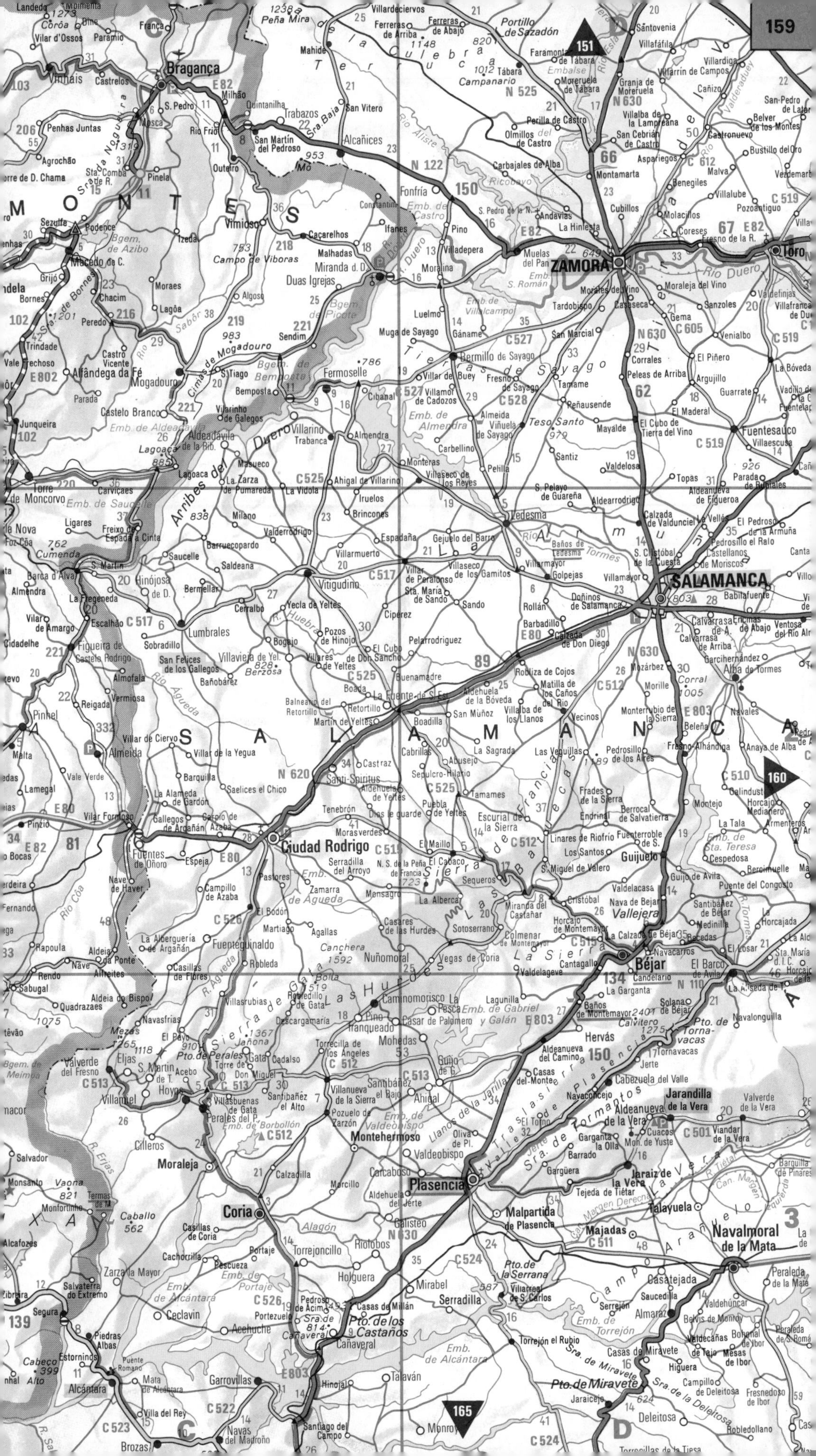
Bragança
Vinhais
Castrelos
França
Paramio
Vilar d'Ossos
Corôa
Milhão
Quintanilha
Trabazos
San Vitero
Alcañices
San Martín del Pedroso
Penhas Juntas
Agrochão
Pinela
Outeiro
Rio Frio
Peña Mira
Villardeciervos
Ferreras de Arriba
Ferreras de Abajo
Mahide
Sierra de la Culebra
Portillo de Sazadón
Tábara
Campanario
Faramontanos de Tábara
Santovenia
Villafáfila
Moreruela de Tábara
Granja de Moreruela
Perilla de Castro
Olmillos de Castro
Villalba de la Lampreana
San Cebrián de Castro
Villardiga
Villarrín de Campos
Cañizo
Castronuevo
San Pedro de Latarce
Belver de los Montes
Bustillo del Oro
Asperiegos
Malva
Vezdemarbán
Montamarta
Carbajales de Alba
Ricobayo
Benegiles
Villalube
Pozoantiguo
Fonfría
Emb. del Castro
Constantim
MONTES
Podence
Macedo de C.
Vimioso
Izeda
Caçarelhos
Ifanes
Pino
Villadepera
S. Pedro de la N.
Andavías
La Hiniesta
Cubillos
Molacillos
Coreses
Fresno de la R.
Toro
Campo de Viboras
Malhadas
Miranda d. D.
Duas Igrejas
Moralina
Muelas del Pan
ZAMORA
Emb. S. Román
Moraleja del Vino
Morales del Vino
Valdefinjas
Villafranca de Duero
Bornes
Grijó
Chacim
Moraes
Algoso
Lagoa
Peredo
Sabor
Sendim
Luelmo
Emb. de Villalcampo
Tardobispo
Casaseca
Gema
Sanzoles
Trindade
Vale Frechoso
Alfândega da Fé
Castro Vicente
Mogadouro
Cimas de Mogadouro
S. Tiago
Bemposta
Bgem. de Bemposta
Bgem. de Picote
Fermoselle
Muga de Sayago
Gáname
Bermillo de Sayago
San Marcial
Corrales
Venialbo
El Piñero
La Bóveda
Parada
Castelo Branco
Vilarinho de Galegos
Villar del Buey
Cibanal
Villamor de Cadozos
Fresno de Sayago
Tamame
Peleas de Arriba
Argujillo
Guarrate
Vadillo de la Guareña
Fuentelapeña
Junqueira
Emb. de Aldeadávila
Aldeadávila de la Rib.
Villarino
Trabanca
Almendra
Emb. de Almendra
Almeida
Viñuela de Sayago
Teso Santo
Peñausende
Mayalde
El Maderal
El Cubo de Tierra del Vino
Fuentesaúco
Villaescusa
Lagoaça
Masueco
Carbellino
Santiz
Valdelosa
Topas
Parada de Rubiales
Torre de Moncorvo
Carviçaes
Emb. de Saucelle
Lagoaca de Pumareda
La Zarza de Pumareda
La Vídola
Ahigal de Villarino
Monteras
Villaseco de los Reyes
Pelilla
S. Pelayo de Guareña
Aldearrodrigo
Aldeanueva de Figueroa
Iruelos
Brincones
Ledesma
Calzada de Valdunciel
La Vellés
El Pedroso de la Armuña
Pedrosillo el Ralo
Castellanos de Moriscos
Ligares
Freixo de Espada à Cinta
Arribes del Duero
Milano
Valderrodrigo
Espadaña
Gejuelo del Barro
Baños de Ledesma
S. Cristóbal de la Cuesta
Cumeda
Barruecopardo
Villarmuerto
Villarmayor
Saucelle
Saldeana
Vitigudino
Villar de Peralonso
Villaseco de los Gamitos
Golpejas
Villamayor
SALAMANCA
Babilafuente
Barca d'Alva
S. Martin
Hinojosa de D.
La Fregeneda
Bermellar
Cerralbo
Yecla de Yeltes
Sta. María de Sando
Sando
Doñinos de Salamanca
Almendra
Vilar de Amargo
Escalhão
Lumbrales
Ciperez
Rollán
Calvarrasa de A.
Encinas de Abajo
Ventosa del Río Almar
Sobradillo
Pozos de Hinojo
Pelarrodríguez
Barbadillo
Calzada de Don Diego
Calvarrasa de Arriba
Cidadelhe
Figueira de Castelo Rodrigo
San Felices de los Gallegos
Villavieja de Yel.
Bogajo
Villares de Yeltes
El Cubo de Don Sancho
Mozárbez
Garcihernández
Alba de Tormes
Almofala
Bañobárez
Berzosa
Buenamadre
Robliza de Cojos
Matilla de los Caños del Río
Morille
Corral
Vermiosa
Boada
Aldehuela de la Bóveda
Villalba de los Llanos
Monterrubio de la Sierra
Pinhel
Reigada
Balneario del Retortillo
Retortillo
La Fuente de S. Esteban
San Muñoz
Vecinos
Beleña
Navales
Martín de Yeltes
Boadilla
Villar de Ciervo
Villar de la Yegua
SALAMANCA
Malta
Almeida
Castraz
Cabrillas
Abusejo
La Sagrada
Las Veguillas
Pedrosillo de los Aires
Fresno-Alhándiga
Anaya de Alba
Vale Verde
Barquilla
Santi-Spíritus
Sepulcro-Hilario
Galindustе
Lamegal
Saelices el Chico
Aldehuela de Yeltes
Tamames
Frades de la Sierra
Horcajo Medianero
Montejo
La Alameda de Gardón
Tenebrón
Dios le guarde
Puebla de Yeltes
Escurial de la Sierra
Endrinal
Berrocal de Salvatierra
La Tala
Armenteros
Pinzio
Vilar Formoso
Gallegos de Argañán
Carpio de Azaba
Morasverdes
Linares de Riofrío
Fuenterroble de S.
Emb. de Sta. Teresa
Ciudad Rodrigo
El Maíllo
Los Santos
Guijuelo
Cespedosa
Fuentes de Oñoro
Espeja
Serradilla del Arroyo
N. S. de la Peña de Francia
El Cabaco
Sierra de Francia
S. Miguel de Valero
Bercimuelle
Nave de Haver
Pastores
Zamarra
Campillo de Azaba
Emb. de Águeda
Monsagro
La Alberca
Sequeros
Valdelacasa
Nava de Béjar
Guijo de Ávila
Puente del Congosto
Vallejera
Santibáñez de Béjar
El Bodón
Martiago
Agallas
Casares de las Hurdes
Sotoserrano
Miranda del Castañar
Cristóbal
Medinilla
La Horcajada
Las Batuecas
La Albergueria de Argañán
Fuenteguinaldo
Horcajo de Montemayor
Colmenar de Montemayor
La Calzada de Béjar
Becedas
El Losar
Aldeia da Ponte
Nave
Alfaiates
Robleda
Canchera
Nuñomoral
Vegas de Coria
La Sierra
Cantagallo
Béjar
Navacarros
El Barco de Ávila
Sta. María d. I. C.
Casillas de Flores
Valdelagеve
Candelario
Horcajo de las Torres
Rendo
Sabugal
Aldeia do Bispo
Villasrubias
Bolla
Robledillo de Gata
Las Hurdes
Caminomorisco
La Pesca
Emb. de Gabriel y Galán
Lagunilla
La Garganta
Baños de Montemayor
Solana de Béjar
La Aliseda de T.
Navalonguilla
Quadrazaes
Descargamaría
Pino franqueado
Casar de Palomero
Calvitero
Pto. de Tornavacas
Navasfrías
Sierra de Gata
Jañona
Mohedas
Hervás
Mezas
El Payo
Torrecilla de los Ángeles
Aldeanueva del Camino
Tornavacas
Valverde del Fresno
Eljas
S. Martín de T.
Pto. de Perales
Gata
Cadalso
Guijo de G.
Jerte
Acebo
Don Miguel
Casas del Monte
Cabezuela del Valle
Villamiel
Hoyos
Santibáñez el Bajo
Santibáñez el Alto
Villanueva de la Sierra
Ahigal
Navaconcejo
Jarandilla de la Vera
Valverde de la Vera
Villasbuenas de Gata
Perales del P.
Pozuelo de Zarzón
Emb. de Valdeobispo
Emb. de Borbollón
Llanos de la Jarilla
Valle del Jerte
Aldeanueva de la Vera
Viandar de la Vera
Cilleros
Montehermoso
El Torno
Oliva de Pl.
Cuacos
Mon. de Yuste
Salvador
Moraleja
Valdeobispo
Sra. de Tormantos
Garganta la Olla
Barrado
Calzadilla
Gargüera
Jaraíz de la Vera
Barquilla de Pinares
Monsanto
Vaona
Marcillo
Carcaboso
Plasencia
Tejeda de Tiétar
La Vera
Termas de M.
Monfortinho
Caballo
Coria
Aldehuela del Jerte
Malpartida de Plasencia
Can. Margen Derecha
Talayuela
Galisteo
Majadas
Navalmoral de la Mata
Alcafozes
Casillas de Coria
Alagón
Riolobos
Campo Arañuelo
Cachorrilla
Pescueza
Portaje
Torrejoncillo
Pto. de la Serrana
Peraleda de la Mata
Zarza la Mayor
Emb. de Portaje
Holguera
Casatejada
Salvaterra do Extremo
Emb. de Alcántara
Mirabel
Villarreal de S. Carlos
Serrejón
Saucedilla
Valdehúncar
Zebreira
Segura
Ceclavín
Pedroso de Acim
Portezuelo
Sra. de
Casas de Millán
Pto. de los Castaños
Serradilla
Almaraz
Emb. de Torrejón
Belvís de Monroy
Peraleda de S. Román
Acehúche
Cañaveral
Valdecañas de Tajo
Bohonal de Ibor
Piedras Albas
Estorninos
Puente Romano
Emb. de Alcántara
Torrejón el Rubio
Sra. de Miravete
Casas de Miravete
Mesas de Ibor
Cabeço Alto
Higuera
Alcántara
Mata de Alcántara
Garrovillas
Hinojal
Talaván
Pto. de Miravete
Sra. de la Deleitosa
Campillo de Deleitosa
Fresnedoso de Ibor
Villa del Rey
Jaraicejo
Deleitosa
Brozas
Navas del Madroño
Santiago del Campo
Monroy
Robledollano
Torrecillas de la Tiesa
151
160
165

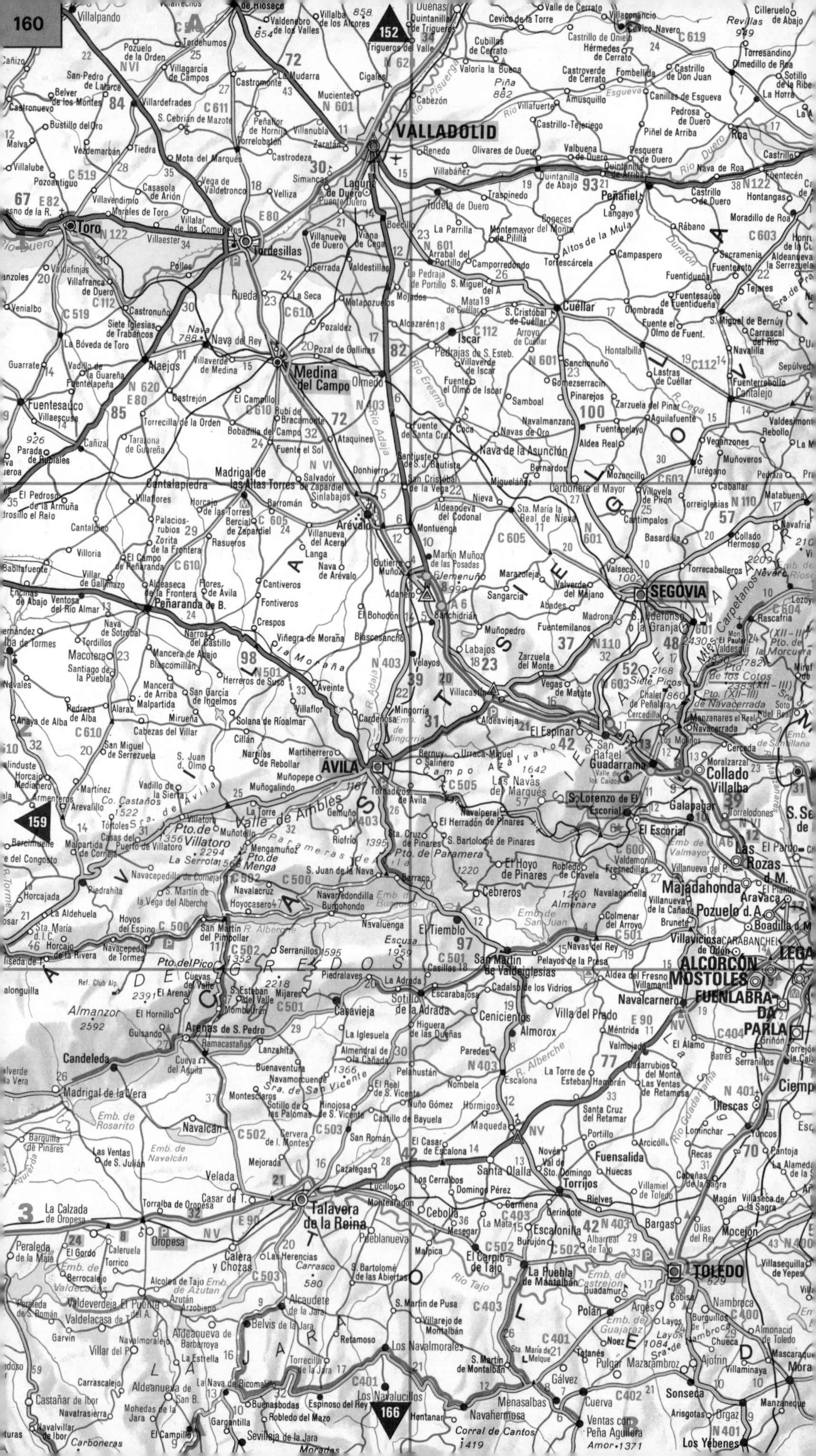

152
159
166
VALLADOLID
SEGOVIA
ÁVILA
TOLEDO
Tordesillas
Toro
Medina del Campo
Arévalo
Peñafiel
Cuéllar
Iscar
Olmedo
Peñaranda de B.
Madrigal de las Altas Torres
Talavera de la Reina
Torrijos
Collado Villalba
Guadarrama
S. Lorenzo de El Escorial
El Escorial
Majadahonda
Las Rozas
Pozuelo d. A.
Aravaca
Boadilla d. M.
ALCORCÓN
MÓSTOLES
FUENLABRADA
PARLA
Navalcarnero
Illescas
Arenas de S. Pedro
Candeleda
Oropesa
Sonseca
Mora
La Calzada de Oropesa
Madrigal de la Vera
San Martín de Valdeiglesias
Cebreros
El Tiembla
Villacastín
Nava del Rey
Alaejos
Fuentesaúco
Simancas
Laguna de Duero
Cantalejo
Turégano
Sta. María la Real de Nieva
Nava de la Asunción
Coca
Rueda
Valle de Amblés
Sierra de Gredos
Almanzor
2592
Campo Azálvaro
Río Duero
Río Tajo
Río Alberche
Río Eresma
Río Adaja
Río Pisuerga

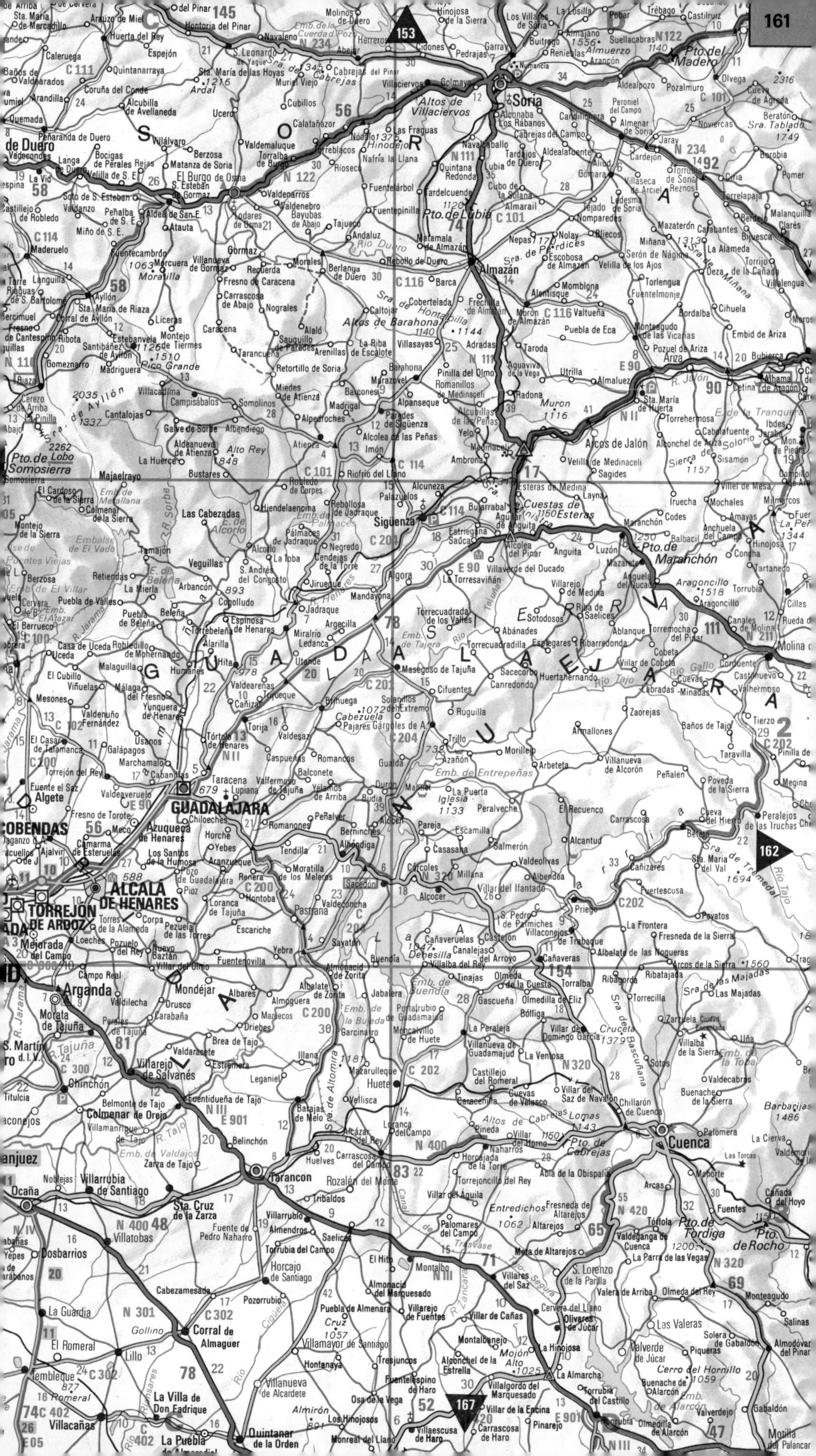

SORIA

GUADALAJARA

CUENCA

ALCALA DE HENARES

TORREJON DE ARDOZ

ARGANDA

Almazán

Sigüenza

Molina

Tarancón

153

162

167

90

2

17

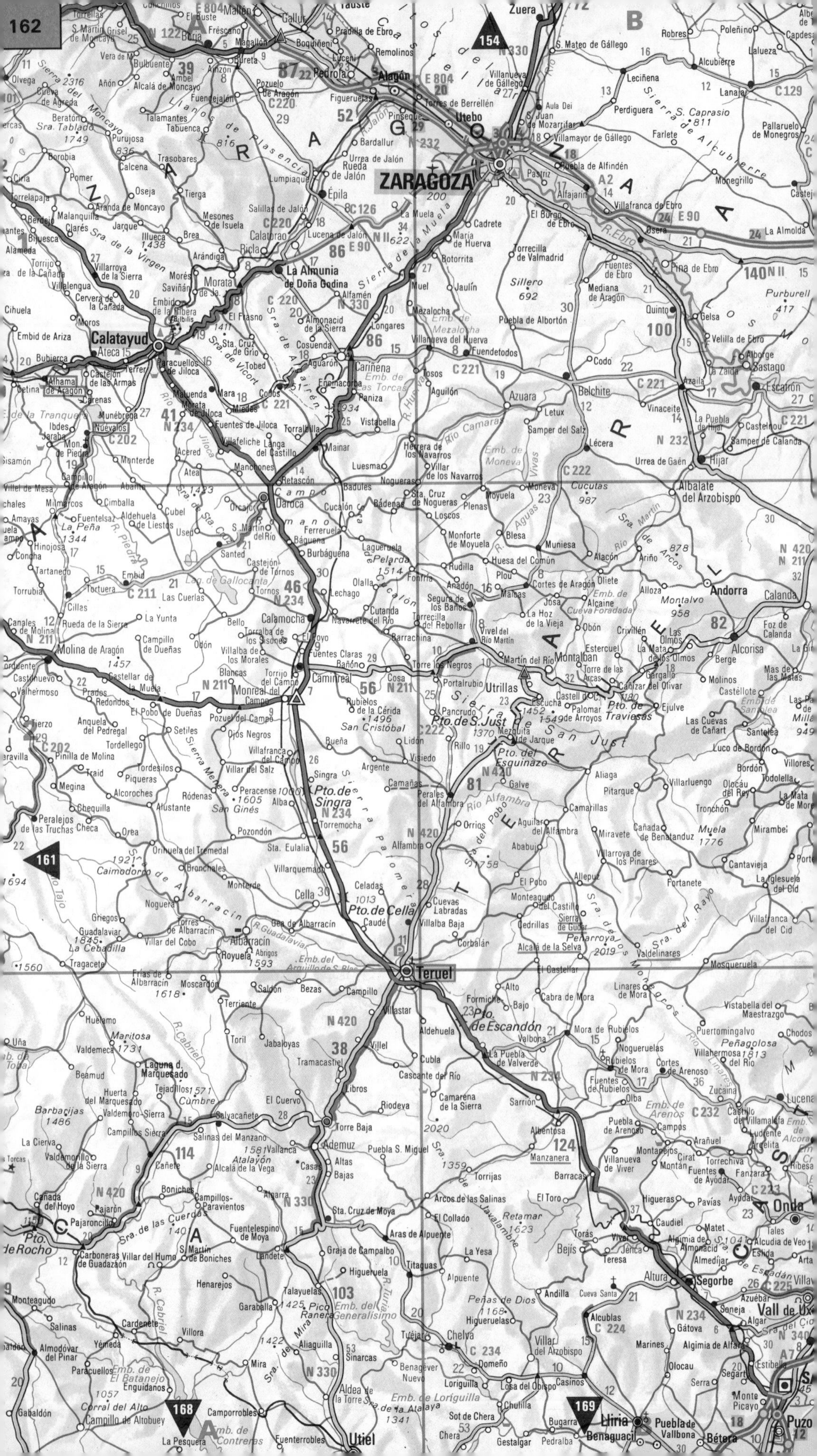

162
A
B
154
Zuera
Tauste
Mallén
Gallur
Pradilla de Ebro
Boquiñeni
Remolinos
Borja
Fréscano
Magallón
Tarazona
Vera de Moncayo
Bulbuente
Ainzón
Añón
Alcalá de Moncayo
Olvega
Cueva de Agreda
Sierra del Moncayo
2316
Pedrola
Alagón
Figueruelas
Pozuelo de Aragón
Fuendejalón
Talamantes
Tabuenca
Beratón
Sra. Tablado
1749
Purujosa
Borobia
Calcena
Trasobares
Pomer
Llanos de Plasencia
Torres de Berrellén
Pinseque
Utebo
Bardallur
Urrea de Jalón
Rueda de Jalón
Lumpiaque
Épila
ZARAGOZA
S. Mateo de Gállego
Villanueva de Gállego
Aula Dei
S. Juan de Mozarrifar
Villamayor de Gállego
Puebla de Alfindén
Pastriz
Alfajarín
Villafranca de Ebro
Leciñena
Perdiguera
Farlete
Sierra de Alcubierre
S. Caprasio
811
Robres
Alcubierre
Poleñino
Lalueza
Lanaja
Capdesaso
Pallaruelo de Monegros
Monegrillo
La Almolda
Castejón de Monegros
Oseja
Tierga
Aranda de Moncayo
Malanquilla
Clarés
Jarque
Mesones de Isuela
Illueca
1438
Brea
Salillas de Jalón
Calatorao
Lucena de Jalón
La Muela
Ricla
Arándiga
Morata de Jalón
Morés
Saviñán
La Almunia de Doña Godina
Sierra de la Muela
Cadrete
María de Huerva
Botorrita
Jaulín
El Burgo de Ebro
Osera
Torrecilla de Valmadrid
Fuentes de Ebro
Pina de Ebro
Mediana de Aragón
Sillero
692
Quinto
Gelsa
Velilla de Ebro
Purburell
417
Berdejo
Bijuesca
Alameda
Torrijo
Villarroya de la Sierra
Sra. de la Virgen
Villalengua
Cervera de la Cañada
Cihuela
Moros
Embid de Ariza
Calatayud
Ateca
Embid de la Ribera
Bilbilis
El Frasno
1411
Sra. de Vicort
Sta. Cruz de Grío
Tobed
Alfamén
Almonacid de la Sierra
Cosuenda
Aguarón
Cariñena
Encinacorba
Paniza
Codos
Muel
Mezalocha
Emb. de Mezalocha
Longares
Villanueva del Huerva
Fuendetodos
Puebla de Albortón
Codo
Belchite
Azuara
Tosos
Aguilón
Emb. de las Torcas
Bubierca
Terrer
Castejón de las Armas
Cetina
Alhama de Aragón
Carenas
Munébrega
Paracuellos de Jiloca
Maluenda
Morata de Jiloca
Mara
Miedes
Fuentes de Jiloca
Villafeliche
Langa del Castillo
Torralbilla
Vistabella
Mainar
Azaila
La Zaida
Sástago
Alborge
Escatrón
Vinaceite
La Puebla de Híjar
Castelnou
Samper de Calanda
Híjar
Urrea de Gaén
Letux
Samper del Salz
Lécera
Emb. de la Tranquera
Ibdes
Jaraba
Nuévalos
Mon. de Piedra
Monterde
Acered
Atea
Manchones
Retascón
Luesma
Herrera de los Navarros
Villar de los Navarros
Río Cámaras
Emb. de Moneva
Moneva
Cucutas
987
Albalate del Arzobispo
Sisamón
Campillo de Aragón
Abanto
Cimballa
Villel de Mesa
Milmarcos
Fuentelsaz
La Peña
1344
Hinojosa
Tartanedo
Aldehuela de Liestos
Cubel
Used
Orcajo
Daroca
Campo Romano
S. Martín del Río
Báguena
Burbáguena
Badules
Cucalón
Ferreruela
Nogueras
Bádenas
Sta. Cruz de Nogueras
Loscos
Plenas
Moyuela
Monforte de Moyuela
Blesa
Muniesa
Alacón
Ariño
878
Río de Arcos
Andorra
Embid
Tortuera
Lag. de Gallocanta
Santed
Castejón de Tornos
Tornos
Lagueruela
Pelarda
1514
Fonfría
Rudilla
Huesa del Común
Plou
Anadón
Segura de los Baños
Maicas
Cortes de Aragón
Oliete
Alloza
Josa
Emb. de Alcaine
Cueva Foradada
Montalvo
958
Calanda
Torrubia
Cillas
Las Cuerlas
Lechago
Olalla
Cutanda
Calamocha
Navarrete del Río
Torrecilla del Rebollar
La Hoz de la Vieja
Obón
Crivillén
Alcorisa
Foz de Calanda
Canales de Molina
Rueda de la Sierra
La Yunta
Bello
Torralba de los Sisones
El Poyo
Barrachina
Vivel del Río Martín
Estercuel
La Mata de los Olmos
Las Olmos
Molina de Aragón
1457
Campillo de Dueñas
Odón
Villalba de los Morales
Fuentes Claras
Bañón
Torre los Negros
Martín del Río
Montalbán
Berge
Castellar de la Muela
Blancas
Torrijo del Campo
Caminreal
Cosa
Portalrubio
Utrillas
Torre de las Arcas
Gargallo
Cañizar del Olivar
Mas de las Matas
Castilnuevo
Valhermoso
Prados Redondos
El Pobo de Dueñas
Monreal del Campo
Rubielos de la Cérida
1496
San Cristóbal
Pancrudo
Pto. de S. Just
Sierra de San Just
Escucha
1452
Palomar de Arroyos
1549
Castell de Cabra
Pto. de Traviesas
Ejulve
Molinos
Castellote
Tierzo
Anquela del Pedregal
Pozuel del Campo
Setiles
Ojos Negros
Bueña
Lidón
Visiedo
Rillo
1370
Mezquita de Jarque
Pto. del Esquinazo
Las Cuevas de Cañart
Santolea
Luco de Bordón
Bordón
Tordellego
Pinilla de Molina
Traid
Megina
Tordesilos
Piqueras
Alcoroches
Alustante
Sierra Menera
Villafranca del Campo
Villar del Salz
Peracense
1605
San Ginés
Ródenas
Alba
Singra
Pto. de Singra
Sierra Palomera
Argente
Camañas
Perales del Alfambra
Galve
Aliaga
Pitarque
Villarluengo
Olocau del Rey
Tronchón
Todolella
Villores
Chequilla
Peralejos de las Truchas
Checa
Orea
Pozondón
Torremocha
Sta. Eulalia
Alfambra
Orrios
Río Alfambra
Aguilar del Alfambra
Camarillas
Miravete
Cañada de Benatanduz
Muela
1776
Mirambel
161
Caimodorro
1921
Orihuela del Tremedal
Bronchales
Monterde
Villarquemado
Celadas
Sierra del Pobo
1758
Ababuj
El Pobo
Villarroya de los Pinares
Allepuz
Fortanete
Cantavieja
La Iglesuela del Cid
Sra. de Albarracín
Noguera
Griegos
Guadalaviar
1845
La Cebadilla
Villar del Cobo
Torres de Albarracín
Gea de Albarracín
Albarracín
Royuela
Cella
1013
Pto. de Cella
Caudé
Cuevas Labradas
Villalba Baja
Corbalán
Monteagudo del Castillo
Sierra de Gúdar
Cedrillas
Alcalá de la Selva
Peñarroya
2019
Valdelinares
Sra. del Rayo
Villafranca del Cid
Tragacete
1560
1593
Abrigos
Emb. del Arquillo de S. Blas
Teruel
El Castellar
Mosqueruela
Frías de Albarracín
1618
Moscardón
Saldón
Bezas
Campillo
Alto
Bajo
Formiche
Cabra de Mora
Linares de Mora
Vistabella del Maestrazgo
Terriente
Villastar
Aldehuela
Pto. de Escandón
Valbona
Mora de Rubielos
Nogueruelas
Puertomingalvo
Peñagolosa
1813
Chodos
Huélamo
Maritosa
1731
Valdemeca
Uña
R. Cabriel
Toril
Jabaloyas
Villel
Cubla
La Puebla de Valverde
Rubielos de Mora
Cortes de Arenoso
Villahermosa del Río
Beamud
Laguna d. Marquesado
Tejadillos
1571
Cumbre
Tramacastiel
Cascante del Río
Fuentes de Rubielos
Zucaina
Huerta del Marquesado
Valdemoro-Sierra
Barbacijas
1486
El Cuervo
Libros
Riodeva
Camarena de la Sierra
2020
Sarrión
Olba
Emb. de Arenós
Castillo de Villamalefa
Lucena
Salvacañete
Campillos Sierra
Torre Baja
Ademuz
Puebla S. Miguel
Albentosa
Puebla de Arenoso
Campos
Ludiente
Argelita
La Cierva
Valdemorillo de la Sierra
Salinas del Manzano
1581
Vallanca
Atalayón
Alcalá de la Vega
Casas Altas
Casas Bajas
1359
Sra. de Javalambre
Torrijas
Manzanera
Villanueva de Viver
Montanejos
Montán
Cirat
Fuentes de Ayódar
Torrechiva
Arañuel
Fanzara
Ribesalbes
Cañete
Boniches
Campillos-Paravientos
Algarra
Arcos de las Salinas
El Toro
Barracas
Higueras
Pavías
Ayódar
Onda
Cañada del Hoyo
Pajarón
Pajaroncillo
Sra. de las Cuerdas
Fuentelespino de Moya
Sta. Cruz de Moya
El Collado
Retamar
1623
Caudiel
Matet
Tales
Alcudia de Veo
Carboneras de Guadazaón
Villar del Humo
S. Martín de Boniches
Landete
Graja de Campalbo
Aras de Alpuente
Titaguas
La Yesa
Torás
Bejís
Viver
Jérica
Teresa
Algimia de Almonacid
Almedíjar
Eslida
Artana
Henarejos
Higueruela
Alpuente
Altura
Segorbe
Monteagudo
Garaballa
Talayuelas
1425
Pico Ranera
Emb. del Generalísimo
103
Peñas de Dios
1168
Higueruelas
Andilla
Cueva Santa
Azuébar
Soneja
Vall de Uxó
Salinas
Cardenete
Yémeda
Villora
1422
Aliaguilla
Tuéjar
Chelva
Alcublas
Villar del Arzobispo
Gátova
Algimia de Alfara
Algar
Almodóvar del Pinar
Paracuellos
Emb. de El Batanejo
Enguídanos
Mira
Sinarcas
Benagéver
Nuevo
Loriguilla
Domeño
Losa del Obispo
Casinos
Marines
Olocau
Estivella
Segart
Serra
1057
Corral del Alto
Campillo de Altobuey
168
Camporrobles
Aldea de la Torre
Emb. de Loriguilla
Sra. de la Atalaya
1341
Chulilla
169
Monte Picayo
Gabaldón
La Pesquera
Emb. de Contreras
Fuenterrobles
Utiel
Sot de Chera
Chera
Gestalgar
Bugarra
Pedralba
Lliria
Benaguacil
Puebla de Vallbona
Bétera
Puzol
ARAGON
TERUEL
CASTELLON
N 122
N 330
N 232
N II
N 211
N 234
N 420
N 340
E 804
E 90
A2
A7
C 220
C 221
C 222
C 224
C 225
C 232
C 234
C 202
C 211
C 126
C 129
C 223

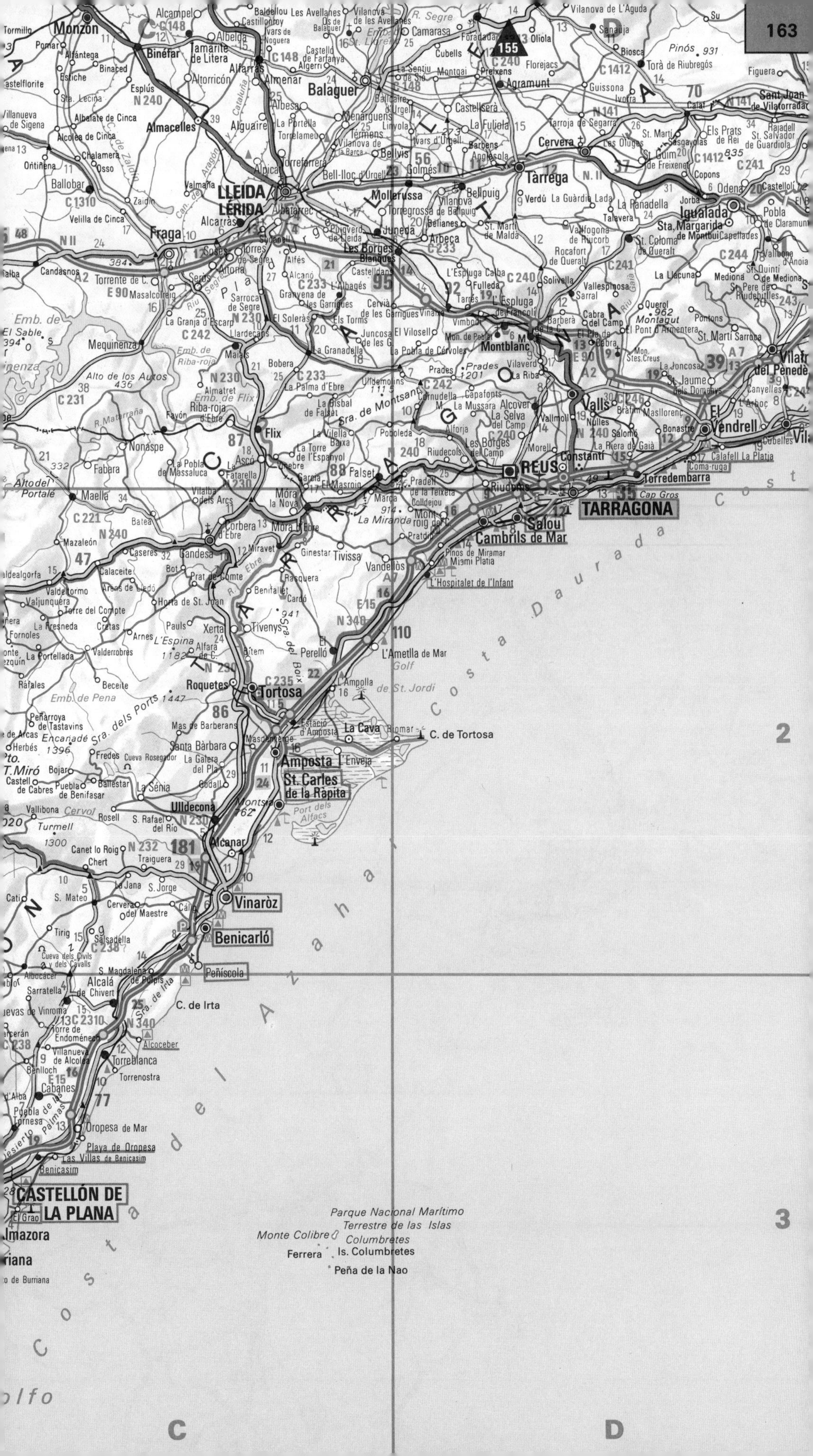

Monzón
Binéfar
Tamarite de Litera
Balaguer
Agramunt
Cervera
Tàrrega
Mollerussa
LLEIDA
LÉRIDA
Fraga
Alcarràs
Almacelles
Les Borges Blanques
Igualada
Sta. Margarida de Montbui
Capellades
Montblanc
Valls
El Vendrell
REUS
TARRAGONA
Salou
Cambrils de Mar
Torredembarra
Mequinenza
Flix
Falset
Móra la Nova
Móra d'Ebre
Gandesa
Maella
Tortosa
Roquetes
Amposta
St. Carles de la Ràpita
Ulldecona
Alcanar
Vinaròz
Benicarló
Peñíscola
C. de Irta
C. de Tortosa
L'Ametlla de Mar
L'Hospitalet de l'Infant
Alcalá de Chivert
Torreblanca
Oropesa de Mar
Benicasim
CASTELLÓN DE LA PLANA
El Grao
Almazora
Costa Daurada
Costa del Azahar
Parque Nacional Marítimo Terrestre de las Islas Columbretes
Monte Colibre
Ferrera
Is. Columbretes
Peña de la Nao
Golfo
C
D
2
3

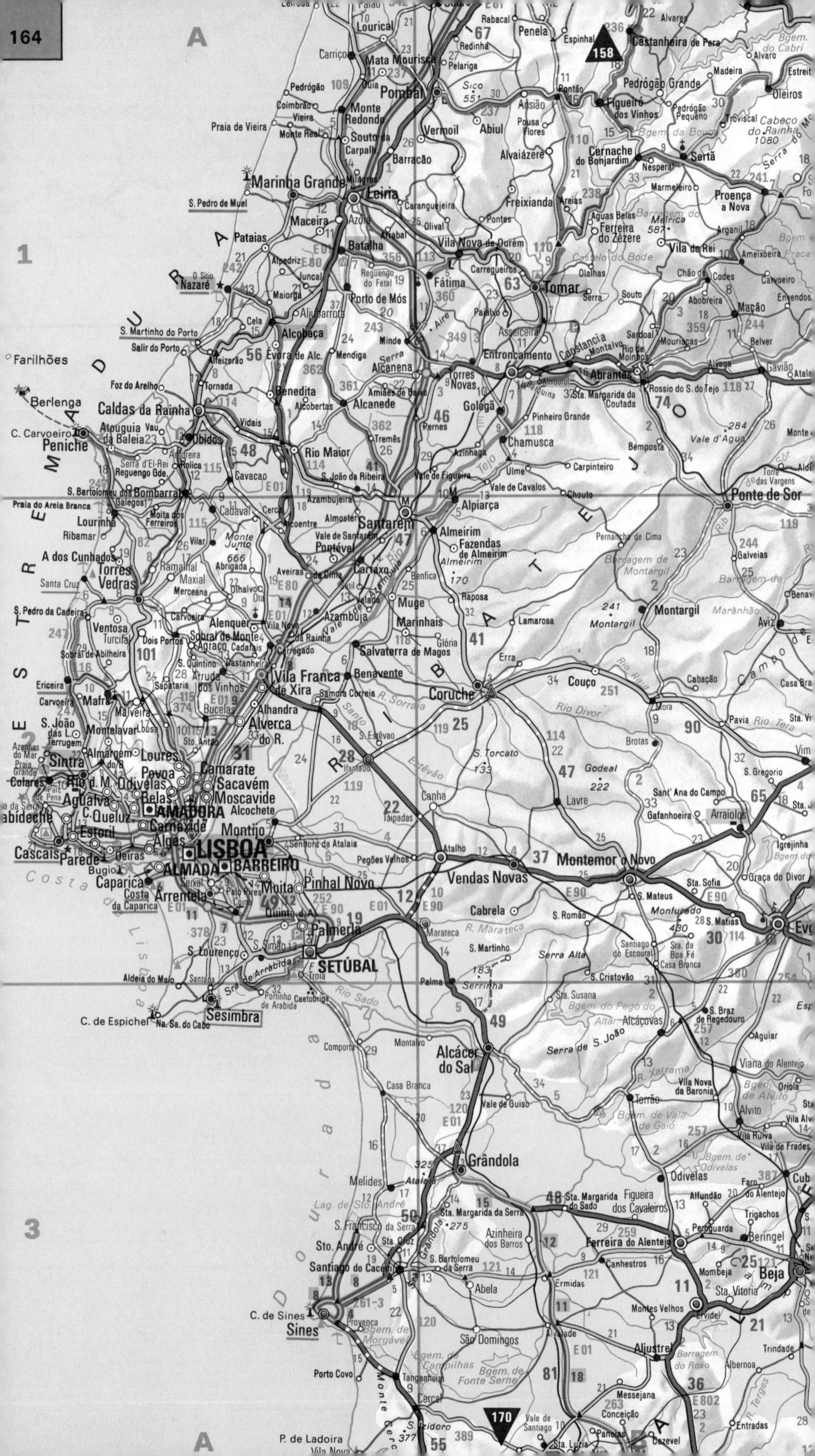
A
1
2
3
158
170
Lourical
Mata Mourisca
Pombal
Carriço
Pedrógão
Monte Redondo
Praia de Vieira
Monte Real
Souto da Carpalh.
Marinha Grande
S. Pedro de Muel
Leiria
Maceira
Batalha
Pataias
Nazaré
Alcobaça
Porto de Mós
S. Martinho do Porto
Salir do Porto
Farilhões
Berlenga
Caldas da Rainha
Peniche
C. Carvoeiro
Atouguia da Baleia
Óbidos
Rio Maior
Bombarral
Lourinhã
Torres Vedras
A dos Cunhados
Santa Cruz
Ericeira
Mafra
Sintra
Colares
Cascais
Estoril
Parede
Oeiras
Amadora
Loures
Odivelas
Sacavém
Moscavide
Alcochete
Montijo
LISBOA
Almada
Barreiro
Caparica
Costa da Caparica
Arrentela
Moita
Pinhal Novo
Palmela
SETÚBAL
Sesimbra
C. de Espichel
Troia
Alverca do R.
Vila Franca de Xira
Alhandra
Alenquer
Azambuja
Cartaxo
Santarém
Almeirim
Alpiarça
Benavente
Salvaterra de Magos
Coruche
Muge
Marinhais
Torres Novas
Golegã
Chamusca
Entroncamento
Tomar
Fátima
Ourém
Vila Nova de Ourém
Alcanena
Constancia
Abrantes
Sertã
Figueiró dos Vinhos
Castanheira de Pera
Oleiros
Proença a Nova
Vila de Rei
Mação
Ponte de Sor
Montargil
Mora
Avis
Arraiolos
Montemor o Novo
Vendas Novas
Évora
Alcácer do Sal
Grândola
Melides
Santiago do Cacém
Sines
C. de Sines
Porto Covo
Cercal
Ferreira do Alentejo
Beja
Aljustrel
Alvito
Viana do Alentejo
Alcáçovas
Torrão
Odivelas
Beringel
Messejana
Serra de Arrábida
Rio Sado
Costa de Lisboa
Costa Dourada
ESTREMADURA
RIBATEJO

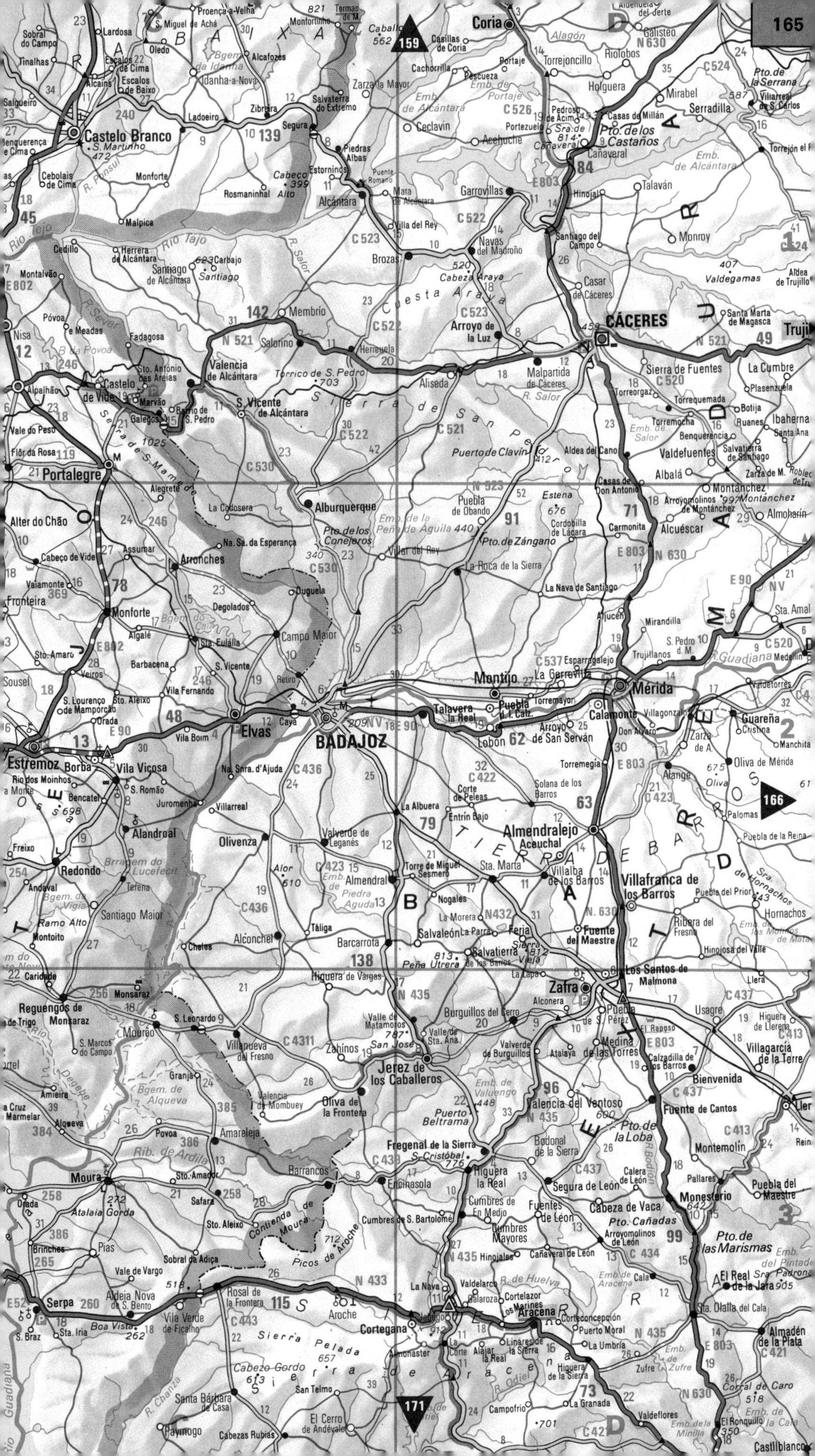

Proença-a-Velha
Termas de M.
Coria
Galisteo
Sobral do Campo
Lardosa
S. Miguel de Aché
Monfortinho
Caballo
159
Casillas de Coria
Alagón
N 630
Tinalhas
Oledo
Alcafozes
Portaje
Torrejoncillo
Riolobos
Escalos de Cima
Escalos de Baixo
Idanha-a-Nova
Cachorrilla
Pescueza
Holguera
Pto. de la Serrana
Alcains
Zarza la Mayor
Emb. de Portaje
Mirabel
Villarreal de S. Carlos
Salvaterra do Extremo
Emb. de Alcántara
C 526
Casas de Millán
Serradilla
Castelo Branco
S. Martinho
Ladoeiro
Zibreira
Segura
Ceclavín
Pedroso de Acím
Pto. de los Castaños
Benquerença
Portezuelo
Sra. de
Acehuche
Cañaveral
Torrejón el R.
Piedras Albas
Cebolais de Cima
R. Ponsul
Monforte
Cabeço Alto
Estorninos
Puente Romano
84
Emb. de Alcántara
Rosmaninhal
Alcántara
Mata de Alcántara
Garrovillas
E 803
Hinojal
Talaván
Malpica
Villa del Rey
C 522
Río Tejo
Rio Tajo
Cedillo
Herrera de Alcántara
R. Salor
C 523
Navas del Madroño
Santiago del Campo
Monroy
Santiago de Alcántara
Carbajo
Santiago
Brozas
Cabeza Araya
Montalvão
E 802
Valdegamas
Aldea de Trujillo
Cuesta Araya
Casar de Cáceres
C 523
Póvoa e Meadas
R. Sever
142
Membrío
C 522
Arroyo de la Luz
CÁCERES
Santa Marta de Magasca
Nisa
Fadagosa
N 521
Salorino
Herreruela
N 521
Trujillo
12
B. da Póvoa
246
Sto. António das Areias
Valencia de Alcántara
Malpartida de Cáceres
Sierra de Fuentes
La Cumbre
Alpalhão
Castelo de Vide
Marvão
Torrico de S. Pedro
Aliseda
C 520
Torreorgaz
Torrequemada
Plasenzuela
Galegos
Barrio de S. Pedro
S. Vicente de Alcántara
Sierra de San Pedro
R. Salor
Botija
Vale do Peso
C 522
C 521
Emb. de Salor
Torremocha
Ruanes
Ibahernando
Benquerencia
Santa Ana
Flôr da Rosa
119
Puerto de Clavín
Aldea del Cano
Valdefuentes
Salvatierra de Santiago
Portalegre
C 530
Zarza de M.
Robledillo de Trujillo
Alegrete
N 523
Albalá
Casas de Don Antonio
Montánchez
Alter do Chão
La Codosera
Alburquerque
Puebla de Obando
Estena
Arroyomolinos de Montánchez
Almoharín
Cordobilla de Lácara
Carmonita
Emb. de la Peña del Águila
Pto. de los Conejeros
91
Alcuéscar
Assumar
Na. Sa. da Esperança
Pto. de Zángano
71
Cabeço de Vide
Arronches
Villar del Rey
E 803
N 630
C 530
La Roca de la Sierra
Vaiamonte
E 90
NV
Fronteira
La Nava de Santiago
Ouguela
Degolados
Monforte
Aljucén
Mirandilla
Sta. Amalia
Bgem. do Caia
E 802
Sta. Eulália
Campo Maior
S. Pedro de M.
C 520
Sto. Amaro
Trujillanos
R. Guadiana
Medellín
Barbacena
S. Vicente
C 537
Esparragalejo
Sousel
Veiros
Retiro
Montijo
La Garrovilla
Mérida
Valdetorres
S. Lourenço de Mamporcão
Sto. Aleixo
Vila Fernando
Talavera la Real
Puebla de la Calzada
Torremayor
Villagonzalo
Guareña
Orada
Caya
Calamonte
Cristina
48
Elvas
BADAJOZ
E 90
Arroyo de San Serván
Don Álvaro
Zarza de A.
Manchita
Estremoz
Borba
Vila Boim
Lobón
62
Oliva de Mérida
13
Vila Viçosa
Torremegía
E 803
Alange
Rio dos Moinhos
S. Romão
C 436
C 422
Oliva
Bencatel
Na. Snra. d'Ajuda
Corte de Peleas
Solana de los Barros
Juromenha
63
166
Villarreal
La Albuera
Entrín Bajo
Palomas
Alandroal
Almendralejo
Puebla de la Reina
Olivenza
79
Aceuchal
Freixo
Valverde de Leganés
TIERRA DE BARROS
Redondo
Brragem do Lucefecit
Torre de Miguel Sesmero
Sta. Marta
Villalba de los Barros
Villafranca de los Barros
Sra. de Hornachos
254
Alor
Almendral
C 423
Emb. de Piedra Aguda
Puebla del Prior
Andaval
Terena
Nogales
Bgem. da Vigia
La Morera
N 432
Hornachos
C 436
Feria
Ribera del Fresno
Santiago Maior
Táliga
La Parra
Salvaleón
Fuente del Maestre
Ramo Alto
Montoito
Cheles
Alconchel
Barcarrota
Sierra Vieja
Salvatierra de los Barros
Peña Utrera
Hinojosa del Valle
138
La Lapa
Los Santos de Maimona
Llera
Caridade
Higuera de Vargas
Monsaraz
N 435
Zafra
256
Reguengos de Monsaraz
Alconera
Usagre
S. Leonardo
Puebla de S. Pérez
Higuera de Llerena
Valle de Matamoros
Burguillos del Cerro
El Raposo
Mourão
Valle de Sta. Ana
S. Marcos do Campo
Villanueva del Fresno
C 4311
E 803
San José
Zahínos
Valverde de Burguillos
Atalaya
Medina de las Torres
Villagarcía de la Torre
Calzadilla de los Barros
Jerez de los Caballeros
Bienvenida
Granja
Bgem. de Alqueva
Degebe
Emb. de Valuengo
96
Amieira
Valencia de Mombuey
Oliva de la Frontera
Valencia del Ventoso
C 437
Fuente de Cantos
Llerena
Marmelar
Alqueva
Puerto Beltrama
N 435
Pto. de la Loba
384
385
Povoa
386
Amareleja
C 413
Fregenal de la Sierra
Bodonal de la Sierra
Montemolín
Rib. de Ardila
S. Cristóbal
Moura
Sto. Amador
Barrancos
C 439
Higuera la Real
C 437
Calera de León
Pallares
Puebla del Maestre
258
Encinasola
Segura de León
Monesterio
Atalaia Gorda
Safara
258
Contienda de Moura
Cumbres de En Medio
Fuentes de León
Cabeza de Vaca
Orada
Sto. Aleixo
Cumbres de S. Bartolomé
Cumbres Mayores
Pto. Cañadas
Arroyomolinos de León
99
Pto. de las Marismas
386
Emb. del Pintado
Brinches
Pias
Picos de Aroche
N 435
Hinojales
Cañaveral de León
C 434
265
Sobral da Adiça
Emb. de Aracena
Cala
El Real de la Jara
Sra. Patrona
Vale de Vargo
R. de Huelva
N 433
Valdelarco
La Nava
Galaroza
Cortelazor
Los Marines
E 52
Serpa
Aldeia Nova de S. Bento
Rosal de la Frontera
115
Aroche
Aracena
Corteconcepción
Sta. Olalla del Cala
Boa Vista
Vila Verde de Ficalho
C 443
Cortegana
Jabugo
Puerto Moral
N 435
Almadén de la Plata
S. Braz
Sta. Iria
Sierra Pelada
Linares de la Sierra
La Umbría
E 803
C 421
Almonaster
La Corte
Alájar
La Real
Zufre
Emb. de Zufre
Cabezo Gordo
Sierra de Aracena
Higuera de la Sierra
73
R. Odiel
Corral de Caro
San Telmo
Santa Bárbara de Casa
171
Campofrío
La Granada
N 630
Emb. de la Cala
R. Chanza
El Cerro de Andévalo
Valdeflores
Emb. de la Minilla
El Ronquillo
Paymogo
Cabezas Rubias
Castilblanco
Guadiana

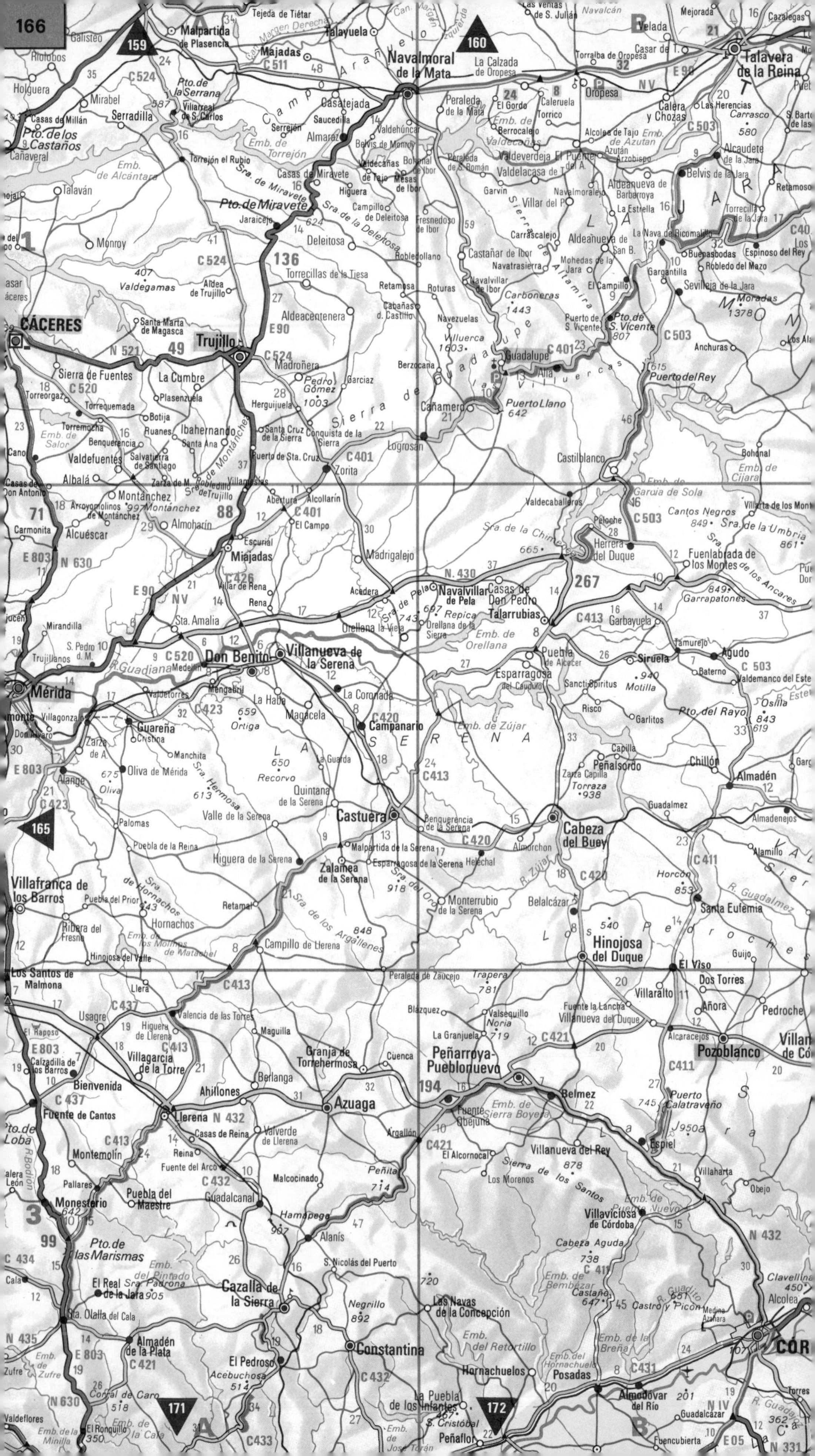

159
160
136
49
88
71
267
194
165
171
172
Malpartida de Plasencia
Tejeda de Tiétar
Talayuela
Majadas
Navalmoral de la Mata
La Calzada de Oropesa
Oropesa
Velada
Mejorada
Talavera de la Reina
Torralba de Oropesa
Casar de T.
Calera y Chozas
Las Herencias
Carrasco
Galisteo
Riolobos
Holguera
Mirabel
Serradilla
Casas de Millán
Pto. de los Castaños
Cañaveral
Pto. de la Serrana
Villarreal de S. Carlos
Campo Arañuelo
Casatejada
Saucedilla
Serrejón
Almaraz
Valdehúncar
Belvís de Monroy
Peraleda de la Mata
El Gordo
Berrocalejo
Caleruela
Torrico
Emb. de Valdecañas
Alcolea de Tajo
Azután
Emb. de Azutan
Arzobispo
Alcaudete de la Jara
Belvis de la Jara
Emb. de Torrejón
Torrejón el Rubio
Emb. de Alcántara
Talaván
Sra. de Miravete
Casas de Miravete
Valdecañas de Tajo
Bohonal de Ibor
Mesas de Ibor
Peraleda de S. Román
Valdeverdeja
El Puente del A.
Valdelacasa de T.
Aldeanueva de Barbarroya
Higuera
Pto. de Miravete
Jaraicejo
Campillo de Deleitosa
Fresnedoso de Ibor
Garvín
Villar del P.
Navalmoralejo
La Estrella
Torrecilla de la Jara
Retamoso
Monroy
Sra. de la Deleitosa
Deleitosa
Robledollano
Castañar de Ibor
Carrascalejo
Aldeanueva de San B.
La Nava de Ricomalillo
Buenasbodas
Espinoso del Rey
Robledo del Mazo
Navatrasierra
Mohedas de la Jara
Sierra de Altamira
Valdegamas
Aldea de Trujillo
Torrecillas de la Tiesa
Retamosa
Roturas
Navalvillar de Ibor
Carboneras
El Campillo
Gargantilla
Sevilleja de la Jara
Moradas
Aldeacentenera
Cabañas d. Castillo
Navezuelas
Villuerca
Puerto de S. Vicente
Pto. de S. Vicente
CÁCERES
Santa Marta de Magasca
Trujillo
Madroñera
Berzocana
Guadalupe
Alía
Anchuras
Sierra de Guadalupe
Las Villuercas
Puerto del Rey
Sierra de Fuentes
La Cumbre
Pedro Gómez
Garciaz
Cañamero
Puerto Llano
Torreorgaz
Torrequemada
Plasenzuela
Herguijuela
Botija
Ruanes
Ibahernando
Santa Ana
Santa Cruz de la Sierra
Conquista de la Sierra
Sierra de Montánchez
Logrosán
Emb. de Salor
Torremocha
Benquerencia
Valdefuentes
Salvatierra de Santiago
Puerto de Sta. Cruz
Zorita
Castilblanco
Bohonal
Emb. de Cíjara
Albalá
Zarza de M.
Robledillo de Trujillo
Villamesías
Casas de Don Antonio
Montánchez
Abertura
Alcollarín
Garcia de Sola
Valdecaballeros
Villarta de los Montes
Arroyomolinos de Montánchez
Cantos Negros
Sra. de la Umbría
Carmonita
Alcuéscar
Almoharín
El Campo
Madrigalejo
Sra. de la Chimenea
Peloche
Herrera del Duque
Fuenlabrada de los Montes
Escurial
Miajadas
Villar de Rena
Rena
Acedera
Sra. de Pela
Navalvillar de Pela
Casas de Don Pedro
Talarrubias
Repica
Orellana de la Sierra
Orellana la Vieja
Emb. de Orellana
Garrapatones
Sra. de los Ancares
Garbayuela
Mirandilla
Sta. Amalia
S. Pedro de M.
Trujillanos
Mérida
Medellín
Don Benito
Villanueva de la Serena
Puebla de Alcocer
Siruela
Tamurejo
Agudo
R. Guadiana
Valdetorres
Mengabril
La Coronada
La Haba
Esparragosa del Caudillo
Sancti-Spíritus
Motilla
Baterno
Valdemanco del Esteras
Villagonzalo
Don Álvaro
Guareña
Cristina
Zarza de A.
Ortiga
Magacela
Campanario
Risco
Garlitos
Pto. del Rayo
Osilla
Emb. de Zújar
La Serena
Manchita
Oliva de Mérida
Oliva
Alange
Sra. Hermosa
Recorvo
La Guarda
Quintana de la Serena
Capilla
Peñalsordo
Zarza Capilla
Torraza
Chillón
Almadén
Guadalmez
Almadenejos
Palomas
Valle de la Serena
Castuera
Benquerencia de la Serena
Almorchón
Cabeza del Buey
Puebla de la Reina
Higuera de la Serena
Malpartida de la Serena
Zalamea de la Serena
Esparragosa de la Serena
Helechal
R. Zújar
Alamillo
Horcón
Villafranca de los Barros
Puebla del Prior
Sra. de Hornachos
Retamal
Sra. del Oro
Monterrubio de la Serena
Belalcázar
Santa Eufemia
R. Guadalmez
Hornachos
Ribera del Fresno
Emb. de los Molinos de Matachel
Sra. de los Argallenes
Campillo de Llerena
Los Pedroches
Hinojosa del Duque
Hinojosa del Valle
Los Santos de Maimona
Llera
Peraleda de Zaucejo
Trapera
El Viso
Guijo
Dos Torres
Villaralto
Añora
Pedroche
Usagre
Higuera de Llerena
Valencia de las Torres
Maguilla
Blázquez
Valsequillo
Noria
Fuente la Lancha
Villanueva del Duque
Alcaracejos
Pozoblanco
El Raposo
Calzadilla de los Barros
Villagarcía de la Torre
Berlanga
Granja de Torrehermosa
Cuenca
La Granjuela
Peñarroya-Pueblonuevo
Bienvenida
Ahillones
Azuaga
Fuente de Cantos
Llerena
Casas de Reina
Valverde de Llerena
Argallón
Fuente Obejuna
Emb. de Sierra Boyera
Belmez
Puerto Calatraveño
Pto. de Loba
R. Bodión
Montemolín
Reina
Fuente del Arco
El Alcornocal
Villanueva del Rey
Sierra de los Santos
Espiel
Villaharta
Obejo
Pallares
Malcocinado
Peñita
Los Morenos
Monesterio
Puebla del Maestre
Guadalcanal
Hamapega
Emb. de Puente Nuevo
Villaviciosa de Córdoba
Alanís
Pto. de las Marismas
Cabeza Aguda
Emb. del Pintado
Sra. Padrona
El Real de la Jara
S. Nicolás del Puerto
Cazalla de la Sierra
Emb. de Bembézar
Castaño
Castro y Picón
R. Guadiato
Clavellinas
Alcolea
Medina Azahara
Cala
Sta. Olalla del Cala
Negrillo
Las Navas de la Concepción
Almadén de la Plata
El Pedroso
Constantina
Emb. del Retortillo
Emb. de la Breña
Emb. de Zufre
Zufre
Acebuchosa
Hornachuelos
Emb. del Hornachuelos
Posadas
Almodóvar del Río
CÓR
Torres
Corral de Caro
La Puebla de los Infantes
S. Cristóbal
Guadalcázar
R. Guadalquivir
Valdeflores
Emb. de la Minilla
El Ronquillo
Emb. de la Cala
Emb. de José Torán
Peñaflor
Fuencubierta
N 521
N 630
N 432
N 430
N 435
NV
N IV
E 90
E 803
E 05
C 524
C 511
C 520
C 401
C 426
C 423
C 420
C 413
C 437
C 432
C 434
C 421
C 433
C 411
C 431
C 503

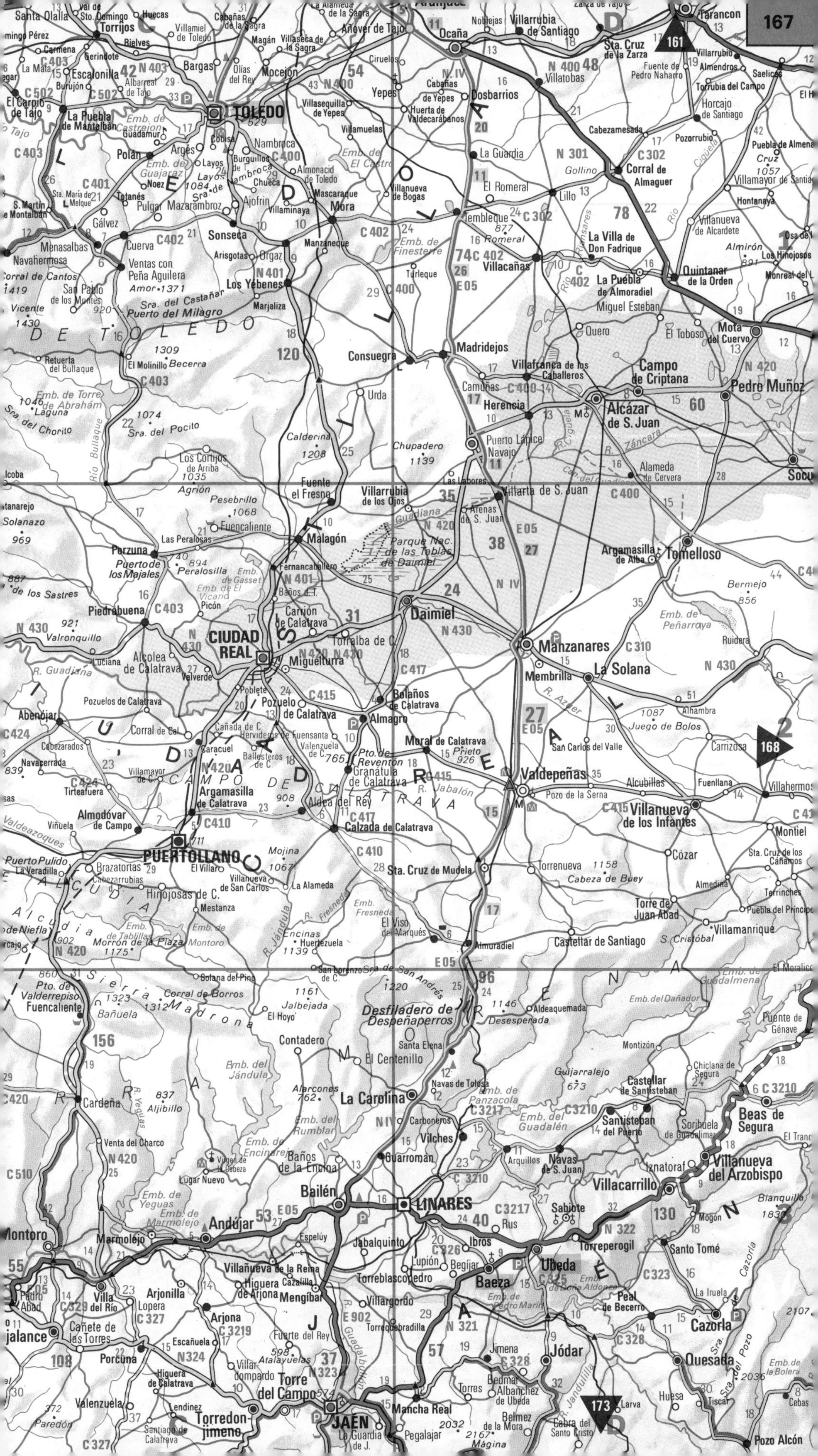

TOLEDO
Torrijos
La Puebla de Montalbán
Polán
Argés
Nambroca
Mocejón
Bargas
Añover de Tajo
Ocaña
Noblejas
Villarrubia de Santiago
Tarancon
Sta. Cruz de la Zarza
Villatobas
Dosbarrios
Yepes
La Guardia
Corral de Almaguer
El Romeral
Lillo
Tembleque
Mora
Sonseca
Orgaz
Los Yébenes
Villacañas
La Villa de Don Fadrique
Quintanar de la Orden
La Puebla de Almoradiel
Mota del Cuervo
Madridejos
Consuegra
Villafranca de los Caballeros
Campo de Criptana
Pedro Muñoz
Alcázar de S. Juan
Herencia
Puerto Lápice
Villarta de S. Juan
Tomelloso
Argamasilla de Alba
Malagón
Fernancaballero
Porzuna
Piedrabuena
CIUDAD REAL
Miguelturra
Daimiel
Manzanares
Membrilla
La Solana
Almagro
Bolaños de Calatrava
Moral de Calatrava
Valdepeñas
Villanueva de los Infantes
Granátula de Calatrava
Argamasilla de Calatrava
Almodóvar de Campo
PUERTOLLANO
Calzada de Calatrava
Sta. Cruz de Mudela
Almuradiel
Castellar de Santiago
Torre de Juan Abad
Montiel
Desfiladero de Despeñaperros
La Carolina
Santa Elena
Vilches
Bailén
LINARES
Andújar
Marmolejo
Montoro
Ubeda
Baeza
Villacarrillo
Villanueva del Arzobispo
Beas de Segura
Santisteban del Puerto
Navas de S. Juan
Cazorla
Quesada
Jódar
Mancha Real
JAEN
Torre del Campo
Torredonjimeno
Martos
Arjona
Arjonilla
Mengíbar
Porcuna
Pozo Alcón
Parque Nac. de las Tablas de Daimiel
MONTES DE TOLEDO
LA MANCHA
CAMPO DE CALATRAVA
Sierra Madrona
SIERRA MORENA
161
168
173

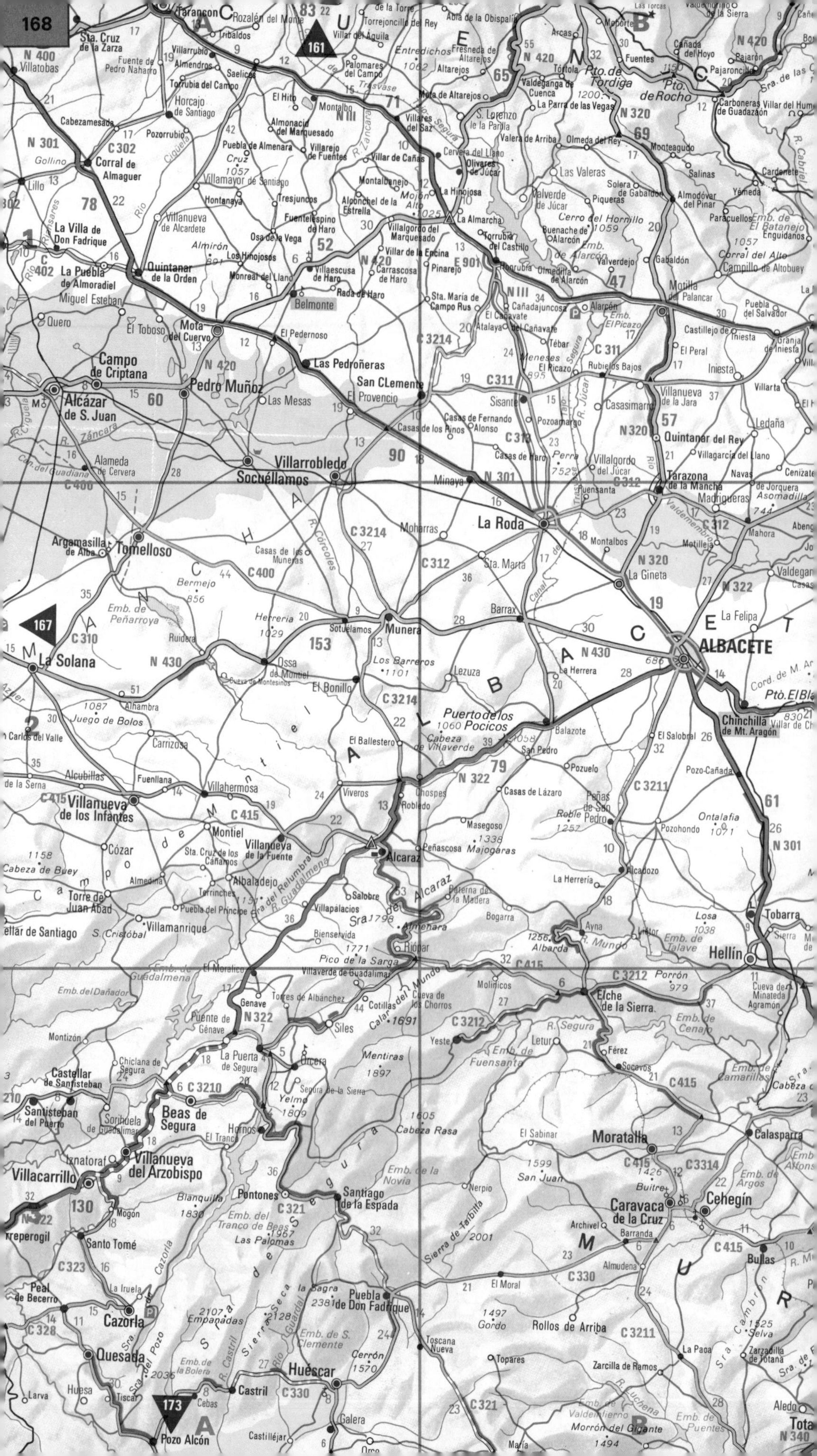

Tarancón
Rozalén del Monte
Tribaldos
Villarrubio
Almendros
Saelices
Villar del Águila
Torrejoncillo del Rey
Abia de la Obispalía
Palomares del Campo
Altarejos
Fresneda de Altarejos
Sta. Cruz de la Zarza
Fuente de Pedro Naharro
Villatobas
Torrubia del Campo
Horcajo de Santiago
Cabezamesada
Pozorrubio
Corral de Almaguer
Lillo
El Hito
Montalbo
Almonacid del Marquesado
Villares del Saz
Villarejo de Fuentes
Villar de Cañas
Puebla de Almenara
Villamayor de Santiago
Hontanaya
Tresjuncos
Montalbanejo
Alconchel de la Estrella
Fuentelespino de Haro
Villanueva de Alcardete
Osa de la Vega
La Villa de Don Fadrique
La Puebla de Almoradiel
Quintanar de la Orden
Los Hinojosos
Monreal del Llano
Villaescusa de Haro
Carrascosa de Haro
Rada de Haro
Belmonte
Villalgordo del Marquesado
Villar de la Encina
Pinarejo
Miguel Esteban
Quero
El Toboso
Mota del Cuervo
El Pedernoso
Las Pedroñeras
San Clemente
El Provencio
Campo de Criptana
Alcázar de S. Juan
Pedro Muñoz
Las Mesas
Alameda de Cervera
Villarrobledo
Socuéllamos
Casas de los Pinos
Minaya
Tomelloso
Argamasilla de Alba
Casas de los Muneras
Munera
Sotuélamos
Ruidera
Ossa de Montiel
Cueva de Montesinos
El Bonillo
La Solana
Alhambra
Carrizosa
Alcubillas
Fuenllana
Villahermosa
Villanueva de los Infantes
Montiel
Cózar
Villanueva de la Fuente
Sta. Cruz de los Cañamos
Albaladejo
Terrinches
Torre de Juan Abad
Puebla del Príncipe
Villamanrique
Almedina
Cabeza de Buey
Alcaraz
Peñascosa
Viveros
Robledo
El Ballestero
Lezuza
Balazote
San Pedro
La Roda
Barrax
Sta. Marta
Montalbos
La Gineta
ALBACETE
La Felipa
La Herrera
Chinchilla de Mt. Aragón
El Salobral
Pozo-Cañada
Pozuelo
Casas de Lázaro
Peñas de San Pedro
Masegoso
Pozohondo
Alcadozo
Ayna
Tobarra
Hellín
Elche de la Sierra
Molinicos
Riópar
Yeste
Letur
Férez
Socovos
Moratalla
Calasparra
Cehegín
Caravaca de la Cruz
Bullas
Barranda
Archivel
Almudena
El Moral
Nerpio
Santiago de la Espada
Pontones
Puebla de Don Fadrique
Huéscar
Castril
Galera
Castilléjar
Orce
Pozo Alcón
Quesada
Cazorla
Peal de Becerro
Santo Tomé
Mogón
Villacarrillo
Villanueva del Arzobispo
Iznatoraf
Sorihuela de Guadalimar
Castellar de Santisteban
Santisteban del Puerto
Chiclana de Segura
Beas de Segura
La Puerta de Segura
Génave
Puente de Génave
Siles
Orcera
Segura de la Sierra
Hornos
El Tranco
Torres de Albánchez
Villaverde de Guadalimar
Bienservida
Villapalacios
Salobre
Bogarra
Cuenca
Honrubia
Motilla del Palancar
Alarcón
Iniesta
Quintanar del Rey
Tarazona de la Mancha
Madrigueras
Mahora
Villalgordo del Júcar
Casasimarro
Villanueva de la Jara
Sisante
El Picazo
Pozoamargo
Tébar
Olmeda del Rey
Almodóvar del Pinar
Campillo de Altobuey
Carboneras de Guadazaón
Cañada del Hoyo
Pajarón
Fuentes
Pto. de Tordiga
Pto. de Rocho
N 400
N 301
N 420
N III
N 320
N 430
N 322
C 3214
C 312
C 400
C 415
C 3212
C 3211
C 321
C 330
161
167
173

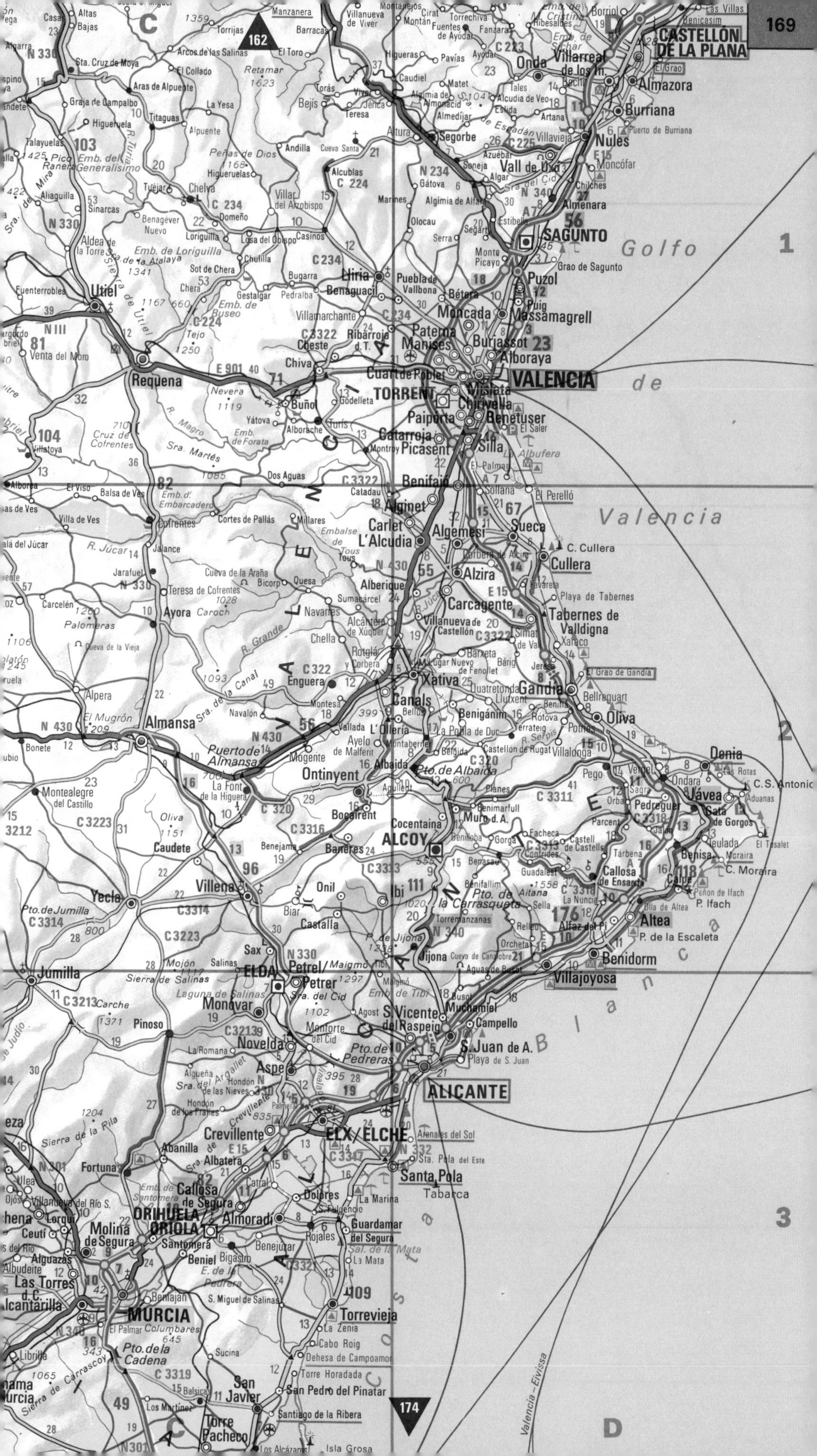
162
CASTELLÓN DE LA PLANA
Villarreal de los In.
Onda
Almazora
Burriana
Nules
Vall de Uxó
Segorbe
Moncófar
Almenara
SAGUNTO
Golfo
Grao de Sagunto
Puzol
Massamagrell
Puig
Burjassot
Alboraya
Moncada
Paterna
Manises
Liria
Benaguacil
Ribarroja d. T.
Cheste
Chiva
VALENCIA
Mislata
Chirivella
TORRENT
Paiporta
Benetuser
Catarroja
Picasent
Silla
El Saler
La Albufera
de
Valencia
Benifayó
Alginet
Carlet
L'Alcudia
Algemesí
Sueca
Cullera
C. Cullera
Alzira
Carcagente
Tabernes de Valldigna
Playa de Tabernes
Villanueva de Castellón
Xativa
Gandía
El Grao de Gandía
Oliva
Canals
L'Olleria
Albaida
Ontinyent
Bocairent
Banyeres
ALCOY
Cocentaina
Ibi
Onil
Castalla
Biar
Villena
Sax
ELDA
Petrel/Petrer
Monóvar
Novelda
Aspe
ALICANTE
S. Vicente del Raspeig
S. Juan de A.
Playa de S. Juan
Campello
Muchamiel
Jijona
Villajoyosa
Benidorm
Altea
Alfaz del Pi
Callosa de Ensarriá
Calpe
P. Ifach
Benisa
Teulada
Moraira
C. Moraira
Jávea
Denia
Ondara
Pedreguer
Pego
Vergel
C.S. Antonio
ELX/ELCHE
Crevillente
Santa Pola
Sta. Pola del Este
Tabarca
Arenales del Sol
Guardamar del Segura
La Marina
Dolores
Almoradí
ORIHUELA/ORIOLA
Callosa de Segura
Torrevieja
La Mata
Cabo Roig
La Zenia
Dehesa de Campoamor
Torre Horadada
San Pedro del Pinatar
San Javier
Santiago de la Ribera
Torre Pacheco
Los Alcázares
Isla Grosa
MURCIA
Molina de Segura
Las Torres d.C.
Santomera
Fortuna
Abanilla
Jumilla
Yecla
Pinoso
Caudete
Almansa
Ayora
Cofrentes
Jalance
Requena
Utiel
Buñol
Turís
Yátova
Venta del Moro
Villatoya
Alpera
Montealegre del Castillo
Enguera
Mogente
Puerto de Almansa
Valencia – Eivissa
Blanca
174

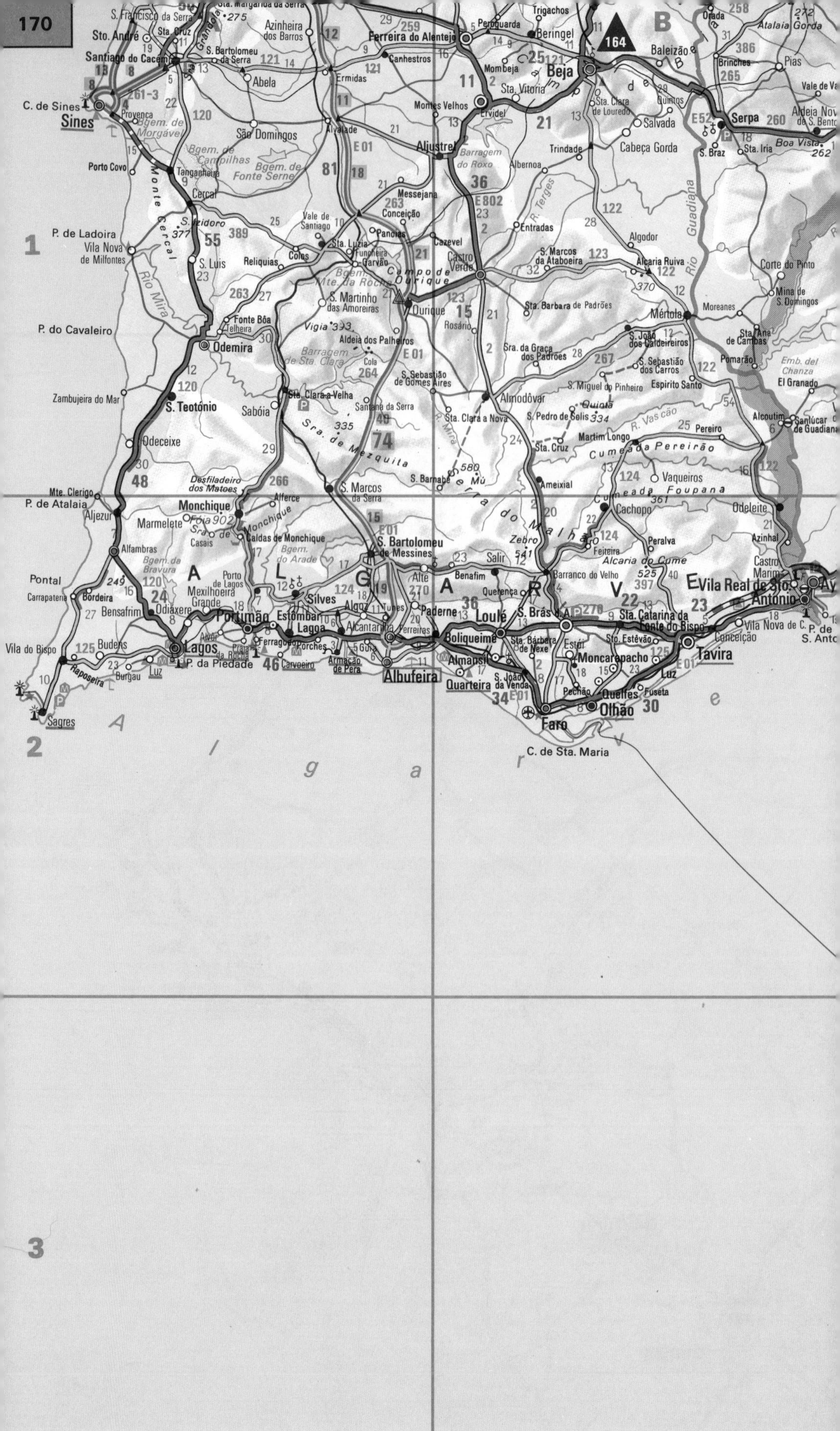
164
A
B
1
2
3
S. Francisco da Serra
Sta. Margarida da Serra
Sto. André
Sta. Cruz
Grândola
Azinheira dos Barros
Ferreira do Alentejo
Peroguarda
Trigachos
Beringel
Baleizão
Ordada
Atalaia Gorda
Santiago do Cacém
S. Bartolomeu da Serra
Abela
Canhestros
Ermidas
Mombeja
Beja
Brinches
Pias
Vale de Vargo
C. de Sines
Sines
Provença
Bgem. de Morgável
São Domingos
Montes Velhos
Ervidel
Sta. Vitória
Sta. Clara de Louredo
Quintos
Salvada
Serpa
Aldeia Nova de S. Bento
Alvalade
Aljustrel
Barragem do Roxo
Trindade
Cabeça Gorda
S. Braz
Sta. Iria
Boa Vista
Porto Covo
Bgem. de Campilhas
Bgem. de Fonte Serne
Tanganheira
Albernoa
Monte Cercal
Cercal
Messejana
Conceição
Vale de Santiago
R. Terges
Entradas
Algodor
Rio Guadiana
S. Izidoro
P. de Ladoira
Vila Nova de Milfontes
S. Luis
Reliquias
Colos
Sta. Luzia
Panoias
Funcheira
Garvão
Cazevel
Castro Verde
Campo de Ourique
S. Marcos da Ataboeira
Alcaria Ruiva
Corte do Pinto
Mina de S. Domingos
Rio Mira
Bgem. da Mte. da Rocha
S. Martinho das Amoreiras
Ourique
Sta. Barbara de Padrões
Mértola
Moreanes
P. do Cavaleiro
Fonte Bôa
Telheira
Vigia
Aldeia dos Palheiros
Rosário
S. João dos Caldeireiros
Sta. Ana de Cambas
Odemira
Barragem de Sta. Clara
Cola
Sra. da Graça dos Padrões
S. Sebastião dos Carros
Pomarão
Emb. del Chanza
S. Sebastião de Gomes Aires
S. Miguel do Pinheiro
Espirito Santo
El Granado
Zambujeira do Mar
S. Teotónio
Sabóia
Sta. Clara-a-Velha
Santana da Serra
Almodôvar
Quinta
S. Pedro de Solis
R. Vascão
Alcoutim
Sanlúcar de Guadiana
Odeceixe
Sra. de Mezquita
Sta. Clara a Nova
R. Mira
Sta. Cruz
Martim Longo
Pereiro
Cumeada Pereirão
Desfiladeiro dos Matoes
S. Barnabé
Serra do Malhão
Ameixial
Vaqueiros
Cumeada Foupana
Mte. Clerigo
P. de Atalaia
Monchique
Alferce
S. Marcos da Serra
Cachopo
Odeleite
Aljezur
Marmelete
Fóia
Sra. do Casais
Monchique
Caldas de Monchique
S. Bartolomeu de Messines
Zebro
Feiteira
Peralva
Azinhal
Alfambras
Bgem. da Bravura
Bgem. do Arade
Salir
Alcaria do Come
Castro Marim
Pontal
Carrapateira
Bordeira
Bensafrim
Mexilhoeira Grande
Porto de Lagos
Silves
Alte
Benafim
Querença
Barranco do Velho
Vila Real de Sto. António
Odiáxere
Portimão
Estombar
Algoz
Tunes
Paderne
Loulé
S. Brás de Alportel
Sta. Catarina da Fonte do Bispo
Vila Nova de Cacela
P. de S. António
Vila do Bispo
Budens
Lagos
Alvor
Praia da Rocha
Ferragudo
Lagoa
Porches
Alcantarilha
Guia
Ferreiras
Boliqueime
Sta. Bárbara de Nexe
Estói
Sto. Estêvão
Conceição
Tavira
Raposeira
Burgau
Luz
P. da Piedade
Carvoeiro
Armação de Pera
Albufeira
Almansil
Quarteira
S. João da Venda
Moncarapacho
Pechão
Quelfes
Fuseta
Luz
Sagres
Faro
Olhão
C. de Sta. Maria
A l g a r v e
A L G A R V E

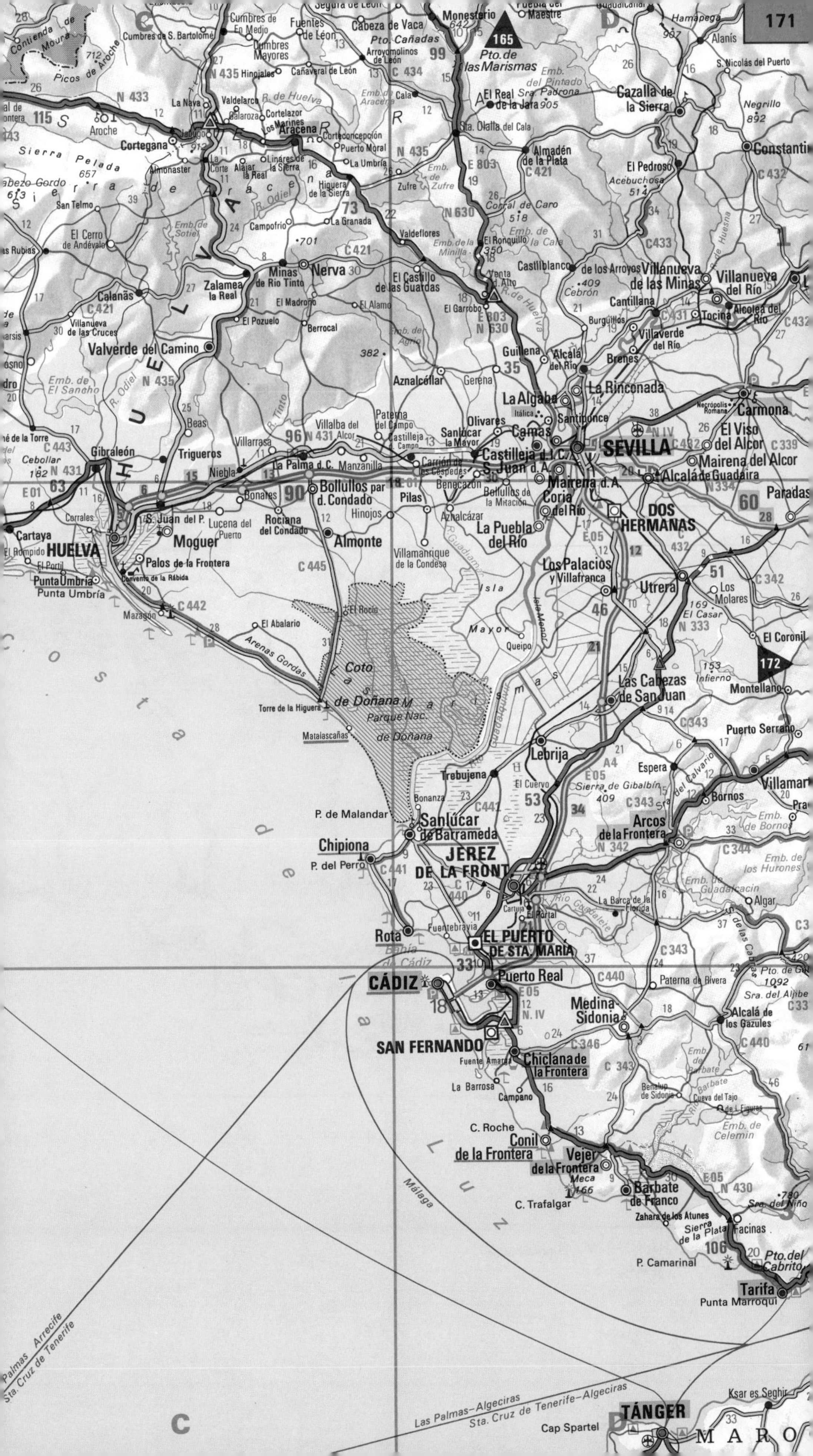

SEVILLA
HUELVA
CÁDIZ
JEREZ DE LA FRONT.
EL PUERTO DE STA. MARÍA
SAN FERNANDO
DOS HERMANAS
TÁNGER
Huelva
Aracena
Nerva
Valverde del Camino
Moguer
Almonte
Palos de la Frontera
Punta Umbría
Cartaya
Gibraleón
Trigueros
Niebla
La Palma d. C.
Bollullos par d. Condado
Castilleja d. l. C.
Camas
Coria del Río
La Puebla del Río
Los Palacios y Villafranca
Utrera
Las Cabezas de San Juan
Lebrija
Sanlúcar de Barrameda
Chipiona
Rota
Puerto Real
Medina Sidonia
Chiclana de la Frontera
Conil de la Frontera
Vejer de la Frontera
Barbate de Franco
Tarifa
Arcos de la Frontera
Carmona
Alcalá de Guadaira
Mairena del Alcor
Cazalla de la Sierra
Constantina
Villanueva de las Minas
Villanueva del Río
Coto de Doñana
Parque Nac. de Doñana
Costa de la Luz
Bahía de Cádiz
C. Trafalgar
Cap Spartel
Ksar es Seghir
MARO

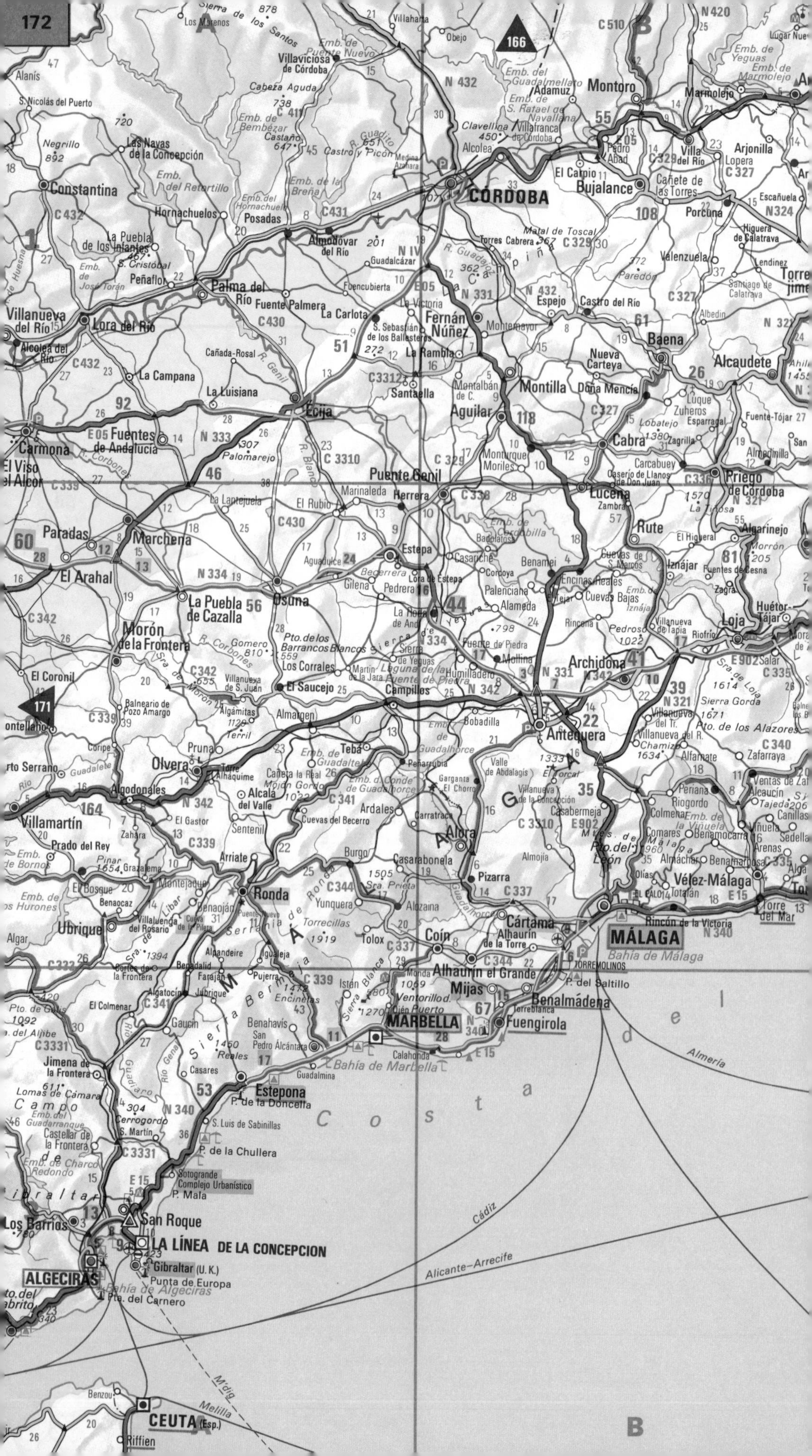
166
171
CÓRDOBA
MÁLAGA
MARBELLA
ALGECIRAS
LA LÍNEA DE LA CONCEPCION
CEUTA (Esp.)
Gibraltar (U.K.)
Punta de Europa
Bahía de Algeciras
Pta. del Carnero
San Roque
Los Barrios
Sotogrande Complejo Urbanístico
P. Mala
P. de la Chullera
S. Luis de Sabinillas
Estepona
P. de la Doncella
Guadalmina
San Pedro Alcántara
Bahía de Marbella
Calahonda
Fuengirola
Torreblanca
Benalmádena
P. del Saltillo
TORREMOLINOS
Bahía de Málaga
Rincón de la Victoria
Torre del Mar
Vélez-Málaga
Costa del Sol
Almería
Cádiz
Alicante–Arrecife
Melilla
Benzou
Riffien
Mijas
Alhaurín el Grande
Alhaurín de la Torre
Cártama
Coín
Tolox
Ronda
Serranía de Ronda
Sierra Bermeja
Jimena de la Frontera
Castellar de la Frontera
Ubrique
Villamartín
Prado del Rey
Grazalema
El Bosque
Benaocaz
Olvera
Algodonales
Zahara
Setenil
Alcalá del Valle
Teba
Campillos
Ardales
Álora
Pizarra
Antequera
Archidona
Loja
Alfarnate
Colmenar
Casabermeja
Pto. del León
Almogía
Valle de Abdalagís
Villanueva de la Concepción
El Torcal
Bobadilla
Mollina
Humilladero
Fuente de Piedra
Alameda
Estepa
Herrera
Puente Genil
Lucena
Rute
Iznájar
Cabra
Priego de Córdoba
Baena
Alcaudete
Montilla
Aguilar
Fernán Núñez
La Rambla
Santaella
Écija
Osuna
El Saucejo
Los Corrales
Marchena
Paradas
El Arahal
La Puebla de Cazalla
Morón de la Frontera
El Coronil
Carmona
Fuentes de Andalucía
La Campana
La Luisiana
Lora del Río
Palma del Río
Fuente Palmera
La Carlota
Posadas
Almodóvar del Río
Hornachuelos
Constantina
Las Navas de la Concepción
Villaviciosa de Córdoba
Obejo
Villaharta
Adamuz
Montoro
Villafranca de Córdoba
Alcolea
El Carpio
Bujalance
Pedro Abad
Villa del Río
Marmolejo
Arjonilla
Lopera
Cañete de las Torres
Porcuna
Valenzuela
Castro del Río
Espejo
Montemayor
Nueva Carteya
Doña Mencía
Zuheros
Luque
Carcabuey
Alcalá la Real
Archidona
Sierra Gorda
Ventas de Zafarraya
Zafarraya
Alcaucín
Canillas
Arenas
Sedella
Periana
Riogordo
Comares
Benamocarra
Almáchar
Totalán
N 331
N 342
N 340
N 321
N 334
N 432
N IV
E 05
E 15
E 902
C 339
C 344
C 337
C 3310
C 430
C 432
C 342
C 341
C 327
C 329
C 3331
Sierra de los Santos
La Campiña
Campo de Gibraltar

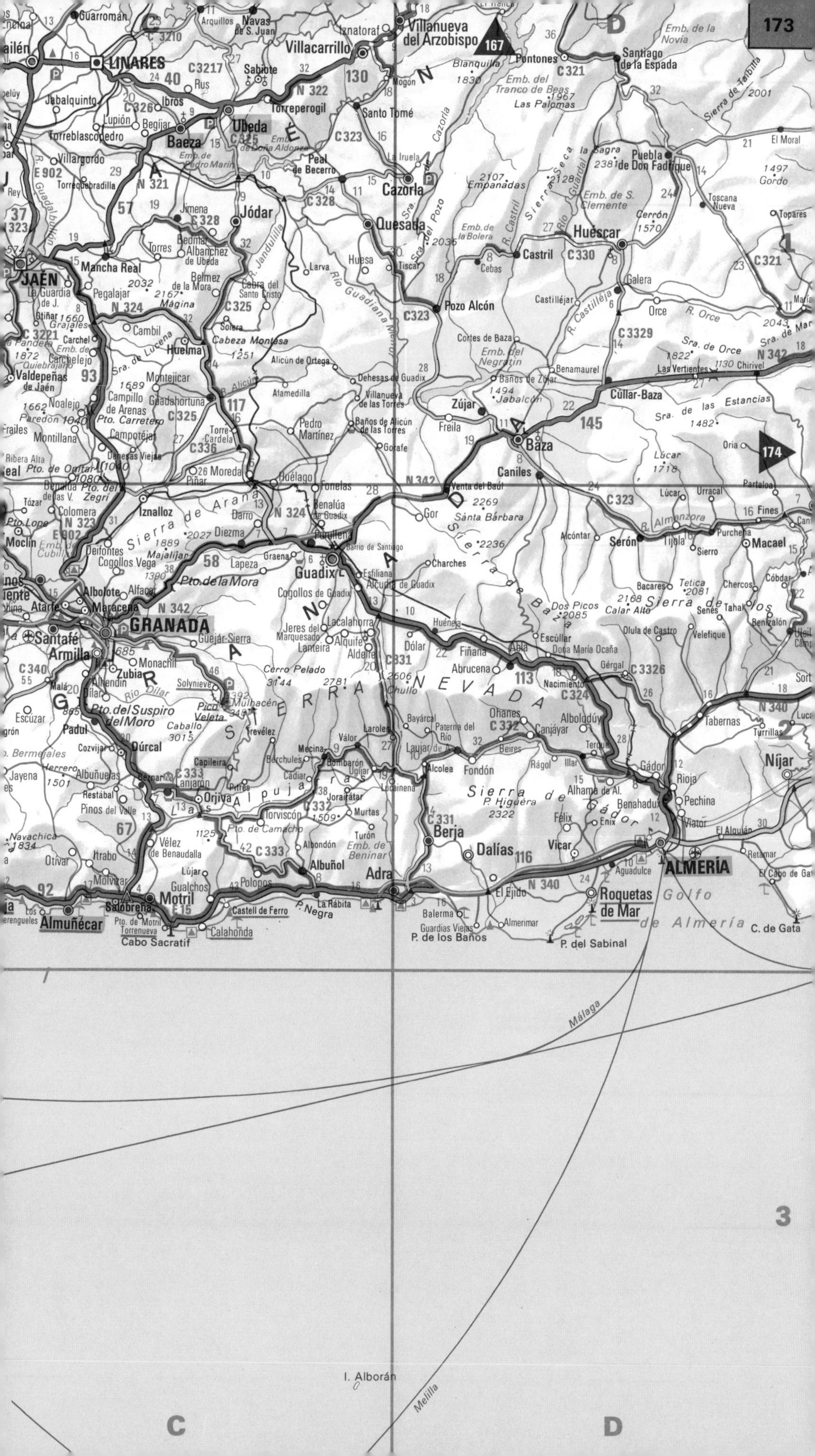
Guarromán
Arquillos
Navas de S. Juan
Iznatoraf
Villanueva del Arzobispo
167
Blanquilla 1830
Pontones
Santiago de la Espada
Emb. de la Novia
D
Bailén
LINARES
C 3217
Sabiote
Villacarrillo
130
Mogón
N
Emb. del Tranco de Beas
1967 Las Palomas
C 321
Sierra de Taibilla
2001
Jabalquinto
C 326
Ibros
Rus
Torreperogil
N 322
Santo Tomé
Cazorla
Lupión
Begíjar
Torreblascopedro
Baeza
Ubeda
C 325
Emb. de Doña Aldonza
C 323
El Moral
Villargordo
E 902
Torrequebradilla
Emb. de Pedro Marín
Peal de Becerro
La Iruela
2107 Empanadas
Sierra Seca
2128
La Sagra 2381
Puebla de Don Fadrique
1497 Gordo
N 321
Jimena
C 328
Jódar
Quesada
Sra. del Pozo
Emb. de S. Clemente
Toscana Nueva
Cerrón 1570
Topares
Río Guadalbullón
Bedmar
Albanchez de Ubeda
R. Jandulilla
Emb. de la Bolera
R. Castril
Huéscar
2035
Torres
Castril
C 330
Cebas
JAÉN
Mancha Real
Larva
Huesa
Tíscar
C 321
Galera
La Guardia de J.
Pegalajar
2032
2167
Mágina
Belmez de la Mora
Cabra del Santo Cristo
Río Guadiana Menor
Pozo Alcón
Castilléjar
R. Castilleja
Orce
R. Orce
N 324
Otíñar
1660
Grajales
C 3221
Carchel
Emb. de Quiebrajano
Carchelejo
La Pandera 1872
Cambil
Huelma
Solera
C 325
Cabeza Montosa 1251
C323
Cortes de Baza
Emb. del Negratín
C 3329
Sra. de Orce
1822
Sra. de María
N 342
Valdepeñas de Jaén
93
Sra. de Lucena
Montejícar
Alicún de Ortega
Dehesas de Guadix
Baños de Zújar
Benamaurel
Las Vertientes
1130 Chirivel
1662 Noalejo
Paredón 1040
Campillo de Arenas
1689
Guadahortuna
Pto. Carretero
R. Alicún
117
Alamedilla
Villanueva de las Torres
1494 Jabalcón
Zújar
Cúllar-Baza
Sra. de las Estancias
1482
Frailes
Montillana
C 325
Campotéjar
Torre-Cardela
Pedro Martínez
Baños de Alicún de las Torres
Freila
145
Ribera Alta
Pto. de Ontar 1080
Dehesas Viejas
C 336
Gorafe
Baza
Lúcar 1718
Oria
174
1040
Moreda
Piñar
Huélago
Fonelas
Caniles
Benalúa de las V.
Pto. del Zegrí
Venta del Baúl
N 342
Partaloa
Tózar
Colomera
Iznalloz
Benalúa de Guadix
N 324
2269
Santa Bárbara
C 323
Lúcar
Urracal
Fines
Pto. Lope
N 323
E 902
Sierra de Arana
Darro
Gor
Moclín
Emb. de Cubillas
2027
Diezma
Purullena
Barrio de Santiago
2236
Alcóntar
Serón
R. Almanzora
Tíjola
Purchena
Sierro
Macael
Deifontes
1889
Majalijar
58
Lapeza
Graena
Guadix
Charches
Sierra de Baza
Cogollos Vega
1390
Esfiliana
Alcudia de Guadix
Pto. de la Mora
Bacares
Tetica 2081
Chercos
Cóbdar
Albolote
Alfacar
Cogollos de Guadix
Dos Picos 2085
2168
Calar Alto
Sierra de los
Atarfe
Maracena
N 342
GRANADA
Jeres del Marquesado
Lacalahorra
Huéneja
Senés
Tahal
Santafé
Güéjar-Sierra
Lanteira
Alquife
Dólar
Fiñana
Abla
Escúllar
Doña María Ocaña
Olula de Castro
Velefique
Benizalón
Armilla
Monachil
Aldeire
C 331
Abrucena
C 340
Zubia
Cerro Pelado 3144
2781
2606
Chullo
Gérgal
C 3326
Malá
Alhendín
Dílar
Río Dílar
Solynieve
3392
Mulhacén 3481
Sierra Nevada
113
Nacimiento
C 324
Sort
Escúzar
Padul
Pto. del Suspiro del Moro
Pico Veleta
Caballo 3015
Trevélez
Bayárcal
Paterna del Río
Ohanes
C 332
Canjáyar
Alboloduy
N 340
Tabernas
Turrillas
Durcal
Cozvíjar
Válor
Laroles
Laujar de A.
Beires
Terque
Bermejales
Jayena
Herrero 1501
Albuñuelas
Capileira
Mecina
Bérchules
Bombarón
Ugíjar
Alcolea
Fondón
Rágol
Illar
Gádor
Rioja
Níjar
Restábal
Pinos del Valle
Béznar
C 333
Lanjarón
Orgiva
Pitres
Alpujarras
Cádiar
Jorairátar
Lucainena
Sierra de Gádor
P. Higuera 2322
Alhama de Al.
Benahadux
Pechina
67
Navachica 1834
Vélez de Benaudalla
Torviscón
C 332
1509
Murtas
C 331
Berja
Félix
Enix
Viator
El Alquián
1125
Pto. de Camacho
Ítrabo
Otívar
42
C 333
Albondón
Turón
Emb. de Beninar
Dalías
116
Vícar
ALMERÍA
Retamar
Lújar
Albuñol
Adra
Aguadulce
El Cabo de Gata
92
Molvízar
Gualchos
Polopos
N 340
El Ejido
Roquetas de Mar
Golfo de Almería
Almuñécar
Los Berengueles
Salobreña
Motril
E 15
Castell de Ferro
La Rábita
P. Negra
Balerma
Pto. de Motril
Torrenueva
Calahonda
Cabo Sacratif
Guardias Viejas
P. de los Baños
Almerimar
P. del Sabinal
C. de Gata
Málaga
3
I. Alborán
Melilla
C
D

168

M
A

Buitre
Cehegín
Archivel
Caravaca
de la Cruz
Barranda
C 415
Bullas
C 330
El Moral
Almudena
23
24
21
C 211
1497
Gordo
Rollos de Arriba
Toscana
Nueva
Topares
La Paca
Zarcilla de Ramos
Sra. de Tolana
1525
Selva
Zarzadilla
de Totana
C 331
1
C 321
Emb. de
Valdeinfierno
Morrón del Gigante
1494
Sra. de María
Maria
Vélez
Blanco
2043
Sra. de la Torrecilla
Vélez Rubio
N 342
1130 Chirivel
18
6
7
22
Puerto Lumbreras
Cabezo Jara
1241
Sra. de Enmedio
C 321
Oria
173
Partaloa
cal
16 Fines
7
Taberno
Albox
N 340
24
47
LORCA
Los Valencianos
C 3211
18
25
882
Sra. de la Almenara
Cantoria
Purchena
Macael
Arboleas
Zurgena
E 15
18
Cuevas del
Almanzora
123
12
Pulpí
Aguilas
Cope
Cabo Cope
Calabardina
S. Juan de
los Terreros
N 332
Chercos
Cóbdar
C 3325
Albánchez
Lubrín
Antas
Bédar
Vera
C 3327
967
Tíjola
Los Gallardos
Garrucha
Benizalón
Hueli del
Campo
93
Turre
Mojácar
P. de Cantal
Sorbas
22
18
N 340
Lucainena de las Torres
22
102
Carboneras
2
Níjar
15
N 332
Turrillas
19
Agua Amarga
El Alquián
30
La Serrata
Las Negras
P. de la Polacra
Retamar
El Cabo de Gata
La Isleta
de Escullos
Sierra de Gata
San José
C. de Gata

Ojós
Ricote
Villanueva del Río S.
1124
19
B
Almoradí
Rojales
Archena
Lorquí
Molina
de Segura
169
ORIHUELA
Bigastro
Benejúzar
E. de la
Pedrera
Ceutí
Campos del Río
Alguazas
Albudeite
Mula
C 415
Las Torres
Alcantarilla
Librilla
Pliego
Sra. de Espuña
1579
S. Miguel de Salinas
MURCIA
El Palmar
Columbares
645
16
42
Benijajan
Pto. de la
Cadena
343
Sucina
San
Javier
San Pedro
Torre Hor.
Alhama
de Murcia
1065
Sierra de Carrascoy
C 3319
Balsicas
49
Los Martínez
Torre
Pacheco
Los Alcázares
Algar
I. Mayor
Mar
de Cristal
La Palma
E 15
Totana
N 340
Aledo
83
20
C 3315
La Aljorra
33
23
Albujón
La Unión
Portmán
Mar
Menor
CARTAGENA
Algarrobo
713
Morata
Mazarrón
Talayón
884
17
Bolnuevo
El Puerto
de Mazarrón
La Azohía
C. Negrete
C. del Agua
Escombreras
C. Tiñoso
Golfo
de Mazarrón

3

A
B

City Approach Maps

Plans de villes synoptiques

Stadtübersichtspläne

Piante di città sinottiche

Planos de ciudades sinópticos

To find the city approach map you want turn to the map on pages 2 and 3, locate the city and turn to the map number shown in the red circle.

Afin de trouver le plan de ville synoptique de la ville desirée, veuillez consulter la carte aux pages 2 et 3, localiser la ville, vous reporter aux numéros de la carte indiqués dans le cercle rouge.

Um die Zufahrtenkarte zur gewünschten Stadt zu finden, suchen Sie zuerst die Stadt auf der Uebersichtskarte Seiten 2-3 und schlagen nachher die Kartennummer auf, welche im roten Kreis angegeben ist.

Afine di trovare la carta dei accessi alla città desiderate, trovate la città sulla carta su pagine 2 e 3 e poi riforitevi alla carta del numero indicato nel cercio rosso.

Para encontrar el mapa de acceso a la ciudad deseada, vaya al mapa en las páginas 2 y 3, localice la ciudad y entonces busque el número del mapa mostrado dentro del círculo rojo.

Legend   Légende   Zeichenerklärung
Leggenda   Signos Convencionales

Motorway
Autoroute
Autobahn
Autostrada
Autopista

Dual carriageway
Semi-autoroute
Autostrasse
Superstrada
Carretera de doble calzada

Through road
Route de transit
Durchgangsstrasse
Strada di attraversamento
Carretera de tránsito

Secondary road
Route de communication
Verbindungsstrasse
Strada di comunicazione
Carretera secundaria

Delft
Centr.
Motorway junction
Sortie d'autoroute
Autobahnanschluss
Uscita dall'autostrada
Salida de la autopista

E 61
A 107
647
Road numbering
Numérotage des routes
Strassennummerierung
Numerazione delle strade
Numeración de carreteras

Railway with station
Chemin de fer avec station
Eisenbahn mit Station
Ferrovia con stazione
Vía férrea con estación

Cable railway, cable car
Funiculaire, téléphérique
Stand- und Luftseilbahn
Funicolare, teleferica
Funicular, teleférico

Car ferry
Bac pour automobiles
Autofahre
Traghetto per automobili
Transbordador de automóviles

State frontier
Frontière d'Etat
Landesgrenze
Frontiera di stato
Frontera entre Estados

Urban area
Terrain bâti
Überbaute Fläche
Terreno costruito
Area urbana

City centre, old part of the city
Cité, vieille ville
Stadtkern, Altstadt
Nucleo urbano, città vecchia
Centro de la ciudad, parte vieja de la ciudad

Park
Parc
Parkanlage
Parco
Parque

Forest
Forêt
Wald
Bosco
Bosque

Nature reserve, country park
Réserve naturelle, parc naturel
Naturschutzgebiet, Naturpark
Regione protezione della natura
Reserva natural, Parque natural

Restricted area
Zone interdite
Sperrzone
Zona proibita
Area restringida

★ Place of interest
Curiosité
Sehenswürdigkeit
Curiosità
Lugar de interés

※ Viewpoint
Point de vue
Aussichtspunkt
Punto panoramico
Punto panorámico

Ⓟ Car park
Possibilité de stationnement (sélection)
Parkmöglichkeit (Auswahl)
Possibilità di parcheggio (selezione)
Parqueadero de automóviles

Ⓡ Motorway restaurant
Restaurant sur autoroute
Restaurant an Autobahn
Ristorante sull'autostrada
Restaurante en la autopista

Ⓣ Motorway petrol station
Station service sur autoroute
Tankstelle an Autobahn
Stazione di servizio sull'autostrada
Gasolinera en la autopista

⊖ Frontier crossing
Passage frontalier
Grenzübergang
Passaggio di frontiera
Cruce de fronteras

✈ Airport
Aéroport
Flughafen
Aeroporto
Aeropuerto

✛ Airfield
Aérodrome
Flugplatz
Campo di aviazione
Campo de aviación

☨ Cathedral, church
Cathédrale, église
Kathedrale, Kirche
Cattedrale, chiesa
Catedral, iglesia

☫ Pilgrimage church, monastery
Eglise de pèlerinage, couvent
Wallfahrtskirche, Kloster
Santuario, convento
Santuario, monasterio

☪ Mosque
Mosquée
Moschee
Moschea
Mezquita

♗ Castle
Château
Schloss, Burg
Castello
Castillo

✪ Fort
Fort
Fort
Forte
Fuerte

☗ Television tower
Tour de télévision
Fernsehturm
Torre di televisiva
Torre de televisión

☀ Lighthouse
Phare
Leuchtturm
Faro
Faro

☓ Windmill
Moulin à vent
Windmühle
Mulino a vento
Molino de viento

⬤ Stadium
Stade
Stadion
Stadio
Estadio

ⓜ Motel
Môtel
Motel
Motel
Motel

⚑ Leisure park
Parc de loisirs
Freizeitpark
Parco di svaghi
Parque de diversiones

🦒 Zoological garden
Jardin zoologique
Zoologischer Garten
Giardino zoologico
Zoológico

♣ Botanical garden
Jardin botanique
Botanischer Garten
Giardino botanico
Jardín botánico

ℹ Tourist information office
Poste d'information
Informationsstelle
Posto d'informazione
Oficina de información turística

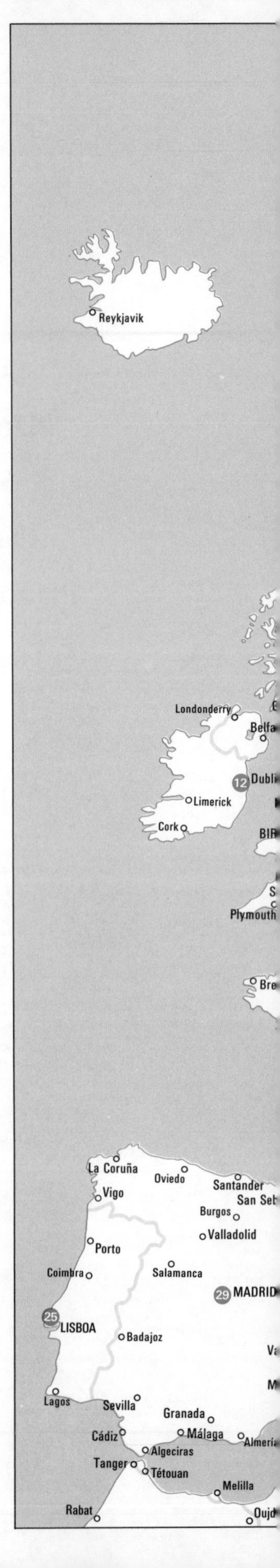

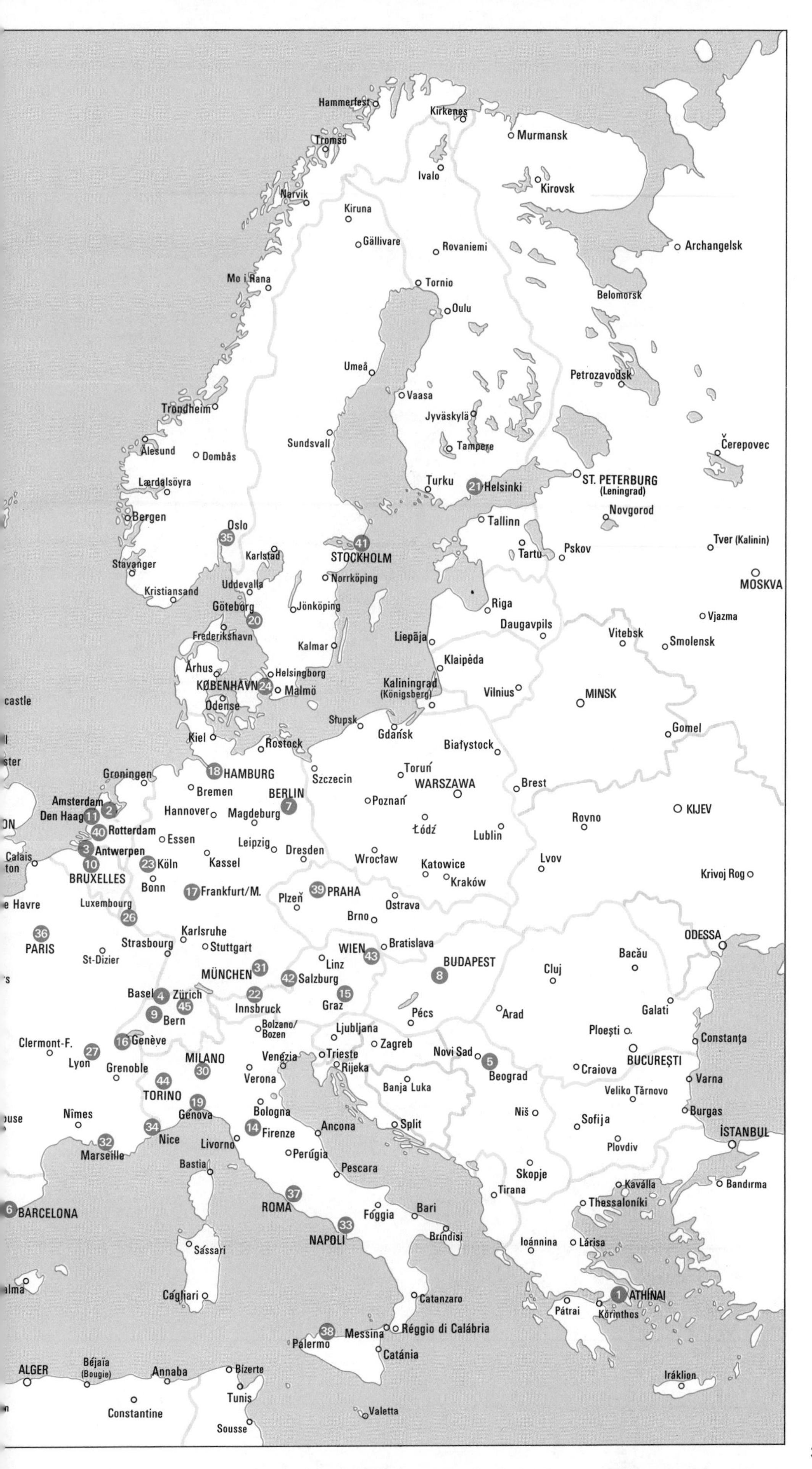
Hammerfest
Kirkenes
Murmansk
Tromsø
Ivalo
Kirovsk
Narvik
Kiruna
Gällivare
Rovaniemi
Archangelsk
Mo i Rana
Tornio
Belomorsk
Oulu
Umeå
Petrozavodsk
Vaasa
Trondheim
Jyväskylä
Sundsvall
Tampere
Čerepovec
Ålesund
Dombås
Lærdalsöyra
Turku
21 Helsinki
ST. PETERBURG
(Leningrad)
Bergen
Novgorod
Tallinn
Oslo
35
41
Tver (Kalinin)
Karlstad
STOCKHOLM
Tartu
Pskov
Stavanger
Norrköping
MOSKVA
Kristiansand
Uddevalla
Göteborg
20
Jönköping
Riga
Vjazma
Frederikshavn
Daugavpils
Vitebsk
Kalmar
Liepāja
Smolensk
Klaipėda
Århus
Helsingborg
KØBENHAVN
24
Malmö
Kaliningrad
(Königsberg)
Vilnius
MINSK
castle
Odense
Słupsk
Gdańsk
Gomel
Kiel
Rostock
Białystock
ster
Groningen
18 HAMBURG
Szczecin
Toruń
Brest
Bremen
WARSZAWA
Amsterdam
2
BERLIN
Poznań
KIJEV
Den Haag 11
Hannover
Magdeburg
7
Rovno
40 Rotterdam
Łódź
Lublin
ON
Essen
Leipzig
Dresden
3 Antwerpen
Kassel
Wrocław
Lvov
Calais
23 Köln
Katowice
ton
10
Kraków
Krivoj Rog
BRUXELLES
Bonn
17 Frankfurt/M.
39 PRAHA
Plzeň
Ostrava
e Havre
Luxembourg
26
Brno
36
Karlsruhe
ODESSA
PARIS
Strasbourg
Stuttgart
WIEN
Bratislava
43
Bacău
St-Dizier
Linz
BUDAPEST
MÜNCHEN 31
Cluj
42 Salzburg
8
Basel 4
Zürich
22
15
45
Innsbruck
Graz
Galati
Arad
9
Bern
Pécs
Bolzano/
Bozen
Ljubljana
Ploeşti
Clermont-F.
16 Genève
Zagreb
Constanţa
27
Venezia
Trieste
Novi Sad
Lyon
MILANO
5
BUCUREŞTI
Grenoble
30
Rijeka
Craiova
Verona
Beograd
Banja Luka
Varna
44
Veliko Tărnovo
TORINO
19
Bologna
Niš
Burgas
Nîmes
Genova
Split
Sofija
34
14 Firenze
Ancona
İSTANBUL
32
Nice
Livorno
Plovdiv
Marseille
Perúgia
Bastia
Pescara
Skopje
Kavála
Bandırma
37
Tirana
ROMA
Thessaloníki
6 BARCELONA
Foggia
Bari
33
NAPOLI
Bríndisi
Ioánnina
Lárisa
Sássari
Cágliari
Catanzaro
1 ATHÍNAI
Pátrai
Kórinthos
38
Messina
Réggio di Calábria
Palermo
Catánia
Béjaïa
(Bougie)
ALGER
Annaba
Bizerte
Iráklion
Tunis
Constantine
Valetta
Sousse

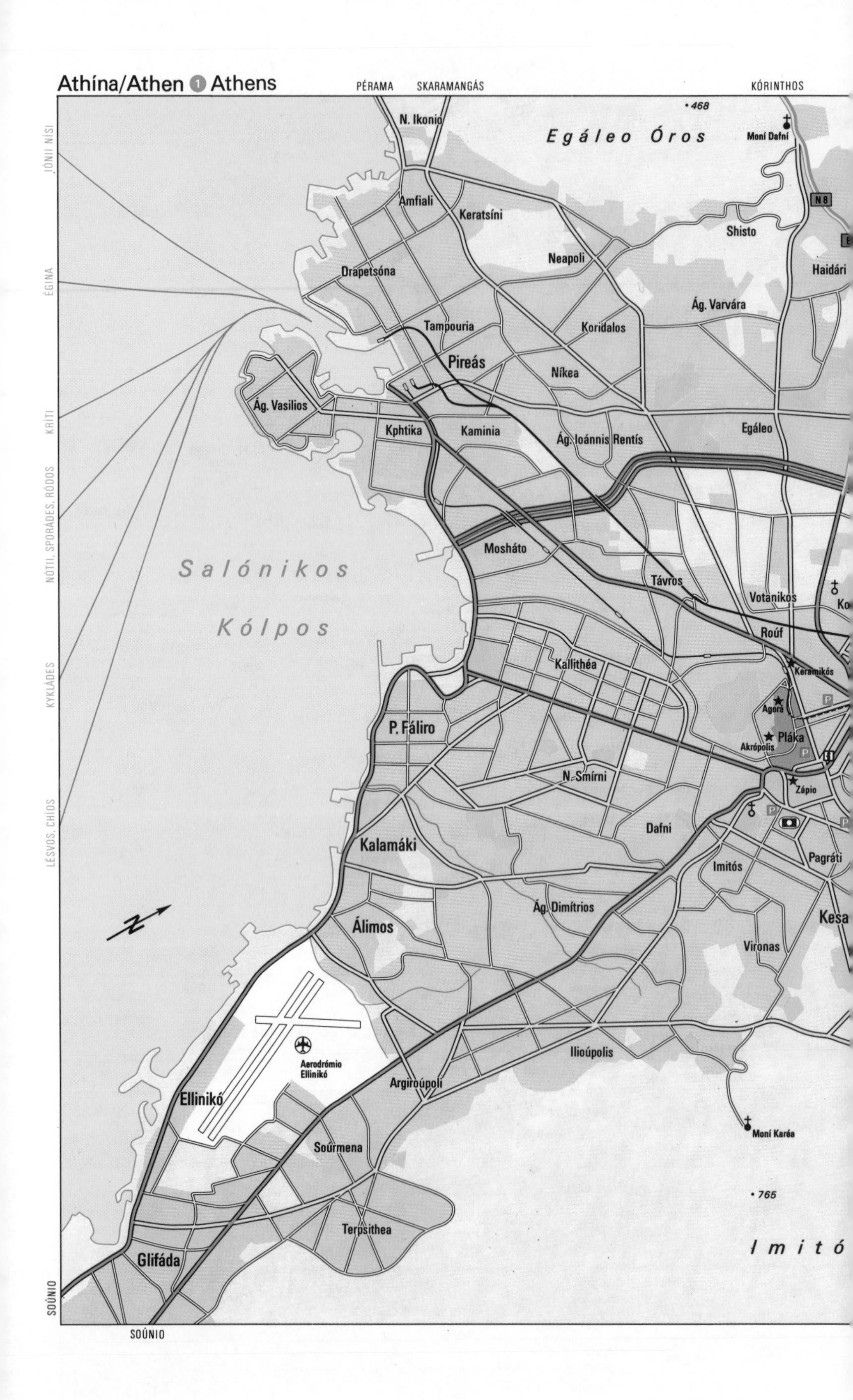

PÉRAMA SKARAMANGÁS

KÓRINTHOS

• 468

N. Ikonío

Egáleo Óros

Moní Dafní

Amfiali

Keratsíni

Shisto

N 8

Drapetsóna

Neapoli

Haidári

Ág. Varvára

Tampouria

Koridalos

Pireás

Níkea

Ág. Vasilios

Kphtika

Kaminia

Ág. Ioánnis Rentís

Egáleo

Salónikos

Kólpos

Mosháto

Távros

Votanikós

Ko

Roúf

Kallithéa

Keramikós

P. Fáliro

Agorá

Pláka

Akrópolis

Zápio

N. Smírni

Dafni

Kalamáki

Pagráti

Imitós

Ág. Dimítrios

Kesa

Álimos

Vironas

Ilioúpolis

Aerodrómio
Ellinikó

Argiroúpoli

Moní Karéa

Ellinikó

Soúrmena

• 765

Terpsithea

Imitó

Glifáda

JÓNII NÍSI | ÉGINA | KRITI | NÓTII, SPORÁDES, RÓDOS | KYKLÁDES | LÉSVOS, CHIOS | SOÚNIO

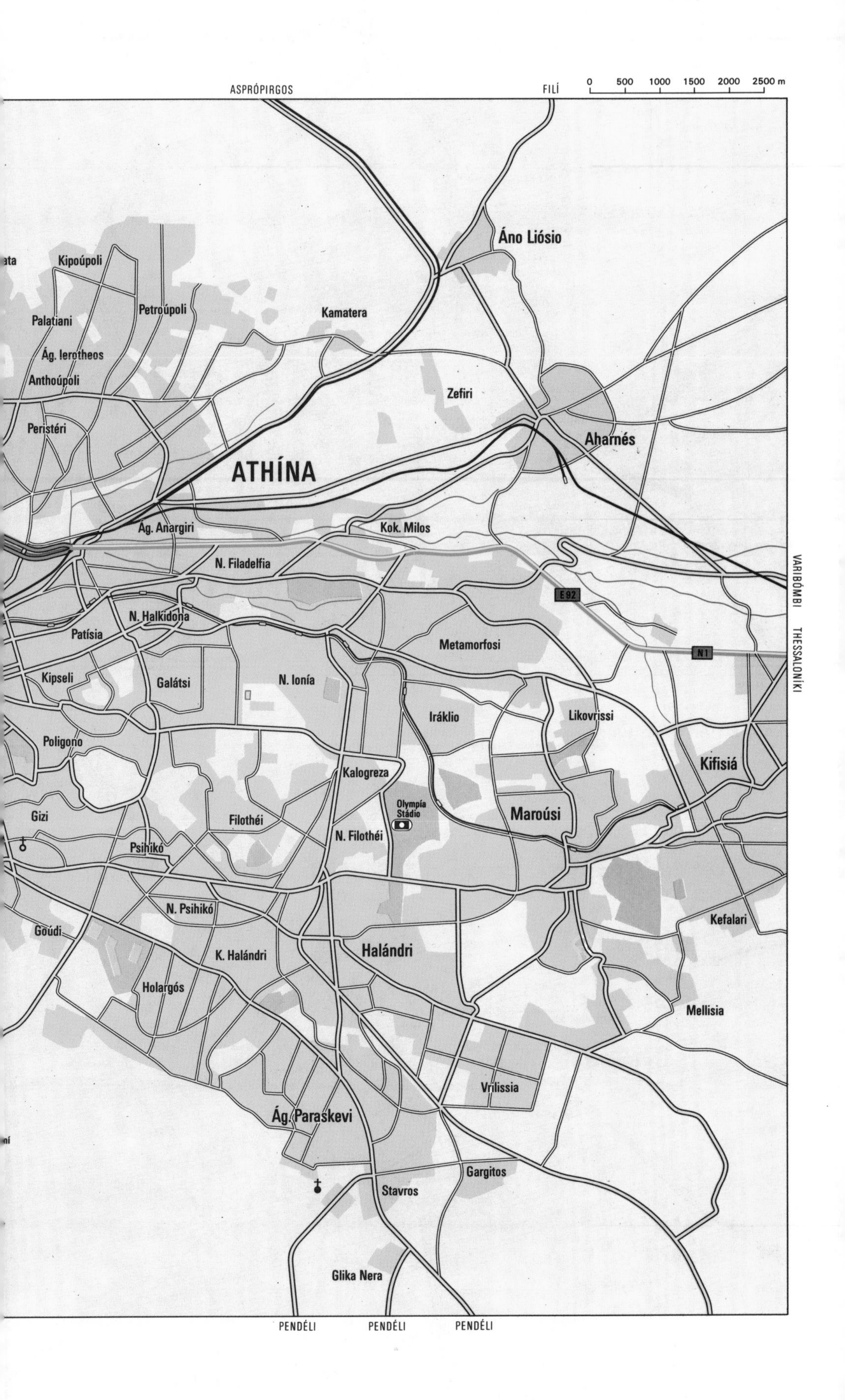

ASPRÓPIRGOS   FILÍ   0   500   1000   1500   2000   2500 m

Áno Liósio

Kipoúpoli

Palatiani   Petroúpoli   Kamatera

Ág. Ierotheos

Anthoúpoli   Zefiri

Peristéri   Aharnés

ATHÍNA

Ág. Anargiri   Kok. Milos

N. Filadelfia

VARIBÓMBI   THESSALONÍKI

N. Halkidona   E 92

Patísia   Metamorfosi

Kipseli   Galátsi   N. Ionía   N1

Poligono   Iráklio   Likovrissi

Kalogreza   Kifisiá

Gizi   Filothéi   Olympía
                                              Stádio   Maroúsi
                              N. Filothéi
Psihikó

                                                                      Kefalari
N. Psihikó

Goúdi   Mellisia
              K. Halándri   Halándri
Holargós

Vrilissia

Ág. Paraskevi

Gargitos

Stavros

Glika Nera

PENDÉLI   PENDÉLI   PENDÉLI

5

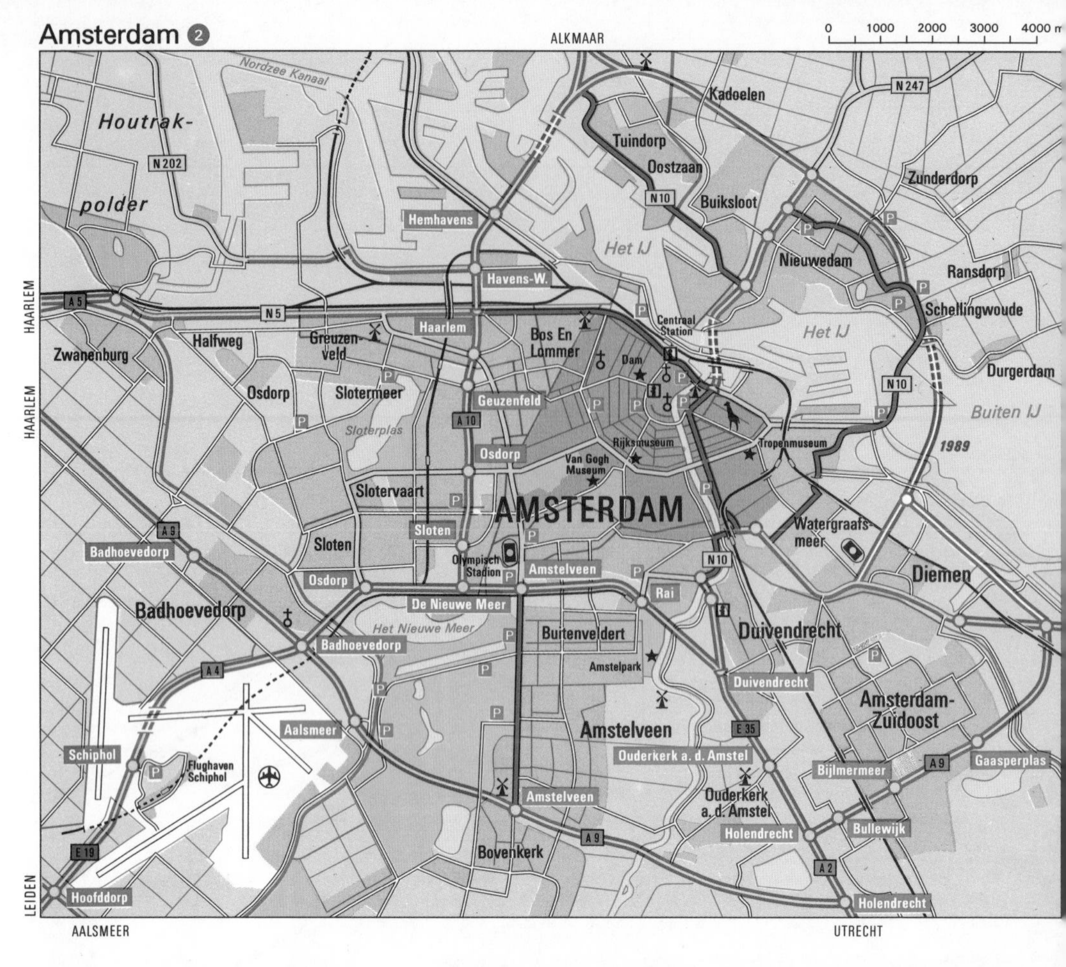

ALKMAAR

0 1000 2000 3000 4000 m

Nordzee Kanaal

Houtrak-polder

N 202

N 247

Kadoelen

Tuindorp
Oostzaan

N 10

Buiksloot

Zunderdorp

Hemhavens

Het IJ

Nieuwedam

Ransdorp

Schellingwoude

Havens-W.

Het IJ

Durgerdam

N 10

Buiten IJ

1989

HAARLEM

A 5

N 5

Halfweg

Greuzen-veld

Haarlem

Bos En Lommer

Centraal Station

Dam

Zwanenburg

Osdorp

Slotermeer

Geuzenveld

Rijksmuseum

Tropenmuseum

A 10

Osdorp

Van Gogh Museum

Slotervaart

AMSTERDAM

Watergraafs meer

A 9

Sloten

Diemen

Badhoevedorp

Sloten

Olympisch Stadion

Amstelveen

N 10

Osdorp

De Nieuwe Meer

Rai

Duivendrecht

Badhoevedorp

Het Nieuwe Meer

Buitenveldert

Duivendrecht

Amsterdam-Zuidoost

A 4

Badhoevedorp

Amstelpark

E 35

Schiphol

Aalsmeer

Ouderkerk a. d. Amstel

Bijlmermeer

A 9

Gaasperplas

Flughaven Schiphol

Amstelveen

Ouderkerk a. d. Amstel

E 19

Bovenkerk

A 9

Holendrecht

Bullewijk

A 2

Hoofddorp

Holendrecht

LEIDEN

HAARLEM

AALSMEER

UTRECHT

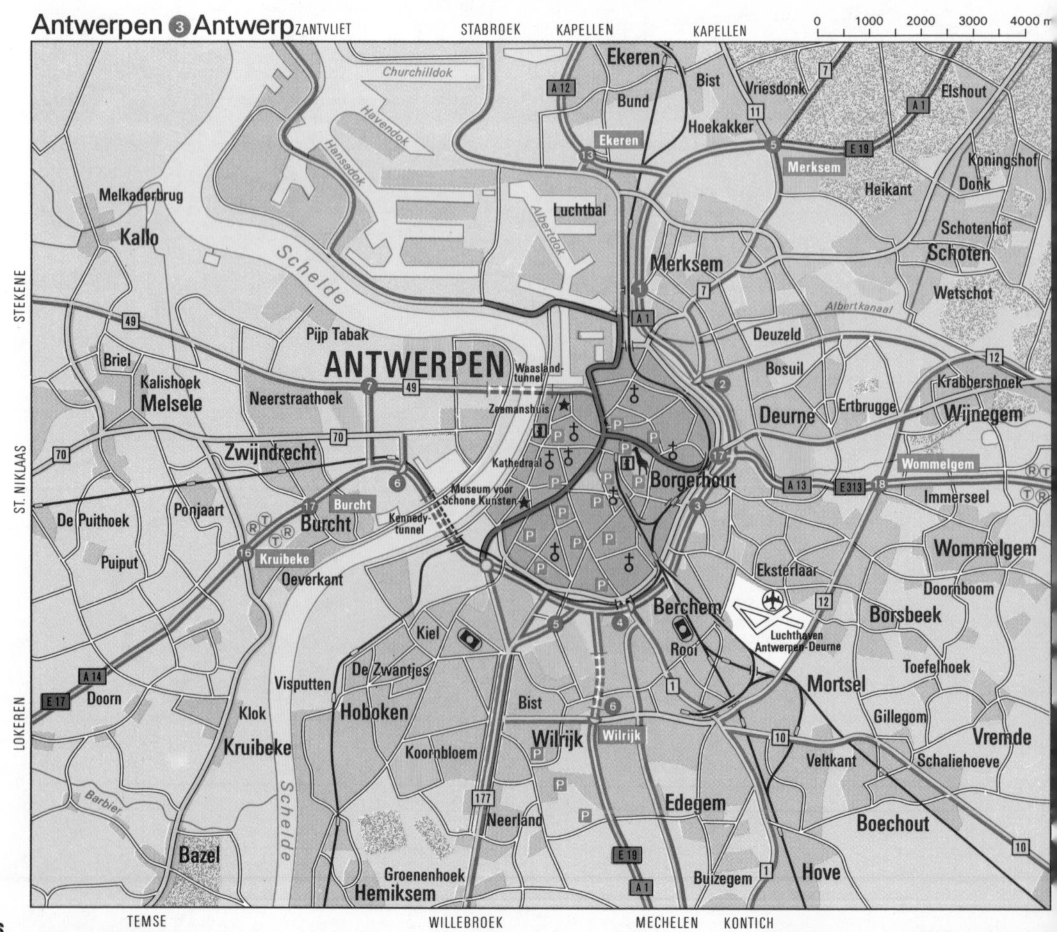

ZANTVLIET   STABROEK   KAPELLEN   KAPELLEN

0 1000 2000 3000 4000 m

Churchilldok

Ekeren

Bist

Vriesdonk

Elshout

A 12

Bund

Hoekakker

7

A 1

Havendok

Ekeren

5

E 19

Koningshof Donk

Hansedok

13

Merksem

Heikant

Schotenhof

Luchtbal

11

Schoten

Melkaderbrug

Schelde

Merksem

Wetschot

Kallo

7

Albertkanaal

49

Deuzeld

Krabbershoek

12

Briel

Pijp Tabak

A 1

Bosuil

Wijnegem

Kalishoek

ANTWERPEN

Waasland-tunnel

Deurne

Ertbrugge

Melsele

Neerstraathoek

7   49

Zeemanshuis

2

Wommelgem

Zwijndrecht

70

Kathedraal

Borgerhout

A 13   E 313

Immerseel

STEKENE

70

6

Museum voor Schone Kunsten

3

Wommelgem

De Puithoek

Ponjaart

Burcht

Kennedy-tunnel

Eksterlaar

Doornboom

Puiput

16

Kruibeke

Berchem

Luchthaven Antwerpen-Deurne

12

Borsbeek

ST. NIKLAAS

Oeverkant

Kiel

4

Rooi

Toefelhoek

A 14

Doorn

De Zwantjes

1

Mortsel

Gillegom

Vremde

E 17

Visputten

Bist

6

Wilrijk

10

Veltkant

Schaliehoeve

Klok

Hoboken

Wilrijk

LOKEREN

Kruibeke

Koornbloem

177

Edegem

Boechout

Barbier

Neerland

1

Bazel

Groenenhoek

E 19

Buizegem

Hove

Hemiksem

A 1

10

TEMSE   WILLEBROEK   MECHELEN   KONTICH

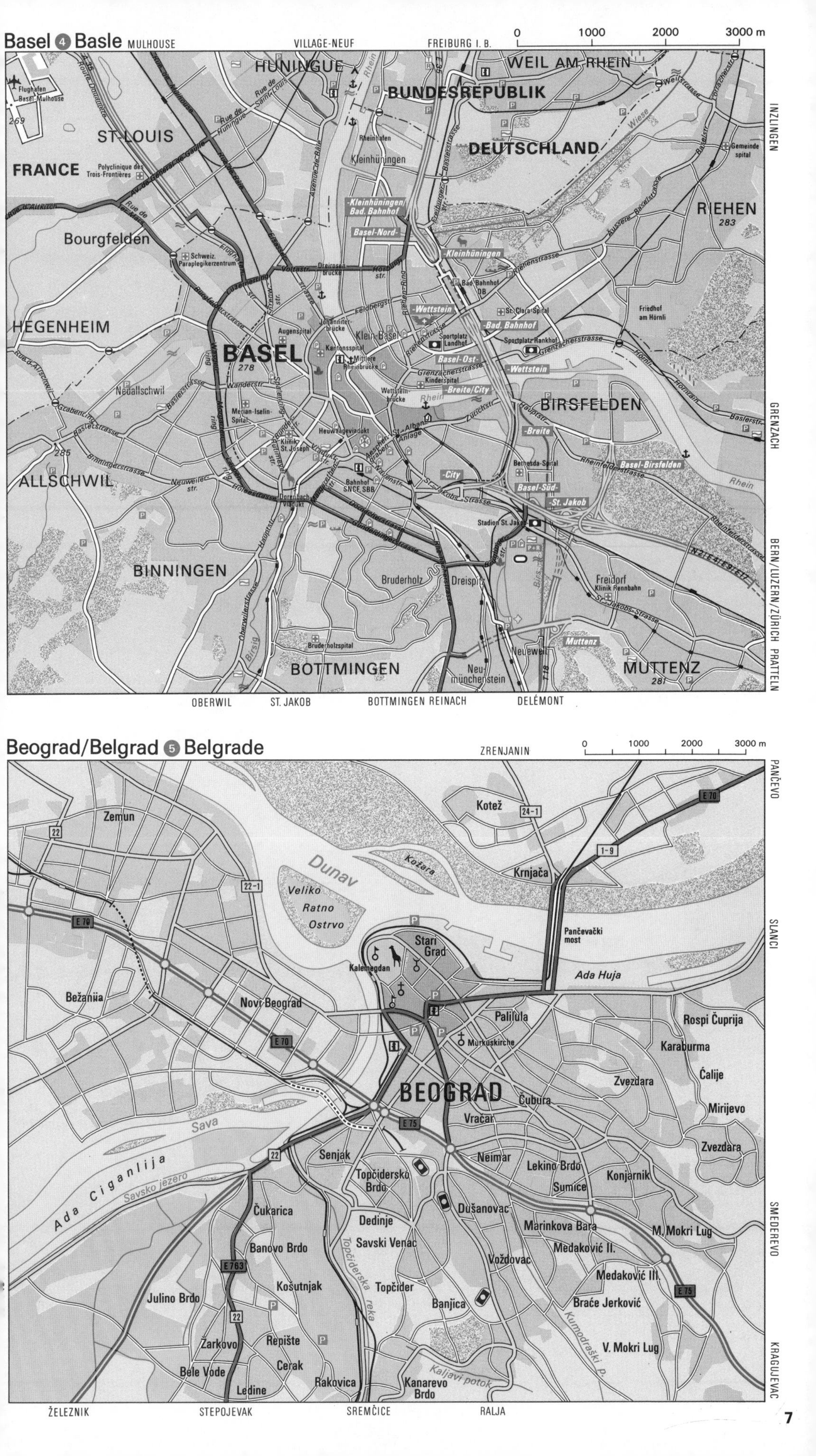

Basel ④ Basle

MULHOUSE   VILLAGE-NEUF   FREIBURG I. B.

0   1000   2000   3000 m

HUNINGUE   WEIL AM RHEIN

BUNDESREPUBLIK

DEUTSCHLAND

ST-LOUIS

FRANCE
Polyclinique des Trois-Frontieres

Kleinhüningen/ Bad. Bahnhof

Basel-Nord

RIEHEN
283

Bourgfelden

Kleinhüningen

Schweiz. Paraplegikerzentrum

HEGENHEIM

Nedallschwil

BASEL
278

St-Clara-Spital

Bad. Bahnhof DB

Friedhof am Hörnli

Augenspital
Kantonsspital

Klein-Basel

Wettstein
Bad. Bahnhof

Sportplatz Landhof
Sportplatz Rankhof

Wettstein

Klinik Merian-Iselin-Spital

Breite/City

Basel-Ost

Grenzacherstrasse
Kinderspital

BIRSFELDEN

Breite

ALLSCHWIL
285

Klinik St. Joseph

City

Bethesda-Spital

Basel-Süd

Basel-Birsfelden

Bahnhof SNCF SBB

St. Jakob

Rhein

BINNINGEN

Stadion St. Jakob

Freidorf
Klinik Rennbahn

Bruderholz

Dreispitz

BOTTMINGEN

Bruderholzspital

Neu-münchenstein

Neuewelt

Muttenz

MUTTENZ
281

OBERWIL   ST. JAKOB   BOTTMINGEN REINACH   DELÉMONT

INZLINGEN

GRENZACH

BERN/LUZERN/ZÜRICH PRATTELN

Beograd/Belgrad ⑤ Belgrade

ZRENJANIN

0   1000   2000   3000 m

Zemun

Kotež

E 70

Dunav

Kotara

Krnjača

Veliko Ratno Ostrvo

Bežanija

Stari Grad
Kalemegdan

Pančevački most

Ada Huja

Novi Beograd

E 70

Paliȟula
Murkuskirche

Rospi Čuprija

Karaburma

Sava

BEOGRAD

Čubura

Vračar

Zvezdara

Čalije

Mirijevo

Zvezdara

E 75

Neimar

Senjak

Lekino Brdo

Konjarnik

Ada Ciganlija

Savsko jezero

Topčidersko Brdo

Sumice

Čukarica

Dušanovac

Marinkova Bara

M. Mokri Lug

Dedinje

E 763

Savski Venac

Medaković II.

Banovo Brdo

Topčider

Voždovac

Medaković III.

Julino Brdo

Košutnjak

Topčider

Banjica

Braće Jerković

E 75

Žarkovo

Repište

Cerak

Kaljavi potok

V. Mokri Lug

Bele Vode

Ledine

Rakovica

Kanarevo Brdo

Kumodraški p.

ŽELEZNIK   STEPOJEVAK   SREMČICE   RALJA

PANČEVO

SLANCI

SMEDEREVO

KRAGUJEVAC

7

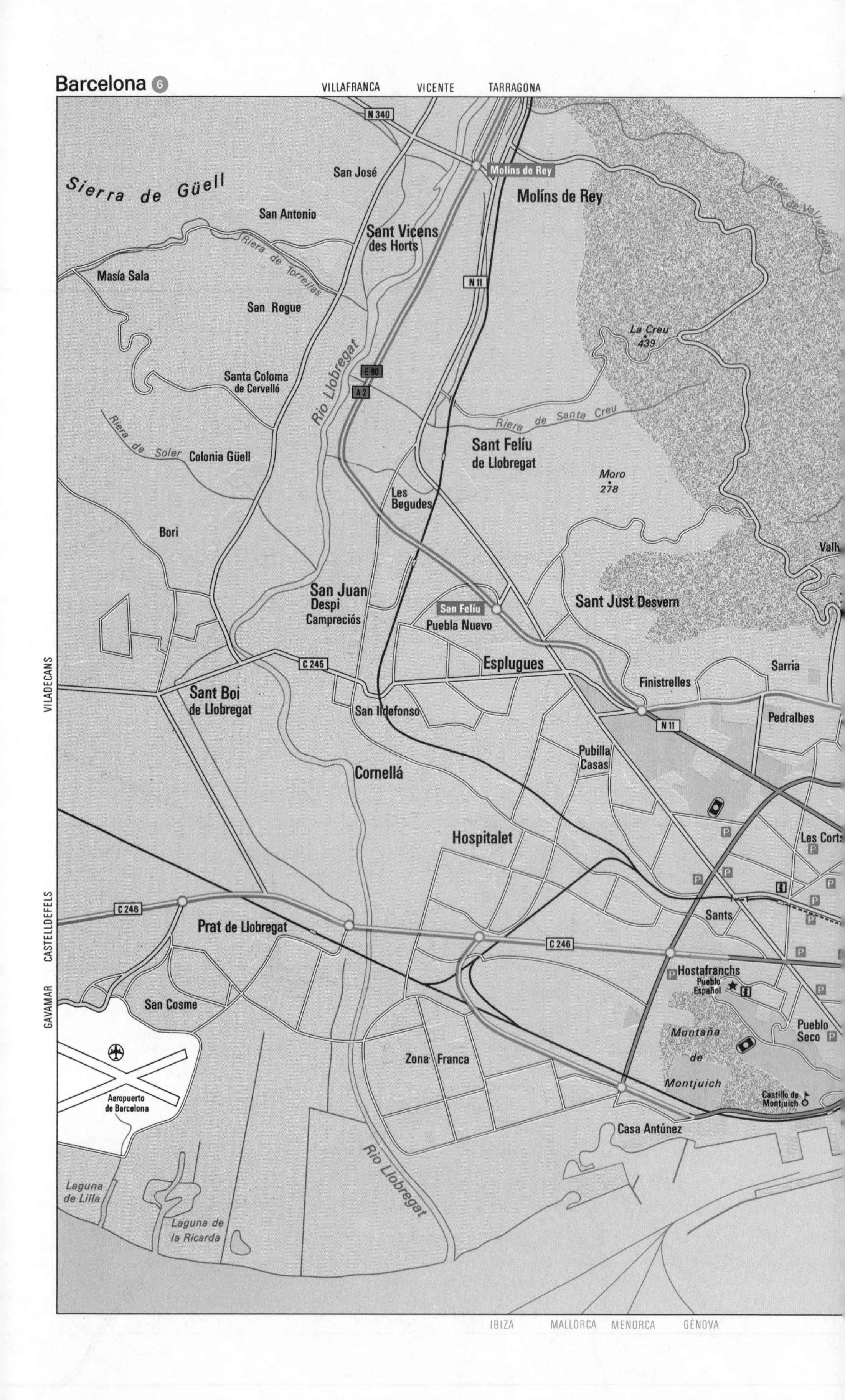

VILLAFRANCA   VICENTE   TARRAGONA

N 340

San José

Molíns de Rey

Molíns de Rey

Sierra de Güell

San Antonio

Riera de Torrelles

Sant Vicens
des Horts

N 11

Masía Sala

San Rogue

Santa Coloma
de Cervelló

Río Llobregat

E 90

A 2

Riera de Santa Creu

La Creu
439

Riera de Soler   Colonia Güell

Sant Felíu
de Llobregat

Moro
278

Bori

Les
Begudes

Valli

San Juan
Despi
Campreciós

San Felíu

Puebla Nuevo

Sant Just Desvern

Esplugues

Sarria

Finistrelles

C 245

Sant Boi
de Llobregat

San Ildefonso

N 11

Pedralbes

Cornellá

Pubilla
Casas

Hospitalet

Les Corts

P

CASTELLDEFELS   VILADECANS

C 246

Prat de Llobregat

C 246

Sants

P

P
i
P

P

GAVAMAR

San Cosme

Hostafranchs
Pueblo
Español ★ i

Pueblo
Seco P

Montaña

de

Zona Franca

Montjuich

Aeropuerto
de Barcelona

Casa Antúnez

Castillo de
Montjuich

Laguna
de Lilla

Laguna de
la Ricarda

Río Llobregat

IBIZA   MALLORCA   MENORCA   GÉNOVA

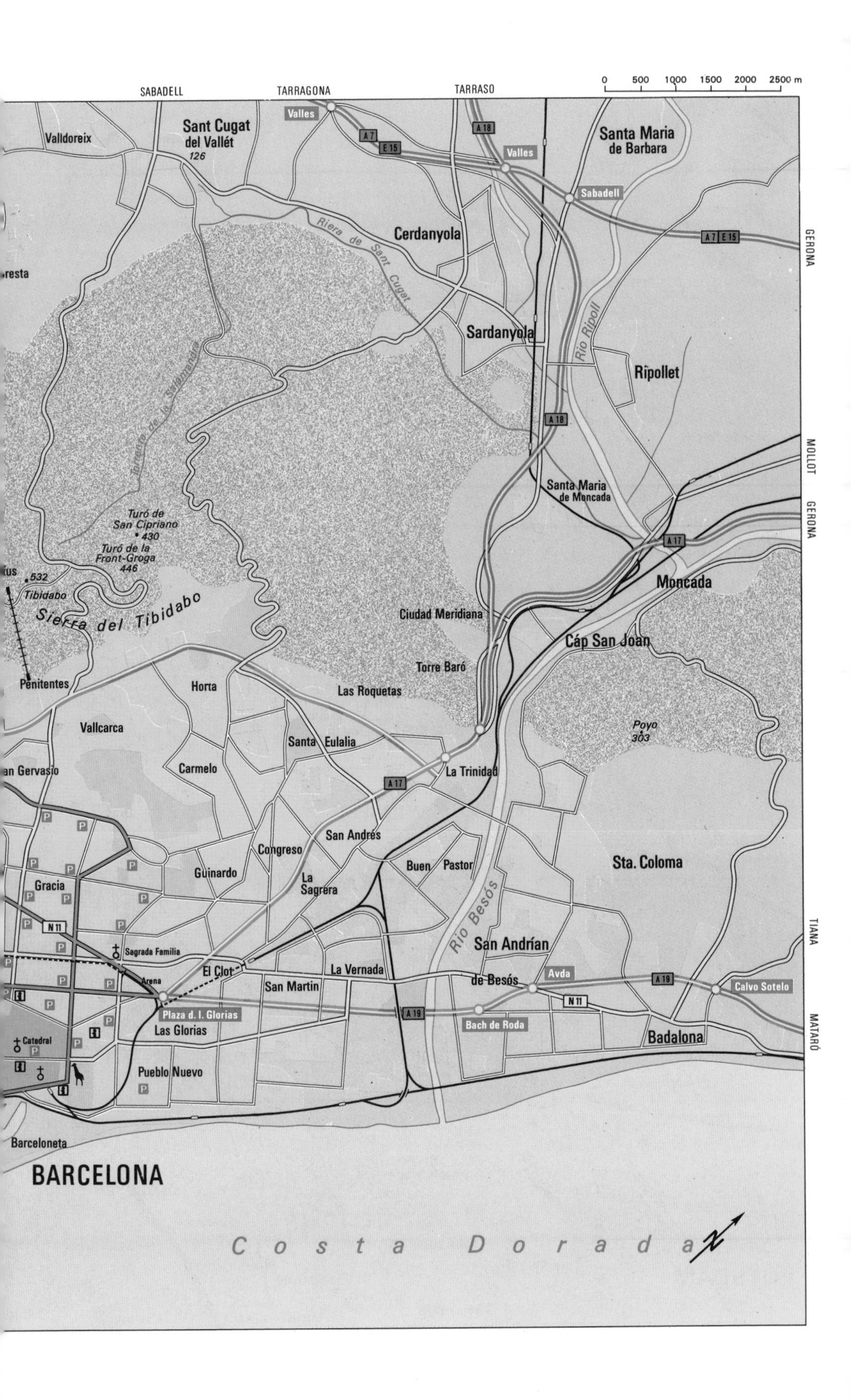

SABADELL   TARRAGONA   TARRASO

0   500   1000   1500   2000   2500 m

Valldoreix

Sant Cugat
del Vallét
126

Valles

Santa Maria
de Barbara

Riera de Sant Cugat

Cerdanyola

Sardanyola

Ripollet

resta

Turó de
San Cipriano
• 430

Turó de la
Front-Groga
446

Santa Maria
de Moncada

Ciudad Meridiana

Moncáda

rius
• 532

Tibidabo

Sierra del Tibidabo

Cáp San Joan

Penitentes

Horta

Las Roquetas

Torre Baró

Poyo
303

Vallcarca

Santa Eulalia

San Gervasio

Carmelo

La Trinidad

Congreso

San Andrés

Gracia

Guinardo

La
Sagrera

Buen   Pastor

Sta. Coloma

N 11

Sagrada Familia

El Clot

La Vernada

San Andrían
de Besós

Avda

Calvo Sotelo

Arena

San Martin

Plaza d. I. Glorias

Las Glorias

Bach de Roda

N 11

Badalona

Catadral

Pueblo Nuevo

A 19

Barceloneta

BARCELONA

Costa   Dorada

Río Ripoll

Río Besós

GERONA

MOLLOT   GERONA

TIANA   MATARÓ

9

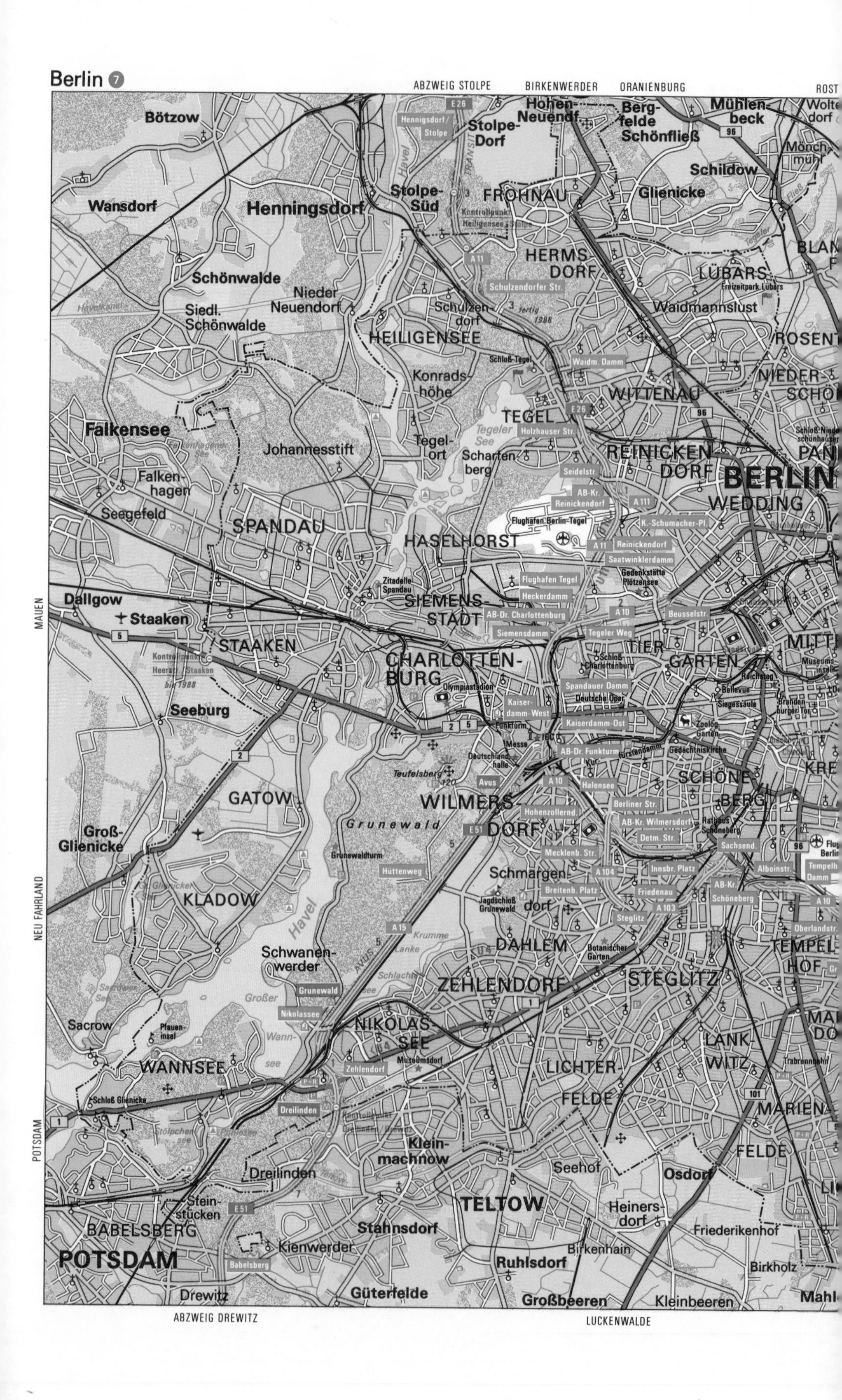

Berlin ⑦

Bötzow

Wansdorf

Henningsdorf

Hohen-Neuendf
Stolpe-Dorf
Schönfließ
Berg-felde

Mühlen-beck
Wolte-dorf
Mönch-mühl

Schildow

Glienicke

BLAN

Stolpe-Süd
FROHNAU

HERMS-DORF
LÜBARS
Freizeitpark Lubars

Schönwalde

Nieder Neuendorf
Siedl. Schönwalde

Schulzen-dorf
Schulzendorfer Str.
fertig 1988
Waidmannslust

ROSEN

Falkensee

Heiligensee

Schloß-Tegel
Waidm. Damm
WITTENAU

Schloß Nieder-schönhauser
NIEDER-SCHÖ

Johannesstift

Konrads-höhe

Tegel
Tegeler See
Holzhauser Str.
REINICKEN-DORF

PAN

Falken-hagen

Tegel-ort
Scharfen-berg
Seidelstr.

BERLIN
WEDDING

Seegefeld

SPANDAU

HASELHORST

AB-Kr. Reinickendorf
A 111
Flughafen Berlin-Tegel
Reinickendorf
K.-Schumacher-Pl
A 10
Beusselstr.

Dallgow

Staaken

Zitadelle Spandau
SIEMENS-STADT
Flughafen Tegel
Heckerdamm
AB-Dr. Charlottenburg
Siemensdamm
Tegeler Weg
Saatwinklerdamm
Gedenkstätte Plötzensee

TIER
GARTEN

MITT
Museums-insel

STAAKEN

Seeburg

CHARLOTTEN-BURG
Olympiastadion
Kaiser-damm-West
Funkturm
Schloß Charlottenburg
Spandauer Damm
Deutsche Oper
Kaiserdamm-Ost
AB-Dr. Funkturm
Reichstag
Bellevue
Siegessäule
Brandenburger Tor
Zoolog. Garten

GATOW

Grunewald
Teufelsberg
Avus
Deutschland-halle
Messe
A 10
Halensee
Hohenzollernd.
Berliner Str.
AB-Kr. Wilmersdorf
Detm. Str.
SCHÖNE-BERG
Gedächtniskirche

KRE

Groß-Glienicke

WILMERS-DORF
Grunewaldturm
Hüttenweg
Mecklenb. Str.
Rathaus Schöneberg
Sachsend.

Flug Berlin
Tempelh Damm
96

KLADOW

Havel
Krumme Lanke
A 15
Schmargen-dorf
Breitenb. Platz
Friedenau
Steglitz
Innsbr. Platz
A 104
AB-Kr. Schöneberg
A 103
A 10
Oberlandstr.

Schwanen-werder

Jagdschloß Grunewald
DAHLEM
Botanischer Garten
TEMPEL-HOF

Sacrow

Grunewald
Nikolassee
Großer Wann-see
Seerose See
ZEHLENDORF
STEGLITZ

MAI DO

WANNSEE

Plauen-insel
Zehlendorf
NIKOLAS-SEE
Museumsdorf
LICHTER-FELDE

LANK-WITZ
Trabrennbahn

Schloß Glienicke
Dreilinden
Stölpchensee
Kleinmachnow
Seehof
Osdorf
MARIEN

FELDE

BABELSBERG

Steinstücken
E 51
Dreilinden
TELTOW
Heiners-dorf
Birkenhain
Friederikenhof

101

LI

POTSDAM

Babelsberg
Kienwerder
Stahnsdorf
Ruhlsdorf
Birkholz

Drewitz
Güterfelde
Großbeeren
Kleinbeeren
Mahl

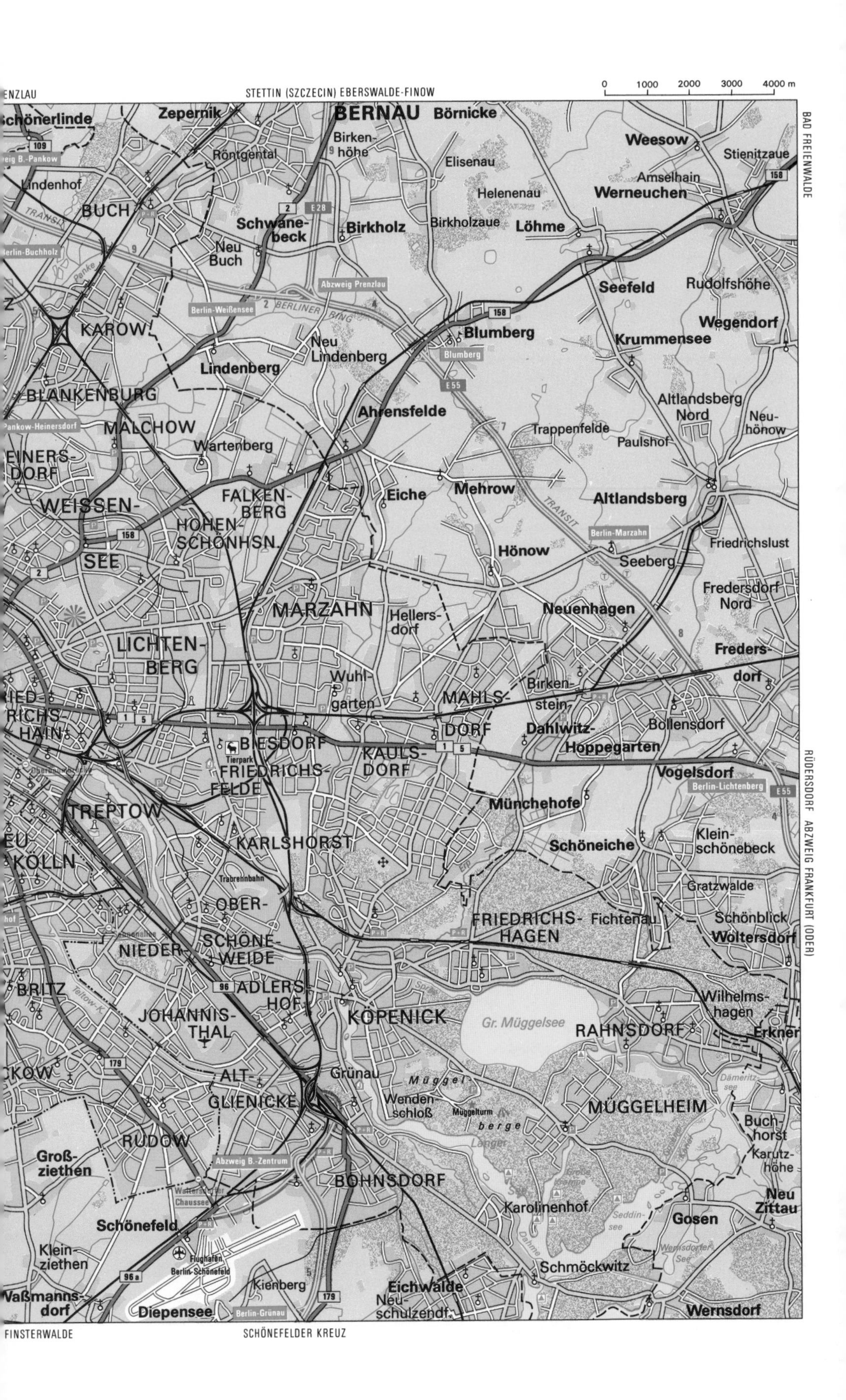

0   1000   2000   3000   4000 m

BAD FREIENWALDE

Schönerlinde

Zepernik

BERNAU

Börnicke

Weesow

Stienitzaue

Birken-
höhe

109

Röntgental

Elisenau

Amselhain

Lindenhof

Helenenau

Werneuchen

Zweig B.-Pankow

BUCH

Schwane-
beck

E 28

Birkholz

Birkholzaue

Löhme

Rudolfshöhe

Berlin-Buchholz

Neu
Buch

Abzweig Prenzlau

Seefeld

KAROW

Berlin-Weißensee

BERLINER RING

158

Blumberg

Krummensee

Wegendorf

Neu
Lindenberg

Blumberg

TRANSIT

BLANKENBURG

Lindenberg

E 55

Altlandsberg
Nord

Neu-
höhow

Pankow-Heinersdorf

MALCHOW

Ahrensfelde

Trappenfelde

Paulshof

EINERS-
DORF

Wartenberg

Eiche

Mehrow

Altlandsberg

Friedrichslust

WEISSEN-

FALKEN-
BERG

Berlin-Marzahn

HOHEN-
SCHÖNHSN.

Hönow

Seeberg

Fredersdorf
Nord

SEE

158

2

MARZAHN

Hellers-
dorf

Neuenhagen

Freders-

LICHTEN-
BERG

Wuhl-
garten

MAHLS-

Birken-
stein

dorf

Bollensdorf

IED-
RICHS-
HAIN

1   5

DORF

1   5

Dahlwitz-
Hoppegarten

BIESDORF

KAULS-
DORF

Tierpark

FRIEDRICHS-
FELDE

Münchehofe

Vogelsdorf

Berlin-Lichtenberg

E 55

TREPTOW

KARLSHORST

Schöneiche

Klein-
schönebeck

EU
KÖLLN

Trabrennbahn

FRIEDRICHS-
HAGEN

Fichtenau

Gratzwalde

Schönblick

Woltersdorf

OBER-
SCHÖNE-
WEIDE

NIEDER-

BRITZ

96

ADLERS-
HOF

Wilhelms-
hagen

Erkner

JOHANNIS-
THAL

KÖPENICK

Gr. Müggelsee

RAHNSDORF

KOW

179

ALT-
GLIENICKE

Grünau

Müggel

Dämeritz
see

Wenden-
schloß

Müggelturm

MÜGGELHEIM

RUDOW

berge

Langer

Buch-
horst

Groß-
ziethen

Abzweig B.-Zentrum

P+R

Karutz-
höhe

Water
Chaussee

BOHNSDORF

Karolinenhof

Seddin-
see

Gosen

Neu
Zittau

Schönefeld

Klein-
ziethen

Flughafen
Berlin-Schönefeld

96 a

Kienberg

179

Eichwalde

Dahme

Wernsdorfer
See

Schmöckwitz

Vaßmanns-
dorf

Diepensee

Berlin-Grünau

Neu-
schulzendf.

Wernsdorf

RÜDERSDORF   ABZWEIG FRANKFURT (ODER)

11

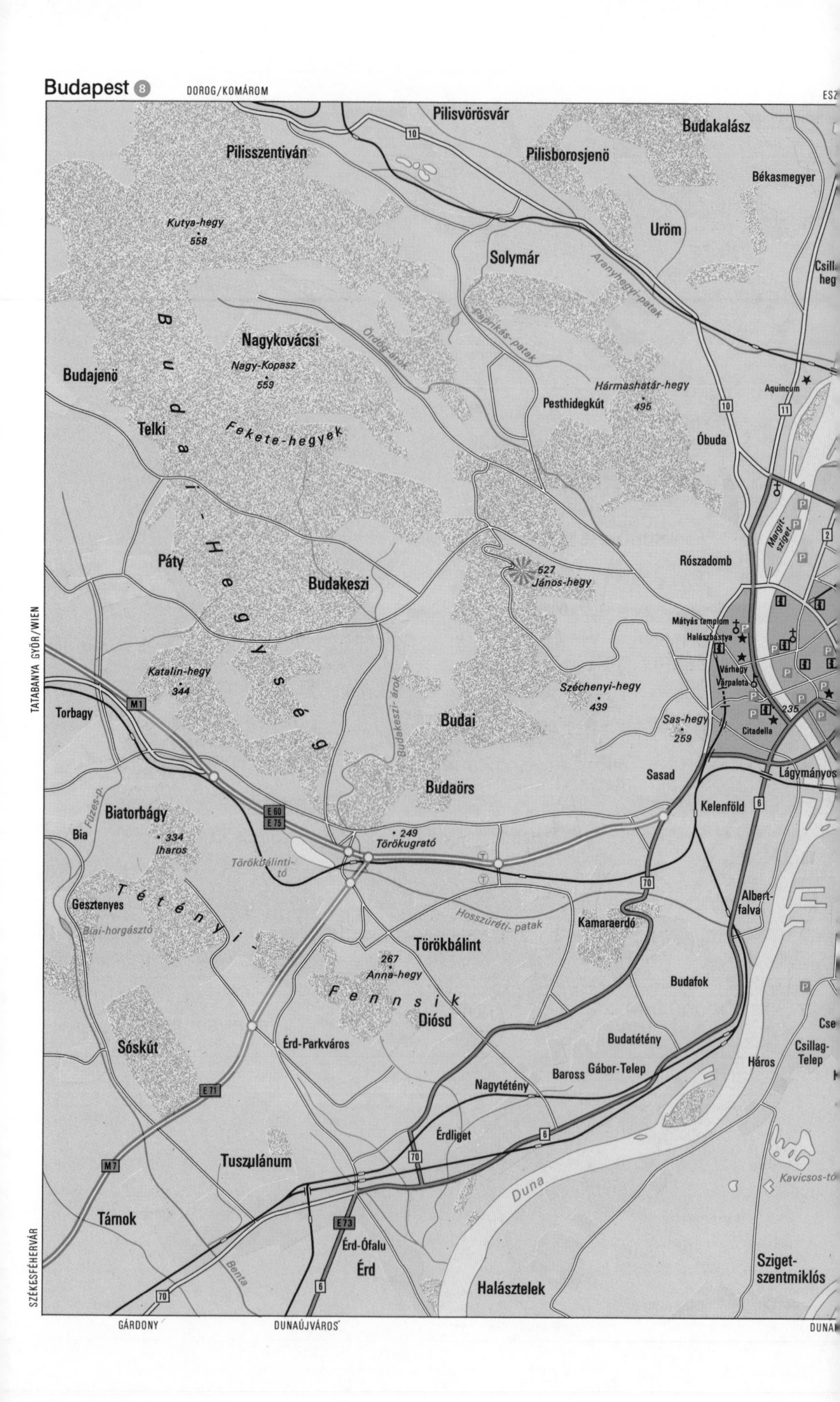

Pilisvörösvár

Pilisszentiván

Budakalász

Békasmegyer

Kutya-hegy
558

Solymár

Uröm

Pilisborosjenö

Csill
heg

Buda

Nagykovácsi

Nagy-Kopasz
559

Hármashatár-hegy
Pesthidegkút 495

Aquincum

Budajenö

Telki

Fekete-hegyek

Óbuda

Páty

Budakeszi

527
János-hegy

Rószadomb

Margit-sziget

Mátyás templom
Halászbástya

Katalin-hegy
344

Budakeszi-árok

Széchenyi-hegy
439

Várhegy
Várpalota
235

Torbagy

M1

Budai

Sas-hegy
259

Citadella

Sasad

Lágymányos

Budaörs

Biatorbágy

E 60
E 75

249
Törökugrató

Kelenföld

6

Bia

334
Iharos

Törökbálinti-tó

Albert-falvá

Gesztenyes

Tétényi-

Biai-horgásztó

Hosszúréti- patak

Kamaraerdő

70

Fennsík

Törökbálint

267
Anna-hegy

Budafok

Cse

Sóskút

Diósd

Érd-Parkváros

Budatétény

Csillag-Telep

Háros

E 71

Baross Gábor-Telep

Nagytétény

Tuszulánum

M7

70

Érdliget

6

Duna

Kavicsos-tó

Tárnok

E 73

Érd-Ófalu
Érd

70

6

Halásztelek

Sziget-szentmiklós

GÁRDONY   DUNAÚJVÁROS   DUNA

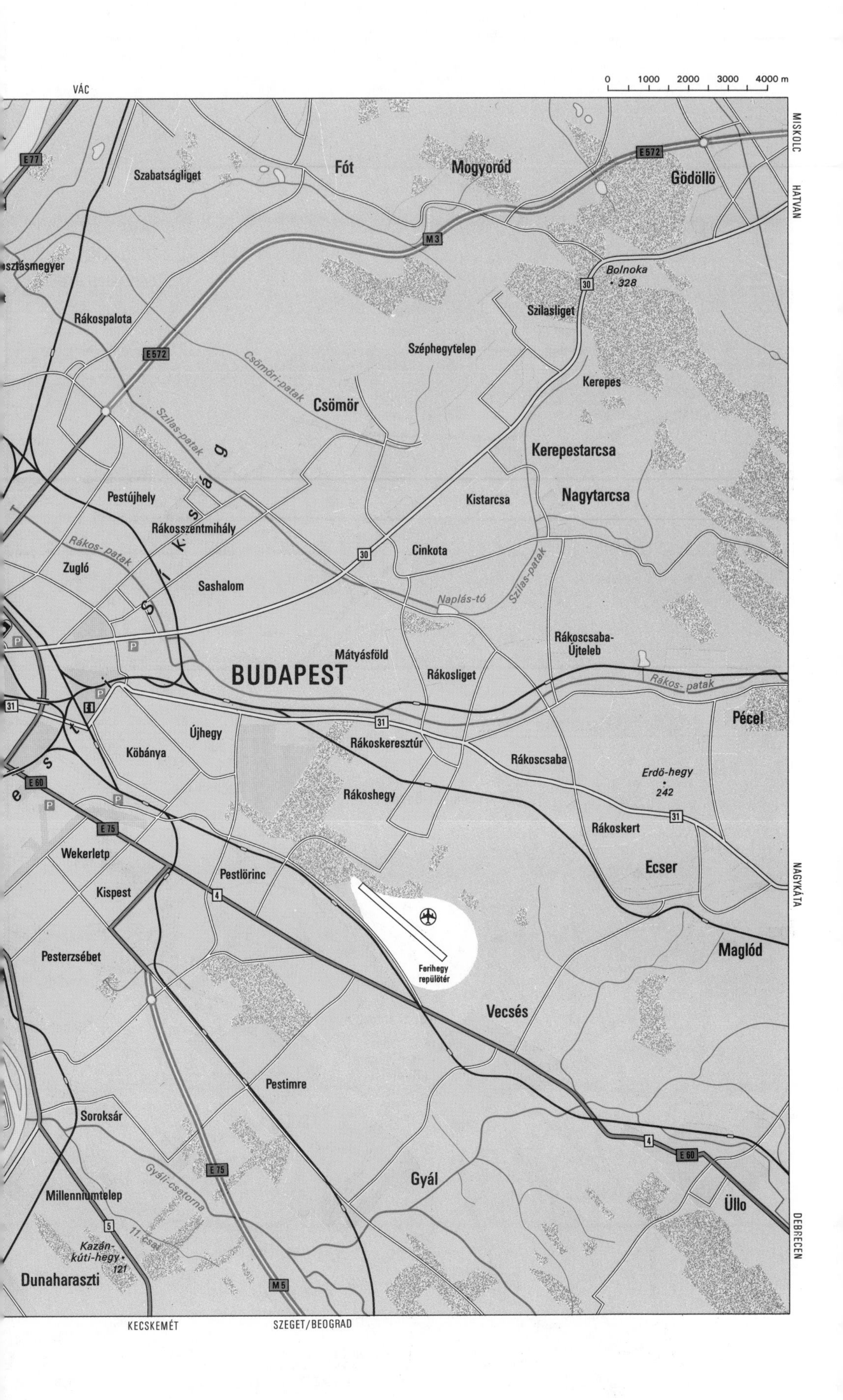

0   1000   2000   3000   4000 m

MISKOLC

E 77

Szabatságliget

Fót

Mogyoród

E 572

Gödöllö

HATVAN

...sztásmegyer

30

Bolnoka
• 328

Rákospalota

Szilasliget

E 572

Széphegytelep

Kerepes

Csömöri-patak

Csömör

Szilas-patak

Kerepestarcsa

Pestújhely

Kistarcsa

Nagytarcsa

Rákosszentmihály

30

Rákos- patak

Cinkota

Zugló

Sashalom

Naplás-tó

Szilas-patak

Rákoscsaba-
Újteleb

P

Mátyásföld

Rákosliget

Rákos- patak

BUDAPEST

31

Pécel

Újhegy

31

Köbánya

Rákoskeresztúr

Rákoscsaba

Erdö-hegy
•
242

E 60

Rákoshegy

Rákoskert

31

P

E 75

Wekerletp

Pestlörinc

Ecser

Kispest

4

NAGYKÁTA

Feríhegy
repülötér

Maglód

Pesterzsébet

Vecsés

Pestimre

Soroksár

Gyáli-csatorna

E 75

Gyál

Üllo

DEBRECEN

Millenniumtelep

5

11. Csat.

Kazán-
kúti-hegy •
121

4

E 60

Dunaharaszti

M 5

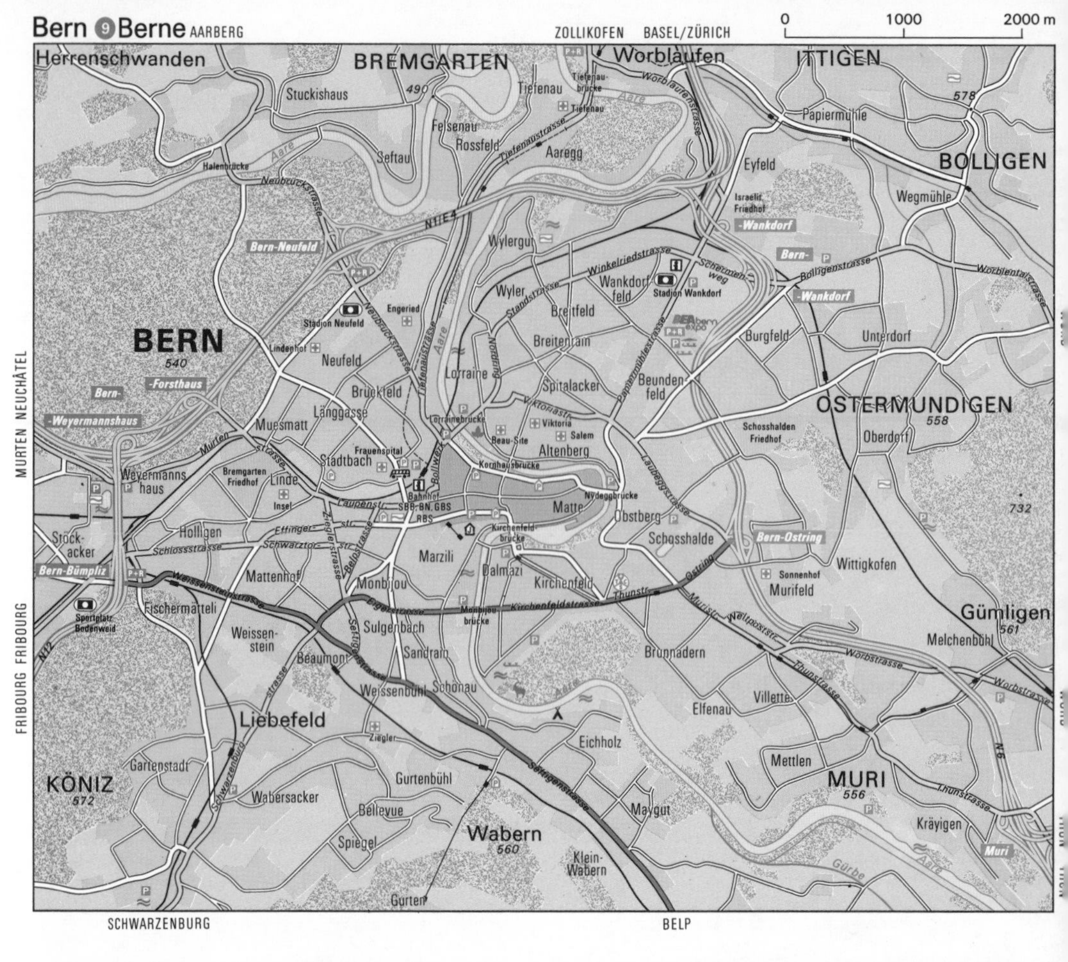

Bern ⑨ Berne

AARBERG • ZOLLIKOFEN • BASEL/ZÜRICH

0   1000   2000 m

Herrenschwanden • BREMGARTEN • Worblaufen • ITTIGEN

Stuckishaus • Tiefenau • Tiefenaubrücke • Tiefenau • Papiermühle • BOLLIGEN

Halenacker • Rossfeld • Seftau • Felsenau • Aaregg • Eyfeld • Wegmühle

Bern-Neufeld • Neubrück • Wylergut • Israelit. Friedhof • Wankdorf

Wyler • Wankdorf feld • Winkelriedstrasse • Schermen weg • Bern-Wankdorf

BERN 540 • Stadion Neufeld • Lindenhof • Neufeld • Lorraine • Breitfeld • Stadion Wankdorf • Burgfeld • Unterdorf

Forsthaus • Bruckfeld • Spitalacker • Breitenrain • Beunden feld

Bern-Weyermannshaus • Langgasse • Viktoria • Salem • Altenberg • Schosshalden Friedhof • Oberdorf • **OSTERMUNDIGEN** 558

Muesmatt • Frauenspital • Stadtbach • Beau-Site • Kornhausbrücke • Nydeggbrücke • 732

Weyermanns haus • Bremgarten Friedhof • Linde • Insel • Bahnhof • SBB-BN GBS • Matte • Obstberg • Bern-Ostring

Stöckacker • Holligen • RBS • Marzili • Kirchenfeld brücke • Schosshalde • Wittigkofen

Bern-Bümpliz • Mattenhof • Schwarztor • Dalmazi • Kirchenfeld • Sonnenhof Friedhof • Murifeld • **Gümligen** 561

Sportplatz Bodenweid • Fischermätteli • Sulgenbach • Sandrain • Schönau • Brunnadern • Elfenau • Villette • Melchenbühl

Weissen stein • Beaumont • Weissenbühl • Eichholz • Mettlen • **MURI** 556 • Kräyigen

KÖNIZ 572 • Gartenstadt • Wabersacker • Ziegler • Gurtenbühl • Maygut • Muri

Liebefeld • Bellevue • Spiegel • **Wabern** 560 • Klein-Wabern • Gurten

SCHWARZENBURG • BELP

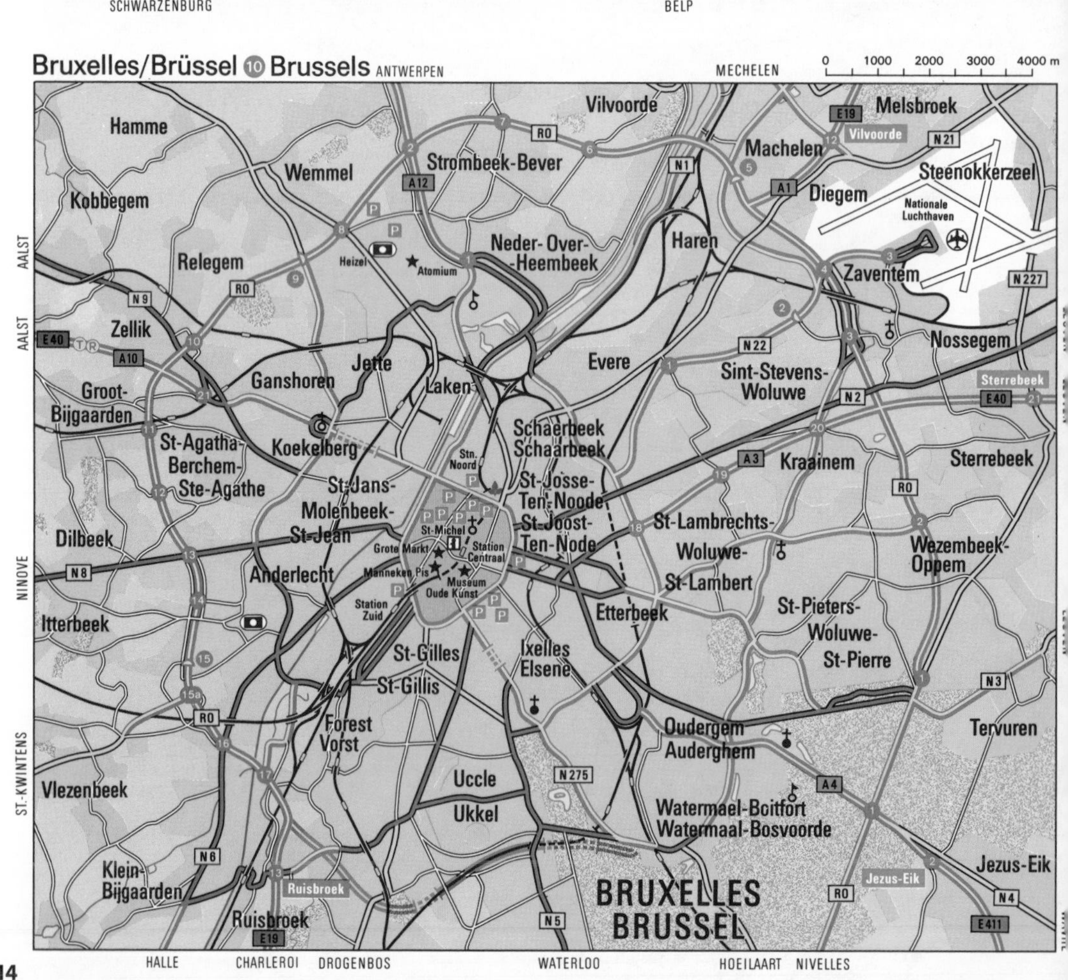

Bruxelles/Brüssel ⑩ Brussels

ANTWERPEN • MECHELEN

0   1000   2000   3000   4000 m

Hamme • Vilvoorde • Melsbroek • E19 • Vilvoorde • N 21

Kobbegem • Wemmel • Strombeek-Bever • A12 • Machelen • Steenokkerzeel • A1 • Diegem

Relegem • Heizel • Neder-Over-Heembeek • Haren • Nationale Luchthaven • Zaventem • N 227

Zellik • E40 • A10 • Atomium • Evere • N 22 • Nossegem

Groot-Bijgaarden • Ganshoren • Jette • Laken • Sint-Stevens-Woluwe • N 2 • Sterrebeek • E40

St-Agatha-Berchem-Ste-Agathe • Koekelberg • Schaerbeek Schaarbeek • Kraainem • RO • Sterrebeek

St-Jans-Molenbeek-St-Jean • Stn. Noord • St-Josse-Ten-Noode St-Joost-Ten-Node • A3 • St-Lambrechts-Woluwe • Wezembeek-Oppem

Dilbeek • Anderlecht • St-Michel • Grote Markt • Station Centraal • Manneken Pis • Museum Oude Kunst • St-Lambert • St-Pieters-Woluwe-St-Pierre

Itterbeek • Station Zuid • N 3

St-Gilles St-Gillis • Ixelles Elsene • Etterbeek • N 275 • Oudergem Auderghem • A4 • Tervuren

Vlezenbeek • Forest Vorst • Uccle Ukkel • Watermael-Boitsfort Watermaal-Bosvoorde • Jezus-Eik • N 3

Klein-Bijgaarden • N 6 • Ruisbroek • N 275 • Jezus-Eik • RO • N 4

Ruisbroek • E19 • **BRUXELLES BRUSSEL** • N 5 • E411

HALLE • CHARLEROI • DROGENBOS • WATERLOO • HOEILAART • NIVELLES

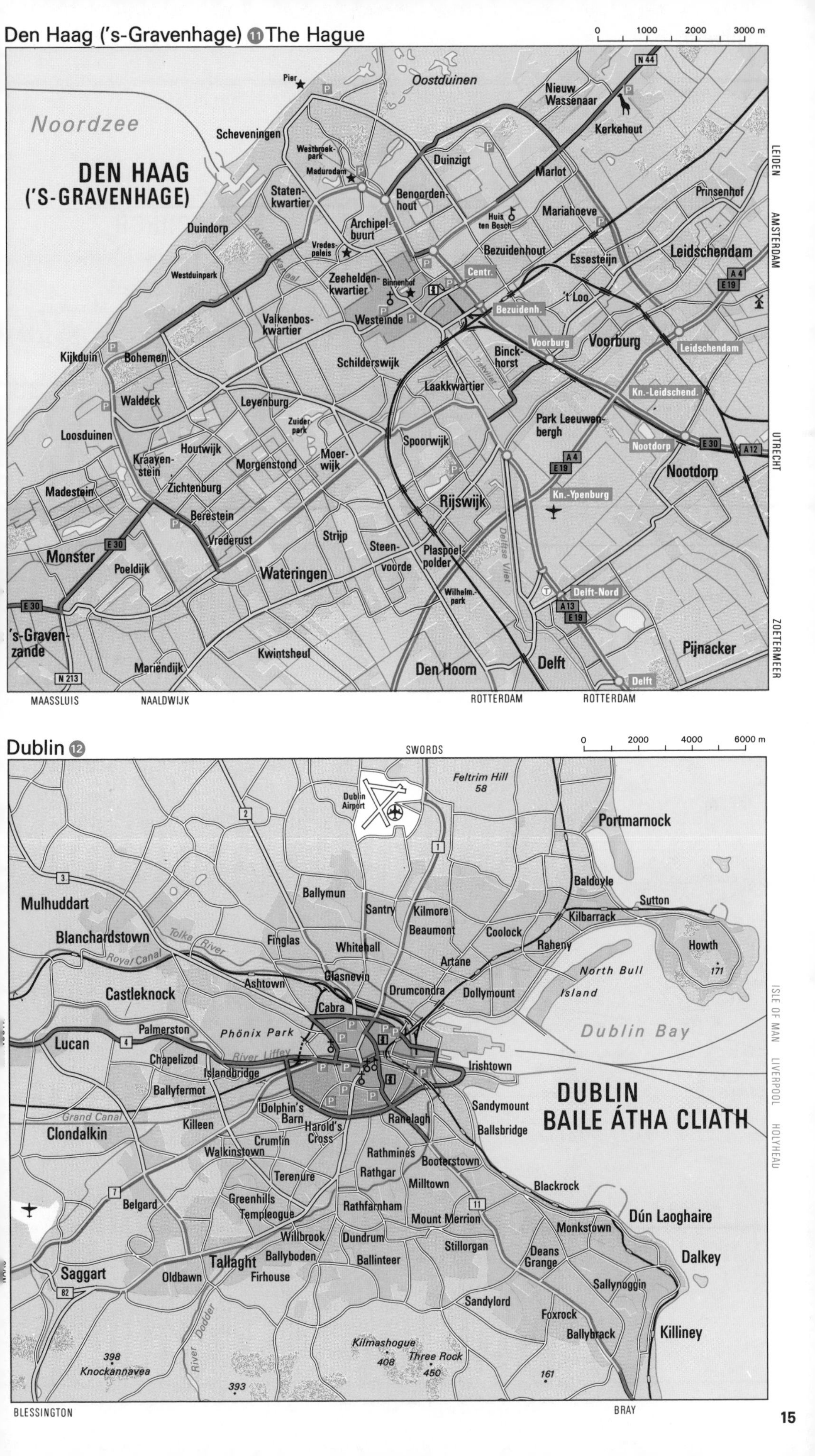

Den Haag ('s-Gravenhage) ⑪ The Hague

0   1000   2000   3000 m

DEN HAAG ('S-GRAVENHAGE)

Noordzee

Oostduinen

N 44

LEIDEN
AMSTERDAM
UTRECHT
ZOETERMEER

Pier

Scheveningen

Westbroek-park
Madurodam

Duinzigt

Nieuw Wassenaar

Kerkehout

Staten-kwartier

Benoorden-hout

Marlot

Prinsenhof

Duindorp

Archipel-buurt

Huis ten Bosch

Mariahoeve

Essesteijn

Leidschendam

A 4
E 19

Vredes-paleis

Bezuidenhout

'tLoo

Westduinpark

Zeehelden-kwartier

Binnenhof

Centr.

Voorburg

Voorburg

Kijkduin

Bohemen

Valkenbos-kwartier

Westeinde

Bezuidenh.

Leidschendam

Kn.-Leidschend.

Waldeck

Schilderswijk

Binck-horst

Loosduinen

Houtwijk

Leyenburg

Zuiderpark

Laakkwartier

Park Leeuwenbergh

Nootdorp

E 30

A 12

Kraayen-stein

Morgenstond

Moer-wijk

Spoorwijk

A 4
E 19

Nootdorp

Madestein

Zichtenburg

Berestein

Rijswijk

Kn.-Ypenburg

Monster

E 30

Vrederust

Strijp

Steen-voorde

Plaspoel-polder

Delfse Vliet

Poeldijk

Wateringen

Wilhelm.-park

Delft-Nord

A 13
E 19

Pijnacker

's-Graven-zande

Mariëndijk

Kwintsheul

Den Hoorn

Delft

Delft

N 213

MAASSLUIS   NAALDWIJK   ROTTERDAM   ROTTERDAM

Dublin ⑫

0   2000   4000   6000 m

SWORDS

Feltrim Hill 58

Dublin Airport

Portmarnock

ISLE OF MAN
LIVERPOOL
HOLYHEAD

Mulhuddart

Ballymun

Santry

Kilmore

Beaumont

Balduyle

Sutton

Blanchardstown

Royal Canal

Tolka River

Finglas

Whitehall

Coolock

Kilbarrack

Raheny

Howth

171

Castleknock

Ashtown

Glasnevin

Drumcondra

Artane

Dollymount

North Bull Island

Dublin Bay

Lucan

Palmerston

Cabra

Phönix Park

River Liffey

Chapelizod

Islandbridge

Irishtown

DUBLIN BAILE ÁTHA CLIATH

Ballyfermot

Grand Canal

Dolphin's Barn

Harold's Cross

Ranelagh

Sandymount

Clondalkin

Killeen

Crumlin

Rathmines

Booterstown

Ballsbridge

Walkinstown

Rathgar

Milltown

Blackrock

Belgard

Terenure

Rathfarnham

Mount Merrion

11

Dún Laoghaire

Greenhills Templeogue

Monkstown

Saggart

Willbrook

Dundrum

Stillorgan

Deans Grange

Dalkey

82

Oldbawn

Tallaght

Ballyboden

Ballinteer

Sallynoggin

Firhouse

Sandylord

Foxrock

Ballybrack

Killiney

398 Knockannavea

393

River Dodder

Kilmashogue

408

Three Rock 450

161

BLESSINGTON   BRAY

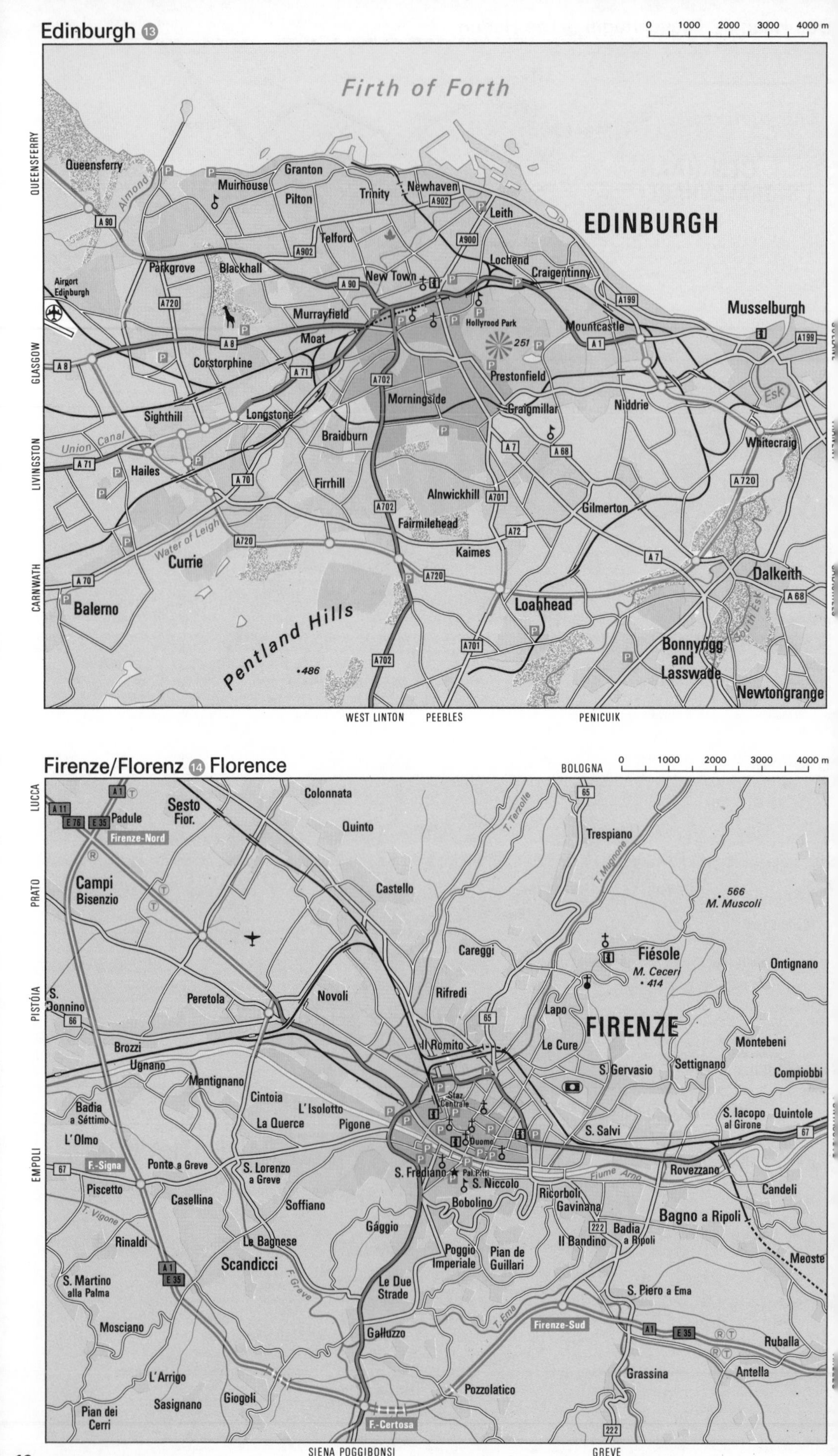

Edinburgh ⑬

Firth of Forth

Queensferry
Muirhouse
Granton
Trinity
Newhaven
Pilton
Leith
EDINBURGH
Telford
Lochend
Craigentinny
Parkgrove
Blackhall
New Town
Mountcastle
Musselburgh
Murrayfield
Hollyrood Park
251
Moat
Prestonfield
Corstorphine
Graigmillar
Niddrie
Sighthill
Morningside
Longstone
Braidburn
Whitecraig
Hailes
Firrhill
Gilmerton
Currie
Fairmilehead
Kaimes
Balerno
Loanhead
Dalkeith
Pentland Hills
·486
Bonnyrigg
and
Lasswade
Newtongrange

QUEENSFERRY
GLASGOW
LIVINGSTON
CARNWATH

Airport
Edinburgh

Union Canal
Water of Leith

WEST LINTON   PEEBLES   PENICUIK

Firenze/Florenz ⑭ Florence

BOLOGNA

Colonnata
Sesto Fior.
Padule
Quinto
Trespiano
Firenze-Nord
566
M. Muscoli
Campi Bisenzio
Castello
Careggi
Fiésole
Ontignano
M. Ceceri
· 414
S. Donnino
Peretola
Novoli
Rifredi
Lapo
FIRENZE
Montebeni
Brozzi
Il Romito
Le Cure
Settignano
Compiobbi
Ugnano
Mantignano
S. Gervasio
Cintoia
L'Isolotto
Staz. Centrale
S. Iacopo al Girone
Quintole
Badia a Séttimo
La Querce
Pigone
Duomo
S. Salvi
L'Olmo
Ponte a Greve
S. Lorenzo a Greve
S. Frediano
S. Niccolo
Rovezzano
Piscetto
Casellina
Soffiano
Bobolino
Ricorboli
Gavinana
Candeli
Rinaldi
Gággio
Poggio Imperiale
Pian de Guillari
Il Bandino
Badia a Ripoli
Bagno a Ripoli
Meoste
Scandicci
Le Due Strade
S. Martino alla Palma
S. Piero a Ema
Mosciano
Galluzzo
Firenze-Sud
Grassina
Ruballa
L'Arrigo
Sasignano
Giogoli
Pozzolatico
Antella
Pian dei Cerri
F.-Certosa

LUCCA
PRATO
PISTOIA
EMPOLI

F.-Signa

Fiume Arno

SIENA POGGIBONSI   GREVE

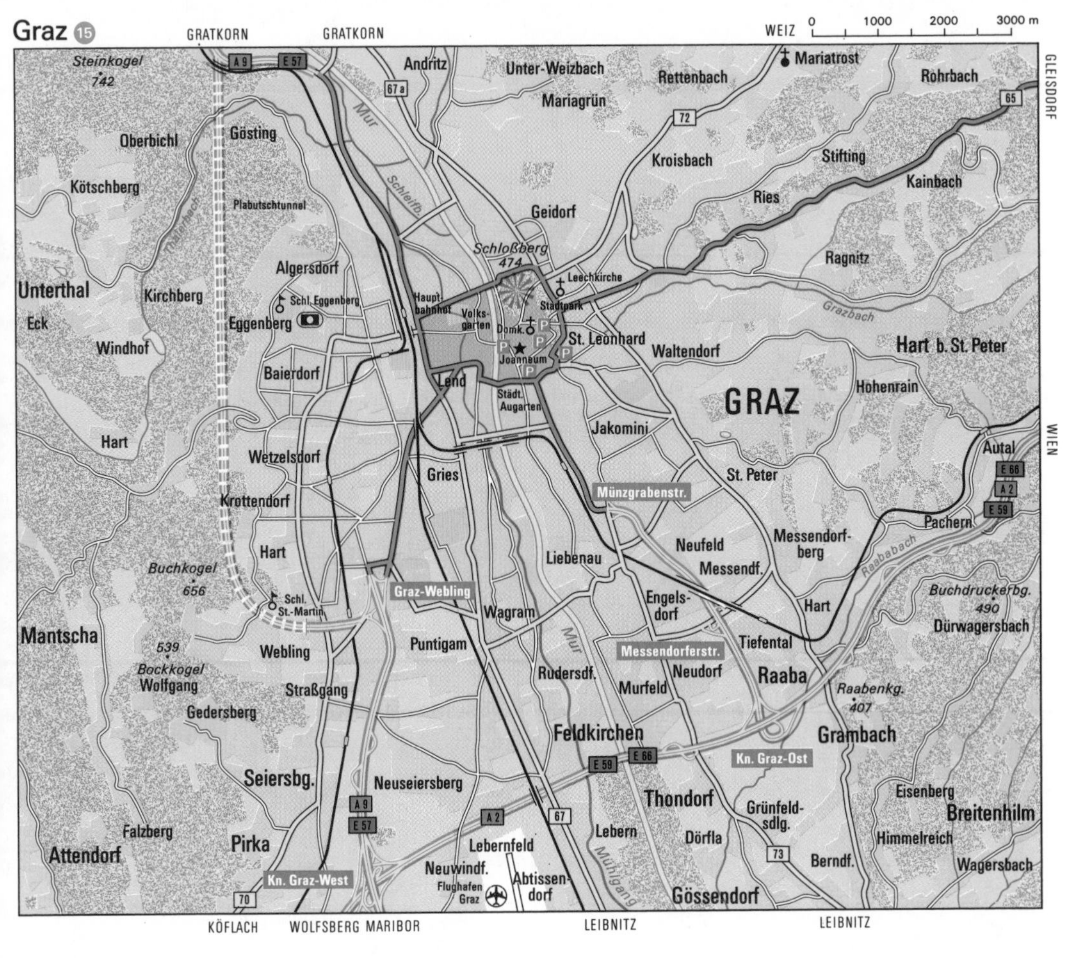

Graz ⑮

GRATKORN   GRATKORN   WEIZ

Steinkogel 742
Oberbichl
Kötschberg
Unterthal
Eck
Windhof
Hart
Kirchberg
Mantscha
Buchkogel 656
Bockkogel Wolfgang
539
Gedersberg
Seiersbg.
Attendorf
Falzberg
Pirka

Andritz
Unter-Weizbach
Rettenbach
Mariagrün
Mariatrost
Rohrbach
Kroisbach
Stifting
Ries
Ragnitz
Kainbach
Gösting
Algersdorf
Schl. Eggenberg
Eggenberg
Baierdorf
Wetzelsdorf
Krottendorf
Hart
Schl. St.-Martin
Webling
Straßgang
Neuseiersberg
Gratkorn
Plabutschtunnel
Schlleuffe
Haupt-bahnhof
Volks-garten
Lend
Gries
Puntigam
Wagram
Lebernfeld
Neuwindf.
Flughafen Graz
Schloßberg 474
Leechkirche
Stadtpark
Domk.
Joanneum
St. Leonhard
Städt. Augarten
Jakomini
Liebenau
Rüdersdf.
Murfeld
Neudorf
Feldkirchen
Thondorf
Lebern
Abtissen-dorf
Gössendorf
Geidorf
Münzgrabenstr.
Graz-Webling
Messendorferstr.
Puntigam
St. Peter
Neufeld
Messendf.
Messendorf-berg
Engels-dorf
Tiefental
Kn. Graz-Ost
Grünfeld-sdlg.
Dörfla
Berndf.
GRAZ
Waltendorf
Hohenrain
Hart b. St. Peter
Autal
Pachern
Buchdruckerbg. 490
Dürwagersbach
Raaba
Raabenkg. 407
Grambach
Eisenberg
Himmelreich
Breitenhilm
Wagersbach

Kn. Graz-West

KÖFLACH   WOLFSBERG MARIBOR   LEIBNITZ   LEIBNITZ

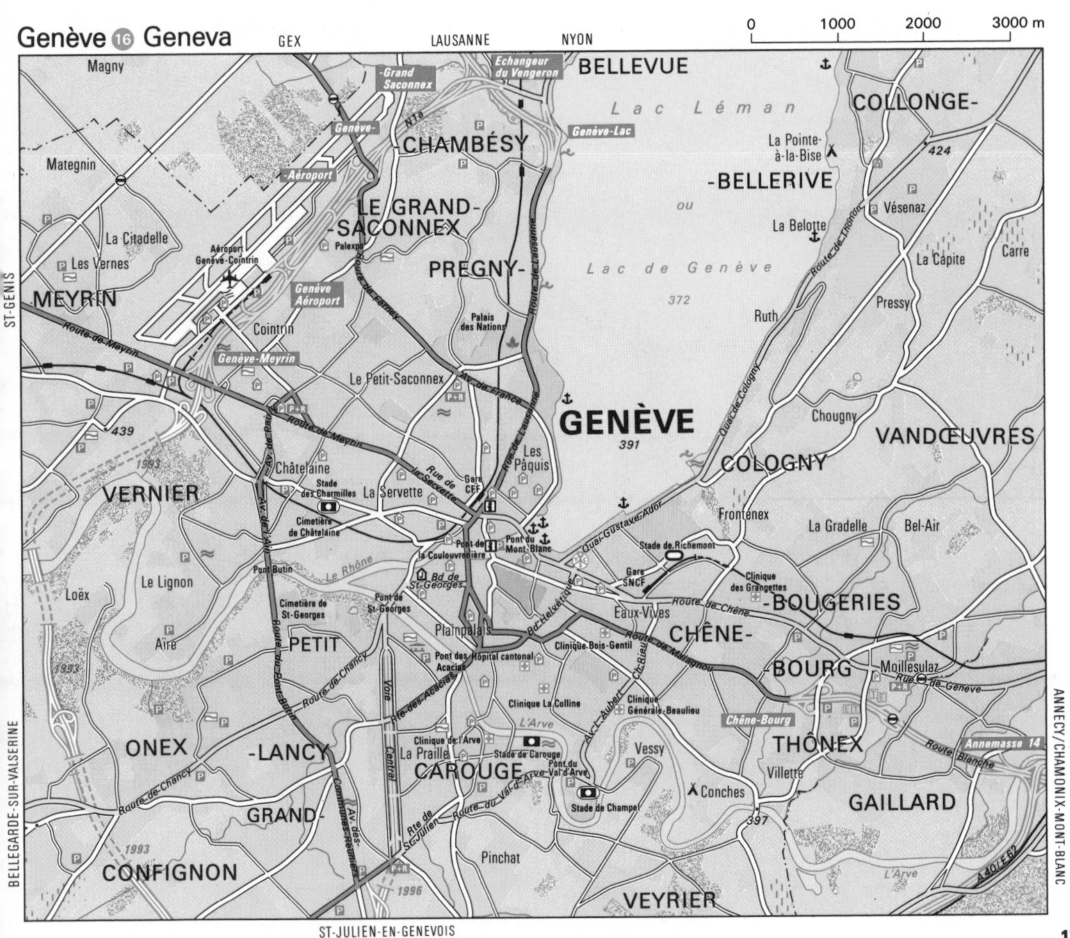

Genève ⑯ Geneva

GEX   LAUSANNE   NYON

Magny
Mategnin
La Citadelle
Les Vernes
MEYRIN
Vernier
Loëx
Le Lignon
Aire
ONEX
GRAND-
CONFIGNON
Grand-Saconnex
Genève-Aéroport
Aéroport Genève-Cointrin
Cointrin
Genève-Meyrin
Châtelaine
Stade de Charmilles
Cimetière de Châtelaine
Pont Butin
Cimetière de St-Georges
Pont de St-Georges
PETIT-LANCY
La Praille
CAROUGE
Pinchat
Échangeur du Vengeron
Grand-Saconnex
Genève-Lac
CHAMBÉSY
LE GRAND-SACONNEX
PREGNY-
Palexpo
Palais des Nations
Le Petit-Saconnex
La Servette
Rue de Lausanne
Gare CFF
Les Pâquis
GENÈVE 391
Plainpalais
Pont du Mont-Blanc
Pont de la Coulouvrenière
Bd de St-Georges
Clinique Bois-Gentil
Clinique La Colline
Clinique de l'Arve
Stade de Carouge
Stade du Val d'Arve
Stade de Champel
L'Arve
Vessy
Villette
Conches
VEYRIER
BELLEVUE
Lac Léman
COLLONGE-
-BELLERIVE
La Pointe-à-la-Bise
La Belotte
ou
Lac de Genève
372
Vésenaz
La Câpite
Carre
Pressy
Ruth
Chougny
VANDŒUVRES
COLOGNY
Frontenex
La Gradelle
Bel-Air
Stade de Richemont
Clinique des Grangettes
BOUGERIES
CHÊNE-
BOURG
Moillesulaz
Chêne-Bourg
THONEX
GAILLARD
Annemasse
Eaux-Vives
Clinique Générale-Beaulieu
Clinique Pinchat

ST-GENIS
BELLEGARDE-SUR-VALSERINE
ST-JULIEN-EN-GENEVOIS
ANNECY/CHAMONIX-MONT-BLANC

Frankfurt 17

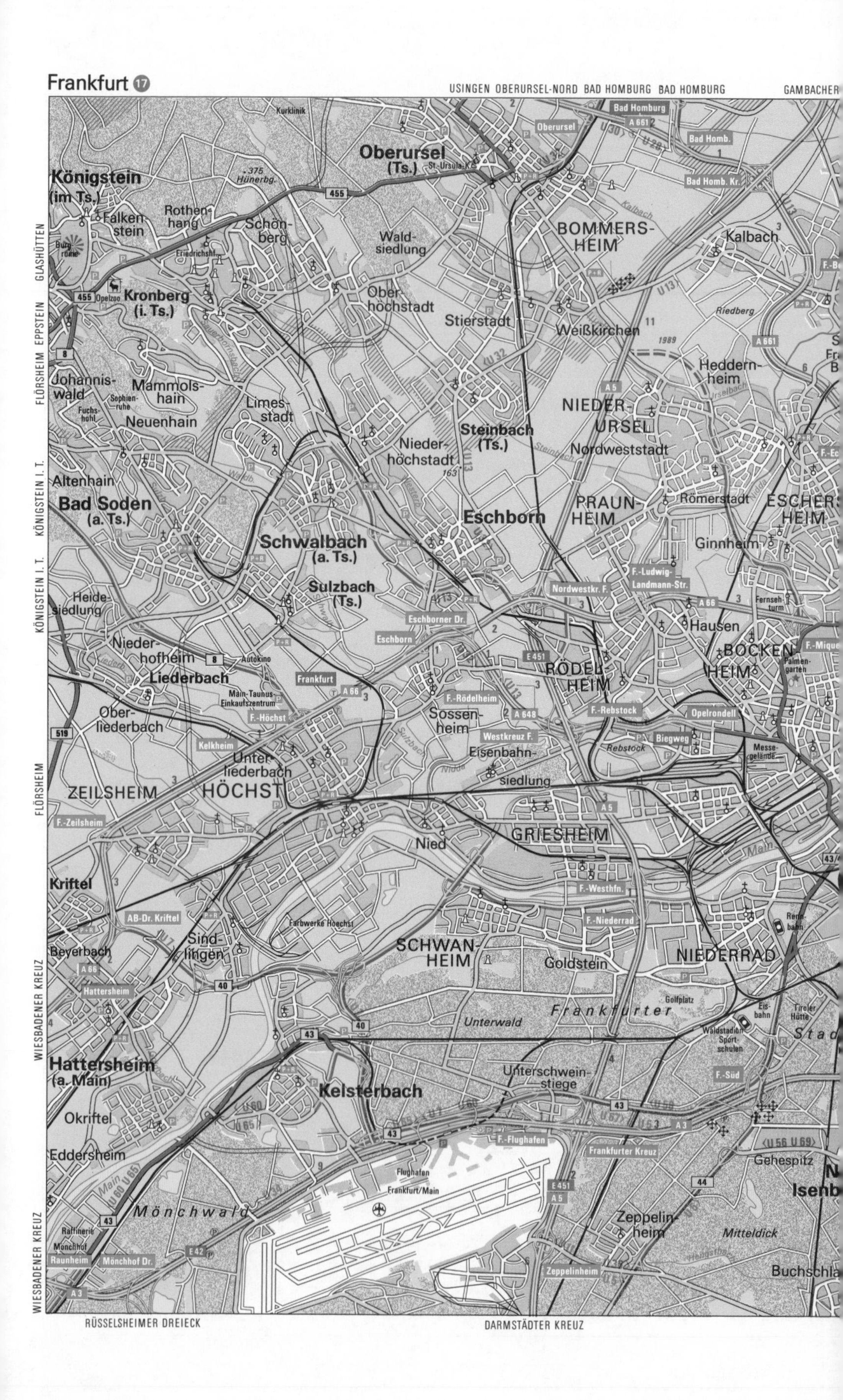

USINGEN
OBERURSEL-NORD
BAD HOMBURG
BAD HOMBURG
GAMBACHER
GLASHÜTTEN
EPPSTEIN
FLÖRSHEIM
KÖNIGSTEIN I. T.
KÖNIGSTEIN I. T.
FLÖRSHEIM
WIESBADENER KREUZ
WIESBADENER KREUZ
RÜSSELSHEIMER DREIECK
DARMSTÄDTER KREUZ
Oberursel (Ts.)
Königstein (im Ts.)
Falkenstein
Rothenhang
Schönberg
Waldsiedlung
Oberhöchstadt
Stierstadt
Weißkirchen
BOMMERSHEIM
Kalbach
Riedberg
Kronberg (i. Ts.)
Opelzoo
Johanniswald
Mammolshain
Neuenhain
Limesstadt
Steinbach (Ts.)
Niederhöchstadt
Heddernheim
NIEDERURSEL
Nordweststadt
Altenhain
Bad Soden (a. Ts.)
Schwalbach (a. Ts.)
Eschborn
PRAUNHEIM
Römerstadt
ESCHERSHEIM
Ginnheim
Heidesiedlung
Sulzbach (Ts.)
Hausen
Niederhofheim
Liederbach
Oberliederbach
BOCKENHEIM
RÖDELHEIM
Sossenheim
Eisenbahnsiedlung
Rebstock
Unterliederbach
ZEILSHEIM
HÖCHST
GRIESHEIM
Nied
Kriftel
Sindlingen
Farbwerke Hoechst
SCHWANHEIM
Goldstein
NIEDERRAD
Beyerbach
Unterwald
Frankfurter Stadtwald
Hattersheim (a. Main)
Kelsterbach
Unterschweinstiege
Okriftel
Eddersheim
Gehespitz
Flughafen Frankfurt/Main
Mönchwald
Zeppelinheim
Mitteldick
Buchschlag
Raunheim
Mönchhof Dr.
Frankfurter Kreuz
F.-Flughafen
Nordwestkr. F.
Westkreuz F.
Eschborner Dr.
Bad Homb. Kr.

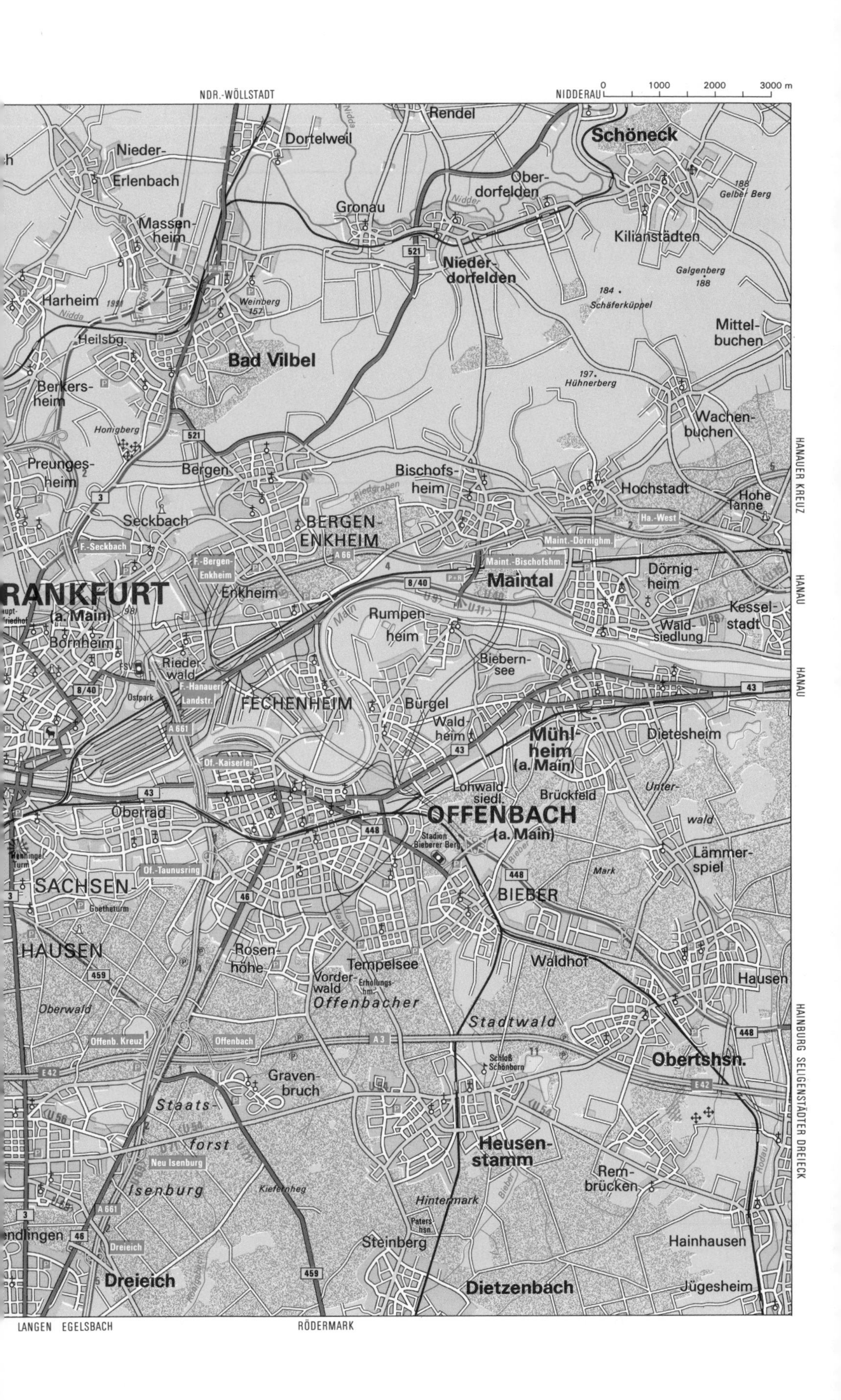

Rendel

Schöneck

Dortelweil

Nieder-
Erlenbach

Ober-
dorfelden

188
Gelber Berg

Gronau

Massen-
heim

521

Kilianstädten

Nieder-
dorfelden

Galgenberg
188

Harheim 199

Weinberg
157

184
Schäferküppel

Mittel-
buchen

Heilsbg.

Bad Vilbel

197
Hühnerberg

Berkers-
heim

Honigberg

521

Wachen-
buchen

Preunges-
heim

Bergen

Bischofs-
heim

Hochstadt

Hohe
Tanne

3

Seckbach

BERGEN-
ENKHEIM

Niedergraben

Ha.-West

F-Seckbach

A 66

Maint.-Dörnigh.

Dörnig-
heim

Kessel-
stadt

F-Bergen-
Enkheim

4

Maint.-Bischofshm.

FRANKFURT
(a. Main)

Enkheim

8/40

Maintal

Wald-
siedlung

Bornheim

Main

Rumpen-
heim

Rieder-
wald

Biebern-
see

F-Hanauer
Landstr.

8/40

Ostpark

FECHENHEIM

Bürgel

Wald-
heim

Mühl-
heim
(a. Main)

Dietesheim

A 661

43

43

Of.-Kaiserlei

Lohwald-
siedl.

Brückfeld

Unter-

wald

43

Oberrad

448

OFFENBACH
(a. Main)

Stadion
Bieberer Berg

Lämmer-
spiel

Henninger
Turm

Of.-Taunusring

Mark

SACHSEN-

46

Goetheturm

BIEBER

448

HAUSEN

459

Rosen-
höhe

Tempelsee

Waldhof

Hausen

Oberwald

Vorder-
wald

Erholungs-
hm.
Offenbacher

Stadtwald

Offenb. Kreuz

Offenbach

A 3

Schloß
Schönborn

11

Obertshsn.

E 42

Gravenbruch

Heusen-
stamm

Staats-

forst

Neu Isenburg

Kiefernheg

Hintermark

Rem-
brücken

Isenburg

A 661

Paters-
hsn.

3

Steinberg

Hainhausen

ndlingen

46

Dreieich

Dreieich

459

Dietzenbach

Jügesheim

19

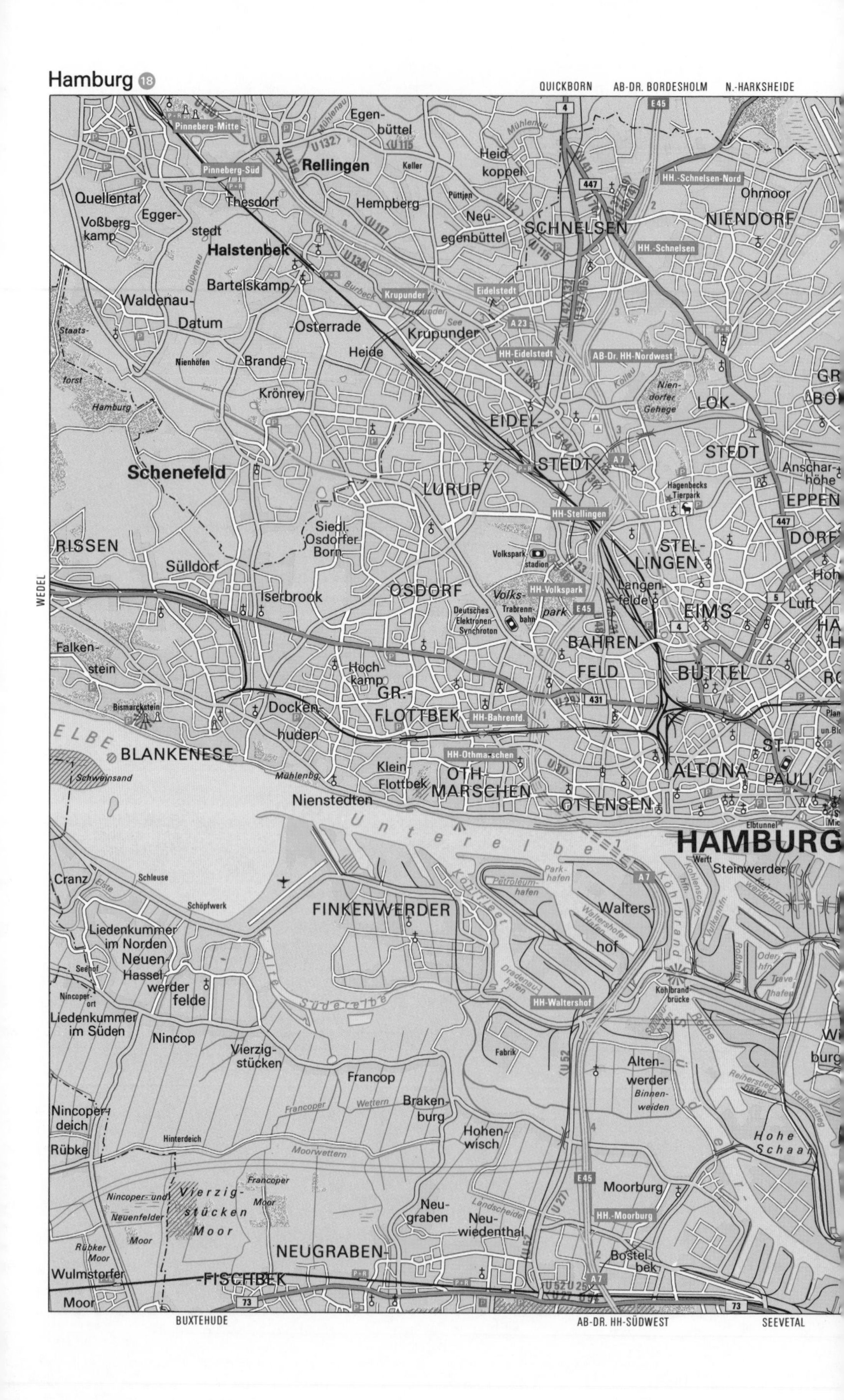
QUICKBORN
AB-DR. BORDESHOLM
N.-HARKSHEIDE
Pinneberg-Mitte
Egenbüttel
Rellingen
Heidkoppel
Pinneberg-Süd
HH.-Schnelsen-Nord
Quellental
Eggerstedt
Thesdorf
Hempberg
Ohmoor
Voßbergkamp
Neu-egenbüttel
SCHNELSEN
NIENDORF
Halstenbek
HH.-Schnelsen
Bartelskamp
Krupunder
Eidelstedt
Waldenau-Datum
Osterrade
Krupunder
HH-Eidelstedt
AB-Dr. HH-Nordwest
Heide
Nienhöfen
Brande
Krönrey
Niendorfer Gehege
LOKSTEDT
EIDELSTEDT
Schenefeld
LURUP
Hagenbecks Tierpark
HH-Stellingen
Siedl. Osdorfer Born
RISSEN
STELLINGEN
Sülldorf
Volkspark-stadion
OSDORF
HH-Volkspark
Langenfelde
Iserbrook
Deutsches Elektronen-Synchroton
Trabrennbahn
EIMSBÜTTEL
BAHRENFELD
Falkenstein
Hochkamp
GR. FLOTTBEK
Bismarckstein
Dockenhuden
HH-Bahrenfd.
ELBE
BLANKENESE
HH-Othmarschen
Schweinsand
Mühlenbg.
Klein-Flottbek
OTHMARSCHEN
ALTONA
ST. PAULI
Nienstedten
OTTENSEN
Elbtunnel
Unterelbe
HAMBURG
Cranz
Schleuse
Werft
Steinwerder
Petroleumhafen
Parkhafen
Schöpfwerk
FINKENWERDER
Waltershof
Liedenkummer im Norden
Neuenfelde
Hasselwerder
Alte Süderelbe
Dradenauhafen
Köhlbrandbrücke
HH-Waltershof
Nincoper-ort
Liedenkummer im Süden
Nincop
Vierzigstücken
Fabrik
Altenwerder
Binnenweiden
Francop
Brakenburg
Nincoperdeich
Hinterdeich
Hohenwisch
Rübke
Moorwettern
Hohe Schaar
Francoper Moor
Vierzigstücken Moor
Nincoper- und Neuenfelder Moor
Moorburg
HH.-Moorburg
Neugraben
Neuwiedenthal
Rübker Moor
NEUGRABEN-FISCHBEK
Bostelbek
Wulmstorfer Moor
WEDEL
BUXTEHUDE
AB-DR. HH-SÜDWEST
SEEVETAL

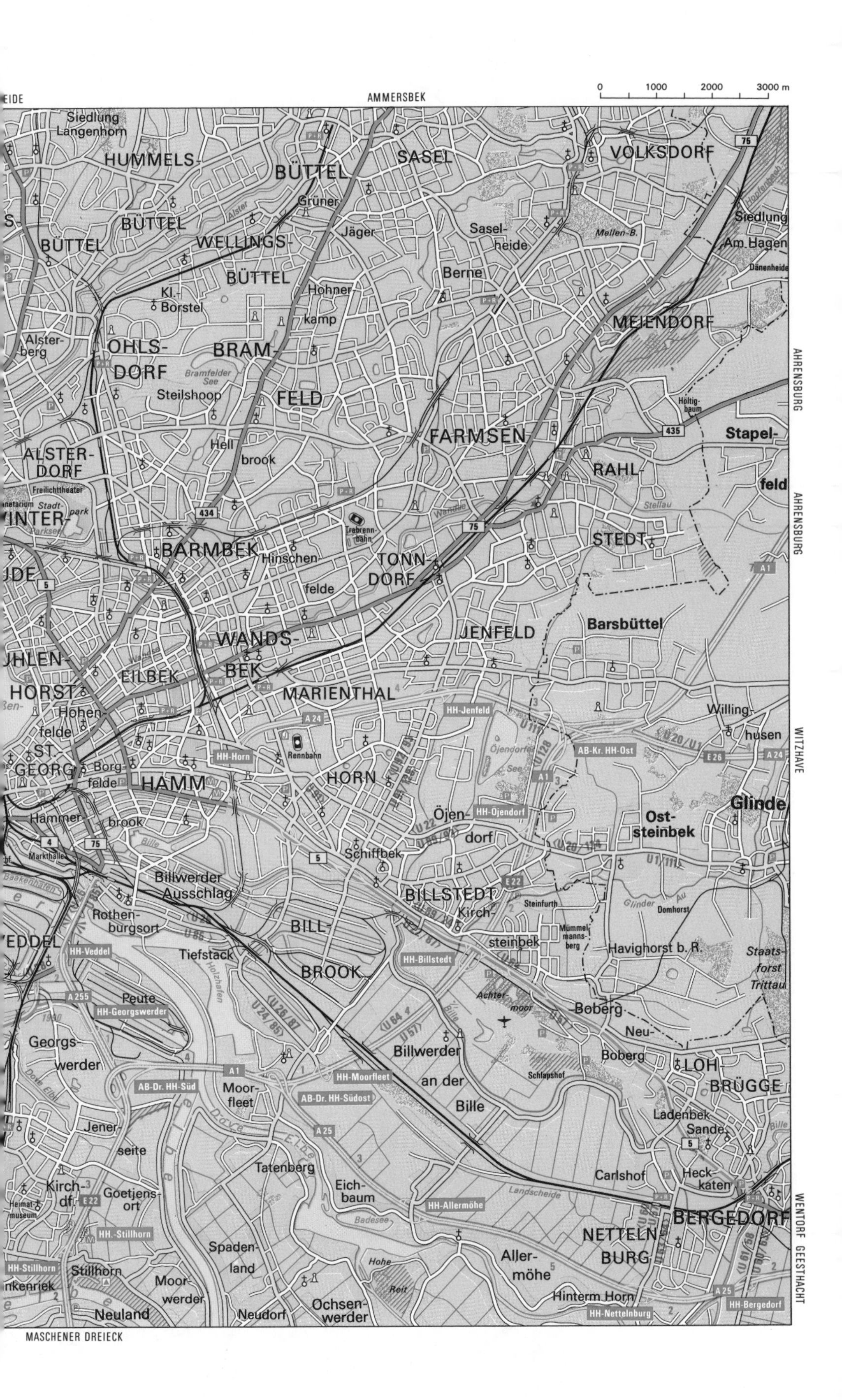

0
1000
2000
3000 m
AMMERSBEK
AHRENSBURG
WITZHAVE
WENTORF
GESTHACHT
MASCHENER DREIECK
Siedlung Langenhorn
HUMMELS-
BÜTTEL
BÜTTEL
BÜTTEL
SASEL
VOLKSDORF
Grüner Jäger
WELLINGS-
BÜTTEL
Sasel-heide
Mellen-B.
Siedlung Am Hagen
Dänenheide
Berne
Kl.-Borstel
Hohner kamp
MEIENDORF
Alster-berg
OHLS-
DORF
BRAM-
FELD
Bramfelder See
Steilshoop
Höltig-baum
FARMSEN
Stapel-
feld
ALSTER-
DORF
Hell brook
RAHL-
STEDT
Freilichttheater
Stadt-park
Stellau
Wandse
Trabrenn-bahn
BARMBEK
Hinschen-felde
TONN-
DORF
WANDS-
BEK
JENFELD
Barsbüttel
EILBEK
HORST
MARIENTHAL
Hohen-felde
HH-Jenfeld
Willing-husen
ST. GEORG
Borg-felde
HH-Horn
Rennbahn
Öjendorfer See
AB-Kr. HH-Ost
HAMM
HORN
Glinde
Hammer-brook
Öjen-dorf
HH-Öjendorf
Ost-steinbek
Markthalle
Schiffbek
Billwerder Ausschlag
BILLSTEDT
Kirch-steinbek
Steinfurth
Glinder Au
Domhorst
Rothen-burgsort
BILL-
BROOK
Mümmel-manns-berg
Havighorst b. R.
Staats-forst Trittau
HH-Veddel
Tiefstack
HH-Billstedt
Achter-moor
Boberg
Neu-Boberg
Peute
HH-Georgswerder
Holzhafen
Georgs-werder
Billwerder an der Bille
Schlapshof
LOH-
BRÜGGE
AB-Dr. HH-Süd
Moor-fleet
HH-Moorfleet
AB-Dr. HH-Südost
Ladenbek
Sande
Jener-seite
Dove Elbe
Tatenberg
Carlshof
Heck-katen
Kirch-df.
Goetjens-ort
Eich-baum
HH-Allermöhe
Landscheide
Heimat-museum
BERGEDORF
HH.-Stillhorn
Badesee
NETTELN-
BURG
Spaden-land
Aller-möhe
HH-Stillhorn
Stillhorn
Moor-werder
Hohe Reit
Hinterm Horn
Neuland
Neudorf
Ochsen-werder
HH-Nettelnburg
HH-Bergedorf
A 1
A 24
A 25
A 255
E 22
E 26
75
435
434

Génova/Genua ⑲ Genoa

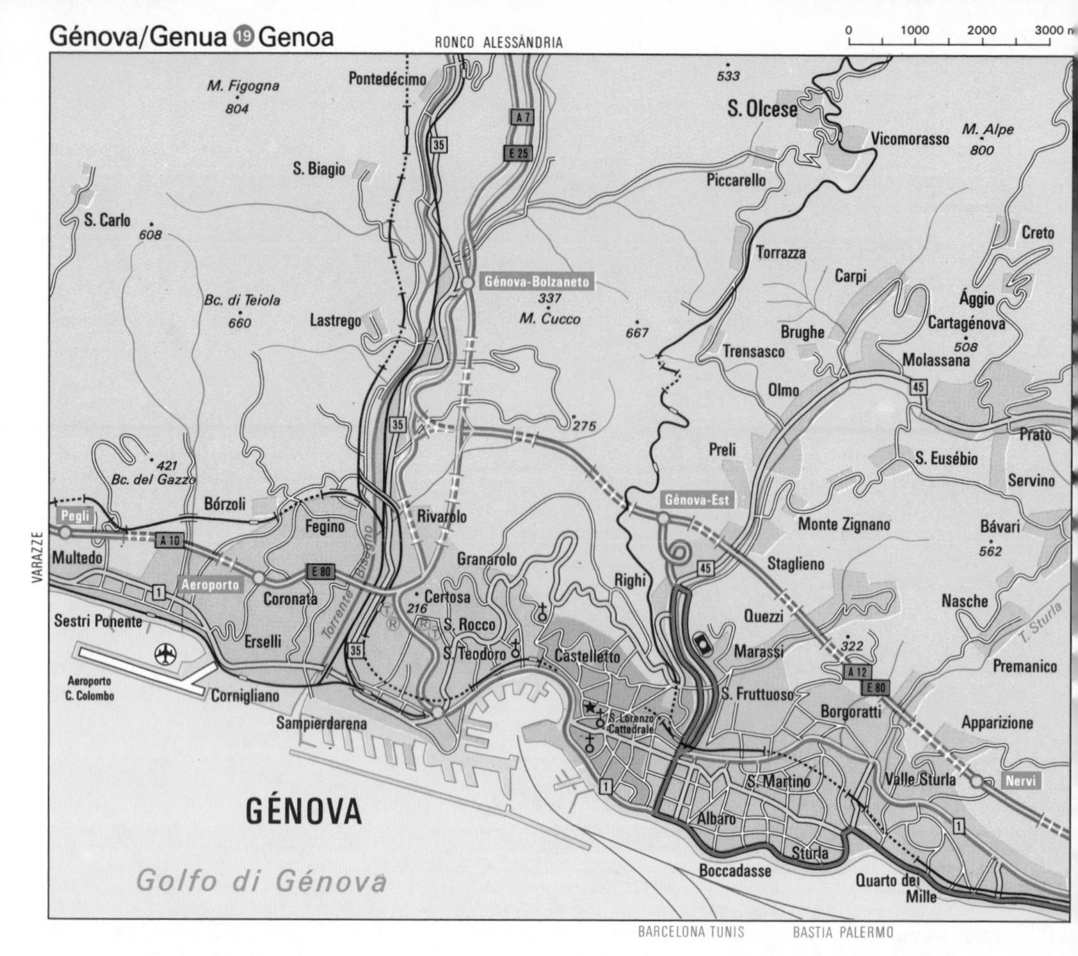

RONCO ALESSÁNDRIA

0   1000   2000   3000 m

M. Figogna 804
Pontedécimo
533
S. Olcese
Vicomorasso
M. Alpe 800

S. Biagio
Piccarello
Creto

S. Carlo 608
Torrazza
Carpi
Àggio
Cartagénova 508

Bc. di Teiola 660
Lastrego
Génova-Bolzaneto 337
M. Cucco
Brughe
Molassana
667
Trensasco
Olmo
Prato

421 Bc. del Gazzo
275
Preli
S. Eusébio
Servino

Pegli
Bórzoli
Rivarolo
Génova-Est
S. Eusébio
Bávari 562

Multedo
Fegino
Granarolo
Righi
Monte Zignano
Staglieno
Nasche

Aeroporto
Coronata
Certosa 216
S. Rocco
Quezzi
Premanico
322

Sestri Ponente
Erselli
S. Teodoro
Castelletto
Marassi
Borgoratti
Apparizione

Aeroporto C. Colombo
Corigliano
Sampierdarena
S. Lorenzo Cattedrale
S. Fruttuoso
Valle Sturla
Nervi

GÉNOVA
S. Martino
Albaro
Stúrla
Quarto dei Mille

Golfo di Génova
Boccadasse

BARCELONA TUNIS   BASTIA PALERMO

Göteborg ⑳ Gothenburg

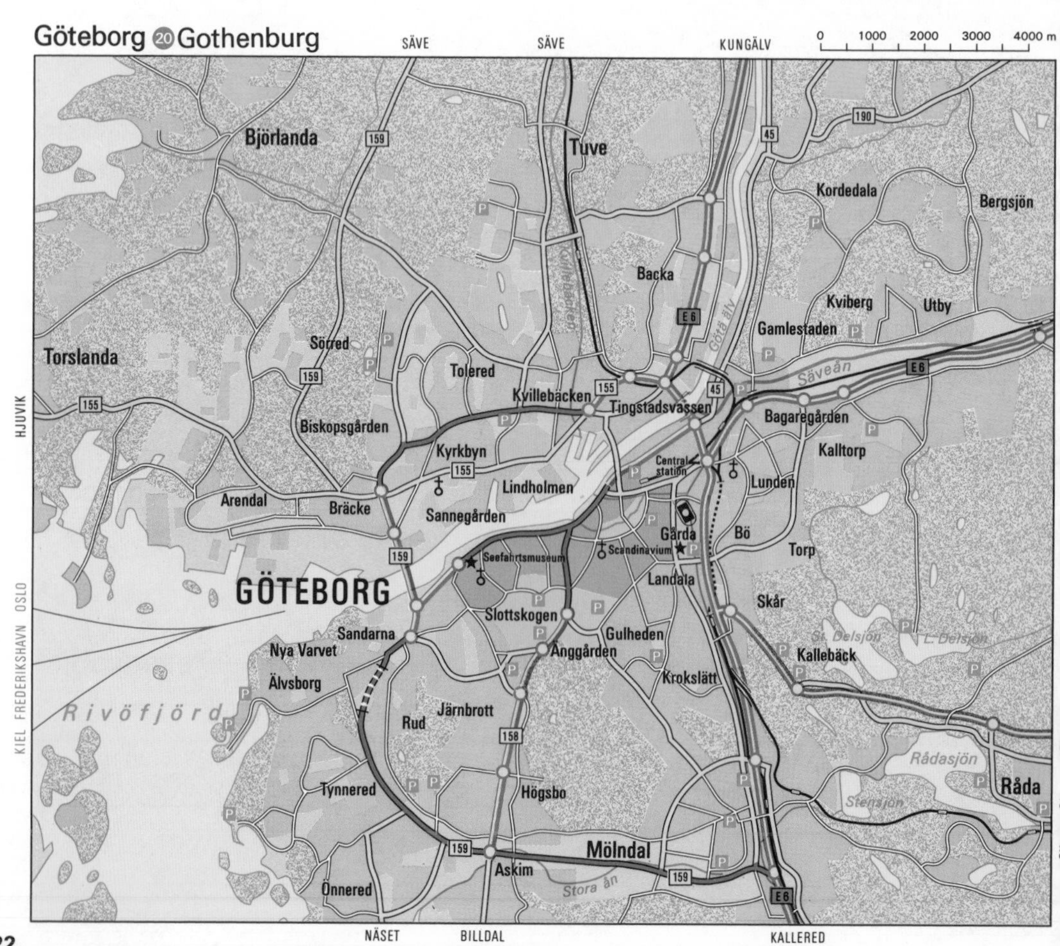

SÄVE   SÄVE   KUNGÄLV

0   1000   2000   3000   4000 m

Björlanda
Tuve
Kordedala
Bergsjön

Torslanda
Backa
Kviberg
Utby
Gamlestaden

Sörred
Tolered
Kvillebäcken
Tingstadsvassen
Bagaregården
Kalltorp

Biskopsgården
Kyrkbyn
Central station
Lundén
Torp

Arendal
Bräcke
Sannegården
Lindholmen
Garda
Scandinàvium
Bö
Skår

GÖTEBORG
Seefahrtsmuseum
Landala
Kallebäck

Sandarna
Slottskogen
Gulheden

Nya Varvet
Änggården
Krokslätt

Älvsborg
Rivöfjörd
Järnbrott
Rud

Tynnered
Högsbo
Rådasjön
Råda

Önnered
Askim
Mölndal

NÄSET   BILLDAL   KALLERED

22

Helsinki ㉑

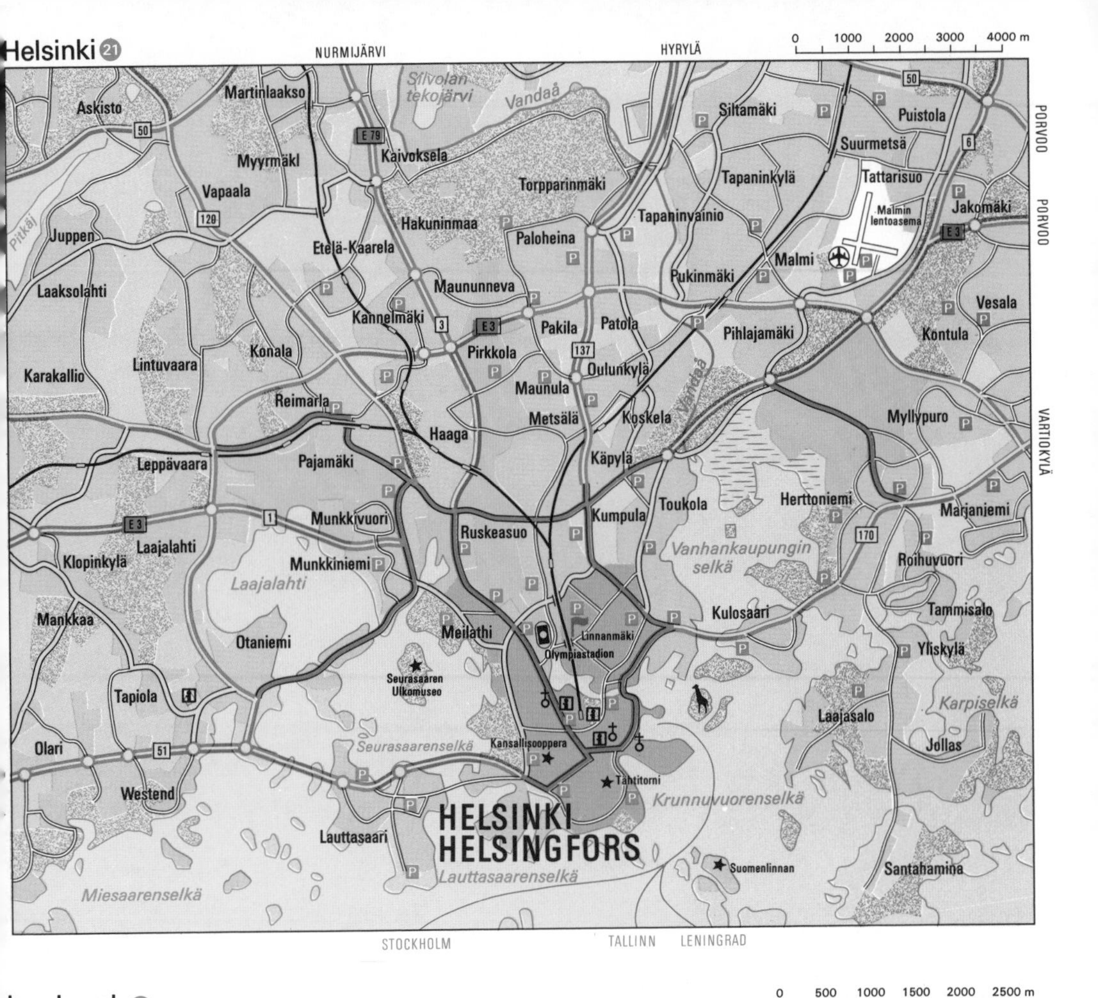

NURMIJÄRVI HYRYLÄ

0 1000 2000 3000 4000 m

Askisto
Martinlaakso
50
Myyrmäkl
E 79
Kaivoksela
Vapaala
120
Etelä-Kaarela
Juppen
Hakuninmaa
Laaksolahti
Kannelmäki
3
E 3
Pakila
Karakallio
Lintuvaara
Reimarla
137
Oulunkylä
Konala
Pirkkola
Maunula
Klopinkylä
Laajalahti
Metsälä
Koskela
Leppävaara
E 3
Pajamäki
Haaga
Käpylä
1
Munkkivuori
Ruskeasuo
Kumpula
Toukola
Herttoniemi
170
Laajalahti
Munkkiniemi
Meiläthi
Linnanmäki
Olympiastadion
Otaniemi
Tapiola
51
Olari
Westend
Seurasaaren
Ulkomuseo
Kansallisooppera
Tähtitorni
Lauttasaari
HELSINKI
HELSINGFORS
Krunnuvuorenselkä
Lauttasaarenselkä
Suomenlinna

STOCKHOLM TALLINN LENINGRAD

NURMIJÄRVI
Vandaå
Siltamäki
Puistola
50
Suurmetsä
6
Torpparinmäki
Tapaninkylä
Tapaninvainio
Tattarisuo
Malmin
lentoasema
Jakomäki
E 3
Paloheina
Pukinmäki
Malmi
Vesala
Kontula
Patola
Pihlajamäki
Myllypuro
Marjaniemi
Roihuvuori
Vanhankaupungin
selkä
Tammisalo
Kulosaari
Yliskylä
Karpiselkä
Laajasalo
Jollas
Santahamina

PORVOO
PORVOO
VARTIOKYLÄ

Innsbruck ㉒

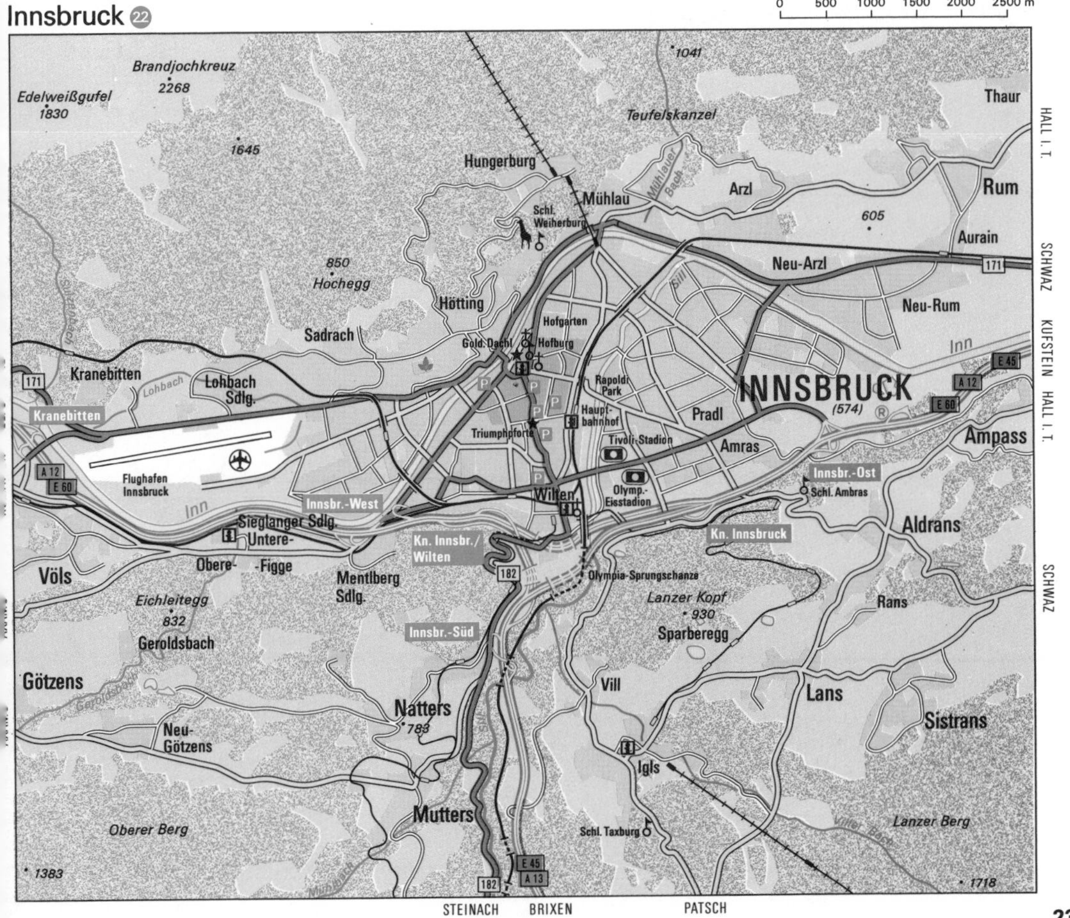

0 500 1000 1500 2000 2500 m

1041
Brandjochkreuz
2268
Edelweißgufel
1830
Thaur
1645
Teufelskanzel
Hungerburg
Mühlau
Arzl
Rum
Schl.
Weiherburg
605
Aurain
850
Hochegg
Neu-Arzl
171
Hötting
Neu-Rum
Kranebitten
Sadrach
Hofgarten
Gold. Dachl
Hofburg
Inn
A 12
E 45
171
Lohbach
Lohbach
Sdlg.
Rapoldi-
Park
INNSBRUCK
(574)
E 60
Kranebitten
Triumphpforte
Haupt-
bahnhof
Pradl
Ampass
Flughafen
Innsbruck
Tivoli-Stadion
Amras
Innsbr.-Ost
A 12
E 60
Inn
Innsbr.-West
Wilten
Olymp.
Eisstadion
Schl. Ambras
Aldrans
Sieglanger Sdlg.
Untere-
Kn. Innsbr./
Wilten
Kn. Innsbruck
Obere- -Figge
Mentlberg
Sdlg.
182
Olympia-Sprungschanze
Rans
Völs
Eichleitegg
832
Innsbr.-Süd
Lanzer Kopf
930
Sparberegg
Lans
Geroldsbach
Vill
Sistrans
Götzens
Natters
789
Neu-
Götzens
Igls
Mutters
Oberer Berg
Schl. Taxburg
Lanzer Berg
1383
E 45
A 13
182
1718
STEINACH BRIXEN PATSCH

HALL I. T.
SCHWAZ
KUFSTEIN
HALL I. T.
SCHWAZ

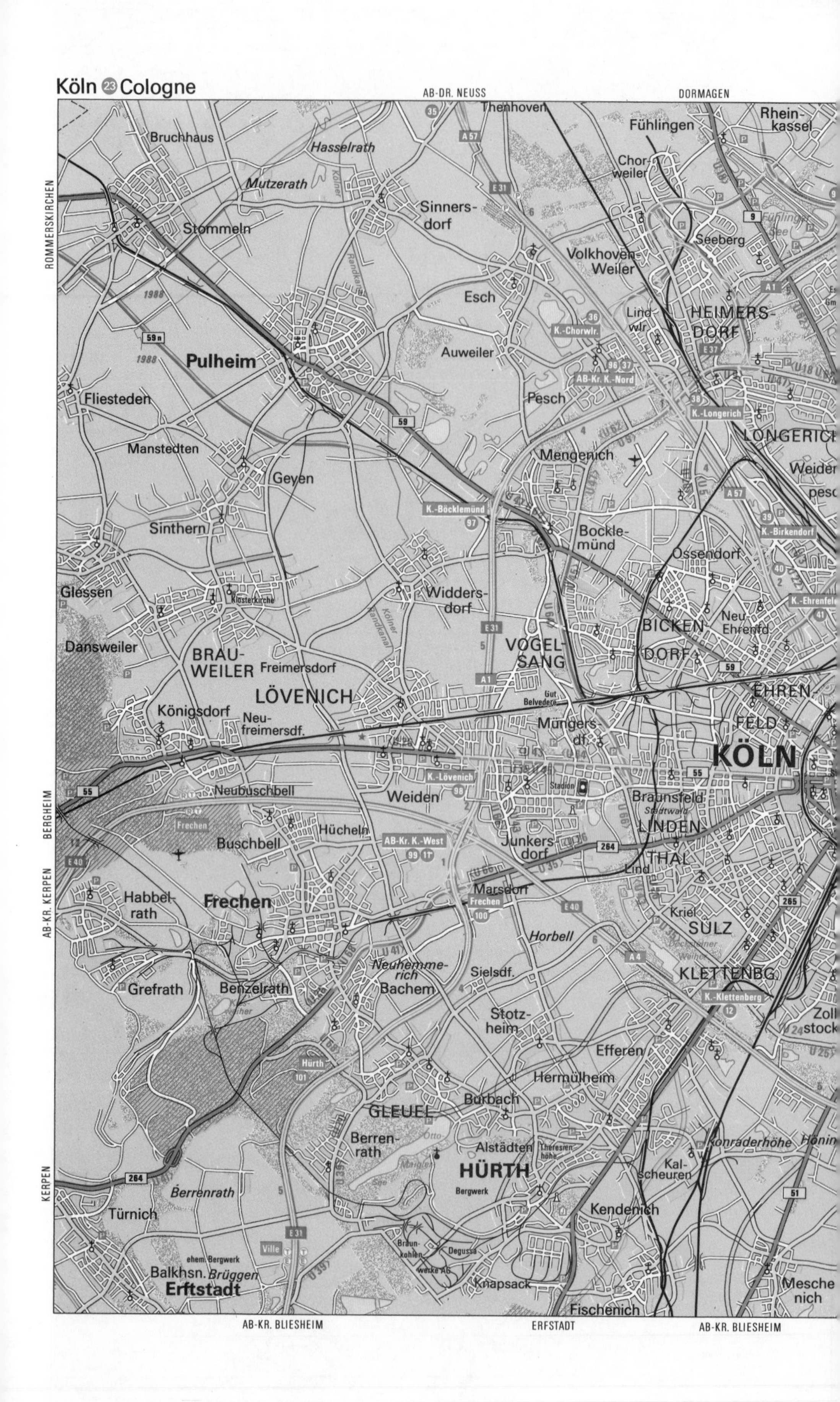

Köln 🅒 Cologne

AB-DR. NEUSS
DORMAGEN
ROMMERSKIRCHEN
BERGHEIM
AB-KR. KERPEN
KERPEN
AB-KR. BLIESHEIM
ERFSTADT
AB-KR. BLIESHEIM
Thenhoven
Fühlingen
Rhein-
kassel
Bruchhaus
Hasselrath
Chor-
weiler
Mutzerath
Sinners-
dorf
Stommeln
Seeberg
Volkhoven-
Weiler
Esch
HEIMERS-
DORF
Pulheim
Auweiler
K.-Chorwlr.
AB-Kr. K.-Nord
Fliesteden
Pesch
K.-Longerich
LONGERICH
Manstedten
Mengenich
Geyen
Weiden
K.-Böcklemünd
Bockle-
münd
K.-Birkendorf
Sinthern
Ossendorf
Glessen
Widders-
dorf
Klosterkirche
BICKEN-
DORF
Neu-
Ehrenfd
K.-Ehrenfeld
Dansweiler
BRAU-
WEILER
Freimersdorf
VOGEL-
SANG
LÖVENICH
Gut
Belvedere
EHREN-
FELD
Königsdorf
Neu-
freimersdf.
Müngers-
df.
Neubuschbell
K.-Lövenich
Weiden
Stadion
Braunsfeld
Stadtwald
LINDEN-
THAL
Frechen
Hücheln
Buschbell
AB-Kr. K.-West
Junkers-
dorf
Lind
Habbel-
rath
Frechen
Marsdorf
Frechen
Kriel
SÜLZ
Horbell
Grefrath
Benzelrath
Neuhemme-
rich
Bachem
Sielsdf.
KLETTENBG.
K.-Klettenberg
Stotz-
heim
Zoll-
stock
Efferen
Hürth
Hermülheim
Burbach
GLEUEL
Berren-
rath
Alstädten
Theresien-
höhe
Konraderhöhe
Kal-
scheuren
HÜRTH
Bergwerk
Berrenrath
Türnich
Kendenich
Ville
Braun-
kohlen-
werke AG
Degussa
ehem. Bergwerk
Balkhsn.
Brüggen
Erftstadt
Knapsack
Fischenich
Mesche-
nich

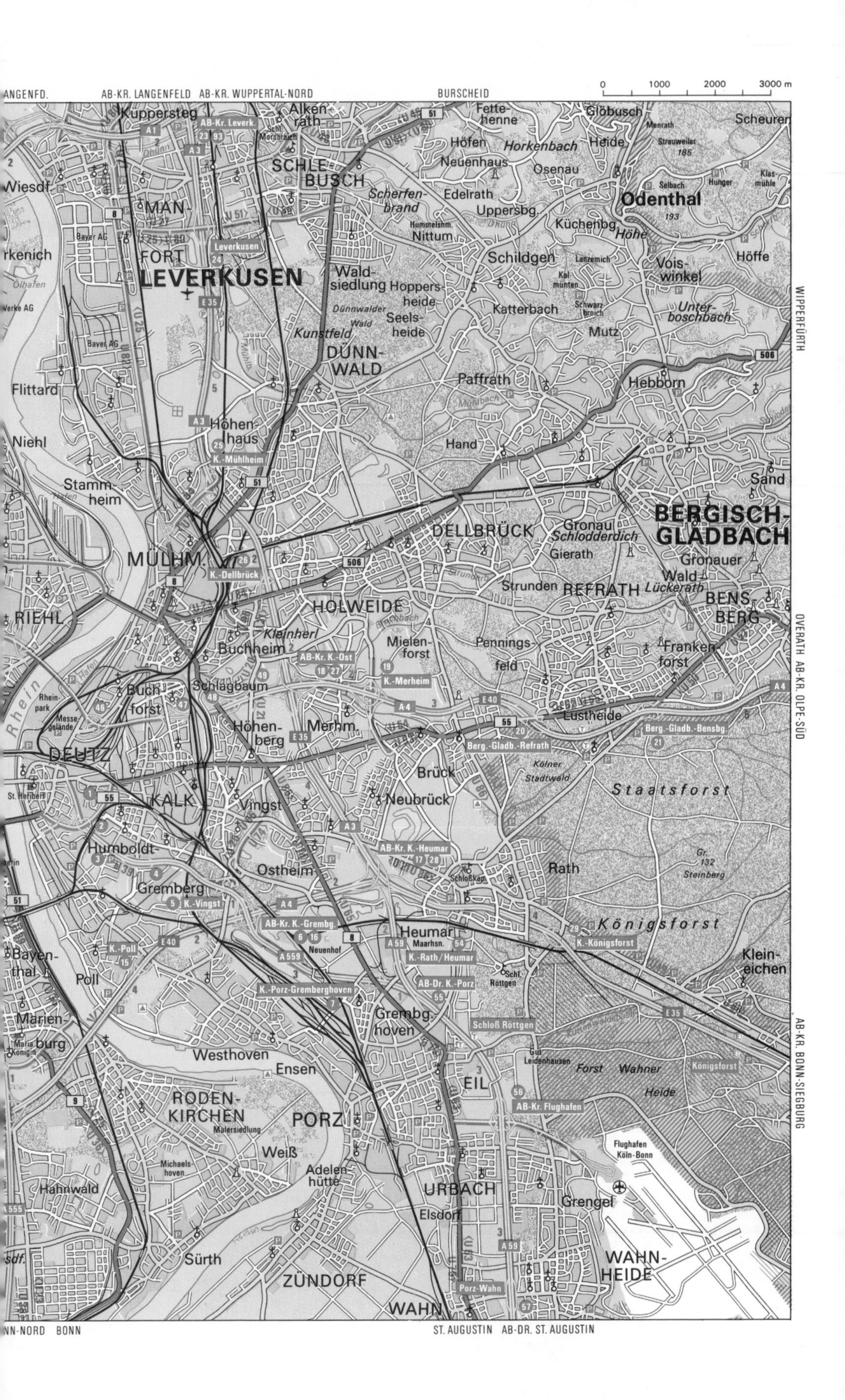
ANGENFD.
AB-KR. LANGENFELD
AB-KR. WUPPERTAL-NORD
BURSCHEID
0 1000 2000 3000 m
LEVERKUSEN
SCHLEBUSCH
MANFORT
Küppersteg
Alkenrath
Fettehenne
Glöbusch
Scheuren
Höfen
Horkenbach
Heide
Neuenhaus
Osenau
Edelrath
Uppersbg.
Odenthal
Küchenbg.
Höhe
Nittum
Schildgen
Voiswinkel
Höffe
Waldsiedlung
Hoppersheide
Seelsheide
Katterbach
Unterboschbach
Mutz
Kunstfeld
DÜNNWALD
Flittard
Paffrath
Hebborn
Höhenhaus
Niehl
Hand
Sand
Stammheim
MÜLHM.
DELLBRÜCK
Gronau
Schlodderdich
Gierath
BERGISCH-GLADBACH
Gronauer Wald
Lückerath
Strunden
REFRATH
BENSBERG
HOLWEIDE
RIEHL
Kleinherl
Buchheim
Mielenforst
Penningsfeld
Frankenforst
Schlagbaum
Buchforst
Rheinpark
Höhenberg
Merhm.
Lustheide
DEUTZ
Kölner Stadtwald
Brück
Neubrück
KALK
Vingst
Staatsforst
Humboldt-
Ostheim
Rath
Gremberg
Heumar
Königsforst
Bayenthal
Poll
Kleineichen
Marienburg
Grembg.hoven
Westhoven
Ensen
Forst
Wahner Heide
EIL
RODENKIRCHEN
PORZ
Weiß
Adelenhütte
Flughafen Köln-Bonn
URBACH
Hahnwald
Grengel
Elsdorf
WAHNHEIDE
Sürth
ZÜNDORF
WAHN
WIPPERFÜRTH
OVERATH AB-KR. OLPE-SÜD
AB-KR. BONN-SIEGBURG
NN-NORD
BONN
ST. AUGUSTIN
AB-DR. ST. AUGUSTIN

København/Kopenhagen ㉔ Copenhagen

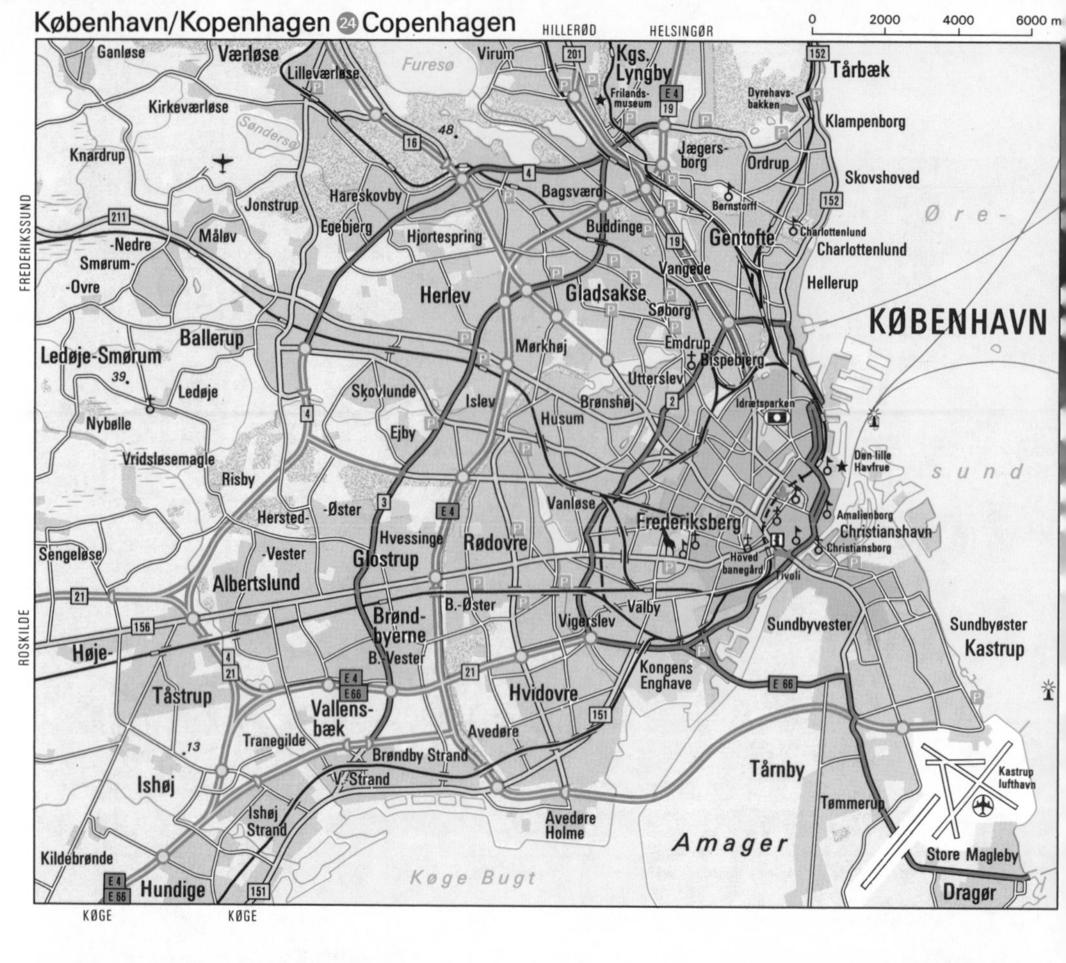

Lisboa/Lissabon ㉕ Lisbon AMADORA

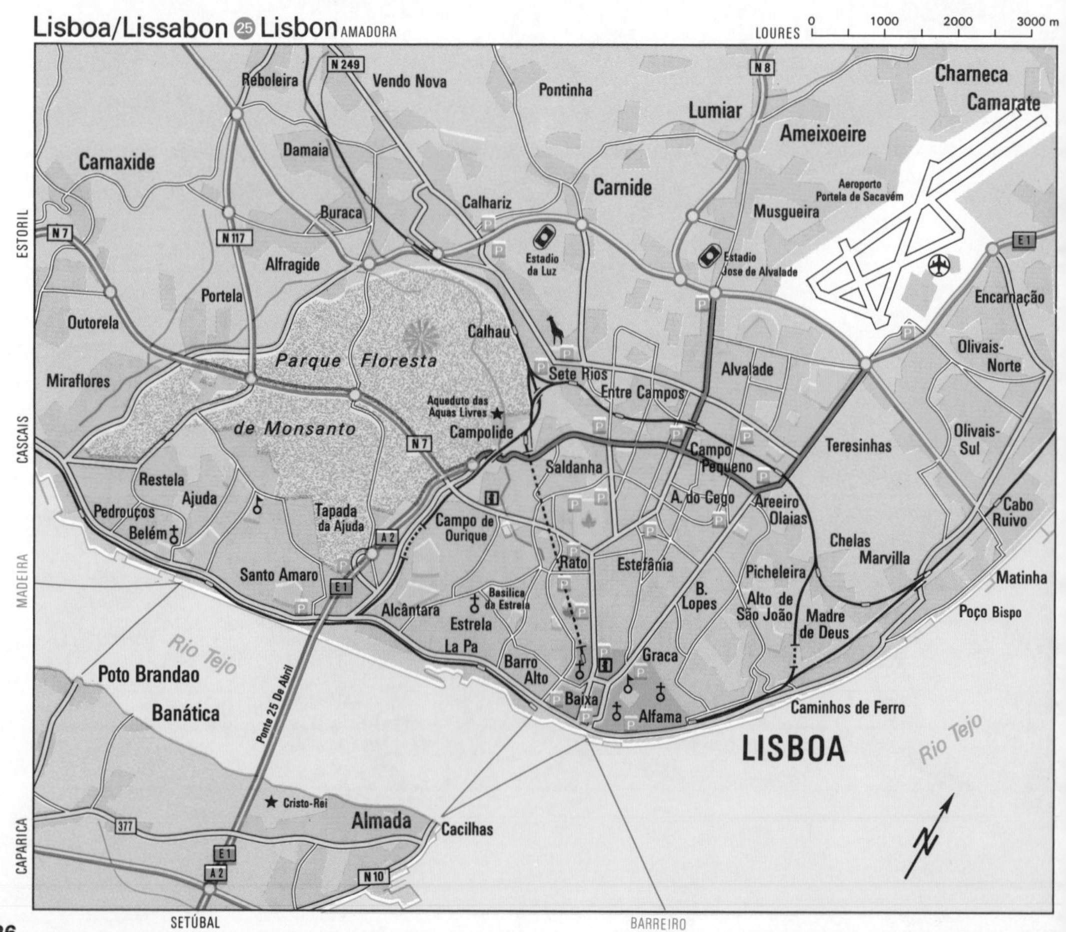

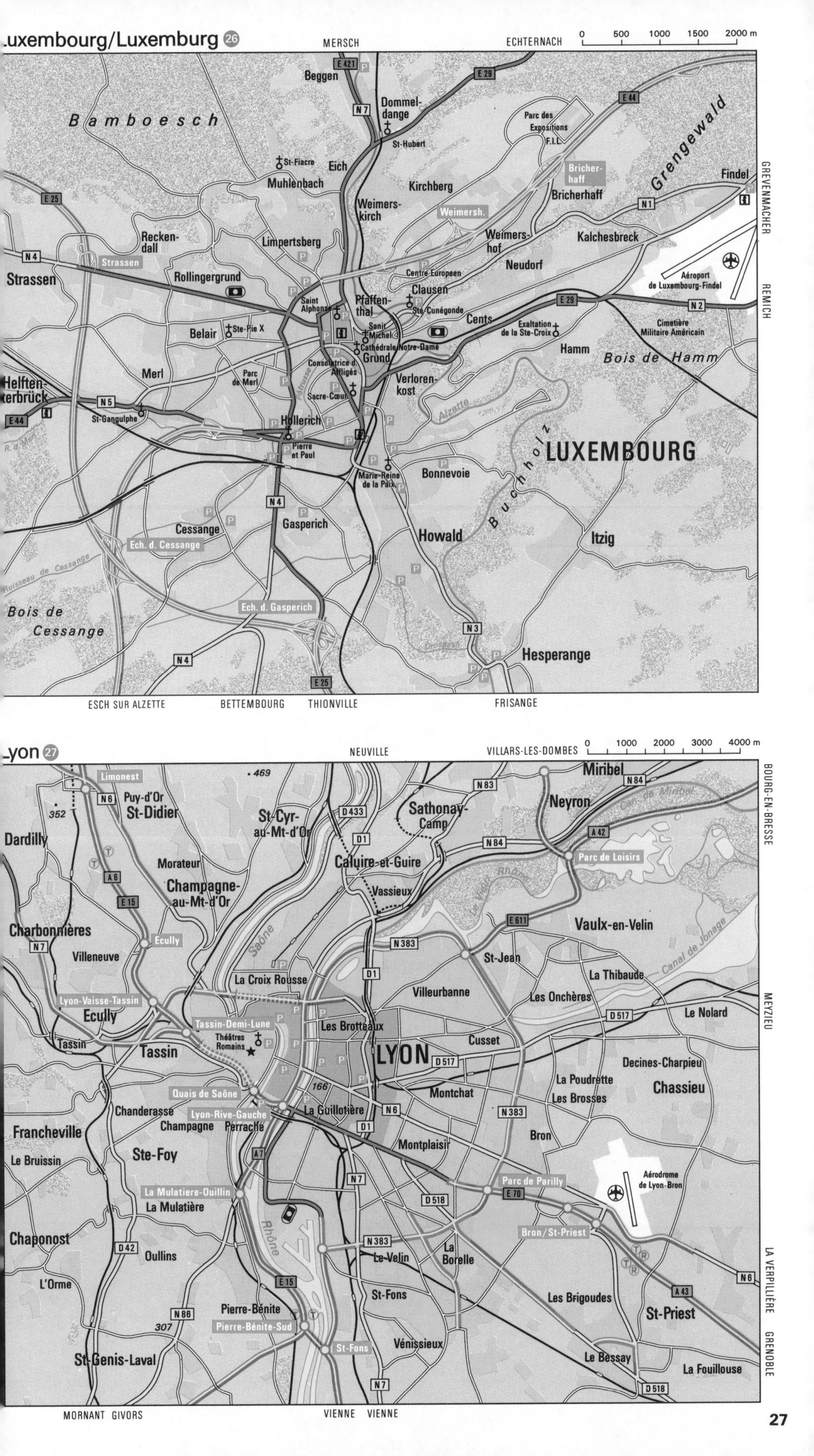

Luxembourg/Luxemburg 26
MERSCH
ECHTERNACH
0 500 1000 1500 2000 m
GREVENMACHER
REMICH
ESCH SUR ALZETTE
BETTEMBOURG
THIONVILLE
FRISANGE
Beggen
Dommeldange
St-Hubert
Bamboesch
Parc des Expositions F.I.L.
Grengewald
St-Fiacre
Eich
Muhlenbach
Kirchberg
Bricherhaff
Findel
Weimerskirch
Weimersh.
Reckendall
Limpertsberg
Weimershof
Kalchesbreck
Strassen
Neudorf
Aéroport de Luxembourg-Findel
Rollingergrund
Centre Europeen
Clausen
Saint Alphonse
Pfaffenthal
Ste-Cunégonde
Cents
Exaltation de la Ste-Croix
Cimetière Militaire Américain
Belair
Ste-Pie X
Saint Michel
Cathédrale Notre-Dame
Grund
Hamm
Bois de Hamm
Merl
Parc de Merl
Consolatrice d'Affligés
Verlorenkost
Helftenterbrück
Sacre-Cœur
St-Gangulphe
Hollerich
Alzette
Pétrusse
Pierre et Paul
Buchholz
LUXEMBOURG
Marie-Reine de la Paix
Bonnevoie
Cessange
Gasperich
Howald
Itzig
Ech. d. Cessange
Ruisseau de Cessange
Bois de Cessange
Ech. d. Gasperich
Hesperange
Drosbach
E 421
E 29
E 44
E 25
N 7
N 1
N 4
N 2
N 5
N 3
Lyon 27
NEUVILLE
VILLARS-LES-DOMBES
0 1000 2000 3000 4000 m
BOURG-EN-BRESSE
MEYZIEU
LA VERPILLIÈRE
GRENOBLE
MORNANT
GIVORS
VIENNE
VIENNE
Limonest
469
Miribel
Neyron
352
Puy-d'Or
St-Didier
St-Cyr-au-Mt-d'Or
Sathonay-Camp
Can. de Miribel
Dardilly
Morateur
Caluire-et-Guire
Parc de Loisirs
Champagne-au-Mt-d'Or
Vassieux
Le Vieux Rhône
Charbonnières
Ecully
Saône
Vaulx-en-Velin
Villeneuve
St-Jean
La Thibaude
Canal de Jonage
La Croix Rousse
Villeurbanne
Les Onchères
Lyon-Vaisse-Tassin
Ecully
Le Nolard
Tassin-Demi-Lune
Les Brotteaux
Tassin
Théâtres Romains
Cusset
Tassin
LYON
Decines-Charpieu
La Poudrette
Quais de Saône
166
Montchat
Chassieu
Les Brosses
Chanderasse
Lyon-Rive-Gauche
La Guillotière
Champagne
Perrache
Francheville
Bron
Montplaisir
Le Bruissin
Ste-Foy
Parc de Parilly
Aérodrome de Lyon-Bron
La Mulatiere-Ouillin
La Mulatière
Bron/St-Priest
Rhône
Chaponost
La Borelle
Oullins
Le Velin
L'Orme
St-Fons
Les Brigoudes
St-Priest
Pierre-Bénite
Pierre-Bénite-Sud
307
St-Fons
Vénissieux
St-Genis-Laval
Le Bessay
La Fouillouse
N 6
A 6
E 15
N 7
D 433
D 1
N 83
N 84
A 42
E 611
N 383
D 517
A 7
D 518
E 70
D 42
N 86
A 43

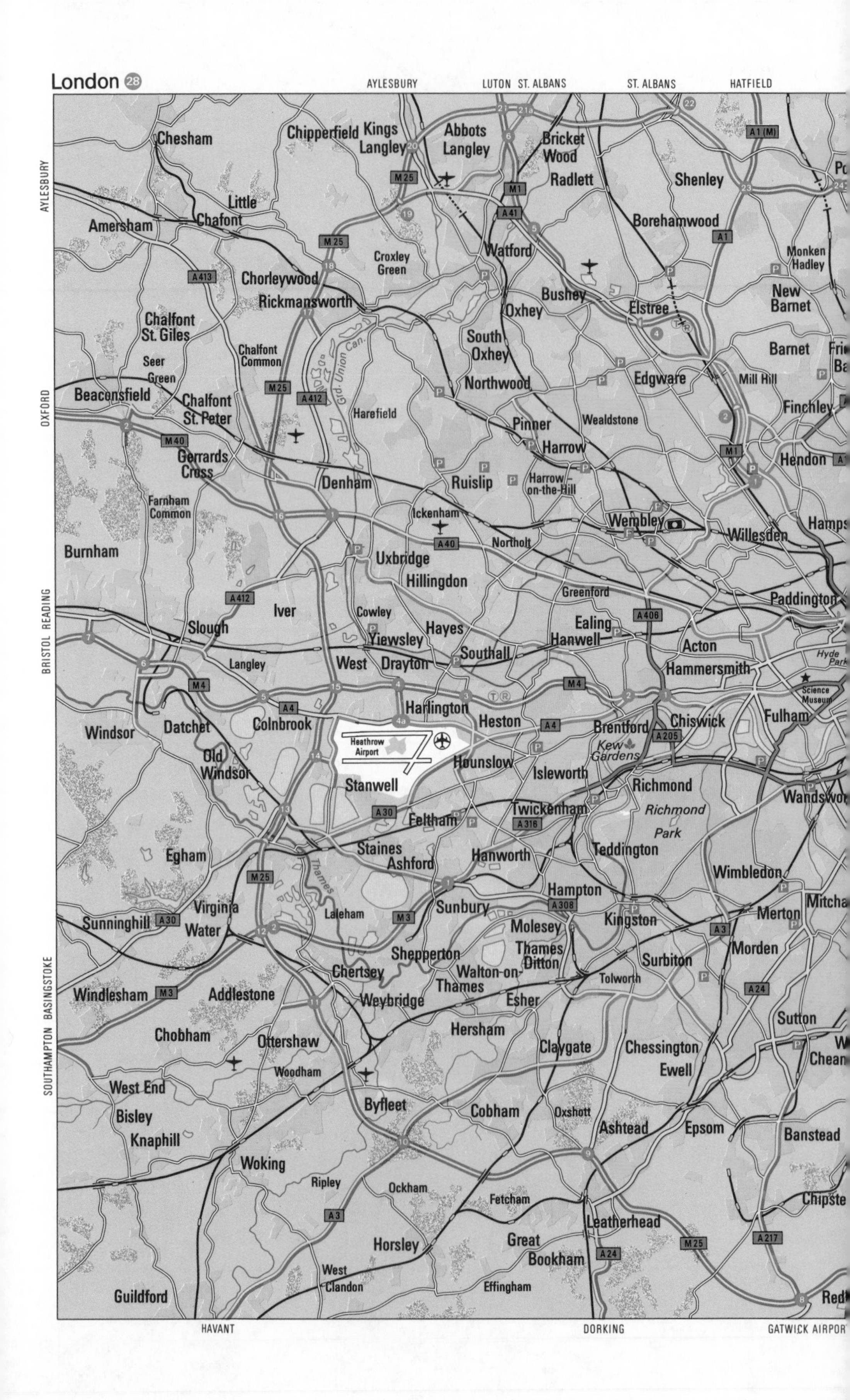

AYLESBURY LUTON ST. ALBANS ST. ALBANS HATFIELD

AYLESBURY

OXFORD

BRISTOL READING

SOUTHAMPTON BASINGSTOKE

Chesham
Chipperfield
Kings Langley
Abbots Langley
Bricket Wood
Radlett
Shenley
Little Chafont
Amersham
Watford
Borehamwood
Monken Hadley
Croxley Green
Chorleywood
Rickmansworth
Bushey
Oxhey
Elstree
New Barnet
Chalfont St. Giles
Seer Green
Chalfont Common
South Oxhey
Northwood
Edgware
Mill Hill
Barnet
Beaconsfield
Chalfont St. Peter
Harefield
Wealdstone
Finchley
Gerrards Cross
Pinner
Harrow
Hendon
Farnham Common
Denham
Ruislip
Harrow-on-the-Hill
Wembley
Willesden
Burnham
Ickenham
Northolt
Hamps
Uxbridge
Hillingdon
Northolt
Greenford
Paddington
Iver
Cowley
Hayes
Ealing
Hanwell
Acton
Slough
Langley
Yiewsley
West Drayton
Southall
Hammersmith
Hyde Park
Windsor
Datchet
Colnbrook
Harlington
Heston
Brentford
Chiswick
Fulham
Science Museum
Old Windsor
Heathrow Airport
Hounslow
Isleworth
Kew Gardens
Richmond
Wandswo
Stanwell
Feltham
Twickenham
Richmond Park
Egham
Staines
Ashford
Hanworth
Teddington
Wimbledon
Mitcha
Sunninghill
Virginia Water
Laleham
Sunbury
Hampton
Kingston
Merton
Morden
Windlesham
Addlestone
Chertsey
Weybridge
Molesey
Thames Ditton
Surbiton
Tolworth
Esher
Sutton
Chobham
Ottershaw
Woodham
Walton-on-Thames
Hersham
Claygate
Chessington
Ewell
Chean
West End
Bisley
Knaphill
Byfleet
Cobham
Oxshott
Ashtead
Epsom
Banstead
Woking
Ripley
Ockham
Fetcham
Leatherhead
Chipste
Horsley
Great Bookham
Red
Guildford
West Clandon
Effingham

HAVANT DORKING GATWICK AIRPOR

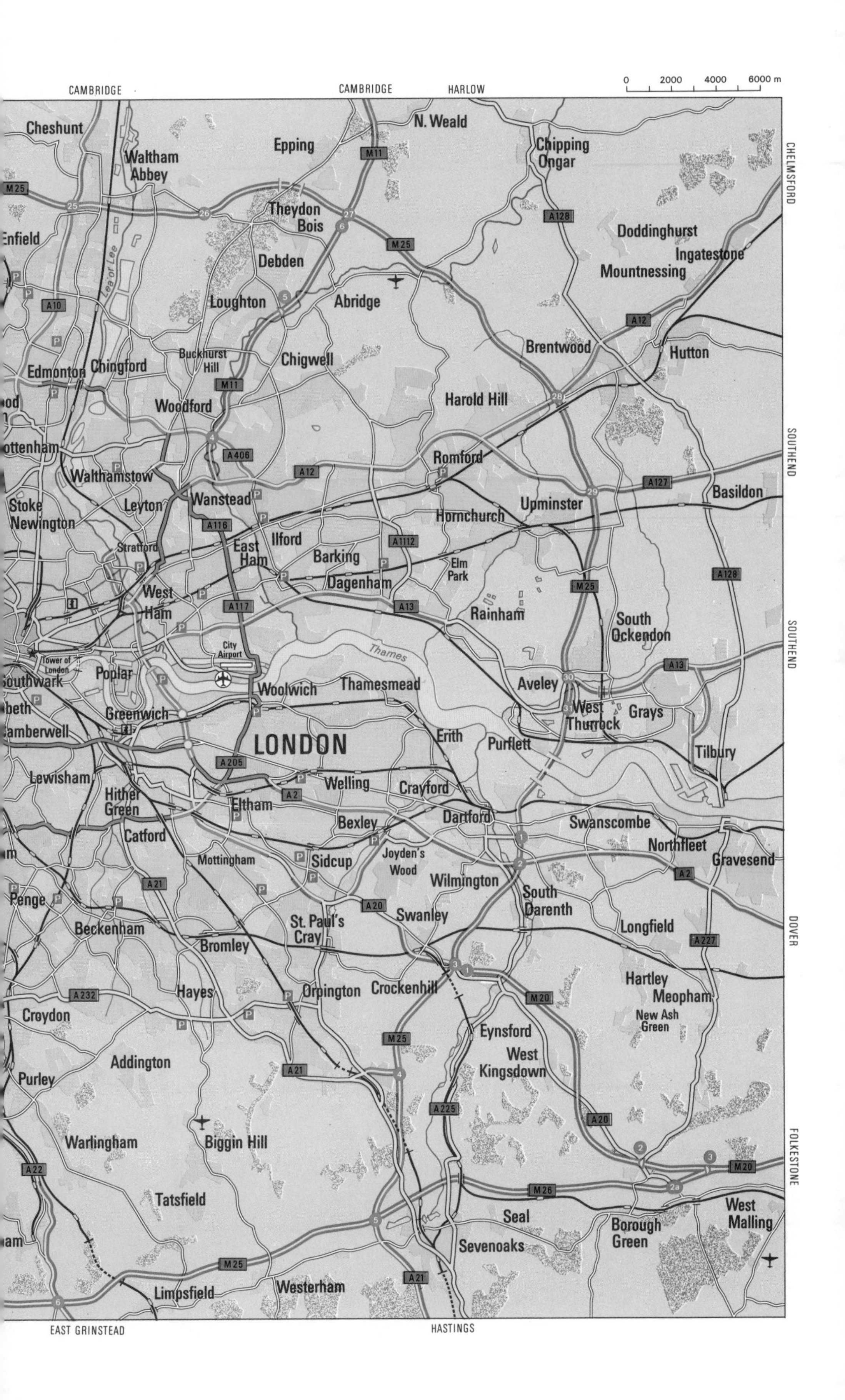

0 2000 4000 6000 m

N. Weald

Cheshunt
Waltham
Abbey
Epping
Chipping
Ongar
CHELMSFORD

Theydon
Bois
Doddinghurst
Ingatestone
Mountnessing

Enfield
Debden
Loughton
Abridge
Brentwood
Hutton

Edmonton Chingford
Buckhurst
Hill
Chigwell
Harold Hill

Woodford
Woolwich

Walthamstow
Leyton
Wanstead
Romford
Upminster
Basildon
SOUTHEND

Stoke
Newington
Stratford
East
Ham
Ilford
Barking
Hornchurch
Elm
Park
South
Ockendon
SOUTHEND

West
Ham
Dagenham
Rainham
Aveley
Grays

Tower of
London
Poplar
City
Airport
Thames

Southwark
Greenwich
Woolwich
Thamesmead
West
Thurrock
Tilbury

beth
Camberwell
LONDON
Erith
Purflett

Lewisham
Hither
Green
Eltham
Welling
Crayford
Dartford
Swanscombe
Northfleet
Gravesend
DOVER

Catford
Bexley
Wilmington
Longfield

Penge
Mottingham
Sidcup
Joyden's
Wood
South
Darenth
Hartley
Meopham

Beckenham
Bromley
St. Paul's
Cray
Swanley
New Ash
Green

Hayes
Orpington
Crockenhill
Eynsford

Croydon
Addington
West
Kingsdown

Purley
Biggin Hill
Warlingham
Seal
Borough
Green
West
Malling

Tatsfield
Sevenoaks

Limpsfield
Westerham

FOLKESTONE

29

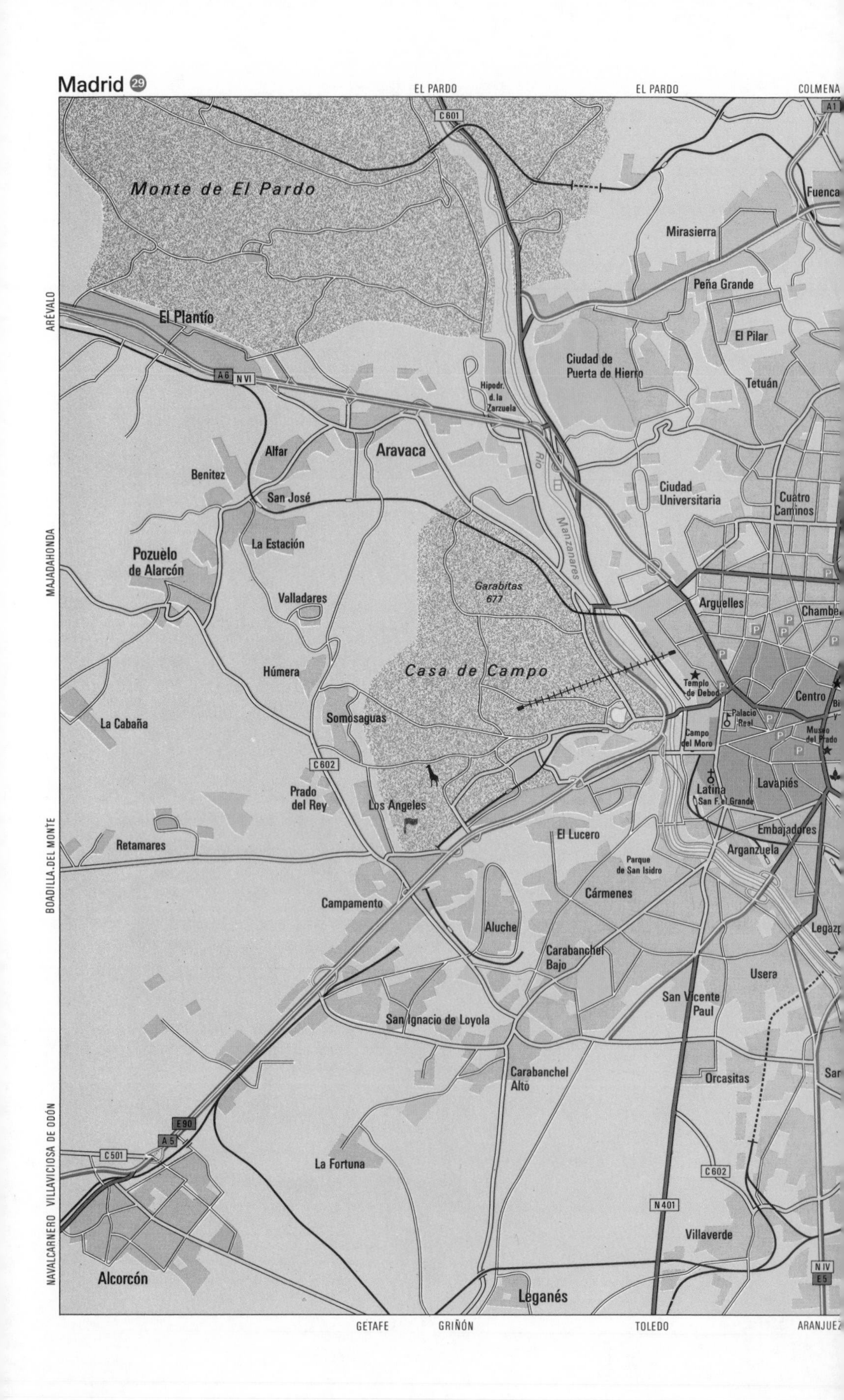

EL PARDO EL PARDO COLMENA

C 601

Monte de El Pardo

Fuenca

Mirasierra

Peña Grande

El Plantío

El Pilar

AREVALO

Ciudad de
Puerta de Hierro

Tetuán

A 6 N VI

Hipodr.
d. la
Zarzuela

Alfar

Aravaca

Benítez

San José

Ciudad
Universitaria

Cuatro
Caminos

La Estación

Pozuelo
de Alarcón

MAJADAHONDA

Valladares

*Garabitas
677*

Arguelles

Chambe

Húmera

Casa de Campo

La Cabaña

Somosaguas

Templo
de Debod

Centro

C 602

Palacio
Real

Museo
del Prado

Prado
del Rey

Campo
del More

Los Angeles

Latina
San F. el Grande

Lavapiés

BOADILLA DEL MONTE

Retamares

El Lucero

Embajadores

Arganzuela

Parque
de San Isidro

Campamento

Cármenes

Legazp

Aluche

Usera

Carabanchel
Bajo

San Vicente
Paul

San Ignacio de Loyola

Orcasitas

Sar

Carabanchel
Alto

VILLAVICIOSA DE ODÓN

E 90

C 501

A 5

La Fortuna

C 602

N 401

NAVALCARNERO

Villaverde

Alcorcón

N IV
E 5

Leganés

GETAFE GRIÑÓN TOLEDO ARANJUEZ

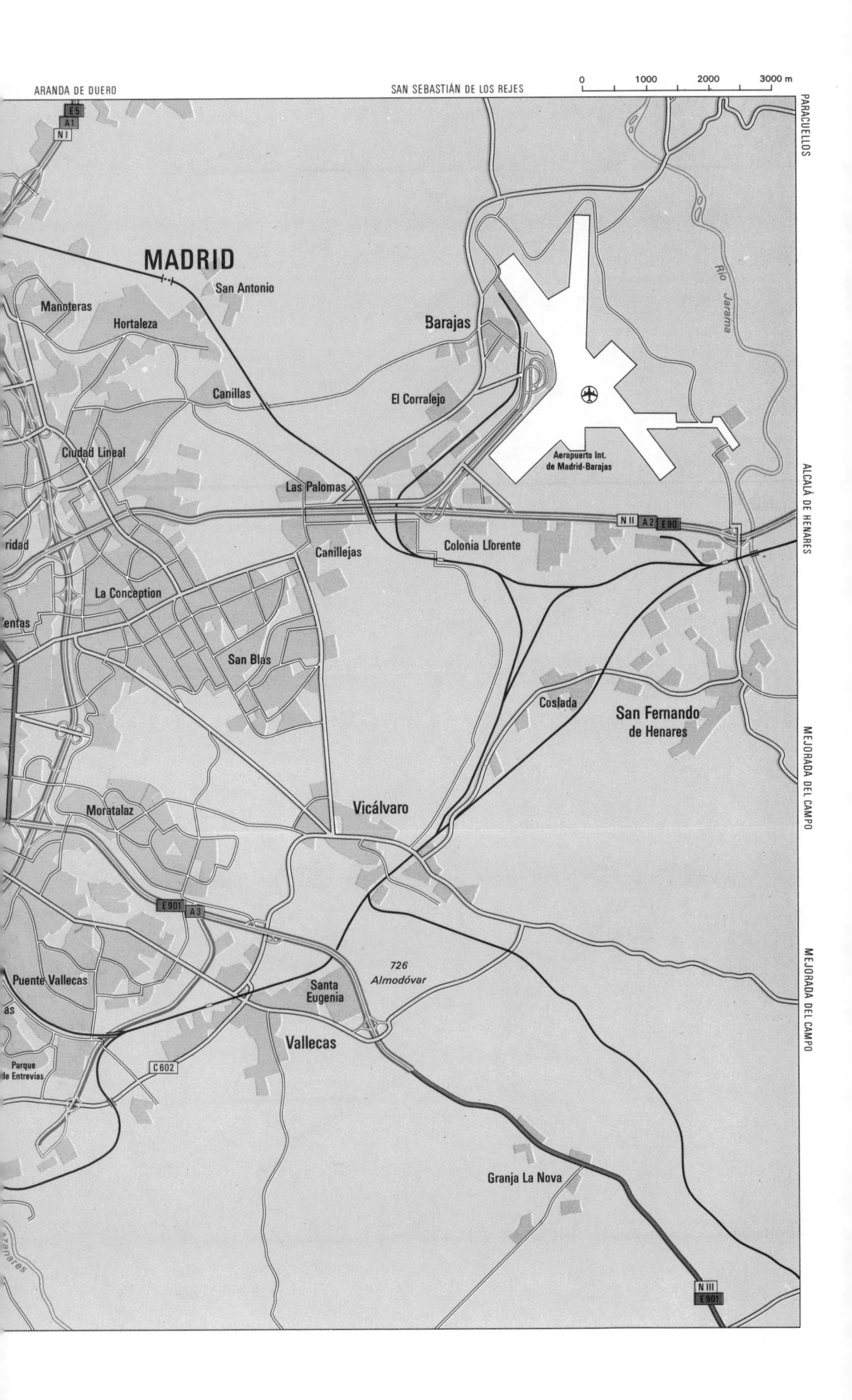

0   1000   2000   3000 m

PARACUELLOS

E5
A1
N I

MADRID

San Antonio

Manoteras

Hortaleza

Barajas

Canillas

El Corralejo

Ciudad Lineal

Las Palomas

Aeropuerto Int.
de Madrid-Barajas

Río Jarama

ALCALÁ DE HENARES

N II A 2 E90

ridad

Canillejas

Colonia Llorente

La Conception

entas

San Blas

Coslada

San Fernando
de Henares

MEJORADA DEL CAMPO

Moratalaz

Vicálvaro

E 901 A 3

726
Almodóvar

MEJORADA DEL CAMPO

Puente Vallecas

Santa
Eugenia

ás

Vallecas

Parque
de Entrevías

C 602

Granja La Nova

anares

N III
E 901

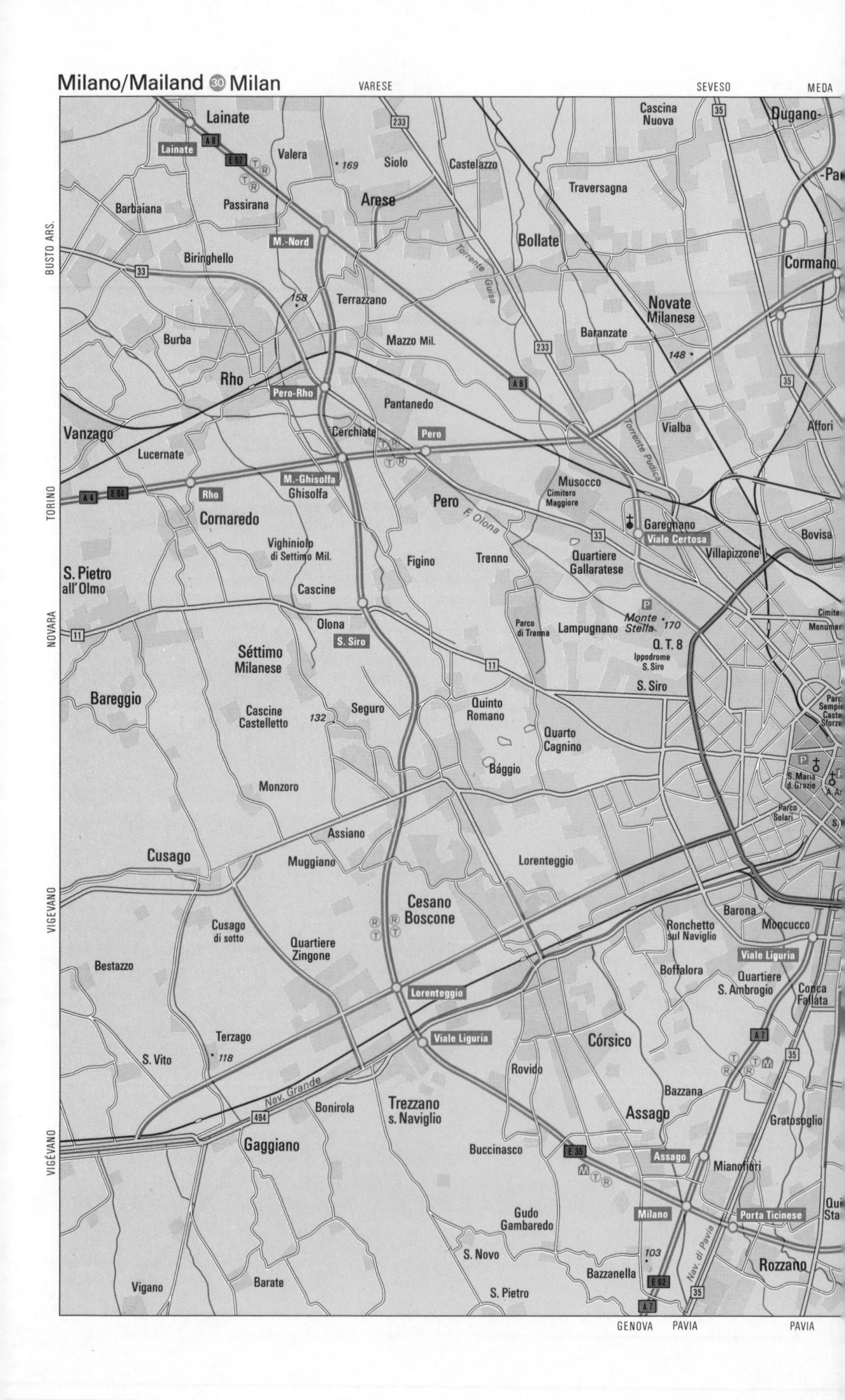
VARESE
SEVESO
MEDA
BUSTO ARS.
TORINO
NOVARA
VIGEVANO
VIGÉVANO
GENOVA
PAVIA
PAVIA
Lainate
Valera
Siolo
Castelazzo
Cascina Nuova
Dugano
Arese
Traversagna
Barbaiana
Passirana
Bollate
Biringhello
Terrazzano
Cormano
Novate Milanese
Baranzate
Burba
Mazzo Mil.
Rho
Pantanedo
Vialba
Affori
Vanzago
Cerchiate
Lucernate
Ghisolfa
Pero
Musocco
Cimitero Maggiore
Cornaredo
Garegnano
Bovisa
Vighiniolo di Settimo Mil.
Figino
Trenno
Quartiere Gallaratese
Villapizzone
S. Pietro all'Olmo
Cascine
Olona
Parco di Trenna
Lampugnano
Monte Stella
Q.T. 8
Ippodrome S. Siro
S. Siro
Séttimo Milanese
Bareggio
Cascine Castelletto
Seguro
Quinto Romano
Quarto Cagnino
Bággio
Monzoro
S. Maria d. Grazie
Parco Solari
Assiano
Cusago
Muggiano
Lorenteggio
Cesano Boscone
Barona
Moncucco
Cusago di sotto
Quartiere Zingone
Ronchetto sul Naviglio
Bestazzo
Boffalora
Quartiere S. Ambrogio
Conca Fallata
Terzago
Córsico
S. Vito
Rovido
Bazzana
Gratosoglio
Nav. Grande
Bonirola
Trezzano s. Naviglio
Assago
Gaggiano
Buccinasco
Mianofiori
Gudo Gambaredo
S. Novo
Nav. di Pavia
Rozzano
Bazzanella
S. Pietro
Vigano
Barate
Lainate
M.-Nord
Pero-Rho
Pero
M.-Ghisolfa
Rho
Viale Certosa
S. Siro
Viale Liguria
Lorenteggio
Viale Liguria
Assago
Milano
Porta Ticinese
A 8
E 62
A 4
E 64
A 7
E 35
E 62
A 7
233
33
11
494
35
169
158
148
170
132
118
103

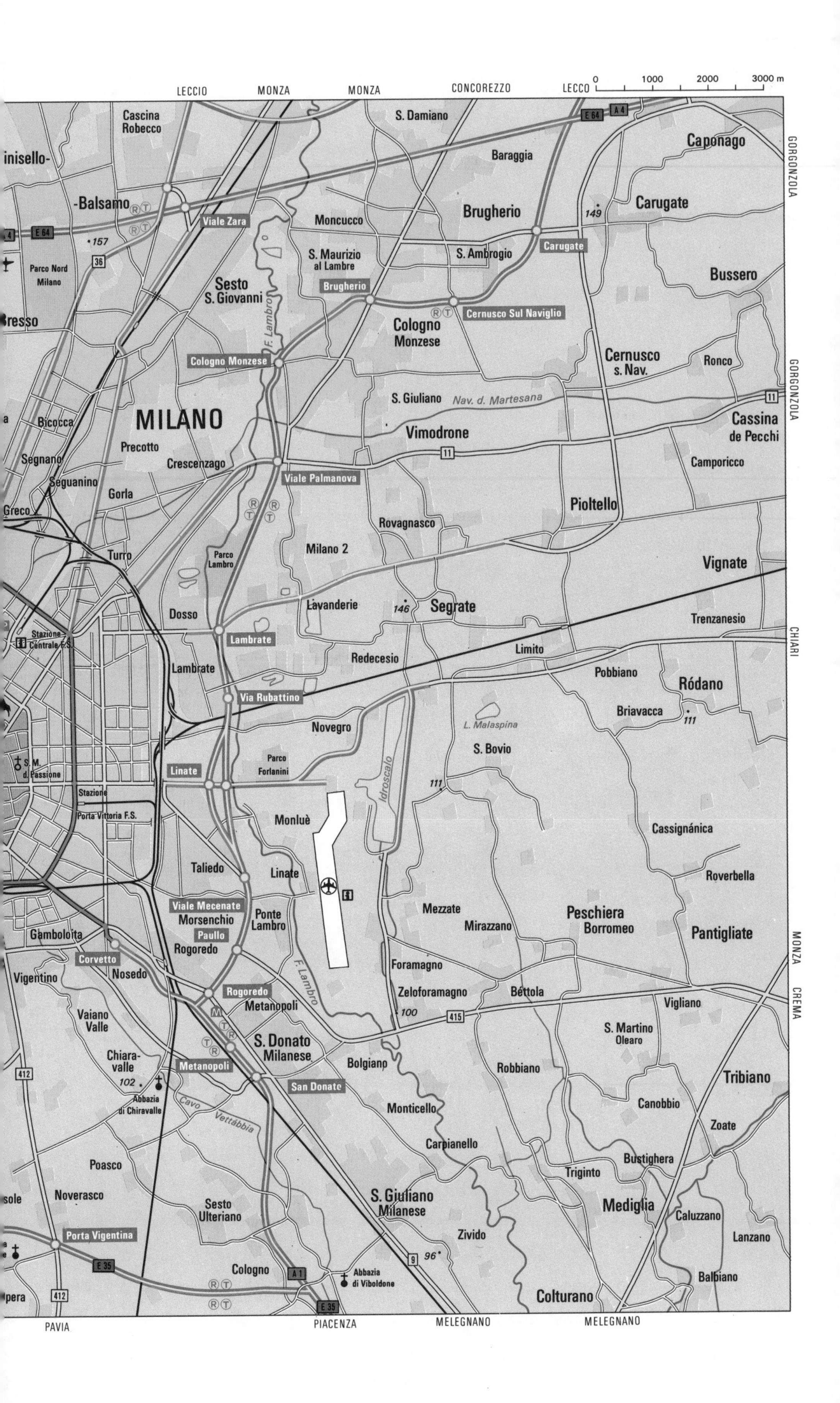

0   1000   2000   3000 m

GORGONZOLA

Cascina
Robecco

S. Damiano

Caponago

Baraggia

inisello-

-Balsamo

E 64   A 4

Viale Zara

Moncucco

Brugherio

149

Carugate

GORGONZOLA

• 157

E 64

S. Maurizio
al Lambre

S. Ambrogio

Carugate

Bussero

Parco Nord
Milano

36

Sesto
S. Giovanni

Brugherio

F. Lambro

Cologno Monzese

Cologno
Monzese

Cernusco Sul Naviglio

Cernusco
s. Nav.

Ronco

11

resso

Cologno Monzese

S. Giuliano

Nav. d. Martesana

GORGONZOLA

MILANO

Vimodrone

Cassina
de Pecchi

Bicocca

11

Segnano

Precotto

Crescenzago

Viale Palmanova

Rovagnasco

Pioltello

Camporicco

Seguanino

Gorla

Milano 2

CHIARI

Greco

Turro

Parco
Lambro

Lavanderie

146

Segrate

Vignate

Trenzanesio

Dosso

Stazione
Centrale F.S.

Lambrate

Lambrate

Redecesio

Limito

Pobbiano

Ródano

Lambrate

Via Rubattino

L. Malaspina

Briavacca

111

S. M.
d. Passione

Novegro

S. Bovio

Linate

Parco
Forlanini

Idroscalo

111

Cassignánica

Stazione
Porta Vittoria F.S.

Monluè

Roverbella

Taliedo

Linate

Mezzate

Peschiera
Borromeo

Pantigliate

Gamboloita

Viale Mecenate

Morsenchio

Ponte
Lambro

Mirazzano

MONZA

Corvetto

Paullo

Rogoredo

F. Lambro

Foramagno

Vigliano

CREMA

Vigentino

Nosedo

Rogoredo

Zeloforamagno

Béttola

Vaiano
Valle

Metanopoli

100

415

S. Martino
Olearo

Chiara-
valle

412

102

Metanopoli

S. Donato
Milanese

Bolgiano

Robbiano

Tribiano

Abbazia
di Chiravalle

San Donate

Canobbio

Zoate

Cavo Vettabbia

Monticello

Poasco

Carpianello

Bustighera

Noverasco

Sesto
Ulteriano

Triginto

Mediglia

Caluzzano

sole

Porta Vigentina

Zivido

Lanzano

E 35

S. Giuliano
Milanese

96°

412

Cologno

A 1

9

Abbazia
di Viboldone

Balbiano

opera

412

E 35

Colturano

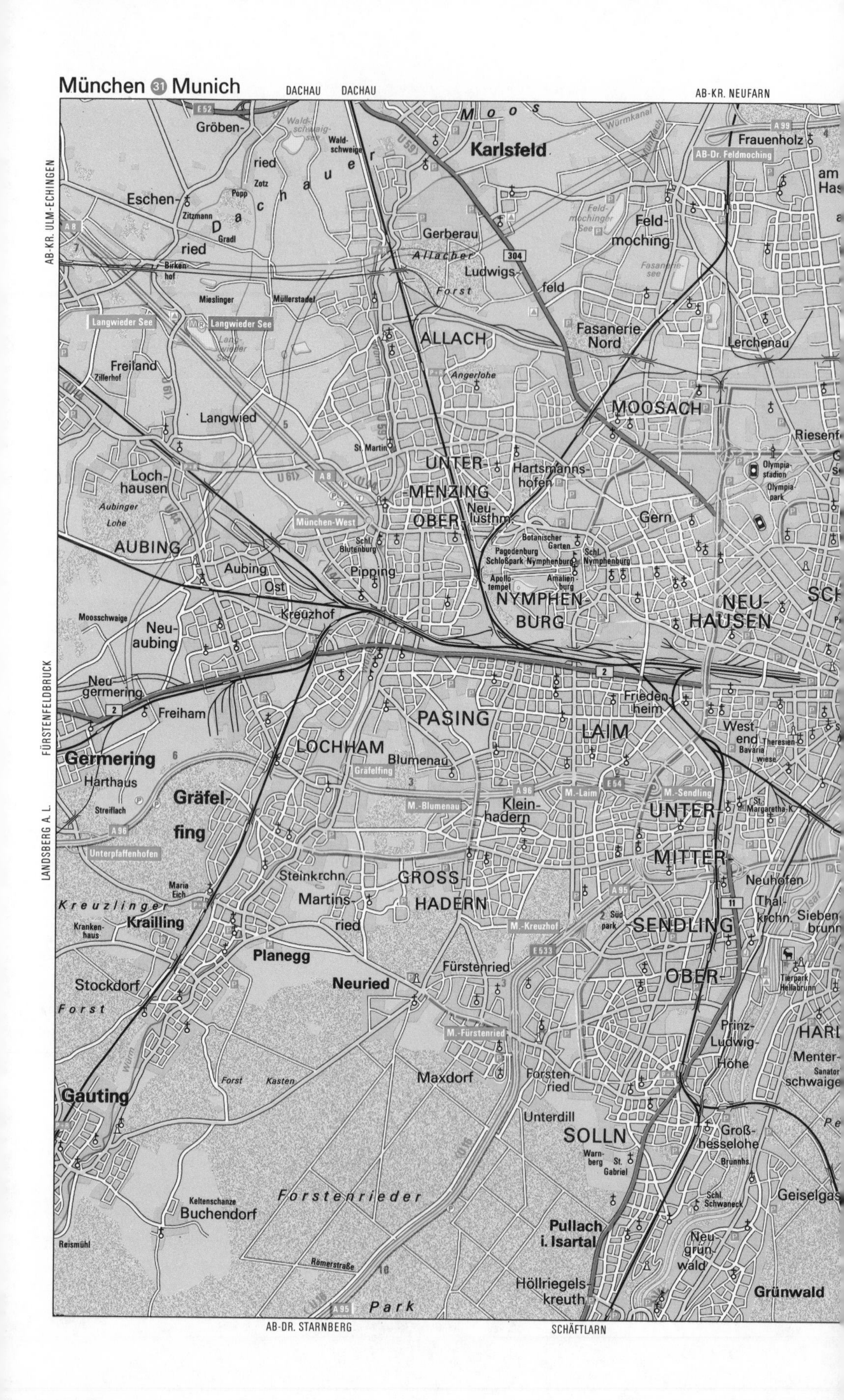

DACHAU   DACHAU   AB-KR. NEUFARN

FÜRSTENFELDBRUCK

LANDSBERG A. L.

Moos

Gröben-
ried

Waldschweige
see

Waldschweige

Karlsfeld

Würmkanal

A 99

Frauenholz

AB-Dr. Feldmoching

am
Has

Eschen-
ried

Popp
Zitzmann
Gradl
Zotz

D

Gerberau

Allacher   304

Ludwigs-
feld

Feld-
moching-
er See

Feld-
moching

Fasanerie
see

Lerchenau

Birken-
hof
Mieslinger
Müllerstadel

Forst

Fasanerie
Nord

Freiland
Zillerhof

Langwieder See   Langwieder See
Lang-
wieder
see

ALLACH

Angerlohe

MOOSACH

Riesen

Langwied

St. Martin

Loch-
hausen
Aubinger
Lohe

Hartsmanns-
hofen

UNTER

München-West

MENZING
OBER

Neu-
lusthm.

Gern

Olympia-
stadion
Olympia-
park

AUBING

Aubing
Ost

Schl.
Blutenburg

Botanischer
Garten
Pagodenburg
Schloßpark Nymphenburg
Apollo-
tempel
Amalien-
burg

Schl.
Nymphenburg

NEU-

NYMPHEN-
BURG

HAUSEN

SCH

Moosschwaige

Kreuzhof

Neu-
aubing

Pipping

Neu-
germering   2
Freiham

Friedens-
heim

West-
end
Bavaria

Theresien
wiese

PASING

LAIM

Germering   6
Harthaus

LOCHHAM

Blumenau
Gräfelfing   3

M.-Laim   E 54

M.-Sendling

St.
Margaretha-K.

UNTER-

Streiflach

Gräfel
fing

A 96

Unterpfaffenhofen

M. Blumenau

Klein-
hadern

MITTER

Maria
Eich

Steinkrchn.

GROSS-

A 95

Neuhofen

Krailling
Krankenhaus

Martins-
ried

HADERN

M.-Kreuzhof

2 Süd
park

SENDLING

Thal-
krchn. Sieben-
brunn

Planegg

Fürstenried

OBER

Tierpark
Hellabrunn

HARL

Stockdorf

Neuried

M.-Fürstenried

Prinz-
Ludwig-
höhe

Menter-
Senator-
schwaige

Forst

Maxdorf

Forsten-
ried

Gauting

Forst   Kasten

Unterdill

SOLLN

Groß-
hesselohe

Kreuzlinger

Wurm

Warnberg   St.
Gabriel

Brunnhs.

Geiselgas

Schl.
Schwaneck

Keltenschanze
Buchendorf

Forstenrieder

Reismühl

Römerstraße   10

Pullach
i. Isartal

Neu-
grün-
wald

Park

Höllriegels-
kreuth

Grünwald

AB-Dr. STARNBERG   SCHÄFTLARN

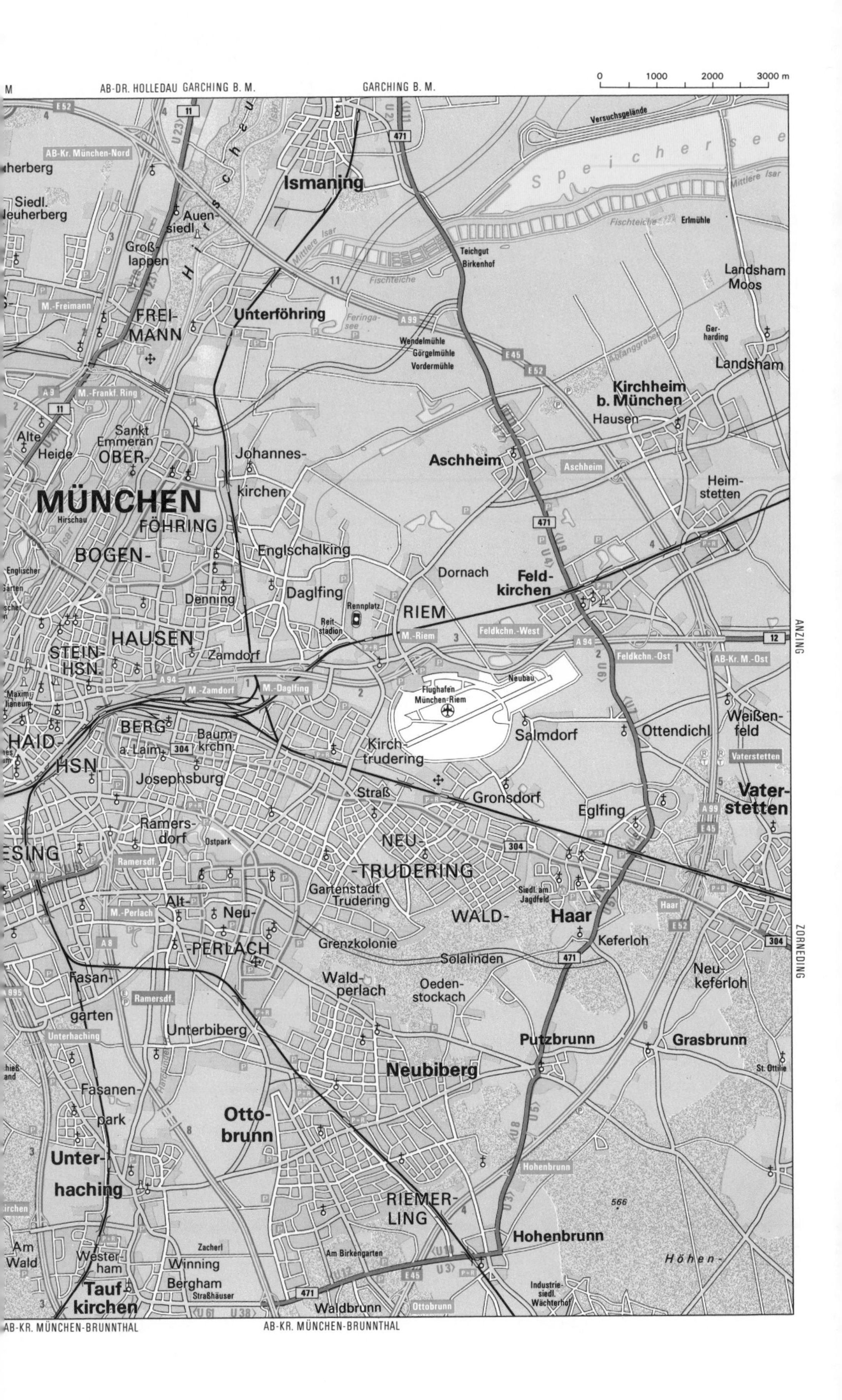

0   1000   2000   3000 m

E 52

AB-Kr. München-Nord

herberg

Siedl.
leuherberg

Siedl.

Groß-
lappen

Auen-
siedl

M.-Freimann

FREI-
MANN

Ismaning

Unterföhring

Feringa-
see

Versuchsgelände

S p e i c h e r s e e

Fischteiche

Mittlere Isar

Erlmühle

Teichgut
Birkenhof

Landsham
Moos

Ger-
harding

Landsham

Mittlere Isar

Fischteiche

A 99

Wendelmühle
Görgelmühle
Vordermühle

E 45

E 52

Schlangengraben

**Kirchheim
b. München**

Hausen

Alte
Heide

Sankt
Emmeran

OBER-

Johannes-

kirchen

Aschheim

Aschheim

Heim-
stetten

A 3

M.-Frankf. Ring

MÜNCHEN

Hirschau

FÖHRING

BOGEN-

Englischer
Garten

Englschalking

Dornach

**Feld-
kirchen**

Denning

Daglfing

Rennplatz.

RIEM

471

Reit-
stadion

M.-Riem

3

Feldkchn.-West

ANZING

12

STEIN-
HSN.

HAUSEN

Zamdorf

A 94

M.-Zamdorf

M.-Daglfing

2

Neubau

Flughafen
München-Riem

Feldkchn.-Ost

AB-Kr. M.-Ost

Weißen-
feld

Ottendichl

Vaterstetten

HAID-

HSN

Maximi-
lianeum

BERG-

a. Laim.

304

Baum-
krchn.

Kirch-
trudering

Salmdorf

**Vater-
stetten**

Josephsburg

Straß

Gronsdorf

A 99

Ramers-
dorf

Ostpark

Eglfing

304

E 45

ESING

Ramersdf.

NEU-

-TRUDERING

Siedl. am
Jagdfeld

Haar

ZORNEDING

M.-Perlach

Alt-

Neu-

Gartenstadt
Trudering

WALD-

Haar

304

A 8

-PERLACH

Grenzkolonie

Keferloh

471

Neu-
keferloh

Solalinden

St. Ottilie

Fasan-

Ramersdf.

Wald-
perlach

Oeden-
stockach

Putzbrunn

Grasbrunn

garten

Unterhaching

Unterbiberg

Neubiberg

Fasanen-

**Otto-
brunn**

Hohenbrunn

park

**Unter-

haching**

kirchen

**RIEMER-
LING**

566

Am
Wald

Wester-
ham

Zacherl

Winning

Hohenbrunn

Höhen-

**Tauf-
kirchen**

Bergham
Straßhäuser

Am Birkengarten

471

U 38

Waldbrunn

E 45

U 3

Ottobrunn

Industrie-
siedl.
Wachterhof

35

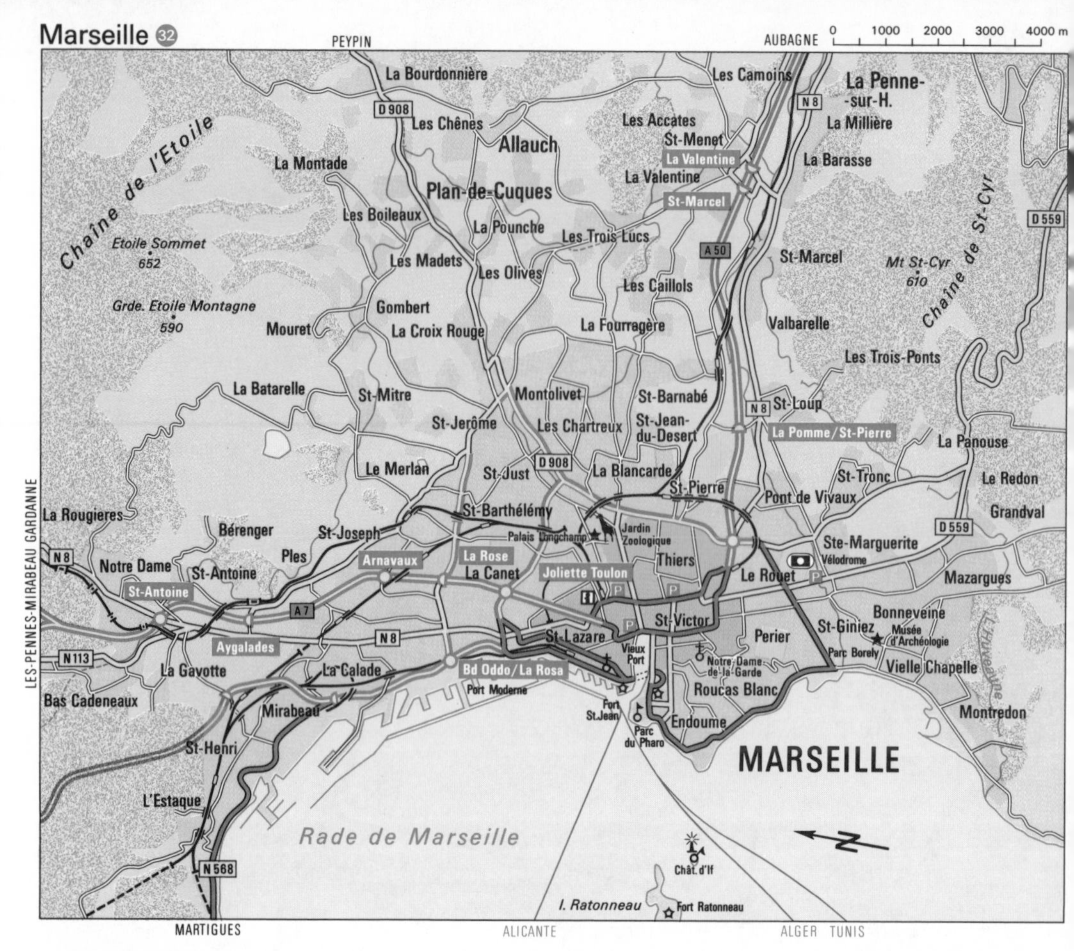

PEYPIN   AUBAGNE   0   1000   2000   3000   4000 m

Chaîne de l'Etoile

La Bourdonnière
Les Chênes
La Montade
D 908
Les Boileaux
Plan-de-Cuques
Les Accates
St-Menet
La Millière
La Penne--sur-H.
La Barasse
N 8
La Valentine
La Valentine
St-Marcel
Allauch
Les Camoins

Etoile Sommet 652
Les Madets
La Pounche
Les Trois-Lucs
Les Olives
Les Caillols
A 50
St-Marcel
Mt St-Cyr 610
Chaîne de St-Cyr
D 559

Grde. Etoile Montagne 590
Gombert
La Croix Rouge
La Fourragère
Valbarelle
Les Trois-Ponts

Mouret
La Batarelle
St-Mitre
Montolivet
St-Barnabé
St-Loup
N 8
La Pomme / St-Pierre
La Panouse

Bérenger
St-Jérôme
Les Chartreux
St-Jean-du-Desert
N 8
St-Tronc
Le Redon

Ples
St-Joseph
Le Merlan
St-Just
La Blancarde
St-Pierre
Pont de Vivaux
D 559
Grandval

Notre Dame
St-Antoine
Arnavaux
D 908
St-Barthélémy
Palais Longchamp
Jardin Zoologique
Thiers
Ste-Marguerite
Vélodrome
Mazargues

St-Antoine
La Rose
La Canet
Joliette Toulon
Le Rouet
St-Giniex
Bonneveine
Vielle Chapelle

LES-PENNES-MIRABEAU GARDANNE
N 8
A 7
N 8
St-Lazare
Vieux Port
St-Victor
Perier
Musée d'Archéologie

Aygalades
Bd Oddo / La Rosa
Port Moderne
Vieux Port
Fort St-Jean
Notre-Dame-de-la-Garde
Roucas Blanc
Montredon

La Gavotte
La Calade
Mirabeau
Endoume
Parc du Pharo
MARSEILLE

Bas Cadeneaux
St-Henri
L'Estaque
N 113
N 568

Rade de Marseille

Chât. d'If
I. Ratonneau
Fort Ratonneau

MARTIGUES   ALICANTE   ALGER TUNIS

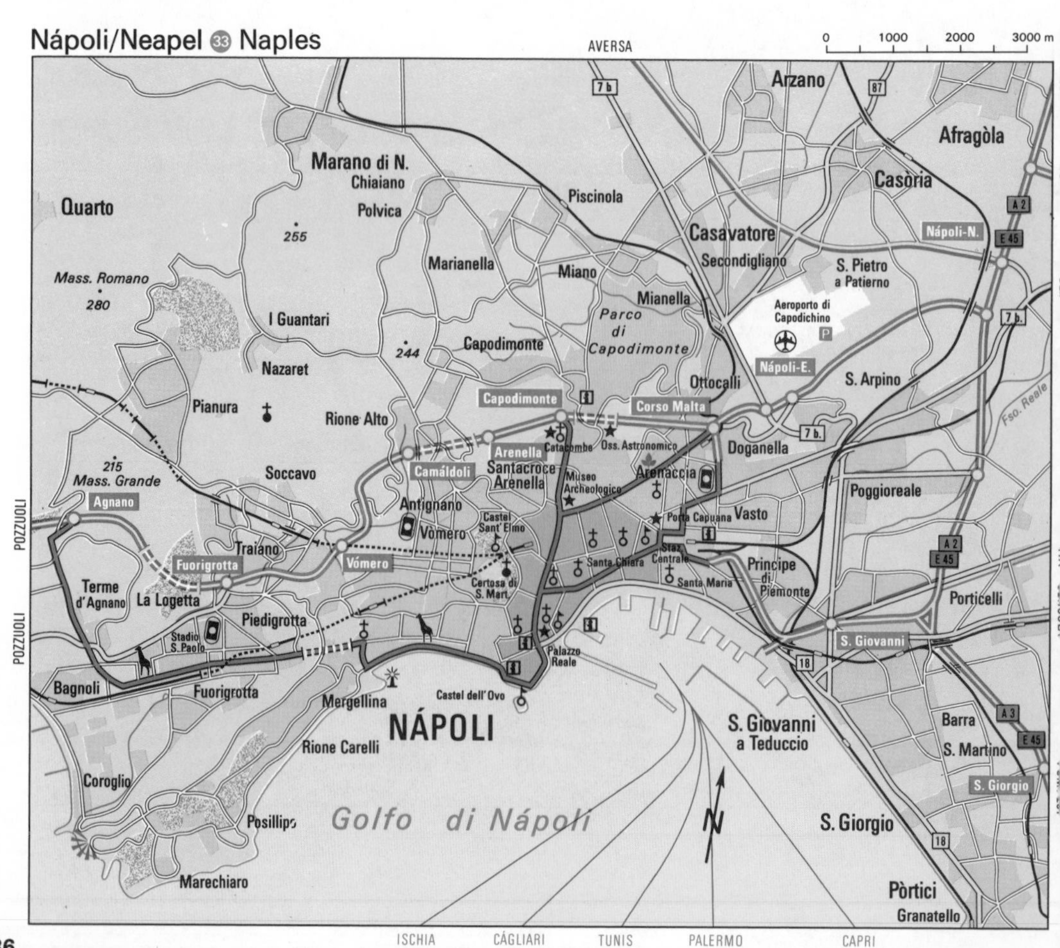

Nápoli/Neapel ③③ Naples

AVERSA   0   1000   2000   3000 m

Arzano
7 b
87

Marano di N.
Chiaiano
Polvica
Piscinola
Casavatore
Afragòla
Casòria
A 2
E 45
Nápoli-N.

Quarto
255
Marianella
Miano
Secondigliano
S. Pietro a Patierno
7 b.

Mass. Romano 280
I Guantari
Mianella
Aeroporto di Capodichino
Nápoli-E.

Nazaret
244
Capodimonte
Parco di Capodimonte
Ottocalli
S. Arpino

Pianura
Rione Alto
Capodimonte
Corso Malta
Doganella
7 b.

215
Mass. Grande
Soccavo
Arenella
Santacroce Arenella
Catacombe
Oss. Astronomico
Museo Archeologico
Arenaccia
Poggioreale

POZZUOLI
Agnano
Camáldoli
Antignano
Castel Sant'Elmo
Porta Capuana
Vasto
A 2
E 45

POZZUOLI
Traiano
Vómero
Santa Chiara
Principe di Piemonte
Porticelli

Terme d'Agnano
La Logetta
Vómero
Certosa di S. Mart.
Santa Maria
S. Giovanni
18

Fuorigrotta
Piedigrotta
Stadio S. Paolo
Palazzo Reale
A 3
E 45

Bagnoli
Fuorigrotta
Mergellina
Castel dell'Ovo
S. Giovanni a Teduccio
Barra
S. Martino

Coroglio
NÁPOLI
Rione Carelli
S. Giorgio

Posillipo
Golfo di Nápoli
S. Giorgio
18

Marechiaro
Pòrtici
Granatello

ISCHIA   CÁGLIARI   TUNIS   PALERMO   CAPRI

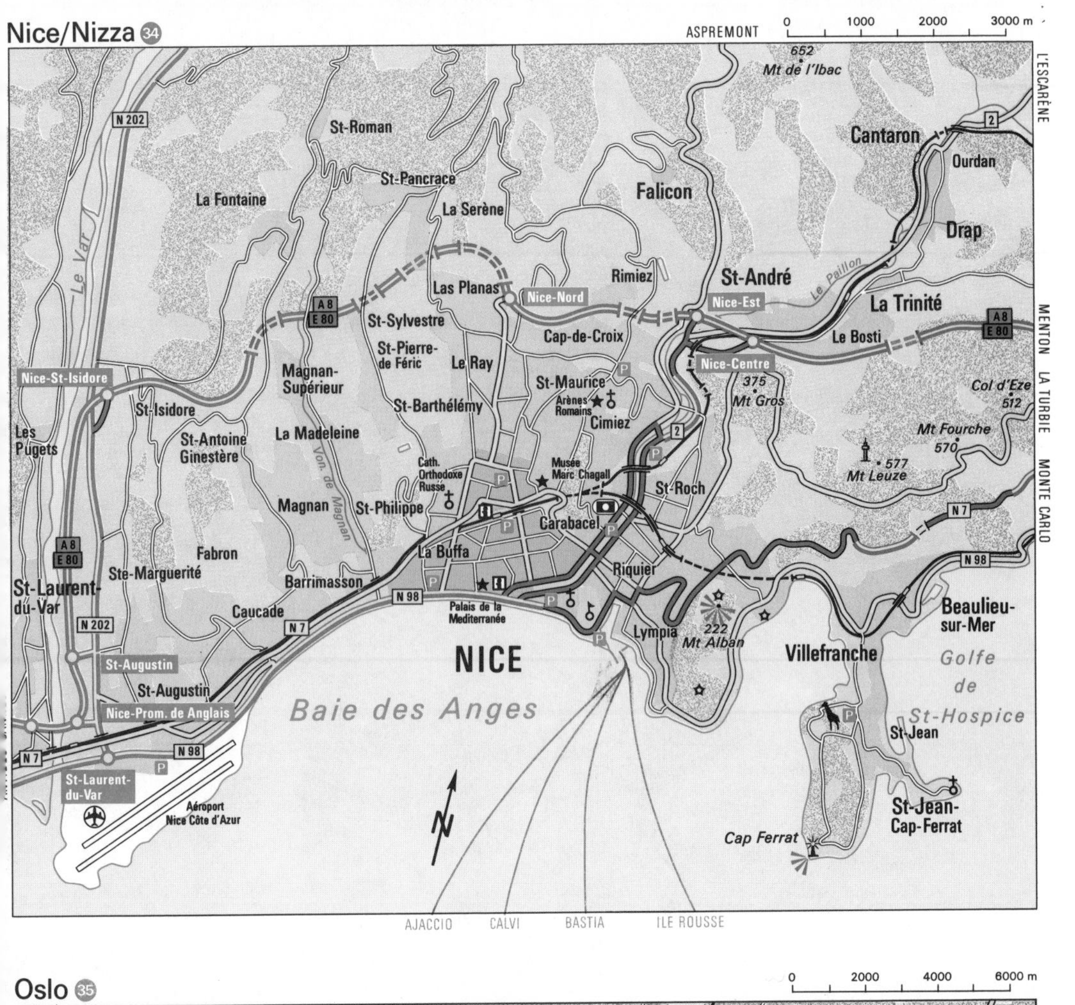

ASPREMONT

0   1000   2000   3000 m

L'ESCARÈNE

652
Mt de l'Ibac

N 202

Cantaron
Ourdan
Drap

2

St-Roman
St-Pancrace
La Fontaine
La Serène
Falicon

MENTON   LA TURBIE   MONTE CARLO

Las Planas
Rimiez
St-André
La Trinité

A8 E80
Nice-Nord
Nice-Est
Le Bosti

A8 E80

Nice-St-Isidore
St-Sylvestre
Cap-de-Croix
Nice-Centre

Les Pugets
St-Pierre-de-Féric
Le Ray

Magnan-Supérieur
St-Maurice
375 Mt Gros
Col d'Eze 512

St-Isidore
St-Barthélémy
Arènes Romains
Cimiez
Mt Fourche 570

St-Antoine Ginestère
La Madeleine
Cath. Orthodoxe Russe
Musée Marc Chagall
577 Mt Leuze

Magnan
St-Philippe
St-Roch

Fabron
Carabacel

N 7

Ste-Marguerite
La Buffa
N 98

Barrimasson
Riquier

Palais de la Méditerranée
Lympia

St-Laurent-du-Var
Caucade
Mt Alban
Villefranche

N 202
N 7

St-Augustin
Beaulieu-sur-Mer

St-Augustin
NICE
Golfe de St-Hospice

Nice-Prom. de Anglais
St-Jean

N 98
N 7

St-Laurent-du-Var
Baie des Anges

Aéroport Nice Côte d'Azur

Cap Ferrat
St-Jean-Cap-Ferrat

N

AJACCIO   CALVI   BASTIA   ILE ROUSSE

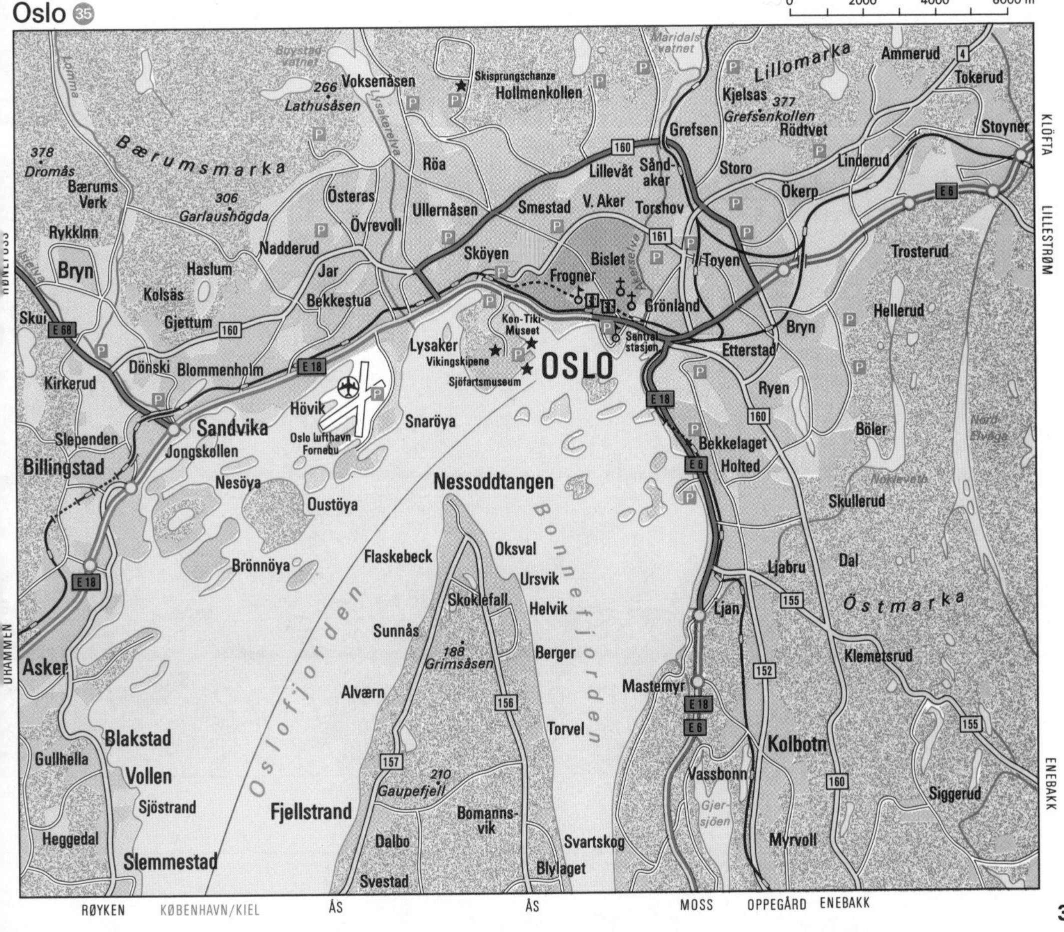

0   2000   4000   6000 m

Maridalsvatnet
Ammerud
Tokerud
4

Bøystad-vatnet
Skisprungschanze
Hollmenkollen
Lillomarka
Kjelsas
377 Grefsenkollen
Stoyner
KLØFTA

266 Voksenåsen
Lathusåsen
Grefsen
Rødtvet

378 Dromås
Bærums-marka
Röa
Lillevåt
Sånd-aker
Storo
Ökern
Linderud

Bærums Verk
306 Garlaushögda
Österas
Ullernåsen
Smestad
V. Aker
Torshov

LILLESTRØM

Rykklnn
Nadderud
Övrevoll
Sköyen
161

Bryn
Haslum
Jar
Bislet
Toyen
Trosterud

Skui
Kolsäs
Bekkestua
Frogner
Grönland
Hellerud

E68
Gjettum
160
Kon-Tiki-Museet
Bryn

Kirkerud
Dönski
Blommenholm
E18
Lysaker
Vikingskipene
Sjöfartsmuseum
Sentral-stasjon
Etterstad
160

Slependen
Hövik
OSLO
Ryen
Böler

Billingstad
Sandvika
Jongskollen
Oslo lufthavn Fornebu
Snaröya
E18
Bekkelaget
Holted
Skullerud

Nesöya
E6

Nessoddtangen
Nord-

Brönnöya
Flaskebeck
Oksval
Ljabru
Dal

Ursvik
Helvik
Ljan
155
Östmarka

Asker
Sunnås
Berger
Mastemyr
Klemetsrud

188 Grimsåsen
E18
152

Blakstad
Alvaern
156
Torvel
E6
Kolbotn
155

Gullhella
Vollen
Sjöstrand
157
210 Gaupefjell
Vassbonn
160
Siggerud

Heggedal
Slemmestad
Fjellstrand
Bomanns-vik
Gjer-sjöen
Myrvoll

Dalbo
Svartskog

Svestad
Blylaget

RØYKEN   KØBENHAVN/KIEL   ÅS   ÅS   MOSS   OPPEGÅRD   ENEBAKK

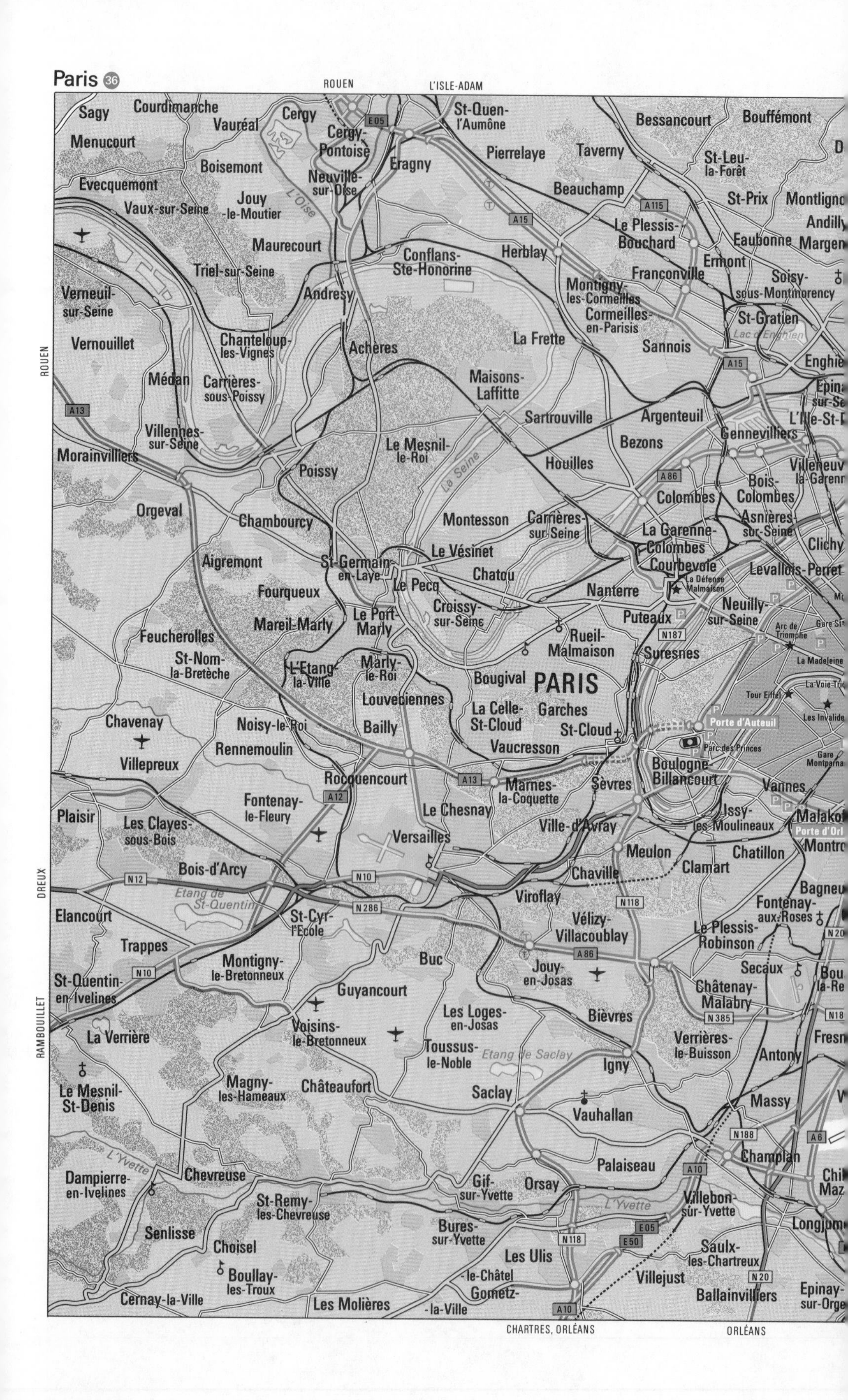

ROUEN   L'ISLE-ADAM

Sagy

Courdimanche

Menucourt

Vauréal

Cergy

Cergy-Pontoise

E05

St-Quen-l'Aumône

Bessancourt

Bouffémont

D

Evecquemont

Boisemont

Neuville-sur-Oise

Eragny

Pierrelaye

Taverny

St-Leu-la-Forêt

St-Prix

Montligno

Vaux-sur-Seine

Jouy-le-Moutier

Beauchamp

A115

Andilly

Eaubonne

Margen

Maurecourt

A15

Le Plessis-Bouchard

Ermont

Triel-sur-Seine

Conflans-Ste-Honorine

Herblay

Franconville

Soisy-sous-Montmorency

Verneuil-sur-Seine

Andresy

La Frette

Montigny-les-Cormeilles

Cormeilles-en-Parisis

Sannois

St-Gratien

Enghie

Vernouillet

Chanteloup-les-Vignes

Achères

Maisons-Laffitte

Lac d Enghien

Epin-sur-Se

Médan

Carrières-sous-Poissy

Le Mesnil-le-Roi

Sartrouville

Argenteuil

Bezons

Gennevilliers

L'Ile-St-l

A13

Villennes-sur-Seine

Poissy

La Seine

Houilles

Colombes

Bois-Colombes

Villeneuv-la-Garenn

Morainvilliers

Orgeval

Chambourcy

Montesson

Carrières-sur-Seine

La Garenne-Colombes

Asnières-sur-Seine

Clichy

Aigremont

Le Vésinet

Courbevoie

Levallois-Perret

Fourqueux

St-Germain-en-Laye

Chatou

Nanterre

La Défense Malmaison

Neuilly-sur-Seine

Mt

Mareil-Marly

Le Pecq

Croissy-sur-Seine

Puteaux

Arc de Triomphe

Gare St

Feucherolles

Le Port-Marly

Rueil-Malmaison

Suresnes

N187

La Madeleine

St-Nom-la-Bretèche

L'Etang-la-Ville

Marly-le-Roi

Bougival

PARIS

Tour Eiffel

La Voie

Les Invalide

Chavenay

Noisy-le-Roi

Louveciennes

La Celle-St-Cloud

Garches

St-Cloud

Porte d'Auteuil

Villepreux

Rennemoulin

Bailly

Vaucresson

Parc des Princes

Gare Montparna

Plaisir

Fontenay-le-Fleury

Rocquencourt

A13

Marnes-la-Coquette

Sèvres

Boulogne-Billancourt

Vannes

Les Clayes-sous-Bois

Le Chesnay

Ville-d'Avray

Issy-les-Moulineaux

Malako

Bois-d'Arcy

A12

Versailles

Meulon

Chatillon

Montro

Porte d'Orl

Elancourt

N12

Etang de St-Quentin

N10

Chaville

Viroflay

Clamart

Bagne

Trappes

St-Cyr-l'Ecole

N286

A118

Le Plessis-Robinson

Fontenay-aux-Roses

N10

Montigny-le-Bretonneux

Buc

Vélizy-Villacoublay

A86

St-Quentin-en-Yvelines

Guyancourt

Jouy-en-Josas

Secaux

Bou la-Re

La Verrière

Voisins-le-Bretonneux

Les Loges-en-Josas

Bièvres

Châtenay-Malabry

N385

N18

Le Mesnil-St-Denis

Magny-les-Hameaux

Châteaufort

Toussus-le-Noble

Etang de Saclay

Igny

Verrières-le-Buisson

Antony

Fresn

Saclay

Vauhallan

Massy

Dampierre-en-Yvelines

Chevreuse

Gif-sur-Yvette

Orsay

Palaiseau

N188

A6

Champlan

Chi Maz

St-Remy-les-Chevreuse

L'Yvette

Villebon-sur-Yvette

A10

Senlisse

Choisel

Bures-sur-Yvette

Longjum

Cernay-la-Ville

Boullay-les-Troux

Les Molières

Gometz--la-Ville

Les Ulis

-le-Châtel

N118

E05

E50

Villejust

Saulx-les-Chartreux

N20

Ballainvilliers

Epinay-sur-Orge

A10

ROUEN

DREUX

RAMBOUILLET

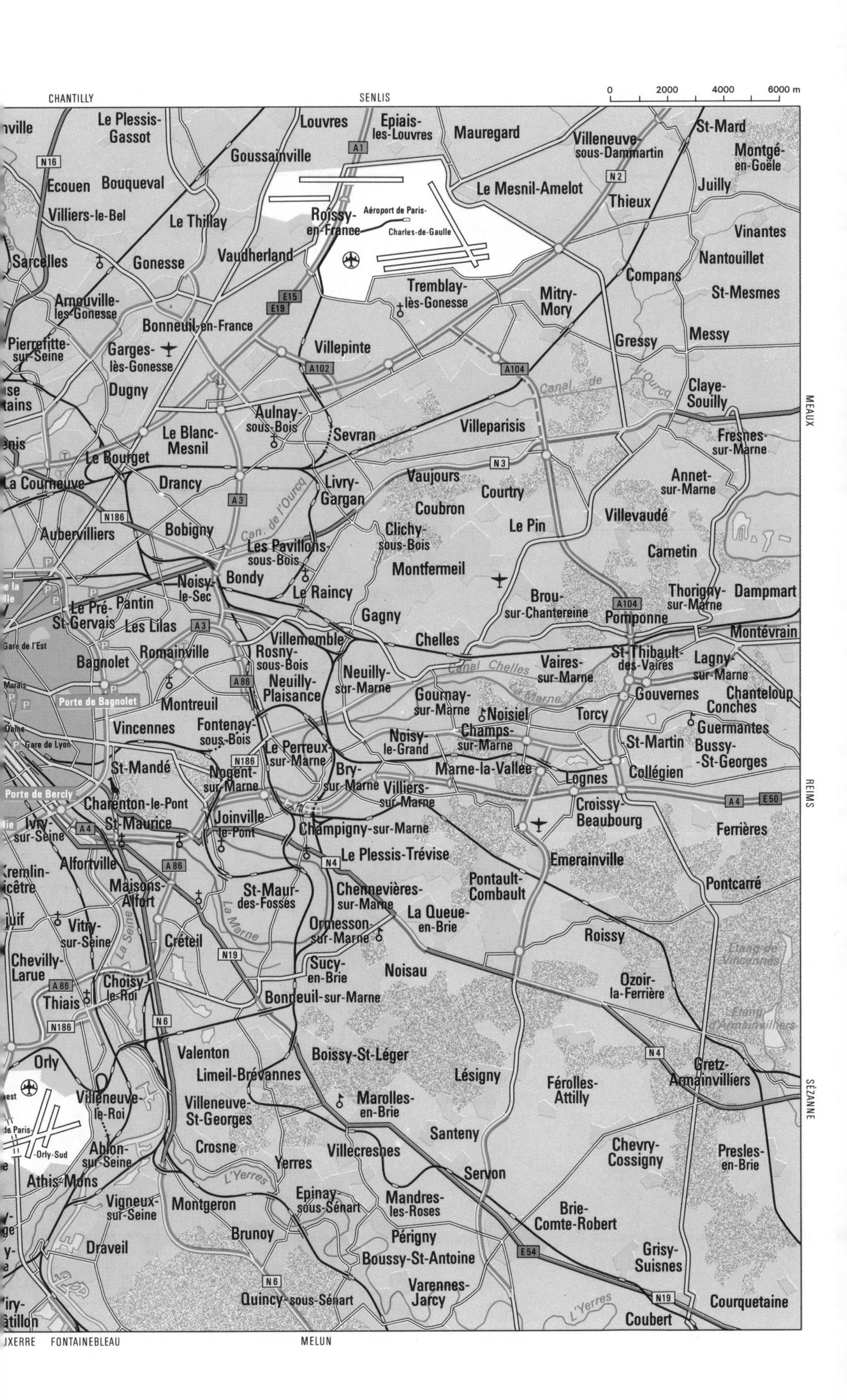

0 2000 4000 6000 m

MEAUX

REIMS

SEZANNE

Le Plessis-Gassot
Louvres
Epiais-les-Louvres
Mauregard
Villeneuve-sous-Dammartin
St-Mard
Montgé-en-Goële
N16
Ecouen
Bouqueval
Goussainville
N2
Thieux
Juilly
Villiers-le-Bel
Le Thillay
Le Mesnil-Amelot
Vinantes
Sarcelles
Gonesse
Vaudherland
Aéroport de Paris-Charles-de-Gaulle
Roissy-en-France
Nantouillet
St-Mesmes
Arnouville-lès-Gonesse
Compans
Pierrefitte-sur-Seine
Garges-lès-Gonesse
Bonneuil-en-France
Tremblay-lès-Gonesse
Mitry-Mory
Gressy
Messy
Dugny
Villepinte
Claye-Souilly
E15
E19
A102
A104
Le Blanc-Mesnil
Aulnay-sous-Bois
Sevran
Villeparisis
Fresnes-sur-Marne
Le Bourget
Drancy
N3
Annet-sur-Marne
La Courneuve
A3
Livry-Gargan
Vaujours
Courtry
Le Pin
Villevaudé
N186
Bobigny
Coubron
Carnetin
Aubervilliers
Les Pavillons-sous-Bois
Clichy-sous-Bois
Thorigny-sur-Marne
Dampmart
Noisy-le-Sec
Bondy
Montfermeil
Brou-sur-Chantereine
A104
Pomponne
Montévrain
Le Pré-St-Gervais
Pantin
Le Raincy
Gagny
St-Thibault-des-Vaires
Lagny-sur-Marne
Les Lilas
A3
Villemomble
Chelles
Canal Chelles
Vaires-sur-Marne
Chanteloup
Gare de l'Est
Romainville
Rosny-sous-Bois
Neuilly-Plaisance
Neuilly-sur-Marne
Gournay-sur-Marne
Marne
Gouvernes
Conches
Bagnolet
Montreuil
Guermantes
Porte de Bagnolet
Vincennes
Fontenay-sous-Bois
Noisiel
Torcy
St-Martin
Bussy-St-Georges
Gare de Lyon
Le Perreux-sur-Marne
Noisy-le-Grand
Champs-sur-Marne
St-Mandé
Nogent-sur-Marne
N186
Bry-sur-Marne
Villiers-sur-Marne
Marne-la-Vallée
Lognes
Collégien
Porte de Bercly
Charenton-le-Pont
Joinville-le-Pont
Croissy-Beaubourg
Ferrières
Ivry-sur-Seine
St-Maurice
Champigny-sur-Marne
A4
A86
N4
Le Plessis-Trévise
Emerainville
Pontcarré
Kremlin-Bicêtre
Maisons-Alfort
St-Maur-des-Fosses
Chennevières-sur-Marne
Pontault-Combault
Alfortville
Ormesson-sur-Marne
La Queue-en-Brie
Roissy
juif
Vitry-sur-Seine
Créteil
N19
Sucy-en-Brie
Noisau
Ozoir-la-Ferrière
Chevilly-Larue
A86
Choisy-le-Roi
Bonneuil-sur-Marne
Thiais
N186
N6
Valenton
Boissy-St-Léger
N4
Gretz-Armainvilliers
Orly
Limeil-Brévannes
Lésigny
Férolles-Attilly
Villeneuve-le-Roi
Villeneuve-St-Georges
Marolles-en-Brie
Aéroport de Paris-Orly-Sud
Crosne
Yerres
Villecresnes
Santeny
Servon
Chevry-Cossigny
Presles-en-Brie
Ablon-sur-Seine
Athis-Mons
Vigneux-sur-Seine
Montgeron
Epinay-sous-Sénart
Mandres-les-Roses
Brie-Comte-Robert
Grisy-Suisnes
Draveil
Brunoy
Périgny
E54
Boussy-St-Antoine
Varennes-Jarcy
N6
Quincy-sous-Sénart
N19
Coubert
Courquetaine

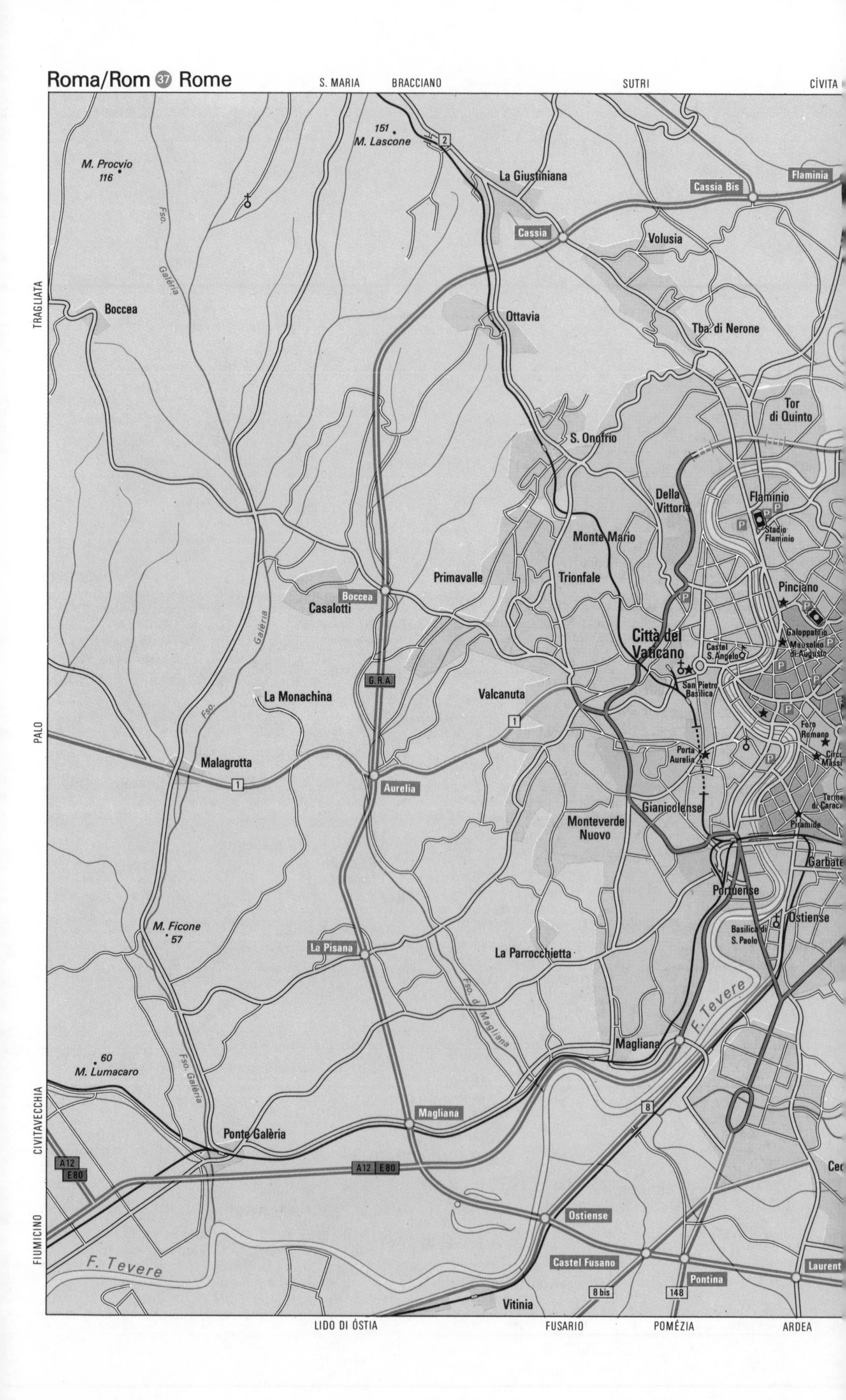
TRAGLIATA

PALO

CIVITAVECCHIA

FIUMICINO

M. Procvio
116

M. Lascone
151

2

La Giustiniana

Cassia Bis

Flaminia

Boccea

Cassia

Volusia

Ottavia

Tba. di Nerone

Tor
di Quinto

S. Onofrio

Della
Vittoria

Flaminio

Stadio
Flaminio

Monte Mario

Primavalle

Trionfale

Pinciano

Boccea

Casalotti

G.R.A.

Galoppatoio

Mausoleo
di Augusto

Città del
Vaticano

Castel
S. Angelo

La Monachina

Valcanuta

San Pietro
Basilica

1

Foro
Romano

Malagrotta

1

Aurelia

Porta
Aurelia

Circo
Massi.

Gianicolense

Terme
di Caraca.

Monteverde
Nuovo

Piramide

M. Ficone
57

Garbate

Portuense

Ostiense

Basilica di
S. Paolo

La Pisana

La Parrocchietta

F. Tevere

60
M. Lumacaro

Magliana

Magliana

8

Ponte Galèria

A12
E80

A12   E80

Ostiense

F. Tevere

Castel Fusano

Pontina

Laurent

8 bis

148

Vitinia

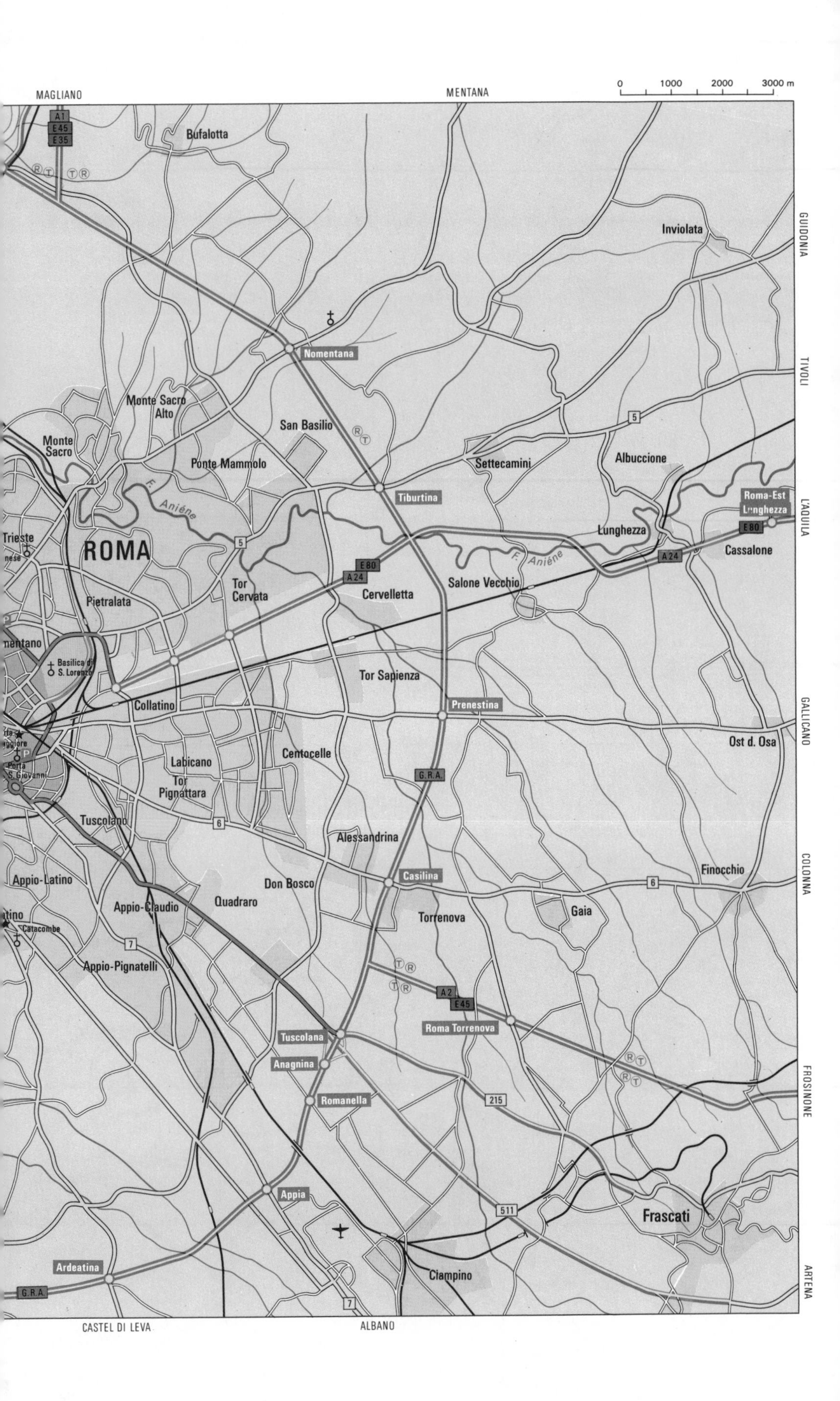

MAGLIANO   MENTANA   0   1000   2000   3000 m

Bufalotta

Inviolata

GUIDONIA

Nomentana

TIVOLI

Monte Sacro
Alto

San Basilio

5

Settecamini

Albuccione

Monte
Sacro

Ponte Mammolo

Roma-Est
Lunghezza

L'AQUILA

Trieste

F. Aniéne

Tiburtina

Lunghezza

E80

A24

Cassalone

ROMA

5

Tor
Cervata

E80
A24

Cervelletta

Salone Vecchio

F. Aniéne

Pietralata

Basilica di
S. Lorenzo

Tor Sapienza

Collatino

Prenestina

Ost d. Osa

GALLICANO

Labicano
Tor
Pignattara

Centocelle

G.R.A.

Porta
S. Giovanni

6

Alessandrina

Finocchio

COLONNA

Tuscolano

Don Bosco

Casilina

6

Appio-Latino

Appio-Claudio

Quadraro

Torrenova

Gaia

tino

Catacombe

7

Appio-Pignatelli

A2
E45

FROSINONE

Tuscolana

Roma Torrenova

Anagnina

Romanella

215

Appia

511

Frascati

Ardeatina

ARTENA

G.R.A.

Ciampino

7

CASTEL DI LEVA   ALBANO

41

Palermo 38

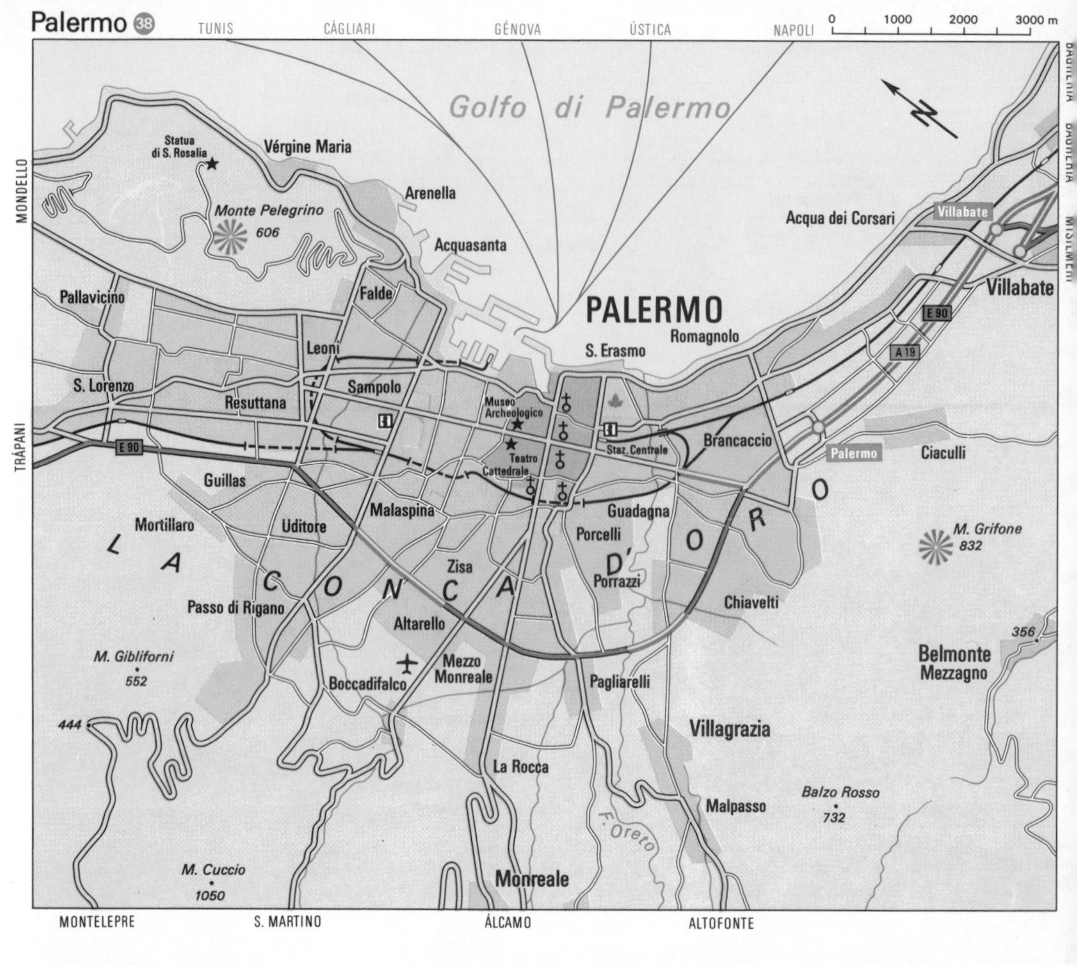

TUNIS
CÁGLIARI
GÉNOVA
ÚSTICA
NAPOLI
0 1000 2000 3000 m
Golfo di Palermo
Statua di S. Rosalia
Vérgine Maria
Arenella
Monte Pelegrino 606
Acquasanta
Acqua dei Corsari
Villabate
Pallavicino
Falde
PALERMO
Romagnolo
S. Erasmo
Leoni
Sampolo
S. Lorenzo
Resuttana
Museo Archeologico
Teatro
Cattedrale
Staz. Centrale
Brancaccio
Palermo
Ciaculli
E 90
A 19
Guillas
Mortillaro
Uditore
Malaspina
Guadagna
Porcelli
M. Grifone 832
LA CONCA D'ORO
Zisa
Porrazzi
Passo di Rigano
Chiavelti
Altarello
356
M. Gibliforni 552
Mezzo Monreale
Boccadifalco
Pagliarelli
Belmonte Mezzagno
444
Villagrazia
La Rocca
Malpasso
Balzo Rosso 732
F. Oreto
M. Cuccio 1050
Monreale
MONDELLO
TRÁPANI
MONTELEPRE
S. MARTINO
ÁLCAMO
ALTOFONTE

Praha/Prag 39 Prague

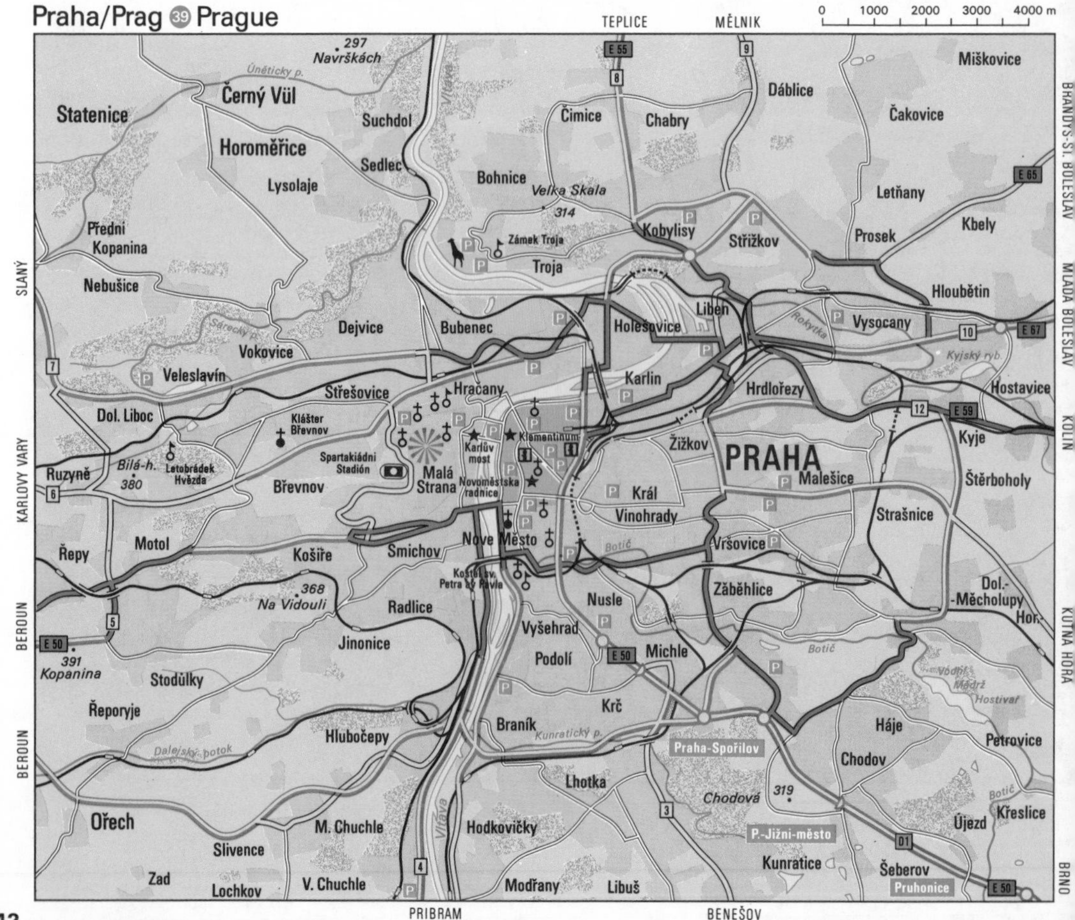

TEPLICE
MĚLNIK
0 1000 2000 3000 4000 m
E 55
9
8
297 Navrškách
Únětický p.
Miškovice
Statenice
Černý Vůl
Suchdol
Čimice
Chabry
Dáblice
Čakovice
Horoměřice
Sedlec
Bohnice
Lysolaje
Velka Skala 314
Letňany
E 65
Kobylisy
Střížkov
Prosek
Kbely
Přední Kopanina
Zámek Troja
Troja
Nebušice
Hloubětin
Libeň
Dejvice
Bubenec
Holešovice
Vysočany
Rokytka
10
E 67
Kyjský ryb.
Vokovice
7
Veleslavín
Karlín
Hrdlořezy
Hostavice
Střešovice
Hradčany
Dol. Liboc
Klášter Břevnov
Klementinum
12
E 59
Žižkov
Kyje
Karlův most
Spartakiádni Stadión
PRAHA
Malešice
Ruzyně
Bílá-h. 380
Letohrádek Hvězda
Malá Strana
Novoměstská radnice
Štěrboholy
6
Břevnov
Král Vinohrady
Strašnice
Motol
Nové Město
Vršovice
Řepy
Košíře
Smíchov
Botič
Kostel sv. Petra a Pavla
368 Na Vidouli
Záběhlice
Nusle
Dol.-Měcholupy
Radlice
5
Hor.
E 50
Vyšehrad
Michle
Jinonice
391 Kopanina
Podolí
Vodní Nádrž Hostivař
Stodůlky
Řeporyje
Krč
Háje
Braník
Kunratický p.
Hlubočepy
Praha-Spořilov
Petrovice
Dalejský potok
Chodov
Lhotka
Chodová
319
Ořech
3
Křeslice
M. Chuchle
Hodkovičky
P.-Jižni-město
Újezd
Vltava
01
Slivence
Kunratice
Zad
4
Šeberov
Lochkov
V. Chuchle
Modřany
Libuš
Pruhonice
SLANÝ
KARLOVY VARY
BEROUN
BRANDÝS-ST. BOLESLAV
MLADÁ BOLESLAV
KOLÍN
KUTNÁ HORA
BRNO
PŘÍBRAM
BENEŠOV

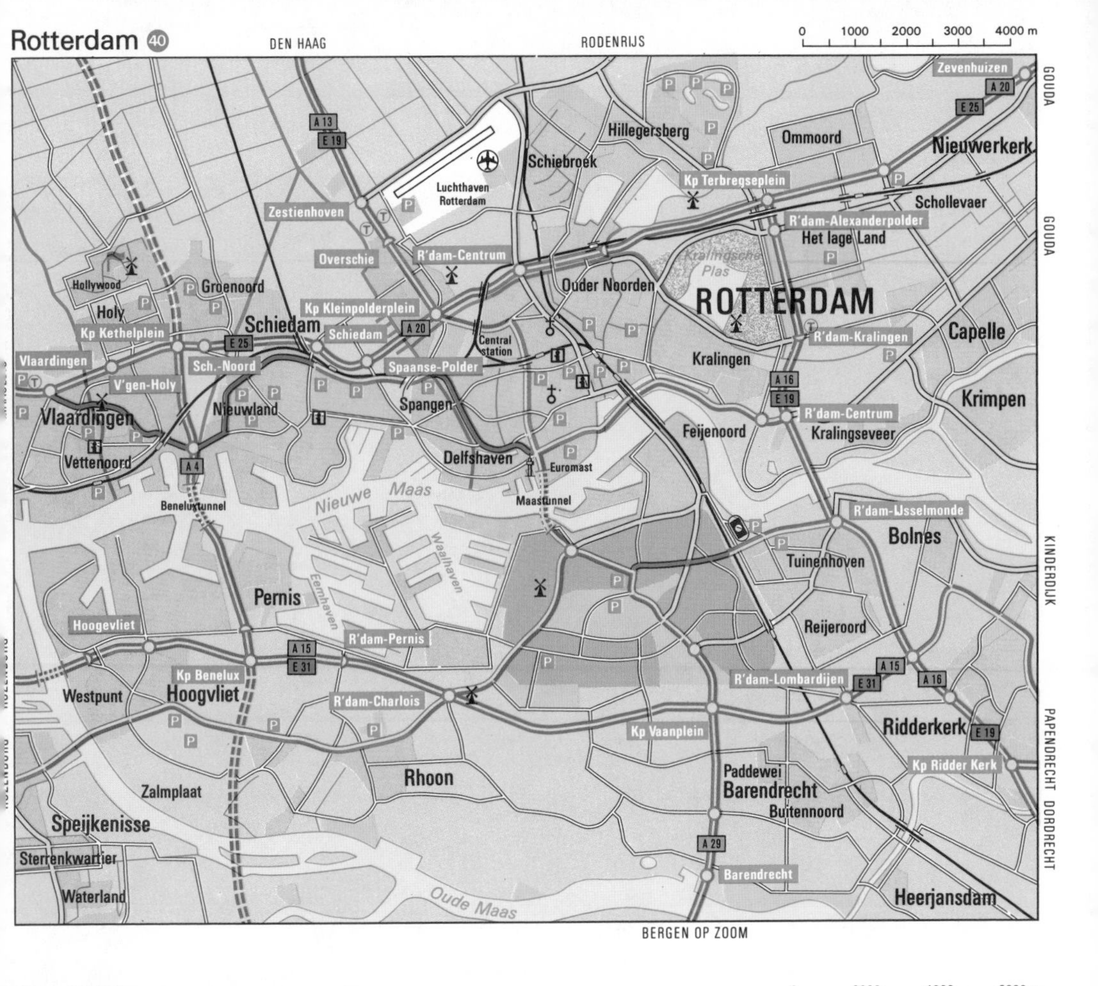

Rotterdam 40
DEN HAAG
RODENRIJS
0 1000 2000 3000 4000 m
GOUDA
GOUDA
KINDERDIJK
PAPENDRECHT
DORDRECHT
BERGEN OP ZOOM
Zevenhuizen
A 20
E 25
A 13
E 19
Hillegersberg
Ommoord
Nieuwerkerk
Schiebroek
Luchthaven Rotterdam
Kp Terbregseplein
Schollevaer
Zestienhoven
R'dam-Alexanderpolder
Het lage Land
Overschie
R'dam-Centrum
Kralingsche Plas
Hollywood
Groenoord
Ouder Noorden
ROTTERDAM
Holy
Kp Kleinpolderplein
Kp Kethelplein
Schiedam
Schiedam
A 20
Central station
R'dam-Kralingen
Capelle
Vlaardingen
E 25
Sch.-Noord
Spaanse-Polder
Kralingen
V'gen-Holy
A 16
E 19
Krimpen
Vlaardingen
Nieuwland
Spangen
R'dam-Centrum
Kralingseveer
Feijenoord
Vettenoord
A 4
Delfshaven
Euromast
Nieuwe Maas
Maastunnel
Beneluxtunnel
R'dam-IJsselmonde
Bolnes
Waalhaven
Tuinenhoven
Pernis
Eemhaven
Hoogevliet
Reijeroord
R'dam-Pernis
A 15
E 31
A 15
Kp Benelux
R'dam-Lombardijen
E 31
A 16
Westpunt
Hoogvliet
R'dam-Charlois
Kp Vaanplein
Ridderkerk
E 19
Kp Ridder Kerk
Rhoon
Paddewei
Zalmplaat
Barendrecht
Buitennoord
Speijkenisse
A 29
Sterrenkwartier
Barendrecht
Waterland
Oude Maas
Heerjansdam

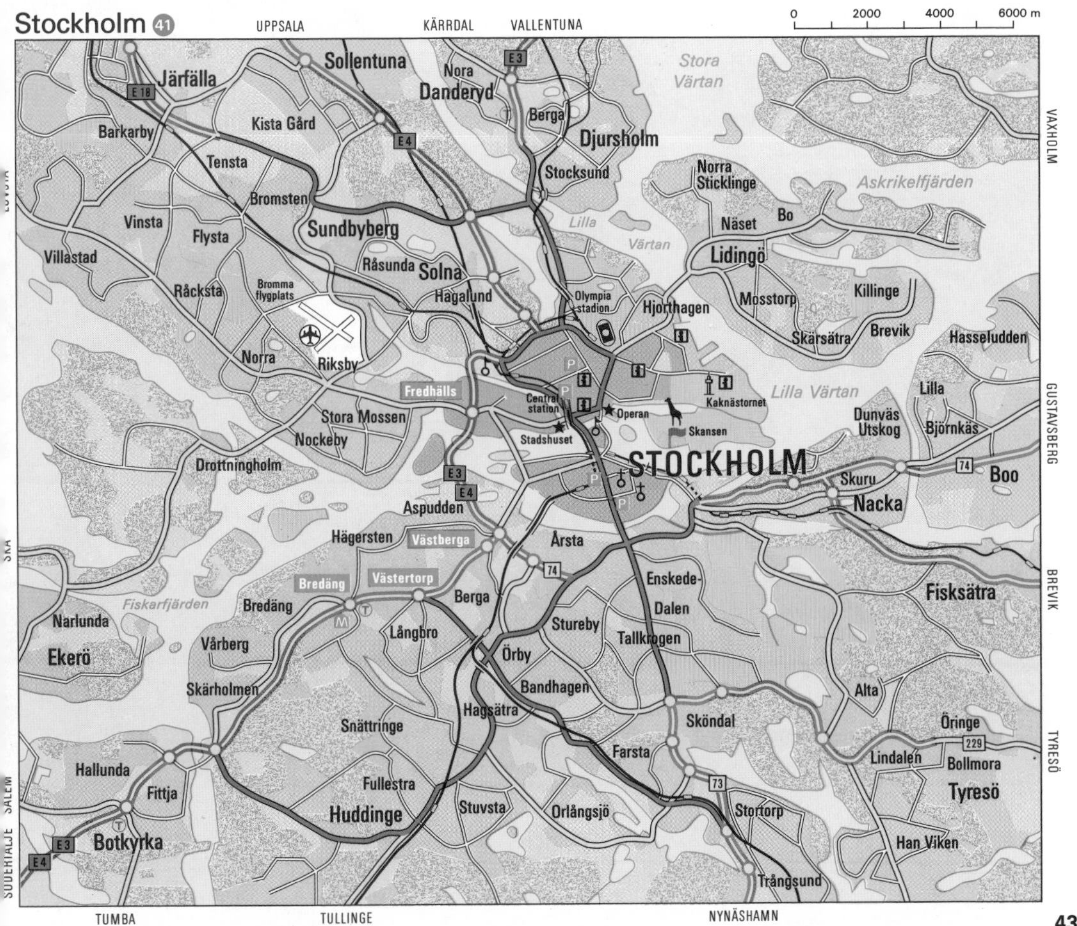

Stockholm 41
UPPSALA
KÄRRDAL
VALLENTUNA
0 2000 4000 6000 m
VAXHOLM
GUSTAVSBERG
BREVIK
TYRESÖ
TUMBA
TULLINGE
NYNÄSHAMN
E 3
Stora Värtan
Sollentuna
Järfälla
Nora
Danderyd
E 18
Berga
Barkarby
Kista Gård
E 4
Djursholm
Tensta
Stocksund
Norra Sticklinge
Askrikelfjärden
Bromsten
Näset
Bo
Vinsta
Sundbyberg
Lilla Värtan
Flysta
Villastad
Råsunda
Solna
Lidingö
Bromma flygplats
Råcksta
Hagalund
Olympia stadion
Killinge
Hjorthagen
Mosstorp
Brevik
Skärsätra
Hasseludden
Norra
Riksby
Fredhälls
Central station
Kaknästornet
Lilla Värtan
Lilla
Operan
Stora Mossen
Dunväs
Utskog
Björnkäs
Stadshuset
Skansen
Nockeby
STOCKHOLM
Drottningholm
74
Boo
Skuru
E 3
Nacka
E 4
Aspudden
Hägersten
Västberga
Årsta
74
Bredäng
Västertorp
Enskede-
Fiskarfjärden
Dalen
Fisksätra
Bredäng
Berga
Narlunda
Stureby
Långbro
Tallkrogen
Vårberg
Ekerö
Örby
Bandhagen
Alta
Skärholmen
Hagsätra
Sköndal
Öringe
Snättringe
229
Farsta
Lindalen
Bollmora
Hallunda
Fittja
Fullestra
73
Tyresö
Huddinge
Stuvsta
Orlångsjö
Stortorp
E 3
Botkyrka
E 4
Han Viken
Trångsund

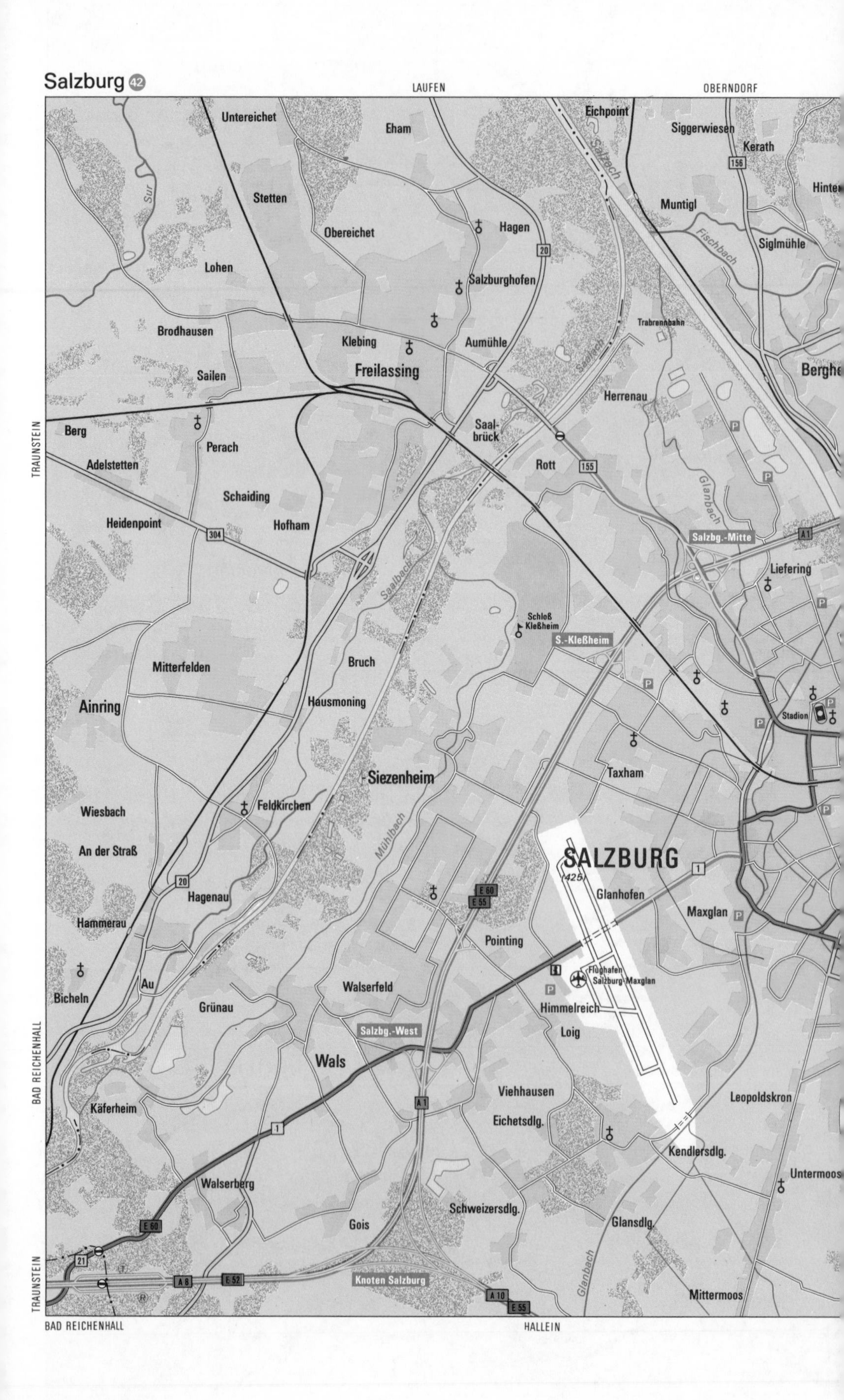

LAUFEN   OBERNDORF

Untereichet

Eham

Eichpoint

Siggerwiesen

Kerath

156

Hinter

Stetten

Obereichet

Hagen

Muntigl

Siglmühle

20

Lohen

Salzburghofen

Brodhausen

Klebing

Aumühle

Trabrennbahn

Berghe

Freilassing

Herrenau

Sailen

Saal-
brück

Berg

Perach

Rott

155

Salzbg.-Mitte

A1

Adelstetten

Glanbach

Liefering

Schaiding

Heidenpoint

304

Hofham

Schloß
Kleßheim

S.-Kleßheim

Mitterfelden

Bruch

Stadion

Ainring

Hausmoning

Taxham

Siezenheim

Wiesbach

Feldkirchen

An der Straß

SALZBURG

20

Hagenau

E 60
E 55

Glanhofen

Maxglan

Hammerau

Pointing

Au

Flughafen
Salzburg-Maxglan

Bicheln

Grünau

Walserfeld

Himmelreich

Salzbg.-West

Loig

Wals

Viehhausen

Leopoldskron

Käferheim

A1

Eichetsdlg.

Kendlersdlg.

Untermoos

1

Walserberg

Schweizersdlg.

Gois

Glansdlg.

E 60

Mittermoos

21

A 8

E 52

Knoten Salzburg

A 10
E 55

BAD REICHENHALL   HALLEIN

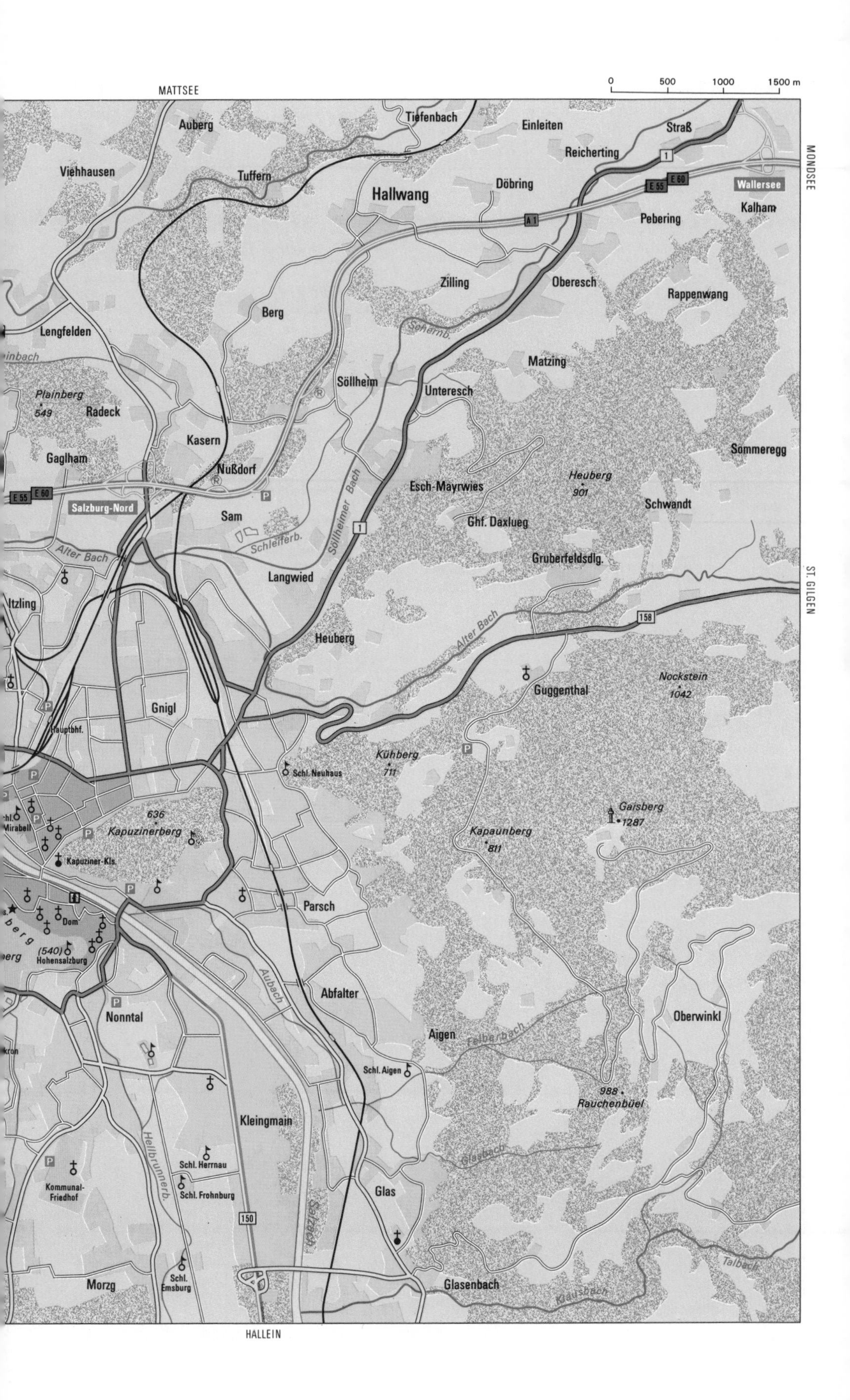

MONDSEE

0   500   1000   1500 m

Auberg
Tiefenbach
Einleiten
Straß
Reicherting
1

Viehhausen
Tuffern
Hallwang
Döbring
E 55   E 60
Wallersee
Pebering
Kalham

Zilling
Oberesch
Rappenwang
A 1

Berg
Matzing

Lengfelden
Schernb.

inbach
Söllheim
Unteresch
Heuberg
901
Schwandt

Plainberg
549
Radeck
Kasern
Esch-Mayrwies
Sommeregg

Gaglham
Nußdorf
Ghf. Daxlueg

E 55   E 60
Gruberfeldsdlg.
Salzburg-Nord
Sam
Schleiferb.
158
1

Alter Bach
Langwied
Alter Bach

Itzling
Heuberg
Guggenthal
Nockstein
1042

Gnigl
Kühberg
711

Hauptbhf.
Schl. Neuhaus
Gaisberg
1287

Mirabell
636
Kapuzinerberg
Kapaunberg
811

Kapuziner-Kls.

Parsch

Dom

(540)
Hohensalzburg
Aubach
Abfalter
Aigen
Oberwinkl

Nonntal
Felberbach

Schl. Aigen
988
Rauchenbüel

Kleingmain
Hellbrunnerb.

Schl. Herrnau
Glasbach

Kommunal-
Friedhof
Schl. Frohnburg
Glas

150
Salzach

Morzg
Schl.
Emsburg
Glasenbach
Talbach

Klausbach

ST. GILGEN

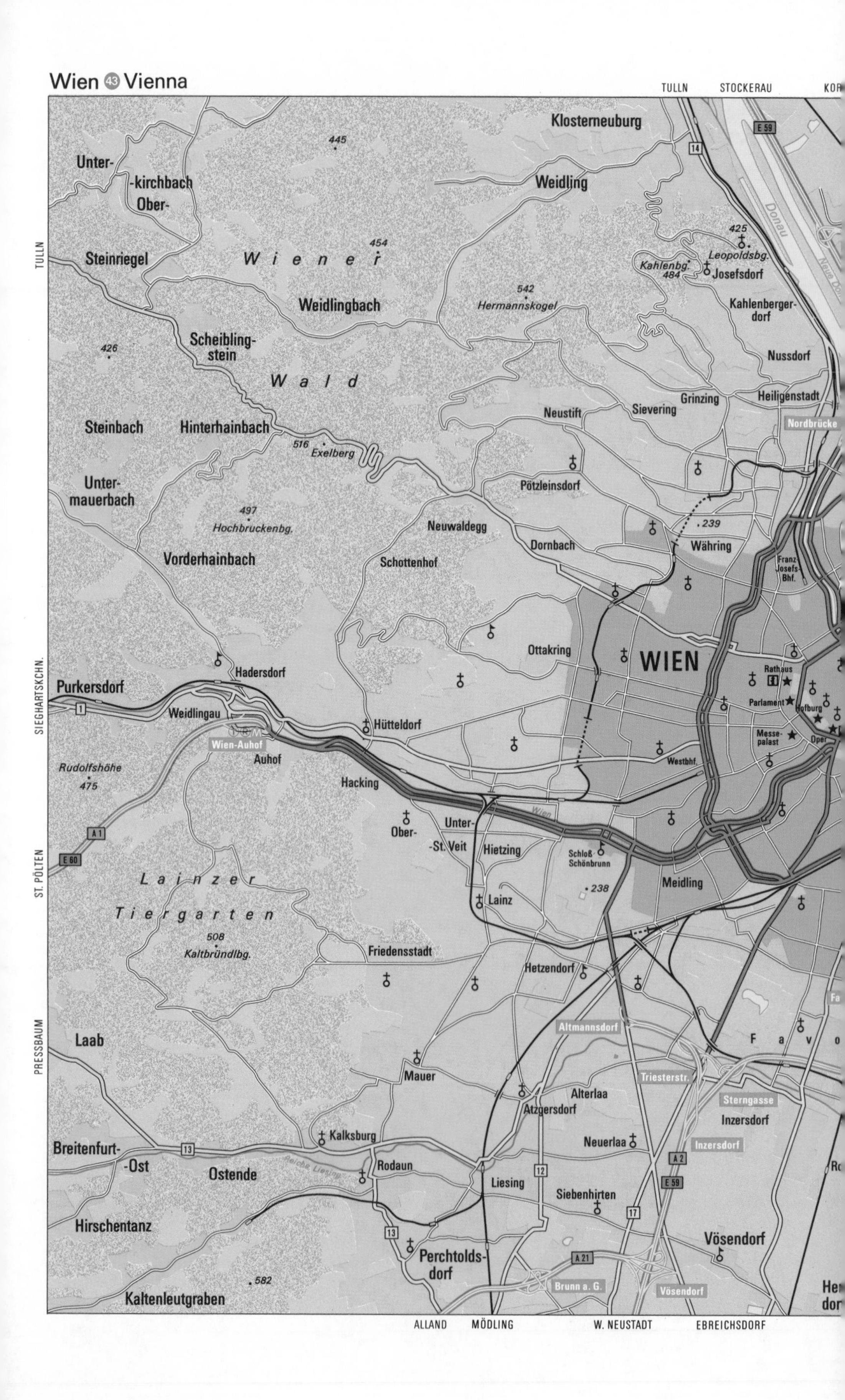

Klosterneuburg

445

Unter-
-kirchbach
Ober-

Weidling

14

Steinriegel

Wiener

454

Weidlingbach

E 59

Donau

425

Kahlenbg. Leopoldsbg.
484

Josefsdorf

Kahlenberger-
dorf

542
Hermannskogel

Nussdorf

Scheibling-
stein

Wald

426

Heiligenstadt

Neustift   Sievering   Grinzing

Nordbrücke

Steinbach   Hinterhainbach

516
Exelberg

Pötzleinsdorf

. 239

497
Hochbruckenbg.

Neuwaldegg

Dornbach   Währing

Franz
Josefs
Bhf.

Unter-
mauerbach

Vorderhainbach

Schottenhof

Ottakring

WIEN

Rathaus
★
Parlament ★   Hofburg

Purkersdorf   Hadersdorf

Weidlingau

1

Hütteldorf

Messe-
palast
★   Oper

Wien-Auhof
Auhof

Hacking

Westbhf.

Rudolfshöhe
475

A 1

Ober-
-St. Veit

Unter-

Hietzing

Schloß
Schönbrunn

Meidling

E 60

ST. PÖLTEN

Lainzer

Lainz

. 238

Tiergarten

508
Kaltbründlbg.

Friedensstadt

Hetzendorf

PRESSBAUM

Laab

Altmannsdorf

Fa   v   o

Mauer

Alterlaa

Triesterstr.

Atzgersdorf

Sterngasse

Inzersdorf

Kalksburg

Neuerlaa

Inzersdorf

Breitenfurt-
-Ost

13

Ostende

Reiche Liesing

Rodaun

Liesing

12

A 2

Ro

E 59

Hirschentanz

Siebenhirten

17

13

. 582

Perchtolds-
dorf

A 21

Vösendorf

He
dor

Kaltenleutgraben

Brunn a. G.

Vösendorf

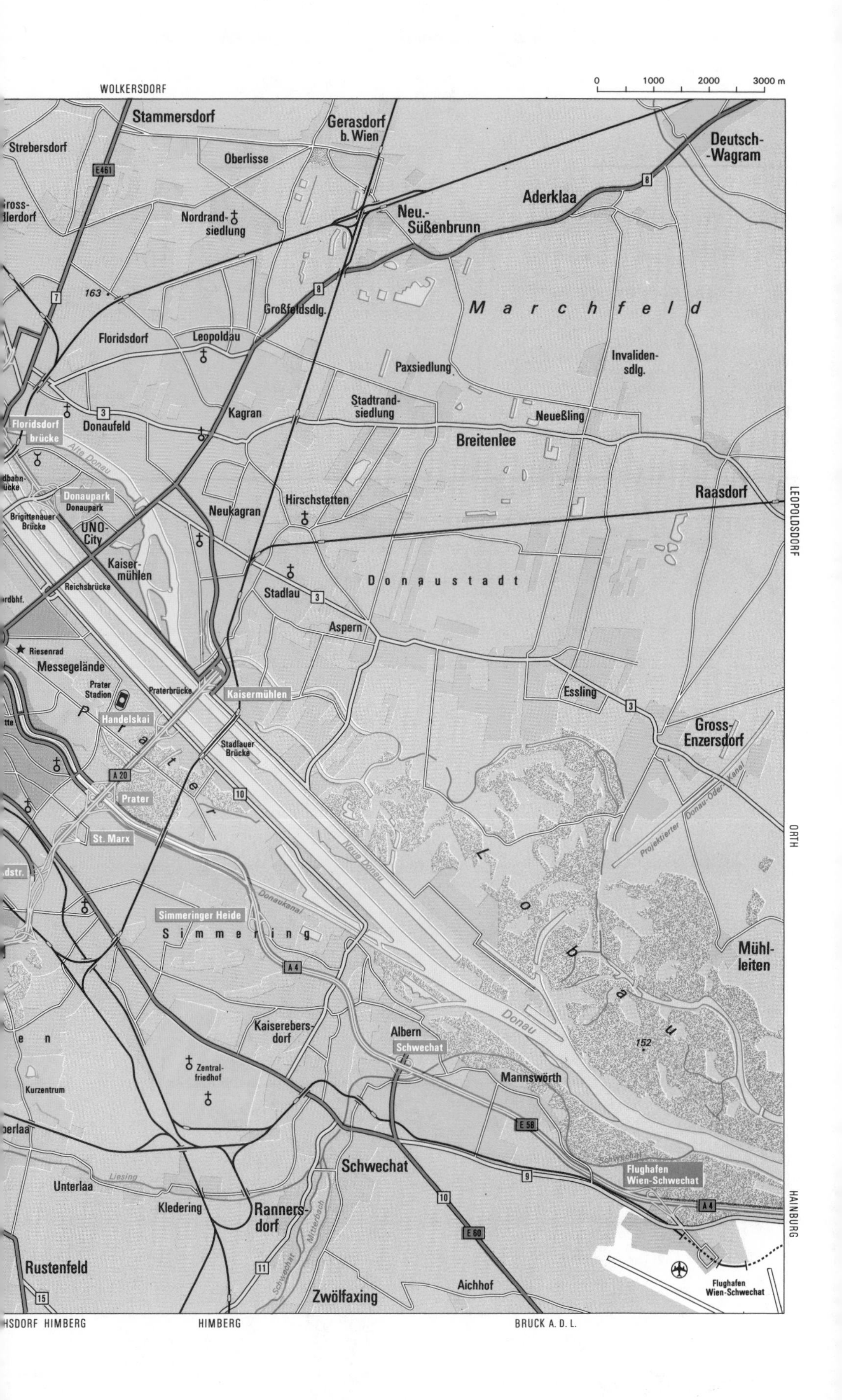

WOLKERSDORF

Stammersdorf

Gerasdorf
b. Wien

Deutsch-
Wagram

Strebersdorf

Oberlisse

E 461

Gross-
llerdorf

Nordrand-
siedlung

Aderklaa

8

Neu.-
Süßenbrunn

7   163

8

Großfeldsdlg.

Marchfeld

Floridsdorf

Leopoldau

Paxsiedlung

Invaliden-
sdlg.

Floridsdorf
brücke

3

Donaufeld

Kagran

Stadtrand-
siedlung

Neueßling

Breitenlee

dbahn-
ücke

Donaupark
Donaupark

Neukagran

Hirschstetten

Raasdorf

LEOPOLDSDORF

Brigittenauer
Brücke

UNO-
City

Kaiser-
mühlen

Donaustadt

Reichsbrücke

rdbhf.

Stadlau

3

Aspern

★ Riesenrad

Messegelände

Prater
Stadion

Praterbrücke

Kaisermühlen

Essling

3

Gross-
Enzersdorf

tte

Handelskai

Stadlauer
Brücke

A 20

10

Prater

Projektierter

Donau-Oder-Kanal

ORTH

St. Marx

Simmeringer Heide

Mühl-
leiten

dstr.

Simmering

A 4

Kaisereebers-
dorf

Albern

Schwechat

Mannswörth

152

Kurzentrum

Zentral-
friedhof

erlaa

E 58

Liesing

Schwechat

E 58

Flughafen
Wien-Schwechat

Unterlaa

Kledering

Ranners-
dorf

9

A 4

Rustenfeld

11

E 60

Aichhof

Flughafen
Wien-Schwechat

15

Zwölfaxing

HSDORF HIMBERG   HIMBERG   BRUCK A. D. L.

HAINBURG

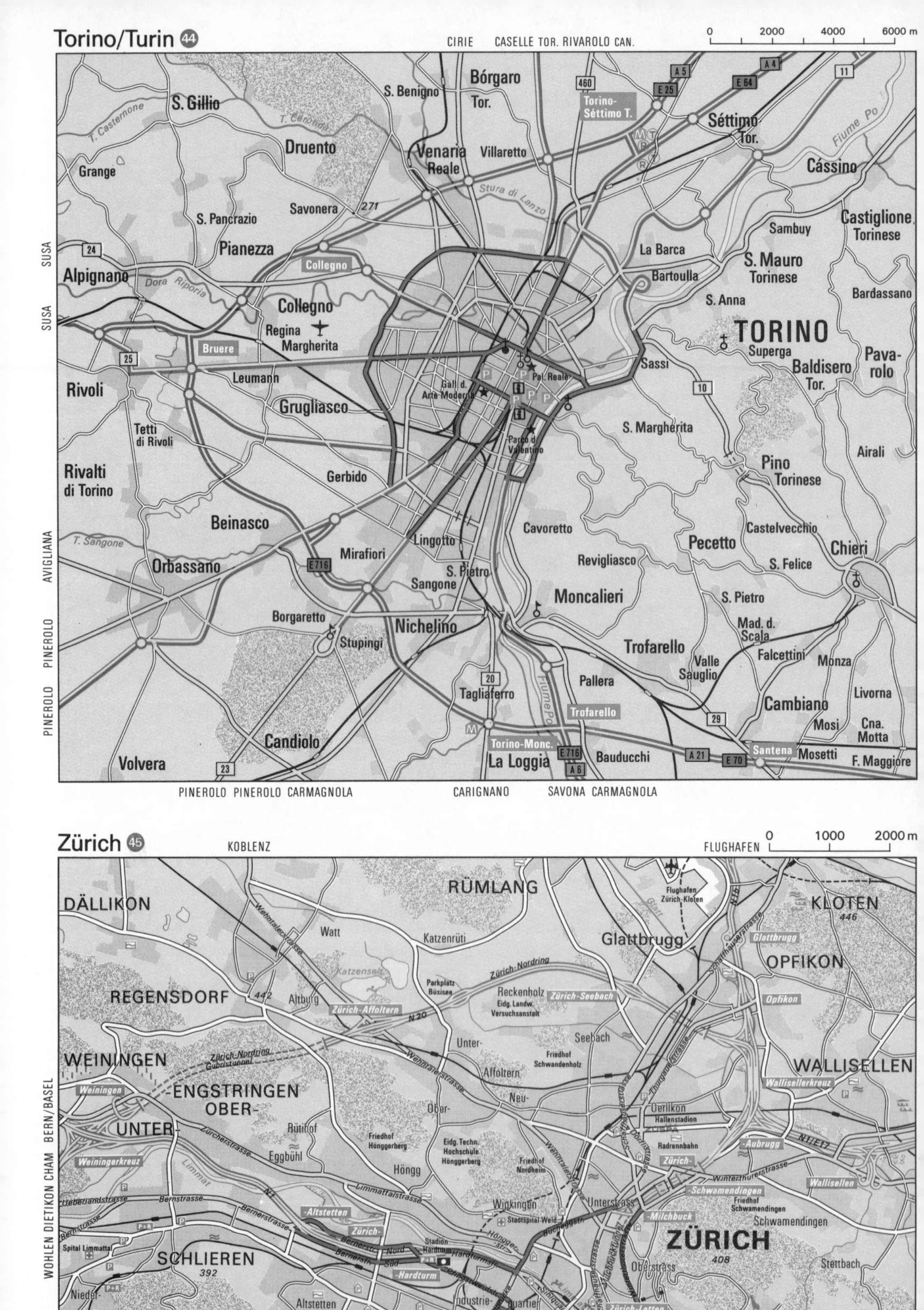

Torino/Turin 44

0   2000   4000   6000 m

S. Gillio
S. Benigno
Bórgaro Tor.
Torino-Séttimo T.
Séttimo Tor.
Fiume Po
Cássino

Grange
Druento
Villaretto
Cástiglione Torinese

Savonera
Venaria Reale
Stura di Lanzo
Sambuy
Bardassano

Pianezza
S. Pancrazio
La Barca
S. Mauro Torinese
Baldisero
Pava-

Alpignano
Collegno
Bartoulla
S. Anna
TORINO

SUSA
Dora Riparia
S. Anna
Superga
Baldisero Tor.
rolo

Collegno
Regina Margherita
Sassi
Airali

Bruere
Gall. d. Arte Moderna
Pal. Reale
S. Margherita
Pino Torinese

Rivoli
Leumann
Grugliasco
Parco di Valentino
Castelvecchio

Tetti di Rivoli
Gerbido
Cavoretto
Revigliasco
S. Felice
Chieri

Rivalti di Torino
Mirafiori
Lingotto
Pecetto
S. Pietro
Mad. d. Scala
Falcettini
Monza

Beinasco
S. Pietro Sangone
Moncalieri
Valle Sauglio

Orbassano
Borgaretto
Nichelino
Trofarello
Cambiano
Livorna

Stupingi
Pallera
Mosi
Cna. Motta

Candiolo
Tagliaferro
Trofarello
Torino-Monc.
Bauducchi
Santena
Mosetti

Volvera
La Loggia
F. Maggiore

Zürich 45

0   1000   2000 m

DÄLLIKON
RÜMLANG
Flughafen Zürich Kloten
KLOTEN

Watt
Katzenrüti
Glattbrugg
OPFIKON

REGENSDORF
Parkplatz Büsisen
Zürich-Seebach
WALLISELLEN

WEININGEN
Unter-
Seebach
Friedhof Schwandenholz
Wallisellerkreuz

ENGSTRINGEN OBER-
Affoltern
Eidg. Techn. Hochschule Hönggerberg
Oerlikon
Aubrugg

UNTER-
Ober-
Neu-
Friedhof Nordheim
Schwamendingen

Eggbühl
Höngg
Winkingen
Schwamendingen

SCHLIEREN
Altstetten
Unterstrass
Milchbuck
ZÜRICH

URDORF
Altstetten
Industrie-Quartier
Zürich-Letten
Fluntern
Stettbach

UITIKON
Friedhof Eichbühl
Aussersihl
Universitäts-spital ETH
Glockhausen

Albisrieden
Enge
Dolder
Hottingen

Triemli
Wiedikon
Hirslanden

Waldegg
Wiedikon
Zürich-
Witikon

Ringlikon
Uetliberg
Brunau
Riesbach

BIRMENSDORF
Landikon
Albisgütli
Zürichsee

48

Index of place names

Localités citées

Ortsverzeichnis

Località citate

Localidades citadas

Place names and other places of interest are in alphabetical order according to the spelling of the country concerned. Each name is followed by a page number referring to the road maps in section 1, and then by the grid reference letter and number.

Example: Lausanne 74 B2 = page 74, grid B2.

Les noms des localités ou d'autres endroits intéressants figurent en ordre alphabétique selon la langue du pays en question. Chaque nom est suivi par le numéro de page se référant aux cartes routières en section 1 et après par la lettre et la chiffre du quadrillage.

Par example: Lausanne 74 B2 = page 74, quadrillage B2.

Namen von Ortschaften und anderen Sehenswürdigkeiten sind in alphabetischer Reihenfolge in der Schreibweise des jeweiligen Landes aufgeführt. Jedem Namen folgt die Seitenzahl einer Strassenkarte in Teil 1 und anschliessend Buchstabe und Ziffer des Rasters.

Beispiel: Lausanne 74 B2 = Seite 74, Raster B2.

Nomi di luoghi ed altri posti di interosse son elencati in ordine alfabetico nella lingus del paese in questione. Ogni nome è seguito dal numero di pagina che si riferisce alle carte stradali in sezione I, e dalla lettere e chifro del quadranto.

Esempio: Lausanne 74 B2 = pagina 74, quadranto B2.

Los nombres de los principales lugares de interés y de otros importantes sitios turísticos están ordenados, alfabéticamente según el país correspondiente. Cada nombre es seguido de un número de página correspondiente al mapa de carreteras en la sección I y por una coordenada conformada por una letra y un número, para la exacta ubicación del lugar.

Ejemplo: Lausana 74 B2 = página 74, coordenada B2.

A

Å 9 C1
Å 8 A3
Å 9 C/D1/2
Å 33 C2
Å 46 B2
Aach 91 B/C3
Aachen 79 D2
Aachen-Eilendorf 79 D2
Aadorf 91 B/C3
Aakoinen 24 B3
Aalen 91 D2
Aalen-Ebnat 91 D2
Aalen-Wasseralfingen 91 D1/2
Aalsmeer 66 A/B3
Aalst 78 B1/2
Aalten 67 C3
Aalter 78 A/B1
Åan 37 C3
Äänekoski 21 D3, 22 A3
Aapajärvi 12 B2
Aapajärvi 17 D2, 18 A1
Aapua 17 D1
Aarau 90 B3, 105 C1
Aarberg 104 B1
Aarbergen 80 B2/3
Aarburg 105 C1
Aardenburg 78 A/B1
Aareavaara 11 C3
Aareschlucht 105 C1/2
Aarschot 79 C1/2
Aatsinki 13 C3
Aavasaksa 17 D2
Aba 128 B1
Ababuj 162 B2
Abades 160 B2
Abadiano 153 D1
Abadín 150 B1
Abadino 153 D1
Abaliget 128 B2
Abalos 153 D2
A Baña 150 A2
Abánades 161 D2
Abanilla 169 C3
Abanto 162 A1/2
Abanto 153 C1
Abarán 169 D3
Abárzuza 153 D2, 154 A2
Abaurrea Alta 108 B3, 155 C2
Abbadía San Salvatore 116 B3
Abbasanta 123 C2
Abbaye 79 B/C2
Abbaye de Chaalis 87 D1
Abbaye de la Réau 101 C2
Abbaye de Montmajour 111 C2
Abbaye de Senanque 111 D2
Abbaye d'Orval 79 C3
Abbaye du Thoronet 112 A3
Abbazia Casamari 119 C2
Abbazia di Fossanova 118 B2
Abbazia di Monte Oliveto Maggiore 115 C3, 116 B2
Abbazia di Montecassino 119 C2
Abbazia di Piona 105 D2, 106 A2
Abbazia di Práglia 107 C3
Abbazia di Valvisciolo 118 B2
Abbazia San Vincenzo al Volturno 119 C2
Abbekås 50 B3
Abbendorf 69 D2
Abbeville 77 D2
Abbey 59 D1, 61 C2
Abbeyfeale 55 C3
Abbey Town 57 C3, 60 A/B1
Abbiategrasso 105 D3
Abborberg 15 C/D3
Abborrträsk 16 A3
Abborrträsk 31 C1
Abbots Bromley 59 D3, 61 C3, 64 A1
Abbotsbury 63 D3
Abbotsford 57 C2
Abbotts Ann 64 A3, 76 A1
Abegondo 150 B1
Abejar 153 C/D3, 161 C1
Abela 164 B3, 170 A1
Abella de la Conca 155 D2/3
Abelnes 42 B3
Abelvær 28 B1
Abenberg 91 D1, 92 A1
Abenberg-Wassermungenau 91 D1, 92 A1
Abengibre 169 B/C2
Abenójar 167 C2
Åbenrå 52 B2
Abensberg 92 A/B2
Abensberg-Offenstetten 92 A/B2
Aberaeron 59 B/C3
Aberargie 57 C1
Aberdare 63 C1
Aberdaron 58 B3
Aberdeen 54 B2
Aberdovey 59 C3
Aberdur 57 C1
Aberfeldy 56 B1
Aberffraw 58 B2
Aberfoyle 56 B1
Abergavenny 63 C1
Abergele 59 C2, 60 A3
Åberget 16 A2
Abergynolwyn 59 C3
Aberlady 57 C1/2
Abernethy 57 C1
Aberporth 62 B1
Abersoch 58 B3
Abersoch 55 D3
Abertillery 63 C1
Abertura 166 A1/2
Aberystwyth 59 C3
Abetone 114 B2, 116 A1
Abiada 152 B1/2
Abia de la Obispalía 161 D3
Abia de las Torres 152 B2
Abide 149 C1
Abiego 155 C3
Abild 49 D2, 50 A1
Abîme du Bramabiau 110 B2
Abingdon 65 C3
Abington 57 B/C2
Abington 54 B3
Abiskojaurestugan 9 D2
Abiskoturiststation 9 D2
Abiul 158 A3, 164 B1
Abla 173 D2
Ablagão 158 A1/2
Ablanque 161 D2
Ablis 87 C2
Ablitas 154 A3
Abmelaseter 4 B3, 10 A/B1
Åbo 28 B3, 33 D1, 34 A1
Åbo 39 D1, 40 A1
Abobreira 164 B1
Aboim 150 A3
A Bola 150 B3
Abondance 104 B2
Abony 129 D1
Åbosjö 30 B2, 35 D1
Åbränna 29 C3, 34 A1
Abrantes 164 B1
Abraur 16 A2
Abraveses 158 B2
Abreiro 158 B1
Abreschwiller 89 D2, 90 A2
Abriès 112 B1
Abrigada 164 A2
Abrigos 162 A2/3
Abrucena 173 D2
Abrud 97 D3, 140 B1
Abtenau 93 C3
Abtsgmünd 91 C/D1/2
Abtsgmünd-Untergröningen 91 C1/2
Abusejo 159 D2
Åby 46 B2
Åbybro 48 B1
Åbyggeby 40 A/B2
Abytorp 46 A1
A Caniza 150 B3
Acate 125 C3
Accadía 120 A2
Accéglio 112 B2
Accettura 120 B3
Acciarella 118 B2
Acciaroli 120 A3
Accous 108 B3, 154 B1/2
Accrington 59 D1/2, 60 B2
Accúmoli 117 D3, 119 B/C1
Acebo 159 C3
Acebuche 171 C2
Acedera 166 A2
Acehuche 159 C3, 165 D1
Acered 162 A1/2
Acerenza 120 B2
Acerno 119 D3, 120 A2
Acerra 119 D3
Aceuchal 165 D2
Ach 92 B2
Acharnaí 147 D2
Achenkirch 92 A3
Achenwald 92 A3
Achern 90 B2
Achern-Wagshurst 90 B2
Acheux-en-Amiénois 78 A3
Achíllion 143 D3
Achíllion 142 A3
Achim 68 A2
Achinós 147 C1
Achladochórion 144 A/B1
Achladókambos 147 C3
Achnacroish 56 A1
Achnasheen 54 A2
Achstetten 91 C2
Aci Castello 125 D2
Aci Catena 125 D2
Acireale 125 D2
Acle 65 D1/2
A Coruna 150 A/B1
Acquacadda 123 C3
Acquacalda 125 C/D1
Acqua-Doria 113 D3
Acquafredda 106 B3
Acqualagna 115 D3, 117 C2
Acquanegra Cremonese 106 A3, 114 A1
Acquanegra sul Chiese 106 B3
Acquapendente 116 B3, 118 A1
Acquarossa [Biasca] 105 D2
Acquasanta Terme 117 D3, 119 C1
Acquasparta 117 C3, 118 B1
Acquaviva 115 C3, 116 B2
Acquaviva delle Fonti 121 C2
Acquaviva Picena 117 D2/3
Acquedolci 125 C2
Acquigny 76 B3, 86 A/B1
Àcqui Terme 113 C1
Acri 122 B1
Ács 95 C3
Acsád 94 B3, 127 D1, 128 A1
Ada 129 D3
Ada 140 A1
Adahuesca 155 C2/3
Adak 16 A3
Adakgruvan 16 A3
Adalsbruk 38 A2
Ådalsvollen 28 B3, 33 D1, 34 A1
Adamuz 167 C3, 172 B1
Adanero 160 A/B2
Adaševci 133 C1
Ädbodarna 39 C1
Addaya 157 C1
Adé 108 B3, 155 C1
Adelboden [Frutigen] 105 C2
Adelebsen 81 C1
Adelfia 121 C2
Ådelfors 51 C1
Adelmannsfelden 91 C/D1
Adelöv 46 A3
Adelsdorf 81 D3
Adelsheim 91 C1
Adelshofen-Tauberzell 91 D1
Adelsö 47 C1
Adelsried 91 D2
Ademuz 163 C3
Adenau 80 A2
Aderstedt 69 C3
Adinkerke 78 A1
Adjud 141 C1
Adliswil 105 C/D1
Admont 93 D3
Ådnekvam 36 A3
Ådneram 42 B2
Adolfsberg (Örebro) 46 A1
Adolfsström 15 C/D2
Adony 129 C1
Adorf 82 B2
A dos Cunhados 164 A2
Adra 173 C/D2
Adradas 161 D1
Adrall 155 C2
Adrano 125 C2
Ádria 115 C1
Aduanas 169 D2
Aduard 67 C1
Adzaneta 162 B3
Aerzen 68 A/B3
Aesch 90 A3
A Estrada 150 A2
Aetós 146 A1
Aetós 146 B3
Aetós 143 C2
Äetsä 24 B1
Åfar 32 B2
Åfarnes 32 A2
Afferden 67 B/C3, 79 D1
Affing 91 D2, 92 A2
Affoltern am Albis 105 C/D1
Áfidnai 147 D2
Afife 150 A3, 158 A1
Áfissos 144 A3
Áfitos 144 A2
Áfitos 148 B1
Aflenz Kurort 94 A3
A Fonsagrada 151 C1
Åfors 16 B3
Afragola 119 D3
Afritz 126 B1/2
Afsluitdijk 66 B2
Aftraet 28 B3, 33 D2
Aga 36 B3
Aga 82 B2
Agallas 159 C2
Ågård 29 C2
Agård 129 B/C1
Ágasegyháza 129 C1
Agay 112 B3
Agazzano 113 D1, 114 A1
Agde 110 B3
Agdenes 28 A3, 33 C1
Agen 109 C2
Ager 155 C3
Agerbæk 48 A3, 52 A1
Agérola 119 D3
Agerskov 52 B1/2
Agger 48 A2
Aggersund 48 B1/2
Àggius 123 D1
Aggösundet 31 C3
Aggsbach Markt 94 A2
Aggstein 94 A2
Agiá 143 D3, 144 A3
Agiá 148 B1
Agía Ánna 147 D1
Agía Marína 147 D3
Agía Marína 147 D2
Agía Marína 147 C1
Agía Paraskeví 142 B2
Agía Pelagía 148 B3
Agía Sofía 147 D1
Agiássos 149 C2
Agía Triás 146 B2
Agía Triás 147 C2
Agići 131 C1
Agighiol 141 D2
Ágii Anárgiri 143 D3
Ágii Apóstoli 147 D2
Ágii Apóstoli 147 D2
Ágii Theódori 147 C2
Agiófillon 143 C3
Agiókambos 143 D3, 144 A3
Ágios Achíllios 142 B1/2
Ágios Andréas 147 C3
Ágios Athanásios 145 C1
Ágios Athanásios 143 C1
Ágios Charálambos 145 C/D1
Ágios Charálambos 149 C1
Ágios Dimítrios 147 C2
Ágios Dimítrios 143 D2
Ágios Efstrátios 145 C3
Ágios Efstrátios 149 C1
Ágios Geórgios 146 B1
Ágios Geórgios 147 D3
Ágios Germanós 143 B/C1
Ágios Harálampos 143 D3
Ágios Ioánnis 144 A3
Ágios Ioánnis 148 B1
Ágios Kírikos 149 C2
Ágios Konstantínos 147 C1
Ágios Loukás 147 D2
Ágios Matthéos 142 A3
Ágios Nikólaos 147 C3
Ágios Nikólaos 142 B3
Ágios Nikólaos 146 A1
Ágios Nikólaos 144 B2
Ágios Nikólaos 147 D1
Ágios Nikolaós 146 B2
Ágios Pandeleímon 143 C1/2
Ágios Pétros 143 D1
Ágios Pétros 147 C3
Ágios Pródromos 144 A2
Ágios Stéfanos 147 D2
Ágios Thomás 147 D2
Ágios Vasílios 147 C3
Ágios Vlásios 146 B1
Ágios Zacharías 142 B2
Agira 125 C2
Aglapsvik 4 A3
Aglasterhausen 91 C1
Aglen 28 B1/2
Agliana 114 B2, 116 A/B1
Agliano 113 C1
Agliè 105 C3
Aglientu 123 D1
Agnana Cálabra 122 A/B3
Ágnanda 142 B3
Ágnanda 148 A1
Agnanderón 143 C3
Agnäs 31 C2
Agnita 140 B1
Agnone 119 D2
Agnone Bagni 125 D3
Agon 85 D1
Agonac 101 D3
Agoncillo 153 D2
Ágordo 107 C2
Agost 169 C3
Ågotnes 36 A3
Ágrafa 146 B1
Agramón 168 B3
Agramunt 155 D3, 163 D1
Ágras 143 C1
Ágreda 153 D3, 154 A3, 162 A1
Agreliá 143 C3
Agri 49 C2/3
Agriá 144 A3
Agrigento 124 B3
Agrínion 146 A1
Agrínion 148 A/B2
Agriovótanon 148 B2
Agriovótanon 147 C/D1
Agrochão 151 C3, 159 C1
Agrón 173 C2
Agrópoli 120 A3
Ågskaret 14 B1
Agua Amarga 174 A2
Aguada de Baixo 158 A2
Aguadulce 173 D2
Aguadulce 172 A2
Agualva 164 A2
A Guardia 150 A3
Aguarón 163 C1
Aguas 154 B2
Aguas Belas 158 A3, 164 B1
Aguas Cándidas 153 C2
Aguas de Busot 169 D2/3
Aguaviva 162 B2
Aguaviva de la Vega 161 D1
A Gudiña 151 C3
Agudo 166 B2
Águeda 158 A2
Agüero 154 B2
Aguessac 110 B2
Aguiar 164 B3
Aguiar da Beira 158 B2
Aguilafuente 160 B1
Aguilar 172 B1
Aguilar de Anguita 161 D2
Aguilar de Bureba 153 C2
Aguilar de Campóo 152 B2
Aguilar de Campos 152 A3
Aguilar de Codés 153 D2
Aguilar del Alfambra 162 B2
Aguilar del Río Alhama 153 D3, 154 A3
Águilas 174 A1
Aguilón 162 A/B1

Aguinaliu 155 C3
Agullent 169 D2
Agunnaryd 50 B2
Agurain 156 A/B1
Aha 15 B/C3
Aha 15 D3
Ahaus 67 C3
Ahaus-Alstätte 67 C3
Ahaus-Ottenstein 67 C3
Ahaus-Wessum 67 C3
Åheim 36 A1
Ahigal 159 D3
Ahigal de Villarino 159 C1/2
Ahillones 166 A3
Ahjola 19 C2
Ahkiolahti 22 B2
Ahlbeck 70 B1
Ahlen 67 D3
Ahlerstedt 68 B1
Ahmas 18 B3
Ahmoo 25 C2
Ahmovaara 23 C/D2
Ahmovaara 23 D1/2
Aho 13 C3
Ahoinen 25 C2
Ahokylä 21 D1, 22 A/B1
Ahola 19 D1
Ahola 19 D2
Ahola 19 D3
Aholahti 27 C1
Aholanvaara 13 C3
Aholming 92 B2
Aho-Nikki 26 B2
Ahonperä 18 A3
Ahorn 81 D2/3, 82 A2
Ahorntal 82 A3
Aho-Västinki 21 D2, 22 A2
Ahrbrück 80 A2
Ahrensbök 53 C3
Ahrensburg 52 B3, 68 B1
Ahrensdorf 70 B3
Ahrenshagen 53 D3
Ähtäri 21 C3
Ähtärinranta 21 C2/3
Ähtävä 20 B1
Ahtiala 25 D2, 26 A2
Ahtopol 141 C/D3
Ahun 102 A2
Åhus 50 B3
Åhus 72 A1/2
Ahvemnen 23 D2
Ahveninen 21 D2, 22 A2
Ahvenisto 26 B1
Ahvensalmi 23 C3
Ahvenselkä 13 C3
Ahvio 26 B2
Å i Åfjord 28 A2, 33 C1
Aibar 155 C2
Aich 93 C3
Aicha 93 C2
Aichach 92 A2
Aichach-Griesbeckerzell 91 D2, 92 A2
Aichstetten 91 D3
Aichtal 91 C2
Aichwald 91 C2
Aiddejavrre 11 C2
Aidenbach 93 C2
Aidone 125 C2
Aidonochórion 144 B1
Aiello Cálabro 122 A2
Aiffres 101 B/C2
Aigen im Mühlkreis 93 C2
Aigle 104 B2
Aignan 108 B2
Aignay-le-Duc 88 B3
Aigre 101 C2
Aigrefeuille-sur-Maine 101 C1
Aigrefeuille-d'Aunis 100 B2
Aiguablava 156 B2
Aiguafreda 156 A3
Aiguebelle 104 A3
Aigueblanche 104 A/B3
Aigueperse 102 B2
Aigues-Mortes 111 C3
Aigues-Vives 110 A3, 156 B1
Aiguilles de Port Colon 84 B3
Aiguilles-en-Queyras 112 B1
Aiguillon 109 C2
Aiguines 112 A2/3
Aigurande-sur-Bouzanne 102 A2
Äijäjoki 11 C2
Äijälä 21 D3, 22 A3
Äijälä 24 B3
Äijävaara 17 C1
Åike 15 C2
Ailefroide 112 A1
Aillant-sur-Tholon 88 A2/3
Aillas 108 B1/2
Aillevillers-et-Lyaumont 89 C/D2/3
Ailly-le-Haut-Clocher 77 D2
Ailly-sur-Noye 77 D3
Aimé 104 B3
Ainali 18 A3
Ainali 21 C1
Aindling 91 D2, 92 A2
Ainhoa 108 A3, 154 A1
Ainring 92 B3
Aínsa 155 C2
Aintala 20 B2
Ainzón 154 A3, 162 A1
Airaines 77 D2
Airaksela 22 B2/3
Airasca 112 B1
Airdrie 56 B2
Aire-sur-l'Adour 108 B2
Aire-sur-la-Lys 77 D2, 78 A2
Airola 119 D3
Airolo 105 D2
Airvault 101 C1
Aísa 154 B2
Aisey-sur-Seine 88 B3
Aissey 89 C/D3, 104 A/B1
Aisy-sur-Armançon 88 B3
Aitakumpu 18 B1
Aitamännikkö 12 A2/3, 17 D1
Aiterhofen 92 B1/2
Aitolahti 25 C1
Aitona 155 C3, 163 C1
Aitoniemi 25 C1
Aitoo 25 C1
Aitrach 91 D3
Aitrang 91 D3
Aittaniemi 13 C3
Aittojärvi 18 B2
Aittojärvi 21 D1, 22 A1
Aittokoski 22 B1
Aittokylä 19 C2
Aittokylä 18 B2
Aittolahti 27 D1
Aittovaara 19 D2
Aittovaara 23 C2
Aiud 97 D3, 140 B1
Aix-en-Othe 88 A2
Aix-en-Provence 111 D3
Aixe-sur-Vienne 101 C2/3
Aix-les-Bains 104 A3
Aix-Noulette 78 A2
Aizarnazabal 153 D1
Aizenay 100 A1
Aizpute 73 C1
Ajac 110 A3, 156 A1
Ajaccio 113 D3
Ajain 102 A2
Ajalvir 161 C2
Ajanki 12 A3, 17 D1/2
Ajankijärvi 12 A3, 17 D1/2
Ajaur 31 C1
Ajaureforsen 15 C3
Ajdovac 134 B3
Ajdovščina 126 B2/3
Ajka 96 B3
Ajnaži 74 A1/2
Ajnovce 138 B1
Ajo 153 C1
Ajofrín 160 B3, 167 C1
Ajos 17 D3, 18 A1
Ajtos 141 C3
Åkarp 50 A3
Äkäsjoensuu 11 C3
Äkäskero 11 C3, 12 A2
Äkäslompolo 11 C3, 12 A2
Akasztó 129 C2
Aken 69 D3
Åker 50 B1
Åkerbäk 20 A1, 31 D2
Åkerbränna 30 A/B2, 35 D1
Åkerby 40 B2
Åkerby 16 B2
Åkerholmen 16 B2
Åkerland 30 A1/2
Åkernäs 15 C3
Åkersberga 47 D1
Åkersjön 29 C/D3, 34 B1
Åkers styckebruk 47 C1
Åkervik 14 B3
Akhisar 149 D2
Åkirkeby 72 A2
Åkirkeby 51 D3
Akkala 23 D3
Akkarfjord 5 C1
Akkarvik 4 B2
Akkastugorna 9 D3
Akkavare 16 A3
Akköy 149 D2
Akkrum 66 B2
Akland 43 C2/3, 44 A2
Akmačići 133 D3, 134 A3
Åknes 42 B2
Akonpohja 27 D1
Åkra 42 A1
Åkra 39 C2
Akrai 125 C3
Åkran 28 B2/3, 33 D1
Akráta 146 B2
Akréfnion 147 C2
Åkrehamn 42 A2
Akrogiáli 144 B1/2
Åkroken 30 B3, 35 D2
Åkroken 16 B3
Akropótamos 144 B1
Aksla 36 A/B2
Aksnes 32 B2
Aktion 146 A1
Aktsestugorna 15 D1, 16 A1
Åkulla 49 D1, 50 A1
Åkullsjön 31 D2
Åkvåg 43 C/D2/3, 44 A2
Åkvisslan 30 B3, 35 D2
Ål 37 C3
Ala 47 D3
Ala 107 B/C3
Ålabodarna 49 D3, 50 A3
Alacón 162 B2
Alà dei Sardi 123 D1/2
Ala di Stura 104 B3
Alaejos 160 A1
Alafors 45 C3
Alagna Valsésia 105 C3
Alagón 154 A/B3, 162 A1
Alahärmä 20 B2
Ala-Honkajoki 24 B1
Alainenjoki 24 B2
Alájar 165 D3, 171 C1
Alajärvi 21 C2
Alajärvi 23 C1
Alajoki 21 D1, 22 A1
Alaköngäs 6 B2
Ala-Kuona 23 C3
Alakylä 12 A2
Alakylä 18 B2
Alakylä 19 C2
Alakylä 24 A/B3
Alakylä 24 A1
Ala-Livo 18 B2
Alalkomenai 146 A2
Alaló 161 C1
A Lama 150 A2
Alameda 172 B2
Alameda de Cervera 167 D1/2, 168 A1/2
Alamedilla 173 C1
Alamillo 166 B2
Álamo 171 C1
Alan 130 B1
Ala-Näljänkä 19 C2
Ala-Nampa 12 B3
Alanäs 30 A2
Alandroal 165 C2
Ålandsbro 35 D2
Alange 165 D2, 166 A2
Alaniemi 18 A1
Alanís 166 A3, 171 D1
Ala-Paakkola 17 D2, 18 A1
Ala-Pitkä 22 B2
Ala-Postojoki 12 B2
Alaraz 160 A2
Alarcón 168 B1
Alar del Rey 152 B2
Alarilla 161 C2
Alaró 157 C2
Alaşehir 149 D2
Ålåsen 29 D2/3, 34 B1
Ala-Siurua 18 B2
Alássio 113 C2
Alastaipale 21 C3
Alastaro 24 B2
Ala-Sydänmaa 18 A3, 21 D1, 22 A1
Ala-Temmes 18 A/B3
Alatoz 169 D2
Alatri 119 C2
Ala-Valli 20 B3
Alavattnet 29 D2, 30 A2, 35 C1
Ala-Vieksi 19 D3
Alavieska 18 A3, 21 C1
Ala-Viirre 21 C1
Alavo 21 C3
Ala-Vuokki 19 D3
Ala-Vuotato 18 B2
Alavus (Alavo) 21 C3
Alayor 157 C1
Alba 163 C2
Alba 113 C1
Alba Adriática 117 D3
Albacete 168 B2
Albacken 35 C2
Alba de Tormes 159 D2
Alba Fucensis 119 C1/2
Albaida 169 D2
Albaina 153 D2
Alba Iulia 140 B1
Ålbæk 44 A/B3, 49 C1
Albala 165 D1/2, 166 A1/2
Albaladejo 167 D2, 168 A2
Albalat dels Sorélls 169 D1
Albalate de las Nogueras 161 D2/3
Albalate de Cinca 155 C3, 163 C1
Albalate de Zorita 161 C3
Albalate del Arzobispo 162 B2
Albalatillo 155 B/C3, 162 B1
Alban 110 A2
Albánchez 173 D2, 174 A2
Albanchez de Ubeda 167 D3, 173 C1
Albanella 120 A3
Albano Laziale 118 B2
Albanyà 156 B2
Albaredo d'Ádige 107 C3
Albarellos 150 B3
Albares 161 C3
Albaron 111 C3
Albarracín 162 A2
Albarreal de Tajo 160 B3, 167 C1
Albas 108 B1/2
Albatana 169 B/C2
Albatàrrec 155 C3, 163 C1
Albatera 169 C3
Albbruck 90 B3
Albedin 172 B1
Albelda 153 D2
Albelda 155 C3
Albendea 161 D2
Albendiego 161 C1
Albenga 113 C2
Albens 104 A3
Albentosa 162 B3
Ålberga 46 B2
Albergaria-a-Nova 158 A2
Albergaria-a-Velha 158 A2
Albergo Val Martello 106 B2
Alberique 169 D2
Alberite 153 D2
Albernoa 164 B3, 170 B1
Albero Alto 154 B3
Albero Bajo 154 B3
Alberobello 121 C2
Alberona 119 D2, 120 A1
Albersdorf 52 B3
Albert 78 A3
Albertacce 113 D3
Albertirsa 129 C1
Albertkázmérpuszta 94 B3
Albertville 104 A/B3
Alberuela de Tubo 155 B/C3
Albesa 155 C3, 163 C1
Albestroff 89 D1, 90 A1
Albi 109 D2, 110 A2
Albias 109 D2
Albidona 120 B3, 122 B1
Albínia 116 B3
Albino 106 A3
Albires 152 A2/3
Albisola Marina 113 C2
Albisola Superiore 113 C2
Alblasserdam 66 A3
Albocácer 163 C2/3
Alböke 51 D1
Albolodúy 173 D2
Albolote 173 C2
Albondón 173 C2
Alborache 169 C1
Alboraya 169 D1
Alborea 169 D1/2
Ålborg 48 B1
Alborge 162 B1
Albosággia 106 A2
Albox 174 A1/2
Albrechtice nad Vltavou 93 D1
Albstadt 91 C2
Albstadt-Ebingen 91 C2
Albstadt-Lautlingen 91 B/C2
Albstadt-Onstmettingen 91 C2
Albstadt-Tailfingen 91 C2
Ålbu 33 C2/3
Albudeite 169 D3
Albufeira 170 A2
Albufereta 169 D3
Albujón 174 B1
Albuñol 173 C2
Albuñuelas 173 C2
Alburquerque 165 C2
Alby 51 D2
Alby 35 C3
Alby-sur-Chéran 104 A3
Alcabideche 164 A2
Alcácer do Sal 164 B3
Alcáçovas 164 B3
Alcadozo 168 B2
Alcafozes 159 C3, 165 C1
Alcaine 162 B2
Alcains 158 B3, 165 C1
Alcala De Chivert 163 C3
Alcalá de Guadaira 171 D1/2
Alcalá de Gurrea 154 B3
Alcalá de Henares 161 C2
Alcalá del Júcar 169 C2
Alcalá de la Selva 162 B2/3
Alcalá de la Vega 162 A3
Alcalá del Río 171 D1
Alcalá del Valle 172 A2
Alcalá del Obispo 154 B3
Alcalá de los Gazules 171 D3
Alcalá de Moncayo 154 A3, 162 A1
Alcalá la Real 173 B/C1
Álcamo 124 A2
Alcampel 155 C3
Alcanadre 153 D2
Alcanar 163 C2
Alcanede 164 A1
Alcanena 164 A/B1
Alcañices 151 D3, 159 C1
Alcañiz 163 B/C2
Alcañizo 160 A3, 166 B1
Alcanó 155 C3, 163 C1
Alcántara 159 C3, 165 C1
Alcántara de Júcar 169 C/D2
Alcantarilha 170 A2
Alcantarilla 169 D3
Alcantud 161 D2
Alcaracejos 166 B3
Alcaraz 168 A2
Alcaria Ruiva 170 B1
Alcarràs 155 C3, 163 C1
Alcaucín 172 B2
Alcaudete 172 B1
Alcaudete de la Jara 160 A3, 166 B1
Alcay 108 A3, 154 B1
Alcázar de San Juan 167 D1, 168 A1
Alcázar del Rey 161 C3
Alcazarén 160 A/B1
Alceda 152 B1
Alcester 64 A2
Alcira 169 D2
Alcoba 167 C1/2
Alcobaça 164 A1
Alcobendas 161 C2
Alcobertas 164 A1
Alcocéber 163 C3
Alcocer 161 D2
Alcochete 164 A2
Alcoentre 164 A2
Alcofra 158 A/B2
Alcolea 166 B3, 172 B1

Alcolea 173 D2
Alcolea de Calatrava 167 C2
Alcolea de Cinca 155 C3, 163 C1
Alcolea del Río 171 D1
Alcolea del Pinar 161 D2
Alcolea de las Peñas 161 C1
Alcolea de Tajo 160 A3, 166 B1
Alcollarín 166 A1/2
Alconaba 153 D3, 161 D1
Alconchel 165 C2/3
Alconchel de Ariza 161 D1
Alconchel de la Estrella 161 D3, 168 A1
Alconera 165 D3
Alcóntar 173 D2
Alcora 162 B3
Alcorcón 160 B2/3
Alcorisa 162 B2
Alcorlo 161 C2
Alcoroches 162 A2
Alcoutim 170 B1
Alcover 163 C1
Alcoy 169 D2
Alcsútdoboz 95 D3, 128 B1
Alcubierre 154 B3, 162 B1
Alcubilla de Avellaneda 153 C3, 161 C1
Alcubillas 167 D2, 168 A2
Alcubillas de las Peñas 161 D1
Alcublas 162 B3, 169 C1
Alcudia 157 C2
Alcudia de Carlet 169 D2
Alcudia de Guadix 173 C2
Alcudia de Veo 162 B3, 169 D1
Alcuéscar 165 D2, 166 A2
Alcuneza 161 D2
Aldbrough 61 D2
Aldeacentenera 166 A1
Aldeadávila de la Ribera 159 C1
Aldeade la Torre 163 C3, 169 D1
Aldea del Cano 165 D1/2, 166 A1/2
Aldea del Fresno 160 B3
Aldea del Rey 167 C2
Aldea de San Esteban 153 C3, 161 C1
Aldea de Trujillo 166 A1
Aldealafuente 153 D3, 161 D1
Aldealpozo 153 D3, 161 D1
Aldeanueva de Atienza 161 C1/2
Aldeanueva de Barbarroya 160 A3, 166 B1
Aldeanueva de Guadalajara 161 C2
Aldeanueva de la Serrezuela 160 B1
Aldeanueva del Camino 159 D3
Aldeanueva de San Bartolomé 160 A3, 166 B1
Aldeanueva de Ebro 153 D2/3, 154 A2
Aldeanueva de la Vera 159 D3
Aldeanueva de Figueroa 159 D1/2, 160 A1/2
Aldeanueva del Codonal 160 B2
Aldeaquemada 167 D3
Aldea Real 160 B1/2
Aldearrodrigo 159 D2
Aldeaseca de la Frontera 160 A2
Aldeavieja 160 B2
Aldeburgh 65 D2
Aldehuela 162 A/B3
Aldehuela de Yeltes 159 C/D2
Aldehuela del Jerte 159 C/D3
Aldehuela de la Bóveda 159 D2
Aldehuela de Liestos 162 A2
Aldeia da Mata 165 B/C1/2
Aldeia da Ponte 159 C2/3
Aldeia do Bispo 159 C3
Aldeia do Maio 164 A2/3
Aldeia dos Palheiros 170 A1
Aldeia Nova de São Bento 165 C3, 170 B1
Aldeire 173 C2
Aldenhoven 79 D2
Aldeno 107 B/C2
Aldernäset 30 A2
Aldersbach 93 C2
Aldershot 64 B3, 76 B1
Aldince 138 B2/3
Aldudes 108 A3, 154 A1
Ale 17 B/C3
Åled 50 A2
Aledo 168 B3, 174 A1
Alegia 153 D1/2
Alegrete 165 C1/2
Aleko 139 D1/2
Aleksandrija 99 D3
Aleksandrija 99 D3
Aleksandrovac 134 B2
Aleksandrovac 134 B3
Aleksin 75 D3
Aleksinac 140 A2/3
Aleksinac 135 C3
Ålem 51 D1
Ålem 72 B1
Ålen 33 D2
Alençon 86 B2
Alenquer 164 A2
Alentisque 161 D1
Aleria 113 D3
Alès 111 C2
Áles 123 C2/3
Aleșd 97 D3, 140 B1
Alesjaurestugorna 9 D2
Alessándria della Rocca 124 B2
Alessándria 113 C1
Alessándria del Carretto 120 B3, 122 B1
Alessano 121 D3
Alesso 107 D2, 126 A2
Ålestrup 48 B2
Ålesund 36 B1
Alet-les-Bains 110 A3, 156 A1
Alevráda 146 A/B1
Alexain 86 A2
Alexándria 143 D2
Alexandria 141 C2
Alexandroúpolis 149 C1
Alexandroúpolis 145 D1, 145 D3
Alf 80 A3
Alfacar 173 C2
Alfajarín 154 B3, 162 B1
Alfambra 162 A/B2
Alfambras 170 A2
Alfamén 155 C3, 163 C1
Alfândega da Fé 159 C1
Alfántega 155 C3, 163 C1
Alfara de Carles dels Ports 163 C2
Alfarela 158 B1
Alfarnate 172 B2
Alfaro 154 A2/3
Alfarrás 155 C3, 163 C1
Alfatar 141 C2
Alfaz del Pi 169 D2
Alfdorf 91 C1/2
Alfedena 119 C2
Alfeizerão 164 A1
Alfeld 92 A1
Alfeld 68 B3
Alfena 158 A1
Alferce 170 A2
Alfés 155 C3, 163 C1
Alfhausen 67 D2
Alfonsine 115 C1/2
Alford 61 D3, 65 C1
Alforja 163 D1
Ålfoten 36 A1
Alfoz 151 B/C1
Alfreites 159 C2/3
Alfreton 61 D3, 65 C1
Alfta 40 A1
Alfundão 164 B3
Algaida 157 C2
Algajola 113 D2
Algalé 165 C2
Algámitas 172 A2
Algar 171 D2
Algar 174 B1
Algar 162 B3, 169 D1
Älgarås 45 D2, 46 A2
Ålgård 42 A2
Algarinejo 172 B2
Algarra 162 A3
Algarrobo 172 B2
Algatocín 172 A3
Algeciras 172 A3
Algemesí 169 D2
Algenstedt 69 C2
Ålgered 35 D3
Algerri 155 C3, 163 C1
Alges 164 A2
Algete 161 C2
Alghero 123 C2
Älghult 51 C1
Älghult 30 B2
Algimia de Alfara 162 B3, 169 D1
Algimia de Almonacid 162 B3, 169 D1
Alginet 169 D1/2
Algodonales 172 A2
Algora 161 D2
Algorta 153 C1
Algoso 159 C1
Algoz 170 A2
Älgsjö 30 B2
Alguaire 155 C3, 163 C1
Alguazas 169 D3
Algueña 169 C3
Algutsrum 51 D2
Algyő 129 D2
Alhadas 158 A3
Alhama de Almería 173 D2
Alhama de Aragón 161 D1, 162 A1
Alhama de Granada 172 B2
Alhama de Murcia 169 C3, 174 B1
Alhambra 167 D2, 168 A2
Alhamn 17 C3
Alhandra 164 A2
Alhaurín de la Torre 172 B2
Alhaurín el Grande 172 B2/3
Alhendín 173 C2
Alhojärvi 25 D1, 26 A1
Ålholm 53 D2
Alhóndiga 161 C2
Ålhus 36 B2
Ália 124 B2
Alía 166 B1
Aliaga 162 B2
Aliaguilla 163 C3, 169 D1
Aliano 120 B3
Alíartos 147 C2
Alibunar 134 B1
Alibunar 140 A2
Alicante 169 D3
Alicún de Ortega 173 C1
Alife 119 D2
Alífira 146 B3
Alijó 158 B1
Alikaí 146 A2
Alikaí 143 D2
Alikí 145 C2
Alikí 146 A1
Alikylä 21 C1
Alimena 125 C2
Alingsås 45 C3
Alíns 155 C2
Alinya 155 D2/3
Aliseda 165 D1
Ališići 131 D1
Alistráti 144 B1
Alì Terme 125 D2
Aliud 153 D3, 161 D1
Alivérion 147 D2
Alixan 111 C/D1
Aljaraque 171 C2
Aljažev dom 126 B2
Aljezur 170 A2
Aljubarrota 164 A1
Aljucén 165 D2, 166 A2
Aljustrel 164 B3, 170 A/B1
Alkkia 20 B3
Alkmaar 66 A/B2
Alkoven 93 C/D2
Allagí 146 B3
Állai 123 C2
Allaines 87 C2
Allaire 85 C3
Allanche 102 B3
Alland 94 A2/3
Allariz 150 B3
Allarmont 89 D2, 90 A2
Alleen 42 B3
Alleghe 107 C2
Allègre 103 C3
Allemagne-de-Provence 112 A2/3
Allemalehto 12 B2
Allemont 112 A1
Allendale Town 57 D3, 60 B1
Allendorf 80 B1/2
Allendorf (Dillkreis) 80 B2
Allentsteig 94 A2
Allepuz 162 B2
Aller 151 D1, 152 A1
Allersberg 92 A1
Allershausen 92 A2
Alleuze 110 B1
Allevard 104 A3
Allex 111 C1
Allgunnen 51 D1
Allingåbro 49 B/C2
Allinge 51 D3
Allinge 72 A2
Allmendingen 91 C2
Allo 153 D2, 154 A2
Alloa 57 B/C1
Allogny 87 D3, 102 A1
Alloluokta kapell 16 A1
Allonnes 87 C2
Allos 112 A2
Alloue 101 C2
Alloway 56 B2
Alloza 162 B2
Allsån 17 C2
Allschwil [Basel SBB] 90 A3
Allstakan 38 B3
Allstedt 82 A1
Allumiere 118 A1
Ally 102 A3
Almacelles 155 C3, 163 C1
Almáchar 172 B2
Almada 164 A2
Almadén 166 B2
Almadén de la Plata 165 D3, 166 A3, 171 D1
Almadenejos 166 B2
Almagro 167 C2
Almajano 153 D3
Almaluez 161 D1
Almansa 169 C2
Almansil 170 B2
Almanza 152 A2
Almarail 153 D3, 161 D1
Almaraz 159 D3, 166 A1
Almargem do Bispo 164 A2
Almargen 172 A2
Almarza 153 D3
Almásfüzitő 95 C3
Almásneszmély 95 C/D3
Almatret 163 C1
Almazán 161 D1
Almazora 163 C3, 169 D1
Almedíjar 162 B3, 169 D1
Almedina 167 D2, 168 A2
Almedinilla 172 B1/2
Almeida 159 D1
Almeida 159 C2
Almeirim 164 A/B2
Almelo 67 C2/3
Almenar 155 C3, 163 C1
Almenara 162 B3, 169 D1
Almenar de Soria 153 D3, 161 D1
Almendra 159 C1
Almendra 159 C2
Almendral 165 C/D2
Almendral de la Cañada 160 A3
Almendralejo 165 D2
Almendros 161 C3, 167 D1, 168 A1
Almería 173 D2
Almesåkra 46 A3
Älmhult 50 B2
Älmhult 72 A1
Almirós 148 B1/2
Almirós 147 C1
Almkerk 66 B3
Almodôvar 170 B1
Almodóvar del Río 166 B3, 172 A1
Almodóvar del Campo 167 C2
Almodóvar del Pinar 161 D3, 162 A3, 168 B1
Almofala 159 C2
Almogía 172 B2
Almoguera 161 C3
Almoharín 165 D2, 166 A2
Almonacid de Toledo 160 B3, 167 C1
Almonacid del Marquesado 161 C/D3, 168 A1
Almonacid de la Sierra 163 B/C1
Almonacid de Zorita 161 C3
Almonaster 165 D3, 171 C1
Almondsbury 63 D1
Almonte 171 C2
Almoradí 169 C3
Almorchon 166 B2
Almorox 160 B3
Almoster 164 A1/2
Almourol 164 B1
Almsele 30 B1/2
Almsjönäs 30 B3, 35 D2
Ämsta 41 C3
Almudévar 154 B3
Almundsryd 51 C2
Almundsryd 72 A1
Almuñécar 173 C2
Almunge 40 B3
Almunia de San Juan 155 C3
Almuniente 154 B3
Almuradiel 167 D2/3
Almurfe 151 D1
Almvik 46 B3
Alnaryd 51 C2
Alnmouth 57 D2
Alnwick 57 D2
Alnwick 54 B3
Alocén 161 C/D2
Aloja 73 D1, 74 A2
Alónia 149 C1
Alónia 145 D2
Alónnisos 147 D1
Alora 172 B2
Alós de Gil 155 D2
Alosno 171 C1
Alozaina 172 A2
Alpalhão 165 C1
Alpandeire 172 A2/3
Alpanseque 161 D1
Alpas 16 B2
Alpbach 92 A/B3, 107 C1
Alpe del Trucco 105 B/C3
Alpe Dévero 105 C2
Alpe di Mera 105 C3
Alpedrinha 158 B3
Alpedriz 164 A1
Alpedroches 161 C1
Alpen 67 C3, 79 D1
Alpens 156 A2
Alpera 169 D2
Alphen aan de Rijn 66 A3
Alpiarça 164 B1/2
Alpignano 112 B1
Alpirsbach 90 B2
Alpua 18 A3
Alpuente 162 A/B3, 169 C1
Alqueva 165 C3
Alquézar 155 C2/3
Alquife 173 C2
Als 49 B/C2
Alsasua 153 D2
Alsdorf 79 D2
Alsdorf-Höngen 79 D2
Alsen 29 C3, 34 B1/2
Alseno 114 A1
Alsenz 80 B3
Alset 28 A3, 33 C1
Alsfeld 81 C2
Alsfeld-Eifa 81 C2
Alsheim 80 B3
Alshult 51 C2
Alsleben 69 C/D3, 82 A1
Alsódabas 129 C1
Alsónémedi 95 D3, 129 C1
Alsónemesapáti 128 A1
Alsóörs 128 B1
Alsószölnök 127 D1
Alstad 50 A/B3
Alstad 8 B2
Ålstad 9 B/C3
Alstadhaug 28 B3, 33 D1
Alstahaug 14 A2
Ålstäket 47 D1
Alsterbro 51 D1
Alsterbro 72 B1

Alstermo 51 C1
Alston 57 C/D3, 60 B1
Alsvik 14 B1
Alta 5 C2
Älta 47 C/D1
Altamura 120 B2
Altare 113 C2
Altarejos 161 D3, 168 B1
Altaussee 93 C3
Altavilla Irpina 119 D3
Altavilla Silentina 120 A2/3
Altdöbern 70 B3, 83 C1
Altdorf 92 A1
Altdorf 105 D1
Altdorf (Landshut) 92 B2
Alt Duvenstedt 52 B2/3
Alte 170 A/B2
Altea 169 D2
Alte Ceccato 107 C3
Altedo 115 B/C1
Alteidet 5 C2
Altena 80 A/B1
Altenahr 80 A2
Altenau 69 B/C3
Altenbeken 68 A3
Altenberge 67 D3
Altenbuch (Marktheidenfeld) 81 C3
Altenburg 82 B1/2
Altenburg 94 A2
Altenglan 80 A3, 90 A1
Altenhagen 70 A1
Altenholz 52 B2/3
Altenkirchen 80 A/B2
Altenmarkt 92 B3
Altenmarkt an der Triesting 94 A2/3
Altenmarkt bei Sankt Gallen 93 D3
Altenmarkt im Yspertal 93 D2
Altenmedingen-Bostelwiebeck 69 C2
Altenmünster-Zusamzell 91 D2
Altenriet 91 C2
Altenstadt 91 D2
Altenstadt 81 C2
Altensteig 90 B2
Altensteig-Berneck 90 B2
Altentreptow 70 A1
Alter do Chão 165 C2
Altfraunhofen 92 B2
Altfriedland 70 B2
Altheim 91 C/D2
Altheim 93 C2
Althofen 126 B1
Althorpe 61 C/D2/3
Althütte 91 C1/2
Altin 28 B2
Altinoluk 149 D1
Altipiani di Arcinazzo 118 B2
Altkirch 89 D3, 90 A3
Altkünkendorf 70 B2
Altlandsberg 70 A/B2
Altlengbach 94 A2
Altlewin 70 B2
Altmannstein 92 A1/2
Altmannstein-Mendorf 92 A1/2
Altmannstein-Pondorf 92 A1
Alt-Meteln 53 C3, 69 C1
Altmünster 93 C3
Altnes 5 C2
Altofonte 124 B2
Altomonte 122 A1
Altomünster 92 A2
Altomünster-Wollomoos 92 A2
Alton 64 B3, 76 A1
Altopáscio 114 B2, 116 A1
Altorricón 155 C3, 163 C1
Altötting 92 B2
Altranft 70 B2
Altrincham 59 D2, 60 B3
Altrip 90 B1
Altruppin 70 A2
Alt Schadow 70 B3
Altscheid 79 D3
Alt-Schönau 69 D1, 70 A1
Altshausen 91 C3
Altstätten 91 C3
Altuna 40 A3
Altura 162 B3, 169 D1
Altusried 91 D3
Altusried-Kimratshofen 91 D3
Altusried-Krugzell 91 D3
Altwarp 70 B1
Altwigshagen 70 B1
Alunda 40 B3
Ålundsby 16 B3
Aluskije 74 A/B2
Alustante 162 A2
Alva 56 B1
Alvaiázere 158 A3, 164 B1
Alvajärvi 21 D1/2, 22 A1/2
Alvalade 164 B3, 170 A1
Alvaneu Bad 106 A1/2
Alvängen 45 C3
Alvarenga 158 A/B2
Alvares 158 A/B3
Alvaro 158 B3
Alvastra 46 A2
Alvdal 33 C3
Älvdalen 39 C1
Alvega 164 B1
Alverca do Ribatejo 164 A2
Alversund 36 A3
Alvesta 51 B/C1
Alvesta 72 A1
Alvettula 25 C2
Älvho 39 D1
Alviano 117 C3, 118 A/B1
Alvignac 109 D1
Alvik 17 C3
Ålvik 36 B3
Alviksträsk 17 C3
Alvito 119 C2
Alvito 164 B3
Älvkarleby 40 B2
Älvkarleö bruk 40 B2
Älvkarlhed 39 D1, 40 A1
Alvnes 15 C1
Alvnes 9 C3
Alvøen 36 A3
Alvôr 170 A2
Alvøy 36 A3
Älvros 38 B1
Älvros 34 B3
Älvsbacka 39 C3, 45 D1
Älvsbacka 16 A2
Älvsbyn 16 B3
Älvsered 49 D1, 50 A1
Älvsnäs 41 B/C3
Ålvundeid 32 B2
Ålvundfoss 32 B2
Alwalton 64 B2
Alwinton 57 D2
Alyth 57 C1
Alytus 73 D2, 74 A3
Alzano Lombardo 106 A3
Alzenau in Unterfranken 81 C3
Alzey 80 B3
Alzo 105 C3
Alzon 110 B2
Alzonne 110 A3, 156 A1
Amadora 164 A2
Amailloux 101 C1
Åmål 45 C1/2
Amalfi 119 D3
Amaliápolis 147 C1
Amaliás 146 A2/3
Amaliás 148 A2
Amance 89 C3
Amancey 104 A1
Amándola 115 D3, 117 D2/3
Amantea 122 A2
Amantia 142 A2
Amárandon 143 C3
Amárandos 142 B2
Amarante 158 B1
Amareleja 165 C3
Amares 150 A/B3, 158 A1
Amárinthos 147 D2
Amaseno 119 C2
Amatrice 117 D3, 119 B/C1
Amaxádes 145 C1
Amayas 161 D2
Ambarès 108 B1
Ambasaguas 152 A2
Ambazac 101 C2
Ambel 154 A3, 162 A1
Ambelákia 143 D3
Ambelákia 147 D2
Ambelakiótissa 146 B1
Ambelón 143 D3
Amberg 82 A3, 92 A/B1
Ambérieu-en-Bugey 103 D2
Ambérieux-en-Dombes 103 D2
Ambert 103 C3
Ambialet 110 A2
Ambierle 103 C2
Ambjörby 39 C2
Amblainville 77 D3, 87 C1
Amble-by-the-Sea 57 D2
Ambleside 59 C/D1, 60 B1
Amblève 79 D2
Ambleville 77 D3, 87 C1
Amboise 86 B3
Ambra 115 C3, 116 B2
Ambrault 102 A1
Ambrières-le-Grand 86 A2
Ambrógio 115 C1
Ambrona 161 D1/2
Ambronay 103 D2
Amdal 28 A/B3, 33 C/D2
Åmdalsverk 43 C2
Amden 105 D1, 106 A1
Ameixial 170 B1/2
Ameixoeira 164 B1
Amel 79 D2
Amélia 117 C3, 118 B1
Amélie-les-Bains-Palalda 156 B2
Amelinghausen 68 B2
Amendolara 120 B3, 122 B1
Amer 156 B2
A Merca 150 B3
America 79 D1
Amerongen 66 B3
Amersfoort 66 B3
Amersham 64 B3
Ames 150 A2
Amesbury 64 A3, 76 A1
Amezketa 153 D1/2
A Mezquita 151 C3
Amfíklia 147 C1
Amfilochía 146 A1
Amfilochía 148 A2
Amfípolis 149 B/C1
Amfípolis 144 B1
Ámfissa 147 B/C2
Ámfissa 148 B2
Amiães de Baixo 164 A1
Amieira 164 B1
Amieira 165 C3
Amiens 77 D2/3
Amigdaléai 143 C2
Amíndeon 143 C2
Åminne 50 B1
Aminne 20 B1
Amiterno 117 D3, 119 C1
Amla 36 B2
Åmli 43 C2
Åmliden 31 C1
Amlwch 58 B2, 60 A3
Ammälä 20 B3
Ammanford 63 C1
Ämmänsaari 19 C/D2
Ammarnäs 15 C2
Ämmätsä 25 C1, 26 A1
Åmmeberg 46 A2
Ammensleben 69 C3
Ammer 35 C2
Ammer 30 A3, 35 C2
Ammerbuch 91 B/C2
Ammern 81 D1
Ammerön 35 C2
Amoeiro 150 B2
Amöneburg 81 C2
Amorbach 81 C3
Amoreanes 170 B1
Amoreira 164 A1
Amorosa 150 A3, 158 A1
Amorosi 119 D3
Åmot 40 A2
Åmot 38 A1/2
Åmot 37 D3
Åmot 43 C1
Amot 36 B2
Åmot 43 D1
Åmotfors 38 B3, 45 C1
Åmotsdal 43 C1
Åmotsdalshytta 33 B/C3, 37 D1
Amou 108 B3, 154 B1
Ampezzo 107 D2, 126 A2
Ampfing 92 B2
Amphiareion 147 D2
Ampiaslantta 16 B1
Amplepuis 103 C2
Amposta 163 C2
Ampthill 64 B2
Ampudia 152 A/B3
Ampuero 153 C1
Ampuis 103 D3
Amriswil 91 C3
Amroth 62 B1
Åmsele 31 C1
Amsteg 105 D1
Amstelveen 66 B2/3
Amsterdam 66 B2/3
Amstetten 93 D2
Amstetten 96 A2/3
Amtzell 91 C3
Amulree 56 B1
Amurrio 153 C1/2
Amusco 152 B3
Amusquillo 152 B3, 160 B1
Åmynnet 31 B/C3
Ån 29 C3, 34 B2
Anacapri 119 C/D3
Anadia 158 A2
Anadón 162 B2
Anafonítria 146 A2
Anagni 118 B2
Añana-Gesaltza 153 C2
Anan'ev 99 C3
Anarisstugan 34 A2
Ånäset 31 D2
Ånäset 31 C2
Åna-Sira 42 A/B3
Anatolí 146 B1
Anatolikón 143 C2
Anattila 19 C3
Anávissos 147 D3
Anávra 147 C1
Anaya de Alba 159 D2, 160 A2
Ançã 158 A3
Ancenis 86 A3
Ancerville-Guë 88 B2
Anché 101 C2
Anchuela del Campo 161 D2
Anchuras 166 B1
Ancín 153 D2
Ancona 117 D2
Ancroft 57 D2
Ancy-le-Franc 88 A/B3
Anda 36 B1
Ándalo 107 B/C2
Åndalsnes 32 A/B2/3
Andaluz 153 C/D3, 161 C1
Andau 94 B3
Andaval 165 C2
Andavias 151 D3, 159 D1
Ändebol 46 B2
Andebu 43 D2, 44 A1
Andeer [Thusis] 105 D2, 106 A2
Andelfingen 90 B3
Andelot 89 C2
Andenes 9 C1
Andenne 79 C2
Anderberget 30 A3, 35 D2
Anderlues 78 B2
Andermatt 105 D2
Andernach 80 A2
Andernos-les-Bains 108 A1
Anderslöv 50 B3
Anderstorp 50 B1
Andijk 66 B2
Andilla 162 B3, 169 C1
Andlau 90 A2
Andoain 153 D1, 154 A1
Andocs 128 B2
Andolsheim 90 A2/3
Andørja 9 C1
Andorra 162 B2
Andorra la Vieja 155 D2, 156 A2
Andosilla 153 D2, 154 A2
Andover 64 A3, 76 A1
Andrå 38 A1
Andraitx 157 C2
Andravída 146 A2
Andreapol' 75 C2
Andrejaš 138 B2
Andrest 108 B3, 155 C1
Andretta 120 A2
Andrezieux 103 C3
Ándria 120 B2, 136 A3
Andrijevci 132 B1
Andrijevica 137 D1, 138 A1
Andrítsena 146 B3
Andrítsena 148 B2
Androniáni 147 D1
Androúsa 146 B3
Andselv (Bardufoss) 4 A3, 9 D1
Andsnes 4 B2
Andújar 167 C3, 172 B1
Anduze 111 B/C2
Andviken 29 D3, 34 B1
Andviken 29 D3, 34 B1
Aneby 46 A3
Åneby 38 A3
Anemorráchi 146 A1
Ænes 42 A1
Ånes 32 B2
Ånessletta 9 C1
Ånestad 38 A2
Anet 87 C1
Anetjärvi 19 C1
Anfo 106 B3
Äng 45 C2
Äng 46 A3
Anga 47 D3
Ånge 15 D2
Ånge 29 C/D3, 34 B1
Ånge 35 C3
Ängebo 35 C3
Angeja 158 A2
Angelbachtal 90 B1
Angelburg-Lixfeld 80 B2
Ängelholm 49 D2, 50 A2
Ängelholm 72 A1
Angeli 6 A3, 11 D1
Angelniemi 24 B3
Angelókastron 142 A3
Angelókastron 147 C3
Angelókastron 146 A1/2
Ängelsberg 40 A3
Angen 28 A2
Anger 127 C/D1
Angera 105 D3
Angermünde 70 B2
Angermünde 72 A3
Angern 69 D3
Angern 94 B2
Angern 107 B/C1
Angers 86 A3
Ängersjö 34 B3
Angervikko 23 C1/2
Angerville 87 C2
Ängesån 17 C1
Ängesbyn 17 C3
Anghiari 115 C3, 117 B/C2
Angístrion 147 D3
Angle 62 B1
Anglès 110 A3
Anglès 156 B2
Anglesola 155 D3, 163 D1
Angles-sur-l'Anglin 101 D1
Anglure 88 A2
Ango 77 C2/3
Ängom 35 D3
Angoulême 101 C3
Ängskär 40 B2
Ängsnäs 40 A2
Ängsö 47 C1
Angüés 155 B/C3
Anguiano 153 C/D2/3
Anguillara Véneta 107 C3, 115 C1
Anguita 161 D2
Angvik 32 B2
Anholt 49 C2
Aniane 110 B2/3
Aniche 78 A2
Anières [Genève] 104 A2
Aniés 154 B2
Anikščiai 73 D2, 74 A3
Ånimskog 45 C2
Anina 135 C1
Anina 140 A2
Anizy-le-Château 78 A/B3
Anjala 26 B2
Anjalankoski-Inkeroinen 26 B2
Anjans fjällstation 29 C3, 34 A1
Anjony 102 A/B3, 110 A1
Anjum 67 C1
Ankaran 126 B3
Ankarede kapell 29 D1
Ankarsrum 46 B3
Ankarsund 15 C/D3
Ankarsvik 35 D3
Ankarvatnet 29 D1

Ankele 22 B3
Ankerlia 4 B3, 10 B1
Anklam 70 A/B1
Anklam 72 A2
Ankum 67 D2
Anlezy 102 B1
Ånn 29 C3, 34 A2
Annaberg 94 A3
Annaberg-Buchholz 82 B2
Annaberg im Lammertal 93 C3
Annaburg 70 A3
Annalong 58 A1
Annamoe 58 A2
Annan 57 C3, 60 A/B1
Anndalsvågen 14 A3
Anneberg 46 A3
Annecy 104 A2/3
Annefors 40 A1
Annemasse 104 A2
Annerstad 50 B2
Annevoie-Rouillon 79 C2
Anneyron 103 D3
Annonay 103 D3
Annonen 18 A3
Annone Véneto 107 D3 126 A3
Annopol 97 C1, 98 A2
Annot 112 A/B2
Annœullin 78 A2
Annula 25 C2
Annweiler am Trifels 90 B1
Anola 27 C2
Añón 154 A3, 162 A1
Áno Porróia 139 D3, 143 D1, 144 A1
Anor 78 B3
Añora 166 B3
Anost 103 C1
Añover de Tajo 160 B3
Anquela del Pedregal 162 A2
Anquela del Ducado 161 D2
Anröchte 80 B1
Ans 48 B2
Ansager 48 A3, 52 A1
Ansbach 91 D1
Anse 103 D2
Ansedónia 116 B3
Anserall 155 D2
Ansfelden 93 D2
Ansião 158 A3, 164 B1
Ansignan 156 B1
Ansjö 30 A3, 35 C2
Ansnes 32 B1
Ansnes 4 A3
Ansó 154 B2
Ansoain 154 A2
Ånstad 8 A3
Anstruther 57 C1
Ansvar 17 C1/2
Antas 158 B2
Antas 174 A2
Antas de Ulla 150 B2
Antegnate 106 A3
Anten 45 C3
Antequera 172 B2
Anterselva/Antholz 107 C/D1
Antey-Saint-André 105 C3
Anthée 79 C2
Anthéor-Cap-Roux 112 B3
Anthering 93 B/C3
Anthótopos 147 C1
Antibes 112 B3
Antícoli Corrado 118 B2
Antignac 102 A/B3
Antignano 114 A3, 116 A2
Antigonea 142 A2
Antigüedad 152 B3
Antillo 125 D2
Antillón 155 B/C3
Antipatra 142 A2
Antnäs 17 C3
Antoing 78 A/B2
Antoñana 153 D2
Antraigues-sur-Volane 111 C1
Antrain 85 D2
Antrefftal 81 C2
Antrim 54 A3, 55 D2
Antrodoco 117 D3, 118 B1
Antronapiana 105 C2
Anttila 6 B3
Anttila 26 B2
Anttola 27 C/D1

Antwerpen 78 B1
Antzuola 153 D1
Anundshogen 40 A3, 47 B/C1
Anutkaski 16 B2
Anversa degli Abruzzi 119 C2
Anvin 77 D2
Anya 155 D3
Anzano di Púglia 120 A2
Anzasco 105 C3
Anzat-le-Luguet 102 B3
Anzi 120 B2/3
Anzin 78 A/B2
Anzing 92 A2
Ánzio 118 B2
Anzola dell'Emília 114 B1
Aoiz 155 C2
Aosta 104 B3
Aoste 103 D3, 104 A3
Aouste-sur-Sye 111 C/D1
Aovaniemi 12 A/B3
Apahida 97 D3, 140 B1
Apaj 129 C1
Apátfalva 129 D2
Apatin 129 C3
Apatóac 127 D2
Apchon 102 B3
Ape 74 A2
Apécchio 115 C3, 117 C2
Apeldoorn 67 B/C3
Apelern 68 B3
Apen 67 D1
Apenburg 69 C2
Apensen 68 B1
A Peroxa 150 B2
Apfelstädt 81 D2, 82 A2
Aphaia 147 D2/3
Ápice 119 D3, 120 A2
Apiés 154 B2
Apiro 115 D3, 117 D2
Apolda 82 A1/2
Apollonía 144 A2
Apollonía 149 C3
Apolonia 142 A1/2
A Pontenova 151 C1
A Porqueira 150 B3
Äppelbo 39 C2
Appelscha 67 C2
Appen 52 B3, 68 B1
Appenweier 90 B2
Appenzell 91 C3, 105 D1, 106 A1
Appiano/Eppan 107 C2
Appignano 115 D3, 117 D2
Appingedam 67 C1
Appleby 57 C/D3, 60 B1
Appledore 62 B2
Appletreewick 59 D1, 61 C2
Appoigny 88 A2/3
Aprelevka 75 D3
Apremont-la-Forêt 89 C1
Aprica 106 B2
Apricena 120 A1
Aprília 118 B2
Ápsalos 143 C1
Apt 111 D2
Aquiléia 126 A3
Aquilónia 120 A2
Aquilué 154 B2
Aquino 119 C2
Ar 47 D2
Arabba 107 C2
Aracena 165 D3, 171 C1
Arachnéon 147 C3
Aráchova 146 B1
Aráchova 147 C2
Aračinovo 138 B2
Arad 97 C3, 140 A1
Arådalens fjällstation 34 B2
Aragona 124 B2/3
Aragoncillo 161 D2
Aragózena 146 B2
Aragúas del Solano 154 B2
Aragüés del Puerto 154 B2
Åraksbø 43 B/C2
Aram 36 A1
Aramaio 153 D1/2
Aramiñon 153 C2
Aramits 108 B3, 154 B1
Aramon 111 C2
Arana-San Bixenti 156 A/B1
Aranaz 108 A3, 154 A1
Arancón 153 D3, 161 D1

Aranda de Duero 153 C3, 161 B/C1
Aranda de Moncayo 154 A3, 162 A1
Arandelovac 133 D2, 134 A/B2
Arandelovac 140 A2
Arándiga 154 A3, 162 A1
Arandilla 153 C3, 161 C1
Aranga 150 B1
Aranjuez 161 C3
Arañuel 162 B3
Aranzueque 161 C2
Arapei 149 D2
Aras 153 D2
Aras de Alpuente 163 C3, 169 D1
Arasluoktastugan 9 C3
Áratos 145 D1
Arauzo de Miel 153 C3, 161 C1
Aravaca 160 B2
Aravissós 143 D1
Arazede 158 A3
Arbancón 161 C2
Arbas 109 C3, 155 D1
Arbatax 123 D2
Arbeca 155 D3, 163 D1
Arbesbach 93 D2
Arbesbach 96 A2
Arbeteta 161 D2
Arbneš 137 D2
Arbo 150 B3
Arboga 46 B1
Arbois 104 A1
Arboleas 174 A1/2
Arbon 91 C3
Arborea 123 C2/3
Arbório 105 C3
Årbostad 9 D1
Årbotten 38 B3
Arbrå 40 A1
Arbroath 57 C1
Arbroath 54 B2
Arbúcies 156 B2/3
Árbus 123 C3
Árbyn 17 C2
Arcachon 108 B1
Arčar 135 D3
Arčar 140 B2
Arcas 161 D3
Arce 155 C2
Arce 119 C2
Arcen 79 D1
Arc-en-Barrois 88 B2
Arces 88 A2
Arc-et-Senans 104 A1
Arcévia 115 D3, 117 C2
Archángelos 139 C3, 143 D1
Archángelos 146 A1
Archánion 146 B1
Archena 169 D3
Arches 89 D2
Archiac 101 C3
Archidona 172 B2
Archivel 168 B3, 174 A1
Arcicóllar 160 B3
Arcidosso 116 B3
Arcille 116 B3
Arcis-sur-Aube 88 A/B2
Arciz 141 D1
Arco 106 B2/3
Arçon 104 A/B1
Arconada 152 B2
Arcos 153 B/C2/3
Arcos de Jalón 161 D1
Arcos de la Frontera 171 D2
Arcos de la Sierra 161 D2/3
Arcos de las Salinas 162 A/B3
Arcos de Valdevez 150 A3, 158 A1
Arc-sur-Tille 89 B/C3
Arcusa 155 C2
Arcy-sur-Cure 88 A3
Årdal 42 A2
Árdala 47 C1/2
Árdales 172 A2
Årdalstangen 37 C2
Árdara 123 C1/2
Ardaúli 123 C2
Ardbeg 56 A2
Ardea 118 B2
Ardee 58 A1
Ardee 54 A3, 55 D2
Arden 48 B2

Ardenicës 142 A1
Ardentes 102 A1
Ardes-sur-Couze 102 B3
Ardez 106 B1
Ardgay 54 A/B2
Ardglass 58 A1
Ardino 140 B3
Ardlussa 56 A1
Ardlussa 54 A2, 55 D1
Ardminish 56 A2
Ardón 151 D2, 152 A2
Ardon 104 A1
Ardore 122 A3
Ardre 47 D3
Ardres 77 D1
Ardrishaig 56 A1
Arduaine 56 A1
Ardvasar 54 A2, 55 D1
Åre 29 C3, 34 A1/2
Areatza 153 C/D1
Areias 158 A3, 164 B1
Aremark 45 B/C1
Arén 155 C2
Arena 122 A2/3
Arenal d'en Castel 157 C1
Arenales del Sol 169 D3
Arenas 172 B2
Arenas de Iguña 152 B1
Arenas del Rey 173 B/C2
Arenas de San Juan 167 D2
Arenas de San Pedro 160 A3
Arendal 43 C3
Arendonk 79 C1
Arendsee 69 C2
Arengosse 108 A/B2
Arenillas 161 C1
Areños 152 B1/2
Aréns de Lledó 163 C2
Arenshausen 81 C/D1
Arenys de Mar 156 B3
Arenys de Munt 156 B3
Arenzano 113 C/D2
Ares 150 B1
Arès 108 B1
Ares del Maestre 163 B/C2
Aresing 92 A2
Arespalditza 153 C1
Äresvik 32 B2
Areta 153 C1
Aréthousa 144 A/B1/2
Aretí 146 A2
Arette 108 B3, 154 B1
Aretxabaleta 153 D1/2
Areu 155 C2
Arevalillo 159 D2, 160 A2
Arévalo 160 A2
Arevattnet 14 B3
Arez 165 B/C1
Arezzo 115 C3, 116 B2
Arfará 146 B3
Arfeuilles 103 C2
Arfons 110 A3
Argalastí 144 A3, 147 C1
Argallón 166 A/B3
Argamasilla de Alba 167 D2, 168 A2
Argamasilla de Calatrava 167 C2
Arganda 161 C3
Arganil 158 B3
Arganil 158 B3, 164 B1
Argantzun 153 C/D2
Arganza 151 C2
Årgård 28 B2
Argásion 146 A2/3
Argecilla 161 C2
Argegno 105 D2/3, 106 A2
Argelaguer 156 B2
Argelès-Gazost 108 B3, 155 C1
Argelès-sur-Mer 156 B2
Argelita 162 B3
Argenbühl-Eglofs 91 C3
Argenschwang 80 A/B3
Argenta 115 C1
Argentan 86 A/B1
Argentat 102 A3, 109 D1
Argente 163 C2
Argentella 113 D2/3
Argentera 112 B2
Argenthal 80 A3
Argentière 104 B2
Argentière-la-Bessée 112 A1
Argentona 156 A/B3

Argenton-Château 100 B1
Argenton-sur-Creuse 101 D1/2
Argentré 86 A2
Argentré-du-Plessis 86 A2
Argent-sur-Sauldre 87 D3
Argeriz 151 B/C3, 158 B1
Argés 160 B3, 167 C1
Argetoaia 135 D2
Argirádes 142 A3
Argiropoúlion 143 D3
Argomariz 153 D2
Árgos 147 C3
Árgos 148 B2
Árgos Orestikón 143 C2
Argostólion 148 A2
Arguedas 154 A2/3
Arguis 154 B2
Argujillo 159 D1
Argy 101 D1
Arhipovka 75 C3
Århus 48 B3
Ariano Ferrarese 115 C1
Ariano Irpino 119 D3, 120 A2
Ariano nel Polésine 115 C1
Arienzo 119 D3
Arild 49 D2, 50 A2
Arilje 133 D3, 134 A3
Arinagour 54 A2, 55 D1
Åringen 14 A2
Aríñiz 153 D2
Ariño 162 B2
Arinthod 103 D2, 104 A2
Arisgotas 160 B3, 167 C1
Arísti 142 B2/3
Aritzo 123 D2
Arive 108 B3, 155 C1/2
Ariz 158 B2
Ariza 161 D1
Årjäng 45 C1
Arjeplog 15 D2
Arjona 167 C3, 172 B1
Arjonilla 167 C3, 172 B1
Arkala 18 B2
Arkelstorp 50 B2
Arkítsa 147 C2
Arkkukari 18 A3
Arklow 58 A3
Arklow 55 D3
Arkösund 47 C2
Årla 46 B1
Årla 47 B/C1
Arlanc 103 C3
Arlanda 40 B3, 47 C1
Arlanzón 153 C2
Arlempdes 110 B1
Arles 111 C2/3
Arles 156 B2
Arleuf 103 C1
Arlon 79 D3
Armação de Pera 170 A2
Armadale 57 B/C2
Arma di Tággia 113 C2
Armagh 54 A3, 55 D2
Armallones 161 D2
Armamar 158 B2
Armasjärvi 17 D2
Arménion 143 D3
Armeno 105 C/D3
Armenteros 159 D2, 160 A2
Armentières 78 A2
Armilla 173 C2
Armintza 153 C1
Armo 122 A3, 125 D2
Armutlu 149 D1
Arnáccio 114 A/B3, 116 A2
Arnac-Pompadour 101 C3
Arnafjord 36 B2/3
Arnage 86 B2/3
Arnager 51 D3
Årnäs 45 D2
Arnäsvall 31 C3
Arnaville 89 C1
Arnavutköy 145 D1/2
Arnay-le-Duc 103 C1
Arnbach 107 D1
Arnberg 31 C1
Arnborg 48 A/B3
Arnbruck 93 B/C1
Arnéa 144 A/B2
Arneberg 38 B2
Arneburg 69 D2
Arnedillo 153 D2/3
Arnedo 153 D2/3

Arnéguy 108 B3, 155 C1
Årnes 28 A2, 33 C1
Arnes 163 C2
Årnes 38 B2/3
Årnes 38 A3
Arnfels 127 C2
Arnhem 66 B3
Árnissa 143 C1
Arnö 47 C1
Arnoga 106 B2
Arnoia 150 B2/3
Arnön 40 B1
Arnoyhamn 4 B2
Arnsberg 80 B1
Arnsberg-Neheim-Hüsten 80 B1
Arnschwang 92 B1
Arnsdorf 83 C1
Arnside 59 D1, 60 B2
Arnstadt 81 D2, 82 A2
Arnstein 81 D3
Arnstorf 92 B2
Arnuero 153 C1
Arnum 52 A/B1
Aroanía 146 B2
Aroche 165 C3, 171 C1
Arões 158 A2
Aroffe 89 C2
Arola 7 C2
Arolla [Sion] 105 C2
Arolsen 81 C1
Arolsen-Mengeringhausen 81 C1
Aron 86 A2
Arona 105 D3
Aronkylä 20 B3
Åros 38 A3, 43 D1, 44 B1
Arosa 106 A1
Årosjåkk 10 A3
Ærøskøbing 53 C2
Årøsund 52 B1
Arouca 158 A2
Årøybukt 4 B3
Åroysund 43 D2, 44 A/B1
Arpáia 119 D3
Arpajon 87 C/D2
Arpajon-sur-Cère 110 A1
Árpás 95 C3
Arpela 17 D2, 18 A1
Arpino 119 C2
Arquà Petrarca 107 C3
Arquata del Tronto 117 D3, 119 B/C1
Arquata Scrívia 113 D1
Arques 77 D1
Arques 110 A3, 156 A/B1
Arques-la-Bataille 76 B2/3
Arquillos 167 D3
Arrabal 158 A3, 164 A/B1
Arrabal del Portillo 160 B1
Arracourt 89 D1/2
Arraiolos 164 B2
Arraiz 108 A3, 154 A1
Arrakoski 25 D1, 26 A1
Arrankorpi 25 C/D2, 26 A2
Arras 78 A2
Arrasate 153 D1
Arraute-Charrite 108 A3, 154 B1
Arrázola 153 D1
Årre 48 A3, 52 A1
Arreau 109 C3, 155 C2
Arredondo 153 C1
Årrenjarka 15 D1
Arrens 108 B3, 154 B1/2
Arrentela 164 A2
Arriate 172 A2
Arrie 50 A3
Arrifana 158 A2
Arrigorriaga 153 C1
Arrild 52 A/B1/2
Arriondas 152 A1
Arro 155 C2
Arroba 167 C2
Arrochar 56 B1
Arromanches-les-Bains 76 B3, 86 A1
Arronches 165 C2
Arróniz 153 D2
Arròs 155 C2
Arroyo de Cuéllar 160 B1
Arroyo de la Luz 165 D1
Arroyo de San Serván 165 D2
Arroyomolinos de Montánchez 165 D2, 166 A2
Arroyomolinos de León 165 D3, 171 C1
Arruda dos Vinhos 164 A2
Års 48 B2
Årsandøy 28 B1
Årsdale 51 D3
Ars-en-Ré 100 A2
Arsiè 107 C2
Arsiero 107 C3
Årslev 53 C1
Arsoli 118 B2
Ars-sur-Formans 103 D2
Ars-sur-Mozelle 89 C1
Årsta havsbad 47 C/D1
Årstein 9 D2
Årsunda 40 A2
Arsuni 123 C/D2
Arsy 78 A3
Árta 146 A1
Artá 157 C1
Árta 148 A1/2
Artajona 154 A2
Artana 162 B3, 169 D1
Arta Terme 107 D2, 126 A2
Artazu 154 A2
Arteaga 153 C/D1
Arteaga 153 D1
Artedó 155 D2, 156 A2
Artegna 126 A2
Arteixo 150 A1
Artemare 104 A2/3
Artemisía 146 B3
Artemísion 147 C1
Arten 107 C2
Artena 118 B2
Artenay 87 C2
Artern 82 A1
Artés 156 A2/3
Artesa de Segre 155 D3
Arthez-d'Asson 108 B3, 154 B1
Arthez de-Béarn 108 B3, 154 B1
Arthon-en-Retz 85 C/D3, 100 A1
Arthonnay 88 B2/3
Articuza 154 A1
Arties 155 C/D2
Artix 108 B3, 154 B1
Artjärvi (Artsjö) 25 D2, 26 A/B2
Artlenburg 69 B/C1
Artotína 146 B1
Artsjö 25 D2, 26 A/B2
Artziniega 153 C1
A Rúa 151 C2
Arundel 76 B1
Arundel Castle 76 B1
Årup 52 B1
Aruskila 23 C2/3
Årvåg 32 B1/2
Arvaja 25 D1, 26 A1
Arvet 39 D1/2
Arveyres 108 B1
Arvidsjaur 16 A3
Arvidsträsk 16 B3
Årvik 36 A1
Årvik 42 A1
Arvika 38 B3, 45 C1
Årviksand 4 B2
Årvikstrand 42 A1
Åryd 51 C1/2
Arzachena 123 D1
Arzacq-Arraziguet 108 B3, 154 B1
Arzano 84 B2/3
Arżano 131 D3, 132 A3
Arzbach 80 B2
Arzberg 82 B3
Arzberg 83 C1
Arzignano 107 C3
Arzon 85 C3
Arzúa 150 B2
Ås 46 A1
Aš 82 B2/3
Ås 29 D3, 34 B2
Ås 33 D2
As 79 C1
Ås 38 B3
Åsa 49 D1, 50 A1
Asa 45 D3
Aså 49 C1
Asamati 142 B1
Åsan 28 B2
Åsäng 35 D2/3
Ašanja 133 D1, 134 A1
Åsarna 34 B2/3
Åsarp 45 D3
Asarum (Karlshamn) 51 C2
Asarum (Karlshamn) 72 A1
Asasp 108 B3, 154 B1
Asbach 80 A2
Åsberget 35 C2
Åsbro 46 A1/2
Asby 46 A3
Ascain 108 A3, 154 A1
Ascha 92 B1
Aschach an der Donau 93 C2
Aschaffenburg 81 C3
Aschau 92 B3
Aschau bei Kraiburg 92 B2
Aschau im Chiemgau 92 B3
Aschau-Sachrang 92 B3
Aschbach Markt 93 D2/3
Ascheberg 67 D3
Ascheberg (Holstein) 53 B/C3
Aschersleben 69 C3
Asciano 115 C3, 116 B2
Asco 113 D2/3
Ascó 163 C1/2
Áscoli Piceno 117 D3
Áscoli Satriano 120 A2
Ascona [Locarno] 105 D2
Ascot 64 B3
Ascoux 87 D2
Ascq 78 A2
Åse 9 C1
Aséa 146 B3
Åseda 51 C1
Åseda 72 B1
Åsele 30 B2
Åselet 16 B3
Asemakylä 18 A2
Asemakylä 18 A/B2
Asemanseutu 21 C3
Åsen 39 C1
Åsen 35 C2
Åsen 9 C/D2
Åsen 28 B3, 33 D1
Åsen 39 C1
Åsen 29 D3, 34 B2
Asendorf (Hoya) 68 A2
Åsenhöga 50 B1
Asenovgrad 140 B3
Åsensbruk 45 C2
Asentopalo 12 B2
Åsenvoll 33 D2/3
Åseral 42 B3
Åserud 38 B3
Asfáka 142 B3
Asfeld 78 B3
Åsgård 33 C3, 37 D1
Åsgårdstrand 43 D2, 44 B1
Åshammar 40 A2
Ashbourne 61 C3, 64 A1
Ashbourne 58 A2
Ashburton 63 C3
Ashby de la Zouch 64 A1
Ashford 65 C3, 77 C1
Ashfordby 64 B1
Ashington 57 D2/3
Ashington 54 B3
Ashkirk 57 C2
Ashton-under-Lyne 59 D2, 60 B3
Asiago 107 C2/3
Asige 49 D2, 50 A1
Asikkala 25 D1/2, 26 A1/2
Asín 154 B2
Asinhal 170 B1
Asíni 147 C3
Ask 50 A/B3
Ask 38 A3
Aska 12 B2
Askainen 24 A2
Askanmäki 19 C2
Askeby 46 B2
Asker 38 A3, 43 D1
Askersund 46 A2
Askesta 40 A/B1
Åskhult 49 D1, 50 A1
Askim 38 A3, 44 B1
Askim (Göteborg) 45 C3, 49 D1
Åskloster 49 D1, 50 A1
Askøby 53 C/D2
Åskogen 17 C2
Askola 25 D2, 26 A2
Asköping 46 B1
Askós 144 A1/2
Askov 48 A/B3, 52 B1
Askøy 36 A3
Askra 147 C2
Askrigg 59 D1, 60 B2
Askvik 42 A2
Askvoll 36 A2
Aslaksrud 43 D1
Aslestad 43 C2
Åsli 37 D3
Åsljunga 50 B2
Åsmark 38 A2
Asmunti 18 B1
Åsnes 38 B2
As Neves 150 A/B3
As Nogais 151 C2
Asnæs 49 C3, 53 C/D1
Asola 106 B3
Ásolo 107 C3
Asón 153 C1
Asopía 147 D2
Ásotthalom 129 D2
Aspa 32 B2
Aspach 91 C1
Aspang Markt 94 A3
Aspariegos 151 D3, 152 A3, 159 D1
Asparn an der Zaya 94 B2
Aspås 29 D3, 34 B2
Aspatria 57 C3, 60 A1
Aspberg 45 D1
Aspe 167 C3
Åspeå 30 B3, 35 D1/2
Aspeboda 39 D2
Aspenes 29 C2
Asperg 91 C1/2
Asperget 38 B2
Asperup 48 B3, 52 B1
Aspet 109 C3, 155 C/D1
Aspli 32 B2
Asplia 28 A2/3, 33 C1
Aspliden 17 B/C2
Aspnäs 35 D2
Aspö 47 C1
Aspö 24 A3
As Pontes de García Rodríguez 150 B1
Aspremont 111 D1
Aspres-sur-Buëch 111 D1, 112 A1/2
Asprochoma 146 B3
Asprogérakas 146 A2
Asprókambos 147 C2
Aspròpirgos 147 D2
Asproválta 144 B1/2
Apsele 30 B2
Assago 105 D3, 106 A3
Assamstadt 91 C1
Asse 78 B1/2
Assebakte 5 D3, 6 A3, 11 D1
Asseiceira 164 B1
Assels 48 A2
Assémini 123 C/D3
Assen 67 C2
Assens 48 B2
Assens 52 B1
Assergi 117 D3, 119 C1
Asseria 131 C2
Assesse 79 C2
Ássiros 143 D1, 144 A1
Assisi 115 D3, 117 C2
Åsskard 32 B2
Asslar 80 B2
Assling 92 B3
Asson 108 B3, 154 B1
Assoro 125 C2
Assumar 165 C2
Astaffort 109 C2
Astakós 146 A1/2
Astakós 148 A2
Åstan 28 A3, 33 C1
Åstdalseter 38 A1
Asteasu 153 D1
Asten 79 C/D1
Åsten 93 D2
Asti 113 C1
Astillero 153 B/C1
Astipálea 149 C3
Aston 59 D2, 60 B3
Astorga 151 D2
Åstorp 49 D3, 50 A2
Åstorp 72 A1
Åstrand 39 C3
Åsträsk 31 C1
Ástros 147 C3
Astudillo 152 B3
Asunta 21 C/D3
Asvestópetra 143 C2
Aszófő 128 B1
Atalaia 164 B1
Atalántí 147 C1
Atalántí 148 B2
Atalaya 165 D3
Atalaya de Cañavate 168 B1
Atalho 164 B2
Atapuerca 153 C2
Ataquines 160 A1
Atarfe 173 C2
Ataun 153 D1/2
Atauta 153 C3, 161 C1
Atea 162 A1/2
Ateca 162 A1
Atei 158 B1
A Teixeira 150 B2
Ateleta 119 C/D2
Atella 120 A/B2
Átena Lucana 120 A3
Atessa 119 D1/2
Ath 78 B2
Atherstone 64 A2
Athíkia 147 C2/3
Athína/Athínai 147 D2
Athína/Athínai 148 B2
Athis-Mons 87 D1/2
Athlone 55 C2
Áthos 144 B2
Athy 55 D3
Atienza 161 C1
Atina 119 C2
Atnbrua 33 C3, 37 D1
Åtniksstugan 14 B3, 29 D1
Atnosen 38 A1
Atostugan 14 B3
Atouguia da Baleia 164 A1
A Toxa 150 A2
Ätrafors 49 D1, 50 A1
Ätran 49 D1, 50 A1
Åträsk 16 B3
Åträsk 31 C/D1/2
Atrå (Tinn) 43 C1
Atri 119 C1
Atripalda 119 D3, 120 A2
Attendorn 80 B1
Attenkirchen 92 A2
Attersee 93 C3
Attersee 96 A3
Attichy 78 A3
Attigliano 117 C3, 118 A/B1
Attigny 79 B/C3
Attleborough 65 C/D2
Attmar 35 D3
Åttonträsk 30 B1
Attre 78 B2
Attu 24 B3
Åtvidaberg 46 B2/3
Atzara 123 D2
Atzendorf 69 C/D3
Au 106 A/B1
Aub 81 D3, 91 C/D1
Aubagnan 108 B2/3
Aubagne 111 D3
Aubange 79 D3
Au bei Bad Aibling 92 A/B3
Aubel 79 D2
Aubenas 111 C1
Aubenton 78 B3
Auberive 88 B3
Auberives-sur-Varèze 103 D3
Auberson, L' [Ste-Croix] 104 B1
Aubeterre-sur-Dronne 101 C3
Aubiet 109 C2/3, 155 C/D1
Aubigny 100 A/B1/2
Aubigny-au-Bac 78 A2
Aubigny-en-Artois 78 A2
Aubigny-sur-Nère 87 D3
Aubin 110 A1
Auboue 89 C1
Aubrac 110 A/B1
Aubusson 102 A2
Auce 73 D1
Auch 109 C2/3, 155 C1
Auchmithie 57 C1
Auchterarder 57 B/C1
Auchtermuchty 57 C1
Auchy-au-Bois 77 D2, 78 A2
Audenge 108 A1
Audenhain 82 B1
Audeux 89 C3, 104 A1
Audierne 84 A2

Audincourt 89 D3, 90 A3
Audlem 59 D2, 60 B3, 64 A1
Audnedal 42 B3
Audresselles 77 D1
Audruicq 77 D1
Audun-le-Roman 89 C1
Aue 82 B2
Auenheim 90 B2
Auerbach 82 A3
Auerbach 82 B2
Auerbach-Michelfeld 82 A3
Auffach 92 B3
Aufsess 82 A3
Aughrim 58 A3
Augsburg 91 D2
Augsburg-Göggingen 91 D2
Augsburg-Haunstetten 91 D2, 92 A2
Augusta 125 D3
Augustdorf 68 A3
Augustenborg 52 B2
Augustów 73 D2/3
Auho 19 C2
Aukra 32 A2
Aukrug 52 B3
Auktsjaur 16 A3
Aulanko 25 C2
Aulendorf 91 C3
Auletta 120 A2/3
Aulis 147 D2
Aulla 114 A2
Aullène 113 D3
Aulnay 101 B/C2
Aulnoye-Aymeries 78 B2
Ault 77 D2
Aultbea 54 A2
Aulus-les-Bains 155 C2
Auma 82 A/B2
Aumale 77 D3
Aumetz 79 D3
Aumont-Aubrac 110 B1
Aunay-en-Bazois 103 C1
Aunay-sur-Odon 86 A1
Aune 28 A/B2
Auneau 87 C2
Auneuil 77 D3, 87 C1
Auning 49 C2
Aups 112 A3
Aura 24 B2
Aura im Sinngrund 81 C2/3
Auran 28 A/B3, 33 C1
Auran asema 24 B2
Auray 85 B/C3
Aure 32 B2
Aurejärvi 21 B/C3
Auriac-sur-Vendinelle 109 D3
Auribeau-sur-Siagne 112 B3
Aurich 67 D1
Aurich-Tannenhausen 67 D1
Aurignac 109 C3, 155 D1
Aurillac 110 A1
Aurland 36 B3
Aurolzmünster 93 C2
Auron 112 B2
Auronzo di Cadore 107 D2
Auros 108 B1
Auroux 110 B1
Aursfjordbotn 4 A3, 9 D1
Aursjøhytta 32 B3, 37 C1
Aurskog 38 A3
Aursmoen 38 A1/2
Aursnes 32 A3, 36 B1
Ausa-Corno 126 A3
Ausejo 153 D2
Ausónia 119 C2
Austad 42 B2
Austafjord 28 B1
Austefjord 32 A3, 36 B1
Austertana (Leirpollen) 7 C1
Austevoll 42 A1
Aústis 123 D2
Austmarka 38 B3
Austnes 32 A2
Austråt 28 A3, 33 C1
Austrumdal 42 A/B2/3
Auterive 109 D3, 155 D1
Autheuil 86 A/B1
Authon 86 B3
Authon 112 A2
Authon-du-Perche 86 B2
Authon-la-Plaine 87 C2
Autio 18 B2/3
Autio 17 C1
Autol 153 D2/3, 154 A2
Autrèche 86 B3
Autreville 89 C2
Autrey-lès-Gray 89 C3
Autricourt 88 B2
Autry-le Châtel 87 D3
Autti 12 B3
Auttoinen 25 D1, 26 A1
Autun 103 C1
Auve 88 B1
Auvers 110 B1
Auvila 27 C1
Auvillars 109 C2
Auxerre 88 A3
Auxey-Duresses 103 D1
Auxi-le-Château 77 D2
Auxon 88 A2
Auxonne 89 C3, 103 D1, 104 A1
Auzances 102 A/B2
Auzat 155 D2
Auzon 102 B3
Åva 24 A2/3, 41 D2
Ava 31 C3
Avaborg 31 D1
Avafors 17 C2
Avaheden 17 B/C2/3
Availles-Limouzine 101 C/D2
Avala 133 D1, 134 A1/2
Avaldsnes 42 A2
Avallon 88 A3
Avan 17 C3
Avanca 158 A2
Åvas 145 D1, 145 D3
Avasjö 30 A/B2
Avaträsk 30 A1/2
Avaviken 16 A3
Avdejevka 99 D1/2
Ávdira 149 C1
Ávdira 145 C1
Avebury Circle 63 D2, 64 A3
A Veiga 151 C2/3
Aveinte 160 A2
Aveiras de Cima 164 A2
Aveiro 158 A2
Avelãs do Caminho 158 A2
Avelengo/Hafling 107 C2
Avelgem 78 A/B2
Avellaneda 153 D3
Avellino 119 D3
Aven Armand 110 B2
Avenches 104 B1
Aven de Marzal 111 C2
Aven d'Orgnac 111 C2
Avène 110 B2
Averbode 79 C1
Avernak By 53 B/C2
Aversa 119 C/D3
Avesnes-le-Comte 78 A2
Avesnes-sur-Helpe 78 B2/3
Avesta 40 A3
Avetrana 121 D3
Avezzano 119 C2
Aviano 107 D2
Avidagos 158 B1
Avigliana 112 B1
Avigliano 120 A/B2
Avignon 111 C2
Avignonet-Lauragais 109 D3, 156 A1
Åvikebruk 35 D3
Ávila 160 A2
Avilés 151 D1
Avilley 89 C/D3
Avintes 158 A2
Avinyó 156 A2
Ávio 106 B3
Avión 150 B2
Avioth 79 C3
Åvist 20 B2
Aviz 164 B2
Avize 88 A1
Avliótai 142 A3
Avlón 147 D2
Avlonárion 147 D2
Avlum 48 A2
Avô 158 B3
Avoca 58 A3
Avoine 86 B3, 101 C1
Ávola 125 D3
Avonmouth 63 D1/2
Avord 102 B1
Avoriaz 104 B2
Avoudrey 104 B1
Avradsberg 39 C2
Avranches 86 A/B1/2
Avren 145 D1
Avricourt 89 D2, 90 A2
Avrillé 100 A2
Avrillé 86 A3
Avtovac 132 B3, 137 C1
Avžže 11 C1
Axat 156 A1
Axbridge 63 D2
Axel 78 B1
Äxelfors 50 A/B1
Axelsvik 17 C/D3
Axiat 155 D2, 156 A1
Axioúpolis 143 D1
Ax-les-Thermes 156 A1
Axmarby 40 A/B2
Axmarsbruk 40 A/B1/2
Axminster 63 C/D2
Axvall 45 D2
Ayamonte 170 B2
Aycliffe 57 D3, 61 C1
Aydin 149 D2
Aydius 108 B3, 154 B1
Ayegui 153 D2, 154 A2
Ayelo de Malferit 169 C/D2
Ayen 101 C3
Ayerbe 154 B2
Ayer [Sierre] 105 C2
Ayguafreda 156 A3
Aylesbury 64 B2/3
Ayllón 161 C1
Aylsham 61 D3, 65 C1
Ayna 168 B2
Aynac 109 D1
Aynho 65 C2
Ayódar 162 B3
Ayora 169 C2
Ayr 56 B2
Ayr 54 A/B3, 55 D1/2
Äyrinmäki 18 A3
Ayron 101 C1
Äyskoski 22 B2
Ay-sur-Moselle 89 C1
Ayton 57 D2
Aytré 100 B2
Ayvacik 149 C1
Ayvalik 149 D1/2
Aywaille 79 C2
Azagra 153 D2, 154 A2
Azaila 162 B1
Azambuja 164 A2
Azambujeira 164 A1/2
Azanja 134 B2
Azannes-et-Soumazannes 89 C1
Azañón 161 D2
Azanúy 155 C3
Azaruja 165 B/C2
Azay-le-Ferron 101 D1
Azay-le-Rideau 86 B3, 101 C1
Azay-sur-Cher 86 B3
Azenhas do Mar 164 A2
Azevo 159 C2
Azinhaga 164 B1
Azinhal 170 B2
Azinheira dos Barros 164 B3
Azkoitia 153 D1
Aznalcázar 171 D2
Aznalcóllar 171 D1
Azóia 158 A3, 164 A1
Azpeitia 153 D1
Azuaga 166 A3
Azuara 162 B1
Azuébar 162 B3, 169 D1
Azuqueca de Henares 161 C2
Azur 108 B2
Azurara 158 A1
Azután 160 A3, 166 B1
Azzano Dézimo 107 D2/3, 126 A2/3

B

Baad 106 B1
Baamonde 150 B1
Baar 105 C/D1
Baarle-Hertog 79 C1
Baarn 66 B3
Babadag 141 D2
Babaevo 75 D1
Babenhausen 81 C3
Babenhausen 91 D2
Babigoszcz 70 B1
Babilafuente 159 D2, 160 A2
Babimost 71 C3
Babina Greda 132 B1
Babin Most 138 B1
Babino Polje 136 B1
Babin Potok 131 B/C1
Babke 70 A1
Babljak 137 D1
Babócsa 128 A2
Babušnica 139 C1
Bač 138 A1
Bač 129 C3
Bacáicoa 153 D2
Bacarés 173 D2
Bacău 141 C1
Baccarat 89 D2
Baceno 105 C2
Bach 109 D2
Bacharach 80 B3
Bačina 134 B3
Bäckan 35 C3
Bačka Palanka 129 C3, 133 C1
Bäckarna 34 B3
Backaryd 51 C2
Bäckaskog 50 B2
Bačka Topola 129 C3
Bačka Topola 140 A1
Backe 30 A2, 35 C1
Bäckebo 51 D1
Båckefors 45 C2
Backgränd 25 C3
Bäckhammar 45 D1, 46 A1
Bački Breg 129 C3
Bački Brestovac 129 C3
Bački Jarak 129 D3, 134 A1
Bački Monoštor 129 C3
Bački Petrovac 129 C3
Backnang 91 C1
Bäcknäs 16 A3
Bačko Gradište 129 D3
Bačko Novo Selo 129 C3, 133 C1
Bačko Petrovo Selo 129 D3
Bacoli 119 C3
Bacqueville-en-Caux 77 C3
Bácsalmás 129 C2
Bácsbokod 129 C2
Bacup 59 D1/2, 60 B2
Bačvani 131 D1
Baczyna 71 C2
Bada 39 B/C3
Bad Abbach 92 B1
Badacsonytomaj 128 A1
Bad Aibling 92 B3
Badajoz 165 C2
Badalona 156 A3
Badalucco 113 C2
Badarán 153 C/D2
Bad Aussee 93 C3
Bad Bentheim 67 C/D2/3
Badbergen 67 D2
Bad Bergzabern 90 B1
Bad Berka 82 A2
Bad Berleburg 80 B1/2
Bad Berleburg-Raumland 80 B1/2
Bad Berleburg-Aue 80 B1/2
Bad Berneck 82 A3
Bad Bertrich 80 A3
Bad Bevensen 69 C2
Bad Bibra 82 A1
Bad Blankenburg 82 A2
Bad Bleiberg ob Villach 126 B2
Bad Bocklet 81 D2
Bad Brambach 82 B2
Bad Bramstedt 52 B3
Bad Breisig 80 A2
Bad Brückenau 81 C2
Bad Buchau 91 C2/3
Bad Camberg 80 B2
Badderen 5 B/C2
Bad Deutsch Altenburg 94 B2
Bad Doberan 53 D3
Bad Driburg 68 A3
Bad Driburg-Neuenheerse 68 A3, 81 C1
Bad Driburg-Dringenberg 68 A3, 81 C1
Bad Düben 82 B1
Bad Düben 72 A3
Bad Dürkheim 80 B3, 90 B1
Bad Dürrenberg 82 B1
Bad Dürrheim 90 B3
Bądecz 71 D1
Bad Eilsen 68 A3
Bad Elster 82 B2
Bad Ems 80 B2
Baden 94 B3
Baden 90 B3
Bádenas 162 A2
Baden-Baden 90 B2
Bad Endbach 80 B2
Badenweiler 90 A3
Baderna 126 B3, 130 A1
Badersleben 69 C3
Bad Essen 68 A3
Bad Feilnbach 92 B3
Bad Feilnbach-Au 92 A/B3
Bad Fischau 94 A/B3
Bad Frankenhausen 82 A1
Bad Freienwalde 70 B2
Bad Freienwalde 72 A3
Bad Friedrichshall 91 C1
Bad Füssing 93 C2
Bad Gandersheim 68 B3
Badgastein 107 D1, 126 A1
Bad Gleichenberg 127 D1
Bad Goisern 93 C3
Bad Gottleuba 83 C2
Bad Grund 68 B3
Bad Hall 93 D3
Bad Harzburg 69 C3
Bad Heilbrunn 92 A3
Bad Herrenalb 90 B2
Bad Hersfeld 81 C2
Bad Hofgastein 107 D1, 126 A1
Bad Homburg von der Höhe 80 B2/3
Bad Honnef 80 A2
Bad Hönningen 80 A2
Badia Calavena 107 C3
Badía Polésine 115 B/C1
Badia Pratáglia 115 C2, 116 B1
Badia Tedalda 115 C2/3, 117 C2
Bad Iburg 67 D3
Bad Imnau 90 B2
Bad Innerlaterns 106 A1
Bad Ischl 93 C3
Bad Ischl 96 A3
Bad Karlshafen 68 B3, 81 C1
Bad Kissingen 81 D2/3
Bad Kleinen 53 C3, 69 C1
Bad Kleinkirchheim 126 B1
Bad Klosterlausnitz 82 A/B2
Bad Kohlgrub 92 A3
Bad König 81 C3
Bad Königshofen 81 D2
Bad Kösen 82 A1
Bad Köstritz 82 B2
Bad Kreuzen 93 D2
Bad Kreuznach 80 B3
Bad Krozingen 90 A3
Bad Laasphe-Holzhausen 80 B2
Bad Laasphe 80 B2
Bad Laer 67 D3
Bad Laer-Glandorf 67 D3
Bad Langensalza 81 D1
Bad Lauchstädt 82 A/B1
Bad Lausick 82 B1
Bad Lauterberg 69 B/C3, 81 D1
Bad Lauterberg-Bartolfelde 81 D1
Bad Liebenstein 81 D2
Bad Liebenwerda 83 C1
Bad Liebenwerda 96 A1
Bad Liebenzell 90 B2
Bad Lippspringe 68 A3
Bad Marienberg 80 B2
Bad Mergentheim 81 C3, 91 C1
Bad Mergentheim-Herbsthausen 91 C1

Bad Mergentheim-Stuppach 91 C1
Bad Münder-Hachmühlen 68 B3
Bad Münder 68 B3
Bad Münder-Bakede 68 B3
Bad Münstereifel-Schönau 79 D2, 80 A2
Bad Münster-Ebernberg 80 B3
Bad Münstereifel 79 D2, 80 A2
Bad Münstereifel-Mutscheid 80 A2
Bad Muskau 83 D1
Bad Nauheim 81 B/C2
Bad Nenndorf 68 B3
Bad Neuenahr-Ahrweiler 80 A2
Bad Neuenahr-Ahrweiler-Ramersbach 80 A2
Bad Neustadt 81 D2
Bad Oeynhausen 68 A3
Badolato 122 B2/3
Badolatosa 172 B2
Bad Oldesloe 53 C3, 68 B1
Badonviller 89 D2, 90 A2
Bad Orb 81 C2/3
Bad Peterstal 90 B2
Bad Pirawarth 94 B2
Bad Pyrmont 68 A/B3
Bad Radkersburg 127 D1/2
Bad Ragaz 105 D1, 106 A1
Bad Rappenau 91 C1
Bad Reichenhall 92 B3
Bad Rippoldsau 90 B2
Bad Saarow-Pieskow 70 B3
Bad Sachsa 81 D1
Bad Säckingen 90 B3
Bad Salzdetfurth-Bodenburg 68 B3
Bad Salzdetfurth 68 B3
Bad Salzschlirf 81 C2
Bad Salzuflen 68 A3
Bad Salzungen 81 D2
Bad Sankt Leonhard im Lavanttal 127 C1
Bad Sassendorf 67 D3, 80 B1
Bad Schallerbach 93 C2
Bad Schandau 83 C2
Bad Schmiedeberg 69 D3, 70 A3, 82 B1
Bad Schönau 94 B3
Bad Schönborn-Langenbrücken 90 B1
Bad Schussenried 91 C3
Bad Schwalbach 80 B3
Bad Schwartau 53 C3
Bad Segeberg 53 B/C3
Bad Soden 80 B3
Bad Soden 81 C2
Bad Soden-Salmünster 81 C2
Bad Sooden-Allendorf 81 C/D1
Bad Steben 82 A2
Bad Sulza 82 A1
Bad Sülze 53 D3
Bad Tatzmannsdorf 94 A/B3, 127 D1
Bad Teinach-Zavelstein 90 B2
Bad Tennstedt 81 D1, 82 A1
Bad Tölz 92 A3
Bad Überkingen 91 C2
Badules 163 C1/2
Bad Urach 91 C2
Bad Vellach 126 B2
Bad Vilbel 81 B/C2/3
Bad Vöslau 94 B3
Bad Waldsee 91 C3
Bad Wiessee 92 A3
Bad Wildungen 81 C1
Bad Wilsnack 69 D2
Bad Wimpfen 91 C1
Bad Windsheim 81 D3, 91 D1
Bad Wörishofen 91 D3
Bad Wurzach-Arnach 91 C3
Bad Wurzach 91 C3
Bad Wurzach-Unterschwarzach 91 C3
Bad Zell 93 D2
Bad Zwischenahn 67 D1
Baélls 155 C3
Baena 172 B1
Baesweiler 79 D2
Baeza 167 D3, 173 C1
Båfjelldalen 14 B3
Bagà 156 A2
Bagaladi 122 A3, 125 D2
Bågede 29 D2
Bâgé-le-Châtel 103 D2
Bagenkop 53 C2
Bagergue 155 D2
Bages 156 B1/2
Baggård 31 C2
Bagheria 124 B2
Bagn 37 D3
Bagnacavallo 115 C2, 117 B/C1
Bagnac-sur-Celé 109 D1, 110 A1
Bagnáia 117 C3, 118 A1
Bagnara Cálabra 122 A3, 125 D1
Bagnasco 113 C2
Bagnères-de-Luchon 155 C2
Bagnères-de-Bigorre 109 B/C3, 155 C1
Bagni 114 A2, 116 A1
Bagni Contursi 120 A2
Bagni di Bórmio 106 B2
Bagni di Lucca 114 B2, 116 A1
Bagni di Másino 106 A2
Bagni di Petriolo 114 B3, 116 B2
Bagni di Rabbi 106 B2
Bagni di Tívoli 118 B2
Bagni di Vinádio 112 B2
Bagno a Rípoli 114 B2, 116 B1/2
Bagno di Romagna 115 C2, 116 B1
Bagnoles-de-l'Orne 86 A2
Bagnoli del Trigno 119 D2
Bagnoli di Sopra 107 C3
Bagnoli Irpino 119 D3, 120 A2
Bagnolo in Piano 114 B1
Bagnolo Mella 106 B3
Bagnolo Piemonte 112 B1
Bagnolo San Vito 114 B1
Bagnols-en-Forêt 112 A/B3
Bagnols-les-Bains 110 B1
Bagnols-sur-Cèze 111 C2
Bagnone 114 A2
Bagnorégio 117 C3, 118 A1
Bagod 128 A1
Bagolino 106 B3
Bagrdan 134 B2
Bagshot 64 B3, 76 B1
Báguena 163 C2
Bagüés 154 B2
Bahabón de Esgueva 153 C3
Bahillo 152 B2
Bahmač 99 D2
Bahrendorf 69 C3
Baia 119 C3
Baia de Aramă 135 D1
Baia de Aramă 140 B2
Báia delle Zágare 120 B1, 136 A3
Baia Domízia 119 C3
Baia Mare 97 D3, 98 A3
Baiano 119 D3
Baião 158 B1/2
Baiardo 113 B/C2
Baia Sardinia 123 D1
Baienfurt 91 C3
Baierbach 92 B2
Baiersbronn-Klosterreichenbach 90 B2
Baiersbronn 90 B2
Baignes-Sainte-Radegonde 101 C3
Baigneux-les-Juifs 88 B3
Băile Herculane 135 C1
Băile Herculane 140 A/B2
Bailén 167 C3
Băile Olănești 140 B2
Băilești 140 B2
Băilești 135 D2
Bailleau-le-Pin 86 A/B2
Bailleul 77 C3
Bailleul 78 A2
Bailo 154 B2
Bain-de-Bretagne 85 D2/3
Bains 110 B1
Bains de Préchacq 108 A2
Bains d'Escouloubre 156 A1
Bains-d'Huchet 108 B2
Bains-les-Bains 89 C/D2
Baio 150 A1
Baiona 150 A3
Bais 86 A2
Baisieux 78 A2
Baiso 114 B1/2
Baixas 156 B1
Baja 129 C2
Baja 96 B3
Bajánsenye 96 A/B3
Bajánsenye 127 D1
Bajgora 138 B1
Bajina Bašta 133 C2
Bajinci 131 D1, 132 A1
Bajmok 129 C2/3
Bajna 95 D3
Bajovo Polje 137 C1
Bajram Curri 138 A2
Bajram Curri 140 A3
Bajša 129 C3
Bajzë 137 D2
Bak 128 A1/2
Bak 96 B3
Bakar 126 B3, 130 B1
Bakarac 126 B3, 130 B1
Bakel 79 C/D1
Bakewell 61 C3, 64 A1
Bakio 153 C/D1
Bække 48 B3, 52 B1
Bakke 42 B3
Bakke 44 B2
Bakkejord 4 A3
Bakken 38 B1/2
Bakken 29 C/D2
Bakken 38 B2
Bakken 32 B1
Bakketun 14 B2/3
Bakko 43 C1
Bækmarksbro 48 A2
Bákoca 128 B2
Bakonybél 128 B1
Bakonycsernye 95 C3, 128 B1
Bakonygyepes 128 A1
Bakonyjákó 128 A/B1
Bakonykoppány 95 C3, 128 B1
Bakonypéterd 95 C3
Bakonysárkány 95 C3, 128 B1
Bakonyszentkirály 95 C3, 128 B1
Bakonyszombathely 95 C3
Bakov nad Jizerou 83 D2
Baksa 128 B2/3
Baksjöliden 30 B2
Baktsjaur 16 A3
Bakum 67 D2, 68 A2
Bakvattnet 29 C/D2/3, 34 B1
Bala 59 C2/3, 60 A3
Balabankoru 145 D3
Balaci 140 B2
Bălăcița 135 D2
Balaguer 155 C/D3, 163 C1
Balaruc-les-Bains 110 B3
Balassagyarmat 95 D2
Balassagyarmat 97 C3
Balata di Baida 124 A2
Balatonakali 128 B1
Balatonalmádi 128 B1
Balatonederics 128 A1
Balatonfőkajár 128 B1
Balatonföldvár 128 B1
Balatonfüred 128 B1
Balatonfüred 96 B3
Balatonfűzfő 128 B1
Balatonkenese 128 B1
Balatonkeresztúr 128 A2
Balatonkeresztúr 96 B3
Balatonlelle 128 B1/2
Balatonmagyaród 128 A2
Balatonszemes 128 B1
Balatonvilágos 128 B1
Bălăușeri 97 D3, 140 B1
Balazote 168 B2
Balbacil 161 D2
Balbigny 103 C2/3
Balboa 151 C2
Balbriggan 58 A2
Balčik 141 D3
Balconete 161 C2
Balcons de la Mescla 112 A2/3
Baldellou 155 C3
Balderschwang 91 D3
Baldichieri d'Asti 113 C1
Baldock 65 B/C2
Baldos 158 B2
Bale 130 A1
Baleira 151 C1/2
Baleisão 165 C3, 170 B1
Baleix 108 B3, 155 B/C1
Balen 79 C1
Balerma 173 D2
Balerno 57 C2
Balestrand 36 B2
Balestrate 124 A2
Balf 94 B3
Balfron 56 B1
Balikesir 149 D1
Bälinge 50 B2
Balingen 90 B2
Balingen-Weilstetten 91 B/C2
Balizac 108 B1
Balje 52 A/B3, 68 A1
Bäljom 29 C3, 34 A1
Balk 66 B2
Balkbrug 67 C2
Ballabani 142 A2
Ballachulish 56 A1
Ballangen 9 C2
Ballangen-Bjørnkåsen 9 C2
Ballan-Miré 86 B3
Ballantrae 56 A/B3
Ballao 123 D3
Ballasalla 58 B1
Ballaugh 58 B1
Ballcaire d'Urgell 155 D3, 163 D1
Balle 49 C2
Ballebro 52 B2
Ballen 49 C3, 53 C1
Ballenstedt 69 C3
Balleroy 76 A/B3, 85 D1, 86 A1
Ballerup 49 D3, 50 A3, 53 D1
Ballestar 163 C2
Ballesteros de Calatrava 167 C2
Ballina 55 C2
Ballinasloe 55 C2/3
Balling 48 A2
Ballingslöv 50 B2
Ballinluig 57 C1
Ballinluig 54 B2
Ballino 106 B2
Ballobar 155 C3, 163 C1
Balloch 56 B1/2
Ballon 86 B2
Ballószög 129 C1
Ballots 85 D2
Ballsh 142 A2
Ballstad 8 B2/3
Ballstädt 81 D1/2
Ballum 52 A2
Ballycanew 58 A3
Ballycarry 56 A3
Ballycastle 54 A3, 55 D2
Ballyclare 56 A3
Ballydonegan 55 C3
Ballygalley 56 A3
Ballygawley 54 A3, 55 D2
Ballygowan 56 A3
Ballyhalbert 56 A3
Ballyhaunis 55 C2
Ballymena 54 A3, 55 D2
Ballynahinch 58 A1
Ballynaskeagh 58 A1
Ballynure 56 A3
Ballyshannon 55 C2
Ballywalter 56 A3
Balmaseda 153 C1
Balme 104 B3
Balmúccia 105 C3
Balneario de Pozo Amargo 172 A2
Balquhidder 56 B1
Balrath 58 A2
Balsa 158 B1
Balsa de Ves 169 D1/2
Balsareny 156 A2/3
Balsby 50 B2
Balsfjord 4 A3, 10 A1
Balsicas 169 C3, 174 B1
Balsièges 110 B1/2
Balsorano 119 C2
Bålsta 40 B3, 47 C1
Balsthal 105 C1
Balta 135 C/D1
Balta 99 C3
Baltanás 152 B3
Baltar 150 B3
Baltasound 54 A1
Baltijsk (Pillau) 73 C2
Baltrum 67 D1
Balugães 150 A3, 158 A1
Bælum 48 B2
Balvano 120 A2
Balve 80 B1
Balvi 74 B2
Balzers [Trübbach] 105 D1, 106 A1
Balzhausen 91 D2
Balzo 117 D3
Bambálion 146 A1
Bamberg 81 D3, 82 A3
Bamble 43 D2, 44 A2
Bamburgh 57 D2
Bampton 63 C2
Bampton 64 A3
Bana 95 C3
Bañares 153 C2
Banatska Palanka 134 B1
Banatsk Aranđelovo 129 D2
Banatski Brestovac 134 B1
Banatski Dvor 129 D3
Banatski Karlovac 134 B1
Banatsko Novo Selo 134 B1
Banbridge 58 A1
Banbury 65 C2
Banchory 54 B2
Bande 150 B3
Bandeira 150 B2
Bandelow 70 B1
Bandholm 53 C2
Bandirma 149 D1
Bando 115 C1
Bandol 111 D3
Băneasa 141 C2
Bañeres 169 C2
Banff 54 B2
Bångbro 39 D3
Bangor 56 A3
Bangor 59 C2, 60 A3
Bangor 84 B3
Bangor 54 A3, 55 D2
Bangor Erris 55 C2
Bangsund 28 B2
Banhos da Curia 158 A2/3
Banie 70 B2
Banja 133 D3, 134 A3, 138 A1
Banja 133 D2, 134 A/B2
Banja 138 B2
Banja 133 C3
Banja Koviljača 133 C2
Banja Luka 131 D1, 132 A1
Banjani 133 D2, 134 A2
Banja Rusanda 129 D3
Banja Vrućica 132 B2
Banjica 138 A1
Banjišta 138 A3
Banjole 130 A1
Banjska 138 B1
Bánk 95 D3
Banka 95 C2
Bankeryd 45 D3, 46 A3
Bankfoot 57 C1
Bankja 139 D1
Banloc 134 B1
Bannalec 84 B2
Bannedsdorf 53 C2
Bannesdorf-Puttgarden 53 C2
Bannockburn 56 B1
Bañobárez 159 C2
Banon 111 D2
Bañón 163 C2
Baños de Alicún de las Torres 173 C1
Baños de Gigonza 171 D3
Baños de Ledesma 159 D2
Baños de la Encina 167 C3
Baños de Molgas 150 B3
Baños de Montemayor 159 D3
Baños de Panticosa 154 B2

Baños de Río Tobía 153 D2
Baños de San Juan 157 D2
Baños de Tus 168 A/B3
Baños de Valdearados 153 C3, 161 C1
Baños de Zújar 173 D1
Baños Fuensante 174 A1
Bánov 95 C2/3
Banova Jaruga 128 A3
Bánovce nad Bebravou 95 C2
Banovići 132 B2
Banská Bystrica 95 D2
Banská Bystrica 97 B/C2
Banská Štiavnica 95 D2
Bansko 139 D3, 143 D1, 144 A1
Bansko 139 D2
Bantheville 88 B1
Bantry 55 C3
Bantzenheim 90 A3
Banyalbufar 157 C2
Banyoles 156 B2
Banyuls-sur-Mer 156 B2
Banzi 120 B2
Baorationovsk 73 C2
Bapaume 78 A2/3
Bapukkåtan 9 D3
Baqueira 155 D2
Bár 129 C2
Bar 137 D2
Barahona 161 D1
Barajas 161 C2
Barajas del Melo 161 C3
Barajevo 133 D1/2, 134 A2
Barakaldo/Baracaldo 153 C1
Baralla 151 C2
Baranbio 153 C1/2
Baranjsko Petrovo Selo 128 B3
Barano d'Íschia 119 C3
Baranoviči 98 B1
Barão de São Miguel 170 A2
Baraolt 141 C1
Bar-ar-Lan 84 A2
Barásoain 154 A2
Barbacena 165 C2
Barbadás 150 B2/3
Barbadillo 159 D2
Barbadillo de Herreros 153 C3
Barbadillo del Mercado 153 C3
Barbadillo del Pez 153 C3
Barban 130 A1
Bárbara 115 D3, 117 C/D2
Barbarano Romano 117 C3, 118 A1
Barbarano Vicentino 107 C3
Barbaros 149 D1
Barbaste 109 C2
Barbastro 155 C3
Barbate de Franco 171 D3
Barbatovac 134 B3, 138 B1
Barbâtre 100 A1
Barbazan 109 C3, 155 C1
Barbele 73 D1, 74 A2
Barbens 155 D3, 163 D1
Barberà de la Conca 163 C1
Barberino di Mugello 114 B2, 116 B1
Barbezieux 101 C3
Bärbo 47 C2
Barbonne-Fayel 88 A2
Barbotan-les-Thérmes 108 B2
Barbués 154 B3
Barbullushi 137 D2
Barbuñales 155 C3
Barby 69 D3
Barca 161 D1
Bárcabo 155 C2
Barca d'Alva 159 C2
Barcarrota 165 C/D2/3
Barcellona Pozzo di Gotto 125 D1/2
Barcelona 156 A3
Barcelonnette 112 A/B2
Barcelos 150 A3, 158 A1
Bárcena del Monasterio 151 C1
Barcheta 169 D2
Barchi 115 D2/3, 117 C2
Barcial 151 D3
Barcillonnette 111 D1/2, 112 A2
Barcina de los Montes 153 C2
Bárcis 107 D2
Barco 158 B3
Barcones 161 C1
Barcos 158 B2
Barcs 128 A2/3
Barcus 108 A/B3, 154 B1
Bard 105 C3
Bardal 14 B2
Bardallur 155 C3, 163 C1
Bardejov 97 C2
Bardi 114 A1
Bardolino 106 B3
Bardonécchia 112 A/B1
Bardowick 68 B1
Bare 133 C3
Bare 133 D2, 134 A/B2
Bare 133 C/D3, 134 A3, 137 D1, 138 A1
Barèges 108 B3, 155 C2
Bärenburg 68 A2
Barendorf 69 C1
Bärenklau 70 B3
Bärenstein 83 B/C2
Bärenstein 83 C2
Barentin 77 C3
Barenton 85 D2, 86 A2
Barfleur 76 B3
Barga 114 A/B2, 116 A1
Bargas 160 B3, 167 C1
Barge 112 B1
Bargemon 112 A3
Bargen [Schaffhausen] 90 B3
Barghe 106 B3
Bargoed 63 C1
Bargrennan 56 B3
Bargteheide 52 B3, 68 B1
Bargum 52 A2
Barham 65 C3, 76 B1
Bari 121 C2, 136 A3
Barič Draga 130 B2
Bárig 169 D2
Barigazzo 114 B2, 116 A1
Bari Santo Spírito 121 C2, 136 A3
Bari Sardo 123 D2
Barisciano 117 D3, 119 C1
Barjac 111 C2
Barjac 110 B1
Barjols 112 A3
Barkarö 40 A3, 46 B1
Barkow 69 D1
Barkowo 71 D1
Barleben 69 C/D3
Bar-le-Duc 88 B1
Barletta 120 B1/2, 136 A3
Barlieu 87 D3
Barlinek 71 C2
Barlinek 72 A3
Barmouth 59 C3
Barmstedt 52 B3, 68 B1
Barnard Castle 57 D3, 61 C1
Bärnau 82 B3
Barneveld 66 B3
Barneville-Carteret 76 A3
Barnewitz 69 D2
Barnoldswick 59 D1, 60 B2
Barnówko 70 B2
Barnsley 61 C2/3
Barnstaple 63 C2
Barnstorf 68 A2
Barntrup-Alverdissen 68 A3
Baron 87 D1
Barone Canavese 105 C3
Baronissi 119 D3
Baronville 89 D1
Barösund 25 C3
Barovo 139 C3, 143 C/D1
Barquilla 159 C2
Barquilla de Pinares 159 D3, 160 A3
Barquinha 164 B1
Barr 56 B2/3
Barr 90 A2
Barra 158 A2
Barracão 158 A3, 164 A/B1
Barracas 162 B3
Barrachina 163 C2
Barraco 160 A/B2
Barrado 159 D3
Barrafranca 125 C2/3
Barrage de Sarrans 110 A1
Barrage de Serre-Ponçon 112 A2
Barrage de Tignes 104 B3
Barrage du Chambon 112 A1
Barranco do Velho 170 B2
Barrancos 165 C3
Barranda 168 B3, 174 A1
Barraqueville 110 A2
Barrax 168 B2
Barrea 119 C2
Barre-des-Cévennes 110 B2
Barreiro 164 A2
Barreiro 158 A/B2
Barreiros 151 C1
Barrême 112 A2
Barrhead 56 B2
Barrhill 56 B3
Barrière-de-Champlon 79 C3
Barrillos 152 A2
Barrio 150 A3, 158 A1
Barrio de San Pedro 165 C1
Barriomartín 153 D3
Barro 152 A1
Barro 150 A2
Barrô 158 B2
Barroca 158 B3
Barrocas e Taias 150 A3
Barromán 160 A2
Barrow-in-Furness 59 C1, 60 A/B2
Barrow-in-Furness 54 B3
Barruecopardo 159 C2
Barruelo de Santullán 152 B2
Barry 63 C2
Bårse 53 D2
Barsebäckshamn 50 A3
Barsinghausen 68 B3
Barssel 67 D1
Barssel-Harkebrügge 67 D1/2
Bar-sur-Aube 88 B2
Bar-sur-Seine 88 B2
Barsviken 35 D3
Bartenheim 90 A3
Barth 53 D2/3
Barth 72 A2
Bartholomä 91 C/D2
Barton 59 D1, 60 B2
Barton-upon-Humber 61 D2
Bartošova Lehôtka 95 D2
Bartoszyce (Bartenstein) 73 C2
Bartow 70 A1
Baruchella 115 B/C1
Barúmini 123 C/D3
Baruth 70 A3
Barvaux 79 C2
Barver 68 A2
Bårvik 5 C1/2
Barwice (Bärwalde) 71 D1
Barwinek 97 C2, 98 A3
Bárzana 151 D1
Bárzio 105 D2/3, 106 A2
Basagliapenta 107 D2, 126 A2
Bašaid 129 D3
Basardilla 160 B2
Basauri 153 C1
Bàscara 156 B2
Baschi 117 C3, 118 A1
Basconcillos del Tozo 152 B2
Basdahl 68 A1
Basedow 53 D3, 69 D1, 70 A1
Basel 90 A3
Baselga di Pinè 107 C2
Basélice 119 D2, 120 A1
Basella 155 C3
Bas-en-Basset 103 C3
Basepohl 70 A1
Båsheim 43 D1
Basiana 133 D1, 134 A1
Basicò 125 D2
Basildon 65 C3
Basingstoke 64 B3, 76 A1
Baška 130 B1
Baška Voda 131 D3, 132 A3
Baskemölla 50 B3
Baške Oštarije 130 B2
Bäskjö 30 B1
Baslow 61 C3, 64 A1
Bäsna 39 D2
Bassacutena 123 D1
Bassai 146 B3
Bassano del Grappa 107 C3
Basse-Bodeux 79 D2
Bassecourt 89 D3, 90 A3, 104 B1
Bassignana 113 C1
Bassilly 78 B2
Bassou 88 A2/3
Bassoues 109 C3, 155 C1
Bassum 68 A2
Bassum-Bramstedt 68 A2
Bassum-Neubruchhausen 68 A2
Båstad 49 D2, 50 A2
Båstad 72 A1
Båstad (Heiås) 38 A3, 44 B1
Bastahovine 133 C2
Bastardo 117 C3
Bastelica 113 D3
Basterud 39 C3
Bastheim 81 D2
Bastia 113 D2
Bastía 107 C3
Bastida 153 C/D2
Bastida 158 A2
Bastogne 79 C/D3
Bastunäs 31 C1/2
Bastuträsk 31 C1
Batajnica 133 D1, 134 A1
Batak 140 B3
Batalha 158 A3, 164 A1
Bátaszék 129 C2
Bátaszék 96 B3
Baté 128 B2
Batea 163 C2
Bateckij 74 B1
Batelov 94 A1
Baterno 166 B2
Bath 63 D2, 64 A3
Bathgate 57 C2
Bathmen 67 C3
Batignano 116 B3
Batina 129 C3
Batlava 138 B1
Batley 61 C2
Batnfjordsøra 32 A/B2
Batočina 134 B2
Bátovce 95 D2
Batres 160 B3
Batrina 132 A/B1
Båtsfjord 7 C1
Båtsfjord 5 C1
Båtsjaur 15 D2
Båtskar 37 C2
Båtskärsnäs 17 C/D2/3
Battáglia Terme 107 C3
Battenberg-Dodenau 80 B1/2
Battice 79 D2
Battipáglia 119 D3, 120 A2
Battle 77 C1
Battonya 97 C3, 140 A1
Baturin 99 D2
Baturino 75 C3
Båtvik 25 C3
Batz-sur-Mer 85 C3
Baud 85 B/C2/3
Baudenbach-Mönchsberg 81 D3
Baudreville 87 C2
Baugé 86 A3
Baugy 102 B1
Bauladu 123 C2
Bauma 91 B/C3, 105 D1
Baume-les-Dames 89 D3, 104 A/B1
Baumgarten 93 B/C2
Baumgarten 69 D1, 70 A1
Baumholder 80 A3
Baunach 81 D3
Baunei 123 D2
Bausendorf 80 A3
Bauska 73 D1, 74 A2
Bautzen 96 A1
Bautzen 83 D1
Bavanište 134 B1
Bavay 78 B2
Bäverhult 31 C1
Bäverträsk 30 B1
Bäverudden 16 B2
Bavorov 93 C1
Bawdeswell 65 C/D1
Bawdsey 63 D1
Bawinkel 67 D2
Bawtry 61 C3
Bayárcal 173 D2
Bayerbach bei Ergoldsbach 92 B2
Bayerdilling 91 D2, 92 A2
Bayerisch Eisenstein 93 C1
Bayeux 76 B3, 86 A1
Bayindir 149 D2
Bayon 89 C/D2
Bayonne 108 A3, 154 A1
Bayramiç 149 C/D1
Bayreuth 82 A3
Bayrischzell 92 B3
Baythorn End 65 C2
Bayubas de Abajo 153 C3, 161 C1
Baza 173 D1
Bazas 108 B1/2
Baziaş 134 B1
Baziaş 140 A2
Baziège 109 D3, 155 D1
Bazoches 88 A1
Bazoches-les-Gallerandes 87 C2
Bazoches-sur-Hoëne 86 B2
Bazoges-en-Paillers 101 C1
Bazolles 103 B/C1
Bazouges-la-Pérouse 85 D2
Bâzovec 135 D3
Bazsi 128 A1
Bazuel 78 B3
Bazzano 114 B1/2
Beaconsfield 64 B3
Beade 150 B2
Beaminster 63 D2
Beamud 161 D3, 162 A3
Beariz 150 B2
Beas 171 C1
Beasain 153 D1/2
Beas de Segura 167 D3, 168 A3
Beateberg 45 D2, 46 A2
Beatenberg [Interlaken] 105 C1/2
Beattock 57 C2
Beattock 54 B3
Beaubery 103 C2
Beaubru 79 C3
Beaucaire 111 C2
Beaucens 108 B3, 155 C1/2
Beaufays 79 C2
Beaufort 104 B3
Beaufort-du-Jura 103 D1/2, 104 A2
Beaufort-en-Vallée 86 A3
Beaufort-sur-Gervanne 111 D1
Beaugency 87 C3
Beaujeu 103 C/D2
Beaulac 108 B2
Beaulieu 76 A1
Beaulieu Abbey 76 A1
Beaulieu-sous-la-Roche 100 A1
Beaulieu-sur-Loire 87 D3
Beaulieu-sur-Dordogne 109 D1
Beaulieu-sur-Mer 112 B3
Beaumarchés 108 B3, 155 C1
Beaumaris 59 C2, 60 A3
Beaumes-de-Venise 111 C/D2
Beaumesnil 86 B1
Beaumetz-lès-Loges 78 A2
Beaumont 109 C1
Beaumont 78 B2
Beaumont-de-Lomagne 109 C2
Beaumont-du-Gâtinais 87 D2
Beaumont-en-Argonne 79 C3
Beaumont-Hague 76 A3
Beaumont-la-Ferrière 88 A3, 102 B1
Beaumont-la-Ronce 86 B3
Beaumont-le-Roger 86 B1
Beaumont-les-Autels 86 B2

Beaumont-sur-Oise 77 D3, 87 D1
Beaumont-sur-Sarthe 86 B2
Beaumont-sur-Vesle 88 B1
Beaune 103 D1
Beaune-la-Rolande 87 D2
Beaupréau 85 D3, 100 B1
Beauraing 79 C3
Beauregard 86 A/B3
Beaurepaire-en-Bresse 103 D1, 104 A1/2
Beaurepaire 103 D3
Beaurières 111 D1
Beauronne 101 C3, 109 C1
Beauvais 77 D3
Beauvallon 112 A3
Beauville 109 C2
Beauvoir-sur-Niort 100 B2
Beauvoir-sur-Mer 100 A1
Beauzée-sur-Aire 89 B/C1
Beba Veche 129 D2
Bebra 81 C2
Bebra-Breitenbach 81 C2
Beccles 65 D2
Becedas 159 D2/3
Beceite 163 C2
Bečej 129 D3
Bečej 140 A1/2
Beceni 141 C2
Becerreá 151 C2
Becerril de Campos 152 B3
Bečvinka 75 D1
Bech 79 D3
Bécherel 85 C2
Bechet 140 B2
Bechhofen 91 D1
Bechhofen (Zweibrücken) 89 D1, 90 A1
Bechí 162 B3, 169 D1
Běchovice 83 D3
Bechyně 93 D1
Bečići 137 C2
Becilla de Valderaduey 152 A3
Beckenried 105 C/D1
Beckhampton 63 D2, 64 A3
Beckingen-Düppenweiler 79 D3, 90 A1
Beckov 95 C2
Beckum 67 D3
Beclean 97 D3, 140 B1
Bécon-les-Granits 86 A3
Bečov nad Teplou 82 B3
Becsehely 128 A2
Becsvölgye 127 D1, 128 A1/2
Bedale 61 C2
Bedale 112 B2
Bédar 174 A2
Bédarieux 110 B3
Bedburg 79 D1/2, 80 A1/2
Bedburg-Hau 67 C3
Bedburg-Kaster 79 D1
Beddgelert 59 C2, 60 A3
Beddingestrand 50 B3
Bédée 85 C2
Bederkesa 52 A3, 68 A1
Bedford 64 B2
Bedlington 57 D3
Bedmar 167 D3, 173 C1
Bednja 127 D2
Bedoin 111 D2
Bédole 106 B2
Bedónia 113 D2, 114 A1
Bedous 108 B3, 154 B1
Bedretto [Airolo] 105 C/D2
Bedrule 57 C2
Bedsted 48 A2
Beduido 158 A2
Bedum 67 C1
Bedworth 64 A2
Beelen 67 D3
Beelitz 70 A3
Beelitz 72 A3, 96 A1
Beendorf 69 C3
Beenz 70 A1
Beerfelde 70 B2
Beerfelden 81 C3, 91 C1
Beerta 67 C1
Beeskow 70 B3
Beeskow 72 A3, 96 A1
Beesten 67 D2
Beetsterzwaag 67 C2
Beetz 70 A2

Beetzendorf 69 C2
Begaljica 133 D1/2, 134 B2
Bégard 84 B1/2
Begejci 129 D3
Begíjar 167 D3, 173 C1
Begis 162 B3, 169 C1
Beg-Meil 84 B2/3
Begna 37 D3
Begndalen 37 D3
Begoml' 74 B3
Begonte 150 B1
Begues 156 A3
Begunicy 74 B1
Begunje 126 B2
Begur 156 B2
Behlow 70 B3
Beho 79 D2
Béhobie 154 A1
Behramkale 149 C1
Behren-Lübchin 53 D3
Behringen 81 D1/2
Beian 28 A3, 33 C1
Beiarn 14 B1
Beichlingen 82 A1
Beidendorf 53 C3, 69 C1
Beijos 158 B2
Beilen 67 C2
Beilngries 92 A1
Beilngries-Paulushofen 92 A1
Beilrode 83 B/C1
Beilstein 80 B2
Beinette 112 B2
Beinwil am See 105 C1
Beire 154 A2
Beires 173 D2
Beisfjord 9 D2
Beith 56 B2
Beitostølen 37 C2
Beiuş 97 D3, 140 B1
Beja 164 B3, 170 B1
Béjar 159 D2/3
Bejís 162 B3, 169 C1
Béke 95 C2/3
Békéscsaba 97 C3, 140 A1
Békéssámson 129 D2
Békésszentandrás 129 D1
Bekkarfjord 6 B1
Bekkelegret 33 C3, 37 D1
Bekken 38 B1
Bekkjarvik 42 A1
Bekkvikdal 32 B1
Belá 95 D1
Bélàbre 101 C2
Bela Crkva 134 B1
Bela Crkva 133 C2
Bela Crkva 140 A2
Belair 108 B3, 154 B1
Belaja Cerkov' 99 C2
Bel'ajevka 141 D1
Belalcázar 166 B2
Bělá nad Radbuzou 82 B3
Belanovce 138 B2
Belanovica 133 D2, 134 A2
Bela Palanka 135 C3, 139 C1
Bela Palanka 140 A/B3
Bělá pod Bezdězem 83 D2
Belas 164 A2
Belascoáin 154 A2
Bélavár 128 A2
Belazaima 158 A2
Belcaire 156 A1
Belchite 162 B1
Bělčice 83 C3, 93 C1
Belčín 139 D2
Belčišta 138 B3, 142 B1
Bel'cy 99 C3
Bełczna 71 C1
Belebelka 75 C2
Belecska 128 B2
Beled 94 B3
Belegiš 133 D1, 134 A1
Belej 130 A1
Beleña 159 D2
Beleña 161 C2
Beleño 152 A1
Bélesta 109 D3, 156 A1
Belev 75 D3
Belfast 54 A3, 55 D2
Belfast 56 A3
Belford 57 D2
Belfort 89 D3, 90 A3
Belgern 83 C1
Bélgida 169 D2

Belgioioso 105 D3, 106 A3, 113 D1
Belgirate 105 D3
Belgodère 113 D2
Belgorod Dnestrovskij 141 D1
Belhade 108 B2
Belianes 155 D3, 163 D1
Beliet 108 A/B1
Beli Iski 139 D2
Beli Manastir 128 B3
Belimel 135 D3
Belin 108 A/B1
Belinchón 161 C3
Beli Potok 135 C3
Belišće 128 B3
Beliševo 139 C1
Bel Iskŭr 139 D2
Beljakovci 139 C2
Beljina 133 D2, 134 A2
Bella 120 A2
Bellac 101 D2
Bellágio 105 D2, 106 A2
Bellano 105 D2, 106 A2
Belláría-Igea Marina 115 C/D2, 117 C1
Belle Croix 79 D2
Bellegarde 111 C2
Bellegarde-du-Loiret 87 D2
Bellegarde-en-Marche 102 A2
Bellegarde-sur-Valserine 104 A2
Belleherbe 89 D3, 104 B1
Belle-Isle-en-Terre 84 B2
Bellême 86 B2
Bellenaves 102 B2
Bellencombre 76 B3
Bellerive-sur-Allier 102 B2
Bellevaux 104 B2
Bellevesvre 103 D1
Belleville 103 D2
Belleville-sur-Vie 100 A/B1
Bellevue 104 B2/3
Bellevue 78 B3
Bellevue-la-Montagne 103 C3
Belley 104 A3
Bellheim 90 B1
Bellicourt 78 A3
Bellingen 90 A3
Bellingham 57 D3
Bellino 112 B1/2
Bellinzona 105 D2
Bellizzi 119 D3, 120 A2
Bell-lloc d'Urgell 155 C/D3, 163 C1
Bello 162 A2
Bellö 46 A/B3
Bellpuig 155 D3, 163 D1
Bellreguart 169 D2
Belluno 107 D2
Bellús 169 D2
Bellver 155 C3, 163 C1
Bellvik 30 A1/2
Bellvis 154 B3, 162 B1
Belm 67 D2/3
Belmez 166 B3
Belmez de la Moraleda 173 C1
Belmont-de-la-Loire 103 C2
Belmonte 158 B3
Belmonte 151 D3
Belmonte 168 A1
Belmonte de Tajo 161 C3
Belmonte de Mezquín 163 C2
Belmont-sur-Rance 110 A2
Belmullet 55 C2
Belo Blato 129 D3, 133 D1, 134 A1
Belo Brdo 134 B3, 138 B1
Belobresca 134 B1
Belogradčik 135 D3
Belogradčik 140 B2
Belœil 78 B2
Beloljin 134 B3, 138 B1
Belo Polje 138 A1
Belorado 153 C2
Belosavci 133 D2, 134 B2
Belotinci 135 D3
Belovo 140 B3
Belp 105 C1
Belpasso 125 C/D2
Belpech 109 D3, 155 D1, 156 A1

Belper 61 C3, 64 A1
Belsey 57 D3
Belsh 142 A1
Beltheim 80 A3
Beltinci 127 D2
Beluša 95 C/D1
Belušić 134 B3
Belvédère du Cirque 112 B1
Belvedere Ostrense 115 D3, 117 D2
Belver 164 B1
Belver de los Montes 152 A3, 159 D1, 160 A1
Belvès 109 C1
Belvis de la Jara 160 A3, 166 B1
Belvis de Monroy 159 D3, 166 A1
Belvoir Castle 61 C/D3, 64 B1
Belyj 75 C2/3
Belyniči 74 B3
Belz 84 B3
Belzig 69 D3
Belzig 72 A3
Bembibre 151 C/D2
Bembridge 76 A1/2
Bemmel 66 B3
Bemposta 164 B1
Bemposta 159 C1
Bempton 61 D2
Benabarre 155 C3
Benacazón 171 D1/2
Benadalid 172 A2/3
Benafigos 162 B3
Benafim 170 A/B2
Benagéver Nuevo 162 A3, 169 C1
Benaguacil 169 C/D1
Benahadux 173 D2
Benahavís 172 A3
Benalmádena 172 B2/3
Benalúa de Guadix 173 C2
Benalúa de las Villas 173 C1/2
Benalup de Sidonia 171 D3
Benamargosa 172 B2
Benamaurel 173 D1
Benamejí 172 B2
Benamocarra 172 B2
Benasal 163 B/C2/3
Benasau 169 D2
Benasque 155 C3
Benátky nad Jizerou 83 D2
Benavent de la Conca 155 D3
Benavente 151 D3
Benavente 164 A2
Benavides 151 D2
Benavila 164 B2
Bencatel 165 C2
Bendeleben 81 D1, 82 A1
Bendery 141 D1
Bendorf 80 A2
Benedikt 127 D2
Benediktbeuren 92 A3
Benedita 164 A1
Benegiles 151 D3, 152 A3, 159 D1
Benejama 169 C2
Benejúzar 169 C3, 174 B1
Benesat 97 D3, 140 B1
Benešov 96 A2
Benešov 83 D3
Benešov nad Ploučnicí 83 D2
Benešov nad Černou 93 D2
Benestare 122 A3
Bénestroff 89 D1
Benet 100 B2
Benetuser 169 D1
Benetutti 123 D2
Bene Vagienna 113 C1/2
Bénévent-l'Abbaye 101 D2, 102 A2
Benevento 119 D3
Benfeld 90 A2
Benfica 164 A/B2
Bengești 135 D1
Bengtsby 25 D3, 26 A3

Bengtsfors 45 C2
Bengtsheden 39 D2, 40 A2
Beniaján 169 C3, 174 B1
Beničanci 128 B3
Benicarló 163 C2
Benicasim 163 C3
Benidorm 169 D2
Beniel 169 C3, 174 B1
Benifallet 163 C2
Benifallim 169 D2
Benifayó 169 D1/2
Beniflá 169 D2
Benigánim 169 D2
Benilloba 169 D2
Benimarfull 169 D2
Benínar 173 C/D2
Benisa 169 D2
Benissalem 157 C2
Benitayo 169 D1/2
Benítsai 142 A3
Benizalón 173 D2, 174 A2
Benkovac 131 C2
Benlloch 59 B/C2, 60 A3
Benlloch 163 C3
Bennebo 40 A3
Benneckenstein 69 C3, 81 D1
Bennekom 66 B3
Bennstedt 82 A1
Bénodet 84 A/B2/3
Bénouville 76 B3, 86 A1
Benquerença de Cima 158 B3, 165 C1
Benquerencia 165 D1, 166 A1
Benquerencia de la Serena 166 A/B2
Bensafrim 170 A2
Bensbyn 17 C3
Bensheim 80 B3
Bensheim-Auerbach 80 B3
Bensjö 35 C2
Benzo 172 A3
Beočin 129 C/D3, 133 C/D1, 134 A1
Beograd 133 D1, 134 A1
Beograd 140 A2
Beram 126 B3, 130 A1
Beranturi 153 C2
Berasáin 154 A1/2
Berastegi 153 D1, 154 A1
Berat 142 A2
Bérat 108 B3, 155 C1
Berat 148 A1
Beratón 154 A3, 161 D1, 162 A1
Beratzhausen-Oberpfraun-dorf 92 A1
Beratzhausen 92 A1
Bérbaltavár 128 A1
Berbegal 155 C3
Berberana 153 C2
Berbinzana 154 A2
Bercedo 153 C1
Berceo 153 C2
Berceto 114 A1
Bercher [Lausanne] 104 A1
Berchidda 123 D1
Berching 92 A1
Berching-Holnstein 92 A1
Berchtesgaden 93 B/C3
Bérchules 173 C2
Bercial de Zapardiel 160 A2
Bercimuel 161 C1
Bercimuelle 159 D2/3
Berck-sur-Mer 77 D2
Bercu 78 A2
Berdal 28 A2, 33 C1
Berdejo 153 D3, 154 A3, 161 D1, 162 A1
Berdičev 99 C2
Berdún 154 B2
Beregovo 97 D2/3, 98 A3
Bereguardo 105 D3, 113 D1
Berek 128 A3
Beremend 128 B3
Berendshagen 53 D3
Bere Regis 63 D2
Berestečko 97 D1/2, 98 B2
Beretinec 127 D2
Berettyóújfalu 97 C3, 140 A1
Beréza 73 D3, 98 B1
Berezan' 99 D2
Berežany 97 D2, 98 B2

Berezino 74 B3, 99 C1
Berezna 99 D2
Berg 29 C2
Berg 14 A3
Berg 28 A3, 33 C1
Berg 29 D3, 34 B1
Berg 126 B1
Berg 34 B2
Berg 30 A3, 35 C2
Berg 51 C1
Berg 29 D3, 34 B1
Berga 51 D1
Berga 50 B1
Berga 51 D2
Berga 156 A2
Berga 81 D1, 82 A1
Berga 82 B2
Bergaland 42 A2
Bergama 149 D2
Bérgamo 106 A3
Bergantino 114 B1
Bergantzu 153 C/D2
Bergara 153 D1
Bergasa 153 D2/3
Bergatreute 91 C3
Bergatreute-Rossberg 91 C3
Bergbacka 16 B3
Bergby 40 A/B2
Berge 67 D2
Berge 34 B2
Berge 69 D2, 70 A2
Berge 162 B2
Berge 35 D3
Berge 43 C2
Bergeby 7 C2
Bergeforsen 35 D3
Bergen 66 A2
Bergen 36 A3
Bergen 69 C2
Bergen 68 B2
Bergen 72 A2
Bergen aan Zee 66 A2
Bergen-Belsen 68 B2
Bergen-Eidsvåg 36 A3
Bergen op Zoom 78 B1
Bergen-Sülze 68 B2
Bergentheim 67 C2
Bergen-Wardböhmen 68 B2
Berger 43 D1, 44 B1
Bergerac 109 C1
Bergères-lès Vertus 88 A1
Bergesserin 103 C2
Berget 38 A1
Berget 28 A3, 33 C1
Berggiesshübel 83 C2
Berghaupten 90 B2
Bergheim 79 D1/2, 80 A1/2
Bergheim-Quadrath-Ichendorf 79 D1/2, 80 A1/2
Berghülen 91 C2
Berg im Gau 92 A2
Bergisch-Gladbach 80 A1/2
Bergisch-Glattbach-Bensberg 80 A1/2
Bergkarlås 39 D2
Bergkvara 51 D2
Bergkvara 72 B1
Bergland 15 C3
Berglen 91 C1/2
Bergli 32 B1
Berglia 29 C2
Berglund 4 B2
Berglund 31 C/D1
Berglunda 31 C1
Bergnäs 30 B1
Bergnäs 15 D3
Bergnäset 17 C3
Bergneustadt 80 A/B1/2
Bergö 20 A2, 31 D3
Bergondo 150 B1
Bergsäng 39 D2
Bergsäng 39 C3
Bergsbotn 9 D1
Bergsfjord 4 B2
Bergshamra 41 C3, 47 D1
Bergsjö 35 D3
Bergsjö 30 A2, 35 C1
Bergsjø 37 C3
Bergsjöåsen 30 A2, 35 C1
Bergsmo 28 B2
Bergsnov 28 A/B1
Berg (Starnberg) 92 A3
Bergstjärn 34 B2
Bergsund 15 C3
Bergsviken 16 B3
Bergtheim 81 D3
Bergua 155 B/C2
Berguenda 153 C2
Bergues 77 D1, 78 A1
Bergün/Bravuogn 106 A2
Bergvik 40 A1
Bergwitz 69 D3
Bergzow 69 D2/3
Berhida 128 B1
Beringel 164 B3, 170 B1
Beringen 79 C1
Berishë i Vënit 138 A2
Berja 173 D2
Berka 81 D2
Berkåk 33 C2
Berkatal-Frankershausen 81 C/D1
Berkeley 63 D1, 64 A3
Berkenbrück 70 B2/3
Berkenthin 53 C3, 69 C1
Berkhamsted 64 B3
Berkheim 91 D2/3
Berknes 36 A/B1
Berkön 17 C3
Berkovica 135 D3, 139 D1
Berkovica 140 B3
Berlanga 166 A3
Berlanga de Duero 161 C1
Berlevåg 7 C1
Berlin (-Ost) 70 A2
Berlin (-Ost) 72 A3
Berlin (West) 72 A3
Berlin (West) 70 A2
Berlstedt 82 A1
Bermellar 159 C2
Bermeo 153 D1
Bermillo de Sayago 159 D1
Bern 105 B/C1
Bernalda 121 C3
Bernardin 126 A/B3
Bernardos 160 B1/2
Bernartice 93 D1
Bernau 70 A2
Bernau 92 B3
Bernau 72 A3
Bernau (Hochschwarzwald) 90 B3
Bernaville 77 D2
Bernay 86 B1
Bernburg 69 D3
Berndorf 94 A3
Berndorf 96 A/B3
Berne 68 A1/2
Berneau 79 C/D2
Bernedo 153 D2
Berneval-le-Grand 76 B2
Berninches 161 C2
Bernkastel-Kues 80 A3
Bernried 92 B1/2
Bernried-Egg 92 B1/2
Bernsdorf 70 A3
Bernsdorf 83 C1
Bernstadt 83 D1
Bernstein 94 B3, 127 D1
Bernués 154 B2
Bernuy-Salinero 160 A/B2
Beromünster 105 C1
Beroun 83 C3
Beroun 96 A2
Berovo 140 B3
Berovo 139 D3
Berra 115 C1
Berre-l'Étang 111 D3
Berrien 84 B2
Berrobi 153 D1, 154 A1
Berrocal 171 C1
Berrocal de Salvatierra 159 D2
Berrocalejo 160 A3, 166 B1
Bersbo 46 B2
Bersenbrück 67 D2
Berthelming 89 D1, 90 A2
Bertincourt 78 A3
Bertinoro 115 C2, 117 C1
Bertogne 79 C3
Bertrix 79 C3
Berven 84 A/B2
Berwang 91 D3
Berwick upon Tweed 57 D2
Berwick upon Tweed 54 B2/3
Berzasca 135 C2
Berzence 128 A2
Berzocana 166 B1
Berzosa 161 C2
Berzosa 153 C3, 161 C1
Berzovia 140 A2
Beša 95 D2
Besalú 156 B2
Besançon 89 C3, 104 A1
Bescanó 156 B2
Besednice 93 D2
Bešenkoviči 74 B3
Besenyszög 129 D1
Běšiny 93 C1
Beška 133 D1, 134 A1
Beskovići 132 B3, 137 C1
Besni Fok 133 D1, 134 A1
Bespén 155 B/C3
Bessaker 28 A2
Bessan 110 B3
Bessarabka 141 D1
Bessay-sur-Allier 102 B2
Bessbrook 58 A1
Besse-en-Chandesse 102 B3
Bessèges 111 C2
Bessé-sur-Braye 86 B3
Bessheim 37 C2
Bessines-sur-Gartempe 101 C2
Besson 102 B2
Best 79 C1
Bestensee 70 A3
Bestorp 46 B2
Bestul 43 D1/2, 44 A1
Bestwig-Nuttlar 80 B1
Bestwig-Ramsbeck 80 B1
Betanzos 150 B1
Bétera 169 D1
Beteta 161 D2
Bétheniville 88 B1
Bethesda 59 C2, 60 A3
Bethmale 109 C3, 155 D2
Béthune 78 A2
Betna 32 B2
Bettelainville 89 C/D1
Bettembourg 79 D3
Betten [Mörel] 105 C2
Bettignies 78 B2
Bettingen 79 D3
Bettmeralp [Mörel] 105 C2
Bettna 46 B2
Bèttola 113 D1, 114 A1
Bettystown 58 A2
Betws-y-Coed 59 C2, 60 A3
Betz 87 D1
Betzdorf 80 B2
Betzenstein 82 A3
Betzenstein-Spies 82 A3
Beuil 112 B2
Beuron 91 C3
Beuvry 78 A2
Beuzeville 77 C3, 86 B1
Bevagna 115 D3, 117 C2/3
Beveren 78 B1
Beverley 61 D2
Bevern 68 B3
Bevernungen-Dalhausen 68 A/B3, 81 C1
Beverstedt 68 A1
Beverungen 68 B3, 81 C1
Beverwijk 66 A2
Bevilácqua 107 C3
Béville-le-Comte 87 C2
Bevtoft 52 B1/2
Bewdley 59 D3, 64 A2
Bex 104 B2
Bexhill 77 C1
Beychac-et-Caillau 108 B1
Beydağ 149 D2
Beynac-et-Cazenac 108 B1
Beynat 102 A3, 109 D1
Bezas 163 C3
Bezau 91 C3
Bezdan 129 C3
Bezděz 83 D2
Bezdružice 82 B3
Bèze 89 C3
Bežeck 75 D2
Bézenet 102 B2
Bezenye 95 B/C3
Béziers 110 B3, 156 B1
Bezmisht 142 B1
Béznar 173 C2
Bezno 83 D2
Bezvěrov 83 B/C3
Bezzecca 106 B2/3
Biała 71 C1
Biała Podlaska 73 D3, 97 D1, 98 A1
Białogard (Belgard) 72 B2
Białośliwie 71 D2
Białowąs 71 D1
Białowieża 73 D3, 98 A1
Białystok 73 D3, 98 A1
Biancavilla 125 C2
Bianco 122 A3
Biandrate 105 C/D3
Biar 169 C2
Biarritz 108 A3, 154 A1
Biarrotte 108 B3, 155 C1
Bias 108 B2
Bias 69 D3
Biasca 105 D2
Biasteri 153 D2
Biatorbágy 95 D3
Biaufond [La Chaux-de-Fonds] 89 D3, 104 B1
Bibbiena 115 C2/3, 116 B2
Bibbona 114 B3, 116 A2
Biberach 90 B2
Biberach 91 C2/3
Biberbach 91 D2
Bibinje 130 B2
Bibione 107 D3, 126 A3
Biblis 80 B3
Biblis-Nordheim 80 B3
Bibury 63 D1, 64 A3
Bicaj 138 A2
Bicaz 141 C1
Bíccari 120 A1
Bicester 65 C2
Bichl 92 A3
Bichlbach 91 D3
Bicorp 169 C2
Bicske 95 D3
Bidache 108 B3, 155 C1
Bidania 153 D1
Bidarray 108 B3, 155 C1
Bidart 108 A3, 154 A1
Bideford 62 B2
Bidjovagge 5 C3, 11 B/C1
Bie 46 B1
Biebergmünd-Bieber 81 C3
Biebersdorf 70 B3
Biebertal 80 B2
Biebertal-Frankenbach 80 B2
Biebesheim 80 B3
Biedenkopf 80 B2
Biedenkopf-Wallau 80 B2
Biedrusko 71 D2
Biegen 70 B3
Biel 154 B2
Biel/Bienne 89 D3, 104 B1
Bielefeld 68 A3
Bielefeld-Senne 68 A3
Bielefeld-Sennestadt 68 A3
Biella 105 C3
Bielle 108 B3, 154 B1
Biellojaure 15 C2/3
Bielmonte 105 C3
Bielsa 155 C2
Bielsko-Biała 97 B/C2
Bielsk Podlaski 73 D3, 98 A1
Bienenbüttel 69 B/C2
Bieniów 71 C3
Bienno 106 B2
Bienservida 168 A2
Biéntina 114 B2/3, 116 A2
Bienvenida 165 D3, 166 A3
Bière 104 A/B2
Biere 69 C/D3
Bierge 155 C2/3
Bierné 86 A3
Bierwart 79 C2
Bierzwnica 71 C1
Bierzwnik 71 C2
Biescas 154 B2
Biesenthal 70 A2
Biessenhofen 91 D3
Bietigheim 90 B1/2
Bietigheim-Bissingen 91 C1
Bièvre 79 C3
Biga 149 D1
Bigadiç 149 D1
Biganos 108 A1
Bigastro 169 C3, 174 B1
Biggar 57 C2
Biggleswade 64 B2
Bignasco [Ponte Brolla] 105 D2
Bigorne 158 B2
Bihać 131 C1
Bijela 132 B1
Bijele Poljane 137 C1/2
Bijeljina 133 C1
Bijelo Polje 137 D1, 138 A1
Bijörnvik 25 D3, 26 B3
Bijuesca 153 D3, 154 A3, 161 D1, 162 A1
Bikova 74 A/B2
Bílá 95 D1
Bilalovac 132 B2
Bilbilis 162 A1
Bilbo/Bilbao 153 C1
Bileća 137 C1
Biłgoraj 97 D1, 98 A2
Bílina 83 C2
Bilisht 142 B2
Bilisht 148 A1
Biljača 139 C2
Biljanovac 134 B3
Bilje 129 C3
Billabona 153 D1, 154 A1
Billdal 45 C3, 49 D1
Billerbeck 67 D3
Billesdon 64 B1/2
Billesholm 50 A2/3
Billiat 104 A2
Billigheim 91 C1
Billinge 50 B3
Billingen 32 B3, 37 C1
Billingsfors 45 C2
Billingshurst 76 B1
Billom 102 B3
Billsta 30 B3
Billund 48 B3, 52 B1
Billy 102 B2
Bílovice 95 C1
Bilshausen 81 D1
Bilston 59 D3, 64 A2
Bilto 4 B3, 10 B1
Bílý Kostel nad Nisou 83 D2
Bilzen 79 C2
Bíňa 95 D3
Binaced 155 C3, 163 C1
Binas 87 C2/3
Binasco 105 D3, 106 A3
Binbrook 61 D3
Binche 78 B2
Bindalseidet 14 A3, 28 B1
Bindlach 82 A3
Bindslev 44 A3, 48 B1
Binéfar 155 C3, 163 C1
Bingen 43 D1
Bingen 91 C2/3
Bingen am Rhein 80 B3
Bingham 61 C3, 64 B1
Bingley 59 D1, 61 C2
Bingsjö 39 D2
Binibeca 157 C1
Binic 85 C2
Biniés 154 B2
Binisafúa 157 C1
Binisalem 157 C2
Binn [Fiesch] 105 C2
Binsfeld 79 D3, 80 A3
Binswangen 91 D2
Bioča 137 D1, 138 A1
Bioče 137 D2
Biograd 130 B2/3
Biol 103 D3
Bionaz 105 B/C3
Biosca 155 C3, 163 C1
Bioska 133 C2
Biota 155 C2
Bippen 67 D2
Birchington 65 C3, 76 B1
Birdlip 63 D1, 64 A2/3
Birgel 79 D2, 80 A2
Birgi 124 A2
Biri 38 A2
Birka 47 C1
Birkeland 43 C3
Birkenfeld (Calw) 90 B1/2
Birkenfeld 80 A3
Birkenhain 81 C2/3
Birkenhead 59 C/D2, 60 B3
Birkenwerder 70 A2
Birkerød 49 D3, 50 A3, 53 D1
Birkestrand 7 C1
Birkfeld 94 A3, 127 C/D1
Bîrlad 141 C1
Birmingham 59 D3, 64 A2

Birnbach 93 C2
Biron 109 C1
Birr 55 C3
Birresborn 79 D2/3, 80 A2/3
Birsay 54 B1
Bîrsești 135 D1
Birstein 81 C2
Biržai 73 D1, 74 A2
Bisáccia 120 A2
Bisacquino 124 B2
Bisaurri 155 C2
Biscarrosse 108 B2
Biscarrués 154 B2
Biscéglie 120 B2, 136 A3
Bischoffen-Niederweidbach 80 B2
Bischofsgrün 82 A3
Bischofsheim 81 D2
Bischofshofen 93 C3
Bischofsmais-Hochdorf 93 C1/2
Bischofswerda 83 C1
Bischofswerda 96 A1
Bischofswiesen 92 B3
Bischofszell 91 C3
Bischwiller 90 B2
Bisegna 119 C2
Bisenti 117 D3, 119 C1
Bishop Auckland 57 D3, 61 C1
Bishop's Castle 59 C/D3
Bishop's Stortford 65 C2/3
Bishops Waltham 76 B1
Bisignano 122 A/B1
Bisingen 91 B/C2
Bisko 131 D3
Biskupiec (Bischofsburg) 73 C2/3
Bismark 69 C2
Bismo 32 B3, 37 C1
Bispberg 39 D2, 40 A2
Bispfors 30 A3, 35 C2
Bispgården 30 A3, 35 C2
Bispingen 68 B2
Bispingen-Wilsede 68 B1/2
Bissendorf 67 D3, 68 A3
Bissingen-Diemantstein 91 D2
Bistagno 113 C1
Bistarac 132 B2
Bistreț 135 D2/3
Bistreț 140 B2
Bistrica 139 D1/2
Bistrica 133 C/D3
Bistrica 139 D2
Bistrica 137 D1
Bistrica 127 C/D2
Bistričak 132 B2
Bistrița 97 D3, 140 B1
Bitburg 79 D3
Bitche 90 A1
Bítem 163 C2
Bitetto 121 C2
Bitola 143 C1
Bitola 148 A/B1
Bitonto 121 C2, 136 A3
Bitschwiller-lès-Thann 89 D3, 90 A3
Bitterfeld 82 B1
Bitti 123 D2
Bivio [St. Moritz] 106 A2
Bivona 124 B2
Bize-Minervois 110 A3, 156 B1
Bizovac 128 B3
Bjåen 42 B1
Bjala 141 C/D3
Bjala 141 C3
Bjännfors 31 D2
Bjærangen 14 B1
Bjäresjö 50 B3
Bjärges 47 D3
Bjärka-Säby 46 B2
Bjarkøy 9 C1
Bjärlöv 50 B2
Bjärnå 24 B3
Bjärnum 50 B2
Bjärred 50 A3
Bjarsjölagard 50 B3
Bjärström 41 C3
Bjärten 31 C2
Bjärtrå 30 B3, 35 D2
Bjästa 30 B3
Bjæverskov 49 D3, 50 A3, 53 D1
Bjelland 42 B3
Bjelovar 128 A3
Bjergby 48 B1
Bjerkreim 42 A3
Bjerkvik 9 D2
Bjernede Kirke 53 C/D1
Bjerre 48 B3, 52 B1
Bjerregård 48 A3
Bjerringbro 48 B2
Bjøberg 37 C3
Bjolderup 52 B2
Bjøllånes 15 C2
Bjølstad 37 D1/2
Bjønnes 43 D2, 44 A1/2
Björbo 39 D2
Björboholm 45 C3
Bjordal 42 B2/3
Bjordal 36 A2
Bjoreidalshytta 37 B/C3
Björholmen 44 B3
Bjørk 37 C2
Bjørkås 10 A1
Björkås 15 C3
Björkbacken 15 C3
Bjorkberg 39 D1
Björkberg 16 B2
Björkberg 30 B1
Björkboda 24 B3
Björke 40 B2
Bjørke 32 A3, 36 B1
Bjørkelangen 38 A/B3
Björketorp 49 D1, 50 A1
Björkfors 46 B3
Björkfors 15 C2/3
Björkfors 17 C/D2
Björkhöjden 30 A3, 35 C1/2
Björkholmen 16 A1
Björkliden 16 A3
Björkliden 9 D2
Bjorklinge 40 B3
Björklinge 40 A/B3
Björklund 16 A3
Bjørkmo 9 C1
Bjørkneset 28 B1
Björkö 24 A3, 41 D2
Björkö 46 A3, 51 C1
Björkö 45 B/C3
Björkö-Arholma 41 C3
Björköby 20 A2, 31 D3
Björkön 35 D3
Björksele 31 B/C1
Björksele 30 B2, 35 D1
Björksjön 39 D3
Björkvattnet 29 C2
Björkvik 46 B2
Björlanda 45 C3, 49 D1
Bjorli 32 B3, 37 C1
Bjørn 14 A2
Björna 31 B/C3
Björnänge 29 C3, 34 A1/2
Bjørnås 32 B2
Bjørnåsbrua 38 A1
Björnbäck 30 B3, 35 D1
Björnbäck 30 B3, 35 D1
Björnberg 35 B/C3
Björnböle 30 B3, 35 D2
Björneborg 45 D1, 46 A1
Björneborg 24 A1
Bjørnes 14 B2
Bjørnestad 42 B3
Bjørnevasshytta 42 B2
Bjørnevatn 7 C2
Bjørnhollia 33 C3, 37 D1
Björnlunda 47 C1
Bjørnset 5 C2
Bjørnset 36 A2
Björnsholm 46 B3
Björnsjö 30 B3
Bjørnskar 4 A2
Bjørnskinn 9 C1
Bjørnsletta 9 D1/2
Björsarv 35 C3
Björsäter 46 B2
Björsjö 39 D3
Bjørsvik 36 A3
Bjurånäs 17 C2
Bjurbekkdalen 14 B2
Bjurberget 38 B2
Bjurfors 31 D1
Bjurholm 31 C2
Bjuröklubb fiskeläge 31 D1
Bjursås 39 D2
Bjurselefors 31 C1
Bjursund 46 B3
Bjurtjärn 45 D1, 46 A1
Bjurträsk 30 B1
Bjurvattnet 31 C2
Bjuv 50 A2
Blace 134 B3
Blackbo 40 A3
Black Bull 58 A2
Blackburn 59 D1/2, 60 B2
Blacke 31 D1
Black Mount 56 B1
Blackpool 59 C1, 60 B2
Blackpool 54 B3
Blackrock 58 A1
Blacksnäs 20 A2/3
Blackstad 46 B3
Blackwater 58 A3
Blackwaterfoot 56 A2
Bladåker 40 B3
Bladon 65 C2/3
Blaenau Ffestiniog 59 C2, 60 A3
Blaenavon 63 C1
Blåfjellhytta 42 B2
Blagaj 131 C1
Blagaj 132 B3, 136 B1
Blagdon 63 D2
Blagnac 108 B2/3, 155 C1
Blagodatnoe 99 D3
Blagoevgrad 140 B3
Blagoevgrad 139 D2
Blagojev Kamen 135 C2
Blåhammaren 28 B3, 33 D2, 34 A2
Blaiken 15 D3
Blain 85 D3
Blairgowrie 57 C1
Blairgowrie 54 B2
Blaise 88 B2
Blaj 97 D3, 140 B1
Blajan 109 C3, 155 C1
Blakeney 65 C/D1
Blakeney 63 D1
Blaker 38 A3
Blaksæter 32 A3, 36 B1
Blakstad 38 A3, 43 D1
Blâmont 89 D2, 90 A2
Blanca 169 D3
Blancas 162 A2
Blancos 150 B3
Blandford Forum 63 D2
Blanes 156 B3
Blangy-sur-Bresle 77 D2
Blankaholm 46 B3
Blankenberge 78 A1
Blankenburg 69 C3
Blankenfelde 70 A3
Blankenhain 82 A2
Blankenheim 79 D2, 80 A2
Blankensee 70 A1
Blansko 94 B1
Blansko 96 B2
Blanzac 101 C3
Blanzy 103 C1
Blascomillán 160 A2
Blascosancho 160 A/B2
Bläse 47 D2
Blåsmark 16 B3
Blatná 93 C1
Blatná na Ostrove 95 C3
Blatné 95 C2
Blatnice 95 C1
Blato 131 D3, 132 A3
Blato 136 A1
Blatten b. Naters [Naters] 105 C2
Blatten (Lötschen) [Goppenstein] 105 C2
Blattnicksele 15 D3
Blaubeuren 91 C2
Blaufelden 91 C1
Blaufelden-Wiesenbach 91 C/D1
Blaustein 91 C2
Blåvand 48 A3, 52 A1
Blåvik 46 A3
Blaye-et-Sainte-Lucie 100 B3, 108 B1
Blaye-les-Mines 109 D2, 110 A2
Blažejovice 93 C1
Blaževac 132 B1
Blaževo 134 B3, 138 B1
Blázquez 166 B3
Bleckede 69 C1
Blecua 155 B/C3
Bled 126 B2
Bledzew 71 C2
Bléharies 78 A/B2
Bleialf 79 D2
Bleibach 90 B2/3
Bleiburg 127 C2
Bleicherode 81 D1
Bleik 9 C1
Bleikvassli 14 B2
Blekendorf 53 C3
Bleket 44 B3
Blendija 135 C3
Bléneau 87 D3
Blenheim Palace 65 C2/3
Blénod-lès-Toul 89 C2
Blera 117 B/C3, 118 A1
Blérancourt 78 A3
Bléré 86 B3
Blerikstugan 15 C3, 29 D1
Blesa 162 B2
Blesje stadmoen 42 B1
Blesle 102 B3
Blesme 88 B1/2
Blessington 58 A2
Blestua 43 D1
Blet 102 B1
Bletchley 64 B2
Bletterans 103 D1, 104 A1
Blickling Hall 61 D3, 65 C1
Blidö 41 C3, 47 D1
Blidsberg 45 D3
Bliecos 153 D3, 161 D1
Blieskastel 89 D1, 90 A1
Blieskastel-Breitfurt 89 D1, 90 A1
Bligny-sur-Ouche 103 C/D1
Blinisht 138 A2
Blinja 127 D3, 131 C1
Blodelsheim 90 A3
Bloemendaal 66 A2
Blois 86 A/B3
Blokhus 33 C2/3
Blokhus 48 B1
Blokzijl 67 B/C2
Blomberg 67 D1
Blomberg 68 A3
Blomberg-Grossenmarpe 68 A3
Blomhöjden 29 D1/2
Blomsholm 44 B2
Blomstermåla 51 D1
Blomvåg 36 A3
Blönsdorf 70 A3
Blonville-sur-Mer 76 B3, 86 A/B1
Blosenberg 82 B2
Bloška Polica 126 B3
Blötberget 39 D3
Błotno 71 C1
Blotzheim 90 A3
Blovice 83 C3, 93 C1
Blowatz 53 C/D3
Blšany 83 C2/3
Bludenz 106 A1
Blumberg 90 B3
Blumberg 70 A2
Blyberg 39 C1/2
Blyth 61 C3
Blyth 57 D3
Blyth 54 B3
Bnin 71 D3
Bo 46 B2
Bø 43 C2
Bø 8 B2
Bø 43 D2, 44 A1
Boada 159 C2
Boadilla 159 C/D2
Boadilla de Ríoseco 152 A3
Boadilla del Monte 160 B2
Boal 151 C1
Boalhosa 150 A3, 158 A1
Boan 137 D1
Bobadilla 153 D2
Bobadilla 172 B2
Bobadilla del Campo 160 A1
Bóbbio 113 D1
Bóbbio Péllice 112 B1
Boberg 30 A3, 35 C2
Böbing 91 D3, 92 A3
Bobingen 91 D2
Böblingen 91 C2
Bobolice 72 B2
Boborás 150 B2
Bobośevo 139 D2
Bobota 129 C3
Bobova 133 C/D2, 134 A2
Bobovdol 139 D2
Bobovdol 140 B3
Böbrach 93 B/C1
Bobrinec 99 D3
Bobrka 97 D2, 98 A2/3
Bobrowice 71 C3
Bobrówko 71 C2
Bobrujsk 99 C1
Bočac 131 D2, 132 A2
Boca do Inferno 164 A2
Bocairente 169 C/D2
Bočar 129 D3
Bocchigliero 122 B1
Boceguillas 161 C1
Bochnia 97 C2
Bocholt 67 C3
Bochov 83 B/C3
Bochum 80 A1
Bocigas de Perales 153 C3, 161 C1
Bockara 51 D1
Bockenem 68 B3
Bockfliess 94 B2
Bockhorn 67 D1
Bockhorn 92 A/B2
Bockhorst 67 D2
Böckstein 107 D1, 126 A1
Bockswiese 68 B3
Bocognano 113 D3
Bocșa 135 C1
Boczów 71 B/C3
Boda 40 A1
Boda 30 A3, 35 C/D2
Boda 45 C1
Boda 39 D2
Böda 51 D1
Böda 72 B1
Bodafors 72 A1
Bodafors 46 A3, 51 C1
Bodajk 95 C3, 128 B1
Bødal 36 B1/2
Bođani 129 C3
Bodåsgruvan 40 A2
Bodbacka 20 A2/3
Bodbyn 20 A1, 31 D2
Boddin 69 C1
Boden 17 B/C2/3
Boden 31 C1
Bodenburg 68 B3
Bodenkirchen 92 B2
Bodenkirchen-Aich 92 B2
Bodenmais 93 C1
Bodenteich 69 C2
Bodenwerder 68 B3
Bodenwöhr 92 B1
Bodiam Castle 77 C1
Bodilis 84 A/B2
Bodin 14 B1
Bodiosa Queirã 158 B2
Bodman 91 C3
Bodmin 62 B3
Bodø 14 B1
Bodom 28 B2, 33 D1
Bodön 17 C3
Bodonal de la Sierra 165 D3
Bodrost 139 D2
Bodrum 149 D2/3
Bodsjö 34 B2
Bodträskfors 16 B2
Boechout 78 B1
Boecillo 152 A/B3, 160 A1
Boek 69 D1, 70 A1
Boën-sur-Lignon 103 C3
Boeza 151 D2
Bofors 46 A1
Bogádmindszent 128 B3
Bogajo 159 C2
Bogan 28 B1
Bogarra 168 B2
Bogatić 133 C1
Bogatynia 83 D2
Bogatynia 96 A1
Boğaz 149 D1
Bogdanci 139 C/D3, 143 D1
Bogdaniec 71 C2
Bogdanovo 75 C3
Bogë 137 D2
Bogen 92 B1/2
Bogen 9 C2
Bogen 38 B3
Bogense 48 B3, 52 B1
Bogetići 137 C/D1
Boggsjö 35 C2
Bogholm 9 D2
Boglárlelle 128 B1/2
Boglárlelle 96 B3
Bognanco Fonti 105 C2
Bognelv 5 C2

Bognes 9 C2
Bogno [Lugano] 105 D2, 106 A2
Bognor Regis 76 B1
Bogodol 132 A3
Bogojevo 129 C3
Bogomila 138 B3
Bogomolje 132 A3, 136 A/B1
Bogorojca 139 C/D3, 143 D1
Bögöte 128 A1
Bogovina 135 C2/3
Bogøy 8 B3
Bøgsetsetran 29 C2
Boguševsk 74 B3
Boguslav 99 D3
Bogutovac 133 D3, 134 A3
Bogutovačka Banja 133 D3, 134 A3
Bogyoszló 94 B3
Bohain-en-Vermandois 78 A/B3
Bohdalice 94 B1
Bohdalov 94 A1
Böheimkirchen 94 A2
Bohinjska Bistrica 126 B2
Böhl-Iggelheim 90 B1
Böhlitz-Ehrenberg 82 B1
Böhmenkirch 91 C2
Böhmfeld 92 A1/2
Bohmte 67 D2, 68 A2/3
Bohmte-Hunteburg 67 D2, 68 A2
Bohonal 166 B1
Bohonal de Ibor 159 D3, 166 A/B1
Böhönye 128 A2
Böhönye 96 B3
Bohunice 95 D2
Bohuslavice u Gottwaldova 95 C1
Boí 155 C/D2
Boiano 119 D2
Boimorto 150 B2
Boiro 150 A2
Bois-d'Amont 104 A2
Boismont 89 C1
Bois Sir Amé 102 A/B1
Boissy-Saint-Léger 87 D1
Boitzenburg 70 A1
Bóixols 155 C2/3
Boizenburg 69 C1
Bojadła 71 C3
Bojana 139 D1
Bojanowo 71 D3
Bojar 163 C2
Bojarka 99 C2
Bojčinovci 135 D3
Bøjden 52 B2
Bojkovice 95 C1
Bojnica 135 C2
Bojtiken 15 C3
Boka 134 B1
Bokel 52 B3, 68 B1
Bokel 68 A1
Bökemåla 51 C2
Bokenäs 44 B2/3
Böklund 52 B2
Bokn 42 A2
Bokod 95 C3
Boksel 16 A3
Böksholm 51 C1
Boksitogorsk 75 C1
Bol 133 D3, 136 A1
Bölan 40 A1
Bolaños de Campos 152 A3
Bolaños de Calatrava 167 C/D2
Bolbec 77 C3
Bölcske 129 C1/2
Bolderslev 52 B2
Böle 17 C2
Böle 29 D3, 34 B2
Böle 34 B3
Bolea 154 B2
Bölebyn 16 B3
Bolemin 71 C2
Bölen 30 A2/3, 35 C1
Böleseter 28 A2
Bolesławiec (Bunzlau) 96 A1
Boleszkowice 70 B2
Bólgheri 114 B3, 116 A2
Bolgrad 141 D1/2
Boliden 31 D1
Boliqueime 170 A/B2

Boljanići 133 C3
Boljetin 135 C2
Boljevac 135 C3
Boljevac 140 A2
Boljevci 133 D1, 134 A1/2
Bolkesjø 43 C/D1, 44 A1
Bölkow 53 D3
Boll 91 C2
Bollate 105 D3, 106 A3
Bollebygd 45 C3, 49 D1
Bollendorf 79 D3
Bollène 111 C2
Bollensdorf 70 A3
Bollerup 50 B3
Bollesetra 5 C2
Bólliga 161 D3
Bollmora 47 D1
Bollnäs 40 A1
Bollstabruk 30 B3, 35 D2
Bollstanäs (Upplands-Väsby) 47 C1
Bollullos de la Mitación 171 D1/2
Bollullos par del Condado 171 C1/2
Bolman 128 B3
Bolmen 50 B1/2
Bolmsö 50 B1
Bolmstad 50 B1
Bologna 114 B1/2
Bologne 88 B2
Bolognetta 124 B2
Bolognola 115 D3, 117 D2/3
Bologoe 75 C1/2
Bologovo 75 C2
Bol'šaja Novinka 75 D1
Bol'šakovo 73 C2
Bolsena 117 B/C3, 118 A1
Bolsover 61 D3, 65 C1
Bolstad 45 C2
Bolsward 66 B2
Boltaña 155 C2
Boltigen 105 B/C2
Bolton 59 D2, 60 B2/3
Bolton Bridge 59 D1, 61 C2
Bolventor 62 B3
Bolvir 156 A2
Bóly 128 B2/3
Bolzaneto 113 D2
Bolzano/Bozen 107 C2
Bomarsund 41 D3
Bomba 119 D2
Bombarón 173 C2
Bombarral 164 A1/2
Bömenzien 69 C2
Bom Jesus 150 A/B3, 158 A1
Bomlitz 68 B2
Bomlitz-Bommelsen 68 B2
Bømlo 42 A1
Bompart 111 D3
Bomsdorf 70 A3
Bomsund 30 A3, 35 C2
Bona 102 B1
Bonaduz 105 D1, 106 A1
Bönan 40 B2
Bonansa 155 C2
Bonanza 171 C/D2
Boñar 152 A2
Bonárcado 123 C2
Bonares 171 C2
Bonäs 39 C/D1/2
Bonäset 29 D2, 35 C1
Bonassola 113 D2, 114 A2
Bonastre 163 D1
Bonboillon 89 C3, 104 A1
Boncourt 89 D3, 90 A3
Bondal 43 C1
Bondalseidet 32 A3, 36 B1
Bondeno 114 B1
Bonderup 48 B1
Bondstorp 45 D3
Bondues 78 A2
Bonefro 119 D2, 120 A1
Bönen 67 D3, 80 B1
Bones 9 D2
Bo'ness 57 C1/2
Bonete 169 D2
Bönhamn 30 B3
Boniches 162 A3
Bonifacio 123 D1
Boniswil 105 C1
Bonn 80 A2
Bonnåsjøen 9 C3

Bonnat 102 A2
Bonn-Bad Godesberg 80 A2
Bonndorf 90 B3
Bønnerup Strand 49 C2
Bonne-sur-Ménoge 104 A/B2
Bonnétable 86 B2
Bonneuil-Matours 101 C1
Bonneval 86 A/B2
Bonneval-sur-Arc 104 B3
Bonneville 104 A/B2
Bonnières-sur-Seine 87 C1
Bonnieux 111 D2
Bonny-sur-Loire 87 D3
Bono 123 D2
Bono 155 C2
Bonorva 123 C2
Bonrepos 109 D2
Bon Secours 78 B2
Bon Secours 79 C2/3
Bønsnes 43 D1
Bønsvig 53 D2
Bontveit 36 A3
Bonyhád 128 B2
Bönyrétalap 95 C3
Boock 70 B1
Boofzheim 90 A2
Booischot 79 C1
Boom 78 B1
Boos 76 B3, 86 A/B1
Boossen 70 B2/3
Boostedt 52 B3
Boothby Graffoe 61 D3, 64 B1
Bootle 59 C/D2, 60 B3
Bootle 59 C1, 60 A2
Bopfingen 91 D1/2
Boppard 80 A/B2
Boqueijón 150 A2
Boquiñeni 155 C3, 163 C1
Bor 135 C2
Bor 50 B1
Bor 82 B3
Bor 140 A2
Borač 133 D2, 134 A/B2
Boraja 131 C3
Borås 45 C3
Borås 72 A1
Borba 165 C2
Borbela 158 B1
Borbona 117 D3, 118 B1
Borča 133 D1, 134 A1
Borchen 68 A3, 81 B/C1
Borci 131 D2, 132 A2
Borculo 67 C3
Bordalba 161 D1
Bordány 129 D2
Bordeaux 108 B1
Bordeira 170 A2
Bordères-Louron 155 C2
Bordes 109 C3, 155 C1
Bordesholm 52 B3
Bordighera 112 B2/3
Bording Stationsby 48 B3
Bordón 162 A2
Bordvedåven 14 B2
Borek Wielkopolski 71 D3
Borello 115 C2, 117 C1
Borelva 15 B/C1
Borensberg 46 A/B2
Borgafjäll (Avasjö) 29 D1
Borgan 28 B1
Bórgaro Torinese 105 C3, 113 B/C1
Borge 44 B1
Borgen 30 B2
Borgentreich 81 C1
Borgentreich-Bühne 81 C1
Börger 67 D2
Borger 67 C2
Borgestad 43 D2, 44 A1
Borggård 46 B2
Borghamn 46 A2
Borghetto 117 C3, 118 B1
Borghetto di Vara 114 A2
Borghetto Santo Spírito 113 C2
Borgholm 51 D1
Borgholm 72 B1
Borgholzhausen 67 D3, 68 A3
Bórgia 122 B2
Borgloon 79 C2
Børglum kloster 48 B1
Borgo alla Collina 115 C2, 116 B1/2

Borgo a Mozzano 114 B2, 116 A1
Borgoforte 114 B1
Borgofranco 105 C3
Borgo Grappa 118 B2
Borgo le Taverne 120 A2
Borgo Libertà 120 A/B2
Borgomanero 105 C/D3
Borgonovo Lígure 113 D2
Borgonovo Val Tidone 113 D1
Borgo Pace 115 C2/3, 117 C2
Borgo Piave 118 B2
Borgoricco 107 C3
Borgorose 119 B/C1
Borgo San Dalmazzo 112 B2
Borgo San Lorenzo 114 B2, 116 B1
Borgosésia 105 C3
Borgo Túfico 115 D3, 117 C/D2
Borgo Val di Taro 114 A1/2
Borgo Valsugana 107 C2
Borgo Vercelli 105 C/D3
Borgsjö 35 C3
Borgsjö 30 B2
Borgstena 45 C/D3
Borgund 37 C2
Borgvattnet 30 A3, 35 C1/2
Borgvik 45 C1
Borhaug 42 B3
Boriç 137 D2
Boričevac 131 C2
Borines 152 A1
Bořislav 83 C1
Borislav 97 D2, 98 A3
Borisov 74 B3
Borispol' 99 D2
Borja 154 A3, 162 A1
Börjelsbyn 17 C2
Börjelslandet 17 C3
Borkan 15 C3, 29 D1
Borken 67 C3
Borken 81 C1/2
Borkenes 9 C2
Borken-Kleinenglis 81 C1
Borken-Weseke 67 C3
Borkheide 70 A3
Borkhusseter 33 C3, 37 D1
Børkop 48 B3, 52 B1
Borkum 67 C1
Borlänge 39 D2
Borlaug 37 C2
Børlia 33 C2
Borlova 135 C1
Borlu 149 C1
Bormes-les-Mimosas 112 A3
Bórmio 106 B2
Born 53 D2/3
Born 69 C2/3
Borna 82 B1
Borne 67 C2/3
Borne 69 C3
Borne 103 C3, 110 B1
Bornem 78 B1
Bornes 159 C1
Bornheim (Bonn) 80 A2
Bornhöved 52 B3
Börnicke 70 A2
Borno 106 B2
Bornos 171 D2
Bornova 149 D2
Bornstedt 82 A1
Borobia 153 D3, 154 A3, 161 D1, 162 A1
Borodjanka 99 C2
Borojevići 127 D3, 131 C1
Borotín 83 D3, 93 D3
Boroughbridge 61 D2
Borovan 140 B2/3
Borovany 93 D1/2
Borovci 135 D3
Borovići 75 C1
Borovnica 126 B2/3
Borovo 129 C3
Borovo Selo 129 C3
Borovsk 75 D3
Borowe 83 D1
Borowina 71 C3
Borrby 50 B3
Borrby 72 A2
Borrby strandbad 50 B3
Borre 53 D2

Borre 43 D2, 44 B1
Borreby 53 C1/2
Borredà 156 A2
Borrentin 70 A1
Börringe 50 B3
Borriol 163 C3
Borris 48 A3
Börrum 46 B2
Børsa 28 A3, 33 C2
Borščev 98 B3
Børselv 5 D2, 6 A2
Borsfa 128 A2
Borsh 142 A2
Borsh 148 A1
Borssele 78 A1
Börssum 69 C3
Borstel 69 D2
Borth 59 C3
Borthwick Castle 57 C2
Bortígali 123 C2
Bort-les-Orgues 102 A/B3
Börtnan 34 B2
Bortnen 36 A1
Borum 48 B2/3
Borup 49 D3, 53 D1
Boruszyn 71 D2
Boryszyn 71 C3
Borzna 99 D2
Borzonasca 113 D2
Bosa 123 C2
Bosa Marina 123 C2
Bosanci 127 C3
Bosanska Dubica 131 D1, 132 A1
Bosanska Gradiška 131 D1, 132 A1
Bosanska Kostajnica 127 D3, 131 C/D1
Bosanska Krupa 131 C1
Bosanska Mezgraja 133 C1/2
Bosanska Rača 133 C1
Bosanski Aleksandrovac 131 D1, 132 A1
Bosanski Brod 132 B1
Bosanski Dubočac 132 B1
Bosanski Kobaš 132 A/B1
Bosanski Novi 131 C1
Bosanski Petrovac 131 C2
Bosanski Šamac 132 B1
Bosansko Grahovo 131 C2
Bosansk Rača 133 C1
Bösárkány 95 C3
Bosau 53 C3
Boscastle 62 B2/3
Bosco 115 C/D3, 117 C2
Bosco Chiesanuova 107 B/C3
Bosco/Gurin [Ponte Brolla] 105 C/D2
Bösel 67 D2
Bösel-Petersdorf 67 D2
Bøseter 38 A1
Bøsetrene 32 B3, 37 C1
Bosilegrad 139 C2
Bosiljevo 127 C3, 130 B1
Bosjökloster 50 B3
Bosjön 39 C2
Boskoop 66 A3
Boskovice 94 B1
Boskovice 96 B2
Bosnek 139 D2
Bošnjace 139 C1
Bošnjaci 133 B/C1
Bosost 155 C2
Bössbo 39 C1
Bossbu 42 B2
Bossolasco 113 C1/2
Bøstad (Borge) 8 B2
Bostan 131 D3, 132 A3
Bostanj 127 C2
Böste 50 B3
Boston 61 D3, 65 C1
Bostrak 43 C2
Bosut 133 C1
Bőszénfa 128 B2
Bot 163 C2
Boteå 30 B3, 35 D2
Botesdale 65 C/D2
Botevgrad 140 B3
Bothel 57 C3, 60 A/B1
Boticas 150 B3, 158 B1
Botija 161 D1, 166 A1
Botley 76 B1
Botn 5 B/C2
Botn 4 A/B2/3
Botn 14 A2

Botn **4** A2
Botngård **28** A3, **33** C1
Botnlia **33** D2
Bötom **20** A3
Botorrita **154** B3, **162** A/B1
Botoš **129** D3, **133** D1, **134** B1
Botoşani **98** B3
Botsmark **31** C/D2
Bottarvegården **47** D3
Bottesford **61** C3, **64** B1
Böttingen (Tuttlingen) **90** B2/3
Bottnaryd **45** D3
Botun **138** B3, **142** B1
Bouayé **85** D3, **100** A1
Boubínský prales (Urwald) **93** C1
Boucau **108** A3, **154** A1
Boucé **86** A2
Bouchain **78** A2
Bouchoir **78** A3
Boucoiran **111** C2
Boucq **89** C1
Boudrac **109** C3, **155** C1
Bouessay **86** A2/3
Bouesse **101** D1/2, **102** A1/2
Bouillon **79** C3
Bouilly **88** B2
Bouin **100** A1
Boujailles **104** A1
Boulay-Moselle **89** D1
Bouleternère **156** B1/2
Bouloc **110** A2
Boulogne-sur-Gesse **109** C3, **155** C1
Boulogne-sur-Mer **77** D1/2
Bouloire **86** B2
Boulouris-sur-Mer **112** B3
Boulzicourt **79** C3
Boumois **86** A3
Bourbon-Lancy **103** C1/2
Bourbonne-les-Bains **89** C2
Bourbourg **77** D1
Bourbriac **84** B2
Bourdeaux **111** D1
Bouresse **101** C2
Bourg-Achard **77** C3, **86** B1
Bourganeuf **102** A2
Bourg-Argental **103** C3
Bourg-de-Péage **111** C/D1
Bourg-de-Visa **109** C2
Bourg-d'Oueil **155** C2
Bourg-en-Bresse **103** D2
Bourges **102** A1
Bourg-et-Comin **78** B3, **88** A1
Bourg-Lastic **102** A/B3
Bourg-Madame **156** A2
Bourgneuf-en-Retz **100** A1
Bourgneuf-en-Mauges **86** A3
Bourgoin-Jallieu **103** D3
Bourg-Saint-Maurice **104** B3
Bourg-Saint-Andéol **111** C2
Bourg-St-Pierre [Orsières] **104** B2
Bourg-sur-Gironde **108** B1
Bourgtheroulde **77** C3, **86** B1
Bourgueil **86** B3, **101** C1
Bourmont **89** C2
Bournazel **110** A1
Bourne **64** B1
Bournemouth **63** D2/3, **76** A1
Bournezeau **101** C1/2
Bouro **150** B3, **158** A1
Bourret **108** B2
Boussac **102** A2
Bousse **89** C1
Bouttencourt **77** D2
Bouvellemont **79** B/C3
Bouvières **111** D1
Bouvron **85** D3
Bouxwiller **90** A2
Bouzonville **89** D1
Bova **122** A3
Bovalino **122** A3
Bovalino Marina **122** A3
Bovallstrand **44** B2
Bova Marina **122** A3
Bovan **135** C3
Bovec **126** A/B2
Bóveda **150** B2
Bóvegno **106** B3
Bovenden **81** C/D1
Bovense **53** C1
Bøverdal **37** C2
Bøverfjord **32** B2
Bóves **112** B2
Boves **77** D2/3
Bovey Tracey **63** C3
Bovik **41** C2/3
Bovino **120** A2
Bøvlingbjerg **48** A2
Bovolenta **107** C3
Bovolone **107** C3
Bovrup **52** B2
Bowes **57** D3, **61** B/C1
Box **63** D2, **64** A3
Box **25** C3
Box **25** D3, **26** A3
Boxberg **81** C3, **91** C1
Boxholm **46** A2/3
Boxmeer **67** B/C3, **79** D1
Boxtel **66** B3, **79** C1
Boyardville **101** C2
Boyle **55** C2
Boynes **87** D2
Božaj **137** D2
Božava **130** B2
Bozcaada **149** C1
Bozdoğan **149** D2
Božejov **93** D1, **94** A1
Bozel **104** B3
Boževac **134** B2
Bozhigradi **142** B2
Božica **139** C1
Božice **94** B1/2
Boží Dar **82** B2
Bozouls **110** A1/2
Bozovici **135** C1
Bozsok **94** B3, **127** D1
Božurište **139** D1
Bózzolo **114** A/B1
Bra **113** C1
Braås **51** C1
Bråbo **51** D1
Brabova **135** D2
Braccagni **116** B3
Bracciano **118** A1/2
Braćevac **135** C2
Bračevci **128** B3
Bracieux **87** C3
Bräcke **35** C2
Brackel **68** B1
Brackenheim **91** C1
Brackley **65** C2
Bracknell **64** B3
Braco **56** B1
Brad **97** D3, **140** B1
Bradford **54** B3
Bradford **61** C2
Bradford on Avon **63** D2, **64** A3
Brädikow **69** D2, **70** A2
Brading **76** B1/2
Brådland **42** A/B2
Bradninch **63** C2
Brædstrup **48** B3
Bradwell Waterside **65** C3
Bradworthy **62** B2
Braemar **54** B2
Brăfim **163** C1
Braga **150** A3, **158** A1
Bragada **150** B3, **158** B1
Bragança **151** C3, **159** C1
Brager **37** D3, **38** A2
Bragin **99** C2
Brahestad **18** A3
Brahetrolleborg **53** C2
Brahmenau **82** B2
Brăila **141** C/D2
Braine-l'Alleud **78** B2
Braine-le-Comte **78** B2
Braintree **65** C2
Brajkovići **132** B2
Brake **68** A1
Brakel **68** A3, **81** C1
Brakel-Bökendorf **68** A3
Brakkstad **28** B1/2
Bräkne-Hoby **51** C2
Brålanda **45** C2
Bralitz **70** B2
Brallo **113** D1
Brálos **147** C1
Brálos **148** B2
Braloştiţa **135** D2
Bramminge **48** A3, **52** A1
Brampton **57** C3, **60** B1
Bramsche **67** D2
Bramsche-Achmer **67** D2
Bramsche-Engter **67** D2
Bramsche-Hesepe **67** D2
Bramsche-Ueffeln **67** D2
Brånaberg **15** C3
Branäs **38** B2
Branca **115** D3, **117** C2
Brancaleone **122** A3
Branchewinda **81** D2, **82** A2
Brand **82** A/B3
Brand **106** A1
Brandal **36** A/B1
Brändåsen **34** A3
Brändberg **16** B2
Brändbo **35** C3
Brandbu **38** A2
Brände **31** C1/2
Brande **48** B3
Brandenberg **92** A3
Brandenburg **69** D2
Brandenburg **72** A3
Brand-Erbisdorf **83** C2
Brandis **82** B1
Brandizzo **105** C3, **113** C1
Brändö **24** A2/3, **41** D2
Brandomil **150** A1/2
Brändön **17** C3
Brandon **65** C2
Brändövik **20** A2, **31** D3
Brandstad **32** B2
Brandstorp **45** D3, **46** A3
Brandval **38** B2/3
Brandvoll **9** D1/2
Brandýsek **83** C2/3
Brandýs nad Labem-Stará Boleslav **83** D2/3
Brandýs nad Labem-Stará Boleslav **96** A2
Braničevo **134** B1/2
Braniewo (Braunsberg) **73** C2
Branišovice **94** B1
Brankovice **94** B1
Brankovina **133** D2, **134** A2
Brännaby **30** A1
Brännåker **30** A1
Brännan **31** D1
Brännäs **16** B3
Brännau **16** A3
Brännberg **16** A3
Branne **108** B1
Brännforsliden **31** C1
Brännland **31** C2
Brännö **45** C3, **49** D1
Brännvattnet **31** D1
Brañosera **152** B2
Branston **61** D3, **64** B1
Brantevik **50** B3
Brantôme **101** C/D3
Branzi **106** A2
Braojos **161** C2
Braskereidfoss **38** B2
Braslav **74** A/B3
Braşov **141** C1/2
Brasparts **84** B2
Brassac **110** A2/3
Brasschaat **78** B1
Bras-sur-Meuse **89** C1
Brassus, Le **104** A2
Brassy **88** A3, **103** C1
Brastad **44** B2
Brataj **142** A2
Bråte **38** A3, **44** B1
Brăteşti **135** D1/2
Bratina **127** D3
Bratislava **94** B2
Bratislava **96** B2/3
Bratronice **83** C3
Brattåker **15** C/D3
Brattås **15** C3, **29** D1
Brattås **14** A3
Brattbäcken **30** A2
Bratten **30** B1
Bratteng **14** B3
Brattfjell **4** A2/3
Brattfjord **94** A3
Brattfors **39** C3, **45** D1
Brattfors **31** C2
Bratthøvollseter **33** C/D2/3
Brattknabben **16** B3
Brattland **14** A/B2
Bråttö **41** D3
Brattsbacka **31** C2
Brattset **32** B2
Brattvåg **32** A2/3
Brattvær **32** B1
Bratunac **133** C2
Bråtveit **42** B1
Braubach **80** A/B2
Braunau am Inn **93** B/C2
Braunlage **69** C3
Braunlage-Hohengeiss **69** C3, **81** D1
Bräunlingen **90** B3
Braunsbach **91** C1
Braunsbedra **82** A/B1
Braunschweig-Waggum **69** C3
Braunschweig **69** C3
Bräunsdorf **83** C2
Braunton **63** B/C2
Braunwald [Linthal] **105** D1, **106** A1
Brauron **147** D2
Bravães **150** A3, **158** A1
Bravsko **131** D2
Bray **58** A2
Bray **55** D2/3
Braye **63** D3
Bray-sur-Seine **87** D2, **88** A2
Bray-sur-Somme **78** A3
Brazatortas **167** C2
Brazey-en-Plaine **103** D1
Brazuelo **151** D2
Brbinj **130** B2
Brčko **133** C1
Brea **154** A3, **162** A1
Brea de Tajo **161** C3
Breared **50** A/B2
Breaza **141** C2
Bréban **88** B2
Brebu Nou **135** C1
Brécey **86** A1
Brechin **54** B2
Breckerfeld **80** A1
Břeclav **94** B2
Břeclav **96** B2
Brecon **63** C1
Brécy **102** B1
Breda **66** A/B3, **79** C1
Bredåker **16** B2
Bredåkra **51** C2
Bredared **45** C3
Bredaryd **50** B1
Bredballe **48** B3, **52** B1
Bredbyn **30** B3, **35** D1
Breddin **69** D2
Bredebro **52** A2
Bredenfelde **70** B1
Bredereiche **70** A1/2
Bredestad **46** A3
Bredevad **52** B2
Bredevoort **67** C3
Bredkälen **29** D2/3, **35** C1
Bredsätra **51** D1/2
Bredsel **16** B2/3
Bredsjö **39** D3
Bredstedt **52** A/B2
Bredsten **48** B3, **52** B1
Bredstrup **48** B3, **52** B1
Bredträsk **31** B/C2
Bredvik **31** C2/3
Bree **79** C1
Breganze **107** C3
Bregenz **91** C3
Breginj **126** A2
Bregovo **135** C/D2
Bregovo **140** B2
Breguzzo **106** B2
Bréhal-Plage **85** D1
Brehna **82** B1
Breidablikk **42** A/B1
Breidenbach **80** B2
Breifonn **42** B1
Breil-sur-Roya **112** B2
Breim **36** B2
Breisach **90** A3
Breistein **36** A3
Breistølen **37** C2/3
Breistrand **9** C2
Breitenbach **81** C2
Breitenbrunn **94** B3
Breitenbrunn **91** D2
Breitenbrunn **92** A1
Breitenfelde **69** C1
Breitengüssbach **81** D3
Breitenworbis **81** D1
Breitscheid **80** B2
Breitstetten **94** B2
Breitungen **81** D2
Breive **42** B1
Breivik **7** C1
Breivik **9** C2
Breivik **8** B2
Breivik **15** C1
Breivik **9** C2
Breivikbotn **5** C1
Breivikeidet **4** A3
Brejning **48** B3, **52** B1
Brejtovo **75** D1
Brekke **36** A2/3
Brekken **14** B2
Brekken **33** D2
Brekkestø **43** C3
Brekkhus **36** B3
Brekksillan **28** B1/2
Breklum **52** A/B2
Brekstad **28** A3, **33** C1
Brélès **84** A2
Bremanger **36** A1
Bremen **68** A2
Bremerhaven **68** A1
Bremervörde **68** A1
Bremervörde-Elm **68** A/B1
Bremervörde-Hesedorf **68** A/B1
Bremgarten **90** B3, **105** C1
Bremnes **42** A1
Bremsdorf **70** B3
Bremsnes **32** A/B2
Brenderup **48** B3, **52** B1
Brenes **171** D1
Brenets, Les [Le Locle] **104** B1
Brenna **8** B2
Brenna **33** D2
Brenna **38** A1
Brennberg-Frauenzell **92** B1
Brénnero/Brenner **107** C1
Brennes **4** B3, **10** A1
Brennfjell **4** B3, **10** A1
Brenngam **6** B1
Brennhaug **33** C3, **37** D1
Brennseter **32** B3, **37** C1
Brennvik **8** B3
Breno **106** B2
Brénod **103** D2, **104** A2
Brensbach **81** C3
Brensvik **5** C/D1, **6** A1
Brentónico **106** B3
Brentwood **65** C3
Brescello **114** B1
Bréscia **106** B3
Bresewitz **53** D2/3
Brésimo **106** B2
Breskens **78** B1
Bresles **77** D3
Bressana Bottarone **113** D1
Bressanone/Brixen **107** C1/2
Bressuire **100** B1
Brest **84** A2
Brest **73** D3, **97** D1, **98** A1
Brestanica **127** C2
Brestova **126** B3, **130** A1
Brestovac **135** C2
Brestovac **128** A/B3
Brestovac **139** C1
Brestovac **139** B/C1
Brestovačka Banja **135** C2
Bretenoux **109** D1
Breteuil **86** B1
Breteuil-sur-Noye **77** D3
Brétignolles-sur-Mer **100** A1/2
Bretningen **37** D1/2, **38** A1
Bretten **90** B1
Brettesnes **8** B2
Bretteville-sur-Laize **86** A1
Breuil-Barret **100** B1
Breuil-Cervínia **105** C2/3
Breuilpont **87** C1
Breuna **81** C1
Brevens bruk **46** B1/2
Brevik **47** D1
Breviken **45** C1
Brévine, La [Les Verrières] **104** B1
Breza **132** B2
Breždje **133** D2, **134** A2
Brezičani **131** D1
Brežice **127** C2/3

Březina 83 B/C2/3
Brezna 133 D3, 134 B3
Breznica 127 D2
Březnice 83 C3, 93 C1
Březnice 96 A2
Breznik 140 B3
Breznik 139 D1
Březno 83 C2
Brezno 97 C2
Brezoi 140 B2
Brézolles 87 B/C1/2
Brezová pod Bradlom 95 C2
Brezovica 134 B3
Brezovica 138 B2
Brezovica 127 D3
Brezovo Polje 133 C1
Briançon 112 A/B1
Briare 87 D3
Briático 122 A2
Bribir 127 C3, 130 B1
Bričany 98 B3
Bricherásio 112 B1
Bricon 88 B2
Bricquebec 76 A3
Brides 62 B1
Brides-les-Bains 104 B3
Bridgend 63 C1/2
Bridgend 54 A2/3, 55 D1
Bridge of Allan 56 B1
Bridge of Cally 57 C1
Bridge of Earn 57 C1
Bridge of Orchy 56 B1
Bridgnorth 59 D3, 64 A2
Bridgwater 63 C/D2
Bridlington 61 D2
Bridport 63 D2/3
Briec 84 B2
Brie-Comte-Robert 87 D1/2
Briedel 80 A3
Brielle 66 A3
Brienne-le-Château 88 B2
Brienon-sur-Armançon 88 A2
Brienz 105 C1
Brienza 120 A3
Brieselang 70 A2
Briesen 70 B3
Brieske 83 C1
Brieskow-Finkenheerd 70 B3
Brietlingen 69 B/C1
Brieva de Cameros 153 C/D3
Brieves 151 C/D1
Briey 89 C1
Brig 105 C2
Brigg 61 D2/3
Brighouse 61 C2
Brightlingsea 65 C/D2/3
Brighton 76 B1
Brignais 103 D3
Brignogan-Plage 84 A1/2
Brignoles 112 A3
Brigstock 64 B2
Brihuega 161 C2
Briksdal 36 B2
Brill 64 B2/3
Brillon-en-Barrois 88 B1/2
Brilon 80 B1
Brilon-Alme 80 B1
Brilon-Messinghausen 80 B1
Brimnes 36 B3
Briñas 153 C/D2
Brinches 165 C3, 170 B1
Brincones 159 C2
Bríndisi 121 D2
Bringsinghaug 36 A1
Brinje 130 B1
Brinon-sur-Beuvron 88 A3, 102 B1
Brinon-sur-Sauldre 87 D3
Brintbodarne 39 C2
Brínzio 105 D2/3
Brión 150 A2
Brione (Verzasca) [Tenero] 105 D2
Brioni 130 A1
Brionne 77 C3, 86 B1
Brion-sur-Ource 88 B2/3
Brioude 102 B3
Briouze 86 A1/2
Briscous 108 B3, 155 C1
Brisighella 115 C2, 116 B1
Brissac-Quincé 86 A3
Brissago [Locarno] 105 D2
Brist 132 A3, 136 B1
Bristol 63 D2
Briton Ferry 63 C1
Brittas 58 A2
Brittas Bay 58 A3
Britvica 132 A3
Britz 70 B2
Brive-la-Gaillarde 101 D3
Briviesca 153 C2
Brixen in Tirol 92 B3
Brixham 63 C3
Brixlegg 92 A3
Bříza 83 C/D2
Brka 133 B/C1
Brlog 130 B1
Brna 136 A1
Brnjica 135 C1/2
Brno 94 B1
Brno 96 B2
Bro 72 B1
Bro 47 C1
Bro 47 D2/3
Bro 44 B2
Broadstairs 65 C3, 76 B1
Broadway 63 D1, 64 A2
Broager 52 B2
Broaryd 50 B1
Broby 50 B2
Broby 72 A1
Broćanac 131 C1
Broc [Broc-Village] 104 B2
Bröckel 68 B2
Brockenhurst 76 A1
Broczyno 71 D1
Brod 133 B/C3
Brod 138 B3
Brod 140 A3
Brodarevo 133 C/D3, 134 A3, 137 D1, 138 A1
Broddbo 40 A3
Broddebo 46 B3
Brodek u Prostějova 94 B1
Brodersby 52 B2
Brodersby-Schönhagen 52 B2
Brodica 135 C2
Brodick 56 A2
Brodick 54 A3, 55 D1
Brod Moravice 127 C3
Brod na Kupi 127 C3
Brodnica 73 C3
Brodosavce 138 B2
Brod Prizrenski 138 B2
Brod Prizrenski 140 A3
Brody 97 D2, 98 B2
Brody 70 B3
Brody 71 C3
Broek 79 D1
Broglie 86 B1
Brójce 71 C3
Brokind 46 B2/3
Brokstedt 52 B3
Brolo 125 C1/2
Bromarv 24 B3
Brome 69 C2
Bromley 65 C3, 76 B1
Bromma 47 C1
Bromma 37 D3
Brommösund 45 D2
Bromnes 4 A2
Bromölla 51 B/C2/3
Bromölla 72 A1
Brompton 61 D2
Brömsebro 51 D2
Bromsgrove 59 D3, 64 A2
Bromyard 59 D3, 63 D1
Bronchales 162 A2
Brønderslev 48 B1
Broni 113 D1
Bronikowo 71 C/D1
Bronkow 70 B3, 83 C1
Brønnøysund 14 A3
Brøns 52 A1/2
Bronte 125 C2
Bronzani Majdan 131 D1, 132 A1
Broons 85 C2
Broquiès 110 A2
Brørup 48 A/B3, 52 A/B1
Brösarp 50 B3
Brösarp 72 A2
Brøske 32 B2
Brossac 101 C3
Brøstadbotn 9 D1
Broșteni 135 D1
Broșteni 140 B2
Brøstrud 37 C3
Brotas 164 B2
Brötjemark 46 A3
Broto 155 C2
Brottby 40 B3, 47 D1
Brøttem 28 A3, 33 C2
Brotterode 81 D2
Brøttingsvåg 32 B1
Brøttum 38 A2
Brou 86 A/B2
Brough 57 D3, 60 B1
Brough 54 B3
Broughshane 56 A3
Broughton 57 C2
Broughton in Furness 59 C1, 60 A/B2
Broughty Ferry 57 C1
Broumov 82 B3
Broumov 96 B1
Brouwersdam 66 A3
Brouwershaven 66 A3
Brouzet-lès-Alès 111 C2
Brovallen 40 A3
Brovary 99 C/D2
Brovès 112 A3
Brovst 48 B1
Brownhills 59 D3, 64 A1/2
Brozas 165 D1
Brozzo 106 B3
Brtnice 94 A1
Brtonigla 126 A/B3, 130 A1
Bru 36 A2
Bru 42 A2
Brua 33 D3
Bruay-en-Artois 78 A2
Brubakk 28 B3, 33 D1
Bruca 124 A2
Bruchhausen-Vilsen 68 A2
Bruchmühlbach-Miesau 90 A1
Bruchsal 90 B1
Bruck 92 B1
Brück 69 D3, 70 A3
Bruck an der Grossglocknerstrasse 107 D1, 126 A1
Bruck an der Mur 94 A3
Bruck an der Leitha 94 B3
Bruck an der Mur 96 A3
Bruck an der Leitha 96 B3
Brücken 80 A3
Brückl 126 B1
Bruckmühl 92 A/B3
Brúcoli 125 D3
Brüel 53 D3, 69 C/D1
Bruère-Allichamps 102 A1
Brués 150 B2
Bruflat 37 D3
Bruges 108 B3, 154 B1
Brugg 90 B3
Brugge 78 A1
Brüggen 79 D1
Brüggen 68 B3
Brühl 80 A2
Bruksvallarna 34 A2/3
Brûlon 86 A2
Brûly 78 B3
Brumath 90 A2
Brummen 67 C3
Brumunddal 38 A2
Brumund sag 38 A2
Bruna 117 C3
Brunau 69 C2
Brunehamel 78 B3
Brunella 123 D1
Brunete 160 B2
Brunflo 34 B2
Brunheda 158 B1
Brunico/Bruneck 107 C1
Bruniquel 109 D2
Brunkeberg 43 C2
Brunna 40 B3
Brunna 47 C1
Brunnbach 93 D3
Brunnberget 39 C2
Brunnen 105 D1
Brunnsberg 39 C1
Brunsbüttel 52 A/B3
Brunskog 38 B3, 45 C1
Brunssum 79 D1/2
Bruntál 96 B2
Bruntveit 42 A1
Bruravik 36 B3
Brus 134 B3
Brusago 107 C2
Brusali 42 A3
Brusand 42 A3
Brušane 130 B2
Brusarci 135 D3
Brusasco 113 C1
Brusino Arsízio [Capolago-Riva s. Vitale] 105 D2/3
Brúsio 106 B2
Brusnik 135 C2
Brusno 95 D1/2
Brusson 105 C3
Brüssow 70 B1
Brutelles 77 D2
Bruton 63 D2, 64 A3
Bruttig-Fankel 80 A3
Bruvik 36 A3
Bruvno 131 C2
Bruvoll 38 A2
Bruxelles/Brussel 78 B2
Bruyéres 89 D2
Bruyères-et-Montbérault 78 B3
Bruzaholm 46 A3
Břvany 83 C2
Brydal 33 D3
Bryn 38 A3, 43 D1
Brynamman 63 C1
Bryne 42 A2
Bryngelhögen 34 B3
Bryn-Hoffnant 62 B1
Brynilen 4 B2
Brynje 29 D3, 34 B2
Brynjegård 29 D3, 35 C2
Brynmawr 63 C1
Bryrup 48 B3
Brzan 134 B2
Brza Palanka 135 C2
Brzeće 134 B3
Brzeg (Brieg) 96 B1
Brzezie 71 D1
Brzozowiec 71 C2
Bua 49 D1, 50 A1
Bua 72 A1
Buais 85 D2, 86 A2
Buan 33 C2
Buarcos 158 A3
Buavåg 42 A1
Bubany 128 A3
Bubari 142 A2/3
Búbbio 113 C1
Bubenreuth 82 A3
Buberget 31 C2
Buberow 70 A2
Bubierca 161 D1, 162 A1
Bubry 84 B2
Bučač 98 B3
Buçaco 158 A2/3
Buccheri 125 C3
Bucchiánico 119 C1
Buccino 120 A2
Bucelas 164 A2
Buchbach 92 B2
Buchbach-Walkersaich 92 B2
Buchboden 106 A/B1
Buchdorf 91 D2
Bücheloh 81 D2, 82 A2
Buchen 81 C3, 91 C1
Büchen 69 C1
Buchenau (Lahn) 80 B2
Buchenbach (Freiburg) 90 B3
Buchenhain 70 A1
Buchères 88 A/B2
Buchholz 70 A3
Buchholz 81 D1, 82 A1
Buchholz in der Nordheide 68 B1
Buchholz-Sprötze 68 B1
Buchloe 91 D3
Buchlov 95 C1
Buchlovice 95 C1
Buchlyvie 56 B1
Buch-Obenhausen 91 D2
Buchs 105 D1, 106 A1
Buchy 76 B3
Bučica 127 D3
Bučin prohod 139 D1
Bučje 135 C3
Bučje 133 C3
Buckden 65 B/C2
Bückeburg 68 A3
Bücken 68 A2
Buckfastleigh 63 C3
Buckhaven 57 C1
Buckie 54 B2
Buckingham 64 B2
Bucklers Hard 76 A1
Buckow 70 B2
Bückwitz 69 D2
Bučovice 94 B1
Bucsu 127 D1
București 141 C2
Bucy-les-Pierrepont 78 B3
Bucz 71 D3
Bud 32 A2
Buda 83 D3
Budakalász 95 D3
Budakeszi 95 D3
Budal 33 C2
Buđanovci 133 D1, 134 A1
Budaörs 95 D3, 129 C1
Budapest 95 D3
Budapest 97 B/C3
Budča 95 D2
Buddbyn 17 B/C2
Büddenstedt-Neu Büddenstedt 69 C3
Buddusò 123 D2
Bude 62 B2
Budeč 94 A1
Büdelsdorf 52 B3
Budenheim 80 B3
Budens 170 A2
Büderich 67 C3, 79 D1, 80 A1
Büderscheid 79 D3
Büdesheim 79 D2
Budești 141 C2
Budia 161 C/D2
Budimlić Japra 131 C1
Büdingen 81 C2
Budišov 94 A1
Budleigh Salterton 63 C3
Budmerice 95 C2
Budogošč' 75 C1
Budoni 123 D1
Búdrio 115 C1
Budva 137 C2
Budyně nad Ohří 83 C2
Budzyń 71 D2
Bue 42 A2/3
Bueña 163 C2
Buenache de la Sierra 161 D3
Buenache de Alarcón 161 D3, 168 B1
Buenamadre 159 C/D2
Buenasbodas 160 A3, 166 B1
Buenaventura 160 A3
Buenavista de Valdavia 152 B2
Buendía 161 C/D2/3
Buer 45 B/C1
Bueu 150 A2
Bugarach 156 A/B1
Bugarra 169 C1
Bugeat 102 A3
Buger 157 C2
Buggerru 123 C3
Buggingen 90 A3
Buglose 108 A2
Bugnara 119 C2
Bugojno 131 D2, 132 A2
Bugøyfjord 7 C2
Bugøynes 7 C2
Bugyi 129 C1
Bühl 90 B2
Bühlertal 90 B2
Bühlertann 91 C1
Bühlerzell 91 C1
Buhuși 141 C1
Búia 126 A2
Builth Wells 63 C1
Buis-les-Baronnies 111 D2
Buitenpost 67 C1
Buitrago 153 D3
Buitrago del Lozoya 161 C2
Bujalance 167 C3, 172 B1
Bujanovac 139 C2
Bujanovac 140 A3
Bujaraloz 155 B/C3, 163 B/C1
Bujarrabal 161 D2
Buje 126 B3, 130 A1
Buk 71 D2/3
Bükköds 128 B2
Bukovac 131 D1, 132 A1
Bukovac 129 C3
Bukova Gora 131 D3, 132 A3
Bukovi 133 D2, 134 A2
Bukovje 126 B3
Buków 71 C3
Bukowiec 71 D2

Bukowiec 71 D3
Bulačani 138 B2
Bülach 90 B3
Bulat-Pestivien 84 B2
Bulbuente 154 A3, 162 A1
Buldan 149 D2
Bulgnéville 89 C2
Bulinac 128 A3
Bulken 36 B3
Bullas 168 B3, 174 A1
Bullay 80 A3
Bulle 104 B2
Büllingen 79 D2
Bulqizë 138 A3
Bultei 123 D2
Bulwell 61 D3, 65 C1
Bumbeşti-Jiu 135 D1
Buna 132 B3, 136 B1
Bünde 68 A3
Bunde 67 D1
Bunessan 56 A1
Bungay 65 D2
Bunge 47 D2
Bunić 131 C2
Buniel 153 B/C2
Bunkeflostrand 50 A3
Bunkris 39 C1
Bunleix 102 A2/3
Bunnerviken 29 C3, 34 A2
Buñol 169 C1
Buntingford 65 C2
Buñuel 154 A3
Bunyola 157 C2
Buollannjargga 5 D3, 6 A3, 11 D1
Buonabitácolo 120 A3
Buonalbergo 119 D3, 120 A2
Buonconvento 115 B/C3, 116 B2
Burbach-Niederdresselndorf 80 B2
Burbage 64 A3, 76 A1
Burbáguena 163 C2
Burcei 123 D3
Bureå 31 D1
Bureåborg 30 B3, 35 D1
Burela 151 B/C1
Büren 80 B1
Büren an der Aare 104 B1
Büren-Steinhausen 80 B1
Bures 65 C2
Bureta 154 A3, 162 A1
Burfjord 5 B/C2
Burford 64 A2/3
Burg 69 D3
Burg 70 B3
Burg 53 C2/3
Burg 52 B3
Burgas 141 C3
Burgau 170 A2
Burgau 127 D1
Burgau 91 D2
Burgbernheim 81 D3, 91 D1
Burgbrohl 80 A2
Burgdorf 68 B2
Burgdorf 105 C1
Burgdorf-Ramlingen-Ehlershausen 68 B2
Burgebrach 81 D3
Bürgel 82 A2
Bürgeln 90 A3
Bürgeln 81 B/C2
Burgelo 153 D2
Burgess Hill 76 B1
Burgh 66 A3
Burghammer 83 D1
Burghaslach 81 D3
Burghaun 81 C2
Burghausen 92 B2
Burgheim 91 D2, 92 A2
Burgh le Marsh 61 D3, 65 C1
Burghley House 64 B1/2
Búrgio 124 B2
Burgkirchen 92 B2
Burgkunstadt 82 A3
Burglengenfeld 92 B1
Burgohondo 160 A2
Burgos 153 C2
Búrgos 123 C/D2
Burgsalach 92 A1
Burgschwalbach 80 B2
Burgsinn 81 C3
Burgstädt 82 B2
Burgstall 69 C/D2/3
Burg-Stargard 70 A1
Burgsteinfurt 67 D3
Burg Strechau 93 D3
Burgsvik 47 D3
Burgsvik 72 B1
Burguete 108 B3, 155 C1/2
Burgui 154 B2
Burguillos 171 D1
Burguillos del Cerro 165 D3
Burguillos de Toledo 160 B3, 167 C1
Burgwald-Ernsthausen 80 B1/2
Burgwedel 68 B2
Burgwedel-Wettmar 68 B2
Burgwindheim 81 D3
Burhaniye 149 D1
Buriasco 112 B1
Burie 101 B/C3
Burjasot 169 D1
Burk 91 D1
Burkardroth 81 D2
Burkardroth-Waldfenster 81 C/D2
Burkersdorf 83 C2
Burkhardsdorf 82 B2
Burlada 154 A2
Burladingen-Stetten 91 C2
Burladingen-Hausen 91 C2
Burladingen 91 C2
Burnham Market 65 C1
Burnham-on-Crouch 65 C3
Burnham-on-Sea 63 C/D2
Burnley 59 D1, 60 B2
Burnley 54 B3
Burntisland 57 C1
Burón 152 A1/2
Buronzo 105 C3
Burøy 32 B1/2
Burøysund 4 A2
Burrel 138 A3
Burriana 163 C3, 169 D1
Burry Port 62 B1
Burs 47 D3
Burscheid 80 A1
Bürserberg 106 A1
Burseryd 50 B1
Bursnäs 34 B3
Burstad 5 D1, 6 A1
Bürstadt 80 B3
Burtenbach 91 D2
Burton 59 D1, 60 B2
Burton Agnes 61 D2
Burtonport 55 C2
Burton upon Trent 61 C3, 64 A1
Burträsk 31 D1
Buru 97 D3, 140 B1
Buruen 38 A1
Burujón 160 B3, 167 C1
Burvik 31 D1
Burwell 65 C2
Burwick 54 B1
Bury 59 D2, 60 B2
Bury Saint Edmunds 65 C2
Burzet 111 C1
Busachi 123 C2
Busalla 113 D1/2
Busana 114 A2, 116 A1
Busca 112 B2
Busche 107 C2
Buseck-Beuern 81 B/C2
Busenberg 90 A/B1
Buseto Palizzolo 124 A2
Buševac 127 D3
Bushat 137 D2
Busigny 78 A/B3
Busjön 31 C1
Busk 97 D2, 98 B2
Buskhyttan 47 C2
Busko-Zdrój 97 C1/2
Bušletić 132 B1
Busot 169 D2/3
Busovača 132 B2
Bussang 89 D2/3, 90 A3
Busset 102 B2
Busseto 114 A1
Bussière-Badil 101 C3
Bussière-Poitevine 101 D2
Bussö 41 D3
Bussolengo 106 B3
Bussoleno 112 B1
Büssü 128 B2
Bussum 66 B3
Bussy [Cugy FR] 104 B1
Bustares 161 C1/2
Bustarviejo 161 B/C2
Bustillo del Páramo 151 D2
Bustillo del Oro 152 A3, 159 D1, 160 A1
Bustnes 14 B2
Busto Arsízio 105 D3
Busto de Bureba 153 C2
Bustos 158 A2
Büsum 52 A3
Butan 140 B2
Butera 125 C3
Bütgenbach 79 D2
Buthroton 142 A3
Butjadingen-Langwarden 52 A3, 67 D1, 68 A1
Butjadingen-Burhave 67 D1, 68 A1
Butjadingen-Eckwarden 67 D1, 68 A1
Butjadingen-Stollhamm 67 D1, 68 A1
Butrinti 142 A3
Bütschwil 91 C3, 105 D1, 106 A1
Buttapietra 107 B/C3
Buttelstedt 82 A1
Buttenheim 82 A3
Buttenwiesen 91 D2
Buttermere 57 C3, 60 A/B1
Buttes 104 B1
Buttlar 81 C/D2
Buttstädt 82 A1
Butzbach 80 B2
Butzen 70 B3
Bützow 53 D3, 69 D1
Buvåg 9 C2
Buvassbrenna 37 C3
Buvatn Fjellstue (Engene Fjellstue) 37 D3
Buvik 28 A3, 33 C2
Buvik 14 B2
Buvik 32 A/B2
Buvika 33 D3
Buxières-les-Mines 102 B2
Buxtehude 68 B1
Buxton 59 D2, 61 C3, 64 A1
Buxy 103 D1
Buzançais 101 D1
Buzancy 79 C3
Buzău 141 C2
Buzet 126 B3, 130 A1
Buziaş 140 A1/2
Byberget 35 C3
Bybjerg 49 D3, 53 D1
Bydalen 34 B2
Bydgoszcz 72 B3
Byerum 51 D1
Byfield 65 C2
Bygd 36 B3
Bygdeå 20 A1, 31 D2
Bygdeträsk 31 D1
Bygdin 37 C2
Bygdsiljum 31 D1/2
Bygget 50 B1/2
Bygland 43 C2
Byglandsfjord 43 B/C2/3
Bygstad 36 A2
Byhleguhre 70 B3
Byholma 50 B2
Byhov 99 C1
Bykle 42 B2
Bylderup 52 B2
Bylnice 95 C1
Byn 35 D3
Byneset 28 A3, 33 C1
Byremo 42 B3
Byrkjedal 42 A/B2
Byrkjelo 36 B2
Byrknes 36 A3
Byrum 49 C1
Byšice-Liblice 83 D2
Byske 31 D1
Býškovice 95 C1
Byssträsk 31 C1/2
Bystrica 97 D2, 98 A3
Bystřice 83 D3
Bystřice nad Pernštejnem 94 B1
Bystřice pod Hostýnem 95 C1
Bytča 95 D1
Bytča 96 B2
Bytnica 71 C3
Bytom 96 B2
Bytom Odrzański (Beuthen) 71 C3
Bytów 72 B2
Bytyń 71 D2
Byvalla 40 A2
Bywell 57 D2/3
Byxelkrok 51 D1
Byxelkrok 72 B1
Bzenec 95 C1
Bzovík 95 D2

C

Cabação 164 B2
Caballar 160 B1/2
Cabana 150 A1
Cabañas 150 B1
Cabañas de Yepes 161 C3, 167 D1
Cabañas de la Sagra 160 B3
Cabañas de Virtus 152 B1/2
Cabañas del Castillo 166 A/B1
Cabanes 163 C3
Cabanillas 161 C2
Cabanillas 154 A3
Cabanne 113 D2
Čabar 127 B/C3
Cabdella 155 D2
Čabdin 127 C/D3
Cabeça Gorda 164 B3, 170 B1
Cabeceiras de Basto 158 B1
Cabeço de Vide 165 C2
Cabella 113 D1
Cabeza del Buey 166 B2
Cabeza de Vaca 165 D3
Cabezamesada 161 C3, 167 D1, 168 A1
Cabezarados 167 C2
Cabezarrubias 167 C2
Cabezas del Villar 160 A2
Cabezas Rubias 171 C1
Cabezón 152 B3, 160 A/B1
Cabezón de la Sal 152 B1
Cabezuela del Valle 159 D3
Cabo de Palos 174 B1
Cabolafuente 161 D1
Cabo Roig 169 C3, 174 B1
Cabourg 76 B3, 86 A1
Cabra 172 B1
Cabra 158 B2
Cabra del Camp 163 C1
Cabra del Santo Cristo 173 C1
Cabra de Mora 162 B3
Cábras 123 C2
Cabredo 153 D2
Cabreiro 150 A3
Cabreiroá 151 B/C3
Cabreiros 150 B1
Cabrejas del Campo 153 D3, 161 D1
Cabrejas del Pinar 153 C/D3, 161 C1
Cabrela 164 B2
Cabrerets 109 D1
Cabril 158 B3
Cabril 158 A/B2
Cabrillanes 151 D2
Cabrillas 159 D2
Cabuérniga 152 B1
Cacabelos 151 C2
Čačak 133 D2, 134 A2/3
Čačak 140 A2
Caçarelhos 151 C/D3, 159 C1
Cáccamo 124 B2
Caccuri 122 B2
Cacela 170 B2
Cáceres 165 D1, 166 A1
Cachopo 170 B2
Cachorrilla 159 C3, 165 D1
Čachrov 93 C1
Čachtice 95 C2
Cacia 158 A2
Čačinci 128 B3
Cadafais 164 A2
Cadalso 159 C3
Cadalso de los Vidrios 160 B3
Cadaqués 156 B2
Cadaval 164 A1/2
Cadavedo 151 C/D1
Čađavica 131 D2, 132 A2
Čadca 95 D1
Čadca 96 B2
Cadelbosco di Sotto 114 B1
Cadelbosco di Sopra 114 B1
Cadenazzo 105 D2
Cadenberge 52 A/B3, 68 A1
Cadenet 111 D2
Cadeo 114 A1
Cadeuil 100 B3
Cádiar 173 C2
Cadillac 108 B1
Cadillon 108 B3, 155 B/C1
Cadima 158 A3
Cádiz 171 D3
Čadjavica 128 B3
Cadolzburg 81 D3, 91 D1, 92 A1
Cadoùin 109 C1
Cadours 109 C2
Cadreita 154 A2
Cadrete 154 B3, 162 B1
Čadyr-Lunga 141 D1
Caen 76 B3, 86 A1
Caër 86 A/B1
Caerano di San Marco 107 C3
Caergwrle 59 C2, 60 B3
Caerlaverock Castle 57 C3, 60 A1
Caerleon 63 C/D1
Caernarfon 59 B/C2, 60 A3
Caerphilly 63 C1
Caersws 59 C3
Caëstre 78 A2
Caetobriga 164 A2/3
Cagli 115 D3, 117 C2
Cágliari 123 D3
Cágliari 123 D3
Čaglin 128 B3
Cagnano Varano 120 B1
Cagnes-sur-Mer 112 B3
Čagoda 75 D1
Cahir 55 C3
Cahors 109 D1/2
Cahuzac-sur-Vère 109 D2
Caiazzo 119 D3
Cain Picafort 157 C2
Caiolo 106 A2
Caión 150 A1
Cairnryan 56 A/B3
Cairnryan 54 A3, 55 D2
Cáiro Montenotte 113 C2
Caister-on-Sea 65 D1/2
Caistor 61 D3
Caivano 119 D3
Cajarc 109 D1
Čajetina 133 C/D3, 134 A3
Čajić 131 D3, 132 A2/3
Čajniče 133 C3
Čakovec 127 D2
Čakovec 96 B3
Cala 165 D3, 166 A3, 171 C/D1
Calabernardo 125 D3
Cala Blanca 157 C1
Cala Blanes 157 C1
Cala Blava 157 C2
Cala Bona 157 C1
Calabor 151 C3
Calaceite 163 C2
Calacuccia 113 D3
Cala d'Oliva 123 C1
Cala d'Or 157 C/D1/2
Caladrones 155 C3
Calaf 155 D3, 156 A3, 163 D1
Calafat 135 D2
Calafat 140 B2
Calafell La Platja 156 A3, 163 D1
Cala Figuera 157 D2
Cala Gonone 123 D2
Cala Grassió 169 D2
Calahonda 172 B3
Calahonda 173 C2
Calahorra 153 D2, 154 A2
Calahorra de Boedo 152 B2
Calais 77 D1

Cala Llonga 157 D3
Calambrone 114 A3, 116 A2
Cala Millor 157 C1
Calamita 124 A2
Calamocha 163 C2
Calamonte 165 D2
Cala Morell 157 C1
Cala Murada 157 C1/2
Calañas 171 C1
Calanda 162 B2
Calangiánus 123 D1
Cala'n Porter 157 C1
Cala Pi 157 D2
Călăraşi 141 C2
Cala Ratjada 157 C1
Cala San Vicente 157 D3
Cala San Vicente 157 C2
Calasanz 155 C3
Calascibetta 125 C2
Calas de Mallorca 157 C1/2
Calasetta 123 C3
Calasparra 168 B3
Calatafimi 124 A2
Calatañazor 153 C/D3, 161 C1
Cala Tarida 169 D2
Calatayud 162 A1
Calatorao 155 C3, 163 C1
Calau 70 B3
Cala Vadella 169 D2
Calavino 106 B2
Calbe 69 D3
Calcena 154 A3, 162 A1
Calcinelli 115 D2, 117 C1/2
Calco 105 D3, 106 A3
Caldaro/Kaltern 107 C2
Caldarola 115 D3, 117 D2
Caldas da Felgueira 158 B2
Caldas da Rainha 164 A1
Caldas de Besaya 152 B1
Caldas de Cavaca 158 B2
Caldas de Monchique 170 A2
Caldas de Nocedo 152 A2
Caldas de Reis 150 A2
Caldas de San Adrián 152 A2
Caldas de Vizela 158 A1
Caldas do Gerez 150 B3, 158 A/B1
Caldbeck 57 C3, 60 B1
Caldelas 150 A/B3, 158 A1
Calden 81 C1
Calderari 125 C2
Calders 156 A3
Caldes de Bohí 155 C/D2
Caldes de Malavella 156 B2/3
Caldes de Montbui 156 A3
Caldetes 156 B3
Caldiero 107 C3
Caldirola 113 D1
Caldonazzo 107 C2
Calella de Mar 156 B3
Calella de Palafrugell 156 B2
Calenzana 113 D2/3
Calera de León 165 D3
Calera y Chozas 160 A3, 166 B1
Caleruega 153 C3, 161 C1
Caleruela 160 A3, 166 B1
Calestano 114 A1
Calgary 56 A1
Cálig 163 C2
Calitri 120 A2
Calivelos 158 B2
Calizzano 113 C2
Callac 84 B2
Callander 56 B1
Calliano 113 C1
Callington 62 B3
Callione 107 B/C2
Callosa de Ensarriá 169 D2
Callosa de Segura 169 C3
Čalma 133 C1
Calne 63 D2, 64 A3
Calolziocorte 105 D3, 106 A3
Calonge de les Gavarres 156 B2
Calore 119 D3, 120 A2
Calov 108 B2
Čalovo 95 C3
Calpe 169 D2
Caltabellotta 124 B2
Caltagirone 125 C3
Caltanissetta 125 B/C2
Caltavuturo 124 B2
Caltojar 161 C/D1
Caluso 105 C3
Calvaire 85 C2/3
Calvarrasa de Abajo 159 D2
Calvarrasa de Arriba 159 D2
Calvello 120 B3
Calvera 155 C2
Calvi 113 D2
Calvia 157 C2
Calvi dell'Úmbria 117 C3, 118 B1
Calvinet 110 A1
Calvisson 111 C2
Calvörde 69 C2/3
Calvos de Randín 150 B3
Calw 90 B2
Calw-Hirsau 90 B2
Calw-Stammheim 90 B2
Calzada de Calatrava 167 C2
Calzada de Don Diego 159 D2
Calzada del Coto 152 A2
Calzada de los Molinos 152 B2
Calzada de Valdunciel 159 D2
Calzadilla 159 C3
Calzadilla de los Barros 165 D3, 166 A3
Calzadilla de la Cueza 152 A/B2
Camaiore 114 A2, 116 A1
Camáldoli 115 C2, 116 B1
Camañas 163 C2
Camarasa 155 D3
Camarate 164 A2
Camarena de la Sierra 162 A/B3
Camarès 110 A2
Camaret-sur-Mer 84 A2
Camargo 152 B1
Camarillas 162 B2
Camariñas 150 A1
Camarma de Esteruelas 161 C2
Camarmeña 152 A1
Camarzana de Tera 151 D3
Camas 171 D1
Cambados 150 A2
Cambeo 150 B2
Camberley 64 B3, 76 B1
Cambil 173 C1
Cambo-les-Bains 108 B3, 155 C1
Camborne 62 A/B3
Cambra 158 A/B2
Cambrai 78 A2/3
Cambre 150 B1
Cambridge 65 C2
Cambrils de Mar 163 D2
Cambron 77 D2
Cambs 53 C/D3, 69 C1
Camburg 82 A1
Cámedo 105 D2
Camelford 62 B3
Camelle 150 A1
Camerino 115 D3, 117 D2
Camerota 120 A3
Camigliatello Silano 122 B1/2
Camin 69 C1
Caminha 150 A3
Caminomorisco 159 C3
Caminreal 163 C2
Camisano Vicentino 107 C3
Cammarata 124 B2
Cammer 69 D3, 70 A3
Cammin 53 D3
Camogli 113 D2
Camoins-les-Bains 111 D3
Camon 109 D3, 156 A1
Campagna 119 D3, 120 A2
Campagne 109 C1
Campagne 108 B2
Campan 109 B/C3, 155 C1
Campana 122 B1
Campanario 166 A2
Campanas 154 A2
Campanet 157 C2
Campano 171 D3
Campaspero 152 B3, 160 B1
Campbeltown 56 A2
Campbeltown 54 A3, 55 D1/2
Campbon 85 C3
Campdevànol 156 A2
Campeã 158 B1
Campello 169 D3
Campello Monti 105 C2/3
Campese 116 A3
Campi Bisénzio 114 B2, 116 B1
Campíglia 105 C3
Campíglia dei Fosci 114 B3, 116 B2
Campíglia Maríttima 114 B3, 116 A2
Campillo 163 C3
Campillo de Deleitosa 159 D3, 166 A1
Campillo de Aragón 161 D1/2, 162 A1/2
Campillo de Altobuey 168 B1
Campillo de Llerena 166 A2/3
Campillo de Dueñas 162 A2
Campillo de Azaba 159 C2
Campillo de Aranda 153 C3, 160 B1
Campillo de Arenas 173 C1
Campillos 172 A2
Campillos-Paravientos 162 A3
Campillos-Sierra 162 A3
Campione 105 D2
Campione del Garda 106 B3
Campisábalos 161 C1
Campi Salentina 121 D3
Campitello 114 B1
Campitello Matese 119 D2
Campli 117 D3, 119 C1
Campmany 156 B2
Campo 155 C2
Campo 105 D2, 106 A2
Campo 165 C3
Campo 158 A1/2
Campobasso 119 D2
Campobecerros 151 C3
Campobello di Licata 124 B3
Campobello di Mazara 124 A2
Campocologno 106 B2
Campodársego 107 C3
Campo de Caso 152 A1
Campo de Criptana 167 D1, 168 A1
Campo di Giove 119 C2
Campo di Trens/Freienfeld 107 C1
Campodolcino 105 D2, 106 A2
Campodónico 115 D3, 117 C2
Campofelice di Roccella 124 B2
Campofelice di Fitália 124 B2
Campofiorito 124 B2
Campofórmido 126 A2
Campotorogna 117 C/D3, 118 B1
Campofrío 165 D3, 171 C1
Campogalliano 114 B1
Campo Lameiro 150 A2
Campolasta/Astfeld 107 C1/2
Campolattaro 119 D2/3
Campo Lígure 113 C/D1/2
Campo Maior 165 C2
Campomanes 151 D1
Campomarino 119 D2, 120 A1
Campomarino 121 C/D3
Campo Molino 112 B2
Cámpora San Giovanni 122 A2
Campo Real 161 C3
Camporeale 124 A/B2
Camporells 155 C3
Camporredondo de Alba 152 A/B2
Camporredondo 160 B1
Camporrobles 163 C3, 169 D1
Campos 162 B2
Campos 150 B3, 158 B1
Camposampiero 107 C3
Camposanto 114 B1
Campos del Puerto 157 C2
Campos del Río 169 D3
Campotéjar 173 C1
Campo Túres/Sand in Tirol 107 C1
Campoverde 118 B2
Camprodón 156 A/B2
Camps-en-Amiénois 77 D2/3
Camucia 115 C3, 116 B2
Camugnano 114 B2, 116 B1
Camuñas 167 D1
Çan 149 D1
Canach 79 D3
Cañada de Calatrava 167 C2
Cañada de Benatanduz 162 B2
Cañada del Hoyo 161 D3, 162 A3
Cañadajuncosa 168 B1
Cañada-Rosal 172 A1
Čanak 131 B/C1/2
Çanakkale 149 C1
Canale 113 C1
Canalejas del Arroyo 161 D2/3
Canales de Molina 161 D2
Canals 169 C/D2
Canal San Bovo 107 C2
Cañamero 166 B1
Canas de Senhorim 158 B2
Cañaveral 159 C3, 165 D1
Cañaveral de León 165 D3, 171 C1
Cañaveras 161 D2/3
Cañaveruelas 161 D2/3
Canazei 107 C2
Cancale 85 C/D1/2
Cancellara 120 B2
Cancello Arnone 119 C3
Cancon 109 C1
Candal 158 A/B2
Candanchú 154 B2
Candasnos 155 C3, 163 C1
Candé 85 D3
Candela 120 A2
Candelario 159 D2/3
Candeleda 160 A3
Candemil 158 B1
Candes-Saint-Martin 86 A/B3, 101 C1
Cándia Lomellina 105 D3, 113 C1
Candilichera 153 D3, 161 D1
Candín 151 C2
Caneças 164 A2
Canelli 113 C1
Canero 151 C1
Canet 156 B1
Canet de Mar 156 B3
Cañete 162 A3
Cañete de las Torres 167 C3, 172 B1
Cañete la Real 172 A2
Canet lo Roig 163 C2
Canet-Plage 156 B1
Canfranc 154 B2
Cangas 150 A2/3
Cangas de Narcea 151 C1
Cangas de Onís 152 A1
Canha 164 B2
Canhestros 164 B3, 170 A1
Canicattì 124 B2/3
Canicattini Bagni 125 D3
Canicosa de la Sierra 153 C3
Caniles 173 D1/2
Canillas de Aceituno 172 B2
Canillas de Esgueva 152 B3, 160 B1
Canillas de Albaida 172 B2
Canillo 155 D2, 156 A2
Canino 116 B3, 118 A1
Cañizal 159 D1/2, 160 A1
Cañizar 161 C2
Cañizar del Olivar 162 B2
Cañizares 161 D2
Cañizo 152 A3, 159 D1, 160 A1
Čanj 137 D2
Canjáyar 173 D2
Ca'N Jordí 157 D3
Canna 120 B3, 122 B1
Canne 120 B2
Cánnero Riviera 105 D2
Cannes 112 B3
Canneto 125 C/D1
Canneto 114 B3, 116 A2
Canneto sul Óglio 106 B3, 114 A/B1
Cannigione 123 D1
Cannóbio 105 D2
Cannock 59 D3, 64 A1
Cano 165 B/C2
Canonbie 57 C3
Canosa di Púglia 120 B2
Canósio 112 B2
Canossa 114 A/B1
Canove 107 C2/3
Canove 113 C1
Can Pastilla 157 C2
Canredondo 161 D2
Cansano 119 C2
Cantagallo 159 D2/3
Cantalapiedra 160 A1/2
Cantalejo 160 B1
Cantallops 156 B2
Cantalojas 161 C1
Cantalpino 159 D2, 160 A2
Cantanhede 158 A2/3
Cantavieja 162 B2
Čantavir 129 D3
Canterbury 65 D3, 77 C1
Cantiano 115 D3, 117 C2
Cantillana 171 D1
Cantimpalos 160 B2
Cantin 78 A2
Cantiveros 160 A2
Cantoral 152 B2
Cantoria 173 D2, 174 A1/2
Cantù 105 D3, 106 A3
Canvey 65 C3
Cany-Barville 77 C3
Canyelles 156 A3, 163 D1
Canyon 5 C2/3
Canzo 105 D3, 106 A2/3
Caoria 107 C2
Cáorle 107 D3, 126 A3
Caorso 114 A1
Caoulet 109 C2
Capaccio 120 A3
Capaci 124 B1/2
Capafóns 163 D1
Capafonts La Mussara 163 D1
Capálbio 116 B3, 118 A1
Capanne 115 C3, 117 C2
Capánnole 115 C3, 116 B2
Capánnoli 114 B3, 116 A2
Capannori 114 B2, 116 A1
Caparde 133 C2
Capareiros 150 A3, 158 A1
Capari 138 B3, 143 B/C1
Caparica 164 A2
Caparroso 154 A2
Capbreton 108 A2/3, 154 A1
Capdenac-Gare 109 D1, 110 A1
Capdepera 157 C1
Cap-de-Pin 108 A2
Capdesaso 155 B/C3, 162 B1
Capel 64 B3, 76 B1
Capela 150 B1
Capel Curig 59 C2, 60 A3
Capel'ka 74 B1/2
Capella 155 C2/3
Capellades 153 D3, 161 D1
Capellen 79 D3
Capendu 110 A3, 156 B1
Capens 108 B3, 155 C1
Capestang 110 A/B3, 156 B1
Capestrano 117 D3, 119 C1
Cap Fréhel 85 C1/2
Capileira 173 C2
Capilla 166 B2
Capillas 152 A3
Capinha 158 B3
Capistrello 119 C2
Čaplje 131 D1/2
Čapljina 132 A3, 136 B1
Capodimonte 116 B3, 118 A1
Capo di Ponte 106 B2

Capo d'Orlando 125 C1/2
Capolago [Capolago-Riva
S. Vitale] 105 D2/3
Capolíveri 116 A3
Čapor 95 C2
Capo Rizzuto 122 B2
Capoterra 123 C/D3
Capovalle 106 B3
Cappadócia 119 B/C2
Cap Pelat 108 B2
Cappelle 119 C1/2
Cappelle sul Tavo 119 C1
Capracotta 119 C/D2
Capráia 114 A3
Capránica 117 C3, 118 A1
Caprarola 117 C3, 118 A1
Caprese Michelángelo
115 C2/3, 117 B/C2
Capri 119 C/D3
Capriati a Volturno 119 C2
Capríccioli 123 D1
Caprile 107 C2
Caprino Bergamasco
106 A3
Caprino Veronese 106 B3
Căpruța 140 A1
Captieux 108 B2
Cápua 119 C/D3
Capurso 121 C2
Capvern 109 C3, 155 C1
Carabaña 161 C3
Carabanchel 160 B2/3
Carabantes 153 D3,
154 A3, 161 D1
Caracal 140 B2
Caracena 161 C1
Caracenilla 161 D3
Caracuel 167 C2
Caradeuc 85 C2
Caráglio 112 B2
Caraman 109 D3, 155 D1
Caramánico Terme 119 C1
Caramulo 158 A/B2
Caranga 151 D1
Caranguejeira 158 A3,
164 A/B1
Caransebeș 140 A/B2
Carantec 84 B1/2
Carasco 113 D2
Carașova 135 C1
Caraula 135 D2
Caravaca de la Cruz 168 B3,
174 A1
Caravággio 106 A3
Carazo 153 C3
Carbajales de Alba 151 D3,
159 D1
Carbajo 165 C1
Carballeda 151 C2
Carballeda de Avia 150 B2
Carballedo 150 B2
Carballiño 150 B2
Carballo 150 A1
Carbellino 159 D1
Carbonara di Po 114 B1
Carbonare di Folgaria
107 C2
Carbon-Blanc 108 B1
Carboneras 174 A2
Carboneras de Guadazaón
162 A3, 168 B1
Carbonero el Mayor
160 B1/2
Carboneros 167 C/D3
Carbónia 123 C3
Carbonin/Schluderbach
107 D2
Carbonne 108 B3, 155 C1
Carbuccia 113 D3
Carcaboso 159 C/D3
Carcabuey 172 B1
Carcagente 169 D2
Carcans 100 B3, 108 A1
Carcans-Plage 101 C3,
108 B1
Cárcar 153 D2, 154 A2
Cárcare 113 C2
Carcassonne 110 A3,
156 A/B1
Carcastillo 154 A2
Carcelén 169 D2
Carcès 112 A3
Carchel 173 C1
Carchelejo 173 C1
Carcóforo 105 C2/3
Cardedeu 156 A/B3
Cardejón 153 D3, 161 D1
Cardeña 167 C3
Cárdenas 153 C/D2
Cardenete 162 A3, 168 B1
Cardeñosa 160 A2
Cardesse 108 B3, 154 B1
Cardiff 63 C2
Cardigan 62 B1
Cardigan 55 D3
Cardó 163 C2
Cardona 155 D3, 156 A2
Carei 97 D3, 98 A3
Carenas 162 A1
Carennac 109 D1
Carentan 76 B3, 86 A/B1
Carentoir 85 C3
Carevdar 127 D2, 128 A2
Carev Dvor 138 B3, 142 B1
Cargèse 113 D3
Carhaix-Plouguer 84 B2
Caria 158 B3
Cariati 122 B1
Caričin Grad 139 C1
Caridade 165 C3
Carignan 79 C3
Carignano 113 B/C1
Carina 142 B1
Cariñena 163 C1
Carini 124 A/B1/2
Cariño 150 B1
Carínola 119 C3
Carisbrooke Castle 76 B1/2
Carisolo 106 B2
Carlentini 125 D3
Carlet 169 D2
Carling 89 D1
Carlingford 58 A1
Carlisle 57 C3, 60 B1
Carlisle 54 B3
Carloforte 123 C3
Carlópoli 122 B2
Carlow 53 C3, 69 C1
Carlow 55 D3
Carlsberg 80 B3, 90 B1
Carlsfeld 82 B2
Carlton-in-Lindrick 61 C3
Carluke 56 B2
Carmagnola 113 B/C1
Carmarthen 62 B1
Carmaux 109 D2, 110 A2
Carmena 160 B3, 167 C1
Cármenes 151 D2, 152 A2
Carmiano 121 D3
Carmona 171 D1, 172 A1
Carmonita 165 D2, 166 A2
Carnac 84 B3
Carnaxide 164 A2
Carnew 58 A3
Carnforth 59 D1, 60 B2
Cárnia 126 A2
Carnlough 56 A3
Carno 59 C3
Carnon-Plage 110 B3
Carnota 150 A2
Carnoules 112 A3
Carnoustie 57 C1
Carnwath 57 C2
Carolei 122 A2
Carolles 85 D1
Carona 106 A2
Caronía 125 C2
Caronia Marina 125 C2
Carovigno 121 D2
Carovilli 119 D2
Carpaneto Piacentino
114 A1
Carpegna 115 C2,
117 C1/2
Carpenédolo 106 B3
Carpentras 111 C/D2
Carpi 114 B1
Carpineti 114 B1/2
Carpineto Romano 118 B2
Cărpiniș 135 D1
Carpino 120 B1
Carpinone 119 D2
Carpinteiro 164 B1/2
Carpio de Azaba 159 C2
Carquefou 85 D3,
100 A/B1
Carqueiranne 112 A3
Carradale 56 A2
Carral 150 A/B1
Carrapateira 170 A2
Carrapichana 158 B2
Carrara 114 A2, 116 A1
Cărrascal del Río 160 B1
Carrascalejo 160 A3,
166 B1
Carrascosa 161 D2
Carrascosa del Campo
161 C/D3
Carrascosa de Abajo
161 C1
Carrascosa de Haro 168 A1
Carratraca 172 A/B2
Carrazeda de Anciães
158 B1
Carrazedo 151 B/C3,
158 B1
Carrbridge 54 B2
Carreço 150 A3, 158 A1
Carrefour-Saint-Jean
86 A/B1
Carregado 164 A2
Carregal do Sal 158 B2
Carrega Lígure 113 D1
Carregueiros 164 B1
Carreña 152 A1
Carreño 151 D1
Carresse 108 A3, 154 B1
Carrickart 55 C/D2
Carrickfergus 56 A3
Carrión de los Condes
152 B2
Carrión de los Céspedes
171 C/D1/2
Carrión de Calatrava
167 C2
Carrizo de la Ribera 151 D2
Carrizosa 167 D2, 168 A2
Carronbridge 57 B/C2
Carrouges 86 A2
Carrù 113 C2
Carry-le-Rouet 111 D3
Carskiey 56 A2
Carsóli 118 B1/2
Carsphairn 56 B2/3
Carstairs 57 B/C2
Carstairs 54 B3
Cartagena 174 B1
Cártama 172 B2
Cartaxo 164 A2
Cartaya 171 C2
Cartelle 150 B2/3
Carteret 76 A3
Cartoceto 115 D3, 117 C2
Carucedo 151 C2
Carúnchio 119 D2
Carvajal 172 B3
Carvalhal 158 B2
Cârvarica 139 D2
Carviçaes 159 C1/2
Carvin 78 A2
Carvoeira 164 A2
Carvoeira 164 A2
Carvoeiro 170 A2
Carvoeiro 164 B1
Caryduff 56 A3
Carzig 70 B2
Casabermeja 172 B2
Casa Branca 164 A3
Casa Branca 164 B2/3
Casa Branca 164 B2
Casacalenda 119 D2,
120 A1
Casa de Uceda 161 C2
Casaio 151 C2
Casais 170 A2
Casa l'Abate 121 D2/3
Casalánguida 119 D1/2
Casalarreina 153 C2
Casalbordino 119 D1
Casalborgone 113 C1
Casalbuono 120 A/B3
Casalbuttano 106 A/B3
Casal Cermelli 113 C1
Casal di Príncipe 119 C3
Casalécchio di Reno
114 B1/2
Casale Monferrato 113 C1
Casalgrande 114 B1
Casalgrasso 112 B1
Casalmaggiore 114 A/B1
Casalmorano 106 A3
Casalnuovo 122 A3
Casalnuovo Monterotaro
119 D2, 120 A1
Casaloldo 106 B3
Casalpusterlengo 106 A3,
113 D1
Casalromano 106 B3
Casalvécchio di Púglia
119 D2, 120 A1
Casalvieri 119 C2
Casamássima 121 C2
Casamícciola Terme 119 C3
Casamozza 113 D2
Casarabonela 172 A2
Casarano 121 D3
Casar de Cáceres 165 D1
Casar de Palomero
159 C/D3
Casar de Talavera 160 A3,
166 B1
Casares 172 A3
Casares de las Hurdes
159 C/D2
Casariche 172 A/B2
Casarrubios del Monte
160 B3
Casarsa della Delízia
107 D2, 126 A2
Casas Altas 163 C3
Casasana 161 D2
Casas Bajas 163 C3
Casasbuenas 160 B3,
167 C1
Casas de Don Antonio
165 D1/2, 166 A1/2
Casas de Don Pedro
166 B2
Casas de Fernando Alonso
168 B1
Casas de Haro 168 B1
Casas de Juan Núñez
168 B2
Casas de Lázaro 168 B2
Casas del Monte 159 D3
Casas de los Pinos 168 B1
Casas de los Muneras
168 A2
Casas del Puerto de Villatoro
160 A2
Casas de Millán 159 C3,
165 D1, 166 A1
Casas de Miravete 159 D3,
166 A1
Casas de Reina 166 A3
Casas de Ves 169 D1/2
Casaseca 159 D1
Casas-Ibáñiez 169 B/C1/2
Casasimarro 168 B1
Casasola de Arión 152 A3,
160 A1
Casasuertes 152 A1
Casatejada 159 D3, 166 A1
Casavieja 160 A3
Casazza 106 A3
Casbas de Huesca
155 B/C2/3
Cascades du Hérisson
104 A2
Cascais 164 A2
Cascante 154 A3
Cascante del Río 162 A/B3
Cascata del Toce 105 C2
Ca'S Catalá 157 C2
Cáscia 117 C/D3, 118 B1
Casciana Terme 114 B3,
116 A2
Cáscina 114 B2/3, 116 A2
Cáseda 155 C2
Case della Marina 123 D3
Case di Giuseppe Garibaldi
123 D1
Casei Gerola 113 D1
Casekow 70 B1/2
Casel 70 B3, 83 C1
Casella 113 D1/2
Caselle in Píttari 120 A3
Caselle Torinese 105 C3,
112 B1
Casemurate 115 C2,
117 C1
Case Perrone 121 C3
Caseres 163 C2
Caserío de Llanos de Don
Juan 172 B1/2
Caserta 119 D3
Caserta vécchia 119 D3
Cashel 55 C3
Cashlie 56 B1
Casillas 160 A/B3
Casillas de Flores 159 C2/3
Casillas de Coria 159 C3
Casina 114 A/B1
Casinina 115 D2, 117 C1
Casinos 162 B3, 169 C1
Časkel 5 D2, 6 A2
Casla 161 B/C1/2
Čáslav 96 A2
Čašniki 74 B3
Cásola Valsénio 115 C2,
116 B1
Cásole d'Elsa 114 B3,
116 A/B2
Cásoli 119 D1
Casória 119 D3
Caspe 163 C1
Caspóggio 106 A2
Caspueñas 161 C2
Cassà de la Selva 156 B2
Cassagnes-Bégonhès
110 A2
Cassana 115 C1
Cassaniouze 110 A1
Cassano allo Iónio
122 A/B1
Cassano d'Adda 106 A3
Cassano delle Murge
121 C2
Cassano Spínola 113 D1
Cássaro 125 C/D3
Cassel 77 D1, 78 A2
Casserres 156 A2
Cassíbile 125 D3
Cassine 113 C1
Cassino 119 C2
Cássio 114 A1
Cassis 111 D3
Cassuéjouls 110 A1
Castagnaro 114 B1
Castagneto Carducci
114 B3, 116 A2
Castaignos-Souslens
108 B3, 154 B1
Castalla 169 C2
Castañar de Ibor 160 A3,
166 B1
Castañares de Rioja 153 C2
Castanheira 164 A2
Castanheira de Pera 158 A3
Castanheira do Vouga
158 A2
Cástano Primo 105 D3
Castasegna [St. Moritz]
106 A2
Castéggio 113 D1
Castejón 154 A2/3
Castejón 161 D2/3
Castejón de Sobrarbe
155 C2
Castejón del Puente 155 C3
Castejón de las Armas
162 A1
Castejón de Valdejasa
154 B3
Castejón de Monegros
154 B3, 162 B1
Castejón de Sos 155 C2
Castejón de Tornos 162 A2
Castel Baronia 120 A2
Castelbelforte 106 B3
Castel Bolognese 115 C2,
116 B1
Castelbuono 125 C2
Castel d'Aiano 114 B2,
116 A/B1
Castel d'Ário 106 B3
Castel de Cabra 162 B2
Casteldelfino 112 B1/2
Castel del Monte 117 D3,
119 C1
Castel del Monte 120 B2,
136 A3
Castel del Piano 116 B3
Castel del Rio 115 B/C2,
116 B1
Castel di Iúdica 125 C2
Castel di Lagopésole
120 A/B2
Castel di Sangro 119 C2
Casteleiro 159 B/C3
Castel Eurialo 125 D3
Castelfiorentino 114 B3,
116 A2
Castelflorite 155 C3,
163 C1
Castelforte 119 C2/3
Castelfranc 108 B1
Castelfranco Emília 114 B1
Castelfranco Véneto
107 C3
Castelfranco in Miscano
119 D2/3, 120 A1/2
Castel Fusano 118 A/B2
Castel Gandolfo 118 B2

Castelgrande 120 A2
Casteljaloux 108 B2
Castellabate 120 A3
Castelladral 156 A2
Castellafiume 119 C2
Castellammare di Stábia 119 D3
Castellammare del Golfo 124 A2
Castellamonte 105 C3
Castellana Grotte 121 C2
Castellane 112 A2
Castellaneta 121 C2
Castellanos de Moriscos 159 D2
Castellarano 114 B1
Castellar de Santisteban 167 D3, 168 A3
Castellar de la Ribera 155 C3
Castellar de la Frontera 172 A3
Castellar de Santiago 167 D2
Castellar del Vallès 156 A3
Castellar de N'Hug 156 A2
Castellar de la Muela 162 A2
Castell'Arquato 114 A1
Castell'Azzara 116 B3
Castellazzo Bormida 113 C1
Castellbó 155 C2
Castelldans 155 C/D3, 163 C1
Castell de Cabres 163 C2
Castell de Castells 169 D2
Castell de Ferro 173 C2
Castelldefels 156 A3
Castelleone 106 A3
Castelletto di Brenzone 106 B3
Castellfollit de la Roca 156 B2
Castellfort 162 B2
Castelli 117 D3, 119 C1
Castellina in Chianti 114 B3, 116 B2
Castellina Maríttima 114 B3, 116 A2
Castelló d'Empúries 156 B2
Castelló de Farfanya 155 C3, 163 C1
Castello di Annone 113 C1
Castello di Fiemme 107 C2
Castello di Quirra 123 D3
Castellolí 155 D3, 156 A3, 163 D1
Castellón de Rugat 169 D2
Castellón de la Plana 163 C3
Castellote 162 B2
Castello Tesino 107 C2
Castellserà 155 D3, 163 D1
Castellterçol 156 A3
Castellúcchio 106 B3, 114 B1
Castellúccio Inferiore 120 B3, 122 A1
Castellúccio de'Sáuri 120 A1/2
Castellúccio Valmaggiore 120 A1/2
Castellúccio Superiore 120 B3, 122 A1
Castell'Umberto 125 C2
Castelluzzo 124 A2
Castel Maggiore 114 B1
Castelmassa 114 B1
Castelmáuro 119 D2
Castelmoron-sur-Lot 109 C2
Castelnau 108 B2
Castelnau 109 D1
Castelnau-Barbarens 109 C3, 155 C1
Castelnau-d'Estrétefonds 108 B2
Castelnaudary 109 D3, 156 A1
Castelnau-de-Médoc 108 A/B1
Castelnau-de-Montmiral 109 D2
Castelnau-Magnoac 109 C3, 155 C1
Castelnau-Montratier 108 B2
Castelnau-Rivière-Basse 108 B3, 155 C1
Castelnou 162 B1
Castelnovo di Sotto 114 B1
Castelnovo ne'Monti 114 A1/2, 116 A1
Castelnuovo di Val di Cécina 114 B3, 116 A2
Castelnuovo Scrívia 113 D1
Castelnuovo della Daúnia 119 D2, 120 A1
Castelnuovo di Garfagnana 114 A2, 116 A1
Castelnuovo Berardenga 115 B/C3, 116 B2
Castelnuovo Don Bosco 113 C1
Castelnuovo del Garda 106 B3
Castelo Branco 159 C1
Castelo Branco 158 B3, 165 C1
Castelo de Paiva 158 A2
Castelo de Vide 165 C1
Castelraimondo 115 D3, 117 D2
Castel San Giovanni 113 D1
Castel San Giórgio 119 D3
Castel San Gimignano 114 B3, 116 A/B2
Castel San Pietro Terme 115 C2, 116 B1
Castelsantángelo 117 D3
Castelsaraceno 120 B3
Castelsardo 123 C1
Castelsarrasin 109 C2
Castelserás 163 B/C2
Casteltérmini 124 B2
Castelvécchio 107 C3
Castelvécchio Subéquo 119 C1
Castelvétere in Valfortore 119 D2, 120 A1
Castelvetrano 124 A2
Castel Volturno 119 C3
Castenédolo 106 B3
Castéra-Verduzan 109 C2
Castets 108 B2
Castiádas 123 D3
Castiello de Jaca 154 B2
Castigaleu 155 C2/3
Castiglioncello 114 A3, 116 A2
Castiglione Olona 105 D3
Castiglione di Garfagnana 114 A2, 116 A1
Castiglione delle Stiviere 106 B3
Castiglione d'Órcia 115 C3, 116 B2/3
Castiglione Chiavarese 113 D2
Castiglione d'Adda 106 A3, 113 D1
Castiglione Messer Marino 119 D2
Castiglione Mantovano 106 B3
Castiglione di Sicília 125 D2
Castiglione della Pescáia 116 A3
Castiglione dei Pépoli 114 B2, 116 B1
Castiglione del Lago 115 C3, 117 B/C2
Castiglion Fibocchi 115 C3, 116 B2
Castiglion Fiorentino 115 C3, 116 B2
Castignano 117 D2/3
Castilblanco de los Arroyos 171 D1
Castilblanco 166 B1/2
Castildelgado 153 C2
Castil de Peones 153 C2
Castilfalé 152 A2/3
Castiliscar 155 C2
Castillazuelo 155 C3
Castilleja del Campo 171 C/D1/2
Castilleja de la Cuesta 171 D1/2
Castilléjar 173 D1
Castillejo de Iniesta 168 B1
Castillejo de Mesleón 161 C1
Castillejo del Romeral 161 D3
Castillejo de Robledo 153 C3, 161 C1
Castillo de Bayuela 160 A3
Castillo de Locubín 173 B/C1
Castillo de Villamalefa 162 B3
Castillon-en-Couserans 109 C3, 155 D1/2
Castillon-la-Bataille 108 B1
Castillonnès 109 C1
Castillonroy 155 C3
Castilnuevo 161 D2, 162 A2
Castilruiz 153 D3
Castione [Castione-Arbedo] 105 D2, 106 A2
Castione della Presolana 106 B2/3
Castions di Strada 126 A2/3
Castlebar 55 C2
Castlebay 54 A2, 55 D1
Castlebellingham 58 A1
Castleblayney 54 A3, 55 D2
Castlebridge 58 A3
Castle Cary 63 D2
Castle Douglas 56 B3, 60 A1
Castleford 61 D2
Castleton 61 C3
Castletown 58 B1
Castletown 58 A3
Castlewellan 58 A1
Casto 106 B3
Castraz 159 C2
Castrejón 160 A1
Castrelo de Miño 150 B2/3
Castrelo do Val 151 B/C3
Castrelos 151 C3, 159 C1
Castres 110 A3
Castricum 66 A2
Castril 168 A3, 173 D1
Castrillo 153 B/C3, 160 B1
Castrillo de la Reina 153 C3
Castrillo de Villavega 152 B2
Castrillo de Duero 152 B3, 160 B1
Castrillo de Murcia 152 B2
Castrillo de Don Juan 152 B3, 160 B1
Castrillo de Onielo 152 B3
Castrillo Matajudíos 152 B2
Castrillón 151 C1
Castrillon 151 D1
Castrillo-Tejeriego 152 B3, 160 B1
Castrocalbón 151 D3
Castro Caldelas 151 B/C2
Castrocaro Terme 115 C2, 116 B1
Castrocontrigo 151 D3
Castro Daire 158 B2
Castro dei Volsci 119 C2
Castro del Río 172 B1
Castro de Rei 151 B/C1
Castrodeza 152 A3, 160 A1
Castrofilippo 124 B2/3
Castrofuerte 151 D2/3, 152 A2/3
Castrojeriz 152 B2
Castro Laboreiro 150 B3
Castro Marim 170 B2
Castromocho 152 A3
Castromonte 152 A3, 160 A1
Castronuevo 151 D3, 152 A3, 159 D1, 160 A1
Castronuño 160 A1
Castropol 151 C1
Castrop-Rauxel 80 A1
Castroreale Terme 125 D1/2
Castro Urdiales 153 C1
Castroverde de Campos 152 A3
Castroverde 151 C1/2
Castroverde de Cerrato 152 B3, 160 B1
Castro Verde 170 B1
Castro Vicente 159 C1
Castrovíllari 120 B3, 122 A1
Castuera 166 A2
Čata 95 D3
Catadau 169 C/D1/2
Çatalca 149 D1
Catane 135 D2
Catánia 125 D2
Catanzaro 122 B2
Catanzaro Lido 122 B2
Catarroja 169 D1
Catelrotto/Kastelruth 107 C2
Catenanuova 125 C2
Cateraggio 113 D3
Caterham 65 C3, 76 B1
Čateške Toplice 127 C2/3
Čatež 127 C2/3
Catí 163 C2
Cá Tiepolo 115 C1
Catignano 119 C1
Catlowdy 57 C3
Catoira 150 A2
Catral 169 C3
Cattaéggio 106 A2
Cattenom 79 D3
Catterick 61 C1/2
Cattólica 115 D2, 117 C1
Cattólica Eraclea 124 B2
Catus 108 B1
Caudé 163 C2
Caudebec-en-Caux 77 C3
Caudete 169 C2
Caudete de las Fuentes 169 D1
Caudiel 162 B3, 169 C/D1
Caudiès-de-Fenouillèdes 156 A/B1
Caudos 108 A1
Caudry 78 A/B2/3
Caujac 109 D3, 155 D1
Caulnes 85 C2
Caulónia 122 B3
Caumont-l'Evente 86 A1
Caunes-Minervois 110 A3, 156 B1
Cauro 113 D3
Caussade 109 D2
Causse-de-la-Selle 110 B2
Čausy 75 C3, 99 C/D1
Cauterets 155 C2
Cauville-sur-Mer 76 B3
Caux [Montreux] 104 B2
Cavacao 164 A1
Cava d'Aliga 125 C3
Cava de Tirreni 119 D3
Cava d'Íspica 125 C3
Cavaglià 105 C3
Cavaillon 111 C/D2
Cavalaire-sur-Mer 112 A3
Cavalese 107 C2
Cavalière 112 A3
Cavallermaggiore 113 B/C1
Cávalo 106 B3
Cavan 54 A3, 55 D2
Cavareno 107 C2
Cavárzere 107 C/D3, 115 C1
Cave del Predil 126 A/B2
Ca'Venier 115 C1
Cavernães 158 B2
Cavezzo 114 B1
Cavignac 101 B/C3, 108 B1
Čavle 126 B3, 130 A/B1
Cavo 116 A3
Cavour 112 B1
Cavtat 137 C2
Caya 165 C2
Caya 165 C2
Cayeux-sur-Mer 77 D2
Caylus 109 D2
Cayres 110 B1
Cayrols 110 A1
Cazalegas 160 A3
Cazalilla 167 C3, 173 B/C1
Cazalla de la Sierra 166 A3, 171 D1
Cazals 108 B1
Cazane 135 C2
Cazaubon 108 B2
Cazaux 108 B1
Cazaux-Savès 109 C3, 155 D1
Cazères-sur-Garonne 109 C3, 155 D1
Cazères-sur-l'Adour 108 B2
Cazevel 164 B3, 170 A/B1
Cazin 131 C1
Čazma 127 D3
Cazorla 167 D3, 168 A3, 173 C/D1
Cazouls-lès-Béziers 110 B3
Cá Zuliani 115 C1
Cdeynia 70 B2
Cdeynia 72 A3
Cea 152 A2
Ceánuri 153 C/D1
Céaucé 86 A2
Cebanico 152 A2
Cebara 131 D3, 132 A3
Cebas 167 D3, 168 A3, 173 D1
Cebolais de Cima 158 B3, 165 C1
Cebolla 160 A/B3, 167 B/C1
Čebovce 95 D2
Cebreros 160 B2
Cebrikovo 141 D1
Cebrones del Río 151 D2/3
Ceccano 119 C2
Cece 129 B/C1/2
Cece 96 B3
Čečersk 99 D1
Čečeviči 99 C1
Čechtice 83 D3
Čechtín 94 A1
Cécina 114 A/B3, 116 A2
Ceclavin 159 C3, 165 D1
Cecos 112 B3
Cedégolo 106 B2
Cedeira 150 B1
Cedillo 158 B3, 165 C1
Cedillo de la Torre 161 C1
Cedovim 158 B2
Cedrillas 162 B2
Cée 150 A2
Cefalù 125 B/C2
Céggia 107 D3, 126 A3
Cegléd 129 D1
Cegléd 97 C3, 140 A1
Céglie Messápico 121 C2
Čegrane 138 B2
Cehegín 168 B3, 174 A1
Cehnice 93 C1
Čehov 75 D3
Ceilhes-et-Rocozels 110 B2
Ceillac 112 B1
Ceinos de Campos 152 A3
Ceira 158 A3
Čejč 94 B1
Čejkovice 94 B1
Čekalin 75 D3
Čekanje 137 C2
Cela 164 A1
Celada de Roblecedo 152 B2
Celadas 163 C2
Čeladná 95 C/D1
Čelákovice 83 D2/3
Celano 119 C1/2
Celanova 150 B3
Celbridge 58 A2
Čelebić 131 D2/3
Celei 135 D1
Čele Kula 135 C3
Celenza Valfortore 119 D2, 120 A1
Čelić 133 C1
Čelije 133 D2, 134 A2
Čelije 140 A2
Čelinac 131 D1/2, 132 A1
Celje 127 C2
Celje 96 A3
Cella 114 B1
Cella 163 C2
Celldömölk 128 A1
Celle 68 B2
Celle-Garssen 68 B2
Celle-Gross Hehlen 68 B2
Celle Lígure 113 C2
Celle-Scheuen 68 B2
Celles-sur-Belle 101 C2
Celles-sur-Ource 88 B2
Celliers 104 A/B3
Cellino San Marco 121 D3

Čelopeci 138 B3
Celorico da Beira 158 B2
Celorico de Basto 158 B1
Céltigos 151 B/C2
Cemaes Bay 58 B2
Cembra 107 C2
Čemerno 132 B3, 137 C1
Cenad 129 D2
Cenarth 62 B1
Cencenighe 107 C2
Cendejas de la Torre 161 C2
Cenicero 153 D2
Cenicientos 160 B3
Cenizate 168 B1/2
Cenlle 150 B2
Cenon 108 B1
Censeau 104 A1
Čenta 133 D1, 134 A1
Centallo 112 B2
Centelles 156 A2/3
Cento 114 B1
Centúripe 125 C2
Cepagatti 119 C1
Čepelare 140 B3
Cépet 109 D2
Čepin 128 B3
Čepinci 145 C1
Čepinski Martinci 128 B3
Cepões 158 B2
Čepovan 126 B2
Ceppo 117 D3, 119 C1
Ceprano 119 C2
Čeralije 128 B3
Cerami 125 C2
Cérans-Foulletourte 86 A/B3
Cëravë 142 B1
Cerbáia 114 B2/3, 116 B2
Cerbère 156 B2
Cercal 164 A1/2
Cercal 164 A/B3, 170 A1
Cerceda 150 A1
Cerceda 160 B2
Cercedilla 160 B2
Cercemaggiore 119 D2
Cerchiara di Calábria 120 B3, 122 B1
Cercs 156 A2
Cercy-la-Tour 103 C1
Cerda 124 B2
Cerdedo 150 A/B2
Cerdeira 158 B3
Cerdeira 159 C2
Cerdeira 158 B3
Cerdido 150 B1
Cérdigo 153 C1
Cerdon-du-Loiret 87 D3
Cerea 107 C3
Ceremošnia 135 C2
Cerenskoe 75 D1
Cerénzia 122 B2
Čerepovec 75 D1
Céres 105 B/C3
Cerese 114 B1
Ceresole Alba 113 C1
Ceresole Reale 104 B3
Céreste 111 D2
Céret 156 B2
Čerević 129 C/D3, 133 C1, 134 A1
Cerezo de Abajo 161 C1
Cerezo de Arriba 161 C1
Cerezo de Riotirón 153 C2
Ceriale 113 C2
Cerignola 120 B2
Čerikov 99 D1
Cérilly 102 B1/2
Čerín 95 D2
Cerisano 122 A2
Cerisiers 88 A2
Cerisy-la-Forêt 76 A3, 85 D1, 86 A1
Cerizay 100 B1
Čerkassy 99 D3
Cerklje 126 B2
Cerknica 126 B3
Cerkno 126 B2
Cerler 155 C2
Cerna 133 B/C1
Cernache do Bonjardim 158 A3, 164 B1
Cernadoi 107 C2
Černá Hora 94 B1
Cernăteşti 135 D2
Cernavodă 141 C/D2
Černá v Pošumaví 93 C/D2
Cernay 89 D3, 90 A3
Cernay-en-Dormois 88 B1
Cerne Abbas 63 D2
Cernégula 153 C2
Černičevo 145 D1
Černigov 99 D2
Černík 95 C2
Cernik 128 A3, 131 D1, 132 A1
Černjahov 99 C2
Černjahovsk (Insterburg) 73 C2
Cernóbbio 105 D3, 106 A3
Černobyl' 99 C2
Černošín 82 B3
Černovcy 98 B3
Černovice 93 D1
Čeřnuc 83 C/D2
Cerollera 163 C2
Cérons 108 B1
Cerósimo 120 B3, 122 B1
Cerovac 127 C3, 131 C1
Cerovac 134 B2
Cerovac 133 C/D1, 134 A1/2
Cerovaćke spilje 131 C2
Cerovlje 126 B3, 130 A1
Cerovo 95 D2
Cerralbo 159 C2
Cerrédolo 114 B2, 116 A1
Cerreto d'Esi 115 D3, 117 C/D2
Cerreto Sannita 119 D2/3
Cërrik 138 A3, 142 A1
Certaldo 114 B3, 116 A/B2
Certosa di Pésio 113 B/C2
Certosa di Pavia 105 D3, 106 A3, 113 D1
Certosa San Lorenzo 120 A3
Cerva 158 B1
Cervantes 151 C2
Cervarolo 114 A/B2, 116 A1
Cervatos 152 B2
Cervatos de la Cueza 152 A/B2
Červen' 99 C1
Červen brjag 140 B3
Červený Kameň 95 C2
Cervera 155 C3, 163 C1
Cervera de Buitrago 161 C2
Cervera del Río Alhama 153 D3, 154 A3
Cervera del Maestre 163 C2
Cervera de los Montes 160 A3
Cervera del Llano 161 D3, 168 A/B1
Cervera de la Cañada 154 A3, 162 A1
Cervera de Pisuerga 152 B2
Cervéteri 118 A2
Cérvia 115 C2, 117 C1
Cervià de les Garrigues 163 C/D1
Cervià de Ter 156 B2
Cervignano del Friuli 126 A3
Cervinara 119 D3
Cervione 113 D3
Cervo 113 C2
Cervo 151 B/C1
Cervon 88 A3, 103 C1
Červonoarmejsk 97 D2, 98 B2
Červonograd 97 D1/2, 98 A2
Červonoznamenka 141 D1
Cerzeto 122 A1
Cesana Torinese 112 B1
Cesarica 130 B2
Cesarò 125 C2
Cesena 115 C2, 117 C1
Cesenático 115 C2, 117 C1
Cēsis 73 D1, 74 A2
Česká Kamenice 83 D2
Česká Kubice 92 B1
Česká Lípa 83 D2
Česká Lípa 96 A1
České Budějovice 96 A2
České Budějovice 93 D1
České Velenice 93 D2
Český Brod 83 D3
Český Dub 83 D2
Český Krumlov 93 D2
Český Krumlov 96 A2
Český Šternberk 83 D3
Český Těšín 96 B2
Češljeva Bara 134 B2
Çeşme 149 C2
Cespedosa 159 D2
Cessalto 107 D3
Cessenon 110 A/B3
Čestereg 129 D3
Čestín 83 D3
Cesuras 150 B1
Cesvaine 74 A2
Cetate 135 D2
Cetina 161 D1
Cetingrad 131 C1
Cetinje 137 C2
Četirci 139 D2
Cetraro 122 A1
Ceutí 169 D3
Ceva 113 C2
Cevico de la Torre 152 B3
Cevico Navero 152 B3
Cevins 104 B3
Cevio [Ponte Brolla] 105 D2
Čevo 137 C2
Ceyrat 102 B3
Ceyzériat 103 D2
Chabanais 101 D2
Chabeuil 111 C/D1
Châble, Le 104 B2
Chablis 88 A3
Chabreloche 103 C2
Chabris 87 C3, 101 D1, 102 A1
Chacim 159 C1
Chaffois 104 A1
Chagny 103 D1
Chaillé-les-Marais 100 B2
Chailley 88 A2
Chailly-en-Brie 87 D1, 88 A1
Chailly-en Bière 87 D2
Chalabre 109 D3, 156 A1
Chalais 101 C3
Chalamera 155 C3, 163 C1
Chalamont 103 D2
Chalandrítsa 146 B2
Chalet de Peñalara 160 B2
Chalíkion 143 B/C3
Chalindrey 89 C3
Chálki 143 D3
Chalkiádes 143 D3
Chalkidón 143 D1/2
Chalkís 147 D2
Chalkís 148 B2
Challain-la-Potherie 85 D3
Challans 100 A1
Challes-les-Eaux 104 A3
Chalmazel 103 C3
Chalonnes-sur-Loire 86 A3
Châlons-sur-Marne 88 B1
Châlons-sur-Vesle 88 A1
Chalon-sur-Saône 103 D1
Châlus 101 D3
Chalusset 101 C3
Cham 105 C/D1
Cham 92 B1
Chamalières-sur-Loire 103 C3
Chamberet 102 A3
Chambéry 104 A3
Chambilly 103 C2
Chamblet 102 B2
Chambley-Bussières 89 C1
Chambly 77 D3, 87 C/D1
Chambois 86 B1
Chambon-Sainte-Croix 102 A2
Chambon-sur-Voueize 102 A2
Chambon-sur-Lac 102 B3
Chambord 87 C3
Chamboulive 102 A3
Chamerau 92 B1
Chamonix-Mont-Blanc 104 B2/3
Chamoux-sur-Gelon 104 A3
Champagnac-de-Belair 101 C/D3
Champagnac-le-Vieux 102 B3
Champagne-Mouton 101 C2
Champagney 89 D3
Champagnole 104 A1
Champaubert 88 A1
Champ de Bataille 77 C3, 86 B1
Champdeniers 101 B/C2
Champdieu 103 C3
Champeaux 87 D2
Champeix 102 B3
Champenoux 89 C/D1
Champéry 104 B2
Champex [Orsières] 104 B2
Champier 103 D3
Champigné 86 A3
Champignelles 87 D3
Champigny-sur-Veude 101 C1
Champillet 102 A2
Champlitte-et-le-Prélot 89 C3
Champoluc 105 C3
Champoly 103 C2
Champorcher 105 C3
Champrond-en-Gatine 87 B/C2
Champs-sur-Tarentaine 102 A/B3
Champtoceaux 86 A/B3
Chamrousse 104 A3, 112 A1
Cham-Thierlstein 92 B1
Chamusca 164 B1
Cham-Windischbergerdorf 92 B1
Chanac 110 B1/2
Chanas 103 D3
Chancy [Pougny-Chancy Ain] 104 A2
Chandai 86 B1
Chandrexa de Queixa 151 B/C2/3
Changy 103 C2
Chaniótis 144 A/B2
Chantada 150 B2
Chantelle 102 B2
Chantelouve 111 D1, 112 A1
Chantemerle 112 A/B1
Chantilly 87 D1
Chantonnay 100 B1
Chão de Codes 164 B1
Chaource 88 A/B2
Chapa 158 B1
Chapaize 103 D2
Chapareillan 104 A3
Chapel-en-le-Frith 59 D2, 61 C3
Chapelle-Royale 86 B2
Charavgí 143 C2
Charavines-les-Bains 103 D3, 104 A3
Charches 173 D2
Chard 63 C/D2
Charenton-du-Cher 102 B1
Charing 65 C3, 77 C1
Charlbury 64 A2/3
Charleroi 78 B2
Charlestown 55 C2
Charleville-Mézières 79 C3
Charlieu 103 C2
Charlottenberg 38 B3
Charly 87 D1, 88 A1
Charmeil 102 B2
Charmes 89 C/D2
Charmes-sur-Rhône 111 C1
Charmoille 89 C3
Charny 87 D2/3
Charny-sur-Meuse 89 C1
Charolles 103 C2
Chârost 102 A1
Charquemont 89 D3, 104 B1
Charritte-de-Bas 108 A3, 154 B1
Charron 100 B2
Charroux 101 C2
Chars 77 D3, 87 C1
Chartres 87 C2
Chásia Óri 143 C3
Chasseneuil-sur-Bonnieure 101 C2/3
Chastellux 88 A3
Château-Arnoux 112 A2
Châteaubourg 86 A/B2
Châteaubriant 86 A3
Château-Chinon 103 C1
Château-d'Oex 104 B2
Château d'Ô 86 B2
Château d'If 111 D3
Château-du-Loir 86 B3
Châteaudun 86 A/B2
Châteaugay 102 B2
Châteaugiron 85 D2
Château-Gontier 86 A3
Château-l'Évêque 101 C/D3
Château-la-Vallière 86 B3
Château-Landon 87 D2
Châteaulin 84 A/B2
Châteaumeillant 102 A1/2
Châteauneuf-sur-Loire 87 C/D2/3
Châteauneuf-en-Thymerais 86 A/B2
Châteauneuf-du Faou 84 B2
Châteauneuf-de-Chabre 111 D2, 112 A2
Châteauneuf 88 B3, 103 C/D1
Châteauneuf 103 C2
Châteauneuf-du-Pape 111 C2
Châteauneuf-sur-Charente 101 C3
Châteauneuf-les-Bains 102 B2
Châteauneuf-la-Forêt 101 D3, 102 A3
Châteauneuf-d'Ille-et-Vilaine 85 C/D2
Châteauneuf-de-Randon 110 B1
Châteauneuf-Val-de-Bargis 88 A3, 102 B1
Châteauneuf-sur-Sarthe 86 A3
Châteauneuf-sur-Cher 102 A1
Château-Porcien 78 B3
Châteauponsac 101 C2
Château-Queyras 112 B1
Château-Renault 86 B3
Châteauredon 112 A2
Châteaurenard 87 D2
Châteaurenard 111 C2
Châteauroux-les-Alpes 112 A1
Châteauroux 101 D1, 102 A1
Château-Salins 89 D1
Château-Thierry 88 A1
Châteauvert 112 A3
Châteauvillain 88 B2
Châtel 104 B2
Châtelaillon-Plage 100 B2
Châtelard, Le [Le Châtelard-Frontière] 104 B2
Châtel-Censoir 88 A3
Châtel-de-Neuvre 102 B2
Châteldon 102 B2
Châtelet 78 B2
Châtel-Guyon 102 B2
Châtelineau 78 B2
Châtellerault 101 C1
Châtel-Montagne 103 C2
Châtel-St-Denis 104 B2
Châtel-sur-Moselle 89 D2
Châtelus-Malvalaix 102 A2
Châtenois 89 C2
Chatham 65 C3, 77 C1
Châtillon-de-Michaille 104 A2
Châtillon-Coligny 87 D3
Châtillon-en-Diois 111 D1
Châtillon-sur-Seine 88 B3
Châtillon-la-Palud 103 D2
Châtillon-sur-Chalaronne 103 D2
Châtillon-sur-Sèvre 100 B1
Châtillon 105 C3
Châtillon-en-Bazois 103 C1
Châtillon-sur-Loire 87 D3
Châtillon-sur-Indre 101 C1
Châtillon-sur-Marne 88 A1
Châtre 101 C3
Chatsworth 61 C3, 64 A1
Chatteris 65 C2
Chauchina 173 C2
Chaudes-Aigues 110 A/B1
Chau de Ventadour 102 A3
Chaudieu 104 A3
Chaudrey 88 B2

Chauffailles 103 C2
Chaulnes 78 A3
Chaumercenne 89 C3, 104 A1
Chaumont 88 B2
Chaumont-en-Vexin 77 D3, 87 C1
Chaumont-sur-Loire 86 A/B3
Chaumont-sur-Tharonne 87 C3
Chaunay 101 C2
Chauny 78 A3
Chaussin 103 D1, 104 A1
Chauvency-le-Château 79 C3
Chauvigny 101 C/D2
Chaux-de-Fonds, La 104 B1
Chavanges 88 B2
Chávarion 146 A2
Chaves 150 B3, 158 B1
Chazelles-sur-Loyn 103 C3
Cheadle 59 D2, 61 B/C3, 64 A1
Cheb 82 B3
Checa 162 A2
Cheddar 63 D2
Chedgrave 65 D2
Chef-Boutonne 101 C2
Cheffois 100 B1
Chéggio 105 C2
Cheles 165 C2/3
Chella 169 C2
Chelle-Debat 109 C3, 155 C1
Chelles 87 D1
Chełm 97 D1, 98 A2
Chelmós 146 B3
Chelmsford 65 C3
Chełmża 73 B/C3
Chełst 71 C2
Cheltenham 63 D1, 64 A2
Chelva 162 B3, 169 C1
Chéméré-le-Roi 86 A2
Chémery-sur-Bar 79 C3
Chemillé 86 A3, 100 B1
Chemillé-sur-Dême 86 B3
Chemin 103 D1
Chemiré-le-Gaudin 86 A/B2/3
Chemnitz 70 A1
Chénérailles 102 A2
Cheniménil 89 D2
Chenoise 87 D2, 88 A2
Chenonceaux 87 B/C3
Chepstow 63 D1
Chequilla 161 D2, 162 A2
Chera 169 C1
Cherain 79 D2/3
Cherasco 113 C1
Cheray 101 C2
Cherbourg 76 A3
Chercos 173 D2, 174 A2
Chérisy 87 C1
Cherónia 147 C2
Chéroy 87 D2
Chert 163 C2
Chertsey 64 B3, 76 B1
Cherveix-Cubas 101 C3
Cheseaux-sur-Lausanne [Lausanne] 104 B2
Chesham 64 B3
Cheshunt 65 C3
Chéssy-les-Mines 103 C/D2
Chessy-les-Près 88 A2
Cheste 169 C1
Chester 59 D2, 60 B3
Chesterfield 61 C3, 64 A/B1
Chester le Street 57 D3, 61 C1
Chesters 57 C2
Chételaudren 85 B/C2
Chevagnes 103 B/C1/2
Chevanceaux 101 C3
Cheverny 87 C3
Chevillon 88 B2
Chevilly 87 C2
Chevreuse 87 C1/2
Chevron 79 C/D2
Chey 101 C2
Cheylade 102 B3
Chezal-Benoît 102 A1
Chézery-Forens 104 A2
Chialamberto 104 B3
Chiampo 107 C3
Chianale 112 B1
Chianciano Terme 115 C3, 116 B2
Chianni 114 B3, 116 A2
Chiappera 112 B2
Chiappi 112 B2
Chiaramonte Gulfi 125 C3
Chiaramonti 123 C1
Chiaravalle 115 D3, 117 D2
Chiaravalle Centrale 122 B2
Chiaréggio 106 A2
Chiari 106 A3
Chiaromonte 120 B3
Chiasso 105 D3
Chiávari 113 D2
Chiavenna 105 D2, 106 A2
Chiché 101 B/C1
Chichester 76 B1
Chiclana de la Frontera 171 D3
Chiclana de Segura 167 D3, 168 A3
Chieming 92 B3
Chieri 113 C1
Chiesa in Valmalenco 106 A2
Chiesina Uzzanese 114 B2, 116 A1
Chieti 119 C1
Chiéuti 120 A1
Chièvres 78 B2
Chigwell 65 C3
Chilbolton 64 A3, 76 A1
Chilches 162 B3, 169 D1
Chilham 65 C/D3, 77 C1
Chilia Veche 141 D2
Chiliomódion 147 C2/3
Chilivani 123 C/D1/2
Chillarón de Cuenca 161 D3
Chilleurs-aux-Bois 87 C2
Chillón 166 B2
Chillon [Villeneuve] 104 B2
Chiloeches 161 C2
Chimay 78 B3
Chimeneas 173 C2
Chinchilla de Monte Aragón 168 B2
Chinchón 161 C3
Chinon 86 B3, 101 C1
Chióggia 107 D3
Chiomonte 112 B1
Chióna 146 B2
Chipiona 171 C2
Chippenham 63 D2, 64 A3
Chipping Campden 64 A2
Chipping Norton 64 A2
Chipping Ongar 65 C3
Chipping Sodbury 63 D1/2, 64 A3
Chiprana 163 B/C1
Chirivel 173 D1, 174 A1
Chirivella 169 D1
Chirk 59 C/D2/3, 60 B3
Chirnside 57 D2
Chisa 113 D3
Chiusa di Pésio 113 B/C2
Chiusaforte 126 A2
Chiusa/Klausen 107 C2
Chiusa Scláfani 124 B2
Chiusi 115 C3, 116 B2
Chiusi della Verna 115 C2/3, 116 B2
Chiva de Morella 163 B/C2
Chivasso 105 C3, 113 C1
Chivy-les-Etouvelles 78 B3
Chizé 101 B/C2
Chlebowo 70 B3
Chludowo 71 D2
Chlumec 83 C2
Chlum u Třeboně 93 D1
Chobienice 71 C3
Chociule 71 C3
Chociwel 71 C1
Chodos 162 B3
Chodov 82 B2
Chodová Planá 82 B3
Chodzież 71 D2
Choisy-le Roi 87 D1
Chojna 70 B2
Chojnice 72 B2/3
Chojno 71 D3
Cholet 100 B1
Chomérac 111 C1
Chomutov 83 C2
Chomutov 96 A1
Chóra 146 B3
Choranche 103 D3, 111 D1
Choreftón 144 A3
Chorges 112 A1/2
Chorin 70 B2
Choristí 144 B1
Chorley 59 D2, 60 B2
Chortiátis 144 A2
Chospes 168 A/B2
Choszczno 71 C1/2
Choszczno 72 A/B3
Chotěšov 83 C2
Chouilly 88 A1
Choumnikón 144 A/B1
Choustiník 93 D1
Chouto 164 B1/2
Chouvigny 102 B2
Choye 89 C3, 104 A1
Chrást 83 C3
Chrastava 83 D2
Chřibská 83 D2
Chříč 83 C3
Chrísafa 147 C3
Chrisochórion 145 C1
Chrisón 147 C2
Chrisoúpolis 145 C1
Christchurch 76 A1
Christiáni 144 B1
Christianón 146 B3
Christiansfeld 52 B1
Chropyně 95 C1
Chróścina 71 D3
Chroúsou 144 B2/3
Chrudim 96 A2
Chrustowo 71 D2
Chrzypsko Wielkie 71 D2
Chudleigh 63 C3
Chueca 160 B3, 167 C1
Chulilla 162 B3, 169 C1
Chulmleigh 63 C2
Chur 106 A1
Church Stretton 59 D3
Churchtown 58 A3
Churwalden [Chur] 106 A1
Chvalovice 94 A2
Chvalšiny 93 D1/2
Chyňava 83 C3
Chynorany 95 C2
Chýnov 93 D1
Chyše 83 C3
Ciadoncha 152 B3
Ciadoux 109 C3, 155 C1
Cianciana 124 B2
Ciano d'Enza 114 A1
Cibanal 159 C1
Cicagna 113 D2
Cicciano 119 D3
Ćićevac 134 B3
Čičevo 137 C1/2
Čičmany 95 D1
Cicognolo 106 B3
Ciconicco 107 D2, 126 A2
Cidadelhe 159 C2
Cidones 153 D3, 161 D1
Ciechanów 73 C3
Ciemnik 71 C1
Ciempozuelos 161 C3
Cierp 109 C3, 155 C2
Cierznie 71 D1
Cieszyn 96 B2
Cieza 169 C3
Cífer 95 C2
Cifuentes 161 D2
Cigales 152 B3, 160 A1
Čigirin 99 D3
Cigliano 105 C3
Cigudosa 153 D3
Cihuela 154 A3, 161 D1
Cîineni 140 B2
Čilipi 137 C2
Cillamayor 152 B2
Cillán 160 A2
Cillas 161 D2, 162 A2
Cilleros 159 C3
Cilleruelo de Arriba 153 C3
Cilleruelo de Abajo 153 B/C3
Cillorigo-Castro 152 B1
Cima Cogna 107 D2
Cimalmotto [Ponte Brolla] 105 C/D2
Cimanes del Tejar 151 D2
Cimballa 162 A2
Ciminna 124 B2
Čimišlija 141 D1
Cimoláis 107 D2
Cîmpeni 97 D3, 140 B1
Cîmpu lui Neag 140 B2
Cîmpu lui Neag 135 D1
Cîmpulung 141 B/C2
Cîmpulung Moldovenesc 141 C1
Cinctorres 162 B2
Cinderford 63 D1
Çine 149 D2
Činěves 83 D2
Ciney 79 C2
Cinfães 158 B2
Cíngia de'Botti 114 A1
Cíngoli 115 D3, 117 D2
Cinigiano 116 B3
Cinisello Bálsamo 105 D3, 106 A3
Cínovec 83 C2
Cinq-Mars-la-Pile 86 B3
Cinquefrondi 122 A3
Cintegabelle 109 D3, 155 D1
Cintrey 89 C3
Cintruénigo 154 A3
Cional 151 D3
Ciordia 153 D2
Cioroiași 135 D2
Ciosaniec 71 C3
Ciovîrnășani 135 D1
Cipérez 159 C/D2
Čiprovci 135 D3
Cirák 94 B3
Cirat 162 B3
Cirauqui 153 D2, 154 A2
Cîrbești 135 D1
Cirella 122 A1
Cirencester 63 D1, 64 A3
Cirey-sur-Vezouze 89 D2, 90 A2
Ciria 153 D3, 154 A3, 161 D1
Ciriè 105 C3, 112 B1
Cirigliano 120 B3
Cîrlibaba 141 B/C1
Cirò 122 B1
Cirò Marina 122 B1/2
Ciron 101 C1/2
Čirpan 141 C3
Cirque d'Archiane 111 D1
Cirque de Consolation 104 B1
Cirque de Gavarnie 155 C2
Cirque de Navacelles 110 B2
Cirque de Troumouse 155 C2
Ciruelos 161 C3, 167 C/D1
Ciry-le-Noble 103 C1/2
Cismon del Grappa 107 C2/3
Cisnădie 140 B1/2
Cisneros 152 A2/3
Čistá 82 B3
Čistá 83 C3
Cisterna di Latina 118 B2
Cisternino 121 C2
Cistierna 152 A2
Ciszkowo 71 D2
Čitluk 135 C3
Čitluk 132 A/B3, 136 B1
Cítov 83 D2
Città della Pieve 115 C3, 117 B/C2/3
Cittadella 107 C3
Cittadella del Capo 122 A1
Città del Vaticano 118 B2
Città di Castello 115 C3, 117 C2
Cittaducale 117 C3, 118 B1
Cittanova 122 A3
Cittareale 117 D3, 118 B1
Città Sant'Ángelo 119 C1
City Airport 65 C3
Ciucea 97 D3, 140 B1
Ciuchesu 123 D1
Ciucurova 141 D2
Ciudadela 157 C1
Ciudad Encantada 161 D3
Ciudad Real 167 C2
Ciudad Rodrigo 159 C2
Ciupercenii-Noi 135 D2/3
Civaux 101 C/D2
Cividale del Friuli 126 A2
Cividate Camuno 106 B2
Cívitacampomarano 119 D2
Cívita Castellana 117 C3, 118 B1
Civitanova del Sánnio 119 D2
Civitanova Marche 117 D2, 130 A3
Civitavécchia 118 A1/2
Civitella Casanova 117 D3, 119 C1
Civitella d'Agliano 117 C3, 118 A1
Civitella del Tronto 117 D3, 119 C1
Civitella di Romagna 115 C2, 116 B1
Civitella Maríttima 114 B3, 116 B2/3
Civitella Roveto 119 C2
Civray 101 C2
Civrieux-d'Azergues 103 D2
Cizur 154 A2
Clachan 56 A2
Clacton-on-Sea 65 C3
Clairac 109 C2
Clairvaux-les-Lacs 104 A2
Clamecy 88 A3
Clapham 59 D1, 60 B2
Clare 65 C2
Clarés 154 A3, 161 D1, 162 A1
Clausholm 48 B2
Clausnitz 83 C2
Clausthal-Zellerfeld 68 B3
Cláut 107 D2
Claviere 112 B1
Clavière 112 B1
Clavijo 153 D2
Claydon 65 D2
Claye-Souilly 87 D1
Cleanov 135 D2
Cleanov 140 B2
Clécy 86 A1
Cleethorpes 61 D2/3
Cleeve Abbey 63 C2
Clefmont 89 C2
Cléguérec 84 B2
Clelles-en-Trièves 111 D1
Clémont 87 D3
Clenze 69 C2
Cleobury Mortimer 59 D3, 64 A2
Cléon-d'Andran 111 C1
Cléré-les Pins 86 B3
Clères 77 C3
Clergoux 102 A3
Clermain 103 C/D2
Clermont 77 D3, 87 D1
Clermont-Créans 86 A/B3
Clermont-en-Argonne 88 B1
Clermont-Ferrand 102 B2/3
Clermont-l'Hérault 110 B3
Clerval 89 D3, 104 B1
Clervaux (Clerf) 79 D3
Cléry-Saint-André 87 C3
Cles 107 B/C2
Clevedon 63 D2
Cleveleys 59 C1, 60 B2
Cley 65 C/D1
Clifden 55 C2
Cliffe 65 C3
Clisson 101 C1
Clitheroe 59 D1, 60 B2
Cliveden 64 B3
Clogherhead 58 A1
Cloghy 56 A3
Clonakilty 55 C3
Clondalkin 58 A2
Clonee 58 A2
Clonmel 55 C/D3
Clophill 64 B2
Clopodia 134 B1
Cloppenburg 67 D2
Cloșani 135 D1
Clough 58 A1
Clough 54 A3, 55 D2
Clovelly 62 B2
Cloyes-sur-le-Loir 86 A/B2
Clue d'Aiglun 112 B2
Clugnat 102 A2
Cluis 102 A1/2
Cluj-Napoca 97 D3, 140 B1
Clun 59 C/D3
Cluny 103 C/D2

Cluses 104 B2
Clusone 106 A/B2/3
Clydebank 56 B2
Clynnog-fawr 58 B2
Coalville 65 C1
Coaña 151 C1
Coarraze 108 B3, 154 B1
Coatbridge 56 B2
Cobadin 141 D2
Cóbdar 173 D2, 174 A2
Cobertelada 161 D1
Cobeta 161 D2
Cobh 55 C3
Cobham 65 C3, 77 C1
Cobisa 160 B3, 167 C1
Cobos de Cerrato 152 B3
Coburg 81 D2, 82 A2
Coburg-Creidlitz 81 D2/3, 82 A2
Coca 160 B1
Cocaali 145 D2
Coccau 126 A/B2
Cocentaina 169 D2
Cochem 80 A3
Cockburnspath 57 D2
Cockermouth 57 C3, 60 A1
Coclois 88 B2
Coculina 152 B2
Codaruina 123 C1
Codes 161 D2
Codigoro 115 C1
Codlea 141 C1/2
Codo 162 B1
Codognè 107 D2/3
Codogno 106 A3, 113 D1, 114 A1
Codos 163 C1
Codróipo 107 D2, 126 A2
Coentral 158 A3
Coesfeld 67 C/D3
Coesfeld-Lette 67 C/D3
Coevorden 67 C2
Cofrentes 169 C2
Cogeces de Monte 152 B3, 160 B1
Coggeshall 65 C2/3
Cognac 101 C3
Cogne 104 B3
Cognin 104 A3
Cogoleto 113 C2
Cogolin 112 A3
Cogollos 153 C3
Cogollos de Guadix 173 C2
Cogollos Vega 173 C2
Cogolludo 161 C2
Cógolo 106 B2
Cohade 102 B3
Coimbra 158 A3
Coimbrão 158 A3, 164 A1
Coín 172 B2
Coirós 150 B1
Coja 158 B3
Čoka 129 D2/3
Col 126 B2/3
Cola 170 A1
Colares 164 A2
Colareț 135 D2
Cölbe 81 B/C2
Cölbe-Bürgeln 81 B/C2
Cölbe-Schönstadt 81 B/C2
Colbitz 69 C/D3
Colchester 65 C2
Coldingham 57 D2
Colditz 82 B1
Coldstream 57 D2
Coleford 63 D1
Colembert 77 D1
Colera 156 B2
Coleraine 54 A3, 55 D2
Coles 150 B2
Coleshill 64 A2
Colfiorito 115 D3, 117 C2
Cólico 105 D2, 106 A2
Coligny 103 D2
Colindres 153 C1
Collado Hermoso 160 B2
Collado Villalba 160 B2
Collagna 114 A2, 116 A1
Collanzo 151 D1, 152 A1
Collarmele 119 C1/2
Colldejou 163 D2
Coll de Nargó 155 C2/3
Collebarucci 114 B2, 116 B1
Collécchio 114 A1
Colle di Tora 117 C3, 118 B1
Colle di Val d'Elsa 114 B3, 116 B2
Colleferro 118 B2
Collegno 112 B1
Colle Isarco/Gossensass 107 C1
Collelongo 119 C2
Collenberg 81 C3
Collepardo 119 C2
Collepasso 121 D3
Collesalvetti 114 A/B3, 116 A2
Colle Sannita 119 D2, 120 A1
Collesano 124 B2
Colletorto 119 D2, 120 A1
Colli a Volturno 119 C2
Colli di Montebove 118 B1/2
Collínas 123 C3
Collinée 85 C2
Cóllio 106 B3
Collioure 156 B2
Collobrières 112 A3
Collon 58 A1
Collonges 104 A2
Colmar 90 A2/3
Colmars 112 A2
Colmberg 91 D1
Colmenar 172 B2
Colmenar de la Sierra 161 C2
Colmenar de Oreja 161 C3
Colmenar de Montemayor 159 D2/3
Colmenar del Arroyo 160 B2
Colmenar Viejo 160 B2
Colmonell 56 B3
Colne 59 D1, 60 B2
Colobraro 120 B3
Cologna 115 C1
Cologna Véneta 107 C3
Cologne-du-Gers 109 C2
Cologno al Sério 106 A3
Cologno Monzese 105 D3, 106 A3
Colombey-les-deux-Eglises 88 B2
Colombey-les-Belles 89 C2
Colombier 104 B1
Colombiès 110 A2
Colomby 76 A3
Colomera 173 C2
Colomers 156 B2
Colonia de San Pedro 157 C1/2
Colonia de Sant Jordi 157 D2
Colonne 113 D1
Colorno 114 A1
Colos 170 A1
Cölpin 70 A1
Colsey 65 C3
Colsterworth 61 D3, 64 B1
Colunga 152 A1
Colungo 155 C2/3
Colwyn Bay 59 C2, 60 A3
Colyton 63 C2
Coma 155 D2/3, 156 A2
Comácchio 115 C1
Comănești 141 C1
Comano Terme 106 B2
Comares 172 B2
Coma-ruga 163 D1
Combarros 151 D2
Combeaufontaine 89 C3
Combe Martin 63 C2
Comber 56 A3
Combles 78 A3
Combourg 85 D2
Combres 87 B/C2
Combronde 102 B2
Comeglians 107 D2, 126 A2
Comillas 152 B1
Cómiso 125 C3
Comlosu Mare 129 D3
Commana 84 B2
Commensacq 108 A/B2
Commentry 102 B2
Commequiers 100 A1
Commerau 83 D1
Commercy 89 C1
Commessággio 114 B1
Como 105 D3, 106 A3
Comorîste 134 B1
Cómpeta 172 B2
Compiègne 78 A3
Comporta 164 A3
Compreignac 101 C2
Comps-sur-Artuby 112 A3
Comrie 56 B1
Comunanza 117 D2/3
Cona 107 C3
Conca 113 D3
Concarneau 84 B2/3
Conceição 164 B3, 170 A1
Conceição 170 B2
Conceição 170 B2
Concerviano 117 C/D3, 118 B1
Concha 161 D2
Conches-en-Ouche 86 B1
Concórdia sulla Sécchia 114 B1
Concots 109 D1/2
Condado 153 C2
Condamine-Châtelard 112 B2
Condat-en-Féniers 102 B3
Condat-lès-Monboissier 102 B3
Condè-en-Brie 88 A1
Condeixa a Nova 158 A3
CONDEON 101 C3
Condé-sur-l'Escaut 78 B2
Condé-sur-Noireau 86 A1
Condé-sur-Vesgre 87 C1/2
Condino 106 B2/3
Condofuri 122 A3
Condom 109 C2
Condove 112 B1
Condrieu 103 D3
Conegliano 107 D2/3
Conflans-en-Jarnisy 89 C1
Conflans-Sainte-Honorine 87 C1
Conflans-sur-Lanterne 89 C3
Conflenti 122 A/B2
Confolens 101 C/D2
Confrides 169 D2
Congleton 59 D2, 60 B3, 64 A1
Congosto de Valdavia 152 B2
Coniale 115 B/C2, 116 B1
Conil de la Frontera 171 D3
Conimbriga 158 A3
Coniston 59 C1, 60 B1/2
Conlie 86 A/B2
Conlig 56 A3
Connah's Quay 59 C2, 60 B3
Connantre 88 A1/2
Connaux 111 C2
Connel 56 A1
Connerré 86 B2
Čonoplja 129 C3
Conques 110 A1
Conques-sur-Orbiel 110 A3, 156 A/B1
Conquista 167 C3
Conquista de la Sierra 166 A1
Consélice 115 C1
Consell 157 C2
Conselve 107 C3
Consenvoye 89 C1
Consett 57 D3, 61 C1
Constancia 164 B1
Constanța 141 D2
Constantí 163 C1/2
Constantim 151 D3, 159 C/D1
Constantina 166 A3, 171 D1, 172 A1
Consuegra 167 D1
Consuma 115 C2, 116 B1/2
Contada 119 D3
Contadero 167 C3
Contarina 115 C1
Contay 78 A3
Contessa Entellina 124 A/B2
Conthil 89 D1
Contigliano 117 C3, 118 B1
Contis-Plage 108 B2
Contres 87 C3
Contrexéville 89 C2
Contrisson 88 B1
Controne 120 A2/3
Contursi 120 A2
Contwig 90 A1
Conty 77 D3
Convento de la Rábida 171 C2
Convento di Fonte Colombo 117 C3, 118 B1
Conversano 121 C2
Conweiler 90 B1/2
Conwy 59 C2, 60 A3
Cookham 64 B3
Coombe Hill 63 D1, 64 A2
Čop 97 C/D2, 98 A3
Copertino 121 D3
Copons 155 D3, 156 A3, 163 D1
Copparo 115 C1
Coppenbrügge 68 B3
Coppet 104 A2
Copplestone 63 C2
Corabia 140 B2
Córaci 122 B2
Corato 120 B2, 136 A3
Coray 84 B2
Corbalán 162 B2/3
Corbeil-Essonnes 87 D2
Corbeilles-du-Gâtinais 87 D2
Corbera de Alcira 169 D2
Corbera d'Ebre 163 C2
Corbie 78 A3
Corbigny 88 A3, 103 C1
Corbridge 57 D3, 61 B/C1
Corby 64 B2
Corchiano 117 C3, 118 B1
Corciano 115 C3, 117 C2
Corcieux 89 D2, 90 A2
Córcoles 161 D2
Corconne 110 B2
Corconte 152 B1/2
Corcova 135 D1/2
Corcoya 172 B2
Corçubión 150 A2
Cordenòns 107 D2, 126 A2
Cordes 109 D2
Cordesse 103 C1
Cordignano 107 D2
Córdoba 166 B3, 172 B1
Córdobilla de Lácara 165 D2
Cordovado 107 D2/3, 126 A3
Corduente 161 D2
Corella 154 A3
Corera 153 D2
Coreses 151 D3, 152 A3, 159 D1
Corga 158 A2
Corgo 151 B/C2
Cori 118 B2
Coria 159 C3
Coria del Río 171 D2
Coriano 115 D2, 117 C1
Corigliano Cálabro 122 B1
Corinaldo 115 D2/3, 117 C/D2
Corinium 131 C2
Coripe 172 A2
Coristanco 150 A1
Cork (Corcaigh) 55 C3
Corlătel 135 D2
Corlay 84 B2
Corleone 124 B2
Corleto Perticara 120 B3
Corlier 103 D2, 104 A2
Çorlu 149 D1
Cormainville 87 C2
Cormatin 103 D2
Cormeilles 77 C3, 86 B1
Corme-Porto 150 A1
Cormery 86 B3, 101 D1
Cormons 126 A2
Cormoz 103 D2
Cornago 153 D3
Cornaredo 105 D3
Cornberg 81 C1
Cornea 135 C1
Corneliano d'Alba 113 C1
Cornella 156 A3
Cornellà del Terri 156 B2
Cornellana 151 D1
Cornereva 135 C1
Corníglio 114 A1/2
Cornimont 89 D2, 90 A3
Corniolo 115 C2, 116 B1
Cornštejn 94 A1
Cornuda 107 C3
Cornudella de Montsant 163 D1
Cornudilla 153 C2
Cornus 110 B2
Corny-sur-Moselle 89 C1
Coronado 158 A1
Çorovoda 142 A/B2
Corpa 161 C2
Corps 111 D1, 112 A1
Corps Nuds 85 D2
Corral de Almaguer 161 C3, 167 D1, 168 A1
Corral de Ayllón 161 C1
Corral de Cal 167 C2
Corrales 159 D1
Corrales 171 C2
Corral-Rubio 169 C2
Corre 89 C2/3
Corredoiras 150 B1/2
Corréggio 114 B1
Corrèze 102 A3
Corridónia 117 D2
Corrie 56 A2
Corsavy 156 B2
Corsham 63 D2, 64 A3
Corsicana 113 D3
Córsico 105 D3, 106 A3
Čortanovci 133 D1, 134 A1
Corte 113 D3
Corteconcepción 165 D3, 171 C1
Corte de Peleas 165 D2
Corte do Pinto 170 B1
Cortegada 150 B3
Cortegada 150 B3
Cortegana 165 C/D3, 171 C1
Cortelazor 165 D3, 171 C1
Cortemaggiore 114 A1
Cortemília 113 C1/2
Córteno Golgi 106 B2
Corteolona 105 D3, 106 A3, 113 D1
Corteraso/Kurzras 106 B1
Cortes 154 A3
Cortes de Aragón 162 B2
Cortes de Arenoso 162 B3
Cortes de Baza 173 D1
Cortes de la Frontera 172 A2/3
Cortes de Pallás 169 C1/2
Cortiguera 151 C2
Cortina d'Ampezzo 107 C/D2
Čortkov 98 B3
Cortona 115 C3, 117 B/C2
Coruche 164 B2
Corullón 151 C2
Coruña del Conde 153 C3, 161 C1
Corvara in Badia 107 C2
Corvera de Asturias 151 D1
Corvey 68 B3
Corwen 59 C2/3, 60 A3
Coryton 65 C3
Corzu 135 D2
Cosa 116 B3
Cosa 163 C2
Cosenza 122 A/B2
Cosham 76 A1
Ćosići 132 A2
Coslada 161 C2
Cosne-d'Allier 102 B2
Cosne-sur-Loire 87 D3
Cospeito 150 B1
Cossato 105 C3
Cossé-le-Vivien 85 D2, 86 A2
Cossonay 104 B2
Costa da Caparica 164 A2
Costa de los Pinos 167 D1
Costa Nova 158 A2
Costaros 110 B1
Costeán 155 C3
Costești 140 B2
Costigliole Saluzzo 112 B1/2
Costigliole d'Asti 113 C1
Costur 163 B/C3
Cosuenda 163 C1
Coswig 69 D3
Coswig 83 C1
Cotehele House 62 B3
Cotillas 168 A3
Cotobade 150 A2
Cotronei 122 B2

Cottanello 117 C3, 118 B1
Cottbus 70 B3
Cottbus 72 A3, 96 A1
Cottendorf 81 D2, 82 A2
Coubert 87 D1/2
Couches-les-Mines 103 C1
Couço 164 B2
Coucouron 110 B1
Coucy-le-Château Auffrigue 78 A3
Coudes 102 B3
Coudons 156 A1
Couflens 155 C2
Couhé 101 C2
Couilly-Pont-aux-Dames 87 D1
Couiza 110 A3, 156 A1
Coulange-la-Vineuse 88 A3
Coulanges-sur-Yonne 88 A3
Coulans-sur-Gée 86 A/B2
Coullons 87 D3
Coulmier-le-Sec 88 B3
Coulmiers 87 C2/3
Coulommiers 87 D1
Coulon 100 B2
Coulonges-en-Tardenois 88 A1
Coulonges-sur-l'Autize 100 B2
Coulport 56 B1
Coupar Angus 57 C1
Couptrain 86 A2
Coura 150 A3
Courances 87 D2
Courcelles-Chaussy 89 D1
Courcelles-sur-Nied 89 C/D1
Courchaton 89 D3
Courchevel 104 B3
Cour-Cheverny 87 C3
Courcité 86 A2
Courcôme 101 C2
Courçon 100 B2
Cour-et-Buis 103 D3
Courgains 86 B2
Courgenard 86 B2
Courgenay 89 D3, 90 A3, 104 B1
Courmangoux 103 D2
Courmayeur 104 B3
Courniou 110 A3
Courpière 103 B/C3
Cours 103 D2
Coursan 110 A/B3, 156 B1
Coursegoules 112 B2/3
Courseulles-sur-Mer 76 B3, 86 A1
Courson-les-Carrières 88 A3
Courtacon 88 A1/2
Courtalain 86 A/B2
Courteilles 86 B1
Courtenay 87 D2
Courthézon 111 C2
Courtomer 86 B2
Courtown Harbour 58 A3
Court-Saint-Étienne 79 B/C2
Courville-sur-Eure 86 A/B2
Cousolre 78 B2
Coussac-Bonneval 101 C3
Coussegrey 88 A2
Coussey 89 C2
Coustellet 111 D2
Coustouges 156 B2
Coutainville-Plage 85 D1
Coutances 85 D1
Couterne 86 A2
Couthenans 89 D3
Coutras 108 B1
Couvent de Corbara 113 D2
Couvent Sainte-Marie 113 D3
Couvet 104 B1
Couvin 78 B3
Couzan 103 C3
Couze-et-Saint-Front 109 C1
Covadonga 152 A1
Covaleda 153 C3
Covanera 153 B/C2
Covarrubias 153 C3
Covas 158 A1
Covasna 141 C1

Coveiu 135 D2
Covelães 150 B3, 158 B1
Covelo 150 A/B2/3
Coventry 64 A2
Coverack 62 B3
Čovići 130 B1
Covide 150 B3, 158 A1
Covigliáio 114 B2, 116 B1
Covilhã 158 B3
Cowbridge 63 C2
Cowdenbeath 57 C1
Cowes 76 B1
Cowley 65 C3
Cox 109 C2
Coxwold 61 D2
Cózar 167 D2, 168 A2
Cozes 100 B3
Cozvíjar 173 C2
Cozzano 113 D3
Craco 120 B3
Crăguesti 135 D1
Craighouse 56 A2
Craighouse 54 A2/3, 55 D1
Craignure 56 A1
Crail 57 C1
Crailsheim 91 D1
Crailsheim-Jagstheim 91 C/D1
Craiova 140 B2
Cranborne 63 D2, 76 A1
Cranbrook 65 C3, 77 C1
Crançot 104 A1/2
Cranleigh 64 B3, 76 B1
Cransac 110 A1
Crans-sur-Sierre [Sierre] 105 C2
Cranwell 61 D3, 64 B1
Craon 85 D2/3, 86 A2/3
Craponne-sur-Arzon 103 C3
Crasna 141 C1
Crassier [Nyon] 104 A2
Craster 57 D2
Crato 165 C1/2
Cravant 87 C3
Craven Arms 59 D3
Crawford 57 C2
Crawinkel 81 D2
Crawley 65 B/C3, 76 B1
Creagorry 54 A2
Crecente 150 B3
Crécy-en-Brie 87 D1
Crécy-en-Ponthieu 77 D2
Crécy-sur-Serre 78 B3
Crediton 63 C2
Creetown 56 B3, 60 A1
Creglingen 81 D3, 91 C/D1
Creil 87 D1
Crema 106 A3
Crémieu 103 D3
Cremlingen 69 C3
Cremona 114 A1
Črensovci 127 D2
Créon 108 B1
Crepaja 133 D1, 134 B1
Crépey 89 C2
Crépy-en-Laonnois 78 A/B3
Crépy-en-Valois 87 D1
Cres 130 A1
Crescentino 105 C3, 113 C1
Crespadoro 107 C3
Crespino 115 C1
Crespos 160 A2
Cressensac 109 D1
Crest 111 C/D1
Cresta, Avers- [Thusis] 106 A2
Cretas 163 C2
Creully 76 B3, 86 A1
Creussen 82 A3
Creussen-Seidwitz 82 A3
Creutzwald 89 D1
Creuzburg 81 D1
Crevalcore 114 B1
Crèvecoeur-le-Grand 77 D3
Crevedia Mare 141 C2
Crevillente 169 C2
Crevola d'Óssola 105 C2
Crewe 59 D2, 60 B3, 64 A1
Crewkerne 63 D2
Crézancy 88 A1
Crianlarich 56 B1
Crianlarich 54 A/B2, 55 D1
Criccieth 59 B/C2/3, 60 A3

Crickhowell 63 C1
Cricklade 63 D1, 64 A3
Crieff 56 B1
Crieff 54 B2
Criel-Plage 76 B2
Criel-sur-Mer 76 B2
Crikvenica 127 C3, 130 B1
Crillon 77 D3
Crimmitschau 82 B2
Crinan 56 A1
Criquetot-l'Esnéval 77 B/C3
Črišnjevo 126 B3, 130 B1
Crispiano 121 C2
Crissolo 112 B1
Cristina 165 D2, 166 A2
Cristóbal 159 D2
Cristuru Secuiesc 141 B/C1
Crivaia 135 C1
Crivillén 162 B2
Crivitz 69 C/D1
Crkvice 137 C2
Črmošnjice 127 C3
Črna 127 C2
Crna Bara 133 C1
Crnac 133 D3, 138 A/B1
Crnac 128 B3
Crna Rijeka 131 D2, 132 A2
Crna Trava 139 C1
Crne Lokve 132 A3
Crniljevo 133 C2
Crni Lug 127 C3, 130 B1
Crni Lug 131 D2
Črni Vrh nad Idrija 126 B2/3
Črnkovći 128 B3
Črnomelj 127 C3
Črnuče 126 B2
Crock 81 D2, 82 A2
Crocketford 56 B3, 60 A1
Crocq 102 A2
Crodo 105 C2
Croft 57 D3, 61 C1
Croglin 57 C3, 60 B1
Croix de Chamrousse 104 A3, 112 A1
Croix-Valmer 112 A3
Crolles 104 A3
Cromarty 54 B2
Cromer 61 D3, 65 C1
Cronat 103 C1
Crook 57 D3, 61 C1
Crookhaven 55 C3
Cropalati 122 B1
Crópani 122 B2
Crópani Marina 122 B2
Cros 102 A3
Crosby 59 C/D2, 60 B3
Crosmières 86 A3
Crosscar 58 A1
Crossmaglen 58 A1
Crossmichael 56 B3, 60 A1
Crotone 122 B2
Crottendorf 82 B2
Croutelle 101 C2
Crowborough 76 B1
Crowland 65 B/C1
Crowle 61 C2
Croxton Kerrial 61 C/D3, 64 B1
Croydon 65 C3, 76 B1
Crozant 101 D2, 102 A2
Crozon 84 A2
Cruas 111 C2
Crúcoli Torretta 122 B1
Crulai 86 B1/2
Cruseilles 104 A2
Crussol 111 C1
Cruz 158 A1
Cruzy 110 A3, 156 B1
Cruzy-le-Châtel 88 B3
Crveni Grm 132 A3, 136 B1
Crvenka 129 C3
Crvljivac 133 C3
Crymmych Arms 62 B1
Csabacsüd 129 D1
Csabrendek 128 A1
Csákánydoroszló 127 D1
Csákberény 95 C/D3, 128 B1
Csákvár 95 D3, 128 B1
Csanytelek 129 D2
Csapod 94 B3
Császár 95 C3
Császártöltés 129 C2
Csávoly 129 C2

Csengőd 129 C2
Csépa 129 D1
Csepreg 94 B3, 128 A1
Cserdi 128 B2
Cserebökény 129 D1/2
Cserkeszőlő 129 D1
Csesztreg 127 D1/2
Csokonyavisonta 128 A2
Csömend 128 A2
Csongrád 129 D2
Csopak 128 B1
Csór 128 B1
Csorna 95 B/C3
Csót 95 C3, 128 A/B1
Csurgó 128 A2
Csurgó 96 B3
Cuacos 159 D3
Cuadros 151 D2, 152 A2
Cualedro 150 B3
Cuart de Poblet 169 D1
Cuatretonda 169 D2
Cuba 164 B3
Cubel 162 A2
Cubel 162 A2
Cubelles 156 A3, 163 D1
Cubells 155 D3
Cubières 156 B1
Cubillas de Cerrato 152 B3, 160 B1
Cubillas de los Oteros 151 D2, 152 A2
Cubillos 153 C3, 161 C1
Cubillos 151 D3, 159 D1
Cubla 162 A/B3
Cubo de Bureba 153 C2
Cubo de la Solana 153 D3, 161 D1
Cucalón 162 B2
Cucho 153 C/D2
Cuckfield 76 B1
Cudillero 151 D1
Čudnov 99 C2
Čudovo 75 C1
Cuéllar 160 B1
Cuenca 166 A3
Cuenca 161 D3
Cuenca de Campos 152 A3
Cuers 112 A3
Cuerva 160 B3, 167 C1
Cueva de Ágreda 154 A3, 161 D1, 162 A1
Cueva de Altamira 152 B1
Cueva de Canalobre 169 D2/3
Cueva de la Vieja 169 D2
Cueva de la Pileta 172 A2
Cueva del Aguila 160 A3
Cueva del Hierro 161 D2
Cueva de los Chorros 168 A/B3
Cueva dels Civils y dels Cavalls 163 C2/3
Cueva de Minateda 168 B3
Cueva de Montesino 167 D2, 168 A2
Cueva de Valporquero 151 D2, 152 A2
Cueva Na Polida 157 C1
Cueva Remigia 163 B/C2
Cueva Rosegador 163 C2
Cueva Santa 162 B3, 169 C1
Cuevas Bajas 172 B2
Cuevas de Amaya 152 B2
Cuevas de Artá 157 C1
Cuevas de Campanet 157 C2
Cuevas del Almanzora 174 A2
Cuevas del Becerro 172 A2
Cuevas del Drach 157 C1/2
Cuevas dels Hams 157 C1/2
Cuevas del Valle 160 A3
Cuevas de Nerja 173 C2
Cuevas de San Clemente 153 C3
Cuevas de San Marcos 172 B2
Cuevas de Santimaminie 153 D1
Cuevas de Velasco 161 D3
Cuevas de Vinromá 163 C3
Cuevas Labradas 161 D2
Cuevas Labradas 162 A/B2
Cuevas Minadas 161 D2
Cuges-les-Pins 111 D3
Cúglieri 123 C2

Cugny 78 A3
Cuijk 66 B3
Cuiseaux 103 D2, 104 A2
Cuisery 103 D2
Cujmir 135 D2
Cujmir 140 B2
Čukljenik 139 C1
Culan 102 A2
Culemborg 66 B3
Culgaith 57 C3, 60 B1
Culine 133 C2
Culjković 133 C3
Culla 162 B3
Cúllar-Baza 173 D1
Cullera 169 D2
Culleredo 150 A1
Cullompton 63 C2
Cully 104 B2
Culoz 104 A3
Cuma 119 C3
Cumbernauld 56 B2
Cumbres de Enmedio 165 D3
Cumbres de San Bartolomé 165 D3
Cumbres Mayores 165 D3, 171 C1
Cumiana 112 B1
Cumieira 158 B1
Cumnock and Holmhead 56 B2
Cumrew 57 C3, 60 B1
Cumwhitton 57 C3, 60 B1
Cunault 86 A3, 101 C1
Cunchillos 154 A3
Cunèges 109 C1
Cúneo 112 B2
Cunewalde 83 D1
Cunfin 88 B2
Cunlhat 103 B/C3
Čunski 130 A2
Cuntis 150 A2
Cuorgnè 105 C3
Cupar 57 C1
Cupello 119 D1/2
Cupra Maríttima 117 D2
Cupramontana 115 D3, 117 D2
Čuprene 135 C/D3
Čuprija 134 B2/3
Curalha 150 B3, 158 B1
Čurilovo 74 B2/3
Curinga 122 A/B2
Curon Venosta/Graun im Vinschgau 106 B1
Curraj i Epërm 138 A2
Curtarolo 107 C3
Curtatone 106 B3, 114 B1
Curtea de Argeș 140 B2
Curtis 150 B1
Curtis-Estación 150 B1
Čurug 129 C3
Cusano Mutri 119 D2
Cuse-et-Adrisans 89 D3
Cushendall 56 A3
Cushendun 56 A3
Cusiano 106 B2
Cusset 102 B2
Cussy-les-Forges 88 A3
Custines 89 C1
Cusy 104 A3
Cutanda 163 C2
Cutigliano 114 B2, 116 A1
Cutro 122 B2
Cutrofiano 121 D3
Cuvilly 78 A3
Cuxac-d'Aude 110 A/B3, 156 B1
Cuxhaven 52 A3, 68 A1
Cuxhaven-Altenbruch 52 A3, 68 A1
Cuxhaven-Altenwalde 52 A3, 68 A1
Cuzzago 105 C2
Cuzzola 123 D1
Cvikov 83 D2
Čvrstec 127 D2, 128 A2
Cwmbran 63 C1
Cybinka 70 B3
Cynwyl Elfed 62 B1
Cysoing 78 A2
Czacz 71 D3
Czaplinek 71 D1
Czarne 71 D1
Czarnków 71 D2
Czarnków 72 B3
Czempiń 71 D3

Czernina 71 D3
Czersk 72 B2/3
Czerwieńsk 71 C3
Czerwona Woda 83 D1
Częstochowa 97 B/C1
Człopa 71 C/D2
Człuchów 72 B3
Czmon 71 D3

D

Daaden 80 B2
Dåasdammen 39 D1
Dabar 130 B1
Dabas 129 C1
Dabel 53 D3, 69 D1
Dąbie 71 C3
Dabilja 139 D3
Dabo 89 D2, 90 A2
Dąbrowa Tarnowska 97 C2
Dąbrówka Wielkopolska 71 C3
Dachau 92 A2
Dachsenhausen 80 B2
Dačice 94 A1
Dad 95 C3
Dädesjö 51 C1
Dadiá 145 D1, 145 D3
Dåfjord 4 A2
Dáfnai 146 B2
Dáfni 144 B2
Dáfni 146 B2/3
Dáfni 149 C1
Dagali 37 C3
Daganzo de Arriba 161 C2
Dagarn 39 D3
Dagda 74 B2
Dagebüll 52 A2
Daggrø 43 C1
Dagmersellen 105 C1
Dagsmark 20 A3
Dahlem 79 D2
Dahlem-Schmidtheim 79 D2
Dahlen 82 B1
Dahlen 70 A1
Dahlen 69 D2
Dahlenburg 69 C1/2
Dahlewitz 70 A3
Dahme 70 A3
Dahme 53 C3
Dahn 90 A/B1
Dähre 69 C2
Dailly 56 B2
Daimiel 167 D2
Dajkanberg 15 C3
Dajkanvik 15 C3
Đakovački Selci 128 B3, 132 B1
Đakovica 138 A2
Đakovica 140 A3
Đakovo 128 B3, 132 B1
Daksbruk (Taalintehdas) 24 B3
Dal 30 B3, 35 D2
Dal 38 A3
Dala 30 B3, 35 D2
Đala 129 D2
Dalaas 106 A/B1
Dalabojegoatte 5 D3, 6 A3, 11 D1
Dalarö 47 D1
Dalåsen 34 B2
Dalasjö 30 A/B1
Dalavardo 15 C2
Dalbeattie 56 B3, 60 A1
Dalboșet 135 C1
Dalby 50 B3
Dalby 38 B2
Dalby 58 B1
Dalby 72 A2
Dalbyn 39 D1/2
Dale 62 B1
Dale 9 C1
Dale 36 A3
Dale 36 A2
Dale 43 C2
Dale 43 C2
Dale 32 A/B2
Dalen 67 C2
Dalen 43 C2
Dalen 33 C3, 37 D1
Dalen 32 B2/3
Dalešice 94 A/B1
Dalfors 39 D1
Dalfsen 67 C2
Dalgard 9 D1
Dâlgopol 141 C3
Dalhem 72 B1
Dalhem 46 B3
Dalhem 47 D3
Dalías 173 D2
Dalj 129 C3
Dalkeith 57 C2
Dalkey 58 A2
Dallgow 70 A2
Dallmin 69 D1/2
Dalmally 56 B1
Dalmellington 56 B2
Dálmine 106 A3
Dalmose 53 C1
Dalry 56 B3
Dalry 56 B2
Dalry 54 B3
Dalrymple 56 B2
Dalseter 37 D2
Dalseter 33 C2
Dalsfjord 36 A/B1
Dals Högen 45 B/C2
Dalsjöfors 45 C/D3
Dals Rostock 45 C2
Dalston 57 C3, 60 B1
Dalstuga 39 D2
Dalsvallen 34 A/B3
Dalton-in-Furness 59 C1, 60 A/B2
Daluis 112 B2
Dalvangen 33 C3, 37 D1
Damásion 143 D3
Damaskinéa 143 B/C2
Damazan 109 C2
Damerow 70 B1
Damice 82 B2
Dammartin-en-Goële 87 D1
Damme 67 D2, 68 A2
Damme 78 A1
Damnatz-Landsatz 69 C2
Dampierre 104 A1
Dampierre 87 C1/2
Dampierre-en-Burly 87 D3
Dampierre-sous-Bouhy 87 D3
Dampierre-sur-Boutonne 101 B/C2
Dampierre-sur-Salon 89 C3
Damp-Zweitausend 52 B2
Damsdorf 53 B/C3
Damsdorf 69 D2/3, 70 A2/3
Damshagen 53 C3
Damüls 106 A1
Damvant [Porrentruy] 89 D3, 90 A3, 104 B1
Damville 87 B/C1
Damvillers 89 C1
Damwoude 67 B/C1
Danasjö 15 C/D3
Danby 61 C1
Dancharinea 108 A3, 154 A1
Dangé 101 C1
Dangeau 86 A/B2
Dangers 86 A/B2
Dangu 77 D3, 87 C1
Danholm 39 D2, 40 A2
Danilovgarad 137 D2
Danków 71 C2
Dannäs 50 B1
Dannemare 53 C2
Dannemarie 89 D3, 90 A3
Dannemora 40 B3
Dannenberg / Elbe 69 C2
Dannenberg-Schaafhausen 69 C2
Dannenwalde 70 A2
Dänschendorf-Westermarkelsdorf 53 C2
Danzé 86 B2/3
Daon 86 A3
Daoulas 84 A2
Darabani 98 B3
Darány 128 A/B2/3
Dáránypuszta 128 B1/2
Dáras 146 B2/3
Darchau 69 C1
Darda 129 B/C3
Dardha 142 B2
Darfo-Boário Terme 106 B2/3
Darlington 57 D3, 61 C1
Darlington 54 B3
Darłowo 72 B2
Darméni 145 D1
Darmstadt 80 B3
Darney 89 C2
Darníus 156 B2
Daroca 162 A2
Darque 150 A3, 158 A1
Darro 173 C2
Dærtahytta 10 A1/2
Dartford 65 C3
Darthus 37 C/D1/2
Dartmouth 63 C3
Dartsel 16 B3
Daruvar 128 A3
Darvel 56 B2
Darwen 59 D2, 60 B2
Darze 69 D1
Dasburg 79 D3
Daševо 99 C3
Daskalovo 139 D1/2
Dassel 68 B3
Dassel-Lauenberg 68 B3
Dassel-Marakoldendorf 68 B3
Dassow 53 C3
Datça 149 D3
D'atlovo 98 B1
Datteln 67 D3, 80 A1
Dáttilo 124 A2
Daugård 48 B3, 52 B1
Daugavpils 74 A2/3
Daumeray 86 A3
Daumitsch 82 A2
Daun 79 D2/3, 80 A2/3
Dautphetal-Allendorf 80 B2
Dautzschen 70 A3, 82 B1
Daventry 65 C2
Daviá 146 B3
David-Gorodok 98 B1
Davle 83 D3
Dávlia 147 C2
Davor 132 A1
Davos Dorf 106 A1
Davos Platz 106 A1
Dawlish 63 C3
Dax 108 A2
Dažnica 132 B1
Deal 65 C3, 76 B1
Deão 150 A3, 158 A1
Deauville 76 B3, 86 B1
Deba 153 D1
Débanos 153 D3, 154 A3
Debar 138 A3
Debar 140 A3
Debeli Lug 135 C2
Debeljača 133 D1, 134 A/B1
Debenham 65 C2
Dębica 97 C2
Dęblin 97 C1, 98 A2
Dębno 70 B2
Debrc 133 D1/2, 134 A2
Debrecen 97 C3, 140 A1
Debrznica 71 C3
Debrzno 71 D1
Dečani 138 A1/2
Decazeville 110 A1
Dechtice 95 C2
Decimomannu 123 C/D3
Děčín 83 C/D2
Děčín 96 A1
Decize 102 B1
Deckenpfronn 90 B2
De Cocksdorp 66 B1/2
Decollatura 122 B2
Decs 129 C2
Dedaj 137 D2
Deddington 65 C2
Dedeleben 69 C3
Dedeli 139 C/D3, 143 D1
Dedelow 70 B1
Dedemsvaart 67 C2
Deetz 69 D2, 70 A2
Deetz 69 D3
Défilé de l'Inzecca 113 D3
Dég 128 B1
Degaña 151 C2
Degeberga 50 B3
Degerby 41 D3
Degerby 25 C3
Degerfors 45 D1, 46 A1
Degerfors 31 C2
Degerhamn 51 D2
Degerndorf 92 B3
Degernes 44 B1
Degerselet 17 C2
Degerträsk 16 B3
Deggendorf 92 B1/2
Deggendorf-Natternberg 92 B2
Deggenhausertal 91 C3
Degolados 165 C2
De Haan 78 A1
De Haar 66 B3
Dehesa de Campoamor 169 C3, 174 B1
Dehesas de Guadix 173 C1
Dehesas Viejas 173 C1
Deibow 69 C1/2
Deidesheim 90 B1
Deifontes 173 C2
Deining 92 A1
Deinste 68 B1
Deinze 78 B1
Déiva Marina 113 D2, 114 A2
Dej 97 D3, 140 B1
Deje 39 C3, 45 D1
Dekani 126 B3
Dekanovec 127 D2
Dekélia 147 D2
Deknepollen 36 A1
De Koog 66 A/B1/2
De Kooi 66 A/B2
De Krim 67 C2
Delary 50 B2
Del'atin 97 D2, 98 A/B3
Delbrück 68 A3
Delbrück-Boke 68 A3, 80 B1
Delbrück-Ostenland 68 A3
Delbrück-Westenholz 68 A3
Delčevo 139 D2
Delčevo 140 B3
Delébio 105 D2, 106 A2
Deleitosa 159 D3, 166 A1
Đelekovec 128 A2
Delémont 90 A3, 104 B1
Delfí 147 C2
Delfí 148 B2
Delft 66 A3
Delfzijl 67 C1
Delgany 58 A2
Délia 124 B2/3
Delianuova 122 A3
Deliblato 134 B1
Deliceto 120 A2
Deligrad 134 B3
Delitzsch 82 B1
Delle 89 D3, 90 A3
Delligsen 68 B3
Delligsen-Grünenplan 68 B3
Dello 106 B3
Delme 89 D1
Delmenhorst 68 A2
Delnice 127 C3, 130 B1
Delvina 142 A2/3
Delvinákion 142 B2/3
Demandice 95 D2
Demetrias 143 D3, 144 A3
Demidov 75 C3
Demigny 103 D1
Demirci 149 D2
Demir Kapija 140 A3
Demir Kapija 139 C3, 143 D1
Demjansk 75 C2
Demmin 72 A2
Demonte 112 B2
Dému 109 B/C2
Denain 78 A2
Denbigh 59 C2, 60 A3
Den Burg 66 A/B2
Dendermonde 78 B1
Denekamp 67 C2
Đeneral Janković 138 B2
Den Haag ('s-Gravenhage) 66 A3
Den Ham 67 C2
Den Helder 66 A/B2
Den Hoorn 66 A/B2
Denia 169 D2
Denkendorf 92 A1
Denklingen (Kaufbeuren) 91 D3
Denneville 76 A3, 85 D1
Denno 107 B/C2
Denny 56 B1/2
Densow 70 A1/2
Dent 59 D1, 60 B2
Dentlein 91 D1
Denzlingen 90 B2/3
De Panne-Bad 78 A1
Deptford 63 D2, 64 A3, 76 A1
Derås 28 B2
Derbent 149 D2
Derborence [Sion] 104 B2
Derby 61 C3, 64 A1
Derenburg 69 C3
Derendingen 105 C1
Dermbach 81 D2
Dermulo 107 B/C2
Derome 49 D1, 50 A1
Deronje 129 C3
Dersenow 69 C1
Deruta 115 C3, 117 C2/3
Dervaig 56 A1
Derval 85 D3
Dervénion 147 C2
Derventa 132 B1
Dérvio 105 D2, 106 A2
Dervíziana 142 B3
Desa 135 D2/3
Desborough 64 B2
Descargamaría 159 C3
Descartes 102 B1
Desenzano del Garda 106 B3
Desfína 147 C2
Dési 143 C3
Desláti 143 C2/3
Dešov 94 A1
Despotovac 134 B2
Despotovac 140 A2
Despotovo 129 C3
Dessau 69 D3
Dessau-Mosigkau 69 D3
Deštná 93 D1
Destriana 151 D2
Désulo 123 D2
Desvres 77 D1/2
Deszk 129 D2
Deta 134 B1
Deta 140 A2
Detčino 75 D3
Detern 67 D1
Detmold 68 A3
Dettelbach 81 D3
Dettingen 91 C2
Dettingen an der Erms 91 C2
Dettmannsdorf 53 D3
Dettwiller 90 A2
Deuerling 92 A/B1
Deurne 79 D1
Deutschfeistritz 127 C1
Deutschkreutz 94 B3
Deutschlands 127 C1
Deutsch Neudorf 83 C2
Deutsch-Wagram 94 B2
Deux-Chaises 102 B2
Deva 140 B1
Devecser 128 A1
Deventer 67 C3
Devesset 103 C3, 111 C1
Devil's Bridge 59 C3
Devín 94 B2
Devin 140 B3
Devínska Nová Ves 94 B2
Devizes 63 D2, 64 A3, 76 A1
Devojački Bunar 134 B1
Devonport 63 B/C3
Devrske 131 C2
Dewsbury 61 C2
Deyá 157 C2
Deza 161 D1
Dezzo 106 B2
Dhërmiu 142 A2
Dhuizon 87 C3
Diablerets, Les 104 B2
Diakoptón 146 B2
Diakovce 95 C2
Diamante 122 A1
Dianalund 49 C3, 53 C/D1
Diano 113 C2
Diano d'Alba 113 C1
Diano Marina 113 C2
Diarville 89 C2
Diavatá 143 D2, 144 A2
Diavolítsion 146 B3
Dicastillo 153 D2, 154 A2
Dichálion 144 B1

Dicomano 115 C2, 116 B1
Didcot 65 C3
Dídima 147 C3
Didimótichon 145 D3
Die 111 D1
Dieburg 81 C3
Diekholzen 68 B3
Diekirch 79 D3
Diélette 76 A3
Dielmissen 68 B3
Dielsdorf 90 B3
Diemelsee-Adorf 81 B/C1
Diemelstadt 81 C1
Diemitz 69 D1/2, 70 A1/2
Dienne 102 B3
Dienstedt 82 A2
Dienten am Hochkönig 93 B/C3, 107 D1, 126 A1
Diepenau-Essern 68 A2
Diepenau-Lavelsloh 68 A2/3
Diepenheim 67 C3
Diepenveen 67 C3
Diepholz 68 A2
Diepholz-Aschen 68 A2
Dieppe 77 C2
Dierberg 70 A2
Dierdorf 80 A/B2
Dieren 67 C3
Diesdorf 69 C2
Diessen am Ammersee 92 A3
Diessenhofen 90 B3
Diessen-Rieden 92 A3
Diest 79 C1/2
Dietenheim 91 D2
Dietenhofen 91 D1
Dietfurt 92 A1
Dietikon 90 B3, 105 C1
Dietingen 90 B2
Dietramszell 92 A3
Dietzenbach 81 B/C3
Dietzhölztal-Ewersbach 80 B2
Dieulefit 111 C/D1
Dieulouard 89 C1
Dieuze 89 D1
Diever 67 C2
Diez 80 B2
Diezma 173 C2
Differdange 79 D3
Digerberg 34 B3
Digerberget 39 D1/2
Digermulen 8 B2
Dignac 101 C3
Dignano 107 D2, 126 A2
Digne 112 A2
Digny 86 A/B2
Digoin 103 C2
Dijon 88 B3
Dikanäs 15 C3
Dikance 138 A/B2
Dikili 149 D2
Diksmuide 78 A1
Dílar 173 C2
Dillenburg 80 B2
Dillingen an der Donau 91 D2
Dillingen/Saar 89 D1
Dima 153 D1
Dimaro 106 B2
Dimbach 93 D2
Dímena 147 C3
Dimitrievka 99 D2
Dimitrovgrad 140 B3
Dimitrovgrad 141 C3
Dimitrovgrad 139 D1
Dimitsána 146 B3
Dimmelsvik 42 A1
Dimovo 135 D3
Dinami 122 A2/3
Dinan 85 C2
Dinant 79 C2
Dinard 85 C1/2
Dinas Mawddwy 59 C3
Dine 151 C3
Dingden 67 C3
Dingelstädt 81 D1
Dingle 44 B2
Dingle 55 C3
Dingolfing 92 B2
Dingtuna 40 A3, 46 B1
Dingwall 54 A/B2
Dinjiška 130 B2
Dinkelsbühl 91 D1
Dinklage 67 D2
Dinslaken-Bottrop 79 D1, 80 A1
Diö 50 B2
Dion 143 D2
Diósjenö 95 D3
Dios le Guarde 159 C2
Diou 103 C2
Dipótamos 145 B/C1
Dippen 56 A2
Dipperz 81 C2
Dippoldiswalde 83 C2
Diragușan 145 D3
Dirdal 42 A2
Dirinella 105 D2
Dirinella [Ranzo-S. Abbondio] 105 D2
Dirleton 57 C1
Dirlewang 91 D3
Dirmstein 80 B3, 90 B1
Dirráchion 146 B3
Dischingen 91 D2
Dischingen-Ballmertshofen 91 D2
Disemont 77 D2
Disenå 38 A/B3
Disentis/Mustér 105 D1/2
Disna 74 B3
Diso 121 D3
Dispílion 143 C2
Diss 65 D2
Dissay-sous-Courcillon 86 B3
Dissen am Teutoburger Wald 67 D3, 68 A3
Distad 36 B2
Distington 57 C3, 60 A1
Dístomon 147 C2
Distos 147 D2
Dístraton 142 B2
Dittelbrunn-Hambach 81 D3
Dittersbach 83 C1
Dittersdorf 82 A2
Dittrichshütte 82 A2
Ditzingen 91 C2
Diustes 153 D3
Divača 126 B3
Diva Slatina 135 D3
Divci 133 D2, 134 A2
Divčibare 133 D2, 134 A2
Dives-sur-Mer 76 B3, 86 A1
Diviakë 142 A1
Dividalshytta 10 A2
Divieto 125 D1
Divion 77 D2, 78 A2
Divišov 83 D3
Divonne-les-Bains 104 A2
Divuša 127 D3, 131 C1
Dixmont 88 A2
Dizy-le-Gros 78 B3
Dizy-Magenta 88 A1
Djäkneböle 31 C2
Djatlovo 98 B1
Djønno 36 B3
Djup 37 C3
Djupa 40 B2/3
Djupdal 30 A1
Djupfjord 9 C2
Djupfors 15 C2
Djuping 9 C3
Djupsjön 29 C3, 34 A1
Djuptjärn 31 C2
Djupvasshytta 32 A3, 36 B1
Djupvik 4 B2/3
Djupvik 9 C3
Djuramåla 51 C2
Djuras 39 D2
Djurö 47 D1
Djurpark 46 B2
Djurröd 50 B2/3
Djursholm 47 C/D1
Dłoń 71 D3
Długa Goślina 71 D2
Długoszyn 71 C2
Dmitrov 75 D2
Dno 74 B2
Doagh 56 A3
Dobanovci 133 D1, 134 A1
Dobbertin 69 D1
Dobbiaco/Toblach 107 D1
Dobele 73 D1
Döbeln 96 A1
Döbeln 83 B/C1
Doberlug-Kirchhain 83 C1
Döbern 83 D1
Dobersberg 94 A1
Doberschütz 82 B1
Dobiegniew 71 C2
Dobiegniew 72 B3
Doboj 132 B1
Dobra 135 C2
Dobra 71 C1
Dobrá Niva 95 D2
Dobřany 83 C3
Dobrá Voda 95 C2
Dobre Miasto (Guttstadt) 73 C2
Dobřen 83 D2
Dobrevo 139 C2
Dobri 127 D2
Dobrica 134 B1
Dobričevo 134 B1
Dobřichovice 83 D3
Dobri Dol 138 B2
Dobrinci 133 D1, 134 A1
Dobrinj 130 B1
Dobříš 83 C/D3
Dobritz 69 D3
Dobrljin 127 D3, 131 C1
Dobrna 127 C2
Dobrnič 127 C3
Dobrodzień 96 B1
Döbrököz 128 B2
Dobromirci 145 C1
Dobro Polje 132 B3
Dobroselica 133 C/D3, 134 A3
Dobro Selo 131 C2
Dobrovice 83 D2
Dobrovnik 127 D2
Dobrun 133 C3
Dobruš 99 D1
Dobruševo 138 B3, 143 C1
Dobrzany 71 C1
Dobrzyń 83 D1
Dockasberg 17 C2
Docking 65 C1
Dockmyr 30 A3, 35 C2
Docksta 30 B3
Dockweiler 79 D2, 80 A2
Doclea 137 D2
Doclin 135 B/C1
Döderhult 51 D1
Dodewaard 66 B3
Dödismorän 34 A3
Dodona 142 B3
Dodóni 142 B3
Dödre 34 B2
Dodro 150 A2
Doesburg 67 C3
Doetinchem 67 C3
Doganović 138 B2
Dogliani 113 C1/2
Dogna 126 A2
Dognecea 135 C1
Dois Portos 164 A2
Dokka 37 D3
Dokkas 16 B1
Dokkum 67 B/C1
Doksany 83 C2
Dokšicy 74 B3
Doksy 83 D2
Dolac 138 A/B1/2
Dolac 132 B2
Dol'any 95 C2
Dólar 173 C/D2
Dolceácqua 112 B2
Dol-de-Bretagne 85 D2
Dôle 103 D1, 104 A1
Dølemo 43 C2/3
Dolenci 138 B3, 142 B1
Dolenja Vas 127 C3
Dolenjske Toplice 127 C3
Dolga Vas 127 D2
Dolgellau 59 C3
Doli 136 B1
Dolianá 142 B3
Dolianá 148 A1
Dolianova 123 D3
Dolice 71 C1/2
Dolina 97 D2, 98 A3
Dolinskaja 99 D3
Dolinskoe 141 D1
Doljane 131 C2
Döllach im Mölltal 107 D1, 126 A1
Dollar 57 B/C1
Dollart-Bunderhammrich 67 D1
Dolle 69 C/D2/3
Döllnitz 82 B1
Dollnstein 91 D1, 92 A1/2
Döllstädt 81 D1
Dolna dikanöa 139 D2
Dolná Poruba 95 C1
Dolné Orešany 95 C2
Dolné Saliby 95 C2
Dolné Vestenice 95 C/D2
Dolni Balvan 139 C2/3
Dolni Bělá 83 C3
Dolni Bogrov 139 D1
Dolní Bousov 83 D2
Dolni Dâbnik 140 B3
Dolní Dvořiště 93 D2
Dolní Kounice 94 B1
Dolni Lom 135 D3
Dolni Poustevna 83 C/D1/2
Dolní Žandov 82 B3
Dolno Cerovene 135 D3
Dolno Ujno 139 C/D2
Dolný Kubín 95 D1
Dolný Kubín 97 C2
Dolný Ohaj 95 C2/3
Dolný Turček 95 D2
Dolo 107 C/D3
Dolores 169 C3
Dolovo 134 B1
Dölsach 107 D1, 126 A1
Dolsk 71 D3
Dołuje 70 B1
Dolus-d'Oléron 101 C2
Domanevka 99 D3
Dománico 122 A2
Domaniža 95 D1
Domanovići 132 B3, 136 B1
Domart-en-Ponthieu 77 D2
Domaševo 137 C1
Domașnea 135 C1
Domaso 105 D2, 106 A2
Domats 87 D2
Domažlice 92 B1
Dombås 32 B3, 37 D1
Dombasle-en-Argonne 89 B/C1
Dombóvár 128 B2
Dombóvár 96 B3
Dombrot-le-Sec 89 C2
Domburg 78 B1
Domène 104 A3, 112 A1
Doménikon 143 C/D3
Domeño 155 C2
Domeño 162 B3, 169 C1
Domèvre-en-Haye 89 C1
Domèvre-sur-Vezouze 89 D2, 90 A2
Domfessel 89 D1, 90 A1
Domfront 86 A2
Domianí 146 B1
Domingo Pérez 160 B3, 167 C1
Dömitz 69 C2
Dommartin 103 C1
Dommartin-Dampierre 88 B1
Dommartin-la-Planchette 88 B1
Dommartin-le-Franc 88 B2
Dommartin-sur-Yèvre 88 B1
Domme 108 B1
Dommitzsch 70 A3, 82 B1
Domnanpirtti 19 D3
Domnítsa 146 B1
Domodóssola 105 C2
Domokós 146 B1
Domoravče 139 B/C2
Dömös 95 D3
Dompaire 89 C2
Dompierre-du-Chemin 86 A2
Dompierre-sur-Besbre 103 C2
Dompierre-sur-Mer 100 B2
Dompierre-sur-Veyle 103 D2
Domptail 89 D2
Domrémy-la-Pucelle 89 C2
Dom Savica 126 B2
Domsjö 31 C3
Dömsöd 129 C1
Dómus de Maria 123 C3
Domusnóvas 123 C3
Domžale 127 B/C2
Donabate 58 A2
Donado 151 D3
Donaghadee 56 A3
Don Álvaro 165 D2, 166 A2
Doña María Ocaña 173 D2
Donamaría 108 A3, 154 A1
Doña Mencía 172 B1
Donaueschingen-Wolterdingen 90 B3
Donaueschingen 90 B3
Donaustauf 92 B1
Donauwörth 91 D2
Don Benito 166 A2
Doncaster 61 C2/3
Donegal 55 C2
Dongen 66 B3, 79 C1
Dongo 105 D2, 106 A2
Donhierro 160 A1/2
Donington 61 D3, 65 B/C1
Doñinos de Salamanca 159 D2
Donja Badanja 133 C2
Donja Bebrina 132 B1
Donja Brela 131 D3, 132 A3
Donja Brezna 137 C1
Donja Bukovica 137 D1
Donja Dubravå 128 A2
Donja Grabovica 132 A/B3
Donja Kamenica 135 C3
Donja Konjščina 127 D2
Donja Ljubata 139 C2
Donja Mutnica 134 B3
Donja Omašnica 134 B3
Donja Sabanta 134 B2
Donja Stubičke Toplice 127 D2
Donja Suvaja 131 C2
Donja Trnava 135 C3
Donje Ljupče 138 B1
Donje Plananjane 131 C3
Donje Vukovije 133 B/C2
Donji Barbeš 135 C3, 139 C1
Donji Dragonožec 127 D3
Donji Dušnik 135 C3, 139 C1
Donji Krčin 134 B3
Donji Lapac 131 C2
Donji Miholjac 128 B3
Donji Milanovac 135 C2
Donji Okrug 131 C3
Donji Rujani 131 D3
Donji Skugrić 132 B1
Donji Svilaj 132 B1
Donji Vakuf 131 D2, 132 A2
Donji Zemunik 130 B2
Donji Žirovac 131 C1
Donkerbroek 67 C2
Donnalucata 125 C3
Donnemarie-Dontilly 87 D2, 88 A2
Donnersbach 93 C/D3
Donnersbachwald 93 C/D3, 126 B1
Donnersdorf 81 D3
Dønnes 14 A2
Dønnesfjord 5 C1
Donorático 114 B3, 116 A2
Donostia/San Sebastián 153 D1, 154 A1
Donovaly 95 D1/2
Donsö 45 C3, 49 D1
Dont 107 C/D2
Dont Forno di Zoldo 107 D2
Donville-les-Bains 85 D1
Donzdorf 91 C2
Donzenac 101 D3
Donzère 111 C1/2
Donzy 87 D3
Dooagh 55 C2
Doorn 66 B3
Dørålseter 33 C3, 37 D1
Đorče Petrov 138 B2
Dorchester 63 D2/3
Dørdal 43 D2, 44 A2
Dordrecht 66 A3
Dörentrup 68 A3
Dörentrup-Bega 68 A3
Dorfen 92 B2
Dorfgastein 107 D1, 126 A1
Dorgali 123 D2
Dorkás 144 A1
Dorking 64 B3, 76 B1
Dormagen 79 D1, 80 A1
Dormans 88 A1

Dornach [Dornach-Arlesheim] 90 A3
Dornauberg 107 C1
Dornberk 126 B2/3
Dornbirn 91 C3
Dornburg 80 B2
Dornburg 82 A1/2
Dorndorf 81 D2
Dornecy 88 A3
Dornelas 150 B3, 158 B1
Dornes 102 B1
Dornoch 54 B2
Dornstadt 91 C2
Dornstetten 90 B2
Dornum 67 D1
Dorog 95 D3
Dorog 96 B3
Dorogobuž 75 C3
Dorohoi 98 B3
Dorotea 30 A2
Dörpen 67 D2
Dörrenbach 90 B1
Dorsten 67 C3, 80 A1
Dorsten-Lembeck 67 C3
Dorsten-Rhade 67 C3
Dorsten-Wulfen 67 C3
Dortan 104 A2
Dortmund 80 A1
Dorum 52 A3, 68 A1
Dörverden 68 A/B2
Dörzbach 91 C1
Dos Aguas 169 C1/2
Dosante 153 B/C1/2
Dosbarrios 161 C3, 167 D1
Dos Hermanas 171 D2
Dósolo 114 B1
Dospat 140 B3
Dos Torres 166 B3
Dötlingen 68 A2
Dotsikón 143 B/C2
Döttingen 80 A2
Douai 78 A2
Douarnenez 84 A2
Doubravník 94 B1
Douchy 87 D2
Doudeville 77 C3
Doué-la-Fontaine 86 A3, 101 C1
Douglas 56 B2
Douglas 58 B1
Douglas 54 A/B3, 55 D2
Doulaincourt 89 B/C2
Doulevant-le-Château 88 B2
Doullens 77 D2
Doune 56 B1
Dounreay 54 B1
Doupov 83 C2
Dourdan 87 C2
Dourgne 110 A3
Douvaine 104 A2
Douvres-la-Délivrande 76 B3, 86 A1
Douzy 79 C3
Dovádola 115 C2, 116 B1
Dover 65 C3, 76 B1
Døvik 42 A2
Döviken 34 B2
Dovre 33 B/C3, 37 D1
Dovregubbens hall 33 C3, 37 D1
Dovsk 99 C1
Dowlais 63 C1
Downham Market 65 C1/2
Downpatrick 58 A1
Doxáton 144 B1
Doyet 102 B2
Dozón 150 B2
Dozulé 76 B3, 86 A/B1
Drac 137 D3
Dračevo 137 C1
Dračevo 138 B2
Drachhausen 70 B3
Drachten 67 C1/2
Drag 9 C2/3
Drag 28 B1
Dragalevci 139 D1
Drăgănești-Vlașca 141 C2
Drăgănești-Olt 140 B2
Draganovo 141 C3
Drăgășani 140 B2
Dragaš 138 A/B2
Draginac 133 C2
Draginje 133 C/D2, 134 A2
Dragland 9 C2
Dragobi 138 A2
Dragocvet 134 B2/3
Dragoištica 139 C/D2
Dragolovci 132 B1
Dragoman 139 D1
Dragomirești 141 C1
Dragoni 119 D2/3
Dragør 49 D3, 50 A3, 53 D1
Dragoš 143 C1
Dragovac 134 B2
Dragovac 139 C1
Dragozetići 130 A1
Dragsfjärd 24 B3
Dragsholm 49 C3, 53 C1
Dragsvik 36 A/B2
Draguignan 112 A3
Drahnsdorf 70 A3
Drahonice 93 C1
Drahovce 95 C2
Drákia 144 A3
Drakótripa 143 C3
Drakótripa 148 B1
Drakšenić 128 A3, 131 D1, 132 A1
Dráma 144 B1
Dramalj 127 B/C3, 130 B1
Drammen 43 D1, 44 A/B1
Drangedal 43 C2, 44 A1
Drängsered 50 A1
Drangstedt 52 A3, 68 A1
Dransfeld 81 C1
Draschwitz 82 B1
Drasenhofen 94 B2
Drašnice 131 D3, 132 A3, 136 B1
Drassburg 94 B3
Drassmarkt 94 B3
Dravagen 34 A/B3
Drávaszabolcs 128 B3
Drávasztára Zaláta 128 B3
Drávasztára 128 B3
Dravískos 144 B1
Dravograd 127 C2
Dravograd 96 A3
Drawno 71 C1/2
Drawsko 71 C2
Drawsko Pomorskie 71 C1
Draž 129 C3
Draženov 82 B3, 92 B1
Draževac 133 D2, 134 A2
Drebkau 70 B3, 83 C/D1
Drée 103 C2
Dreetz 69 D2
Drégelypalánk 95 D2/3
Dreglin 73 C3
Drehna 70 A/B3
Dreieich-Sprendlingen 80 B3
Dreileben 69 C3
Dreis (Wittlich) 79 D3, 80 A3
Drejø 53 C2
Dren 138 B1
Drena 106 B2
Drénchia 126 A/B2
Drenovac 139 C1
Drenovci 133 C1
Drenovec 135 D3
Drenovo 139 C3, 143 C1
Drensteinfurt 67 D3
Drensteinfurt-Rinkerode 67 D3
Dresden 83 C1
Dresden 96 A1
Dreux 86 A/B1
Drevdalen 38 B1
Drevja 14 B2
Dřevohostice 95 C1
Drevsjø 33 D3
Drewen 69 D2
Drewitz 69 D3
Drezdenko 71 C2
Drezdenko 72 B3
Drežnica 130 B1
Drhovy 83 C/D3
Driebergen 66 B3
Driebes 161 C3
Driedorf 80 B2
Dries 78 B1/2
Drijber 67 C2
Drimnin 56 A1
Drimós 143 D1, 144 A1
Drinjača 133 C2
Drionville 77 D1/2
Drist 137 D2
Drivstua 33 C3, 37 D1
Drlače 133 C2
Drnholec 94 B1/2
Drniš 131 C3
Drò 106 B2
Drøbak 38 A3, 44 B1
Drobeta-Turnu Severin 135 C/D2
Drobeta-Turnu Severin 140 B2
Drobin 73 C3
Drobrovo 126 A2
Drochtersen 52 B3, 68 B1
Drochtersen-Assel 52 B3, 68 B1
Drogeham 67 C1
Drogheda 58 A1/2
Drogheda 55 D2
Drogičin 73 D3, 97 D1, 98 B1
Drogobyč 97 D2, 98 A3
Drogomin 71 C2
Drögsnäs 46 B3
Droisy 86 A/B1
Droitwich 59 D3, 64 A2
Drokija 99 C3
Dromara 58 A1
Drömme 30 B3
Dromod 55 C2
Dromore 56 A3, 58 A1
Dronero 112 B2
Dronfield 61 C3, 64 A/B1
Dronninglund 49 B/C1
Dronten 66 B2
Drosáton 139 D3, 143 D1, 144 A1
Drosendorf Stadt 94 A1/2
Drösing 94 B2
Drosopigí 143 C2
Drosopigí 143 B/C3
Drøsselbjerg 49 C3, 53 C1
Drottningholm 47 C1
Drottningskär 51 C2
Droué 87 B/C2
Drożków 71 C3, 83 D1
Dr Petru Groza 97 D3, 140 B1
Drubravice 131 C2/3
Druento 112 B1
Druid 59 C2/3, 60 A3
Druja 74 B2/3
Drulingen 89 D1, 90 A1/2
Drumgoft 58 A2/3
Drummore 56 B3
Drummore 54 A3, 55 D2
Drusenheim 90 B2
Druten 66 B3
Druyes-les-Belles-Fontaines 88 A3
Družba 99 D1
Družba 141 C/D3
Đružetići 133 D2, 134 A2
Druževo 139 D1
Drvenik 132 A3, 136 B1
Dryburgh Abbey 57 C2
Drymen 56 B1
Drynaholmen 32 A2
Drzonowo 71 D1
Dualchi 123 C2
Duas-Igrejas 159 C1
Dub 137 C2
Dub 133 C2
Dubá 83 D2
Dubac 137 C1/2
Dubci 133 D2, 134 A2/3
Duben 70 B3
Dübendorf 90 B3, 105 D1
Dubica 128 A3, 131 D1, 132 A1
Dubin 71 D3
Dublin (Baile Átha Cliath) 58 A2
Dublin (Baile Átha Cliath) 55 D2
Dublje 133 C1
Dubna 75 D2
Dub nad Moravou 95 B/C1
Dubňany 94 B1
Dubnica nad Váhom 95 C1
Dubník 95 D3
Dubno 98 B2
Dubočac 132 B1
Dubossary 141 D1
Duboštica 132 B2
Dubovac 134 B1
Dubovo 139 C1
Dubraja 131 C2
Dubrava 127 D3
Dubrava 131 D1/2, 132 A1
Dubrava 137 C1/2
Dubravčak 127 D3
Dubravica 134 B1/2
Dubrovica 98 B2
Dubrovka 74 B2
Dubrovka 99 B/C2
Dubrovnik 137 C1/2
Ducaj 137 D2
Ducey 86 A2
Duchcov 83 C2
Ducherow 70 B1
Duči 73 D1
Duclair 77 C3
Dudar 95 C3, 128 B1
Duddington 64 B2
Dudelange 79 D3
Dudeldorf 79 D3, 80 A3
Duderstadt 81 D1
Duderstadt-Mingerode 81 D1
Dudeștii Vechi 129 D2
Düdingen 104 B1
Dudley 59 D3, 64 A2
Dueñas 152 B3
Duerne 103 C3
Dueso 152 A1
Duesund 36 A3
Dueville 107 C3
Duffel 79 B/C1
Duffield 61 C3, 64 A1
Duga Poljana 133 D3, 134 A3, 138 A1
Duga Resa 127 C3
Dugenta 119 D3
Dugo Selo 127 D3
Duhovščina 75 C3
Duinbergen 78 A1
Duingen 68 B3
Duingt 104 A3
Duino-Aurisina 126 A/B3
Duisburg 79 D1, 80 A1
Duisburg-Rheinhausen 79 D1, 80 A1
Duisburg-Walsum 79 D1, 80 A1
Dukati 142 A2
Dukovany 94 A/B1
Dukštas 74 A3
Dulantzi 153 D2
Duleek 58 A2
Dulje 138 B2
Dülmen 67 D3
Dülmen-Buldern 67 D3
Dülmen-Merfeld 67 D3
Dulovo 141 C2
Dulpetorpet 38 B2
Dulverton 63 C2
Dumača 133 C/D1, 134 A1
Dumbarton 56 B2
Dumbarton 54 A/B2/3, 55 D1
Dumbrava de Sus 135 D2
Dumbría 150 A2
Dumfries 57 C3
Dumfries 54 B3
Dummer 65 C3, 76 B1
Dümmer 69 C1
Dümpelfeld 80 A2
Duna 28 B2
Dunaalmás 95 C/D3
Dunaföldvár 129 C1
Dunaföldvár 96 B3
Dunaharaszti 95 D3, 129 C1
Dunajevcy 98 B3
Dunajská Streda 96 B3
Dunajská Streda 95 C3
Dunakeszi 95 D3
Dunakömlőd 129 C2
Dunapataj 129 C2
Dunaszekcső 129 C2
Dunaszentgyörgy 129 C2
Dunaújváros 129 C1
Dunaújváros 96 B3
Dunavățu de Jos 141 D2
Dunavci 135 D2/3
Dunbar 57 C1/2
Dunblane 56 B1
Duncombe 59 D1, 60 B2
Dundalk 58 A1
Dundalk 54 A3, 55 D2
Dundee 54 B2
Dundee 57 C1
Dundonald 56 A3
Dundrum 58 A1
Dunfermline 57 C1
Dunfermline 54 B2
Dungannon 54 A3, 55 D2
Dungarvan 55 C/D3
Dunholme 61 D3, 64 B1
Dunières 103 C3
Đunis 134 B3
Dunje 139 C3, 143 C1
Dunkeld 57 C1
Dunker 47 C1
Dunkerque 77 D1, 78 A1
Dún Laoghaire 58 A2
Dún Laoghaire 55 D2/3
Dunleer 58 A1
Dun-le-Palestel 101 D2, 102 A2
Dunlop 56 B2
Dunmore 55 C2
Dunmurry 56 A3
Dunningen 90 B2
Dunoon 56 B1/2
Dunoon 54 A2/3, 55 D1
Duns 54 B3
Duns 57 D2
Dunshaughlin 58 A2
Dunstable 64 B2
Dunster 63 C2
Dun-sur-Auron 102 B1
Dun-sur-Meuse 89 B/C1
Dunwich 65 D2
Đurakovac 138 A1
Durance 109 B/C2
Durango 153 D1
Duras 109 B/C1
Đuravci 137 D2
Durban-Corbières 110 A3, 156 B1
Durbe 73 C1
Durbuy 79 C2
Dúrcal 173 C2
Durdat-Larequille 102 B2
Đurđevac 128 A2
Đurđevi Stupovi 137 D1, 138 A1
Đurđevića Tara 133 C3, 137 D1
Đurđevo 129 D3, 134 A1
Düren 79 D2
Düren-Gürzenich 79 D2
Durfort 108 B2
Durham 57 D3, 61 C1
Durham 54 B3
Đurinci 133 D2, 134 A/B2
Đurmanec 127 D2
Đurmanec 96 A3
Dürmentingen 91 C2/3
Durmersheim 90 B1
Durness 54 A1
Dürnfeld 126 B1
Dürnkrut 94 B2
Dürnstein 94 A2
Durón 161 C/D2
Dürrboden [Dovos-Platz] 106 A1
Dürrenboden [Schwyz] 105 D1
Durrës 137 D3, 142 A1
Durrow 55 D3
Dürrwangen 91 D1
Dursley 63 D1, 64 A3
Durston 63 C/D2
Dursunbey 149 D1
Durtal 86 A3
Duruelo de la Sierra 153 C3
Dushman 137 D2, 138 A2
Dušikrava 130 B1/2
Dusina 132 B2
Dusnok 129 C2
Düsseldorf 79 D1, 80 A1
Düssnitz 70 A3
Dussoi 107 D2
Duszniki 71 D2
Dutovlje 126 B3
Duvberg 34 B3
Duved 29 C3, 34 A1/2
Duvno 131 D3, 132 A3
Duži 136 B1
Duži 137 C1
Dužica 127 D3
Dvärsätt 29 D3, 34 B2
Dverberg 9 C1
Dvor 131 C1
Dvorníky 95 C2
Dvorovi 133 C1
Dvory nad Žitavou 95 C3
Dwingeloo 67 C2
Dybbøl 52 B2
Dybvad 49 B/C1
Dymchurch 77 C1
Dymer 99 C2

Dynäs 30 B3, 35 D2
Dypfest 28 A3, 33 C1
Dyranut 37 B/C3
Dyreborg 52 B2
Dyrnesvågen 32 B1
Džanići 132 B3
Džep 139 C1
Džepčište 138 B2
Dzeržinsk 98 B1
Działdowo 73 C3
Džigolj 135 B/C3
Džurin 99 C3

E

Ea 153 D1
Eándion 147 D2
Eaní 143 C2
Eardisley 63 C1
Earith 65 C2
Earls Colne 65 C2
Earlston 57 C2
Easdale 56 A1
Easington 61 D1
Easington 61 D2
Easingwold 61 D2
East Aberthaw 63 C2
Eastbourne 77 B/C1
Eastchurch 65 C3, 77 C1
East Cowes 76 B1
East Dereham 65 C1
East Grinstead 65 C3, 76 B1
East Harling 65 C2
East Kilbride 56 B2
Eastleigh 76 B1
East Linton 57 C1/2
East-Looe 62 B3
East Retford 61 C3, 64 B1
Eastry 65 C3, 76 B1
Eastwood 61 D3, 65 C1
Eaton Socon 64 B2
Eaux-Bonnes 108 B3, 154 B1/2
Eauze 108 B2
Ebbw Vale 63 C1
Ebeleben 81 D1
Ebelsbach 81 D3
Ebeltoft 49 C2/3
Ebenfurth 94 B3
Ebensee 93 C3
Ebensee 96 A3
Ebensfeld 81 D3, 82 A3
Ebenweiler 91 C3
Eberbach 81 C3, 91 C1
Ebergötzen 81 D1
Eberhardzell 91 C3
Ebermannsdorf 92 B1
Ebermannstadt 82 A3
Ebern 81 D3
Eberndorf 127 B/C2
Ebersbach 83 D1/2
Ebersbach 96 A1
Ebersbach-Musbach 91 C3
Ebersberg 92 A/B2/3
Ebersburg-Schmalnau 81 C2
Eberschwang 93 C2
Ebersdorf 68 A1
Eberstein 126 B1
Eberswalde-Finow 70 B2
Eberswalde-Finow 72 A3
Ebnat (-Kappel) [Ebnat-Kappel] 105 D1, 106 A1
Éboli 119 D3, 120 A2
Ebrach 81 D3
Ebreichsdorf 94 B3
Ébreuil 102 B2
Ebsdorfergrund-Dreihausen 81 C2
Ebstorf 69 B/C2
Ecclefechan 57 C3, 60 A/B1
Eccleshall 59 D3, 60 B3, 64 A1
Eceabat 149 C1
Echalar 108 A3, 154 A1
Echallens [Lausanne] 104 B2
Echarren 153 D2, 154 A1/2
Echarri-Aranaz 153 D2
Échauffour 86 B1/2
Echevarría 153 D1
Eching 92 B2
Échiré 101 B/C2
Échourgnac 101 C3, 109 C1
Echt 79 D1
Echtenerbrug 66 B2
Echternach 79 D3
Echzell 81 C2
Écija 172 A1
Ečka 129 D3, 133 D1, 134 A1
Eckartsberga 82 A1
Eckental 82 A3
Eckental-Eschenau 82 A3, 92 A1
Eckernförde 52 B2
Eckerö 41 C3
Eckington 61 D3, 65 C1
Ecommoy 86 B3
Écouché 86 A1/2
Ecouen 87 D1
Écouis 77 D3, 87 C1
Écouviez 79 C3
Écs 95 C3
Écueillé 101 C1
Ed 30 B3, 35 D2
Eda 38 B3
Eda glasbruk 38 B3
Edalund Milla 46 B2
Edam 66 B2
Edane 38 B3, 45 C1
Eddelak 52 B3
Edderitz 69 D3, 82 A/B1
Eddleston 57 C2
Eddystone Lighthouse 62 B3
Ede 35 D3
Ede 29 D3, 35 C1
Ede 66 B3
Edebäck 39 C3
Edefors 16 B2
Edefors 29 D3, 35 C1
Edefors Harads 16 B2
Edeköy 145 D1, 145 D3
Edelschrott 127 C1
Edelsfeld 82 A3, 92 A1
Edemissen 68 B2/3
Eden 30 A/B2, 35 D1
Edenbridge 65 C3, 76 B1
Edenkoben 90 B1
Edermünde-Besse 81 C1
Edertal 81 C1
Edertal-Gellershausen 81 C1
Edertal-Hemfurth-Edersee 81 C1
Edertal-Mehlen 81 C1
Édessa 143 C1
Édessa 148 B1
Edevik 29 C2, 34 A1
Edewecht 67 D1/2
Edinburgh 57 C2
Edinburgh 54 B2/3
Edincy 98 B3
Edincy 98 B3
Edingen 78 B2
Edipsós 147 C1
Edirne 145 D2
Edirne 141 C3
Edland 42 B1
Edlitz im Burgenland 127 D1
Edlitz Markt 94 A/B3
Édolo 106 B2
Edremit 149 D1
Edsbro 40 B3
Edsbruk 46 B3
Edsbyn 39 D1, 40 A1
Edsele 30 A3, 35 C1/2
Edshult 46 A3
Edsleskog 45 C1/2
Edsvalla 45 D1
Eefde 67 C3
Eeklo 78 B1
Eelde-Paterswolde 67 C1/2
Eemshaven 67 C1
Eferding 93 C2
Eferding 96 A2
Effeltrich 82 A3
Effiat 102 B2
Efira 146 A/B2
Efkarpía 139 D3, 143 D1, 144 A1
Eforie Sud 141 D2
Efpálion 146 B2
Efringen-Kirchen 90 A3
Efteløt 43 D1, 44 A1
Egebjerg 49 D3, 53 D1
Egebjerg Gård 49 B/C3, 53 C1
Egeln 69 C3
Egeløkke 53 C2
Egenäs 45 C1
Eger 97 C3
Egernsund 52 B2
Egersund 42 A3
Egervár 128 A1
Egeskov 53 C1/2
Egestorf 68 B1/2
Egestorf-Evendorf 68 B2
Egg 91 C3
Eggan 28 A3, 33 C1/2
Eggenburg 94 A2
Eggenthal 91 D3
Eggesin 70 B1
Eggingen 90 B3
Eggkleiva 28 A3, 33 C2
Egglham 93 B/C2
Eggstätt 92 B3
Eggum 8 B2
Egham 64 B3
Eghezée 79 C2
Égina 147 D3
Égina 148 B2
Eging am See 93 C2
Egínion 143 D2
Égion 146 B2
Égion 148 B2
Égletons 102 A3
Egling 91 D2, 92 A2
Egling 92 A3
Egling-Endlhausen 92 A3
Eglisau 90 B3
Égliseneuve-d'Entraigues 102 B3
Egloffstein 82 A3
Egmond aan Zee 66 A2
Egna/Neumarkt 107 C2
Egnázia 121 C2
Egósthena 147 C2
Egremont 57 C3, 60 A1
Égreville 87 D2
Egton 61 C/D1
Egtved 48 B3, 52 B1
Éguilly-sous-Bois 88 B2
Éguzon 101 D2, 102 A2
Egyházasrádóc 127 D1, 128 A1
Egyptinkorp 23 C1
Ehäjärvi 26 B2
Ehekirchen 92 A2
Ehingen 91 C2
Ehningen 91 B/C2
Ehra-Lessien 69 C2
Ehrenberg 81 D2
Ehrenburg 68 A2
Ehrenburg-Schweringhausen 68 A2
Ehrenfriedersdorf 82 B2
Ehrenhain 82 B2
Ehrenhausen 127 C1/2
Ehrenkirchen-Kirchhofen 90 A3
Ehringshausen 80 B2
Ehrwald 91 D3
Ehtamo 24 B2
Eibar 153 D1
Eibau 83 D1/2
Eibenstock 82 B2
Eibergen 67 C3
Eibesbrunn 94 B2
Eibiswald 127 C1/2
Eibiswald 96 A3
Eichelsachsen 81 C2
Eichenberg 81 D2
Eichenbrunn 94 B2
Eichendorf 92 B2
Eichendorf-Kröhstorf 92 B2
Eichenzell 81 C2
Eichholz 83 C1
Eichow 70 B3
Eichstätt 92 A1/2
Eichstetten 90 A2/3
Eichwalde 70 A2/3
Eich (Worms) 80 B3
Eicklingen 68 B2
Eid 32 A2/3
Eidbukta 14 B2
Eide 42 A/B3
Eide 32 A2
Eidem 14 A3
Eidet 28 A3, 33 C2
Eidet 125 D2
Eidfjord 36 B3
Eidhaugen 14 B2
Eiđi 55 C1
Eidkjosen 4 A3
Eidsborg 43 C1/2
Eidsbotn 36 A3
Eidsbugarden 37 C2
Eidsdal 32 A3, 36 B1
Eidsfjord 8 B2
Eidsfoss 43 D1, 44 A1
Eidshaug 28 B1
Eidslandet 36 A3
Eidsøra 32 B2
Eidssund 42 A2
Eidstå 43 C2
Eidsvåg 32 B2
Eidsvoll 38 A2/3
Eidsvoll verk 38 A2/3
Eidvågeid 5 C1/2
Eigeltingen 91 B/C3
Eikanger 36 A3
Eikefjord 36 A2
Eiken 42 B3
Eikenes 36 A2
Eiksund 36 A/B1
Eilenburg 82 B1
Eimisjärvi 23 D3
Eimke 68 B2
Eina 38 A2
Einbeck 68 B3
Einbeck-Salzderhelden 68 B3
Einbeck-Wenzen 68 B3
Eindhoven 79 C1
Eines 28 B3, 33 D1
Einsiedeln 105 D1
Einvika 28 A/B2
Einville-au-Jard 89 D2
Eisdorf 68 B3
Eiselfing 92 B2/3
Eisenach 81 D1/2
Eisenbach-Schollach 90 B3
Eisenberg 80 B3, 90 B1
Eisenberg 82 A/B1/2
Eisenerz 93 D3
Eisenerz 96 A3
Eisenhüttenstadt 72 A3, 96 A1
Eisenhüttenstadt 70 B3
Eisenkappel 126 B2
Eisenkappel 96 A3
Eisenstadt 96 B3
Eisenstadt 94 B3
Eisfeld 81 D2, 82 A2
Eisgarn 93 D1/2
Eisleben 82 A1
Eisleben-Helfta 82 A1
Eislingen 91 C2
Eisriesenwelt 93 C3
Eitensheim 92 A2
Eiteråga 14 B2
Eiterelvmoen 9 C/D2
Eiterfeld 81 C2
Eitorf 80 A2
Eivik 14 B1
Eixo 158 A2
Eizeringen 78 B2
Ejby 52 B1
Ejea de los Caballeros 155 C3
Ejheden 39 D1
Ejsing 48 A2
Ejstrup 48 B3
Ejulve 162 B2
Ekáli 147 D2
Ekängen 46 B2
Ekeberg 45 D3
Ekeby 40 B3
Ekeby 50 A3
Ekebyholm 40 B3
Ekedalen 45 D3
Ekenäs 45 D2
Ekenässjön 46 A3, 51 C1
Ekenäs/Tammisaari 24 B3
Ekeren 78 B1
Ekerö 47 C1
Eketånga 49 D2, 50 A2
Ekfors 17 C/D2
Ekkerøy 7 C/D2
Eknäs 24 B3
Ekne 28 B3, 33 D1
Ekolsund 40 B3, 47 C1
Ekora 153 D2
Ekorrsele 31 C1
Ekorrsjö 31 C1
Ekorrträsk 31 C1
Ekra 32 B3, 37 C1
Ekshärad 39 C3
Eksingedal 36 A3
Eksjö 46 A3
Eksjö 72 A/B1
Ekträsk 31 C1
El Abalario 171 C2
Eläinpuisto 18 B1
El Álamo 160 B3
El Alcornocal 166 B3
El Almendro 171 B/C1
El Almicerán 167 D3, 168 A3, 173 D1
El Alquián 173 D2
Elämäjärvi 21 D1/2, 22 A1/2
Elanec 99 D3
Elantxobe 153 D1
El Arahal 171 D2, 172 A2
El Arenal 157 C2
El Arenal 160 A3
Elassón 143 D3
Elassón 148 B1
Elateia 147 C1
Eláti 143 C3
Elátia 147 C1
Elátia 143 D3
Elatochórion 142 B3
El Ballestero 168 A/B2
El Barco de Avila 159 D2/3
Elbasan 138 A3, 142 A1
El Berrón 151 D1, 152 A1
El Berrueco 161 C2
Elbeuf 77 C3, 86 B1
Elbingerode 69 C3
Elbląg (Elbing) 73 C2
El Bodón 159 C2
El Bohodón 160 A2
El Bonillo 168 A2
El Bosque 172 A2
El Bruc 156 A3, 163 D1
El Brull 156 A2/3
Elburg 66 B2
El Burgo 172 A2
El Burgo de Ebro 154 B3, 162 B1
El Burgo de Osma 153 C3, 161 C1
El Burgo Ranero 152 A2
El Buste 154 A3
El Cabaco 159 D2
El Cabo de Gata 173 D2, 174 A2
El Campillo 160 A1
El Campillo 166 B1
El Campo 166 A2
El Campo de Peñaranda 160 A2
El Cañavate 168 B1
El Cardoso de la Sierra 161 C2
El Carpio 167 C3, 172 B1
El Carpio de Tajo 160 B3, 167 C1
El Casar de Talamanca 161 C2
El Casar de Escalona 160 B3
El Castellar 162 B2/3
El Castillo de las Guardas 171 D1
El Centenillo 167 C3
El Cerro de Andévalo 171 C1
Elche 169 C3
Elche de la Sierra 168 B2/3
Elcili 145 D3
Elcóaz 155 C2
El Collado 162 A/B3, 169 C1
El Collado 153 D3
El Colmenar 172 A3
El Coronil 171 D2
El Cubillo 161 C2
El Cubo de Don Sancho 159 C2
El Cubo de Tierra del Vino 159 D1
El Cuervo 171 D2
El Cuervo 163 C3
Elda 169 C2/3
Eldagsen 68 B3
Eldalsosen 36 B2
Eldena 69 C1
Eldforsen 39 C2
Eléa 146 B3
Elefsís 147 D2
Elefsís 148 B2
Elefthériani 146 B1/2

Elefthérion **143** D3
Eleftherochórion **143** C2
Eléftheron **142** B2
Eleftheroúpolis **144** B1
Eleja **73** D1, **74** A2
El Ejido **173** D2
Elektrénai **73** D2, **74** A3
Elemir **129** D3
Elena **141** C3
Elenheimen **5** C1/2
Eleochória **144** A2
Eleoúsa **142** B3
El Escorial **160** B2
El Espinar **160** B2
El Estanyol **157** D2
Eleutherai **147** D2
El Formigal **154** B2
El Frago **154** B2
El Franco **151** C1
El Frasno **154** A3, **162** A1
Elgå **33** D3
Elgå **33** D3
El Garrobo **171** D1
El Gastor **172** A2
Elgeta **153** D1
Elgin **54** B2
Elgoibar **153** D1
El Gordo **160** A3, **166** B1
Elgorriaga **108** A3, **154** A1
El Grado **155** C2/3
El Granado **170** B1
El Grao **169** D1
El Grao de Gandía **169** D2
Elgsnes **9** C1
El Herradón **160** B2
El Herrumblar **168** B1
El Higueral **172** B2
El Hito **161** C/D3, **168** A1
El Horcajo **167** C2/3
El Hornillo **160** A3
Elhovo **141** C3
El Hoyo **167** C3
El Hoyo de Pinares **160** B2
Elíaen **38** B1
Elie **57** C1
Elijärvi **17** D2/3, **18** A1
Elimäenkylä **21** C/D3
Elimäki **26** B2
Elin Pelin **140** B3
Elis **146** A2
Elisejna **139** D1
Elizondo **108** A3, **154** A1
Eljaröd **50** B3
Ełk (Lyck) **73** D2/3
Elland **59** D2, **61** C2
Ellefsplass **33** D3
Ellenberg **91** D1
Ellesmere **59** D2/3, **60** B3
Ellesmere Port **59** D2, **60** B3
Elling **49** C1
Ellingen **91** D1, **92** A1
Ellinikón **147** D2
Ellmau **92** B3
Ellös **44** B3
El Losar **159** D2/3
Ellrich **81** D1
Ellwangen **91** D1
Ellwangen-Rindelbach **91** D1
Ellzee **91** D2
El Maderal **159** D1
El Madroño **171** C1
El Maillo **159** D2
El Masnou **156** A3
El Masroig **163** C1/2
Elmelunde **53** D2
El Molar **161** C2
El Molinillo **167** C1
El Moral **168** B3, **173** D1, **174** A1
El Moralico **168** A2/3
Elmshorn **52** B3, **68** B1
Elmstein **90** B1
El Musel **151** D1, **152** A1
Elne **156** B1/2
Elnesvågen **32** A2
Elorrio **153** D1
Elorz **154** A2
Előszállás **129** C1
El Palmar **169** D3
El Palmar **169** D1/2
El Palo **172** B2
El Payo **159** C3
El Pedernoso **168** A1
El Pedroso **166** A3, **171** D1
El Pedroso de la Armuña **159** D2, **160** A2
El Peral **168** B1
El Perello **163** C2
El Perelló **169** D1/2
El Picazo **168** B1
El Piñero **159** D1
El Pla de Cabra **163** C1
El Plantío **160** B2
El Pobo **162** B2
El Pobo de Dueñas **162** A2
El Pont d'Armentera **163** C1
El Portal **171** D2/3
El Port de la Selva **156** B2
El Portil **171** C2
El Poyo **163** C2
El Pozuelo **171** C1
El Prat de Llobregat **156** A3
El Provencio **168** A1
El Puente del Arzobispo **160** A3, **166** B1
El Puerto de Santa María **171** D2/3
El Quintanar **153** C/D3
El Raposo **165** D3, **166** A3
El Rasillo **153** D3
El Real de la Jara **165** D3, **166** A3, **171** D1
El Real de San Vicente **160** A3
El Recuenco **161** D2
El Redal **153** D2
El Rocío **171** C2
El Rompido **171** C2
El Ronquillo **171** D1
El Royo **153** D3
El Rubio **172** A2
El Sabinar **168** B3
El Saler **169** D1
El Salobral **168** B2
El Saucejo **172** A2
Elsdorf **79** D2, **80** A2
Elsegårde **49** C2/3
Elsenborn **79** D2
Elsenfeld **81** C3
El Serrat **155** D2, **156** A1/2
Elsfjord **14** B2
Elsfleth **68** A1
Elsfleth-Moorriem **67** D1, **68** A1
Elshø **38** B1
Elsloo **67** C2
El Soleràs **163** C1
Elspe-Cobbenrode **80** B1
Elspeet **66** B3
Els Prats de Rei **155** D3, **156** A3, **163** D1
Elsrud **37** D3
Elst **66** B3
Elster **70** A3
Elsterberg **82** B2
Elsterwerda **83** C1
Els Torms **163** C1
Elstra **83** C1
Eltdalen **38** B1
El Tejar **172** B2
Eltendorf **127** D1
El Tiemblo **160** B2
El Toboso **167** D1, **168** A1
El Tormillo **155** C3
El Torno **159** D3
El Toro **162** B3
El Tosalet **169** D2
El Tranco **168** A3
Eltravåg **42** A1
Eltville am Rhein **80** B3
Eltziego **153** D2
El'uja **75** C3
Elva **74** A1
Elva **112** B1/2
Elvanfoot **57** C2
Elvas **165** C2
Elvåsen **28** B1
Elvdal **38** B1
Elve **42** B3
Elvebakken **6** B1
Elvekrok **6** B1
Elven **85** C3
El Vendrell **156** A3, **163** D1
Elvenes **7** C/D2
Elveng **28** A3, **33** C1
Elverum **38** A/B2
Elveseter **37** C2
Elvestad **38** A3, **44** B1
Elvevollen **4** A/B3, **10** A1
El Villar **167** C2
El Villar de Arnedo **153** D2
El Vilosell **163** D1
El Viso **169** D1/2
El Viso **166** B2/3
El Viso del Alcor **171** D1/2
Elvran **28** B3, **33** D1
Elxleben **81** D2, **82** A2
Elxleben **81** D1, **82** A1
Ely **65** C2
Elz **80** B2
Elzach **90** B2
Elzach-Prechtal **90** B2
Elze **68** B3
Emådalen **39** D1
Embesós **146** A1
Embid **162** A2
Embid de Ariza **161** D1
Embid de la Ribera **154** A3, **162** A1
Embleton **57** D2
Emborion **149** C3
Embrun **112** A1/2
Embún **154** B2
Emden **67** C/D1
Emersacker **91** D2
Emkarby **41** C3
Emkendorf **52** B3
Emlichheim **67** C2
Emmaboda **51** C2
Emmaboda **72** B1
Emmaljunga **50** B2
Emmeloord **66** B2
Emmelshausen **80** A3
Emmen **105** C1
Emmen **67** C2
Emmenbrücke **105** C1
Emmendingen **90** A/B2
Emmer-Compascuum **67** C2
Emmerich **67** C3
Emmerich-Elten **67** C3
Emmersdorf an der Donau **94** A2
Emmerthal **68** B3
Emmerthal-Emmern **68** B3
Emmerthal-Grohnde **68** B3
Emmerting **92** B2
Emolahti **21** D1, **22** A1
Emospohja **21** D2, **22** A2
Empo **24** B3
Émpoli **114** B2, **116** A2
Emptinne **79** C2
Emsbüren **67** D2
Emsbüren-Elbergen **67** D2
Emsdetten **67** D3
Emsfors **51** D1
Emskirchen **81** D3, **91** D1
Emstal **81** C1
Emstek **67** D2, **68** A2
Emsworth **76** A/B1
Ena **154** B2
Enafors **28** B3, **33** D2, **34** A2
Enånger **40** A/B1
Enanlahti **27** D1
Enare **6** B3
Enarsvedjan **29** C/D3, **34** B1
Enåsen **35** C3
Encamp **155** D2, **156** A2
Encausse-les-Thermes **109** C3, **155** C1
Encinacorba **163** C1
Encinas de Abajo **159** D2, **160** A2
Encinasola **165** C/D3
Encinas Reales **172** B2
Encío **153** C2
Enciso **153** D3
Endalsetra **33** C2
Endelave By **49** B/C3, **53** B/C1
Enden **37** D1/2, **38** A1
Enden **37** C1
Éndine **106** A/B3
Endingen **90** A2
Endorf **92** B3
Endre **47** D3
Endresplass **14** B3, **29** C1
Endrinal **159** D2
Enebakk **38** A3, **44** B1
Enebakkneset **38** A3
Eneby **46** B3
Enériz **154** A2
Enese **95** C3
Enez **145** D1/2
Enez **149** C1
Enfield **65** C3
Engan **14** A2
Engdal **32** B2
Engelberg **105** C1
Engelhartszell **93** C2
Engelhartszell **96** A2
Engelia **37** D3, **38** A2
Engeln **68** A2
Engelskirchen **80** A1/2
Engelskirchen-Ründeroth **80** A1/2
Engelsviken **44** B1
Engen **90** B3
Engen-Talmühle **90** B3
Enger **68** A3
Engerda **82** A2
Engerdal **38** B1
Engerdalssetra **33** D3
Engerneset **38** B1
Enghien (Edingen) **78** B2
Engjan **32** B2
Englefontaine **78** B2
Engstingen-Grossengstingen **91** C2
Enguera **169** C2
Enguídanos **162** A3, **168** B1
Engvik **4** A2
Enix **173** D2
Enkenbach-Alsenborn **80** B3, **90** B1
Enkhuizen **66** B2
Enkirch **80** A3
Enklinge **24** A3, **41** D2
Enköping **40** A/B3, **47** C1
Enmoerr **33** C2
Enna **125** C2
Ennepetal **80** A1
Ennezat **102** B2
Ennigerloh **67** D3
Ennigerloh-Enniger **67** D3
Ennigerloh-Westkirchen **67** D3
Enningdal **44** B2
Ennis **55** C3
Enniscorthy **55** D3
Enniskean **55** C3
Enniskerry **58** A2
Enniskillen **54** A3, **55** C/D2
Ennistimon **55** C3
Enns **96** A2/3
Enns **93** D2
Eno **23** D2
Enokunta **25** C1
Enonekiö **11** C2, **12** A1
Enonkoski **23** C3
Enonkylä **18** B3
Enonlahti **26** B1
Enontekiö/Hetta **11** C2, **12** A1
Ens **66** B2
Enschede **67** C3
Ensdorf **92** A/B1
Ensisheim **89** D2/3, **90** A3
Enskogen **35** C3
Enstaberga **47** C2
Enter **67** C3
Entlebuch **105** C1
Entrácque **112** B2
Entradas **164** B3, **170** B1
Entraigues **111** D1, **112** A1
Entrains-sur-Nohain **88** A3
Entrambasmestas **152** B1
Entraunes **112** B2
Entraygues-sur-Truyère **110** A1
Entrechaux **111** D2
Entrena **153** D2
Entre-os-Rios **158** A2
Entrevaux **112** B2
Entrèves **104** B3
Entrimo **150** B3
Entrín Bajo **165** D2
Entroncamento **164** B1
Entzheim **90** A2
Envendos **164** B1
Envermeu **76** B2/3
Enviken **39** D2, **40** A2
Enying **128** B1
Enzersdorf im Thale **94** B2
Enzinger Boden **107** D1, **126** A1
Enzklösterle **90** B2
Eosazia **113** D3
Épaignes **77** C3, **86** B1
Épannes **100** B2
Epanomí **143** D2, **144** A2
Epanomí **148** B1
Epároz **155** C2
Epe **67** B/C2/3
Épernay **88** A1
Épernon **87** C2
Epfig **90** A2
Ephesos **149** D2
Epidamnus **137** D3, **142** A1
Epidauros (Hieron Asklepiou) **147** C3
Epidauros (Hieron Asklepiou) **148** B2
Epidaurum **137** C2
Épierre **104** A3
Épila **155** C3, **163** C1
Épinal **89** D2
Episcopía **120** B3, **122** A1
Epískepsis **142** A3
Episkopí **147** D3
Epitálion **146** A/B3
Époisses **88** A/B3
Epoo/Ebbo **25** D3, **26** A3
Épouville **77** B/C3
Eppelborn **90** A1
Eppelheim **90** B1
Eppenbrunn **90** A1
Eppendorf **83** C2
Epping **65** C3
Eppingen **91** B/C1
Eppingen-Richen **91** B/C1
Eppishausen-Mörgen **91** D2
Épreville **77** C3
Eptachórion **142** B2
Eptálofos **147** C1/2
Epworth **61** C2/3
Eques **154** A2
Équi Terme **114** A2, **116** A1
Eracléa **107** D3, **126** A3
Eraclea Mare **107** D3, **126** A3
Eraclea Minoa **124** B2/3
Eräjärvi **25** C1
Eräjärvi **27** C1
Erásmion **145** C1
Eratiní **146** B2
Eratinón **145** C1
Erátira **143** C2
Erba **105** D3, **106** A3
Erbach **81** C3
Erbach **91** C2
Erbach-Ebersberg **81** C3
Erbalunga **113** D2
Erbendorf **82** B3
Erbendorf-Grötschenreuth **82** B3
Ercé **155** C2
Ercheu **78** A3
Érchie **121** D3
Ercolano **119** D3
Ercsi **129** C1
Ercsi **96** B3
Érd **96** B3
Érd **95** D3, **129** C1
Erdek **149** D1
Erdevik **133** C1
Erding **92** A/B2
Erding-Langengeisling **92** A/B2
Erdut **129** C3
Éréac **85** C2
Éremo dei Cárceri **115** D3, **117** C2
Eresfjord **32** B2
Eretria **147** D2
Erétria **147** D2
Erezée **79** C2
Erfde **52** B3
Erftstadt **79** D2, **80** A2
Erfurt **81** D1/2, **82** A1/2
Ergersheim-Ermetzhofen **81** D3, **91** D1
Ergersheim-Neuherberg **81** D3, **91** D1
Ērgli **73** D1, **74** A2
Ergolding **92** B2
Ergoldsbach **92** B2
Érice **124** A2
Ericeira **164** A2
Eriksberg **46** B2
Eriksbu **43** C/D1
Erikslund **35** C3
Eriksmåla **51** C2
Eriksvik **47** D1
Erímanthos Óros **146** B2
Eringsboda **51** C2
Erithraí **147** C/D2
Érize-la-Petite **89** B/C1

Erkelenz 79 D1
Erkheim 91 D3
Erkner 70 A/B2/3
Erkrath 80 A1
Erla 154 B3
Erlangen 82 A3
Erlau 81 D2
Erlenbach (am Main) 81 C3
Erlensee 81 C3
Erli 113 C2
Erlsbach 107 D1
Ermelo 66 B2/3
Ermenoville 87 D1
Ermidas 164 B3, 170 A1
Ermióni 147 C/D3
Ermióni 148 B2
Ermoúpolis 149 C2
Ermsleben 69 C3
Ermua 153 D1
Erndtebrück 80 B1/2
Ernée 85 D2, 86 A2
Ernestinovo 129 B/C3
Ernsgaden 92 A2
Ernstbrunn 94 B2
Eroles 155 C/D2/3
Erolzheim 91 D2/3
Erpfendorf 92 B3
Erquy 85 C1/2
Erra 164 B2
Errazu 108 A3, 154 A1
Errenteria 153 D1, 154 A1
Errezil 153 D1
Errindlev 53 C/D2
Erro 108 A3, 154 A1/2
Ersekë 142 B2
Ersekë 148 A1
Érsekvadkert 95 D3
Ershausen 81 D1
Ersmark 31 D1
Ersnäs 17 C3
Erstein 90 A2
Erstfeld 105 D1
Ersvik 14 B1
Ertebølle 48 B2
Ertenvåg 14 B1
Ertingen 91 C2/3
Erto 107 D2
Ertsjärv 17 C1/2
Ervalla 46 A/B1
Ervas Tenras 159 B/C2
Ervasti 19 C2
Ervedal 158 B2/3
Ervedal 164 B2
Ervedosa 158 B1/2
Ervenik 131 C2
Ervidel 164 B3, 170 B1
Ervik 36 A1
Ervik 32 B2
Ervillers 78 A2
Ervy-le-Châtel 88 A2
Erwitte 80 B1
Erwitte-Bad Westernkotten 68 A3, 80 B1
Erxleben 69 C3
Esbjerg 48 A3, 52 A1
Escalada 153 B/C2
Escalaplano 123 D3
Escalhão 159 C2
Escaló 155 C2
Escalona 160 B3
Escalonilla 160 B3, 167 C1
Escalos de Baixo 158 B3, 165 C1
Escalos de Cima 158 B3, 165 C1
Escamilla 161 D2
Es Caná 157 D3
Escañuela 167 C3, 172 B1
Escarabajosa 160 B3
Escariche 161 C2
Escároz 154 A/B2
Escarrilla 154 B2
Escatrón 162 B1
Eschach 91 C3
Eschau 81 C3
Eschede 68 B2
Eschede-Starkshorn 68 B2
Eschede-Weyhausen 68 B2
Eschenbach in der Oberpfalz 82 A3
Eschenburg-Eibelshausen 80 B2
Eschenlohe 92 A3
Eschershausen 68 B3
Esch-sur-Alzette 79 D3
Esch-sur-Sûre 79 D3
Eschwege 81 D1
Eschweiler 79 D2
Escó 154 B2
Escobosa de Almazán 161 D1
Escombreras 174 B1
Escos 108 A3, 154 B1
Escosse 109 D3, 155 D1, 156 A1
Escource 108 A2
Es Cubells 169 D2
Escucha 162 B2
Escúllar 173 D2
Escurial 166 A2
Escurial de la Sierra 159 D2
Esens 67 D1
Esens-Bensersiel 67 D1
Esfiliana 173 C2
Esgos 150 B2
Esgueira 158 A2
Esher 64 B3, 76 B1
Eskdale 59 C1, 60 A1/2
Eskeland 42 A1
Eskelinkosi 22 B2
Eskiköy 145 D3
Eskilsäter 45 C/D2
Eskilstrup 53 D2
Eskilstuna 46 B1
Eskola 21 C1
Eskön 40 B2
Eskoriatza 153 D1/2
Eslarn 82 B3, 92 B1
Eslava 154 A2
Eslida 162 B3, 169 D1
Eslohe 80 B1
Eslohe-Reiste 80 B1
Eslöv 50 B3
Eslöv 72 A1/2
Esnanoes 100 B2
Espadaña 159 C2
Espalion 110 A1
Esparragal 172 B1
Esparragalejo 165 D2
Esparragosa de Caudillo 166 B2
Esparragosa de la Serena 166 A2
Esparreguera 156 A3
Esparron 111 D3, 112 A3
Espeja 159 C2
Espejo 153 C2
Espejo 172 B1
Espejón 153 C3, 161 C1
Espeland 36 A3
Espelette 108 A3, 154 A1
Espelkamp 68 A2/3
Espelúy 167 C3, 173 C1
Espera 171 D2
Espéraza 110 A3, 156 A1
Espergærde 49 D3, 50 A2/3
Espéria 119 C2
Esperstoft 52 B2
Espiel 166 B3
Espierba 155 C2
Espinama 152 A/B1
Espinhal 158 A3
Espinho 158 A2
Espinilla 152 B1/2
Espinosa de Cerrato 152 B3
Espinosa de Cervera 153 C3
Espinosa de Villagonzalo 152 B2
Espinosa de Henares 161 C2
Espinosa de los Monteros 153 C1
Espinoso del Rey 160 A3, 166 B1
Espirito Santo 170 B1
Esplantas 110 B1
Esplegares 161 D2
Esplús 155 C3, 163 C1
Espolla 156 B2
Espondeilhan 110 B3
Esponellá 156 B2
Espoo/Esbo 25 C3
Esporles 157 C2
Esposende 150 A3, 158 A1
Espot 155 D2
Esprels 89 D3
Espronceda 153 D2
Es Pujols 157 D3
Esquedas 154 B2
Esquivias 160 B3
Esrange 10 B3
Essai 86 B2
Esse (Ähtävä) 20 B1
Essen 80 A1
Essen 78 B1
Essen-Kettwig 80 A1
Esserteaux 77 D3
Essertenne-et-Cecey 89 C3
Essing 92 A1
Essingen 91 C/D2
Esslingen 91 C2
Essômes-sur-Marne 88 A1
Essoyes 88 B2
Essvik 35 D3
Estació d'Amposta 163 C2
Estada 155 C3
Estadilla 155 C3
Estagel 156 B1
Estaing 110 A1
Estaires 78 A2
Estallenchs 157 C2
Estang 108 B2
Estavayer-le-Lac 104 B1
Este 107 C3
Estebanvela 161 C1
Estela 158 A1
Estella 153 D2, 154 A2
Estensvoll 33 C3, 37 D1
Estepa 172 A2
Estépar 152 B2/3
Estepona 172 A3
Esterasa de Medina 161 D1/2
Estercuel 162 B2
Estérencuby 108 B3, 155 C1
Esternay 88 A1
Esterri d'Àneu 155 C2
Estertal-Bösingfeld 68 A3
Esterwegen 67 D2
Esterzili 123 D2
Esthal 90 B1
Estibella 162 B3, 169 D1
Estiche 155 C3, 163 C1
Estissac 88 A2
Estivareilles 102 B2
Estoi 170 B2
Estômbar 170 A2
Estopiñán 155 C3
Estorf 68 A/B1
Estoril 164 A2
Estorninos 159 C3, 165 C1
Estrées-Saint-Denis 78 A3
Estreito 158 B3, 164 B1
Estremera 161 C3
Estremoz 165 C2
Estriégana 161 D2
Estuna 41 C3
Estvad 48 A/B2
Esztergom 95 D3
Esztergom 96 B3
Étables 101 C1
Étables-sur-Mer 85 C1/2
Étagnac 101 D2
Étain 89 C1
Étais-la Sauvin 88 A3
Etalle 79 C3
Étampes 87 C2
Étang-sur-Arroux 103 C1
Étaples 77 D2
Étaules 100 B3
Étauliers 100 B3
Étel 84 B3
Eteläinen 25 C2
Etelälahti 18 A3, 21 D1, 22 A1
Etelämaa 24 A1
Etelä-Vartsala 24 A2, 41 D2
Etelhem 47 D3
Étival-Clairefontaine 89 D2, 90 A2
Etnedal 37 D2/3
Etnesjøen 42 A1
Étoges 88 A1
Etolikón 146 A2
Eton 64 B3
Étréaupont 78 B3
Étréchy 87 C/D2
Étrépagny 77 D3, 87 C1
Étretat 77 B/C3
Etropole 140 B3
Étroubles 104 B3
Ettal 92 A3
Ettelbrück 79 D3
Ettenheim 90 A/B2
Etten-Leur 79 C1
Ettenstatt 91 D1, 92 A1
Ettington 64 A2
Ettlingen 90 B1
Ettringen 91 D2
Étuz 89 C3, 104 A1
Etxebarri 153 D1
Etxebarri 110 A3, 156 B1
Etyek 95 D3, 129 C1
Etzenricht 82 B3
Eu 77 C/D2
Euerdorf 81 D3
Eugénie-les-Bains 108 B2
Eúgenikon 145 D3
Eugmo 20 B1
Eugui 108 A3, 154 A1/2
Eulate 153 D2
Eupen 79 D2
Eura 24 B2
Eurajoki 24 A1/2
Eurasburg 92 A2
Eursinge 67 C2
Euskirchen 79 D2, 80 A2
Eutin 53 C3
Eutresis 147 C2
Eväjärvi 25 C1, 26 A1
Evanger 36 A/B3
Évaux-les-Bains 102 A/B2
Evenesdal 15 C1
Évenos 111 D3, 112 A3
Evenskjær 9 C2
Evenstad 38 A1
Evergem 78 B1
Ȩvermov 83 C3
Everöd 50 B3
Everswinkel 67 D3
Evertsberg 39 C1/2
Evesham 63 D1, 64 A2
Évians-les-Bains 104 B2
Evijärvi 21 C2
Evinochórion 146 B2
Evínos 146 B2
Évisa 113 D3
Evitskog 25 C3
Evje 43 C3
Evjen 14 B1
Evolène [Sion] 105 C2
Evora 164 B2
Évora de Alcobaça 164 A1
Evoramonte 165 C2
Évran 85 C2
Évrange 79 D3
Évrecy 86 A1
Évreux 86 B1
Évron 86 A2
Évropos 139 C3, 143 C/D1
Evrostína 147 B/C2
Evry 87 D2
Évzoni 139 C/D3, 143 D1
Ewijk 66 B3
Exaplátanos 143 C/D1
Exaplátanos 145 C1
Éxarchos 147 C1/2
Excideuil 101 D3
Exeter 63 C2/3
Exmes 86 B1
Exmouth 63 C3
Exochí 144 B1
Extertal 68 A3
Extremo 150 A3
Eydehamn 43 C3
Eye 65 C2
Eye 65 B/C1/2
Eyemouth 57 D2
Eyguians 111 D2, 112 A2
Eyguières 111 C/D2
Eygurande 102 A3
Eygurande-et-Gardefeuil 101 C3, 108 B1
Eylie 155 D2
Eymet 109 C1
Eymoutiers 102 A3
Eysteinkyrkja 33 C3, 37 D1
Eystrup 68 A/B2
Ézaro 150 A2
Ezcaray 153 C2
Ezcurra 154 A1
Ezeriș 135 C1
Ezerišče 74 B2/3
Ezine 149 C1

F

Fabara 163 C1/2
Fabas 109 C3, 155 D1
Fåberg 37 D2, 38 A1
Fåbergstølen 36 B2
Fabero 151 C2
Fabian 155 C2
Fäbodliden 30 B1
Fåborg 53 B/C2
Fabrègues 110 B3
Fabrezan 110 A3, 156 B1
Fabriano 115 D3, 117 C2
Fabrízia 122 A/B3
Facha 150 A3, 158 A1
Facheca 169 D2
Facinas 171 D3
Facture 108 A1
Fadagosa 165 C1
Fadd 129 C2
Faédis 126 A2
Faenza 115 C2, 116 B1
Faeto 120 A1/2
Fafe 158 A/B1
Făgăraș 140 B1
Fågelberget 29 D2
Fågelfors 51 C/D1
Fågelmara 51 D2
Fågelsjö 39 D1
Fågelsta 46 A2
Fågelsundet 40 B2
Fågelvik 47 B/C3
Fagerhaug 33 C2
Fagerhøi 37 D2
Fagerholt 44 B1/2
Fagerhult 44 B2
Fagerhult 51 C1
Fagernes 4 A3
Fagernes 37 D2/3
Fagersanna 45 D2, 46 A2
Fagersta 39 D3, 40 A3
Fagerstrand 38 A3, 44 B1
Fagervik 25 C3
Fagervika 14 A2
Făget 140 A/B1
Fäggeby 39 D2, 40 A2
Fåglavik 45 C/D3
Fagnano Castello 122 A1
Fago 154 B2
Fahrenhorst 68 A2
Fahrenzhausen-Grossnöbach 92 A2
Fahrland 70 A2
Fahy [Porrentruy] 89 D3, 90 A3
Faia 158 B1
Fai della Paganella 107 B/C2
Faido 105 D2
Faimes 79 C2
Fairford 64 A3
Fairlie 56 B2
Faissault 78 B3
Fajão 158 B3
Fakenham 65 C1
Fåker 34 B2
Fakovići 133 C2
Fakse 53 D1
Fakse Ladeplads 53 D1/2
Falaise 86 A1
Falaise d'Aval 76 B3
Fålasjö 30 B3, 35 D2
Falcade 107 C2
Falces 154 A2
Falconara Maríttima 115 D3, 117 D2
Falcone 125 D1/2
Faleide 32 A3, 36 B1
Falerna 122 A2
Falerum 46 B3
Falešty 99 C3
Falešty 141 C1
Falirákion 149 D3
Falkenberg 72 A1
Falkenberg 82 B3
Falkenberg 49 D2, 50 A1
Falkenberg 92 B2
Falkenberg 83 C1
Falkenhagen 69 D1/2
Falkenhain 82 B1
Falkenrehde 70 A2
Falkensee 70 A2
Falkenstein 82 B2
Falkenstein 92 B1
Falkenthal 70 A2
Falkirk 57 B/C1/2
Falkland 57 C1
Falköping 45 D3
Fall 37 D3, 38 A2
Fallet 34 A/B3
Fällfors 20 A1, 31 D2
Fällfors 16 B3
Fallingbostel 68 B2

Fallingbostel-Dorfmark **68** B2
Fällkäl **30** B2, **35** D1
Fällkäl **30** B2, **35** D1
Fällsvikshamnen **30** B3
Falltorp **38** B2
Falmouth **62** B3
Falset **163** C/D1/2
Falstone **57** C/D2/3
Fălticeni **141** C1
Fältjägarstugan **34** A2
Falträsk **31** B/C1
Falun **39** D2
Fana **36** A3
Fanano **114** B2, **116** A1
Fanári **147** C/D3
Fanárion **143** C3
Fanárion **145** C1
Fanefjord Kirke **53** D2
Fangel **53** C1
Fanghetto **112** B2
Fanjeaux **109** D3, **156** A1
Fankel **80** A3
Fannrem (Orkanger) **28** A3, **33** C2
Fano **115** D2, **117** C/D1
Fanø Vesterhavsbad **52** A1
Fantoft **36** A3
Fanzara **162** B3
Fão **150** A3, **158** A1
Fara **127** C3
Farád **95** B/C3
Fara in Sabina **118** B1
Farajàn **172** A2/3
Faramontanos de Tábara **151** D3, **159** D1
Fara Novarese **105** C/D3
Fara San Martino **119** C/D1/2
Farasdués **154** B2
Fårbo **51** D1
Fårbo **72** B1
Farchant **92** A3
Farcheville **87** D2
Fardella **120** B3
Færder **44** B1/2
Fareham **76** B1
Fårentuna **47** C1
Fårevejle **49** C3, **53** C1
Fargau-Pratjau **53** C3
Färgelanda **45** C2
Faringdon **64** A3
Faringe **40** B3
Färingtofta **50** B2/3
Farini d'Olmo **113** D1, **114** A1
Färjestaden **51** D2
Färjestaden **72** B1
Farkadón **143** C3
Farlete **154** B3, **162** B1
Färlöv **50** B2/3
Farná **95** D3
Färnäs **39** D2
Farnborough **65** C3, **76** B1
Farnborough **64** B3, **76** B1
Farnese **116** B3, **118** A1
Farnham **64** B3, **76** B1
Farningham **65** C3, **77** B/C1
Farnworth **59** D2, **60** B2/3
Fårö **47** D2
Faro **170** B2
Faro do Alentejo **164** B3
Fårösund **47** D2
Fårösund **73** C1
Farra d'Alpago **107** D2
Farrington Gurney **63** D2
Farrou **109** D1/2
Fársala **143** D3
Fársala **148** B1/2
Farsaliótis **143** C/D3
Farsø **48** B2
Farstad **32** A2
Farsund **42** B3
Farum **49** D3, **50** A3, **53** D1
Fårup **48** B2
Fasano **121** C2
Fassberg **68** B2
Fassberg-Müden **68** B2
Fåssjö **35** B/C3
Fasterholt **48** B3
Fastov **99** C2
Fátima **164** A/B1
Fatmomakke **29** D1
Fättjaur **15** C3
Faucogney **89** D3
Faugères **110** B3
Fauguerolles **109** C1/2
Faulenrost **69** D1, **70** A1
Faulquemont **89** D1
Faulungen **81** D1
Fauquembergues **77** D2
Făurei **141** C1/2
Fauske **15** C1
Fauville-en-Caux **77** C3
Fauvillers **79** C3
Fåvang **37** D2, **38** A1
Favara **124** B3
Favareta **169** D2
Faverges **104** A3
Faverney **89** C3
Faverolles **87** C1/2
Faversham **65** C3, **77** C1
Favignana **124** A2
Favone **113** D3
Fawley **76** B1
Fay-aux-Loges **87** C2/3
Fay-de-Bretagne **85** D3
Fayence **112** A/B3
Fayet **110** A2
Fayl-Billot **89** C3
Fayón **163** C1
Fay-sur-Lignon **111** C1
Fažana **130** A1
Fazendas de Almeirim **164** B2
Fécamp **77** C3
Feces de Abajo **151** B/C3, **158** B1
Feda **42** B3
Fedje **36** A3
Fefor **37** D2
Fegen **50** A1
Fégréac **85** C3
Fegyvernek **129** D1
Fehérvárcsurgó **95** C3, **128** B1
Fehrbellin **69** D2, **70** A2
Fehring **127** D1
Feichten **106** B1
Feigefossen **36** B2
Feios **36** B2
Feira **158** A2
Feiring **38** A2
Feistritz am Wechsel **94** A3
Feiteira **170** B2
Feitos **150** A3, **158** A1
Feketić **129** C/D3
Fekjan **37** D3
Felanitx **157** C2
Felchow **70** B2
Feldbach **127** D1
Feldbach **96** A3
Feldberg **90** B3
Feldberg **70** A1
Felde **52** B3
Feldkirch **106** A1
Feldkirchen in Kärnten **126** B1/2
Feldkirchen-Westerham **92** A3
Feldkirchen in Kärnten **96** A3
Felgueiras **158** A/B1
Feliceto **113** D2
Felina **114** A/B1/2
Félines-Termenès **110** A3, **156** B1
Felino **114** A1
Felísio **115** C2, **116** B1
Felitto **120** A3
Félix **173** D2
Felixstowe **65** C2
Felizzano **113** C1
Fell **79** D3, **80** A3
Fellbach **91** C2
Felletin **102** A2
Fellingfors **14** B3
Fellingsbro **46** B1
Felsberg **81** C1
Felsőrajk **128** A2
Felsőszentiván **129** C2
Felsted **52** B2
Felton **57** D2
Feltre **107** C2
Femanger **42** A1
Femsjö **50** B1
Femundsenden **33** D3
Femundshytta **33** D3
Fendeille **109** D3, **156** A1
Fene **150** B1
Fenékpuszta **128** A2
Fener **107** C2/3
Fenes **9** C1
Fenestrelle **112** B1
Fénétrange **89** D1, **90** A1/2
Fengersfors **45** C2
Fenny Stratford **64** B2
Fensmark **53** D1
Feolin Ferry **56** A2
Feragen **33** D2/3
Ferchland **69** D2
Ferdinandovac **128** A2
Ferdinandshof **70** B1
Fère-Champenoise **88** A1
Fère-en-Tardenois **88** A1
Ferentillo **117** C3, **118** B1
Ferentino **119** B/C2
Férento **117** C3, **118** A1
Férez **168** B3
Feria **165** D2
Feričanci **128** B3
Ferla **125** C/D3
Ferlach **126** B2
Fermignano **115** D2/3, **117** C2
Fermo **117** D2
Fermoselle **159** C1
Fermoy **55** C3
Fernancaballero **167** C2
Fernán Núñez **172** B1
Ferney-Voltaire **104** A2
Fernhurst **76** B1
Ferns **58** A3
Ferragudo **170** A2
Férrai **145** D1, **145** D3
Férrai **149** C1
Ferrals-les-Corbières **110** A3, **156** B1
Ferrandina **120** B3
Ferrara **115** C1
Ferrara di Monte Baldo **106** B3
Ferreira do Alentejo **164** B3, **170** A/B1
Ferreira do Zêzere **158** A3, **164** B1
Ferreiros **150** A3, **158** A1
Ferreras de Abajo **151** D3
Ferreras de Arriba **151** D3
Ferrerías **157** C1
Ferreruela **163** C2
Ferret [Orsières] **104** B2/3
Ferrette **89** D3, **90** A3
Ferriere **113** D1
Ferrière-Larçon **101** D1
Ferrières **100** B2
Ferrières **108** B3, **154** B1
Ferrières-en-Gâtinais **87** D2
Ferrières-Saint-Mary **102** B3
Ferrières-sur-Sichon **103** C2
Ferring **48** A2
Ferrol **150** B1
Fertília **123** C1/2
Fertőd **94** B3
Fertőszentmiklós **94** B3
Fervença **158** B1
Ferwerd **66** B1
Festøy **32** A3, **36** B1
Festvåg **8** B2
Festvåg **8** B3
Fetești **141** C/D2
Fetsund **38** A3
Feucht **92** A1
Feuchtwangen **91** D1
Feudingen **80** B2
Feugarolles **109** C2
Feurs **103** C3
Fevåg **28** A3, **33** C1
Fevik **43** C3
Ffestiniog **59** C2/3, **60** A3
Fiamignano **117** D3, **118** B1
Fiane **43** C3
Fiano **105** C3, **112** B1
Fiastra **115** D3, **117** D2
Ficarolo **115** B/C1
Fichtelberg **82** A3
Fichtenau-Wildenstein **91** D1
Fichtenberg **91** C1
Fichtenwalde **70** A3
Ficulle **117** C3
Fidenza **114** A1
Fidjeland **42** B2
Fiè allo Scíliar/Völs am Schlern **107** C2
Fieberbrunn **92** B3
Fienvillers **77** D2
Fier **142** A1/2
Fier **148** A1
Fiera di Primiero **107** C2
Fierbinți Tîrg **141** C2
Fierbinți **141** C2
Fiesch **105** C2
Fiésole **114** B2, **116** B1
Figalía **146** B3
Figeac **109** D1
Figeholm **51** D1
Figline Valdarno **115** B/C3, **116** B2
Figueira da Foz **158** A3
Figueira de Castelo Rodrigo **159** C2
Figueira dos Cavaleiros **164** B3
Figueiredo de Alva **158** B2
Figueiro **158** B2
Figueiró dos Vinhos **158** A3, **164** B1
Figueiró do Campo **158** A3
Figuera **155** D3, **156** A3, **163** D1
Figueral **157** D3
Figueres **156** B2
Figuerola d'Orcau **155** D2/3
Figueruelas **155** C3, **163** B/C1
Fiholm **47** B/C1
Fiksdal **32** A2/3
Filadélfia **122** A/B2
Filadélfion **144** A1/2
Filáki **143** D3, **147** C1
Filákion **145** D2/3
Filákion **141** C3
Filaktí **143** C3
Filettino **119** C2
Filey **61** D2
Filí **147** D2
Fília **146** B3
Fília **148** B2
Filiași **140** B2
Filiași **135** D2
Filiátai **142** B3
Filiatrá **146** B3
Filiatrá **148** A/B2
Filipjakov **130** B2
Filipstad **39** C3, **45** D1
Filiriá **143** D1
Filitosa **113** D3
Fillan **32** B1
Fillingsnes **32** B1
Fillsta **29** D3, **34** B2
Filótas **143** C2
Filottrano **115** D3, **117** D2
Filskov **48** A/B3, **52** B1
Filsum **67** D1
Filton **63** D1/2
Filtvet **44** B1
Filzmoos **93** C3
Finale di Rero **115** C1
Finale Emília **114** B1
Finale Lígure **113** C2
Fiñana **173** D2
Finbo **41** C2
Finby **41** D3
Findon **76** B1
Fines **173** D1/2, **174** A1/2
Finja **50** B2
Finnanger **28** B1/2
Finnart **56** B1
Finnäs **30** B1
Finnbacka **39** D2
Finnberget **39** C1
Finnbyen **8** A2/3
Finneby **35** C3
Finneidfjord **14** B2
Finnemisj kapell **5** C/D2, **6** A2
Finnentrop **80** B1
Finnerödja **45** D2, **46** A2
Finnes **9** C/D1
Finnes **14** B1
Finnfjordeidnet **9** D1
Finngruvan **39** C2
Finnhamn **47** D1
Finning **91** D2/3, **92** A3
Finnjord **4** A3, **10** A1
Finnkroken **4** A2
Finnmyren **16** B3
Finnøy **42** A2
Finnøy **9** C3
Finnsäter **29** C3, **34** B1
Finnset **32** B3, **37** C1
Finnskog **38** B2
Finnsnes **9** D1
Finntorp **45** C1
Finnträsk **16** B3
Finnvik **42** A1/2
Finnvik **5** C1
Finnvollan **29** C1
Fino Mornasco **105** D3, **106** A3
Fins **78** A3
Finsand **37** D3
Finse **37** B/C3
Finsjö **51** D1
Finsland **42** B3
Finspång **46** B2
Finstad **33** D3
Finstad **38** B2
Finsterwalde **70** A/B3, **83** C1
Finsterwalde **72** A3, **96** A1
Finström **41** C2/3
Fintel **68** B1/2
Fintry **56** B1
Fionnay [Le Châble] **104** B2
Fionnphort **54** A2, **55** D1
Fiorano Modenese **114** B1
Fiorenzuola d'Arda **114** A1
Fiquefleur **77** C3
Firenze **114** B2, **116** B1/2
Firenzuola **117** C3, **118** B1
Firenzuola **114** B2, **116** B1
Firminy **103** C3
Firmo **122** A1
Firovo **75** C2
Fiscal **155** C2
Fischach **91** D2
Fischamend Markt **94** B2
Fischamend Markt **96** B3
Fischbach **94** A3
Fischbach **90** A1
Fischbach (Birkenfeld) **80** A3
Fischen **91** D3
Fishguard **62** B1
Fishguard **55** D3
Fiskåhaugen **28** B1
Fiskarheden **39** C2
Fiskari/Fiskars **25** B/C3
Fiskbæk **48** B2
Fiskebäckskil **44** B3
Fiskebøl **8** B2
Fiskeby **46** B2
Fiskefjord **9** C2
Fiskeläge **31** D1
Fiskevollen **33** D3
Fiskö **24** A2/3, **41** D2
Fiskøy **9** C2
Fisksätra **47** D1
Fisksjölandet **35** C2
Fisktjønnmoen **14** B2
Fismes **88** A1
Fisterra **150** A2
Fitero **154** A3
Fitíai **146** A1
Fitjar **42** A1
Fiuggi **118** B2
Fiuggi Fonte **118** B2
Fiumalbo **114** B2, **116** A1
Fiumata **117** D3, **118** B1
Fiumefreddo di Sicília **125** D2
Fiumefreddo Brúzio **122** A2
Fivizzano **114** A2, **116** A1
Fix-Saint-Geneys **103** C3, **110** B1
Fjågesund **43** C2
Fjäl **29** D3, **34** B2
Fjälbyn **31** D1
Fjälkinge **50** B2/3
Fjällandet **29** D3, **35** C2
Fjällåsen **10** A3
Fjällbacka **44** B2
Fjällbosjö **15** D3
Fjällnäs **33** D2, **34** A2/3
Fjällsjönäs **15** D3
Fjällskäfte **46** B1
Fjälltuna **30** B2, **35** D1
Fjand Gårde **48** A2
Fjæra **42** A/B1
Fjärås **49** D1, **50** A1
Fjärdhundra **40** A3
Fjære **43** C3
Fjærland **36** B2
Fjelberg **42** A1
Fjell **36** A3

Fjell **28** B2
Fjellerup **49** C2
Fjellkjøsa **28** A3, **33** C1/2
Fjellsrud **38** A3
Fjellstad **9** D1
Fjellstøl **43** C1
Fjellvær **32** B1
Fjelstrup **52** B1
Fjerritslev **48** B1
Fjølvika **28** B1
Fjørtoft **32** A2
Fjugesta **46** A1
Flå **37** D3
Flå **28** A3, **33** C2
Flaach [Henggart] **90** B3
Fladungen **81** D2
Flaka **41** D3
Flakaträsk **15** D3
Flakaträsk **31** B/C2
Flakk **28** A3, **33** C1
Flakkebjerg **53** C1
Flakstad **8** A/B2/3
Flåm **36** B3
Flamatt **104** B1
Flammersfeld **80** A2
Flåmseter **33** C3, **37** D1
Flärke **31** C2/3
Flarken **31** D1/2
Flassans-sur-Issole **112** A3
Flata **5** D2, **6** A2
Flatabø **42** A/B1
Flatdal **43** C1
Flåte **42** A1
Flateby **38** A3
Flateland **42** B2
Flaten **43** C3
Flåten **4** B2
Flatford Mill **65** C/D2
Flatholmen **44** B3
Flatøydegard **37** D2/3
Flatråker **42** A1
Flått **28** B1
Flattach **107** D1, **126** A1
Flattnitz **126** B1
Flatval **32** B1
Flatvoll **37** D3
Flauenskjold **49** B/C1
Flavigny-sur-Moselle **89** C2
Flawil **91** C3
Flayat **102** A2/3
Flechtingen **69** C3
Fleckeby **52** B2
Flecken Zechlin **69** D1/2, **70** A1/2
Fleet **64** B3, **76** B1
Fleetmark **69** C2
Fleetwood **59** C/D1, **60** B2
Flekke **36** A2
Flekkefjord **42** B3
Flemløse **52** B1
Flen **39** D2/3
Flen **46** B1
Flensburg **52** B2
Flenstad **28** A2, **33** C1
Fléres/Pflersch **107** C1
Flermoen **38** B1
Flers **86** A1
Flesberg **43** D1
Flesje **36** B2
Flesnes **9** C2
Flessau **69** C/D2
Flesvik **33** B/C1
Fleurance **109** C2
Fleuré **101** C2
Fleurey-lès-Faverney **89** C3
Fleurie **103** D2
Fleurier **104** B1
Fleurus **79** B/C2
Fleurville **103** D2
Fleury **77** D3, **87** C1
Fleury-en-Bière **87** D2
Fleury-sur-Andelle **76** B3, **86** B1
Flez **88** A3
Flickerbäcken **38** B1
Flieden **81** C2
Flims Dorf [Trin] **105** D1, **106** A1
Flims Waldhaus [Valendas-Sagogn] **105** D1, **106** A1
Flines-les-Râches **78** A2
Flins-sur-Seine **87** C1
Flint **59** C2, **60** B3
Flintbek **52** B3
Flirsch **106** B1
Flisa **38** B2
Flisby **46** A3
Fliseryd **51** D1
Flivik **46** B3
Flix **163** C1
Flize **79** C3
Flø **36** A1
Floby **45** D3
Floda **31** C/D1
Floda **45** C3
Floda **46** B1
Floda **39** D2
Flogny **88** A2
Flöha **83** B/C2
Floirac **108** B1
Flor **34** B3
Flora **28** B3, **33** D1
Florac **110** B2
Flôr da Rosa **165** C1/2
Florejachs **155** C3, **163** C1
Florennes **79** B/C2
Florensac **110** B3
Florentin **135** D2
Florenville **79** C3
Flores de Ávila **160** A2
Florídia **125** D3
Flórina **143** C1/2
Florínas **123** C1/2
Florø **36** A2
Flörsbach **81** C3
Flörsbachtal **81** C3
Florstadt-Niederflorstadt **81** C2
Florvåg **36** A3
Floss **82** B3
Flossenbürg **82** B3
Flosta **43** C3
Flostrand **14** B2
Flötningen **33** D3
Fløttumsetra **33** C2
Flovika **8** B2
Fluberg **37** D3, **38** A2
Flüelen **105** D1
Flüh **90** A3
Flumet **104** B3
Flúmini **123** D3
Fluminimaggiore **123** C3
Flums **105** D1, **106** A1
Fluorn-Winzeln **90** B2
Flurkmark **31** C/D2
Flyggsjö **31** C2
Flyinge **50** B3
Flykälen **29** D2/3, **34** B1
Flyn **30** A2, **35** C1
Flystveit **42** B3
Flytsåsen **39** D1
Fobello **105** C2/3
Foča **133** C3
Foça **149** D2
Fochabers **54** B2
Focşani **141** C1/2
Foeni **140** A1/2
Fogdö **47** C1
Fóggia **120** A1
Foglianise **119** D3
Föglö **41** D3
Fogueteiro **164** A2
Fohnsdorf **127** C1
Foiano della Chiana **115** C3, **116** B2
Foiano Valfortore **119** D2, **120** A1
Foix **109** D3, **155** D1/2, **156** A1
Fojnica **132** B2
Fojnica **132** B3, **137** C1
Fokovci **127** D1/2
Fokstua **33** B/C3, **37** D1
Foldereid **28** B1
Foldingbro **52** A/B1
Fole **47** D2/3
Folelli **113** D2/3
Folgaria **107** C2/3
Folgosa **158** B1/2
Folgoso de la Ribera **151** D2
Folgoso do Caurel **151** C2
Foligno **115** D3, **117** C2/3
Folkärna **40** A3
Folkestad **36** A/B1
Folkestone **65** C3, **76** B1
Folkingham **61** D3, **64** B1
Follafoss **28** B2, **33** D1
Follandsvangen **33** C3, **37** D1
Folldalsverk **33** C3, **37** D1
Follebu **37** D2, **38** A1
Follina **107** C/D2
Föllinge **29** D3, **34** B1
Follónica **116** A3
Fombelaux **101** D3
Fombellida **152** B3, **160** B1
Foncea **153** C2
Foncine-le-Bas **104** A2
Foncouverte **110** A2
Fondamente **110** B2
Fondi **119** C2
Fondo **107** C2
Fondón **173** D2
Fonelas **173** C1/2
Fonfría **162** A/B2
Fonfría **151** D3, **159** D1
Fonn **36** B2
Fonnebostsjøn **36** A3
Fonnes **36** A3
Fonni **123** D2
Fonó **128** B2
Fons **111** C2
Fontainebleau **87** D2
Fontaine-Chalendray **101** C2
Fontaine-de-Vaucluse **111** D2
Fontaine-Française **89** C3
Fontaine Henry **76** B3, **86** A1
Fontaine-la-Soret **77** C3, **86** B1
Fontaine-le-Dun **77** C3
Fontaine-sur-Coole **88** B1
Fontana Liri **119** C2
Fontanarejo **167** C2
Fontane **113** C2
Fontanellato **114** A1
Fontanelle **114** A1
Fontanelle **107** D3
Fontanetto Po **105** C3, **113** C1
Fontaniva **107** C3
Fontannes **103** C3
Fontanosas **167** C2
Fonte Blanda **116** B3
Fonte Bôa **170** A1
Fontécchio **117** D3, **119** C1
Fontellas **154** A3
Fontenay-le-Comte **100** B2
Fontenay-sur-Loing **87** D2
Fontenay-Trésigny **87** D1/2
Fontet **108** B1
Fontevrault-l'Abbaye **86** A/B3, **101** C1
Fontfroide **110** A3, **156** B1
Fontgombault **101** D1
Fontibre **152** B1/2
Fonti del Clitunno **117** C3
Fontiveros **160** A2
Font Romeu **156** A2
Fontvieille **111** C2
Fonyód **128** A1/2
Fonz **155** C3
Fonzaleche **153** C2
Fonzaso **107** C2
Fóppolo **106** A2
Föra **51** D1
Foradada **155** D3
Foradada de Tosca **155** C2
Foråsen **29** D3, **34** B1
Forbach **90** B2
Forbach **89** D1, **90** A1
Forbach-Schönmünzach **90** B2
Förby **24** B3
Forcall **162** B2
Forcalqueiret **112** A3
Forcalquier **111** D2, **112** A2
Forcarey **150** A/B2
Force **117** D2/3
Forchheim **82** A3
Forchheim **83** C2
Forchtenau **94** B3
Forchtenberg **91** C1
Førde **36** B2
Førde **36** A2
Førde **42** A1
Förderstedt **69** C/D3
Fordingbridge **76** A1
Fordongiánus **123** C2
Fore **14** B1
Forenza **120** B2
Foresta Búrgos **123** C/D2
Forest-Montiers **77** D2
Føresvik **42** A2
Forfar **57** C1
Forfar **54** B2
Forges-les-Eaux **77** D3
Forheim-Aufhausen **91** D2
Foria **120** A3
Forío **119** C3
Forjães **150** A3, **158** A1
Førland **42** B3
Forlì **115** C2, **117** B/C1
Forlì del Sánnio **119** C2
Forlimpópoli **115** C2, **117** C1
Formby **59** C2, **60** B2/3
Formerie **77** D3
Fórmia **119** C3
Formiche Alto **162** B3
Formiche Bajo **162** B3
Formiche di Grosseto **116** A3
Formícola **119** C/D3
Formigal **154** B2
Formigaleso **155** C2
Formígine **114** B1
Formigliana **105** C3
Formignana **115** C1
Formiguères **156** A1/2
Fornalutx **157** C2
Fornebu **38** A3
Fornelli **123** C1
Fornells **157** C2
Fornells **157** C1
Fornells de la Muntanya **156** A2
Fornelos de Montes **150** A2
Fornes **173** C2
Fornes **9** C2
Fornes **9** C1/2
Fornes **9** D1
Forneset **4** A3
Forni Avoltri **107** D2, **126** A2
Forni di Sopra **107** D2
Forni di Sotto **107** D2, **126** A2
Forno **112** B1
Forno Allione **106** B2
Forno Alpi Gráie **104** B3
Forno di Zoldo **107** D2
Fórnoles **163** C2
Fornols **155** D2, **156** A2
Fornos de Algedres **158** B2
Fornovo di Taro **114** A1
Forradal **28** B3, **33** D1
Forráskút **129** D2
Fors **40** A3
Fors **31** B/C3
Forsa **40** A1
Forsand **42** A2
Forsbacka **15** D2/3
Forsed **30** B3, **35** D2
Forserum **46** A3
Forshaga **45** D1
Forsheda **50** B1
Forsland **14** A2
Förslövsholm **49** D2, **50** A2
Forsmark **40** B2
Forsmark **15** C3
Forsmo **30** A2/3, **35** C1
Forsmo **30** A2/3, **35** C1
Forsmo **30** B3, **35** D2
Forsnacken **15** C3
Forsnäs **30** A/B2
Forsnäs **16** A2
Forsnäs **16** B2
Forsnes **32** B1
Forsøl **5** C1, **6** A1
Forssa **25** C2
Forssjö **46** B2
Forst **70** B3
Forst **72** A3, **96** A1
Forstau **93** C3, **126** A/B1
Forsvik **46** A2
Fortanete **162** B2
Fort Augustus **54** A2, **55** D1
Forte dei Marmi **114** A2, **116** A1
Forte di Bibbona **114** A/B3, **116** A2
Förtha **81** D2
Fortingall **56** B1
Fortino **120** A/B3
Fort la Latte **85** C1/2
Fort-Mahon-Plage **77** D2
Fortun **37** C2
Fortuna **169** C3
Fortuneswell **63** D3
Fort William **54** A2, **55** D1
Forvik **14** A3
Fos **155** C2
Fosdinovo **114** A2
Foskros **34** A3
Fosmark **42** A2
Fosnavåg **36** A1
Foss **33** C2
Foss **28** B2
Fossacésia **119** D1
Fossacésia Marina **119** D1
Fossano **113** B/C1/2
Fossbakken **33** C3
Fossbakken **9** D2
Fossbua **10** A2
Fosse **37** D2
Fossé **86** A/B3
Fossemagne **101** D3, **109** C1
Fosser **38** A3
Fosses-la-Ville **79** C2
Fossestølen **36** A3
Fossestrand **5** D2, **6** A2
Fosseter **33** C3, **37** D1
Fossheim **37** C/D2
Fossholt **37** D3
Fossli **36** B3
Fosso Ghiáia **115** C2, **117** C1
Fóssoli **114** B1
Fossombrone **115** D2/3, **117** C2
Fos-sur-Mer **111** C3
Fót **95** D3
Fotheringhay **64** B2
Fotolívos **144** B1
Foucarmont **77** D3
Fouesnant **84** B2/3
Fougères **86** A/B2
Fougères-sur-Bièvre **86** A/B3
Fougerolles **89** D2/3
Foulain **89** B/C2
Foulsham **65** C/D1
Fountains Abbey **61** C2
Fouras **100** B2
Fourchambault **102** B1
Fourfourás **149** C3
Foúrka **142** B2
Fourmies **78** B3
Fourná **146** B1
Fournels **110** B1
Fournols **103** B/C3
Fourques **156** B1/2
Fourquet **109** C2
Fours **103** C1
Fours **112** A/B2
Fovant **63** D2, **76** A1
Foz **151** C1
Foz de Arouce **158** A3
Foz de Calanda **162** B2
Foz do Arelho **164** A1
Frabosa Soprana **113** C2
Fraddon **62** B3
Frades **150** B1/2
Frades de la Sierra **159** D2
Fraeyming-Merlebach **89** D1, **90** A1
Frafjord **42** A2
Fraga **155** C3, **163** C1
Fragagnano **121** C3
Fragneto Monforte **119** D2/3
Frahier-et-Chatebier **89** D3
Frailes **173** C1
Fraire **78** B2
Fraize **89** D2, **90** A2
Frameries **78** B2
Framlingham **65** C2
Främlingshem **40** A2
Frammersbach **81** C3
Främmestad **45** C2/3
Framnäs **16** A1
França **151** C3
Francardo **113** D3
Francavilla Fontana **121** C/D2/3
Francavilla di Sicília **125** D2
Francavilla al Mare **119** C/D1
Francavilla in Sinni **120** B3, **122** A1
Franco **158** B1
Francofonte **125** C3
Francorchamps **79** D2
Frändefors **45** C2

Franeker 66 B1
Frangy 104 A2
Frankenau 81 C1
Frankenberg 81 B/C1
Frankenberg 83 B/C2
Frankenburg am Hausruck 93 C2/3
Frankenfels 94 A3
Frankenfels 96 A3
Frankenhardt-Gründelhardt 91 C1
Frankenheim 81 D2
Frankenmarkt 93 C3
Frankenstein 90 B1
Frankenthal 80 B3, 90 B1
Frankershausen 81 C/D1
Frankfurat-Markendorf 70 B3
Frankfurt 70 B3
Frankfurt 72 A3
Frankfurt am Main 80 B3
Frankrike 29 C3, 34 A/B1
Frånö 30 B3, 35 D2
Fránscia 106 A/B2
Fränsta 35 C3
Františkovy Lázně 82 B3
Frascati 118 B2
Frascineto 120 B3, 122 A/B1
Fraserburgh 54 B2
Frashëri 142 B2
Frasne 104 A3
Frasnes-lez-Buissenal 78 B2
Fratel 165 B/C1
Frauenau 93 C1
Frauenfeld 91 B/C3
Frauenkirchen 94 B3
Frauenstein 83 C2
Fraugde 53 C1
Frayssinet 109 D1
Frayssinet-le-Gélat 108 B1
Frechas 159 B/C1
Frechen 79 D2, 80 A2
Frechilla 152 A3
Frechilla de Almazán 161 D1
Freden 68 B3
Fredensborg 49 D3, 50 A3
Fredericia 48 B3, 52 B1
Frederiksberg 53 C/D1
Frederikshavn 49 C1
Frederiksoord 67 C2
Frederikssund 49 D3, 50 A3, 53 D1
Frederikssund 72 A1/2
Frederiksværk 49 D3, 50 A3
Fredes 163 C2
Fredrika 30 B2
Fredriksberg 39 C3
Fredriksdal 46 A3
Fredrikshamn 26 B2
Fredrikstad 44 B1
Fredros 38 B3
Fredvang 8 A2/3
Fregenal de la Sierra 165 D3
Freginals 163 C2
Frehne 69 D1
Frei 32 B2
Freiamt-Ottoschwanden 90 B2
Freiberg 83 C2
Freiberg 96 A1
Freiberg am Neckar 91 C1
Freiburg 52 B3, 68 A/B1
Freiburg im Breisgau 90 A/B3
Freiburg-Tiengen 90 A3
Freiensteinau 81 C2
Freigericht 81 C3
Freihung 82 A/B3
Freila 173 D1
Freiland 94 A3
Freilassing 93 B/C3
Freilingen 80 B2
Freisen 80 A3, 90 A1
Freising 92 A2
Freistadt 93 D2
Freistadt 96 A2
Freistatt 68 A2
Freital 83 C1/2
Freixedas 159 B/C2
Freixenet de Segarra 155 C3, 163 C1
Freixianda 158 A3, 164 B1

Freixiosa 158 B2
Freixo 165 C2
Freixo de Espada a Cinta 159 C2
Fréjus 112 A/B3
Frekhaug 36 A3
Frelsdorf 68 A1
Fremdingen 91 D1
Frensdorf 81 D3
Frenštát pod Radhoštěm 95 C1
Freren 67 D2
Fréscano 154 A3
Freshwater 76 A1/2
Fresnay-sur-Sarthe 86 A/B2
Fresneda de Altarejos 161 D3, 168 B1
Fresneda de la Sierra 161 D2/3
Fresneda de la Sierra Tirón 153 C2
Fresnedillas 160 B2
Fresnedo 151 C2
Fresnedoso de Ibor 159 D3, 166 A/B1
Fresne-Saint-Mamès 89 C3
Fresnes-en-Woëvre 89 C1
Fresnes-sur-Apance 89 C2/3
Fresnes-sur-Escaut 78 B2
Fresnillo de las Dueñas 153 C3, 161 B/C1
Fresno-Alhandiga 159 D2
Fresno de Cantespino 161 C1
Fresno de Caracena 161 C1
Fresno de la Ribera 151 D3, 152 A3, 159 D1
Fresno de Riotirón 153 C2
Fresno de Sayago 159 C1
Fresno de Torote 161 C2
Fresnoy-Folny 77 C/D2/3
Fressonneville 77 D2
Fresvik 36 B2
Frétigney-et-Velloreille 89 C3
Frettes 89 C3
Freudenberg 82 A/B3, 92 B1
Freudenberg 80 B2
Freudenberg 81 C3
Freudenstadt 90 B2
Frévent 77 D2
Freyburg 82 A1
Freyenstein 69 D1
Freystadt 92 A1
Freystadt-Burggriesbach 92 A1
Freyung 93 C2
Frías 153 C2
Frías de Albarracín 162 A3
Fribourg/Freiburg 104 B1
Frick 90 B3
Frickenhausen 91 C2
Frickenhausen am Main 81 D3
Frickingen 91 C3
Fridafors 51 C2
Fridaythorpe 61 D2
Fridingen 91 B/C3
Fridolfing 93 B3
Frieda 81 D1
Friedberg 81 B/C2
Friedberg 91 D2, 92 A2
Friedberg 94 A3
Friedburg 93 C3
Friedeburg 82 A1
Friedeburg 67 D1
Friedeburg-Horsten 67 D1
Friedenfels 82 B3
Friedenshorst 69 D2, 70 A2
Friedersdorf 83 C1
Friedersdorf 70 A/B3
Friedewald (Bad Hersfeld) 81 C2
Friedland 81 C/D1
Friedland 70 B3
Friedland 70 A1
Friedland-Stockhausen 81 C/D1
Friedrichroda 81 D2
Friedrichsbrunn 69 C3
Friedrichshafen 91 C3
Friedrichshain 83 D1
Friedrichskoog 52 A3

Friedrichsluga 70 A3, 83 C1
Friedrichsruhe 69 D1
Friedrichstadt 52 A/B2/3
Friedrichsthal 89 D1, 90 A1
Friedrichsthal 70 B1/2
Friedrichswalde 70 A/B2
Frielendorf 81 C1/2
Friesach 126 B1
Friesach 96 A3
Friesack 69 D2
Friesenheim 90 B2
Friesenried 91 D3
Friesoythe 67 D2
Friesoythe-Edewechter-damm 67 D1/2
Friesoythe-Gehlenberg 67 D2
Friesoythe-Markhausen 67 D2
Friesoythe-Neuscharrel 67 D2
Friggesby 25 C3
Friggesund 35 C3
Friitala 24 A1
Frijsenborg 48 B2
Frilandsmuseum Hjerl Hede 48 A2
Frillesås 49 D1, 50 A1
Frillesås 49 D1, 50 A1
Frillesås 72 A1
Frinnaryd 46 A3
Frinton 65 C2/3
Friockheim 57 C1
Friol 150 B1/2
Fristad 45 C/D3
Fristad 15 D3
Fritsla 45 C3, 49 D1
Fritzlar 81 C1
Froan 32 B1
Frodba 55 C1
Fröderyd 51 C1
Frödinge 46 B3
Frogner 38 A3
Frognerseteren 38 A3
Frohburg 82 B1
Frohnhausen (Dillkreis) 80 B2
Frohnleiten 127 C1
Frohnleiten 96 A3
Froidos 88 B1
Froissy 77 D3
Fröjel 47 D3
Fröjel 72 B1
Froland 43 C3
Frome 63 D2, 64 A3
Fromentel 86 A1/2
Fromentine 100 A1
Frómista 152 B2/3
Frönäs 20 A2/3
Fronhausen-Bellnhausen 81 B/C2
Fronreute-Blitzenreute 91 C3
Fronsac 108 B1
Fronteira 165 C2
Frontenay-Rohan-Rohan 100 A1
Frontenex 104 A3
Frontenhausen 92 B2
Frontignan 110 B2
Fronton 108 B2
Frøsendal 28 B2
Frosinone 119 C2
Frosolone 119 D2
Frosta 28 A3, 33 C1
Frostavallen 50 B3
Frostkåge 31 D1
Frostup 48 A/B1
Frövi 46 B3
Frøyrak 43 B/C2
Fruges 77 D2
Frunzovka 141 D1
Frutak 137 D2
Frutigen 105 C2
Frýdek-Místek 96 B2
Frýdlant 96 A1
Frýdlant 83 D2
Fryele 50 B1
Fryksås 39 C/D1
Fryksta 45 D1
Frymburk 93 D2
Fryšták 95 C1
Fthiotís 146 B1
Fubine 113 C1
Fucécchio 114 B2, 116 A1/2

Fuencalderas 154 B2
Fuencaliente 167 C3
Fuencaliente 167 C2
Fuencarral 161 B/C2
Fuencubierta 172 A1
Fuendejalón 154 A3, 162 A1
Fuendetodos 162 B1
Fuengirola 172 B3
Fuenlabrada 160 B3
Fuenlabrada de los Montes 166 B2
Fuenllana 167 D2, 168 A2
Fuenmayor 153 D2
Fuensalida 160 B3
Fuensanta 168 B1/2
Fuensanta de Martos 173 B/C1
Fuente-Álamo 169 C2
Fuente-Álamo de Murcia 174 B1
Fuentealbilla 168 B1/2
Fuente Amarga 171 D3
Fuentebravia 171 D2/3
Fuentecambrón 153 C3, 161 C1
Fuentecén 152 B3, 160 B1
Fuente de Cantos 165 D3, 166 A3
Fuente del Arco 166 A3
Fuente del Maestre 165 D2
Fuente de Pedro Naharro 161 C3, 167 D1, 168 A1
Fuente de Piedra 172 B2
Fuente de Santa Cruz 160 A/B3
Fuente el Fresno 167 C2
Fuente el Olmo de Iscar 160 B1
Fuente el Olmo de Fuentidu-eña 160 B1
Fuente el Saz 161 C2
Fuente el Saz de Jarama 161 C2
Fuente el Sol 160 A1
Fuenteguinaldo 159 C2
Fuente la Higuera 169 C2
Fuente la Lancha 166 B3
Fuentelárbol 153 D3, 161 C1
Fuentelespino de Haro 161 D3, 168 A1
Fuentelespino de Moya 162 A3, 169 C1
Fuentelmonje 161 D1
Fuentelsaz 161 D2, 162 A2
Fuentemilanos 160 B2
Fuentenovilla 161 C2/3
Fuente Obejuna 166 B3
Fuente Palmera 172 A1
Fuentepelayo 160 B1
Fuentepinilla 153 D3, 161 C1
Fuenterrebollo 160 B1
Fuenterroble de Salvatierra 159 D2
Fuenterrobles 169 D1
Fuentes 161 D3
Fuente Salvage 169 B/C2
Fuente Santa 151 D1, 152 A1
Fuentesaúco de Fuentidu-eña 160 B1
Fuentesaúco 159 D1, 160 A1
Fuentes Claras 163 C2
Fuentes de Andalucía 172 A1
Fuentes de Ayódar 162 B3
Fuentes de Cesna 172 B2
Fuentes de Ebro 154 B3, 162 B1
Fuentes de Jiloca 162 A1
Fuentes de León 165 D3
Fuentes de Magaña 153 D3
Fuentes de Nava 152 A/B3
Fuentes de Oñoro 159 C2
Fuentes de Ropel 151 D3, 152 A3
Fuentes de Rubielos 162 B3
Fuentes de Valdepero 152 B3
Fuentesoto 160 B1
Fuentespina 153 C3, 161 B/C1
Fuente-Tójar 172 B1

Fuentidueña de Tajo 161 C3
Fuentidueña 160 B1
Fuerte del Rey 167 C3, 173 C1
Fuertescusa 161 D2
Fugelsta 30 A3, 35 C2
Fügen 92 A3, 107 C1
Fuglafjørdhur 55 C1
Fugleberg 9 C1/2
Fuglebjerg 53 C/D1
Fuglefjell 5 D1
Fuglefjell 4 B2
Fuglefjell 28 B1
Fuglefjell 4 B2
Fuglefjell 8 A3
Fuglefjell 7 D1
Fuglefjell 5 B/C1
Fuglefjell 7 C1
Fuglefjell 4 A/B2
Fuglefjell 7 C/D2
Fuglefjell 6 B1
Fuglefjell 7 C/D1
Fuglefjell 8 A3
Fuglefjell 5 D1, 6 B1
Fuglefjell 6 B1
Fuglefjell 7 C1
Fuglefjell 7 D1
Fuglefjellet 14 A2
Fuglem 28 A/B3, 33 D2
Fuglstad 29 C1
Fuglvik 32 B2
Fulda 81 C2
Fuldera [Zernez] 106 B2
Fulleda 155 D3, 163 D1
Fullerö 40 A3, 46 B1
Fullsjön 30 A3, 35 C1
Fullsjön 30 A3, 35 C1
Fülöpszállás 129 C1
Fulpmes 107 C1
Fulunäs 39 B/C1
Fumay 79 C3
Fumel 109 C1
Funäs 34 B2
Funäsdalen 34 A3
Funcheira 170 A1
Fundão 158 B2
Fúndres/Pfunders 107 C1
Fundulea 141 C2
Funes 154 A2
Fünfstetten 91 D2
Funtana 126 A/B3, 130 A1
Furadouro 158 A2
Furci 119 D2
Fure 36 A2
Furenes 36 A3
Furnace 56 A1
Furnes 38 A2
Fürstenau 68 A/B3
Fürstenau 67 D2
Fürstenau-Schwagstorf 67 D2
Fürstenberg 70 A1/2
Fürstenfeldbruck 92 A2
Fürstenfeld 96 A/B3
Fürstenstein 93 C2
Fürstenwalde 70 B2/3
Fürstenwalde 72 A3
Fürstenwerder 70 A1
Fürstenzell 93 C2
Fürstenzell-Sandbach 93 C2
Fürth 81 B/C3
Fürth 82 A3, 91 D1, 92 A1
Fürth 92 B2
Furth im Wald 92 B1
Furtwangen 90 B3
Furuberg 35 C3
Furudal 39 D1
Furudalseter 28 B2
Furuflaten 4 A/B3, 10 A1
Furuhult 35 D2
Furunäs 16 B2
Furuögrund 31 D1
Furusjö 45 D3
Furusund 41 C3, 47 D1
Furutangvik 29 C1
Furuvik 40 B2
Fuscaldo 122 A1
Fusch an der Grossglock-nerstrasse 107 D1, 126 A1
Fuseta 170 B2
Fushë Arrëz 138 A2
Fushë Muhur 138 A3
Fush Krujë 137 D3

Fusine Laghi 126 B2
Fúsio [Ponte Brolla] 105 D2
Füssen 91 D3
Fussy 87 D3, 102 A1
Fustiñana 154 A3
Futog 129 C/D3, 133 C1, 134 A1
Futrikelv 4 A2
Füzesabony 97 C3
Fužine 127 C3, 130 B1
Fynshav 52 B2
Fyns Hoved 49 C3, 53 C1
Fyrås 29 D3, 35 C1
Fyresdal 43 C2
Fyrkat 48 B2

G

Gaaldorf 127 B/C1
Gabaldón 161 D3, 168 B1
Gabarret 108 B2
Gabas 108 B3, 154 B2
Gabasa 155 C3
Gabbro 114 A/B3, 116 A2
Gabčíkovo 95 C3
Gabela 136 B1
Gabellino 114 B3, 116 A/B2
Gaber 139 D1
Gabicce Mare 115 D2, 117 C1
Gablingen 91 D2
Gabøl 52 B1
Gabriac 110 A1/2
Gabrica 140 A3
Gabrovac 135 C3
Gabrovo 141 C3
Gaby 105 C3
Gacé 86 B1
Gacko 132 B3, 137 C1
Gadbjerg 48 B3, 52 B1
Gäddede 29 C/D2
Gäddträsk 31 C1
Gadebusch 53 C3, 69 C1
Gædgenjarga 6 B2
Gadmen [Meiringen] 105 C1/2
Gádor 173 D2
Gádoros 129 D2
Gadžin Han 135 C3, 139 C1
Gaël 85 C2
Gaerwen 58 B2, 60 A3
Găeşti 141 C2
Gaeta 119 C3
Gafanha da Nazaré 158 A2
Gafanhoeira 164 B2
Gáfete 165 C1
Gaflenz 93 D3
Gagarin 75 D3
Gägelow 53 C3
Gaggenau 90 B2
Gaggi 125 D2
Gággio Montano 114 B2, 116 A1
Gagliano Castelferrato 125 C2
Gagliano del Capo 121 D3
Gagnef 39 D2
Gagsmark 16 B3
Gahro 70 A/B3
Gaibana 115 C1
Gæidno 7 B/C2
Gaienhofen-Hemmenhofen 91 C3
Gaildorf 91 C1
Gailey 59 D3, 64 A1
Gailingen 90 B3
Gaillac 109 D2
Gaillefontaine 77 D3
Gaillon 76 B3, 86 A/B1
Gainsborough 61 C/D3
Gaiole in Chianti 115 B/C3, 116 B2
Gairloch 54 A2
Gáiro 123 D2
Gáiro Scalo 123 D2
Gais 91 C3, 105 D1, 106 A1
Gaishorn 93 D3
Gaj 128 A3
Gaj 134 B1
Gajary 94 B2
Gajewo 71 D2
Gajsin 99 C3
Gajvoron 99 C3
Gakovo 129 C3
Gala 158 A3
Galambok 128 A2
Galan 109 C3, 155 C1
Galanito 11 C1
Galanta 95 C2
Galapagar 160 B2
Galápagos 161 C2
Galar 154 A2
Galaroza 165 D3, 171 C1
Galashiels 57 C2
Galashiels 54 B3
Galatás 148 B2
Galatás 147 D3
Galaţi 141 C/D2
Galatina 121 D3
Galatiní 143 C2
Galátista 144 A2
Galátone 121 D3
Galaxídion 147 B/C2
Galbarra 153 D2
Galdakao 153 C1
Galeata 115 C2, 116 B1
Galegos 165 C1
Galenbeck 70 A/B1
Galera 168 A3, 173 D1
Galeria 113 D3
Galgojavrre 4 B3, 10 B1
Galič 97 D2, 98 B3
Galicea Mare 135 D2
Galičnik 138 A/B3
Galíndez 153 C2
Galinduste 159 D2
Galipsós 144 B1
Galisteo 159 C/D3
Galižana 130 A1
Gallarate 105 D3
Gallardon 87 C2
Gällared 49 D1, 50 A1
Gallareto 113 C1
Gallegos de Argañán 159 C2
Gallejaur 16 A3
Galliate 105 D3
Gallicano 114 A/B2, 116 A1
Gällinge 49 D1, 50 A1
Gállio 107 C2/3
Gallipienzo 155 C2
Gallípoli 121 D3
Gällivare 16 B1
Gallneukirchen 93 D2
Gällö 35 C2
Gallo 115 D2, 117 C1/2
Gallspach 93 C2
Gällstad 45 D3
Gallúccio 119 C2
Gallur 155 C3
Galovac 130 B2
Gålsjö bruk 30 B3, 35 D2
Galston 56 B2
Galtabäck 49 D1, 50 A1
Galtby 24 A3
Galten 33 D3
Galten 5 C1
Galten 48 B3
Galtisjaur 15 D2
Gåltjärn 35 D2
Galtström 35 D3
Galtür 106 B1
Galugnano 121 D3
Galve 162 B2
Galve de Sorbe 161 C1
Galveias 164 B2
Galven 40 A1
Gálvez 160 B3, 167 C1
Galway (Gaillimh) 55 C2/3
Gama 153 C1
Gamaches 77 D2
Gamarde-les-Bains 108 A2
Gambach (Friedberg) 80 B2
Gámbara 106 B3
Gambarana 113 C/D1
Gambárie 122 A3
Gambassi Terme 114 B3, 116 A2
Gambatesa 119 D2, 120 A1
Gambolò 105 D3, 113 D1
Gamfoss 15 C1
Gamil 150 A3, 158 A1
Gaming 93 D3
Gaming 96 A3
Gaminiz 153 C1
Gamlakarleby 20 B1
Gamleby 46 B3
Gamleby 72 B1
Gammalvallen 34 A/B3
Gammelboliden 16 B3
Gammelby 25 D2, 26 A2
Gammel Estrup 49 B/C2
Gammel Skagen 44 B3
Gammelstad (Nederluleå) 17 C3
Gammelvær 5 B/C2
Gammertingen 91 C2
Gams bei Hieflau 93 D3
Gams [Haag-Gams] 105 D1, 106 A1
Gamvik 5 C1
Gamvik 7 C1
Gamvik 5 C2
Gamzigrad 135 C2/3
Gâmzovo 135 D2
Gan 108 B3, 154 B1
Gáname 159 D1
Ganceviči 98 B1
Ganda di Martello/Gand 106 B2
Ganddal 42 A2
Ganderkesee-Brink 68 A2
Ganderkesee 68 A2
Gandesa 163 C2
Gandía 169 D2
Gandino 106 A3
Gandra 150 A3, 158 A1
Gándria [Lugano] 105 D2
Gandvik 7 C2
Gangelt 79 D1/2
Ganges 110 B2
Gånghester 45 C/D3
Gangi 125 C2
Gangkofen 92 B2
Gankofen-Obertrennbach 92 B2
Gan'kovo 75 C1
Gannat 102 B2
Gannay-sur-Loire 103 C1
Gånsager 52 A1
Gansdalen 38 A3
Gänserndorf 94 B2
Gänserndorf 96 B2/3
Gånsvik 35 D2/3
Gánt 95 D3, 128 B1
Ganthem 47 D3
Ganton 61 D2
Gaočići 133 C2
Gap 112 A1/2
Gapohytta 4 B3, 10 A1
Gara 129 C2
Garaballa 163 C3, 169 D1
Garaguso 120 B2/3
Gara Hitrino 141 C3
Garaño 151 D2
Gara Pirin 139 D3
Garavan 112 B2/3
Garbagna 113 D1
Garbayuela 166 B2
Garbom 25 D2, 26 A2
Garbsen 68 B2/3
Garching 92 B2
Garching bei München 92 A2
García 163 C1/2
Garcíaz 166 A1
Garcihernández 159 D2, 160 A2
Garcinarro 161 C/D3
Garda 106 B3
Gardanne 111 D3
Gärdås 39 C2
Gårdby 51 D2
Gärde 29 C3, 34 B1
Garde 47 D2
Garde 154 B2
Gardelegen 69 C2
Gardermoen 38 A3
Gardíkion 146 B1
Gardíkion 142 B3
Gardíkion 143 C3
Garding 52 A2/3
Gardinovci 129 D3, 133 D1, 134 A1
Gärdnäs 29 D2
Gardno 70 B1
Gardone Riviera 106 B3
Gardone Val Trómpia 106 B3
Gardonne 109 C1
Gárdony 129 B/C1
Gardouch 109 D3, 155 D1
Gårdsby 51 C1
Gardsenden 32 B3, 37 D1
Gårdsjö 45 D2, 46 A2
Gardsjönäs 15 C3
Gårdskär 40 B2
Gärdslösa 51 D1/2
Garein 108 B2
Garelochhead 56 B1
Garešnica 128 A3
Garéssio 113 C2
Gargaliáni 146 B3
Gargaliáni 148 A/B2/3
Gargallo 162 B2
Garganta El Chorro 172 A2
Garganta la Olla 159 D3
Gargantiel 166 B2
Gargantilla 166 B1
Gargellen 106 A/B1
Garggogæcce 7 B/C1
Gargia 5 C2/3
Gargilesse-Dampierre 101 D2, 102 A2
Gargjaur 15 D3
Gargnano 106 B3
Gargnås 15 D3
Gárgoles de Abajo 161 D2
Gargüera 159 D3
Gargždai 73 C2
Garijp 67 B/C1/2
Garitz 69 D3
Garkleppvollen 33 D2
Garlasco 105 D3, 113 D1
Garlieston 56 B3, 60 A1
Garlin 108 B3, 154 B1
Garlitos 166 B2
Gârljano 139 C/D2
Garlstorf 68 B1
Garmisch-Partenkirchen 92 A3
Garmisch-Partenkirchen-Griesen 91 D3, 92 A3
Garnat-sur-Engièvre 103 C1/2
Garpenberg 40 A2
Garphytte nationalpark 46 A1
Garrafe de Torío 151 D2, 152 A2
Garralda 108 B3, 155 C1/2
Garray 153 D3, 161 D1
Garrel 67 D2
Garrigil 57 D3, 60 B1
Garriguella 156 B2
Garristown 58 A2
Garrovillas 159 C3, 165 D1
Garrow 56 B1
Garrucha 174 A2
Gars am Inn 92 B2
Gars am Kamp 94 A2
Garsås 39 D2
Gärsnäs 50 B3
Garstang 59 D1, 60 B2
Garten 28 A3, 33 C1
Garth 63 C1
Gartow 69 C2
Gartz 70 B1/2
Garvão 170 A1
Garve 54 A/B2
Garvín 160 A3, 166 B1
Garwolin 73 C3, 97 C1, 98 A1/2
Garzyn 71 D3
Gasa 15 D3
Gåsborn 39 C3
Gåsbu 32 B3, 37 C1
Gaschurn 106 B1
Gascueña 161 D3
Gåsenstugan 34 A2
Gåsholma 40 B2
Gaskashytta 10 A2
Gaskeluokt 15 D3
Gasny 87 C1
Gaspoltshofen 93 C2
Gassano 114 A2, 116 A1
Gasselsdorf 127 C1/2
Gasselte 67 C2
Gássino Torinese 113 C1
Gässjön 30 A3, 35 C2
Gasteiz/Vitoria 153 D2
Gasteren 67 C2
Gastoúni 146 A2
Gastoúrion 142 A3
Gata de Gorgos 169 D2
Gatčina 74 B1
Gatehouse of Fleet 56 B3, 60 A1
Gateshead 57 D3, 61 C1
Gateshead 54 B3
Gátova 162 B3, 169 D1
Gattendorf 94 B3
Gatteo al Mare 115 C/D2, 117 C1
Gattières 112 B2/3
Gattinara 105 C3
Gau-Algesheim 80 B3
Gaucín 172 A3
Gaukheihytta 42 B2
Gau-Odernheim 80 B3
Gaupne 36 B2
Gausdal 37 D2
Gautefall 43 C2
Gautelishytta 9 D3
Gauting 92 A2/3
Gautsbu 32 B3, 37 C1
Gautsjø 32 B3, 37 C1
Gavà 156 A3
Gavaloú 146 B1/2
Gavardo 106 B3
Gavarnie 155 C2
Gavi 113 D1
Gavião 164 B1
Gavirate 105 D3
Gävle 40 B2
Gavnø 53 D1/2
Gavoi 123 D2
Gavorrano 114 B3, 116 A2/3
Gavrákia 146 B1
Gavray 86 A/B1
Gávrion 149 C2
Gávros 143 B/C2
Gavsele 30 B2, 35 D1
Gävunda 39 C2
Gaweinstal 94 B2
Gawroniec 71 C1
Gåxsjö 29 D3, 35 B/C1
Gazoldo degli Ippóliti 106 B3
Gázoros 144 B1
Gazzuolo 114 B1
Gbelce 95 D3
Gdańsk (Danzig) 73 B/C2
Gdov 74 B1
Gdynia 72 B2
Gea de Albarracín 163 C2
Geaune 108 B2/3, 154 B1
Geay 101 C1
Gebhardshain-Elkenroth 80 B2
Gebhardshain 80 B2
Gebra 81 D1
Gebra 81 D1
Gedern 81 C2
Gedinne 79 C3
Gedney Drove End 61 D3, 65 C1
Gèdre 155 C2
Gedser 53 D2
Gedsted 48 B2
Gedved 48 B3
Geel 79 C1
Geertruidenberg 66 B3
Geeste 67 D2
Geeste-Dalum 67 C/D2
Geeste-Gross-Hespe 67 C/D2
Geeste-Osterbrock 67 D2
Geesthacht 68 B1
Gefell 82 A2
Géfira 143 D1/2
Gefíria 143 D3
Gefrees 82 A3
Gehrden 68 B3
Gehren 81 D2, 82 A2
Geijersholm 39 C3
Geilenkirchen 79 D1/2
Geilo 37 C3
Geiranger 32 A3, 36 B1
Geisa 81 C/D2
Geiselhöring 92 B2
Geiselwind 81 D3
Geisenfeld 92 A2
Geisenhausen 92 B2
Geisenheim 80 B3
Geising 83 C2
Geisingen 90 B3
Geislingen 91 C2
Geisnes 28 B1
Geistthal 127 C1
Geitastrand 28 A3, 33 C1/2
Geiterygghytta 37 C3
Geithain 82 B1
Geithus 43 D1

Gejuelo del Barro **159** D2
Gela **125** C3
Geldermalsen **66** B3
Geldern **79** D1
Geldrop **79** C1
Geleen **79** D1/2
Gelenau **82** B2
Gelibolu **149** C/D1
Gelida **156** A3
Gellershausen **81** C1
Gel'm'azov **99** D2
Gelnhausen **81** C2/3
Gelsa **162** B1
Gelse **128** A2
Gelsenkirchen **80** A1
Gelsted **52** B1
Geltendorf **91** D2, **92** A2
Gelting **52** B2
Gema **159** D1
Gembloux **79** C2
Gemenc **129** C2
Gémenos **111** D3
Gemert **79** C/D1
Gémir **109** D2
Gemla **51** C1/2
Gemona del Friuli **126** A2
Gémozac **100** B3
Gemünden **81** C2
Gemünden **80** A3
Gemünden am Main **81** C3
Gemünden am Main-Wernfeld **81** C3
Gemünden-Ehringshausen **81** C2
Gemuño **160** A2
Genarp **50** B3
Génave **168** A3
Genazzano **118** B2
Gençay **101** C2
Gendrey **89** C3, **104** A1
Gendringen **67** C3
Génelard **103** C1/2
Genemuiden **67** C2
Generalski Stol **127** C3, **130** B1
General-Toševo **141** C/D2
Genestoso **151** C/D1/2
Genêts **85** D1/2
Genevad **50** A2
Genève **104** A2
Gengenbach **90** B2
Génicourt-sur-Meuse **89** C1
Genillé **87** B/C3, **101** D1
Genk **79** C1/2
Genlis **89** B/C3, **103** D1
Gennep **67** B/C3
Genner **52** B2
Gennes **86** A3
Gennes-sur-Glaize **86** A3
Genola **112** B1/2
Génolhac **110** B2
Genouilly **103** C1
Génova **113** D2
Génova-Dória **113** D2
Génova-Nervi **113** D2
Génova-Pegli **113** D2
Génova-Voltri **113** C/D2
Gensingen **80** B3
Gent **78** B1
Genthin **69** D2/3
Gentioux **102** A2/3
Genzano di Lucánia **120** B2
Genzano di Roma **118** B2
Geolooginen tutkimusasema **12** B1
Georgenthal **81** D2
Georgítsion **146** B3
Georgsheil **67** D1
Georgsmarienhütte **67** D3
Gepatschhaus **106** B1
Ger **108** B3, **155** C1
Ger **108** B3, **155** C1
Ger **86** A1/2
Ger **156** A2
Gera **82** B2
Geraardsbergen **78** B2
Gerabronn **91** C1
Gerace **122** A3
Gerakaroú **144** A2
Gerakiní **144** A2
Gerakiní **148** B1
Gera Lário **105** D2, **106** A2
Gérardmer **89** D2, **90** A2/3
Geras **94** A2
Gerb **155** C/D3, **163** C1
Gerbéviller **89** D2
Gerbini **125** C2
Gerbstedt **69** C/D3, **82** A1
Gerca **98** B3
Gerdau **69** B/C2
Gereméas **123** D3
Gerena **171** D1
Geretsried **92** A3
Gérgal **173** D2
Gergei **123** D3
Gerhardshofen-Birnbaum **81** D3
Geria **158** A3
Gerichshain **82** B1
Gerindote **160** B3, **167** C1
Geringswalde **82** B1
Gerlé **109** C3, **155** C1/2
Gerlos **107** C1
Germaringen **91** D3
Germay **89** C2
Germering-Unterpfaffenhofen **92** A2
Germersheim **90** B1
Germigny-des-Prés **87** D3
Germont **79** C3
Gernay-la-Ville **87** C1/2
Gernika Lumo **153** D1
Gernrode **69** C3
Gernsbach **90** B2
Gernsheim **80** B3
Gerola Alta **106** A2
Geroldsbach-Strobenried **92** A2
Geroldsgrün **82** A2
Geroldstein **80** B3
Gerolimín **148** B3
Gerolzhofen **81** D3
Geroplátanos **142** B2/3
Gerovo **127** B/C3
Gerri de la Sal **155** D2
Gersau **105** C/D1
Gersfeld **81** C/D2
Gersheim **89** D1, **90** A1
Gersten **67** D2
Gerstetten **91** C/D2
Gersthofen **91** D2
Gerstungen **81** D2
Gerswalde **70** A/B1/2
Gerthausen **81** D2
Gerwisch **69** D3
Gerzen (Vilsbiburg) **92** B2
Gescher **67** C3
Geseke **68** A3, **80** B1
Gésera **154** B2
Geslau **91** D1
Gessertshausen **91** D2
Gestalgar **169** C1
Gesté **85** D3, **100** B1
Gesten **48** B3, **52** B1
Gesualdo **119** D3, **120** A2
Gesunda **39** C/D2
Geta **41** C2
Getafe **160** B3
Getan **29** C3, **34** A/B1
Getan **29** C3, **34** B1
Getaria **153** D1
Getbo **39** D3
Getinge **49** D2, **50** A1/2
Getinge **72** A1
Gettorf **52** B2/3
Getxo **153** C1
Gevelsberg **80** A1
Gevgelija **139** C3, **143** D1
Gevrey-Chambertin **88** B3, **103** D1
Gex **104** A2
Geyer **82** B2
Gföhl **94** A2
Ghedi **106** B3
Gheorghe Georghiu-Dej **141** C1
Gheorghieni **141** C1
Gherla **97** D3, **140** B1
Ghiffa **105** D2
Ghigo **112** B1
Ghilarza **123** C2
Ghirla **105** D2/3
Ghislarengo **105** C3
Ghisonaccia **113** D3
Ghisoni **113** D3
Ghyvelde **78** A1
Giáltra **147** C1
Giâmos **33** D2
Giannitsá **143** D1
Giants Ring **56** A3
Giardinetto **120** A1/2
Giardini-Náxos **125** D2
Giarole **113** C1
Giarratana **125** C3
Giarre **125** D2
Giat **102** A/B2/3
Giaveno **112** B1
Giazza **107** C3
Giba **123** C3
Gibellina **124** A2
Gibostad **9** D1
Gibraleón **171** C1/2
Gibraltar **172** A3
Gic **95** C3, **128** B1
Gic **96** B3
Gideå **31** C2/3
Giebelstadt **81** C/D3
Gieboldehausen **81** D1
Giekerk **66** B1
Gielow **69** D1, **70** A1
Gien **87** D3
Giengen **91** D2
Giens **112** A3
Gières **104** A3, **112** A1
Giessen **80** B2
Giessübel **81** D2, **82** A2
Gieten **67** C2
Giethoorn **67** C2
Gievnjegoikka **5** C3, **11** C1
Giffaumont **88** B2
Gifford **57** C2
Gifhorn **69** C2
Gifhorn-Kästorf **69** C2
Gifhorn-Wilsche **69** B/C2
Gif-sur-Yvette **85** C1/2
Gige **128** A/B2
Gigean **110** B3
Gigen **140** B2
Gíglio Porto **116** A3
Gignac **110** B2/3
Gijón **151** D1, **152** A1
Gil **155** D2
Gilău **97** D3, **140** B1
Gildeskål **14** B1
Gilena **172** A2
Gillberga **45** C1
Gilleleje **49** D3, **50** A2
Gilleleje **72** A1
Gillenfeld **80** A3
Gillhovs Kapell **34** B2
Gillingham **63** D2
Gillingham **65** C3, **77** C1
Gillstad **45** C2
Gilserberg **81** C2
Gilserberg-Moischeid **81** C2
Gimat **109** C2
Gimdalen **30** A3, **35** C2
Gimigliano **122** B2
Gimileo **153** C/D2
Gimnón **147** C2/3
Gimo **40** B3
Gimont **109** C2/3, **155** C/D1
Gimsøy **8** B2
Ginasservis **111** D2/3, **112** A3
Ginestar **163** C2
Ginestra degli Schiavoni **119** D2/3, **120** A2
Ginosa **121** C2
Ginostra **125** D1
Gioi **120** A3
Gióia dei Marsi **119** C2
Gióia del Colle **121** C2
Gióia Sannítica **119** D2/3
Gióia Táuro **122** A3
Gioiosa Iónica **122** B3
Gioiosa Marea **125** C1/2
Giornico **105** D2
Giovinazzo **121** B/C2, **136** A3
Gîrbovu **135** D1
Girecourt-sur-Durbion **89** D2
Girifalco **122** B2
Gîrnic **135** C1
Giromagny **89** D3, **90** A3
Girona/Gerona **156** B2
Gironella **156** A2
Gironnville-sous-les-Côtes **89** C1
Girvan **56** B2
Girvan **54** A3, **55** D2
Gisburn **59** D1, **60** B2
Gisira Pagana **125** C3
Gislaved **50** B1
Gislaved **72** A1
Gislev **53** C1/2
Gisløy **9** B/C1
Gisors **77** D3, **87** C1
Gisselås **29** D3, **35** C1
Gisselfeld **53** D1
Gissi **119** D2
Gisslarbo **39** D3, **40** A3, **46** B1
Gissträsk **31** C1
Gistad **46** B2
Gistain **155** C2
Gistel **78** A1
Gistrup **48** B1/2
Giswil **105** C1
Gíthion **148** B3
Gittelde **68** B3
Giubega **135** D2
Giubega **140** B2
Giulești **140** B2
Giulianova **119** C1
Giurgeni **141** C/D2
Giurgiu **141** C2
Giussano **105** D3, **106** A3
Give **48** B3, **52** B1
Givet **79** C2/3
Givors **103** D3
Givry **78** B2
Givry **103** D1
Givry-en-Argonne **88** B1
Givskud **48** B3, **52** B1
Gizdavac **131** C/D3
Gizeux **86** B3
Giżycko (Lötzen) **73** C2
Gizzeria **122** A2
Gizzeria Lido **122** A2
Gjælen **14** B1
Gjæsingen **28** B2
Gjendebu **37** C2
Gjendesheim **37** C2
Gjengedal **36** A2
Gjengstøa **32** B1
Gjerdvik **36** A2
Gjerlev **48** B2
Gjermundshamn **42** A1
Gjern **48** B2/3
Gjerrild **49** C2
Gjerstad **43** C2
Gjersvik **29** C1
Gjesås **38** B2
Gjestal **42** A2
Gjesvær **5** D1
Gjevillvasshytta **33** C2
Gjeving **43** C/D3, **44** A2
Gjirokaster **142** A2
Gjirokaster **148** A1
Gjøl **48** B1
Gjølme **28** A3, **33** C2
Gjøra **32** B3
Gjorslev **50** A3, **53** D1
Gjøvdal **43** C2
Gjøvik **38** A2
Gjøvik **9** D1
Gjueševo **139** C2
Gjueševo **140** A/B3
Gla (Arne) **147** C2
Gladdenstedt **69** C2
Gladenbach **80** B2
Gladstad **14** A3
Glaisin **69** C1
Glamis **57** C1
Glamis Castle **57** C1
Glamoč **131** D2, **132** A2
Glamsbjerg **52** B1
Glandieu **104** A3
Glan-Münchweiler **80** A3, **90** A1
Glanshammar **46** B1
Glarus **105** D1, **106** A1
Glasgow **56** B2
Glasgow **54** B2/3, **55** D1
Glashütte **83** C2
Glashütten **127** C1
Glassdrummond **58** A1
Glastonbury **63** D2
Glauchau **82** B2
Glava **45** C1
Glava Glasbruk **45** C1
Glavanovci **139** C1
Glavatičevo **132** B3
Glavnik **138** B1
Gledić **134** B3
Gleđica **133** D3, **134** A3
Gleichen-Bremke **81** D1
Glein **14** A2
Gleina **82** A1
Gleinstätten **127** C1
Gleisdorf **127** C/D1
Gleisdorf **96** A3
Gleissenberg **92** B1
Glen **34** A/B2
Glenariffe **56** A3
Glenarm **56** A3
Glenbarr **56** A2
Glencoe **56** A/B1
Glencolumbkille **55** C2
Glendalough **58** A2
Glenluce **56** B3
Glenrothes **57** C1
Glenties **55** C2
Gleschendorf **53** C3
Glesne **43** D1
Gletsch **105** C2
Glienicke **70** B3
Glífa **147** C1
Glífa **148** B2
Glifáda **148** B2
Glifáda **147** D2
Glikí **142** B3
Glimåkra **50** B2
Glimminge **50** B2
Glimmingehus **50** B3
Glina **127** D3, **131** C1
Glinka **71** D3
Glissjöberg **34** B3
Glitterheim **37** C2
Gliwice (Gleiwitz) **96** B2
Globino **99** D3
Globočica **138** B2
Glod'any **99** B/C3
Gloggnitz **94** A3
Glogovac **138** B1
Glogovica **135** C2
Glogovnica **127** D2
Głogów (Glogau) **71** C/D3
Głogów (Glogau) **96** A/B1
Glomfjord **14** B1
Glommen **49** D2, **50** A1
Glommen **72** A1
Glommersträsk **16** A3
Glömminge **51** D2
Glonn **92** A3
Glória **164** A/B2
Glösa **29** C/D3, **34** B1/2
Gløshaug **29** B/C2
Glos-la-Ferrière **86** B1
Glóssa **147** D1
Glössbo **40** A1
Glossop **59** D2, **61** B/C3
Glöte **34** A3
Gløtleger **33** C3, **37** D1
Glottertal **90** B2/3
Gløtvola **33** D3
Gloucester **63** D1, **64** A2
Glöwen **69** D2
Gložan **129** C3, **133** C1
Głubczyce (Leobschütz) **96** B2
Glubokoe **74** B3
Głuchowo **71** D3
Glücksburg **52** B2
Glückstadt **52** B3, **68** B1
Glud **48** B3, **52** B1
Gluggvatnet **14** B3
Gluha Bukovica **132** A/B2
Gluhov **99** D1/2
Glumsø **53** D1
Glun **111** C1
Glušci **133** C1
Glusk **99** C1
Glyngøre **48** A2
Glynn **56** A3
Glypha **146** B2
Gmünd **126** A/B1
Gmünd **93** D2
Gmünd **96** A2
Gmund am Tegernsee **92** A3
Gmunden **93** C3
Gmunden **96** A3
Gnarp **35** D3
Gnarrenburg-Kuhstedt **68** A1
Gnarrenburg-Karlshöfen **68** A1
Gnarrenburg **68** A1
Gnas **127** D1
Gnesta **47** C1
Gnevsdorf **69** D1
Gniew **73** B/C2/3
Gniezno **72** B3
Gnisvärd **47** C/D3
Gnjilane **138** B2
Gnjilane **140** A3
Gnocchetta **115** C1
Gnoien **53** D3
Gnosjö **50** B1

Goathland 61 D1
Goatteluobbal 10 B1/2
Goč 134 B3
Goce Delčev 140 B3
Goch 67 C3, 79 D1
Gochsheim 81 D3
Göd 95 D3
Göda 83 D1
Godall 162 B2
Godalming 64 B3, 76 B1
Godby 41 C/D3
Godeč 139 D1
Godeč 140 B3
Godegård 46 A2
Godejord 29 C2
Godelleta 169 C1
Goderville 77 C3
Godiascò 113 D1
Godisa 128 B2
Godmanchester 65 B/C2
Gödöllő 97 C3
Godovič 126 B2
Gödre 128 B2
Godshill 76 B2
Godstone 65 C3, 76 B1
Godus 133 C2
Goes 78 B1
Góglio 105 C2
Gogolewo 71 C1
Göhlsdorf 69 D2/3, 70 A2/3
Göhrde 69 C2
Göhren 82 B2
Goirle 79 C1
Góis 158 A/B3
Góito 106 B3
Goizueta 153 D1, 154 A1
Gojan i Epërm 138 A2
Gokels 52 B3
Göksholm 46 B1
Gol 37 C/D3
Golå 37 D2
Gola 128 A2
Golada 150 B2
Gołańcz 71 D2
Gölby 41 C/D3
Golchen 70 A1
Golczewo 71 B/C1
Gołdap 73 C/D2
Goldbach 81 D1/2
Goldbeck 69 D2
Goldberg 69 D1
Goldelund 52 B2
Goldenbaum 70 A1
Goldenstedt 68 A2
Golegã 164 B1
Golemo Selo 139 C1
Golenice 70 B2
Goleniów (Gollnow) 70 B1
Goleniów (Gollnow) 72 A3
Golfe Juan 112 B3
Golfo Aranci 123 D1
Gölle 128 B2
Göllersdorf 94 A/B2
Gollhofen 81 D3, 91 D1
Gollin 70 A2
Golling an der Salzach 93 C3
Göllingen 81 D1, 82 A1
Gollmitz 70 A/B1
Gollonboc 142 B1
Golmayo 153 D3, 161 D1
Golmés 155 D3, 163 D1
Golpejas 159 D2
Golssen 70 A3
Golubac 135 B/C2
Golubac 140 A2
Golubinći 133 D1, 134 A1
Golubinja 132 B2
Golubovec 127 D2
Golzow 69 D3
Golzow 70 B2
Golzow 70 B2
Gomadingen 91 C2
Gomagoi 106 B2
Gómara 153 D3, 161 D1
Gomaringen 91 C2
Gombrén 156 A2
Gomel' 99 C/D1
Gomesende 150 B3
Gomeznarro 161 C1
Gomezserracín 160 B1
Gommern 69 D3
Gomolava 133 C/D1, 134 A1
Gompertshausen 81 D2
Gomphoi 143 C3
Gonçalo Bocas 159 B/C2
Goncelin 104 A3
Gondelsheim 90 B1
Gondershausen 80 A3
Gondifelos 158 A1
Gondo [Brig] 105 C2
Gondomar 158 A1/2
Gondomar 150 A3
Gondrecourt-le-Château 89 C2
Gönen 149 D1
Gonesse 87 D1
Gonfaron 112 A3
Goni 123 D3
Gonnesa 123 C3
Gönnheim 90 B1
Gónni 143 D3
Gonnord 86 A3, 100 B1
Gónnos 143 D3
Gonnosfanádiga 123 C3
Gonnosnó 123 C2/3
Gontinhães 150 A3, 158 A1
Gönyű 95 C3
Gonzaga 114 B1
Goodwood House 76 B1
Goole 61 C2
Goor 67 C3
Göpfritz an der Wild 94 A2
Goppenstein 105 C2
Göppingen 91 C2
Goppollen 38 A1
Gopshus 39 C2
Gor 173 D2
Góra 71 D3
Gora 127 D3, 131 C1
Goračići 133 D2/3, 134 A3
Gorafe 173 C/D1
Goraiolo 114 B2, 116 A1/2
Goraiolo 114 B2, 116 A1
Góra Kalwaria 73 C3, 97 C1
Goražde 133 C3
Görcsöny 128 B2/3
Gördalen 38 B1
Gordaliza del Pino 152 A2
Gordes 111 D2
Gördes 149 D2
Górdola 105 D2
Gordon 57 C2
Gordona 105 D2, 106 A2
Gordoncillo 152 A3
Gordoxola 153 C1
Gorebridge 57 C2
Gorey 63 D3, 85 C1
Gorey 58 A3
Gorga 169 D2
Gorga 118 B2
Gorges de Daluis 112 B2
Gorges de Galamus 156 B1
Gorges de Kakouetta 108 A/B3, 154 B1
Gorges de l'Asco 113 D2/3
Gorges de l'Ardèche 111 C2
Gorges de la Restonica 113 D3
Gorges du Daoulas 84 B2
Gorges du Fier 104 A2/3
Gorges du Lot 110 A1
Gorges du Toul Gonlic 84 B2
Gorges Supérieures du Cians 112 B2
Görgeteg 128 A2
Gorgómilos 142 B3
Gorgonzola 105 D3, 106 A3
Gorgopótamos 147 B/C1
Gorica 130 B2
Gorica 131 D3, 132 A3
Goričan 127 D2, 128 A2
Goriče 126 B2
Goricy 75 D2
Gorinchem 66 B3
Goring 65 C3
Gorino Ferrarese 115 C1
Göritz 69 D3
Göritz 70 B1
Gorízia 126 A/B2
Gorki 75 C3
Gorleben 69 C2
Gorleston 65 D1/2
Gørlev 49 C3, 53 C1
Gorlice 97 C2
Görlitz 96 A1
Görlitz 83 D1
Gormaz 153 C3, 161 C1
Gorna Koznica 139 D2
Gorni Cibâr 135 D3
Gornja Briska 137 D2
Gornja Bukovica 133 C/D2, 134 A2
Gornja Čadjavica 133 C1
Gornjak 134 B2
Gornja Klina 138 B1
Gornja Ljubovida 133 C2
Gornja Ljuta 132 B3
Gornjane 135 C2
Gornja Radgona 127 D2
Gornja Radgona 96 A3
Gornja Stubičke Toplice 127 D2
Gornja Toplica-Vrujci 133 D2, 134 A2
Gornja Trepča 133 D2, 134 A2/3
Gornja Tuzla 133 B/C2
Gornje Gadimlje 138 B2
Gornje Jelenje 127 B/C3, 130 B1
Gornje Morakovo 137 D1
Gornje Zimlje 132 B3
Gornji Banjani 133 D2, 134 A2
Gornji Grad 127 C2
Gornji Hrgovi 132 B1
Gornji Klasnić 127 D3, 131 C1
Gornji Kneginec 127 D2
Gornji Kokoti 137 D2
Gornji Komarevo 127 D3, 131 C1
Gornji Kosinj 130 B1/2
Gornji Lapac 131 C2
Gornji Malovan 131 D2/3, 132 A2
Gornji Milanovac 133 D2, 134 A2
Gornji Podgradci 131 D1, 132 A1
Gornji Ribnik 131 D2, 132 A2
Gornji Šeher 131 D1, 132 A1
Gornji Vakuf 132 A2
Gornji Žabar 132 B1
Gorno Nerezi 138 B2
Goro 115 C1
Gorodec 98 B2
Gorodenka 98 B3
Gorodišče 99 D3
Gorodnja 99 D1/2
Gorodok 98 B3
Gorodok 97 D2, 98 A2/3
Gorohov 97 D1, 98 B2
Górowo Iławeckie (Landsberg) 73 C2
Gorredijk-Kortezwaag 67 C2
Gorron 86 A2
Gorsium 128 B1
Gorssel 67 C3
Gortyn 146 B3
Görvik 30 A2/3, 35 C1
Görzke 69 D3
Górzna 71 D1
Gorzów Wielkopolski (Landsberg) 71 C2
Gorzów Wielkopolski (Landsberg) 72 A3
Górzyca 70 B2
Gorzyń 71 C2
Gosaldo 107 C2
Gosau 93 C3
Göschenen 105 D1/2
Goscikowo 71 C3
Gościm 71 C2
Gosdorf 127 D1/2
Gosforth 59 C1, 60 A1
Gösing an der Mariazellerbahn 94 A3
Goslar 69 B/C3
Goslar-Hahndorf 69 B/C3
Goslar-Hahnenklee 68 B3
Goslar-Oker 69 B/C3
Gospić 130 B2
Gospođinci 129 D3
Gosport 76 B1
Gossa 69 D3, 82 B1
Gössäter 45 D2
Gossau 91 C3
Gössenheim 81 C3
Gössl 93 C3
Gössnitz 82 B2
Gössweinstein 82 A3
Gössweinstein-Behringersmüle 82 A3
Gostivar 138 B2/3
Gostivar 140 A3
Göstling an der Ybbs 96 A3
Göstling an der Ybbs 93 D3
Gostomia 71 D1/2
Gostyń 71 D3
Gostyń 72 B3, 96 B1
Goszczanowo 71 C2
Göta 45 C3
Götafors 50 B1
Göteborg 45 C3
Göteborg 72 A1
Götene 45 D2
Gotha 81 D2
Gothem 47 D3
Gotlunda 46 B1
Gottby 41 C3
Gotthun 69 D1, 70 A1
Göttingen 81 C/D1
Gottlob 129 D2/3
Gottne 30 B3
Gottröra 40 B3
Gottsbüren 81 C1
Gottwaldov 95 C1
Gottwaldov 96 B2
Götzendorf an der Leitha 94 B3
Götzis 91 C3, 106 A1
Gouarec 84 B2
Gouda 66 A3
Goudargues 111 C2
Gouesnou 84 A2
Gouffre de Padirac 109 D1
Goulaine 86 A/B3, 101 C1
Gouméi 146 B2
Gouménissa 143 D1
Goumois 89 D3, 104 B1
Gouneau 109 C2
Goúra 147 B/C2
Gourdon 108 B1
Gourin 84 B2
Gournay 87 D1
Gournay-en-Bray 77 D3
Gournay-sur-Aronde 78 A3
Gourock 56 B1/2
Gouveia 158 B2
Gouveias 159 B/C2
Gouviá 142 A3
Gouvinhas 158 B1/2
Gouzon 102 A2
Govedarci 139 D2
Govedari 136 B1
Govérnolo 114 B1
Goviller 89 C2
Goyatz 70 B3
Gozd 126 B2
Gozdnica 83 D1
Gozdowice 70 B2
Gozée 78 B2
Gozón 151 D1
Gozzano 105 C/D3
Grab 133 C3, 137 D1
Grab 137 C2
Gräben 69 D3
Graben-Neudorf 90 B1
Grabenstätt 92 B3
Gråbo 45 C3
Gråborg 51 D2
Grabovac 131 D3, 132 A3
Grabovac 133 D1/2, 134 A2
Grabovci 133 D1, 134 A1
Grabovica 135 C2
Grabovica 131 D3, 132 A3
Grabow 69 C1
Grabowhöfe 69 D1, 70 A1
Grabowno 71 D1/2
Grabrovnica 128 A2/3
Gračac 131 C2
Gračac 134 B3
Graça do Divor 164 B2
Gračanica 138 B1/2
Gračanica 132 B1
Gračanica 133 C2
Graçay 102 A1
Grad 127 D1
Gradac 132 A3, 136 B1
Gradac 133 D3, 134 A3
Gradac 133 C3
Gradačac 132 B1
Građani 137 D2
Gradara 115 D2, 117 C1
Graddis fjellstue 15 C1
Gräddö 41 C3
Gradec 127 D2/3
Gradec 135 D2
Gradefes 152 A2
Grades 126 B1
Gradevo 139 D2
Gradignan 108 B1
Grădinari 135 B/C1
Gradine 139 D1
Gradisca d'Isonzo 126 A2/3
Gradišče 127 D2
Gradište 128 B3
Gradište 133 B/C1
Gradište 139 C2
Gradižsk 99 D3
Grado 126 A3
Grado 151 D1
Grádoli 116 B3, 118 A1
Gradsko 139 C3
Gradskovo 135 C2
Graena 173 C2
Gräfelfing 92 A2/3
Grafenau 93 C1/2
Grafenau-Haus 93 C2
Gräfenberg 82 A3
Gräfenhainichen 69 D3
Grafenhausen 90 B3
Grafenrheinfeld 81 D3
Gräfenroda 81 D2
Grafenschlag 93 D2, 94 A2
Gräfentonna 81 D1
Grafenwöhr 82 A/B3
Graffer 32 B3, 37 C1
Grafing 92 A/B2/3
Gräfsnäs 45 C3
Gráglia 105 C3
Gragnano 119 D3
Grahovo 126 B2
Grahovo 137 C1/2
Graine 65 C3
Graja de Campalbo 163 C3, 169 D1
Grajal de Campos 152 A2
Grajewo 73 D3, 98 A1
Gram 52 B1
Gramada 135 C/D3
Gramais 106 B1
Gramat 109 D1
Gramkow 53 C3
Grammatikón 147 D2
Gramméni Oxiá 146 B1
Grammichele 125 C3
Grampound 62 B3
Gramsbergen 67 C2
Gramsh 142 A/B1
Gramzow 70 B1/2
Gran 38 A2
Granabeg 58 A2
Granada 173 C2
Granås 15 C3
Granåsen 30 A2, 35 C/D1
Granátula de Calatrava 167 C2
Granberget 31 D2
Granberget 30 A1/2
Granbergsliden 16 A3
Granbergsträsk 16 A3
Granboda 41 D3
Grancey-le-Château 88 B3
Grandas de Salime 151 C1
Grandcamp-les-Bains 76 A3, 86 A1
Grand Canyon du Verdon 112 A2/3
Grand Champ 85 C3
Grand-Couronne 77 C3, 86 B1
Grand Croix 104 B3, 112 B1
Grandes Grottes 84 A2
Grand-Fougeray 85 D3
Grândola 164 B3
Grand Phare 84 B3
Grandrieu 110 B1
Grand-Rozoy 88 A1
Grands Goulets 111 D1
Grandson 104 B1
Grandvillars 89 D3, 90 A3
Grandvilliers 77 D3
Grane 14 B3
Grañén 154 B3
Granera 156 A3
Grangärde 39 D3
Grangemouth 57 B/C1/2
Grange-over-Sands 59 C/D1, 60 B2
Grängesberg 39 D3

Granges-de-Crouhens 109 C3, 155 C1/2
Granges-sur-Vologne 89 D2
Granges-sur-Aube 88 A2
Grängshyttan 39 D3
Grängsjö 35 D3
Grängsjö 40 A1
Granheim 37 C3
Granhult 51 C1
Granhult 17 C1
Granieri 125 C3
Graninge 30 A/B3, 35 D2
Gräningen 69 D2
Granítsa 146 B1
Granja 158 A2
Granja 165 C3
Granja de Iniesta 168 B1
Granja de Moreruela 151 D3, 159 D1
Granja de Torrehermosa 166 A3
Granjinha 158 B2
Grankulla 25 C3
Grankullavik 51 D1
Granliden 31 D1
Gränna 46 A3
Grannäs 15 C3
Grannäs 15 D3
Granollers 156 A3
Grañón 153 C2
Granön 31 C2
Granön 29 D2, 30 A1
Granschütz 82 B1
Granschütz-Grimma 82 B1
Gransee 70 A2
Gransee 72 A3
Gränsgård 15 D3
Gransherad 43 C1, 44 A1
Gransjö 30 A3, 35 D2
Gransjö 30 B1
Gransjö 16 B2
Gransjön 38 B2/3
Gransjöriset 30 B1
Gränssjö 15 B/C3
Grantham 61 D3, 64 B1
Grantown-on-Spey 54 B2
Granträsk 17 C2
Granträsk 16 B3
Granträskmark 16 B3
Grantshouse 57 D2
Granvik 24 B3
Granvika 33 D3
Granville 85 D1
Granvin 36 B3
Granyena de les Garrigues 155 C3, 163 C1
Grao de Sagunto 162 B3, 169 D1
Grasbakken 7 C2
Gräsberg 39 D3
Grasellenbach-Wahlen 81 C3
Gräsgård 51 D2
Grasleben 69 C3
Grasleben-Twülpstedt 69 C2/3
Gräslotten 29 C3, 34 A/B1
Gräsmark 38 B3
Grasmere 57 C3, 60 B1
Gräsmyr 31 C2
Gräsö 40 B2
Grassano 120 B2
Grassau 92 B3
Grasse 112 B3
Gråssjö 35 C2
Græsted 49 D3, 50 A2
Gråsten 52 B2
Grästorp 45 C2
Gratangen 9 D2
Gratens 109 C3, 155 D1
Gråtneset 14 B2
Gråträsk 16 A3
Gratteri 124 B2
Gratwein 127 C1
Graulhet 109 D2
Graus 155 C2/3
Graustein 83 D1
Grautheller 42 B2
Grávalos 153 D3, 154 A3
Gravanes 32 A3, 36 B1
Gravberget 38 B2
Gravdal 8 B2
Gravdal 42 A3
Grave 66 B3
Gravedona 105 D2, 106 A2
Gravéggia 105 C/D2
Graveide 43 C1
Gravelines 77 D1
Gravellona Toce 105 C/D2/3
Gravelotte 89 C1
Gravendal 39 C/D3
Grävenwiesbach 80 B2
Gravesend 65 C3
Gravfjorden 14 A3, 29 B/C1
Graviá 147 C1
Gråvika 36 A3
Gravina di Catánia 125 D2
Gravina in Púglia 120 B2
Gravmark 20 A1, 31 D2
Gravoúna 145 C1
Gray 89 C3
Grayan-et-l'Hôpital 100 B3
Grays 65 C3
Graz 127 C1
Graz 96 A3
Grazalema 172 A2
Grčarice 127 C3
Grdelica 139 C1
Gréalou 109 D1
Great Ayton 61 C1
Great Driffield 61 D2
Great Dunmow 65 C2/3
Great Harwood 59 D1, 60 B2
Great Malvern 63 D1, 64 A2
Great Missenden 64 B3
Great Rowsley 61 C3, 64 A1
Great Shelford 65 C2
Great Torrington 63 B/C2
Great Witley 59 D3, 64 A2
Great Yarmouth 65 D1/2
Grebbestad 44 B2
Grebenac 134 B1
Grebenau 81 C2
Grebenstein 81 C1
Gréccio 117 C3, 118 B1
Greda 127 D2
Greding 92 A1
Greding-Kraftsbuch 92 A1
Gredstedbro 52 A1
Greencastle 58 A1
Greenlaw 57 C/D2
Greenloaning 56 B1
Greenock 56 B2
Greenock 54 A2/3, 55 D1
Greenore 58 A1
Grefrath 79 D1
Grefsgård 37 C3
Gréggio 105 C3
Greifenburg 126 A1
Greifenstein-Allendorf 80 B2
Greiffenberg 70 B2
Greifswald 72 A2
Greillenstein 94 A2
Grein 93 D2
Grein 96 A2/3
Greipstad 43 B/C3
Greiz 82 B2
Gremersdorf 53 C3
Grenå 49 C2
Grenade 108 B2
Grenade-sur-l'Adour 108 B2
Grenås 29 D3, 35 C1
Grenåskilen 29 D3, 30 A2, 35 C1
Grenchen 105 B/C1
Grenier-Montgon 102 B3
Greningen 29 D3, 35 C2
Grenoble 104 A3
Grense-Jakobselv 7 D2
Gréoux-les-Bains 111 D2, 112 A2/3
Gresenhorst 53 D3
Gressåmoen 29 C2
Gresse 69 C1
Gresslivollen 33 D2
Gressoney-la Trinité 105 C3
Gressoney-Saint-Jean 105 C3
Gressvik 44 B1
Gresten 93 D3
Gretna Green 57 C3, 60 B1
Grettstadt 81 D3
Greussen 81 D1, 82 A1
Greux 89 C2
Grevbäck 45 D2, 46 A2
Greve 114 B3, 116 B2
Greven 69 C1
Greven 67 D3
Grevená 143 C2
Grevená 148 A/B1
Grevenbroich-Gustorf 79 D1, 80 A1
Grevenbroich 79 D1, 80 A1
Greveníton 142 B3
Grevenka 99 D2
Grevenmacher 79 D3
Greven-Reckenfeld 67 D3
Grevesmühlen 53 C3, 69 C1
Greve Strand 49 D3, 50 A3, 53 D1
Grevie 49 D2, 50 A2
Grey Abbey 56 A3
Greystoke 57 C3, 60 B1
Greystones 58 A2
Grez-en-Bouère 86 A2/3
Grèzes 109 D1
Grgar 126 B2
Grieben 69 D2
Griegos 162 A2
Gries 126 A1
Griesalp [Reichenbach im Kandertal] 105 C2
Gries am Brenner 107 C1
Griesbach 93 C2
Griesen 91 D3, 92 A3
Griesheim 80 B3
Gries in Sellrain 107 C1
Grieskirchen 93 C2
Griesstätt 92 B3
Griffen 127 C1/2
Grignan 111 C1/2
Grigno 107 C2
Grignols 108 B2
Grigoriopol' 141 D1
Grijó 159 C1
Grijó 158 A2
Grijota 152 B3
Grijpskerk 67 C1
Grillby 40 B3, 47 C1
Grimaldi 122 A/B2
Grimaud 112 A3
Grimdalen 43 C2
Grimentz [Sierre] 105 C2
Grime's Grave 65 C2
Grimeton 49 D1, 50 A1
Grimma 82 B1
Grimmared 49 D1, 50 A1
Grimmialp, Kurheim [Oey-Diemtigen] 105 C2
Grimsås 50 B1
Grimsbu 33 C3, 37 D1
Grimsby 61 D2/3
Grimsdalshytta 33 C3, 37 D1
Grimslöv 51 B/C2
Grimsmark 31 D1/2
Grimsmyrheden 39 C2
Grimstad 43 C3
Grimstad 32 B2
Grindaheim 37 C2
Grinde 36 B2
Grindelwald 105 C2
Grinder 38 B2
Grindheim 42 B3
Grindjord 9 D2
Grindsted 48 A3, 52 A/B1
Grinkiškis 73 D2
Grinneröd 45 C3
Griñón 160 B3
Grip 32 A/B2
Gripenberg 46 A3
Gripport 89 C2
Gripsholm 47 C1
Grisel 154 A3
Grisignano di Zocco 107 C3
Grisolles 108 B2
Grisslehamn 41 C3
Grisvåg 32 B2
Grizzana 114 B2, 116 B1
Grjaznovo 75 D3
Grljan 135 C3
Grljevac 131 D3
Grøbæk 48 B2
Gröbenzell 92 A2
Gröbers 82 B1
Grobjina 73 C1
Gröbming 93 C3
Gröbzig 69 D3, 82 A/B1
Grocka 133 D1, 134 B1/2
Grödby 47 C1
Grödig 93 B/C3
Grödinge 47 C1
Gröditsch 70 B3
Gröditz 83 C1
Grodno 73 D2/3, 98 A1
Grodzisk Mazowiecki 73 C3, 97 C1
Grodzisk Wielkopolski 71 D3
Groenlo 67 C3
Groesbeek 67 B/C3
Grohote 131 C3
Groitzsch 82 B1
Groix 84 B3
Grójec 73 C3, 97 C1
Grolanda 45 D3
Groléjac 108 B1
Grolloo 67 C2
Grömbach 90 B2
Grömitz 53 C3
Grömitz-Cismar 53 C3
Gromo Santa Maria 106 A2
Grøna 32 B3, 37 C1
Grönahög 45 D3
Gronau 67 C3
Gronau-Epe 67 C3
Gronau (Leine) 68 B3
Grönbo 16 B3
Grønbua 37 C2
Grøndal 36 A2
Grøndalen 38 A/B1
Gröndalen 33 D2, 34 A2
Grönenbach 91 D3
Grong 28 B2
Grönhögen 51 D2
Grönhögen 72 B1
Gröningen 91 C/D1
Groningen 67 C1
Gröningen 69 C3
Grønlia 14 B3
Grønligrotten 14 B2
Grønnes 32 A2
Grønningen 28 A3, 33 C1
Grono [Castione-Arbedo] 105 D2, 106 A2
Grønøysetra 33 C3, 37 D1
Grönskåra 51 C1
Grönskåra 72 B1
Grønvik 42 A2
Grönviken 35 C2
Grønvollfoss 43 C/D1, 44 A1
Groomsport 56 A3
Grootegast 67 C1
Gropello Cairoli 105 D3, 113 D1
Groppo San Giovanne 114 A1
Grorud 43 D2, 44 A1
Grosbois-en-Montagne 88 B3
Grosbreuil 100 A2
Grósio 106 B2
Grošnica 134 B2
Grossa 113 D3
Grossalmerode 81 C1
Grossalsleben 69 C3
Grossarl 126 A1
Grossbodungen 81 D1
Grossbothen 82 B1
Grossbottwar 91 C1
Gross Buchholz 69 D2
Grossdobritz 83 C1
Gross-Dölln 70 A2
Grossefehn 67 D1
Grossefehn-Bagband 67 D1
Grossefehn-Strackholt 67 D1
Grossenbrode 53 C2/3
Grossenehrich 81 D1, 82 A1
Grossengottern 81 D1
Grossenhain 83 C1
Grossenhain 96 A1
Grossenkneten 67 D2, 68 A2
Grossenkneten-Sage 67 D2, 68 A2
Grossenlüder 81 C2
Grossenlupnitz 81 D1/2
Grossensee 68 B1
Grossenstein 82 B2
Grossenwiehe 52 B2
Gross-Enzersdorf 94 B2
Grossereix 101 C2
Grosserlach 91 C1
Grosser Rachel 93 C1
Grosseto 116 B3
Grossfurra 81 D1
Gross Gastrose 70 B3
Gross-Gerau 80 B3
Gross-Gerungs 93 D2
Grosshansdorf 53 B/C3, 68 B1
Grossharthau 83 C1
Grosshartmannsdorf 83 C2
Grosshartmannsdorf 127 D1
Grossheide 67 D1
Grossheimschuh 127 C1
Grossheubach 81 C3
Grosshöchstetten 105 C1
Grosskayna 82 A/B1
Grosskirchheim 107 D1, 126 A1
Gross Köris 70 A3
Gross-Kreutz 69 D2/3, 70 A2/3
Grosskrut 94 B2
Gross-Leine 70 B3
Gross Lieskow 70 B3
Grosslittgen 79 D3, 80 A3
Grossmehring 92 A2
Gross-Miltzow 70 A1
Grossmugl 94 B2
Grossnaundorf 83 C1
Gross-Nemerow 70 A1
Gross Oesingen 69 B/C2
Gross-Ossnig 70 B3, 83 D1
Grossostheim 81 C3
Gross-Pankow 69 D2
Grosspertholz 93 D2
Grosspetersdorf 127 D1
Grossraming 93 D3
Grossräschen 83 C1
Grossreifling 93 D3
Gross Reken 67 C3
Gross Rietz 70 B3
Grossrinderfeld 81 C3
Grossröhrsdorf 83 C1
Grossrosenburg 69 D3
Grossrosseln 89 D1, 90 A1
Gross-Salitz 53 C3, 69 C1
Gross Sankt Florian 127 C1
Gross Särchen 83 C/D1
Grossschirma 83 C2
Gross Schönebeck 70 A2
Grossschönau 83 D2
Grossschweinbarth 94 B2
Gross Schwülper 69 B/C3
Gross-Siegharts 94 A2
Grosssölk 93 C3
Grosssolt 52 B2
Grossthiemig 83 C1
Gross-Umstadt 81 C3
Grosswarasdorf 94 B3
Gross Warnow 69 C1
Grossweikersdorf 94 A2
Gross-Welle 69 D2
Gross-Welzin 69 C1
Gross-Werzin 69 D2
Grosswilfersdorf 127 D1
Gross-Wittensee 52 B2/3
Gross Wokern 53 D3, 69 D1
Grosswudicke 69 D2
Gross-Ziethen 70 B2
Grostenquin 89 D1
Grosuplje 127 B/C2/3
Grøtavær 9 C1
Grøtfjord 4 A2
Grötingen 35 C2
Grotli 32 A/B3, 37 C1
Grötlingbo 47 D3
Grøtnesdalen 4 A2
Grotta Azzurra 119 C/D3
Grotta di Bossea 113 C2
Grotta di Nettuno 123 C2
Grotta di Tibério 119 C3
Grottáglie 121 C2/3
Grottaminarda 119 D3, 120 A2
Grottammare 117 D2/3
Grotta Zinzulusa 121 D3
Grotte 124 B2/3
Grotte de Clamouse 110 B2
Grotte de Dargilan 110 B2
Grotte de l'Apothicairerie 84 B3
Grotte de la Sainte Baume 111 D3
Grotte de Labouiche 109 D3, 155 D1, 156 A1

Grotte de Médous 109 B/C3, 155 C1
Grotte de Niaux 155 D2, 156 A1
Grotte de Pech Merle 109 D1
Grotte des Demoiselles 110 B2
Grotte di Catullo 106 B3
Grotte di Castro 116 B3, 118 A1
Grotte du Loup 108 B3, 155 C1
Grotteria 122 A/B3
Grotte Santo Stéfano 117 C3, 118 A1
Grottes de Bétharram 108 B3, 155 B/C1
Grottes de Crozon 84 A2
Grottes de Trabuc 110 B2
Grottes d'Oxocelhaya 108 B3, 155 C1
Grøttingen 28 A2, 33 C1
Gróttole 120 B2
Grouw 66 B1/2
Grova 40 A1
Grøvdalsbu 32 B2/3
Gröveldalsvallen 34 A3
Grövels fjellstation 34 A3
Grovfjord 9 C/D2
Grøvseter 37 C2
Grožnjan 126 B3, 130 A1
Grua 38 A3
Grubbe 40 A1
Grubbe 30 B2, 35 D1
Grubben 14 B3
Gruben 33 D3
Grubišno Polje 128 A3
Grubo 69 D3
Gruda 137 C2
Grude 131 D3, 132 A3
Grudovo 141 C3
Grudziądz 73 B/C3
Grue Finnskog 38 B2
Gruffelingen 79 D2
Gruissan 110 B3, 156 B1
Gruja 135 D2
Grumbach 83 C1/2
Grumento Nova 120 B3
Grumo Áppula 121 C2
Grums 45 C/D1
Grünau im Almtal 93 C3
Grünbach am Schneeberg 94 A3
Grünberg 81 C2
Grünburg 93 D3
Grundagssätern 34 A3
Grundfors 15 C3, 29 D1
Grundfors 30 B1
Grundforsen 38 B1
Grundsjö 35 C3
Grundsjö 30 A2
Grundsund 44 B3
Grundsunda 31 C3
Grundsunda 41 D3
Grundtjärn 30 B3, 35 D1
Grundträsk 16 B3
Grundträsk 16 A3
Grundträsk 16 A3
Grundträskliden 16 A3
Grundvattnet 16 B2/3
Grüneberg 70 A2
Grünendeich 68 B1
Grünewald 83 C1
Grünewalde 83 C1
Grungedal 42 B1
Grünhain 82 B2
Grünheide 70 B2/3
Grünkraut 90 A3
Grunnfarnes 9 C1
Grunnfjord 4 A2
Grunnførfjorden 8 B2
Grunow 70 B3
Grünsfeld 81 C3
Grünstadt 80 B3, 90 B1
Grüntal 70 A/B2
Gruomba 15 D1/2
Grupčin 138 B2
Grutness 54 A1
Gruvberget 40 A1/2
Gruyères 104 B2
Gruža 134 B2/3
Grycksbo 39 D2
Gryfice 72 A/B2
Gryfino 72 A3
Gryfino 70 B1
Gryllefjord 9 C1

Grymyr 38 A2/3
Grynberget 30 A2
Gryt 47 C2/3
Gryta 32 B1
Gryte 28 B3, 33 D1
Grytgöl 46 B2
Grythyttan 39 C/D3
Grytnäs 47 C2
Grytsjö 29 D1
Grytstorp 46 B2
Grzebienisko 71 D2
Grzmiąca 71 D1
Gschwend 91 C1
Gstaad 104 B2
Gsteig b. Gstaad [Gstaad] 104 B2
Guadahortuna 173 C1
Guadalajara 161 C2
Guadalaviar 162 A2/3
Guadalcanal 166 A3
Guadalcázar 172 A1
Guadalest 169 D2
Guadalix de la Sierra 161 B/C2
Guadalmez 166 B2
Guadalmina 172 A3
Guadalupe 166 B1
Guadamur 160 B3, 167 C1
Guadarrama 160 B2
Guadix 173 C2
Guagno 113 D3
Guájar Alto 173 C2
Gualachulain 56 A/B1
Gualchos 173 C2
Gualda 161 D2
Gualdo Tadino 115 D3, 117 C2
Gualtieri 114 B1
Guarcino 119 C2
Guarda 158 B2
Guardamar del Segura 169 C3, 174 B1
Guardamíglio 113 D1, 114 A1
Guardas Viejas 173 D2
Guardavalle 122 B3
Guardea 117 C3, 118 A/B1
Guárdia 120 A2
Guardia de Ares 155 C2
Guardia de Noguera 155 D3
Guardiagrele 119 C/D1
Guardialfiera 119 D2, 120 A1
Guárdia Perticara 120 B3
Guárdia Sanframondi 119 D2/3
Guardiola de Berga 156 A2
Guardistallo 114 B3, 116 A2
Guardo 152 A2
Guareña 165 D2, 166 A2
Guarrate 159 D1, 160 A1
Guarromán 167 C/D3
Guasa 154 B2
Guasila 123 D3
Guastalla 114 B1
Gúbbio 115 D3, 117 C2
Gubbträsk 15 D3
Guberevac 134 B3
Gubin 70 B3
Gubin 72 A3, 96 A1
Guča 133 D3, 134 A3
Guča Gora 132 A/B2
Guchen 155 C2
Gúdar 162 B2
Gudavac 131 C1
Guddal 36 A2
Gudensberg 81 C1
Gudhem 45 D2/3
Gudhjem 51 D3
Gudhjem 72 A2
Gudme 53 C2
Gudmuntorp 50 B3
Gudow 69 C1
Gudsø 48 B3, 52 B1
Gudumbro 48 A2
Gudvangen 36 B3
Guebwiller 89 D2/3, 90 A3
Gué-d'Hossus 78 B3
Guéhenno 85 C2/3
Güéjar-Sierra 173 C2
Guémar 90 A2
Guémené-Penfao 85 D3
Guémené-sur-Scorff 84 B2
Güeñes 153 C1
Guer 85 C2/3

Guérande 85 C3
Guéret 102 A2
Guérigny 102 B1
Güesa 154 B2
Guéthary 108 A3, 154 A1
Gueugnon 103 C1/2
Gúglia 114 B2, 116 A/B1
Güglingen 91 C1
Guglionesi 119 D2, 120 A1
Gugutka 145 D1, 145 D3
Gühlen Glienicke 69 D2, 70 A2
Guia 170 A2
Guia 158 A3, 164 A1
Guichen 85 D2
Guide Post 57 D2/3
Guidizzolo 106 B3
Guidónia-Montecélio 118 B2
Guíglia 114 B1/2, 116 A/B1
Guignes 87 D2
Guijo 166 B2/3
Guijo de Ávila 159 D2
Guijuelo 159 D2
Guildford 64 B3, 76 B1
Guillaumes 112 B2
Guillena 171 D1
Guillestre 112 A/B1
Guimara 153 B/C3
Guimarães 158 A1
Guimiliau 84 B2
Guînes 77 D1
Guingamp 84 B2
Guintanilla 151 D2
Guipavas 84 A2
Guipry 85 D3
Guirguillano 153 D2, 154 A2
Guisando 160 A3
Guisborough 61 C1
Guiscard 78 A3
Guise 78 B3
Guisséry 84 A1/2
Guissona 155 C3, 163 C1
Guitíriz 150 B1
Guîtres 108 B1
Gujan-Mestras 108 A1
Gulbene 74 A2
Gulboviken 34 B2
Guldborg 53 D2
Gulen 36 A2/3
Gulgofjorden 7 C1
Gullabo 51 C/D2
Gullane 57 C1
Gullänget 31 C3
Gullaskruv 51 C1
Gullbrø 36 B3
Gulleråsen 39 C2
Gullholmen 9 C2
Gullholmen 44 B3
Gullön 16 A3
Gullringen 46 B3
Gullspång 45 D2, 46 A1/2
Gullstein 32 B2
Güllük 149 D2
Gulpen 79 D2
Gulsele 30 B2, 35 D1
Gulsvik 37 D3
Gültz 70 A1
Gülze 69 C1
Gülzow 53 D3, 69 D1
Gumboda 31 D2
Gumiel de Hizán 153 C3, 161 B/C1
Gummark 31 D1
Gummarksnoret 31 D1
Gümmenen 104 B1
Gummersbach 80 A1/2
Gummersbach-Derschlag 80 A/B1/2
Gumpelstadt 81 D2
Gumpersdorf 92 B2
Gumpoldskirchen 94 B2/3
Gumtow 69 D2
Gümüldür 149 D2
Gunarasfürdő 128 B2
Gundelfingen 91 D2
Gundelsheim 91 C1
Gundertshausen 93 B/C2/3
Gundheim 80 B3
Gundinci 132 B1
Gunnarn 30 B1
Gunnarsberg 15 D3
Gunnarsbyn 17 C2
Gunnarskog 38 B3

Gunnarvattnet 29 C/D2
Gunnebo 46 B3
Gunnilbo 39 D3, 40 A3
Günselsdorf 94 B3
Gunsleben 69 C3
Gunsta 40 B3
Güntersberge 69 C3, 81 D1, 82 A1
Guntersblum 80 B3
Guntersdorf 94 A2
Guntín de Pallares 150 B2
Guntramsdorf 94 B2/3
Günzburg 91 D2
Gunzenhausen 91 D1
Günzerode 81 D1
Gurahonţ 97 D3, 140 A/B1
Gura Humorului 141 C1
Guralätsch-Alp [Ilanz] 105 D2, 106 A2
Gura Văii 135 C1/2
Gura Zlata 135 D1
Gurgazo 113 D3, 123 D1
Guri i zi 137 D2
Gurk 126 B1
Gurrea de Gállego 154 B3
Gurs 108 B3, 154 B1
Gusborn 69 C2
Gušće 127 D3, 131 C/D1
Gusendos de los Oteros 152 A2
Gusev 73 C/D2
Gusinje 137 D2, 138 A1/2
Gusmar 142 A2
Gúspini 123 C3
Gussago 106 B3
Gusselby 39 D3, 46 A/B1
Güssing 127 D1
Gussola 114 A1
Gusswerk 94 A3
Gustav Adolf 39 C3
Gustavsberg 45 C2
Gustavsberg 47 D1
Gustavsfors 45 C1
Güsten 69 C/D3
Gustorf 79 D1, 80 A1
Güstrow 53 D3, 69 D1
Gusum 46 B2
Gütenbach 90 B2/3
Gutengermendorf 70 A2
Gutenstein 94 A3
Gütersloh 68 A3
Gutierre Muñoz 160 A/B2
Guttannen [Innertkirchen] 105 C2
Guttaring 126 B1
Guvåg 8 B2
Guyhirn 65 C1/2
Gvardejsk (Tapiau) 73 C2
Gvarv 43 C/D2, 44 A1
Gvozd 137 D1
Gwda Wielka 71 D1
Gwieżdzin 71 D1
Gy 89 C3
Gyál 95 D3, 129 C1
Gyékényes 128 A2
Gyldensten 48 B3, 52 B1
Gyljen 17 C2
Gyllene Uttern 46 A3
Gylling 48 B3, 52 B1
Gyltvik 9 C3
Gyömrő 129 C1
Gyöngyös 97 C3
Gyönk 128 B2
Győr 95 C3
Győr 96 B3
Győrvár 128 A1
Gysinge 40 A2/3
Gyttorp 46 A1
Gyula 97 C3, 140 A1
Gyulafirátót 128 B1
Gyulakeszi 128 A1
Gyülevész 128 A1
Gyvasshytta 42 B2

H

Haacht 79 C1/2
Häädemeeste 74 A1
Haag 92 B2
Haag 93 D2/3
Haag am Hausruck 93 C2
Haahainen 22 B1

Haaksbergen 67 C3
Haan 80 A1
Haapajärvi 21 D1, 22 A1
Haapajärvi 27 C2
Haapa-Kimola 25 D2, 26 B2
Haapakoski 20 B2
Haapakoski 22 B3
Haapakumpu 13 C2/3
Haapala 26 B2
Haapala 27 C1
Haapalahti 23 D2
Haapaloso 23 D3
Haapaluoma 20 B3
Haapamäki 21 D1/2, 22 A1/2
Haapamäki 21 C3
Haapamäki 22 B3
Haapamäki 23 C3
Haaparanta 13 C3
Haapasaari 26 B3
Haapasalmi 23 D3
Haapavaara 23 D1
Haapavesi 18 A3, 21 D1, 22 A1
Haapovaara 23 D2/3
Haapsalu 74 A1
Haar 92 A2/3
Haaraaoja 18 B3
Haarada 21 D2, 22 A2
Haarajoki 22 B3
Haarajoki 25 D2, 26 A2
Haarasaajo 12 A3, 17 D2
Haarbach 93 C2
Haarinka 21 D2, 22 A2
Haarlem 66 A2
Haaroinen 24 B2
Haataja 19 C1
Haavisto 25 C2
Habach 92 A3
Habartice 83 D1/2
Habas 108 A3, 154 B1
Habay-la-Neuve 79 C3
Habkern [Interlaken-West] 105 C1/2
Hablingbo 47 D3
Habo 45 D3
Hábol 45 C2
Habsburg [Schinznach Bad] 90 B3
Habscheid 79 D2/3
Håby 44 B2
Hachenburg 80 B2
Hacinas 153 C3
Hackås 34 B2
Häckeberga 50 B3
Hadamar 80 B2
Hädänberg 30 B2/3, 35 D1
Haddenham 65 C2
Haddington 57 C1/2
Haddon Hall 61 C3, 64 A1
Hademstorf 68 B2
Hadersdorf am Kamp 94 A2
Haderslev 52 B1
Haderup 48 A/B2
Hadleigh 65 C/D2
Hadmersleben 69 C3
Hadrian's Wall 57 C/D3, 60 B1
Hadsel 8 B2
Hadselsand 8 B2
Hadsten 48 B2
Hadsund 48 B2
Hadžići 132 B2/3
Haedington 65 C3
Haeggeriset 38 B1
Haelen 79 D1
Haffkrug-Scharbeutz 53 C3
Hafslo 36 B2
Hafstad 32 B2
Haga 38 A2
Haga 34 B2
Hagafoss 37 C3
Haganj 127 D2/3
Hagaström 40 A/B2
Hagby 51 D2
Hage 33 C2
Hage 67 D1
Hagebök 53 C/D3
Hægebostad 42 B3
Hægeland 43 B/C3
Hagelstadt 92 B1/2
Hagen 80 A1
Hagen 67 D3
Hagen 68 A1
Hagen-Hohenlimburg 80 A2

Hagenow 69 C1
Hagenwerder 83 D1
Hagétaubin 108 B3, 154 B1
Hagetmau 108 B2/3
Hagfors 39 C3
Häggås 30 A1
Häggåsen 30 B3, 35 D2
Häggdånger 35 D3
Häggenås 29 D3, 34 B1/2
Häggnäset 29 D2
Häggsåsen 34 B2
Häggsjöbränna 29 C3, 34 A1
Häggsjömon 30 B2, 35 D1
Häggsjön 29 D2, 34 B1
Haglebu 37 D3
Hagley 59 D3, 64 A2
Hagnillseter 33 C3
Hagondange 89 C1
Hagshult 50 B1
Hagsta 40 A/B2
Haguenau 90 A/B2
Håhellerhytta 42 B2
Hahn 80 A3
Hahnbach 82 A3, 92 A1
Hahnenklee-Bockswiese 68 B3
Hahót 128 A2
Haiger 80 B2
Haigerloch 90 B2
Häijää 24 B1
Haikela 23 D1
Hailsham 77 B/C1
Hailuoto 18 A2
Haina-Löhlbach 81 C1
Hainburg an der Donau 94 B2
Hainburg an der Donau 96 B2/3
Hainfeld 96 A3
Hainfeld 94 A2/3
Hainichen 83 B/C2
Hajala 24 B2/3
Hajdúböszörmény 97 C3
Hajdučica 134 B1
Hajnówka 73 D3, 98 A1
Hajós 129 C2
Hakadal 38 A3
Håkafot 29 D2
Håkantorp 45 C2/3
Hakasuo 19 C3
Hakenberg 70 A2
Hakenstedt 69 C3
Håkjerringnes 9 D1
Hakkas 16 B1
Hakkenpää 24 A2
Häkkilä 21 D2, 22 A2
Häkkilä 22 B3
Häkkiskylä 21 C3
Hakkstabben 5 C2
Håknäs 31 C2/3
Hakokylä 19 D3
Hakulinranta 18 B2
Halaesa 125 C2
Hålaforsen 30 A2/3, 35 D1
Halámky 93 D1/2
Hålandsosen 42 A/B2
Halastelki iskola 129 C/D2
Halászi 95 C3
Halbe 70 A/B3
Halbenrain 127 D1/2
Hålberg 16 A3
Halberstadt 69 C3
Halblech-Buching 91 D3
Halblech-Trauchgau 91 D3
Halbturn 94 B3
Halbturn 96 B3
Hald Ege 48 B2
Halden 44 B1
Haldensleben 69 C3
Haldenwang 91 D3
Halesworth 65 D2
Halfing 92 B3
Hälgö 47 C2
Halhjem 42 A1
Halifax 59 D1/2, 61 C2
Halikarnassos 149 D2/3
Halikko 24 B3
Hälilä 23 C1
Haljala 74 A1
Halk 52 B1/2
Halkia 25 D2, 26 A2
Halkivaha 24 B2
Halkokumpu 22 B3
Halkosaari 20 B2
Hall 47 D2
Hälla 30 B2, 35 D1
Hällabrottet 46 A1
Hålland 29 C3, 34 A2
Hallapuro 21 C2
Hallaryd 50 B2
Hallaskar 36 B3
Hallavaara 19 C2/3
Hallbergmoos 92 A2
Hällbo 40 A1
Hällbybrunn 46 B1
Hälle 44 B1/2
Halle 82 B1
Halle 68 A3
Halle 78 B2
Hällefors 39 C/D3
Hälleforsnäs 46 B1
Halle-Hörste 67 D3, 68 A3
Hallein 93 C3
Hällekis 45 D2
Hallen 29 C/D3, 34 B2
Hallen 29 D3, 30 A2, 35 C1
Hallen 34 B2
Hallenberg 80 B1
Hallenberg-Hesborn 80 B1
Hallencourt 77 D2
Halle-Neustadt 82 A/B1
Hallerud 45 D2, 46 A2
Hällesjö 30 A3, 35 C2
Hällestad 46 B2
Hällevadsholm 44 B2
Hällevik 51 C2/3
Hälleviksstrand 44 B3
Hållfjället 29 C3, 34 A2
Hällfors 16 B3
Halli 25 C1, 26 A1
Hallila 25 D2, 26 A2
Hallingby 37 D3
Hallingskeid 36 B3
Hällinmäki 22 B3
Hall in Tirol 107 C1
Hällnäs 15 D2
Hällnäs 40 B2
Hällnäs 31 C1/2
Hallsberg 46 A1
Hallschlag 79 D2
Hallshuk 47 D2
Hällsjö 30 B3, 35 D2
Hällstad 45 D3
Hallstahammar 40 A3, 46 B1
Hallstatt 93 C3
Hallstatt 96 A3
Hallstavik 41 B/C3
Hällstugan 39 C1
Halltal 107 C1
Halluin 78 A2
Hällvattnet 30 A2, 35 C1
Hallviken 29 D3, 35 C1
Halma 79 C3
Halmeniemi 26 B1/2
Halmeperä 21 D1, 22 A1
Halmeu 97 D3, 98 A3
Halmrast 37 D3, 38 A2
Halmstad 49 D2, 50 A2
Halmstad 72 A1
Halna 45 D2, 46 A2
Halne 37 C3
Halos 147 C1
Halosenniemi 18 A2
Hals 32 B2
Hals 49 B/C1/2
Hals 9 C1
Hals 28 B2
Halsa 14 B1
Halsanaustan 32 B2
Hälsingfors 31 C2
Halskov 53 C1
Halsnøykloster 42 A1
Halstead 65 C2
Halstedkloster 53 C2
Halstenbek 52 B3, 68 B1
Halsua 21 C1/2
Hålta 45 C3
Haltdalen 33 D2
Haltern 67 C/D3
Haltern-Hamm 67 C/D3
Halttula 18 A1/2
Haltwhistle 57 C/D3, 60 B1
Hälvä 27 D1
Halver 80 A1
Ham 78 A3
Hämäläinen 12 B2
Hamar 38 A2
Hamarhaug 42 A1
Hamarinperä 18 A1
Hamarneset 14 B2
Hamarøy 14 A/B2
Hamarøy 9 C2/3
Hambergen 68 A1
Hambühren 68 B2
Hamburg 68 B1
Hamburg-Kirchwerder 68 B1
Hamburgsund 44 B2
Hambye 86 A/B1
Hamdorf 52 B3
Hämeenkyrö (Tavastkyrö) 24 B1
Hämeenlinna (Tavastehus) 25 C2
Hämelerwald 68 B3
Hameln 68 B3
Hamersleben 69 C3
Hamidiye 145 D3
Hamilton 56 B2
Hamina (Fredrikshamn) 26 B2
Haminalahti 22 B2
Haminanmäki 25 D1, 26 A/B1
Hamlagrø 36 A/B3
Hamlagrøosen 36 A/B3
Hamleperä 21 D1, 22 A1
Hamm 67 D3, 80 B1
Hammar 46 A2
Hammarby 40 A2
Hammarland 41 C3
Hammarn 39 C/D3, 45 D1
Hammarnäs 29 D3, 34 B2
Hammarö 45 D1
Hammarsbyn 39 C2
Hammarstrand 30 A3, 35 C2
Hammaslahti 23 D3
Hamm-Bockum-Hövel 67 D3, 80 B1
Hamme 78 B1
Hammel 48 B2/3
Hammelburg 81 C/D3
Hammelburg-Gauaschach 81 C/D3
Hammelspring 70 A2
Hamme-Mille 79 C2
Hammenhög 50 B3
Hammer 28 B2, 33 D1, 34 A1
Hammer 28 B2
Hammer 28 B2
Hammerdal 29 D3, 35 C1
Hammerfest 5 C1, 6 A1
Hammershøj 48 B2
Hammershus 51 D3
Hammerum 48 A/B3
Hamm-Heessen 67 D3, 80 B1
Hamminkeln 67 C3
Hamminkeln-Brünen 67 C3
Hamminkeln-Dingden 67 C3
Hamm-Pelkum 67 D3, 80 B1
Hamn 32 B1
Hamnbukt 5 D2, 6 A2
Hamneidet 4 B2
Hamnes 28 B2
Hamnes 4 B2/3
Hamningberg 7 D1
Hamnøy 8 A3
Hamnsund 9 C2/3
Hamnsundet 14 A3
Hamnvågernes 4 A3, 9 D1, 10 A1
Hamnvik 9 C/D2
Hamoir 79 C2
Hampetorp 46 B1
Hamra 39 D1
Hamrångefjärden 40 A/B2
Hamremoen 43 D1
Hamstreet 77 C1
Hamula 22 A/B2
Hamula 22 B2
Hamzali 139 D3
Hån 45 C1
Hana 7 C2
Hanau 81 C3
Hanau-Grossauheim 81 C3
Hanau-Steinheim 81 C3
Handen 47 C/D1
Handewitt 52 B2
Handlová 95 D2
Handlová 96 B2
Handog 29 D3, 34 B2
Handöl 29 B/C3, 34 A2
Handrup 67 D2
Handsjö 34 B3
Handstein 14 A2
Handsverk 37 C/D2
Hanerau-Hademarschen 52 B3
Hanestad 33 D3
Hangaskylä 20 B3
Hangasmäki 25 C2
Hangastenmaa 26 B1
Hangelsberg 70 B2/3
Hånger 50 B1
Hanhikoski 12 B3
Hanhimaa 11 D3, 12 A1/2
Hanhivirta 23 C3
Hanho 21 C3
Haniá/Chaniá 149 B/C3
Hani i Hotit 137 D2
Hankamäki 23 C2
Hankamäki 22 B3
Hankasalmen asema 22 A/B3
Hankasalmi 22 A3
Han Knežica 131 D1
Hankø bad 44 B1
Hanko/Hangö 24 B3
Hannäs 46 B3
Hännilä 27 C1
Hännilä 21 D3, 22 A2/3
Hänninen 19 D1
Hänniskylä 21 D3, 22 A3
Hannover 68 B2/3
Hannukainen 11 C3, 12 A2
Hannumäki 17 C1
Hannusperä 18 B2
Hannusranta 19 C3
Hannut 79 C2
Hanö 51 C2/3
Hanøy kapell 9 B/C2
Han Pijesak 133 C2
Hanshagen 53 C3, 69 C1
Hansjö 39 C/D1/2
Hansnes 4 A2
Hanstedreservatet 48 A1
Hanstedt (Harburg) 68 B1
Hanstedt-Velgen 68 B2
Hanstholm 48 A1
Han-sur-Lesse 79 C2/3
Han-sur-Nied 89 D1
Häntälä 24 B2
Hantháza 129 C/D1
Haou 108 A3, 154 B1
Haparanda / Haaparanta 17 D2/3, 18 A1
Haparanda hamn 17 D3, 18 A1
Häppälä 21 D3, 22 A3
Hapträsk 16 B2
Hara 39 C3
Hara 74 A1
Häradsbygden 39 D2
Haranes 28 B1
Haras du Pin 86 B1
Harbach 93 D2
Harbak 28 A2
Härbergsdalen 29 D1
Harbo 40 B3
Harboøre 48 A2
Harburg 91 D2
Harburg-Ebermergen 91 D2
Hårby 52 B1/2
Harcourt 77 C3, 86 B1
Hardegarijp 67 B/C1
Hardegsen 68 B3, 81 C1
Hardelot-Plage 77 D2
Hardenberg 67 C2
Harderwijk 66 B2/3
Hardeshøj 52 B2
Hardheim 81 C3
Hardheim-Bretzingen 81 C3, 91 C1
Hardom 25 D2, 26 A/B2
Hardt (Rottweil) 90 B2
Hareid 36 A/B1
Harelbeke 78 A2
Haren 67 C/D2
Haren 67 C1/2
Haren-Rütenbrock 67 C2
Haren-Wesuwe 67 C/D2
Hareskov 49 D3, 50 A3, 53 D1
Harestad 45 C3
Harestua 38 A3
Harewood 61 C2
Harewood House 61 C2
Harfleur 77 B/C3
Harg 40 B3
Hargnies 79 C3
Hargshamn 40 B3
Harhala 25 C1
Haringvlietdam (Uitwateringssluizen) 66 A3
Harivaara 23 D2
Harjakangas 24 A/B1
Harjakopski 24 B1
Harjankylä 20 B3
Härjänvatsa 25 C3
Harjavalta 24 B1
Harjula 18 B1
Harjumaa 26 B1
Harjunkylä 20 A/B2
Harjunmaa 22 B3
Harjunpää 24 A1
Harjunsalmi 25 D1, 26 A1
Härkäneva 21 C1
Harkány 128 B3
Härkeberga 40 A/B3
Härkinvaara 23 C2/3
Härkmeri 20 A3
Härkmyran 16 B2
Härkönen 17 D2, 18 A1
Harlech 59 C3, 60 A3
Harleston 65 C2
Hårlev 50 A3, 53 D1
Harlingen 66 B1/2
Harlösa 50 B3
Harlow 65 C3
Härlunda 51 B/C2
Härmä 20 B2
Härmä 19 D1
Harmaalamranta 21 D2, 22 A2
Harmainen 25 D1, 26 A1
Harmanec 95 D1/2
Harmånger 35 D3
Härmänkylä 19 D3
Harmanli 141 C3
Härmänmäki 19 C3
Hármas 129 C1
Harmer Hill 59 D3
Harndrup 48 B3, 52 B1
Harnekop 70 B2
Hårnes 28 A2
Hårnes 32 A2
Härnösand 35 D2/3
Haro 153 C2
Háromfa 128 A2
Härpe 25 D3, 26 A3
Harpefoss 37 D2
Harpenden 64 B2/3
Harplinge 49 D2, 50 A2
Harpstedt 68 A2
Harrejaure 16 B1
Harrelv 7 C1/2
Harrogate 61 C2
Harrogate 54 B3
Harrold 64 B2
Harrow 64 B3
Harrsjö 15 C3
Harrsjöhöjden 29 D2, 30 A1
Harrsjön 29 D2
Harrström 20 A2/3
Harrvik 15 C3
Härryda 45 C3, 49 D1
Harsa 39 D1, 40 A1
Harsefeld 68 B1
Harsewinkel 67 D3, 68 A3
Hårsjøen 33 D2/3
Harskirchen 89 D1, 90 A1
Harsleben 69 C3
Harsprånget 16 A/B1
Harstad 9 C2
Harsum 68 B3
Harsvik 28 A2
Harta 129 C2
Hartberg 127 D1
Hartberg 96 A3
Hårte 35 D3
Hartenholm 52 B3
Hartennes-et-Taux 88 A1
Hartha 82 B1
Hartland 62 B2
Hartlepool 61 D1
Hartmannsdorf 82 B2
Hartola 25 D1, 26 A1
Hartola 26 B2
Hartosenpää 26 B1
Harvaluoto 24 B3
Harvasstua 14 B3, 29 D1
Harwich 65 C2
Harzgerode 82 A1
Hasborn 80 A3

Haseldorf 68 B1
Häselgehr 106 B1
Haselund 52 B2
Haselünne 67 D2
Håsjö 30 A3, 35 C2
Håsjö Gamla 30 A3, 35 C2
Haskovo 141 C3
Haslach 90 B2
Haslach an der Mühl 93 C2
Hasle 51 D3
Hasle [Hasle-Rüegsau] 105 C1
Haslemere 64 B3, 76 B1
Haslemoen 38 B2
Haslev 53 D1
Haslev 72 A2
Hasmark 49 C3, 53 C1
Hasnon 78 A2
Hasparren 108 B3, 155 C1
Hassel 35 C/D3
Hassela 35 C/D3
Hasselfelde 69 C3, 81 D1, 82 A1
Hasselfors 46 A1
Hassel (Hoya) 68 A/B2
Hasselö 47 B/C3
Hasselt 79 C1/2
Hasselt 67 C2
Hasselvik 28 A3, 33 C1
Hassfurt 81 D3
Hassi 25 D1, 26 A1
Hässjö 35 D3
Hassleben 81 D1, 82 A1
Hässleholm 50 B2
Hässleholm 72 A1
Hasslerör 45 D2
Hasslö 51 C2
Hassloch 90 B1
Hæstad 14 A2
Hästbacka 21 B/C1
Hästbo 40 A/B2
Hastersboda 41 D3
Hästholmen 46 A2
Hastière-Lavaux 79 C2
Hastings 77 C1
Hästö 24 B3
Hästveda 50 B2
Hasvik 5 C2
Hatě 94 A2
Hateg 140 B1/2
Hatfield 61 C2/3
Hatfield 65 B/C3
Hatherleigh 63 C2
Hathersage 61 C3, 64 A1
Hatsola 27 C1
Hattem 67 C2
Hatten 90 B1/2
Hatten-Kirchhatten 67 D2, 68 A2
Hattevik 32 B1
Hattfjelldal 14 B3
Hatting 48 B3, 52 B1
Hattingen 80 A1
Hattlinghus 28 B2
Hattstedt 52 A/B2
Hattula 25 C2
Hattuselkonen 23 D1
Hattuvaara 23 D2
Hattuvaara 23 D1
Hatulanmäki 22 B1
Hatvan 97 C3
Hatzfeld 80 B1/2
Haubourdin 78 A2
Haudères, Les [Sion] 105 C2
Haudo 24 A2
Hauenstein 90 B1
Haugastøl 37 C3
Hauge 42 A3
Haugen 37 D2
Haugen 33 D3
Haugesund 42 A2
Haugfoss 43 D1
Haugfoss 43 C2
Haughom 42 B3
Haugnes 9 C1
Haugsdorf 94 A2
Haugseter 37 C/D2
Hauho 25 C2
Haukå 36 A2
Haukanmaa 21 D3, 22 A3
Haukedal 36 B2
Haukeland 36 A3
Haukeligrend 42 B1
Haukeliseter 42 B1
Haukijärvi 24 B1
Haukijärvi 19 C2

Haukilahti 21 C2
Haukilahti 19 D3
Haukimäki 22 B1/2
Haukiniemi 23 B/C2
Haukipudas 18 A2
Haukitaipale 12 A3, 18 A/B1
Haukivouri asema 22 B3
Haukivuori 22 B3
Hauklappi 27 C1
Hauknes / Andfiska 14 B2
Haundorf-Obererlbach 91 D1
Haunetal 81 C2
Haunia 24 B1
Haurida 46 A3
Haus 36 A3
Haus 93 C3
Hausach 90 B2
Häusern 90 B3
Hausham 92 A3
Hausjärvi 25 C/D2, 26 A2
Hauske 42 A2
Hausmannstätten 127 C1
Haustreisa 14 B3
Hausvik 42 B3
Hautajärvi 13 C3
Hautakylä 21 C2
Hautecombe 104 A3
Hautefort 101 C3
Hauteluce 104 B3
Haute-Nendaz [Sion] 104 B2
Hauterives 103 D3
Hauteville-Lompnès 103 D2, 104 A2
Hautjärvi 25 D2, 26 A2
Hautmont 78 B2
Hautomäki 22 B2
Hauzenberg 93 C2
Hauzenberg-Germannsdorf 93 C2
Hauzenberg-Oberneureuth 93 C2
Havant 76 A1
Håvberget 39 D3
Havdhem 67 C3
Havdrup 49 D3, 50 A3, 53 D1
Havelange 79 C2
Havelberg 69 D2
Havelte 67 C2
Havelterberg 67 C2
Håven 39 D1
Haverdal 49 D2, 50 A2
Haverfordwest 62 B1
Haverfordwest 55 D3
Haverhill 65 C2
Haverö 35 B/C3
Håverödal 41 B/C3
Håverud 45 C2
Håvilsrud 38 B3
Havířov 96 B2
Havixbeck 67 D3
Hävla 46 B2
Havlíčkův Brod 96 A2
Hävlingstugan 34 A3
Havnbjerg 52 B2
Havndal 48 B2
Havneby 52 A2
Havnsø 49 C3, 53 C1
Havnsund 32 A3
Havola 27 B/C2
Havøysund 5 D1, 6 A1
Havsa 141 C3
Havsnäs 30 A2
Havsnäs 30 A2, 35 C1
Havstenssund 44 B2
Havtorsbygget 39 C1
Havumäki 21 D3, 22 A3
Hawarden 59 C/D2, 60 B3
Hawes 59 D1, 60 B2
Hawick 57 C2
Hawick 54 B3
Hawkhurst 77 C1
Haworth 59 D1, 61 B/C2
Hayange 89 C1
Haydon Bridge 57 D3, 60 B1
Hayfield 59 D2, 61 B/C3
Hayingen 91 C2
Hayle 62 B2
Hay-on-Wye 63 C1
Haywards Heath 76 B1
Hazas de Cesto 153 C1
Hazebrouck 78 A2
Hazlov 82 B3

Headcorn 65 C3, 77 C1
Heager 48 A3
Heanor 61 D3, 65 C1
Heathfield 77 B/C1
Heathrow 64 B3
Hebnes 42 A2
Heby 40 A3
Hèches 109 C3, 155 C1
Hechingen 91 C2
Hecho 154 D2
Hechtel 79 C1
Hechthausen 52 B3, 68 A/B1
Heckelberg 70 B2
Heckington 61 D3, 64 B1
Hecklingen 69 C3
Hedalen 37 D3
Hedared 45 C3
Hédauville 78 A3
Hedberg 16 A3
Hedby 39 D2
Heddal 43 C/D1, 44 A1
Hedderen 42 B2
Hede 34 A3
Hede 45 B/C2
Hédé 85 D2
Hedehusene 49 D3, 50 A3, 53 D1
Hedemora 40 A2/3
Heden 15 D3
Hedenäset 17 D2
Hedensted 48 B3, 52 B1
Hedersleben 82 A1
Hedersleben 69 C3
Hédervár 95 C3
Hedesunda 40 A2
Hedeviken 34 A/B3
Hedlo 36 B3
Hedmark 30 B1
Hedon 61 D2
Hee 48 A3
Heede 67 D2
Heek 67 C3
Heemstede 66 A2/3
Heer 79 C/D2
Heer-Agimont 79 C2/3
Heerbrugg 91 C3
Heerde 67 C2
Heerenveen 66 B2
Heerhugowaard 66 A/B2
Heerlen 79 D2
Heesch 66 B3
Heeslingen 68 B1
Heestrand 44 B2
Heeze 79 C1
Hegge 37 C/D2
Heggenes 37 D2
Heggmo 14 B2
Heggstad 28 B2, 33 D1
Hegræ 28 B3, 33 D1
Hegset 33 D2
Hegyeshalom 94 B3
Hegyfalu 94 B3, 128 A1
Heia 4 A3, 9 D1, 10 A1
Heia 28 B2
Heidal 37 D1/2
Heiddorf 69 C1/2
Heide 52 A/B3
Heideck 92 A1
Heidelberg 90 B1
Heiden 67 C3
Heiden 91 C3
Heidenau 68 B1
Heidenau 83 C1/2
Heidenheim 91 D2
Heidenheim (Gunzenhausen) 91 D1
Heidenheim-Hechlingen 91 D1
Heidenreichstein 93 D1/2, 94 A1/2
Heidenrod 80 B3
Heidenrod-Geroldstein 80 B3
Heidenrod-Laufenselden 80 B2/3
Heiderscheid 79 D3
Heigenbrücken 81 C3
Heikendorf 52 B2/3
Heikkilä 19 D1
Heikkurila 27 C1
Heiland 43 C2
Heilbronn 91 C1
Heiligenberg 91 C3
Heiligenblut 107 D1, 126 A1
Heiligengrabe 69 D1/2

Heiligenhafen 53 C2/3
Heiligenhaus 80 A1
Heiligenkreuz im Lafnitztal 127 D1
Heiligenkreuz 94 A/B2/3
Heiligenstadt-Burggrub 82 A3
Heiligenstadt 81 D1
Heiligkreuzsteinach 81 B/C3, 90 B1
Heiloo 66 A2
Heilsbronn 91 D1
Heiltz-le-Maurupt 88 B1
Heim 32 B1
Heimbach 80 A3
Heimbach (Schleiden) 79 D2
Heimburg 69 C3
Heimdal 28 A3, 33 C1/2
Heimertingen 91 D2/3
Heimola 13 B/C2
Heinäaho 22 B2
Heinälammi 25 B/C1
Heinämaa 25 D2, 26 A2
Heinäperä 22 B1
Heinäpohja 21 D2, 22 A2
Heinävaara 23 C2
Heinävaara 23 D2
Heinäveden asema 23 C3
Heinävesi 23 C3
Heinersdorf 70 B2
Heinersreuth (Bayreuth) 82 A3
Heiniemi 26 B1
Heinijärvi 18 A3
Heinikoski 18 A1
Heinisuo 18 B1
Heinjoki 24 B2
Heinlahti 26 B2/3
Heino 67 C2
Heinola 25 D1/2, 26 A1/2
Heinolan maalaiskunta 25 D1/2, 26 B1/2
Heinolanperä 18 A3
Heinoniemi 23 C3
Heinoo 24 B1
Heinsberg 79 D1
Heinsberg-Karken 79 D1
Heinsburg-Randerath 79 D1
Heintaival 22 A/B2/3
Heist-op-den-Berg 79 C1
Heitersheim 90 A3
Heituinlahti 26 B2
Hejde 47 D3
Hejlsminde 52 B1
Hejnice 83 D2
Hejnsvig 48 A/B3, 52 A/B1
Hejnum 47 D2
Hekal 142 A2
Hel 73 B/C2
Helags fjällstation 34 A2
Helbra 82 A1
Heldburg 81 D2
Helden 79 D1
Heldrungen 82 A1
Helechal 166 B2
Helfenberg 93 C/D2
Helfštýn 95 C1
Helgådalen 28 B3, 33 D1
Helgeli 4 B2/3
Helgenäs 46 B3
Helgenäs Kirke 49 C3
Helgeroa 43 D2, 44 A2
Helgheim 36 B2
Helgøy 4 A2
Helgøy 38 A2
Helgum 30 A3, 35 D2
Helgum 30 A/B3, 35 D2
Heligfjäll 30 A1
Heliport (Scilly Isles) 62 A3
Hell 28 A/B3, 33 C/D1
Hella 36 B2
Helland 32 B2
Helland 32 A2/3
Helland 42 A2
Helland 9 C3
Hellandsbygd 42 B1
Hellanmaa 20 B2
Hellarmo 15 C1
Helle 43 D2, 44 A2
Helle 42 B2
Helle 8 A3
Helle 42 A2
Helleland 42 A3

Hellemobotn 9 C3
Hellendoorn 67 C2
Hellenthal 79 D2
Hellenthal-Hollerath 79 D2
Hellenthal-Losheim 79 D2
Hellenthal-Reifferscheid 79 D2
Hellesøy 36 A3
Hellested 50 A3, 53 D1
Hellesvik 14 A2
Hellesylt 32 A3, 36 B1
Hellevad 52 B2
Hellevik 36 A2
Hellevoetsluis 66 A3
Helligvær 8 B3
Hellín 168 B2/3
Hellmonsödt 93 D2
Hellnes 4 B2
Hellsö 24 A3, 41 D3
Hellvik 42 A3
Helmbrechts 82 A2/3
Helmdon 65 C2
Helmond 79 C1
Helmsdale 54 B1/2
Helmsley 61 C2
Helmstedt 69 C3
Helnæs By 52 B2
Helnessund 8 B3
Helppi 12 A2, 17 D1
Helsingborg 49 D3, 50 A2/3
Helsingborg 72 A1
Helsinge 49 D3, 50 A2/3
Helsingør 49 D3, 50 A2/3
Helsingør 72 A1
Helsinki 24 A2
Helsinki/Helsingfors 25 C/D3, 26 A3
Helsinki-Kivenlahti 25 C3
Helsinki-Soukka 25 C3
Helsinki-Tapiola 25 C3
Helsinki-Vuosaari 25 D3, 26 A3
Helston 62 A/B3
Heltersberg 90 A1
Helvécia 129 C1
Hemau 92 A1
Hemel Hempstead 64 B3
Hemer 80 B1
Hemfurt-Edersee 81 C1
Hemhofen 81 D3, 82 A3
Héming 89 D1/2, 90 A2
Hemingbrough 61 C2
Hemling 31 B/C2
Hemmesta 47 D1
Hemmet 48 A3, 52 A1
Hemmingen 68 B3
Hemmingen 31 C1
Hemmingsmark 16 B3
Hemmonranta 23 B/C2
Hemmoor 52 A/B3, 68 A1
Hemnebygda 36 B1
Hemnes 38 A3, 44 B1
Hemnesberget 14 B2
Hemsbach 80 B3
Hemse 47 D3
Hemse 72 B1
Hemsedal 37 C3
Hemsjö 35 C2
Hemsjö 51 C2
Hemslingen 68 B2
Hemsön 35 D2
Henån 85 B/C3
Hénanbihen 85 C2
Henarejos 162 A3, 169 B/C1
Hendaye 154 A1
Hendset 32 B2
Hendy 63 C1
Hengelo 67 C2
Hengelo 67 C3
Hengersberg 93 B/C2
Hénin-Liétard 78 A2
Henley-in-Arden 64 A2
Henley on Thames 64 B3
Hennan 35 C3
Henndorf am Wallersee 93 C3
Henneberg 81 D2
Hennebont 84 B3
Hennef 80 A2
Hennef-Uckerath 80 A2
Henne Strand 48 A3, 52 A1
Hennickendorf 70 A3
Hennigsdorf 70 A2
Henning 28 B2, 33 D1
Henningen 69 C2

Henningsvær 8 B2
Hennstedt 52 B3
Hennstedt 52 B3
Hénoville 77 D2
Henri-Chapelle 79 D2
Henrichemont 87 D3
Henriksfjäll 15 C3, 29 D1
Hensås 37 C2
Henstedt-Ulzburg 52 B3, 68 B1
Henstridge 63 D2
Henvålen 34 A2
Hepolanperä 17 D3, 18 A1
Heppenheim 80 B3
Herad 42 B3
Heradsbygd 38 A/B2
Heraion 147 C2
Heraion 147 C3
Herajärvi 25 C/D1, 26 A1
Herajoki 25 C2
Herajoki 23 D2
Heraklea 143 C1
Herálec 94 A1
Herand 36 B3
Heraniemi 23 D2
Herbault 86 A/B3
Herbertingen 91 C2/3
Herbés 163 C2
Herbesthal 79 D2
Herbignac 85 C3
Herbitzheim 89 D1, 90 A1
Herbolzheim 90 A/B2
Herborn 80 B2
Herbrechtingen-Hausen 91 D2
Herbrechtingen 91 D2
Herbstein 81 C2
Herce 153 D2/3
Herceg Novi 137 C2
Hercegovac 128 A3
Hercegszántó 129 C2/3
Herdla 36 A3
Herdorf 80 B2
Herdwangen-Schönach 91 C3
Héréchou 109 C3, 155 C1
Hereford 63 D1
Herefoss 43 C3
Herencia 167 D1
Herend 128 B1
Herentals 79 C1
Hérépian 110 B3
Herfølge 50 A3, 53 D1
Herford 68 A3
Herguijuela 166 A2
Héricourt 89 D3
Héricourt-en-Caux 77 C3
Hérimoncourt 89 D3, 90 A3
Heringen 81 D1, 82 A1
Heringen-Widdershausen 81 D2
Heringsdorf 53 C3
Herisau 91 C3, 105 D1
Hérisson 102 B2
Herk-de-Stad 79 C1/2
Herland 36 A2
Herleshausen-Nesselröden 81 D1/2
Herleshausen 81 D1/2
Herlufmagle 53 D1
Hermagor 126 A2
Hermannsburg 68 B2
Hermannshof 53 D3
Hermansjö 30 B3, 35 D1
Hermansjö 30 B3, 35 D1
Hermansverk 36 B2
Hérmedes de Cerrato 152 B3, 160 B1
Herment 102 A/B3
Hermeskeil 80 A3
Hermisende 151 C3
Hermitage Castle 57 C2
Hermsdorf 82 A/B2
Hermsdorf 83 C2
Hernani 153 D1, 154 A1
Herne 80 A1
Herne Bay 65 D3, 77 C1
Hernes 28 A3, 33 C1
Herning 48 A/B3
Heroldsberg 82 A3, 92 A1
Heroldstatt-Ennabeuren 91 C2
Herøy 14 A2
Herpf 81 D2
Herråkra 51 C1
Herrala 25 D2, 26 A2
Herramélluri 153 C2
Herräng 41 C3
Herraskylä 21 C3
Herre 43 D2, 44 A1
Herredsgrensen 14 B1
Herrenberg 91 B/C2
Herrenchiemsee 92 B3
Herrera 172 A/B2
Herrera de Alcántara 165 C1
Herrera del Duque 166 B2
Herrera de los Navarros 162 A/B1
Herrera de Pisuerga 152 B2
Herrera de Valdecañas 152 B3
Herreros 153 D3, 161 C/D1
Herreros 151 D2/3
Herreros de Suso 160 A2
Herreruela 165 C1
Herrestad 45 C2
Herrhamra 47 C1/2
Herrieden 91 D1
Herrieden-Neunstetten 91 D1
Herringbotn 14 B2/3
Herrischried 90 B3
Herritslev 53 D2
Herrljunga 45 C3
Herrnhut 83 D1/2
Herrö 34 B3
Herröskatan 41 D3
Herrsching 92 A3
Herrskog 30 B3, 35 D2
Herrstein 80 A3
Herrvik 47 D3
Herry 87 D3, 102 B1
Hersbruck 82 A3, 92 A1
Herschbach 80 B2
Herschbach 80 B2
Herscheid 80 B1
Herselt 79 C1
Hersin-Coupigny 78 A2
Herstal 79 C2
Herstmonceux Castle 77 C1
Hersvik 36 A2
Herte 40 A1
Herten 67 C/D3, 80 A1
Hertford 65 C3
Hervás 159 D3
Hervideros de Fuensanta 167 C2
Herxheim 90 B1
Herxheim 80 B3, 90 B1
Herzberg 68 B3, 81 D1
Herzberg 70 A3, 83 C1
Herzberg 69 D1
Herzberg 70 A2
Herzberg 72 A3, 96 A1
Herzberg-Scharzfeld 81 D1
Herzberg-Sieber 69 B/C3, 81 D1
Herzebrock 67 D3, 68 A3
Herzfelde 70 B2
Herzlake 67 D2
Herzogenaurach 81 D3, 91 D1, 92 A1
Herzogenbuchsee 105 C1
Herzogenburg 94 A2
Herzsprung 69 D2
Hesdin 77 D2
Hesel 67 D1
Heskestad 42 A/B3
Hesnæs 53 D2
Hesperange 79 D3
Hessdalen 33 D2
Hesselagergård 53 C2
Hessen 69 C3
Hesseneck-Kailbach 81 C3, 91 C1
Hessisch Lichtenau 81 C1
Hessisch Oldendorf-Hemeringen 68 A/B3
Hessisch Oldendorf 68 A/B3
Hessisch Oldendorf-Fischbeck 68 A/B3
Hessvik 42 A1
Hestedt 69 C2
Hestenesøyri 36 A/B1
Hestmon 14 A2
Hestnes 32 B1
Hestøy 14 A2
Hestra 50 B1
Hestra 46 A3
Hestvika 32 B1
Hetekylä 18 B2
Hetlevik 36 A3
Hettstedt 69 C3, 82 A1
Hetzerath 79 D3, 80 A3
Heubach 91 C2
Heubach 81 D2, 82 A2
Heudebouville 76 B3, 86 A/B1
Heusden 79 C1
Heustreu 81 D2
Heusweiler 89 D1, 90 A1
Heves 97 C3
Hévíz 128 A1/2
Hevlín 94 B2
Hevosoja 26 B2
Hexham 57 D3, 60 B1
Hexham 54 B3
Heyrieux 103 D3
Heysham 59 C/D1, 60 B2
Heysham 54 B3
Heytesbury 63 D2, 64 A3
Hidasnémeti 97 C2
Hiddenhausen 68 A3
Hieflau 93 D3
Hiendelaencina 161 C2
Hiersac 101 C3
Hiers-Brouage 100 B2
Hietakangas 13 B/C2
Hietakylä 22 B3
Hietama 21 D3, 22 A3
Hietana 25 D2, 26 A/B2
Hietanen 26 B1
Hietanen 17 D1
Hietaniemi 13 C2
Hietaniemi 19 C1
Hietaniemi 11 D2/3, 12 B1
Hietaniemi 26 B1
Hietaperä 19 D3
Hietoinen 25 D2, 26 A2
Hiettanen 17 D1
Higham Ferrers 64 B2
Highworth 64 A3
High Wycombe 64 B3
Higrav 8 B2
Higuera 159 D3, 166 A1
Higuera de Arjona 167 C3, 172 B1
Higuera de Calatrava 167 C3, 172 B1
Higuera de la Serena 166 A2
Higuera de la Sierra 165 D3, 171 C1
Higuera de las Dueñas 160 A/B3
Higuera de Llerena 165 D3, 166 A3
Higuera de Vargas 165 C2/3
Higuera la Real 165 D3
Higueras 162 B3
Higueruela 169 C2
Higueruela 163 C3, 169 D1
Higueruelas 162 B3, 169 C1
Hihnavaara 13 C2
Hiidenkirnut 12 A3
Hiidenkylä 21 D1, 22 A1
Hiilinki 21 C/D2
Hiirikylä 23 C1
Hiirola 26 B1
Hiisijärvi 19 C3
Hiiskoski 23 D2
Hiitelä 25 D2, 26 A2
Híjar 162 B1/2
Hikiä 25 C/D2, 26 A2
Hilchenbach 80 B1/2
Hildburghausen 81 D2
Hilden 80 A1
Hilders 81 D2
Hildesheim 68 B3
Hilgertshausen-Tandern-Hilgertshausen 92 A2
Hilgertshausen-Tandern 92 A2
Hillared 45 D3
Hille 68 A3
Hillebola 40 B2
Hillegom 66 A2/3
Hiller 28 B1
Hillerød 49 D3, 50 A3
Hillerød 72 A1/2
Hillerse 68 B2/3
Hillerstorp 50 B1
Hilleshamn 9 D2
Hillesheim 79 D2, 80 A2
Hillestad 43 D1, 44 A1
Hilli 21 C1
Hillilä 21 C1
Hillmersdorf 70 A3
Hillosensalmi 26 B2
Hillringsberg 45 C1
Hillsborough 56 A3
Hilltown 58 A1
Hilpoltstein 92 A1
Hilter 67 D3
Hiltunen 19 D1
Hilvarenbeek 79 C1
Hilversum 66 B3
Hilzingen 90 B3
Himalansaari 27 B/C1
Himanka 21 C1
Himankakylä 21 C1
Himara 142 A2
Himberg 94 B2/3
Himbergen 69 C2
Himesháza 128 B2
Himki 75 D2
Himmelberg 126 B1
Himmelpforten 68 B1
Hinckley 65 C2
Hindås 45 C3
Hindås 72 A1
Hindelang 91 D3
Hindelbank 105 C1
Hindeloopen 66 B2
Hindenberg 70 A2
Hindersby 25 D2, 26 B2
Hindersön 17 C3
Hinderwell 61 C1
Hindhead 64 B3, 76 B1
Hindley 59 D2, 60 B2/3
Hindon 63 D2, 64 A3
Hindrem 28 A3, 33 C1
Hindseter 37 C2
Hinganmaa 12 B2
Hingham 65 C/D2
Hinkaperä 18 B3, 21 D1, 22 A1
Hinnerjoki 24 A/B2
Hinnerup 48 B2
Hinneryd 50 B2
Hinojal 159 C3, 165 D1, 166 A1
Hinojales 165 D3, 171 C1
Hinojos 171 C/D2
Hinojosa 161 D2, 162 A2
Hinojosa de la Sierra 153 D3
Hinojosa de Duero 159 C2
Hinojosa de San Vicente 160 A3
Hinojosa del Valle 165 D2/3, 166 A2/3
Hinojosa del Duque 166 B2/3
Hinojosas de Calatrava 167 C2
Hinova 135 D2
Hinrichshagen 53 D3
Hinrichshagen 70 A1
Hinte 67 C/D1
Hinte-Loppersum 67 C/D1
Hinterhornbach 91 D3, 106 B1
Hinterrhein [Thusis] 105 D2, 106 A2
Hinterriss 92 A3
Hintersee 93 C3
Hintersee 70 B1
Hinterstoder 93 C/D3
Hinterthal 92 B3, 126 A1
Hintertux 107 C1
Hinterzarten 90 B3
Hinthaara/Hindhår 25 D2/3, 26 A3
Hinx 108 A2
Hio 150 A2/3
Hippolytushoef 66 B2
Hîrlău 141 C1
Hirrlingen 91 B/C2
Hirschaid 81 D3, 82 A3
Hirschau 82 A/B3, 92 A/B1
Hirschbach 82 A3, 92 A1
Hirschberg 82 A2
Hirschfelde 83 D2
Hirschhorn 91 B/C1
Hirsilä 25 C1
Hirsingue 89 D3, 90 A3
Hirsjärvi 25 C2
Hirson 78 B3
Hîrșova 141 C/D2
Hirtshals 44 A3, 48 B1
Hirvaanmäki 21 D2, 22 A2
Hirvas 12 A3
Hirvaskoski 19 C2
Hirvaskylä 21 D3, 22 A3
Hirvasperä 18 A2/3
Hirvasvaara 13 C3
Hirveäkuaru 12 B2
Hirvelä 18 B2
Hirvelä 19 D3, 23 D1
Hirvelä 26 B2
Hirvenlahti 25 D1, 26 B1
Hirvensalmi 26 B1
Hirviäkuru 12 B2
Hirvihaara 25 D2, 26 A2
Hirvijärvi 20 B3
Hirvijärvi 25 C1
Hirvijärvi 22 B1
Hirvijärvi 17 C2
Hirvijoki 20 B2
Hirvikylä 21 C3
Hirvilahti 22 B2
Hirvimäki 21 D3, 22 A3
Hirvirangas 21 D3, 22 A3
Hirvisalo 25 D1/2, 26 B1/2
Hirvivaara 23 D2
Hirvlax 20 B2
Hirwaun 63 C1
Hirzenhain 81 C2
Hisar 149 D2
Hishult 50 B2
Hisøy 43 C3
Hissjön 31 C/D2
Hita 161 C2
Hitchin 64 B2
Hitis/Hiittinen 24 B3
Hittarp 49 D3, 50 A2
Hitterdal 33 D2
Hittisau 91 C/D3
Hitzacker 69 C2
Hitzendorf 127 C1
Hitzkirch 105 C1
Hiukkajoki 27 D1
Hjåggsjö 31 C2
Hjallerup 48 B1
Hjältanstorp 35 C3
Hjältevad 46 A/B3
Hjardemal Klit 48 A1
Hjartdal 43 C1
Hjelle 37 C2
Hjelle 32 A3, 36 B1
Hjelle 36 B1
Hjellebotn 28 B2
Hjellestad 36 A3
Hjelmelandsvågen 42 A2
Hjelmset 14 A3, 28 B1
Hjerkinn 33 C3, 37 D1
Hjerm 48 A2
Hjerpsted 52 A2
Hjerting 48 A3, 52 A1
Hjo 45 D2/3, 46 A2
Hjøllund 48 B3
Hjølmo 36 B3
Hjørring 48 B1
Hjorte 52 B1
Hjorted 46 B3
Hjortkvarn 46 B2
Hjortnäs 39 D2
Hjortsberga 51 B/C1
Hjortskarmoen 14 B3
Hjulsjö 39 D3
Hlinky 82 B3
Hlohovec 95 C2
Hlohovec 96 B2
Hluboká nad Vltavou 93 D1
Hluboš 83 C3
Hluk 95 C1
Hmel'nickij 98 B3
Hmelnik 99 C3
Hnanice 94 A2
Hoberg 29 C3, 34 A1
Hobøl 38 A3, 44 B1
Hobro 48 B2
Hoburgen 47 C/D3
Höchberg 81 C/D3
Hochdonn 52 B3
Hochdorf 105 C1
Höchenschwand 90 B3
Höchenschwand-Tiefenhäusern 90 B3
Hochfelden 90 A2
Hochfilzen 92 B3
Höchheim-Irmelshausen 81 D2
Hochkirch 83 D1
Hochosterwitz 126 B1
Hochsölden 107 B/C1
Hochspeyer 90 B1

Höchst **81** C3
Hochstadt **90** B1
Höchstädt **91** D2
Höchstädt **82** B3
Höchstadt an der Aisch **81** D3
Höchstenbach **80** B2
Hochwolkersdorf **94** B3
Hockenheim **90** B1
Hockeroda **82** A2
Hocksjö **30** A2, **35** C1
Hodal **33** D3
Hoddesdon **65** C3
Hoddevika **36** A1
Hodenhagen **68** B2
Hodkovice nad Mohelkou **83** D2
Hódmezővásárhely **129** D2
Hódmezővásárhely **97** C3, **140** A1
Hodnet **59** D3, **60** B3
Hodonín **94** B1/2
Hodonín **96** B2
Hodorov **97** D2, **98** A3
Hodoš **96** A/B3
Hodoš **127** D1
Hodošan **127** D2, **128** A2
Hoedekenskerke **78** B1
Hoek van Holland **66** A3
Hoemsbu **32** B3
Hoenderloo **66** B3
Hoensbroek **79** D2
Hof **82** A/B2
Hof **80** B2
Hof **38** B2
Hof am Leithagebirge **94** B3
Hofbieber **81** C2
Hofbieber-Kleinsassen **81** C2
Höfer **68** B2
Hofgeismar **81** C1
Hofgeismar-Hümme **81** C1
Hofheim **81** D3
Hofheim **80** B3
Hofkirchen im Mühlkreis **93** C2
Hofles **28** B1
Hofors **40** A2
Höganäs **49** D2/3, **50** A2
Höganäs **72** A1
Högberget **16** A3
Högbo **40** A2
Hogboda **45** C1
Högby **51** D1
Högby **72** B1
Högbynäs **29** D2, **30** A2
Högerud **45** C1
Högfjällshotellet **39** C1
Högfors **39** D3
Högfors **40** A3
Höggnabba **21** B/C1/2
Högheden **15** D2
Högheden **16** A3
Höghult **46** B3
Högklint **47** D3
Högkulla **31** C1
Högland **31** C2
Höglekardalen **34** B2
Höglunda **30** A3, **35** C2
Högnäset **30** A1
Hogndalen **15** B/C1
Hognerud **45** C1
Hognes **28** B1
Hognfjord **9** C2
Högsåra **24** B3
Högsäter **38** B3
Högsäter **45** C1
Högsäter **45** C2
Högsby **51** D1
Högsby **72** B1
Høgset **32** A/B2
Högsjö **46** B1
Högsta **29** C/D3, **34** B2
Högvålen **34** A3
Hőgyész **128** B2
Hohberg **90** B2
Hohburg **82** B1
Höheinöd **90** A1
Hohenaltheim **91** D2
Hohenaspe **52** B3
Hohenau **94** B2
Hohenberg **94** A3
Hohenberg-Krusemark **69** D2
Hohenbrünzow **70** A1
Hohenbucko **70** A3
Hohenburg **92** A1
Hohenburg-Mendorferbuch **92** A1
Hohenems **91** C3, **106** A1
Hohenfels **92** A1
Hohenfurch **91** D3
Hohengüstow **70** B1
Hohenhameln **68** B3
Höhenkirchen **92** A3
Hohenleipisch **83** C1
Hohenleuben **82** B2
Hohenlinden **92** A/B2
Hohenlockstedt **52** B3
Hohenmölsen **82** B1
Hohen Neuendorf **70** A2
Hohenpeissenberg **91** D3, **92** A3
Hohenpolding-Sulding **92** B2
Hohenpriessnitz **82** B1
Hohenroda **81** C/D2
Hohensaaten **70** B2
Hohenschwangau **91** D3
Hohenseeden **69** D3
Hohenseefeld **70** A3
Hohenstein-Bernloch **91** C2
Hohenstein-Ernstthal **82** B2
Hohentauern **93** D3
Hohenthann **92** B2
Hohenwarsleben **69** C3
Hohenwarth **92** B1
Hohenwarth **94** A2
Hohenwarthe **69** D3
Hohenwart (Schrobenhausen) **92** A2
Hohenwestedt **52** B3
Hohenziatz **69** D3
Hohn **52** B3
Höhn **80** B2
Hohne **68** B2
Höhnstedt **82** A1
Hohnstein **83** C1/2
Hohnstorf **69** C1
Höhr-Grenzhausen **80** A/B2
Hohwacht **53** C3
Hoilola **23** D3
Hoisko **21** C2
Højby **49** C/D3
Højer **52** A2
Højerup **50** A3, **53** D1
Hojniki **99** C1/2
Hojreby **53** C2
Højslev Stationsby **48** B2
Hojsova Stráž **93** C1
Hok **45** D3, **46** A3, **50** B1
Hökåsen **40** A3, **46** B1
Hokka **26** B1
Hokkaskylä **21** C3
Hokksund **43** D1
Hökmark **31** D1
Hökön **50** B2
Hököpinge **50** A3
Hokovce **95** D2
Hokstad **28** B3, **33** D1
Hol **37** C3
Hol **45** C3
Holaforsen **30** A2/3, **35** D1
Holand **15** B/C1
Holand **29** C2
Holand **14** A/B2
Holand **9** C2
Holbæk **49** D3, **53** D1
Holbeach **61** D3, **65** C1
Holckenhavn **53** C1
Holdorf **67** D2
Holdorf-Gramke **67** D2
Høle **42** A2
Hole **43** D1
Holeby **53** C2
Hølen **44** B1
Holen **33** C3, **37** D1
Holešov **95** C1
Holevik **36** A2
Holguera **159** C3, **165** D1, **166** A1
Holíč **94** B2
Hölick **40** B1
Holja **25** C1
Höljäkkä **23** C2
Höljes **38** B2
Holkestad **8** B3
Hollabrunn **94** A2
Hollabrunn **96** A/B2
Holland-on-Sea **65** C3
Hollandsche Veld **67** C2
Hollandse brug **66** B2/3
Hollås **28** B2, **33** D1
Holle **68** B3
Holleben **82** A/B1
Høllen **43** B/C3
Hollenbach **92** A2
Hollenegg **127** C1
Hollenstedt **68** B3
Hollenstedt **68** B1
Hollfeld **82** A3
Hollingsholm **32** A2
Hölloch **105** D1
Hollola **25** D2, **26** A2
Hollsand **29** D2
Hollum **66** B1
Höllviksnäs **50** A3
Holm **57** C2
Holm **20** B1/2
Holm **14** B2
Holm **35** C2
Holm **30** B3, **35** D1/2
Holm **9** B/C1/2
Holm **52** B2
Holm **14** A3, **28** B1
Holm **32** A2
Holm **75** C2
Holmajärvi **10** A3
Holmbukt **4** B2
Holme **36** A/B1/2
Holme **65** B/C2
Holmec **127** C2
Holmedal **42** A1
Holmegård **53** D1
Holmegil **45** B/C1
Holmen **37** D3, **38** A2
Holmen **4** B3, **10** B1
Holmenkollen **38** A3
Holmes Chapel **59** D2, **60** B3, **64** A1
Holmesletta **4** A2
Holmestrand **43** D1/2, **44** A/B1
Holmfirth **61** C2/3
Holmfors **16** B3
Holmisperä **21** D2, **22** A2
Holmön **20** A1, **31** D2
Holmsbu **43** D1, **44** B1
Holmsjö **51** C2
Holmsjö **30** B2, **35** D1
Holmsta **30** A3, **35** C/D2
Holmstad **8** B2
Holmstrand **30** A3, **35** C/D2
Holmsund **20** A1, **31** D2
Holmsvattnet **31** D1
Holmsveden **40** A1
Holmträsk **30** B2, **35** D1
Holmträsk **31** C1
Holmträsk **31** C1
Holmträsk **16** B3
Holmvassdalen **14** B3
Holm-Žirkovskij **75** C3
Hölö **47** C1/2
Holopeniči **74** B3
Holøydal **33** D3
Holsbybrunn **46** A3, **51** C1
Holsen **36** B2
Holsengsetra **28** B2
Holsljunga **49** D1, **50** A1
Holstebro **48** A2
Holsted **48** A3, **52** A/B1
Holsteinborg **53** C1/2
Holsworthy **62** B2
Holt **65** D1
Holt **59** D2, **60** B3
Holte **49** D3, **50** A3, **53** D1
Holten **67** C3
Holtet **38** B2
Holtet **44** B2
Holtinkylä **18** B2
Holubov **93** D1/2
Holum **42** B3
Holungen **81** D1
Holungsøyi **33** B/C3, **37** D1
Holvik **28** B2
Holvik **43** C1
Holwerd **66** B1
Holyhead **58** B2
Holyhead **55** D2/3
Holywell **59** C2, **60** A/B3
Holywood **56** A3
Holzappel **80** B2
Holzdorf **70** A3
Holzengel **81** D1, **82** A1
Holzgau **106** B1
Holzgerlingen **91** C2
Holzhausen (Hofgeismar) **81** C1
Holzheim **91** D2
Holzkirchen **92** A3
Holzminden **68** B3
Holzminden-Neuhaus **68** B3
Holzthaleben **81** D1
Holzweissig **82** B1
Homberg **79** D1, **80** A1
Homberg **81** C1/2
Homberg **81** C2
Hombornes **14** A3
Homburg **89** D1, **90** A1
Homburg-Einöd **89** D1, **90** A1
Homesh **138** A3
Hommelstø **14** A3
Hommelvik **28** A/B3, **33** C1
Hommersåk **42** A2
Homps **110** A3, **156** B1
Homstad **28** B2
Hondarribia **154** A1
Hondón de las Nieves **169** C3
Hondón de los Frailes **169** C3
Hondschoote **78** A1
Hønefoss **38** A3, **43** D1
Honfleur **77** B/C3
Høng **49** C3, **53** C1
Hongsand **28** A2
Hongset **14** A3
Honigsee **52** B3
Honiton **63** C2
Honkajärvi **20** A3
Honkajoki **20** B3
Honkakoski **24** B1
Honkakoski **22** B1/2
Honkalahti **27** C2
Honkamukka **13** C2
Honkaranta **21** D2, **22** A2
Honkilahti **24** B2
Honko **20** B3
Honkola **25** B/C2
Honningsvåg **36** A1
Honningsvåg **5** D1, **6** B1
Honnstad **32** B2
Hönö **45** B/C3, **49** C/D1
Honrubia **168** B1
Honrubia de la Cuesta **153** C3, **161** B/C1
Hønseby **5** C1/2
Hontalbilla **160** B1
Hontanar **160** B3, **167** C1
Hontanaya **161** C3, **167** D1, **168** A1
Hontangas **153** B/C3, **160** B1
Hontianska Vrbica **95** D2
Hontianske Nemce **95** D2
Hontianske Nemce **96** B2/3
Hontianske Tesáre **95** D2
Hontoba **161** C2
Hontomín **153** C2
Höntönvaara **23** D2
Hontoria de la Cantera **153** C3
Hontoria del Pinar **153** C3, **161** C1
Hönttö **23** D2
Hoofddorp **66** A2/3
Hoogersmilde **67** C2
Hoogeveen **67** C2
Hoogezand-Sappemeer **67** C1
Hoogkerk **67** C1
Hoog-Soeren **66** B3
Hoogstede **67** C2
Hoogstraten **79** C1
Hook **64** B3, **76** A/B1
Höör **50** B3
Höör **72** A1/2
Hoorn **66** B2
Hopelandsjøen **36** A3
Hopen **32** B1
Hopen **9** C3
Hopen **28** A2
Hoppegarten **70** B2
Hoppenrade **53** D3, **69** D1
Hopperstad **36** B2
Hoppula **12** B3
Hopseidet **6** B1
Hopsten **67** D2
Hopsten-Schale **67** D2
Hoptrup **52** B1/2
Hora Svatého Šebestiána **83** C2
Horažďovice **93** C1
Horb am Neckar **90** B2
Horb-Dettingen **90** B2
Horbelev **53** D2
Hørby **49** C1
Hörby **50** B3
Hörby **72** A1/2
Horcajada de la Torre **161** D3
Horcajo de las Torres **160** A2
Horcajo de los Montes **166** B1
Horcajo de la Rivera **159** D2/3, **160** A2/3
Horcajo de Montemayor **159** D2/3
Horcajo de Santiago **161** C3, **167** D1, **168** A1
Horcajo-Medianero **159** D2, **160** A2
Horche **161** C2
Horda **50** B1
Hordabø **36** A3
Hořelice **83** C/D3
Hořesedly **83** C3
Høreslia **37** D3
Horezu **140** B2
Horgen **105** D1
Hörgertshausen **92** A/B2
Horgoš **129** D2
Horgoš **140** A1
Horhausen **80** A2
Horia **141** D2
Hořice na Šumavě **93** C/D2
Höringhausen **81** C1
Horjul **126** B2
Horka **83** D1
Hörken **39** D3
Horley **65** B/C3, **76** B1
Hormakumpu **11** D3, **12** A2
Hormigos **160** B3
Hormilleja **153** D2
Hormisto **24** A/B1
Horn **46** B3
Horn **14** A2
Horn **14** A3
Horn **37** D3, **38** A2
Horn **94** A2
Horn **96** A2
Hornachos **165** D2, **166** A2
Hornachuelos **166** B3, **172** A1
Horná Mariková **95** C1
Horná Štubňa **95** D1/2
Hornbach **89** D1, **90** A1
Horn-Bad Meinberg **68** A3
Hornbæk **49** D3, **50** A2
Hornberg **90** B2
Hornberga **39** C/D1
Hornburg **69** C3
Horncastle **61** D3, **65** C1
Horndal **40** A2/3
Horndal **9** C3
Horndean **76** A1
Horne **52** B2
Horneburg **68** B1
Hörnefors **31** C2
Horné Lefantouce **95** C2
Hornhausen **69** C3
Horní Bečva **95** C1
Horní Bobrová **94** A/B1
Horní Cerekev **94** A1
Horní Jiřetín **83** C2
Horní Lideč **95** C1
Horní Lomná **95** D1
Hornindal **32** A3, **36** B1
Hørning **48** B3
Hörningsholm **47** C1
Horní Planá **93** C2
Horní Slavkov **82** B3
Horní Stropnice **93** D2
Horní Vltavice **93** C1
Hornmyr **30** B1
Hornnes **43** B/C3
Horno **70** B3
Hornos **168** A3
Hornoy **77** D3
Hornsea **61** D2
Hornsjø **38** A1
Hörnsjö **31** C2
Hornslet **49** B/C2
Hornsved **49** D3
Hornu **78** B2
Hörnum **52** A2

Hornum 48 B2
Horný Tisovník 95 D2
Horo 20 A3
Horol 99 D2
Horonkylä 21 D2, 22 A2
Hořovice 83 C3
Hořovičky 83 C3
Horred 49 D1, 50 A1
Horrmundsvalla 39 C1
Horschen Althorschen 81 C1
Horsdal 14 B1
Horsens 48 B3, 52 B1
Horsforth 61 C2
Horsgard 32 A/B2
Horsham 76 B1
Horsham Saint Faith 65 C1
Hørsholm 49 D3, 50 A3, 53 D1
Hörsingen 69 C3
Horská Kvilda 93 C1
Horsmaanaho 23 C2
Horsnes 4 A/B3, 10 A1
Horšovský Týn 82 B3, 92 B1
Horst 79 D1
Horst 52 B3, 68 B1
Hörstel 67 D2/3
Hörstel-Dreierwalde 67 D2/3
Horstmar 67 D3
Horta 158 B2
Horta de Sant Joan 163 C2
Horten 43 D2, 44 B1
Hortigüela 153 C3
Hortlax 16 B3
Horton 59 D1, 60 B2
Horton 63 C/D2
Hørve 49 C3, 53 C1
Hörvik 51 C2/3
Hosanger 36 A3
Hösbach 81 C3
Hoscheid 79 D3
Hosen 28 A2
Hosenfeld 81 C2
Hosenfeld-Hainzell 81 C2
Hosingen 79 D3
Hosio 18 B1
Hosjö 39 D2, 40 A2
Hospental 105 D2
Hospice de France 155 C2
Hospital 155 C2
Hospital de Órbigo 151 D2
Hospitalet de Llobregat 156 A3
Hossa 19 D2
Hossa 11 D3, 12 A2
Hossegor 108 A2/3
Hössjö 31 C2
Hössjön 30 A2, 35 C1
Hossmo 51 D2
Hössna 45 D3
Hostalric 156 B3
Höstanäs 25 C3
Hostens 108 B1
Hostěradice 94 B1
Hosterias de Ordesa 155 C2
Hostikka 27 C2
Hostomice 83 C3
Hoston 28 A3, 33 C2
Höstoppen 29 D2, 35 C1
Hostouň 82 B3, 92 B1
Hostrup 48 B1
Hotagen 29 D2, 34 B1
Hotedršica 126 B2/3
Hötensleben 69 C3
Hotimsk 99 D1
Hotin 98 B3
Hoting 30 A2
Hotkovo 75 D2
Hotton 79 C2
Hou 49 C1
Houdain 78 A2
Houdan 87 C1
Houdelaincourt-sur-Ornair 89 C2
Houdremont 79 C3
Houécourt 89 C2
Houeillès 108 B2
Houffalize 79 C/D3
Houghton le Spring 57 D3, 61 C1
Houlgate 76 B3, 86 A/B1
Hourtin 100 B3
Hourtin-Plage 101 C3
Houthalen 79 C1
Houtsala 24 A3
Houtskär 24 A3, 41 D3
Houtskari 24 A3, 41 D3
Hov 48 B3
Hov 46 A2
Hov 14 A2
Hova 45 D2, 46 A2
Høvåg 43 C3
Hovdala 50 B2
Hovde 43 C2/3
Hovden 8 B1/2
Hovden 42 B1/2
Hove 48 A2
Hove 76 B1
Hovedgård 48 B3
Hövelhof 68 A3
Hoven 48 A3, 52 A1
Hovenäset 44 B2
Hoverport 77 D1
Hovet 42 B2
Hovet 37 C3
Hovězí 95 C1
Höviksnäs 45 C3
Hoviland 37 D3, 38 A2
Hovin 43 C1
Hovlös 17 C2
Hovmantorp 51 C2
Hovmantorp 72 A/B1
Høvreslia 37 D3
Hovslätt 45 D3, 46 A3
Howard 61 C2
Howden 61 C2
Howth 58 A2
Höxter 68 B3
Höxter-Fürstenau 68 A/B3
Höxter-Godelheim 68 B3, 81 C1
Hoya 68 A2
Hoya-Gonzalo 168 B2
Hoya Gonzalo 160 B2
Høyanger 36 A/B2
Høydal 36 B1
Høydal 36 A2
Høydalsmo 43 C1/2
Hoyerswerda 83 C/D1
Hoyerswerda 96 A1
Høyholm 14 A3
Höykkylä 21 C2
Hoylake 59 C2, 60 A/B3
Høylandet 28 B1/2
Hoym 69 C3
Hoyocasero 160 A2
Hoyos 159 C3
Hoyos del Espino 160 A2/3
Höytiä 21 D3, 22 A3
Hoyuelos de la Sierra 153 C3
Hrachoviště 93 D1
Hradec Králové 96 A2
Hrádek 94 B2
Hrádek nad Nisou 83 D2
Hranice 82 B2
Hranice 95 C1
Hranice 96 B2
Hrasnica 132 B3
Hrastnik 127 C2
Hrastovlje 126 B3
Hřensko 83 D2
Hrge 132 B2
Hrob 83 C2
Hroboňovo 95 C3
Hronov 95 D1/2
Hronská Dúbrava 95 D2
Hronský Beňadik 95 D2
Hrotovice 94 A1
Hroznětín 82 B2
Hrtkovci 133 C/D1, 134 A1
Hrubieszów 97 D1, 98 A2
Hrubý Šúr 95 C2
Hrušovany nad Jevišovkou 94 B1/2
Hrustovača pećina 131 D1/2
Hrvace 131 D3
Huaröd 50 B3
Huarte Araquil 153 D2, 154 A1/2
Hubberholme 59 D1, 60 B2
Huben 107 D1
Hückelhoven 79 D1
Hückeswagen 80 A1
Hucknall 61 D3, 65 C1
Hucksjöåsen 30 A3, 35 C2
Hucqueliers 77 D2
Huddersfield 61 C2
Huddinge 47 C1
Huddunge 40 A3
Hude 68 A2
Hude-Wüsting 68 A2
Hudiksvall 40 B1
Huecas 160 B3
Huedin 97 D3, 140 B1
Huélago 173 C1/2
Huélamo 162 A3
Huelgoat 84 B2
Huelma 173 C1
Huelva 171 C2
Huelves 161 C3
Huéneja 173 D2
Huercal-Overa 174 A1/2
Huérmeces 153 B/C2
Huerta de Arriba 153 C3
Huerta del Marquesado 162 A3
Huerta del Rey 153 C3, 161 C1
Huerta de Valdecarábanos 161 C3, 167 C/D1
Huertahernando 161 D2
Huérteles 153 D3
Huertezuela 167 C2/3
Huerto 155 B/C3
Huesa 167 D3, 168 A3, 173 C1
Huesa del Común 162 B2
Huesca 154 B3
Huéscar 168 A3, 173 D1
Huete 161 D3
Huétor-Tájar 172 B2
Hüfingen 90 B3
Huglfing 92 A3
Hugulia 37 D2
Huhdasjärvi 26 B2
Huhmarkoski 20 B2
Huhtamo 24 B2
Huhtiankylä 21 D3
Huhtilampi 23 D3
Huhus 23 D2
Huikko 21 D3, 22 A3
Huikola 18 B3
Huissinkylä 20 B2
Huittinen 24 B2
Huizen 66 B3
Hukanmaa 11 C3
Hukkajärvi 23 D1
Hukkula 23 C2
Hulån 39 C2
Hulín 95 C1
Huljala 25 D2, 26 A2
Hullaryd 46 A3
Hüllhorst-Schnathorst 68 A3
Hullsjön 35 C/D3
Hulsig 44 B3, 49 C1
Hulst 78 B1
Hulsund 28 A3, 33 C1
Hult 46 A3
Hulta 41 D2/3
Hultafors 45 C3
Hultanäs 51 C1
Hulterstad 51 D2
Hultsbruck 46 B2
Hultsfred 46 B3, 51 C/D1
Hultsjö 51 C1
Hum 135 C3
Hum 137 C1
Humada 152 B2
Humalajoki 21 C2
Humanes 161 C2
Humbécourt 88 B2
Humble 53 C2
Humenné 97 C2, 98 A3
Humes 89 C2/3
Humilladero 172 B2
Humlebæk 49 D3, 50 A3
Humlum 48 A2
Hummelholm 31 C2
Hummelshain 82 A2
Hummeltal 82 A3
Hummelvik 32 B1
Hummelvik 4 B2
Humppi 21 C/D2
Humppila 24 B2
Hundåla 14 A2
Hundberg 4 A3, 10 A1
Hundeidvik 32 A3, 36 B1
Hundeluft 69 D3
Hundested 49 D3
Hundested 72 A1
Hundholmen 9 C2
Hundisburg 69 C3
Hundorp 37 D2
Hundslund 48 B3
Hundsnes 42 A2
Hundvik 36 A1
Hundvin 36 A3
Hunedoara 140 B1/2
Hünengräber 67 D2, 68 A2
Hünfeld 81 C2
Hünfelden 80 B2
Hünfelden-Kirberg 80 B2
Hunge 35 B/C2
Hungen 81 C2
Hungen-Villingen 81 C2
Hungerford 64 A3
Huningue 90 A3
Hunmanby 61 D2
Hunnebostrand 44 B2
Hunnes 36 A1
Hunstanton 65 C1
Huntingdon 65 B/C2
Huntly 54 B2
Hünxe 67 C3, 79 D1, 80 A1
Huopanankoski 21 D2, 22 A2
Huorso 9 C3
Huotari 22 B1
Hüpstedt 81 D1
Hurbanovo 95 C3
Hurdal 38 A2
Hures-la-Parade 110 B2
Hurezani 140 B2
Huriel 102 A/B2
Hurissalo 27 C1
Hurskaala 22 B3
Hurst Green 77 C1
Hürtgenwald 79 D2
Hürth 80 A2
Hurttala 27 C2
Huruksela 26 B2
Hurum 37 C2
Hurup 48 A2
Hurva 50 B3
Huså 29 C3, 34 A1
Husaby 45 D2
Husbands Bosworth 64 B2
Husby 40 A2
Husby 14 A2
Husby-Långhundra 40 B3
Huși 141 C/D1
Husinec 93 C1
Huskasnäs 35 C3
Husnes 42 A1
Husøy 36 A2
Hust 97 D2/3, 98 A3
Hustad 32 A2
Hustopeče 94 B1
Husu 27 C2
Husum 31 C3
Husum 52 A/B2
Husvik 28 B2
Husvika 14 A2/3
Hutisko Solanec 95 C1
Hutovo 136 B1
Hüttau 93 C3
Hüttenberg 127 B/C1
Hüttenberg-Rechtenbach 80 B2
Hutthurm 93 C2
Hutton Cranswick 61 D2
Hutton Rudby 61 D1
Hüttschlag 126 A1
Huttula 27 B/C1
Huttula 27 C2
Huttula 21 D3
Huttwil 105 C1
Hutunvaara 23 D2
Huuhanaho 27 B/C1
Huuhkaala 27 C1
Huuki 11 C3
Huutijärvi 25 C1
Huutokoski 22 B3
Huutokoski 23 C2
Huutoniemi 6 B3
Huuvari 25 D2, 26 A2
Huy 79 C2
Hvalba 55 C1
Hvalpsund 48 B2
Hvar 131 C3, 136 A1
Hvaščevka 75 D3
Hverringe 49 C3, 53 C1
Hvidbjerg 48 A2
Hvide Sande 48 A3
Hvitsten 38 A3, 44 B1
Hvittingfoss 43 D1/2, 44 A1
Hvojnaja 75 C/D1
Hvožďany 83 C3, 93 C1
Hycklinge 46 B3
Hyde 59 D2, 60 B3
Hyen 36 A2
Hyenville 85 D1
Hyères 112 A3
Hylestad 42 B2
Hylla 28 B2/3, 33 D1
Hyllekrog 53 C/D2
Hyllestad 36 A2
Hyllinge 53 D1
Hyllinge 50 A2
Hyllingsvollen 33 D2
Hyltebruk 50 B1
Hyltebruk 72 A1
Hynnekleiv 43 C3
Hyödynkylä 21 D2, 22 A2
Hyönölä 25 C2/3
Hypämäki 23 C3
Hypiö 12 B3
Hyppeln 44 B3
Hyrakäs 18 B2/3
Hyrlä 25 D3, 26 A3
Hyrov 97 D2, 98 A3
Hyry 18 A/B1
Hyrynsalmi 19 C3
Hyssna 45 C3, 49 D1
Hythe 77 C1
Hythe 76 A1
Hytölä 21 D3, 22 A3
Hytti 27 C2
Hyttikoski 18 B3
Hyttön 40 B2
Hyväniemi 19 C1
Hyvikkälä 25 C2
Hyvinkää (Hyvinge) 25 C2, 26 A2
Hyvölänranta 18 B3
Hyypiänniemi 23 C3
Hyypiö 12 B3
Hyyppä 20 B3
Hyyrylä 25 C1

I

Iacobeni 141 C1
Iam 134 B1
Iași 141 C1
Íasmos 145 C1
Ibahernando 166 A1
Ibarrangelu 153 D1
Ibbenbüren 67 D3
Ibdes 161 D1, 162 A1
Ibeas de Juarros 153 C2
Ibestad 9 C/D2
Ibi 169 C/D2
Ibieca 155 B/C2/3
Ibiza 157 D3
Ibriktepe 145 D3
Ibros 167 D3, 173 C1
Ichenhausen 91 D2
Ichtershausen 81 D2, 82 A2
Ickworth House 65 C2
Ičnja 99 D2
Idanha a Nova 159 B/C3, 165 C1
Idar-Oberstein 80 A3
Idbacka 30 A2
Idd 44 B1/2
Iden 69 D2
Idiazabal 153 D1/2
Idivuoma 10 B2
Idkerberget 39 D2
Idoméni 139 C3, 143 D1
Ídra 147 D3
Ídra 148 B2
Idre 34 A3
Idrija 126 B2
Idse 42 A2
Idstein 80 B2/3
Idstein-Wörsdorf 80 B2/3
Idvattnet 30 B1
Idvor 133 D1, 134 A/B1
Iecava 73 D1, 74 A2
Ielsi 119 D2, 120 A1
Ieper 78 A2
Ierissós 144 B2
Ierissós 149 B/C1
Ieropigí 142 B2
Iérzu 123 D2
Ieșelnița 135 C1/2
Iesi 115 D3, 117 D2
Ifanes 151 D3, 159 C/D1
Iffeldorf 92 A3
Iffezheim 90 B2
Ifjord 6 B1

Ifta 81 D1
Igal 128 B2
Igalo 137 C2
Iga Vas 126 B3
Igea 153 D3, 154 A3
Igelfors 46 B2
Igensdorf 82 A3
Igerøy 14 A3
Iggelheim 90 B1
Iggesund 40 A/B1
Iggön 40 B2
Iglesias 152 B2
Iglésias 123 C3
Igling 91 D2/3
Igls 107 C1
Ignaberga 50 B2
Igorre 153 C/D1
Igoumenítsa 142 A/B3
Igoumenítsa 148 A1
Igrane 131 D3, 132 A3, 136 B1
Igrejinha 164 B2
Igrexa 151 B/C1
Igriés 154 B2
Igualada 155 D3, 156 A3, 163 D1
Igualeja 172 A2/3
Igüeña 151 D2
Iguerande 103 C2
Ihamaniemi 23 C3
Iharosberény 128 A2
Ihlienworth 52 A3, 68 A1
Ihlow 67 D1
Ihode 24 A2
Iholdy 108 B3, 155 C1
Ihotunlahti 22 B1
Ihringen 90 A2/3
Ii 18 A2
Iijärvi 6 B3
Iinattijärvi 19 C2
Iironranta 21 C2
Iiruu 21 C2
Iisalmi 22 B1
Iisvesi 22 B3
Iittala 25 C2
Iitti 26 B2
Iitto 10 B2
Iittula 24 B3
Iivantiira 19 D3
IJmuiden 66 A2
IJsselmuiden 67 B/C2
IJzendijke 78 B1
Ika 126 B3, 130 A1
Ikaalinen 24 B1
Ikast 48 B3
Ikervár 128 A1
Ikkala 21 C3
Ikkala 25 C2/3
Ikkeläjärvi 20 B3
Ikornnes 32 A3, 36 B1
Ikosenniemi 18 B2
Ilandža 134 B1
Ilanz 105 D1, 106 A1
Ilava 95 C1
Ilavainen 24 A1/2
Iława 73 C3
Il Bívio 114 B2, 116 B1
Il Castagno 114 B3, 116 A2
Ilche 155 C3
Ilchester 63 D2
Ile d'Aix 101 C2
Ilfracombe 63 B/C2
Ílhavo 158 A2
Ilia 140 B1
Il'ičevsk 141 D1
Ilidža 132 B2/3
Iliókastron 147 C/D3
Ilirska Bistrica 126 B3
Iljanvaara 23 D1
Iljino 75 C2
Ilkeston 61 D3, 65 C1
Ilkley 59 D1, 61 C2
Illana 161 C3
Illano 151 C1
Illar 173 D2
Illats 108 B1
Illereichen-Altenstadt 91 D2
Illerkirchberg 91 C/D2
Illertissen 91 D2
Illescas 160 B3
Ille-sur-Têt 156 B1
Illfeld-Wiegersdorf 81 D1
Illfurth 89 D3, 90 A3
Illiers 86 A/B2
Illingen 91 B/C1
Illkirch Graffenstaden 90 A2
Illmitz 94 B3
Illo 24 B1/2
Illora 173 B/C2
Illueca 154 A3, 162 A1
Ilmajoki 20 B2/3
Ilmenau 81 D2, 82 A2
Ilminster 63 D2
Ilmola 17 D2, 18 A1
Ilmolahti 21 D2, 22 A2
Ilok 129 C3, 133 C1
Ilola/Illby 25 D2/3, 26 A2/3
Ilomantsi 23 D2/3
Ilosjoki 21 D2, 22 A2
Iłowa 83 D1
Iłowiec 71 D1
Ilsede 68 B3
Ilsenburg 69 C3
Ilseng 38 A2
Ilshofen 91 C1
Ilskov 48 B2/3
Ilvesjoki 20 B3
Ilveskorpi 18 A3
Ilz 127 D1
Imatra 27 C2
Imeno 127 C2
Imera 124 B2
Ímera 143 C2
Ímeron 145 C1
Imfors 30 A2/3, 35 C1
Imingen 37 C3
Immala 27 C1/2
Immeln 50 B2
Immenhausen-Holzhausen 81 C1
Immenreuth 82 A3
Immenstaad 91 C3
Immenstadt 91 D3
Immingham 61 D2
Ímola 115 C2, 116 B1
Imón 161 C/D1/2
Imotski 131 D3, 132 A3
Impéria 113 C2
Imphy 102 B1
Impiö 19 B/C1
Impruneta 114 B2/3, 116 B2
Imsenden 38 A1
Imst 106 B1
Ina 21 C2
Inari 23 D2
Inari (Anar) 6 B3
Inarinköngäs 5 D3, 6 A3, 11 D1
Inca 157 C2
Inchenhofen 92 A2
Incisa in Val d'Arno 115 B/C2/3, 116 B2
Incisioni rupestri (Parco Nazionale) 106 B2
Indal 35 D3
Inden 79 D2
Inderdalen 14 B2
Inđija 133 D1, 134 A1
Inđija 140 A2
Indre Arna 36 A3
Indre Billefjord 5 D2, 6 A1/2
Indre Brenna 5 D1/2, 6 A/B1
Indre Fræna 32 A2
Indre Leirpollen 5 D2, 6 A1/2
Indre Matre 42 A1
Ineu 97 C3, 140 A1
Infantado 164 A2
Ingå/Inkoo 25 C3
Ingå station 25 C3
Ingatestone 65 C3
Ingatorp 46 A/B3
Ingdalen 28 A3, 33 C1
Ingedal 44 B1
Ingelfingen 91 C1
Ingelheim 80 B3
Ingelmunster 78 A1/2
Ingelstad 51 C2
Ingelstad 72 A/B1
Ingersheim 89 D2, 90 A2/3
Ingleton 59 D1, 60 B2
Ingliston 57 C2
Ingolstadt 92 A2
Ingolstadt-Dünzlau 92 A2
Ingolstadt-Unsernherrn 92 A2
Ingøy 5 C1
Ingrandes-sur-Loire 85 D3, 86 A3
Inguiniel 84 B2
Ingulec 99 D3
Ingulsvatn 29 C1/2
Ingurtosu 123 C3
Ingvallsbenning 39 D3, 40 A2/3
Ingwiller 90 A1/2
Inha 21 C3
Iniesta 168 B1
Iniö 24 A3, 41 D2
Inke 128 A2
Inkee 19 C1
Inkere 24 B2/3
Inkerilä 26 B2
Innala 21 C3
Innansjön 31 D1
Inndyr 14 B1
Innerkrems 126 B1
Innerleithen 57 C2
Innertällmo 30 B2, 35 D1
Innertavle 20 A1, 31 D2
Innerthal [Siebnen-Wangen] 105 D1
Innertkirchen 105 C1/2
Innervillgraten 107 D1
Innfjorden 32 A3
Innhavet 9 C3
Innsbruck 107 C1
Innset 33 C2
Innset 9 D2
Inntorget 14 A3
Innvik 32 A3, 36 B1
Inói 147 D2
Inowrocław 72 B3
Ins 104 B1
Inseros 45 C3, 49 D1
Insingen 91 D1
Insjön 39 D2
Insjön 30 B1
Ińsko 71 C1
Instefjord 36 A2/3
Însurăţei 141 C2
Interlaken 105 C1/2
Întorsura Buzăului 141 C1/2
Intra 105 D2/3
Intróbio 105 D2, 106 A2
Inveraray 56 A/B1
Inveraray 54 A2, 55 D1
Invergarry 54 A2, 55 D1
Inverkeilor 57 C1
Inverkeithing 57 C1
Inverness 54 B2
Inveruno 105 D3
Inverurie 54 B2
Inviken 29 D2
Inzell 92 B3
Inzersdorf im Kremstal 93 C3
Ioánnina 142 B3
Ioánnina 148 A1
Ioniškis 73 D1
Íos 149 C3
Ipáti 146 B1
Ipazter 153 D1
Ipel'ský Sokolec 95 D2/3
Iphofen 81 D3
Ipolytarnóc 97 C2/3
İpsala 149 C1
İpsala 145 D1, 145 D3
Ipsheim 81 D3, 91 D1
Ípsos 142 A3
Ipsoús 146 B3
Ipswich 65 C2
Iráklia 139 D3, 144 A1
Iráklio/Iráklion 149 C3
Irañeta 153 D2, 154 A1/2
Irdning 93 C/D3
Iregszemcse 128 B2
Irig 133 D1, 134 A1
Irinovac 131 C1
Irissarry 108 B3, 155 C1
Irixo 150 B2
Irixoa 150 B1
Irjanne 24 A1/2
Irninniemi 19 D1
Ironbridge 59 D3, 64 A1/2
Irrel 79 D3
Iršava 97 D2/3, 98 A3
Irschenberg 92 A/B3
Irsina 120 B2
Iruecha 161 D1/2
Iruelos 159 C2
Irún 154 A1
Irura 153 D1, 154 A1
Irurita 108 A3, 154 A1
Irurzun 154 A1/2
Irvine 56 B2
Irxleben 69 C3
Isaba 154 B2
Isaccea 141 D2
Isane 36 A1
Ísaris 146 B3
Isbister 54 A1
Isbre 5 B/C2
Iscar 160 B1
Isca sullo Iónio 122 B2
Ischgl 106 B1
Íschia 119 C3
Íschia di Castro 116 B3, 118 A1
Ischitella 120 B1
Iscroni 135 D1
Isdes 87 D3
Ise 44 B1
Iselle 105 C2
Iseltwald 105 C1/2
Isenbüttel 69 C2/3
Iseo 106 A/B3
Isérables [Riddes] 104 B2
Iserlohn 80 B1
Iserlohn-Letmathe 80 A/B1
Isernhagen 68 B2
Isérnia 119 C/D2
Isfjorden 32 B2/3
Ishëm 137 D3
Isigny-sur-Mer 76 A3, 85 D1
Ísili 123 D2/3
Iskola 24 A2/3
Iskrec 139 D1
Iskrovci 139 D1
Iškuras 5 D3, 6 A3, 11 D1
Isla Canela 170 B2
Isla Cristina 170 B2
Isla Ravena 157 C1/2
Isle of Whithorn 56 B3, 60 A1
Isle of Whithorn 54 A/B3, 55 D2
Isles-sur-Suippes 88 B1
Ismaning 92 A2
Ismantorpsborg 51 D2
Isnäs 25 D2/3, 26 A3
Isnestoften 5 C2
Isny 91 D3
Iso-Äiniö 25 D1/2, 26 A1/2
Iso-Evo 25 C/D2, 26 A2
Isohaara 17 D2/3, 18 A1
Isohalme 13 C3
Isojoki (Storå) 20 B3
Isokumpu 19 C1/2
Isokylä 20 B2
Isokylä 18 A/B3
Isokylä 17 C1
Isokylä 13 B/C3
Isokylä 21 C2
Isokyrö (Storkyrö) 20 B2
Isola 112 B2
Isoláccia 106 B2
Ísola d'Asti 113 C1
Ísola del Cantone 113 D1
Ísola del Gran Sasso d'Itália 117 D3, 119 C1
Ísola del Liri 119 C2
Ísola della Scala 107 B/C3
Ísola delle Fémmine 124 B1
Ísola di Capo Rizzuto 122 B2
Ísola Dovarese 106 B3
Ísola Fossara 115 D3, 117 C2
Ísola Rossa 123 C1
Isona 155 D3
Isoniemi 20 B3
Isoperä 24 B2
Iso-Rahi 24 A2, 41 D2
Isorella 106 B3
Isòvol 156 A2
Ispagnac 110 B2
Isperih 141 C2
Íspica 125 C/D3
Ispra 105 D3
Ispringen 90 B1/2
Issakka 23 B/C1
Isselburg 67 C3
Isselburg-Werth 67 C3
Issenheim 89 D2/3, 90 A3
Issigeac 109 C1
Issime 105 C3
Issogne 105 C3
Issoire 102 B3
Issoncourt 89 C1
Issoudun 102 A1
Issum 79 D1
Is-sur-Tille 88 B3
Issy-l'Évêque 103 C1
Ist 130 B2
Istán 172 A3
İstanbul 149 D1
Istarske Toplice 126 B3, 130 A1
Isterberg-Wengsel 67 C/D2/3
Isthmía 147 C2
Ístia d'Ombrone 116 B3
Istiaia 147 C1
Istibanja 139 C2
Istiéa 147 C1
Istok 138 A1
Istra 75 D2
Isträsk 16 B2/3
Istres 111 C/D3
Istunmäki 22 A/B2/3
Istvándi 128 A/B2
Isuerre 154 B2
Itä-Ähtäri 21 C2/3
Itä-Aure 21 B/C3
Itä-Karttula 22 B2
Itäkoski 22 B1/2
Itäkylä 21 C2
Itálica 171 D1
Itäranta 19 B/C3, 22 B1
Itéa 147 C2
Itéa 143 D3
Itháki (Vathí) 146 A2
Itháki (Vathí) 148 A2
Íti 147 B/C1
Íti Óros 146 B1
Ítrabo 173 C2
Itri 119 C2/3
Ittenhausen 91 C2
Ittenheim 90 A2
Itterbeck 67 C2
Ittervoort 79 D1
Ittireddu 123 C/D2
Íttiri 123 C1/2
Itzehoe 52 B3
Itzgrund-Kaltenbrunn 81 D3, 82 A3
Ivacevići 98 B1
Ivajlovgrad 141 C3
Ivajlovgrad 145 D3
Ivalon Matti 11 D2, 12 B1
Iván 94 B3, 128 A1
Ivančice 94 B1
Ivančici 132 B2
Ivanec 127 D2
Ivangorod 74 B1
Ivangrad 137 D1, 138 A1
Ivanić Grad 127 D3
Ivanjci 127 D2
Ivanjica 133 D3, 134 A3
Ivanjica 140 A2
Ivanjska 131 D1, 132 A1
Ivanka pri Nitre 95 C2
Ivankovo 129 B/C3, 132 B1
Ivano-Frankovsk 97 D2, 98 B3
Ivanovice na Hané 94 B1
Ivanovka 141 D1
Ivanovo 97 D1, 98 B1
Ivanovo Selo 128 A3
Ivanska 128 A3
Ivarrud 14 B3
Ivars de Noguera 155 C3
Ivars d'Urgell 155 D3, 163 D1
Iveland 43 C3
Iven 70 A1
Ivenack 70 A1
Iversfjord 7 B/C1
Ívira 144 B1
Ivje 74 A3
Ivla 50 B2
Ivorra 155 C3, 163 C1
Ivoy-le-Pré 87 D3
Ivrea 105 C3
Ivry-en-Montagne 103 C/D1
Ivry-la-Bataille 87 C1
Ivybridge 63 C3
Iwuy 78 A2
Ixworth 65 C2
Izalzu 108 A3, 154 B2
Izarra 153 C2
Izbište 134 B1

Izborsk 74 B2
Izeda 151 C3, 159 C1
Izegem 78 A1/2
Izjaslav 98 B2
Izmail 141 D2
Izmir 149 D2
Iznájar 172 B2
Iznalloz 173 C1/2
Iznatoraf 167 D3, 168 A3
Izola 126 A/B3
Izsák 129 C1
Iž Veli 130 B2
Izvor 139 C2
Izvor 139 D2
Izvor 139 C3
Izvor 138 B3
Izvor 140 A3
Izvor 140 A3
Izvor Buna 132 B3, 137 B/C1
Izzetiyve 145 D3

J

Jäähdyspohja 21 C3
Jääjoki 21 C/D2
Jääkärikämppä 18 B1
Jaakonvaara 23 D2
Jaala 26 B2
Jaalanka 19 C2
Jaalanka 19 B/C3
Jaama 23 D3
Jaama 74 B1
Jääskönkylä 12 A2/3, 17 D1
Jaatila 12 A3
Jabalera 161 C/D3
Jabaloyas 163 C3
Jabalquinto 167 C3, 173 C1
Jabarella 154 B2
Jabbeke 78 A1
Jablanac 130 B1/2
Jablan Do 137 C2
Jablanica 132 A/B3
Jablanica 135 C3
Jablanovac 127 D2/3
Jablonec nad Nisou 83 D2
Jablonica 95 C2
Jabłonna 71 D3
Jablonné v Podještědí 83 D2
Jablonov 97 D2, 98 B3
Jabugo 165 D3, 171 C1
Jabuka 133 D1, 134 A/B1
Jabuka 133 C3
Jabukovac 135 C2
Jabukovac 127 D3, 131 C1
Jabukovik 139 C1
Jaca 154 B2
Jachenau 92 A3
Jáchymov 82 B2
Jackarby 25 D3, 26 A3
Jäckvik 15 D2
Jade 67 D1, 68 A1
Jäder 47 B/C1
Jäderfors 40 A2
Jade-Schweiburg 67 D1, 68 A1
Jädraås 40 A2
Jadraque 161 C2
Jaén 167 C3, 173 C1
Jagel 52 B2
Jægerspris 49 D3, 53 D1
Jægervatn 4 A2/3
Jagnjilo 134 B2
Jagodzin 83 D1
Jagotin 99 D2
Jagow 70 B1
Jagsthausen 91 C1
Jagstzell 91 D1
Jahkola 25 C/D2, 26 A2
Jahnsfelde 70 B2
Jahodná 95 C2/3
Jahorina 132 B3
Jahroma 75 D2
Jajce 131 D2, 132 A2
Ják 127 D1
Jakabszállás 129 C1/2
Jäkälävaara 19 C1
Jakimovo 135 C3
Jakkukylä 18 B2
Jakkula 20 B2

Jäkna 16 A2
Jákó 128 A2
Jakobsbakken 15 C1
Jakobsberg 47 C1
Jakobstad/Pietarsaari 20 B1
Jakokoski 23 D2/3
Jakoruda 140 B1
Jakovo 139 D3
Jakšić 128 B3
Jalance 169 C2
Jalasjärvi 20 B3
Jalasjoki 24 B2
Jalhay 79 D2
Jaligny 103 B/C2
Jalkala 22 B3
Jallais 86 A3, 100 B1
Jalón 169 D2
Jaluna 22 B2
Jamali 23 D2
Jämäs 19 D3, 23 C1
Jambol 141 C3
Jameln 33 D2
Jamena 133 C1
Jametz 79 C3
Jämijärven asema 24 B1
Jämijärvi 24 B1
Jamikow 70 B1/2
Jäminkipohja 25 C1
Jämjö 51 C/D2
Jämjö 72 B1
Jamm 74 B1
Jammerdal 38 B3
Jamnička Kiselica 127 D3
Jämnvallen 34 B3
Jamoigne 79 C3
Jampol' 98 B2
Jampol' 99 C3
Jämpsä 19 D1
Jämsä 25 D1, 26 A1
Jämsä 21 C1
Jämsänkoski 25 D1, 26 A1
Jämshög 51 B/C2
Jämtkrogen 35 C2/3
Jämtön 17 C2/3
Jamu Mare 134 B1
Janakkala 25 C2
Janče 138 A/B3
Jandelsbrunn 93 C2
Jäniskylä 26 B1
Janiszowice 71 C3
Janj 131 D2, 132 A2
Janja 133 C1/2
Janjevo 138 B1/2
Janjina 136 B1
Jänkä 21 C2
Jänkälä 13 C2
Jänkänalusta 10 A3
Jänkisjärvi 17 C2
Jankkila 7 C2/3
Jankov 83 D3
Jánoshalma 129 C2
Jánoshalma 97 C3
Jánosháza 96 B3
Jánosháza 128 A1
Jánossomorja 94 B3
Janova Lehota 95 D2
Janovice nad Úhlavou 93 C1
Janów Lubelski 97 C/D1, 98 A2
Jänschwalde 70 B3
Jansjö 30 A/B3, 35 D1
Jansjö 30 A/B3, 35 D1
Jänsmässholmen 29 C3, 34 B1
Janzé 85 D2
Jäpåsen 39 D1/2
Jäppilä 22 B3
Jaraba 161 D1, 162 A1/2
Jaraco 169 D2
Jarafuel 169 C2
Jaraicejo 159 D3, 166 A1
Jaraiz de la Vera 159 D3
Jarak 133 C/D1, 134 A1
Jarandilla de la Vera 159 D3
Jaray 153 D3, 161 D1
Järbo 40 A2
Jarcevo 75 C3
Jard-sur-Mer 100 A2
Jaren 38 A2
Jarfjordbotn 7 D2
Jargeau 87 C2/3
Jarhoinen 12 A3, 17 D1
Jarkovac 134 B1
Järkvissle 35 C/D2
Järlåsa 40 B3

Jarlovo 139 D2
Jarmolincy 98 B3
Järna 39 C2
Järna 47 C1
Jarnac 101 C3
Järnäs 31 C3
Järnäsklubb 31 C3
Järnboås 39 D3, 46 A1
Järnforsen 51 C1
Järnmalm gruvor 10 B3
Järnskog 38 B3, 45 C1
Jarny 89 C1
Jarocin 72 B3, 96 B1
Jaroměř 96 A/B1/2
Jaroměřice 94 A1
Jaroslavice 94 B2
Jaroslaw 97 D2, 98 A2
Jarošov nad Nežárkou 93 D1
Järpås 45 C2
Järpen 29 C3, 34 A/B2
Järpliden 38 B2
Jarplund 52 B2
Jarplund-Weding 52 B2
Jarque 154 A3, 162 A1
Jarrow 57 D3, 61 C1
Järsnäs 46 A3
Järvberget 30 B2, 35 D1
Järvelä 25 D2, 26 A2
Järvelänranta 19 D3
Järvenpää 25 D2, 26 A2
Järvenpää 20 A/B3
Järvenpää 22 B1
Järvenpää 25 C1
Järvenpää 27 C1
Järvenpää 23 C2
Järvenpää 23 C2
Järvenpää 11 C3, 12 A2
Järvensuu 7 C3
Järvikylä 18 B3
Järvikylä 21 C/D1
Järvikylä 21 C1
Järvinen 25 D2, 26 A/B2
Järvirova 12 A2, 17 D1
Järvsjö 30 B1
Järvsö 40 A1
Järvtjärn 31 D1
Jarże 86 A3
Jasaksö 41 C2
Jasenak 127 C3, 130 B1
Jasenica 131 C1
Jasenice 131 C2
Jasenjani 132 B3
Jasenovac 128 A3, 131 D1, 132 A1
Jasenovo 133 D3, 134 A3
Jasenovo 134 B1
Jasień 71 C3
Jasika 134 B3
Jasin'a 97 D2, 98 A3
Jaskyňa Izbica 95 D1/2
Jasło 97 C2
Jastrebarsko 127 C/D3
Jastrowie 71 D1
Jastrowie 72 B3
Jastrzębie-Zdrój 96 B2
Jászalsószentgyörgy 129 C1
Jászberény 97 C3
Jászladány 129 D1
Jatabe 153 C1
Játar 173 B/C2
Jativa 169 D2
Jättendal 35 D3
Jättensjö 35 C3
Jättölä 25 C3
Jatuni 11 C2
Jatznik 70 B1
Jauge 108 B1
Jaulín 154 B3, 162 B1
Jaulnay 101 C1
Jaunay-Clan 101 C1
Jaun [Broc-Fabrique] 104 B2
Jaunjelgava 73 D1, 74 A2
Jaunpiebalga 74 A2
Jaunsaras 154 A1
Jaurakainen 18 B2
Jaurakkajärvi 19 C2
Jaurrieta 155 C2
Jausiers 112 A/B2
Jåvall 38 A/B3, 44 B1
Javarus 12 B3
Jávea 169 D2
Jävenitz 69 C2
Javerlhac 101 C3
Javier 155 C2

Javierregay 154 B2
Javierrelatre 154 B2
Javorani 131 D2, 132 A1/2
Javorov 97 D2, 98 A2
Jävre 16 B3
Jävrebodarna 16 B3
Javron 86 A2
Jawor (Jauer) 96 B1
Jaworzno 97 B/C2
Jayena 173 C2
Jazak 133 C/D1, 134 A1
Jazbina 127 D2
Jaželbicy 75 C1/2
Jebjerg 48 A/B2
Jedburgh 57 C2
Jedburgh 54 B3
Jedlina 82 B3
Jedl'ové Kostol'any 95 D2
Jedovnice 94 B1
Jędrzejów 97 C1
Jedrzychowice 71 D3
Jeesiö 11 D3, 12 B2
Jeesiöjärvi 11 D3, 12 A2
Jegunovce 138 B2
Jekabpils 74 A2
Jekimoviči 75 C3
Jektevik 42 A1
Jelah 132 B1/2
Jelašnica 135 C3
Jelenec 95 C3
Jelenia Góra (Hirschberg) 96 A1
Jelenin 71 C3
Jelgava 73 D1, 74 A2
Jelling 48 B3, 52 B1
Jels 52 B1
Jelsa 42 A2
Jelsa 136 A1
Jelšane 126 B3
Jemappes 78 B2
Jemgum 67 D1
Jemgum-Ditzum 67 D1
Jemnice 94 A1
Jena 82 A2
Jenbach 92 A3
Jeneč 83 C/D3
Jenikowo 71 C1
Jenlain 78 B2
Jenneret 79 C2
Jensåsvoll 33 D2
Jenzat 102 B2
Jeppo/Jepua 20 B2
Jeresa 169 D2
Jeres del Marquesado 173 C2
Jerez de la Frontera 171 D2
Jerez de los Caballeros 165 D3
Jerggul (Holmestrand) 5 D3, 6 A3, 11 D1
Jergucati 142 A/B2/3
Jérica 162 B3, 169 C/D1
Jerichow 69 D2
Jerka 71 D3
Jerši 75 C/D3
Jerslev 48 B1
Jerstad 8 B2
Jerte 159 D3
Jerup 44 B3, 49 C1
Jerxheim 69 C3
Jesberg 81 C1/2
Jesenice 126 B2
Jesenice 83 D3
Jesenice 83 C3
Jesenice 96 B2
Jesenice 96 A3
Jeseník 96 B2
Jeseritz 69 C2
Ješín 83 C/D2
Jésolo 107 D3
Jessen 70 A3
Jessheim 38 A3
Jessnitz 69 D3, 82 B1
Jesteburg 68 B1
Jestřebí 83 D2
Jetnemsstugan 29 D1
Jettingen 90 B2
Jettingen-Scheppach 91 D2
Jetzendorf 92 A2
Jeumont 78 B2
Jevenstedt 52 B3
Jever 67 D1
Jevišovice 94 A1
Jevnaker 38 A3
Jevremovac 133 C1, 134 A1/2

Jezerane 130 B1
Jezerce 138 B2
Jezero 131 D2, 132 A2
Jezersko 126 B2
Jiana 135 D2
Jibou 97 D3, 140 B1
Jičín 96 A1/2
Jieprenjåkkstugan 9 D2
Jieznas 73 D2, 74 A3
Jihlava 96 A2
Jihlava 94 A1
Jijona 169 D2/3
Jillesnåle 15 D2/3
Jílové u Prahy 83 D3
Jiltjer 15 D3
Jimbolia 140 A1
Jimena 167 D3, 173 C1
Jimena de la Frontera 172 A3
Jince 83 C3
Jindřichovice 82 B2
Jindřichovice pod Smrkem 83 D1/2
Jindřichův Hradec 93 D1
Jindřichův Hradec 96 A2
Jinošov 94 B1
Jiřetín pod Jedlovou 83 D2
Jiříkov 83 D1/2
Jirkov 83 C2
Jirueque 161 C2
Jistebnice 83 D3, 93 D1
Joachimshof 69 D2
Joachimsthal 70 A/B2
Joachimsthal 93 D2
Jochberg 92 B3
Jock 17 C1
Jockas 27 C1
Jódar 167 D3, 173 C1
Jodoigne 79 C2
Joensuu 23 D3
Joesjö 14 B3
Joeström 15 C3
Jögeva 74 A1
Johannelund 31 C1/2
Johannestorp 16 B2
Johanngeorgenstadt 82 B2
Johannisfors 40 B2
Johannisholm 39 C2
Johanniskirchen 92 B2
Johansfors 51 C2
Johnsbach 93 D3
Johnstone 56 B2
Johovac 132 B1
Jöhstadt 83 B/C2
Joigny 88 A2
Joinville 88 B2
Jokela 25 C/D2, 26 A2
Jokela 25 C1, 26 A1
Jokela 12 A3, 17 D1
Jokela 12 B3
Jokela 22 B1
Jøkelfjord 5 B/C2
Jokijärvi 22 B2
Jokijärvi 19 C2
Joki-Kokko 18 B2
Jokikunta 25 C2/3
Jokikylä 18 A1
Jokikylä 21 D1, 22 A1
Jokikylä 20 A2, 31 D3
Jokikylä 21 C1
Jokikylä 19 C3
Jokikylä 20 B3
Jokilampi 19 C1
Jokiniemi 25 C2
Jokioinen 25 B/C2
Jokiperä 20 B2
Jokipii 20 B3
Jokitörmä 6 B3
Jokivarsi 21 C3
Jokkmokk 16 A/B1/2
Jokue 25 D2, 26 B2
Jolanda di Savóia 115 C1
Jolanki 12 A3, 17 D1
Jøldalshytta 33 C2
Joloskylä 18 B2
Jomala 41 C/D3
Jømna 38 B2
Jönåker 47 B/C2
Jonasvollen 33 D3
Jonava 73 D2, 74 A3
Jonchery-sur-Vesle 88 A1
Joncy 103 C1/2
Jondal 36 B2
Jönköping 45 D3, 46 A3
Jönköping-Huskvarna 45 D3, 46 A3

Jönköping-Norahammar 45 D3
Jönköping 72 A1
Jönköping-Huskvarna 72 A1
Jonku 19 C2
Jonquières 111 C2
Jons 103 D2/3
Jonsa 22 B2
Jonsberg 47 C2
Jonstorp 49 D2, 50 A2
Jonzac 100 B3
Jorairátar 173 C2
Jorba 155 D3, 156 A3, 163 D1
Jordbru 9 B/C3
Jordbru 47 C/D1
Jordbrugrotten 14 B2
Jördenstorf 53 D3
Jordet 38 B1
Jordfallet 5 C2
Jorgastak 5 D3, 6 A3, 11 D1
Jork 68 B1
Jörlanda 45 C3
Jormlien 29 C1
Jormua 19 C3
Jormvattnet 29 C/D1
Joroinen 22 B3
Jørpeland 42 A2
Jorquera 169 B/C2
Jørstad 28 B2
Josa 162 B2
Jošanica 135 C3
Jošanica 134 B2
Jošanička Banja 134 B3
Josipdol 127 C3, 130 B1
Josipovac 128 B3
Josnes 87 C3
Jössefors 38 B3, 45 C1
Josselin 85 C2
Jossgrund-Burgjoss 81 C2/3
Jøssinghamn 42 A/B3
Jøssund 28 A/B2
Jøssund 28 A2/3, 33 C1
Jostedal 36 B2
Jøstølen 32 B1/2
Jotkajavrre 5 C/D2/3, 6 A2
Jou 158 B1
Joucou 156 A1
Joué-sur-Erdre 85 D3
Jouet-sur-l'Aubois 102 B1
Jougné-Remouchamps 79 C/D2
Joukio 27 D1
Joukokylä 19 C2
Joure 66 B2
Jöusen 20 B1
Jou-sous-Monjou 110 A1
Joutsa 25 D1, 26 A/B1
Joutsenmäki 23 C3
Joutseno 27 C2
Joutsijärvi 13 C3
Joux-la-Ville 88 A3
Jouy-le-Châtel 87 D1/2, 88 A1/2
Jouy-le-Potier 87 C3
Jovan 30 B1
Jøvik 4 A3
Joyeuse 111 C1/2
Juånäset 35 C3
Juankoski 23 C2
Juan-les-Pins 112 B3
Jübek 52 B2
Jubera 153 D2
Jublains 86 A2
Jubrique 172 A3
Jüchen 79 D1
Jüchsen 81 D2
Judaberg 42 A2
Judenau 94 A2
Judenburg 127 B/C1
Judenburg 96 A3
Judinsalo 25 D1, 26 A1
Juelsminde 48 B3, 52 B1
Juf [Thusis] 106 A2
Juggijaur 16 B1
Jugon 85 C2
Jugorje 127 C3
Juhnov 75 D3
Juhtimäki 25 B/C1
Juillac 101 C3
Juist 67 C1
Jukajärvi 27 C1
Jukkasjärvi 10 A/B3
Juktfors 15 D3

Jukua 19 C1
Julåsen 35 C3
Jule 29 C2
Jülich 79 D2
Juliénas 103 D2
Julita 46 B1
Julmatt lammit 21 D2, 22 A2
Jumaliskylä 19 D3
Jumeaux 102 B3
Jumesniemi 24 B1
Jumièges 77 C3
Jumilhac-le-Grand 101 D3
Jumilla 169 D2/3
Juminen 22 B1/2
Jumisko 13 C3
Jumkil 40 B3
Juncal 164 A1
Juncosa de les Garrigues 163 C1
Juneda 155 C/D3, 163 C/D1
Jung 45 C/D2
Jungdalshytta 37 C3
Junget 48 B3, 52 B1
Jungfraujoch BE/VS 105 C2
Jungsund 20 A2, 31 D3
Junik 18 A2
Juniville 78 B3, 88 B1
Junkerdal 15 C1
Junkerträsk 16 B2
Junnikkala 27 C1
Junnonoja 18 B3
Junosuando 11 B/C3
Junqueira 159 C1
Junsele 30 A/B2, 35 D1
Junttilanvaara 19 D2
Juntusranta 19 D2
Juojärvi 23 C2
Juoksengi 17 D1/2
Juoksenki 12 A3, 17 D1/2
Juokslahti 26 A1
Juokuanvaara 17 D2/3, 18 A1
Juonto 19 D3
Juorkuna 18 B2
Juornaankylä 25 D2, 26 A2
Juotasniemi 12 B3
Jurançon 108 B3, 154 B1
Juratiški 74 A3
Jurbarkas 73 D2
Juré 103 C2
Jurilovca 141 D2
Jurjevo 130 B1
Jürmala 73 D1, 74 A2
Jurmo 24 A2, 41 D2
Jurmo 24 A3
Jurmu 19 C2
Juromenha 165 C2
Jur pri Bratislave 95 B/C2
Jurques 86 A1
Jurunbron 15 C1
Jurva 20 B2/3
Jurvala 27 C2
Jurvansalo 21 D2, 22 A2
Jussac 110 A1
Jussey 89 C3
Juta 128 B2
Jüterbog 70 A3
Jüterbog 72 A3, 96 A1
Jutis 15 D2
Jutrosin 71 D3
Juujärvi 12 B3
Juuka 23 C2
Juuma 13 C3
Juupajoki 25 C1
Juupakylä 21 B/C3
Juurikka 23 D3
Juurikkalahti 23 C1
Juurikkamäki 23 C2/3
Juustovaara 12 A2, 17 D1
Juutinen 22 B1
Juutinva A 19 D3
Juva (Jockas) 27 C1
Juvigny-le-Tertre 85 D1/2, 86 A1/2
Juvigny-sous-Andaine 86 A2
Juvola 23 C3
Juvvasshytta 37 C2
Juzennecourt 88 B2
Jyderup 49 C3, 53 C1
Jylängänjoki 21 D1, 22 A1
Jylhä 22 A/B2
Jylhä 21 C1

Jylhämä 18 B3
Jyllinge 49 D3, 50 A3, 53 D1
Jyllinkoski 20 B3
Jyrkänkoski 19 D1
Jyrkkä 22 B1
Jyväskylä 21 D3, 22 A3

K

Kaakamo 17 D2/3, 18 A1
Kaalimaa 11 D2, 12 B1
Kaamanen 6 B3
Kaamasen Kievari 6 B3
Kaamasmukka 6 B3
Kaanaa 25 C1
Kaanaa 25 D2, 26 A2
Kääpälä 26 B2
Kaarakkala 22 B1
Kaaresuvanto 11 B/C2
Kaarina 24 B2/3
Käärmelehto 12 A/B2
Kaarnalampi 23 C3
Kaarnijärvi 12 B3
Kaarssen 69 C1/2
Kaarst 79 D1, 80 A1
Kaartilankoski 27 C1
Kaava 6 B2
Käävänkulä 26 B2
Kaavi 23 C2
Kabböle 25 D3, 26 A/B3
Kåbdalis 16 A/B2
Kabelvåg 8 B2
Kać 129 D3, 133 D1, 134 A1
Kačanička Klisura 138 B2
Kačanik 138 B2
Kačarevo 133 D1, 134 B1
Kačikol 138 B1
Kácov 83 D3
Kaczkowo 71 D3
Kaczory 71 D2
Kadaň 83 C2
Kadarkút 128 A/B2
Kåddis 31 C/D2
Kadrifakovo 139 C2/3
Käenkoski 23 D2
Kåfjord 5 C2
Kåfjord 5 D1, 6 A/B1
Kåfjord 4 B3
Kåfjordbotn 4 B3, 10 B1
Kagarlyk 99 D2
Kåge 31 D1
Kågeröd 50 A2/3
Kagul 141 D1
Kahl 81 C3
Kahla 82 A2
Kähtävä 18 A3, 21 C1
Kaiáfas 146 B3
Kaibing 127 D1
Kaidankylä 25 C1
Kainach bei Voitsberg 127 C1
Kainasto 20 B3
Kaindorf 127 D1
Kainulasjärvi 17 C1
Kainuunkylä 17 D2
Kainuunmäki 22 B1
Kaipiainen 26 B2
Kaipola 25 D1, 26 A1
Kairala 12 B2
Kaisajoki 17 D2, 18 A1
Kaisepakte 10 A2
Kaisers 106 B1
Kaisersbach 91 C1
Kaisersesch 80 A2/3
Kaiserslautern 90 A/B1
Kaiserstuhl [Weiach-Kaiser-stuhl] 90 B3
Kaiser-Wilhelm-Koog 52 A3
Kaisheim 91 D2
Kaitainen 27 C2
Kaitainen 22 B3
Kaitainsalmi 19 C3
Kaitajärvi 12 A3, 17 D2
Kaitjärvi 26 B2
Kaitsor 20 B2
Kaitum 10 A3
Kaitumjaurestugorna 9 D3
Kaivanto 19 B/C3
Kaivomäki 26 B1
Kajaani 19 C3

Kajama 21 D2, 22 A2
Kajanki 11 C2/3
Kajava 19 D1
Kajo 23 C2
Kakanj 132 B2
Kakavi 142 B3
Käkelä 19 C2
Kakerbeck 69 C2
Käkilahti 18 B3
Kąkolewo 71 D3
Kakoúri 147 B/C3
Kakóvatos 146 B3
Kakriala 26 B1
Kakskerta 24 B3
Kälä 25 D1, 26 B1
Kalače 138 A1
Kalak 6 B1
Kalakoski 20 B3
Kalamákion 143 D3, 144 A3
Kalamákion 144 A3
Kalamariá 143 D2, 144 A2
Kalámata 146 B3
Kalámata 148 B2/3
Kalambáka 148 B1
Kalambáka 143 C3
Kalambákion 144 B1
Kalamítsion 144 B2
Kálamos 147 D2
Kálamos 146 A1
Kalándra 144 A2/3
Kalándra 148 B1
Kalá Nerá 144 A3
Kalanti 24 A2
Kalapódion 147 C1
Kalaraš 141 D1
Kälarne 30 A3, 35 C2
Kalávrita 146 B3
Kalávrita 148 B2
Kalawa 71 C2/3
Kalax 20 A3
Kalbach-Veitsteinbach 81 C2
Kalbe 69 C2
Kalce 126 B2/3
Káld 128 A1
Kaldfarnes 9 C1
Kaldfjord 4 A3
Kaldhusseter 32 A3, 36 B1
Kaldjord 9 B/C2
Kaldvåg 9 C2/3
Kalefeld-Echte 68 B3
Kalek 83 C2
Kaleköy 149 C1
Kalela 24 B2
Kälen 35 C3
Kaléndzion 146 B2
Kaléndzion 142 B3
Kalenić 134 B3
Kalesija 133 C2
Kaleva 24 B2/3
Kalhovd 43 C1
Kalí 143 C/D1
Kali 130 B2
Kaliáni 147 C2
Kalindría 139 D3, 143 D1, 144 A1
Kalinin 75 D2
Kaliningrad (Königsberg) 73 C2
Kalinkoviči 99 C1
Kalinovik 132 B3
Kalinovka 99 C3
Kalisz 72 B3, 96 B1
Kalisz Pomorski 71 C1
Kalíves 145 C1/2
Kalívia 146 B2/3
Kalix 17 C2/3
Kalixforsbron 10 A3
Kaljazin 75 D2
Kalje 127 C2
Kaljula 27 C1
Kaljunen 27 D1
Kalkar 67 C3
Kalkar-Grieth 67 C3
Kalkberget 30 A2
Kalkbruk 25 D3, 26 A3
Kalkhorst 53 C3
Kalkkiainen 13 B/C3
Kalkkimaa 17 D2, 18 A1
Kalkkinen 25 D1, 26 A1
Kall 79 D2
Kall 29 C3, 34 A1
Källa 51 D1
Kallax 17 C3
Kallbäck 25 D3, 26 A3

Källby 45 D2
Källebäcken 45 D3, 46 A3
Kallenhardt 80 B1
Kållered 45 C3, 49 D1
Källerstad 50 B1
Källeryd 50 B1
Kalletal 68 A3
Kalletal-Langenholzhausen 68 A3
Kallinge 51 C2
Kallioaho 22 A3
Kalliokylä 21 D1, 22 A/B1
Kalliola 25 D2, 26 A2
Kallioniemi 21 D2, 22 A2
Kalliosalmi 12 B3
Kallipéfki 143 D2/3
Kallislahti 27 C1
Kallithéa 143 C/D3
Kallithéa 144 A2
Kallithéa 146 B3
Kallmora 39 D1
Kallmünz 92 A/B1
Kallmünz-Rohrbach 92 A/B1
Kallo 11 D3, 12 A2
Källom 30 B3, 35 D2
Kallön 15 D3
Kalloní 147 C/D3
Kalloní 149 C1/2
Kallrör 29 C3, 34 A1
Kallsedet 29 C3, 34 A1
Källsjö 49 D1, 50 A1
Kallsta 29 D3, 34 B1/2
Kallträsk 20 A3
Källunge 47 D3
Kallunki 13 C3
Källvik 47 C2
Källvik 40 B1
Kallvik 9 C2
Kallviken 31 D1/2
Kalmankaltio 11 D2, 12 A1
Kalmar 51 D2
Kalmar 72 B1
Kalmari 21 D2
Kalmavirta 21 D3, 22 A3
Kalmomäki 23 B/C1
Kalmthout 78 B1
Kalna 135 C3
Kálna nad Hronom 95 D2
Kalnciems 73 D1, 74 A2
Kalnik 127 D2
Kalø 49 C2
Kalochórion 143 B/C2
Kalocsa 129 C2
Kalocsa 96 B3
Kalógria 146 A2
Kalókastron 144 A1
Kalonérion 143 C2
Kalón Nerón 146 B3
Kalótichon 145 C1
Kalotina 139 D1
Kalovka 75 C2
Káloz 128 B1
Kalpáki 142 B3
Kalpio 19 C3
Kals 107 D1, 126 A1
Kalsdorf bei Graz 127 C1
Kälsjärv 17 C2
Kalsk 71 C3
Kaltbrunn 105 D1, 106 A1
Kaltenkirchen 52 B3, 68 B1
Kaltennordheim 81 D2
Kaluđerovo 134 B1
Kaludra 138 A1
Kaluga 75 D3
Kalundborg 49 C3, 53 C1
Kaluš 97 D2, 98 A/B3
Kalvåg 36 A1/2
Kalvarija 73 D2
Kalvatn 32 A3, 36 B1
Kalvbäcken 30 B2, 35 D1
Kalvehave 53 D2
Kalvhögen 30 A2, 35 C1
Kälviä 21 B/C1
Kalvitsa 26 B1
Kalvola 25 C2
Kalvsvik 51 C2
Kalvträsk 31 C1
Kalwang 93 C3
Kalydon 146 B2
Kám 128 A1
Kämäränkylä 19 D3, 23 C/D1
Kamári 21 D2, 22 A2
Kamári 143 D3, 144 A3
Kamarína 146 A1
Kamen 67 D3, 80 A/B1

Kamen' **74** B3
Kamenari **137** C2
Kámena Voúrla **147** C1
Kamenec **73** D3, **98** A1
Kamenec-Podol'skij **98** B3
Kamenica **133** C/D2, **134** A2
Kamenica **135** C3
Kamenica **139** C/D2
Kamenica **138** B1/2
Kamenice nad Lipou **93** D1
Kamenický Šenov **83** D2
Kameničná **95** C3
Kamenka **99** C3
Kamenka **99** D3
Kamenka **141** D1
Kamenka-Bugskaja **97** D2, **98** A/B2
Kamen'-Kaširskij **73** D3, **97** D1, **98** B2
Kamenný Újezd **93** D1/2
Kameno Pole **140** B3
Kamenščak **127** D2
Kamensko **131** D3, **132** A3
Kamensko **128** A3
Kamenz **83** C1
Kami **21** B/C1
Kamienica **71** D2
Kamieniec **71** D3
Kamień Pomorski **72** A2
Kamlunge **17** C2
Kammela **24** A2, **41** D2
Kämmenniemi **25** C1
Kammerforst **81** D1
Kamnik **127** B/C2
Kamnik **96** A3
Kamøyvær **5** D1, **6** B1
Kampen **52** A2
Kampen **66** B2
Kampevoll **9** D1
Kamp-Lintfort **79** D1, **80** A1
Kampor **130** B1
Kamsjön **31** C1/2
Kamula **21** D1, **22** A1
Kamýk nad Vltavou **83** D3
Kanal **126** A/B2
Kanala **21** C1/2
Kanália **143** D3, **144** A3
Kanálion **146** A1
Kanallákion **146** A1
Kanan **15** C3
Kandel **90** B1
Kandern **90** A3
Kandersteg **105** C2
Kandestederne **44** A/B3, **49** C1
Kándia **147** C3
Kandíla **146** A1
Kandíla **147** B/C3
Kanev **99** D2/3
Kanfanar **130** A1
Kangaasvieri **21** C1
Kangádion **146** A/B2
Kangas **18** A3, **21** C1
Kangas **20** B2
Kangasaho **21** C2
Kangasala **25** C1
Kangashäkki **21** D3, **22** A3
Kangaskylä **18** B3
Kangaskylä **21** C1
Kangaskylä **21** C/D2
Kangaslahti **23** B/C2
Kangaslampi **23** C3
Kangasniemi **22** A/B3
Kangasvieri **21** C1
Kangosfors **11** C3
Kangosjärvi **11** C3
Kania **71** C1
Kanina **142** A2
Kanjiža **129** D2
Kankaankylä **21** C1
Kankaanpää **24** B1
Kankaanpää **21** C3
Kankainen **22** B3
Kankainen **21** D3, **22** A3
Kankari **18** B3
Kankari **20** B3
Kankenseter **38** B2
Kånna **50** B2
Kännäkkä **19** C1
Kannas **19** C/D2
Kannonkoski **21** D2, **22** A2
Kannonsaha **21** D2, **22** A2
Kannus **21** C1
Kannusjärvi **26** B2
Kannuskoski **26** B2
Kanona **133** D3, **134** A3
Kanpezu-Santi Kurtz **153** D2
Känsäkangas **21** C1
Kanstad **9** C2
Kantala **22** B3
Kanteemaa **24** B2
Kantokylä **18** A3, **21** C1
Kantola **19** C3
Kantomaanpää **12** A3, **17** D2
Kantornes **4** A3, **10** A1
Kantti **20** B3
Kantvik **25** C3
Kanunki **24** B2
Kánya **128** B2
Kaonik **132** B2
Kapandrítion **147** D2
Kaparéllion **147** C2
Kapela **128** A2/3
Kapellen **94** A3
Kapellen **78** B1
Kapelln **94** A2
Kapfenberg **94** A3
Kapfenberg **96** A3
Kapfenstein **127** D1
Kapitan Andreevo **145** D2
Kaplice **93** D2
Kaplice **96** A2
Kaporin **134** B2
Kaposfő **128** A/B2
Kaposszekcső **128** B2
Kaposvár **128** B2
Kaposvár **96** B3
Kapp **38** A2
Kapparmora **47** D1
Kappel **53** C2
Kappel **80** A3
Kappel am Albis [Baar] **105** C/D1
Kappel-Grafenhausen **90** A2
Kappeln **52** B2
Kappelshamn **47** D2
Kappelshamn **73** B/C1
Kappelskär **41** C3
Kapperapalo **11** D2, **12** A1
Kappl **106** B1
Kåpponis **16** B2
Kaprun **107** D1, **126** A1
Kápsas **147** B/C3
Kapsochóra **144** A/B2
Káptalanfa **128** A1
Kaptol **128** B3
Kapusta **12** A3, **17** D2
Kapuvár **94** B3
Kapuvár **96** B3
Käpylä **18** A3
Käpysalo **22** B2
Karabiga **149** D1
Karaburun **149** C/D2
Karacabey **149** D1
Karacasu **149** D2
Karaincirli **145** D2
Karakasim **145** D3
Karan **133** D2, **134** A2/3
Karankamäki **22** B1
Karaova **149** D2/3
Karasjok **5** D3, **6** A3, **11** D1
Karatmanovo **139** C2/3
Karats **16** A1
Karatu **25** C3
Káravos **147** D2
Karavukovo **129** C3
Karbäcken **30** A1/2
Karben **81** B/C2/3
Karbenning **40** A3
Kårberg **46** A1/2
Kårböle **35** C3
Karby **48** A2
Karcag **97** C3, **140** A1
Kardámila **149** C2
Kardašova Řečice **93** D1
Kardeljevo (Ploče) **136** B1
Karden **80** A2/3
Kardis **17** D1
Kardítsa **143** C3
Kardítsa **148** B1
Kardoskút **129** D2
Kårdžali **141** C3
Kåremo **51** D1/2
Karesuando **11** B/C2
Kargowa **71** C3
Kårhamn **5** C1/2
Karhe **25** B/C1
Karhi **21** B/C1
Karhila **21** C3
Karhujärvi **13** C3
Karhukangas **18** A3
Karhula **26** B2
Karhulankylä **21** C3
Karhunoja **24** B2
Karhunpesäkivi **6** B3
Kariá **143** D2/3
Kariá **147** C2
Kariá **146** A1
Kariá **147** C3
Kariaí **147** C1
Kariaí **144** B2
Kariaí **147** C3
Kariani **144** B1/2
Karifaí **144** B1
Karigasniemi **5** D3, **6** A/B3, **11** D1
Karihaug **9** C2
Karijoki **20** A3
Karilanmaa **25** D1, **26** A1
Karinainen **24** B2
Käringön **44** B3
Karinkanta **18** A2
Karinusbua **38** A/B1
Karise **50** A3, **53** D1
Karisjärvi **25** C2/3
Karis/Karjaa **25** C3
Karítena **146** B3
Karítsa **143** D3, **144** A3
Karjala **24** A/B2
Karjalaisenniemi **19** C1
Karjalohja **25** C3
Karjanlahti **20** B2
Kärjenkoski **20** A3
Kärjenniemi **25** C1/2
Karjula **25** C1
Kärkäjoki **12** B2
Karkalmpi **25** D1, **26** A1
Karkaloú **146** B3
Karkaloú **148** B2
Kärkiskylä **21** C1
Kärkkäälä **21** D3, **22** A3
Karkkila (Högfors) **25** C2
Karkku **24** B1
Kärkölä **25** C2
Kärkölä **25** D2, **26** A2
Karlå **20** A3
Karlby **24** A3, **41** D3
Karlebotn **7** C2
Karleby/Kaarlela **20** B1
Karlholmsbruck **40** B2
Karl-Marx-Stadt (Chemnitz) **82** B2
Karlobag **130** B2
Karlovac **127** C3
Karlovásion **149** D2
Karlovčić **133** D1, **134** A1
Karlovo **140** B3
Karlovy Vary **82** B2/3
Karlsbäck **31** C2
Karlsbad-Langensteinbach **90** B1/2
Karlsberg **39** D1
Karlsborg **17** C2/3
Karlsborg **46** A2
Karlsby **46** A2
Karlsfeld **92** A2
Karlshamn **51** C2
Karlshamn **72** A1
Karlshausen **79** D3
Karlshöfen **68** A1
Karlshuld **92** A2
Karlskoga **46** A1
Karlskron **92** A2
Karlskrona **51** C2
Karlskrona **72** B1
Karlskron-Pobenhausen **92** A2
Karlslunde Strand **49** D3, **50** A3, **53** D1
Karlsøy **4** A/B2
Karlsro **16** B2
Karlsruhe **90** B1
Karlstad **45** D1
Karlstadt **4** A3, **9** D1
Karlstadt **81** C3
Karlstadt-Wiesenfeld **81** C3
Karlstein **94** A1/2
Karlštejn **83** C/D3
Karlsten **15** D3
Karlstift **93** D2
Karlstift **96** A2
Karmacs **128** A1
Karmanovo **75** D2/3
Karmansbo **39** D3
Kärnä **21** D2, **22** A2
Kärnä **21** C2
Kårnare **140** B3
Karnevaara **11** C3
Karnin **70** B1
Karnobat **141** C3
Karoro **126** A3
Karow **69** D1
Kärpänkylä **19** D1
Karpenísion **146** B1
Karperón **143** C2/3
Kärra **49** D1, **50** A1
Karrantza **153** C1
Kärrbo **40** A3, **47** B/C1
Karrebæksminde **53** D1/2
Kärrgruvan **40** A3
Karsaikkovvara **22** B1
Kärsämä **18** B3
Kärsämäki **21** D1, **22** A1
Karsanlahti **22** B2
Kärsava **74** B2
Karsbo **51** D2
Karsikas **21** D1, **22** A1
Karsko **71** C2
Kårsta **40** B3, **47** D1
Karstädt **69** D2
Kårstø **42** A2
Karstorp **51** C2
Karstula **21** C2
Kartavoll **42** A3
Kartérion **142** B3
Kårtjevuolle **9** D3
Karttula **22** B2
Kartuzy **72** B2
Karuna **24** B3
Karungi **17** D2, **18** A1
Karunki **17** D2, **18** A1
Karup **48** B2
Karvala **21** C2
Karvaselkä **11** D2, **12** B1
Kärväskylä **21** D2, **22** A2
Kårvatn **32** B2
Karvia **20** B3
Karvik **9** D1
Karvik **4** B2
Karvila **23** C3
Karvio **23** C3
Karvoskylä **21** D1, **22** A1
Karvsor **20** B2
Kås **48** B1
Kasala/Kasaböle **20** A3
Käsatakka **9** C3
Kåseberga **50** B3
Kasejovice **83** C3, **93** C1
Kasendorf **82** A3
Kasfjord **9** C1/2
Kašin **75** D2
Kašina **127** D2/3
Kasiniemi **25** C1, **26** A1
Kaskei **27** C2
Kasker **15** D2
Kaskii **27** C1
Kaskinen (Kaskö) **20** A3
Kaskö **20** A3
Käsmä **19** C/D1
Kasnäs **24** B3
Káspakas **145** C3
Kašperské Hory **93** C1
Kassa **17** D1
Kassándria **144** A2
Kassel **81** C1
Kässijärvi **7** C3
Kassiópi **142** A3
Kassiterá **145** D1
Kassope **146** A1
Kastanéa **143** D2
Kastanéa **143** C/D2
Kastanéa **147** B/C2
Kastanéa **147** B/C2
Kastanéa **143** C3, **146** B1
Kastanéa **148** B2
Kastanéa **148** B2
Kastanéa **148** B1/2
Kastanéai **145** D2
Kastaní **142** B3
Kastav **126** B3, **130** A1
Kastellaun **80** A3
Kastéllion **147** C1
Kaštel Stari **131** C3
Kastélyosdombó **128** A/B2/3
Kasterlee **79** C1
Kastl **92** A1
Kastlösa **51** D2
Kastorf **53** C3, **69** C1
Kästorf (Gifhorn) **69** C2
Kastoría **143** C2
Kastoría **148** A/B1
Kastórion **146** B3
Kastrákion **147** C2
Kástron **147** D1
Kástron **147** C2
Kástron tís Oréas **143** D3
Kastrup **49** D3, **50** A3, **53** D1
Kasukkala **27** C2
Kaszczor **71** C/D3
Katafa **127** D1, **128** A1
Katajamäki **23** C1/2
Katajamäki **22** B3
Katajamäki **22** B2
Katákolon **146** A3
Katákolon **148** A2
Kataloinen **25** C/D2, **26** A2
Katápola **149** C3
Kåtaselet **16** A/B3
Katavothra **143** C3
Katelbogen **53** D3, **69** D1
Kateríni **143** D2
Katerma **19** D3, **23** D1
Katholm **49** C2
Katinhäntä **24** A2
Kätkäsuvanto **11** C2/3
Kätkävaara **12** A3, **17** D2
Kätkesuando **11** C2/3
Katlanovo **139** C2
Katlanovska Banja **139** C2
Káto Achaïa **146** B2
Káto Achaïa **148** A/B2
Káto Alepochórion **143** D3, **144** A3
Kató Alepochórion **147** C2
Káto Almirí **147** C2
Katochí **146** A2
Káto Drosíni **145** D1
Káto Figália **146** B3
Káto Gotzéa **144** A3
Káto Klinaí **143** C1
Káto Makrinoú **146** B2
Káto Nevrokópion **144** B1
Káto Orfaná **143** D3
Káto Tithoréa **147** C1
Katoúna **146** A1
Káto Vérmion **143** C2
Katovice **93** C1
Katowice **96** B2
Katrineberg **40** A1/2
Katrineholm **46** B1/2
Kats **66** A3, **78** B1
Katsikás **142** B3
Katsikko **12** B2
Kattarp **49** D2/3, **50** A2
Kättbo Norra **39** C2
Kattelus **21** C3
Katthammarsvik **47** D3
Kattila-aho **23** D3
Kattilainen **26** B2
Kattilanmäki **23** C3
Kattilasaari **17** D2
Kattisavan **30** B1
Kattisberg **31** C1
Kattisträsk **31** C1
Katunci **139** D3
Katusice **83** D2
Katwijk **66** A3
Katymár **129** C2
Katzelsdorf **94** B2
Katzenelnbogen **80** B2
Katzhütte **82** A2
Katzweiler **80** A/B3, **90** A1
Kaub **80** B3
Kaufbeuren **91** D3
Kaufbeuren-Neugablonz **91** D3
Kaufering **91** D2/3
Kaufungen **81** C1
Kauhajärvi **21** B/C2
Kauhajärvi **20** B3
Kauhajoki **20** B3
Kauhava **20** B2
Kaukalampi **25** D2, **26** A2
Kauklahti **25** C3
Kaukola **21** B/C3
Kaukola **24** B3
Kaukonen **11** D3, **12** A2
Kaukuri **24** B3
Kaulinranta **17** D2
Kaulio **26** B2
Kaulsdorf **82** A2
Kaunas **73** D2, **74** A3
Kauniainen/Grankulla **25** C3
Kaunissaari **26** B3
Kaupanger **36** B2
Kauppila **20** A3
Kauppila **22** A/B3

Kauppilanmäki **22** B1
Kaurajärvi **20** B2
Kaurissalo **24** A2, **41** D2
Kauronkylä **19** D3
Kausala **25** D2, **26** B2
Kaušany **141** D1
Kaustby **21** C1
Kaustinen (Kaustby) **21** C1
Kautokeino **11** C1
Kauttua **24** B2
Kautzen **94** A1
Kavadarci **139** C3, **143** C1
Kavadarci **140** A3
Kavajë **137** D3
Kavak **149** D1
Kavála **149** C1
Kavála **144** B1
Kavarna **141** D3
Kavcik **145** D3
Kävlinge **50** A3
Kávos **142** A3
Kavoúri **147** D2
Kawcze **71** D3
Kaxås **29** C3, **34** B1
Kaxholmen **45** D3, **46** A3
Käylä **13** C3
Käymäjärvi **11** C3
Kayna **82** B1/2
Käyrämö **12** B2
Käyrämö **12** B3
Kaysersberg **89** D2, **90** A2
Kazanci **131** D2
Kažani **138** B3, **143** B/C1
Kazanlâk **141** C3
Kazatin **99** C2/3
Kazincbarcika **97** C2/3
Kaźmierz **71** D2
Kbely **83** D3
Kdyně **93** B/C1
Kéa **149** C2
Kebnekaise fjällstation **9** D3
Kecel **129** C2
Kecskemét **129** C/D1
Kecskemét **97** C3, **140** A1
Kédainiai **73** D2, **74** A3
Kédange-sur-Canner
  89 C/D1
Kédros **143** C3, **146** B1
Kędzierzyn-Koźle **96** B2
Kefalárion **147** C2
Kefalárion **147** C3
Kéfalos **149** D3
Kefenrod **81** C2
Kefermarkt **93** D2
Kehl **90** A/B2
Kehl-Bodersweier **90** B2
Kehl-Goldscheuer **90** A/B2
Kehnert **69** D3
Kehrig **80** A2
Kehrigk **70** B3
Kehro **25** B/C2
Keighley **59** D1, **61** C2
Keihärinkoski **21** D2, **22** A2
Keihäskoski **24** B2
Keikyä **24** B1/2
Keila **74** A1
Keills **56** A1/2
Keimola **25** C3, **26** A3
Keinäsperä **18** B2
Keipene **73** D1, **74** A2
Keisala **21** C2
Keisanmäki **26** B2
Keistiö **24** A3, **41** D2
Keitele **21** D2, **22** A2
Keitelepohja **21** D2, **22** A2
Keith **54** B2
Kekäleniemi **27** D1
Kekkilä **21** D2, **22** A2
Kelankylä **18** B1
Kelberg **80** A2
Kelbra **81** D1, **82** A1
Kelč **95** C1
Kelchsau **92** B3
Kêlcyrë **142** A2
Kêlcyrë **148** A1
Keléd **128** A1
Kelevíz **128** A2
Kelheim **92** A/B1
Kelheim-Weilenburg
  92 A1/2
Keljonkangas **21** D3, **22** A3
Kelkheim (Taunus) **80** B3
Kelkkala **24** B3
Kell **80** A3
Kella **81** D1
Kélla **143** C1/2
Kellahti **24** A1

Kellarpelto **27** C1
Kellenhusen **53** C3
Kellinghusen **52** B3
Kellmünz **91** D2
Kello **18** A2
Kellokoski **25** D2, **26** A2
Kelloniemi **13** B/C3
Kelloselkä **13** C3
Kelmé **73** D2
Kelontekemä **11** D3,
  12 A/B2
Kelottijärvi **10** B2
Kelso **57** C/D2
Kelsterbach **80** B3
Kelstrup Strand **52** B1
Keltiäinen **25** C2
Keltti **26** B2
Kelujärvi **12** B2
Kelvä **23** D2
Kelvedon **65** C2/3
Kemberg **69** D3
Kembs **90** A3
Kemence **95** D2/3
Kemeneshőgyész **95** C3,
  128 A1
Kemer **149** D2
Kémes **128** B3
Kemi **17** D3, **18** A1
Kemihaaran rajavartioasema
  13 C1
Kemijärvi **12** B3
Kemilä **19** D1
Keminmaa **17** D2/3, **18** A1
Kemin maalaiskunta
  17 D2/3, **18** A1
Keminvaara **19** C2
Kemnath **92** B1
Kemnath **82** A3
Kempele **18** A/B2
Kempen-Hülsd **79** D1
Kempenich **80** A2
Kempen-Niederrhein **79** D1
Kempfeld-Katzenloch
  80 A3
Kempten (Allgäu) **91** D3
Kempten-Sankt Mang
  91 D3
Kemptthal **90** B3
Kendal **59** D1, **60** B1/2
Kendal **54** B3
Kenderes **129** D1
Kendríkon **139** D3, **143** D1,
  144 A1
Kéndron **146** A/B2
Kenespahta **6** B2
Kengis **17** C/D1
Kengyel **129** D1
Kenilworth **64** A2
Kenmare **55** C3
Kenmore **54** B2
Kenmore **56** B1
Kennacraig **56** A2
Kenraalinkylä **23** D3
Kentford **65** C2
Kenton **63** C3
Kenzingen **90** A/B2
Kępno **96** B1
Kepsut **149** D1
Keramídion **143** D3,
  144 A3
Keramítsa **142** B3
Keramotí **145** C1
Keräntöjärvi **11** C3
Keraséa **143** C2
Kerasóna **142** B3
Keräs-Sieppi **11** C2/3,
  12 A1
Keratéa **147** D2/3
Kerava (Kervo) **25** D3,
  26 A3
Kérazan **84** A3
Kerdílion Óros **144** A/B1
Kerekegyháza **129** C1
Kerepes **95** D3
Kerimäki **27** D1
Keriniemi **27** C1
Kériolet **84** B2/3
Keríon **146** A3
Keríon **148** A2
Kerisalo **22** B3
Kerjean **84** A/B2
Kerken-Nieukerk **79** D1
Kerkétion Óros **143** C3
Kerkhove **78** B2
Kerkineon **143** D3
Kerkíni **139** D3, **144** A3
Kérkira **142** A3

Kérkira **148** A1
Kerkkoo **25** D2/3, **26** A2/3
Kerkola **24** B2
Kerkonkoski **22** B2
Kerkrade **79** D2
Kerma **23** C3
Kermaria **85** B/C1/2
Kernascléden **84** B2
Kernhof **94** A3
Kernovo **74** B1
Kerns [Kerns-Kägiswil]
  105 C1
Kernuz **84** A3
Kerpen **79** D2, **80** A2
Kerpen-Blatzheim **79** D2,
  80 A2
Kerpen-Türnich **79** D2,
  80 A2
Kershopefoot **57** C3
Kersilö **12** B2
Kerta **128** A1
Kerteminde **53** C1
Kértezi **146** B2
Kerttuankylä **21** B/C2
Kervo **25** D3, **26** A3
Kesälahti **27** D1
Keşan **145** D3
Keşan **149** C/D1
Kesäranta **27** C1
Kesariani **147** D2
Keselyüs **129** C2
Kesilö **25** D1, **26** B1
Keskijärvi **23** D3
Keskikylä **18** A2/3
Keskikylä **21** C2
Keskikylä **20** B3
Keskikylä **18** B3
Keskikylä **18** A3
Keskinen **19** D3
Keskipiiri **18** A2
Keski-Posio **19** C1
Kes'ma **75** D1
Kesova Gora **75** D2
Kesseli **23** D1
Kesti **20** A/B3
Kestilä **18** B3
Kestilä **18** A2
Keswick **57** C3, **60** B1
Keswick **54** B3
Keszeg **95** D3
Keszthely **128** A1/2
Keszthely **96** B3
Ketomella **11** C2, **12** A1
Keträvaara **19** D2
Kętrzyn (Rastenburg)
  73 C2
Ketsch **90** B1
Kettering **64** B2
Kettershausen **91** D2
Kettlewell **59** D1, **60** B2
Kéty **128** B2
Ketzin **70** A2
Keula **81** D1
Keuruu **21** C3
Kevelaer **67** C3, **79** D1
Kevelaer-Winnekendonk
  67 C3, **79** D1
Kevi **129** D3
Kevo **6** B2
Keynsham **63** D2
Keyritty **23** B/C2
Kežmarok **97** C2
Kianí **145** D1, **145** D3
Kiannanniemi **19** D2
Kiáton **147** C2
Kiáton **148** B2
Kibæk **48** A3
Kiberg **7** D2
Kičevo **138** B3
Kičevo **140** A3
Kidderminster **59** D3,
  64 A2
Kidlington **65** C2/3
Kidwelly **62** B1
Kiefersfelden **92** B3
Kiehtäjä **19** C2
Kiekinkoski **23** D1
Kieksiäisvaara **17** C/D1
Kiel **52** B3
Kielajoki **6** B3
Kielce **97** C1
Kielder **57** C2
Kiellatupa **6** B3
Kienberg **92** B3
Kienitz **70** B2
Kiental [Reichenbach im
  Kandertal] **105** C2

Kieri **17** D2
Kierinki **12** A/B2
Kierspe **80** A/B1
Kierun **15** C/D1
Kiesen **105** C1
Kiesilä **26** B1/2
Kiesima **22** A/B2
Kietävälä **27** D1
Kietävälä **27** C1
Kietz **70** B2
Kiev **99** C2
Kifino Selo **132** B3, **137** C1
Kifisiá **147** D2
Kifisiá **148** B2
Kífisos **148** B2
Kífisos **147** C2
Kifjord **6** B1
Kihlanki **11** C3
Kihniö **20** B3
Kihniön asema **20** B3
Kiihtelysvaara **23** D3
Kiikala **25** C2/3
Kiikka **24** B1
Kiikoinen **24** B1
Kiilisjärvi **17** C2
Kiilopään-Eräkeskus **12** B1
Kiimavaara **19** D3
Kiiminki **18** B2
Kiiskilä **21** C1
Kiiskilä **27** C1
Kiistala **11** D3, **12** A1/2
Kijevo **132** B3
Kijevo **131** C2
Kijevo **138** B1/2
Kikinda **129** D3
Kikinda **140** A1
Kikorze **71** C1
Kil **46** A1
Kil **45** D1
Kil **43** D2, **44** A2
Kila **46** B2
Kila **45** D1
Kilafors **40** A1
Kila/Kiila **24** B3
Kilane **43** C/D2, **44** A1/2
Kilás **147** C3
Kilb **94** A2
Kilberget **16** B3
Kilberry **56** A2
Kilboghamn **14** B2
Kilbotn **9** C2
Kilbride **58** A2
Kilchattan **56** A/B2
Kilchrenan **56** A1
Kilcreggan **56** B1/2
Kilcullen **55** D3
Kile **44** B2
Kilebygd **43** D2, **44** A1
Kilen **43** C2
Kilija **141** D2
Kilingi-Nömme **74** A1
Kilkee **55** C3
Kilkeel **58** A1
Kilkenny **55** D3
Kilkinkylä **26** B1
Kilkís **143** D1, **144** A1
Killarney **55** C3
Killearn **56** B1
Killeberg **50** B2
Killin **56** B1
Killiney **58** A2
Killingi **10** A3
Killíni **146** A2
Killinkoski **21** C3
Killnick **58** A3
Killorglin **55** C3
Killough **58** A1
Killyleagh **58** A1
Kilmacolm **56** B2
Kilmaluag **54** A2
Kilmarnock **54** A/B3, **55** D1
Kilmarnock **56** B2
Kilmartin **56** A1
Kilmelford **56** A1
Kilmory **56** A2
Kilmory **56** A2
Kilmuckridge **58** A3
Kilninver **56** A1
Kilpisjärvi **10** B1
Kilpua **18** A3
Kilsmo **46** B1
Kilsyth **56** B1/2
Kilvakkala **24** B1
Kilvenaapa **18** B2
Kilvo **16** B1
Kilwinning **56** B2
Kimbolton **64** B2

Kími **147** D1
Kími **149** B/C2
Kiminki **21** C2
Kimito/Kemiö **24** B3
Kimméria **145** C1
Kimo **20** B2
Kimola **25** D2, **26** B2
Kimonkylä **25** D2, **26** B2
Kimry **75** D2
Kimstad **46** B2
Kinahmo **23** C2
Kincardine on Forth
  57 B/C1
Kindberg **94** A3
Kindelbrück **81** D1, **82** A1
Kinderåsen **34** B2
Kinding **92** A1
Kinéta **147** D2
Kineton **64** A2
Kingarth **56** A/B2
Kinghorn **57** C1
Kingisepp **74** B1
Kingsbarn **57** C1
Kingsberg **40** A2'
Kingsbridge **63** C3
Kingsclere **65** C3, **76** B1
King's Lynn **65** C1
Kings Thorn **63** D1
Kingston **64** B3, **76** B1
Kingston upon Hull **61** D2
Kingswear **63** C3
Kington **59** C/D3, **63** C1
Kinisjärvi **12** A2, **17** D1
Kinkton **56** A1
Kinloch **54** A2, **55** D1
Kinlochleven **54** A2, **55** D1
Kinloch Rannoch **54** B2,
  55 D1
Kinn **37** D3
Kinn **9** C1
Kinna **49** D1, **50** A1
Kinna **72** A1
Kinnared **50** A/B1
Kinnarp **45** D3
Kinnarumma **45** C3, **49** D1
Kinna-Skene **49** D1, **50** A1
Kinna-Skene **72** A1
Kinnegad **55** D2
Kinni **26** B1
Kinnula **21** C/D2
Kinnulanlahti **22** B2
Kinrooi-Kessenich **79** D1
Kinross **57** C1
Kinsale **55** C3
Kinsarvik **36** B3
Kintaus **21** D3, **22** A3
Kintus **24** B1
Kiónion **146** A2
Kiosque **155** C2
Kiparissía **146** B3
Kipárissos **143** D3
Kipfenberg **92** A1
Kípi **142** B3
Kipiná **18** B2
Kipouríon **143** C2/3
Kippel [Goppenstein]
  105 C2
Kippford **56** B3, **60** A1
Kippinge **53** C2
Kirakkajärvi **7** C2/3
Kirakkaköngäs **6** B3
Kirakka-Olli **7** C2
Kirazli **149** D1
Kirbymoorside **61** C2
Kirchardt **91** C1
Kirchbach **126** A2
Kirchbach in Steiermark
  127 C1
Kirchberg **91** C/D1
Kirchberg **80** A3
Kirchberg **82** B2
Kirchberg am Wagram
  94 A2
Kirchberg am Wechsel
  94 A3
Kirchberg am Walde **93** D2
Kirchberg an der Pielach
  94 A2/3
Kirchberg an der Raab
  127 C/D1
Kirchberg in Tirol **92** B3
Kirchberg [Kirchberg-Al-
  chenflüh] **105** C1
Kirchberg (Regen) **93** C1/2
Kirchdorf **68** A2
Kirchdorf **93** B/C2
Kirchdorf **94** A3, **127** C1

Kirchdorf 53 C3
Kirchdorf an der Krems 93 C/D3
Kirchdorf an der Krems 96 A3
Kirchdorf (Freising) 92 A2
Kirchdorf im Wald 93 C1
Kirchehrenbach 82 A3
Kirchendemenreuth 82 B3
Kirchenlamitz 82 A/B3
Kirchen-Sieg 80 B2
Kirchhain 81 C2
Kirchheilingen 81 D1
Kirchheim 91 C1
Kirchheim 81 C3
Kirchheim-Bolanden 80 B3
Kirchheim (Hersfeld) 81 C2
Kirchheim im Innkreis 93 C2
Kirchheim unter Teck 91 C2
Kirchhundem 80 B1
Kirchhundem-Oberhundem 80 B1
Kirchhundem-Rahrbach 80 B1/2
Kirchhundem-Albaum 80 B1
Kirchlauter 81 D3
Kirchlinteln-Sehlingen 68 B2
Kirchlinteln 68 B2
Kirchroth 92 B1
Kirchschlag in der Buckligen Welt 94 B3
Kirchweidach 92 B2/3
Kirchzarten 90 B3
Kircubbin 56 A3
Kiriákion 147 C2
Kiriši 75 C1
Kirjais 24 A/B3
Kirjakkala 24 B3
Kirjala 24 B3
Kirkağaç 149 D2
Kirkambeck 57 C3, 60 B1
Kirkbride 57 C3, 60 A/B1
Kirkby in Ashfield 61 D3, 65 C1
Kirkby Lonsdale 59 D1, 60 B2
Kirkby Stephen 57 D3, 60 B1
Kirkcaldy 57 C1
Kirkcaldy 54 B2
Kirkcolm 56 A3
Kirkconnel 56 B2
Kirkcowan 56 B3
Kirkcudbright 56 B3, 60 A1
Kirkeby 52 A2
Kirkeby 28 B3, 33 D1
Kirkehamn 42 B3
Kirkehavn 53 C1/2
Kirke Hvalsø 49 D3, 53 D1
Kirkenær 38 B2
Kirkenes (Kirkkoniemi) 7 C/D2
Kirkham 59 D1, 60 B2
Kírki 145 D1
Kirkintilloch 56 B2
Kirkjubøur 55 C1
Kirkkonummi/Kyrkslätt 25 C3
Kirkkopahta 11 C3, 12 A2
Kirk Michael 58 B1
Kirknesvågen 28 B2, 33 D1
Kirkoswald 57 C3, 60 B1
Kirkoswald 56 B2
Kirkpatrick 57 C3, 60 B1
Kirkton 57 C2
Kirkton of Largo 57 C1
Kirkvollen 33 D2
Kirkwall 54 B1
Kirkwhelpington 57 D3
Kirn 80 A3
Kirnički 141 D1/2
Kirnujärvi 17 C1
Kirov 75 D3
Kirovograd 99 D3
Kirovsk 75 C1
Kirra 147 C2
Kirriemuir 57 C1
Kirton-in-Lindsey 61 D3
Kirtorf 81 C2
Kiruna 10 A3
Kiruna-Tuolluvaara 10 A3
Kisa 46 B3
Kisbér 95 C3
Kisbér 96 B3
Kisela Voda 138 B2
Kiseljak 132 B2
Kiseljak 133 C2
Kishajmás 128 B2
Kisiljevo 134 B1/2
Kišinëv 141 D1
Kiskassa 128 B2/3
Kisko 25 B/C3
Kiskomárom 128 A2
Kiskőrös 129 C2
Kiskőrös 97 C3
Kiskundorozsma 129 D2
Kiskunfélegyháza 129 D1/2
Kiskunfélegyháza 97 C3, 140 A1
Kiskunhalas 97 C3, 140 A1
Kiskunhalas 129 C2
Kiskunlacháza 129 C1
Kiskunmajsa 129 C/D2
Kiskunmajsa 97 C3, 140 A1
Kismaros 95 D3
Kisoroszi 95 D3
Kissakoski 26 B1
Kissala 27 D1
Kissámos (Kastéllion) 148 B3
Kissanlahti 23 C1/2
Kisslegg 91 C3
Kisslegg-Waltershofen 91 C3
Kistanje 131 C2
Kistelek 129 D2
Kisterenye 97 C3
Kistrand 5 D2, 6 A1
Kisújszállás 129 D1
Kisújszállás 97 C3, 140 A1
Kisurisstugan 9 D3
Kisvárda 97 C/D2/3, 98 A3
Kiszkowo 71 D2
Kiszombor 129 D2
Kitee 23 D3
Kiteenlahti 23 D3
Kitinoja 20 B2
Kitka 19 C/D1
Kitkiöjärvi 11 C3
Kitkiojoki 11 C3
Kitrinópetras 145 D1, 145 D3
Kítros 143 D2
Kitsi 23 D2
Kittelfjäll 15 C3, 29 D1
Kittilä 11 D3, 12 A2
Kittlitz 83 D1
Kittsee 94 B2/3
Kitula 25 C3
Kituperä 18 B3, 22 B1
Kitzbühel 92 B3
Kitzingen 81 D3
Kitzscher 82 B1
Kiukainen 24 B1/2
Kiuruvesi 22 B1
Kivarinjärvi 19 C2
Kivercy 98 B2
Kivérion 147 C3
Kivesjärvi 19 C3
Kiveslahti 19 B/C3
Kivijärvi 21 D2, 22 A2
Kivijärvi 18 B2
Kivik 50 B3
Kivik 72 A2
Kivikangas 21 C2
Kivikylä 24 A2
Kivilahti 23 D2
Kivilompolo 12 A3, 17 D2
Kiviniemi 26 B2/3
Kiviöli 74 A/B1
Kivipaja 27 C1
Kiviperä 19 D1
Kiviranta 19 D1
Kivisuo 26 A1
Kivivaara 23 D1
Kivivaara 19 C2
Kivivaara 23 D3
Kivotós 143 C2
Kjækan 5 C2/3
Kjårnes 9 C3
Kjeldebotn 9 C2
Kjeldobu 37 B/C3
Kjellerup 48 B2
Kjengsnes 9 C2
Kjennsvasshytta 14 B2
Kjerrengvoll 33 D2
Kjerret 38 B3
Kjerringøy 8 B3
Kjerringvåg 32 B1
Kjerringvik 9 C2
Kjerringvik 43 D2, 44 A/B1/2
Kjerringvik 28 B3, 33 D1
Kjerstivika 28 B2
Kjevik 43 C3
Kjølen 44 B1
Kjøli turisthytte 33 D2
Kjøllefjord 6 B1
Kjølsdal 36 A1
Kjølstad 28 B1
Kjoltan 15 C1
Kjøpmannskjer 43 D2, 44 B1
Kjøpsvik 9 C2/3
Kjørsvik 32 B1
Kjorvihytta 15 C1
Kjosen 43 C2, 44 A1
Kjul 14 A3
Kjulaås 47 B/C1
Kjustendil 139 D2
Kjustendil 140 B3
Klåbu 28 B2
Kl'ačno 95 D1
Kladanj 133 B/C2
Kläden 69 C/D2
Klädesholmen 44 B3
Kladnica 133 D3, 134 A3
Kladnica 139 D1/2
Kladnice 131 C3
Kladno 83 C3
Kladno 96 A2
Kladovo 135 C/D2
Kladruby 82 B3
Klagenfurt 126 B2
Klagenfurt 96 A3
Klågerup 50 A/B3
Klagstorp 50 B3
Klaipėda (Memel) 73 C2
Klaksvík 55 C1
Klamila 26 B2
Klampenborg 49 D3, 50 A3, 53 D1
Klana 126 B3
Klanac 130 B2
Klanjec 127 D2
Klanxbüll 52 A2
Kläppe 34 B2
Kläppen 16 A3
Kläppsjö 30 B2, 35 D1
Kläppsjö 30 B2, 35 D1
Klarabro 38 B2
Klarup 48 B1/2
Klašnice 131 D1, 132 A1
Klašterec 83 C2
Kláštor pod Znievom 95 D1
Klatovy 93 C1
Klatovy 96 A2
Klaukkala 25 C3
Klaus an der Pyhrnbahn 93 C/D3
Klausenleopoldsdorf 94 A2/3
Klauvnes 4 B2
Klazienaveen 67 C2
Kleemola 21 C1
Klegod 48 A3
Kleinarl 126 A1
Kleinau 69 C2
Klein Bademeusel 70 B3, 83 D1
Klein Berssen 67 D2
Kleinblittersdorf 89 D1, 90 A1
Kleingiesshübel 82 A2
Kleinglödnitz 126 B1
Kleinhaugsdorf 94 A2
Klein-Koschen 83 C1
Kleinkrausnik 70 A3
Klein Lüben 69 D2
Klein-Machnow 70 A2/3
Klein-Muckrow 70 B3
Klein-Mühlingen 69 D3
Kleinmünchen 93 D2
Klein Oschersleben 69 C3
Kleinpaschleben 69 D3
Kleinrinderfeld 81 C3
Kleinsaubernitz 83 D1
Kleinwelka 83 D1
Kleinwusterwitz 69 D2
Kleiv 37 D3
Kleiva 9 B/C2
Kleive 32 A/B2
Kleivegrend 43 C2
Klek 129 D3
Klek 136 B1
Klemensker 51 D3
Klemetinvaara 19 C3
Klemetsrud 38 A3
Klemetstad 5 D2, 6 A2
Klenak 133 C1, 134 A1
Klenči 92 B1
Klenica 71 C3
Klenike 139 C2
Klenovica 130 B1
Klepci 132 A/B3, 136 B1
Klepp 42 A2
Kleppen 28 B3, 33 D1, 34 A1
Kleppestø 36 A3
Kleptow 70 B1
Kletnja 99 D1
Klettbach 82 A2
Klettgau-Bühl 90 B3
Klettgau-Erzingen 90 B3
Klettwitz 83 C1
Klevar 43 D1, 44 A1
Kleve 67 C3
Klevshult 50 B1
Kličev 99 C1
Kličevac 134 B1
Kliening 127 C1
Klietz 69 D2
Klimatiá 142 B3
Kliment 141 C2/3
Klimoviči 99 D1
Klimovo 99 D1
Klimovsk 75 D3
Klimpfjäll 29 D1
Klin 75 D2
Klina 138 A1
Klinča Selo 127 D3
Klincy 99 D1
Klinga 28 B2
Klingenberg 9 C3
Klingenmünster 90 B1
Klingenthal 82 B2
Klintebjerg 49 C3, 53 C1
Klintehamn 47 D3
Klintehamn 72 B1
Klintholm 53 D2
Kliplev 52 B2
Klippan 50 A2
Klippan 72 A1
Klippen 15 C2
Klis 131 C/D3
Klisoúra 143 C2
Klisoúra 142 B3
Klisoúra 148 A1
Klisura 139 C1
Klisura 139 D2
Klitmøller 48 A1/2
Klitten 83 D1
Klitten 39 C1
Kljaci 131 C3
Kljajićevo 129 C3
Kljake 131 C3
Kljasticy 74 B2/3
Ključ 131 D2, 132 A2
Klobouky 94 B1
Kłobuck 96 B1
Klobuk 131 D3, 132 A3, 136 B1
Klockarberg 39 D2
Klockow 69 D1, 70 A1
Klockow 70 A/B1
Klockrike 46 A/B2
Kłodawa 71 C2
Klöden 70 A3
Kłodzko (Glatz) 96 B1/2
Kløfta 38 A3
Klokkarstua 38 A3, 43 D1, 44 B1
Klokočevac 135 C2
Klokočevci 128 B3
Klokočov 95 D1
Klokot 138 B2
Kloosterburen 67 C1
Kloosterhaar 67 C2
Kloosterzande 78 B1
Kłopot 70 B3
Klos 138 A3
Klöse 31 C2
Kloštar 128 A2/3
Kloštar Ivanić 127 D3
Kloster-Birnau 91 C3
Klosterfelde 70 A2
Klostermansfeld 82 A1
Klosterneuburg 94 B2
Klosterreichenbach 90 B2
Klosters 106 A1
Kloster Sankt Trudpert 90 A/B3
Kloster Zinna 70 A3
Kloten 39 D3
Kloten 90 B3
Klotten 80 A3
Klötze 69 C2
Klovborg 48 B3
Kløven 32 B1
Klöverträsk 16 B3
Klöveskog 45 C2
Kløvfors 14 B3
Klövsjö 34 B3
Klubbfors 16 B3
Klubbukt 5 C/D1/2, 6 A1
Kluczbork 96 B1
Kluczewo 71 C/D1
Kluess 53 D3, 69 D1
Klukshåckren 29 C3, 34 A/B2
Klupe 132 A1/2
Klüsserath 80 A3
Klutmark 31 D1
Klütz 53 C3
Knaben gruver 42 B2/3
Knåda 39 D1, 40 A1
Knaften 31 C1
Knap-dale 56 A2
Knapstad 38 A3, 44 B1
Knäred 50 B2
Knaresborough 61 C2
Knarrevik 36 A3
Knarsdale 57 C3, 60 B1
Knarvik 36 A3
Knebel 49 C2/3
Kneippbyn 47 D3
Knetzgau 81 D3
Kneža 140 B2/3
Knežak 126 B3
Kneževi Vinogradi 129 C3
Kneževo 128 B3
Knežina 133 B/C2
Kněžmost 83 D2
Knić 134 B2/3
Knićanin 129 D3, 133 D1, 134 A1
Knighton 59 C/D3
Knin 131 C2
Knislinge 50 B2
Knittelfeld 127 C1
Knittelfeld 96 A3
Knittlingen 90 B1
Knivsta 40 B3
Knížecí Pláně 93 C1
Knjaževac 135 C3
Knjaževac 140 A2
Knock 57 C/D3, 60 B1
Knokke-Heist 78 A1
Knoppe 35 D3
Knott End 59 C/D1, 60 B2
Knowle 64 A2
Knüllwald 81 C1/2
Knüllwald-Remsfeld 81 C1/2
Knutby 40 B3
Knuthenborg 53 C/D2
Knutsford 59 D2, 60 B3, 64 A1
Knutsvik 42 A2
Koarholanmäki 19 C3, 22 B1
Kobarid 126 A/B2
Kobbevåg 4 A3, 10 A1
Kobbfoss 7 C3
København 49 D3, 50 A3, 53 D1
København 72 A2
Kobenz 127 C1
Koberg 45 C3
Kobern-Gondorf 80 A2
Koblenz 80 A/B2
Koblenz 90 B3
Kobrin 73 D3, 97 D1, 98 A/B1
Kobylanka 70 B1
Kobylin 71 D3
Kočani 139 C2
Kočani 140 A/B3
Koceljevo 133 D2, 134 A2
Kočerin 132 A3
Kočerinovo 139 D2
Kočerov 99 C2
Kočevje 127 C3
Kočevska Reka 127 C3
Kochel am See 92 A3
Kochel-Walchensee 92 A3
Kočov 82 B3
Kocs 95 C3
Kocsér 129 D1
Kocsola 128 B2
Kodal 43 D2, 44 A1

Kode 45 C3
Kodër Shëngjergij 137 D2, 138 A2
Kodesjärvi 20 B3
Kodiksalm 24 A/B2
Kodisjoki 24 A2
Ködnitz 82 A3
Koekange 67 C2
Köfering (Regensburg) 92 B1
Köflach 127 C1
Köflach 96 A3
Køge 72 A2
Køge 49 D3, 50 A3, 53 D1
Kogel 69 D1
Kohiseva 22 B3
Kohlberg 82 B3
Kohma 23 C2
Kohtavaara 23 C1/2
Koijärvi 25 C2
Koikkala 27 C1
Koikul 16 B2
Köinge 49 D1, 50 A1
Koirakoski 22 B1
Koiramännikkö 12 A2/3
Koiravaara 23 C1
Koisjärvi 25 C3
Koitila 19 C1
Koitsanlahti 27 D1
Koivistonkylä 21 D3, 22 A3
Koivu 18 A1
Koivula 13 C2
Koivumaa 12 A2/3, 17 D1
Koivumäki 21 C2
Koivumäki 23 C3
Koivumäki 22 B2
Koivuniemi 18 A/B1
Koivuvaara 23 D2/3
Koja 10 A3
Köjan 29 C3, 34 A2
Kojanlahti 23 C2/3
Kojetín 95 C1
Kojola 20 B2
Kojonperä 24 B2
Kojsko 126 A/B2
Kökar 24 A3, 41 D3
Kokašice 82 B3
Kokava nad Rimavicou 97 C2
Kokelv 5 D1, 6 A1
Kokemäki (Kumo) 24 B1/2
Kokheden 16 B2
Kokin Brod 133 D3, 134 A3
Kokkila 24 B3
Kokkila 25 C2
Kókkini Ekklisía 143 B/C3
Kokkinókastro 147 D1
Kókkino Neró 143 D3, 144 A3
Kokkinopilós 143 D2
Kokkokylä 18 B1
Kokkola 25 C1
Kokkolahti 23 C3
Kokkola/Karleby 20 B1
Kokkoniemi 19 D2
Kokkosenlahti 27 B/C1
Kokkovaara 12 A2
Koklë 142 B1
Köklot 20 A2, 31 D3
Kokonvaara 23 C2
Kokořín 83 D2
Kokory 95 C1
Kokra 126 B2
Kokseby 53 D2
Koksijde-Bad 78 A1
Kokträsk 16 A3
Köla 38 B3
Kola 131 D1/2, 132 A1
Kolan 130 B2
Kolari 134 B2
Kolari 12 A2
Kolárovo 95 C3
Kolárovo 96 B3
Kolåsen 29 C3, 34 A1
Kolašin 137 D1
Kolbäck 40 A3, 46 B1
Kołbaskowo 70 B1
Kolbermoor 92 B3
Kolbnitz 126 A1
Kolbu 38 A2
Kolby Kås 49 C3, 53 C1
Kolchikón 144 A1/2
Koldby 48 A2
Kolding 48 B3, 52 B1
Koler 16 B3
Kolerträsk 16 B3
Kölesd 128 B2
Kolho 21 C3
Koli 23 D2
Kolín 83 D3
Kolín 96 A2
Kolind 49 C2
Kolindrós 143 D2
Kolinec 93 C1
Kölingared 45 D3
Kolka 73 C/D1
Kolkanranta 27 C1
Kolkku 21 D2, 22 A2
Kolkonjärvi 19 C1
Kolkonpää 27 C1
Kolkontaipale 23 B/C3
Kolkwitz 70 B3
Kollaja 18 B2
Kölleda 82 A1
Kollerschlag 93 C2
Kollerud 39 B/C3
Kollínai 147 B/C3
Kolltveit 36 A3
Kollum 67 C1
Kolma 22 B3
Kolmikanta 18 B3
Kölmjärv 17 C2
Kolm-Saigurn 107 D1, 126 A1
Köln 80 A2
Kolno 73 C3, 98 A1
Köln-Porz 80 A2
Köln-Rondorf 80 A2
Koło 73 B/C3, 96 B1
Kołobrzeg (Kolberg) 72 B2
Kolodistoe 99 C3
Kolomyja 97 D2, 98 B3
Kolonjë 142 A2
Koloveč 83 B/C3, 93 C1
Kolovrat 133 C3
Kolpino 75 B/C1
Kolppi 20 B1
Kolsätter 34 B3
Kölsillre 35 B/C3
Kölsjön 35 C3
Kolsko 71 C3
Kølstrup 53 C1
Kolsva 39 D3, 40 A3, 46 B1
Kolta 95 D3
Kolu 21 C2/3
Kolunić 131 C2
Kolvaa 24 B2
Kolvereid 28 B1
Kølvrå 48 B2
Komádi 97 C3, 140 A1
Komagfjord 5 C2
Komagvær 7 D2
Komagvik 4 A2
Koman 137 D2, 138 A2
Komarin 99 C2
Komárno 96 B3
Komárno 95 C3
Komárom 95 C3
Komárom 96 B3
Kombótion 146 A1
Komen 126 B3
Komi 25 B/C1
Komin 127 D2
Komiža 136 A1
Komjatice 95 C2
Komló 128 B2
Kömlöd 95 C3
Kommelhaug 9 C2
Komménon 146 A1
Kommerniemi 27 C1
Kommíná 143 C2
Komninón 143 C2
Komoran 138 B1/2
Komorniki 71 D3
Komossa 20 B2
Kompakka 23 D3
Kompelusvaara 17 C1
Kömpöc 129 D2
Komrat 141 D1
Komsomol'skoe 99 C2/3
Komu 21 D1, 22 A1
Komula 23 C1
Komulanköngäs 19 C3
Konak 134 B1
Konakovo 75 D2
Konarevo 133 D3, 134 A/B3
Konäs 29 C3, 34 A1
Končanica 128 A3
Kondiás 145 C3
Kondopoúli 145 C3
Kondovázena 146 B2/3
Kondrovo 75 D3
Koněprusy 83 C3
Køng 53 D2
Konga 51 C2
Köngäs 5 D3, 6 A/B3, 11 D1
Köngäs 6 B2
Köngäs 12 B3
Köngäs 11 D3, 12 A1/2
Kongasmäki 19 C3
Kongens gruve 43 D1, 44 A1
Kongenshus Hede 48 B2
Kongensvoll 28 A3, 33 C1
Kongeparken 42 A2
Konginkangas 21 D2, 22 A2
Kongsberg 43 D1, 44 A1
Kongsbergseter 43 C1
Kongselva 9 B/C2
Kongsfjord 7 C1
Kongsli 10 A1
Kongsmoen 29 B/C1
Kongsness 36 B2
Kongsvinger 38 B3
Kongsvoll 33 C3, 37 D1
Koniarovce 95 C2
Königerode 82 A1
Königsberg 81 D3
Königsbronn 91 D2
Königsbrück 83 C1
Königsbrunn 91 D2
Königsdorf 92 A3
Königsee 82 A2
Königsfeld im Schwarzwald 90 B2
Königshütte 69 C3
Königslutter 69 C3
Königsmoos-Wagenhofen 92 A2
Königstein 80 B2/3
Königstetten 94 A/B2
Königswartha 83 D1
Königswiesen 93 D2
Königswinter 80 A2
Königswinter-Oberpleis 80 A2
Königs-Wusterhausen 70 A3
Königs-Wusterhausen 72 A3
Konin 72 B3, 96 B1
Koningsbosch 79 D1
Konispoli 142 A3
Kónitsa 142 B2
Kónitsa 148 A1
Konjavo 139 D2
Konjevrate 131 C3
Konjic 132 B3
Konjsko 137 C1/2
Konken 80 A3, 90 A1
Könnern 69 D3, 82 A1
Konnersreuth 82 B3
Konnerud 43 D1, 44 A1
Konnevesi 21 D3, 22 A3
Könni 20 B2
Konnuslahti 22 B3
Könölä 17 D2, 18 A1
Konolfingen 105 C1
Konopiště 83 D3
Konopište 139 C3, 143 C1
Konotop 71 C3
Konotop 71 C1
Konotop 99 D2
Konradsreuth 82 A2
Końskie 97 C1
Konsko 139 C3, 143 D1
Konsmo 42 B3
Konstanz 91 C3
Konstanz-Dettingen 91 C3
Kontich 78 B1
Kontinjoki 19 C3, 22 B1
Kontiolahti 23 D2
Kontiomäki 19 C3
Kontiomäki 22 B3
Kontioranta 23 D2/3
Kontiovaara 23 D2
Kontiovaara 23 D2
Kontkala 23 C3
Kontojärvi 12 A3
Kontókalion 142 A3
Konttajärvi 12 A3, 17 D1
Konttila 18 B1
Konttimäki 21 D3
Konz 79 D3
Konzell 92 B1
Köörtilä 24 A1
Kopačevo 129 C3
Kopanica 71 C3
Kopardal 14 A2
Koparnes 36 A1
Koper 126 B3
Köpernitz 70 A2
Kopervik 42 A2
Kópháza 94 B3
Kopidlno 83 D2
Kopilovci 135 D3
Köping 46 B1
Köpinge 50 B3
Köpingebro 50 B3
Köpingsvik 51 D1
Kopisto 18 A3
Koplik 137 D2
Köpmanholmen 31 B/C3
Köpmannebro 45 C2
Koporice 138 B1
Koposperä 21 D1, 22 A1
Koppang 38 A1
Koppangen 4 B3
Kopparberg 39 D3
Koppelo 23 C1
Kopperå 28 B3, 33 D1
Koppom 38 B3, 45 C1
Kopravaara 23 C/D2
Koprivna 132 B1
Koprivnica 128 A2
Koprivnica 135 C2
Koprivnica 96 B3
Koprivnik 127 C3
Kopsa 18 A3
Kopti 99 D2
Koraće 132 B1
Korahosenniemi 19 C/D1
Koraj 133 C1
Korakiána 142 A3
Korapela 11 D3, 12 A1
Koravenkylä 21 C1
Korbach 81 C1
Korbevac 139 C1/2
Korbovo 135 D2
Korbulič 138 B2
Korçë 142 B2
Korçë 148 A1
Korčula 136 B1
Korczyców 71 B/C3
Kordel 79 D3, 80 A3
Korec 98 B2
Korentokylä 19 C2
Korentovaara 23 D1
Kórfos 147 C2/3
Korgen 14 B2
Koria 26 B2
Koridallós 143 C3
Korifí 143 C2
Korinth 53 C2
Kórinthos 147 C2
Kórinthos 147 C2
Kórinthos 148 B2
Koriseva 23 D2
Korissós 143 C2
Korita 136 B1
Korita 137 C1
Koríthion 146 A2
Koritnica 135 C3, 139 C1
Koritnik 133 D3, 134 A3
Korjukovka 99 D1/2
Korkana 19 D3
Korkatti 18 A3
Korkea 23 D1
Korkeakangas 23 D3
Korkeakoski 25 C1
Korkeaoja 24 B1
Korkeela 25 C/D1, 26 A1
Korkeporten 5 D1
Korkiamaa 17 D2, 18 A1
Körle 81 C1
Körmend 127 D1
Körmend 96 B3
Kormu 25 C2
Kormu 18 B3
Korneuburg 94 B2
Kórnik 71 D3
Kornsjø 45 B/C2
Kornstad 32 A2
Kornwestheim 91 C1/2
Környe 95 C/D3
Koromačno 130 A1
Koróni 148 B3
Korónia 147 C2
Koronisiá 146 A1
Koronoúda 143 D1, 144 A1
Koronowo 72 B3
Koropíon 148 B2
Koropíon 147 D2
Kőröshegy 128 B1
Korospohja 25 D1, 26 A1
Korosten' 99 C2
Kőröstetétlen 129 D1
Korostyšev 99 C2
Korotovo 75 D1
Korovatiči 99 C1
Korpela 11 D3, 12 A1
Körperich 79 D3
Korpi 21 C1
Korpi 24 A2
Korpi 24 B2
Korpijärvi 26 B1
Korpijoki 21 D1, 22 A1
Korpikå 17 C2
Korpikoski 26 B1
Korpikylä 17 D2, 18 A1
Korpilahti 21 D3, 22 A3
Korpilombolo 17 C1
Korpilompolo 12 A3, 17 D1
Korpimäki 23 C2
Korpinen 22 B2
Korpiperä 21 C2
Korpo/Korppoo 24 A3
Korpoström 24 A3
Korppinen 21 D2, 22 A2
Kors 32 B3, 37 C1
Korså 40 A2
Korsbäck 20 A2
Korsberga 45 D2/3, 46 A2
Korsberga 51 C1
Korsbyn 31 B/C2
Korsen 28 B2
Korsfjord 5 C2
Korshamn 42 B3
Korshavn 44 B1/2
Korsholm/Mustasaari 20 A2
Korsmo 38 A/B3
Korsmyrbränna 29 D3, 35 C1/2
Korsnäs 39 D2
Korsnäs 20 A2
Korsnes 9 C2
Korsö 24 A2/3, 41 D2
Korsør 53 C1
Korssjøen 33 D3
Korssjön 31 D1/2
Korsträsk 16 B3
Korsu 23 D1
Korsun'-Ševčenkovskij 99 D3
Korsveien 28 A3, 33 C2
Korte 21 B/C3
Kortejärvi 21 C2
Kortekangas 22 B1
Kortesalmi 25 D1, 26 B1
Kortesjärvi 20 B2
Kortevaara 19 D3, 23 D1
Kortgene 78 B1
Kortrijk 78 A2
Kortteinen 23 C2
Kor'ukovka 99 D1/2
Korvala 12 B3
Korvanniemi 19 C3
Korvenkylä 18 A/B2
Korvenkylä 21 C1
Korweiler 80 A3
Koryčany 94 B1
Korytnica-kúpele 95 D1
Kos 149 D3
Kosančić 139 C1
Košava 135 D2
Kösching 92 A2
Kościan 71 D3
Kościan 72 B3, 96 B1
Kościerzyna 72 B2
Kose 74 A1
Kosel 138 B3, 142 B1
Košetice 83 D3, 93 D1
Košice 83 D3
Košice 97 C2
Kosieczyn 71 C3
Kosierz 71 C3
Kosjerić 133 D2, 134 A2
Kosjerić 140 A2
Koška 128 B3
Koskama 11 D3, 12 A/B2
Koskeby/Koskenkylä 20 B2
Koskela 18 B3
Koskenjoki 21 D1, 22 A/B1
Koskenkorva 20 B2/3
Koskenkylä/Forsby 25 D2, 26 A2
Koskenkylä 24 B2
Koskenkylä 25 B/C2

Koskenkylä **17** D2, **18** A1
Koskenlaskupaikka **19** D3
Koskenmäki **19** D3
Koskenmylly **25** D1, **26** A/B1
Koskenniska **6** B3, **11** D1
Koskenpää **21** D3, **22** A3
Koskenperä **21** D1, **22** A1
Koski **24** B2
Koski **24** B3
Koski **25** D2, **26** A2
Koski **25** C3
Koskimäki **20** B2/3
Koskue **20** B3
Koskullskulle **16** B1
Kosman **133** C3
Kosmás **147** C3
Kosmonosy **83** D2
Kosola **20** B2
Kosola **27** C/D1
Kosov **97** D2, **98** B3
Kosovo Polje **138** B1
Kosovrasti **138** A3
Kosovska Kamenica **138** B1/2
Kóspallag **95** D3
Kossdorf **83** C1
Kössen **92** B3
Kost **83** D2
Kosta **51** C1/2
Kósta **147** C3
Kosta **72** B1
Kostajnica **127** D3, **131** C/D1
Košťálkov **94** A1
Kostamo **12** B3
Kostanjevac **127** C3
Kostanjevica **127** C3
Kostebrau **83** C1
Kostelec **93** D1
Kostelec na Hané **94** B1
Kostelec nad Černými Lesy **83** D3
Kostelec nad Labem **83** D2/3
Kostenec **140** B3
Koštice **83** C2
Kostinbrod **139** D1
Kostojevići **133** C2, **134** A2
Kostolac **134** B1/2
Kostrina **97** D2, **98** A3
Kostrzyn **70** B2
Kostrzyn **71** D2/3
Kosťukoviči **99** D1
Kosturino **139** C/D3, **143** D1
Kosula **23** C3
Koszalin (Köslin) **72** B2
Kőszeg **94** B3, **127** D1
Koszyce **71** D1/2
Kotajärvi **19** D3, **23** D1
Kotajärvi **18** B2
Kotala **13** C2
Kotala **21** C3
Kotalanperä **18** B2
Kotamaa **12** B2
Kótas **143** B/C2
Kotasalmi **23** B/C2
Kotel **141** C3
Köthen **69** D3
Kotikylä **22** B2
Kotila **19** C3
Kotiranta **19** D2
Kotka **26** B2/3
Kotor **137** C2
Kotoriba **128** A2
Kotorsko **132** B1
Kotor Varoš **131** D2, **132** A1/2
Kotovsk **99** C3
Kotovsk **141** D1
Kotrónia **145** D1, **145** D3
Kötschach **107** D1/2, **126** A1/2
Köttsjön **30** A3, **35** C2
Kötz **91** D2
Kötzting **92** B1
Koufália **143** D1
Koufós **144** B2/3
Kouhi **21** D3, **22** A3
Koukounariés **147** D1
Koúkoura **147** C2
Koúmanis **146** B2/3
Koura **20** B2/3
Kouřim **83** D3
Kouroútas **146** A2/3
Koutaniemi **19** C3
Koutojärvi **17** D2
Koutsochéra **146** B2/3
Koutsócheron **143** D3
Koutus **12** A3, **17** D1
Kouva **19** C1
Kouvola **26** B2
Kovačevci **139** D2
Kovačica **133** D1, **134** A/B1
Kovačica **140** A2
Kovářská **83** B/C2
Kovel' **97** D1, **98** B2
Kovelahti **24** B1
Kovero **23** D3
Kovero **24** A2
Kovero **24** B1
Koversada **130** A1
Kovilj **129** D3, **133** D1, **134** A1
Kovin **134** B1
Kovin **140** A2
Kovjoki **20** B1/2
Kövra **34** B2
Köyceğiz **149** D3
Köyhäjoki **21** C1
Köyhänperä **21** D1, **22** A1
Köyliö **24** B2
Köyliönkylä **24** B2
Kozáni **143** C2
Kozáni **148** B1
Kozarac **129** B/C3
Kozarac **131** D1, **132** A1
Kozármisleny **128** B2
Kozelec **99** D2
Kozel'sk **75** D3
Kozica **131** D3, **132** A3, **136** B1
Kozienice **97** C1, **98** A2
Kozí Hrádek **93** D1
Kozina **126** B3
Kozje **127** C2
Kožlany **83** C3
Kozluk **133** C2
Kozly **83** C2
Kozmice **83** D3
Kozojedy **83** C3
Kozolupy **83** C3
Kożuchów **71** C3
Kožuhe **132** B1
Krääkkiö **24** B1/2
Kräckelbäcken **39** C1
Krackow **70** B1
Kraddsele **15** C/D2/3
Kraftsdorf **82** A/B2
Kragenæs **53** C2
Kragerø **43** D2, **44** A2
Krągi **71** D1
Kragujevac **134** B2
Kragujevac **140** A2
Krahne **69** D3
Kraiburg **92** B2
Kraichtal **90** B1
Krajenka **71** D1
Krajková **82** B2/3
Krajkovac **135** B/C3
Krajn **137** D2
Krajné **95** C2
Krajnik Dolny **70** B2
Kråkberget **8** B2
Kråken **31** C3
Krakhella **36** A2
Krækkjahytta **37** C3
Kräklingbo **47** D3
Kråklivollen **33** C2
Kråkmo **9** C3
Krakovec **83** C3
Kraków **97** C2
Krakow am See **53** D3, **69** D1
Kråkshult **46** B3
Kråkstad **38** A3, **44** B1
Králíky **96** B2
Kraljëa Sutjeska **132** B2
Kraljevica **126** B3, **130** B1
Kraljevo **134** B3
Kraljevo **140** A2
Kraľovany **95** D1
Kráľov Brod **95** C2/3
Kralovice **83** C3
Kralupy nad Vltavou **83** D2/3
Kralupy nad Vltavou **96** A2
Králův Dvůr **83** C3
Kramfors **30** B3, **35** D2
Kramnitse **53** C2
Krampen **94** A3
Krampenes **7** C/D2
Krampfer **69** D2
Kråmvik **43** C1
Kramvik **7** D2
Kranéa **143** C3
Kranéa Deskátis **143** C2/3
Kranenburg **67** B/C3
Kranevo **141** D3
Krångede **30** A3, **35** C2
Kranichfeld **82** A2
Kranídion **147** C3
Kranj **126** B2
Kranj **96** A3
Kranjska Gora **96** A3
Kranjska Gora **126** B2
Kransvik **14** B1
Krąpiel **71** C1
Krapina **127** D2
Krapinske Toplice **127** D2
Krapkowice **96** B1/2
Kraselov **93** C1
Krašic **127** C3
Krasilov **98** B3
Krāslava **74** A/B2/3
Kraslice **82** B2
Krásná Hora **83** D3
Krásná Lípa **83** D2
Kraśnik **97** C/D1, **98** A2
Krásno **82** B3
Krasnoe **75** C3
Krasnogorodskoe **74** B2
Krasnoil'sk **98** B3
Krasnoje Selo **74** B1
Krásno nad Kysucou **95** D1
Krasnopole **99** D1
Krasnopolje **74** B3
Krasno Polje **130** B1
Krasnye Okny **141** D1
Krasnyj **75** C3
Krasnyj Holm **75** D1
Krasnystaw **97** D1, **98** A2
Kratovo **140** A3
Kratovo **139** C2
Kraubath **127** C1
Krauchenwies **91** C3
Krautheim **91** C1
Krautscheid (Prüm) **79** D3
Kravaře **83** D2
Kravarsko **127** D3
Krčedin **133** D1, **134** A1
Kreba **83** D1
Krefeld **79** D1, **80** A1
Kreien **69** D1
Kreien **69** D1
Kreiensen **68** B3
Kreischa **83** C2
Krej Lura **138** A2
Krekilä **21** C1
Křelovice **83** D3, **93** D1
Kremenčug **99** D3
Kremenec **98** B2
Kremenica **143** C1
Kremges **99** D3
Kremikovci **139** D1
Kremincy **97** D2, **98** A/B3
Kremmen **70** A2
Kremna **133** C2/3
Kremnica **95** D2
Krems an der Donau **94** A2
Krems an der Donau **96** A2
Kremsbrücke **126** A/B1
Kremsmünster **93** C/D2/3
Křemže **93** D1
Krepoljin **135** B/C2
Krępsko **71** D1
Kreševo **132** B2/3
Kresna **139** D2/3
Kressberg-Mariäkappel **91** D1
Kressbronn **91** C3
Krestcy **75** C1
Kréstena **146** B3
Kretinga **73** C2
Kreuth **92** A3
Kreuzau **79** D2
Kreuzen **126** A/B2
Kreuzen **93** D2
Kreuzenstein **94** B2
Kreuzlingen **91** C3
Kreuztal **80** B2
Kreuztal-Krombach **80** B2
Kreuzwirt **94** A3, **127** D1
Kría Vrísi **143** D2
Kričev **99** D1
Kričevci **127** D2
Kriebstein **82** B1
Krieglach **94** A3
Kriegsfeld **80** B3
Krien **70** A1
Kriezá **147** D2
Krimml **107** D1
Krimpen aan de Lek **66** A3
Křinec **83** D2
Kringlevasshytta **42** B2
Krionéri **146** B2
Krionérion **147** C2
Kripan **153** D2
Kristallopigí **142** B2
Kristdala **51** D1
Kristdala **72** B1
Kristianopel **72** B1
Kristianopel **51** D2
Kristiansand **43** C3
Kristiansand-Randesund **43** C3
Kristianstad **50** B2/3
Kristianstad **72** A1
Kristiansund **32** A/B2
Kristiinankaupunki **20** A3
Kristineberg **39** B/C1
Kristineberg **16** A3
Kristinefors **38** B2
Kristinehamn **45** D1, **46** A1
Kristinehov **50** B3
Kristinestad (Kristiinankaupunki) **20** A3
Kristóni **143** D1, **144** A1
Kristvalla **51** D1/2
Kristvik **28** A/B3, **33** C/D1
Kriva Feja **139** C1/2
Krivajevići **132** B2
Kriváň **97** C2
Kriva Palanka **140** A3
Kriva Palanka **139** C2
Krivelj **135** C2
Krivi Vir **135** C3
Krivodol **135** D3
Krivoe Ozero **99** C3
Krivogaštani **138** B3, **143** C1
Krivoj Rog **99** D3
Křivoklát **83** C3
Krivolak **139** C3
Križ **127** D3
Křižanov **94** A/B1
Križevci **127** D2
Križevci **127** D2
Križišče **127** B/C3, **130** B1
Krk **130** B1
Krka **127** C3
Krmčine **130** B2
Krnjeuša **131** C1/2
Krnjevo **134** B2
Krnov **96** B2
Krobia **71** D3
Krobielewko **71** C2
Krøderen **43** D1
Krögis **83** C1
Krognes **7** D1
Krogsbølle **49** C3, **53** C1
Krokan **43** C1
Krokedal **38** A3, **44** B1
Krokek **46** B2
Krokelv **5** D1, **6** A1
Kroken **14** B3
Kroken **4** A3
Kroken **36** B2
Kroken **43** C/D2, **44** A2
Kroken **36** B2
Kroken **33** D3
Krokfors **15** C3
Krokhaug **33** C3, **37** D1
Kroknäs **34** B3
Krokom **29** D3, **34** B2
Kroksätra **38** B2
Krokselvmoen **14** B2
Kroksjö **31** C/D2
Kroksjö **30** B1
Krokstad **28** A3, **33** C2
Krokstadelva **43** D1, **44** A1
Krokstrand **44** B2
Krokträsk **17** C2
Krokvåg **30** A3, **35** C2
Krokvik **10** A3
Krolevec **99** D2
Krölpa **82** A2
Kroměříž **95** C1
Kroměříž **96** B2
Krompachy **97** C2
Kronach **82** A2/3
Kronberg **80** B2/3
Kronburg **91** D3
Kronoberg **51** C1
Kronoby/Kruunupyy **20** B1
Kronogård **16** A3
Kronogård **16** A2
Kronsågen **16** A/B1
Kronshagen **52** B3
Kronstorf **93** D2
Kröpelin **53** D3
Kropp **52** B2/3
Kroppenstedt **69** C3
Kropstädt **69** D3, **70** A3
Krościenko **97** D2, **98** A3
Krośniewice **73** C3, **97** B/C1
Krosno **97** C2, **98** A2/3
Krosno Odrzańskie (Crossen) **72** A3, **96** A1
Krosno Odrzańskie (Crossen) **71** C3
Krossbu **37** C2
Krostitz **82** B1
Krotoszyn **96** B1
Kröv **80** A3
Krovíli **145** D1
Krpimen **138** B1
Krrabë **138** A3, **142** A1
Kršan **126** B3, **130** A1
Krško **127** C2
Krstac **137** C1
Krstatice **131** D3, **132** A3
Krstinja **127** D3, **131** C1
Krstu **129** D2
Křtiny **94** B1
Krüden **69** C/D2
Kruë i Fushës **137** D2
Kruft **80** A2
Kruishoutem **78** B1/2
Krujë **137** D3, **138** A3
Krumbach **91** D2
Krumbach Markt **94** A/B3
Krummesse **53** C3, **69** C1
Krummhörn **67** C1
Krummhörn-Greetsiel **67** C1
Krummhörn-Rysum **67** C1
Krün **92** A3
Krupa **131** C2
Krupa **131** D2, **132** A1/2
Krupac **139** D1
Krupaja **135** B/C2
Krupanj **133** C2
Krupina **95** D2
Krupište **139** C2
Krupka **83** C2
Krupki **74** B3
Kruså **52** B2
Krušćica **132** B2
Kruščica **134** B1
Kruščica **131** D2, **132** A2
Kruse **137** D2
Krušedol Selo **133** D1, **134** A1
Kruševac **134** B3
Kruševac **140** A2
Kruševo **138** B3, **143** C1
Krutå **14** B3
Kruth **89** D2/3, **90** A3
Krutvatn **14** B3
Kruusila **25** B/C3
Kryckeltjärn **31** C2
Krylbo **40** A3
Krynica **97** C2
Krystallgrotten **14** B2
Krzęcin **71** C2
Krzemieniewo **71** D1
Krzepielow **71** C/D3
Krzeszyce **71** C2
Krzystkowice **71** C3
Krzywin **71** D3
Krzyz **71** C2
Książ Wielkopolski **71** D3
Kšinná **95** C/D2
Kuaejoki **21** C2
Kubbe **30** B3, **35** D1
Kubinka **75** D3
Küblis **106** A1
Kubrat **141** C2
Kučevo **140** A2
Kučevo **135** C2
Kuchen **91** C2
Kuchl **93** C3
Kuçi **142** A2
Kućište **138** A1
Kuddby **46** B2
Kuerlinkant **11** C3, **12** A2
Kufstein **92** B3
Kuggeboda **51** C2
Kuggören **40** B1
Kuha **18** B1

Labinot-Fushë 138 A3, 142 A1
La Bisbal d'Empordà 156 B2
La Bisbal de Falset 163 C1
Lablachère 111 C1/2
Lábod 128 A2
Laboe 52 B2/3
Labouheyre 108 A2
La Bouille 77 C3, 86 B1
La Bourboule 102 B3
Laboutarié 109 D2, 110 A2
La Bouteille 78 B3
La Bóveda de Toro 159 D1, 160 A1
Labrède 108 B1
La Bresse 89 D2, 90 A3
La Bretagne 77 C3, 86 B1
La Bretesche 85 C3
La Brillanne 111 D2, 112 A2
Labrit 108 B2
Labroye 77 D2
Labruguière 110 A3
L'Absie 100 B1/2
Laburgade 109 D2
Laç 137 D3
La Cabrera 161 C2
La Caillère 100 B1/2
La Caletta 123 C3
La Caletta 123 D1/2
Lacalm 110 A1
La Calmette 111 C2
La Calzada de Béjar 159 D2/3
La Calzada de Oropesa 160 A3, 166 B1
La Campana 172 A1
La Canal 169 D2
Lacanau 108 A1
Lacanau-Océan 108 B1
La Canourgue 110 B1/2
La Canya 156 B2
La Capelle 78 B3
Lacapelle-Marival 109 D1
Laćarak 133 C1
La Carlota 172 A1
La Carolina 167 D3
Lacarre 108 B3, 155 C1
Lacaune 110 A2
La Cava 163 C2
La Cavalerie 110 B2
Lacave 109 D1
La Caze 110 B2
Lacco Ameno 119 C3
Lacedónia 120 A2
La Celle 102 A3
La Celle-en-Morvan 103 C1
La Cellera de Ter 156 B2
La Celle-Saint-Avant 101 C1
La Cerca 153 C2
La Chaise-Dieu 103 C3
La Chaize-le-Vicomte 101 C1
La Chamba 103 C3
La Chambre 104 A3
Lachamp 101 D3, 102 A3
Lachanás 144 A1
Lachanás 148 B1
La Chapelaude 102 A/B2
La Chapelle-Gauthier 87 D2
La Chapelle-Saint Blaise 86 B3, 101 C1
La Chapelle-en-Serval 87 D1
La Chapelle-Glain 86 A/B3
La Chapelle-Laurent 102 B3
La Chapelle 79 C3
La Chapelle d'Angillon 87 D3
La Chapelle-la-Reine 87 D2
La Chapelle 85 C2/3
La Chapelle-en-Vercors 111 D1
La Chapelle-sur-Erde 85 D3, 100 A1
La Chapelle-en-Valgaude-mard 112 A1
La Chapelle-Rainsouin 86 A2
La Chapelle-Saint-Laurent 100 B1
Lachapelle-sous-Rouge-mont 89 D3, 90 A3
Láchar 173 C2
La Charce 111 D1/2
La Charité-sur-Loire 87 D3, 102 B1
La Chartre-sur-le-Loir 86 B3
La Châtaigneraie 100 B1
La Châtre 102 A1/2
La Chaussée-sur-Marne 88 B1
La Cheminée 89 D3, 104 B1
Lachen 105 D1
Lachendorf 68 B2
La Cheppe 88 B1
La Chèze 85 C2
La Cierva 161 D3, 162 A3
La Ciotat 111 D3
Laćisled 134 B3
La Cité 110 A3, 156 A/B1
Läckeby 51 D2
Läckö 45 D2
La Clayette 103 C2
La Clusaz 104 A/B2/3
La Cluse-et-Mijoux 104 A/B1
Lacock 63 D2, 64 A3
La Codoñera 163 B/C2
La Codosera 165 C2
La Colle-Saint-Michel 112 A2
La Coma 155 D2/3, 156 A2
Lacona 116 A3
Láconi 123 D2
La Coquille 101 D3
La Coronada 166 A2
La Corte 165 D3, 171 C1
La Côte-Saint-André 103 D3
La Couarde 100 A/B2
La Coucourde 111 C1
La Couronne 111 C/D3
Lacourt 108 B3, 155 C1/2
La Courtine-le Trucq 102 A3
La Couvertoirade 110 B2
Lacq 108 B3, 154 B1
La Crèche 101 C2
La Croisière 101 C2
Lacroix-Bàrrez 110 A1
La Croix-Haute 111 D1
La Croixille 85 D2
La Croix-Laurent 85 D3
La Croix-Saint-Ouen 87 D1
La Crosetta 107 D2
Lacrouzette 110 A2/3
La Cumbre 165 D1, 166 A1
Lacunza 153 D2, 154 A1/2
La Cure 104 A2
Lad 128 A/B2
Ladánybene 129 C1
Ladapeyre 102 A2
Ladbergen 67 D3
Ladby 53 C1
Låddejåkkstugan 9 C3
Ladelund 52 A/B2
Ladenburg 80 B3, 90 B1
Ladendorf 94 B2
Ladero 153 D2
Ladignac-le-Long 101 D3
Ladíspoli 118 A2
Ladne Vode 134 B2
Ladoeiro 158 B3, 165 C1
Ladon 87 D2
Ladoye-sur-Seille 104 A1
La Drée 103 C1
Laer 67 D3
Laerru 123 C1
La Espina 151 D1
La Estrella 160 A3, 166 B1
La Fajolle 156 A1
La Farga de Moles 155 D2
La Fatarella 163 C1/2
La Felguera 151 D1, 152 A1
La Felipa 168 B2
La Fère 78 A3
La Ferrière-sous-Jougne 104 A/B1
La Ferrière 101 C1
La Ferrière-sur-Risle 86 B1
La Ferrière-en-Parthenay 101 C1
La Ferté-Alais 87 D2
La Ferté-Bernard 86 B2
La Ferté-Beauharnais 87 C3
La Ferté-Fresnel 86 B1
La Ferté-Gaucher 88 A1
La Ferté-Imbault 87 C3
La Ferté-Macé 86 A2
La Ferté-Milon 87 D1, 88 A1
La Ferté-Saint-Aubin 87 C3
La Ferté-Saint-Cyr 87 C3
La Ferté-sous Jouarre 87 D1, 88 A1
La Ferté-Vidame 86 B2
La Feuillie 77 D3
Laffrey 111 D1, 112 A1
La Flèche 86 A3
La Florida 151 C/D1
Lafnitz 94 A3, 127 D1
La Fotelaie 76 A3, 85 D1
La Fouillade 109 D2
La Fourche 86 B2
Lafrançaise 108 B2
La Franqui 110 A/B3, 156 B1
La Fregeneda 159 C2
La Fresneda 163 C2
La Frette 103 D3
La Frontera 161 D2/3
La Frua 105 C2
La Fuliola 155 D3, 163 D1
La Gacilly 85 C3
La Galera del Pla 163 C2
Laganadi 122 A3, 125 D1/2
La Garde 110 B1
La Garde-Freinet 112 A3
Lagares 158 B2/3
Lagares 158 A2
La Garganta 159 D3
La Garnache 100 A1
Lagaro 114 B2, 116 B1
La Garonnette 112 A/B3
La Garriga 156 A3
La Garrovilla 165 D2
Lage 68 A3
La Gendretière 87 C3, 101 D1, 102 A1
Lageosa 158 B2
Lägerdorf 52 B3, 68 B1
Lagfors 35 D2
Laggars 20 B2
Laginá 143 D1/2, 144 A1/2
La Ginebrosa 163 B/C2
La Gineta 168 B2
Lagnieu 103 D2
Lagny-sur-Morin 87 D1
Lago 122 A2
Lagôa 170 A2
Lagôa 159 C1
Lagoaça 159 C1/2
Lagonegro 120 B3
Lagonísi 147 D2/3
Lagor 108 B3, 154 B1
Lagorce 111 C1/2
Lagos 170 A2
Lagosanto 115 C1
Łagów 71 C3
La Grafouillère 102 A3, 109 D1
Lagran 153 D2
La Granada 165 D3, 171 C1
La Granadella 163 C1
La Grand'Combe 111 B/C2
La Grand Croix 103 C3
La Grande Motte 111 C3
La Granja d'Escarp 163 C1
La Granjuela 166 B3
Lagrasse 110 A3, 156 B1
La Grave-en-Oisans 112 A1
La Gravelle 85 D2
La Groise 78 B3
Lägsta 30 B2, 35 D1
La Guarda 166 A2
La Guàrdia Lada 155 C3, 163 C1
La Guardia 161 C3, 167 D1
La Guardia de Jaén 173 C1
Laguarres 155 C2/3
Laguarta 155 C2
Laguenne 102 A3
Laguépie 109 D2
La Guerche-de-Bretagne 86 A2/3
Lagueruela 163 C2
Laguiole 110 A1
Laguna de Cameros 153 D3
Laguna de Duero 152 A/B3, 160 A1
Laguna del Marquesado 162 A3
Laguna de Negrillos 151 D2/3
Lagunarrota 155 C3
Lagunilla 159 D3
Lagunilla del Jubera 153 D2
La Haba 166 A2
La Haye-Descartes 101 C/D1
La Haye-du-Puits 76 A3, 85 D1
La Haye-Pesnel 86 A/B1
Lähdejänkkä 12 A3, 17 D2
Lähden 67 D2
Lahdenkylä 21 C3
Lahdenperä 21 C/D2
Lahenpää 17 C1
La Hermida 152 B1
La Herrería 167 D3, 168 A3
La Herrería 168 B2
Laheycourt 88 B1
La Higuera 169 D2
La Hiniesta 151 D3, 159 D1
La Hinojosa 161 D3, 168 A/B1
Lahn 67 D2
Lahnajärvi 17 C1
Lahnajärvi 25 C3
Lahnakoski 21 B/C1
Lahnalahti 22 B3
Lahnanen 21 D1, 22 A1
Lahnasjärvi 22 B1
Lahnasuando 17 C1
Lahntal 80 B2
Lahntal-Caldern 80 B2
Laholm 50 A2
Laholm 72 A1
Laholuoma 20 B3
La Horcajada 159 D2, 160 A2
La Horra 152 B3, 160 B1
La Houssoye 77 D3, 87 C1
Lahovaara 23 C2
La Hoz de la Vieja 162 B2
Lahr-Reichenbach 90 B2
Lahr/Schwarzwald 90 B2
Lahstedt 68 B3
Lähteenkylä 24 B2
Lahti 25 D2, 26 A2
Lahti 24 A2
Lahtiranta 18 A3
Lahtolahti 23 C2
La Huerce 161 C1/2
La Hulpe 78 B2
La Hutte 86 B2
Laichingen 91 C2
Laichingen-Feldstetten 91 C2
Laichingen-Machtolsheim 91 C2
L'Aigle 86 B1
La Iglesuela 160 A3
La Iglesuela del Cid 162 B2
Laignes 88 B3
Laiguéglia 113 C2
L'Aiguillon-sur-Mer 101 C2
Laihia 20 B2
Laikko 27 D1
Laimbach am Ostrong 93 D2
Laimoluokta 10 A2
Lainate 105 D3
Lainio 10 B3
Lairg 54 A/B1/2
La Iruela 167 D3, 168 A3, 173 C/D1
Laisbäck 15 D3
La Isla 152 A1
La Isleta de Escullos 174 A2
Laissac 110 A2
Laisstugan 15 C2
Laïsta 142 B2/3
Laisvall 15 D2
Laisvallsby 15 D2
Laiterla 24 B3
Laitiala 25 D2, 26 A2
Laitikkala 25 C1/2
Laitila 24 A2
Laivajärvi 17 D2, 18 A1
Laives 103 D1
Láives/Leifers 107 C2
La Jana 163 C2
La Javie 112 A2
Lajkovac 133 D2, 134 A2
Lajksjö 30 A2
La Jonchère-Saint-Maurice 101 D2
La Joncosa 163 C1
La Jonquera 156 B2
Lajosmizse 129 C1
Lakaluoma 21 B/C2
Lakaniemi 21 C2
Lakasjö 30 B2, 35 D1
Lakatnik 139 D1
Lakaträsk 16 B2
Lakavica 139 C3
Łąkie 71 D1
Lákion 149 D2/3
Lákka 142 A3
Lakkópetra 146 A/B2
Lakócsa 128 B3
Lakolk 52 A1/2
Lakomäki 21 D2, 22 A2
Laksåvik 32 B1
Lakselv 5 D2, 6 A2
Lakshola 9 C3
Laktaši 131 D1, 132 A1
La Lantejuela 172 A2
La Lapa 165 D2/3
Lálas 146 B3
L'Albagés 155 C3, 163 C1
L'Albenc 103 D3
Lalbenque 109 D2
La Léchère 105 C2/3
Lalić 129 C3
La Lima 114 B2, 116 A1
Lalín 150 B2
Lalinci 133 D2, 134 A2
Lalinde 109 C1
La Línea de la Concepcion 172 A3
La Llacuna 155 D3, 156 A3, 163 D1
Lalley 111 D1
Lalling 93 C1/2
Lalm 37 D1
La Lóggia 113 B/C1
La Losilla 153 D3
La Loupe 86 B2
Lalouvesc 103 C3, 111 C1
La Louvière 78 B2
L'Alpe-d'Huez 112 A1
Laluenga 155 C3
Lalueza 154 B3, 162 B1
La Luisiana 172 A1
Laluque 108 A2
Lam 93 B/C1
Lama 150 A3, 158 A1
La Machine 102 B1
La Maddalena 123 D1
Lama dei Peligni 119 C2
Lamagistère 109 C2
Lamaids 102 A2
La Maielletta 119 C1
La Mailleraye-sur-Seine 77 C3
La Malène 110 B2
Lamalou-les-Bains 110 A/B3
Lama Mocogno 114 B2, 116 A1
Lamanère 156 B2
Lamanon 111 D2
Lamarche 89 C2
La Marina 169 C3
Lamarosa 164 B2
Lamarque 100 B3, 108 B1
La Martella 120 B2
Lamas de Mouro 150 B3
Lamas d'Olo 158 B1
Lamastre 111 C1
La Mata 160 B3, 167 C1
La Mata 169 C3, 174 B1
La Mata de los Olmos 162 B2
La Mata de Monteagudo 152 A2
La Mata de Morella 162 B2
La Matilla 160 B1/2
La Maucarrière 101 C1
Lambach 93 C2/3
Lamballe 85 C2
Lambesc 111 D2/3
Lámbia 146 B2
Lámbia 148 B2
Lamborn 39 D2, 40 A2

Lambourn **64** A3
Lambrecht **90** B1
Lamegal **159** C2
Lamego **158** B2
La Membrolle-sur-Choisille **86** B3
L'Ametlla de Mar **163** C/D2
L'Ametlla de Montsec **155** C/D3
Lamézia Terme **122** A/B2
Lamía **147** C1
La Mierla **161** C2
La Mine **76** A/B3, **85** D1, **86** A1
Lamington **57** C2
Lamland **41** C/D3
Lamlash **56** A2
Lammasaho **22** B2
Lammasperä **21** C3
Lammhult **51** C1
Lammhult **72** A1
Lammi **21** C2
Lammi **25** C/D2, **26** A2
Lamminmäki **22** B3
Lamminperä **18** B1/2
Lammu **23** C3
La Molina **156** A2
La Mongie **109** B/C3, **155** C2
La Monnerie-le-Montel **103** B/C2
La Morera **165** D2
La Morte **111** D1, **112** A1
Lamorteau **79** C3
La Mothe **110** B1/2
La Mothe-Achard **100** A1/2
Lamothe-Cassel **109** D1
La Mothe-Saint-Héraye **101** C2
Lamotte-Beuvron **87** C3
La Motte-Chalancon **111** D1
La Motte-du-Caire **112** A2
Lampaanjärvi **22** B2
Lampaluoto **24** A1, **41** D1
Lampaul **84** A2
Lampeland **43** D1
Lamperila **22** B2
Lampertheim **80** B3
Lampeter **63** C1
Lampinsaari **18** A3
Lampiselkä **12** B2
L'Ampolla **163** C2
Lamposaari **27** C2
Lamppi **24** A1
Lamprechtshausen-Kirchendorf **92** B3
Lämsänkylä **19** D1
Lamsfeld **70** B3
Lamspringe **68** B3
Lamstedt **52** A/B3, **68** A1
Lamstedt-Grossenhain **68** A1
Lamu **18** B3, **21** D1, **22** A1
La Muda **107** C/D2
La Mudarra **152** A3, **160** A1
La Muela **154** A/B3, **162** A1
La Mure **111** D1, **112** A1
Lamure-sur-Azergues **103** C2
La Musara **163** D1
Lana **107** C2
Lanabukt **7** D2
Lanaja **154** B3, **162** B1
Lanarce **111** B/C1
Lanark **57** B/C2
La Nava **165** D3, **171** C1
La Nava de Ricomalillo **160** A3, **166** B1
La Nava de Santiago **165** D2
Láncara **151** C2
Lancaster **59** D1, **60** B2
Lancaster **54** B3
Lanchester **57** D3, **61** C1
Lanciano **119** D1
Lancin **103** D3
Landåsen **37** D3, **38** A2
Landau **92** B2
Landau in der Pfalz **90** B1
Landcross **62** B2
Landeck **106** B1
Landedo **151** C3
Landensberg **91** D2
Landerneau **84** A2
Landersfjorden **6** B1
Landeryd **50** B1
Landesbergen **68** A2
Landete **163** C3, **169** D1
Landévant **84** B3
Landin **69** D2
Landivisiau **84** A/B2
Landivy **85** D2
Landkirchen **53** C2
Landl **92** B3
Landön **29** D3, **34** B1
Landquart **106** A1
Landrecies **78** B2/3
Landres **89** C1
Landriano **105** D3, **106** A3
Landsberg **82** B1
Landsberg am Lech **91** D2/3
Landsbro **51** C1
Landshut **92** B2
Landskrona **49** D3, **50** A3
Landskrona **72** A1/2
Landstuhl **90** A1
Landvetter **45** C3, **49** D1
Lanestosa **153** C1
La Neuville **78** A2
Laneuville-sur-Meuse **79** C3
Langa **160** A2
Långå **34** A3
Langå **48** B2
Langadás **144** A1/2
Langa de Duero **153** C3, **161** C1
Langa del Castillo **163** C1
Langádia **146** B3
Langadíkia **144** A2
Långåminne **20** A2
Langangen **43** D2, **44** A1/2
Långared **45** C3
Långaröd **50** B3
Långås **49** D1/2, **50** A1
Långasjö **51** C2
Langau **94** A1/2
Langayo **152** B3, **160** B1
Långbäcken **30** B1/2
Langballig **52** B2
Långban **39** C3
Långbergsöda **41** D2/3
Långbo **39** D1, **40** A1
Langdorf **93** C1
Langeac **102** B3, **110** B1
Langeais **86** B3
Langebæk **53** D2
Langedijk **66** A/B2
Långedrag **45** C3, **49** D1
Längelmäki **25** C1
Langelsheim **68** B3
Langen **80** B3
Langen **52** A3, **68** A1
Langen **106** B1
Langen **33** D3
Langenaltheim **91** D1/2, **92** A1/2
Langenargen **91** C3
Langenau **91** D2
Langenbach (Freising) **92** A2
Langenberg **68** A3
Langenburg **91** C1
Langeneichstädt **82** A1
Langenenslingen **91** C2
Langenes **8** B1
Langenfeld **80** A2
Langenfeld **80** A1
Langenfeld (Scheinfeld) **81** D3
Längenfeld **106** B1
Langenhagen **68** B2
Langenhahn **80** B2
Langenhorn **52** A2
Langenlois **94** A2
Langenmosen **92** A2
Langen-Neuenwalde **52** A3, **68** A1
Langenneufnach **91** D2
Langenselbold **81** C2/3
Langenthal **105** C1
Langenwang **94** A3
Langenwetzendorf **82** B2
Langenzenn **81** D3, **91** D1
Langeoog **67** D1
Langernyw **59** C2, **60** A3
Langerwehe **79** D2
Langesi **36** A1
Langeskov **53** C1
Langesø **53** B/C1
Langesund **43** D2, **44** A2
Langevåg **36** B1
Langevåg **42** A1
Langewahl **70** B3
Langewiesen **81** D2, **82** A2
Langfjell **14** B2
Langfjord **5** C2
Langfjordbotn **7** C2
Långflon **38** B2
Långforsselet **17** C2
Langhamn **9** D1
Långhed **40** A1
Langhirano **114** A1
Langholm **57** C3
Langholm **54** B3
Langhuso **36** B3
Länglingen **30** A2, **35** C1
Långlöt **51** D2
Långnäs **40** A2
Långnäs **41** D3
Langnes **9** D1
Langø **53** C2
Langogne **110** B1
Langon **108** B1
Langør **49** C3
Langport **63** D2
Langquaid **92** B2
Langraiz **153** C/D2
Langreo **151** D1
Langres **89** C3
Långron **31** C3
Langrune-sur-Mer **76** B3, **86** A1
Långsådalen **29** C3, **34** A1
Langsåvoll **28** B3, **33** D1
Langschlag **93** D2
Långsel **17** C2
Långsel **17** C2
Långsele **30** A1
Långsele **31** C/D1
Långsele **30** B3, **35** D1
Långsele **30** B3, **35** D1
Långsele **30** A/B3, **35** D2
Långserud **45** C1
Långset **14** A/B2
Långshyttan **40** A2
Långsjön **16** B2
Långsjön **47** D1
Långskog **35** D3
Langstrand **5** C1
Långträsk **16** B3
Längträsk **31** C1
Långträsk **17** B/C3
Långträsk **17** D2
Långudden **15** D2
Languidic **84** B3
Languilla **161** C1
Langula **81** D1
Langvatn **14** B3
Långvattnet **15** D3
Långvattnet **30** B2, **35** D1
Långvattnet **31** C1
Langvattnet **31** C2
Långvik **25** C3
Långviksmon **31** C2
Långvinds bruk **40** B1
Langwedel **68** A2
Langwedel-Etelsen **68** A2
Langweid **91** D2
Langwies **106** A1
Lanhezes **150** A3, **158** A1
Lanildut **84** A2
Lanivet **62** B3
Lanjarón **173** C2
Lånke **28** A/B3, **33** C/D1
Länkipohja **25** C1, **26** A1
Lanklaar **79** C/D1
Lankojärvi **12** A3, **17** D1
Lankoori **24** A1
Lanmeur **84** B1/2
Länna **47** C1
Lanna **46** A1
Lännahom **40** B3
Lannavaara **10** B3
Lannéanou **84** B2
Lannemezan **109** C3, **155** C1
Lannevesi **21** D3, **22** A3
Lannilis **84** A2
Lannion **84** B1
La Nocle-Maulaix **103** C1
Lanouaille **101** C3
Lansån **17** C2
Länsi-Aure **21** B/C3
Länsikoski **19** D1
Länsikoski **17** D2, **18** A1
Länsikylä **21** C2
Länsi-Teisko **25** C1
Länsi-Vuokko **23** C2
Lansjärv **17** C1
Lanslebourg-Mont-Cenis **104** B3
Lanslevillard **104** B3
Lanta **109** D3, **155** D1
Lantadilla **152** B2
Lantto **19** D3
Lanuéjols **110** B2
La Nuncia **169** D2
Lanusei **123** D2
Lanvéoc **84** A2
Lanvollon **85** B/C1/2
Lány **83** C3
Lanz **69** C2
Lanz **108** A3, **154** A1
Lanza **150** B1/2
Lanzahita **160** A3
Lanžhot **94** B2
Lanzo d'Intelvi **105** D2, **106** A2
Lanzo Torinese **105** C3
Laon **78** B3
Laons **86** A/B1/2
La Paca **168** B3, **174** A1
La Pacaudière **103** C2
Lapad **137** C1
Lápafő **128** B2
Lapajärvi **13** C3
Lapalisse **103** C2
La Pallice **101** C2
Lapalluoto **18** A3
La Palma del Condado **171** C1/2
Lapalud **111** C2
La Palud-sur-Verdon **112** A2/3
Lapani **142** B2
La Parra **165** D2
La Parra de las Vegas **161** D3, **168** B1
La Parrilla **152** B3, **160** B1
Lápas **146** A/B2
La Patte-d'Oie **87** C/D1
La Pedraja de Portillo **160** A/B1
La Pedriza **173** B/C1/2
La Peraleja **161** D3
Laperdiguera **155** C3
La Pernelle **76** B3
La Péruse **101** C2
La Pesquera **168** B1
La Petite-Pierre **89** D1, **90** A1/2
La Petrízia **122** B2
Lapeyrade **108** B2
Lapeyrouse **103** D2
Lapeza **173** C2
Lapford **63** C2
Lapinhelvetti **11** C3
La Pinilla **161** C2
Lapinjärvi/Lappträsk **25** D2, **26** B2
Lapinjärvi **21** D2, **22** A2
Lapinjoki **24** A1/2
Lapinkylä **25** C3
Lapinlahti **22** B2
Lapinneva **20** B3
La Plagne **104** B3
La Plama **174** B1
La Plama d'Ebre **163** C1
La Platja d'Aro **156** B2/3
La Plaza **151** D1
Lapleau **102** A3
Laplje Selo **138** B1/2
Laplume **109** C2
Lapoblación **153** D2
La Pobla de Cérvoles **163** D1
La Pobla de Lillet **156** A2
La Pobla de Massaluca **163** C1/2
La Pobletta de Bellveí **155** D2
La Pola de Gordón **151** D2, **152** A2
La Portella **155** C3, **163** C1
La Portellada **163** C2
Lapoutroie **89** D2, **90** A2
La Póveda de Soria **153** D3
Lapovo **134** B2
Lappago/Lappach **107** C1
Lappajärvi **21** C2
Lappalaisten kesätuvat **11** C2
Läppe **46** B1
Lappea **17** D1
Lappeenranta (Villmanstrand) **27** C2
Lappers **25** C3
Lappersdorf **92** B1
Lappersdorf-Hainsacker **92** B1
Lappfjärd/Lappväärtti **20** A3
Lappfors **20** B1/2
Lapphaugen **9** D2
Lappi **24** A2
Lappi **19** D2
Lappila **25** D2, **26** A2
Lappo **20** B2
Lappo **24** A3, **41** D2
Lappohja/Lappvik **24** B3
Lappoluobbal **5** C3, **11** C1
Lapporten **9** D2, **10** A2
Lappträsk **16** A3
Lappvattnet **31** D1
Laprade **110** A3
Lapradelle **156** A1
La Preste **156** A/B2
La Primaube **110** A2
Laprugne **103** C2
Lâpseki **149** D1
Lapua (Lappo) **20** B2
La Puebla **157** C2
La Puebla de los Infantes **166** B3, **172** A1
La Puebla de Montalbán **160** B3, **167** C1
La Puebla de Valdavia **152** B2
La Puebla de Híjar **162** B1
La Puebla de Fantova **155** C2
La Puebla de Roda **154** B2
La Puebla de Cazalla **171** D2
La Puebla de Almoradiel **167** D1, **168** A1
La Puebla de Valverde **162** B3
La Puebla del Río **171** D2
La Puerta **161** D2
La Puerta de Segura **168** A3
La Punta **113** D3
La Punta **123** C3
Lăpușna **141** C1
Lăpușnicel **135** C1
La Puye **101** D1
Lapväärtti **20** A3
Łapy **73** D3, **98** A1
Laqueuille **102** B3
L'Áquila **117** D3, **119** C1
La Rábita **173** C2
Laracha **150** A1
Laragh **58** A2
Laragne-Montéglin **111** D2, **112** A2
La Rambla **172** B1
Larbert **56** B1/2
L'Arboç **156** A3, **163** D1
L'Arbresle **103** C/D2/3
Lärbro **47** D2
Lärbro **73** B/C1
Larceveau-Arros-Cibits **108** A3, **154** B1
Larchant **87** D2
Larche **101** D3, **109** D1
Larche **112** B2
Lårdal **43** C2
Lærdalsøyri **37** B/C2
Lardaro **106** B2
Larderello **114** B3, **116** A2
Lardero **153** D2
Lárdos **149** D3
Lardosa **158** B3
La Reale **123** C1
Laredo **153** C1
Laredorte **87** C1
Laredorte **110** A3, **156** B1
La Regeserie **86** A3
Laren **67** C3
Laren **66** B3
La Réole **108** B1
Largentière **111** C1
Largs **56** B2
La Riaille **112** B1
Lariano **118** B2
La Riba **163** C1
La Riba de Escalote **161** C1
La Riera de Gaià **163** C1/2
Lárimna **147** C/D1/2

La Rinconada 171 D1
Larino 119 D2, 120 A1
Lárisa 143 D3
Lárisa 148 B1
La Rixouse 104 A2
Larkhall 56 B2
Larkollen 44 B1
L'Armentera 156 B2
Larmor-Plage 84 B3
Larne 56 A3
Larne 54 A3, 55 D2
La Robla 151 D2, 152 A2
La Roca de la Sierra 165 D2
La Roche-aux-Fées 86 A/B2/3
La Rochebeaucourt-et-Argentine 101 C3
La Roche-Bernard 85 C3
La Roche-Chalais 101 C3
La Rochecourbon 100 B2/3
La Roche-Derrien 84 B1
La Roche-des-Arnauds 111 D1, 112 A1/2
La Roche-en-Brénil 88 A/B3
La Roche-en-Ardenne 79 C2/3
La Rochefoucauld 101 C3
La Roche-Jagu 84 B1
La Rochelle 101 C2
La Roche-Posay 101 D1
La Rochepot 103 C/D1
La Rocherolle 101 D1, 102 A1
La Roche-sur-Yon 100 A/B1
La Roche-sur-Foron 104 A2
La Rochette 104 A3
Larochette 79 D3
La Roche-Vineuse 103 D2
La Roda 168 B2
La Roda 151 C1
La Roda de Andalucía 172 A/B2
La Roë 85 D2
Laroles 173 C/D2
La Romana 169 C3
La Romieu 109 C2
Laroquebrou 109 D1, 110 A1
Laroque-d'Olmes 109 D3, 156 A1
La Roque-Sainte-Marguerite 110 B2
Laroque-Timbaut 109 C2
Larouco 151 C2
Larraga 154 A2
Larraona 153 D2
Larrasoaña 108 A3, 154 A2
Larrate 153 C2
Larrau 108 A3, 154 B1
Larrazet 109 C2
Larrêt 89 C3
Larseng 4 A3
Larsmo/Luoto 20 B1
Larsnes 36 A1
Larumbe 154 A1/2
Laruns 108 B3, 154 B1/2
Larv 45 C/D3
Larva 167 D3, 168 A3, 173 C1
Larvik 43 D2, 44 A1/2
Larvik 42 A2
Lärz 69 D1, 70 A1
La Sabina 157 D3
La Sagrada 159 D2
La Sainte-Baume 111 D3
Lasalle 110 B2
La Salvetat-sur-Agout 110 A3
La Salvetat-Peyralès 110 A2
Läsänkoski 26 B1
Las Arenas 152 A/B1
Lasarte 153 D1, 154 A1
La Saulce 111 D1/2, 112 A2
La Sauve-Majeure 108 B1
Las Bordas 155 C2
Låsby 48 B3
Las Cabezadas 161 C2
Las Cabezas de San Juan 171 D2
Las Caldas 151 D1
Las Casas 154 B3
Lascaux (fermées) 108 B1
Lascellas 155 C3
Lascelle 110 A1
Lascuarre 155 C2/3
Las Cuerlas 162 A2
Las Cuevas de Cañart 162 B2
La Seca 160 A1
Lasel 79 D3
La Selle-sur-le-Bied 87 D2
La Selva 119 C2
La Selva 163 C1
La Sénia 163 C2
La Sentiu de Suó 155 D3, 163 C/D1
La Serre 102 A3
La Seu d'Urgell 155 D2
La Seyne-sur-Mer 111 D3, 112 A3
Las Fraguas 153 D3, 161 C/D1
Lasgraisses 109 D2
Las Herencias 160 A3, 166 B1
Las Illas 156 B2
Lasinja 127 D3
Łasko 71 C2
Laško 127 C2
Las Labores 167 D1/2
Las Machorras 110 B3
Las Majadas 161 D3
Las Mesas 168 A1
Las Navas del Marqués 160 B2
Las Navas de la Concepción 166 A/B3, 172 A1
Las Negras 174 A2
La Solana 167 D2, 168 A2
La Source 87 C3
La Souterraine 101 D2
Lasovo 135 C3
Las Parras de Castellote 162 B2
Laspaúles 155 C2
Las Pedroñeras 168 A1
Las Pedrosas 154 B3
Las Peralosas 167 C2
La Spézia 114 A2
Las Preses 156 B2
Las Rotas 169 D2
Las Rozas 152 B2
Las Rozas de Madrid 160 B2
Lassahn 69 C1
Lassay 86 A2
Lassee 94 B2
Lassekrog 35 C3
Lasseube 108 B3, 154 B1
Lassigny 78 A3
Lassila 24 B1
Lassing 93 D3
Lassnitz 126 B1
Lasswade 57 C2
Lastanosa 155 C3, 163 B/C1
Lastebasse 107 C2/3
Lastic 102 A/B3
Las Torcas 161 D3
Lastours 110 A3, 156 A/B1
Lastovo 136 A1
Lastra a Signa 114 B2, 116 B1/2
Lastras de Cuéllar 160 B1
Lastres 152 A1
Lästringe 47 C2
Lastrup 67 D2
Lastukoski 23 C2
Lastva 137 C1
La Suze-sur-Sarthe 86 A/B2/3
Las Veguillas 159 D2
Las Ventas 153 C2
Las Ventas con Peña Aguilera 167 C1
Las Ventas de San Julián 160 A3
Las Ventas de Retamosa 160 B3
Las Vertientes 173 D1
Las Vilás de Tubó 155 C2
Las Villas de Benicasim 163 C3
La Tala 159 D2
La Talaudière 103 C3
La Terrasse-sur-Dorlay 103 C/D3
Laterza 121 C2
La Teste 103 C/D3
La Teste 108 B1
Lathen 67 D2
Latheron 54 B1
La Thuile 104 B3
Lathus 101 D2
Latiana 121 D2/3
Latikberg 30 B1
Latillé 101 C1/2
Latina 118 B2
Latisana 107 D3, 126 A3
La Toba 161 C2
Latorps-bruk 46 A1
La Torre 160 A2
La Torre de Esteban Hambrán 160 B3
La Torre de Cabdella 155 D2
La Torre de l'Espanyol 163 C1/2
La Torresaviñan 161 D2
La Tour-Blanche 101 C3
La Tour-d'Aigues 111 D2
La Tour-d'Auvergne 102 B3
Latour-de-France 156 B1
La Tour-du-Pin 103 D3, 104 A3
Latovaino 25 B/C2
La Tranche-sur-Mer 100 A/B2
La Tremblade 101 C3
Latresne 108 B1
La Trimouille 101 D2
La Trinité-sur-Mer 85 B/C3
La Trinité-Porhoët 85 C2
La Trinité 63 D3, 85 C1
La Trique 100 B1
Latrónico 120 B3, 122 A1
Latronquière 109 D1, 110 A1
Latschau 106 A1
Latterbach [Oey-Diemtigen] 105 C2
Lattuna 13 C2
La Tuca 155 C/D2
La Turballe 85 C3
Latva 18 A/B3
Latva 19 B/C2
Latvaset 21 D1, 22 A1
Lau 47 D3
Laubach 80 A3
Laubach 81 C2
Laubrières 85 D2
Laubsdorf 70 B3, 83 D1
Laucha 82 A1
Lauchhammer 83 C1
Lauchhammer 96 A1
Lauda-Königshofen 81 C3, 91 C1
Laudal 42 B3
Lauder 57 C2
Laudio 153 C1
Lauenbrück 68 B1/2
Lauenburg 69 C1
Lauenen [Gstaad] 104 B2
Lauf 82 A3, 92 A1
Laufach 81 C3
Laufen 90 A3
Laufen 92 B3
Laufenburg 90 B3
Laufenburg 90 B3
Lauffen am Neckar 91 C1
Laugerie 109 C1
Laugharne 62 B1
Laugnac 109 C2
Lauhankylä 24 B1/2
Lauhovd 43 C1
Lauingen 91 D2
Laujar de Andarax 173 D2
Laukaa 21 D3, 22 A3
Laukansalo 23 C3
Lauker 16 A/B3
Laukka 18 B2/3
Laukka-aho 23 C2
Laukkala 22 A/B2
Laukuluspa 10 A3
Laukvik 8 B3
Laukvik 4 A2
Laukvik 8 B2
Laukvik 5 C2
La Umbría 165 D3, 171 C1
Launceston 62 B3
La Unión 174 B1
La Unión de Campos 152 A3
Launois 78 B3
Launonen 25 C2
Laupen 104 B1
Laupheim 91 C2
Laurbjerg 48 B2
Laureana di Borrello 122 A3
Laurenburg 80 B2
Laurenzana 120 B3
Lauria 120 B3, 122 A1
Laurière 101 D2
Laurino 120 A3
Lauris-sur-Durance 111 D2
Laurito 120 A3
Lauritsala 27 C2
Lausanne 104 B2
Lauscha 82 A2
Laussonne 111 B/C1
Lauta 83 C1
Lautamaa 17 D2, 18 A1
Lautaporras 25 C2
Lautela 25 B/C2
Lautenbach 89 D2, 90 A3
Lautenbach 90 B2
Lauter 47 D2
Lauter 82 B2
Lauterbach 81 C2
Lauterbourg 90 B1
Lauterbrunnen 105 C2
Lauterecken 80 A3
Lauterhofen 92 A1
Lauterhofen-Traunfeld 92 A1
Lauterstein 91 C2
Lautertal 81 D2, 82 A2
Lautertal 81 C2
Lautertal-Gadernheim 81 B/C3
Lautiosaari 17 D3, 18 A1
Lautrec 109 D2, 110 A2
Lauttakulma 25 C1
Lauttavaara 19 C2
Lauvareid 42 A1
Lauvåsen 37 D2
Lauvåsen 37 D2
Lauve 43 D2, 44 A1/2
Lauvnes 42 B3
Lauvøy 28 A2, 33 C1
Lauvsjølia 29 C2
Lauvsnes 28 B2
Lauvstad 36 A/B1
Lauvuskylä 23 C1
Lauzerte 108 B2
Lauzun 109 C1
La Vachey 104 B3
Lavagna 113 D2
La Vaivre-de-Seveux 89 C3
Laval 86 A2
Lavala 19 D2
Laval-Atger 110 B1
Lavamünd 127 C2
Lavamünd 96 A3
Lavangen 9 D2
La Vansa 155 D2
Lávara 145 D1, 145 D3
Lavardac 109 C2
Lavardin 86 B3
Lavau 87 D3
Lavaur 109 D2
Lavaveix-les-Mines 102 A2
La Vecilla 152 A2
La Vega 152 B1
Lavelanet 109 D3, 156 A1
La Vellés 159 D2
Lavello 120 B2
Laven 48 B3
Lavena-Ponte Tresa 105 D2
Lavenham 65 C2
Laveno-Mombello 105 D2/3
La Ventosa 161 D3
La Veredilla 167 C2
Lavergne 108 B1
La Verna 115 C2/3, 116 B2
Lavezzola 115 C1
Lavia 24 B1
Laviana 151 D1, 152 A1
Laviano 120 A2
La Victoria 172 A/B1
La Vid 153 C3, 161 C1
Lavid de Ojeda 152 B2
La Vídola 159 C1/2
La Vieille-Lyre 86 B1
Lavik 36 A/B3
Lavik 36 A2
Lavik 9 D1
La Vilella Baixa 163 C1
La Villa 116 A3
La Villa 107 C2
La Villa de Don Fadrique 167 D1, 168 A1
La Villa/Stern 107 C2
La Villedieu-en-Fontenette 89 C3
La Villedieu 101 C2
La Villedieu 102 A3
La Villedieu-du-Clain 101 C2
La Villetelle 102 A2
Lavínio Lido di Enea 118 B2
Lavis 107 C2
La Visaille 104 B3
Lavit 109 C2
Låvong 14 A/B2
Lavos 158 A3
La Voulte-sur-Rhône 111 C1
Lavoûte-Chilhac 102 B3
Lavra 159 C1
Lavre 164 B2
Lávrion 147 D3
Lávrion 149 B/C2
Lavry 74 B2
Lavsjö 30 A2
La Wantzenau 90 A/B2
Ławy 71 B/C2
Laxå 46 A1/2
Laxbäcken 30 A1
Laxe 150 A1
Laxede 16 B2
Laxenburg 94 B2/3
Laxey 58 B1
Laxo 54 A1
Laxsjö 29 D3, 34 B1
Laxsjön 35 D2
Laxtjärn 39 C3
Laxton 61 C3, 64 B1
Laxvik 49 D2, 50 A2
Laxviken 29 D3, 34 B1
Layana 155 C2
La Yesa 162 B3, 169 C1
Läyliäinen 25 C2
Layna 161 D2
Layos 160 B3, 167 C1
Layrac 109 C2
Laytown 58 A2
La Yunta 162 A2
Laz 84 B2
Laza 150 B3
La Zaida 162 B1
Lazarádes 143 C2
Lazarevac 133 D2, 134 A2
Lazarevo 129 D3, 134 A1
Lazaropole 138 A/B3
La Zarza de Pumareda 159 C1/2
La Zenia 169 C3, 174 B1
Lazići 133 C2/3
Lazise 106 B3
Lazkao 153 D1/2
Lázně-Kynžvart 82 B3
Laznica 135 C2
Lazonby 57 C3, 60 B1
Lazzaro 122 A3, 125 D2
Leadenham 61 D3, 64 B1
Leadhills 57 B/C2
Leányvár 95 D3
Leatherhead 64 B3, 76 B1
Łeba 72 B2
Lebach 89 D1, 90 A1
Le Ballon 86 A/B2
Lebane 139 C1
Le Barcarès 156 B1
Le Barp 108 B1
Lebbeke 78 B1
Le Béage 111 C1
Le Beausset 111 D3, 112 A3
Le Bec-Hellouin 77 C3, 86 B1
Lebeña 152 B1
Lébénymiklós 95 C3
Lebesby 6 B1
Le Bettex 104 B3
Le Biot 86 A1/2
Le Biot 104 B2
Le Blanc 101 C1
Le Bleymard 110 B1/2
Le Bois 104 B3
Le Boisle 108 B2
Le Bonhomme 89 D2, 90 A2
Le Boréon 112 B2

Lębork (Lauenburg) 72 B2
Le Boulou 156 B2
Le Bourg 109 D1
Le Bourg-d'Oisans 112 A1
Le Bourget 87 D1
Le Bourget-du-Lac 104 A3
Le Bourgneuf-la-Forêt 85 D2, 86 A2
Le Bourg-Saint-Léonard 86 B1
Le Breuil 103 C2
Lebrija 171 D2
Le Brugeron 103 C3
Le Bugue 109 C1
Le Buisson 110 B1
Le Buisson-Cussac 109 C1
Lebus 70 B2/3
Le Busseau 100 B1/2
Leca da Palmeira 158 A1
Le Canadel-sur-Mer 112 A3
Le Castella 122 B2
Le Cateau 78 B3
Le Catelet 78 A3
Le Caylar 110 B2
Lecce 121 D3
Lecco 105 D3, 106 A2/3
Lece 138 B1
Lécera 162 B1
Lech 106 B1
Lechago 163 C2
L'Échalp 112 B1
Le Chambon-Feugerolles 103 C3
Le Chambon-sur-Lignon 103 C3, 111 C1
Le Champ-Saint-Père 101 C2
Le Château-d'Oléron 101 C2
Le Châtelard 104 A3
Le Châtelet-en-Brie 87 D2
Le Châtelet-en-Berry 102 A1
Le Châtellier 86 A1/2
Lechbruck 91 D3
Lechená 146 A2
Le Cheylard 111 C1
Le Chiáviche 114 B1
Lechlade 64 A3
Lechovice 94 B1/2
Leči 73 C1
Leciñena 154 B3, 162 B1
Leck 52 A/B2
Le Collet-de-Dèze 110 B2
Le Colombier 111 C1
Le Conquet 84 A2
Le Creusot 103 C1
Le Croisic 85 C3
Le Crotoy 77 D2
Lectoure 109 C2
Lecumberri 153 D1/2, 154 A1
Lecumberry 108 B3, 155 C1
Łęczyca 71 C1
Łęczyca 73 C3, 97 B/C1
Ledaña 168 B1
Ledanca 161 C2
Ledbury 63 D1, 64 A2
Ledeč nad Sázavou 83 D3
Ledenika 135 D3, 139 D1
Lederzeele 77 D1
Le Désert 112 A1
Ledesma 159 D2
Ledesma de Soria 153 D3, 161 D1
Ledeuix 108 B3, 154 B1
Lédignan 111 C2
Leding 31 B/C3
Lednice 94 B2
Lednické Rovne 95 C1
Le Donjon 103 C2
Le Dorat 101 D2
Lędyczek 71 D1
Lee 48 B2
Leeds 61 C2
Leeds 54 B3
Leegebruch 70 A2
Leek 59 D2, 61 B/C3, 64 A1
Leek 67 C1/2
Leenane 55 C2
Leende 79 C1
Leer 67 D1
Leerbeek 78 B2
Leerdam 66 B3

Leer-Loga 67 D1
Leese 68 A2
Leeuwarden 66 B1
Leezen 52 B3, 68 B1
Le Faou 84 A2
Le Faouët 84 B2
Le Ferriere 118 B2
Lefinnlia 32 B3, 37 C1
Lefka 145 D2
Lefkadítion 146 B1
Lefkás 146 A1
Lefkás 148 A2
Lefkímmi 148 A1
Lefkímmi 142 A3
Lefkón 139 D3, 144 A1
Léfktra 146 B3
Léfktrá 147 C2
Lefktra 148 A/B2
Le Fleix 109 C1
Le Folgoët 84 A2
Le Fond-de-France 104 A3
Le Fossat 109 D3, 155 D1
Le Fromental 110 B1
Leganes 108 B2/3
Leganiel 161 C3
Legarda 153 D2
Legarda 154 A2
Legau 91 D3
Le Gault-Perche 86 B2
Legazpi 153 D1/2
Legden 67 C3
Légé 100 A1
Legionowo 73 C3
Legnago 107 C3
Legnano 105 D3
Legnica (Liegnitz) 96 B1
Légny 103 C/D2
Legoland 48 B3, 52 B1
Legorreta 153 D1
Legrad 128 A2
Le Grand-Bourg 101 D2, 102 A2
Le Grand-Lemps 103 D3
Le Grand-Lucé 86 B2/3
Le Grand-Pressigny 101 D1
Le Grau-du-Roi 111 C3
Legrená 147 D3
Le Gua 100 B3
Léguevin 108 B3, 155 C1
Legutio 153 D2
Le Havre 76 B3
Lehčevo 135 D3
Le Hérie-la-Viéville 78 B3
Lehesten 82 A2
Lehmäjoki 20 B2
Lehmen 80 A2
Lehmikumpu 17 D2, 18 A1
Lehmivaara 23 C1
Lehmo 23 D3
Lehndorf 82 B2
Lehnice 95 C2/3
Lehnin 69 D3, 70 A3
Le Hohwald 89 D2, 90 A2
Le Houga 108 B2
Lehrberg 91 D1
Lehre 69 C3
Lehre-Flechtorf 69 C3
Lehrte 68 B2/3
Lehrte-Hämelerwald 68 B3
Lehrte-Immensen 68 B2/3
Lehtimäki 21 C2
Lehtiniemi 13 C3
Lehtoi 23 D3
Lehtola 19 C/D3
Lehtoperä 21 D1/2, 22 A1/2
Lehtovaara 19 C1/2
Lehtovaara 12 B2
Lehtovaara 23 D2, 23 D1
Lehtovaara 19 D2
Lehtovaara 19 C3, 22 B1
Lehva 98 B1
Leibnitz 96 A3
Leibnitz 127 C1
Leicester 65 C1/2
Leiden 66 A3
Leidenborn 79 D3
Leiferde 69 B/C2/3
Leigh 59 D2, 60 B3
Leighton Buzzard 64 B2
Leikanger 36 A1
Leikanger 36 A1
Leikanger 36 B2
Leimen 90 B1
Leimrieth 81 D2

Leine 37 C2
Leinefelde 81 D1
Leinesodden 14 A2
Leinfelden-Echterdingen 91 C2
Leingarten 91 C1
Leini 105 C3, 113 B/C1
Leino 19 C2
Leino 27 C2
Leinovaara 23 C/D3
Leinstrand 28 A3, 33 C1/2
Leioa 153 C1
Leipämäki 23 C3
Leipheim 91 D2
Leipivaara 19 C2
Leipojärvi 16 B1
Leipzig 82 B1
Leira 32 B2
Leira 28 A3, 33 C1
Leira 37 D2/3
Leiranger 8 B3
Leirbakk 29 C2
Leirbotn 5 C2
Leiret 38 A/B2
Leirfjord 14 A2
Leiria 158 A3, 164 A1
Leiro 150 B2
Leirosa 158 A3
Leirosen 14 A/B2
Leirvåg 9 C1
Leirvassbu 37 C2
Leirvik 36 A2
Leirvik 28 B1
Leirvik 28 A2/3, 33 C1
Leirvik 42 A1
Leirvík 55 C1
Leirvika 14 B2
Leisnig 82 B1
Leissigen 105 C2
Leiston 65 D2
Leith 57 C1/2
Leitzersdorf 94 B2
Leitzkau 69 D3
Leivonmäki 26 A/B1
Leivonmäki 23 C3
Leixlip 58 A2
Leiza 153 D1, 154 A1
Leizen 69 D1
Leka 14 A3, 28 B1
Lekåsa 45 C3
Lekeitio 153 D1
Lekenik 127 D3
Lekeryd 46 A3
Leknes 32 A3, 36 B1
Leknes 8 B2
Łęknica 83 D1
Leksand 39 D2
Leksberg 45 D2
Leksvik 28 A3, 33 C1
Lekvattnet 38 B3
Le Lardin 101 C3, 108 B1
Le Lauzet-Ubaye 112 A2
Le Lavandou 112 A3
Lel'čicy 99 C2
Le Levancher 104 B2
Le Liège 87 B/C3, 101 D1
Le Lion-d'Angers 86 A3
Lelkendorf 53 D3, 69 D1, 70 A1
Lellainen 24 B2
Le Locle 104 B1
Le Logis du Pin 112 A2/3
Le Lonzac 102 A3
Le Loroux-Bottereau 86 A3, 101 C1
Le Louroux-Béconnais 85 D3, 86 A3
Le Luc 112 A3
Le Lude 86 B3
Lelystad 66 B2
Lem 48 A3
Lem 48 A2
Le Malzieu-Ville 110 B1
Le Mans 86 B2
Le Mas 112 B2
Le Mas-d'Agenais 109 B/C2
Le Mas-d'Azil 108 B3, 155 C1
LEMASNAUMA 110 A2
Le Mayet-de-Montagne 103 C2
Le May-sur-Evre 85 D3, 86 A3, 100 B1
Lembach 90 A/B1
Lemberg 89 D1, 90 A1
Lemberk 83 D2

Lembeye 108 B3, 155 C1
Lembruch 68 A2
Le Mechenin 101 C3
Le Mêle-sur-Sarthe 86 B2
Le Ménil 89 C2
Le Merlerault 86 B1/2
Lemesjö 31 C2
Le Mesnil-Herman 86 A/B1
Lemförde 68 A2
Lemgo 68 A3
Lemgow-Schmarsau 69 C2
Lemi 27 C2
Lémie 104 B3, 112 B1
Lemierzyce 71 B/C2
Le Mirandol 109 D1
Lemke (Nienburg-Weser) 68 A2
Lemlahti 24 A1
Lemland 41 D3
Lemmenjoki 6 B3, 11 D2
Lemmer 66 B2
Lemnia 141 C1
Le Moline 113 D1, 114 A1
Le Monastier-sur-Gazeille 111 B/C1
Le Monêtier-les-Bains 112 A1
Le Monêtier-Allemont 111 D2, 112 A2
Le Mont-Dore 102 B3
Le Montenvers 104 B2/3
Le Montet 102 B2
Le Mont-Saint-Michel 85 D1/2
Le Moustier 109 C1
Lempäälä 25 C1
Lempdes 102 B3
Lempyy 22 B3
Lemu 24 A/B2
Le Muret 108 A/B1/2
Le Muy 112 A3
Lemvig 48 A2
Lena 38 A2
Lena 151 D1
Lenart 127 D2
Lencloître 101 C1
Lencouacq 108 B2
Lend 107 D1, 126 A1
Lendinara 115 C1
Lendinez 167 C3, 172 B1
Lendrup Strand 48 B2
Lendum 49 B/C1
Le Neubourg 77 C3, 86 B1
Lengau 92 B3, 107 D1
Lengdorf 92 B2
Lengefeld 83 C2
Lengefeld 81 D1
Lengenfeld 94 A2
Lengenfeld 82 B2
Lengenwang 91 D3
Lengerich 82 B2
Lengerich 67 D2
Lengerich 67 D2
Lenggries 92 A3
Lenggries-Vorderriss 92 A3
Lengronne 86 A1
Lengyeltóti 128 A/B2
Lenhovda 51 C1
Lenhovda 72 B1
Lenk im Simmental 105 C2
Lenkovcy 98 B2
Lennartsfors 45 C1
Lennestadt-Altenhundem 80 B1
Lennestadt-Elspe 80 B1
Lennestadt-Kirchveischede 80 B1
Lenningen-Schopfloch 91 C2
Lennoxtown 56 B1/2
Leno 106 B3
Lénola 119 C2
Le Nouvion-en-Thiérache 78 B3
Lenovac 135 C3
Lens 78 A2
Lens 78 A2
Lensahn 53 C3
Lensvik 28 A3, 33 C1
Lenti 127 D2
Lentiira 19 D3
Lenting 92 A2
Lentini 125 D3
L'Enveja 163 C2
Lenvik 9 D1

Lenzburg 90 B3, 105 C1
Lenzen 69 C2
Lenzerheide/Lai [Tiefencastel] 106 A2
Lenzkirch 90 B3
Leoben 93 D3, 127 C1
Leoben 96 A3
Leobersdorf 94 B3
Leofreni 118 B1
Leogang 92 B3
Léognan 108 B1
Leominster 59 D3
Léon 108 B2
León 151 D2, 152 A2
Leonberg 91 C2
Léoncel 111 D1
Leondárion 146 B3
Leonding 93 D2
Leonessa 117 C/D3, 118 B1
Leonforte 125 C2
Leonídion 147 C3
Leonídion 148 B2/3
Leonstein 93 D3
Leonte 150 B3, 158 A/B1
Leontion 146 B2
Leopoldov 95 C2
Leopoldsburg 79 C1
Leopoldshagen 70 B1
Leovo 141 D1
Leoz 154 A2
Lepaa 25 C2
Le Palais 84 B3
Le Paly 85 C2
Le Pas 110 A2
Lepe 171 C2
Le Péage-de-Roussillon 103 D3
Lepel' 74 B3
Lepenski Vir 135 C2
Le Perray-en-Yvelines 87 C1/2
Le Perrier 100 A1
Le Perron 86 B2
Le Perthus 156 B2
Lepetane 137 C2
Lepikkomäki 23 C3
Lepikontorppa 22 B2
L'Épine 88 B1
Le Pin-en-Mauges 85 D3, 86 A3, 100 B1
Le Pin-la-Garenne 86 B2
Lepistönmäki 20 B2
Le Planey 104 B3
Le Plessis-Belleville 87 D1
Lepoglava 127 D2
Le Poiré-sur-Vie 100 A1
Le Pondy 102 B1
Le Pont-de-Beauvoisin 104 A3
Le Pont-de-Claix 111 D1
Le Pont-de-Montvert 110 B2
Le Pont du Travo 113 D3
Le Pontet 100 B3
Le Pontet 111 C2
Le Pontet 104 A3
Le Ponthou 84 B2
Le Porge 108 A1
Le Port-Boulet 86 B3, 101 C1
Le Portel 77 D1/2
Leposavići 138 B1
Le Pouldu 84 B3
Le Pouliguen 85 C3, 100 A1
Lépoura 147 D2
Lépoura 149 B/C2
Le Pouzin 111 C1
Leppäjärvi 11 C2
Leppäkoski 25 C1, 26 A1
Leppäkoski 25 C2
Leppälä 27 C2
Leppälä 6 B2
Leppälahti 23 C3
Leppälahti 22 B2
Leppälahti 21 D3, 22 A3
Leppälänkylä 21 C2
Leppämäki 23 B/C3
Leppärinne 23 D1
Leppäselkä 21 D2, 22 A2
Leppävesi 21 D3, 22 A3
Leppävirta 22 B3
Leppiaho 18 B1
Leppin 69 C2
Leppiniemi 18 B2/3
Le Prada 109 B/C2

Lépreon 146 B3
Lepşa 141 C1
Lepsala 25 D1, 26 B1
Lepsény 128 B1
Leptokariá 143 D2
Le Puy 110 B1
Le Puy-Notre-Dame 101 C1
Le Quesnoy 78 B2
Léquile 121 D3
Lerbäck 46 A1/2
Lerberg 43 D1
Lerberget 49 D2/3, 50 A2
Lercara Friddi 124 B2
Lerchenborg 49 C3, 53 C1
Lerdal 45 C2
Lerdala 45 D2
L'Erée 63 D3
Le Repas 85 D1
Lerga 154 A2
Lérici 114 A2
Lérida / Lleida 155 C3, 163 C1
Lerín 153 D2, 154 A2
L'Erkelsbrugge 77 D1, 78 A1/2
Lerkil 49 D1, 50 A1
Lerma 153 B/C3
Lermon 29 C2
Lermoos 91 D3
Lerna 147 C3
Le Rocher-Mézangers 86 A2
Lérouville 89 C1
Le Roux 112 B1
Le Rozier 110 B2
Lerrain 89 C2
Lerum 45 C3
Lerum 72 A1
Le Russey 89 D3, 104 B1
Lerwick 54 A1
Les 155 C2
Les Abrets 103 D3, 104 A3
Lesaca 108 A3, 154 A1
Les Aix-d'Angillon 87 D3, 102 B1
Les Ajustons 110 B1
Lešak 134 B3, 138 B1
Les Ancizes-Comps 102 B2
Les Andelys 77 C/D3, 87 C1
Lešani 138 B3, 142 B1
Les Arcs 104 B3
Les Arcs-sur-Argens 112 A3
Le Saret 108 B3, 155 C1
Les Aubiers 100 B1
Le Sauze 112 A/B2
Les Avellanes 155 C3
Les Baux 111 C2
Les Bertins 87 D3, 102 B1
Les Billaux 108 B1
Les Bordes 87 D3
Les Borges Blanques 155 D3, 163 C/D1
Les Borges del Camp 163 D1/2
Les Bouchoux 104 A2
Lesbury 57 D2
Les Cabanes-de-Lapalme 110 A/B3, 156 B1
Les Cabannes 155 D2, 156 A1
Les Cabòries 156 A3
L'Escala 156 B2
Les Calanche 113 D3
Les Cammazès 109 D3
Lescar 108 B3, 154 B1
L'Escarène 112 B2
Lesce 126 B2
Lešće 127 C3, 130 B1
Les Clots 112 A1
Les Contamines-Montjoie 104 B3
Les Cortalets 156 B2
Lescun 108 B3, 154 B1/2
Les Deux Alpes 112 A1
Les Eaux-Chaudes 108 B3, 154 B1/2
Les Échelles 104 A3
Le Sel-de-Bretagne 85 D2
Lesencefalu 128 A1
Les Escaldes 155 D2, 156 A2
Les Essarts 101 C1
Les Estables 111 C1
Les Étangs 89 C/D1
Les Eyzies-de-Tayac 109 C1
Les Farguettes 110 A2
Les Fins 104 B1
Les Forges 85 D2
Les Forges 85 C2
Les Fourgs 104 B1
Les Gets 104 B2
Les Goudes 111 D3
Les Halles 103 C3
Les Hayons 76 B3
Les Herbiers 100 B1
Les Hôpitaux-Neufs 104 A/B1
Lésina 120 A1
Les Islettes 88 B1
Lesja 32 B3, 37 C1
Lesjaskog 32 B3, 37 C1
Lesjaverk 32 B3, 37 C1
Lesjöfors 39 C3
Leskelä 18 B3
Leskova 138 A1
Leskovac 139 C1
Leskovac 140 A3
Leskovice 83 D3, 93 D1, 94 A1
Leskovik 135 C3
Leskoviku 142 B2
Les Lèches 109 C1
Leslie 57 C1
Les Llosses 156 A2
Les Lucs-sur-Boulogne 100 A1
Lesmahagow 56 B2
Les Matelles 110 B2
Les Mazures 79 B/C3
Les Mées 111 D2, 112 A2
Les Ménuires 104 B3
Les Mesnuls 87 C1
Lesmont 88 B2
Les Moutiers-les-Mauxfaits 100 A/B2
Leśna 83 D1/2
Lešná 95 C1
Lešnica 133 C1/2
Leśniów Wielki 71 C3
Lesnoe 141 D1
Lesnoe 75 D1
Les Ollières-sur-Eyrieux 111 C1
Les Oluges 155 C3, 163 C1
Les Ormes 101 C1
Lesovaara 19 D2
Les Pargots 104 B1
Lesparre-Médoc 100 B3
L'Espérou 110 B2
Les Pieux 76 A3
Les Pilles 111 D2
Les Planes d'Hostoles 156 B2
L'Espluga Calba 155 D3, 163 D1
L'Espluga de Francolí 163 D1
Les Ponts-de-Cé 86 A3
L'Espunyola 156 A2
Les Quatre-Bras 78 B2
Lesquin 78 A2
L'Esquirol 156 A/B2
Les Riceys-Haut 88 B2
Les Rochers 86 A2
Les Rosaires 85 C2
Les Rosiers 86 A3
Les Rousses 104 A2
Les Sables-d'Olonne 100 A2
Lessach 126 B1
Les Salles-du-Gardon 111 B/C2
Les Salles-sur-Verdon 112 A2/3
Lessay 76 A3, 85 D1
Lessebo 51 C2
Lessebo 72 A/B1
Les Settons 88 A3, 103 C1
Les Sièges 88 A2
Lessines 78 B2
Les Sorinières 85 D3, 100 A1
L'Estany 156 A2
L'Estartit 156 B2
Lestelle-Bétharram 108 B3, 154 B1
Les Ternes 110 A/B1
Lesterps 101 D2
Les Thilliers-en-Vexin 77 D3, 87 C1
Lestijärvi 21 C1
L'Estréchure 110 B2
Les Trois Moutiers 101 C1
Lesund 32 B2
Lesura 135 D3
Les Vans 111 C2
Les Vignes 110 B2
Leszno 71 D3
Leszno 72 B3, 96 B1
L'Etac 63 D3, 85 C1
Letchworth 65 B/C2
Le Teil 111 C1
Le Teilleul 85 D2, 86 A2
Le Temple-de-Médoc 108 A1
Le Temple-de-Bretagne 85 D3
Letenye 128 A2
Le Theil-sur-Huisne 86 B2
Le Thillot 89 D2/3
Le Thor 111 C/D2
Le Thoronet 112 A3
Letičev 99 B/C3
Letino 119 C/D2
Letkés 95 D3
Letku 25 C2
Le Touquet-Paris-Plage 77 D2
Le Tourne 108 B1
Le Touvet 104 A3
Letovanić 127 D3
Letovice 94 B1
Le Translay 77 D2
Le Trayas 112 B3
Le Tréport 76 B2
Le Truel 110 A2
Letsbo 35 C3
Letschin 70 B2
Letter 68 B2/3
Letterkenny 55 C/D2
Lettingsvollan 33 D3
Letur 168 B3
Letuš 127 C2
Letux 162 B1
Letzlingen 69 C2
Leuben 83 C1
Leubingen 82 A1
Léuca 121 D3
Leuchars 57 C1
Leuglay 88 B3
Leugnies 78 B2
Leukerbad [Leuk] 105 C2
Leuk Stadt 105 C2
Leuna 82 B1
Leušen' 141 D1
Leutenbach 91 C1/2
Leutenberg 82 A2
Leutershausen 91 D1
Leutkirch 91 C/D3
Leutkirch-Friesenhofen 91 D3
Leutkirch-Gebrazhofen 91 C/D3
Leutkirch-Herlazhofen 91 C/D3
Leutschach 127 C2
Leuven 79 C2
Leuze 78 B2
Levadiá 147 C2
Levajok fjellstue 6 B2
Leväkylä 22 B3
Le Val André 85 C2
Le Val Richer 76 B3, 86 B1
Levan 142 A2
Lévane 115 C3, 116 B2
Levänen 27 C2
Levang 43 D2, 44 A2
Levanger 28 B3, 33 D1
Levanjska Varoš 128 B3, 132 B1
Levanpelto 24 B1
Levanto 25 D2, 26 A2
Lévanto 113 D2, 114 A2
Lévanzo 124 A2
Leväranta 12 B3
Leväsjoki 24 A1
Leveld 37 C3
Leven 57 C1
Leven 54 B2
Levene 45 C2
Levens 112 B2
Levens Hall 59 D1, 60 B2
Leverano 121 D3
Leveråsvallen 34 B3
Le Verdon-sur-Mer 100 B3
Leverkusen 80 A1/2
Leverkusen-Opladen 80 A1
Le Vernet 112 A2
Le Vernet-la-Varenne 102 B3
Levet 102 A1
Le Veurdre 102 B1
Levice 95 D2
Levice 96 B2/3
Lévico Terme 107 C2
Levide 47 D3
Levídion 146 B3
Levie 113 D3
Levier 104 A1
Le Vieux Bourg 85 C/D2
Le Vigan 110 B2
Le Vigean 108 B1
Le Vigen 101 C3
Lévignac 108 B2/3
Levignen 87 D1
Levijoki 21 C2
Le Ville 115 C3, 117 C2
Le Vivier-sur-Mer 85 D2
Levonperä 21 C/D1, 22 A1
Levo oja 18 B2
Levroux 101 D1, 102 A1
Levski 141 B/C3
Lewes 76 B1
Lewice 71 C2
Leyburn 59 D1, 61 C2
Leyburn 54 B3
Leymen 90 A3
Leysin 104 B2
Leżajsk 97 C/D2, 98 A2
Lezama 153 C1/2
Lezardrieux 84 B1
Lézat-sur-Lèze 108 B3, 155 C1
Lezay 101 C2
Lezhë 137 D3
Lézignan-Corbières 110 A3, 156 B1
Ležimir 133 C1
Lézinnes 88 A/B3
Lezo 153 D1, 154 A1
Lezoux 102 B2/3
Lezuza 168 B2
LGuardia 150 A3
L'Herbaudière 100 A1
L'Herbergement 101 C1
L'Hermet 110 A2
L'Hôpital-du-Grosbois 89 C3, 104 A1
L'Hospitalet 156 A1/2
L'Hospitalet de l'Infant 163 D2
Lia 28 B3, 33 D1
Lia 9 B/C1/2
Liabø 32 B2
Liabygda 32 A3, 36 B1
Liancourt 87 D1
Lianokládian 146 B1
Liapádes 142 A3
Liart 78 B3
Liarvåg 42 A2
Liatorp 50 B2
Liatorp 72 A1
Liaunet 28 B1
Libáň 83 D2
Libčeves 83 C2
Liběchov 83 D2
Libeliče 127 C2
Liber 151 C2
Liberec 83 D2
Liberec 96 A1
Liběšice 83 D2
Líbeznice 83 D2/3
Libin 79 C3
Libochovice 83 C2
Libofshë 142 A1
Libohova 142 A/B2
Libourne 108 B1
Liboussou 109 C1
Librazhd 138 A3, 142 B1
Librilla 169 D3
Libros 163 C3
Libuň 83 D2
Lič 127 C3, 130 B1
Licata 124 B3
Licenza 118 B1/2
Liceras 161 C1
Lich 81 B/C2
Lichás 147 C1
Lichères-près-Aigremont 88 A3
Lichfield 64 A1
Lichtenau 94 A2
Lichtenau 90 B2
Lichtenau 81 C1
Lichtenau-Atteln 81 B/C1
Lichtenau-Kleinenberg 81 C1
Lichtenberg 82 A2
Lichtenborn 79 D3
Lichtenegg 94 A/B3
Lichtenfels-Goddelsheim 81 B/C1
Lichtenfels 82 A3
Lichtenfels-Sachsenberg 81 B/C1
Lichtensteig 105 D1, 106 A1
Lichtenstein-Unterhausen 91 C2
Lichtenstein 82 B2
Lichtenstein 91 C2
Lichtenvoorde 67 C3
Lička Kaldrma 131 C2
Lički Jasenica 130 B1
Lički Osik 130 B2
Ličko Lešće 130 B1
Ličko Petrovo Selo 131 C1
Licodía Eubéa 125 C3
Licq-Atherey 108 A3, 154 B1
Licques 77 D1
Lid 42 B1
Lid 39 C3
Lida 73 D2, 74 A3
Lidar 37 C/D2
Liden 35 D2
Liden 30 A1
Lidgatu 30 A/B3, 35 D1/2
Lidhult 50 B1/2
Lidhult 72 A1
Lidice 83 C/D3
Lidingö 47 C/D1
Lidköping 45 D2
Lido Azzurro 121 C3
Lido degli Estensi 115 C1
Lido dei Pini 118 B2
Lido delle Nazioni 115 C1
Lido di Camaiore 114 A2, 116 A1
Lido di Copanello 122 B2
Lido di Jésolo 107 D3, 126 A3
Lido di Metaponto 121 C3
Lido di Mortelle 122 A3, 125 D1
Lido di Portonuovo 120 B1, 136 A2/3
Lido di Siponto 120 B1
Lido di Tarquínia 118 A1
Lido di Volano 115 C1
Lidón 162 A2
Lidoríkion 146 B1/2
Lido Silvana 121 C3
Lidsjöberg 29 D2
Lidzbark Warmiński (Heilsberg) 73 C2
Liebenau 93 D2
Liebenau (Nienburg-Weser) 68 A2
Liebenthal 70 A2
Liebenwalde 70 A2
Liebertswolkwitz 82 B1
Lieboch 127 C1
Liebschütz 82 A2
Liebstadt 83 C2
Liechtensteinklamm 126 A1
Liedakkala 17 D2, 18 A1
Liédena 155 C2
Liedenpohja 21 C3
Liedon asema 24 B2
Lieg 80 A3
Liège 79 C2
Liehittäjä 17 C/D2
Liekokylä 18 B1
Lieksa 23 D2
Lielax 24 B3
Lien 29 C3, 34 B1
Lienen 67 D3
Lienen-Kattenvenne 67 D3
Lienz 107 D1, 126 A1
Liepāja 73 C1
Liepimä 11 C3, 12 A1
Liepimäjärvi 11 C3, 12 A1
Lièpvre 89 D2, 90 A2
Lier 79 B/C1
Lierbyen 43 D1
Liérganes 153 B/C1
Lierstall 80 A2
Liesa 154 B2/3
Liesborn 67 D3, 68 A3, 80 B1

Liesjärvi 21 C3
Lieskau 83 C1
Lieskovec 95 D2
Lieso 25 C2, 26 A2
Liesse 78 B3
Liessel 79 D1
Liestal 90 A3
Liești 141 C3
Lieteksavo 10 A3
Lietlahti 22 B3
Lieto 24 B2
Liétor 168 B2
Lietzen 70 B2
Lieurey 77 C3, 86 B1
Lieusaint 87 D2
Lievestuore 21 D3, 22 A3
Lievikoski 24 B1
Lievoperä 18 B3
Liezen 93 D3
Liezen 96 A3
Liffol-le-Grand 89 C2
Lifjell Turisthotell 43 C1/2,
  44 A1
Lifton 62 B3
Ligardes 109 C2
Ligares 159 C2
Ligatne 73 D1, 74 A2
Ligescourt 77 D2
Lignan 105 C3
Lignano Pineta 126 A3
Lignano Sabbiadoro
  126 A3
Ligné 86 A3
Ligneuville 79 D2
Lignières 102 A1
Ligny-en-Barrois 89 C1/2
Ligny-en-Brionnais 103 C2
Ligny-le-Châtel 88 A2/3
Ligny-le-Ribault 87 C3
Ligónchio 114 A2, 116 A1
Ligoúrion 147 C3
Ligueil 101 D1
Lihjamo 21 C3
Lihme 48 A2
Lihostavl' 75 D2
Lihula 74 A1
Liikasenvaara 13 C/D3
Liikavaara 16 B1
Liimattala 22 B3
Liinamaa 20 B2
Liinanki 12 A3, 17 D1/2
Liipantönkkä 20 B2
Liitonjoki 21 D2, 22 A2
Liittoperä 21 D1, 22 A1
Lijeva Rijeka 137 D1/2
Likenäs 39 B/C2
Liléa 147 C1
L'Île Bouchard 101 C1
L'Île Rousse 113 D2
Lilienfeld 94 A2/3
Lilienthal 68 A2
Lilienthal-Worpswede
  68 A1/2
Liljanovo 139 D3
Liljedal 45 C/D1
Liljendal 25 D2, 26 A2
Lillå 16 B2
Lilla Edet 45 C3
Lillåfors 16 B2
Lilland 9 C2
Lillby 20 B1/2
Lille 78 A2
Lillebonne 77 C3
Lillefjord 5 D1, 6 A1
Lillehammer 38 A1/2
Lillehamn 42 B3
Lilleidet 8 B2
Lille Lerresfjord 5 C2
Lilleng 9 C2
Lillerød 49 D3, 50 A3,
  53 D1
Lillers 77 D2, 78 A2
Lillesand 43 C1
Lille Skensved 49 D3,
  50 A3, 53 D1
Lillestrøm 38 A3
Lillevollen 28 B3, 33 A3
Lillholmsjön 29 D3, 34 B1
Lillholmträsk 31 C1
Lillkågeträsk 31 D1
Lillkyro 20 B2
Lillmälö 24 B3
Lillmörtsjö 35 C3
Lillo 161 C3, 167 D1,
  168 A1
Lillögda 30 B1/2
Lillpite 16 B3

Lillsaivis 17 C2
Lillselet 17 C1/2
Lillström 35 D3
Lillsved 47 D1
Lillviken 15 C2
Lillviken 29 D2, 30 A2
Lima 39 C2
Limanowa 97 C2
Limátola 119 D3
Limay 87 C1
Limbach (Mosbach) 81 C3,
  91 C1
Limbach-Oberfrohna 82 B2
Limbaži 73 D1, 74 A2
Limburg an der Lahn 80 B2
Limedsforsen 39 C2
Limenária 145 B/C2
Limenária 149 C1
Limerick (Luimneach)
  55 C3
Limes 106 B2
Limhamn 50 A3
Limín 144 B1
Liminka 18 A2/3
Limín Litochórou 143 D2
Liminpuro 19 B/C3
Limmared 45 D3
Limmared 72 A1
Limmen 66 A2
Límni 147 C/D1
Límni Ilíki 147 C/D2
Límni Ioánninon 144 A1/2
Límni Kerkínis 139 D3,
  144 A1
Limoges 101 C2/3
Limogne 109 D1/2
Limoise 102 B1
Limone Piemonte 112 B2
Limonest 103 D2/3
Limone sul Garda 106 B3
Limours 87 C2
Limoux 110 A3, 156 A1
Limpias 153 C1
Lin 138 A/B3, 142 B1
Lina älv 16 B1
Linanäs 47 D1
Linards 101 D3
Linares 167 D3, 173 C1
Linares de la Sierra 165 D3,
  171 C1
Linares de Mora 162 B3
Linares de Riofrío 159 D2
Linás de Broto 155 B/C2
Lincluden Abbey 57 C3
Lincoln 61 D3, 64 B1
Linda 82 A2
Lindärva 45 D2
Lindås 36 A3
Lindåskroken 43 D1, 44 A1
Lindau 69 D3
Lindau 52 B2/3
Lindau (Bodensee) 91 C3
Linde 48 A2
Lindelse 53 C2
Linden 81 D2
Lindenberg im Allgäu
  91 C3
Lindenborg 48 B2 .
Lindenfels 81 B/C3
Lindenhayn 82 B1
Lindern 67 D2
Linderöd 50 B3
Lindesberg 39 D3, 46 A/B1
Lindesnäs 39 C/D2/3
Lindesnes 42 B3
Lindfors 39 C3, 45 D1ء
Lindholmen 40 B3,
  47 C/D1
Lindholm Høje 48 B1
Lindisfarne 57 D2
Lindlar 80 A1/2
Lindö 46 B2
Lindome 45 C3, 49 D1
Líndos 149 D3
Lindoso 150 B3, 158 A/B1
Lindow 70 A2
Lindsdal 51 D2
Lindwedel-Hope 68 B2
Líně 83 C3
Lingbo 40 A1/2
Linge 32 A3, 36 B1
Lingen 67 D2
Lingen-Brögbern 67 D2
Lingen-Estringen 67 D2
Linghed 39 D2, 40 A2
Lingslätö (Barnens ö)
  41 C3

Linguaglossa 125 D2
Linhamari 25 C3
Linkenheim-Hochstetten
  90 B1
Linkka 17 D2
Linköping 46 B2
Linkuva 73 D1, 74 A2
Linlithgow 57 C1/2
Linna 21 C/D3
Linnankylä 20 B3
Linnankylä 21 D2/3,
  22 A2/3
Linnerud 38 A/B2
Linneryd 51 C2
Linnes 38 B1
Linnes 29 C/D2, 34 B1
Linnés Hammarby 40 B3
Linnich 79 D1/2
Linsell 34 B3
Linthal 105 D1, 106 A1
Linthe 69 D3, 70 A3
Linton 65 C2
Lintorpet 38 B2
Lintula 11 D3, 12 A1/2
Linxe 108 B2
Linyola 155 D3, 163 D1
Linz 93 D2
Linz 96 A2
Linz am Rhein 80 A2
Lion 76 B3, 86 A1
Lioni 120 A2
Lípari 125 C/D1
Lipe 134 B2
Lipenec 83 C2
Liperi 23 C3
Lipiany 71 B/C2
Lipica 126 B3
Lipik 128 A3
Lipinki Łużyckie 71 C3,
  83 D1
Lipinvaara 23 C1
Lipka 71 D1
Lipkany 98 B3
Lipkovo 138 B2
Lipljan 138 B2
Lipník nad Bečvou 95 C1
Lipno 71 D3
Lipno 73 C3
Lipno nad Vltavou 93 D2
Lipolist 133 C1
Lipomo 105 D3, 106 A3
Liposthey 108 A2
Lipova 140 A1
Lipovac 135 C3
Lipovac 133 C1
Lipovec 99 C3
Lipovo Polje 130 B1/2
Lippetal 67 D3, 80 B1
Lippetal-Herzfeld 67 D3,
  80 B1
Lippetal-Lipporg 67 D3,
  80 B1
Lippó 128 B3
Lippstadt 68 A3, 80 B1
Lippstadt-Benninghausen
  67 D3, 68 A3, 80 B1
Lippstadt-Hörste 68 A3,
  80 B1
Liptál 95 C1
Liptovská Lúžna 95 D1
Liptovská Osada 95 D1
Liptovská Teplá 95 D1
Liptovský Mikuláš 97 C2
Lipůvka 94 B1
Liqenas 142 B1/2
Liria 162 B3, 169 C/D1
Lírkia 147 C3
Lis 138 A3
Lisac 132 A2
Lisboa 164 A2
Lisburn 56 A3
Lisburn 54 A3, 55 D2
Liseleje 49 D3
Liselund 53 D2
Lísen 94 B1
Lisiera 107 C3
Lisieux 77 B/C3, 86 B1
Lisina 134 B3
Liskeard 62 B3
L'Isle-Adam 87 C/D1
L'Isle d'Abeau 103 D3
L'Isle-de-Noé 109 C3,
  155 C1
L'Isle-en-Dodon 109 C3,
  155 C/D1
L'Isle-Jourdain 101 C/D2

L'Isle-Jourdain 109 C2/3,
  155 D1
L'Isle-sur-la-Sorgue
  111 C/D2
L'Isle-sur-le-Doubs 89 D3
L'Isle-sur-Serein 88 A3
Lisle-sur-Tarn 109 D2
Lisma 11 D2, 12 A/B1
Lismanaapa 12 B2
Lišnja 131 D1, 132 A1
Lišov 93 D1
Lisovići 132 B1/2
Lispeszentadorján 127 D2,
  128 A2
Lisse 66 A3
Lisskogsåsen 39 C2
Lissus 137 D3
List 52 A2
Lísta 142 B3
Listed 51 D3
Listerby 51 C2
Lištica 132 A3
Listrac-Médoc 100 B3,
  108 A/B1
Lit 29 D3, 34 B2
Litava 95 D2
Litcham 65 C1
Litchfield 65 C3, 76 B1
Liteň 83 C3
Lit-et-Mixe 108 B2
Lithakiá 146 A3
Litíf 143 D1/2, 144 A1/2
Litice 83 C3
Litija 127 C2
Litlos 42 B1
Litmaniemi 23 C2/3
Litobratřice 94 B1
Litóchoron 143 D2
Litoměřice 83 C2
Litoměřice 96 A1
Litschau 93 D1
Litslena 40 B3, 47 C1
Litsnäset 29 D3, 34 B2
Littiäinen 17 D2
Littlehampton 76 B1
Little Moreton Hall 59 D2,
  60 B3, 64 A1
Little Petherick 62 B3
Littleport 65 C2
Little Walsingham 65 C1
Litvínov 83 C2
Litvínov 96 A1
Liubcova 135 C2
Liukkunen 23 C2
Liumseter 37 D2
Livaderón 143 C2
Livádion 144 A2
Livádion 143 C/D2
Livanátai 147 C1
Livarot 86 B2
Livártzion 146 B2
Livata 118 B2
Livek 126 A/B2
Liverá 143 C2
Livernon 109 D1
Liverpool 59 C/D2, 60 B3
Livigno 106 B2
Livingston 57 C2
Liviöjärvi 17 C1
Livno 131 D3, 132 A2/3
Livo 18 B2
Livø 48 B2
Livold 127 C3
Livonniska 19 C1
Livonsaari 24 A2
Livorno 114 A3, 116 A2
Livorno Antignano 114 A3,
  116 A2
Livorno Ferráris 105 C3
Livorno Quercianella
  114 A3, 116 A2
Livron-sur-Drôme 111 C1
Livry-Gargan 87 D1
Lixheim 89 D1, 90 A2
Lizartza 153 D1, 154 A1
Lizoáin 154 A2
Lizy-sur-Ourcq 87 D1
Lizzano 121 C3
Lizzano in Belvedere
  114 B2, 116 A1
Lizzola 106 A/B2
Ljady 74 B1
Ljig 133 D2, 134 A2
Ljønes 15 C1
Ljørdal 38 B1
Ljøsheim 38 A1/2

Ljosland 42 B2
Ljuban' 75 C1
Ljubaništa 142 B1
Ljubaševka 99 C3
Ljuben 140 B3
Ljubija 131 D1
Ljubimec 145 D2
Ljubimec 141 C3
Ljubin 138 B2
Ljubina 132 B2
Ljubinić 133 D2, 134 A2
Ljubinje 137 C1
Ljubiš 133 D3, 134 A3
Ljubljana 126 B2
Ljubno 127 C2
Ljubojno 143 B/C1
Ljubojno 148 A1
Ljuboml' 97 D1, 98 A2
Ljuboml' 97 D1, 98 A2
Ljubostinja 134 B3
Ljubovija 133 C2
Ljubuški 132 A3, 136 B1
Ljubytino 75 C1
Ljudinovo 75 D3
Ljugarn 73 B/C1
Ljugarn 47 D3
Ljung 45 C/D3
Ljungå 35 C2
Ljungaverk 35 C3
Ljungby 50 B1/2
Ljungby 72 A1
Ljungbyhed 50 A/B2/3
Ljungbyholm 51 D2
Ljungbyholm 72 B1
Ljungdalen 34 A2
Ljungsarp 45 D3
Ljungsbro 46 B2
Ljungskile 45 C3
Ljuså 17 B/C2
Ljusfallshammar 46 B2
Ljusfors 46 B2
Ljusliden 15 C3, 29 D1
Ljusne 40 A/B1
Ljusnedalen 34 A3
Ljusterö 47 D1
Ljustorp 35 D2/3
Ljusträsk 16 A/B2
Ljusvattnet 31 D1
Ljutice 133 D2, 134 A2
Ljutoglava 138 B2
Ljutomer 127 D2
Lladorre 155 C2
Lladurs 155 D3, 156 A2
Llafranc 156 B2
Llagostera 156 B2/3
Llamas de la Ribera 151 D2
Llanarmon Dyffryn Ceiriog
  59 C3, 60 A3
Llanbadarn-Fynydd 59 C3
Llanberis 59 C2, 60 A3
Llancà 156 B2
Llandeilo 63 C1
Llandinabo 63 D1
Llandovery 63 C1
Llandrindod Wells 59 C3
Llandudno 59 C2, 60 A3
Llandyssul 62 B1
Llanelli 63 B/C1
Llanera 151 D1
Llanerchymedd 58 B2
Llanes 152 A/B1
Llanfaethlu 58 B2
Llanfair Caereinion 59 C3
Llanfairfechan 59 C2,
  60 A3
Llanfarian 59 C3
Llanfihangel Ystrad
  63 B/C1
Llanfyllin 59 C3
Llangadock 63 C1
Llangefni 58 B2
Llangoed 59 C2, 60 A3
Llangollen 59 C2/3,
  60 A/B3
Llangranog 62 B1
Llangurig 59 C3
Llanidloes 59 C3
Llanrhystyd 59 C3
Llanrwst 59 C2, 60 A3
Llansteffan 62 B1
Llanthaedr ym Mochnant
  59 C3, 60 A3
Llanthony Priory 63 C1
Llantrisant 63 C1/2
Llanwrda 63 C1
Llanwrtyd Wells 63 C1
Llanymynech 59 C3

Llardecans 163 C1
Llavorsí 155 C2
Lledó 156 B2
Lleida/Lérida 155 C3, 163 C1
Llera 165 D2/3, 166 A3
Llerena 165 D3, 166 A3
Llers 156 B2
Lles 155 D2, 156 A2
Llessui 155 D2
Llimiana 155 D3
Llinars de l'Aigua d'Ora 155 D2/3, 156 A2
Llivia 156 A2
Lloret de Mar 156 B3
Lloseta 157 C2
Llovio 152 A1
Llubi 157 C2
Llucmajor 157 C2
Llwyngwril 59 C3
Llyswen 63 C1
Lnáře 83 C3, 93 C1
Lo 30 B3, 35 D2
Lo 78 A1
Löa 39 D3
Loanhead 57 C2
Loano 113 C2
Loarre 154 B2
Löbau 83 D1
Löbau 96 A1
Lobbach-Waldwimmersbach 91 B/C1
Lobbæk 51 D3
Lobeira 150 B3
Löbejün 69 D3, 82 A/B1
Lobenstein 82 A2
Lobera de Onsella 154 B2
Löberöd 50 B3
Łobez 71 C1
Lobios 150 B3
Lobn'A 75 D2
Löbnitz 82 B1
Löbnitz 53 D3
Lobón 165 D2
Lobor 127 D2
Loburg 69 D3
Łobżenica 71 D1
Locana 105 B/C3
Locarno 105 D2
Locate di Triulzi 105 D3, 106 A3
Lochaline 56 A1
Lochaline 54 A2, 55 D1
Lochboisdale 54 A2, 55 D1
Lochbuie 56 A1
Lochcarron 54 A2
Lochdonhead 56 A1
Lochearnhead 56 B1
Lochem 67 C3
Loches 101 D1
Lochgelly 57 C1
Lochgilphead 56 A1
Lochgilphead 54 A2, 55 D1
Lochgoilhead 56 B1
Lochinver 54 A1/2
Lochmaben 57 C3
Lochmaddy 54 A2
Łochowice 71 C3
Lochranza 56 A2
Lochwinnoch 56 B2
Lockerbie 57 C3
Lockne 34 B2
Locknevi 46 B3
Löcknitz 70 B1
Locksta 30 B2
Locmaria 84 B3
Locmariaquer 85 C3
Locminé 85 C2/3
Locorotondo 121 C2
Locri 122 A/B3
Locri Epizefiri 122 A3
Locronan 84 A2
Loctudy 84 A2/3
Lodares de Osma 153 C3, 161 C1
Lodby 46 B2
Löddeköpinge 50 A3
Lødding 28 B1
Lodè 123 D2
Lodenau 83 D1
Loděnice 83 C3
Lodersleben 82 A1
Löderup 50 B3
Loderups strandbad 50 B3
Lodève 110 B2
Lodi 106 A3
Lødingen 9 C2
Lodosa 153 D2
Lödöse 45 C3
Łódź 73 C3, 97 C1
Loeches 161 C2/3
Loen 32 A3, 36 B1
Loenen 67 B/C3
Løfallstrand 42 A1
Lofer 92 B3
Löffingen 90 B3
Lofsdalen 34 A3
Loftahammar 47 B/C3
Lofthouse 59 D1, 61 C2
Lofthus 36 B3
Lofthus 9 C3
Loftus 61 C1
Loga 42 B3
Logatec 126 B2/3
Lögdeå 31 C2/3
Logišin 98 B1
Logodaš 139 D2
Lögow 69 D2
Log pod Mang 126 A/B2
Lograto 106 A/B3
Logron 86 A/B2
Logroño 153 D2
Logrosán 166 A/B1
Logstein 28 A3, 33 C1
Løgstør 48 B2
Loguivy-Plougras 84 B2
Løgumkloster 52 A/B2
Lohals 53 C2
Lohärad 41 B/C3
Lohberg 93 C1
Lohéac 85 C/D2/3
Lohiaanta 19 C1
Lohijärvi 12 A3, 17 D2
Lohijoki 21 D1, 22 A1
Lohikoski 27 C1
Lohiniva 12 A2, 17 D1
Lohja (Lojo) 25 C3
Lohjan asema 25 C3
Lohmar 80 A2
Lohmar-Wahlscheid 80 A2
Lohmen 83 C1/2
Lohmen 53 D3, 69 D1
Löhnberg 80 B2
Löhnberg-Niederhausen 80 B2
Löhne 68 A3
Lohne 67 D2, 68 A2
Lohnsburg 93 C2
Lohnsfeld 80 B3, 90 B1
Loholm 15 D2
Lohr 81 C3
Lohra 80 B2
Lohsa 83 D1
Lohtaja 21 C1
Lohvica 99 D2
Loiano 114 B2, 116 B1
Loiching 92 B2
Loiching-Wendelskirchen 92 B2
Loimaa 24 B2
Loimaan maalaiskunta 24 B2
Lóiri 123 D1
Loivos 150 B3, 158 B1
Loja 172 B2
Lojev 99 C/D1/2
Lojsta 47 D3
Løjt Kirkeby 52 B2
Loka Brunn 39 C/D3, 45 D1, 46 A1
Lokakylä 21 D2, 22 A2
Lokalahti 24 A2
Lokca 95 D1
Loke 34 B2
Løken 37 D2
Løken 38 A3
Løkeng 5 B/C2
Loker 78 A2
Lokeren 78 B1
Loket 82 B2/3
Lokka 13 C2
Løkken 28 A3, 33 C2
Løkken 48 B1
Lokkiperä 21 C1
Loknja 74 B2
Loksa 74 A1
Lokve 126 B2
Lokve 127 C3, 130 B1
Lollar 80 B2
Lom 37 C1
Lom 135 D3
Lom 140 B2
Lomajärvi 11 D3, 12 B2
Lomåsen 29 D3, 34 B1
Lomåsen 29 D3, 34 B1
Lombardore 105 C3, 113 B/C1
Lombez 109 C3, 155 D1
Lombheden 17 C2
Lomello 113 D1
Lomen 37 C2
Lominchar 160 B3
Lomma 50 A3
Lommatzsch 83 C1
Lomme 78 A2
Lommel 79 C1
Lomnice 82 B2/3
Lomnice nad Lužnicí 93 D1
Lompolo 11 D2/3, 12 A1
Lomsjö 30 A/B2
Łomża 73 C/D3, 98 A1
Lonato 106 B3
Lončari 132 B1
Lončarica 128 A3
Londinières 76 B3
London 65 C3
Londonderry (Derry) 54 A3, 55 D2
Lonevåg 36 A3
Longaníkos 146 B3
Longaníkos 148 B2
Longare 107 C3
Longares 163 C1
Longarone 107 D2
Long Compton 64 A2
Long Eaton 61 D3, 65 C1
Longeau 89 C3
Longega/Zwischenwasser 107 C1/2
Longeville 100 A2
Longeville-les-Saint-Avold 89 D1
Longford 55 C/D2
Longformacus 57 C2
Longhorsley 57 D2
Longjumeau 156 A1
Longlaville 79 C/D3
Longleat House 63 D2, 64 A3
Longlier 79 C3
Long Melford 65 C2
Longnes 87 C1
Longnor 59 D2, 61 C3, 64 A1
Longny-au-Perche 86 B2
Longobucco 122 B1
Longpont 87 D1, 88 A1
Longpré-les-Corps-Sainte 77 D2
Longré 101 C2
Longridge 59 D1, 60 B2
Longroiva 159 B/C2
Long Stratton 65 C2
Long Sutton 65 C1
Longton 59 D2, 60 B3, 64 A1
Longtown 57 C3, 60 B1
Longué 86 A3
Longueville-sur-Scie 77 C3
Longuyon 79 C3
Longvic 88 B3, 103 D1
Longwy 79 C/D3
Lonigo 107 C3
Lonin 28 A2
Löningen 67 D2
Löningen-Wachtum 67 D2
Lonja 128 A3, 131 D1
Lonkka 19 D2
Lönnewitz 83 C1
Lonny 79 B/C3
Lönsboda 50 B2
Lönsboda 72 A1
Lønsdal 15 C1
Lønset 33 C2/3
Lønset 32 A2
Lons-le-Saunier 103 D1, 104 A1/2
Lønstrup 48 B1
Loon op Zand 66 B3, 79 C1
Loon-Plage 77 D1
Loosdorf 94 A2
Lopar 130 B1
Lopare 133 C1/2
Lopătari 141 C2
Lopatica 138 B3, 143 C1
Lopera 167 C3, 172 B1
Loporzano 154 B2/3
Loppa 4 B2
Loppersum 67 C1
Loppi 25 C2
Loqueffret 84 B2
Lora de Estepa 172 A/B2
Lora del Río 171 D1, 172 A1
Loranca del Campo 161 D3
Loranca de Tajuña 161 C2
Lorås 29 D3, 35 C1
Lorca 174 A1
Lorch 91 C2
Lorch 80 B3
Lordosa 158 B2
Loreley 80 B3
Lorentzweiler 79 D3
Lorenzago di Cadore 107 D2
Lorenzana 151 D2, 152 A2
Lorenzo 113 D3
Loreo 115 C1
Loreto 117 D2, 130 A3
Loreto Aprutino 119 C1
Lórév 129 C1
Lorgues 112 A3
Lórica 122 B2
Lorient 84 B3
Loriga 158 B3
Loriguilla 162 B3, 169 C1
Loriol-sur-Drôme 111 C1
Lormes 88 A3, 103 C1
Loro Ciuffenna 115 C3, 116 B2
Loro Piceno 115 D3, 117 D2
Lorqui 169 D3
Lorquin 89 D1/2, 90 A2
Lörrach 90 A3
Lorrez-le-Bocage 87 D2
Lorris 87 D2/3
Lorsch 80 B3
Lörudden 35 D3
Lorup 67 D2
Lorvão 158 A3
Los 39 D1
Losa del Obispo 162 B3, 169 C1
Los Alares 166 B1
Los Alcázares 174 B1
Los Aranoñes 154 B2
Los Arcos 153 D2
Los Balbases 152 B2/3
Los Barrios de Bureba 153 C2
Los Barrios 172 A3
Los Berengueles 173 C2
Los Cerralbos 160 A/B3
Los Corrales 172 A2
Los Corrales de Buelna 152 B1
Los Cortijos 167 C1/2
Loscos 162 A/B2
Løset 38 A1
Loshamn 42 B3
Losheim 79 D3, 80 A3, 90 A1
Los Hinojosos 167 D1, 168 A1
Loshult 50 B2
Los Marines 165 D3, 171 C1
Los Martínez 169 C3, 174 B1
Los Molares 171 D2
Los Molinos 160 B2
Los Morenos 166 B3
Los Navalmorales 160 A/B3, 166 B1
Los Navalucillos 160 A/B3, 166 B1
Løsning 48 B3, 52 B1
Los Olmos 162 B2
Losomäki 23 C2
Losovaara 19 C2
Los Palacios y Villafranca 171 D2
L'Ospedale 113 D3
Los Rábanos 153 D3, 161 D1
Lossa / Finne 82 A1
Los Santos 159 D2
Los Santos de la Humosa 161 C2
Los Santos de Maimona 165 D2/3
Lossburg 90 B2
Losse 108 B2
Losser 67 C3
Lossiemouth-Branderburgh 54 B2
Lössnitz 82 B2
Lossvik 9 C3
Lostwithiel 62 B3
Los Valencianos 174 A/B1
Los Villares 173 C1
Los Villares de Soria 153 D3
Los Yebenes 167 C1
Löt 51 D1
Lote 36 B1
Loten 42 A2
Løten 38 A2
Lotorp 46 B2
Lotte 67 D2/3
Lottefors 40 A1
Löttorp 51 D1
Lotyń 71 D1
Lotzorai 123 D2
Louargat 84 B2
Loubeyrat 102 B2
Loučeň 83 D2
Loučim 93 C1
Loučka 95 C1
Loudéac 85 C2
Loudes 103 C3, 110 B1
Loudun 101 C1
Loué 86 A2
Loue 17 D2, 18 A1
Louejärvi 12 A3
Louejoki 12 A3, 17 D2
Loughborough 65 C1
Loughbrickland 58 A1
Loughgall 58 A1
Loughor 63 C1
Lougratte 109 C1
Louhans 103 D1
Louhossoa 108 B3, 155 C1
Loukee 26 B1
Loukeinen 23 C2
Loukkojärvi 18 B2
Louko 20 B3
Loukolampi 22 B3
Loukusa 19 C1
Loulay 100 B2
Loulé 170 B2
Louny 83 C2
Louny 96 A1/2
Lourdes 108 B3, 155 C1
Lourdios-Ichère 108 B3, 154 B1
Louredo 150 B3, 158 A/B1
Lourenzá 151 C1
Loures 164 A2
Loures-Barousse 109 C3, 155 C1
Lourical 158 A3
Lourinhã 164 A1/2
Loúros 146 A1
Lourosa 158 B3
Lourosa 158 A2
Loury 87 C2
Lousã 158 A3
Lousa 164 A2
Lousada 158 A1
Lousame 150 A2
Louth 58 A1
Louth 61 D3
Loutrá 145 D2
Loutrá 144 A/B2/3
Loutrá 144 A1/2
Loutrá Aridéas 143 C1
Loutrá Edipsoú 147 C1
Loutrá Eleftherón 144 B1/2
Loutrá Eleftherón 149 C1
Loutrá Ipátis 146 B1
Loutrá Irmínis 146 A2
Loutrá Kaïtsis 146 B1
Loutrá Kaiáfas 146 B3
Loutrá Kaiáfas 148 A/B2
Loutrá Killínis 146 A2
Loutrákion 147 C2
Loutrákion 146 A1
Loutrá Sidirókastrou 139 D3, 144 A1
Loutrá Smokóvou 146 B1
Loutrá Vólvis 144 A2
Loutrón 146 A1
Loutrón Elénis 147 C2
Loutrós 145 D1, 145 D3
Loutrós 143 D3
Loútsa 147 D2
Louveigné 79 C/D2
Louvie-Juzon 108 B3, 154 B1
Louviers 76 B3, 86 B1
Louvigné du-Désert 86 A/B2
Louvois 88 A/B1

Louvres 87 D1
Lövånger 31 D1
Lovanperä 21 D1, 22 A1
Lövås 30 B2
Løvås 43 D1/2, 44 A1
Lovasbereny 95 D3, 128 B1
Lövåsen 30 A3, 35 C2
Lovászpatona 95 C3, 128 A/B1
Lövberg 29 D1
Lövberga 30 A2, 35 C1
Lövdalen 34 A/B2
Loveč 140 B3
Løvenborg 49 C/D3, 53 C/D1
Lóvere 106 B3
Lóvero 106 B2
Lövestad 50 B3
Loviisa/Lovisa 25 D2/3, 26 B2/3
Lovinac 131 C2
Lovište 136 A/B1
Lövnäs 39 C1
Lövnäs 30 A1
Lövõ 94 B3
Lovosice 83 C2
Løvøyen 33 D2
Lovran 126 B3, 130 A1
Lovreč 126 B3, 130 A1
Lovreć 131 D3, 132 A3
Lovrenc na Pohorju 127 C2
Løvrødsvollen 33 C/D2
Lövsjön 39 D2/3
Lövsta 35 B/C2
Lövstabruk 40 B2
Lövstrand 30 A1
Lövtjärn 40 A2
Lovund 14 A2
Lövvattnet 31 D1
Lövvik 35 D2
Lövvik 30 A2
Lövvik 35 D2
Lowdham 61 C3, 64 B1
Löwenberg 70 A2
Löwenstein 91 C1
Lowestoft 65 D2
Łowicz 73 C3, 97 C1
Łowicz Wałecki 71 C1
Loxstedt 68 A1
Loxstedt-Bexhövede 68 A1
Loxstedt-Dedesdorf 68 A1
Loxstedt-Stotel 68 A1
Löytana 21 D2, 22 A2
Löytövaara 19 C1
Löyttymäki 25 C/D2, 26 A2
Löytynmäki 22 B2
Lož 126 B3
Lozen 139 D1
Łozice 70 B2
Loznica 133 C2
Loznicy 75 C2
Lozöac 131 C3
Lozovik 134 B2
Lozoya 160 B2
Lozoyuela 161 C2
Lozzo di Cadore 107 D2
Luarca 151 C1
Lubań (Lauban) 83 D1
Lubań (Lauban) 96 A1
Lubanowo 70 B2
L'ubar 99 C2
Lübars 69 D3
Lubartów 97 D1, 98 A2
Lubasz 71 D2
Lübbecke 68 A3
Lübben 70 B3
Lübben 72 A3, 96 A1
Lübbenau 70 B3
Lubczyna 70 B1
Lübeck 53 C3, 69 C1
Lübeck-Travemünde 53 C3
Lubenec 83 C3
Lubersac 101 C3
Lubia 153 D3, 161 D1
Lubiatowo 71 C1/2
Lubiesz 71 C/D1
Lubieszewo 71 C1
Lubiń 71 D3
Lubin 96 B1
Lublin 97 D1, 98 A2
Lubliniec 96 B1
Lubniewice 71 C2
Lubno 71 D1
Lubny 99 D2
Lubochňa 95 D1
Luboń 71 D2/3
Lubosz 71 C/D2
Łubowo 71 D1
Lubrín 174 A2
Lubrza 71 C3
Lubsko 71 B/C3
Lübtheen 69 C1
Luby 82 B2
Lübz 69 D1
Lucainena 173 C/D2
Lucainena de las Torres 173 D2, 174 A2
Lucan 58 A2
Lúcar 173 D1/2
Luçay-le-Mâle 101 D1
Lucca 114 A/B2, 116 A1
Luče 127 C2
Lucelle [Alle] 89 D3, 90 A3
Lucena 172 B1/2
Lucena de Jalón 155 C3, 163 B/C1
Lucena del Cid 162 B3
Lucena del Puerto 171 C2
Lucenay-l'Évêque 103 C1
Luc-en-Diois 111 D1
Lučenec 97 C2/3
Luceni 155 C3, 163 B/C1
Lucens 104 B1/2
Lucera 120 A1
Luchente 169 D2
Luché-Pringé 86 A/B3
Lüchow 69 C2
Luciana 167 C2
Lučice 133 D3, 134 A/B3
Lucignano 115 C3, 116 B2
Lucillo 151 D2
Lucillos 160 A/B3
Lucito 119 D2
Luck 97 D1, 98 B2
Lucka 82 B1
Luckau 70 A/B3
Luckau 72 A3, 96 A1
Luckenwalde 72 A3, 96 A1
Luckenwalde 70 A3
Lucksta 35 D3
Lückstedt 69 C2
Lúčky Kúpele 95 D1
Luco de Bordón 162 B2
Luco dei Marsi 119 C2
Luçon 101 C2
Ludbreg 127 D2
Lüdenscheid 80 A/B1
Lüderitz 69 D2
Lüdersdorf 53 C3, 69 C1
Lüdge-Elbrinxen 68 A/B3
Lüdge-Rischenau 68 A/B3
Ludgershall 64 A3, 76 A1
Ludgo 47 C2
Ludiente 162 B3
Lüdinghausen 67 D3
Ludlow 59 D3
Ludomy 71 D2
Luduș 97 D3, 140 B1
Ludvika 39 D3
Ludwigsau 81 C2
Ludwigsau-Ersrode 81 C2
Ludwigsburg 91 C1/2
Ludwigschorgast 82 A3
Ludwigsdorf 83 D1
Ludwigsfelde 70 A3
Ludwigshafen am Rhein 80 B3, 90 B1
Ludwigshafen am Bodensee 91 C3
Ludwigslust 69 C1
Ludwigsstadt 82 A2
Ludza 74 B2
Luelmo 159 D1
Luesia 154 B2
Luesma 163 C1/2
Lug 137 C1
Lug 129 C3
Lug 133 C1
Luga 74 B1
Lugagnano Val d'Arda 114 A1
Lugán 152 A2
Lugano 105 D2
Lugar Nuevo 167 C3
Lugar Nuevo de Fenollet 169 D2
Lugau 82 B2
Lügde 68 A/B3
Lugendorf 94 A2
Ługi 71 C2
Lugnano in Teverina 117 C3, 118 A/B1
Lugnarohögen 50 A2
Lugnås 45 D2
Lugnvik 30 B3, 35 D2
Lugnvik 29 D3, 34 B2
Lugny 103 D2
Lugo 115 C2, 116 B1
Lugo 150 B2
Lugoj 140 A1/2
Lugones 151 D1
Lugros 173 C2
Lugueros 152 A2
Lugugnana 107 D3, 126 A3
Luhačovice 95 C1
Luhalahti 24 B1
Luhanka 25 D1, 26 A1
Luhe-Wildenau 82 B3, 92 B1
Luhtapohja 23 D2
Luhtikylä 25 D2, 26 A2
Luikonlahti 23 C2
Luino 105 D2
Luiro 13 B/C2
Luisenthal 81 D2
Lújar 173 C2
Luka 132 B3
Lúka 95 C2
Luka 136 B1
Luka 136 B1
Luka 130 B2
Luka 135 C2
Luka-Barskaja 99 C3
Lukácsháza 94 B3, 127 D1
Lukare 133 D3, 138 A1
Lukavac 132 B2
Lukavac 132 B3, 137 C1
Lukavec 83 D3, 93 D1
Lukavica 132 B1
Lukićevo 129 D3, 134 A1
Lukkarila 22 B2
Lukkaroinen 18 A3
Lukovica 127 C2
Lukovit 140 B3
Lukovo 135 C3
Lukovo 134 B3, 138 B1
Lukovo 138 A3, 142 B1
Lukovo-Šugarje 130 B2
Lukovska Banja 134 B3, 138 B1
Łuków 73 D3, 97 C/D1, 98 A1/2
Luksefjell 43 D2, 44 A1
Lula 123 D2
Luleå 17 C3
Lumbarda 136 B1
Lumbier 155 C2
Lumbrales 159 C2
Lumbreras 153 D3
Lumbres 77 D1/2
Lumijoki 18 A2/3
Lumio 113 D2
Lummelunda 47 D2
Lummelunds bruk 47 D2
Lummimetsä 18 A3
Lummukka 21 B/C2
Lumparland 41 D3
Lumpiaque 155 C3, 163 C1
Lumsheden 40 A2
Luna 154 B2/3
Lunano 115 C2, 117 C1/2
Lunas 110 B2
Lund 50 A/B3
Lund 28 B1
Lund 53 D1/2
Lund 72 A2
Lunda 40 B3, 47 C1
Lundbäck 31 D1
Lunde 30 B3, 35 D2
Lunde 37 D2
Lunde 43 C/D2, 44 A1
Lunde 37 D3
Lunde 36 B2
Lundeborg 53 C2
Lundeby 44 B1
Lundebyvollen 38 B2
Lunden 52 A/B3
Lundenes 9 C1
Lunderseter 38 B3
Lunderskov 48 B3, 52 B1
Lundkälen 29 D3, 34 B2
Lundmoen 37 D2/3
Lundsberg 45 D1, 46 A1
Lundsbrunn 45 D2
Lundsjön 29 D3, 34 B1
Lünebach 79 D3
Lüneburg 68 B1
Lunel 111 C2/3
Lünen 67 D3, 80 A1
Lunestedt 68 A1
Lunéville 89 D2
Lungern 105 C1
Lungro 122 A1
Lungsjön 30 A3, 35 C1
Luninec 98 B1
Lunkkaus 13 C2
Lunnäset 34 A3
Lunndörsstugan 34 A2
Lünne 67 D2
Lunow 70 B2
Lunz am See 93 D3
Luogosanto 123 D1
Luoma-aho 21 C2
Luopa 20 B3
Luopajärvi 20 B3
Luopioinen 25 C1
Luoppoperä 19 C2
Luostanlinna 23 C2
Luosu 11 C3, 12 A2
Luotola 27 B/C2
Luovankylä 20 A/B3
Lupac 135 C1
Lupeni 135 D1
Lupeni 140 B2
Lupiac 109 B/C2/3
Lupiana 161 C2
Lupiñen 154 B2/3
Lupión 167 D3, 173 C1
Lupoglav 127 D3
Lupoglav 126 B3, 130 A1
Luppa 82 B1
Luque 172 B1
Lúras 123 D1
Lurbe-Saint-Christau 108 B3, 154 B1
Lurçy-Lévy 102 B1
Lure 89 D3
Lureuil 101 D1
Lurgrotte 127 C1
Luri 113 D2
Lurøy 14 A2
Lury-sur-Arnon 102 A1
Lušci Palanka 131 C1/2
Lüsens 107 C1
Luserna San Giovanni 112 B1
Lusévera 126 A2
Lushnjë 142 A1
Lushnjë 148 A1
Lusi 25 D1, 26 A/B1
Lusiana 107 C3
Lusignan 101 C2
Lusigny-sur-Barse 88 B2
Lus-la-Croix-Haute 111 D1
Lusminki 19 D1
Luso 158 A2/3
Lusón/Lüsen 107 C1
Luspa 10 B2
Luss 56 B1
Lussac 108 B1
Lussac-les-Châteaux 101 C/D2
Lussac-les-Eglises 101 C2
Lussan 111 C2
Lustad 28 B2, 33 D1, 34 A1
Lustenau 91 C3
Luštěnice 83 D2
Luster 36 B2
Lutago/Luttach 107 C1
Lutherstadt-Wittenberg 69 D3
Lutherstadt-Wittenberg 72 A3
Lütjenburg 53 C3
Lutnes 38 B2
Lutol Suchy 71 C3
Luton 64 B2
Luton Hoo 64 B2/3
Lutry 104 B2
Lutta 24 A2
Lütte 69 D3
Lutter am Barenberge 68 B3
Lutterworth 65 C2
Lutzelbourg 89 D1, 90 A2
Lützen 82 B1
Lutzerath 80 A3
Lutzmannsburg 94 B3
Lützow 53 C3, 69 C1
Luujoki 18 A1
Luukkola 27 C1
Luukkonen 27 C1
Luumäen asema 27 C2
Luumäki 27 B/C2
Luupujoki 22 B1
Luupuvesi 22 B1
Luusniemi 22 B3
Luusua 12 B3
Luutalahti 23 D3
Luvia 24 A1
Luvos 16 A1
Luxembourg 79 D3
Luxeuil-les-Bains 89 D3
Luxey 108 B2
Luyego 151 D2
Luyères 88 B2
Luynes 86 B3
Luz 170 B2
Luz 170 A2
Lužani 132 A/B1
Luzarches 87 D1
Luzás 155 C2/3
Luzenac 155 D2, 156 A1
Luzern 105 C1
Lužki 74 B3
Luzo 158 A2/3
Luzón 161 D2
Luz-Saint-Sauveur 155 C2
Luzy 103 C1
Luzzara 114 B1
Luzzi 122 A/B1
L'vov 97 D2, 98 A2
Lwówek 71 C/D2
Lychen 70 A1/2
Lycke 45 B/C3
Lyckeby 51 C2
Lyčkovo 75 C1/2
Lycksele 31 C1
Lydd 77 C1
Lydham 59 C/D3
Lydney 63 D1
Lye 47 D3
Lyestad 45 D2, 46 A2
Lygna 38 A2
Lykintö 23 C1
Lykkja 37 C2
Lykkja 37 C3
Lykosoura 146 B3
Lyly 25 C1
Lylykylä 19 C2
Lylyvaara 23 D2
Lyme Regis 63 C/D2/3
Lymington 76 A1
Lyndhurst 76 A1
Lyne 48 A3, 52 A1
Lyngdal 43 D1
Lyngdal 42 B3
Lyngør 43 C/D3, 44 A2
Lyngseidet 4 B3
Lyngsnes 28 B1
Lyngvær 8 B2
Lynton 63 C2
Lyø 52 B2
Lyökki 24 A2, 41 D2
Lyon 103 D3
Lyons-la-Forêt 77 D3, 87 C1
Lysá nad Labem 83 D2/3
Lysá pod Makytou 95 C1
Lysebotn 42 B2
Lysekil 44 B2/3
Lyseklöster 36 A3
Lysnes 9 D1
Lysøysund 28 A2/3, 33 C1
Lyss 104 B1
Lystrup 48 B2/3
Lysvik 39 C3
Lysvoll 9 C2
Lytham 59 C/D1/2, 60 B2
Lytham Saint Anne's 59 C1/2, 60 B2
Lyxaberg 30 B1

M

Maakeski 25 D1, 26 A1
Maalahti 20 A2, 31 D3
Maalismaa 18 B2
Maam Cross 55 C2
Maaninka 22 B2
Maaninkavaara 13 C3
Maanselkä 23 C1
Maarala 27 C1
Maaria 24 B2
Maarianhamina 41 C/D3
Maarianvaara 23 C2
Maarlanperä 21 D1, 22 A1
Maarssen 66 B3

Maaseik 79 D1
Maaselka 19 D3
Maasholm 52 B2
Maasholm-Maasholm-Bad 52 B2
Maasmechelen 79 C/D1/2
Maassluis 66 A3
Maastricht 79 C/D2
Määttälä 21 C1
Määttälänvaara 19 D1
Maavesi 22 B3
Mablethorpe 61 D3, 65 C1
Macael 173 D2, 174 A1/2
Mação 164 B1
Maccagno 105 D2
Macchiagódena 119 D2
Macchiareddu 123 D3
Macclesfield 59 D2, 60 B3, 64 A1
Maceda 150 B2/3
Macedo de Cavaleiros 151 C3, 159 C1
Maceira 158 B2
Maceira 158 A3, 164 A1
Macelj 127 D2
Macerata 117 D2
Macerata Féltria 115 C2, 117 C1
Machault 88 B1
Machecoul 100 A1
Macherádon 146 A2/3
Machilly 104 A/B2
Machliny 71 D1
Machrihanish 56 A2
Machynlleth 59 C3
Macieira 158 A1
Măcin 141 D2
Macinaggio 113 D2
Mácine 115 D3, 117 D2
Mačkat 133 C/D3, 134 A3
Macken 80 A2/3
Mackenrode 81 D1
Mačkovci 127 D1
Macocha 94 B1
Macomér 123 C2
Mâcon 103 D2
Macon 78 B3
Macotera 160 A2
Macquenoise 78 B3
Macroom 55 C3
Macugnaga 105 C2
Mačul'niki 75 C3
Macure 131 C2
Madängsholm 45 D3
Madaras 129 C2
Maddalena 112 B1
Maddalena Spiággia 123 D3
Maddaloni 119 D3
Made 66 A/B3
Madeira 158 B3, 164 B1
Madekoski 18 B2
Maderuelo 161 C1
Madésimo 105 D2, 106 A2
Madetkoski 12 B1/2
Madlan 42 A2
Madona 74 A2
Madonna del Bosco 115 C1
Madonna delle Grázie 112 B2
Madonna della Neve 117 D3, 118 B1
Madonna della Pace 118 B2
Madonna di Campíglio 106 B2
Madonna di Ponte [Brissago] 105 D2
Madonna di Tirano 106 B2
Madrid 161 B/C2/3
Madridejos 167 D1
Madrid El Pardo 160 B2
Madrigal 161 C1
Madrigal de la Vera 159 D3, 160 A3
Madrigal de las Altas Torres 160 A2
Madrigalejo 166 A2
Madrigalejo del Monte 153 C3
Madriguera 161 C1
Madrigueras 168 B1/2
Madrona 160 B2
Madroñera 166 A1
Madžarovo 145 D2
Maella 163 C1/2
Mäenkylä 21 C/D3
Mäentaka 24 B2
Maesteg 63 C1
Maeztu 153 D2
Mafalda 119 D2
Mafjordhamn 5 C1
Mafra 164 A2
Magacela 166 A2
Magalas 110 B3
Magallón 154 A3, 162 A1
Magán 160 B3, 167 C1
Magaña 153 D3
Magasa 106 B3
Magaz de Cepeda 151 D2
Magdala 82 A2
Magdeburg 69 C/D3
Magenta 105 D3
Magerholm 32 A3, 36 B1
Magesq 108 B2
Maggia [Ponte Brolla] 105 D2
Maghera 54 A3, 55 D2
Magione 115 C3, 117 C2
Maglaj 132 B2
Maglavit 135 D2
Magleby 53 C2
Maglehem 50 B3
Magliano de'Marsi 119 C1/2
Magliano in Toscana 116 B3
Magliano Sabina 117 C3, 118 B1
Maglić 133 D3, 134 A3
Máglie 121 D3
Magnac-Laval 101 C2
Magnières 89 D2
Magnor 38 B3
Magny-Cours 102 B1
Magny-en-Vexin 77 D3, 87 C1
Mágocs 128 B2
Magolsheim 91 C2
Magouládes 142 A3
Maguelone 110 B3
Maguilla 166 A3
Magura 135 C/D3
Magura 138 B2
Magusteiro 150 B3, 158 B1
Magyaratád 128 B2
Magyaregregy 128 B2
Magyarfalva 94 B3
Magyarkeszi 128 B1/2
Magyarmecske 128 B2/3
Magyarnándor 95 D3
Magyarszék 128 B2
Mahide 151 D3, 159 C1
Mahlsdorf 69 C2
Mahora 168 B2
Mahovo 127 D3
Mähring 82 B3
Maials 163 C1
Măicănești 141 C2
Maicas 162 B2
Maîche 89 D3, 104 B1
Máida 122 B2
Máida Marina 122 A/B2
Maiden Castle 63 D2/3
Maidenhead 64 B3
Maiden Newton 63 D2
Maidstone 65 C3, 77 C1
Maienfeld 106 A1
Maiero 115 C1
Măieruș 141 C1
Maignelay 78 A3
Maijanen 12 A2/3, 17 D1
Mailhac-sur-Benaize 101 C2
Maillat 103 D2, 104 A2
Maillezais 100 B2
Mailly-la-Ville 88 A3
Mailly-le-Camp 88 B2
Mainar 163 C1
Mainburg 92 A2
Mainburg-Lindkirchen 92 A2
Mainhardt 91 C1
Mainiemi 26 B1
Mainleus 82 A3
Mainleus-Buchau 82 A3
Mainsat 102 A2
Maintenon 87 C2
Mainua 19 C3, 22 B1
Mainz 80 B3
Maiorca 158 A3
Maiorga 164 A1
Maiori 119 D3
Mairena del Aljarafe 171 D1/2
Mairena del Alcor 171 D1/2
Mairos 151 C3, 158 B1
Maisach 92 A2
Maisey-le-Duc 88 B3
Maison Forestière 113 D2/3
Maison-Rouge 87 D2, 88 A2
Maisons-Laffitte 87 C1
Maissau 94 A2
Maisse 87 D2
Maissin 79 C3
Maitenbeth 92 B2
Maivala 27 C1
Maizières-lès-Vic 89 D1/2
Maizières-lès-Metz 89 C1
Maja 127 D3, 131 C1
Majadahonda 160 B2
Majadas 159 D3, 166 A1
Majaelrayo 161 C2
Majava 19 C1
Majavasuvanto 13 C2
Majavatn 14 B3, 29 C1
Majdan 129 D2
Majdanpek 135 C2
Majilovac 134 B1/2
Majkić Japra 131 C1
Majovakylä 18 B1
Makarska 131 D3, 132 A3, 136 A/B1
Makeevskoe 75 D2
Mäkelä 25 D2, 26 A2
Mäkikylä 21 C3
Makkola 21 D3, 22 A3
Makó 129 D2
Makó 97 C3, 140 A1
Makole 127 C/D2
Makov 95 D1
Makov 96 B2
Makovac 138 B1
Makovo 139 B/C3, 143 C1
Makrakómi 146 B1
Makrakómi 148 B2
Mákri 145 D1
Makríammos 145 C1/2
Makrinoú 146 B2
Makriráchi 146 B1
Maksamaa 20 B2
Maksatiha 75 D2
Maksniemi 17 D3, 18 A1
Mæl 43 C1
Malå 16 A3
Malá 173 C2
Mala Bršljanica 128 A3
Mala Čista 131 C2/3
Malacky 94 B2
Malacky 96 B2
Málaga 172 B2
Málaga del Fresno 161 C2
Malagón 167 C2
Malaguilla 161 C2
Malahide 58 A2
Malahvianvaara 19 D3
Malaja Višera 75 C1
Malaja Viska 99 D3
Mala Kladuša 131 C1
Mala Krsna 134 B2
Malalbergo 115 C1
Mala Mitrovica 133 C1
Malanquilla 154 A3, 161 D1, 162 A1
Malarby 24 B3
Mälarhusens strandbad 50 B3
Mäläskä 18 B3
Mala Subotica 127 D2
Malaucène 111 D2
Malaunay 77 C3
Mälävaara 13 C3
Malax (Maalahti) 20 A2, 31 D3
Malborghetto 126 A2
Malbork (Marienburg) 73 C2
Malborn 80 A3
Malbuisson 104 A1
Malcésine 106 B3
Malchin 69 D1, 70 A1
Malching 93 C2
Malchow 69 D1
Malcocinado 166 A3
Maldegem 78 B1
Maldon 65 C3
Malè 106 B2
Malefougasse 111 D2, 112 A2
Malemort-sur-Corrèze 101 D3
Mælen 28 B2
Malente 53 C3
Måleràs 51 C1
Malesco 105 C/D2
Malesherbes 87 D2
Malesína 147 C1
Malestroit 85 C3
Maletićevo 134 B1
Malexander 46 A3
Malfa 125 C1
Malga Mare 106 B2
Malgrat de Mar 156 B3
Malhadas 151 D3, 159 C1
Malham 59 D1, 60 B2
Malhu 21 D3
Mali Borak 133 D2, 134 A2
Malicorne-sur-Sarthe 86 A3
Mali Đerdap 135 C1/2
Mali Iđoš 129 C/D3
Malijai 112 A2
Målilla 51 C/D1
Målilla 72 B1
Mali Lošinj 130 A/B2
Malín 83 D3
Malin 99 C2
Malingsbo 39 D3
Malinska 130 B1
Maliq 142 B1/2
Mališevo 138 B2
Maliskylä 21 D1, 22 A1
Mali Zvornik 133 C2
Maljasalmi 23 C2/3
Maljevac 127 D3, 131 C1
Maljovica 139 D2
Malkara 149 D1
Malkenes 42 A1
Malkkila 23 C3
Malko Gradište 145 D2
Malko Tărnovo 141 C3
Mallaig 54 A2, 55 D1
Mållångssta 39 D1, 40 A1
Mallemort 111 D2
Mallén 154 A3
Mallersdorf-Pfaffenberg 92 B2
Málles Venosta/Mals 106 B1/2
Malling 48 B3
Mallinkainen 25 C2, 26 A2
Malliss 69 C1/2
Mallnitz 126 A1
Mallow 55 C3
Mallusjoki 25 D2, 26 A2
Malm 28 B2
Malmåsen 38 B1
Malmbäck 46 A3
Malmberget 16 B1
Malmédy 79 D2
Malmesbury 63 D1, 64 A3
Malmköping 47 B/C1
Malmö 50 A3
Malmö 72 A2
Malmön 44 B2
Malmslätt 46 B2
Malnate 105 D3
Malnes 8 B2
Malo 107 C3
Malojaroslavec 75 D3
Maloja [St.-Moritz] 106 A2
Malo Konjari 138 B3, 143 C1
Malo-les-Bains 77 D1, 78 A1
Malonty 93 D2
Malorita 73 D3, 97 D1, 98 A2
Malovătu 135 D1/2
Måløy 36 A1
Malpartida 160 A2
Malpartida de Cáceres 165 D1
Malpartida de la Serena 166 A2
Malpartida de Plasencia 159 D3
Malpartida de Corneja 159 D2, 160 A2
Malpas 59 D2, 60 B3
Malpica 160 B3, 167 B/C1
Malpica 158 B3, 165 C1
Malpica de Arba 154 A/B2
Malpica de Bergantiños 150 A1
Malsch 90 B1/2
Malschwitz 83 D1
Målselv 4 A3, 9 D1
Målsetsløl 36 B2/3
Malsfeld 81 C1
Malšice 93 D1
Malsjö 45 C1
Målsnes 4 A3, 9 D1
Målsryd 45 C/D3
Malstedt 68 A/B1
Malta 126 A/B1
Malta 159 C2
Maltat 103 C1
Maltbränna 31 C1
Maltby 61 D3
Malterdingen 90 A/B2
Malterhausen 70 A3
Maltesholm 50 B3
Malton 61 C2
Maluenda 162 A1
Mælum 43 D2, 44 A1
Malung 39 C2
Malungen 35 D3
Malungen 38 A2
Malungsfors 39 C2
Małuszów 71 C2/3
Malva 152 A3, 159 D1, 160 A1
Malveira 164 A2
Malveira da Serra 164 A2
Malvik 28 A3, 33 C1/2
Malý Krtíš 95 D2
Malženice 95 C2
Mamaia Băi 141 D2
Mamarrosa 158 A2
Mambrillas de Lara 153 C3
Mamers 86 B2
Mammendorf 92 A2
Mamming 92 B2
Mámmola 122 A/B3
Mamoiada 123 D2
Mamolar 153 C3
Mamone 123 D2
Mamonovo (Heiligenbeil) 73 C2
Mamuras 137 D3
Manacor 157 C/D2
Manacore 120 B1
Manamansalo 19 B/C3
Mañaria 153 D1
Manasija 134 B2
Mănăstirea Tismana 135 D1
Manastir Morača 137 D1
Mancera de Arriba 160 A2
Mancera de Abajo 160 A2
Mancha Real 167 D3, 173 C1
Manchester 59 D2, 60 B3
Manchita 165 D2, 166 A2
Manchones 162 A1/2
Manciano 116 B3, 118 A1
Manciet 108 B2
Mancourt-sur-Orne 89 C1
Mandal 42 B3
Måndalen 32 A3
Mandanici 125 D2
Mándas 123 D3
Mandatoríccio 122 B1
Mandayona 161 C/D2
Mandello del Lário 105 D2/3, 106 A2/3
Manderscheid 80 A3
Mandling 93 C3, 126 A/B1
Mandø 52 A1
Mandoúdion 147 D1
Mándras 147 D2
Mandres-la-Côte 89 C2
Mandrica 145 D1, 145 D3
Mandúria 121 D3
Mane 111 D2
Mane 109 C3, 155 D1
Manerba del Garda 106 B3
Mañeru 154 A2
Måneset 28 B1
Mánesis 146 B3
Manětín 83 C3
Manevići 98 B2
Mánfa 128 B2
Manfredónia 120 B1
Mangalia 141 D2
Mángana 145 C1
Mangen 38 B3
Mångsbodarna 39 C2
Mangskog 38 B3, 45 C1

Mangualde 158 B2
Manhay 79 C2
Manheulles 89 C1
Maniago 107 D2, 126 A2
Maninghem-au-Mont 77 D2
Manisa 149 D2
Manises 169 D1
Manjärv 16 B3
Manjaur 31 C1
Mank 94 A2
Mankala 25 D2, 26 B2
Månkarbo 40 B3
Mankila 18 A/B3
Manlleu 156 A2
Mánna 147 C2
Mannersdorf an der Rabnitz 94 B3
Mannersdorf am Leithagebirge 94 B3
Mannervaara 23 D3
Mannheim 80 B3, 90 B1
Männikkö 17 C1
Männikkövaara 19 B/C1
Mannila 24 B2
Manningtree 65 D2
Mannseterbakken 33 D3
Manojlovac slap 131 C2
Manolás 146 A2
Manoppello 119 C1
Manosque 111 D2, 112 A2
Manresa 156 A3
Mansares 158 A2
Månsåsen 34 B2
Manschnow 70 B2
Mansfeld 82 A1
Mansfield 61 D3, 65 C1
Mansilla 153 C3
Mansilla de las Mulas 152 A2
Mansle 101 C2
Mansoniemi 24 B1
Månsta 39 C1
Månsträsk 16 A3
Manteigas 158 B2/3
Mantel 82 B3
Mantes 87 C1
Mantgum 66 B1/2
Manthelan 101 D1
Mantiel 161 D2
Mantila 20 B3
Mantineia 147 B/C3
Mäntlahti 26 B2
Mantorp 46 A/B2
Måntorp 30 A1
Mántova 106 B3, 114 B1
Mäntsälä 25 D2, 26 A2
Mänttä 21 C3
Mäntyharju 26 B1
Mäntyharjun asema 26 B1
Mäntyjärvi 19 C1
Mäntyjärvi 12 A3, 17 D1
Mäntylahti 22 B2
Mäntylänperä 18 A3
Mäntylärvi 23 C2
Mäntyluoto 24 A1, 41 D1
Mäntypää 12 B1
Mäntyvaara 17 C1
Manzac-sur-Vern 101 C3, 109 C1
Manzalvos 151 C3
Manzanal de Arriba 151 C/D3
Manzanares 167 D2
Manzanares el Real 160 B2
Manzaneda 151 C2
Manzaneque 160 B3, 167 C1
Manzanera 162 B3
Manzanilla 171 C1/2
Manzat 102 B2
Manziana 118 A1
Maoča 132 B1
Maqellarë 138 A3
Maqueda 160 B3
Mara 162 A1
Maracena 173 C2
Maradik 133 D1, 134 A1
Maråkerby 40 A/B1
Maranchón 161 D2
Maranello 114 B1
Marano 114 B2, 116 A/B1
Marano di Nápoli 119 C/D3
Marano Lagunare 126 A3
Marans 100 B2
Mărășești 141 C1
Marateca 164 A/B2
Marathéa 143 C3
Marathías 146 B2
Marathón 147 D2
Marathópolis 146 B3
Maraye-en-Othe 88 A2
Marazion 62 A3
Marazoleja 160 B2
Marazovel 161 C/D1
Marbach 91 C1
Marbach an der Donau 93 D2, 94 A2
Marbache 89 C1
Mårbacka 39 C3
Marbella 172 A3
Marboz 103 D2
Mårbu 43 C1
Marburg 81 B/C2
Marburg-Cappel 81 B/C2
Marby 34 B2
Marc 155 D2
Marça 163 C1/2
Marcali 128 A2
Marcaltő 95 C3, 128 A1
Marčana 130 A1
Marcaria 114 B1
Marcelová 95 C3
Marcén 154 B3
Marcena 107 B/C2
Marcenais 101 C3, 108 B1
Marcenat 102 B3
Mârčevo 135 D3
March 65 C2
Marchais 78 B3
Marchamalo 161 C2
Marchaux 89 C3, 104 A1
Marche-en-Famenne 79 C2/3
Marchegg 94 B2
Marchegg 96 B2/3
Marchena 172 A2
Marchenoir 86 A/B3
Marcheprime 108 A/B1
March-Hugstetten 90 A/B2/3
Marchiennes 78 A2
Marchtrenk 93 C/D2
Marciac 109 B/C3, 155 C1
Marciana 116 A3
Marciana Marina 116 A3
Marcianise 119 D3
Marcigny 103 C2
Marcilhac-sur-Celé 109 D1
Marcillac-la-Croze 109 D1
Marcillac-la-Croisille 102 A3
Marcillac-Vallon 110 A1/2
Marcillat-en-Combraille 102 B2
Marcilloles 103 D3
Marcilly-en-Gault 87 C3
Marcilly-sur-Eure 86 A/B1
Marcilly-sur-Seine 88 A2
Marck 77 D1
Marckolsheim 90 A2
Marco 107 B/C3
Marco de Canaveses 158 A/B1/2
Marcoing 78 A2/3
Mårdaklev 50 A1
Mar de Cristal 174 B1
Marden 63 D1
Mardie 87 C2/3
Mårdsel 16 B2
Mårdsjö 30 A1/2
Mårdsund 29 C/D3, 34 B2
Mære 28 B2, 33 D1
Marécottes, Les 104 B2
Marèges 102 A3
Mareilly-en-Villette 87 C3
Mareilly-le-Hayer 88 A2
Marennes 100 B2/3
Maresquel 77 D2
Maretz 78 A/B3
Mareuil 101 C3
Mareuil-en-Brie 88 A1
Mareuil-le-Port 88 A1
Mareuil-sur-Ourcq 87 D1
Mareuil-sur-Ay 88 A1
Mareuil-sur-Arnon 102 A1
Mareuil-sur-Lay 101 C2
Marevo 75 C2
Margam 63 C1
Margarítion 142 B3
Margate 65 C3, 76 B1
Margaux 108 B1
Margerie 88 B2
Margès 103 D3
Margherita di Savóia 120 B1, 136 A3
Marghita 97 D3, 140 B1
Margone 104 B3, 112 B1
Margonin 71 D2
Margut 79 C3
María 173 D1, 174 A1
Maria Alm am Steinernen Meer 92 B3, 126 A1
María de Huerva 154 B3, 162 B1
María de la Salud 157 C2
Maria Elend 126 B2
Mariager 48 B2
Maria Laach 80 A2
Marialva 159 B/C2
Maria Neustift 93 D3
Marianka 94 B2
Mariannelund 46 B3
Mariannelund 72 B1
Marianópoli 124 B2
Mariánské Lázně 82 B3
Mariapfarr 126 B1
Maria Saal 126 B1/2
Maria Taferl 93 D2, 94 A2
Maria-ter-Heide 79 B/C1
Maria Wörth 126 B2
Mariazell 94 A3
Mariazell 96 A3
Maribo 53 C/D2
Maribor 127 C/D2
Maribor 96 A3
Marica 141 C3
Marieberg 17 C2
Marieberg 46 A1
Marieby 34 B2
Mariedamm 46 A2
Mariefred 47 C1
Mariehamn (Maarianhamina) 41 C/D3
Marieholm 50 A/B3
Marieholm 50 B1
Marielyst 53 D2
Mariembourg 78 B3
Marienberg 83 C2
Marienborg 53 D2
Marienhagen 68 B3
Marienheide 80 A1
Marienmünster Bredenborn 68 A3
Marienmünster 68 A3
Mariental 69 C3
Mariënvelde 67 C3
Mariestad 45 D2
Marifjøra 36 B2
Marignane 111 D3
Marigny 86 A/B1
Marigny-le-Châtel 88 A2
Marija Bistrica 127 D2
Marikostinovo 139 D3, 144 A1
Marín 150 A2
Marina 131 C3
Marina del Cantone 119 D3
Marina di Alberese 116 A/B3
Marina di Amendolara 120 B3, 122 B1
Marina di Andora 113 C2
Marina di Badolato 122 B2/3
Marina di Belvedere 122 A1
Marina di Castagneto Donorático 114 B3, 116 A2
Marina di Carrara 114 A2
Marina di Camerota 120 A3
Marina di Campo 116 A3
Marina di Castellaneta 121 C3
Marina di Cécina 114 A/B3, 116 A2
Marina di Chiéuti 119 D2, 120 A1
Marina di Fuscaldo 122 A1
Marina di Gáiro 123 D2
Marina di Gioiosa Iónica 122 B3
Marina di Grosseto 116 A3
Marina di Lícola 119 C3
Marina di Mancaversa 121 D3
Marina di Maratea 120 A/B3, 122 A1
Marina di Massa 114 A2, 116 A1
Marina di Nováglie 121 D3
Marina di Orosei 123 D2
Marina di Palma 124 B3
Marina di Pisa 114 A2/3, 116 A2
Marina di Pietrasanta 114 A2, 116 A1
Marina di Ragusa 125 C3
Marina di Sant'António 122 B3
Marina di Sorso 123 C1
Marina di Torre Grande 123 C2
Marina di Vasto 119 D1/2
Mar'ina Gorka 99 C1
Marina San Giovanni 121 D3
Marina San Vito 119 D1
Marina Schiavonea 122 B1
Marine d'Albo 113 D2
Marine de Meria 113 D2
Marine De Porticciolo 113 D2
Marine de Sisco 113 D2
Marineo 124 B2
Marines 77 D3, 87 C1
Marines 162 B3, 169 D1
Mæringsdalen 33 B/C2
Maringues 102 B2
Marinha Grande 158 A3, 164 A1
Marinhais 164 A/B2
Marinkainen 21 B/C1
Marino 118 B2
Mariol 102 B2
Mariotto 120 B2
Maristova 37 C2
Marjaliza 167 C1
Märjamaa 74 A1
Marjaniemi 18 A2
Marjoniemi 25 D1, 26 A1/2
Marjotaipale 25 D1, 26 B1
Marjovaara 23 D3
Mark 30 A1
Marka 14 B1
Markabygd 28 B3, 33 D1
Markaryd 50 B2
Markaryd 72 A1
Markdorf 91 C3
Markee 70 A2
Markelo 67 C3
Marken 20 B2
Markersdorf 82 B2
Market Deeping 64 B1
Market Drayton 59 D2/3, 60 B3, 64 A1
Market Harborough 64 B2
Markethill 58 A1
Market Rasen 61 D3
Market Weighton 61 D2
Markgrafneusiedl 94 B2
Markgrafpieske 70 B3
Markgröningen 91 C1/2
Markina Xemein 153 D1
Markiniz 153 D2
Märkisch Buchholz 70 A/B3
Markitta 17 B/C1
Markkina 10 B2
Mark-Kleeberg 82 B1
Markkleeberg 82 B1
Markkula 21 C1
Marklohe-Lemke 68 A2
Marknesse 66 B2
Markneukirchen 82 B2
Márkó 128 B1
Markópoulon 147 D2
Markovac 134 B1
Markovac 134 B2
Markovgrad 138 B3, 143 C1
Markovićevo 134 B1
Markranstädt 82 B1
Marksuhl 81 D2
Markt Allhau 127 D1
Marktbergel 81 D3, 91 D1
Markt Berolzheim 91 D1
Markt Bibart 81 D3
Markt Erlbach 81 D3, 91 D1
Marktheidenfeld 81 C3
Markt Indersdorf 92 A2
Marktjärn 35 C2/3
Marktl 92 B2
Marktleugast 82 A2/3
Marktleuthen 82 B3
Markt Nordheim-Herbolzheim 81 D3, 91 D1
Marktoberdorf 91 D3
Marktoberdorf-Leuterschach 91 D3
Markt Piesting 94 A/B3
Marktredwitz 82 B3
Markt Rettenbach 91 D3
Marktrodach 82 A2
Markt Sankt Martin 94 B3
Markt Sankt Florian 93 D2
Markt Schwaben 92 A/B2
Markušica 129 B/C3
Markvarec 94 A1
Marl 67 C3, 80 A1
Marlborough 64 A3
Marle 78 B3
Marlieux 103 D2
Marlishausen 81 D2, 82 A2
Marlow 64 B3
Marlow 53 D3
Marma 40 B2
Marmagne 103 C1
Marmande 109 B/C1
Marmara 149 D1
Marmaris 149 D3
Marmaverken 40 A1
Marmeleiro 158 B3, 164 B1
Marmelete 170 A2
Marmirolo 106 B3
Marmolejo 167 C3, 172 B1
Marmorbyn 46 B1
Marmore 117 C3, 118 B1
Marmoutier 89 D1/2, 90 A2
Marnach 79 D3
Marnay 89 C3, 104 A1
Marne 52 A3
Marne-la-Vallée 87 D1
Mårnes 14 B1
Marnheim 80 B3
Marnitz 69 D1
Maroilles 78 B2/3
Maroldsweisach 81 D2/3
Marolles-les-Braults 86 B2
Maromme 77 C3
Marone 106 B3
Marónia 145 C/D1
Mårosjö 30 A3, 35 C2
Maroslele 129 D2
Maróstica 107 C3
Marotta 115 D2, 117 D1/2
Måröyfjord 6 B1
Marpingen 80 A3, 90 A1
Marquartstein 92 B3
Marquion 78 A2
Marquise 77 D1
Marradi 115 C2, 116 B1
Marrasjärvi 12 A3, 17 D1
Marraskoski 12 A3
Marratxi 157 C2
Mars 111 C1
Marsac-en-Livradois 103 C3
Marságlia 113 D1
Marsala 124 A2
Marsango 107 C3
Marsannay-la-Côte 88 B3, 103 D1
Marsanne 111 C1
Marsberg-Bredelar 81 B/C1
Marsberg-Essentho 81 B/C1
Marsberg-Meerhof 81 C1
Marsberg-Westheim 81 C1
Marsciano 117 C3
Marseillan 110 B3
Marseille 111 D3
Marseille-en-Beauvaisis 77 D3
Marseilles-les-Aubigny 102 B1
Marshfield 63 D1/2, 64 A3
Mársia 117 D3
Mársico 120 A/B3
Mársico Nuovo 120 A/B3
Marsjärv 17 C2
Mars-la-Tour 89 C1
Marsliden 29 D1
Maršovice 83 D3
Marssac-sur-Tarn 109 D2
Märsta 40 B3, 47 C1
Marstal 53 C2
Marstein 32 B3, 37 C1
Marstrand 44 B3
Marsvinsholm 50 B3
Märsylä 21 C1

Marszow 71 C3, 83 D1
Marta 116 B3, 118 A1
Martano 121 D3
Martel 109 D1
Martelange 79 C/D3
Mártély 129 D2
Mårtensboda 31 D1
Martfeld 68 A2
Martfű 129 D1
Marthon 101 C3
Martiago 159 C2
Martignacco 126 A2
Martigné 86 A2
Martigné-Briand 86 A3, 101 B/C1
Martigné-Ferchaud 86 A3
Martigny 104 B2
Martigny-les-Bains 89 C2
Martigues 111 C/D3
Martiherrero 160 A2
Martikkala 22 B2
Martim Longo 170 B1
Martimo 17 D2, 18 A1
Martímporra 151 D1, 152 A1
Martin 95 D1
Martin 96 B2
Martina Franca 121 C2
Martina (Martinsbruck) [Scuol-Tarasp] 106 B1
Martinci 133 C1
Martín de la Jara 172 A2
Martín del Río 162 B2
Martín de Yeltes 159 C/D2
Martinet 155 D2, 156 A2
Martínez 160 A2
Martín Muñoz de las Posadas 160 A/B2
Martinniemi 18 A2
Martínon 147 C1/2
Martinroda 81 D2, 82 A2
Martinsberg 93 D2, 94 A2
Martinšćica 130 A1
Martinsicuro 117 D3
Martinska 131 C3
Mártis 123 C1
Martizay 101 D1
Martjanci 127 D1/2
Mart'janovo 75 B/C2
Martock 63 D2
Martofte 49 C3, 53 C1
Martonoš 129 D2
Martonvaara 23 C2
Martonvásár 95 D3, 129 C1
Martorell 156 A3
Martos 172 B1
Martres-de-Veyre 102 B3
Martres-Tolosane 109 C3, 155 D1
Martron 101 C3
Martti 13 C2
Marttila 25 C2
Marttila 24 B2
Marttisenjärvi 22 B1
Marum 67 C1/2
Marunowo 71 D2
Marvão 165 C1
Marvejols 110 B1
Marvik 42 A2
Marxheim 91 D2, 92 A2
Marxwalde 70 B2
Marxzell 90 B1/2
Märy 24 B2/3
Maryport 57 C3, 60 A1
Maryport 54 B3
Marzabotto 114 B2, 116 B1
Marzahna 69 D3, 70 A3
Marzahne 69 D2
Marzocca 115 D2/3, 117 D2
Masalcolreig 155 C3, 163 C1
Masamagrell 169 D1
Mas-Cabardes 110 A3, 156 A/B1
Máscali 125 D2
Mascalucia 125 D2
Mascaraque 160 B3, 167 C1
Mascarenhas 151 C3, 159 C1
Mas de Barberans 163 C2
Mas de las Matas 162 B2
Masdenverge 163 C2
Masegoso 168 B2
Masegoso de Tajuña 161 D2
Maselheim 91 C2
Masella 156 A2
Måsenes 5 D1, 6 B1
Masera 105 C2
Masevaux 89 D3, 90 A3
Masfjorden 36 A3
Masham 61 C2
Masi 5 C3, 11 C1
Maside 150 B2
Masi Torello 115 C1
Måskenåive 15 D3
Maskjok 7 C2
Masku 24 A/B2
Maslacq 108 B3, 154 B1
Maslenica 131 B/C2
Maslinica 131 C3
Masllorenç 163 D1
Maso Corto 106 B1
Masomäki 21 D2, 22 A2
Måsøy 5 D1, 6 A1
Masquefa 156 A3
Massa 114 A2, 116 A1
Massa Fiscáglia 115 C1
Massafra 121 C2
Massagettes 102 B3
Massa Lombarda 115 C1/2, 116 B1
Massa Lubrense 119 D3
Massalubrense 119 D3
Massa Maríttima 114 B3, 116 A2
Massa Martana 117 C3, 118 B1
Massanet de la Selva 156 B3
Massanet de Cabrenys 156 B2
Massarosa 114 A2, 116 A1
Massat 155 C2
Massay 87 C3, 102 A1
Massbach-Poppenlauer 81 D2/3
Massello 112 B1
Masseret 101 D3
Masseria 107 C1
Masseria/Maiern 107 C1
Masseria Piede Rocca 119 C2
Masseube 109 C3, 155 C1
Massiac 102 B3
Massing 92 B2
Mässlingen 34 A2
Mästerby 47 D3
Masterelv 5 D1, 6 A1
Mästocka 50 B2
Masua 123 C3
Masueco 159 C1/2
Masungsbyn 10 B3
Måsvik 4 A2
Maszewo 71 B/C3
Maszewo 71 C1
MATABUENA 160 B2
Mata de Alcántara 159 C3, 165 C/D1
Mata de Cuéllar 160 B1
Matala 18 A1
Matalalahti 22 B1
Matalascañas 171 C2
Matamala de Almazán 153 D3, 161 D1
Mata Mourisca 158 A3, 164 A1
Matanza 152 A2/3
Matanza de Soria 153 C3, 161 C1
Matapozuelos 160 A1
Matara 23 C2
Mataramäki 22 B3
Mataraselkä 12 B2
Mataró 156 B3
Matarredonda 172 A1/2
Mataruška Banja 133 D3, 134 A/B3
Mätäsvaara 23 C2
Matejče 139 B/C2
Matélica 115 D3, 117 C/D2
Matera 121 B/C2
Materija 126 B3
Mateševo 137 D1
Mátészalka 97 D3, 98 A3
Matet 162 B3, 169 D1
Mateus 158 B1
Matfen 57 D3, 61 B/C1
Matfors 35 D3
Matha 101 C2
Mathay 89 D3
Mathildedal 24 B3
Mathopen 36 A3
Mathry 62 B1
Máti 147 D2
Matignon 85 C2
Matilla de los Caños del Río 159 D2
Matino 121 D3
Mátion 145 D3
Mátion 147 B/C2/3
Matka 138 B2
Matkakoski 17 D2, 18 A1
Matkaniva 18 A3
Matkavaara 19 C3
Matku 25 B/C2
Matlock 61 C3, 64 A1
Matnäset 34 B2
Matočina 145 D2
Matojärvi 17 D2
Matos 158 A3
Matosinhos 158 A1/2
Matour 103 C2
Matrand 38 B3
Matre 36 A3
Matrei am Brenner 107 C1
Matreier Tauernhaus 107 D1
Matrei in Osttirol 107 D1
Mätsäkansa 25 C1/2
Matsdal 15 C3
Mattaincourt 89 C2
Mattarello 107 C2
Matteröd 50 B2
Mattersburg 94 B3
Mattighofen 93 C2/3
Mattila 19 D1
Mattilanmäki 13 C3
Mattilanperä 18 A3
Mattinata 120 B1
Mattinen 24 A2
Mattisudden 16 B1/2
Mattmar 29 C3, 34 B2
Mattön 40 A2/3
Mattsmyra 39 D1
Måttsund 17 C3
Matulji 126 B3, 130 A1
Matute 153 C/D2
Matvejevskaja-Harčevn'a 75 C1
Maubeuge 78 B2
Maubourguet 108 B3, 155 C1
Maubranche 102 A/B1
Mauchline 56 B2
Mauer 90 B1
Mauerkirchen 93 C2
Mauern 92 A/B2
Mauguio 111 B/C3
Maukkula 23 D3
Maula 17 D2, 18 A1
Maulbronn 90 B1
Maulde 78 A/B2
Maule 87 C1
Mauléon-Licharre 108 A3, 154 B1
Maulévrier 100 B1
Maunola 27 C1
Maunu 10 B2
Maunu 10 B2
Maunujärvi 12 A2
Maunula 18 A/B2
Maura 38 A3
Maurach 92 A3, 107 C1
Maure-de-Bretagne 85 C2/3
Maureilhan 110 B3, 156 B1
Mauriac 102 A3
Maurnes 9 C2
Mauron 85 C2
Maurs 110 A1
Maurset 36 B3
Maurstad 36 A1
Mauru 18 B1
Maurumaa 24 A2, 41 D2
Maury 156 B1
Mausoléo 113 D2
Maussac 102 A3
Maussane 111 C2
Mausundvær 32 B1
Mautern an der Donau 94 A2
Mauterndorf 126 B1
Mauterndorf 96 A3
Mautern in Steiermark 93 D3, 127 C1
Mauth 93 C1/2
Mauthausen 93 D2
Mauth-Finsterau 93 C1
Mauvezin 109 C2
Mauzé-sur-le-Mignon 100 B2
Mauzun 102 B3
Mavas 15 C1
Mavrélion 143 C3
Mavrodéndrion 143 C2
Mavrothálassa 144 B1
Mavrovi Hanovi 138 B3
Mavrovo 138 B3
Mavrovoúnion 143 D3
Maxhütte-Haidhof 92 B1
Maxial 164 A2
Maxmo (Maksamaa) 20 B2
Mayalde 159 D1
Maybole 56 B2
Mayen 80 A2
May-en-Multien 87 D1
Mayenne 86 A2
Mayerhofen 107 D1, 126 A1
Mayet 86 B3
Mayorga 152 A3
Mäyränperä 18 A3
Mayrhofen 107 C1
Mäyry 21 C2
Mazagón 171 C2
Mazaleón 163 C2
Mazamet 110 A3
Mazara del Vallo 124 A2
Mazarákia 142 B3
Mazarambroz 160 B3, 167 C1
Mazarete 161 D2
Mazaricos 150 A2
Mazarulleque 161 C/D3
Mázaszászvár 128 B2
Mazaterón 153 D3, 161 D1
Maze 86 A3
Mažeikiai 73 C/D1
Mazères 109 D3, 155 D1, 156 A1
Mazérolles 108 B3, 154 B1
Mazeyrolles 109 C1
Mazières-en-Gâtine 101 C2
Mazin 131 C2
Mázion 142 B2
Mazirbe 73 C/D1
Mazsalaca 73 D1, 74 A2
Mazuecos 161 C3
Mazuelo de Muñó 152 B2/3
Mažurani 130 B2
Mazzarino 125 C3
Mazzarrá Sant'Andrea 125 D2
Mazzarrone 125 C3
Mchy 71 D3
Mealhada 158 A2/3
Méan 79 C2
Meana Sardo 123 D2
Meaño 150 A2
Meåstrand 30 A3, 35 C2
Meathas Truim (Edgeworthstown) 55 C/D2
Meaulne 102 B1/2
Meaux 87 D1
Meåvollan 33 D2
Mebygda 29 C2
Mecerreyes 153 C3
Mechelen 78 B1
Mechernich 79 D2, 80 A2
Mecina 173 C2
Meckenbeuren 91 C3
Meckenheim 80 A2
Mecklenburg 53 C3, 69 C1
Meco 161 C2
Mêda 158 B2
Medak 131 B/C2
Medåker 46 B1
Meddo 67 C3
Mede 113 C/D1
Medebach 80 B1
Međeja 126 B3, 130 A1
Medelby 52 B2
Medelim 159 B/C3
Medellín 165 D2, 166 A2
Medemblik 66 B2
Medena Selišta 131 D2
Měděnec 83 C2
Medesano 114 A1
Medevi 46 A2
Medewitz 69 D3
Medgidia 141 D2
Medhamn 45 D1
Mediana 135 C3
Mediana de Aragón 154 B3, 162 B1
Mediaş 97 D3, 140 B1
Medicina 115 C1/2
Medina Azahara 166 B3, 172 A1
Medinaceli 161 D1/2
Medina de las Torres 165 D3
Medina del Campo 160 A1
Medina de Pomar 153 C2
Medina de Ríoseco 152 A3
Medina-Sidonia 171 D3
Medinci 128 B3
Medinilla 159 D2
Mediona 155 D3, 156 A3, 163 D1
Medjurečje 133 D3, 134 A3
Medkovec 135 D3
Medle 31 D1
Médole 106 B3
Medrano 153 D2
Medskogen 38 B2
Medskogsbygget 34 A3
Medstugan 29 B/C3, 33 D1, 34 A1
Medulin 130 A1
Međumajdan 131 C1
Meduno 107 D2, 126 A2
Medveđa 134 B3
Medveđa 139 B/C1
Medveđa 140 A3
Medved'ov 95 C3
Medviđa 131 C2
Medvode 126 B2
Medvodje 126 B2
Medyn' 75 D3
Medzibrod 95 D1/2
Medzilaborce 97 C2, 98 A3
Medžitlija 143 C1
Meeder 81 D2, 82 A2
Meerane 82 B2
Meerbeck 68 A3
Meerbusch 79 D1, 80 A1
Meerle 79 C1
Meersburg 91 C3
Meerssen 79 C/D2
Mefjordbotn 9 D1
Megála Kalívia 143 C3
Megáli Panagiá 144 B2
Megáli Vólvi 144 A1/2
Megalochórion 143 C3
Megalopolis 146 B3
Mégara 147 D2
Mégara 148 B2
Mégaron 143 C2
Mégève 104 B3
Megina 161 D2, 162 A2
Meglecy 75 D1
Mehadia 135 C1
Mehamn 7 B/C1
Mehedeby 40 B2
Méhoudin 86 A2
Mehringen 69 C3
Mehring (Trier) 80 A3
Mehrstetten 91 C2
Mehun-sur-Yèvre 87 C/D3, 102 A1
Mehus 9 C1
Meigle 57 C1
Meijel 79 D1
Meilen 105 D1
Meilhan 108 B2
Meillant 102 A/B1
Meimoa 159 B/C3
Méina 105 D3
Meine 69 C2/3
Meinersen 68 B2
Meinerzhagen 80 A/B1
Meinerzhagen-Valbert 80 B1
Meineweh 82 B1
Meinhardt-Frieda 81 D1
Meiningen 81 D2
Meira 151 C1
Meiringen 105 C1/2
Meis 150 A2
Meisburg 79 D3, 80 A3
Meisenheim 80 A/B3
Meisingset 32 B2
Meissen 83 C1
Meissen 96 A1

Meitingen   **Mielslahti**

Meitingen **91** D2
Mejorada **160** A3
Mejorada del Campo **161** C2/3
Mel **107** C/D2
Melago/Melag **106** B1
Melaje **133** D3, **138** A1
Melalahti **19** C3
Melangseidet **4** A3, **9** D1, **10** A1
Melás **143** C2
Melbeck **68** B1/2
Melbourne **61** C3, **64** A/B1
Melbu **8** B2
Melby **49** D3
Meldal **33** C2
Méldola **115** C2, **117** C1
Meldorf **52** A/B3
Melegnano **105** D3, **106** A3
Melen **29** B/C3, **34** A1
Melen **29** B/C3, **34** A1
Melenci **129** D3
Melendugno **121** D3
Meleta **114** B3, **116** A/B2
Meleti **114** A1
Mélezet **112** A/B1
Melfi **120** A/B2
Melfjorden **14** B2
Melgaço **150** B3
Melgar de Arriba **152** A2/3
Melgar de Fernamental **152** B2
Melgar de Tera **151** D3
Melgar de Yuso **152** B2/3
Melhus **32** B2
Melhus **28** A3, **33** C2
Melick **79** D1
Mélida **154** A2
Melide **150** B2
Melides **164** A3
Meligalás **146** B3
Melíki **143** D2
Melilli **125** D3
Mélisey **89** D3
Mélissa **145** C1
Melíssi **143** C2/3
Melissourgós **144** A2
Melíti **143** C1
Mélito di Porto Salvo **122** A3, **125** D2
Melívia **145** C1
Melívia **143** D3, **144** A3
Melk **94** A2
Melk **96** A2/3
Melkoniemi **27** D1
Melksham **63** D2, **64** A3
Mellajärvi **12** A3, **17** D2
Mellakoski **12** A3, **17** D2
Mellansel **30** B3
Mellansjö **35** C3
Mellansjö **17** C3
Mellansvartbäck **31** C2
Mellbystrand **50** A2
Melle **68** A3
Melle **101** C2
Melle-Buer **68** A3
Mellen **69** C2
Melle-Neuenkirchen **68** A3
Mellensee **70** A3
Melleray **86** B2
Melle-Riemsloh **68** A3
Mellerud **45** C2
Mellerup **48** B2
Mellifont Abbey **58** A1/2
Mellilä **24** B2
Mellingen **82** A2
Mellingen **90** B3
Mellingsmoen **29** C1
Mellösa **46** B1
Mellrichstadt **81** D2
Mellrichstadt-Bahra **81** D2
Melnica **134** B2
Melnice **130** B1
Mělnické Vtelno **83** D2
Mělník **83** D2
Melnik **139** D3
Mělník **96** A1/2
Melo **158** B2
Melón **150** B2/3
Melpers **81** D2
Melrand **84** B2
Melrose **57** C2
Melsomvik **43** D2, **44** A/B1
Melsträsk **16** B3
Melsungen **81** C1
Meltaus **12** A3

Meltausjoki **12** A/B3
Meltingen **28** A/B3, **33** C1
Meltola **25** C3
Meltola **27** C2
Melton Mowbray **64** B1
Meltosjärvi **12** A3, **17** D2
Melun **87** D2
Melun-Sénart **87** D2
Melvich **54** B1
Mélykút **129** C2
Melzo **105** D3, **106** A3
Mem **46** B2
Memaliaj **142** A2
Membrilla **167** D2
Membrio **165** C1
Memëlishti **142** B1
Memmelsdorf **81** D3, **82** A3
Memmingen **91** D3
Memmingen-Steinheim **91** D3
Memurubu **37** C2
Menággio **105** D2, **106** A2
Menai Bridge **59** B/C2, **60** A3
Menàrguens **155** C3, **163** C1
Menars **86** A/B3
Menasalbas **160** B3, **167** C1
Menat **102** B2
Menata **115** C1
Mendavia **153** D2
Mende **110** B1
Mende **129** C1
Menden **80** B1
Mendenítsa **147** C1
Menden-Lendringsen **80** B1
Mendibieu **108** A/B3, **154** B1
Mendig **80** A2
Mendiga **164** A1
Mendigorría **154** A2
Mendrisio **105** D2/3
Ménéac **85** C2
Menemen **149** D2
Menen **78** A2
Menetou-Salon **87** D3, **102** A/B1
Ménétréol-sur-Sauldre **87** D3
Ménétréol-sur-Sancerre **87** D3
Menfi **124** A2
Ménfőcsanak **95** C3
Mengabril **166** A2
Mengamuñoz **160** A2
Mengara **115** D3, **117** C2
Mengen **91** C3
Mengerskirchen **80** B2
Mengeš **126** B2
Mengíbar **167** C3, **173** C1
Mengkofen-Weichshofen **92** B2
Menídion **146** A1
Menigoute **101** C2
Menkijärvi **21** C2
Mennecy **87** D2
Menonen **25** B/C2
Mens **111** D1, **112** A1
Mensignac **101** C3
Menslage **67** D2
Mentana **118** B2
Menthon-Saint-Bernard **104** A3
Menton **112** B2/3
Méntrida **160** B3
Menz **70** A2
Méounes-les-Montrieux **112** A3
Meppel **67** C2
Meppen **67** D2
Meppen-Helte **67** D2
Meppen-Versen **67** C/D2
Mequinenza **163** C1
Mer **87** C3
Mera **150** B1
Meråker **28** B3, **33** D1
Meranges **156** A2
Merano/Meran **107** C1/2
Merasjärvi **11** C3
Merasjärvi **10** B3
Merate **105** D3, **106** A3
Mercadal **157** C1
Mercatale **115** C3, **117** C2

Mercatino Conca **115** C/D2, **117** C1
Mercato San Severino **119** D3
Mercato Saraceno **115** C2, **117** C1
Merceana **164** A2
Mercus **155** D2, **156** A1
Merdrignac **85** C2
Mere **63** D2, **64** A3
Merelim **150** A3, **158** A1
Merenlahti **27** C2
Mérens-les-Vals **156** A1/2
Méréville **87** C2
Mergozzo **105** C/D2
Méribel-les-Allues **104** B3
Meriç **145** D3
Mérida **165** D2, **166** A2
Mérigon **108** B3, **155** C1
Merijärvi **18** A3
Merikarvia **24** A1
Meriläinen **21** C1/2
Merimasku **24** A2
Měřín **94** A1
Mering **91** D2, **92** A2
Merjärv **20** B1
Merkenes **15** C1
Merkine **73** D2, **74** A3
Merklín **83** C3, **93** C1
Merlara **107** C3, **115** B/C1
Merlimont-Plage **77** D2
Mern **53** D2
Mernye **128** B2
Merošina **135** C3
Mersch **79** D3
Merseburg **82** B1
Mersevát **128** A1
Mers-les-Bains **76** B2
Mertajärvi **10** B2
Mertendorf **82** A1
Merthyr Tydfil **63** C1
Mertingen **91** D2
Mértola **170** B1
Merton **63** C2
Mertzwiller **90** A1/2
Méru **77** D3, **87** C1
Merufe **150** A/B3
Mervans **103** D1
Merville **78** A2
Merxheim **80** A3
Méry-sur-Oise **87** C/D1
Méry-sur-Seine **88** A2
Merzamemi **125** D3
Merzdorf **70** A3
Merzenich **79** D2
Merzenstein **93** D2
Merzig **79** D3, **80** A3
Merzig-Besseringen **79** D3
Merzig-Brotdorf **79** D3, **80** A3
Mes **137** D2
Mesagne **121** D2/3
Mesão Frio **158** B1/2
Mesas de Ibor **159** D3, **166** A/B1
Meschede **80** B1
Meschede-Calle **80** B1
Meschede-Eversberg **80** B1
Meschede-Freienohl **80** B1
Meschede-Remblinghausen **80** B1
Meschers-sur-Gironde **100** B3
Mescoules **109** C1
Mešćovsk **75** D3
Mesegar **160** B3, **167** C1
Mešeišta **138** B3, **142** B1
Meselefors **30** A/B1
Mesenikólas **143** C3
Mesía **150** B1
Mesić **134** B1
Mesinge **49** C3, **53** C1
Meskjer **4** A3, **9** D1
Meskusvaara **19** C/D1
Meslay-du-Maine **86** A2
Mesnalien **38** A1/2
Mesnières-en-Bray **76** B3
Mesocco [Castione-Arbedo] **105** D2, **106** A2
Mesochóra **143** C3
Mésola **115** C1
Mesolóngion **146** A/B2
Mesón do Vento **150** A/B1
Mesones **161** C2
Mesones de Isuela **154** A3, **162** A1
Mesopótamon **142** B3

Mesoraca **122** B2
Mespelbrunn **81** C3
Messac **85** D3
Messaure **16** B1
Messdorf **69** C2
Messei **86** A1/2
Messejana **164** B3, **170** A1
Messel **81** B/C3
Messelt **38** A1
Messene **146** B3
Méssia **144** B1
Messigny **88** B3
Messina **122** A3, **125** D1
Messina Divieto **125** D1
Messina Mili Marina **122** A3, **125** D2
Messina Sparta **122** A3, **125** D1
Messina Torre Faro **122** A3, **125** D1
Messíni **146** B3
Messíni **148** B2/3
Messkirch **91** C3
Messkirch-Rohrdorf **91** C3
Messtetten **91** C2
Mestanza **167** C2
Mestilä **24** B2
Mestlin **69** D1
Město-Touškov **83** C3
Mestrino **107** C3
Mesvres **103** C1
Metajna **130** B2
Metaljka **133** C3
Metallikón **143** D1, **144** A1
Metamórfosis **144** A/B2
Metanópoli **105** D3, **106** A3
Metapontum **121** C3
Metaxás **143** C2
Metelen **67** C/D3
Meteóra **143** C3
Méthana **147** D3
Methil **57** C1
Methóni **143** D2
Methven **57** C1
Metković **136** B1
Metlika **127** C3
Metnitz **126** B1
Metnitz **96** A3
Mętno **70** B2
Metóchion **146** A2
Metovnica **135** C2
Metsäkylä **19** C2
Metsäkylä **25** C2
Metsäkylä **18** A3
Metsäkylä **26** B2
Metsälä **19** C1/2
Metsälä **20** A3
Metsämaa **24** B2
Metsolahti **21** D3, **22** A3
Métsovon **143** B/C3
Mettälä **26** B2
Mettendorf (Bitburg) **79** D3
Mettet **79** C2
Mettingen **67** D2/3
Mettlach **79** D3
Mettlach-Orscholz **79** D3
Mettlach-Weiten **79** D3
Mettmann **80** A1
Metz **89** C1
Metzdorf **70** B2
Metzervisse **89** C1
Metzingen **91** C2
Meucon **85** C3
Meulan **87** C1
Meung-sur-Loire **87** C3
Meurville **88** B2
Meuselwitz **82** B1
Mevagissey **62** B3
Mevassvika **28** B2
Mexborough **61** D3
Mexilhoeira Grande **170** A2
Meximieux **103** D2
Meyenburg **69** D1
Meymac **102** A3
Meyrargues **111** D2/3
Meyrin [Vernier-Meyrin] **104** A2
Meyrueis **110** B2
Meyssac **102** A3, **109** D1
Mezalocha **154** A/B3, **162** A/B1
Mezdra **140** B3
Mèze **110** B3
Mežgorje **97** D2, **98** A3
Mézidon **86** A1

Mézières-en-Brenne **101** C1
Mézières-sur-Issoire **101** D2
Mézilhac **111** C1
Mézilles **87** D3, **88** A3
Mézin **109** C2
Mezőberény **97** C3, **140** A1
Mezőcsokonya **128** A/B2
Mezőfalva **129** C1
Mezőhék **129** D1
Mezőkövesd **97** C3
Mezőörs **95** C3
Mezőszilas **128** B1
Mezőtúr **129** D1
Mezőtúr **97** C3, **140** A1
Mezquita de Jarque **162** B2
Mezzana **106** B2
Mezzani **114** A1
Mezzano **107** C2
Mezzaselva/Mittewald **107** C1
Mezzoiuso **124** B2
Mezzoldo **106** A2
Mezzolombardo **107** B/C2
Miajadas **166** A2
Mialet **101** D3
Miami Platja **163** D2
Miasteczko Krajeńskie **71** D2
Miastko **72** B2
Michalovce **97** C2, **98** A3
Michalovy Hory **82** B3
Michelau im Steigerwald **81** D3
Michelau in Oberfranken **82** A2/3
Michelbach Markt **94** A2
Micheldorf in Oberösterreich **93** C/D3
Michelfeld (Schwäbisch Hall) **91** C1
Michelsneukirchen **92** B1
Michelstadt **81** C3
Michendorf **70** A3
Michíon **146** B2
Michorzewo **71** D2/3
Mickelsträsk **31** C/D2
Mičurin **141** C/D3
Mid-Calder **57** C2
Middalsbu **42** B1
Middelburg **78** B1
Middelfart **48** B3, **52** B1
Middelharnis **66** A3
Middelharnis-Sommelsdijk **66** A3
Middelkerke-Bad **78** A1
Middelstum **67** C1
Middenmeer **66** B2
Middleham **59** D1, **61** C2
Middlesbrough **61** D1
Middleton **59** D1, **60** B2
Middleton **59** D2, **60** B2/3
Middleton-in-Teesdale **57** D3, **60** B1
Middleton Stoney **65** C2
Middlewich **59** D2, **60** B3, **64** A1
Midéa **147** C3
Midhurst **76** B1
Midlum **52** A3, **68** A1
Midões **158** B2/3
Midsund **32** A2
Midtgulen **36** A1/2
Midtleger **42** B1
Midtli **38** B1/2
Midtskogberget **38** B1/2
Midvágur **55** C1
Mid Yell **54** A1
Miechów **97** C1/2
Miedes **162** A1
Miedes de Atienza **161** C1
Międzybórz **71** D1
Międzychód **71** C2
Międzyrzecz **71** C2
Międzyrzec Podlaski **73** D3, **97** D1, **98** A1
Międzyzroczj **72** A/B3
Miehikkälä **27** C2
Miehlen **80** B2/3
Miejska Górka **71** D2
Miekojärvi **17** C2
Miélan **109** C3, **155** C1
Mielec **97** C2
Mielęcin **71** D2
Mielęcin **71** B/C2
Mielslahti **19** C3

Mieluskylä 18 A3, 21 D1
Miengo 152 B1
Mierasjärvi 6 B2/3
Mieraslompolo 6 B2
Miercurea-Ciuc 141 C1
Mieres 156 B2
Mieres 151 D1
Mierlo 79 C1
Miesakjaurestugan 9 D2
Miesbach 92 A3
Mieste 69 C2
Miesterhorst 69 C2
Mieszkowice 70 B2
Mietingen 91 C2
Mietinkylä 27 C1/2
Mieto 20 B3
Mietoinen 24 A2
Miettilä 27 D1
Mifol 142 A2
Migennes 88 A2
Migliarino 114 A2, 116 A1/2
Migliaro 115 C1
Migliónico 120 B2/3
Migné 101 C1
Migueláñez 160 B1/2
Miguel Esteban 167 D1, 168 A1
Miguelturra 167 C2
Mihai-Viteazu 141 D2
Mihajlovac 134 B2
Mihajlovac 135 C2
Mihajlovgrad 135 D3
Mihal'kovo 75 D1
Mihályfa 128 A1
Mihályi 94 B3
Mihla 81 D1
Miiluranta 21 D1, 22 A1
Mijares 160 A3
Mijas 172 B2/3
Mijoux 104 A2
Mikaševiči 99 B/C1
Mikínai 147 C3
Mikkeli (Sant Michel) 26 B1
Mikkelvik 4 A2
Mikkola 12 B2
Mikleuš 128 B3
Míkonos 149 C2
Mikosszéplak 128 A1
Mikrevo 139 D3
Mikrókambos 143 D1, 144 A1
Mikromiliá 144 B1
Mikrón Chórion 146 B1
Mikrón Dérion 145 D1, 145 D3
Mikrópolis 144 B1
Mikrothívai 143 D3, 147 C1
Mikróvalton 143 C2
Mikulášovice 83 D1/2
Mikulincy 98 B3
Mikulino 75 D2
Mikulov 96 B2
Mikulov 94 B2
Mikulov 83 C2
Mikulovice 96 B2
Milagres 158 A3, 164 A1
Milagro 154 A2
Miłaków 71 C3
Milano 159 C2
Milano 105 D3, 106 A3
Milano Maríttima 115 C2, 117 C1
Milâs 149 D2
Milatovac 135 C2
Milazzo 125 D1
Milborne Port 63 D2
Mildenhall 65 C2
Miléai 144 A3
Milena 124 B2
Mileševo 133 C/D3
Miletići 130 B2
Mileto 122 A2
Miletos 149 D2
Milevsko 83 D3, 93 D1
Milford 64 B3, 76 B1
Milford Haven 62 B1
Milford Haven 55 D3
Milhão 151 C3, 159 C1
Míli 147 C3
Míli 147 D1
Milići 133 C2
Milíčín 83 D3
Milín 83 C3
Milína 147 C1
Mílis 123 C2
Militello in Val di Catánia 125 C3
Miljutino 74 B1
Mill 66 B3
Millana 161 D2
Millançay 87 C3
Millares 169 C1/2
Millas 156 B1
Millau 110 B2
Millésimo 113 C2
Millevaches 102 A3
Millisle 56 A3
Millom 59 C1, 60 A/B2
Millom 54 B3
Millport 56 B2
Millstatt 126 A/B1
Milly 87 D2
Milmarcos 161 D2, 162 A2
Milmersdorf 70 A2
Milna 131 C/D3
Milna 131 C/D3, 136 A1
Milnathort 57 C1
Milngavie 56 B2
Milnthorpe 59 D1, 60 B2
Miločer 137 C2
Milohnić 130 A/B1
Mílos 149 C3
Miloševac 132 B1
Miloševa Kula 135 C2
Miloševa Kula 140 A2
Milošev Do 133 D3, 134 A3, 137 D1
Miloševo 135 C2
Miloslavci 139 C1
Milot 137 D3
Milovidy 98 B1
Milow 69 D2
Miltach 92 B1
Miltenberg 81 C3
Milton Keynes 64 B2
Milutinovac 135 C2
Milverton 63 C2
Mimizan 108 B2
Mimizan-Plage 108 B2
Mimoň 83 D2
Minack Theatre 62 A3
Mina de São Domingos 170 B1
Miñana 153 D3, 161 D1
Minas de Oro Romanas 151 C1
Minas de Rio Tinto 171 C1
Mînăstirea 141 C2
Minaya 168 B1/2
Minde 164 A/B1
Mindelheim 91 D2/3
Minden 68 A3
Mindin 85 C3, 100 A1
Mindnes 14 A3
Mindszent 129 D2
Mindtangen 14 A2/3
Minehead 63 C2
Mineo 125 C3
Minerbe 107 C3
Minérbio 115 B/C1
Minerbio 113 D2
Minerve 110 A3, 156 B1
Minervino Murge 120 B2
Minfeld 90 B1
Minglanilla 168 B1
Mingorría 160 A/B2
Miniato 114 B2/3, 116 A2
Minićevo 135 C3
Minkiö 25 B/C2
Minne 35 B/C3
Minnesund 38 A2
Miño 150 B1
Miño de San Esteban 153 C3, 161 C1
Minsk 74 B3
Mińsk Mazowiecki 73 C3, 97 C1, 98 A1
Minster 65 C3, 76 B1
Minsterley 59 D3
Minturnae 119 C3
Minturno 119 C3
Miodnica 71 C3
Miokovićevo 128 A3
Miolans 104 A3
Mionica 133 D2, 134 A2
Mionnay 103 D2
Mios 108 A1
Mira 107 D3
Míra 143 D3
Mira 162 A3, 169 C1
Mira 158 A2
Mirabeau 111 D2
Mirabel 159 C/D3, 165 D1, 166 A1
Mirabella 119 D3, 120 A2
Mirabella Imbáccari 125 C3
Mirador Fito 152 A1
Miradoux 109 C2
Miraflores de la Sierra 160 B2
Miralrío 161 C2
Miramar 158 A2
Miramare 115 D2, 117 C1
Miramas 111 C/D3
Mirambeau 100 B3
Mirambel 162 B2
Miramont-de-Guyenne 109 C1
Miranda de Arga 154 A2
Miranda de Ebro 153 C2
Miranda del Castañar 159 D2
Miranda do Corvo 158 A3
Miranda do Douro 159 C/D1
Mirande 109 C3, 155 C1
Mirandela 159 B/C1
Mirandilla 165 D2, 166 A2
Mirándola 114 B1
Mirano 107 C/D3
Mirantes 151 D2
Miravci 139 C3, 143 D1
Miraveche 153 C2
Miravet 163 C2
Miravete 162 B2
Miré 86 A3
Mirebeau-en-Poitou 101 C1
Mirebeau-sur-Bèze 89 C3
Mirecourt 89 C2
Mirepoix 109 D3, 156 A1
Mireval 110 B3
Mirgorod 99 D2
Miribel 103 D2/3
Mířkov 82 B3
Mirna 127 C2/3
Mirna Peč 127 C3
Mironovka 99 D2/3
Mirosławiec 71 C1
Mirošov 83 C3
Mirotice 93 C1
Mirovice 83 C3, 93 C1
Mirow 69 D1, 70 A1
Mirtíski 145 D1
Mirto Crosia 122 B1
Mirtófiton 144 B1
Mirueña 160 A2
Misano Adriático 115 D2, 117 C1
Misburg 68 B2/3
Misi 12 B3
Misilmeri 124 B2
Miske 129 C2
Miskolc 97 C3
Miškovići 130 B2
Mislata 169 D1
Mislina 136 B1
Mišnjak 130 B1/2
Missanello 120 B3
Missilä 22 B1
Missillac 85 C3
Mistelbach 94 B2
Mistelbach 96 B2
Misten 8 B3
Misterbianco 125 D2
Misterhem 33 D3
Misterhult 46 B3, 51 D1
Mistorf 53 D3, 69 D1
Mistrás 147 B/C3
Mistrás 148 B2/3
Mistretta 125 C2
Místros 147 D2
Misurina 107 D2
Misvær 15 C1
Mitanderfors 38 B3
Mítikas 146 A1
Mitilíni 149 C/D2
Mitrašinci 139 D2/3
Mitrópolis 143 C3
Mitrovac 133 C2
Mittådalen 34 A2
Mittelberg 106 B1
Mittelberg 91 D3, 106 B1
Mittelbiberach 91 C2/3
Mittel-Neufnach 91 D2
Mittenwald 92 A3
Mittenwalde 70 A3
Mittenwalde 70 A/B1/2
Mitterbach am Erlaufsee 94 A3
Mitterding 93 C2
Mitterdorf an der Raab 127 C1
Mitterndorf im Steir.Salzkammergut 93 C3
Mittersheim 89 D1, 90 A1/2
Mittersill 107 D1
Mitterteich 82 B3
Mitterweissenbach 93 C3
Mittet 32 A/B2
Mittewald an der Drau 107 D1, 126 A1
Mittweida 82 B1/2
Mitwitz 82 A2
Mizil 141 C2
Mjällby 51 C2/3
Mjällom 30 B3
Mjåvatn 43 C2
Mjåvatn 43 C3
Mjöbäck 49 D1, 50 A1
Mjøensetra 33 C3
Mjöhult 49 D2/3, 50 A2
Mjölan 17 C2
Mjölby 46 A2
Mjølfjell 36 B3
Mjølkarlia 14 B3
Mjölkbäcken 15 B/C2
Mjømna 36 A3
Mjøndalen 43 D1, 44 A1
Mjørlund 38 A2
Mjösebo 51 D1
Mjösjöby 31 C2
Mjösund 24 B3
Mjöträsk 17 C2
Mladá Boleslav 83 D2
Mladá Boleslav 96 A1/2
Mladá Vožice 83 D3, 93 D1
Mladenovac 133 D2, 134 B2
Mladenovac 140 A2
Mladenovo 129 C3, 133 C1
Mladikovine 132 B2
Mlado Nagoričane 139 C2
Mladotice 83 C3
Mława 73 C3
Mlini 137 C1/2
Mlinište 131 D2, 132 A2
Mnich 93 D1
Mnichov 82 B3
Mnichovice 83 D3
Mnichovo Hradiště 83 D2
Mníšek 83 C2
Mníšek pod Brdy 83 D3
Mo 30 A3, 35 C1
Mo 44 B2
Mo 32 B3
Mo 30 A3, 35 D2
Mo 45 C1/2
Mo 36 A3
Mo 37 D2, 38 A1/2
Mo 43 C1/2
Mo 38 A/B2
Moan 29 C3, 34 B2
Moaña 150 A2/3
Moarottaja 19 C1
Moat of Urr 56 B3, 60 A1
Moča 95 D3
Mocejón 160 B3, 167 C1
Mochales 161 D2
Mochov 83 D3
Mochtín 93 C1
Mochy 71 C/D3
Möckern 69 D3
Mockfjärd 39 D2
Möckmühl 91 C1
Möckmühl-Züttlingen 91 C1
Mockrehna 82 B1
Mockträsk 17 B/C3
Moclín 173 C2
Modane 104 B3, 112 A/B1
Modbury 63 C3
Módena 114 B1
Módica 125 C3
Modigliana 115 C2, 116 B1
Mödling 94 B2/3
Modra 95 C2
Modran 132 B1
Modřany 83 D3
Modrava 93 C1
Modriča 132 B1
Modrište 138 B3
Modruš 130 B1
Modrý Kameň 95 D2
Modrze 71 D3
Modugno 121 C2
Moeche 150 B1
Moelingen 79 C/D2
Moelv 38 A2
Moen 28 B3, 33 D1, 34 A1
Moen 28 B3, 33 D1
Moen 4 A3, 9 D1
Moena 107 C2
Moers 79 D1, 80 A1
Mofalla 45 D2, 46 A2
Moffat 57 C2
Mogadouro 159 C1
Møgeltønder 52 A2
Mogen 43 C1
Mogente 169 C2
Móggio Udinese 126 A2
Mögglingen 91 C2
Mogila 138 B3, 143 C1
Mogilev 74 B3
Mogilëv-Podol'skij 99 C3
Móglia 114 B1
Mogliano Véneto 107 D3
Moglica 142 B1/2
Mogón 167 D3, 168 A3, 173 C/D1
Mogor 150 B1
Mogorić 131 B/C2
Mógoro 123 C3
Moguer 171 C2
Mohács 129 B/C2/3
Moharras 168 B2
Moheda 51 C1
Mohedas 159 D3
Mohedas de la Jara 166 B1
Mohelnice 96 B2
Möhkö 23 D1
Möhne-Günne 80 B1
Möhnesee-Körbecke 80 B1
Moholm 45 D2, 46 A2
Mohorn 83 C1/2
Mohorte 161 D3
Mohrkirch 52 B2
Moi 42 B3
Moi 42 B3
Moi 135 D1
Moià 156 A2/3
Móie 115 D3, 117 D2
Moikipää 20 A2, 31 D3
Moimenta 151 C3
Moimenta da Beira 158 B2
Moimenta de Mac Dão 158 B2
Mo i Rana 14 B2
Moirans 103 D3, 104 A3
Moirans-en-Montagne 104 A2
Mõisaküla 74 A1
Moisdon-la-Rivière 86 A3
Moisiovaara 19 D3
Moissac 109 C2
Moisselles 87 D1
Moisund 43 B/C3
Moïta 113 D3
Moita 164 A2
Moita 158 A/B3
Moita dos Ferreiros 164 A1/2
Möja 47 D1
Mojácar 174 A2
Mojados 160 A/B1
Mojkovac 137 D1
Mojstrana 126 B2
Møklevika 29 C1
Möklinta 40 A3
Mokošica 137 C1
Mokra Gora 133 C3
Mokreš 135 D3
Mokrice 127 C/D3
Mokrin 129 D2/3
Mokro 132 B2
Mokronog 127 C2/3
Mokro Polje 131 C2
Mokrós 144 B1
Möksy 21 C2
Mol 129 D3
Mol 79 C1
Molacillos 151 D3, 159 D1
Mola di Bari 121 C2
Molare 113 C1
Molaretto 104 B3, 112 B1
Molat 130 B2
Molbergen 67 D2
Mold 59 C2, 60 B3

Moldava v Krušných horách
  83 C2
Molde 32 A2
Moldøra 28 A2/3, 33 C1
Moldova Nouă 135 C1/2
Moldova Nouă 140 A2
Moldova Veche
  135 B/C1/2
Møldrup 48 B3, 52 B1
Moldvik 5 B/C2
Molesme 88 B2/3
Molesworth 64 B2
Molezuelas de la Carballeda
  151 D3
Molfetta 121 B/C2, 136 A3
Moliden 30 B3
Molières 108 B2
Moliets-et-Maa 108 B2
Molina Aterno 119 C1
Molina de Aragón 161 D2,
  162 A2
Molina de Segura 169 D3
Molina di Ledro 106 B2/3
Molinella 115 C1
Molinicos 168 B2/3
Molini di Túres/Mühlen
  107 C1
Molino 112 B3
Molinos 162 B2
Molinos de Duero
  153 C/D3
Molins de Rei 156 A3
Moliterno 120 B3
Molitg 156 A/B1/2
Molivdosképastos 142 B2
Möljeryd 51 C2
Molkojärvi 12 A2
Molkoköngäs 12 A2/3,
  17 D1
Molkom 39 C3, 45 D1
Mollans-sur-Ouveze
  111 D2
Möllbrücke 126 A1
Mölle 49 D2, 50 A2
Møllebogen 28 B1
Molledo 152 B1
Möllenbeck 70 A1
Möllenhagen 70 A1
Mollerussa 155 D3,
  163 C/D1
Mollet del Vallès 156 A3
Móllia 105 C3
Molliens-Vidame 77 D2/3
Mollina 172 B2
Mollišjok 5 D3, 6 A2
Mollis [Näfels-Mollis]
  105 D1, 106 A1
Mölln 69 C1
Molló 156 A/B2
Mollösund 44 B3
Mölltorp 45 D2, 46 A2
Molnári 128 A2
Mølnarodden 8 A3
Mölnbo 47 C1
Mølnbukt 28 A3, 33 C1
Mölndal (Göteborg) 45 C3,
  49 D1
Mölndal (Göteborg) 72 A1
Mölnlycke 45 C3, 49 D1
Molodečno 74 A3
Mólos 147 C1
Moloy 88 B3
Molpe (Moikipää) 20 A2,
  31 D3
Molschleben 81 D1/2
Molsheim 90 A2
Molunat 137 C2
Molve 128 A2
Molveno 106 B2
Molvízar 173 C2
Mománo 112 B3
Momarken 38 A3, 44 B1
Mombaróccio 115 D2,
  117 C1
Mombaruzzo 113 C1
Mombeja 164 B3, 170 B1
Mombeltrán 160 A3
Momblona 161 D1
Mömbris 81 C3
Mombuey 151 D3
Momčilgrad 141 C3
Mömlingen 81 C3
Mommark 52 B2
Mommila 25 D2, 26 A2
Momo 105 D3
Momrak 43 C2
Momyr 28 A2

Monà 20 B2
Monachil 173 C2
Monaco 112 B2/3
Monaghan 54 A3, 55 D2
Monamolin 58 A3
Monäs 20 B1/2
Monasterace Marina
  122 B3
Monasterio de Rodilla
  153 C2
Monasterio de Cristo
  151 C1
Monasterio de Lluc 157 C2
Monasterio de Poblet
  163 D1
Monasterio de Yuste
  159 D3
Monasterio de las Huelgas
  153 C2
Monasterio de Vega
  152 A2/3
Monasterio de Leyre
  155 C2
Monasterio de Piedra
  161 D1, 162 A1
Monasterio El Paular
  160 B2
Monasterio Montserrat
  156 A3
Monasterio San Salvador
  157 C2
Monasterio Santes Creus
  163 C1
Monasterio San Miguel de
  Escalade 152 A2
Monastir 123 D3
Monastirákion 146 A1
Monastyriska 97 D2, 98 B3
Monbahus 109 C1
Monbrun 109 C2/3
Moncada 169 D1
Moncalieri 113 B/C1
Moncalvillo de Huete
  161 D3
Moncalvo 113 C1
Monção 150 A3
Moncarapacho 170 B2
Monceau 78 B2
Mönchdorf 93 D2
Mönchengladbach 79 D1
Mónchio delle Corti
  114 A2, 116 A1
Monchique 170 A2
Monchy-Humières 78 A3
Monclar-de-Quercy
  109 D2
Moncófar 163 B/C3,
  169 D1
Moncontour-de-Bretagne
  85 C2
Moncontour-de-Poitou
  101 C1
Moncoutant 100 B1
Monda 172 A/B2/3
Mondariz 150 A2/3
Mondariz-Balneario
  150 A3
Mondéjar 161 C3
Mondicourt 77 D2, 78 A2
Mondim de Basto 158 B1
Mondolfo 115 D2,
  117 D1/2
Mondoñedo 151 B/C1
Mondorf-les-Bains 79 D3
Mondoubleau 86 B2
Mondoví 113 C2
Mondragon 111 C2
Mondragone 119 C3
Mondsee 93 C3
Monéglia 113 D2
Monegrillo 154 B3, 162 B1
Monein 108 B3, 154 B1
Monemvasía 148 B3
Moneo 153 C2
Monesi 113 C2
Monesíglio 113 C2
Monesterio 165 D3,
  166 A3
Monestier-de-Clermont
  111 D1
Monestiès 109 D2, 110 A2
Moneva 162 B1/2
Monfalcone 126 A3
Monfero 150 B1
Monflanquin 109 C1
Monfort 109 C2
Monforte 165 C2

Monforte 158 B3, 165 C1
Monforte de Lemos 150 B2
Monforte de Moyuela
  162 B2
Monforte del Cid 169 C3
Monforte San Giórgio
  125 D1/2
Monghidoro 114 B2,
  116 B1
Mongiana 122 A/B3
Mongiardino Lígure
  113 D1
Mongstad 36 A3
Monguelfo/Welsberg
  107 C/D1
Monguillem 108 B2
Monheim 80 A1
Moní Agías Lávras 146 B2
Moniaive 56 B2/3
Monica 133 D2, 134 A2
Moní Chiliandaríou 144 B2
Mönichkirchen 94 A3
Mon Idée 78 B3
Moní Elónis 147 C1
Monifieth 57 C1
Moniga del Garda 106 B3
Moní Ikosifiníssis 144 B1
Monikie 57 C1
Moní Loukoú 147 C3
Moní Megístis Lávras
  144 B2
Moní Osíou Louká 147 C2
Monistrol 156 A3
Monistrol-d'Allier 110 B1
Monistrol-sur-Loire 103 C3
Mönkebude 70 B2
Monmouth 63 D1
Monnai 86 B1
Monnaie 86 B3
Mönni 23 D2/3
Monni 25 C2, 26 A2
Monnickendam 66 B2
Monninkylä 25 D2, 26 A2
Monó Ágios Ioánnis
  144 A/B1
Monola 27 B/C2
Monópoli 121 C2
Monor 129 C1
Monor 97 C3, 140 A1
Monóvar 169 C3
Monpazier 109 C1
Monreal 154 A2
Monreal 80 A2
Monreal del Campo 163 C2
Monreal del Llano 168 A1
Monreale 124 B2
Monroy 165 D1, 166 A1
Monroyo 163 C2
Mons 78 B2
Mons 112 A/B3
Monsagro 159 C/D2
Monsanto 159 C3
Monsaraz 165 C3
Monschau 79 D2
Monschau-Imgenbroich
  79 D2
Monschau-Kalterherberg
  79 D2
Monségur 108 B1
Monsélice 107 C3
Monsheim 80 B3
Mönsheim 91 B/C1/2
Monsols 103 C2
Mønsted 48 B2
Mönsterås 51 D1
Mönsterås 72 B1
Monsteroy 42 A2
Monsummano Terme
  114 B2, 116 A1
Montabaur 80 B2
Montaberner 169 D2
Montagnac 110 B3
Montagnana 107 C3
Montagny 103 C2
Montagut de Fluvià 156 B2
Montaigu 101 C2
Montaigu-de-Quercy
  109 C2
Montaiguët-en-Forez
  103 C2
Montaigut-en-Combraille
  102 B2
Montaigut-sur-Save
  108 B2
Montalba-d'Amélie 156 B2
Montalba-le-Château
  156 B1

Montalbán 162 B2
Montalbán de Córdoba
  172 B1
Montalbanejo 161 D3,
  168 A/B1
Montalbano Elicona
  125 D2
Montalbano Iónico 120 B3
Montalbo 161 D3, 168 A1
Montalbos 168 B2
Montalcino 115 B/C3,
  116 B2
Montaldo di Cósola 113 D1
Montalegre 150 B3,
  158 B1
Montalivet-les-Bains
  101 C3
Montallegro 124 B2/3
Montalto delle Marche
  117 D2/3
Montalto di Castro 116 B3,
  118 A1
Montalto Marina 116 B3,
  118 A1
Montalto Pavese 113 D1
Montalto Uffugo 122 A1
Montalvão 165 C1
Montalvo 164 B1
Montalvo 164 A/B3
Montamarta 151 D3,
  159 D1
Montán 162 B2
Montañana 155 C2/3
Montanara 106 B3, 114 B1
Montanaro 105 C3, 113 C1
Montana [Sierre] 105 C2
Montánchez 165 D2,
  166 A2
Montanejos 162 B3
Montaner 108 B3, 155 C1
Montano Antília 120 A3
Montargil 164 B2
Montargis 87 D2
Montari 25 D2, 26 A2
Montastruc 109 C3,
  155 C1
Montastruc-la-Conseillère
  109 D2
Montauban 108 B2
Montauban-de-Bretagne
  85 C2
Montauriol 109 D3,
  155 C1
Montázzoli 119 D2
Montbard 88 B3
Montbazens 110 A1
Montbazon 86 B3,
  101 C/D1
Montbéliard 89 D3
Montbenoît 104 B1
Montblanc 163 C1
Montbovon 104 B2
Montbozon 89 C/D3
Montbras 89 C2
Montbrison 103 C3
Montbron 101 C3
Montbrun 101 D3
Montbrun-les-Bains
  111 D2
Montceau-les-Mines
  103 C1
Montceaux-les-Provins
  88 A1/2
Montcenis 103 C1
Montchanin-les-Mines
  103 C1
Montcornet 78 B3
Montcuq 108 B2
Montdardier 110 B2
Mont-de-Marsan 108 B2
Montdidier 78 A3
Monteagudo 161 D3,
  162 A3, 168 B1
Monteagudo 154 A3
Monteagudo de las Vicarías
  161 D1
Monteagudo del Castillo
  162 B2
Montealegre 152 A3
Montealegre del Castillo
  169 C2
Montearagón 160 A/B3,
  166 B1
Monte Argentário 116 B3
Montebello Iónico 122 A3,
  125 D2

Montebello Veronese
  107 C3
Montebelluna 107 C/D3
Montébilloy 87 D1
Montebourg 76 B3
Montebruno 113 D1/2
Montecalvo Irpino 119 D3,
  120 A2
Monte Carlo 112 B2/3
Montecarotto 115 D3,
  117 D2
Montecastrilli 117 C3,
  118 B1
Montecatini Terme 114 B2,
  116 A1
Montecatini Val di Cécina
  114 B3, 116 A2
Montécchio Emília
  114 A/B1
Montécchio Maggiore
  107 C3
Montécchio 115 D2,
  117 C1
Monte Cerignone 115 C2,
  117 C1
Montech 108 B2
Montechiaro d'Asti 113 C1
Monte Claro 165 C1
Monte Clerigo 170 A2
Monte Colombo 115 D2,
  117 C1
Montecorvino Rovella
  119 D3, 120 A2
Montecreto 114 B2,
  116 A1
Monte da Pedra 165 B/C1
Montederramo 150 B2/3
Montederramo 150 B2/3
Monte de Trigo 165 C3
Monte di Prócida 119 C3
Montedoro 124 B2
Montefalco 117 C3
Montefalcone di Val Fortore
  119 D2, 120 A1/2
Montefalcone nel Sánnio
  119 D2
Montefano 117 D2
Montefiascone 117 B/C3,
  118 A1
Montefiorino 114 B2,
  116 A1
Monteflávio 118 B1/2
Monteforte d'Alpone
  107 C3
Monteforte Irpino 119 D3
Montefrío 172 B2
Montegalda 107 C3
Montegiordano Marina
  120 B3, 122 B1
Montegiórgio 117 D2
Monte Gordo 158 B3,
  165 B/C1
Montegranaro 117 D2,
  130 A3
Montegrotto Terme 107 C3
Montehermoso 159 C3
Montejaque 172 A2
Montejicar 173 C1
Montejo 153 C2
Montejo 159 D2
Montejo De la Vega
  153 C3, 161 B/C1
Montejo de la Sierra 161 C2
Montejo de Tiermes 161 C1
Montelánico 118 B2
Montelavar 164 A2
Montel-de-Gelat 102 B2
Monteleone di Púglia
  120 A2
Monteleone d'Orvieto
  117 B/C3
Monteleone di Spoleto
  117 C/D3, 118 B3
Montelepre 124 A/B2
Montélimar 111 C1
Montella 119 D3, 120 A2
Montellano 171 D2,
  172 A2
Montelupo Fiorentino
  114 B2, 116 A/B1/2
Montemaggiore Belsito
  124 B2
Montemagno 113 C1
Montemarano 119 D3,
  120 A2
Montemarcello 114 A2
Montemayor 172 B1

Montemayor de Pililla 152 B3, 160 B1
Montemboeuf 101 C3
Montemerano 116 B3, 118 A1
Montemésola 121 C2/3
Montemiletto 119 D3, 120 A2
Montemilone 120 B2
Montemolín 165 D3, 166 A3
Montemónaco 117 D3
Montemor o Novo 164 B2
Montemor-o-Velho 158 A3
Montemurlo 114 B2, 116 A/B1
Montemurro 120 B3
Montendre 101 B/C3
Montenegro de Cameros 153 D3
Montenero 114 A3, 116 A2
Montenero di Bisáccia 119 D2, 120 A1
Montenero Sabino 117 C3, 118 B1
Montepiano 114 B2, 116 B1
Monte Picayo 162 B3, 169 D1
Montépilloy 87 D1
Montepulciano 115 C3, 116 B2
Monteras 159 C/D1/2
Monterchi 115 C3, 117 C2
Monterde 162 A1/2
Monterde 162 A2
Monte Real 158 A3, 164 A1
Montereale 117 D3, 119 B/C1
Montereale Valcellina 107 D2, 126 A2
Montereau-Faut-Yonne 87 D2
Monte Redondo 158 A3, 164 A1
Monterénzio 114 B2, 116 B1
Monteriggioni 114 B3, 116 B2
Monte Romano 116 B3, 118 A1
Monteroni d'Árbia 114 B3, 116 B2
Monteroni di Lecce 121 D3
Monterosi 118 A/B1
Monterosso al Mare 114 A2
Monterosso Almo 125 C3
Monterotondo 118 B1/2
Monterotondo Maríttimo 114 B3, 116 A2
Monterrei 151 B/C3
Monterroso 150 B2
Monterrubio de Demanda 153 C3
Monterrubio de la Serena 166 B2
Monterrubio de la Sierra 159 D2
Monterubbiano 117 D2
Montesa 169 C2
Monte Salgueiro 150 B1
Monte San Biágio 119 C2
Monte San Giovanni Incárico 119 C2
Montesano Salentino 121 D3
Montesano Scalo 120 A/B3
Montesano sulla Marcellana 120 A/B3
Monte San Savino 115 C3, 116 B2
Monte Sant'Ángelo 120 B1
Monte San Vito 115 D3, 117 D2
Montesárchio 119 D3
Montescaglioso 121 B/C2/3
Montesclaros 160 A3
Montese 114 B2, 116 A1
Montesilvano Marina 119 C1
Montespértoli 114 B3, 116 A/B2
Montespluga 105 D2, 106 A2
Montesquieu-Volvestre 108 B3, 155 C1
Montesquiou-sur-Losse 109 C3, 155 C1
Montes Velhos 164 B3, 170 A/B1
Monteux 111 C/D2
Montevarchi 115 C3, 116 B2
Montevécchio 123 C3
Montevécchio 123 C3
Monteverde 120 A2
Monteverdi Maríttimo 114 B3, 116 A2
Montezémolo 113 C2
Montfaucon 85 D3, 100 B1
Montfaucon 88 B1
Montfaucon-en-Velay 103 C3
Montferrat 112 A3
Montfleur 103 D2, 104 A2
Montfort 79 D1
Montfort-en-Chalosse 108 A/B2
Montfort-l'Amaury 87 C1
Montfort-sur-Boulzane 156 A1
Montfort-sur-Meu 85 C2
Montfort-sur-Risle 77 C3, 86 B1
Montfranc 110 A2
Montgai 155 D3, 163 D1
Montgaillard 108 B3, 155 C1
Montgenèvre 112 A/B1
Montgomery 59 C3
Montguyon 101 C3
Monthermé 79 C3
Monthey 104 B2
Monthois 88 B1
Monthureux-sur-Saône 89 C2
Monti 123 D1
Montícchio Bagni 120 A2
Monticelli d'Ongina 114 A1
Monticelli Terme 114 A1
Montichiari 106 B3
Monticiano 114 B3, 116 B2
Montiel 167 D2, 168 A2
Montier-en-Der 88 B2
Montieri 114 B3, 116 A/B2
Montiers-sur-Saulx 89 C2
Montíglio 113 C1
Montignac 101 C3, 108 B1
Montigny 89 D2, 90 A2
Montigny-le-Roi 89 C2
Montigny-sur-Canne 103 C1
Montigny-sur-Aube 88 B2
Montijo 165 D2
Montijo 164 A2
Montilla 172 B1
Montillana 173 C1
Montivilliers 77 B/C3
Montizón 167 D3, 168 A3
Montjay 111 D2
Montjean-sur-Loire 86 A3
Montlhéry 87 D2
Montlieu-la-Garde 101 C3
Mont-Louis 156 A2
Montluçon 102 B2
Montluel 103 D2
Montmarault 102 B2
Montmartin-sur-Mer 85 D1
Montmédy 79 C3
Montmélian 104 A3
Montmeyan 112 A3
Montmeyran 111 C1
Montmirail 86 B2
Montmirail 88 A1
Montmirey-le-Château 89 C3, 103 D1, 104 A1
Montmoreau-Saint-Cybard 101 C3
Montmorency 87 D1
Montmorillon 101 D2
Montmort 88 A1
Montmuran 85 C/D2
Montóggio 113 D1/2
Montoir-de-Bretagne 85 C3
Montoire-sur-le-Loir 86 B3
Montoito 165 C2/3
Montolieu 110 A3, 156 A1
Montorio 153 B/C2
Montório al Vomano 117 D3, 119 C1
Montório nei Frentani 119 D2, 120 A1
Montoro 167 C3, 172 B1
Montpellier-le-Vieux 110 B2
Montpellier 110 B3
Montpézat 109 C3, 155 D1
Montpezat 111 C2
Montpezat-de-Quercy 109 D2
Montpezat-sous-Bauzon 111 C1
Montpon-Ménestérol 109 B/C1
Montpont-en-Bresse 103 D2
Montŕdon-Labessonnié 110 A2
Montréal 110 A3, 156 A1
Montréal-de-Gers 109 B/C2
Montréjeau 109 C3, 155 C1
Montrésor 86 A/B3, 101 C1
Montresta 123 C2
Montret 103 D1
Montreuil-aux-Lions 87 D1, 88 A1
Montreuil-Bellay 101 C1
Montreuil-sur-Mer 77 D2
Montreux 104 B2
Montrevault 85 D3, 100 B1
Montrevel-en-Bresse 103 D2
Montrichard 86 A/B3
Montricoux 109 D2
Montroc 104 B2
Mont-roig del Camp 163 D2
Montrond 104 A1
Montrond-les-Bains 103 C3
Montrose 54 B2
Montrottier 104 A2/3
Montroy 169 C/D1
Mont-Saint-Vincent 103 C1
Montsalvy 110 A1
Montsauche 88 A3, 103 C1
Montsaunès 109 C3, 155 D1
Mont-Saxonnex 104 B2
Montsecret 86 A1
Montségur 156 A1
Montseny 156 A/B3
Montsoreau 86 A/B3, 101 C1
Mont-sous-Vaudrey 103 D1, 104 A1
Monts-sur-Guesnes 101 C1
Montsûrs 86 A2
Montuenga 160 A/B2
Montuiri 157 C2
Monturque 172 B1
Monumento a Colón 171 C2
Monza 105 D3, 106 A3
Monze 110 A3, 156 B1
Monzón 155 C3
Monzón de Campos 152 B3
Moorenweis 92 A2
Moormerland-Warsingsfehn 67 D1
Moormerland 67 D1
Moormerland-Oldersum 67 D1
Moormerlland-Neermoor 67 D1
Moosbach 82 B3
Moosbrunn 94 B3
Moosburg 92 A/B2
Moosinning 92 A2
Moos-Langenisarhofen 92 B2
Moosthenning 92 B2
Mór 95 C3, 128 B1
Mór 96 B3
Mora 160 B3, 167 C1
Mora 164 B2
Mora 39 C/D2
Mora 39 D2
Moracz 70 B1
Móra d'Ebre 163 C2
Mora de Rubielos 162 B3
Mora de Santa Quiteria 168 B2
Moradillo de Roa 153 B/C3, 160 B1
Moraes 159 C1
Moraġ 73 C2
Mórahalom 129 D2
Moraira 169 D2
Moraïtika 142 A3
Moral 161 C1
Móra la Nova 163 C2
Moral de Calatrava 167 D2
Moral de la Reina 152 A3
Moraleda de Zafayona 172 B2
Moraleja 159 C3
Moraleja del Vino 159 D1
Morales 161 C1
Morales del Vino 159 D1
Morales de Toro 152 A3, 160 A1
Morales de Valverde 151 D3
Moralina 159 D1
Moralzarzal 160 B2
Moraña 150 A2
Morannes 86 A3
Morano Cálabro 120 B3, 122 A1
Morano sul Po 105 C3, 113 C1
Mörarp 49 D3, 50 A2
Morasverdes 159 C/D2
Morata 174 B1
Morata de Jalón 154 A3, 162 A1
Morata de Jiloca 162 A1
Morata de Tajuña 161 C3
Moratalla 168 B3
Moratilla de los Meleros 161 C2
Moravče 127 C2
Moraviţa 134 B1
Moravská Nová Ves 94 B2
Moravské Budějovice 94 A1
Moravské Budějovice 96 A2
Moravské Lieskové 95 C1/2
Moravske Toplice 127 D1/2
Moravský Ján 94 B2
Moravský Krumlov 94 B1
Morbach 80 A3
Morbach-Gonzerath 80 A3
Morbegno 106 A2
Mörbisch am See 94 B3
Mörbylånga 51 D2
Mörbylånga 72 B1
Morcenx 108 A2
Morciano di Romagna 115 D2, 117 C1
Morcillo 159 C3
Morcone 119 D2
Morcote 105 D2/3
Morcuera 161 C1
Mordelles 85 D2
Morecambe 59 D1, 60 B2
Moreda 173 C1/2
Morée 86 A/B2/3
Morehampstead 63 C3
Moreira 158 A1
Moreira do Rei 158 A/B1
Mørekvam 37 C2/3
Morella 163 B/C2
Moreni 141 C2
Moreruela de Tábara 151 D3, 159 D1
Morés 154 A3, 162 A1
Móres 123 C2
Morestel 103 D3, 104 A3
Moreton in Marsh 64 A2
Moret-sur-Loing 87 D2
Moretta 112 B1
Moreuil 78 A3
Morez 104 A2
Morfasbukten 9 D2/3
Morfasso 113 D1, 114 A1
Mórfion 142 B3
Morgat 84 A2
Morgedal 43 C1/2
Morges 104 B2
Morgex 104 B3
Morgins [Troistorrents] 104 B2
Morgny 77 D3, 87 C1
Morgongåva 40 A3
Morgovejo 152 A2
Morhange 89 D1
Mørholmen 43 C3
Mori 106 B3
Moriani-Plage 113 D3
Møriaunet 28 A2, 33 C1
Morienval 87 D1
Moriles 172 B1/2
Morillas Zubilana 153 C2
Morille 159 D2
Morillejo 161 D2
Morillo de Monclus 155 C2
Morin 138 A2
Morina 138 A2
Morina 140 A3
Moringen 68 B3, 81 C1
Moringen-Fredelsloh 68 B3
Moripen 43 C3
Moritzburg 83 C1
Moriville 89 D2
Morjärv 17 C2
Morkarla 40 B3
Mørke 49 C2
Morken 28 A2, 33 C1
Morkkaperä 12 B3
Mörkö 47 C1/2
Mørkøv 49 C3, 53 C/D1
Morkovice 95 B/C1
Mörkret 38 B1
Mørkri 37 B/C2
Morl 82 A/B1
Morlaàs 108 B3, 154 B1
Morlaix 84 B2
Morlanne 108 B3, 154 B1
Mörlen 80 B2
Morley 61 C2
Mörlunda 51 C/D1
Mörlunda 72 B1
Mormanno 120 B3, 122 A1
Mormant 87 D2
Mornant 103 D3
Mornay-Berry 102 B1
Mornesi 113 C/D1
Mörnsheim 91 D1/2, 92 A1/2
Moročno 98 B2
Mörön 17 C3
Morón de Almazán 161 D1
Morón de la Frontera 172 A2
Moror 155 C/D3
Moros 161 D1, 162 A1
Morosaglia 113 D2/3
Morović 133 C1
Morozzo 113 B/C2
Morpeth 57 D2/3
Morpeth 54 B3
Morrfällsviken 30 B3
Morriston 63 C1
Mörrum 51 C2
Morsains 88 A1
Morsbach 80 B2
Mörsch 90 B1
Mörsil 29 C3, 34 A/B2
Mørsvikbotn 9 C3
Mortagne-au-Perche 86 B2
Mortagne-sur-Sèvre 100 B1
Mortagne-sur-Gironde 100 B3
Mortágua 158 A2/3
Mortain 85 D1/2, 86 A1/2
Mortara 105 D3, 113 C/D1
Mörtberg 16 B2
Morteau 104 B1
Mortegliano 126 A2
Mortemart 101 D2
Mortenshals 4 A3, 9 D1
Mortensjordet 5 D1, 6 A/B1
Mortenslund 29 C2
Mörtfors 46 B3, 51 D1
Mortrée 86 B2
Mörtsjön 29 D3, 34 B1
Mortsund 8 B2/3
Mörtträsk 16 B2
Morup 49 D2, 50 A1
Morups Tånge 49 D2, 50 A1
Moryń 70 B2
Morzine 104 B2
Morzyczyn 71 B/C1
Mos 150 A3
Mosa 26 B2

Mosätt 34 B3
Mosbach 91 C1
Mosbach-Neckarelz 91 C1
Mosby 43 C3
Mosca 151 C3, 159 C1
Moscardón 162 A3
Moscavide 164 A2
Mošćenička Draga 126 B3, 130 A1
Moschendorf 127 D1
Moschófiton 143 C3
Moschopótamos 143 D2
Mosel 82 B2
Mosina 71 D3
Mosiny 71 D1
Mosjøen 14 A/B2/3
Moskaret 33 C3, 37 D1
Moskog 36 A/B2
Moskosel 16 A2
Moskuvaara 12 B2
Moskva 75 D2/3
Moso in Passíria/Moos in Passeiert. 107 C1
Mosonmagyaróvár 95 B/C3
Mosonmagyaróvár 96 B3
Mosonszolnok 94 B3
Mošorin 129 D3, 133 D1, 134 A1
Mošovce 95 D1
Mosqueruela 162 B2/3
Moss 44 B1
Mossala 24 A3
Mossaträsk 30 B2, 35 D1
Mossebo 50 B1
Mossiberg 39 C1
Mössingen 91 C2
Mössingen-Bad Sebastiansweiler 91 C2
Mosso Santa Maria 105 C3
Møsstrand 43 C1
Most 83 C2
Most 96 A1
Mostad 8 A3
Mostar 132 B3
Moste 126 B2
Moster 42 A1
Mosterhamn 42 A1
Mosterøy 42 A2
Mostiska 97 D2, 98 A2
Most na Soči 126 B2
Mostøl 42 B1
Móstoles 160 B3
Mostrim 55 C/D2
Mosty 73 D3, 98 B1
Mosty 71 B/C1
Mosty u Jablunkova 95 D1
Mosvik 28 B3, 33 D1
Mota de Altarejos 161 D3, 168 B1
Mota del Cuervo 167 D1, 168 A1
Mota del Marqués 152 A3, 160 A1
Motala 46 A2
Motešice 95 C1/2
Motherwell 56 B2
Möthlow 69 D2, 70 A2
Motilla del Palancar 168 B1
Motilleja 168 B2
Mötingselberget 30 A/B1
Motjärnshyttan 39 C3
Motnik 127 C2
Motovun 126 B3, 130 A1
Motril 173 C2
Motru 135 D1
Motta 107 C3
Motta di Livenza 107 D3
Motta Montecorvino 119 D2, 120 A1
Motta San Giovanni 122 A3, 125 D2
Motta Visconti 105 D3
Motten-Kothen 81 C2
Möttingen 91 D2
Móttola 121 C2
Möttönen 21 C2
Mötzing-Schönach 92 B1/2
Mou 48 B2
Mouchamps 100 B1
Mouchan 109 C2
Mouchard 104 A1
Moudon 104 B1/2
Moúdros 145 C3
Mouflers 77 D2
Mougon 101 C2
Mouhijärvi 24 B1
Mouilleron-en-Pareds 100 B1
Moulay 86 A2
Mouleydier 109 C1
Mouliherne 86 A/B3
Moulin-Mage 110 A2
Moulin-Neuf 109 D3, 156 A1
Moulins 102 B1/2
Moulins-Engilbert 103 C1
Moulins-la-Marche 86 B2
Moulismes 101 D2
Moult 86 A1
Mountain Ash 63 C1
Moura 165 C3
Mourão 165 C3
Moure 150 A3, 158 A1
Mourenx 109 C3, 155 C1
Mourèze 110 B3
Mouriés 139 D3, 143 D1, 144 A1
Mouriès 111 C2/3
Mouríkion 147 D2
Mouriscas 164 B1
Mourmelon-le-Grand 88 B1
Mouronho 158 B3
Mourujärvi 13 C3
Mouscron (Moeskroen) 78 A2
Moussey 89 D1/2, 90 A2
Moustey 108 B2
Moustier 109 C1
Moustiers-Sainte-Marie 112 A2
Mouthe 104 A1/2
Mouthier-Haute-Pierre 104 A1
Mouthoumet 110 A3, 156 B1
Moutier 104 B1
Moûtiers 104 B3
Moutiers-au-Perche 86 B2
Mouton 100 B3
Moux 88 A/B3, 103 C1
Moux 110 A3, 156 B1
Mouy-de-l'Oise 77 D3, 87 D1
Mouzákion 146 B2/3
Mouzákion 143 C3
Mouzay 79 C3
Mouzon 79 C3
Møvik 36 A3
Moville 54 A3, 55 D2
Moxhe 79 C2
Moyenvic 89 D1
Moyeuvre-Grande 89 C1
Möykky 20 B3
Möykkylä 18 A3
Möykkylänperä 18 B3
Moyuela 162 B1/2
Možajsk 75 D3
Mozárbez 159 D2
Mozgovo 135 C3
Mózia 124 A2
Mozirje 127 C2
Mozoncillo 160 B1/2
Mozyr' 99 C1
Mozzánica 106 A3
Mrągowo 73 C2/3
Mrakovica 131 D1, 132 A1
Mramor 135 C3
Mramorak 134 B1
Mratinje 133 C3, 137 C1
Mrazovac 131 C1
Mrčajevci 133 D2, 134 A2/3
Mrežičko 139 C3, 143 C1
Mrkalji 133 C2
Mrkonjić Grad 131 D2, 132 A2
Mrkopalj 127 C3, 130 B1
Mrzla Vodice 127 C3, 130 B1
Mšec 83 C2/3
Mšené-lázně 83 C2
Mšeno 83 D2
Mstislavl' 75 C3
Mszczonów 73 C3, 97 C1
Múccia 115 D3, 117 C/D2
Much 80 A2
Muchamiel 169 D3
Mücheln 82 A1
Much Wenlock 59 D3
Mucientes 152 A/B3, 160 A1
Mücka 83 D1
Mücke-Flensungen 81 C2
Mücke-Nieder-Ohmen 81 C2
Mudanya 149 D1
Mudau 81 C3, 91 C1
Müddersheim 79 D2, 80 A2
Müden (Aller) 68 B2
Muel 154 A/B3, 162 A/B1
Muelas del Pan 151 D3, 159 D1
Mués 153 D2
Muga de Sayago 159 C/D1
Mugaire 108 A3, 154 A1
Mugardos 150 B1
Muge 164 A/B2
Mügeln 83 B/C1
Mügeln 70 A3
Muggensturm 90 B1/2
Múggia 126 B3
Muğla 149 D2/3
Mugron 108 B2
Mühlacker 90 B1
Mühlbach am Hochkönig 93 C3, 107 D1, 126 A1
Muhlbach-sur-Munster 89 D2, 90 A3
Mühlbeck 69 D3, 82 B1
Mühlberg 83 C1
Mühlberg 81 D2
Mühldorf 94 A2
Mühldorf 92 B2
Mühlen Eichsen 53 C3, 69 C1
Mühlhausen (Höchstadt) 81 D3
Mühlhausen 81 D2
Mühlhausen (Neumarkt) 92 A1
Mühlhausen 81 D1
Mühlingen 91 C3
Mühltal 80 B3
Mühltroff 82 A/B2
Muhola 21 D2, 22 A2
Muhos 18 B2/3
Muhr 126 A1
Muhr 91 D1
Muiden 66 B2/3
Muides-sur-Loire 87 C3
Muiños 150 B3
Muirkirk 56 B2
Muir of Ord 54 A/B2
Muittan 21 D2/3
Mujdžići 131 D2, 132 A2
Mujejärvi 23 C1
Mukačevo 97 D2, 98 A3
Mukařov 83 D3
Mukkajärvi 17 C1/2
Mukkavaara 16 B1
Mukkavaara 13 C2
Mula 14 B2
Mula 169 B/C3, 174 A/B1
Mulda 83 C2
Mulfingen 91 C1
Mülheim 80 A1
Mulhouse 89 D3, 90 A3
Muljula 23 D3
Mulkwitz 83 D1
Mullaghboy 56 A3
Mullerup 49 C3, 53 C1
Müllheim 90 A3
Mullhyttan 46 A1
Mullingar 55 D2
Müllrose 70 B3
Mullsjö 45 D3
Mullsjö 31 C2
Mulrany 55 C2
Mulsanne 86 B2/3
Multia 21 C3
Multra 30 B3, 35 D2
Munakka 20 B2
Munapirtti 26 B2/3
Münchberg 82 A2/3
Müncheberg 70 B2
Müncheberg 72 A3
München 92 A2
Münchenbernsdorf 82 A/B2
Münchhausen (Marburg) 80 B2
Münchsmünster 92 A2
Münchweiler an der Rodalbe 90 A1
Mundaca 153 D1
Mundal 36 B2
Münden 81 C1
Münden-Hedemünden 81 C1
Munderfing 93 C2/3
Munderkingen 91 C2
Mundesley 65 D1
Mundford 65 C2
Mundheim 42 A1
Mune 126 B3
Munébrega 162 A1
Munera 168 A2
Mungia 153 C1
Muniesa 162 B2
Munilla 153 D3
Munka-Ljungby 50 A2
Munkbyn 35 C3
Munkedal 45 B/C2
Munkedals bruk 45 B/C2
Munkflohögen 29 D3, 34 B1
Munkfors 39 C3
Munktorp 40 A3, 46 B1
Munne 26 B2
Münnerstadt 81 D2
Muñogalindo 160 A2
Muñopedro 160 B2
Muñopepe 160 A2
Muñotello 160 A2
Muñoveros 160 B1/2
Munsala 20 B2
Münsingen 91 C2
Münsingen 105 C1
Münsingen-Bremelau 91 C2
Münsingen-Buttenhausen 91 C2
Munsö 47 C1
Munster 68 B2
Münster 67 D3
Münster 105 C2
Munster 89 D2, 90 A2/3
Munster-Alvern 68 B2
Munster-Breloh 68 B2
Münster-Hiltrup 67 D3
Münstermaifeld 80 A2
Münster-Nienberge 67 D3
Munster-Oerrel 68 B2
Münster-Sprakel 67 D3
Münstertal 90 B3
Münster-Wolbeck 67 D3
Munsvattnet 29 D2
Muntele Mic 135 C1
Münzkirchen 93 C2
Muodoslompolo 11 C3
Muonio 11 C3, 12 A1
Muotkajärvi 11 C2
Muotkan Ruoktu 6 B3
Muotkavaara 11 C3, 12 A1/2
Murakeresztúr 128 A2
Murakka 25 D1, 26 A/B1
Muráň 97 C2
Muras 150 B1
Muraszemenye 127 D2
Murat 102 B3, 110 A1
Murata 119 C2
Muratli 149 D1
Murat sur-Vèbre 110 A2
Murau 126 B1
Murau 96 A3
Muravera 123 D3
Murazzano 113 C2
Murazzo 112 B2
Murça 159 B/C2
Murça 158 B1
Murchante 154 A3
Murci 116 B3, 118 A1
Murcia 169 C3, 174 B1
Mur-de-Barrez 110 A1
Mur-de-Bretagne 85 B/C2
Mur-de-Sologne 87 C3
Mureck 127 D1/2
Mureşenii Bîrgăului 97 D3, 140 B1
Muret 108 B3, 155 C1
Murg 105 D1, 106 A1
Murgaševo 138 B3, 143 C1
Murgeni 141 C/D1
Murgia 153 C/D2
Muri 105 C1
Murias de Paredes 151 D2
Muriel Viejo 153 C3, 161 C1
Murieta 153 D2
Murillo de Gállego 154 B2
Murillo de Río Leza 153 D2
Murillo el Fruto 154 A2
Murino 137 D1, 138 A1
Mürlenbach 79 D2/3, 80 A3
Murnau am Staffelsee 92 A3
Muro 157 C2
Muro 113 D2
Muro de Aguas 153 D3
Muro de Alcoy 169 D2
Muro en Cameros 153 D2/3
Murol 102 B3
Murole 25 C1
Muro Lucano 120 A2
Muron 100 B2
Muros 150 A2
Muros de Nalón 151 D1
Murowana Goślina 71 D2
Murrë 138 A3
Murrhardt 91 C1
Murronkylä 18 B3
Murska Sobota 127 D1/2
Murska Sobota 96 A/B3
Mursko Središće 127 D2
Murtas 173 C2
Murtede 158 A2/3
Murten 104 B1
Murter 131 C3
Murtfü 129 D1
Murtino 139 D3, 143 D1, 144 A1
Murto 18 B2
Murtoinen 22 A/B3
Murtolahti 22 B2
Murtomäki 22 B1
Murtomäki 22 A/B2
Murtosa 158 A2
Murtovaara 19 D1
Murueta 153 D1
Murum 45 D3
Muruvik 28 A/B3, 33 C/D1
Murvica 130 B2
Murviel-les-Beziers 110 B3
Mürzsteg 94 A3
Murzynowo 71 C2
Mürzzuschlag 94 A3
Mürzzuschlag 96 A3
Müsch 79 D2, 80 A2
Muşeteşti 135 D1
Musetrene 37 D2
Museums-Jernbane 28 A3, 33 C2
Musile di Piave 107 D3
Muskiz 153 C1
Muskö 47 C/D1/2
Mušov 94 B1
Mussalo 26 B2/3
Musselburgh 57 C2
Musselkanaal 67 C2
Mussidan 109 C1
Mussomeli 124 B2
Mussy-sur-Seine 88 B2
Mustafa Kemalpaşa 149 D1
Müstair [Zernez] 106 B2
Mustajärvi 21 C3
Mustajärvi 20 B3
Mustajärvi 25 D1/2, 26 A1/2
Mustajoki 24 B1
Mustamaa 20 B2
Mustamaa 18 B3
Mustavaara 19 C2
Mustila 26 B2
Mustinlahti 23 C2/3
Mustio 25 C3
Mustion asema 25 C3
Mustla 74 A1
Mustolanmäki 23 C1
Mustolanmutka 19 C3, 23 B/C1
Mustvee 74 A/B1
Mušutište 138 B2
Muta 127 C2
Mutala 25 C1
Mutalahti 23 D3, 23 D1/2
Mutanj 133 D2, 134 A2
Mutriku 153 D1
Mutterstadt 90 B1
Mutzig 90 A2
Mutzschen 82 B1
Muuga 74 A1
Muurame 21 D3, 22 A3
Muurasjärvi 21 D1, 22 A1
Muurikkala 27 C2
Muurla 24 B3
Muurola 12 A3
Muurola 27 B/C2
Muuruvesi 23 C2

Muusko 12 B3
Muxagata 159 B/C2
Muxía 150 A1
Muzillac 85 C3
Mužla 95 D3
Mužlja 129 D3, 134 A1
Muzzana del Turgnano 126 A3
Mycielin 71 C3
Myckelasen 34 B2
Myckelgensjö 30 B2/3, 35 D1
Myckelsjö 35 D2/3
Myckle 31 D1
Mycklebostad 9 D1
Myckling 35 D3
Myennes 87 D3
Myggenäs 45 B/C3
Myggsjö 39 C/D1
Myhinpää 22 B3
Myjava 95 C2
Mykenai 147 C3
Mykland 36 B2
Mykland 43 C3
Myklebostad 8 B3
Myklebust 36 B2
Myllperä 21 D2, 22 A2
Myllyklä 25 C2
Myllykoski 26 B2
Myllykoski 20 B2
Myllykylä 25 C3
Myllykylä 12 B2
Myllylahti 19 D2
Myllymaa 24 B1
Myllymäki 21 C3
Myllyperä 18 A3
Myllyperä 21 D2, 22 A2
Mynämäki 24 A/B2
Mynttilä 26 B1
Myössäjärvi 6 B3
Myran 38 B3, 45 C1
Myrdal 36 B3
Myre 8 B1
Myreng 37 D2
Myrheden 16 B2
Myrheden 16 B3
Myrholen 39 D2
Myrkky 20 A3
Myrland 9 C2
Myrland 8 A/B2
Myrlandshaugen 9 D2
Myrlia 4 A3, 10 A1
Myrmoen 33 D2
Myrskylä/Mörskom 25 D2, 26 A2
Myrvang 9 C2
Myrviken 34 B2
Mysen 44 B1
Myślenice 97 C2
Myślibórz 70 B2
Myssjö 34 B2
Myssjön 35 D3
Mysuseter 37 D1/2
Mýto 83 C3

N

Nå 36 B3
Naamanka 19 C1/2
Naamankylä 18 B3
Naamijoki 12 A3, 17 D1
Naantali (Nådendal) 24 A/B2/3
Naappila 25 C1
Naarajärvi 22 B3
Naarden 66 B2/3
Näärinki 27 B/C1
Naarjoki 24 A/B2
Naartijärvi 17 D2
Naarva 23 D2
Naas 55 D2/3
Näätämö 7 C2
Näätänmaa 23 C3
Näätävaara 19 D2
Naatula 24 B2
Nabbelund 51 D1
Nabburg 82 B3, 92 B1
Načeradec 83 D3
Náchod 96 A/B1/2
Nacimiento 173 D2
Nacka 47 D1
Näckådalen 39 C1
Näcksåsen 29 D2
Nădab 97 C3, 140 A1
Nadalj 129 D3
Nadarzyce 71 D1
Nádasdladány 128 B1
Naddvik 37 C2
Nadela 150 B2
Nådendal 24 A/B2/3
Nădlac 140 A1
Nadrljan 129 D2
Nadvornaja 97 D2, 98 A/B3
Näfels [Näfels-Mollis] 105 D1, 106 A1
Náfpaktos 146 B2
Náfplion 147 C3
Náfplion 148 B2
Nafría la Llana 153 D3, 161 C1
Naggen 35 C3
Nago 106 B2/3
Nagold 90 B2
Nagold-Hochdorf 90 B2
Nagu/Nauvo 24 A3
Nagyargencs 95 C3, 128 A1
Nagyatád 128 A2
Nagyatád 96 B3
Nagybajom 128 A2
Nagybaracska 129 C2
Nagycenk 94 B3
Nagydorog 129 B/C2
Nagygyimót 95 C3, 128 A/B1
Nagyhalász 97 C3, 98 A3
Nagyharsány 128 B3
Nagyigmánd 95 C3
Nagykanizsa 128 A2
Nagykanizsa 96 B3
Nagykapornak 128 A1
Nagykáta 129 C/D1
Nagykáta 97 C3, 140 A1
Nagykónyi 128 B2
Nagykőrös 129 C/D1
Nagykörű 129 D1
Nagylak 129 D2
Nagylengyel 128 A1/2
Nagymágocs 129 D2
Nagymaros 95 D3
Nagyoroszi 95 D3
Nagyszénás 129 D2
Nagyvázsony 128 B1
Naharros 161 D3
Nahrstedt 69 C/D2
Nahwinden 82 A2
Naidăş 135 B/C1
Naila 82 A2
Nailloux 109 D3, 155 D1, 156 A1
Nailsworth 63 D1, 64 A3
Nairn 54 B2
Naisjärv 17 C2
Naizin 85 C2
Najac 109 D2
Nájera 153 D2
Näkkälä 11 C2
Naklo 126 B2
Nakło nad Notecią 72 B3
Nakovo 129 D3
Nakskov 53 C2
Nalda 153 D2
Nälden 29 D3, 34 B2
Näljänkä 19 C2
Nalkki 19 C3
Nálles/Nals 107 C2
Nalliers 100 B2
Naltijärvi 11 D2, 12 A1
Nalzen 109 D3, 155 D1/2, 156 A1
Nalžovské Hory 93 C1
Namborn 80 A3, 90 A1
Nambroca 160 B3, 167 C1
Namdalseid 28 B2
Nämdö 47 D1
Náměšť nad Oslavou 94 A/B1
Namlos 91 D3, 106 B1
Namnå 38 B2
Nampont-Saint-Martin 77 D2
Namsos 28 B2
Namsvassgardan 29 C1
Namur 79 C2
Namysłów 96 B1
Nancy 89 C1/2
Nandlstadt 92 A2
Nangis 87 D2
Nannestad 38 A3
Nans-les-Pins 111 D3
Nantes 85 D3, 100 A1
Nanteuil-le-Haudoin 87 D1
Nantiat 101 C2
Nantrow 53 D3
Nantua 103 D2, 104 A2
Nantwich 59 D2, 60 B3, 64 A1
Náousa 143 C/D2
Náousa 148 B1
Napajedla 95 C1
Napapiiri 12 A3
Nápola 124 A2
Nápoli 119 C/D3
Napp 8 A/B2
Nárai 127 D1
Narberth 62 B1
Nårbo 42 A2/3
Nærbø 42 A2/3
Narbonne 110 A/B3, 156 B1
Narbonne-Plage 110 B3, 156 B1
Narbuvollen 33 D3
Narcao 123 C3
Narcy 87 D3, 102 B1
Nard 128 B3
Nardò 121 D3
Närhilä 21 D2, 22 A2
Narila 22 B3
Narkaus 12 B3
Narken 17 C1
Narni 117 C3, 118 B1
Naro 124 B3
Naroč' 74 A3
Narodiči 99 C2
Naro-Fominsk 75 D3
Narón 150 B1
Nærøy 28 B1
Nåroy 36 B3
Nærøy 36 B3
Närpes (Närpiö) 20 A3
Närpiö 20 A3
Narppa 21 C1
Narrillos de Rebollar 160 A2
Narros del Castillo 160 A2
Närsäkkälä 27 D1
Närsen 39 C2/3
Nærsnes 38 A3, 43 D1, 44 B1
Narta 128 A3
Närtesalo 27 C1
Nårunga 45 C3
Naruska 13 C2
Narva 25 B/C1
Närvä 25 D1, 26 A1
Narva 74 B1
Närvijoki 20 A3
Narvik 9 D2
Narvik-Ankenes 9 D2
Narzole 113 C1/2
Näs 41 C/D2
Näs 34 B2
Näs 30 A/B3, 35 D2
Næs 53 D2
Näsåker 30 A3, 35 D1/2
Năsăud 97 D3, 140 B1
Näsberg 39 D1
Näs bruk 40 A3
Näsby 51 D2
Našec 138 A/B2
Näset 35 C3
Näset 29 D2
Näset 45 C3, 49 D1
Näset 39 D1
Näshult 51 C1
Našice 128 B3
Näske 30 B3
Näsland 31 C2
Naso 125 C1/2
Nassau 80 B3
Nassenfels 92 A2
Nassenheide 70 A2
Nassereith 91 D3, 106 B1
Nässja 46 A2
Nässjö 46 A3
Nässjö 30 A2/3, 35 C1
Nässjö 72 A1
Nässundet 45 D1, 46 A1
Nastan 136 A1
Nästangsjö 30 A1
Nastätten 80 B2/3
Nästelsjö 34 B3
Nästi 24 A2
Nastola 25 D2, 26 A2
Næstved 53 D1/2
Näsum 51 B/C2
Näsviken 40 A1
Natalinci 134 B2
Naters 105 C2
Nattavaara by 16 B1
Nattavaara station 16 B1
Nattheim 91 D2
Nättraby 51 C2
Naturno/Naturns 107 B/C1/2
Naturreservatet 49 C2
Naucelle 110 A2
Nauders 106 B1
Nauen 70 A2
Nauen 72 A3
Naul 58 A2
Naulaperä 19 C2
Naulavaara 23 C1
Naumburg 82 A1
Naumburg 81 C1
Naundorf 83 C2
Naundorf 70 A3, 82 B1
Naunhof 82 B1
Naurua 18 B2
Naustbukt 4 A2
Naustbukta 28 B1
Naustdal 36 A2
Nauste 32 B2
Nausterstøa 33 C3
Naustvilla 32 B3, 37 C1
Nauthella 42 A1
Nautijaur 16 A1
Nautsund 36 A2
Nauviale 110 A1
Näva 38 B3, 45 C1
Nava 151 D1, 152 A1
Navacarros 159 D2/3
Navacepeda de Tormes 160 A2/3
Navacepedilla de Corneja 160 A2
Navacerrada 167 C2
Navacerrada 160 B2
Navaconcejo 159 D3
Nava de Arévalo 160 A2
Nava de Béjar 159 D2
Nava de la Asunción 160 B1/2
Nava del Rey 160 A1
Nava de Roa 152 B3, 160 B1
Nava de Sotrobal 160 A2
Navafría 160 B2
Navahermosa 160 B3, 167 C1
Naval 155 C2/3
Navalacruz 160 A2
Navalagamella 160 B2
Navalcaballo 153 D3, 161 D1
Navalcán 160 A3
Navalcarnero 160 B3
Navaleno 153 C3, 161 C1
Navales 159 D2, 160 A2
Navalilla 160 B1
Navalmanzano 160 B1
Navalmoral de la Mata 159 D3, 166 A/B1
Navalmoralejo 160 A3, 166 B1
Navalón 169 C2
Navalonguilla 159 D3
Navalperal de Pinares 160 B2
Navalpino 167 B/C2
Navaluenga 160 A2
Navalvillar de Ibor 166 B1
Navalvillar de Pela 166 A/B2
Navamorcuende 160 A3
Navan (An Uaimh) 55 D2
Navarcles 156 A3
Navardún 155 C2
Navares de las Cuevas 160 B1
Navarredondilla 160 A2
Navarrenx 108 B3, 154 B1
Navarrés 169 C2
Navarrete 153 D2
Navarrete del Río 163 C2
Navás 156 A2
Navasa 154 B2
Navascués 154 A/B2
Navas de Estena 167 C1
Navas de Jorquera 168 B1/2
Navas del Madroño 165 D1
Navas del Rey 160 B2/3
Navas de Oro 160 B1
Navas de San Juan 167 D3
Navas de Tolosa 167 D3
Navasfrías 159 C3
Navata 156 B2
Navatrasierra 166 B1
Nave 106 B3
Nave 159 C2/3
Nave de Haver 159 C2
Nävekvarn 47 C2
Navelli 117 D3, 119 C1
Navelsaker 32 A3, 36 B1
Nåverdal 33 C2
Näverede 29 D3, 35 C2
Näverkärret 39 D3, 46 B1
Näverliden 16 A3
Näverrys 18 B1
Naverstad 44 B2
Naves 104 B3
Navès 155 D3, 156 A2
Naves 102 A3
Naveta d'Es Tudóns 157 C1
Navezuelas 166 B1
Navia 151 C1
Navia de Suarna 151 C2
Navilly 103 D1
Navioci 133 B/C1/2
Navis 107 C1
Navit 5 B/C2/3
Năvodari 141 D2
Na Xamena 169 D2
Náxos 149 C2/3
Nay 108 B3, 154 B1
Nayland 65 C2
Nazaré 164 A1
Nazija 75 C1
Nazilli 149 D2
Ndërfushë 137 D3, 138 A2/3
Ndroq 137 D3, 142 A1
Néa Anchíalos 143 D3, 144 A3
Néa Artáki 147 D2
Néa Epídavros 147 C3
Néa Fókea 144 A2
Néai Kariaí 143 D3
Néa Iraklítsa 144 B1
Néa Kallikrátia 144 A2
Néa Kallísti 145 C1
Néa Karváli 145 B/C1
Néa Kerdília 144 B1
Néa Máditos 144 A/B2
Néamákri 147 D2
Néa Messángala 143 D2/3
Néa Michanióna 143 D2, 144 A2
Néa Moudaniá 144 A2
Néa Moudaniá 148 B1
Néant-sur-Yvel 85 C2
Néa Péramos 144 B1
Néa Plagiá 144 A2
Neápolis 143 C2
Neápolis 148 A/B1
Néa Potídea 144 A2
Néa Psará 147 D2
Néa Psará 148 B2
Néa Róda 144 B2
Néa Sánda 145 D1
Néa Sánda 149 C1
Néa Skióni 144 A2/3
Néa Ténedos 144 A2
Neath 63 C1
Néa Tríglia 144 A2
Néa Víssi 145 D2/3
Néa Zíchni 144 B1
Néa Zíchni 149 B/C1
Nebel 52 A2
Nebelin 69 C/D2
Nebljusi 131 C2
Nebolči 75 C1
Nebra 82 A1
Nebreda 153 C3
Nečemice 83 C2
Neckarbischofsheim 91 C1
Neckargemünd 90 B1
Neckargerach 91 C1
Neckarsulm 91 C1
Neckartailfingen 91 C2
Neckenmarkt 94 B3
Necrópoli Etrusca 114 B2, 116 B1
Necrópoli Pantálica 125 D3
Necrópolis Romana 171 D1
Nečtiny 83 C3
Nečujam 131 C3
Neda 150 B1

Nedalens turisthytta 33 D2
Nedansjö 35 D3
Nedaški 99 C2
Neded 95 C3
Nedelišće 127 D2
Nederbrakel 78 B2
Nederby 48 A/B2
Nedervetil/Alaveteli 21 B/C1
Nederweert 79 C/D1
Nedlitz 69 D3
Nedre Eggedal 43 D1
Nedre Flåsjön 17 C2
Nedrefosshytta 5 B/C3, 10 B1
Nedre Gärdsjö 39 D2
Nedre Heimdalen 37 C/D2
Nedre Kuouka 16 B1/2
Nedre Parakka 10 B3
Nedre Soppero 10 B3
Nedre Tollådal 15 B/C1
Nedre Voljakkala 17 D2, 18 A1
Nedstrand 42 A2
Neede 67 C3
Needham Market 65 D2
Neerpelt 79 C1
Nees By 48 A2
Neetze 69 C1
Nefyn 58 B2/3
Negádes 142 B3
Negenborn 68 B3
Negorci 139 C3, 143 D1
Negotin 135 C2
Negotin 140 B2
Negotino 139 C3
Negovanovci 135 D2
Negredo 161 C2
Negreira 150 A2
Nègrepelisse 109 D2
Negrești-Oaș 97 D3, 98 A3
Negru Vodă 141 D2
Nehvonniemi 23 D1/2
Neiden 7 C2
Neila 153 C3
Neistenkangas 12 A3, 17 D1
Neitisuando 10 B3
Neittävä 18 B3
Nejdek 82 B2
Neksø 51 D3
Neksø 72 A/B2
Nelas 158 B2
Nelidovo 75 C2
Neljäntuulen tupa 6 B3
Nellimö 7 C3
Nellingen 91 C2
Nellingen 91 C2
Nelson 59 D1, 60 B2
Nelvik 32 B1/2
Neman (Ragnit) 73 C2
Němčice 93 B/C1
Neméa 147 C2/3
Neméa 147 C2/3
Nemesszalók 128 A1
Nemesvid 128 A2
Németkér 129 C2
Nemila 132 B2
Nemirov 99 C3
Nemours 87 D2
Nemšová 95 C1
Nenagh 55 C3
Nendeln 106 A1
Nennhausen 69 D2
Nensjö 30 B3, 35 D2
Nentershausen 81 C/D1/2
Nentershausen 80 B2
Nenthead 57 D3, 60 B1
Nenzing 106 A1
Neochórion 143 C3
Neochórion 146 A2
Neochórion 144 A3
Neochórion 146 A2
Neochórion 145 D1, 145 D3
Néon Ginekókastron 143 D1, 144 A1
Néon Kavaklíon 145 C1
Néon Monastírion 143 D3, 146 B1
Néon Petrítsi 139 D3, 144 A1
Néos Marmarás 144 B2
Neós Páos 146 B2
Nepas 153 D3, 161 D1
Nepi 117 C3, 118 B1
Nepomuk 83 C3, 93 C1
Nepomuk 96 A2
Nérac 109 C2
Neráïda 143 C2
Neráïda 142 B3
Neratovice 83 D2
Nerău 129 D2/3
Nerdal 32 B2
Néré 101 C2
Neresheim 91 D2
Neresnica 135 C2
Nereta 73 D1, 74 A2
Nereto 117 D3
Nerezine 130 A2
Nerežišće 131 D3
Neringa 73 C2
Néris-les-Bains 102 B2
Nerja 173 C2
Nerkoo 22 B2
Nermo 38 A1
Néronde 103 C2/3
Nérondes 102 B1
Nerpio 168 B3
Nersingen 91 D2
Nerskogen 33 C2
Nerva 171 C1
Nervesa della Battáglia 107 D3
Nes 36 A/B2
Nes 38 A2
Nes 9 C2
Nes 29 B/C2
Nes 66 B1
Nes 37 D3
Nes 37 D3
Nes 36 B2
Nes 38 A3
Nes 29 C2
Nes 42 A1/2
Nes 32 B2
Nes 55 C1
Nesan 29 C1
Nesaseter 29 C1
Nesbøsjøen 36 A3
Nesbyen 37 D3
Neschholz 69 D3, 70 A3
Neschwitz 83 D1
Nesebâr 141 C3
Neset 4 B2
Nesflaten 42 B1
Nesheim 36 B3
Nesland 43 C2
Nesland 42 B2
Nesland 8 A3
Neslandsvatn 43 C/D2, 44 A2
Nesna 14 A/B2
Nesodden 38 A3
Nesoddtangen 38 A3
Nesperal 158 A/B3, 164 B1
Nespereira 158 A/B2
Nespereira 150 B2
Nes Røstlandet 8 A3
Nesseby 7 C2
Nesselwang 91 D3
Nesse-Nessmersiel 67 D1
Nesso 105 D2/3, 106 A2
Nestáni 147 C3
Nestar 152 B2
Nestavoll 33 C3, 37 D1
Nestelbach bei Graz 127 C1
Nesterov 97 D2, 98 A2
Neštin 129 C3, 133 C1
Neston 59 C2, 60 B3
Nestórion 142 B2
Nestórion 148 A1
Nesttun 36 A3
Nesviž 98 B1
Neteka 131 C2
Netlandsnes 42 B3
Netolice 93 D1
Netphen 80 B2
Netretić 127 C3
Nettancourt 88 B1
Nettersheim-Tondorf 79 D2, 80 A2
Nettersheim 79 D2, 80 A2
Nettetal 79 D1
Nettetal-Kaldenkirchen 79 D1
Nettetal-Lobberich 79 D1
Nettlebed 64 B3
Nettuno 118 B2
Netvořice 83 D3
Netzschkau 82 B2
Neualbenreuth 82 B3
Neubörger 67 D2
Neubrandenburg 70 A1
Neubrandenburg 72 A3
Neubrück 70 B3
Neubrunn (Marktheidenfeld) 81 C3
Neu Büddenstedt 69 C3
Neubukow 53 D3
Neubulach 90 B2
Neuburg 92 A2
Neuburg am Inn 93 C2
Neuburg-Zell 92 A2
Neuburxdorf 83 C1
Neuchâtel 104 B1
Neudau 127 D1
Neudenau 91 C1
Neudingen 90 B3
Neudorf 82 B2
Neudorf-Platendorf 69 C2
Neudrossenfeld 82 A3
Neuenbürg 90 B1/2
Neuendettelsau 91 D1
Neuendorf 79 D2
Neuenhagen 70 A/B2
Neuenhaus 67 C2
Neuenkirchen 68 A2
Neuenkirchen 67 D2
Neuenkirchen 68 B2
Neuenkirchen 67 D3
Neuenkirchen-Vörden 67 D2
Neuenkirchen 52 A3
Neuenmarkt 82 A3
Neuenrade 80 B1
Neuensalz 82 B2
Neuenstein 91 C1
Neuenstein-Aua 81 C2
Neuental-Zimmersrode 81 C1/2
Neuenweg 90 A/B3
Neuerburg 79 D3
Neue Schleuse 69 D2
Neufahrn 92 B2
Neufahrn (Freising) 92 A2
Neufahrn-Piegendorf 92 B2
Neuf-Brisach 90 A3
Neufchâteau 89 C2
Neufchâteau 79 C3
Neufchâtel-en-Bray 77 D3
Neufchâtel-sur-Aisne 78 B3
Neufelden 93 C2
Neugattersleben 69 D3
Neugersdorf 83 D1/2
Neuharlingersiel 67 D1
Neuhaus 82 A3
Neuhaus 52 A/B3, 68 A1
Neuhaus 69 C1
Neuhaus 82 A2
Neuhausen 83 C2
Neuhausen am Rheinfall 90 B3
Neuhausen ob Eck 91 B/C3
Neuhaus-Schierschnitz 82 A2
Neuhof 81 C2
Neuhofen an der Krems 93 D2
Neuillé-Pont-Pierre 86 B3
Neuilly-le-Réal 102 B2
Neuilly-l'Evêque 89 C2/3
Neuilly-Saint-Front 87 D1, 88 A1
Neu-Isenburg 80 B3
Neukalen 69 D1, 70 A1
Neukirch 83 D1
Neukirchen 52 A2
Neukirchen 81 C2
Neukirchen am Walde 93 C2
Neukirchen an der Enknach 93 B/C2
Neukirchen bei Sulzbach-Rosenberg 82 A3, 92 A1
Neukirchen bei Heilig Blut 92 B1
Neukirchen-Balbini 92 B1
Neukirchen-Vluyn 79 D1, 80 A1
Neukloster 53 D3, 69 C/D1
Neu Kosenow 70 A/B1
Neulengbach 94 A2
Neulietzegöricke 70 B2
Neulikko 19 C2
Neulingen-Bauschlott 90 B1
Neulise 103 C2
Neu Lübbenau 70 B3
Neulussheim 90 B1
Neum 136 B1
Neumagen-Dhron 80 A3
Neumarkt 92 A1
Neumarkt am Wallersee 93 C3
Neumarkt an der Ybbs 93 D2
Neumarkt an der Raab 127 D1
Neumarkt im Mühlkreis 93 D2
Neumarkt im Hausruckkreis 93 C2
Neumarkt in Steiermark 126 B1
Neumarkt-Sankt Veit 92 B2
Neu-Moresnet 79 D2
Neumünster 52 B3
Neunagelberg 93 D2
Neunburg 92 B1
Neunburg-Kemnath 92 B1
Neung-sur-Beuvron 87 C3
Neunkirch 90 B3
Neunkirchen 94 A3
Neunkirchen 80 B2
Neunkirchen 81 C3
Neunkirchen-Seelscheid 80 A2
Neunkirchen-Wiebelskirchen 89 D1, 90 A1
Neunkirchen 89 D1, 90 A1
Neunkirchen am Brand 82 A3
Neunkirchen 96 A/B3
Neuötting 92 B2
Neupetershain 83 C1
Neupölla 94 A2
Neureichenau-Altreichenau 93 C2
Neuried-Ichenheim 90 A/B2
Neuruppin 69 D2, 70 A2
Neuruppin 72 A3
Neusäss 91 D2
Neuschoo 67 D1
Neuschwanstein 91 D3
Neusiedl am See 94 B3
Neuss 79 D1, 80 A1
Neussargues 102 B3, 110 A/B1
Neustadt 81 C2
Neustadt 81 C3
Neustadt 53 C3
Neustadt 80 A2
Neustadt 83 C/D1/2
Neustadt 82 A2
Neustadt 69 D2
Neustadt am Rennsteig 81 D2, 82 A2
Neustadt am Rübenberge-Schneeren 68 B2
Neustadt am Rübenberge-Mandelsloh 68 B2
Neustadt am Rübenberge-Mardorf 68 A/B2
Neustadt am Rübenberge 68 B2
Neustadt am Kulm 82 A3
Neustadt am Rübenberge-Eilvese 68 B2
Neustadt am Rübenberge-Dudensen 68 B2
Neustadt an der Waldnaab 82 B3
Neustadt an der Weinstrasse 90 B1
Neustadt an der Donau 92 A2
Neustadt an der Aisch 81 D3
Neustadt bei Coburg 82 A2
Neustadt-Geinsheim 90 B1
Neustadt-Glewe 69 C1
Neustift im Stubaital 107 C1
Neu St. Johann [Nesslau-Neu St. Johann] 105 D1, 106 A1
Neustrelitz 70 A1
Neustrelitz 72 A3
Neustupov 83 D3
Neu-Ulm 91 C/D2
Neu-Ulm-Pfuhl 91 C/D2
Neuves-Maisons 89 C2
Neuveville, La 104 B1
Neuvic 101 C3, 109 C1
Neuvic-d'Ussel 102 A3
Neuville 78 B2/3
Neuville-aux-Boix 87 C2
Neuville-de-Poitou 101 C1
Neuville-en-Condroz 79 C2
Neuville-lès-Decize 102 B1
Neuville-sur-Saône 103 D2
Neuville-sur-Ain 103 D2
Neuvilly-en-Argonne 88 B1
Neuvola 22 B3
Neuvosenniemi 19 C3
Neuvy-Pailloux 102 A1
Neuvy-Saint-Sépulchre 102 A1/2
Neuvy-Sautour 88 A2
Neuvy-sur-Barangeon 87 D3
Neuvy-sur-Loire 87 D3
Neu-Wendischthun 69 C1
Neuwied 80 A2
Neuwiller 90 A2
Neu Wulmstorf 68 B1
Neuzelle 70 B3
Neu-Zittau 70 A/B2/3
Névache 112 A1
Nevade 140 A2
Nevegal 107 D2
Neveklov 83 D3
Nevel' 74 B2
Nevernes 14 A3
Nevers 102 B1
Nevesinje 132 B3, 137 C1
Nevest 131 C3
Neviano 121 D3
Neviano degli Arduini 114 A1
Nevlunghavn 43 D2, 44 A2
New Abbey 57 C3, 60 A1
New Alresford 65 C3, 76 B1
Newark-on-Trent 61 C/D3, 64 B1
Newbiggin-by-the-Sea 57 D2/3
Newborough 58 B2
Newbridge 63 C1
Newbridge-on-Wye 59 C3, 63 C1
Newburgh 57 C1
Newbury 65 C3, 76 B1
Newby Bridge 59 C/D1, 60 B2
Newcastle 58 A1
Newcastle 58 A2
Newcastle Emlyn 62 B1
Newcastleton 57 C2/3
Newcastle-under-Lyme 59 D2, 60 B3, 64 A1
Newcastle upon Tyne 57 D3, 61 C1
Newcastle upon Tyne 54 B3
New Cumnock 56 B2
Newenden 77 C1
Newent 63 D1, 64 A2
New Galloway 56 B3
Newgrange 58 A1/2
Newhaven 76 B1
New Holland 61 D2
New Luce 56 B3
Newlyn East 62 B3
Newmarket 65 C2
New Mills 59 D2, 61 B/C3
Newnham 63 D1, 64 A2/3
Newport 62 B1
Newport 59 D3, 64 A1
Newport 65 C2
Newport 63 C/D1
Newport 76 B1/2
Newport-on-Tay 57 C1
Newport Pagnell 64 B2
Newquay 62 B3
New Quay 58 B3, 62 B1
New Radnor 59 C3
New Romney 77 C1
New Ross 55 D3
Newry 54 A3, 55 D2
Newry 58 A1
New Scone 57 C1
Newstead Abbey 61 D3, 65 C1
Newton 59 D2, 60 B3
Newtonabbey 56 A3
Newton Abbot 63 C3

Newton Ferrers 63 C3
Newton Hamilton 58 A1
Newtonmore 54 B2, 55 D1
Newton Stewart 54 A/B3, 55 D2
Newton Stewart 56 B3
Newtown 59 C3
Newtownards 56 A3
Newtownbutler 54 A3, 55 D2
Nexon 101 C3
Nezavertajlovka 141 D1
Nežin 99 D2
Nianfors 40 A1
Niannoret 40 A1
Niaux 155 D2, 156 A1
Nibbiano 113 D1
Nibe 48 B1/2
Nicaj-Shalë 137 D2, 138 A2
Nicastro 122 A/B2
Niccone 115 C3, 117 C2
Nice 112 B3
Nichelino 112 B1
Nickelsdorf 94 B3
Nickelsdorf 96 B3
Nicolinț 134 B1
Nicolosi 125 D2
Nicosia 125 C2
Nicótera 122 A2/3
Nicótera Marina 122 A2/3
Nidda 81 C2
Nidda-Eichelsdorf 81 C2
Nidderau 81 C2/3
Nideck 89 D2, 90 A2
Nideggen 79 D2
Nidrí 146 A1
Nidríon 146 A1
Nidzica (Neidenburg) 73 C3
Niebla 171 C1/2
Niebüll 52 A2
Niederaichbach 92 B2
Niederanven 79 D3
Niederaula 81 C2
Niederbipp 105 C1
Niederbobritzsch 83 C2
Niederbronn-les-Bains 90 A1
Niederfell 80 A2
Niederfeulen 79 D3
Niederfinow 70 B2
Niedergurig 83 D1
Niederheimbach 80 B3
Niederkassel 80 A2
Niederkrüchten 79 D1
Niederlahnstein 80 A/B2
Niederlandin 70 B2
Niedernai 90 A2
Niederndodeleben 69 C3
Nieder-Olm 80 B3
Niederorschel 81 D1
Nieder-Ramstadt 80 B3
Niedersachswerfen 81 D1
Nieder-Seifersdorf 83 D1
Niederstetten 91 C1
Niederstotzingen 91 D2
Niedersulz 94 B2
Niederurnen [Nieder- und Oberurnen] 105 D1, 106 A1
Niederviehbach-Lichtensee 92 B2
Niederwölz 126 B1
Niederzier 79 D2
Niederzissen 80 A2
Niedoradz 71 C3
Niegosław 71 C2
Nieheim 68 A3
Niekursko 71 D2
Niel 78 B1
Niella Tánaro 113 C2
Niemegk 69 D3, 70 A3
Niemelä 13 C3
Niemelä 6 B2
Niemelä 7 B/C2
Niemenkylä 20 B2/3
Niemenkylä 24 B1
Niemi 24 A1, 41 D1
Niemica 71 B/C1
Niemis 17 D2
Niemisel 17 C2
Niemisjärvi 21 D3, 22 A3
Niemistenkylä 25 D1, 26 A/B1
Niemisvesi 21 C3
Nienborstel 52 B3
Nienburg 68 A/B2
Nienburg 69 D3
Nienburg-Holtorf 68 A/B2
Nienburg-Langendamm 68 A/B2
Nienhagen 68 B2
Niepart 71 D3
Niepruszewo 71 D2/3
Nierstein 80 B3
Niesi 12 B2/3
Niesky 83 D1
Niesky 96 A1
Niestetal 81 C1
Nietsak 16 B1
Nieul 101 C2
Nieul-le-Dolent 100 A1/2
Nieul-sur-l'Autise 100 B2
Nieuw-Amsterdam 67 C2
Nieuweburg 66 B2
Nieuwe-Pekela 67 C2
Nieuwerbrug 66 A/B3
Nieuwerkerk 66 A3, 78 B1
Nieuweschans 67 C/D1
Nieuw-Heeten 67 C2/3
Nieuwkoop 66 A/B3
Nieuwleusen 67 C2
Nieuwolda 67 C1
Nieuwpoort 66 B3
Nieuwpoort 78 A1
Nieuwpoort-Bad 78 A1
Nieuw-Schoonebeek 67 C2
Nieva 160 B2
Niewisch 70 B3
Nigrán 150 A3
Nigríta 144 A1
Nigríta 148 B1
Nihajlovgrad 140 B2/3
Nihajlovgrad 135 D3
Niinikoski 25 D2, 26 A2
Niinilahti 21 D2, 22 A2
Niinimäki 23 C3
Niinimäki 21 D1, 22 A1
Niinisaari 27 C1
Niinisalo 24 B1
Niinivesi 22 A/B2
Niirala 23 D3
Niittylahti 23 D3
Niitynpää 24 B2
Níjar 173 D2, 174 A2
Nijbroek 67 C2/3
Nijemci 133 C1
Nijeveen 67 C2
Nijkerk 66 B3
Nijmegen 66 B3
Nijverdal 67 C2/3
Nikaranperä 21 D3, 22 A3
Níkea 143 D3
Níki 143 D3
Nikifóros 144 B1
Nikinci 133 D1, 134 A1
Nikísiani 144 B1
Nikísiani 149 C1
Nikítas 144 B2
Nikitsch 94 B3
Nikkala 17 D2/3, 18 A1
Nikkaluokta 10 A3
Nikkaroinen 25 D1, 26 A1
Nikkeby 4 B2
Nikkilä 25 D3, 26 A3
Nikolaev 97 D2, 98 A3
Nikolaevo 74 B1
Nikoličevo 135 C2
Nikolince 134 B1
Nikol'skoe 75 D1
Nikopol 140 B2
Nikopolis 146 A1
Nikópolis 144 A1
Nikopolis 146 A1
Nikšić 137 C/D1
Nilakkavuoma 10 A3
Nilivaara 17 B/C1
Nilivaara 11 D3, 12 A2
Nilsebu 42 B2
Nilsiä 23 B/C2
Nîmes 111 C2
Nímis 126 A2
Nin 130 B2
Nine 158 A1
Ninfa 118 B2
Ninove 78 B2
Niort 100 B2
Nipen 9 C2
Nipivatn 5 C2
Niš 135 C3
Niš 140 A3
Nisa 165 C1
Nisákion 142 A3
Niscemi 125 C3
Niška Banja 135 C3
Niskalehto 19 C1
Niskankorpi 21 C1
Niskanpää 17 D2
Niskanperä 12 A/B3
Niska-Pietilä 27 C/D1/2
Nisko 97 C1/2, 98 A2
Niskos 20 B3
Nissan-lez-Enserune 110 B3, 156 B1
Nissedal 43 C2
Nissinvaara 19 D1
Niton 76 B2
Nitra 95 C2
Nitra 96 B2/3
Nitrianske Pravno 95 D1/2
Nitrianske Rudno 95 D2
Nitry 88 A3
Nittedal 38 A3
Nittel 79 D3
Nittenau 92 B1
Nittendorf-Etterzhausen 92 B1
Nittkvarn 39 D3
Nittsjö 39 D2
Nittylahti 22 B2
Niukkala 27 D1
Nivå 49 D3, 50 A3
Niva 19 D3
Niva 18 B2
Nivala 21 C/D1
Nivala 12 B2
Nivankylä 12 A/B3
Nivelles 78 B2
Nivnice 95 C1
Niwica 83 D1
Niwiska 71 C3
Nizy-le-Comte 78 B3
Nizza Monferrato 113 C1
Njakaure 16 B2
Njallejaur 16 A/B3
Njavve 15 D1, 16 A1
Njeguševo 129 C/D3
Njetsavare 16 B1
Njivice 126 B3, 130 B1
Njunjes 16 A1
Njunjesstugan 15 D1
Njurundabommen 35 D3
Njutånger 40 A/B1
Noailles 77 D3, 87 C/D1
Noailles 101 D3, 109 D1
Noáin 154 A2
Noasco 104 B3
Nöbbele 51 C2
Noblejas 161 C3
Nocé 86 B2
Noceda 151 C/D2
Nocera Inferiore 119 D3
Nocera Tirinese 122 A2
Nocera Umbra 115 D3, 117 C2
Noceto 114 A1
Nochten 83 D1
Noci 121 C2
Nocíglia 121 D3
Nocina 153 C1
Nocito 154 B2
Nódalo 153 D3, 161 C/D1
Nodeland 43 C3
Nödinge 45 C3
Nods 104 A/B1
Noépoli 120 B3, 122 B1
Noeux-les Mines 78 A2
Noevci 139 D1
Noez 160 B3, 167 C1
Nofuentes 153 C2
Nogales 165 D2
Nogara 107 B/C3
Nogaro 108 B2
Nogent-en-Bassigny 89 C2
Nogent-l'Artaud 88 A1
Nogent-le-Roi 87 C2
Nogent-le-Rotrou 86 B2
Nogent sur Oise 87 D1
Nogent-sur-Seine 88 A2
Nogent-sur-Vernisson 87 D3
Nógrád 95 D3
Nograles 161 C1
Nogueira de Ramuin 150 B2
Noguera 162 A2
Nogueras 162 A/B1/2
Nogueruelas 162 B3
Nohant 102 A1
Nohfelden 80 A3
Noia 150 A2
Noidans-le-Ferroux 89 C3
Noirétable 103 C2/3
Noirmont, Le 89 D3, 104 B1
Noirmoutier-en-l'Ile 100 A1
Noja 153 C1
Nojamaa 27 C1
Nojewo 71 D2
Nokia 25 B/C1
Nokka 25 D1, 26 B1
Nol 45 C3
Nola 119 D3
Nolay 153 D3, 161 D1
Nolay 103 C/D1
Noli 113 C2
Nolmyra 40 B3
Nolvik 15 C3
Nombela 160 B3
Nomécourt 88 B2
Noméný 89 C1
Noméxy 89 D2
Nomparedes 153 D3, 161 D1
Nompatelize 89 D2, 90 A2
Nonancourt 86 A/B1
Nonant-le-Pin 86 B1/2
Nonántola 114 B1
Nonaspe 163 C1
None 112 B1
Nonnenhorn 91 C3
Nonnweiler 80 A3
Nonnweiler-Primstal 80 A3, 90 A1
Nontron 101 C/D3
Nonza 113 D2
Noordbergum 67 B/C1
Noordeinde 66 B2
Noordwijk 66 A3
Noordwijkerhout 66 A3
Noordwolde 67 C2
Noormarkku (Norrmark) 24 A1
Nopala 26 B2
Nopankylä 20 B2/3
Noposenaho 21 C2
Noppo 25 C2
Nor 40 A1
Nor 35 C2
Nor 38 B2/3
Nora 30 B3, 35 D2
Nora 46 A1
Nora 123 D3
Nørager 48 B2
Norainkylä 20 B3
Norberg 40 A3
Nórchia 116 B3, 118 A1
Nórcia 117 D3
Nordagutu 43 D2, 44 A1
Nordana 35 D2
Nordanå 35 D3
Nordanåker 30 A3, 35 C1/2
Nordanås 15 C3
Nordanås 30 B2
Nordanholen 39 D2
Nordankäl 30 A2, 35 C1
Nordansjö 30 A1
Nordansjö 30 A1
Nordausques 77 D1
Nordberg 32 B3, 37 C1
Nordborg 52 B2
Nordbotn 32 B1
Nordby 38 A/B1
Nordby 48 A3, 52 A1
Nordby 49 C3
Nordby Bruk 38 A3
Nördbyn 16 B3
Norddal 32 A3, 36 B1
Norddal 36 A2
Norddyrøy 32 B1
Nordeide 36 A/B2
Norden 16 A/B2
Norden 67 C/D1
Nordendorf 91 D2
Nordenham 68 A1
Nordenham-Esenshamm 68 A1
Norden-Norddeich 67 C1
Norderåsen 29 D3, 34 B1
Norderhov 38 A3, 43 D1
Norderney 67 C1
Norderö 29 D3, 34 B2
Norderstapel 52 B2/3
Norderstedt 52 B3, 68 B1
Nordfjordbotn 4 A3, 9 D1, 10 A1
Nordfjordeid 36 A/B1
Nordfold 9 B/C3
Nord-Frøya 32 B1
Nordgard 33 D3
Nordhalben 82 A2
Nordhallen 29 C3, 34 A1
Nordhallen 29 C3, 34 A1
Nordhastedt 52 B3
Nordhausen 81 D1
Nordheim 32 B2
Nordheim vor der Rhön 81 D2
Nordholz 52 A3, 68 A1
Nordholz-Spieka 52 A3, 68 A1
Nordhorn 67 C2
Nordhorn-Brandlecht 67 C2
Nordhus 5 C2
Nordingrå 30 B3
Nordkisa 38 A3
Nordkjosbotn 4 A3, 10 A1
Nordkrekling 28 B1
Nordland 8 A3
Nordlandskorsen 28 B1
Nord-Lenangen 4 B2
Nordli 14 B3
Nördlingen 91 D1/2
Nordlysobservatoriet 4 A3
Nordmaling 31 C2/3
Nordmannset 5 D1, 6 A1
Nordmannset 5 D1, 6 B1
Nordmannvik 6 B1
Nordmark 39 C3
Nordmela 9 C1
Nordnesøy 14 A1/2
Nord-Odal 38 A/B2
Nordomsjön 39 C1
Nordre Osen 38 B1
Nordsand 9 C1
Nord-Sel 33 C3, 37 D1
Nordseter 38 A1
Nordsinni 37 D3
Nordsjö 40 A1
Nordsjö 40 A1
Nordsjö 30 A2, 35 C1
Nordsjona 14 B2
Nordskaget 32 B1
Nordskot 8 B3
Nord-Statland 28 B2
Nordstemmen 68 B3
Nörd-Stensvattnet 30 A2, 35 C1
Nordstrand-Süden 52 A2
Nordstrand-Süderhafen 52 A2
Nordvågen 5 D1, 6 B1
Nordværnes 14 B1
Nordvik 24 B3
Nordvik 14 A2
Nordvik 32 B1
Nordvika 32 B1
Nordwalde 67 D3
Nore 43 C1
Norg 67 C2
Norges-la-Ville 88 B3
Norham 57 D2
Norheimsund 36 A/B3
Nørholm 43 C3
Norinkylä 20 B3
Norma 118 B2
Nornäs 39 C1
Noroy-le-Bourg 89 C/D3
Norppa 21 C1
Norra Bergnäs 15 D2
Norra Drängsmark 31 D1
Norra Finnskoga 38 B2
Norra Fjällnäs 15 C3
Norra Flymen 51 C2
Norra Hede 34 A3
Norra Holmnäs 16 A3
Norråker 29 D2, 30 A1
Norra Klagshamn 50 A3
Norra Kölviken 45 C1
Norrala 40 A/B1
Norra Möckleby 51 D2
Norra Nordsjö 31 C2
Norra Ny 39 C2
Norra polcirkeln 17 C2
Norra Rörum 50 B2/3
Norra Sandsjö 46 A3, 51 C1
Norra Sunderbyn 17 C3
Norra Tannflo 30 A/B3, 35 D1/2

Norra Tresund 30 A1
Norra Umstrand 15 D3
Norra Unnaryd 45 D3
Norra Vallgrund 20 A2, 31 D3
Norra Vånga 45 D2/3
Norrbäck 30 B1
Norrbacka 16 A3
Norrboda 40 B2
Norrboda 39 D1/2
Norrboda 41 D3
Norrby 30 B1
Norrby 31 C1
Norrbyn 39 D1
Norrbyn 31 B/C3
Norrbyn 31 C2/3
Nørre Åby 52 B1
Nørre Alslev 53 D2
Nørre Arup 48 A/B1/2
Nørre Broby 53 B/C1
Nørre Knudstrup 48 B2
Nørre Nebel 48 A3, 52 A1
Nørre Snede 48 B3
Nørresundby 48 B1
Nørre Vorupør 48 A2
Norrfjärden 16 B3
Norrfjärden 20 A1, 31 D2
Norrfjärden 35 D3
Norrfors 31 C2
Norrfors 30 B2
Norrgård 31 C1
Norrhult-Klavreström 51 C1
Norrhult-Klavreström 72 A/B1
Norriån 17 C2
Norrköping 46 B2
Norrmark 24 A1
Norrmesunda 30 B3, 35 D1
Norrmjöle 31 C2
Norrnäs 20 A3
Norrow Water Castle 58 A1
Norrsjö 29 D2
Norrskedika 40 B2/3
Norrsunda 40 B3, 47 C1
Norrsundet 40 A/B2
Norrtälje 41 C3
Norrvik 30 B1
Nors 48 A1/2
Norsholm 46 B2
Norsjö 31 C1
Norsjövallen 31 C1
Norsminde 49 B/C3
Nørstedalsseter 37 C2
Nörten-Hardenberg 81 C/D1
Northallerton 61 C1/2
Northam 62 B2
Northampton 64 B2
North Berwick 57 C1
Northeim 68 B3, 81 C/D1
Northeim-Hohnstedt 68 B3
Northeim-Sudheim 68 B3, 81 C/D1
Northleach 63 D1, 64 A2/3
North Newbald 61 D2
North Petherton 63 C/D2
North Somercotes 61 D3
North Sunderland 57 D2
North Tawton 63 C2
North Tidworth 64 A3, 76 A1
North Walsham 61 D3, 65 C1
Northwich 59 D2, 60 B3, 64 A1
Northwold 65 C2
Nortorf 52 B3
Nortrup 67 D2
Nort-sur-Erde 85 D3
Norvalahti 12 A/B3
Norvasalmi 12 B3
Nörvenich 79 D2, 80 A2
Norwich 65 C1/2
Nos 32 A3, 36 B1
Nøsen 37 C/D3
Nøsenseter 37 C3
Nosovka 99 D2
Nøss 9 C1
Nossa Senhora da Esperança 165 C2
Nossa Senhora do Cabo 164 A3
Nossa Senhora d'Ajuda 165 C2
Nossebro 45 C3
Nössemark 45 C1
Nossen 83 C1
Nossentiner Hütte 69 D1
Nösund 44 B3
Noszlop 128 A1
Notaresco 117 D3, 119 C1
Nötbolandet 31 C3
Notmarkskov 52 B2
Nötö 24 A3
Noto 125 D3
Noto Antica 125 D3
Notodden 43 D1, 44 A1
Notre Dame 112 B2
Notre-Dame de la Salette 111 D1, 112 A1
Notre-Dame-de-Monts 100 A1
Notre-Dame-d'Aspres 86 B1/2
Notre-Dame-du Mai 111 D3, 112 A3
Notre-Dame-de-Sanilhac 101 D3, 109 C1
Notre-Dame des Fontaines 113 B/C2
Nøtterøy 43 D2, 44 B1
Nottingham 61 D3, 65 C1
Nottuln 67 D3
Nottuln-Appelhülsen 67 D3
Nottuln-Darup 67 D3
Nouan-le-Fuzelier 87 C3
Nouans-les-Fontaines 101 C1
Nougaroulet 109 C2
Nousiainen 24 B2
Nousu 13 C2
Nouvion-en-Ponthieu 77 D2
Nova 127 D1/2, 128 A2
Nová Baňa 95 D2
Nova Breznica 138 B2
Nova Bukovica 128 B3
Nová Bystřice 93 D1, 94 A1
Novaci 133 D2, 134 A2
Novaci 143 C1
Novaci 140 B2
Nova Crnja 129 D3
Nová Dubnica 95 C1
Novaféltria 115 C2, 117 C1
Nova Gorica 126 B2
Nova Gradiška 128 A3, 131 D1, 132 A1
Nová Hospoda 93 C1
Novaja Praga 99 D3
Novaja Ušica 98 B3
Nova Kasaba 133 C2
Nováky 95 D2
Novales 154 B3
Nova Levante/Welschnofen 107 C2
Novalja 130 B2
Nova Pazova 133 D1, 134 A1
Nová Pec 93 C2
Nova Ponente/Deutschnofen 107 C2
Novara 105 D3
Novara di Sicilia 125 D2
Nová Říše 94 A1
Nova Sela 132 A3, 136 B1
Nova Siri 120 B3
Nova Siri Stazione 121 B/C3
Novate Mezzola 105 D2, 106 A2
Nova Topola 131 D1, 132 A1
Nova Varoš 133 D3, 134 A3
Nova Vas 126 B3
Nova Zagora 141 C3
Nové Hrady 93 D2
Novelda 169 C3
Novellara 114 B1
Nové Mesto nad Váhom 95 C2
Nové Město pod Smrkem 83 D2
Nové Mesto nad Váhom 96 B2
Nové Mitrovice 83 C3, 93 C1
Noventa di Piave 107 D3
Noventa Vicentina 107 C3
Novés 160 B3
Nové Sady 95 C2
Nové Strašecí 83 C3
Nové Zámky 95 C3
Nové Zámky 96 B3
Novgorod 75 C1
Novgorodka 99 D3
Novgorodka 74 B2
Novgorod-Severskij 99 D1
Novi-Bečej 129 D3
Novi di Módena 114 B1
Novi-Dojran 139 D3, 143 D1, 144 A1
Noviercas 153 D3, 161 D1
Novigrad 126 A/B3, 130 A1
Novigrad 131 B/C2
Novigrad Podravski 128 A2
Novi Iskâr 139 D1
Novij Bug 99 D3
Novi Karlovci 133 D1, 134 A1
Novi Kneževac 129 D2
Novi Lígure 113 D1
Novillas 155 C3
Novi Marof 127 D2
Novi Marof 96 A/B3
Novion-Porcien 78 B3
Novi Pazar 133 D3, 138 A1
Novi Pazar 140 A3
Novi Pazar 141 C3
Novi Sad 140 A2
Novi Sad 129 D3, 133 D1, 134 A1
Novi Šeher 132 B2
Novi Slankamen 133 D1, 134 A1
Novi Vinodolski 130 B1
Novoarhangel'sk 99 D3
Novo Brdo 138 B1
Novograd-Volynskij 99 B/C2
Novogrudok 98 B1
Novo Korito 135 C3
Nóvoli 114 B2, 116 B1
Novo Mesto 127 C3
Novo Miloševo 129 D3
Novomirgorod 99 D3
Novopetrovskoe 75 D2
Novopolock 74 B3
Novoržev 74 B2
Novoselë 142 A2
Novoselica 98 B3
Novo Selo 135 D2
Novo Selo 139 D3
Novosokol'niki 74 B2
Novoukrainka 99 D3
Novovolynsk 97 D1, 98 A2
Novozavidovskij 75 D2
Novo Zvečevo 128 A3
Novozybkov 99 D1
Novska 128 A3, 131 D1
Nový Bor 83 D2
Nový Hrozenkov 95 C1
Nový Jičín 96 B2
Nový Knín 83 D3
Nový Přerov 94 B2
Novy Rychnov 94 A1
Nowa Dęba 97 C1/2, 98 A2
Nowa Sól (Neusalz) 72 B3, 96 A1
Nowa Sól (Neusalz) 71 C3
Nowe 73 B/C3
Nowe Bielawy 71 C3
Nowe Biskupice 70 B3
Nowe Miasteczko 71 C3
Nowe Warpno 70 B1
Nowe Worowo 71 C1
Nowiny Wielkie 71 C2
Nowogard 71 C1
Nowogard 72 A2/3
Nowogród Bobrżanski 71 C3
Nowy Dwór Gdański 73 C2
Nowy Dwór Mazowiecki 73 C3
Nowy Sącz 97 C2
Nowy Tomyśl 71 C/D3
Noyal 85 C2
Noyalo 85 C3
Noyant 86 B3
Noyant-de-Touraine 101 C1
Noyant-la-Plaine 86 A3, 101 B/C1
Noyelles-sur-Mer 77 D2
Noyen-sur-Sarthe 86 A2/3
Noyers 88 A3
Noyers-sur-Cher 86 A/B3, 101 C1
Noyers-sur-Jabron 111 D2, 112 A2
Noyon 78 A3
Nozay 85 D3
Nozeroy 104 A1
Nuaillé 100 B1
Nuasjärvi 12 A3, 17 D1
Nuasniemi 12 A3, 17 D1
Nueil-sur-Argent 100 B1
Nuenen 79 C1
Nueno 154 B2
Nuestra Señora de Cura 157 C2
Nuestra Señora de la Peña de Fra 159 D2
Nueva 153 C1
Nueva 152 A1
Nueva Carteya 172 B1
Nuévalos 162 A1
Nuevo Baztán 161 C2/3
Nughedu Santa Vittória 123 C/D2
Nuijamaa 27 C2
Nuits 88 B3
Nuits-Saint-Georges 103 D1
Nukari 25 C/D2, 26 A2
Nules 163 B/C3, 169 D1
Nulles 163 C1
Nulvi 123 C1
Numana 117 D2, 130 A3
Numancia 153 D3, 161 D1
Numansdorp 66 A3
Nümbrecht 80 A2
Nummela 25 C3
Nummenkylä 25 C2
Nummenpää 25 C2/3
Nummi 25 C3
Nummi 24 A/B2
Nummijärvi 20 B3
Nummikoski 20 B3
Numminen 25 D2, 26 A2
Nummi-Pusula 25 C2/3
Nünchritz 83 C1
Nuneaton 64 A2
Nunnanen 11 D2, 12 A1
Nunnanlahti 23 C2
Nunnington 61 C2
Nuño Gómez 160 A/B3
Nuñomoral 159 C/D2/3
Nunsdorf 70 A3
Nunspeet 66 B2
Nuojua 18 B3
Nuoksujärvi 17 C1
Nuoramoinen 25 D1, 26 A1
Nuorgam (Njuorggam) 6 B2
Nuoritta 18 B2
Núoro 123 D2
Nuorpiniemi 6 B2
Nuortikon 16 B1
Nuorunka 19 C1
Nuottionranta 17 D2
Nuraghe Seruci 123 C3
Nuraghe su Nuraxi 123 C/D3
Nurágus 123 D2/3
Nurallao 123 D2
Nuráminis 123 D3
Núria 156 A2
Nurmaa 26 B1
Nurmes 23 C1
Nurmesklyä 23 C1
Nurmesperä 21 D1, 22 A1
Nurmijärvi 23 D1/2
Nurmijärvi 25 C2/3, 26 A2/3
Nurmo 20 B2
Nürnberg 82 A3, 91 D1, 92 A1
Nürnberg-Fischbach 92 A1
Nürnberg-Katzwang 91 D1, 92 A1
Nurri 123 D2/3
Nürtingen 91 C2
Nus 105 C3
Nusco 119 D3, 120 A2
Nusfjord 8 A/B2/3
Nusnäs 39 D2
Nusplingen 91 B/C2
Nussdorf am Inn 92 B3
Nuštar 129 C3, 133 C1
Nüsttal-Morles 81 C2
Nutheim 43 C1
Nuttuperä 21 D1, 22 A1
Nuuatila 18 B3
Nuuksujärvi 11 B/C3
Nuupas 18 B1
Nuutajärvi 25 B/C2
Nuutilanmäki 27 B/C1
Nuvsvåg 5 C2
Nuvvus 6 B2
Nvutånger 40 A/B1
Nya Bastuselet 16 A3
Nyadal 35 D2
Nyåker 31 C2
Nyåkern 34 B3
Nyåkerstjärn 31 C2
Nyalka 95 C3
Nyárlőrinc 129 D1
Nybäck 31 D1
Nybble 45 D1, 46 A1
Nybergsund 38 B1
Nyborg 53 C1
Nybro 51 D2
Nybro 72 B1
Nyby 29 D3, 35 B/C2
Nyby 30 B1/2
Nyby 20 A2
Nyby 53 D2
Nybyn 30 B3, 35 D2
Nybyn 17 C2
Nydala 50 B1
Nye 51 C1
Nyergesújfalu 95 D3
Nygård 38 A2
Nygård 9 D1
Nygard 38 A1
Nygården 14 B3
Nyhammar 39 D3
Nyhamnsläge 49 D2, 50 A2
Ny Hellesund 43 C3
Nyhem 30 A3, 35 C2
Ny Hesselager 53 C1/2
Nyhyttan 39 D3, 46 A1
Nyírabrány 97 C/D3, 98 A3, 140 A/B1
Nyirád 128 A1
Nyírbátor 97 C/D3, 98 A3
Nyíregyháza 97 C3
Nykälä 22 B3
Nykarleby (Uusikaarlepyy) 20 B1
Nyker 51 D3
Nykirke 37 D3, 38 A2
Nykirke 43 D2, 44 B1
Nykøbing 53 D2
Nykøbing 48 A2
Nykøbing 49 D3
Nyköping 47 C2
Nykrogen 40 A3
Nykroppa 39 C3, 45 D1, 46 A1
Nyksund 8 B1
Nykvåg 8 B2
Nykvarn 47 C1
Nyland 30 B3, 35 D2
Nyland 31 C3
Nyland 31 C2
Nyland 30 B3, 35 D2
Nyliden 31 C2
Nymburk 83 D2/3
Nymindegab 48 A3, 52 A1
Nymo 4 B2
Nymoen 38 B1
Nymoen 14 B2
Nynäshamn 47 C2
Nyon 104 A2
Nyons 111 D2
Nyord 53 D2
Nýřany 83 C3
Nyrolä 21 D3, 22 A3
Nýrsko 93 C1
Nyrud 7 C3
Nysa (Neisse) 96 B1/2
Nysäter 45 C1
Nysätern 34 A2/3
Nyseter 37 D2
Nyseter 32 B3, 37 C1
Nyseter 33 C2/3
Nyseter 38 B1
Nyskoga 38 B2
Nyskolla 38 A1
Nyslott 27 C1
Nysø 53 D2
Nystad 24 A2, 41 D2
Nysted 53 D2
Nystrand 16 B3
Nysund 45 D1, 46 A1
Nytjärn 30 B2, 35 D1
Nytorp 17 C1
Nyträsk 31 D1
Nyúl 95 C3
Nyvik 30 A3, 35 C2

Nyvik 29 C1
Nyvoll 5 C2

O

Oakengates 59 D3, 64 A1
Oakham 64 B1/2
Oanes 42 A2
Obalj 132 B3
Oban 56 A1
Oban 54 A2, 55 D1
Obanos 154 A2
O Barco 151 C2
Obbola 20 A1, 31 D2
Obdach 127 C1
Obejo 166 B3
Oberammergau 92 A3
Oberasbach 82 A3, 91 D1, 92 A1
Oberau 92 A3
Oberaula 81 C2
Oberaurach-Kirchaich 81 D3
Oberaurach-Unterschleichach 81 D3
Oberbergkirchen 92 B2
Oberbodnitz 82 A2
Ober-Cunnersdorf 83 D1/2
Oberdachstetten 91 D1
Oberderdingen-Flehingen 90 B1
Oberdrauburg 107 D1, 126 A1
Oberelsbach 81 D2
Oberfeistritz 127 C/D1
Obergrafendorf 94 A2
Obergünzburg 91 D3
Obergurgl 107 B/C1
Oberhaching 92 A3
Oberharmersbach 90 B2
Oberhausen 80 A1
Oberhof 81 D2
Oberhofen am Thunersee 105 C1/2
Oberiberg [Schwyz] 105 D1
Oberkappel 93 C2
Oberkirch 90 B2
Oberkochen 91 D2
Oberkotzau 82 A/B2
Oberlahnstein 80 A/B2
Oberland 81 C2
Oberlungwitz 82 B2
Obermassfeld-Grimmenthal 81 D2
Obermehler 81 D1
Obermodern 90 A1/2
Obernai 90 A2
Obernberg am Brenner 107 C1
Obernberg am Inn 93 C2
Obernburg 81 C3
Oberndorf 90 B2
Oberndorf 52 A/B3, 68 A1
Oberndorf am Lech 91 D2
Oberndorf an der Melk 94 A2/3
Oberndorf bei Salzburg 92 B3
Obernkirchen 68 A3
Obernzenn 81 D3, 91 D1
Oberoderwitz 83 D1/2
Oberort 93 D3
Oberpframmern 92 A3
Oberpöring 92 B2
Ober-Ramstadt 81 B/C3
Oberreute 91 C/D3
Oberriet 106 A1
Oberröblingen 82 A1
Oberrot 91 C1
Oberschweinbach 92 A2
Obersinn 81 C2/3
Oberstaufen 91 C/D3
Oberstdorf 91 D3
Oberstenfeld 91 C1
Obersulm 91 C1
Obersüssbach-Obermünchen 92 A/B2
Obertilliach 107 D1/2, 126 A1/2
Obertrubach 82 A3
Obertrum am See 93 C3
Oberursel 80 B2/3
Obervellach 126 A1
Oberviechtach 82 B3, 92 B1
Oberwart 127 D1
Oberwart 96 A/B3
Oberweiler (Bitburg) 79 D3
Oberweissbach 82 A2
Oberwesel 80 B3
Oberweser-Gieselwerder 81 C1
Oberweser-Oedelsheim 81 C1
Oberwiesenthal 82 B2
Oberwölz 126 B1
Obidos 164 A1
Obilić 138 B1
Obing 92 B3
Obing-Frabertsham 92 B3
Objaljai 74 A2
Objat 101 D3
Obladis 106 B1
Obljaj 127 D3, 131 C1
Obninsk 75 D3
Obod 137 D2
Obodovka 99 C3
O Bolo 151 C2
Obón 162 B2
Oborniki 71 D2
Oborniki 72 B3
Obornjača 129 D3
Oborovo 127 D3
Obory 83 C/D3
Obra 71 C3
Obrenovac 133 D1/2, 134 A2
Obrenovac 140 A2
Obrež 133 D1, 134 A1
Obrigheim 91 C1
Obrov 126 B3
Obrovac 131 C2
Obrovac 131 D3
Obrovac 129 C3, 133 C1
Obršani 138 B3, 143 C1
Obrtići 133 C2/3
Obryta 71 B/C1/2
Obrzycko 71 D2
Obsteig 106 B1
Obudovac 132 B1
Obuhov 99 C/D2
Ocaña 161 C3, 167 D1
Ocana 113 D3
Occhiobello 115 C1
Occimiano 113 C1
Očevlja 132 B2
Ochagavía 108 A3, 154 B2
Ochandiano 153 D1/2
Ochiltree 56 B2
Ochla 71 C3
Ochsenfurt 81 D3
Ochsenfurt-Hopferstadt 81 D3
Ochsenhausen 91 C2/3
Ochtendung 80 A2
Ochtrup 67 C/D3
Očihov 83 C2/3
Ockelbo 40 A2
Öckerö 44 B3
Ockholm 52 A2
Ocrkavlje 132 B3
Ócsa 95 D3, 129 C1
Öcsény 129 C2
Öcsöd 129 D1
Octeville 76 A3
Octeville-sur-Mer 76 B3
Öd 34 B2
Ödåkra 49 D3, 50 A2
Odda 42 B1
Odden 4 B3
Odder 48 B3
Oddesund 48 A2
Ödeborg 45 C2
Odeceixe 170 A1
Odeleite 170 B2
Odelzhausen 92 A2
Odemira 170 A1
Ödemiș 149 D2
Odén 155 D2/3
Òdena 155 D3, 156 A3, 163 D1
Odensbacken 46 B1
Odensberg 45 D3
Odense 53 C1
Odensjö 50 B1/2
Oderberg 70 B2
Odernheim 80 A/B3
Oderzo 107 D3
Ödeshög 46 A2
Odessa 141 D1
Odestugu 45 D3, 46 A3
Odiáxere 170 A2
Odiham 64 B3, 76 A/B1
Ødis 52 B1
Odivelas 164 A2
Odivelas 164 B3
Odkarby 41 C/D2/3
Ödkarby 41 C/D2/3
Odlandstø 42 A3
Odoev 75 D3
Odón 162 A2
Odoorn 67 C2
Odorheiu Secuiesc 141 C1
Odra 127 D3
Ødsted 48 B3, 52 B1
Odžaci 129 C3
Odžak 133 C3, 137 D1
Odžak 132 B1
Oebisfelde 69 C2
Oechsen 81 D2
Oed 93 D2
Oederan 83 C2
Oeffelt 67 B/C3
Oegstgeest 66 A3
Oeiras 164 A2
Oelde 67 D3
Oelde-Stromberg 67 D3, 68 A3
Oelsig 70 A3, 83 C1
Oelsnitz 82 B2
Oelsnitz 82 B2
Oelze 81 D2, 82 A2
Oelzschau 82 B1
Oensingen 105 C1
Oer-Erkenschwick 67 D3, 80 A1
Oettingen 91 D1
Oetzen-Stöcken 69 C2
Ofärne 40 A1
Ofena 117 D3, 119 C1
Offenbach 90 B1
Offenbach am Main 81 B/C3
Offenbach-Hundheim 80 A3
Offenberg 92 B1/2
Offenburg 90 B2
Offenhausen 82 A3, 92 A1
Offenseealm 93 C3
Offerberg 40 A1
Offerdal 29 C/D3, 34 B1
Offersøy 9 C2
Offida 117 D2/3
Offingen 91 D2
Ofte 43 C1/2
Ofte 42 B3
Ofterschwang 91 D3
Oftringen [Aarburg-Oftringen] 105 C1
Ogardy 71 C2
Ogéviller 89 D2
Oggevatn 43 C3
Oggiono 105 D3, 106 A3
Ogliara 119 D3, 120 A2
Ogliastro Cilento 120 A3
Ogna 42 A3
Ognica 70 B2
Ogoja 139 D1
Ogorele 75 C1
Ogradena 135 C1/2
Ogre 73 D1, 74 A2
Ogrosen 70 B3
O Grove 150 A2
Ogulin 127 C3, 130 B1
Ohanes 173 D2
Ohensaari 24 A/B2
Ohey 79 C2
Ohkola 25 D2, 26 A2
Ohlstadt 92 A3
Öhn 29 D2, 30 A2, 35 C1
Ohrdruf 81 D2
Ohrid 138 B3, 142 B1
Öhringen 91 C1
Ohtaanniemi 23 C2
Ohtanajärvi 17 C1
Ohtinen 25 C2
Ohtola 21 C3
Oia 150 A3
Oiã 158 A2
Oiartzun 153 D1, 154 A1
Oijärvi 18 B1
Oijusluoma 19 D1
Oikarainen 12 B3
Oikemus 21 C1
Oímbra 150 B3
Oinaala 25 C2
Oinas 12 B3
Oinasjärvi 25 C2
Oinasjärvi 22 B1
Oinaskylä 21 D2, 22 A2
O Incio 151 C2
Oiniadai 146 A2
Oinoskylä 21 C/D2
Oion 153 D2
Oiron 101 C1
Oirschot 79 C1
Oiselay-et-Grachaux 89 C3
Oisemont 85 C1/2
Oitti 25 C/D2, 26 A2
Oittila 21 D3
Oix 156 B2
Öja 20 B1
Öja 47 D3
Ojakkala 25 C3
Ojakylä 21 D1, 22 A1
Ojakylä 21 D1, 22 A1
Ojakylä 18 A/B3
Ojakylä 18 A2
Ojakylä 18 A3, 21 C1
Ojakylä 18 B3
Ojala 21 B/C2
Ojanpera 18 B3
Ojanperä 21 D1, 22 A1
Öjarn 29 D2, 35 B/C1
Öje 39 C2
Öjebyn 16 B3
Ojén 172 A3
Ojós 169 D3
Ojos Negros 162 A2
Öjung 39 D1
Ojurås 39 D2
Okehampton 63 C2/3
Okkelberg 28 B3, 33 D1
Okkenhaug 28 B3, 33 D1
Oklaj 131 C2/3
Öknö 51 D1
Okol 137 D2, 138 A2
Okoli 127 D3
Okonek 71 D1
Okruglica 139 C1
Oksajärvi 11 B/C3
Oksakoski 21 C2
Oksava 21 D1, 22 A1
Oksbøl 48 A3, 52 A1
Oksby 48 A3, 52 A1
Økseidet 11 C1
Øksendalsøra 32 B2
Øksendrup 53 C1/2
Øksengard 15 C1
Øksfjord 5 C2
Øksna 38 A2
Øksnes 8 B1
Øksnes 28 B2
Øksneshamn 9 B/C2
Okstad 28 A/B3, 33 C/D2
Oksvoll 28 A3, 33 C1
Okt'abr'skij 99 C1
Okučani 128 A3, 131 D1, 132 A1
Okulovka 75 C1
Olalhas 164 B1
Olalla 163 C2
Olargues 110 A3
Olazagutía 153 D2
Olba 162 B3
Olbernhau 83 C2
Olbersdorf 83 D2
Olbersleben 82 A1
Ólbia 123 D1
Olby 102 B3
Olching 92 A2
Oldeboorn 66 B2
Oldebroek 66 B2
Oldeide 36 A1
Oldemarkt 67 B/C2
Olden 36 B1
Oldenburg 67 D1, 68 A1/2
Oldenburg 53 C3
Oldenswort 52 A2/3
Oldenzaal 67 C2/3
Olderbakken 4 B3, 10 A1
Olderdalen 4 B3
Olderfjord 5 D1/2, 6 A1
Oldernes 5 D2, 6 A1
Oldervik 4 A3, 9 D1, 10 A1
Oldervik 14 B2
Oldervik 4 A2/3
Oldham 59 D2, 60 B2/3
Oldisleben 82 A1
Oldsum 52 A2
Oleby 39 B/C3
Oledo 158 B3
Oléggio 105 D3
Oleiros 158 B3, 164 B1
Oleiros 150 A2
Oleiros 150 B1
Ølen 42 A1
Olesa de Montserrat 156 A3
Oleśnica (Oels) 96 B1
Oletta 113 D2
Olette 156 A2
Olevsk 99 B/C2
Olfen 67 D3, 80 A1
Ølgod 48 A3, 52 A1
Olhain 78 A2
Olhalvo 164 A2
Olhão 170 B2
Olhava 18 A2
Oliana 155 C3
Olías 172 B2
Olías del Rey 160 B3, 167 C1
Olib 130 B2
Oliena 123 D2
Oliete 162 B2
Olígirtos 143 D3
Olimbiás 143 C2
Olimpiás 144 B2
Olimpiás 143 C2
Olingen 79 D3
Olingskog 39 C1
Oliola 155 C3
Olite 154 A2
Olius 155 D3, 156 A2
Oliva 169 D2
Oliva de la Frontera 165 C3
Oliva de Mérida 165 D2, 166 A2
Oliva de Plasencia 159 D3
Olivadi 122 B2
Olival 158 A3, 164 B1
Olivarella 125 D1/2
Olivares 171 D1
Olivares de Duero 152 B3, 160 B1
Olivares de Júcar 161 D3, 168 B1
Oliveira de Frades 158 A/B2
Oliveira de Azeméis 158 A2
Oliveira do Bairro 158 A2
Oliveira do Hospital 158 B3
Olivella 156 A3
Olivenza 165 C2
Olivèse 113 D3
Olivet 87 C2/3
Olivone [Biasca] 105 D2
Olkamangi 17 D1
Olkkajärvi 12 B3
Olkusz 97 C2
Olla de Altea 169 D1
Ollebacken 29 D3, 34 B1
Ollería 169 C/D2
Ollerton 61 C3, 64 B1
Olli 21 C2
Olliergues 103 C3
Ollikkala 26 B1
Ollila 25 B/C2
Ollila 13 C3
Ollilanniemi 19 C/D3
Öllölä 23 D3
Ollsta 29 D3, 35 B/C1
Ollsta 29 D3, 35 B/C1/2
Ölme 45 D1, 46 A1
Olmeda de la Cuesta 161 D3
Olmeda del Rey 161 D3, 168 B1
Olmedilla de Alarcón 168 B1
Olmedilla de Eliz 161 D3
Olmedillo de Roa 152 B3, 160 B1
Olmedo 160 A/B1
Olmedo 123 C1/2
Olmi Cappella 113 D2
Olmillos de Sasamón 152 B2
Olmillos de Castro 151 D3, 159 D1
Olmo 115 C3, 116 B2
Olmo al Brembo 106 A2
Olmos de la Picaza 152 B2
Olney 64 B2
Olocau 162 B3, 169 D1
Olocáu del Rey 162 B2
Olofsbo 49 D2, 50 A1
Olofsfors 31 C2/3
Olofström 51 B/C2
Olofström 72 A1

Olombrada 160 B1
Olomouc 96 B2
Olonne-sur-Mer 100 A2
Olonzac 110 A3, 156 B1
Oloron-Sainte-Marie 108 B3, 154 B1
Olost 156 A2
Olot 156 B2
Olovo 132 B2
Olpe 80 B1/2
Olšany u Prostějova 94 B1
Olsäter 39 C3, 45 D1
Olsberg 80 B1
Olsberg-Bigge 80 B1
Olsborg 4 A3, 9 D1
Olsbrücken 80 A/B3, 90 A1
Olsene 78 A/B1/2
Olseröd 50 B3
Ölserud 45 C/D2
Olshammar 46 A2
Olší 94 B1
Olsker 51 D3
Olsrud 4 A3, 10 A1
Olst 67 C2/3
Olsvik 14 A3, 28 B1
Olsztyn (Allenstein) 73 C2/3
Oltedal 42 A2
Olten 90 B3, 105 C1
Oltenița 141 C2
Oltre Vara 114 A2
Oltyně 93 D1
Olula de Castro 173 D2
Olvasjärvi 18 B2
Ølve 42 A1
Olvega 153 D3, 154 A3, 161 D1
Olveiroa 150 A2
Olvenstedt 69 C3
Olvera 172 A2
Olvés 162 A1
Olympia 146 B3
Olynthos 144 A2
Olzai 123 D2
Omagh 54 A3, 55 D2
Ombersley 59 D3, 64 A2
Omeath 58 A1
Omegna 105 C2/3
Omellóns 155 D3, 163 D1
Omenamäki 23 C1
Omiš 131 D3
Omišalj 126 B3, 130 B1
Ommen 67 C2
Omoljica 133 D1, 134 B1
Omonville-la-Rogue 76 A3
Ömossa/Metsalä 20 A3
Omsjö 30 B2/3, 35 D1
Omurtag 141 C3
Ön 34 B3
Øn 36 A2
Oña 153 C2
Onano 116 B3, 118 A1
Onara 107 C3
Oñati 153 D1/2
Onchan 58 B1
Onda 162 B3, 169 D1
Ondara 169 D2
Ondarroa 153 D1
Ondřejov 83 D3
Ondres 108 A3, 154 A1
Onéglia 113 C2
Onesse-et-Laharie 108 A2
Ongstad 8 B2
Önhult 46 B3
Onil 169 C2
Onís 152 A1
Onkamaa 26 B2
Onkamo 23 D3
Onkamo 13 C3
Onkeroinen 25 D2, 26 A2
Onkijoki 24 B2
Onkiniemi 25 D1, 26 A/B1
Onnaing 78 B2
Önnesmark 31 D1
Önnestad 50 B2/3
Önningeby 41 C/D3
Onno 105 D2/3, 106 A2
Onøy 14 A2
Onsaker 37 D3, 38 A2/3
Onsevig 53 C2
Önskan 30 B3, 35 D1
Onslunda 50 B3
Onšovice 94 A1
Onstwedde 67 C2
Ontaneda 152 B1
Onteniente 169 C/D2
Ontiñena 155 C3, 163 C1
Ontojoki 19 C/D3, 23 C1
Onttola 23 C/D3
Ontur 169 B/C2
Önusberg 16 B3
Onzonilla 151 D2, 152 A2
Oombergen 78 B2
Ooperi 20 B2
Oostburg 78 B1
Oost-Cappel 78 A1/2
Oostduinkerke-Bad 78 A1
Oostende 78 A1
Oosterbeek 66 B3
Oosterend 66 B1
Oosterhesselen 67 C2
Oosterhout 66 A/B3, 79 C1
Oosterwolde 67 C2
Oosthuizen 66 B2
Oostkamp 78 A1
Oostmalle 79 C1
Oostvleteren 78 A1/2
Oostvoorne 66 A3
Oostwold 67 C1
Ootmarsum 67 C2
Opalenica 71 D3
Opaljenik 133 D3, 134 A3
Opatija 126 B3, 130 A1
Opatovac 129 C3, 133 C1
Opatovská Vez 95 D2
Opava 96 B2
Ope 29 D3, 34 B2
Openica 138 B3, 142 B1
Opi 119 C2
O Pino 150 B2
Oplenac 133 D2, 134 B2
Opočka 74 B2
Opole (Oppeln) 96 B1
Opoul-Périllos 156 B1
Opovo 133 D1, 134 A1
Oppach 83 D1
Oppbodarna 34 B3
Oppdal 33 C2/3
Oppeano 107 C3
Oppeby 46 B3
Oppeby (Nyköping) 47 C2
Oppegård 38 A2
Oppegård 38 A3, 44 B1
Oppeid 9 C2/3
Oppenau 90 B2
Oppenheim 80 B3
Opphaug 28 A3, 33 C1
Oppheim 36 B3
Opphus 38 A1
Óppido Lucano 120 B2
Óppido Mamertina 122 A3
Oppin 82 B1
Opponitz 93 D3
Oppsjö 30 B3, 35 D2
Oppstryn 32 A3, 36 B1
Oppurg 82 A2
Oprişor 135 D2
Oprtalj 126 B3, 130 A1
Opshaugvik 32 A3, 36 B1
Ópusztaszer 129 D2
Opuzen 136 B1
Ör 51 C1
ØR 44 B1/2
Öra 45 D3
Øra 4 B2
Ora/Auer 107 C2
Orada 165 C2
Orada 165 C3
Oradour-sur-Glane 101 D2
Oradour-sur-Vayres 101 D3
Orago 105 D3
Orahova 131 D1, 132 A1
Orahovac 138 A/B2
Orahovac 140 A3
Orahovica 128 B3
Oraison 111 D2, 112 A2
Orajärvi 12 A3, 17 D1
Orajärvi 12 B2
Orakylä 12 B2
Orange 111 C2
Orani 123 D2
Oranienbaum 69 D3
Oranienburg 70 A2
Oranienburg 72 A3
Orašac 139 C1
Orašac 137 B/C1
Orašac 133 D2, 134 A/B2
Orasi 137 D2
Orasi 113 D3
Orašje 133 B/C1
Orăştie 140 B1
Oratoire 112 A1
Orava 20 B2
Oravais/Oravainen 20 B2
Oravala 26 B2
Oravankylä 21 D1, 22 A1
Oravasaan 21 D3, 22 A3
Oravi 23 C3
Oravikoski 22 B3
Oravisalo 23 C3
Oravița 135 C1
Oravița 140 A2
Oravivaara 19 C3
Oravská Lesná 95 D1
Oravská Polhora 95 D1
Oravská Polhora 97 C2
Oravské Veselé 95 D1
Oravský Podzámok 95 D1
Orba 169 D2
Orbaiceta 108 B3, 155 C1/2
Ørbæk 53 C1
Orbaneja del Castillo 153 B/C2
Orbassano 112 B1
Orbe 104 B1/2
Orbec 86 B1
Örberga 46 A2
Orbetello 116 B3
Örby 49 D1, 50 A1
Orca 158 B3
Orcajo 162 A2
Orcau 155 D2/3
Orce 173 D1
Orcera 168 A3
Orchamps 103 D1, 104 A1
Orchamps-Vennes 104 B1
Orches 101 C1
Orcheta 169 D2
Orchies 78 A2
Orchomenós 147 C2
Orchomenos 147 B/C3
Orchomenos 147 C2
Orcières 112 A1
Orcines 102 B2/3
Orcival 102 B3
Ordes 150 A/B1/2
Ordino 155 D2, 156 A2
Ordizia 153 D1/2
Ordona 120 A1/2
Ore 42 B3
Öre 31 C2/3
Ore 39 D1/2
Orea 162 A2
Orebić 136 B1
Örebro 46 A1
Orebygård 53 C/D2
Oredež 74 B1
Öregcsertő 129 C2
Öreglak 128 A/B2
Öregrund 40 B2/3
Orehoved 53 D2
Oreí 147 C1
Orellana de la Sierra 166 A/B2
Orellana la Vieja 166 A/B2
Ören 149 D2/3
Oreovica 134 B2
Öreryd 50 B1
Orés 154 B2
Oreškovica 134 B2
Orestiás 145 D3
Öretjärndalen 30 A3, 35 C2
Orford 65 D2
Organya 155 C2
Orgaz 160 B3, 167 C1
Orgeev 141 D1
Orgelet-le Bourget 103 D2, 104 A2
Ørgenvika 37 D3
Orgères-en-Beauce 87 C2
Orgiano 107 C3
Orgon 111 C/D2
Orgósolo 123 D2
Orgovány 129 C1/2
Orhaneli 149 D1
Ória 121 D2/3
Oria 173 D1, 174 A1
Orient 157 C2
Origny-Sainte-Benoite 78 A/B3
Orihuela 169 C3, 174 B1
Orihuela del Tremedal 162 A2
Orikon 142 A2
Oriku 142 A2
Orimattila 25 D2, 26 A2
Oriniemi 24 B2
Oriniemi 23 C/D2
Orinnoro 22 B3
Orio 153 D1
Oriola 164 B3
Oriolo 120 B3, 122 B1
Oripää 24 B2
Oristano 123 C2
Őriszentpéter 127 D1
Oriveden asema 25 C1
Orivesi 25 C1
Orjães 158 B3
Orjahovo 140 B2
Orjasjärvi 17 D2
Ørjavik 32 A2
Ørje 45 B/C1
Orjiva 173 C2
Orkanger 28 A3, 33 C2
Örkelljunga 50 B2
Örkelljunga 72 A1
Orkelsjøhytta 33 C3
Örkény 129 C1
Örkény 97 C3, 140 A1
Orkland 28 A3, 33 C2
Orlamünde 82 A2
Ørland 28 A3, 33 C1
Orlate 138 B2
Orléans 87 C2/3
Orlec 130 A1
Orlík nad Vltavou 83 C/D3, 93 C/D1
Orljane 135 C3, 139 C1
Orljani 138 B1
Orlovat 129 D3, 133 D1, 134 A/B1
Orlu 156 A1
Órma 143 C1
Ormaiztegi 153 D1/2
Ormaryd 46 A3
Ormea 113 C2
Ormemyr 43 C/D1, 44 A1
Orménion 145 D2
Ormes 87 C2/3
Ormhult 50 B2
Ormília 144 A2
Órmos 143 D2, 144 A2
Órmos Panagiás 144 B2
Órmos Prínou 145 B/C1/2
Ormož 127 D2
Ormskirk 59 D2, 60 B2/3
Ornaisons 110 A3, 156 B1
Ornans 104 A1
Ornäs 39 D2
Ørnes 14 B1
Orneta 73 C2
Ørnhøj 48 A2/3
Ornö 47 D1
Örnsköldsvik 31 C3
Oroix 108 B3, 155 C1
Orolik 129 C3, 133 C1
Orom 129 D2/3
Orón 153 C2
Oron-la-Ville [Oron] 104 B2
Oropesa 160 A3, 166 B1
Oropesa de Mar 163 C3
Ororbia 154 A2
Orosei 123 D2
Orosháza 129 D2
Orosháza 97 C3, 140 A1
Oroso 150 A/B2
Oroszlány 95 C/D3
Oroszló 128 B2
Orotelli 123 D2
Oroz-Betelu 108 B3, 155 C2
Orozko 153 C1
Orphin 87 C2
Orpierre 111 D2
Orrefors 51 C1/2
Orrefors 72 B1
Orrestad 42 A3
Orrios 162 B2
Orroli 123 D2/3
Orrskog 40 B2
Orrviken 34 B2
Orsa 39 D1/2
Orša 74 B3
Orsago 107 D2/3
Orsara di Púglia 120 A1/2
Orsay 87 C/D1/2
Örsbäck 31 C2
Örsebo 46 B3
Orsennes 101 D2, 102 A2
Örserum 46 A3
Orsia 105 C3
Orsières 104 B2
Örsjö 51 C2
Ørslev 49 C3, 53 C1
Ørslevkloster 48 B2
Ørsnes 32 A2/3
Orsogna 119 C/D1
Orsoja 135 D3
Orsomarso 120 B3, 122 A1
Orșova 135 C1/2
Orșova 140 A/B2
Örspuszta 128 B1
Ørsta 36 B1
Ørsted 52 B1
Ørsted 49 B/C2
Örsundsbro 40 B3
Orta 105 C3
Ortaklar 149 D2
Orta Nova 120 A/B1/2
Orte 117 C3, 118 B1
Ortenberg-Selters 81 C2
Ortenburg-Iglbach 93 C2
Ortenburg-Wolfachau 93 C2
Orth an der Donau 94 B2
Orth an der Donau 96 B3
Orthez 108 A/B3, 154 B1
Orthovoúnion 143 C3
Ortigosa 153 D3
Ortigueira 150 B1
Ortilla 154 B2/3
Ortisei/Sankt Ulrich 107 C2
Orțișoara 140 A1
Ortnevik 36 B2
Orto 113 D3
Ortolano 117 D3, 119 C1
Örtomta 46 B2
Orton 57 C3, 60 B1
Ortona 119 D1
Ortona dei Marsi 119 C2
Ortrand 83 C1
Örträsk 31 C2
Ortsjö 35 D3
Ortueri 123 C/D2
Orubica 131 D1, 132 A1
Ørum 49 C2
Ørum 48 B2
Orune 123 D2
Orusco 161 C3
Ørvella 43 C1, 44 A1
Orvieto 117 C3, 118 A1
Orville 89 B/C3
Orvínio 118 B1
Orzinuovi 106 A3
Osa 36 B3
Osa de la Vega 161 C/D3, 168 A1
Osanica 135 C2
Osann-Monzel 80 A3
Os Anxeles 150 A2
Osara 24 B1
O Saviñao 150 B2
Osbruk 50 B1
Osburg 79 D3, 80 A3
Osby 50 B2
Osby 72 A1
Oščadnica 95 D1
Oschatz 83 B/C1
Oschatz 96 A1
Oschersleben 69 C3
Óschiri 123 D1
Osdalssetter 38 A/B1
Os de Balaguer 155 C3
Ose 42 B2
Øse 48 A3, 52 A1
Osečina 133 C2
Osečná 83 D2
Oseja 154 A3, 162 A1
Oseja de Sajambre 152 A1
Osek 83 C2
Osenovo 139 D2
Osera 154 B3, 162 B1
Oset 38 A1
Oset 37 C/D3
Osidda 123 D2
Osieczna 71 D3
Osiek nad Notecią 71 D2
Osíglia 113 C2
Osijek 129 B/C3
Osilnica 127 C3
Ósilo 123 C1
Ósimo 117 D2
Osinów Dolny 70 B2
Osipaonica 134 B2
Osipoviči 99 C1
Osječenica 137 C1
Oskar 51 C/D2
Oskarshamn 51 D1
Oskarshamn 72 B1
Oskarström 72 A1
Oskarström 50 A1/2

Oslany 95 D2
Oslättfors 40 A2
Oslavany 94 B1
Oslavička 94 A1
Osli 94 B3
Oslo 38 A3
Øsløs 48 A/B1/2
Osma 12 A/B2/3
Osma 153 C2
Osmakova 135 C3
Os Milagres do Medo 150 B3
Os'mino 74 B1
Ošmjany 74 A3
Ösmo 47 C1/2
Osnabrück 67 D3
Osnäs 24 A2, 41 D2
Ośno Lubuskie 70 B2
Osoppo 107 D2, 126 A2
Osor 130 A1/2
Osor 156 B2
Osorno 152 B2
Ospedaletti 113 B/C2/3
Ospitale di Cadore 107 D2
Ospitaletto 106 B3
Oss 66 B3
Ossa 144 A1
Ossa de Montiel 168 A2
Ossauskoski 18 A1
Össeby-Garn 40 B3, 47 D1
Ossès 108 B3, 155 C1
Ossi 123 C1/2
Ossiach 126 B2
Ossmannstedt 82 A1/2
Osso 155 C3, 163 C1
Ossun 108 B3, 155 C1
Östanå 50 B2
Östanbäck 31 D1
Östanberg 24 B3
Östanbjörke 39 C3
Östansjö 15 D2
Östansjö 39 C1
Östansjö 16 A2
Östansjö 46 A1
Östansjö 40 A/B1
Östanvik 39 D1
Oštarije 127 C3, 130 B1
Ostaškov 75 C2
Ostatija 133 D3, 134 A3
Östavall 35 C3
Ostbevern 67 D3
Østbirk 48 B3
Östbjörka 39 D2
Östby 30 B2, 35 D1
Østby 38 B1
Östbyn 35 C3
Östbyn 35 C2
Östbyn 31 D2
Osted 49 D3, 53 D1
Osteel 67 D1
Ostellato 115 C1
Ostelsheim 90 B2
Ostenfeld 52 B2
Ostenholz 68 B2
Østerbø 37 B/C3
Osterburg 69 D2
Osterburken 91 C1
Østerby 53 C2
Østerby 48 A3
Österby 49 C1
Österbybruk 40 B3
Österbymo 46 A3
Österbymo 72 B1
Ostercappeln 67 D2/3, 68 A2/3
Österdalsisen 14 B2
Österfärnebo 40 A2/3
Österforse 30 A/B3, 35 D2
Östergraninge 30 B3, 35 D2
Österhaninge 47 D1
Österhankmo 20 B2
Osterheide-Osternholz 68 B2
Osterhofen 93 B/C2
Osterhofen-Obergessenbach 92 B2
Osterholz-Scharmbeck 68 A1
Øster Hurup 49 B/C2
Østerhus 42 A/B2
Østerild 48 A1/2
Øster Jølby 48 A2
Øster Karup 50 A2
Østerlars 51 D3
Øster Løgum 52 B2
Österlövsta 40 B2
Østermarie 51 D3
Östermark 20 A3
Ostermiething 92 B3
Österneret 30 B2
Österö 20 B2
Osterode 68 B3
Osterode-Dorste 68 B3, 81 D1
Oster-Ohrstedt 52 B2
Öster Ritjemjåkk 9 D3
Östersele 31 C2
Öster Själevad 31 B/C3
Österslöv 50 B2
Öster Sönnarslöv 50 B3
Östersträsjö 35 C3
Österstrand 30 B2
Österström 35 C/D2/3
Östersund 29 D3, 34 B2
Östersundom 25 D3, 26 A3
Österunda 40 A/B3
Östervåla 40 B3
Östervallskog 38 B3, 45 C1
Øster Vrå 48 B1
Osterwieck 69 C3
Osterzell 91 D3
Ostffyasszonyfa 94 B3, 128 A1
Ostfildern 91 C2
Östhammar 40 B2/3
Ostheim 81 D2
Osthofen 80 B3
Óstia 118 A/B2
Ostiano 106 B3
Ostíglia 114 B1
Ostiz 108 A3, 154 A2
Östloning 35 D2/3
Östmark 38 B2/3
Östmarkum 30 B3
Ostnäs 20 A1, 31 D2
Östomsjön 39 C1
Ost'or 99 C/D2
Ostoróg 71 D2
Ostra 115 D3, 117 D2
Östra Ämtervik 39 C3, 45 C/D1
Östraby 50 B3
Ostrach 91 C3
Ostrach-Habsthal 91 C2/3
Östra Ed 47 B/C3
Östra Eknö 47 B/C3
Östra Frölunda 50 A1
Östra Galåbodarna 34 B2
Östra Grevie 50 A3
Östra Hjoggböle 31 D1
Östra Husby 46 B2
Östra Karup 50 A2
Östra Ljungby 50 A2
Östra Malmagen 33 D2/3, 34 A2/3
Östra Näsberget 39 C2
Östrand 16 B2/3
Östra Ny 46 B2
Östra Ryd 46 B2
Östra Sjulsmark 31 D2
Östra Stugusjö 35 C2/3
Östra Torsås 51 C1/2
Ostrau 83 C1
Ostrau 82 B1
Ostrava 96 B2
Oštrelj 131 C2
Ostriconi 113 D2
Östringen 90 B1
Ostritz 83 D1/2
Ostróda (Osterode) 73 C3
Ostrog 98 B2
Ostrołęka 73 C3, 98 A1
Östromsjön 39 C1
Ostropole 71 D1
Ostrošickij Gorodok 74 B3
Ostrov 74 B2
Ostrov 141 C2
Ostrov 82 B2
Ostrovačice 94 B1
Ostrov nad Oslavou 94 A1
Ostrov u Macochy 94 B1
Ostrowice 71 C1
Ostrowiec 70 B2
Ostrowiec Świętokrzyski 97 C1
Ostrów Mazowiecka 73 C3, 98 A1
Ostrów Wielkopolski 96 B1
Ostrožac 131 C1
Ostružnica 133 D1, 134 A1/2
Ostryna 73 D2/3, 74 A3, 98 B1
Ostseebad Ahrenshoop 53 D2/3
Ostseebad Boltenhagen 53 C3
Ostseebad Dierhagen 53 D3
Ostseebad Graal-Müritz 53 D3
Ostseebad Kühlungsborn 53 D3
Ostseebad Nienhagen 53 D3
Ostseebad Prerow 53 D2/3
Ostseebad Prerow 72 A2
Ostseebad Rerik 53 D3
Ostseebad Wustrow 53 D3
Ostseebad Zingst 53 D2/3
Ostuni 121 C/D2
Ostvik 31 D1
Østvika 29 C1
Osuna 172 A2
Oswestry 59 C3, 60 B3
Oszkó 128 A1
Osztopán 128 B2
Ota 164 A2
Otalampi 25 C3
Otamo 24 A1
Otanmäki 18 B3, 22 B1
Otava 26 B1
Otavice 131 C3
Oteiza 153 D2, 154 A2
Oteo 153 C1/2
Oteren 4 A3, 10 A1
Oterma 18 B3
Otero de Bodas 151 D3
Otero de las Dueñas 151 D2
Oterstranda 14 B1
Otervik 14 A3, 28 B1
Oteševo 142 B1
Othery 63 D2
Otiñar 173 C1
Otívar 173 C2
Otley 61 C2
Otlo 28 A/B3, 33 C/D1
Otnes 38 A1
Otočac 130 B1
Otočec 127 C3
Ötofta 50 A/B3
Otok 133 C1
Otoka 131 C1
Otorowo 71 D2
Otrokovice 95 C1
Otrokovice 96 B2
Otta 37 D1/2
Ottana 123 D2
Ottaviano 119 D3
Ottenby 72 B1
Ottendorf-Okrilla 83 C1
Ottenhöfen 90 B2
Ottenschlag 94 A2
Ottensheim im Mühlkreis 93 D2
Ottenstein 68 B3
Otterbach 80 B3, 90 A/B1
Otterbäcken 45 D2, 46 A1/2
Otterberg 80 B3, 90 A/B1
Otterburn 57 D2
Otterburn 54 B3
Otter Ferry 56 A1/2
Otterfing 92 A3
Otterlo 66 B3
Otterndorf 52 A3, 68 A1
Ottersberg 68 A2
Ottersøy 28 B1
Ottersweier 90 B2
Otterup 49 C3, 53 C1
Ottervattnet 31 C2
Ottervik 28 B2
Ottery Saint Mary 63 C2
Öttevény 95 C3
Ottmarsheim 90 A3
Ottnang 93 C2/3
Ottobeuren 91 D3
Ottobiano 105 D3, 113 D1
Ottobrunn 92 A2/3
Ottone 113 D1
Ottonträsk 31 C2
Ottrau 81 C2
Ottsjö 29 C3, 34 A2
Ottsjön 29 D3, 34 B1
Ottweiler 89 D1, 90 A1
Otvöskónyi 128 A2
Otxandio 153 D1/2
Otyń 71 C3
Otzberg-Lengfeld 81 C3
Ötztal-Bahnhof 106 B1
Ouanne 88 A3
Ouarville 87 C2
Oucques 86 A/B3
Ouddorp 66 A3
Oudega 67 B/C1/2
Oudenaarde 78 B2
Oude-Pekela 67 C1/2
Oudeschild 66 B2
Oudeschoot 67 B/C2
Oudewater 66 B3
Oudon 86 A3
Ougney 89 C3, 103 D1, 104 A1
Ouguela 165 C2
Ouistreham 76 B3, 86 A1
Oulainen 18 A3
Oulanka 13 C3
Oulchy-le-Château 88 A1
Oulins 87 C1
Oullins 103 D3
Oulujoki 18 A/B2
Oulunsalo 18 A2
Oulu (Uleåborg) 18 A/B2
Oulx 112 B1
Oundle 64 B2
Oura 150 B3, 158 B1
Ouranópolis 144 B2
Ourense 150 B2
Ourique 170 A1
Ourol 150 B1
Ourondo 158 B3
Ouroux-en-Morvan 88 A3, 103 C1
Ouroux-sur-Saône 103 D1
Ourville-en-Caux 77 C3
Ousse 108 B3, 154 B1
Ousson-sur-Loire 87 D3
Outakoski 6 B2
Outarville 87 C2
Outeiro 151 C3, 159 C1
Outeiro 151 B/C1
Outeiro 150 A3, 158 A1
Outeiro de Rei 150 B1
Outes 150 A2
Outokumpu 23 C2/3
Outovaara 12 B3
Ouville-la-Rivière 77 C2/3
Ouzouer-le-Marché 87 C2/3
Ouzouer-sur-Loire 87 D3
Ovada 113 C1
Ovágen 36 A3
Ovanåker 39 D1, 40 A1
Ovanmyra 39 D2
Ovar 158 A2
Ovča 133 D1, 134 A/B1
Ovčar Banja 133 D2, 134 A2/3
Ovče Polje 139 C2/3
Övedskloster 50 B3
Ovelgönne 68 A1
Ovelgönne-Oldenbrock 68 A1
Överälve 35 C3
Överammer 30 A3, 35 C2
Överäng 29 C3, 34 A1
Øverås 32 B2
Overath 80 A2
Overby 49 C3
Øverbygd 10 A1
Överenhörna 47 C1
Over Feldborg 48 A2
Overgård 48 B2
Øvergård 4 A3, 10 A1
Överhogdal 34 B3
Overijse 79 B/C2
Over Jerstal 52 B1/2
Överkalix 17 C2
Överlännäs 30 B3, 35 D2
Överlida 49 D1, 50 A1
Overloon 79 D1
Övermalax 20 A2
Övermark (Ylimarkku) 20 A3
Overmere 78 B1
Överö 41 D3
Over Simmelkær 48 A/B2
Överste Nyland 31 C2
Overton 59 C/D2/3, 60 B3
Övertorneå 17 D2
Övertorneå 17 D2
Överturingen 34 B3
Överum 46 B3
Ovesholm 50 B3
Ovidiopol' 141 D1
Ovidiu 141 D2
Oviedo 151 D1
Ovíglio 113 C1
Oviken 34 B2
Ovíndoli 119 C1
Övitsby 25 C3
Ovodda 123 D2
Övra 30 A2, 35 C/D1
Övre Åbyn 31 D1
Øvre Årdal 37 C2
Øvre Åstbru 38 A1
Övre Björknäs 15 C3
Øvrebo 43 B/C3
Øvrebø 43 B/C3
Övre Brännträsk 16 B2
Øvrebygd 42 A2/3
Øvre Espedal 42 A2
Övre Granberg 16 B3
Övre Grundsel 16 B3
Øvre Kildal 4 B3
Övre Långträsk 16 A3
Øvre Moen 42 B2
Øvrenes 5 D2, 6 A2
Övre Nyland 31 C2
Övre Parakka 10 B3
Øvre Rendal 33 D3
Øvre Sirdal 42 B2
Övre Soppero 10 B2/3
Övre Svartlå 16 B2
Övre Tväråselet 16 B3
Ovronnaz [Riddes] 104 B2
Ovruč 99 C2
Øvstebo 42 A1
Øvstestøl 32 A3, 37 B/C1
Ovtočići 137 C/D2
Ovtrup 48 A3, 52 A1
Owen 91 C2
Owingen (Überlingen) 91 C3
Owinska 71 D2
Owschlag 52 B2/3
Öxabäck 49 D1, 50 A1
Oxberg 39 C1/2
Oxelösund 47 C2
Oxford 65 C3
Oxie 50 A3
Oxílithos 147 D1/2
Oxkangar 20 B2
Öxnered 45 C2
Oxsjön 35 C3
Øy 43 C2
Oyace 104 B3
Øyan 33 C/D3
Øyangen 28 A3, 33 C1
Oyarzún 153 D1, 154 A1
Øye 32 B2
Øye 32 A3, 36 B1
Øyenkilen 44 B1
Øyer 37 D2, 38 A1
Øyestranda 42 B3
Øyfjell 43 C1
Øyhelle 8 B2
Øyjord 8 B3
Oy-Mittelberg 91 D3
Øynan 37 C2/3
Øynes 9 C2
Øynes 15 C1
Oyonnax 104 A2
Øyra 5 C2
Oyrières 89 C3
Oysang 43 D2, 44 A2
Øyslebø 42 B3
Øystad Moskusgård 9 D2
Øystese 36 B3
Oyten 68 A2
Oyten-Bassen 68 A2
Oyten-Schanzendorf 68 A2
Oyteti Stalin (Kuçovë) 142 A1
Øyungen 38 A1
Øyvatnet 9 C2
Oza dos Ríos 150 B1
Ozalj 127 C3
Ozariči 99 C1
Ózd 97 C2/3
Ozeta 153 D2
Ozieri 123 C/D2
Ozora 128 B1/2
Ozzano Monferrato 113 C1

P

Pääaho 19 C2
Pääjärvi 21 C2

Paaki 19 C3
Paakkila 23 C2
Paakkola 17 D2, 18 A1
Paalasmaa 23 C2
Påarp 49 D3, 50 A2/3
Pääsinniemi 25 D1, 26 A1
Paaso 25 D1, 26 B1
Paatela 27 C1
Paattinen 24 B2
Paatus 6 B2
Paavola 18 A3
Paavonvaara 23 D3
Pabianice 97 C1
Pabillónis 123 C3
Pabneukirchen 93 D2
Påbo 45 D3
Pabradė 74 A3
Paceco 124 A2
Pacentro 119 C1/2
Pachino 125 D3
Pačir 129 C3
Pack 127 C1
Paço de Sousa 158 A1/2
Paços de Ferreira 158 A1
Pacov 83 D3, 93 D1
Pacsa 128 A1/2
Pacy-sur-Eure 86 B1
Padankoski 25 C1, 26 A1
Padasjoki 25 D1, 26 A1
Padborg 52 B2
Padej 129 D3
Pađene 131 C2
Padenghe sul Garda 106 B3
Paderborn 68 A3, 81 B/C1
Paderborn-Sande 68 A3
Paderborn-Schloss Neuhaus 68 A3, 80 B1
Paderborn-Wewer 68 A3, 80 B1
Padern 156 B1
Paderne 170 A2
Paderne 150 B1
Paderne de Allariz 150 B2/3
Padiham 59 D1, 60 B2
Padina 133 D1, 134 B1
Padina 141 C2
Padinska Skela 133 D1, 134 A1
Padirac 109 D1
Pádola 107 D2
Pádova 107 C3
Padragkút 128 A/B1
Padrela 150 B3, 158 B1
Padrenda 150 B3
Pádria 123 C2
Padron 150 A2
Padru 123 D1
Padstow 62 B3
Padul 173 C2
Padula 120 A/B3
Paduli 119 D3, 120 A2
Padva 24 B3
Paesana 112 B1
Paese 107 D3
Paestum 120 A3
Pag 130 B2
Pagánica 117 D3, 119 C1
Pagánico 114 B3, 116 B2/3
Pagny-sur-Meuse 89 C1/2
Pagode-de-Chanteloup 86 B3
Pagoúria 145 C1
Pago Veiano 119 D2/3, 120 A2
Paguera 157 C2
Paharova 17 C1
Páhi 129 C2
Pahkakoski 18 B2
Pahkakumpu 13 C3
Pahkala 21 C1
Pahkasalo 18 A3
Pähl 92 A3
Pahtaoja 18 A1
Pahuvaara 19 D2
Paialvo 164 B1
Paião 158 A3
Paide 74 A1
Paijärvi 26 B2
Pailhès 109 D3, 155 D1
Paillart 77 D3
Paimbœf 85 C3, 100 A1
Paimio (Pemar) 24 B2/3
Paimpol 84 B1
Paimpont 85 C2
Painsalo 22 B1
Painswick 63 D1, 64 A2/3
Painten 92 A1
Paio Pires 164 A2
Paipórta 169 D1
Paisco 106 B2
Paisley 56 B2
Paistivuoma 12 A2, 17 D1
Paisua 22 B1
Paittasjärvi 11 C2
Päiväjoki 12 B3
Päiväkunta 21 D3, 22 A3
Päiviälä 23 C3
Pajala 17 C1
Pajares 153 D3
Pajares 161 C2
Pajares de los Oteros 152 A2
Pajarón 162 A3, 168 B1
Pajaroncillo 162 A3, 168 B1
Pajujärvi 22 B2
Pajukoski 23 C1
Pajulankylä 26 B1
Pajuniemi 18 A2
Pajuskylä 22 B2
Páka 127 D2, 128 A2
Pakaa 25 D2, 26 A2
Pakarila 22 A/B3
Pakinainen 24 A3
Pakisvaara 12 A3, 17 D2
Pakkala 25 C1
Pakola 12 A2
Pakosław 71 D3
Pakoštane 131 B/C2/3
Pákozd 128 B1
Pakrac 128 A3
Paks 129 C2
Paks 96 B3
Paksumaa 6 B3
Paksuniemi 10 A/B3
Palacios de Benaver 152 B2
Palacios de la Sierra 153 C3
Palacios de Sanabria 151 C3
Palacios del Sil 151 C/D2
Palaciosrubios 160 A2
Paladru 103 D3, 104 A3
Palafrugell 156 B2
Palagiano 121 C2
Palagonía 125 C3
Paláia 114 B3, 116 A2
Palaiseau 87 C/D1/2
Palamás 143 C/D3
Palamonastíri 143 C3
Palamós 156 B2/3
Påläng 17 C2/3
Palanga 73 C1/2
Palanzano 114 A1/2, 116 A1
Palárikovo 95 C2/3
Palas de Rei 150 B2
Palata 119 D2, 120 A1
Palatítsia 143 D2
Palatna 138 B1
Palau 123 D1
Palau Sverdera 156 B2
Palavas-les-Flots 110 B3
Palazuelos 161 C/D2
Palazzo Adriano 124 B2
Palazzo del Pero 115 C3, 117 B/C2
Palazzolo Acréide 125 C/D3
Palazzolo sull'Óglio 106 A3
Palazzolo Vercellese 105 C3, 113 C1
Palazzo San Gervásio 120 B2
Palazzuolo sul Sénio 115 C2, 116 B1
Pålböle 20 A1, 31 D2
Paldiski 74 A1
Pale 132 B2/3
Paleá Epídavros 147 C3
Palena 119 C2
Palencia 152 B3
Palenciana 172 B2
Palenzuela 152 B3
Paleochóra 148 B3
Paleochórion 144 B2
Paleokastrítsa 142 A3
Paleokastrítsa 148 A1
Paleómonastiri 143 C3
Paleópirgos 146 B2
Paleópolis 145 C/D2
Palermo 124 B1/2
Palermo Ácqua dei Corsari 124 B2
Palermo-Mondello 124 B1
Páleros 146 A1
Palestrina 118 B2
Palheiros 158 B1
Palheiros da Tocha 158 A3
Palheiros de Quiaios 158 A3
Palhoça 158 A2
Páli 94 B3
Pali 125 C2
Paliano 118 B2
Palič 129 C/D2
Palikkala 24 B2
Palinges 103 C2
Palinuro 120 A3
Palionéllini 143 D2
Paliouriá 143 C2/3
Palioúrion 144 B2/3
Palioúrion 148 B1
Paliseul 79 C3
Palivuk 132 A2
Paljakanpuisto 19 C3
Paljakka 19 C3
Paljakka 19 C2
Paljakka 26 B1/2
Paljakka 19 D1
Paljakka 30 A/B3, 35 D2
Påljorda 14 A/B3
Pälkäne 25 C1
Pålkem (Vitträsk) 17 B/C2
Palkisoja 12 B1
Pallagorío 122 B2
Pallanza 105 D2/3
Pallares 165 D3, 166 A3
Pallaruelo de Monegros 155 B/C3, 162 B1
Pallastunturi 11 C3, 12 A1
Palling 92 B3
Pallíni 147 D2
Pallonen 23 D2
Palma 164 B2/3
Palma Campánia 119 D3
Pálmaces de Jadraque 161 C2
Palma del Río 172 A1
Palma de Mallorca 157 C2
Palma di Montechiaro 124 B3
Palmanova 126 A2/3
Palma Nova 157 C2
Palmela 164 A2
Palmeral de Elche 169 C3
Palmi 122 A3
Palmižana 131 C3, 136 A1
Pålnostugan 9 D2
Palo 12 A3, 17 D1
Palo 113 C2
Palo del Colle 121 C2
Palojärvi 11 C2
Palojärvi 12 A3, 17 D1
Palojärvi 12 B3
Palojoensuu 11 C2
Palokangas 22 B3
Palokastër 142 A2
Palokki 23 C3
Palolompolo 12 A3, 17 D1
Palomaa 6 B3
Palomäki 23 C2
Palomar de Arroyos 162 B2
Palomares del Campo 161 D3
Palomas 165 D2, 166 A2
Palombara Sabina 118 B1/2
Palomera 161 D3
Palonselkä 11 D3, 12 A2
Palonurmi 23 C2
Paloperä 13 C3
Paloperä 11 C3, 12 A2
Palos de la Frontera 171 C2
Paloselkä 11 D3, 12 A2
Palosenjärvi 22 B1
Palosenmäki 21 D3, 22 A3
Palovaara 18 B1
Pals 156 B2
Palsasuo 10 B2
Palsasuo 6 B3
Pålsboda 46 A/B1
Pålsböle 25 C3
Palsgård 48 B3, 52 B1
Palsselkä 12 B2
Paltamo 19 C3
Paltanen 22 B3
Paltaniemi 19 C3
Păltsastugorna 10 A1
Palù di Férsina 107 C2
Palus 24 A/B1
Paluzza 107 D2, 126 A2
Påmark 24 A/B1
Pambukovica 133 D2, 134 A2
Pamhagen 94 B3
Pamiątkowo 71 D2
Pamiers 109 D3, 155 D1, 156 A1
Pamilo 23 D2
Pamparato 113 C2
Pampelonne 110 A2
Pampilhosa 158 B3
Pampilhosa do Botão 158 A3
Pamplona/Iruñea 154 A2
Panagiá 147 D2
Panagía 145 C1/2
Panagjurište 140 B3
Panajë 142 A2
Panassac 109 C3, 155 C1
Pancalieri 112 B1
Pančarevo 139 D1
Pančevo 133 D1, 134 A/B1
Pančevo 140 A2
Pancorbo 153 C2
Pancrudo 162 A/B2
Pandino 106 A3
Pandrup 48 B1
Panelia 24 A/B1/2
Panenský Týnec 83 C2
Panes 152 B1
Panevéggio 107 C2
Panevėžys 73 D2, 74 A2/3
Pangbourne 64 B3
Paničište 139 D2
Panillo 155 C2
Panissières 103 C2/3
Paniza 163 C1
Panka 22 B2
Pankajärvi 23 D1/2
Pankakoski 23 D2
Pankasz 127 D1
Panker 53 C3
Panni 120 A2
Pannonhalma 95 C3
Panoias 159 B/C2
Panoias 164 B3, 170 A1
Panórama 144 A2
Päntäne 20 B3
Panticosa 154 B2
Pantoja 160 B3
Pantón 150 B2
Panttila 20 B3
Páola 122 A1/2
Pápa 95 C3, 128 A1
Pápa 96 B3
Páparis 146 B3
Paparotti 126 A2
Papasídero 120 B3, 122 A1
Pápateszér 95 C3, 128 B1
Papenburg 67 D2
Papenburg-Aschendorf 67 D2
Papinniemi 23 D3
Pappás 139 D3, 144 A1
Pappenheim 91 D1, 92 A1
Pappenheim 81 D2
Pappilanvaara 19 C3
Pappinen 25 D1, 26 A1
Pappinen 24 B2
Papraća 133 C2
Papradno 95 C/D1
Papusuo 18 B3, 22 B1
Parábita 121 D3
Paraćin 134 B3
Paraćin 140 A2
Paracuellos de Jiloca 162 A1
Paracuellos 162 A3, 168 B1
Paracuellos de Jarama 161 C2
Parada de Cunhos 158 B1
Parada de Rubiales 159 D1/2, 160 A1/2
Parada do Sil 150 B2
Paradas 171 D2, 172 A2
Paradaseca 151 C2
Paradela 150 B2
Paradela 150 B3, 158 B1
Paradísia 146 B3
Paralía 143 D2
Paralía 146 B2
Paralía Avlídos 147 D2
Paralía Iríon 147 C3
Paralía Kímis 147 D1
Paralía Skotínis 143 D2
Paralía Tiroú 147 C3
Parálion Ástros 147 C3
Parálion Ástros 148 B2
Paralovo 138 B1/2
Paramé 85 C1/2
Paramio 151 C3
Paramithiá 142 B3
Páramo 150 B2
Páramo del Sil 151 C2
Paranéstion 145 B/C1
Paranhos 158 B2
Parantala 21 D3, 22 A3
Parapótamos 142 B3
Paravóla 146 B1
Paray-le-Monial 103 C2
Parcent 169 D2
Parcé-sur-Sarthe 86 A3
Parchen 69 D2/3
Parchim 69 D1
Parcoul 101 C3
Parczew 73 D3, 97 D1, 98 A2
Pardilla 153 C3, 161 B/C1
Pardubice 96 A2
Parede 164 A2
Paredes 160 B3
Paredes 158 A1/2
Paredes de Coura 150 A3
Paredes de Nava 152 B3
Paredes de Sigüenza 161 C/D1
Paredes de Viadores 158 A/B2
Pareja 161 D2
Parentis-en-Born 108 A2
Parey 69 D2/3
Párga 142 B3
Párga 148 A1
Pargas 24 B3
Pargas/Parainen 24 B3
Pargny-sur-Saulx 88 B1
Parhalahti 18 A3
Parigné-l'Évêque 86 B2/3
Parikkala 27 D1
Paris 87 D1
Parisot 109 D2
Parissavaara 23 D2
Pärjänsuo 19 B/C2
Parkajoki 11 C3
Parkalompolo 11 C3
Parkano 20 B3
Parkkila 19 C2
Parkkila 26 B1
Parkkila 21 D1, 22 A1
Parkkima 21 D1, 22 A1
Parkku 25 C1
Parkstetten 92 B1/2
Parkua 19 C3, 22 B1
Parla 160 B3
Pärlan 16 A1/2
Parma 114 A1
Parma-San Pancrázio 114 A1
Parndorf 94 B3
Párnica 95 D1
Pärnu 74 A1
Pärnu-Jaagupi 74 A1
Parola 25 C2
Parona di Valpolicella 106 B3
Páros 149 C2/3
Parowa 83 D1
Parque da Pena 164 A2
Parracombe 63 C2
Pårraskårsa 10 A3
Parres 152 A/B1
Parsau 69 C2
Parsberg 92 A1
Parsberg-Willenhofen 92 A1
Parsdorf 92 A2
Parsęcko 71 D1
Parsów 70 B1
Parstein 70 B2
Partaharju 22 B3
Partakko 6 B3
Partakoski 27 C1/2
Partaloa 173 D1/2, 174 A1
Partanna 124 A2
Partenen 106 B1
Partenstein 81 C3
Parthenay 101 C1
Parthénion 147 C3
Partille (Göteborg) 45 C3
Partinello 113 D3

Partinico 124 A/B2
Partizani 133 D2, 134 A2
Partizanske Vode 133 C3, 134 A3
Partizánske 95 C/D2
Partoș 134 B1
Pårup 48 B3
Parviainen 19 C2
Pârvomaj 141 B/C3
Påryd 72 B1
Påryd 51 D2
Parzán 155 C2
Pasaia 153 D1, 154 A1
Paşaköy 145 D1, 145 D3
Pasala 21 D2, 22 A2
Paşayiğit 145 D3
Pașcani 141 C1
Pas de Cère 110 A1
Pas-en-Artois 78 A2
Pasewalk 70 B1
Pasewalk 72 A3
Pasi 26 B2
Pasiano di Pordenone 107 D2/3
Pasikovci 128 A3, 131 D1
Påskallavik 51 D1
Påskallavik 72 B1
Pasmajärvi 12 A2, 17 D1
Pašman 130 B2
Passail 127 C1
Passais 86 A2
Passau 93 C2
Passau 96 A2
Passau-Heining 92 B2
Passetto 115 C1
Passignano sul Trasimeno 115 C3, 117 C2
Passô 158 B2
Passopisciaro 125 D2
Passos 158 B1
Passow 69 D1
Passow 70 B1/2
Passugg [Chur] 106 A1
Pástena 119 D2
Pástena 119 C2
Pasto 20 B3
Pastorello 114 A1
Pastores 159 C2
Pastoriza 151 C1
Pastow 53 D3
Pastrana 161 C2
Pastricciola 113 D3
Pastriz 154 B3, 162 B1
Pasvalis 73 D1, 74 A2
Pata 95 C2
Pataholm 51 D1
Pataias 164 A1
Patajoki 25 D1, 26 A1
Patana 21 C2
Pătaș 135 C1
Patay 87 C2
Pateley Bridge 61 C2
Pateniemi 18 A2
Patergassen 126 B1
Patergassen 96 A3
Paterna 169 D1
Paterna del Campo 171 C1
Paterna de la Madera 168 B2
Paterna del Río 173 D2
Paterna de Rivera 171 D3
Paternion 126 B1/2
Paternò 125 C2
Paternópoli 119 D3, 120 A2
Patersdorf 93 B/C1
Pathhead 57 C2
Patiní 143 B/C3, 146 A1
Patiópoulon 146 A1
Pătîrlagele 141 C2
Patitírion 147 D1
Patokoski 12 A3
Patoniemi 13 C3
Patoniva 6 B2
Patos 142 A2
Patos 148 A1
Patosh Fshat 142 A2
Pátra/Pátrai 146 B2
Pátra/Pátrai 148 B2
Pátrica 119 B/C2
Patrikka 23 D3
Patrington 61 D2
Pattada 123 D2
Pattensen 68 B3
Pattensen-Schulenburg 68 B3
Patterdale 57 C3, 60 B1
Patti 125 C/D1/2
Pattijoki 18 A3
Pättikkä 10 B2
Pättikkäkoski 10 B2
Pătulele 135 D2
Páty 95 D3
Pau 108 B3, 154 B1
Pauillac 100 B3
Paukarlahti 22 B3
Paukkaja 23 D2
Paul 158 B3
Pauland 30 B1
Paularo 107 D2, 126 A2
Paulhac-en-Margeride 110 B1
Paulhaguet 103 B/C3
Paulhan 110 B3
Paulilátino 123 C2
Paulinenaue 69 D2, 70 A2
Paull 61 D2
Paullo 105 D3, 106 A3
Pauls 163 C2
Pausa 82 A/B2
Pausele 30 B1
Pauträsk 30 B1
Pauvres 78 B3
Pavia 105 D3, 106 A3, 113 D1
Pavia 164 B2
Pavías 162 B3, 169 D1
Pavilly 77 C3
Pavilosta 73 C1
Pávliani 147 B/C1
Pavlica 133 D3, 134 A/B3
Pavlikeni 141 C3
Pavlíkov 83 C3
Pávlos 147 C1/2
Pavlovsk 74 B1
Pavullo nel Frignano 114 B2, 116 A1
Päwesin 69 D2, 70 A2
Pawłowice 71 D3
Pawłowo Zońskie 71 D2
Payerne 104 B1
Paymogo 165 C3, 170 B1
Payrac 109 D1
Pazardžik 140 B3
Pazin 126 B3, 130 A1
Paziols 156 B1
Pazo de Irijoa 150 B1
Pazos de Borbén 150 A2/3
Peacehaven 76 B1
Peal de Becerro 167 D3, 168 A3, 173 C1
Peanía 147 D2
Péaule 85 C3
Peć 138 A1
Peć 140 A3
Pećane 131 C2
Péccioli 114 B3, 116 A2
Pécel 95 D3
Pečenjevce 139 C1
Pechão 170 B2
Pechea 141 C1/2
Pechern 83 D1
Pechina 173 D2
Peći 131 C2
Pećigrad 131 C1
Pećinci 133 D1, 134 A1
Pecka 133 C2
Peckatel 70 A1
Pečky 83 D3
Pęcław 71 D3
Pecorara 113 D1
Pecorone 120 B3, 122 A1
Pečory 74 B2
Pécs 128 B2
Pećska Banja 138 A1
Pécsvárad 128 B2
Pečurice 137 D2
Pedaso 117 D2
Pederoa 107 C1/2
Pederobba 107 C2/3
Pedersöre/Pietarsaaren maalaiskunta 20 B1
Pederstrup 53 C2
Pedescala 107 C3
Pedorido 158 A2
Pedrafita do Cebreiro 151 C2
Pedra Furada 158 A1
Pedrajas 153 D3, 161 D1
Pedrajas de San Esteban 160 B1
Pedralba 169 C1
Pedralva de la Pradería 151 C3
Pedras Salgadas 150 B3, 158 B1
Pedraza 160 B1/2
Pedraza de Alba 159 D2, 160 A2
Pedreguer 169 D2
Pedreira 150 B1
Pedreña 153 B/C1
Pedrera 172 A2
Pedro Abad 167 C3, 172 B1
Pedroche 166 B3
Pedrógão Grande 158 A/B3, 164 B1
Pedrógão Pequeno 158 A/B3, 164 B1
Pedrógão 165 C3
Pedrogão 159 B/C3
Pedrógão 158 A3, 164 A1
Pedrola 155 C3, 163 C1
Pedro Martínez 173 C1
Pedro Muñoz 167 D1, 168 A1
Pedrosa de Duero 152 B3, 160 B1
Pedrosa del Rey 152 A2
Pedrosillo de los Aires 159 D2
Pedrosillo el Ralo 159 D2
Pedroso 153 D2
Pedroso de Acim 159 C3, 165 D1
Peebles 57 C2
Peel 58 B1
Peel 54 A3, 55 D2
Peera 10 B1/2
Pefkíon 147 C1
Pefkotón 139 C3, 143 C1
Pega 159 C2
Pegalajar 173 C1
Pegau 82 B1
Peggau 127 C1
Pegnitz 82 A3
Pego 169 D2
Pegões Velhos 164 A/B2
Pegolotte 107 C3
Pehčevo 139 D2/3
Pehula 24 B1
Peine 68 B3
Peine-Stederdorf 68 B3
Peinikanniemi 19 D1
Péio 106 B2
Peipohja 24 B1/2
Peïra-Cava 112 B2
Peisey-Nancroix 104 B3
Peissen 69 D3
Peissenberg 92 A3
Peiting 91 D3
Peitz 70 B3
Pekankylä 19 D3
Pekanpää 17 D2
Pekkala 12 B3
Pekkula 23 D3
Peklino 99 D1
Pelahustán 160 A/B3
Pelariga 158 A3
Pelarrodríguez 159 D2
Pelasgía 147 C1
Pelayos de la Presa 160 B2/3
Pełczyce 71 C2
Peleas de Arriba 159 D1
Pélekas 142 A3
Peletá 147 C3
Pelhřimov 83 D3, 94 A1
Pelhřimov 96 A2
Pelilla 159 D1/2
Pelinnaion 143 C3
Pelkkikangas 21 B/C2
Pelkoperä 18 A/B3
Pelkosenniemi 12 B2
Pella 44 B1
Pella 143 D1/2
Pélla 143 D1/2
Pellegrino Parmense 114 A1
Pellegrue 108 B1
Pellérd 128 B2
Pellesmäki 22 B2
Pellevoisin 101 D1
Pellingen 79 D3, 80 A3
Pellinki/Pellinge 25 D3, 26 A3
Pello 12 A3, 17 D1
Pello 12 A3, 17 D1
Pellosniemi 26 B1
Pellossalo 27 C/D1
Pellworm-Ostersiel 52 A2
Pellworm-Waldhusen 52 A2
Peloche 166 B2
Pelso 18 B3
Peltokangas 21 C2
Peltosalmi 22 B1
Peltovuoma 11 C2, 12 A1
Pélussin 103 D3
Pemar 24 B2/3
Pembridge 59 D3
Pembroke 62 B1
Pembroke 55 D3
Pembroke Dock 62 B1
Pemfling-Grafenkirchen 92 B1
Pempelijärvi 17 C1
Penacova 158 A3
Peñafiel 152 B3, 160 B1
Penafiel 158 A1/2
Peñaflor 172 A1
Peñaflor de Hornija 152 A3, 160 A1
Penagos 153 B/C1
Penaguião 158 B1/2
Peñalba 155 C3, 163 C1
Peñalba de San Esteban 153 C3, 161 C1
Peñalén 161 D2
Peñalsordo 166 B2
Penalva do Castelo 158 B2
Peñalver 161 C2
Penamacor 159 B/C3
Peñaranda de Duero 153 C3, 161 C1
Peñaranda de Bracamonte 160 A2
Peñarroya-Pueblonuevo 166 B3
Peñarroya de Tastavíns 163 C2
Peñarrubia 172 A2
Penarth 63 C2
Peñascosa 168 A/B2
Peñas de San Pedro 168 B2
Peñausende 159 D1
Penc 95 D3
Pencader 62 B1
Penchard 87 D1
Pendagií 146 B1/2
Pendálofos 143 B/C2
Pendápolis 144 B1
Pendine 62 B1
Pendueles 152 B1
Penedono 158 B2
Penela 158 A3
Pénestin 85 C3
Pengerjoki 21 D3
Penhale 62 A/B3
Penhas Juntas 151 C3, 159 C1
Peniche 164 A1
Penicuik 57 C2
Penig 82 B2
Peninki 21 D1/2, 22 A1/2
Peñíscola 163 C2/3
Penistone 61 C2/3
Penkridge 59 D3, 64 A1
Penkun 70 B1
Penmaenmawr 59 C2, 60 A3
Penmarch 84 A3
Pennabilli 115 C2, 117 C1
Pennala 25 D2, 26 A2
Pennapiedimonte 119 C1
Penne 117 D3, 119 C1
Penne 42 B3
Penningby 41 C3
Peno 75 C2
Peæon de Ifach 169 D2
Penrhyndeudraeth 59 C2/3, 60 A3
Penrith 57 C3, 60 B1
Penrith 54 B3
Penryn 62 B3
Pensala 20 B2
Pentinniemi 18 B1
Penttäjä 17 C/D1
Pentti 26 B2
Penttilänlahti 22 B2
Penttilänvaara 19 D1
Pen-y-groes 58 B2, 60 A3
Penzance 62 A3
Penzberg 92 A3
Pénzesgyőr 128 B1
Penzlin 70 A1
Pepelište 139 C3
Pépinster 79 D2
Pępowo 71 D3
Peqin 142 A1
Pér 95 C3
Pera Boa 158 B3
Peracense 162 A2
Perachóra 147 C2
Perafita 158 A1
Perafita 156 A2
Perä-Hyyppä 20 B3
Peral 158 B3, 165 B/C1
Perälä 20 A3
Peralada 156 B2
Peralbillo 167 C2
Peral de Arlanza 152 B3
Peraleda de la Mata 159 D3, 160 A3, 166 B1
Peraleda de Zaucejo 166 A2/3
Peraleda de San Román 159 D3, 160 A3, 166 B1
Peralejos de las Truchas 161 D2, 162 A2
Perales del Alfambra 162 B2
Perales del Puerto 159 C3
Perales de Tajuña 161 C3
Peralta 154 A2
Peralta de Alcofea 155 C3
Peralta de la Sal 155 C3
Peraltilla 155 C3
Peralva 170 B2
Peralveche 161 D2
Pérama 147 D2
Pérama 142 B3
Peramola 155 C3
Perä-Musko 23 D3
Peranka 19 D2
Peränkylä 24 A1
Perä-Posio 19 C1
Perarolo 107 C3
Perarolo di Cadore 107 D2
Perarrúa 155 C2
Peräseinäjoki 20 B3
Peräsilta 25 C1
Perast 137 C2
Perat 142 B2
Perat 148 A1
Perazancas 152 B2
Perbál 95 D3
Perchtoldsdorf 94 B2
Percy 86 A/B1
Perdasdefogu 123 D3
Perdiguera 154 B3, 162 B1
Pérdika 142 B3
Pérdika 147 D3
Pérdika 142 B3
Peréa 143 D2, 144 A2
Perečin 97 D2, 98 A3
Peredo 159 C1
Pereg 129 C1
Pereiro 170 B1
Pereiro de Aguiar 150 B2
Perejaslav-Hmel'nickij 99 D2
Perelhal 150 A3, 158 A1
Peremyšl' 75 D3
Peremyšl'any 97 D2, 98 A/B2/3
Perevolok 74 B1
Pérfugas 123 C1
Perg 93 D2
Perga 99 C2
Pérgine Valdarno 115 C3, 116 B2
Pérgine Valsugana 107 C2
Pérgola 115 D3, 117 C2
Pergusa 125 C2
Perho 21 C2
Peri 106 B3
Periam 140 A1
Periana 172 B2
Périers 76 A3, 85 D1
Pérignac 100 B3
Périgné 101 C2
Périgueux 101 D3
Períklia 139 C3, 143 D1
Perilla de Castro 151 D3, 159 D1
Perillo 150 A/B1
Perino 113 D1
Perișor 135 D2
Peristerá 144 A2
Perithórion 144 B1
Perivol 139 C/D2
Perivólion 142 B2/3

Perjasica **127** C3, **131** B/C1
Perkam **92** B1/2
Perkáta **129** C1
Perkiömäki **20** B2
Perkupa **97** C2
Perl **79** D3
Perl-Borg **79** D3
Perleberg **69** D2
Perlez **129** D3, **133** D1, **134** A1
Perlez **140** A2
Perly [Genève] **104** A2
Permantokoski **12** B3
Përmeti **142** B2
Pernancha de Cima **164** B2
Pernå/Pernaja **25** D2/3, **26** A2/3
Pernarec **83** B/C3
Pernek **94** B2
Pernes **164** A/B1
Pernes-les-Fontaines **111** C/D2
Pernik **139** D1/2
Pernik **140** B3
Pernink **82** B2
Perniö (Bjärnå) **24** B3
Perniön asema **24** B3
Pernitz **94** A3
Pernitz **96** A3
Pernoo **26** B2
Pernu **19** C1
Peroguarda **164** B3
Peroniel del Campo **153** D3, **161** D1
Péronne **78** A3
Perorrubio **161** B/C1
Perosa Argentina **112** B1
Pérouges **103** D2
Perpignan **156** B1
Perranporth **62** B3
Perrecy-les-Forges **103** C1/2
Perrero **112** B1
Perreux **103** C2
Perrigny-sur-Loire **103** C2
Perros-Guirec **84** B1
Persac **101** C/D2
Persberg **39** C3, **45** D1
Persenbeug **93** D2
Pershagen **47** C1
Pershore **63** D1, **64** A2
Persi **113** D1
Persnäs **51** D1
Persön **17** C3
Perštejn **83** B/C2
Perstorp **50** B2
Perstorp **72** A1
Pertengo **105** C/D3, **113** C1
Perth **57** C1
Perth **54** B2
Perthes **88** B2
Pertisau **92** A3
Perttaus **12** A/B2/3
Pertteli **24** B2/3
Perttula **25** C2/3
Pertuis **111** D2/3
Pertunmaa **26** B1
Pertusa **155** B/C3
Peruc **83** C2
Peručac **133** C2
Perúgia **115** C3, **117** C2
Perunkajärvi **12** B3
Perušić **130** B2
Péruwelz **78** B2
Pervijze **78** A1
Pervomajsk **99** D3
Perwez **79** C2
Pesadas de Burgos **153** C2
Pésaro **115** D2, **117** C1
Pescantina **106** B3
Pesčanyj Brod **99** C/D3
Pescara **119** C/D1
Pescasséroli **119** C2
Péschici **120** B1
Peschiera del Garda **106** B3
Péscia **114** B2, **116** A1
Pescina **119** C2
Pescolanciano **119** D2
Pescopagano **120** A2
Pescopennataro **119** D2
Pesco Sannita **119** D3, **120** A2
Pescueza **159** C3, **165** D1
Peshkëpija **142** A2
Peshkopi **138** A3

Peshkopi **140** A3
Pesiökylä **19** C2
Pesiönranta **19** C2
Pesmes **89** C3, **103** D1, **104** A1
Pesočani **138** B3, **142** B1
Pesoz **151** C1
Pesquera de Duero **152** B3, **160** B1
Pessac **108** B1
Pessalompolo **12** A3, **17** D2
Pessani **145** D1, **145** D3
Pessegueiro do Vouga **158** A2
Pessione **113** C1
Pessoux **79** C2
Pestá **142** B3
Peštani **142** B1
Pesteana Jiu **135** D1
Peštera **140** B3
Peštişani **135** D1
Pestovo **75** D1
Pešurići **132** C2/3
Peszéradacs **129** C1
Petacciato Marina **119** D2
Petäiskylä **23** C1
Petäjäjärvi **18** B1
Petäjäkangas **18** B2
Petäjäkylä **21** D2, **22** A2
Petäjämäki **22** B3
Petäjäskoski **12** A3
Petäjäskoski **18** A3
Petäjavaara **19** C3
Petäjävesi **21** D3, **22** A3
Petalax (Petolahti) **20** A2, **31** D3
Pétange **79** D3
Petanjci **127** D2
Petar u Sumi **126** B3, **130** A1
Pétas **146** A1
Petäys **22** B1
Peteranec **128** A2
Peterborough **65** B/C2
Peterhead **54** B2
Peterlee **61** D1
Petersberg-Marbach **81** C2
Petersborg **4** A3, **10** A1
Petersfield **76** A/B1
Petershagen-Ovenstädt **68** A2/3
Petershagen-Windheim **68** A2/3
Petershagen **68** A2/3
Petershagen **70** B2/3
Petershausen **92** A2
Peterstow **63** D1
Petiknäs **31** C1
Petikträsk **16** A3
Petília Policastro **122** B2
Petín **151** C2
Petit-Fossard **87** D2
Petit-Mars **85** D3
Petkula **12** B2
Petkus **70** A3
Petlovača **133** C1
Petolahti **20** A2, **31** D3
Pétra **143** D2
Petra **157** C2
Petragalla **120** B2
Petralía Soprana **125** C2
Petralía Sottana **125** C2
Petrálona **144** A2
Petraná **143** C2
Petrčane **130** B2
Petrel **126** C2/3
Petrele **137** D3, **138** A3, **142** A1
Petrella Liri **119** B/C2
Petrella Salto **117** D3, **118** B1
Petrella Tifernina **119** D2
Petreto-Bicchisano **113** D3
Petrič **139** D3, **144** A1
Petrijanec **127** D2
Petrijevci **128** B3
Petrikov **99** C1
Petrinja **127** D3
Petrodvorec **74** A/B1
Petröec **139** B/C2
Petrokrepost' **75** C1
Pétrola **168** B2
Petronà **122** B2
Petronell-Carnuntum **94** B2
Petroşani **140** B2
Petroúlion **143** C3

Petroússa **144** B1
Petrovaara **23** C2
Petrovac **134** B2
Petrovac **137** C/D2
Petrovac **140** A2
Petrovaradin **129** D3, **133** D1, **134** A1
Petrovčić **133** D1, **134** A1
Petrovice **83** D3, **93** D1
Petrovice **83** C2
Petrovice **93** C1
Petrovice **83** C3, **93** C1
Petrovo **75** D1
Petrovo Selo **135** C2
Petruma **23** C3
Petřžalka **94** B2
Petsáki **146** B2
Petschow **53** D3
Petsmo **20** A/B2
Petsund **38** A3
Pettäikkö **18** B3
Pettbol **40** B3
Pettenbach **93** C3
Petting **92** B3
Pettorano sul Gízio **119** C2
Pettorazza Grimani **107** C3, **115** C1
Petworth **76** B1
Peuerbach **93** C2
Peuerbach **96** A2
Peulje **131** C2
Peura **18** A1
Peurajärvi **18** B1
Peuralinna **21** C2
Peurasuvanto **12** B2
Peuravaara **19** C3
Peutaniemi **19** C2
Pevensey **77** C1
Pewsey **64** A3, **76** A1
Peyrat-le-Château **102** A2/3
Peyrebrune **109** D1
Peyrehorade **108** A3, **154** B1
Peyrolles-en-Provence **111** D2/3
Pézenas **110** B3
Pezinok **95** B/C2
Pezuela de las Torres **161** C2
Pfaffendorf **70** B3
Pfaffenhofen **91** D2
Pfaffenhofen-Tegernbach **92** A2
Pfaffenhofen **92** A2
Pfaffenhofen **107** B/C1
Pfaffenhoffen **90** A1/2
Pfäffikon **105** D1
Pfäffikon **90** B3, **105** D1
Pfaffing **92** B2/3
Pfaffing-Springlbach **92** B2/3
Pfafflar **106** B1
Pfalzgrafenweiler **90** B2
Pfarrkirchen **92** B2
Pfatter **92** B1
Pfatter-Geisling **92** B1
Pfeffenhausen **92** A/B2
Pfinztal-Berghausen **90** B1
Pförring-Forchheim **92** A1/2
Pforzheim **90** B1/2
Pfreimd **82** B3, **92** B1
Pfronstetten-Tigerfeld **91** C2
Pfronten **91** D3
Pfullendorf **91** C3
Pfullendorf-Denkingen **91** C3
Pfullingen **91** C2
Pfungstadt **80** B3
Pfyn [Felben-Wellhausen] **91** B/C3
Phalsbourg **89** D1, **90** A2
Phare de Cordouan **101** C3
Phare de Pertusato **123** D1
Pheneos **146** B2
Pherai **143** D3
Philippeville **78** B2
Phílippi **144** B1
Philippsburg **90** B1
Philippsreut **93** C1/2
Philippsreut **96** A2
Philippsthal-Heimbolds-hausen **81** C/D2
Philippsthal (Werra) **81** C/D2

Phlious **147** C2
Phoenike **142** A3
Phyäselkä **23** D3
Phyhämaa **24** A2, **41** D2
Physkeis **146** B2
Piacenza **113** D1, **114** A1
Piádena **106** B3, **114** A1
Piagge **115** D2, **117** C1/2
Piamprato **105** C3
Piana **113** D3
Piana Crixia **113** C2
Piana degli Albanesi **124** B2
Pianazzo **105** D2, **106** A2
Piancáldoli **115** B/C2, **116** B1
Pian Castagna **113** C1/2
Piancastagnáio **116** B3
Piandelagotti **114** B2, **116** A1
Pian della Mussa **104** B3
Piandimeleto **115** C2, **117** C2
Pianella **119** C1
Pianella **114** B3, **116** B2
Pianello Val Tidone **113** D1
Pianezza **112** B1
Piano del Re **112** B1
Piano Laceno **119** D3, **120** A2
Pianoro **114** B2, **116** B1
Pianottoli-Caldarello **113** D3
Pians **106** B1
Piansano **116** B3, **118** A1
Pias **165** C3, **170** B1
Piasecznik **71** C1
Piaseczno **70** B2
Piasek **70** B2
Piaski **71** D3
Piastre **114** B2, **116** A1
Piatra-Neamt **141** C1
Piazza **107** C2
Piazza al Sérchio **114** A2, **116** A1
Piazza Armerina **125** C2/3
Piazza Brembana **106** A2
Piazze **116** B3
Piazzola sul Brenta **107** C3
Pibrac **108** B2/3, **155** C1
Pićan **126** B3, **130** A1
Picão **158** B2
Picão **158** B2
Picasent **169** D1
Piccovagia **113** D3
Picerno **120** A2
Picher **69** C1
Pickering **61** C/D2
Pico **119** C2
Picón **167** C2
Picquigny **77** D2
Piecnik **71** D1
Piedicavallo **105** C3
Piédicorte-di-Gaggio **113** D3
Piedicroce **113** D3
Piediluco **117** C3, **118** B1
Piedimonte Etneo **125** D2
Piedimonte Matese **119** D2
Piedimulera **105** C2
Piedipaterno **117** C3, **118** A1
Piedivalle **117** D3
Pie di Via **104** A1
Piedrabuena **167** C2
Piedrafita **151** D2
Piedrahíta **160** A2
Piedralaves **160** A3
Piedras Albas **159** C3, **165** C1
Piedratajada **154** B3
Piegaro **115** C3, **117** C2/3
Piehinki **18** A3
Pieksämäki **22** B3
Pieksänlahti **27** C1
Pielavesi **22** B2
Pielppajärven lapin kirkko **6** B3
Pielungo **107** D2, **126** A2
Piène-Basse **112** B2
Pieńsk **83** D1
Pienza **115** C3, **116** B2
Piera **156** A3, **163** D1
Pierowall **54** B1
Pierowall **54** B1
Pierre **103** D1
Pierre-Buffière **101** C3

Pierrefeu-du-Var **112** A3
Pierrefitte-Nestalas **108** B3, **155** C1/2
Pierrefitte-sur-Aire **89** C1
Pierrefonds **87** D1
Pierrefontaine-les-Varans **89** D3, **104** B1
Pierrefort **110** A1
Pierrelatte **111** C2
Pierroton **108** B1
Piertinjaure **16** A1/2
Piesaskylä **21** D3, **22** A3
Piesau **82** A2
Piesjoki **6** B2/3
Pieski **71** C2/3
Piešt'any **95** C2
Piešt'any **96** B2
Pietracamela **117** D3, **119** C1
Pietralba **113** D2
Pietra Lígure **113** C2
Pietralunga **115** C/D3, **117** C2
Pietramelara **119** C/D2/3
Pietramontecorvino **119** D2, **120** A1
Pietraperzía **125** C2
Pietrapórzio **112** B2
Pietraróia **119** D2
Pietrasanta **114** A2, **116** A1
Pieve al Toppo **115** C3, **116** B2
Pieve del Cáiro **113** D1
Pieve di Bono **106** B2
Pieve di Cadore **107** D2
Pieve di Livinallongo **107** C2
Pieve di Soligo **107** D2/3
Pieve di Teco **113** C2
Pievepélago **114** B2, **116** A1
Pieve Santo Stéfano **115** C2/3, **117** B/C2
Pieve Tesino **107** C2
Pieve Torina **115** D3, **117** C/D2
Pieve Vécchia **106** B3
Pigaí **145** C1
Pigaí **143** C3
Pigaí **148** A/B1
Pigna **113** B/C2
Pignataro Maggiore **119** C3
Pignola **120** B2/3
Pihkainmäki **22** B2
Pihkala **18** B3
Pihlajalahti **27** C1
Pihlajalahti **25** C1
Pihlajamäki **19** C3
Pihlajavaara **23** D2, **23** D1
Pihlajaveden-asema **21** C3
Pihlajavesi **21** C3
Pihlava **24** A1
Pihtipudas **21** D2, **22** A2
Pihtisulku **21** C3
Pihtšoskordši **4** B3, **10** B1
Piikkiö (Pikis) **24** B2/3
Piilijärvi **10** B3
Piilo **23** D2
Piippola **18** B3, **22** A1
Piipsjärvi **18** A3
Piispa **23** C2
Piispajärvi **19** C2
Piittisjärvi **18** B1
Pikajärvi **12** A/B3
Pikalevo **75** C1
Pikalji **137** D2
Pikis **24** B2/3
Pikkarala **18** B2
Pikkavaaraa **13** C3
Pikkujaakko **16** B1
Pikku-Kulus **12** B3
Pila **115** C/D1
Pila **104** B3
Pila Canale **113** D3
Pilas **171** D2
Piła (Schneidemühl) **71** D1/2
Piła (Schneidemühl) **72** B3
Pilastri **114** B1
Pilat-Plage **108** B1
Piléa **143** D2, **144** A2
Pilgrimstad **34** B2
Pili **147** D2
Pílion **147** C2
Pílion Óros **143** D3, **144** A
Pilis **129** C1
Piliscsaba **95** D3

Pilisszentkereszt **95** D3
Pilisvörösvár **95** D3
Piłka **71** C2
Pille-l'Ardit **108** B2
Pillingsdorf **82** A2
Piloña **152** A1
Pilorí **143** C2
Pilpala **25** C2
Pilsach-Dietkirchen **92** A1
Pilštanj **127** C2
Pilsting **92** B2
Pilträsk **16** A/B2/3
Piña de Campos **152** B2/3
Pina de Ebro **154** B3, **162** B1
Piñar **173** C1/2
Pinarejo **168** A/B1
Pinarejos **160** B1
Pinarello **113** D3
Pinarhisar **141** C3
Pinay **103** C2
Píncara **115** C1
Pincehely **128** B2
Pineda **161** D3
Pineda de la Sierra **153** C2/3
Pineda de Mar **156** B3
Pinela **151** C3, **159** C1
Piñel de Arriba **152** B3, **160** B1
Pinell de Solsonés **155** D3
Pinerolo **112** B1
Pineto **119** C1
Piney **88** B2
Pinggau **94** A3
Pinhal Novo **164** A2
Pinhão **158** B1/2
Pinheiro **150** B3, **158** A1
Pinheiro Grande **164** B1
Pinhel **159** C2
Pinilla de los Barruecos **153** C3
Pinilla del Olmo **161** D1
Pinilla de los Moros **153** C3
Pinilla de Molina **161** D2, **162** A2
Pinjainen/Billnäs **25** C3
Pinkafeld **94** A3, **127** D1
Pinneberg **52** B3, **68** B1
Pino **151** D3, **159** D1
Pino **113** D2
Pino del Río **152** A/B2
Pino do Val **150** A2
Pinofranqueado **159** C3
Pinols **102** B3, **110** B1
Piñor **150** B2
Pinos de Miramar **163** D2
Pinoso **169** C3
Pinos Puente **173** C2
Pinsaguel **108** B3, **155** C1
Pinseque **154** A/B3, **162** A/B1
Pinsk **98** B1
Pintamo **19** C2
Pintano **154** B2
Pinto **161** B/C3
Pinzano al Tagliamento **107** D2, **126** A2
Pinzio **159** C2
Pinzolo **106** B2
Piòbbico **115** C/D3, **117** C2
Piojärvi **27** C1
Piombino **116** A3
Pionsat **102** B2
Pioppo **124** B2
Pióraco **115** D3, **117** C/D2
Piossasco **112** B1
Piotrków Trybunalski **97** C1
Piove di Sacco **107** C3
Piovene-Rocchette **107** C3
Pióvera **113** C/D1
Pioz **161** C2
Pipriac **85** C/D3
Piqerasi **142** A2
Piqueras **162** A2
Piqueras **161** D3, **168** B1
Piran **126** A/B3
Píras **123** D1/2
Pirciato **125** C1
Pireás/Pireéfs **147** D2
Pireás/Pireéfs **148** B2
Pirgadíkia **144** B2
Pírgi **144** B1
Pirgi **143** C2
Pirgí **149** C2
Pírgos **146** A/B3
Pírgos **143** D2, **144** A2
Pírgos **147** B/C1
Piriac-sur-Mer **85** C3
Pirin **139** D3
Pirjatin **99** D2
Pirkkala **25** C1
Pirmasens **90** A1
Pirna **83** C2
Pirna **96** A1
Pirok **138** B2
Pirompré **79** C3
Pirot **135** C/D3, **139** C/D1
Pirot **140** B3
Pirovac **131** C3
Pirrttikoski **12** B3
Pirsógianni **142** B2
Pirsógianni **148** A1
Pirttijärvi **24** A1
Pirttijärvi **23** D3
Pirttikoski **18** A3
Pirttikoski **25** C2
Pirttikylä **20** A2/3
Pirttikylä **21** C3
Pirttimäki **23** B/C1
Pirttimäki **22** B1
Pirttimäki **22** B2
Pirttinen **20** B2
Pirttiniemi **21** C1
Pirttiniemi **17** C1
Pirttivaara **19** D2
Pirttivaara **23** D2/3
Pirttivuopio **10** A3
Pisa **12** A3
Pisa **23** C2
Pisa **114** A2, **116** A1/2
Pisak **131** D3, **132** A3
Pisana **107** C3
Pisany **100** B3
Pisarovina **127** D3
Pisa Tirrénia **114** A3, **116** A2
Pišča **73** D3, **97** D1, **98** A2
Pisciatello **113** D3
Pisciotta **120** A3
Piscu Vechi **135** D2/3
Písek **93** C/D1
Písek **96** A2
Pishkash **138** A3, **142** B1
Písia **147** C2
Piškorevci **128** B3, **132** B1
Pisodérion **143** C1/2
Pisogne **106** B3
Pissos **108** B2
Pisticci **120** B3
Pisto **19** D2
Pistóia **114** B2, **116** A1
Pisz (Johannisburg) **73** C3, **98** A1
Pitäjänmäki **21** D1, **22** A1
Pitarque **162** B2
Piteå **16** B3
Pite-Altervattnet **16** B3
Piteå-Munksund **16** B3
Pitești **140** B2
Pithagórion **149** D2
Pithiviers **87** C/D2
Pitigliano **116** B3, **118** A1
Pitillas **154** A2
Pitkäaho **26** B1
Pitkäjärvi **24** B2
Pitkälä **27** C/D1
Pitkälahti **22** B2
Pitkälahti **23** C3
Pitkälahti **27** C1
Pitkälahti **22** B2/3
Pitkäluoto **24** A2, **41** D2
Pitkäsalo **21** C2
Pitlochry **54** B2
Pitomača **128** A2/3
Pitres **173** C2
Pitsund **16** B3
Pittenweem **57** C1
Pitvaros **129** D2
Pivka **126** B3
Pivnica **128** A3
Pivnice **129** C3
Pivski Manastir **133** C3, **137** C1
Pizarra **172** B2
Pizzighettone **106** A3
Pizzo **122** A2
Pizzolato **124** A2
Pizzoli **117** D3, **119** B/C1
Pjätteryd **50** B2
Pjelax **20** A3
Pjesker **16** A3
Pjesörn **31** C1
Plaaz **53** D3, **69** D1
Plabennec **84** A2
Pla de San Tirs **155** C2
Plaffeien [Fribourg] **104** B1
Plaisance **110** A2
Plaisance-du-Gers **108** B3, **155** C1
Pláka **147** C3
Plameira **150** A2
Plan **155** C2
Plana **137** C1
Planá **82** B3
Plána **144** B2
Planá nad Lužnicí **93** D1
Plaňany **83** D3
Pláncios **107** C1/2
Plancoët **85** C2
Plan-de-Baix **111** D1
Plandište **134** B1
Plan d'Orgon **111** C/D2
Plan-du-Lac **104** B2
Plan-du-Var **112** B2
Planes **169** D2
Planfoy **103** C3
Planica **126** B2
Plánice **93** C1
Planina **127** C2
Planina **126** B3
Planina **126** B2
Planinica **135** C3
Plankenfels **82** A3
Planoles **156** A2
Plános **146** A2
Plans-sur-Bex, Les [Bex] **104** B2
Plasencia **159** D3
Plasencia del Monte **154** B2
Plasenzuela **165** D1, **166** A1
Plasiá **143** D3
Plaški **130** B1
Plassen **38** B1/2
Plášťovce **95** D2
Plasy **83** C3
Plat **137** C1/2
Platak **126** B3
Platamón **143** D2
Platamón **145** B/C1
Platamona Lido **123** C1
Platania **122** A/B2
Plataniá **147** C/D1
Plataniá **144** B1
Plataniá **148** B2
Plátanos **148** B3
Plátanos **147** C1
Plátanos **143** D2
Plátanos **146** B1
Plátanos **146** B3
Platanótopos **144** B1
Platanoúsa **142** B3
Platanóvrisi **146** B3
Platariá **142** A/B3
Plate **69** C1
Plateaí **147** C/D2
Platí **143** D2
Platì **122** A3
Platí **145** C3
Platičevo **133** C/D1, **134** A1
Platíkambos **143** D3
Platíschis **126** A2
Platístomon **146** B1
Platta (Medel) [Disentis/Mustér] **105** D1/2
Plattling **92** B2
Plau **69** D1
Plau **72** A3
Plaue **81** D2, **82** A2
Plauen **82** B2
Plav **138** A1
Plava Laguna **126** A/B3, **130** A1
Plavca **130** B1
Plave **126** A/B2
Plavecký Mikuláš **95** C2
Plavișevița **135** C2
Plavna **135** C2
Plavnica **137** D2
Pławce **71** D3
Playa de Oropesa **163** C3
Playa de Pineda **163** C2
Playa de San Juan **169** D3
Playa de Tabernes **169** D2
Pleaux **102** A3, **110** A1
Pleine-Fougères **85** D2
Pleinfeld **91** D1, **92** A1
Pleiskirchen **92** B2
Plélan-le-Grand **85** C2
Plélan-le-Petit **85** C2
Plémet **85** C2
Plenas **162** B2
Pléneuf-Val-André **85** C2
Plenița **135** D2
Plérin **85** C2
Pleš **134** B3
Pleščenicy **74** B3
Plešin **133** D3, **134** A3
Plessé **85** C/D3
Plestin-les Grèves **84** B1/2
Pleszew **72** B3, **96** B1
Pleterje **127** C3
Pleternica **128** B3, **132** B1
Plettenberg **80** B1
Pleubian **84** B1
Pleumartin **101** D1
Pleuron **146** B2
Pleurs **88** A1/2
Pleven **140** B3
Pleyben **84** B2
Pleystein **82** B3
Pliego **169** B/C3, **174** A/B1
Pliešovce **95** D2
Pliezhausen **91** C2
Plitvice **131** C1
Plitvička Jezera **131** C1
Plitvički Ljeskovac **131** C1
Pljavinjas **73** D1, **74** A2
Pljevlja **133** C3
Ploaghe **123** C1/2
Plobsheim **90** A2
Plochingen **91** C2
Płock **73** C3
Ploemeur **84** B3
Ploërmel **85** C2
Ploiești **141** C2
Plomárion **149** C2
Plombières-les-Bains **89** D2
Plomin **130** A1
Plön **53** C3
Plonéour-Lanvern **84** A2/3
Plonévez-du-Faou **84** B2
Płońsk **73** C3
Płońsko **71** C2
Plössberg **82** B3
Plössberg-Schönficht **82** B3
Ploștina **135** D1
Płoty **71** C1
Plou **162** B2
Plouagat **85** B/C2
Plouaret **84** B2
Plouay **84** B2
Ploubalay **85** C2
Plœuc-sur-Lié **85** C2
Ploudalmézeau **84** A2
Plouescat **84** A1/2
Plouézec **85** B/C1
Plougasnou **84** B1/2
Plougastel-Daoulas **84** A2
Plougonven **84** B2
Plouguenast **85** C2
Plouguerneau **84** A2
Plouha **85** C1/2
Plouharnel **84** B3
Plouhinec **84** A2
Plouigneau **84** B2
Ploumanach **84** B1
Plouray **84** B2
Plovdiv **140** B3
Plozevet **84** A2
Plumelec **85** C3
Plumlov **94** B1
Plumpton **57** C3, **60** B1
Plungė **73** C1/2
Pluvigner **85** B/C3
Plužina **135** C3
Plužine **133** C3, **137** C1
Plymouth **63** B/C3
Plzeň **83** C3
Plzeň **96** A2
Pniewy **72** B3
Pniewy **71** D2
Pobar **153** D3
Poběžovice **82** B3, **92** B1
Pobla de Claramunt **155** D3, **156** A3, **163** D1
Pobla del Duc **169** D2
Pobla de Segur **155** D2
Pobladura del Valle **151** D3
Poblete **167** C2
Poboleda **163** C/D1
Pobrdje **133** D3, **134** A3, **138** A1
Počátky **94** A1
Počep **99** D1
Pöchlarn **94** A2
Počinok **75** C3
Počitelj **132** A/B3, **136** B1
Pockau **83** C2
Pocking **93** C2
Pöcking **92** A3
Pocklington **61** C/D2
Poco do Inferno **158** B2/3
Poćuta **133** C/D2, **134** A2
Podberez'je **75** B/C2
Podbořanský Rohozec **83** C2/3
Podbořany **83** C2/3
Podborove **75** C/D1
Podbro **126** B2
Podčetrtek **127** C2
Poděbrady **83** D3
Poděbrady **96** A2
Podence **151** C3, **159** C1
Podensac **108** B1
Podersdorf am See **94** B3
Podgajci Posavski **133** C1
Podgajcy **97** D2, **98** B3
Podgaje **71** D1
Podgora **131** D3, **132** A3, **136** B1
Podgorač **128** B3
Podgorac **135** C2/3
Podgorić **128** A3
Podgorica **127** B/C2
Podgorje **126** B3
Podgrab **133** B/C3
Podgrad **126** B3
Podhum **131** D3, **132** A3
Podivín **94** B1/2
Podkoren **126** B2
Podkova **145** C1
Podlapača **131** C2
Podlugovi **132** B2
Podnanos **126** B3
Podnovlje **132** B1
Podochórion **144** B1
Podol'sk **75** D3
Podpeč **126** B2/3
Podrašnica **131** D2, **132** A2
Podravska Moslavina **128** B3
Podravska Slatina **128** B3
Podravske Sesvete **128** A2
Podromanija **133** B/C2
Podsreda **127** C2
Podsused **127** D3
Podturen **127** D2
Podujevo **138** B1
Podujevo **140** A3
Podvelež **132** B3
Podvinje **132** B1
Podvoločisk **98** B3
Podvrška **135** C2
Pogar **132** B2
Poggiardo **121** D3
Poggibonsi **114** B3, **116** B2
Póggio a Caiano **114** B2, **116** A/B1
Poggiodomo **117** C3, **118** B1
Póggio Mirteto **117** C3, **118** B1
Póggio Moiano **118** B1
Póggio Renático **115** B/C1
Póggio Rusco **114** B1
Póggio Valleversa **113** C1
Pöggstall **94** A2
Pogny **88** B1
Pogonianí **142** B2
Pogorzela **71** D3
Pogradec **142** B1
Pogradec **148** A1
Pohja **25** C1
Pohja **21** D2, **22** A2
Pohjalahti **18** B1
Pohjalahti **25** C1
Pohja-Lankila **27** C1
Pohjankylä **24** B3
Pohjansaha **24** A1
Pohja/Pojo **25** B/C3
Pohjasenvaara **12** A2
Pohjaslahti **21** C3
Pohjois-Ii **18** A2
Pohjoislahti **21** C3
Pohjoisranta **18** A1/2
Pohjola **25** D1, **26** A1

Pohořelice 94 B1
Pohořelice 96 B2
Pohoří na Šumavě 93 D2
Pohtimolampi 12 A3
Poiana Mare 135 D2/3
Poiana Teiului 141 C1
Poiares 158 A3
Poijula 19 C2
Poikajärvi 12 A/B3
Poikelus 25 C1
Poikko 24 A2/3
Poikmetsä 25 C/D2, 26 A2
Point Sublime 110 A2
Poio 150 A2
Poirino 113 C1
Poisieuy 102 A1
Poissy 87 C1
Poitiers 101 C1/2
Poix 77 D3
Poix-Terron 79 B/C3
Pojan 142 A1/2
Pojanluoma 20 B2/3
Pojate 134 B3
Pokka 11 D2, 12 B1
Pokkola 24 B2
Pokljuka 126 B2
Pokupsko 127 D3
Pol 151 C1
Pola 75 C1/2
Polače 136 B1
Pola de Allande 151 C1
Pola de Somiedo 151 D1
Połajewo 71 D2
Poláky 83 C2
Polán 160 B3, 167 C1
Polari 130 A1
Polch 80 A2
Połczyn-Zdrój 71 C1
Połczyn-Zdrój 72 B2/3
Poleñino 154 B3
Polesella 115 C1
Polessk (Labiau) 73 C2
Polesskoe 99 C2
Polgár 97 C3
Polgárdi 96 B3
Polgárdi 128 B1
Polhov Gradec 126 B2
Polia 122 A/B2
Polianí 146 B3
Poliçan 142 A2
Poliçani 142 B2
Poliçani 148 A1
Policastrello 122 A1
Police 70 B1
Polichnitos 149 C2
Policko 71 C2
Poličnik 130 B2
Policoro 121 C3
Polídendron 143 D2
Polígiros 144 A2
Polígiros 148 B1
Polignac 103 C3, 110 B1
Polignano a Mare 121 C2
Poligny 104 A1
Políkastron 143 D1
Políkastron 148 B1
Polístena 122 A3
Politiká 147 D1/2
Polizzi Generosa 124 B2
Pölja 22 B2
Poljak 130 B2
Poljana 134 B2
Poljana 127 C2
Poljana 128 A3
Poljanak 131 C1
Poljane Gorenja Vas 126 B2
Poljčane 127 C2
Polje 132 B1
Poljica 136 A1
Poljice 132 B2
Poljice Popovo 137 C1
Polla 120 A2/3
Pölläkkä 22 B3
Pölläkkä 23 C3
Pöllau 94 A3, 127 D1
Polle 68 B3
Polleben 82 A1
Pollença 157 C2
Pollenfeld 92 A1
Pollenzo 113 C1
Pollfoss 32 B3, 37 C1
Pollhagen 68 A2/3
Póllica 120 A3
Polling 92 B2
Polling 92 A3
Pollos 160 A1
Pöllwitz 82 B2

Polmak (Pulmanki) 7 B/C2
Polná 94 A1
Polne 71 D1
Polock 74 B3
Polonkylä 19 D1/2
Polonnoe 99 B/C2
Polopos 173 C2
Polperro 62 B3
Polruan 62 B3
Polsingen-Döckingen 91 D1
Polski Gradec 141 C3
Polski Trâmbeš 141 C3
Polso 21 C2
Pöls ob Judenburg 126 B1
Pöltsamaa 74 A1
Polttila 24 A2
Polusperä 18 A3
Polvela 23 C2
Polvenkylä 20 B3
Polverigi 115 D3, 117 D2
Polvijärvi 23 C2
Polviniemi 19 C2
Polz 69 C2
Polzela 127 C2
Pomar 155 C3, 163 C1
Pomarance 114 B3, 116 A2
Pomarão 170 A1
Pomarez 108 A/B2/3, 154 B1
Pomárico 120 B2/3
Pomarkku (Påmark) 24 A/B1
Pomáz 95 D3
Pombal 158 A3, 164 B1
Pomer 154 A3, 161 D1, 162 A1
Pomézia 118 B2
Pomezí nad Ohří 82 B3
Pomigliano d'Arco 119 D3
Pömiö 18 A1
Pommersfelden 81 D3
Pomorie 141 C3
Pomošnaja 99 D3
Pomoy 89 C/D3
Pompei 119 D3
Pompei Scavi 119 D3
Pompignan 110 B2
Pomssen 82 A1
Poncé-sur-le-Loir 86 B3
Poncin 103 D2
Pondisménon 139 D3, 144 A1
Pondokeraséa 139 D3, 144 A1
Ponferrada 151 C2
Poniec 71 D3
Ponikovica 133 D2, 134 A2/3
Pons 100 B3
Ponsa 25 C1
Ponsacco 114 B3, 116 A2
Ponso 107 C3
Pont 104 B3
Pontacq 108 B3, 155 C1
Pontailler-sur-Saône 89 C3, 104 A1
Pont-à-Marcq 78 A2
Pont-à-Mousson 89 C1
Pontão 158 A3, 164 B1
Pontardawe 63 C1
Pontarion 102 A2
Pontarlier 104 A3
Pontassieve 115 B/C2, 116 B1/2
Pontaubault 86 A/B2
Pont-Audemer 77 C3, 86 B1
Pontaumur 102 B2
Pont-Authou 77 C3, 86 B1
Pont-Aven 84 B2/3
Pontavert 78 B3
Pont Canavese 105 C3
Pont-Carral 108 B1
Pontcharra 104 A3
Pontchâteau 85 C3
Pont-Croix 84 A2
Pont-d'Ain 103 D2
Pont d'Arc 111 C2
Pont-de-Dore 102 B2/3
Pont-de-Labeaume 111 C1
Pont-de-la-Maye 108 B1
Pont-de-l'Arche 76 B3, 86 B1
Pont-de-l'Isère 111 C1
Pont de Molins 156 B2

Pont-de-Pany 88 B3
Pont-de-Rhodes 109 D1
Pont-de-Roide 89 D3, 104 B1
Pont-de-Salars 110 A2
Pont d'Espagne 155 C2
Pont de Suert 155 C2
Pont de Tréboul 110 A1
Pont-de-Vaux 103 D2
Pont-de-Veyle 103 D2
Pont-d'Ouilly 86 A1
Pont-du-Château 102 B2/3
Pont-du-Gard 111 C2
Pont-du-Loup 112 B3
Pont du Roi 155 C2
Ponte 105 C/D2
Ponte a Elsa 114 B2/3, 116 A2
Ponte a Moriano 114 A/B2, 116 A1
Ponte Arche 106 B2
Ponteareas 150 A3
Pontebba 126 A2
Ponte Cáffaro 106 B3
Pontecagnano 119 D3, 120 A2
Ponte-Caldelas 150 A2
Ponte Castirla 113 D3
Ponteceno di sopra 113 D1, 114 A1
Ponte-Ceso 150 A1
Pontecesures 150 A2
Pontecorvo 119 C2
Ponte da Barca 150 A3, 158 A1
Pontedássio 113 C2
Ponte de Lima 150 A3, 158 A1
Ponte dell'Ólio 113 D1, 114 A1
Pontedera 114 B2/3, 116 A2
Ponte de Sor 164 B1/2
Pontedeume 150 B1
Pontedeva 150 B3
Ponte di Barbarano 107 C3
Ponte di Ferro 117 C3
Ponte di Legno 106 B2
Ponte di Nava 113 C2
Ponte di Piave 107 D3
Pontefract 61 D2
Pontegrande 105 C2
Pontelagoscuro 115 C1
Ponteland 57 D3, 61 C1
Pontelandolfo 119 D2/3
Ponte Leccia 113 D2/3
Pontelongo 107 C3
Ponte Nelle Alpi 107 D2
Ponte Nossa 106 A2/3
Pont-en-Royans 103 D3, 111 D1
Ponte-Nuovo 113 D2/3
Pontenure 114 A1
Pontenx-les-Forges 108 A2
Pontepetri 114 B2, 116 A1
Ponterwyd 59 C3
Pontes 158 A3, 164 B1
Ponte Sampaio 150 A2
Ponte San Nicolò 107 C3
Ponte San Pietro 106 A3
Pontesbury 59 D3
Pont-et-Massène 88 B3
Ponte Tresa 105 D2
Pontevedra 150 A2
Pontével 164 A2
Pontevico 106 B3
Pont-Farcy 85 D1, 86 A1
Pontfaverger-Moronvilliers 88 B1
Pontgibaud 102 B2/3
Pont-Hébert 76 B3, 86 A/B1
Ponthierry 87 D2
Ponticino 115 C3, 116 B2
Pontigny 88 A2/3
Pontijou 86 A/B3
Pontínia 118 B2
Pontinvrea 113 C2
Pöntiö 21 C1
Pontivy 85 B/C2
Pont-l'Abbé 84 A2/3
Pont, Le 104 A/B1/2
Pont-l'Evêque 76 B3, 86 B1
Pontlevoy 86 A/B3
Pontoise 87 C1

Ponton 106 B3
Pontones 168 A3
Pontons 155 D3, 156 A3, 163 D1
Pontonx-sur-l'Adour 108 A2
Pontorson 85 D2
Pontrémoli 114 A2
Pontresina 106 A2
Pontrhydfendigaid 59 C3
Pontrieux 84 B1/2
Pontrilas 63 D1
Ponts 155 C3
Pont-Sainte-Maxence 87 D1
Pont-Saint-Esprit 111 C2
Pont-Saint-Martin 105 C3
Pont-Saint-Pierre 76 B3, 86 A/B1
Ponts-de-Martel, Les 104 B1
Ponts-de-Sains 78 B3
Pöntsö 11 D3, 12 A1
Pöntsönlahti 23 C/D3
Pont-sur-Yonne 87 D2, 88 A2
Pontvallain 86 B3
Pontypool 63 C1
Pontypridd 63 C1
Ponza 118 B3
Ponzone 113 C1/2
Poola 20 A/B2
Poole 63 D2/3, 76 A1
Popel'n'a 99 C2
Poperinge 78 A2
Pópoli 119 C1
Popovac 134 B2/3
Popovača 127 D3
Popova Šapka 138 B2
Popovica 135 C2
Popovica 140 B3
Popovo 141 C3
Popowo Kościelne 71 D2
Poppel 79 C1
Poppenhausen 81 D3
Poppenhausen 81 C2
Poppi 115 C2, 116 B2
Poprad 97 C2
Pópulo 158 B1
Populónia 114 A/B3, 116 A2/3
Poraovaara 13 B/C3
Porches 170 A2
Porčia 107 D2
Porcuna 167 C3, 172 B1
Pordenone 107 D2
Pordic 85 C2
Poreč 126 A/B3, 130 A1
Poreč'je 75 D2/3
Porhov 74 B2
Pori (Björneborg) 24 A1
Poříčí nad Sázavou 83 D3
Porjus 16 A/B1
Pörkenäs 20 B1
Porkkakylät 21 D3
Porkkala 25 C3
Pörknäs 20 B1
Porla 46 A1
Porlammi 25 D2, 26 A2
Porlezza 105 D2, 106 A2
Porlock 63 C2
Pornainen 25 D2/3, 26 A2/3
Pornássio 113 C2
Pörnbach 92 A2
Pornic 85 C3, 100 A1
Pornichet 85 C3, 100 A1
Pornóapáti 127 D1
Porokylä 23 C1
Pörölänmäki 22 B3
Póros 147 D3
Porozina 130 A1
Porras 25 C2
Porraskoski 25 C/D1/2, 26 A1/2
Porrassalmi 26 B1
Porrentruy 89 D3, 90 A3
Porreres 157 C2
Porretta Terme 114 B2, 116 A/B1
Porriño 150 A3
Porsangmoen 5 D2, 6 A2
Pörsänmäki 22 B2
Porsgrunn 43 D2, 44 A1
Porsgrunn-Brevik 43 D2, 44 A1/2

Porsgrunn-Eidanger 43 D2, 44 A1
Porsgrunn-Heistad 43 D2, 44 A1/2
Porsifors 16 B2
Porspoder 84 A2
Portadown 58 A1
Portadown 54 A3, 55 D2
Portaferry 54 A3, 55 D2
Portaferry 58 A1
Portaje 159 C3, 165 C1
Portalegre 165 C1/2
Portalrubio de Guadamajud 161 D3
Portalrubio 162 A/B2
Portals Vells 157 C2
Port Appin 56 A1
Portariá 143 D3, 144 A3
Portás 150 A2
Port Askaig 56 A2
Port Askaig 54 A2/3, 55 D1
Porta Westfalica-Barkhausen 68 A3
Portbail 76 A3, 85 D1
Port Barcarès 156 B1
Portbou 156 B2
Port Camargue 111 C3
Port Carlisle 57 C3, 60 A/B1
Port d'Agres 110 A1
Port-de-Bouc 111 C3
Port-de-la-Meule 100 A1
Port-de-Lanne 108 B3, 155 C1
Port-de-Piles 101 C1
Port de San Miguel 157 D3
Port Dinorwic 59 B/C2, 60 A3
Porté 156 A2
Porte de la Creu 157 D3
Portel 165 C3
Portel-des-Corbières 110 A3, 156 B1
Portell de Morella 162 B2
Port Ellen 56 A2
Port Ellen 54 A3, 55 D1
Port-en-Bessin 76 B3, 86 A1
Port'Ércole 116 B3
Port Erin 58 B1
Port Erin 54 A3, 55 D2
Portese 106 B3
Portet-d'Aspet 109 C3, 155 C/D1/2
Portets 108 B1
Port-Eynon 62 B1
Portezuelo 159 C3, 165 D1
Port Glasgow 56 B2
Port-Grimaud 112 B3
Porthcawl 63 C1/2
Porthleven 62 A/B3
Porth Mellin 62 A/B3
Porticcio 113 D3
Pórtici 119 D3
Pórtico di Romagna 115 C2, 116 B2
Porţile de fier (Eisernes Tor) 135 C1/2
Portilla de la Reina 111 C3
Portillo 160 B3
Portimão 170 A2
Portimo 18 B1
Portimojärvi 17 D2
Portinatx 157 D3
Portinho da Arabida 164 A2/3
Portishead 63 D1/2
Port-Joinville 100 A1
Port Lamont 56 A/B2
Port-la-Nouvelle 110 A/B3, 156 B1
Port Laoise 55 D3
Port-Leucate 156 B1
Port Logan 56 A/B3
Port-Louis 84 B3
Portmadoc 59 C2/3, 60 A3
Portman 174 B1
Portmarnock 58 A2
Portnacroish 56 A1
Portnaguran 54 A1
Portnahaven 54 A3, 55 D1
Port Navalo 85 C3
Porto 113 D3
Porto 151 C3
Porto 158 A1/2
Porto Azzurro 116 A3
Porto Botte 123 C3

Portobuffolè 107 D2/3
Pórto Cárras 144 B2
Porto Cerésio 105 D2/3
Porto Cervo 123 D1
Porto Cesáreo 121 D3
Pórto Chéli 147 C3
Porto-Colom 157 C1/2
Porto Conte 123 C2
Porto Covo 164 A3,
 170 A1
Porto Cristo 157 C1
Porto d'Áscoli 117 D2/3
Porto de Lagos 170 A2
Porto de Mós 164 A1
Porto di Brenzone 106 B3
Porto do Son 150 A2
Porto Empédocle 124 B3
Portoferráio 116 A3
Portofino 113 D2
Port of Menteith 56 B1
Port of Ness 54 A1
Porto Garibaldi 115 C1
Portogruaro 107 D3,
 126 A3
Pórto Lágo 145 C1
Porto Levante 115 C1
Porto Levante 125 C/D1
Portomaggiore 115 C1
Porto Mantovano 106 B3
Portomarín 150 B2
Porto Maurízio 113 C2
Portomouro 150 A2
Pòrtom (Pirttikylä) 20 A2/3
Porto Palma 123 C3
Porto Palo 124 A2
Portopalo 125 D3
Porto Petro 157 D2
Porto-Pollo 113 D3
Porto Potenza Picena
 117 D2, 130 A3
Pórto Ráfti 147 D2
Porto Recanati 117 D2,
 130 A3
Portorož 126 A/B3
Porto San Giórgio 117 D2,
 130 A3
Porto Sant'Elpídio 117 D2,
 130 A3
Porto Santo Stéfano
 116 B3
Portoscuso 123 C3
Porto Tolle 115 C1
Porto Tórres 123 C1
Porto-Vecchio 113 D3
Portovénere 114 A2
Portovesme 123 C3
Portpatrick 56 A3
Portree 54 A2
Port-Sainte-Marie 109 C2
Port-Saint-Louis-du-Rhône
 111 C3
Port Saint Mary 58 B1
Port-Saint-Père 85 D3,
 100 A1
Pörtschach am Wörther See
 126 B2
Portsmouth 76 A1
Port Soderick 58 B1
Portsonachan 56 A1
Port-sur-Saône 89 C2
Port Talbot 63 C1
Porttikoski 12 B2
Portugalete 153 C1
Portumna 55 C3
Portunhos 158 A3
Port-Vendres 156 B2
Port William 56 B3
Porvoo/Borgå 25 D3,
 26 A3
Porzuna 167 C2
Posada 152 A1
Posada 123 D1/2
Posada de Valdeón 152 A1
Posadas 166 B3, 172 A1
Posav Bregi 127 D3
Poschiavo 106 B2
Posedarje 131 B/C2
Poseídon 147 D3
Poshnjë 142 A1
Pósina 107 C3
Posio 19 C1
Positano 119 D3
Possagno 107 C3
Possåsen 38 B2
Possendorf 83 C2
Pössneck 82 A2

Posta 117 D3, 118 B1
Póstal 107 C2
Posta Piana 120 B2
Postau 92 B2
Postavy 74 A3
Postbauer-Heng 92 A1
Postiglione 120 A2/3
Postioma 107 D3
Postira 131 D3
Post-mawr 62 B1
Postneset 6 B1
Postojna 126 B3
Postojnska Jama 126 B3
Postoloprty 83 C2
Postřižin 83 D2
Posušje 131 D3, 132 A3
Poteaux 79 D2
Potenza 120 B2
Potenza Picena 117 D2,
 130 A3
Potes 152 B1
Potka 4 B3
Potkraj 131 D3, 132 A3
Potoci 131 D2
Potok 127 D3
Potós 145 C2
Potríes 169 D2
Potsdam 70 A2/3
Potsdam 72 A3
Pottendorf 94 B3
Pottenstein 94 A3
Pottenstein 82 A3
Pöttmes 92 A2
Potton 65 B/C2
Potůčky 82 B2
Pouancé 86 A3
Pouan-les-Vallées 88 A/B2
Pougny 104 A2
Pougues-les-Eaux 102 B1
Pouillé 100 B2
Pouilley-les-Vignes 89 C3,
 104 A1
Pouillon 108 A3, 154 B1
Pouilly-en-Auxois 88 B3,
 103 C1
Pouilly-sous-Charlieu
 103 C2
Pouilly-sur-Loire 87 D3,
 102 B1
Pouilly-sur-Saône 103 D1
Poulaines 87 C3, 101 D1,
 102 A1
Pouldreuzic 84 A2
Poule-lès-Écharmeaux
 103 C2
Poúlithra 147 C3
Poullaouen 84 B2
Poulton-le-Fylde 59 C/D1,
 60 B2
Pourcieux 111 D3, 112 A3
Pourión 144 A3
Pourrain 88 A3
Pouru 21 C3
Pousa Flores 158 A3,
 164 B1
Poussu 19 D1
Pouttula 20 B2
Pouxeux 89 D2
Pouyastruc 109 B/C3,
 155 C1
Pouy-de-Touges 109 C3,
 155 D1
Pouzauges 100 B1
Pouzilhac 111 C2
Považská Bystrica 95 D1
Považská Bystrica 96 B2
Poveda de la Sierra 161 D2
Povíglio 114 B1
Povino Polje 133 C3,
 137 D1
Povlja 131 D3, 132 A3
Povljana 130 B2
Povoa 165 C3
Póvoa de Lanhoso 150 B3,
 158 A1
Póvoa de Santo Adrião
 164 A2
Póvoa de Varzim 158 A1
Póvoa e Meadas 165 C1
Powalice 71 C1
Powerscourt Gardens
 58 A2
Poyatos 161 D2
Pöylä 24 B3
Pöyry 26 B1
Poysdorf 94 B2
Pöytä 24 B2

Poza de la Sal 153 C2
Poza de la Vega 152 A/B2
Pozal de Gallinas 160 A1
Pozaldez 160 A1
Pozalmuro 153 D3, 161 D1
Pozán de Vero 155 C3
Požarevac 134 B2
Požarevac 140 A2
Pozdeň 83 C2
Požega 133 D2/3,
 134 A2/3
Požega 140 A2
Požeranje 138 B2
Poznań 71 D2/3
Poznań 72 B3
Pozo Alcón 173 D1
Pozoamargo 168 A3
Pozoantiguo 152 A3,
 159 D1, 160 A1
Pozoblanco 166 B3
Pozo-Cañada 168 B2
Pozo de Guadalajara
 161 C2
Pozo de la Serna 167 D2,
 168 A2
Pozohondo 168 B2
Pozo-Lorente 169 B/C2
Pozondón 162 A2
Pozoříce 94 B1
Pozorrubio 161 C3,
 167 D1, 168 A1
Pozos de Hinojo 159 C2
Pożrzadło 71 C3
Pozuel de Ariza 161 D1
Pozuel del Campo 162 A2
Pozuelo 168 B2
Pozuelo de Aragón 154 A3,
 162 A1
Pozuelo de Alarcón 160 B2
Pozuelo de Calatrava
 167 C2
Pozuelo de la Orden
 152 A3, 160 A1
Pozuelo de Zarzón 159 C3
Pozuelos de Calatrava
 167 C2
Pozza di Fassa 107 C2
Pożzadło Wielke 71 C1
Pozzallo 125 C3
Pozzolengo 106 B3
Pozzomaggiore 123 C2
Pozzo San Nicola 123 C1
Pozzuoli 119 C3
Pozzuolo 115 C3, 116 B2
Prača 133 B/C3
Prachatice 93 C1
Prachatice 96 A2
Pracht 80 A/B2
Prackenbach 92 B1
Prada 151 C2
Prádanos de Ojeda 152 B2
Pradejón 153 D2
Pradell de la Teixeta
 163 C/D1/2
Pradelles 110 B1
Prades 163 D3
Prades 156 A/B1/2
Prades-le-Lez 110 B2
Pradiélis 126 A2
Pradilla de Ebro 155 C3
Pradillo 153 D3
Pradléves 112 B2
Prado del Rey 171 D2,
 172 A2
Pradoluengo 153 C2
Prados Redondos 162 A2
Pragelato 112 B1
Pragersko 127 C/D2
Prägraten 107 D1
Praha 83 D3
Praha 96 A2
Prahecq 101 B/C2
Prahovo 135 C2
Práia a Mare 120 B3,
 122 A1
Praia da Rocha 170 A2
Praia de Mira 158 A2
Praia de Vieira 158 A3,
 164 A1
Praia do Areia Branca
 164 A1/2
Praia do Guincho 164 A2
Praia Grande 164 A2
Pralboino 106 B3
Pralognan-la-Vanoise
 104 B3

Pra Loup 112 A2
Prámanda 142 B3
Prameny 82 B3
Pranjani 133 D2, 134 A2
Prapatnica 131 C3
Praranger 104 B3
Prarayé 105 C2/3
Prasiá 146 A/B1
Prášily 93 C1
Prästkulla 24 B3
Prästö 41 D3
Præstø 53 D2
Præstø 72 A2
Pratau 93 D2
Prat de Comte 163 C2
Pratdip 163 C/D2
Prat-et-Bonrepaux 109 C3,
 155 D1
Prati di Tivo 117 D3,
 119 C1
Pratjau 53 C3
Prato 114 B2, 116 B1
Prato all'Isarco/Blumau
 107 C2
Prato Cárnico 107 D2,
 126 A2
Prato della Résia 126 A2
Prátola 119 D3, 120 A2
Prátola Peligna 119 C1/2
Pratolino 114 B2, 116 B1
Pratomagno/Prastmann
 107 C/D1
Prato Nevoso 113 C2
Prats de Lluçanès 156 A2
Prats-de-Mollo-la-Preste
 156 B2
Prauthoy 89 C3
Pravdinsk (Friedland)
 73 C2
Pravia 151 D1
Prazzo 112 B2
Prebl 127 C1
Přebuz 82 B2
Préchac 108 B2
Prechtal 90 B2
Précigné 86 A3
Přečistoe 75 C3
Précy-sous-Thil 88 B3
Predáppio 115 C2,
 117 B/C1
Predazzo 107 C2
Preddvor 126 B2
Predeal 141 C2
Predejane 139 C1
Predešti 135 C2
Predgrad 127 C3
Předín 94 A1
Preding 127 C1
Predlitz 126 B1
Predlitz 96 A3
Predmier 95 D1
Přední Výtoň. 93 C/D2
Predoje 137 C1
Predosa 113 C1
Predošćca 130 A1
Pré-en-Pail 86 A2
Preetz 53 B/C3
Préfailles 85 C3, 100 A1
Pregarten 93 D2
Pregarten 96 A2
Pregnana 105 D3
Pregrada 127 D2
Preignac 108 B1
Preili 74 A2
Preixens 155 D3, 163 D1
Préjano 153 D3
Prekaja 131 C/D2
Preko 130 B2
Prekonoška Pećina 135 C3
Preljina 133 D2, 134 A2/3
Prelog 127 D2
Premana 105 D2, 106 A2
Premantura 130 A1
Premeno 105 D2
Prémery 88 A3, 102 B1
Premià de Mar 156 A/B3
Premnitz 69 D2
Prémontré 78 A3
Premuda 130 B2
Prenčov 95 D2
Prenjas 138 A3, 142 B1
Prenzlau 70 B1
Prenzlau 72 A3
Přerov 96 B2
Přerov 95 C1
Pré-Saint-Didier 104 B3
Prescot 59 D2, 60 B3

Prese, Le 106 B2
Preševo 139 B/C2
Presicce 121 D3
Presjeka 137 C1
Preslav 141 C3
Prešov 97 C2
Prespa 128 A3
Pressac 101 C2
Pressath 82 A/B3
Pressath-Hessenreuth
 82 A/B3
Pressbaum 94 A2
Presseck 82 A2/3
Pressel 82 B1
Pressig 82 A2
Prestatyn 59 C2, 60 A3
Presteigne 59 C/D3
Prestesetra 29 C2
Přeštice 83 C3, 93 C1
Přeštice 96 A2
Preston 59 D1/2, 60 B2
Prestwick 56 A3
Pretor 142 B1
Pretoro 119 C1
Prettin 70 A3, 82 B1
Pretzier 69 C2
Pretzsch 70 A3
Pretzschendorf 83 C2
Preuilly-sur-Claise 101 D1
Preussisch-Oldendorf-
 Holzhausen 68 A3
Preussisch-Oldendorf
 68 A3
Preusslitz 69 D3
Prévenchères 110 B1
Préveranges 102 A2
Préveza 146 A1
Préveza 148 A2
Prezelle 69 C2
Prezid 126 B3
Prez-vers-Noréaz [Rosé]
 104 B1
Prgomet 131 C3
Priaranza del Bierzo 151 C2
Priay 103 C2
Pribeta 95 C/D3
Priboj 133 C3
Priboj 139 C1
Priboj 133 C1/2
Příbovce 95 D1
Příbram 83 C3
Příbram 96 A2
Prichsenstadt 81 D3
Prichsenstadt-Neuses
 81 D3
Pričinović 133 C1, 134 A1
Pridvorci 132 B3
Pridvorica 133 D3, 134 A3
Pridvorica 138 B1
Priego 161 D2
Priego de Córdoba
 172 B1/2
Priekopa 95 D1
Priekule 95 C1
Prienai 73 D2
Prien am Chiemsee 92 B3
Prieros 70 A/B3
Priestewitz 83 C1
Prievidza 95 D2
Prievidza 96 B2
Prignano Cilento 120 A3
Prigradica 136 A1
Prigrevica 129 C3.
Prijeboj 131 C1
Prijedor 131 D1
Prijepolje 133 C3
Prilep 138 B3, 143 C1
Prilike 133 D3, 134 A3
Priluka 131 D3, 132 A3
Priluki 99 D2
Přimda 82 B3
Primel-Trégastel 84 B1
Primišlje 127 C3, 131 B/C1
Primolano 107 C2
Primorsko 141 C3
Primošten 131 C3
Princetown 63 C3
Prinsehytta 37 C/D2
Prinzersdorf 94 A2
Príolo Gargallo 125 D3
Prioro 152 A2
Prisad 139 B/C3, 143 C1
Přísečnice 83 C2
Prisjan 139 C1
Prismala 20 B3
Prisoje 131 D3, 132 A3
Prissac 101 C2

Priština 138 B1
Priština 140 A3
Prittriching 91 D2
Pritzerbe 69 D2
Pritzier 69 C1
Pritzwalk 69 D1/2
Privas 111 C1
Priverno 118 B2
Privlaka 130 B2
Privlaka 133 C1
Prizren 138 B2
Prizren 140 A3
Prizzi 124 B2
Prnjavor 132 A/B1
Prnjavor 133 C1
Probištip 139 C2
Probstzella 82 A2
Prócchio 116 A3
Prócida 119 C3
Prodo 117 C3, 118 A/B1
Pródromos 143 D1
Pródromos 146 A1
Pródromos 147 C2
Proença a Nova 158 B3, 164 B1
Proença-a-Velha 158 B3
Proevska Banja 139 C2
Profitis 144 A2
Prohor Pčinjski 139 C2
Prokópion 147 D1
Prokuplje 135 B/C3, 139 B/C1
Prokuplje 140 A3
Prolom 138 B1
Prómachi 143 C1
Promachón 139 D3, 144 A1
Promajna 131 D3, 132 A3
Promírion 147 C/D1
Promona 131 C2
Pronstorf 53 C3
Propiac-les-Bains 111 D2
Propriano 113 D3
Prosek 138 A3
Prosigk 69 D3, 82 B1
Prosiměřice 94 A/B1
Proskinás 147 C1
Prosotsáni (Pirsópolis) 144 B1
Prosotsáni (Pirsópolis) 149 B/C1
Prossedi 119 B/C2
Prosselsheim 81 D3
Prostějov 94 B1
Prostějov 96 B2
Protići 131 D2, 132 A2
Protivanov 94 B1
Protivín 93 D1
Prottes 94 B2
Prötzel 70 B2
Prousós 146 B1
Provadija 141 C3
Provatón 145 D1, 145 D3
Provença 164 A3, 170 A1
Provenchères-lès-Darney 89 C2
Provenchères-sur-Fave 89 D2, 90 A2
Provés/Proveis 107 B/C2
Provins 88 A2
Provo 133 D1, 134 A1/2
Prozor 132 A2/3
Prozoroki 74 B3
Prudhoe 57 D3, 61 C1
Prudnik (Neustadt) 96 B2
Prulláns 155 D2, 156 A2
Prüm 79 D2
Prun 106 B3
Pruna 172 A2
Prunelli di-Fiumorbo 113 D3
Prunéřov 83 C2
Prunetta 114 B2, 116 A1
Prunişor 135 D2
Prusac 131 D2, 132 A2
Pruśce 71 D2
Pruszków 73 C3, 97 C1
Prut 141 D1
Prutting 92 B3
Prutz 106 B1
Pružany 73 D3, 98 B1
Prüzen 53 D3, 69 D1
Pružina 95 D1
Przasnysz 73 C3
Przechlewo 71 D1
Przelewice 71 C2
Przemęt 71 D3

Przemocze 71 B/C1
Przemyśl 97 D2, 98 A2
Przewóz 83 D1
Pržno 137 C2
Przybiernów 70 B1
Przybychowo 71 D2
Przybymierz 71 C3
Przyłęg 71 C2
Przytoczna 71 C2
Psača 139 C2
Psachná 147 D1/2
Psárion 146 B3
Psárion 147 C2
Psathópirgos 146 B2
Pskov 74 B2
Pšov 83 C3
Pšovlky 83 C3
Pszczew 71 C2
Ptaszkowo 71 D3
Pteleós 147 C1
Ptéri 146 B2
Ptič' 99 C1/2
Ptoïon 147 C/D2
Ptolemaïs 143 C2
Ptolemaïs 148 B1
Ptuj 96 A3
Ptuj 127 D2
Ptujska Gora 127 D2
Puanunsuo 19 D1
Pucarevo 132 A2
Puchberg am Schneeberg 94 A3
Puchheim 92 A2
Púchov 95 C/D1
Púchov 96 B2
Pucioasa 141 C2
Pučišća 131 D3
Puck 72 B2
Puckeridge 65 C2
Pudarica 130 B1/2
Pudasjärvi Kurenalus 18 B2
Puddletown 63 D2
Puderbach (Neuwied) 80 A/B2
Puebla de Alcocer 166 B2
Puebla de Alfindén 154 B3, 162 B1
Puebla de Almenara 161 C3, 167 D1, 168 A1
Puebla de Albortón 162 B1
Puebla de Arenoso 162 B3
Puebla de Beleña 161 C2
Puebla de Benifasar 163 C2
Puebla de Brollón 151 B/C2
Puebla de Don Rodrigo 167 B/C2
Puebla de Don Fadrique 168 A3, 173 D1
Puebla de Eca 161 D1
Puebla de Guzmán 171 B/C1
Puebla de la Calzada 165 D2
Puebla de la Reina 165 D2, 166 A2
Puebla del Caramiñal 150 A2
Puebla de Lillo 152 A1/2
Puebla del Maestre 165 D3, 166 A3
Puebla del Príncipe 167 D2, 168 A2
Puebla del Prior 165 D2, 166 A2
Puebla del Salvador 168 B1
Puebla de Obando 165 D2
Puebla de Parga 150 B1
Puebla de Sanabria 151 C3
Puebla de Sancho Pérez 165 D3
Puebla de Trives 151 C2
Puebla de Valles 160 B3
Puebla de Vallbona 169 C/D1
Puebla de Yeltes 159 D2
Pueblanueva 160 A3, 166 B1
Puebla San Miguel 163 C3
Puebla Tornesa 163 C3
Puéchabon 110 B2
Puendeluña 154 B2/3
Puente-Almuhey 152 A2
Puente de Domingo Flórez 151 C2
Puente de Génave 167 D3, 168 A3

Puente de la Reina 154 A2
Puente del Congosto 159 D2
Puente de Montañana 155 C2/3
Puente Duero 152 A3, 160 A1
Puentedura 153 C3
Puente Genil 172 A/B1/2
Puentenansa 152 B1
Puente Nuevo 172 A2
Puente Romano 159 C3, 165 C/D1
Puentevea 150 A2
Puente-Viesgo 152 B1
Puerto Cabrera 157 D2
Puerto de Alcudia 157 C2
Puerto de Andratx 157 C2
Puerto de Burriana 163 C3, 169 D1
Puerto de Campos 157 D2
Puerto de Motril 173 C2
Puerto de Pollença 157 C2
Puerto de Santa Cruz 166 A1
Puerto de San Vicente 166 B1
Puerto de Sóller 157 C2
Puerto de Vega 151 C1
Puerto Lápice 167 D1
Puertollano 167 C2
Puerto Lumbreras 174 A1
Puertomingalvo 162 B3
Puerto Moral 165 D3, 171 C1
Puerto Real 171 D3
Puerto Serrano 171 D2, 172 A2
Puget-Théniers 112 B2
Puget-Ville 112 A3
Pugnac 100 B3, 108 B1
Puhos 23 D3
Puhos 19 C2
Puichéric 110 A3, 156 B1
Puig 169 D1
Puigcerdà 156 A2
Puigpuñent 157 C2
Puig-reig 156 A2
Puigverd de Lleida 155 C3, 163 C1
Puiseaux 87 D2
Puisieux 78 A2/3
Puisserguier 110 A/B3, 156 B1
Puivert 109 D3, 156 A1
Pujerra 172 A2/3
Pujols-sur-Dordogne 108 B1
Pukaro/Pockar 25 D2, 26 B2
Pukavik 51 C2
Pukè 138 A2
Pukiš 133 C1
Pukkila 25 D2, 26 A2
Pula 130 A1
Pula 123 C/D3
Pulaj 137 D2/3
Puławy 97 C1, 98 A2
Pulborough 76 B1
Púlfero 126 A2
Pulgar 160 B3, 167 C1
Pulheim 79 D1/2, 80 A1/2
Pulheim-Sinnersdorf 79 D1, 80 A1/2
Pulheim-Stommeln 79 D1, 80 A1/2
Pulju 11 D2, 12 A1
Pulkau 94 A2
Pulkkaviita 13 C2
Pulkkila 18 B3
Pulkkila 25 D1/2, 26 A1/2
Pulkkinen 21 C2
Pulkonkoski 22 B2
Pullach 92 A2/3
Pullenreuth 82 A/B3
Pulliala 26 B1
Pulpi 174 A1
Pulsa 27 C2
Pulsano 121 C3
Pulsnitz 83 C1
Pułtusk 73 C3
Pułtusk 97 C1, 98 A2
Pulversheim 89 D3, 90 A3
Pumpsaint 63 C1
Punat 130 B1
Punkaharju 27 D1
Punkaharjun asema 27 D1

Punkalaidun 24 B2
Punkasalmi 27 D1
Punkka 26 B1
Punta Ala 116 A3
Punta Križa 130 A/B2
Punta Secca 125 C3
Punta Skala 130 B2
Punta Umbría 171 C2
Punt-Chamues-ch, La 106 C2
Punxín 150 B2
Puokio 19 C3
Puolakkavaara 12 B2
Puolanka 19 C2
Puolitaival 11 C2
Puoliväli 22 B2
Puoltikasvaara 10 B3
Puolusperä 18 A3
Puotila 24 A2
Puottaure 16 B2
Pupnatska Luka 136 A/B1
Puračić 132 B2
Puralankylä 21 D2, 22 A2
Puranuvaara 19 C1
Puras 19 D2
Purchena 173 D2
Pürgen-Stoffen 91 D3
Pürgg 93 C/D3
Purgstall 93 D2/3, 94 A2/3
Purkersdorf 94 A/B2
Purkijaur 16 A1
Purmerend 66 B2
Purmo 20 B1/2
Purmojärvi 21 B/C2
Purnumukka 12 B1
Purnuvaara 10 B3
Purontaka 21 C1
Purroy de la Solana 155 C3
Purujosa 154 A3, 162 A1
Purullena 173 C2
Puschwitz 83 D1
Puškin 74 B1
Puškinskie 74 B2
Püspökladány 97 C3, 140 A1
Pussay 87 C2
Pussemange 79 C3
Pusterwald 126 B1
Pustevny 95 C/D1
Pustoška 74 B2
Pusula 25 C2/3
Puszczykowo 71 D3
Pusztamagyaród 128 A2
Pusztamérges 129 C/D2
Pusztaszabolcs 129 C1
Pusztaszames 128 B1/2
Pusztavám 95 C3, 128 B1
Putaja 24 B1
Putanges-Pont-Écrepin 86 A1
Puthossalo 23 D3
Putifígari 123 C2
Putignano 121 C2
Putikko 27 D1
Putivl' 99 D2
Putkela 23 D2/3
Putkilahti 25 D1, 26 A1
Putkivaara 18 B1
Putlitz 69 D1
Putna 98 B3
Putous 6 B2
Putte 78 B1
Puttelange-les-Farschwiller 89 D1, 90 A1
Putten 66 B3
Püttlingen 89 D1, 90 A1
Putula 25 D2, 26 A2
Putzu Idu 123 C2
Puukari 23 C1
Puukkoinen 25 D1, 26 A1
Puukkokumpu 18 A1
Puuluoto 17 D2/3, 18 A1
Puumala 27 C1
Puuppola 21 D3, 22 A3
Puutikkala 25 C1
Puutossalmi 22 B2/3
Puutteenperä 17 D3, 18 A1
Puydrouard 100 B2
Puy-Guillaume 102 A2
Puylagarde 109 D2
Puylaroque 109 D2
Puylaurens 109 D3
Puy-l'Évêque 108 B1
Puymiclan 109 C1
Puymirol 109 C2
Puyôô 108 A3, 154 B1
Puyravault 100 B2

Puzol 169 D1
Pwllheli 58 B3
Pwllheli 55 D3
Pyhäjärvi 12 B2/3
Pyhäjärvi 21 D1, 22 A1
Pyhäjärvi 6 A/B3, 11 D1
Pyhäjoki 24 B2
Pyhäjoki 18 A3
Pyhäkylä 19 C2
Pyhältö 26 B2
Pyhänkoski 18 A3
Pyhäntä 18 B3, 21 D1, 22 A1
Pyhäntä 19 C3
Pyhäntaka 25 D2, 26 A2
Pyhäportti 18 A/B1
Pyhäranta 24 A2, 41 D2
Pyhäsalmi 21 D1, 22 A1
Pyhäselkä 23 D3
Pyhra 94 A2
Pyhtää/Pyttis 26 B2/3
Pylälahti 21 D2, 22 A2
Pyle 63 C1/2
Pylkönmäki 21 C3
Pylvänälä 22 A/B3
Pyntäinen 24 A/B1
Pyöli 24 B2
Pyöli 25 C3
Pyöree 22 B1
Pyörni 20 B2/3
Pyrbaum 92 A1
Pyrrönperä 21 D1, 22 A1
Pyrzyce 70 B1/2
Pyšely 83 D3
Pytalovo 74 B2
Pyttbua 32 B3, 37 C1
Pyydyskylä 21 D2/3, 22 A2/3
Pyykkölänvaara 19 C/D3
Pyyli 23 C3
Pyyrinlahti 21 D2, 22 A2/3

Q

Qeparoi 142 A2
Quadrazaes 159 C3
Quaglietta 120 A2
Quakenbrück 67 D2
Qualiano 119 C3
Quarré-les-Tombes 88 A3
Quart 105 B/C3
Quart d'Onyar 156 B2
Quarteira 170 A/B2
Quarto d'Altino 107 D3
Quartu Sant'Élena 123 D3
Quédillac 85 C2
Quedlinburg 69 C3
Queensferry 57 C1/2
Queijada 150 A/3, 158 A1
Queipo 171 D2
Queis 82 B1
Quejo 153 C1
Quel 153 D2/3
Quelaines 86 A2
Quelfes 170 B2
Quellendorf 69 D3
Queluz 164 A2
Quemada 153 C3, 161 C1
Quend 77 D2
Quenstedt 69 C3, 82 A1
Queralbs 156 A2
Quercianella 114 A3, 116 A2
Querença 170 B2
Querfurt 82 A1
Quérigut 156 A1
Quero 167 D1, 168 A1
Querol 163 C1
Quéron 85 C2
Querschied 89 D1, 90 A1
Quesa 169 C2
Quesada 167 D3, 168 A3, 173 C1
Quesnoy-sur-Deûle 78 A2
Questembert 85 C3
Quettehou 76 B3
Quetzdölsdorf 82 B1
Queyrac 100 B3
Quiaios 158 A3
Quiberon 84 B3
Quiberville 77 C2/3
Quickborn 52 B3, 68 B1
Quiévrain 78 B2

Quiévrechain **78** B2
Quiliano **113** C2
Quillan **156** A1
Quillebeuf-sur-Seine **77** C3
Quimerch **84** A/B2
Quimper **84** A/B2
Quimperlé **84** B2/3
Quincoces de Yuso **153** C2
Quinéville **76** B3
Quingey **104** A1
Quinson **112** A3
Quinta do Anjo **164** A2
Quintana de la Serena **166** A2
Quintana del Puente **152** B3
Quintana del Marco **151** D3
Quintanaloranco **153** C2
Quintanapalla **153** C2
Quintanar de la Sierra **153** C3
Quintanar del Rey **168** B1
Quintanar de la Orden **167** D1, **168** A1
Quintana Redonda **153** D3, **161** D1
Quintanarraya **153** C3, **161** C1
Quintana y Congosto **151** D2/3
Quintanilha **151** C3, **159** C1
Quintanilla de Trigueros **152** B3
Quintanilla de Arriba **152** B3, **160** B1
Quintanilla de la Mata **153** B/C3
Quintanilla Sobresierra **153** C2
Quintanilla de las Torres **152** B2
Quintanilla de San García **153** C2
Quintanilla de Abajo **152** B3, **160** B1
Quintela de Leirado **150** B3
Quintin **85** C2
Quinto **162** B1
Quintos **165** C3, **170** B1
Quinzano d'Óglio **106** A/B3
Quiroga **151** C2
Quirra **123** D3
Quissac **111** B/C2
Quistello **114** B1
Qukës **138** A3, **142** B1
Qytet Stalin (Kuçovë) **142** A1
Qytet Stalin (Kuçovë) **148** A1

R

Raaattama **11** C2/3, **12** A1
Raab **93** C2
Raabs an der Thaya **94** A1/2
Raahe (Brahestad) **18** A3
Raajärvi **12** B3
Raakku **13** C3
Rääkkylä **23** C/D3
Raalte **67** C2
Raanujärvi **12** A3, **17** D1
Raappananmäki **19** C3
Raate **19** D2/3
Raattama **11** C2/3, **12** A1
Raatti **23** C2
Rab **130** B1/2
Rabac **130** A1
Rabacal **158** A3
Råbäck **45** D2
Rábade **150** B1
Rábafüzes **127** D1
Rábahidvég **128** A1
Rabanal del Camino **151** D2
Rabanera del Pinar **153** C3
Rábano **152** B3, **160** B1
Rábano de Sanabria **151** C3
Rabastens **109** D2
Rabastens-de-Bigorre **109** B/C3, **155** C1
Rabbalshede **44** B2
R'abcevo **75** C3
Rabenau **81** C2
Rabenstein **94** A2/3
Råberg **30** B1
Rabí **93** C1
Rąbino **71** C1
Rabiša **135** C/D3
Råbjerg Mile **44** A/B3, **49** C1
Rabka **97** C2
Rabrovo **134** B2
Rabrovo **139** C/D3, **143** D1
Rabštejn **94** A/B1
Rabuiese **126** B3
Råby-Rönö **47** C2
Rača **94** B2
Rača **134** B2
Rača **133** C2
Rača **138** B1
Rácale **121** D3
Racalmuto **124** B2
Răcarii de Sus **135** D2
Răcășdia **135** B/C1
Racconigi **113** C1
Rače **127** C/D2
Ráchai **147** C1
Rachecourt-sur-Marne **88** B2
Râches **78** A2
Racibórz (Ratibor) **96** B2
Racimierz **70** B1
Račinovci **133** C1
Račišće **136** A/B1
Račja vas **126** B3
Ráckeve **129** C1
Racksund **15** D2
Racot **71** D3
Råda **39** C3
Råda **45** C/D2
Rada de Haro **168** A1
Radalj **133** C2
Radanovići **137** C2
Rădăuți **98** B3
Radawnica **71** D1
Radcliffe **59** D2, **60** B2/3
Radda in Chianti **114** B3, **116** B2
Raddusa **125** C2
Råde **44** B1
Radeberg **83** C1
Radebeul **83** C1
Radeburg **83** C1
Radeče **127** C2
Radęcin **71** C2
Radehov **97** D1/2, **98** B2
Rådelsbråten **38** B2
Radenbeck (Gifhorn) **69** C2
Radenci **127** D2
Radenthein **126** B1
Radevormwald **80** A1
Radiče **139** C/D3
Radicófani **116** B3
Radicóndoli **114** B3, **116** A/B2
Radijovce **138** B2
Radimlije **132** B3, **136** B1
Radiumbad Brambach **82** B2/3
Radlje ob Dravi **127** C2
Radljevo **133** D2, **134** A2
Rådmansö **41** C3
Radmer an der Hasel **93** D3
Radmirje **127** C2
Radnevo **141** C3
Radnica **71** C3
Radnice **83** C3
Radoboj **127** D2
Radoinja **133** C/D3, **134** A3
Radolfzell **91** C3
Rådom **30** A3, **35** D2
Radom **97** C1
Radomir **139** D1/2
Radomsko **97** C1
Radomyšl' **99** C2
Radomyšl **93** C1
Radona **161** D1
Radonice **83** C2
Radošina **95** C2
Radošovce **95** B/C2
Radoszyce **97** C2, **98** A3
Radotín **83** D3
Radovesice **83** C2
Radovići **137** C2
Radoviš **139** C3
Radoviš **140** A/B3
Radovljica **126** B2
Radovnica **139** C2
Radowo Wielkie **71** C1
Radstadt **93** C3, **126** A1
Radstock **63** D2, **64** A3
Raduč **131** C2
Răducăneni **141** C/D1
Radujevac **135** D2
Radun' **73** D2, **74** A3
Raduša **138** B2
Radviliškis **73** D2
Radwanow **71** C3
Radzyń Podlaski **73** D3, **97** D1, **98** A1/2
Raesfeld **67** C3
Ráfales **163** C2
Raffadali **124** B2/3
Rafína **147** D2
Rafjord **7** C1
Rafnes **43** C2
Rafsbotn **5** C2
Raftsjöhöjden **29** D3, **34** B1
Ragazzola **114** A1
Rågeleje **49** D3, **50** A2
Rägelin **69** D2, **70** A2
Raggsjö **31** C1
Raggsteinhytta **37** C3
Raglan **63** D1
Raglicy **75** B/C1
Rágol **173** D2
Ragösen **69** D3
Ragow **70** B3
Rågsveden **39** C2
Raguhn **69** D3
Ragunda **30** A3, **35** C2
Ragusa **125** C3
Råhällan **40** A2
Rahden **68** A2
Rahikka **20** B3
Rahikkala **27** C1
Rahkonen **21** C1
Rahnlavaara **23** C2
Råholt **38** A3
Rahov **97** D2/3, **98** A3
Rahula **26** B1
Raiano **119** C1/2
Raijala **24** B2
Raikuu **23** C3
Räimä **22** B2
Rain **91** D2, **92** A2
Rainbach im Mühlkreis **93** D2
Rain-Bayerdilling **91** D2, **92** A2
Raippaluoto **20** A2, **31** D3
Raippo **27** C2
Rairiz de Veiga **150** B3
Räisälä **13** C3
Raisdorf **52** B3
Raisio (Reso) **24** B2/3
Raisjavrre **5** C3, **11** B/C1
Raiskio **18** B1
Raistimäki **21** D3, **22** A3
Raitapera **21** C2
Raitoo **25** C2
Raittijärvi **10** B1
Raiutula **6** B3
Rajac **133** D3, **134** A3
Rajadell **155** D3, **156** A3, **163** D1
Raja-Jooseppi **13** C1
Rajala **12** B2
Rajalahti **24** B3
Rajamäki **25** C2
Rajavartioasema **19** D1
Rajcza **95** D1
Rajë **138** A2
Rajec **95** D1
Rájec-Jestřebí **94** B1
Rajhrad **94** B1
Rajić **128** A3, **131** D1, **132** A1
Rajka **95** B/C3
Raka **127** C2/3
Rakalj **130** A1
Rakeie **38** B3
Rakek **126** B3
Rakicke **142** B1/2
Rakita **139** D1
Rakitnica **128** A2
Rakkestad **44** B1
Rakneset **14** A2
Rákos **129** D2
Rakov **74** A/B3
Raková **95** D1
Rakova Bara **135** C2
Rakovac **132** A1
Rakovica **131** C1
Rakovica **135** C3
Rakovník **83** C3
Rakovník **96** A2
Rakovski **140** B3
Råkvåg **28** A3, **33** C1
Rakvere **74** A1
Raldon **107** B/C3
Ralja **133** D1/2, **134** A/B2
Ralsko **83** D2
Ram **134** B1
Ramacastañas **160** A3
Ramacca **125** C2/3
Rämälä **26** B1
Ramales de la Victoria **153** C1
Ramalhal **164** A2
Ramanj **15** D1/2
Ramatuelle **112** A3
Ramberg **8** A2/3
Ramberg **90** B1
Rambervillers **89** D2
Rambo **31** C2
Rambouillet **87** C2
Rambucourt **89** C1
Ramerupt **88** B2
Rameški **75** D2
Ramin **70** B1
Ramirás **150** B3
Ramkvilla **51** C1
Ramlingen-Ehlershausen **68** B2
Rämmen **39** C3
Rammsjö **30** A3, **35** C2
Ramnäs **40** A3
Rämne **44** B2
Ramnous **147** D2
Rampillon **87** D2
Ramså **9** C1
Ramsau **92** B3
Ramsberg **39** D3
Ramsbottom **59** D2, **60** B2
Ramsele **30** A2/3, **35** C1
Ramsele **31** C2
Ramsen **80** B3, **90** B1
Ramsey **58** B1, **60** A1/2
Ramsey **65** C2
Ramsey **54** A/B3, **55** D2
Ramsgate **65** C3, **76** B1
Rämshyttan **39** D2/3
Rämshyttan-turist station **39** D2/3
Ramsjö **35** C3
Rämsöö **24** B1
Ramstadlandet **28** A/B1
Ramstein-Miesenbach **90** A1
Ramsund **9** C2
Ramsvik **8** B3
Ramundberget **34** A2
Ramvik **35** D2
Ramygala **73** D2, **74** A3
Råna **42** A3
Råna **9** C2
Råna **9** C3
Ranalt **107** C1
Rånäs **40** B3
Rånåsfoss **38** A3
Rance **78** B2/3
Ránchio **115** C2, **117** C1
Rancířov **94** A1
Randaberg ferjekai **42** A2
Randabygd **32** A3, **36** B1
Rândalen **34** A3
Randalsvollen **15** C2
Randan **102** B2
Randazzo **125** C/D2
Randbøl **48** B3, **52** B1
Randbøl Hede **48** B3, **52** B1
Randegg **93** D3
Randen **32** B3, **37** C/D1
Randers **48** B2
Randijaur **16** A1
Randín **150** B3
Randsfjord **38** A3
Randsundet **34** A3
Randsverk **37** C/D2
Råneå **17** C2
Ranemsletta **28** B2
Ranes **32** B2
Rånes **86** A2
Ranft **105** C1
Rangendingen **91** B/C2
Rangsby **20** A3
Rangsdorf **70** A3
Ranhados **158** B2
Ranheim **28** A3, **33** C1
Ranis **82** A2
Rankinen **18** A3
Rankovići **132** A/B2
Rankweil **106** A1
Rannankylä **21** D1, **22** A1
Ranna-Pungerja **74** B1
Rännelanda **45** C2
Rannoch Station **56** B1
Rannungen **81** D3
Ranovac **134** B2
Ransarstugan **14** B3, **29** D1
Ransäter **39** C3, **45** D1
Ransbach-Baumbach **80** B2
Ransjö **34** B3
Ransta **40** A3
Ranstadt **81** C2
Ranta **6** B3
Rantajärvi **17** D1
Rantakangas **21** C2
Rantakylä **26** B1
Rantala **26** B2
Rantasalmen asema **23** C3
Rantasalmi **23** C3
Rantsila **18** B3
Ranttila **5** D3, **6** A3, **11** D1
Rantum **52** A2
Rantzau **53** C3
Ranua **18** B1
Ranum **48** B2
Rånvassbotn **9** C2
Ranzo **113** C2
Rao **151** C2
Raon-l'Etape **89** D2, **90** A2
Rapakkojoki **22** B1
Rapala **25** D1, **26** A1
Rapallo **113** D2
Rapla **74** A1
Rapolano Terme **115** C3, **116** B2
Rapolla **120** A/B2
Raposa **164** B2
Raposeira **170** A2
Rapoula **159** C2/3
Rapperswil **105** D1
Räpplinge **51** D1/2
Rappy **109** D3, **156** A1
Rapsáni **143** D3
Rapukkåtan **9** C/D3
Ras **133** D3, **134** A3, **138** A1
Rasal **154** B2
Räsälä **22** B2/3
Rasbo **40** B3
Rascafría **160** B2
Rasdorf **81** C2
Raseborg **25** C3
Raseiniai **73** D2
Raševica **134** B3
Rasimäki **22** B1
Rasines **153** C1
Rasinkylä **19** C2/3
Rasinperä **18** B3
Rasivaara **23** D3
Råsjö **35** C3
Raška **133** D3, **134** A/B3
Raška **140** A2/3
Raskršće **132** B2/3
Raslina **131** C3
Rasno **132** A3
Rasovo **135** D3
Rasquera **163** C2
Rássina **115** C2/3, **116** B2
Rast **135** D2/3
Rastabynes **5** C2
Rastatt **90** B1/2
Rasteby **4** A/B3, **10** A1
Rastede **67** D1, **68** A1
Rastenfeld **94** A2
Rasteš **138** B3
Rasti **11** D3, **12** A2
Rasti **23** D3
Rastičevo **131** D2, **132** A2
Rastina **129** C2/3
Rastinkylä **23** C/D1
Rastovac **137** C/D1
Rastow **69** C1
Råstrand **15** D3
Rasueros **160** A2
Rasvåg **42** B3
Ratan **20** A1, **31** D2
Rätan **34** B3
Ratasjärvi **12** A3, **17** D2

Ratasvuoma 12 A3, 17 D2
Rateče 126 B2
Ratekau 53 C3
Rathcoole 58 A2
Rathdrum 58 A2/3
Rathenow 69 D2
Rathfriland 58 A1
Rath Luirc (Charleville) 55 C3
Rathnew 58 A2
Rathsweiler 80 A3
Ratibořské Hory 83 D3, 93 D1
Ratikylä 20 B3
Ratingen 80 A1
Ratíškovice 94 B1
Ratkovo 129 C2
Ratno 73 D3, 97 D1, 98 A/B2
Ratoath 58 A2
Rattelsdorf 81 D3
Rattenberg 92 A/B3
Rattendorf 126 A2
Rattersdorf 94 B3
Rattersdorf 96 B3
Rattosjärvi 12 A3, 17 D1
Rättvik 39 D2
Ratu 20 A1, 31 D2
Ratula 25 D2, 26 A/B2
Ratula 26 B2
Ratzdorf 70 B3
Ratzeburg 53 C3, 69 C1
Rätzlingen 69 C2/3
Raubling 92 B3
Raudanjoki 12 B3
Raudaskylä 21 C1
Raudasmäki 21 C1
Raudeberg 36 A1
Raudnes 42 A1/2
Rauduskylä 11 D3, 12 A1/2
Raufoss 38 A2
Rauha 27 C2
Rauhala 11 C3, 12 A1/2
Rauhaniemi 27 C1
Rauhellern 37 C3
Rauhenebrach-Untersteinbach 81 D3
Rauland 43 C1
Rauland fjellstoge 43 C1
Raulhac 110 A1
Rauma (Raumo) 24 A2
Raumo 24 A2
Rauris 107 D1, 126 A1
Rauscedo 107 D2, 126 A2
Rauschenberg (Marburg) 81 C2
Rausjødalssetra 33 D3
Raustøl 43 C3
Rautajärvi 25 C1
Rautalampi 22 B3
Rautaperä 7 C3
Rautas 10 A3
Rautasluspe 10 A2/3
Rautavaara 23 C1/2
Rautila 24 A2
Rautio 18 A3, 21 C1
Rautionmäki 21 D2/3, 22 A2/3
Rautjärvi 27 C/D1
Rautu 24 B1
Rautuvaara 11 C3, 12 A2
Rauvantaipalle 23 C2
Rauvatn 14 B2
Rauville-la-Bigot 76 A3
Rava 130 B2
Ravadasköngäs 11 D2
Ravan 132 B2
Ravanica 134 B2
Ravanusa 124 B3
Rava-Russkaja 97 D2, 98 A2
Ravatn 14 B3
Ravattila 27 C2
Ravča 131 D3, 132 A3, 136 B1
Ravel 102 B2/3
Ravello 119 D3
Ravelsnes 4 B2
Raven 127 D2
Ravenglass 59 C1, 60 A1/2
Ravenhorst 53 D3
Ravenna 115 C2, 117 C1
Ravenna Casal Borsetti 115 C1
Ravenna Ghibullo 115 C2, 117 C1

Ravenna Lido di Sávio 115 C2, 117 C1
Ravenna Lido di Classe 115 C2, 117 C1
Ravenna Marina Romea 115 C1
Ravenna Marina di Ravenna 115 C1/2
Ravenna Mezzano 115 C1/2
Ravenna Punta Marina 115 C1/2, 117 C1
Ravenna Sant'Alberto 115 C1
Ravensburg-Eschach 91 C3
Ravensburg-Weingarten 91 C3
Ravensburg-Weingarten-Taldorf 91 C3
Ravijoki 27 B/C2
Ravioskorpi 25 D1, 26 A1
Rävlanda 45 C3, 49 D1
Ravna Dubrava 139 C1
Ravna Gora 127 C3, 130 B1
Ravnastua 5 D3, 6 A2/3
Ravne na Koroškem 127 C2
Ravni 132 B3
Ravniš 134 B3
Ravnje 133 C1
Ravno 131 D3, 132 A2/3
Ravnstrup 48 B2
Ravsted 52 B2
Rawa Mazowiecka 73 C3, 97 C1
Rawicz 96 B1
Rawtenstall 59 D1/2, 60 B2
Rayleigh 65 C3
Räyrinki 21 C2
Räyskälä 25 C2
Ražana 133 D2, 134 A2
Ražanac 130 B2
Razboj 131 D1, 132 A1
Razbojna 134 B3
Razdel'naja 141 D1
Razdol 140 B3
Razdol 139 D3
Razdrto 126 B3
Razgrad 141 C2/3
Ražice 93 C/D1
Razlog 139 D2
Razlog 140 B3
Răzvani 141 C2
Re 105 D2
Reading 64 B3
Real 158 A2
Réalmont 110 A2
Réaumur 100 B1
Réaup 109 B/C2
Rebais 87 D1, 88 A1
Rébénacq 108 B3, 154 B1
Rebild 48 B2
Rebild Bakker Nat. Park 48 B2
Rebirechioulet 109 C3, 155 C1
Rebolledo de la Torre 152 B2
Rebollo de Duero 161 C/D1
Rebollosa de Jadraque 161 C2
Rebordelo 151 C3, 159 B/C1
Recanati 117 C2
Rečane 75 C2
Recas 160 B3
Recco 113 D2
Recea 135 D2
Recey-sur-Ource 88 B3
Rechnitz 94 B3, 127 D1
Rečica 127 C/D3
Rečica 99 C1
Recke 67 D2
Reckendorf 81 D3
Recklinghausen 67 C/D3, 80 A1
Recław 70 B1
Recoaro Terme 107 C3
Recogne 79 C3
Recologne 89 C3, 104 A1
Recoules-Prévinquières 110 A/B2
Recuerda 161 C1
Reculver 65 C3, 76 B1

Recz 71 C1
Redalen 38 A2
Redange 79 D3
Redcar 61 C1
Redditch 59 D3, 64 A2
Redefin 69 C1
Redekin 69 D2
Redessan 111 C2
Redhill 65 B/C3, 76 B1
Redice 137 D1
Rédics 127 D2
Rédics 96 B3
Redinha 158 A3
Redon 85 C3
Redondela 150 A2/3
Redondo 165 C2
Redruth 62 A/B3
Redslared 50 A1
Reedham 65 D2
Rees 67 C3
Reeth 59 D1, 61 B/C1/2
Reetz 69 D3
Reetz 69 D1/2
Reffannes 101 C2
Reftele 50 B1
Refugio Club Alpino 160 A3
Regalbuto 125 C2
Regen 93 C1
Regensburg 92 B1
Regenstauf 92 B1
Reggello 115 C2/3, 116 B2
Réggio di Calábria Catafório 122 A3, 125 D2
Réggio di Calábria 122 A3, 125 D1/2
Réggio di Calábria Péllaro 122 A3, 125 D2
Reggiolo 114 B1
Réggio nell'Emília 114 B1
Reghin 97 D3, 140 B1
Regis Breitingen 82 B1
Regna 46 B2
Regnitzlosau 82 B2
Regny 103 C2
Régua 158 B1/2
Reguengo de Fetal 158 A3, 164 A1
Reguengo Grande 164 A1/2
Reguengos de Monsaraz 165 C3
Rehau 82 B2
Rehberg 69 D2
Rehburg-Loccum 68 A/B2
Rehburg-Loccum-Bad Rehburg 68 A/B2
Rehden 68 A2
Rehlingen 89 D1
Rehlingen-Biringen 79 D3
Rehna 53 C3, 69 C1
Rehula 27 C2
Reichelsheim 81 C3
Reichenau 91 C3
Reichenau an der Rax 94 A3
Reichenau [Reichenau-Tamins] 105 D1, 106 A1
Reichenbach im Kandertal 105 C2
Reichenbach 82 B2
Reichenbach (Roding) 92 B1
Reichenbach-Steegen 80 A3, 90 A1
Reichenbach 83 D1
Reichenberg 70 B2
Reichenberg (Würzburg) 81 C/D3
Reichenfels 127 C1
Reichenthal 93 D2
Reichertshausen 92 A2
Reichertshofen 92 A2
Reichmannsdorf 82 A2
Reichshof-Denklingen 80 A/B2
Reichshof-Eckenhagen 80 B1/2
Reichshoffen 90 A1
Reigada 159 C2
Reigate 65 B/C3, 76 B1
Reignac 100 B3
Reignac 101 C3
Reijolanmäki 23 D3
Reila 24 A2, 41 D1/2
Reillo 161 D3, 162 A3, 168 B1

Reims 88 A1
Rein 28 A3, 33 C1
Reina 166 A3
Reinach 105 C1
Reinbek 68 B1
Reine 8 A3
Reinfeld 53 C3, 69 B/C1
Reinfjord 4 B2
Reingard 14 B1
Reinhardshagen-Veckerhagen 81 C1
Reinhardtsgrimma 83 C2
Reinheim 33 C3, 37 D1
Reinheim 81 B/C3
Reinli 37 C3
Reinosa 152 B1/2
Reinøysund 7 C/D2
Reinsfeld 80 A3
Reinskar 4 A2
Reinskareng 14 B3
Reinsnos 42 B1
Reinsvoll 38 A2
Reisbach 92 B2
Reisbach-Haberskirchen 92 B2
Reischach (Altötting) 92 B2
Reisjärvi 21 C1
Reiskirchen 81 B/C2
Reistad 38 A3, 43 D1
Reitan 32 B3, 37 C1
Reitan 33 D2
Reitano 125 C2
Reite 9 D1/2
Reit im Winkl 92 B3
Reitkalli 26 B2
Reittiö 22 B2
Reitzenhain 83 C2
Rejas 153 C3, 161 C1
Rejmyre 46 B2
Rejsby 52 A1
Rekeland 42 A3
Reken 67 C3
Rekhulet 17 C2
Rekijoki 25 B/C2/3
Rekikoski 24 B2
Rekivaara 23 D3
Rekovac 134 B3
Rekowo 70 B1
Rekvik 4 A2/3
Reliquias 170 A1
Reljinac 134 B3
Relletti 18 A3
Relleu 169 D2
Remagen 80 A2
Rémalard 86 B2
Remchingen 90 B1
Remda 82 A2
Remdalen 14 B3, 29 D1
Remeskylä 21 D1, 22 A/B1
Remich 79 D3
Remiremont 89 D2
Remmarbäcken 30 B2/3, 35 D1
Remmaren 30 B2, 35 D1
Remmen 34 B3
Remolinos 155 C3, 163 B/C1
Remollon 112 A2
Remoulins 111 C2
Remplin 53 D3, 69 D1, 70 A1
Remscheid 80 A1
Rémuzat 111 D2
Rena 38 A1/2
Rena 166 A2
Renaison 103 C2
Renålandet 29 D2, 35 C1
Renåseter 38 A1
Renazé 85 D3
Renchen 90 B2
Rendal 32 B2
Rendalen fjellstue 38 A1
Rende 122 A1/2
Rendína 144 A/B2
Rendína 146 B1
Rendo 159 C2/3
Rendsburg 52 B3
Renedo 152 B3, 160 A/B1
Renedo de Valdavia 152 B2
Renera 161 C2
Renescure 77 D1, 78 A2
Renesse 66 A3
Renfors 31 C1
Renfrew 56 B2
Rengínion 147 C1
Rengonkylä 20 B3

Rengsdorf 80 A2
Rengsjö 40 A1
Reni 141 D2
Renieblas 153 D3, 161 D1
Renko 25 C2
Renkomäki 25 D2, 26 A2
Renkum 66 B3
Rennebu 33 C2
Rennerod 80 B2
Rennertshofen 91 D2, 92 A2
Rennertshofen-Ammerfeld 91 D2, 92 A2
Rennes 85 D2
Rennes-les-Bains 110 A3, 156 A1
Renningen 91 B/C2
Rennweg 126 A/B1
Rens 52 B2
Rensjön 30 A3, 35 C1
Rensjön 10 A2/3
Rensved 34 B2
Rentjärn 16 A3
Renträsk 16 A3
Renvallen 16 A3
Renviken 16 A3
Reocín 152 B2
Répcelak 94 B3, 128 A1
Repki 99 D1/2
Replot/Raippaluoto 20 A2, 31 D3
Repojoki 11 D2, 12 B1
Reposaari 24 A1, 41 D1
Reppen 14 B1
Repušnica 135 C3
Repvåg 5 D1, 6 A/B1
Requejo 151 C3
Requena 169 C1
Réquista 110 A2
Reriz 158 B2
Resana 107 C3
Resanovci 131 C2
Resarö 47 D1
Resavica 135 B/C2
Resavska-pećina 135 C2
Resele 30 B3, 35 D1/2
Resen 138 B3, 142 B1
Resende 158 B2
Résia 106 B1
Résia/Reschen 106 B1
Reşita 135 C1
Reşita 140 A2
Resko 71 C1
Resmo 51 D2
Resnik 133 D1, 134 A1/2
Resö 44 B2
Reso 24 B2/3
Ressons-sur-Matz 78 A3
Restábal 173 C2
Restad 45 C2
Restelica 138 A/B2
Resuttano 125 B/C2
Retamal 166 A2
Retamar 173 D2, 174 A2
Retamosa 166 A/B1
Retamoso 160 A3, 166 B1
Retascón 163 C1/2
Rethel 78 B3
Rethem 68 B2
Réthimnon 149 C3
Retiendas 161 C2
Retiers 86 A2/3
Retiro 165 C2
Retjons 108 B2
Retkovci 129 B/C3, 132 B1
Retortillo 159 C2
Retortillo de Soria 161 C1
Retournac 103 C3
Rétság 95 C3
Rettenberg 91 D3
Rettenegg 94 A3
Retuerta 153 C3
Retuerta de Bullaque 167 C1
Retunen 23 C2
Retz 94 A2
Retzow 69 D1
Reuden 69 D3
Reudnitz 82 B2
Reugny 86 B3
Reugny 102 B2
Reuilly 102 A1
Reus 163 D1/2
Reusel 79 C1
Reuterstadt Stavenhagen 70 A1

Reuti (Hasliberg) [Brünig-Hasliberg] **105** C1/2
Reutlingen **91** C2
Reutlingen-Gönningen **91** C2
Reutte **91** D3
Reutuaapa **18** B1
Rev **51** D2
Revel **109** D3
Reventin-Vaugris **103** D3
Révere **114** B1
Revest-du-Bion **111** D2
Révfülöp **128** A/B1
Revholmen **44** B1
Revigny-sur-Ornain **88** B1
Revilla del Campo **153** C2/3
Revin **79** B/C3
Revine **107** D2
Revište **95** D2
Revlingen **33** D3
Řevnice **83** C/D3
Revò **107** B/C2
Revonlahti **18** A3
Revsnes **36** B2
Revsnes **9** C2
Revsnes **28** A2, **33** C1
Revsneshamn **5** D1, **6** A1
Revsund **35** B/C2
Rexbo **39** D2
Reynel **89** C2
Řezekne **74** B2
Rezepin **72** A3
Rezepin **70** B3
Rezina **99** C3
Reznos **153** D3, **161** D1
Rezzato **106** B3
Rezzo **113** C2
Rezzoáglio **113** D1/2
Rgošte **135** C3
Rgotina **135** C2
Rgotina **140** A/B2
Rhade **67** C3
Rhälänmäki **22** B1
Rhauderfehn-Westrhauderfehn **67** D1/2
Rhauderfehn-Burlage **67** D2
Rhauderfehn-Collinghorst **67** D1
Rhaunen **80** A3
Rhayader **59** C3
Rheda-Wiedenbrück **68** A3
Rhede **67** C3
Rhede (Ems) **67** D2
Rheden **67** C3
Rheinau [Altenburg-Rheinau] **90** B3
Rheinau-Freistett **90** B2
Rheinbach **80** A2
Rheinbach-Hilberath **80** A2
Rheinberg **79** D1, **80** A1
Rheinberg-Borth **67** C3, **79** D1, **80** A1
Rheinböllen **80** A/B3
Rheine **67** D3
Rheineck **91** C3
Rheine-Mesum **67** D3
Rheinfelden **90** A/B3
Rheinfelden **90** A/B3
Rheinhausen **90** A2
Rheinsberg **70** A2
Rheinstetten-Mörsch **90** B1
Rheinzabern **90** B1
Rhêmes-Notre-Dame **104** B3
Rhenen **66** B3
Rhens **80** A/B2
Rhiconich **54** A1
Rhinow **69** D2
Rho **105** D3
Rhosllanerchrugog **59** C/D2, **60** B3
Rhumspringe **81** D1
Rhyl **59** C2, **60** A3
Riace **122** B3
Riace Marina **122** B3
Riaguas de San Bartolomé **161** C1
Riákia **143** D2
Riala **41** B/C3, **47** D1
Rialb de Noguera **155** C2
Riaño **152** A2
Rians **111** D2/3
Rianxo **150** A2
Riaza **161** C1

Ribadavia **150** B2/3
Ribadelago **151** C3
Ribadeo **151** C1
Riba de Saelices **161** D2
Ribadesella **152** A1
Ribadumia **150** A2
Ribaflecha **153** D2
Ribaforada **154** A3
Ribagorda **161** D2/3
Ribamar **164** A2
Ribarce **140** B3
Ribarci **139** C2
Ribare **134** B3
Riba-roja d'Ebre **163** C1
Ribarredonda **161** D2
Ribarroja **169** C/D1
Ribarroja del Turia **169** C/D1
Ribarska Banja **134** B3
Ribas **155** C2/3
Ribas **152** B3
Ribas de Sil **151** C2
Ribatajada **161** D2/3
Ribchester **59** D1, **60** B2
Ribe **52** A1
Ribeauvillé **89** D2, **90** A2
Ribécourt **78** A3
Ribeira **150** A2
Ribeira de Fraguas **158** A2
Ribeira de Pena **158** B1
Ribeira de Piquín **151** C1
Ribeiradio **158** A2
Ribemont **78** A/B3
Ribera **124** B2
Ribera Alta **173** C1
Ribérac **101** C3
Ribera de Cardós **155** C2
Ribera del Fresno **165** D2, **166** A2
Ribesalbes **162** B3
Ribes de Freser **156** A2
Ribnica **132** B2
Ribnica **127** C3
Ribnica **126** B3
Ribnica na Pohorju **127** C2
Ribnik **131** B/C2
Ribnik **127** C3
Ribnitz-Damgarten **53** D3
Ribnitz-Damgarten **72** A2
Ribolla **114** B3, **116** A/B2/3
Ribota **161** C1
Ricadi **122** A2
Říčany **95** C2
Riccall **61** C2
Ríccia **119** D2, **120** A1
Ríccio **115** C3, **117** B/C2
Riccione **115** D2, **117** C1
Richelieu **101** C1
Rich Hill **58** A1
Richisau [Glarus] **105** D1
Richmond **61** C1
Rickenbach-Willaringen **90** B3
Rickleå **20** A1, **31** D2
Rickling **52** B3
Rickmansworth **64** B3
Ricla **155** C3, **163** C1
Ricote **169** D3
Ridasjärvi **25** C/D2, **26** A2
Riddarhyttan **39** D3
Riddes **104** B2
Ridica **129** C2/3
Ridsdale **57** D2/3
Riebnesluspen **15** D2
Riečnica **95** D1
Riec-sur-Bélon **84** B3
Riedau **93** C2
Riede **68** A2
Riedenburg **92** A1
Riedenburg-Meihern **92** A1
Riedenhaim **81** C/D3, **91** C1
Rieden-Vilshofen **92** B1
Riedhausen **91** C3
Ried im Innkreis **93** C2
Ried im Innkreis **92** A2/3
Ried im Oberinntal **106** B1
Riedlingen **91** C2
Riedstadt-Wolfskehlen **80** B3
Riegelsberg **89** D1, **90** A1
Riegersburg **127** D1
Riegersburg **94** A1/2
Riegersdorf **126** B2
Riego de la Vega **151** D2

Riekofen-Taimering **92** B1/2
Rielasingen-Worblingen **90** B3
Riello **151** D2
Rielves **160** B3, **167** C1
Riemst **79** C2
Rieneck **81** C3
Riénsena **152** A1
Rieponlahti **22** B2
Riepsdorf **53** C3
Riesa **83** C1
Riesa **96** A1
Rieschweiler-Mühlbach **90** A1
Rieseby **52** B2
Riese Pio X **107** C3
Riesi **125** C2
Riessen **70** B3
Rieste **67** D2
Riestedt **82** A1
Rietavas **73** C2
Rietbad [Nesslau-Neu St. Johann] **105** D1, **106** A1
Rietberg **68** A3
Rietberg-Mastholte **68** A3
Rietheim-Weilheim **90** B3
Rieti **117** C3, **118** B1
Rietschen **83** D1
Rieumes **109** C3, **155** D1
Rieupeyroux **110** A2
Rieutord **111** C1
Rieutort-de-Randon **110** B1
Rieux **108** B3, **155** C1
Rieux-Minervois **110** A3, **156** B1
Rievaulx Abbey **61** C2
Riez **112** A2
Riezlern **91** D3, **106** B1
Rifiano/Riffian **107** C1/2
Rifúgio del Teodulo **105** C2
Riga **73** D1, **74** A2
Rigács **128** A1
Riggisberg [Thurnen] **105** C1
Rignac **110** A1/2
Rignano Flamínio **118** B1
Rignano Gargánico **120** A1
Rigney **89** C3, **104** A1
Rigny-Ussé **86** B3, **101** C1
Rigolato **107** D2, **126** A2
Rihtniemi **24** A2, **41** D1/2
Riihikoski **24** B2
Riihimäki **25** C2, **26** A2
Riihiniemi **25** D1, **26** B1
Riihivaara **23** D1
Riihivaara **19** D3, **23** D1
Riihivalkama **25** C2
Riihivuori **21** D3, **22** A3
Riiho **24** B1
Riiho **21** C3
Riikonkumpu **11** D3, **12** A2
Riipi **12** B2
Riipi **20** A/B3
Riipisenvaara **12** A3, **17** D1
Riisikkala **25** C2
Riisipere **74** A1
Riistavesi **23** B/C2
Riitiala **24** B1
Rijeka **126** B3, **130** A1
Rijeka **127** C3, **131** C1
Rijeka Crnojevića **137** D2
Rijssen **67** C2/3
Riksgränsen **9** D2
Rila **139** D2
Rillé **86** B3
Rillo **162** B2
Rilly-sur-Loire **86** A/B3
Rilski Manastir **139** D2
Rilski Manastir **140** B3
Rima **105** C2
Rimala **20** A/B2
Rimasco **105** C3
Rimaucourt **89** C2
Rimavská Sobota **97** C2
Rimbach (Kötzting) **92** B1
Rimbo **40** B3
Rimeize **110** B1
Rimella **105** C2/3
Rimforsa **46** B3
Rímini **115** D2, **117** C1
Rímini-Viserba **115** D2, **117** C1
Rimmilä **25** C2
Rîmnicu Sărat **141** C2
Rîmnicu Vîlcea **140** B2

Rimont **108** B3, **155** C1
Rimpar **81** C/D3
Rimske Toplice **127** C2
Rincón de la Victoria **172** B2
Rincón de Soto **154** A2
Rindal **33** B/C2
Rindarøy **32** A2
Rinde **36** B2
Rinella **125** C1
Ringarum **46** B2
Ringe **53** C1
Ringebu **37** D2
Ringelai **93** C2
Ringen **28** A3, **33** C2
Ringkøbing **48** A3
Ringmer **76** B1
Ringnäs **39** C1
Ringnes **37** D3
Ringselet **15** D2
Ringsted **49** D3, **53** D1
Ringvattnet **29** D2
Ringwood **76** A1
Rinkaby **50** B3
Rinna **46** A2
Rinøyvåg **9** C2
Rintala **20** B2
Rinteln **68** A3
Rinteln-Steinbergen **68** A3
Río **151** C2
Riobianco/Weissenbach **107** C1
Riocavado de la Sierra **153** C3
Riocerezo **153** C2
Rio de Mel **158** B2
Rio de Moinhos **164** B1
Rio de Mouro **164** A2
Riodeva **163** C3
Rio di Pusteria/Mühlbach **107** C1
Rio dos Moinhos **165** C2
Riofrío **172** B2
Ríofrío **160** A2
Rio Frio **151** C3, **159** C1
Riofrío del Llano **161** C1/2
Riogordo **172** B2
Rioja **173** D2
Riola di Vergato **114** B2, **116** B1
Riola Sardo **123** C2
Riolobos **159** C/D3, **165** D1, **166** A1
Riolo Terme **115** C2, **116** B1
Riom **102** B2
Riomaggiore **114** A2
Rio Maior **164** A1
Riomar **163** C/D2
Rio Marina **116** A3
Rio Mau **158** A1
Riom-ès-Montagnes **102** B3
Ríon **146** B2
Ríon **148** B2
Rion-des-Landes **108** A2
Ríonegro del Puente **151** D3
Rionero in Vúlture **120** A/B2
Rionero Sannítico **119** C2
Riópar **168** A2/3
Riós **151** C3
Riosa **151** D1
Rio Saliceto **114** B1
Ríoscuro **151** D2
Ríoseco **153** C/D3, **161** C1
Ríoseco de Tapia **151** D2
Riospaso **151** D1/2
Riotord **103** C3
Riotorto **151** C1
Rio Torto **151** C3, **158** B1
Riovéggio **114** B2, **116** B1
Rioz **89** C3
Říp **83** C/D2
Ripač **131** C1
Ripacándida **120** A/B2
Ripanj **133** D1/2, **134** A2
Riparbella **114** B3, **116** A2
Ripatransone **117** D2
Ripley **61** D3, **65** C1
Ripley **61** C2
Ripoll **156** A2
Ripon **61** C2
Ripon **54** B3
Riposto **125** D2
Rippig **79** D3

Ripsa **47** C1/2
Riqueval **78** A3
Risan **137** C2
Risarven **39** D1, **40** A1
Risbäck **30** B2/3, **35** D1
Risbäck **29** D1, **30** A1
Risberg **39** C2
Risberg **31** C1
Risbrunn **34** B3
Risca **63** C1
Riscle **108** B2/3
Risco **166** B2
Rise **29** D3, **34** B1
Riseberga kloster **46** A1
Risede **29** D2
Riseley Common **64** B3, **76** A/B1
Risliden **31** C1
Risnes **36** A2
Risnes **42** B3
Risnes **36** A3
Rišňovce **95** C2
Risögrund **17** C2/3
Risöhäll **20** B1
Risør **43** D2/3, **44** A2
Risøyhamn **9** C1
Rispéscia **116** B3
Rissna **35** C2
Ristedt **69** C2
Risteli **23** C1
Risti **74** A1
Ristiina **26** B1
Ristijärvi **19** C3
Ristijärvi **25** C1, **26** A1
Ristikangas **22** A3
Ristilä **13** C3
Ristilampi **12** B3
Ristinge **53** C2
Ristinkylä **23** C3
Ristniemi **24** B3
Ristonmännikkö **12** B2
Ristovac **139** C2
Risträsk **20** A1, **31** D2
Risträsk **30** B1
Risretu **135** D2/3
Risretu **140** B2
Risudden **17** D2
Risulahti **27** C1
Risum-Lindholm **52** A2
Risuperä **21** C2
Ritakoski **6** B3
Rítíni **143** D2
Ritopek **133** D1, **134** B1
Rittarylä **19** C3
Ritterhude **68** A1/2
Rittersdorf **79** D3
Rittersgrün **82** B2
Ritzerow **70** B1
Ritzleben **69** C2
Riudecols **163** D1/2
Riudóms **163** D1/2
Riutta **21** C1
Riuttala **24** B1
Riuttala **22** B2
Riuttaskylä **21** C3
Riutula **6** B3
Riva-Bella **76** B3, **86** A1
Riva del Garda **106** B2/3
Riva di Túres/Rain-Taufers **107** C1
Rivalta di Torino **112** B1
Rivanazzano **113** D1
Rivarolo Canavese **105** C3
Rivarolo Mantovano **114** A/B1
Rive-de-Gier **103** C/D3
Riverbukt **5** C2
Rivergaro **113** D1, **114** A1
Rives **103** D3, **104** A3
Rivesaltes **156** B1
Rivières-le-Bois **89** C3
Rivière-sur-Tarn **110** B2
Rivignano **107** D2/3, **126** A3
Rivisóndoli **119** C2
Rívoli **112** B1
Rivolta d'Adda **106** A3
Rixheim **90** A3
Rixö **44** B2
Rízai **147** C3
Rizárion **143** C1
Rízoma **143** C3
Rizómata **143** D2
Rjukan **43** C1
Rljeća **132** B2
Rö **35** D2
Roa **38** A3

Røa 38 B1
Roa 152 B3,160 B1
Roade 64 B2
Roaldkvam 42 A1
Roan 28 A2
Röån 30 A2, 35 C/D1
Roana 107 C2/3
Roanne 103 C2
Roasjö 45 C3, 49 D1
Roavvegiedde 6 B2
Röbäck 31 C/D2
Róbbio 105 D3
Robecco d'Óglio 106 A/B3
Röbel 69 D1, 70 A1
Röbel 72 A3
Røberg 28 A3, 33 C1
Robert-Espagne 88 B1
Robertsfors 31 D2
Robič 126 A/B2
Robin Hood's Bay 61 D1
Rob Koy's Cave 56 B1
Robleda 159 C2/3
Robledillo de Gata 159 C3
Robledillo de Mohernando
  161 C2
Robledillo de Trujillo
  165 D1/2,166 A1/2
Robledo 168 A/B2
Robledo 151 C2
Robledo de Chavela 160 B2
Robledo de Corpes 161 C2
Robledo del Mazo 160 A3,
  166 B1
Robledollano 166 A/B1.
Robles 151 D2,152 A2
Röblingen 82 A1
Robliza de Cojos 159 D2
Robregordo 161 C2
Robres 154 B3
Robres del Castillo
  153 D2/3
Roč 126 B3,130 A1
Rocafort de Queralt
  155 C3,163 C1
Rocamadour 109 D1
Roccabianca 114 A1
Roccadáspide 120 A3
Rocca di Mezzo 119 C1
Rocca di Neto 122 B2
Rocca di Papa 118 B2
Roccafranca 106 A3
Roccagorga 118 B2
Roccalbegna 116 B3
Roccalumera 125 D2
Rocca Mássima 118 B2
Roccamena 124 A/B2
Roccamonfina 119 C2/3
Roccanova 120 B3
Rocca Pia 119 C2
Rocca Priora 115 D2/3,
  117 D2
Roccaraso 119 C2
Rocca San Casciano
  115 C2,116 B1
Roccasecca 119 C2
Roccasicura 119 C/D2
Rocca Sinibalda 117 C3,
  118 B1
Roccastrada 114 B3,
  116 B2
Roccaverano 113 C1/2
Roccavione 112 B2
Roccella Iónica 122 B3
Roccelletta del Véscovo di
  Sqvillace 122 B2
Rocchetta Sant'António
  120 A2
Rocha 170 A2
Rochdale 59 D2, 60 B2
Rochebloine 111 C1
Roche-Bonne 111 C1
Rochebrune 104 B3
Rochechouart 101 D2/3
Roche d'Oëtre 86 A1
Rochefort 79 C2/3
Rochefort-en-Terre 85 C3
Rochefort-en-Yvelines
  87 C2
Rochefort-Montagne
  102 B3
Rochefort-sur-Loire 86 A3
Rochefort-sur-Mer 100 B2
Roche, La [Bulle] 104 B1/2
Rochemaure 111 C1
Rochemolles 112 B1
Rochers de Ham 85 D1,
  86 A1

Rocheservière 100 A1
Rochester 65 C3, 77 C1
Rochetaillée-sur-Aujon
  88 B3
Rochetaillée 103 D2
Rochford 65 C3
Rochlitz 82 B1
Rociana del Condado
  171 C2
Rockanje 66 A3
Rockcliffe 56 B3, 60 A1
Rockenhausen 80 B3
Rockesholm 46 A1
Rockhammar 46 B1
Rockmyrheden 15 D3
Rockneby 51 D1/2
Ročov 83 C2
Rocroi 78 B3
Rød 28 B1
Róda 142 A3
Rodach 81 D2
Rodach-Mährenhausen
  81 D2
Roda de Isábena 155 C2
Roda de Ter 156 A2
Rodal 32 B2
Rodalben 90 A1
Rödånäs 31 C2
Rodange 79 D3
Rødberg 28 A3, 33 C1
Rødberg 37 C/D3
Rødby 53 C2
Rødbyhavn 53 C2
Rødding 48 A2
Rødding 52 B1
Rödeby 51 C2
Rodeiro 150 B2
Rødekro 52 B2
Rodel 54 A2
Rodellar 155 C2
Rodelund 48 B3
Roden 67 C1/2
Ródenas 162 A2
Rødenes 38 A/B3, 44 B1
Rodenkirchen 68 A1
Rodenkirchen-Rondorf
  80 A2
Rödental-Oeslau 82 A2
Rödermark-Ober-Roden
  81 B/C3
Rodewisch 82 B2
Rodez 110 A2
Rodheim vor der Höhe
  80 B2
Rødhus 48 B1
Rodiá 143 D2
Rodiá 146 B3
Rodiezmo 151 D2, 152 A2
Rodi Gargánico 120 B1
Roding 92 B1
Rödingbäck 15 C2
Rödinghausen 68 A3
Rödinghausen-Bieren
  68 A3
Roding-Neubäu 92 B1
Rödingträsk 16 B2
Rödingträsk 31 B/C1
Rødkærsbro 48 B2
Rodleben 69 D3
Rödmyra 40 A1
Rodolívos 144 B1
Rödön 29 D3, 34 B2
Rodópolis 139 D3, 143 D1,
  144 A1
Ródos 149 D3
Rødøy 14 A/B1
Rødsand 9 C1
Rødsjøseter 28 A3, 33 C1
Rødsvollen 33 D3
Rødtangen 43 D1, 44 B1
Rødungstøl 37 C3
Rödvattnet 30 B2, 35 D1
Rødven 32 A2
Rødvig 53 D1
Roermond 79 D1
Roeselare 78 A1/2
Roetgen 79 D2
Ro Ferrara 115 C1
Röfors 46 A1/2
Rogač 131 C3
Rogaća 133 D2, 134 A2
Rogačev 99 C1
Rogačica 139 C1/2
Rogačica 133 C2
Rogalin 71 D3
Rogäsen 69 D3
Rogaška Slatina 127 C2

Rogatec 127 C/D2
Rogatica 133 C3
Rogatin 97 D2, 98 A/B3
Rogätz 69 D3
Rogenstugan 34 A3
Roggel 79 D1
Roggenburg 91 D2
Roggiano Gravina 122 A1
Rogliano 122 A/B2
Rognan 32 B1/2
Rognan 15 C1
Rogne 32 A2
Rognes 33 C2
Rogny 87 D3
Rógoi 146 A1
Rogoznica 131 C3
Rogoźno 71 D2
Rogsta 34 B2
Rogsta 40 B1
Rohan 85 C2
Rohr 92 A/B2
Rohr 81 D2
Rohrau 94 B2/3
Rohrbach an der Lafnitz
  94 A3,127 D1
Rohrbach in Oberösterreich
  93 C2
Rohrbach in Oberösterreich
  96 A2
Rohrbach-les-Bitche
  89 D1, 90 A1
Rohrbach-les-Dieuze
  89 D1, 90 A1/2
Rohrbeck 70 A3
Rohrdorf 90 B2
Röhrnbach 93 C2
Roigheim 91 C1
Rois 150 A2
Roisel 78 A3
Roismala 24 B1
Roitzsch 82 B1
Roitzsch 82 B1
Roivanen 12 B1
Rojales 169 C3,174 B1
Röjan 34 B3
Rojas 153 C2
Röjdåfors 38 B2
Röjdåsen 38 B2/3
Röjeråsen 39 D2
Röjtökmuzsaj 94 B3
Rok 46 A2
Röke 50 B2
Rokitnica 71 C3
Røkkum 32 B2
Røkland 15 C1
Roknäs 16 B3
Rokovci 129 C3,133 B/C1
Rokowo Szczecinskie
  71 D1
Röksta 30 B3
Rokuankansallispuisto
  18 B3
Rokycany 83 C3
Rokycany 96 A2
Rokytnice 95 C1
Rolampont 89 C2
Rolandstorpet 29 C/D1/2
Rold 48 B2
Røldal 42 B1
Rolde 67 C2
Rolfs 17 C2/3
Rolfstorp 49 D1, 50 A1
Rolica 164 A1
Rollag 43 D1
Rollán 159 D2
Rolle 104 A/B2
Rolleville 77 B/C3
Rollos de Arriba 168 B3,
  174 A1
Rollot 78 A3
Rollset 28 B3, 33 D2
Rolsvåg 36 A3
Rølvåg 14 A2
Rolvsøy 44 B1
Roma 47 D3
Roma 118 B2
Roma 72 B1
Roma-Fiumicino 118 A2
Roma-Focene 118 A2
Roma-Fregene 118 A2
Romagnano Sésia 105 C3
Romakloster 47 D3
Romaldkirk 57 D3,
  61 B/C1
Roma-Lido di Castel Fusano
  118 A/B2

Roma-Lido di Óstia
  118 A/B2
Roman 141 C1
Romana 123 C2
Romancos 161 C2
Romanillos de Medinaceli
  161 D1
Romano Alto 107 C3
Romanones 161 C2
Romanshorn 91 C3
Romans-sur-Isère 103 D3,
  111 C/D1
Romedal 38 A2
Romenay 103 D2
Romeral 161 C3,167 D1
Römerstein 91 C2
Romfo 32 B2/3
Romhány 95 D3
Römhild 81 D2
Romilly-sur-Seine 88 A2
Rommenäs 38 B3, 45 C1
Romny 99 D2
Romont 104 B1/2
Romorantin-Lanthenay
  87 C3
Romppala 23 D2
Romrod 81 C2
Romsey 76 A1
Romsila 24 B3
Rømskog 38 B3, 45 C1
Romstad 28 B2
Røn 37 C/D2
Rönäs 14 B2/3
Roncade 107 D3
Roncal 154 B2
Roncegno 107 C2
Ronce-les-Bains 101 C2/3
Roncesvalles 108 B3,
  155 C1
Ronchamp 89 D3
Ronchi dei Legionari
  126 A2
Ronciglione 117 C3,
  118 A1
Ronco 115 C2,117 C1
Ronco Canavese 105 C3
Ronco Scrívia 113 D1
Ronda 172 A2
Rondablikk 37 D1/2
Rondanina 113 D1/2
Rønde 49 C2
Rondelli 114 B3,116 A2/3
Rondvassbu 33 C3, 37 D1
Ronehamn 47 D3
Ronfe 158 A1
Rong 36 B3
Rongesund 36 A3
Ronkaisperä 21 D1, 22 A1
Rönkönvaara 23 C3
Rönnäng 44 B3
Rönnäs 16 A3
Rönnberg 16 A3
Rønne 51 D3
Rønne 72 A2
Ronneburg 82 B2
Ronneby 51 C2
Ronneby 72 A/B1
Ronnebyhamn 51 C2
Rønnede 53 D1
Rönneshytta 46 A2
Rönnholm 31 C3
Rönnholm 20 A2
Rönninge 47 C1
Rönnliden 16 A3
Rönnön 29 C3, 34 B1
Ronnynklä 21 D2, 22 A2
Rönö 47 B/C2
Ronsberg 91 D3
Ronse 78 B2
Rønsvik 32 B1/2
Ronta 115 B/C2,116 B1
Rontsa 23 C2
Roodeschool 67 C1
Röölä 24 A3
Roosendaal 78 B1
Roosinpohja 21 C3
Ropeid 42 A1/2
Ropenkåtan 15 B/C3
Roperuelos del Páramo
  151 D2/3
Ropinsalmi 10 B2
Ropotovo 138 B3
Roppen 106 B1
Roquebillière 112 B2
Roquebrun 110 A/B3
Roquecourbe 110 A2/3
Roquefort 108 B2

Roquefort-sur-Soulzon
  110 A/B2
Roquemaure 111 C2
Roquesteron 112 B2
Roquetaillade 108 B1
Roquetas de Mar 173 D2
Roquetes 163 C2
Roquevaire 111 D3
Rörbäck 17 C2/3
Rörbäcksnäs 38 B1/2
Rørby 49 C3, 53 C1
Rore 131 D2
Roreto Chisone 112 B1
Rørholt 43 D2, 44 A2
Röron 44 B3
Rörön 34 B2
Røros 33 D2/3
Rørøy 14 A3
Rorschach 91 C3
Rørstad 9 B/C3
Rörvattnet 29 C/D2, 34 B1
Rørvig 49 D3
Rörvik 51 C1
Rørvik 28 B1
Rørvik 28 A3, 33 C1
Rosà 107 C3
Rosal 150 A3
Rosala 24 B3
Rösa, La [Ospizio Bernina]
  106 B2
Rosal de la Frontera
  165 C3,171 B/C1
Rosans 111 D2
Rosário 170 B1
Rosarno 122 A3
Roscanvel 84 A3
Rosche 69 C2
Roscoff 84 B1
Roscommon 55 C2
Roscrea 55 C/D3
Rose 122 A/B1
Rose 137 C2
Rosegg 126 B2
Rosell 163 C2
Roselle 116 B3
Rosenberg 91 C/D1
Rosenburg 94 A2
Rosendahl 67 C/D3
Rosendahl-Darfeld 67 D3
Rosendahl-Holtwick
  67 C/D3
Rosendahl-Höpingen
  67 D3
Rosendahl-Osterwick
  67 C/D3
Rosendal 42 A1
Rosendal 28 B1
Rosenfeld 90 B2
Rosenfors 51 C/D1
Rosengarten 91 C1
Rosengarten 68 B1
Rosenheim 92 B3
Rosenholm 49 B/C2
Rosenow 70 A1
Rosenthal 81 C2
Rosenthal 83 C2
Rosentorp 39 D1
Rosersberg 40 B3, 47 C1
Roses 156 B2
Roseto degli Abruzzi
  119 C1
Roseto Valfortore 119 D2,
  120 A1
Rosheim 90 A2
Rósia 114 B3, 116 B2
Rosia Jiu 135 D1
Rosice 94 B3
Rosières-en-Blois 89 C2
Rosières-en-Santerre 78 A3
Rosiers-d'Égletons 102 A3
Rosignano Maríttimo
  114 A/B3,116 A2
Rosignano Solvay
  114 A/B3,116 A2
Rosinedal 31 C2
Rosiorii de Vede 140 B2
Rositz 82 B1/2
Roskilde 49 D3, 50 A3,
  53 D1
Roskilde 72 A2
Roški slap 131 C2/3
Rosko 71 D2
Roskovec 142 A1/2
Röslau 82 A/B3
Roslavl' 75 C3
Roslev 48 A/B2
Roslin 57 C2

Rosmaninhal 159 C3, 165 C1
Røsnæs Kloster 49 C3, 53 C1
Rosnay-l'Hopital 88 B2
Rosny-sur-Seine 87 C1
Rosolina 115 C1
Rosolina Mare 107 D3, 115 C1
Rosolini 125 C/D3
Rosoman 139 C3
Rosporden 84 B2
Rösrath 80 A2
Rossa [Castione-Arbedo] 105 D2, 106 A2
Rossano 122 B1
Rossas 158 A2
Rossenes 36 A3
Rossfjord 4 A3, 9 D1
Rosshaupten 91 D3
Rosshyttan 40 A3
Rossiglione 113 C1/2
Rossillon 103 D2, 104 A3
Rossio do São do Tejo 164 B1
Rossla 81 D1, 82 A1
Rossland 36 A3
Rosslare 58 A3
Rosslare Harbour 58 A3
Rosslare Harbour 55 D3
Rosslau 69 D3
Rossleben 82 A1
Rossleithen 93 D3
Rossön 30 A2, 35 C1
Ross-on-Wye 63 D1
Rossow 69 D2
Rossow 70 A1
Røssvik 9 C3
Rosswein 83 C1
Røst 36 A1
Rostadalen 10 A1
Rostahytta 10 A1
Röstånga 50 B2/3
Rostarzewo 71 D3
Rostassac 108 B1
Roštín 95 B/C1
Rostock 53 D3
Rostock 72 A2
Rostock-Petersdorf 53 D3
Rostock-Warnemünde 53 D3
Rostrenen 84 B2
Rostrevor 58 A1
Rostrup 48 B2
Rostudel 84 A2
Rösund 25 C3
Røsvassbukt 14 B2
Røsvik 9 C3
Rosvik 17 B/C3
Rosvoll 32 B2
Röszke 129 D2
Rot 39 C1
Rot 91 C/D3
Rota 9 C3
Rota 171 C/D2/3
Rota Greca 122 A1
Rot am See 91 C/D1
Rot am See-Brettheim 91 D1
Roteberg 39 D1, 40 A1
Rotello 119 D2, 120 A1
Rot-Ellwangen 91 C3
Rotenburg 81 C1/2
Rotenburg 68 B2
Rotenburg-Mulmshorn 68 A/B1/2
Rotglá 169 C/D2
Roth 79 D2
Roth 80 B2
Roth 92 A1
Rötha 82 B1
Rotha 82 A1
Rothbury 57 D2
Röthelstein 94 A3, 127 C1
Rothemühl 70 B1
Röthenbach (Allgäu) 91 C/D3
Röthenbach im Emmental [Signau] 105 C1
Rothenbuch 81 C3
Rothenburg 83 D1
Rothenburg ob der Tauber 91 D1
Rothenfels 81 C3
Rothenklempenow 70 B1
Rothenthurm 127 B/C1
Rotherham 61 D3
Rothesay 56 A/B2
Rothesay 54 A2/3, 55 D1
Rotonda 120 B3, 122 A1
Rotondella 120 B3
Rótova 169 D2
Rotsjö 30 A3, 35 C2
Rotsund 4 B2/3
Rott 92 B3
Rott 91 D3, 92 A3
Rottach-Egern 92 A3
Røttangen 9 C3
Rottås 32 B2
Röttenbach 91 D1, 92 A1
Rottenbach 82 A2
Rottenbuch 91 D3, 92 A3
Rottenburg 92 B2
Rottenburg 91 B/C2
Rottenburg-Bad Niedernau 91 B/C2
Rottenburg-Ergenzingen 90 B2
Rottendorf (Würzburg) 81 D3
Rottenmann 93 D3
Rotterdam 66 A3
Rotthalmünster 93 C2
Röttingen 81 C/D3, 91 C1
Rottleberode 81 D1, 82 A1
Rottmersleben 69 C3
Rottne 51 C1
Rottnemon 38 B3
Rottneros 39 B/C3
Rottofreno 113 D1, 114 A1
Rottweil 90 B2
Roturas 166 A/B1
Rötviken 29 C/D2, 34 B1
Rötz 92 B1
Roubaix 78 A2
Rouchovany 94 A/B1
Roudnice nad Labem 83 C/D2
Roudouallec 84 B2
Rouen 77 C3
Rouffach 89 D2, 90 A3
Rouffignac 101 D3, 109 C1
Rougé 85 D3
Rougemont 89 D3
Roughsike 57 C3
Rougnac 101 C3
Rouillac 101 C2/3
Roujan 110 B3
Roukala 21 C1
Roukalahti 23 C3
Roulans 89 C3, 104 A1
Roundwood 58 A2
Roupy 78 A3
Rouravaara 11 D3, 12 A1/2
Rousínov 94 B1
Roussac 101 C2
Rouvignies 78 A/B2
Rouvray 88 A/B3
Rouvroy-sur-Audry 78 B3
Rouy 103 B/C1
Rovakka 17 D1
Rovala 13 C2
Rovala 12 B3
Rovaniemi 12 A/B3
Rovanjska 131 B/C2
Rovanpää 11 D3, 12 A/B2
Rovanpää 12 A3, 17 D1
Rovanperä 11 D3, 12 A2
Rovastinaho 18 B1
Rovato 106 A/B3
Rovensko pod Troskou 83 D2
Roverbella 106 B3
Roveredo in Piano 107 D2, 126 A2
Roveredo [Lugano] 105 D2
Rovereto 107 B/C2/3
Róvere Veronese 107 B/C3
Rövershagen 53 D3
Roverud 38 B3
Roviaí 147 C1
Rovigo 115 C1
Rovinari 135 D1
Rovinj 130 A1
Rovinjsko Selo 130 A1
Rovišće 128 A2/3
Rovisuvanto 5 D3, 6 A/B3, 11 D1
Rovno 98 B2
Rovon 103 D3, 104 A3
Rów 70 B2
Rowardennan 56 B1
Roxburgh 57 C2
Roxenbaden 46 B2
Roxförde 69 C2
Royal Leamington Spa 64 A2
Royal Tunbridge Wells 65 B/C3, 76 B1
Royan 100 B3
Royat 102 B3
Roybon 103 D3
Roye 78 A3
Royères-de-Vassivières 102 A2
Røyken 38 A3, 43 D1, 44 B1
Røykenvik 38 A2
Röykkä 25 C2/3
Røymoen 32 B3
Røyrvik 29 C1
Røysheim 37 C1/2
Røysing 28 B2
Royston 65 C2
Röyttä 17 D3, 18 A1
Røytvoll 14 A3, 28 B1
Royuela 162 A2/3
Rožaj 138 A1
Rožaj 140 A3
Rozalén del Monte 161 C3
Różan 73 C3, 98 A1
Różanki 71 C2
Róża Wielka 71 D1/2
Rozay-en-Brie 87 D1/2
Rožďalovice 83 D2
Roženski manastir 139 D3
Rozières-sur-Mouzon 89 C2
Rozkoš 94 A1
Rožmberk nad Vltavou 93 D2
Rožmitál pod Třemšínem 83 C3
Rožňava 97 C2
Rožnov 98 B3
Rožnov pod Radhoštěm 95 C1
Rozoy-sur-Serre 78 B3
Roztoky 83 D2/3
Rozvadov 82 B3
Rrëshen 138 A2/3
Rrogozhinë 137 D3, 142 A1
Ruabon 59 C/D2/3, 60 B3
Ruanes 165 D1, 166 A1
Rubbestad 9 D1
Rubbestadneset 42 A1
Rübenau 83 C2
Rubeži 137 C/D1
Rubiá 151 C2
Rubián 150 B2
Rubí de Bracamonte 160 A1
Rubielos Bajos 168 B1
Rubielos de la Cérida 163 C2
Rubielos de Mora 162 B3
Rubiera 114 B1
Rubik 137 D3
Rubjerg Knude 48 B1
Rublacedo de Abajo 153 C2
Rucava 73 C1
Ruchocice 71 D3
Ruda 51 D1
Rudanka 132 B1
Rudanmaa 24 B1
Rudbøl 52 A2
Ruddington 61 D3, 65 C1
Rude 127 C/D3
Ruden 127 C2
Rüdenhausen 81 D3
Rüdersdorf 70 A/B2
Rüdersdorf 72 A3
Ruderting 93 C2
Rüdesheim 80 B3
Rüdesheim-Assmannshausen 80 B3
Rudíkov 94 A1
Rudilla 162 B2
Rudina 135 D1
Rüdingsdorf 70 A3
Rudinice 137 C1
Rudki 97 D2, 98 A2/3
Rudkøbing 53 C2
Rudná 83 C/D3
Rudna Glava 135 C2
Rudnica 133 C3
Rudnica 134 B3, 138 B1
Rudnik 133 D2, 134 A2
Rudnik 138 B1
Rüdnitz 70 A2
Rudnja 75 C3
Rudo 133 C3
Rudolstadt 82 A2
Rudozem 140 B3
Rudsgrend 43 C1
Rudskoga 45 D1/2, 46 A1
Ruds Vedby 49 C3, 53 C1
Rue 77 D2
Rueda 160 A1
Rueda de Jalón 155 C3, 163 C1
Rueda de la Sierra 161 D2, 162 A2
Rueil-Malmaison 87 C/D1
Ruelle-sur-Touvre 101 C3
Ruerrero 152 B2
Ruesta 154 B2
Ruffano 121 D3
Ruffec 101 C2
Ruffieu 104 A2
Ruffieux 104 A3
Rúfina 115 B/C2, 116 B1
Rugby 65 C2
Rugeley 59 D3, 64 A1
Ruggstorp 51 D1
Rugles 86 B1
Rugsund 36 A1
Ruguilla 161 D2
Ruhällen 40 A3
Rühen 69 C2
Ruhkaperä 21 D1, 22 A1
Ruhla 81 D2
Rühlow 70 A1
Ruhmannsfelden 93 B/C1
Ruhpolding 92 B3
Ruhpolding-Seehaus 92 B3
Ruhstorf 93 C2
Ruhstorf-Schmidham 93 C2
Ruhvana 27 D1
Ruidera 167 D2, 168 A2
Ruínas 123 C2
Ruinen 67 C2
Ruinerwold 67 C2
Ruines-en-Margeride 110 B1
Ruissalo 24 B2/3
Ruivães 150 B3, 158 B1
Rūjiena 74 A1/2
Ruka 19 D1
Rukajärvi 19 D1
Rukkisenperä 18 A3
Rullbo 39 D1
Rülzheim 90 B1
Rum 128 A1
Ruma 133 D1, 134 A1
Ruma 140 A2
Rumburk 96 A1
Rumburk 83 D2
Rumenka 129 D3, 133 C/D1, 134 A1
Rumigny 78 B3
Rumilly 104 A2/3
Rumilly-en-Cambrésis 78 A2/3
Rummukkala 23 C3
Rumo 23 C1
Rumont 89 C1
Rumpu 27 C2
Rumšiškes 73 D2, 74 A3
Runcorn 59 D2, 60 B3
Runde 36 A1
Rundhaug 4 A3, 9 D1, 10 A1
Rundmoen 15 B/C2
Rundvik 31 C3
Runemo 40 A1
Rungsted 49 D3, 50 A3, 53 D1
Runkaus 18 A1
Runni 22 B1
Runsten 51 D2
Ruohokangas 13 C1
Ruohola 18 B1/2
Ruokojärvi 12 A2, 17 D1
Ruokojärvi 17 C1/2
Ruokolahti 27 C1/2
Ruokotaipale 27 C1
Ruolahti 25 D1, 26 A1
Ruoms 111 C1/2
Ruona 21 C2
Ruona 18 B1
Ruonajärvi 12 A2/3, 17 D1
Ruoppakögäs 11 C/D3, 12 A1
Ruopsa 12 B3
Ruorasmäki 25 D1, 26 B1
Ruosniemi 24 A1
Ruotanen 21 D1, 22 A1
Ruoti 120 A/B2
Ruotinkulä 21 D3, 22 A3
Ruotsalo 21 B/C1
Ruotsinkylä 26 B2
Ruotsinpyhtää/Strömfors 26 B2
Ruotten 19 B/C2
Ruovesi 21 C3
Rupa 126 B3
Rupakivi 13 C3
Rupea 141 B/C1
Ruppendorf 83 C2
Ruppichteroth 80 A2
Rupt-sur-Moselle 89 D2/3
Rus 167 D3, 173 C1
Rušani 128 A3
Rúscio 117 C3, 118 B1
Rusdal 42 B3
Ruše 127 C2
Ruse 141 C2
Rusele 30 B1
Rușețu 141 C2
Ruševo 128 B3, 132 B1
Rushden 64 B2
Rushtë 138 A2
Rusi 25 D1, 26 A/B1
Rusinowo 71 C1
Rusinowo 71 D1/2
Ruskamen 131 D3
Ruske 30 A/B2, 35 D1
Ruskeala 25 D1, 26 A1
Ruskeala 25 C3
Ruski Krstur 129 C3
Rusko 24 B2
Ruskola 24 B3
Rusko Selo 129 D3
Rusksele 31 C1
Ruskträsk 31 C1
Rusovce 94 B2/3
Rüsselsheim 80 B3
Russeluft 5 C2
Russelv 4 B2
Russenes 5 D1/2, 6 A1
Russhaugen 9 C2
Russi 115 C2, 117 B/C1
Russkaja 98 B3
Rust 94 B3
Rustefjelbma 7 C1/2
Rusteseter 32 B3, 37 C1
Rustrel 111 D2
Ruszów 83 D1
Rutalahti 21 D3, 22 A3
Rutalahti 25 D1/2, 26 A2
Rutava 24 B2
Rute 172 B2
Rutesheim 91 B/C2
Rüthen 80 B1
Rutherglen 56 B2
Ruthin 59 C2, 60 A3
Ruthwell 57 C3, 60 A1
Rüti 105 D1
Rutigliano 121 C2
Rutino 120 A3
Rutledal 36 A2
Rutna 16 B1
Ruto 20 B2
Rutvik 17 C3
Ruuhijärvi 25 D2, 26 A2
Ruuhijärvi 12 A3, 17 D1
Ruuhimäki 21 D3, 22 A3
Ruukki 18 A3
Ruunaa 23 D2
Ruunala 25 B/C2
Ruurlo 67 C3
Ruutana 22 B1
Ruutana 25 C1
Ruuvaoja 13 C2
Ruvallen 34 A2
Ruvanaho 13 C3
Ruvaslahti 23 C2
Ruvo del Monte 120 A2
Ruvo di Púglia 120 B2, 136 A3
Ruza 75 D2/3
Ružany 73 D3, 98 B1
Ružić 131 C3
Ružin 99 C2/3
Ružinci 135 D3
Ružomberok 95 D1
Ružomberok 97 C2
Ry 48 B3

Rybnica 99 C3
Rybnik 96 B2
Rychnov 83 D2
Rychtářov 94 B1
Ryczywół 71 D2
Rydaholm 50 B1
Rydal 45 C3, 49 D1
Rydboholm 45 C3, 49 D1
Ryde 76 B1/2
Rydet 49 D1, 50 A1
Rydland 38 A1
Rydöbruk 50 A/B1
Rydsgård 50 B3
Rydsnäs 46 A3
Rydzyna 71 D3
Rye 48 B3
Rye 77 C1
Rygg 36 B1/2
Rygge 44 B1
Ryggefjord 5 D1, 6 A1
Ryggesbo 39 D1, 40 A1
Ryhälä 27 C1
Rykene 43 C3
Rykroken 33 C3, 37 D1
Rymättylä 24 A3
Ryningsnäs 51 D1
Rynkäinen 20 B3
Rynkänpuoli 18 B1
Rynoltice 83 D2
Ryönanjoki 22 B1
Ryphusseter 33 C3, 37 D1
Rypin 73 C3
Ryppefjord 5 C1, 6 A1
Ryr 45 C2
Rysjedalsvåg 36 A2
Ryssa 39 C/D2
Ryssby 50 B1/2
Ryssdal 36 B1/2
Rytilahti 13 C3
Rytinki 19 C1
Rytky 22 B1/2
Rytkynperä 18 A3, 21 D1, 22 A1
Ryttylä 25 C2, 26 A2
Ryumgård 49 C2
Rzeczenica 71 D1
Rzęśnica 70 B1
Rzeszów 97 C2, 98 A2
Rżev 75 C/D2

S

Sääksjärvi 21 C2
Sääksjärvi 25 D2, 26 A2
Sääksjärvi 20 B1/2
Sääksjärvi 24 B1
Sääksjärvi 25 D2, 26 B2
Sääksmäki 25 C2
Saal 53 D3
Saal 92 A/B1
Saalbach 92 B3, 126 A1
Saalburg 82 A2
Saaldorf 82 A2
Saaldorf-Surheim 92 B3
Saales 89 D2, 90 A2
Saalfeld 82 A2
Saalfelden am Steinernen Meer 92 B3
Saanen 104 B2
Säänjärvi 27 B/C2
Saaramaa 26 B2
Saarbrücken-Dudweiler 89 D1, 90 A1
Saarbrücken 89 D1, 90 A1
Saarburg 79 D3
Saarela 23 D1
Saarenkirkko 27 D1
Saarenkylä 21 D2, 22 A2
Saarenmaa 24 A1/2
Säärenperä 18 A2
Saaresmäki 22 B1
Saari 27 D1
Saari 25 D2, 26 A2
Saariharju 19 B/C1
Saarijärvi 24 B1
Saarijärvi 21 D2/3, 22 A2/3
Saari-Kämä 18 B1
Saarikas 21 D3, 22 A3
Saarikoski 10 B2
Saarikoski 18 A3
Saarikylä 19 D2
Saarilampi 21 D3, 22 A3
Saarimäki 23 C1
Saario 23 D3
Saaripudas 11 C3
Saariselkä 12 B1
Saarivaara 19 D3
Saarivaara 23 C2
Saarivaara 23 D3
Saarlouis 89 D1, 90 A1
Saarmund 70 A3
Saarwellingen 89 D1, 90 A1
Saas Almagell [Stalden-Saas] 105 C2
Saasenheim 90 A2
Saas Fee [Stalden-Saas] 105 C2
Saas Grund [Stalden-Saas] 105 C2
Sääskilahti 19 B/C1
Säävälä 18 B2
Šabac 133 C1, 134 A1
Šabac 140 A2
Sabadell 156 A3
Săbăoani 141 C1
Sabarat 108 B3, 155 C1
Sabáudia 118 B2/3
Sabbioneta 114 B1
Sabero 152 A2
Sabile 73 D1
Sabiñánigo 154 B2
Sabinov 97 C2
Sabiote 167 D3, 173 C1
Šabla 141 D2/3
Sables-d'Or-les-Pins 85 C1/2
Sablé-sur-Sarthe 86 A3
Sablonnières 88 A1
Sæbø 32 A3, 36 B1
Sabóia 170 A1
Sæbø (Øvre Eidfjord) 36 B3
Sæbøvik 42 A1
Sabres 108 B2
Sabrosa 158 B1
Sabugal 159 C3
Sæby 49 C1
Sacavém 164 A2
Sacecorbo 161 D2
Sacedón 161 C/D2
Saceruela 167 B/C2
Sachsenbrunn 81 D2, 82 A2
Sachsendorf 70 B2
Sachsenhagen 68 A/B2/3
Sachsenheim 91 C1
Sachsenheim-Hohenhaslach 91 C1
Sachy 79 C3
Sacile 107 D2
Sacra di San Michele 112 B1
Sacramenia 152 B3, 160 B1
Săcueni 97 C/D3, 140 A/B1
Sada 150 B1
Sádaba 155 C2
Sada de Sangüesa 155 C2
Sadelkow 70 A1
Sadjem 16 B1
Sadovec 140 B3
Sądów 70 B3
Sadská 83 D3
Sädvaluspen 15 D2
Sady 71 D2
Saelices 161 C3, 167 D1, 168 A1
Saelices de Mayorga 152 A2/3
Saelices del Río 152 A2
Saelices el Chico 159 C2
Saepinum 119 D2
Saerbeck 67 D3
Saetre 38 A3, 43 D1, 44 B1
Saeul 79 D3
Safara 165 C3
Šafárikovo 97 C2
Säffle 45 C1
Saffron Walden 65 C2
Safonovo 75 C3
Šafov 94 A1/2
Säfsnäs 39 C3
Saga 28 A3, 33 C1
Sagar 83 D1
S'Agaró 156 B3
Sågen 39 C3
Sagiáda 142 A3
Sagides 161 D1/2
Sågliden 34 A3
Sågmyra 39 D2
Sagone 113 D3
Sagra 169 D2
Sagrado 126 A3
Sagres 170 A2
Sagu 24 B3
Sagunto 162 B3, 169 D1
Sagvåg 42 A1
Ságvár 128 B1
Sahagún 152 A2
Sahalahti 25 C1
Sahankylä 20 B3
Sahinpuro 23 B/C2
Sahloinen 21 D3, 22 A3
Šahovskaja 75 D2
Sahrajärvi 21 D3
Sahún 155 C2
Šahy 95 D2/3
Šahy 96 B3
Saignelégier 89 D3, 104 B1
Saignes 102 A3
Saija 13 C2/3
Säijä 25 C1
Saikari 22 B2
Saillagouse 156 A2
Saillans 111 D1
Säimen 23 C3
Sain-Bel 103 C/D2/3
Sains-du-Nord 78 B3
Saint-Affrique 110 A2
Saint-Agnan-en-Vercors 111 D1
Saint-Agnant 100 B2
Saint Agnes 62 B3
Saint-Agrève 111 C1
Saint-Aignan-sur-Cher 86 A/B3, 101 C1
Saint-Aignan 109 C2
Saint-Aigulin 101 C3
Saint-Alban-sur-Limagnole 110 B1
Saint Albans 64 B3
Saint-Alvère 109 C1
Saint-Amand-les-Eaux 78 A/B2
Saint-Amand-de-Vendôme 86 B3
Saint-Amand-sur-Fion 88 B1
Saint-Amand-Mont-Rond 102 A/B1
Saint-Amand-en-Puisaye 87 D3
Saint-Amans-des-Cots 110 A1
Saint-Amans-la-Lozère 110 B1
Saint-Amans-Soult 110 A3
Saint-Amant-Roche-Savine 103 C3
Saint-Amant-Tallende 102 B3
Saint-Amant-de-Boixe 101 C2/3
Saint-Amarin 89 D2/3, 90 A3
Saint-Ambroix 111 C2
Saint-Amé 89 D2
Saint-Amour 103 D2
Saint-Andiol 111 C2
Saint-André-d'Hébertot 77 B/C3, 86 B1
Saint-André-de-Valborgne 110 B2
Saint-André-de-Najac 109 D2
Saint-André-les-Alpes 112 A2
Saint-André-de-l'Eure 86 A/B1
Saint-André-sur-Cailly 76 B3
Saint-André-le-Bouchoux 103 D2
Saint-André-de-Corcy 103 D2
Saint-André-de-Cubzac 108 B1
Saint-André-de-Sangonis 110 B2/3
Saint Andrews 57 C1
Saint Andrews 54 B2
Saint-Angel 102 A3
Saint Anne 63 D3
Saint-Anthème 103 C3
Saint-Antoine-de-Ficalba 109 C2
Saint-Antoine 108 B1
Saint-Antoine 113 D3
Saint-Antonin-Noble-Val 109 D2
Saint-Août 102 A1
Saint-Arcons-d'Allier 103 B/C3, 110 B1
Saint-Arnoult-en-Yvelins 87 C2
Saint Asaph 59 C2, 60 A3
Saint-Astier 101 C3
Saint-Auban-sur-l'Ouvèze 111 D2
Saint-Auban 112 A/B2
Saint-Aubin-du-Cormier 86 A/B2
Saint-Aubin-sur-Aire 89 C1/2
Saint-Aubin-de-Blaye 100 B3
Saint-Aubin-sur-Mer 76 A/B2/3
Saint-Aubin-d'Aubigné 85 D2
Saint-Augustin 102 A3
Saint-Aulaye 101 C3
Saint Austell 62 B3
Saint Austell-Fowey 62 B3
Saint-Avit 102 A/B2
Saint-Avold 89 D1
Saint-Aygulf 112 A/B3
Saint-Bard 102 A2
Saint-Bauzille-de-Putois 110 B2
Saint-Béat 109 C3, 155 C2
Saint-Beauzély 110 A2
Saint Bees 57 C3, 60 A1
Saint-Benin-d'Azy 102 B1
Saint-Benoît-en-Woëvre 89 C1
Saint-Benoît-du-Sault 101 C2
Saint-Benoît-en-Diois 111 D1
Saint-Benoît-en-Woëvre 87 D1
Saint-Bertrand-de-Comminges 109 C3, 155 C1
Saint-Blaise-la-Roche 89 D2, 90 A2
Saint Blazey 62 B3
Saint-Blin 89 C2
Saint-Bonnet-le-Froid 103 C3
Saint-Bonnet-le-Courreau 103 C3
Saint-Bonnet-près-Riom 102 B2
Saint-Bonnet-le-Château 103 C3
Saint-Bonnet-de-Joux 103 C2
Saint-Bonnet-en-Champsaur 112 A1
Saint-Bonnet-de-Bellac 101 D2
Saint-Bonnet-sur-Gironde 100 B3
Saint Boswells 57 C2
Saint-Branchs 86 B3, 101 D1
Saint Brelade 63 D3, 85 C1
Saint-Brévin-les-Pins 85 C3, 100 A1
Saint-Briac-sur-Mer 85 C1/2
Saint-Brice-en-Coglès 86 A2
Saint-Brieuc 85 C2
Saint-Broing-les-Moines 88 B3
Saint-Calais 86 B2/3
Saint-Cannat 111 D2/3
Saint-Caradec 85 C2
Saint-Cast 85 C1/2
Saint-Céré 109 D1
Saint-Cernin 102 A3, 110 A1
Saint-Cézaire-sur-Siagne 112 B3
Saint-Chamant 102 A3
Saint-Chamas 111 C/D3
Saint-Chamond 103 C3
Saint-Chély-d'Aubrac 110 A1
Saint-Chély-d'Apcher 110 B1
Saint-Chéron 87 C2
Saint-Chinian 110 A3
Saint-Christophe-en-Brionnais 103 C2
Saint-Christoly-Médoc 100 B3
Saint-Christophe-du-Ligneron 100 A1
Saint-Christol-lès-Alès 111 C2
Saint-Christophe-le-Chaudry 102 A1/2
Saint-Christophe-le-Jajolet 86 A/B1/2
Saint-Christophe-en-Bazelle 87 C3, 101 D1, 102 A1
Saint-Ciers-sur-Gironde 100 B3
Saint-Cirq-Lapopie 109 D1
Saint-Clair-sur-Epte 77 D3, 87 C1
Saint-Clar 109 C2
Saint-Clar-de-Rivière 108 B3, 155 C1
Saint-Claud-sur-le-Son 101 C2
Saint-Claude-sur-Bienne 104 A2
Saint Clears 62 B1
Saint Colombier 85 C3
Saint-Côme-d'Olt 110 A1
Saint-Constant 110 A1
Saint-Cosme-en-Vairais 86 B2
Saint-Cricq-Chalosse 108 B2/3, 154 B1
Saint-Cyprien 109 C1
Saint-Cyprien-Plage 156 B1/2
Saint-Cyr-du-Vaudreuil 76 B3, 86 A/B1
Saint-Cyr-en-Talmondais 101 C2
Saint-Cyr-l'Ecole 87 C1
Saint-Cyr-les-Vignes 103 C3
Saint-Cyr-sur-Menthon 103 D2
Saint-Cyr-sur-Mer 111 D3
Saint-Dalmas-le-Selvage 112 B2
Saint David's 62 A/B1
Saint David's 55 D3
Saint Day 62 B3
Saint-Denis-de-Gastines 85 D2, 86 A2
Saint-Denis 110 A3, 156 A1
Saint-Denis-sur-Sarthon 86 A2
Saint-Denis 85 C1
Saint-Denis-d'Oléron 101 C2
Saint-Denis-en-Bugey 103 D2
Saint-Denis-d'Anjou 86 A3
Saint-Didier-sur-Chalaronne 103 D2
Saint-Didier-en-Velay 103 C3
Saint-Dié 89 D2, 90 A2
Saint-Dier-d'Auvergne 102 B3
Saint-Disdier 111 D1, 112 A1
Saint-Dizier 88 B2
Saint-Dizier-Leyrenne 102 A2
Saint Dogmaels 62 B1
Saint-Donat 102 B3
Saint-Dyé-sur-Loire 87 C3
Sainte-Adresse 76 B3
Sainte-Anne-d'Auray 85 C3
Sainte-Anne 86 B2
Sainte-Bazeille 108 B1
Sainte-Cécile 103 C/D2
Sainte-Croix 111 D1
Sainte-Croix-Volvestre 108 B3, 155 C1
Sainte-Croix-en-Plaine 90 A3
Sainte-Engrâce 108 A/B3, 154 B1
Sainte-Énimie 110 B2

Sainte-Eulalie-en-Born **108** B2

Sainte-Feyre **102** A2

Sainte-Foy-de-Longas **109** C1

Sainte-Foy-l'Argentière **103** C3

Sainte-Foy-la-Grande **109** B/C1

Sainte-Gauburge-Sainte-Colombe **86** B1/2

Sainte-Gemme-la-Plaine **100** B2

Sainte-Geneviève-sur-Argence **110** A1

Sainte-Hélène **108** A/B1

Sainte-Hermine **100** B2

Sainte-Jalle **111** D2

Sainte-Livrade-sur-Lot **109** C2

Saint-Élix-Theux **109** C3, **155** C1

Sainte-Lucie-di-Tallano **113** D3

Sainte-Marguerite **77** C2/3

Sainte-Marie-de-Ré **101** C2

Sainte-Marie-de-Vars **112** A/B1

Sainte-Marie-aux-Mines **89** D2, **90** A2

Sainte-Marie-de-Campan **109** C3, **155** C1

Sainte-Marie-et-Sicché **113** D3

Sainte-Maure-de-Touraine **101** C1

Sainte-Maxime-sur-Mer **112** A3

Sainte-Menehould **88** B1

Sainte-Mère-Eglise **76** B3

Saint-Émilion **108** B1

Sainte-Montaine **87** D3

Sainte-Odile **90** A2

Saintes **100** B3

Sainte-Sévère-sur-Indre **102** A2

Saintes-Maries-de-la-Mer **111** C3

Saint-Esteben **108** B3, **155** C1

Saint-Estèphe **100** B3

Sainte-Suzanne **86** A2

Sainte-Thorette **102** A1

Saint-Étienne-de-Montluc **85** D3, **100** A1

Saint-Étienne-en-Dévoluy **111** D1, **112** A1

Saint-Étienne-les-Orgues **111** D2, **112** A2

Saint-Étienne-de-Baïgorry **108** B3, **155** C1

Saint-Étienne-du-Grès **111** C2

Saint-Étienne-de-Saint-Geoirs **103** D3

Saint-Étienne-de-Tinée **112** B2

Saint-Étienne-de-Lugdarès **110** B1

Saint-Étienne-Vallée-Française **110** B2

Saint-Étienne **103** C3

Saint-Fargeau **87** D3

Saint-Félicien **103** C/D3, **111** C1

Saint-Félix-Lauragais **109** D3

Saint-Félix **100** B2

Saint-Félix-de-Sorgues **110** A/B2

Saint-Fiacre **84** B2

Saintfield **56** A3

Saint Fillans **56** B1

Saint-Firmin-en-Valgodemard **112** A1

Saint-Florent **113** D2

Saint-Florent-le-Vieil **85** D3

Saint-Florent-sur-Cher **102** A1

Saint-Florentin **88** A2

Saint-Florent-des-Bois **101** C1/2

Saint-Flour **110** B1

Saint-Flovier **101** D1

Saint-Fort-sur-le-Né **101** C3

Saint-Fort-sur-Gironde **100** B3

Saint-François-Longchamp **104** A/B3

Saint-Front-sur-Lémance **109** C1

Saint-Fulgent **101** C1

Saint-Gabriel-Brécy **76** B3, **86** A1

Saint-Galmier **103** C3

Saint-Gaudens **109** C3, **155** C1

Saint-Gaultier **101** D1

Saint-Gein **108** B2

Saint-Gély-du-Fesc **110** B2

Saint-Genès-Champespe **102** B3

Saint-Genest-Malifaux **103** C3

Saint-Gengoux-le-National **103** C/D1/2

Saint-Geniès-de-Malgoirès **111** C2

Saint-Geniez-d'Olt **110** A/B1/2

Saint-Genis-Laval **103** D3

Saint-Genis-de-Saintonge **100** B3

Saint-Genis-Pouilly **104** A2

Saint-Génis-des-Fontaines **156** B1

Saint-Genix-sur-Guiers **104** A3

Saint-Geoire-en-Valdaine **104** A3

Saint-Georges-sur-Loire **86** A3

Saint-Georges-de-Luzençon **110** A/B2

Saint-Georges-en-Couzan **103** C3

Saint-Georges-du-Vièvre **77** C3, **86** B1

Saint-Georges de Didonne **100** B3

Saint-Georges-sur-la-Prée **87** C3, **102** A1

Saint-Georges-du-Bois **86** B2

Saint-Georges-de-Reneins **103** D2

Saint-Geours-de-Maremme **108** B2/3

Saint-Gérand-le-Puy **102** B2

Saint-Gérard **79** C2

Saint-Germain-de-Confolens **101** C/D2

Saint-Germain-de-Joux **104** A2

Saint-Germain-l'Herm **103** B/C3

Saint-Germain-de-Calberte **110** B2

Saint-Germain-Laval **103** C2/3

Saint-Germain-Lembron **102** B3

Saint-Germain-des-Fossés **102** B2

Saint-Germain-du-Plain **103** D1

Saint-Germain-du-Bois **103** D1

Saint-Germain-lès-Arlay **103** D1, **104** A1

Saint-Germain-Lespinasse **103** C2

Saint-Germain-les-Belles **101** D3

Saint-Germain-en-Laye **87** C1

Saint Germans **62** B3

Saint-Germé **108** B2/3

Saint-Germer-de-Fly **77** D3

Saint-Gervais-sur-Mare **110** A/B2/3

Saint-Gervais-d'Auvergne **102** B2

Saint-Gervais-les-Bains **104** B2/3

Saint-Gildas-de-Rhuys **85** C3

Saint-Gildas-des-Bois **85** C3

Saint-Gilles **111** C2/3

Saint-Gilles-Croix-de-Vie **100** A1

Saint-Gingolph **104** B2

Saint-Girons **108** B3, **155** C1/2

Saint-Girons **108** B2

Saint-Gobain **78** A3

Saint-Goin **108** B3, **154** B1

Saint-Gondon **87** D3

Saint-Gorgon-Main **104** A/B1

Saint-Gravé **85** C3

Saint-Guénolé **84** A3

Saint-Guilhem-le-Désert **110** B2

Saint-Héand **103** C3

Saint Helens **59** D2, **60** B3

Saint Helier **63** D3, **85** C1

Saint-Herbot **84** A2

Saint-Hilaire **110** A3, **156** A1

Saint-Hilaire-de-Court **87** C3, **102** A1

Saint-Hilaire-du-Harcouët **85** D2

Saint-Hilaire-de-Villefranche **100** B2/3

Saint-Hilaire-des-Loges **100** B2

Saint-Hilaire-Fontaine **103** C1

Saint-Hilaire-Cottes **77** D2, **78** A2

Saint-Hilaire-le-Grand **88** B1

Saint-Hilaire-Bonneval **101** C3

Saint Hippolyte **89** D3, **104** B1

Saint-Hippolyte-du-Fort **110** B2

Saint-Honorat **112** B3

Saint-Honoré-les-Bains **103** C1

Saint-Hubert **79** C3

Saint Ives **62** A3

Saint Ives **65** C2

Saint-James **86** A2

Saint-Jaques **105** C3

Saint-Jean-aux-Bois **87** D1

Saint-Jean-Brévelay **85** C2/3

Saint-Jean-de-Luz **108** A3, **154** A1

Saint-Jean-de-Verges **109** D3, **155** D1, **156** A1

Saint-Jean-d'Angle **100** B2/3

Saint-Jean-de-Bournay **103** D3

Saint-Jean-d'Angély **100** B2

Saint-Jean-de-Côle **101** D3

Saint-Jean-de-Losne **103** D1

Saint Jean-de-Daye **76** B3, **86** A/B1

Saint-Jean-de-Monts **100** A1

Saint-Jean-d'Illac **108** A/B1

Saint-Jean-du-Doigt **84** B1/2

Saint-Jean-du-Gard **110** B2

Saint-Jean-du-Bruel **110** B2

Saint-Jean-de-Sixt **104** A/B2/3

Saint-Jean-de-Maurienne **104** A/B3

Saint-Jean de Barrou **110** A3, **156** B1

Saint-Jean-de-Maruéjols **111** C2

Saint-Jean-de-Linières **86** A3

Saint-Jean-de-Fos **110** B2

Saint-Jean-en-Royans **111** D1

Saint-Jean-le-Centenier **111** C1

Saint-Jean-le-Priche **103** D2

Saint-Jean-le-Thomas **85** D1

Saint-Jean-les-Deux-Jumeaux **87** D1

Saint-Jean-la-Bussière **103** C2

Saint-Jean-Poutge **109** C2

Saint-Jean-Pied-de-Port **108** B3, **155** C1

Saint-Jean-Rohrbach **89** D1, **90** A1

Saint-Jean-Soleymieux **103** C3

Saint-Jean-sur-Erve **86** A2

Saint-Jeoire **104** B2

Saint-Jeure-d'Ay **103** D3

Saint John **63** D3, **85** C1

Saint John's Chapel **57** D3, **60** B1

Saint Johns **58** B1

Saint Jores **76** A3, **85** D1

Saint-Jouan-de-l'Isle **85** C2

Saint-Jouin-de-Marnes **101** C1

Saint-Julien Boutières **111** C1

Saint-Julien-l'Ars **101** C2

Saint-Julien-du-Sault **88** A2

Saint-Julien-en-Quint **111** D1

Saint-Julien-Molin-Molette **103** C/D3

Saint-Julien-en-Genevois **104** A2

Saint-Julien-de-l'Escap **100** B2

Saint-Julien-sur-le-Suran **103** D2, **104** A2

Saint-Julien-Beychevelle **100** B3

Saint-Julien-le-Faucon **86** B1

Saint-Julien-Chapteuil **111** C1

Saint-Julien-en-Born **108** B2

Saint-Julien-en-Beauchêne **111** D1

Saint-Junien **101** D2

Saint Just **62** A3

Saint-Just-en-Chevalet **103** C2

Saint-Just-en-Chaussée **77** D3

Saint-Juste-Ibarre **108** A3, **154** B1

Saint-Justin **108** B2

Saint-Just-sur-Loire **103** C3

Saint Keverne **62** B3

Saint-Lambert-du-Lattay **86** A3, **100** B1

Saint-Lary **155** C2

Saint-Lary **109** C2

Saint-Laurent-en-Grandvaux **104** A2

Saint-Laurent-sur-Saône **103** D2

Saint-Laurent-des-Eaux **87** C3

Saint-Laurent-du-Pont **104** A3

Saint-Laurent-de-Mûre **103** D3

Saint-Laurent-sur-Gorre **101** D3

Saint-Laurent **89** D2

Saint-Laurent-sur-Mer **76** A/B3, **86** A1

Saint-Laurent-d'Aigouze **111** C2/3

Saint-Laurent-en-Caux **77** C3

Saint-Laurent-de-Neste **109** C3, **155** C1

Saint-Laurent-de-la-Cabrerisse **110** A3, **156** B1

Saint-Laurent-de-Chamousset **103** C3

Saint-Laurent-des-Autels **86** A/B3, **101** C1

Saint-Laurent-de-Cerdans **156** B2

Saint-Laurent-et-Benon **100** B3

Saint-Laurent-sur-Sèvre **100** B1

Saint-Laurent-les-Bains **110** B1

Saint-Laurent-de-la-Salanque **156** B1

Saint-Laurent-en-Gâtines **86** B3

Saint-Léger-sous-Beuvray **103** C1

Saint-Léger-sous-Cholet **85** D3, **100** B1

Saint-Léger-en-Yvelines **87** C1/2

Saint-Léger-des-Vignes **102** B1

Saint-Léger-sur-Dheune **103** C/D1

Saint-Léon **109** D3, **155** D1

Saint-Léonard-de-Noblat **101** C/D3

Saint-Léonard-des-Bois **86** A2

Saint Leonards **77** C1

Saint-Leu-d'Esserent **77** D3, **87** D1

Saint-Lizier **108** B3, **155** C1

Saint-Lô **85** D1

Saint-Louis **90** A3

Saint-Loup-de-Fribois **86** A/B1

Saint-Loup-de-la-Salle **103** D1

Saint-Loup-de-Naud **87** D2, **88** A2

Saint-Loup-du-Dorat **86** A2/3

Saint-Loup-sur-Semouse **89** C/D2/3

Saint-Lunaire **85** C1/2

Saint-Lys **108** B3, **155** C1

Saint-Macaire **108** B1

Saint-Maclou **77** C3, **86** B1

Saint-Magne **108** B1

Saint-Maixent-l'École **101** C2

Saint-Malo **85** C1/2

Saint-Mamest **109** C1

Saint-Mamet-la-Salvetat **110** A1

Saint-Marcel **103** D1

Saint-Marcel-de-Careiret **111** C2

Saint-Marcellin **103** D3

Saint-Marcet **109** C3, **155** C1

Saint-Marc-sur-Seine **88** B3

Saint-Mard-de-Réno **86** B2

Saint-Mars-la-Jaille **86** A/B3

Saint-Martain-la-Rivière **101** C/D2

Saint-Martial-d'Artenset **109** B/C1

Saint-Martin-Osmonville **76** B3

Saint-Martin-de-Ré **101** C2

Saint-Martin-en-Campagne **76** B2

Saint-Martin-en-Haut **103** C3

Saint-Martin-d'Estréaux **103** C2

Saint-Martin-d'Auxigny **87** D3, **102** A1

Saint-Martin **110** B2/3

Saint-Martin-d'Ablois **88** A1

Saint-Martin-du-Puy **88** A3

Saint-Martin-en-Bresse **103** D1

Saint-Martin-de-Londres **110** B2

Saint-Martin-de-Valamas **111** C1

Saint-Martin-de-Seignanx **108** B3, **155** C1

Saint-Martin-de-Crau **111** C2/3
Saint-Martin-Valmeroux **102** A3, **110** A1
Saint-Martin-la-Méanne **102** A3
Saint-Martin-sur-Ouanne **87** D3
Saint-Martin-d'Ardèche **111** C2
Saint-Martin-Vésubie **112** B2
Saint-Martin-des-Besaces **85** D1, **86** A1
Saint-Martin-du-Var **112** B2
Saint-Martin-d'Oney **108** B2
Saint-Martin-d'Oydes **109** D3, **155** D1, **156** A1
Saint-Martin-de-Boscherville **77** C3
Saint-Martin-d'Entraunes **112** B2
Saint-Martory **109** C3, **155** D1
Saint-Mathieu **101** D3
Saint-Mathieu **84** A2
Saint-Mathurin **86** A3
Saint-Matré **108** B2
Saint-Maurice-Navacelles **110** B2
Saint-Maurice-sur-Aveyron **87** D3
Saint-Maurice-de-Ventalon **110** B2
Saint-Maurice-les-Charencey **86** B2
Saint-Maurice-sur-Moselle **89** D2/3, **90** A3
Saint-Maurin **109** C2
Saint Mawes **62** B3
Saint-Maximin-la-Sainte-Baume **111** D3, **112** A3
Saint-Médard-de-Guizières **108** B1
Saint-Médard-en-Jalles **108** B1
Saint-Méen-le-Grand **85** C2
Saint-Menoux **102** B1/2
Saint-Mesmin **100** B1
Saint Michael's Mount **62** A3
Saint-Michel-en-Grève **84** B1/2
Saint-Michel-Chef-Chef **85** C3, **100** A1
Saint-Michel-de-Castelnau **108** B2
Saint-Michel-de-Maurienne **104** B3, **112** A1
Saint-Michel-en-l'Herm **101** C2
Saint-Michel-Mont Mercure **100** B1
Saint-Michel **109** C3, **155** C1
Saint-Mihiel **89** C1
Saint-Montant **111** C1/2
Saint-Nazaire **85** C3, **100** A1
Saint-Nazaire-le-Désert **111** D1
Saint-Nazaire-en-Royans **103** D3, **111** D1
Saint-Nectaire **102** B3
Saint Neots **64** B2
Saint-Nicolas-du-Pélem **84** B2
Saint-Nicolas-de-la-Grave **109** C2
Saint-Nicolas-de-Port **89** C/D2
Saint-Nicolas-de-Redon **85** C3
Saint-Omer **77** D1
Saint-Pair-sur-Mer **85** D1
Saint-Palais **108** A3, **154** B1
Saint-Palais-sur-Mer **100** B3
Saint-Papoul **109** D3, **156** A1
Saint-Pardoux-la-Rivière **101** D3

Saint-Parres-lès-Vaudes **88** B2
Saint-Paul-Cap-de-Joux **109** D2/3
Saint-Paul-de-Fenouillet **156** B1
Saint-Paul-de-Jarrat **109** D3, **155** D1/2, **156** A1
Saint-Paul-de-Varax **103** D2
Saint-Paul-des-Landes **110** A1
Saint-Paul-et-Valmalle **110** B2/3
Saint-Paulien **103** C3, **110** B1
Saint-Paul-lez-Durance **111** D2
Saint-Paul-le-Jeune **111** C2
Saint-Paul-lès-Dax **108** A2
Saint-Paul-sur-Ubaye **112** B2
Saint-Paul-Trois-Châteaux **111** C2
Saint-Pé-de-Bigorre **108** B3, **155** B/C1
Saint-Pée-sur-Nivelle **108** A3, **154** A1
Saint-Péravy-la-Colombe **87** C2
Saint-Péray **111** C1
Saint-Père **88** A3
Saint-Père-en-Retz **85** C3, **100** A1
Saint Peter Port **63** D3
Saint-Péver **84** B2
Saint-Pey-d'Armens **108** B1
Saint Philbert-de-Bouaine **100** A1
Saint-Philbert-de-Grand-Lieu **100** A1
Saint-Pierre-sur-Dives **86** A/B1
Saint-Pierre **110** A2
Saint-Pierre-en-Port **77** C3
Saint-Pierre-les-Bois **102** A1
Saint-Pierre-le-Moûtier **102** B1
Saint-Pierre-Église **76** B3
Saint-Pierre-de-Fursac **101** D2
Saint-Pierre-du-Chemin **100** B1
Saint-Pierre-de-la-Fage **110** B2
Saint-Pierre-des-Nids **86** A2
Saint-Pierreville **111** C1
Saint-Pierre-de-Chignac **101** D3, **109** C1
Saint-Pierre-de-Chartreuse **104** A3
Saint-Pierre-sur-Mer **110** B3, **156** B1
Saint-Pierre-Toirac **109** D1
Saint-Pierre-de-Boeuf **103** D3
Saint-Pierre-d'Entremont **104** A3
Saint-Pierre-d'Oléron **101** C2
Saint-Pierre-Chérignat **101** D2, **102** A2
Saint-Pierre-sur-Orthe **86** A2
Saint-Pierre-Quiberon **84** B3
Saint-Pierre-à-Champ **101** B/C1
Saint-Plancard **109** C3, **155** D1
Saint-Pois **85** D1
Saint-Poix **85** D2
Saint-Pol-de-Léon **84** B1/2
Saint-Polgues **103** C2
Saint-Pol-sur-Ternoise **77** D2
Saint-Pol-sur-Mer **77** D1, **78** A1
Saint-Pons **110** A3
Saint-Porchaire **100** B2/3

Saint-Pourçain-sur-Besbre **103** C2
Saint-Pourçain-sur-Sioule **102** B2
Saint-Priest-des-Champs **102** B2
Saint-Priest-Laprugne **103** C2
Saint-Privat **102** A3
Saint-Privat-d'Allier **110** B1
Saint-Privé **87** D3
Saint-Prix **111** C1
Saint-Puy **109** C2
Saint-Quay-Portrieux **85** C1/2
Saint-Quentin-les-Anges **85** D3, **86** A3
Saint-Quentin **78** A3
Saint-Rambert-en-Bugey **103** D2, **104** A2
Saint-Rambert-sur-Loire **103** C3
Saint-Rambert-d'Albon **103** D3
Saint-Raphaël **112** B3
Saint-Remèze **111** C2
Saint-Rémy-du-Plain **85** D2
Saint-Rémy-sur-Dore **103** B/C2
Saint-Rémy-de-Provence **111** C2
Saint-Rémy **86** A1
Saint-Rémy **109** B/C1
Saint Renan **84** A2
Saint-René **85** C2
Saint-Revèrien **88** A3, **102** B1
Saint-Riquier **77** D2
Saint-Romain-de-Colbosc **77** C3
Saint-Romain-de-Jalionas **103** D3
Saint-Romans **103** D3, **111** D1
Saint-Rome-de-Cernon **110** A/B2
Saint-Rome-de-Tarn **110** A2
Saint-Saëns **76** B3
Saint-Samson-la-Poterie **77** D3
Saint-Satur **87** D3
Saint-Saturnin **102** B3
Saint-Saturnin-d'Apt **111** D2
Saint-Saud-Lacoussière **101** D3
Saint-Saulge **102** B1
Saint-Sauves-d'Auvergne **102** B3
Saint-Sauveur-de-Montagut **111** C1
Saint-Sauveur-le-Vicomte **76** A3
Saint-Sauveur **100** A1
Saint-Sauveur-en-Puisaye **87** D3, **88** A3
Saint-Sauveur-Lendelin **85** D1
Saint-Sauveur-sur-Tinée **112** B2
Saint-Savin **100** B3
Saint-Savin **101** D1/2
Saint-Savin **108** B3, **155** C1/2
Saint-Savinien **100** B2
Saint-Seine-en-Bâche **103** D1, **104** A1
Saint-Seine-l'Abbaye **88** B3
Saint-Sernin-sur-Rance **110** A2
Saint-Servan-sur-Mer **85** C1/2
Saint-Sever **108** B2
Saint-Sever-Calvados **85** D1
Saint-Séverin **101** C3
Saint-Soupplets **87** D1
Saint-Sulpice **109** D2
Saint-Sulpice-sur-Lèze **108** B3, **155** C1
Saint-Sulpice-de-Favières **87** C/D2

Saint-Sulpice-les-Feuilles **101** C2
Saint-Sylvestre-sur-Lot **109** C2
Saint-Symphorien **108** B1/2
Saint-Symphorien-d'Ancelles **103** D2
Saint-Symphorien-de-Lay **103** C2
Saint-Symphorien-sur-Coise **103** C3
Saint-Symphorien-d'Ozon **103** D3
Saint-Thégonnec **84** B2
Saint-Thibault **88** B3
Saint-Thibéry **110** B3
Saint-Thiébault **89** C2
Saint-Trivier-de-Courtes **103** D2
Saint-Trivier-sur-Moignans **103** D2
Saint-Trojan-les-Bains **101** C2/3
Saint-Tropez **112** A3
Saint-Urcize **110** A/B1
Saint-Vaast-la-Hougue **76** B3
Saint-Valéry-en-Caux **77** C2/3
Saint-Valéry-sur-Somme **77** D2
Saint-Vallier **103** D3
Saint-Vallier-de-Thiey **112** B3
Saint-Vaury **102** A2
Saint-Venant **78** A2
Saint-Véran **112** B1
Saint-Vincent-de-Connezac **101** C3
Saint-Vincent **105** C3
Saint-Vincent-de-Tyrosse **108** B2/3
Saint-Vincent-sur-Jabron **111** D2
Saint-Vit **89** C3, **104** A1
Saint-Vivien-de-Médoc **100** B3
Saint-Wandrille **77** C3
Saint-Yan **103** C2
Saint-Ybars **108** B3, **155** C1
Saint-Yorre **102** B2
Saint-Yrieix-la-Perche **101** C3
Saint-Yrieix-le-Déjalat **102** A3
Saint-Yvy **84** B2
Saint-Zacharie **111** D3
Sainville **87** C2
Sairakkala **25** D2, **26** A2
Sairinen **24** A2
Saissac **110** A3, **156** A1
Saivomuotka **11** C2/3
Sajaniemi **25** C2
Šajkaš **129** D3, **133** D1, **134** A1
Säjvis **17** D2/3
Säkäjärvi **27** B/C2
Sakarétsi **146** A1
Šakiai **73** D2
Säkinmäki **22** A/B3
Säkkilä **13** C3
Sakrihei **14** B2
Saksala **24** B2
Saksenvik **15** C1
Sakskøbing **53** D2
Saksnes **32** B2
Saksumdal **37** D2, **38** A1/2
Säkylä **24** B2
Sala **40** A3
Šal'a **95** C2
Salacgrīva **73** D1, **74** A2
Salach **91** C2
Sala Consilina **120** A3
Salahmi **22** B1
Salamajärvi **21** C2
Salamanca **159** D2
Salamís **147** D2
Salandra **120** B2/3
Salanki **11** D2, **12** A1
Salantai **73** C1/2
Salaparuta **124** A2
Salar **172** B2
Salardú **155** D2
Salas **151** D1
Salás **155** D2

Salaš **135** C2
Salas Altas **155** C3
Salas de los Infantes **153** C3
Salaspils **73** D1, **74** A2
Salau **155** C2
Salavaux [Avenches] **104** B1
Salberg **31** C2
Salberget **31** C1
Salbertrand **112** B1
Salbohed **40** A3
Salbris **87** C3
Salceda de Caselas **150** A3
Salching **92** B2
Salcia **135** D2
Šalčininkai **73** D2, **74** A2
Salcombe **63** C3
Sălcuța **135** D2
Saldaña **152** A/B2
Saldeana **159** C2
Saldón **162** A3
Saldus **73** C/D1
Sale **59** D2, **60** B3
Sale **113** D1
Saleby **45** C/D2
Salem **91** C3
Salemertal **91** C3
Salemi **124** A2
Salen **56** A1
Salen **28** B1
Sälen **39** C1
Salen **54** A2, **55** D1
Salen **54** A2, **55** D1
Salenpää **26** B2
Salernes **112** A3
Salerno **119** D3
Salers **102** A/B3, **110** A1
Salettes **110** B1
Salford **59** D2, **60** B3
Salgen-Hausen **91** D2
Salgótarján **97** C3
Salgueiro **158** B3, **165** C1
Salgüero de Juarros **153** C2
Salhus **36** A3
Sali **130** B2/3
Sálice Salentino **121** D3
Sálice Terme **113** D1
Salientes **151** D2
Saliers **111** C2
Salies-de-Béarn **108** A3, **154** B1
Salies-du-Salat **109** C3, **155** D1
Salignac **108** B1
Salihli **149** D2
Salillas **154** B3
Salillas de Jalón **155** C3, **163** B/C1
Salinas **151** D1
Salinas **161** D3, **162** A3, **168** B1
Salinas **169** C2/3
Salinas **155** C2
Salinas de Hoz **155** C2/3
Salinas de Jaca **154** B2
Salinas del Manzano **162** A/3
Salinas de Léniz **153** D2
Salinas de Oro **153** D2, **154** A2
Salinas de Pisuerga **152** B2
Salin-de-Giraud **111** C3
Saline di Volterra **114** B3, **116** A2
Salinillas de Bureba **153** C2
Sälinkää **25** D2, **26** A2
Salin-les-Thermes **104** B3
Salins-les-Bains **104** A1
Salir **170** B2
Salir do Porto **164** A1
Salisbury **76** A1
Salizzole **107** C3
Salka **95** D3
Sälkastugorna **9** D3
Salla **13** C3
Salla **127** C1
Sallanches **104** B2/3
Sallent **156** A2/3
Sallent de Gállego **154** B2
Salles **108** A/B1
Salles-Curan **110** A2
Salles-sous-Bois **111** C1/2
Salles-sur-l'Hers **109** D3, **155** D1, **156** A1
Sallgast **83** C1
Sallingsund **48** A2

Sällsjö 29 C3, 34 B2
Salmchâteau 79 D2
Salmenkylä 22 B3
Salmentaka 25 C1
Salmerón 161 D2
Salmi 21 B/C2
Salmiech 110 A2
Salmijärvi 11 C3, 12 A2
Salmijärvi 19 C2
Salminen 19 C/D1
Salminen 22 B2/3
Salmivaara 13 C3
Salmtal 80 A3
Salò 106 B3
Salo 24 B3
Salobre 168 A2
Salobrena 173 C2
Saloinen 25 C2, 26 A2
Saloinen 18 A3
Salo-Issakka 27 C2
Salokylä 23 C3
Salo-Miehikkälä 26 B2
Salomó 163 C1
Salona 131 C/D3
Salon-de-Provence 111 D2/3
Saloníki 142 B3
Salonta 97 C3, 140 A1
Saloranta 27 C1
Salorino 165 C1
Salornay-sur-Guye 103 C/D2
Salorno/Salurn 107 C2
Salou 163 C2
Salpakangas 25 D2, 26 A2
Salreu 158 A2
Salsadella 163 C2
Salsán 34 B2
Salsbruket 28 B1
Salses 156 B1
Salsomaggiore Terme 114 A1
Salsta 40 B3
Salt 156 B2
Saltash 62 B3
Saltburn-by-the-Sea 61 C1
Saltbuvik 28 B2
Saltcoats 56 B2
Saltfleet 61 D3
Saltoluokta fjällstation 9 D3
Saltsjöbaden 47 D1
Saltum 48 B1
Saltveit 42 A1/2
Saltvik 40 B1
Saltvik 51 D1
Saltvik 41 C/D2/3
Saludécio 115 D2, 117 C1
Salussola 105 C3
Saluzzo 112 B1
Salvacañete 162 A3
Salvada 165 B/C3, 170 B1
Salvador 159 C3
Salvador de Zapardiel 160 A1/2
Salvages 110 A2/3
Salvagnac 109 D2
Salvaleón 165 D2/3
Salvaterra de Miño 150 A3
Salvaterra de Magos 164 A2
Salvaterra do Extremo 159 C3, 165 C1
Salvatierra de Santiago 165 D1, 166 A1/2
Salvatierra de Esca 154 B2
Salvatierra de los Barros 165 D2/3
Salviac 108 B1
Sælvig 49 C3, 53 C1
Salzbergen 67 D2/3
Salzburg 93 B/C3
Salzderhelden 68 B3
Salzfurtkapelle 69 D3, 82 B1
Salzgitter 68 B3
Salzgitter Bad 68 B3
Salzgitter-Gebhardshagen 68 B3
Salzgitter-Lebenstedt 68 B3
Salzgitter-Thiede 69 B/C3
Salzhausen 68 B1
Salzhemmendorf 68 B3
Salzhemmendorf-Lauenstein 68 B3
Salzkotten 68 A3, 80 B1
Salzmünde 82 A1
Salzwedel 69 C2
Salzweg 93 C2
Sama de Langreo 151 D1, 152 A1
Samadet 108 B2/3, 154 B1
Samarína 142 B2
Samassi 123 C3
Samatan 109 C3, 155 D1
Sambiase 122 A/B2
Sambin 86 A/B3
Samboal 160 B1
Sambor 97 D2, 98 A2
Sambuca di Sicília 124 A/B2
Sambuci 118 B2
Samedan 106 A2
Samekappelet 6 B1
Samer 77 D2
Sámi 146 A2
Sámi 148 A2
Samikón 146 B3
Sammakko 17 B/C1
Sammakkovaara 23 C2
Sammakkovaara 23 C1
Sammaljoki 24 B1/2
Såmmarlappastugan 15 D1
Sammatti 25 C3
Sammichele di Bari 121 C2
Samminmaja 24 B1
Samnanger 36 A3
Samnaun [Scuol-Tarasp] 106 B1
Samobor 127 C/D3
Samodreža 138 B1
Samoëns 104 B2
Samokov 138 B3
Samokov 138 B3
Samokov 139 D2
Samokov 140 B3
Samone 105 C3
Samora Correia 164 A2
Šamorín 95 C2/3
Samoš 134 B1
Samos 151 C2
Sámos 149 D2
Samothráki (Chora) 145 C/D2
Samper de Calanda 162 B1/2
Samper del Salz 162 B1
Sampéyre 112 B1/2
Sampieri 125 C3
Sämsjölandet 30 A/B2
Samswegen 69 C3
Samugheo 123 C/D2
San Adrián 153 D2, 154 A2
San Adrián de Juarros 153 C2/3
San Agustín 161 C2
San Agustín de Llusanés 156 A2
San Amaro 150 B2
San Andrés del Rabanedo 151 D2, 152 A2
San Andrés del Congosto 161 C2
San Aniol de Finestres 156 B2
San Antolín 151 C1/2
San Antonio Abad 169 D2
San Asensio 153 D2
Sanaüja 155 C3
San Bartolomé de Pinares 160 B2
San Bartolomeo al Mare 113 C2
San Bartolomeo in Galdo 119 D2, 120 A1
San Bartolomé de las Abiertas 160 A3, 166 B1
San Bartolomé de la Torre 171 C1
San Baudilio de Llusanés 156 A2
San Benedetto 118 B2
San Benedetto in Alpe 115 C2, 116 B1
San Benedetto del Tronto 117 D2/3
San Benedetto Po 114 B1
San Benito 166 B2
San Bernardino [Castione-Arbedo] 105 D2, 106 A2
San Biágio Platani 124 B2
San Biágio di Callalta 107 D3
San Biase 119 D2
San Biase 120 A3
San Bonifácio 107 C3
San Bou 157 C1
San Bruno 119 D2
San Carlo 124 B2
San Carlos 157 D3
San Carlos del Valle 167 D2, 168 A2
San Carlo (Val Bavona) [Ponte Brolla] 105 D2
San Casciano in Val di Pesa 114 B2/3, 116 B2
San Casciano dei Bagni 116 B3
San Cassiano 107 C2
San Cassiano/Sankt Kassian 107 C2
San Cataldo 124 B2
San Cataldo 121 D3
San Cataldo 119 C2
San Cebrián de Mazote 152 A3, 160 A1
San Cebrián de Castro 151 D3, 159 D1
San Cebrián de Mudá 152 B2
San Cebrián de Campos 152 B3
Sancelles 157 C2
Sancergues 87 D3, 102 B1
Sancerre 87 D3
San Cesáreo 118 B2
San Cesário di Lecce 121 D3
Sancey-le-Grand 89 D3, 104 B1
Sancheville 87 C2
Sanchidrián 160 A/B2
San Chírico Raparo 120 B3
San Chírico Nuovo 120 B2
Sanchonuño 160 B1
San Cipirello 124 A/B2
San Ciprián 150 B1
San Ciprián de Viñas 150 B2/3
San Cipriano Picentino 119 D3, 120 A2
San Cipriano d'Aversa 119 C3
San Claudio al Chienti 117 D2
San Clemente 115 B/C2, 116 B1
San Clemente 157 C1
San Clemente 168 A/B1
Sancoins 102 B1
San Colombano al Lambro 106 A3, 113 D1
San Costantino Albanese 120 B3, 122 A/B1
San Cristóbal de Cuéllar 160 B1
San Cristóbal de Cea 150 B2
San Cristóbal de la Cuesta 159 D2
San Cristóbal de Entreviñas 151 D3, 152 A3
San Cristóbal de la Polantera 151 D2
San Cristóbal 157 C1
San Cristóbal de la Vega 160 A/B2
Sancti-Spíritus 159 C2
Sancti-Spíritus 166 B2
Sand 31 C2
Sand 42 A1/2
Sand 38 A3
Sanda 43 C2
Sanda 41 D3
Sandaméri 146 B2
San Damiano d'Asti 113 C1
San Damiano Macra 112 B2
Sandane 36 B1/2
San Daniele Po 114 A1
San Daniele del Friuli 107 D2, 126 A2
Sandanski 139 D3
Sandanski 139 D3
Sandanski 140 B3
Sandared 45 C3
Sandarne 40 B1
Sandås 30 B1
Sandau 69 D2
Sandbach 59 D2, 60 B3, 64 A1
Sandbäckshult 51 D1
Sandbank 56 B1/2
Sandberg 81 D2
Sandbukt 4 B2
Sandbukta 28 A/B2, 33 C/D1
Sandby 51 D2
Sandby 53 C2
Sanddal 36 B2
Sande 36 A2
Sande 43 D1, 44 A1
Sande 36 B1/2
Sande 36 B1/2
Sande 37 B/C2
Sande 67 D1
Sandefjord 43 D2, 44 A/B1
Sandeggen 4 A3
Sande-Gödens 67 D1
Sandeid 42 A1
Sandemar 47 D1
San Demétrio ne'Vestini 117 D3, 119 C1
San Demétrio Corone 122 B1
Sandersdorf 69 D3, 82 B1
Sandersleben 69 C3, 82 A1
Sanderstølen 37 D3
Sandfors 31 D1
Sandgate 65 C3, 76 B1
Sandhamn 47 D1
Sandhaug 42 B1
Sandhead 56 A/B3
Sandhem 45 D3
Sandiás 150 B3
Sandillon 87 C3
Sandim 151 C3, 159 B/C1
Sandim 158 A2
Sandl 93 D2
Sandland 4 B2
Sandmo 29 C2
Sandnäset 35 C2
Sandnäset 34 B2
Sandnes 8 B2
Sandnes 9 C2
Sandnes 9 C1
Sandnes 42 A2
Sandnessjøen 14 A2
Sandö 30 B3, 35 D2
Sando 159 D2
Sandomierz 97 C1, 98 A2
San Dónaci 121 D3
San Donà di Piave 107 D3
San Donato Val di Comino 119 C2
Sándorfalva 129 D2
Sandøsund 43 D2, 44 B1/2
Sandoval de la Reina 152 B2
Sandown 76 B2
Sandøy 32 A2
Sandrigo 107 C3
Sandringham 65 C1
Sandsbråten 43 D1
Sandsbro (Vaxjö) 51 C1
Sandsele 15 D3
Sandset 8 B2
Sandshamn 36 A1
Sandsjö 39 D1
Sandsjö 15 D3
Sandsjö 30 B1
Sandslån 30 B3, 35 D2
Sandstad 32 B1
Sandstedt 68 A1
Sandtangen 7 C2
Sandtorg 9 C2
Sandur 55 C1
Sandvarp 30 B3, 35 D2
Sandvatn 42 B3
Sandve 42 A2
Sandvig 51 C3, 51 D3
Sandvik 9 D1
Sandvik 46 A3
Sandvik 4 A3
Sandvik 51 D1
Sandvika 38 A3, 43 D1
Sandvika 32 B2
Sandvika fjellstue 28 B3, 33 D1, 34 A1
Sandvika fjellstue 28 B3, 33 D1, 34 A1
Sandvika (Nordli) 29 C2
Sandviken 29 C2/3, 34 A1
Sandviken 40 A2
Sandviken 29 D3, 34 B1
Sandviken 16 A1
Sandvikvåg 42 A1
Sandwich 65 C3, 76 B1
Sandy 64 B2
San Emiliano 151 D2
Såner 44 B1
San Esteban de Pravia 151 D1
San Esteban de Gormaz 153 C3, 161 C1
San Esteban de Nogales 151 D3
San Esteban del Valle 160 A3
San Esteban de Valdueza 151 C2
San Esteban del Molar 151 D3, 152 A3
San Fele 120 A2
San Felice Circeo 118 B3
San Felice sul Panaro 114 B1
San Felice/Sankt Felix 107 C2
San Felices 153 D3
San Felices de los Gallegos 159 C2
San Ferdinando 122 A3
San Ferdinando di Púglia 120 B1/2
San Fernando de Henares 161 C2
San Fernando 171 D3
San Fernando 157 D3
San Fili 122 A1/2
San Foca 121 D3
San Francesco 117 C3, 118 B1
San Francesco 119 D1
San Francisco Javier 157 D3
San Fratello 125 C2
San Fulgencio 169 C3, 174 B1
Sånga 30 B3, 35 D2
San Gabriele 115 C1
San Galgano 114 B3, 116 B2
San García de Ingelmos 160 A2
Sangarcía 160 B2
Sangarrén 154 B3
Sångas 147 C3
Sangatte 77 D1
San Gavino Monreale 123 C3
San Gémini 117 C3, 118 B1
San Genésio 105 D3, 106 A3, 113 D1
Sangerhausen 82 A1
San Germano Vercellese 105 C3
San Giácomo delle Segnate 114 B1
San Giácomo d'Acri 122 B1
San Giácomo/Sankt Jakob 107 C1
San Giácomo 112 B2
San Giácomo di Véglia 107 D2
San Gimignano 114 B3, 116 A/B2
San Ginésio 115 D3, 117 D2
Sanginjoki 18 B2
Sanginjoki 18 B2
Sanginkylä 18 B2
San Giórgio di Lomellina 105 D3, 113 D1
San Giórgio di Livenza 107 D3, 126 A3
San Giórgio della Richinvelda 107 D2, 126 A2
San Giórgio Lucano 120 B3
San Giórgio del Sánnio 119 D3, 120 A2
San Giorgio a Cremano 119 D3
San Giórgio di Piano 114 B1
San Giórgio in Bosco 107 C3
San Giórgio Iónico 121 C3
San Giórgio 115 D2, 117 C1
San Giórgio la Molara 119 D2/3, 120 A2
San Giórgio di Nogaro 126 A3

San Giovanni in Persiceto 114 B1
San Giovanni Bianco 106 A2/3
San Giovanni a Piro 120 A3
San Giovanni Suérgiu 123 C3
San Giovanni 107 C1
San Giovanni in Fiore 122 B2
San Giovanni Ilarione 107 C3
San Giovanni Rotondo 120 B1
San Giovanni/Sankt Johann 107 C1
San Giovanni Sínis 123 C2
San Giovanni Reatino 117 C3, 118 B1
San Giovanni in Croce 114 A1
San Giovanni 107 C2
San Giovanni Gémini 124 B2
San Giovanni Valdarno 115 C3, 116 B2
Sangis 17 D2
San Giuliano Terme 114 A/B2, 116 A1/2
San Giuseppe Jato 124 B2
San Giustino 115 C3, 117 C2
San Giusto Canavese 105 C3
San Godenzo 115 C2, 116 B1
San Gregório 117 D3, 119 C1
San Gregório da Sássola 118 B2
San Gregório Magno 120 A2
San Gregorio 150 B3
Sangüesa 155 C2
San Guido 114 B3, 116 A2
Sanguinet 108 A1
Sanguinetto 107 C3
Saní 144 A2
Sanica Gornja 131 D2
San Ignacio de Loyola 153 D1
San Ildefonso o la Granja 160 B2
Sanitz 53 D3
San Javier 169 C3, 174 B1
San Joan de Villatorrada 156 A3
San Jorge 163 C2
San Jorge 169 D2
San José 172 B1
San José 174 A2
San José 169 D2
San Juan Bautista 152 B3
San Juan Bautista 157 D3
San Juan de Nieve 151 D1
San Juan de la Peña 154 B2
San Juan de los Terreros 174 A1/2
San Juan de la Nava 160 A2
San Juan de Aznalfarache 171 D1/2
San Juan de Mozarrifar 154 B3, 162 B1
San Juan de Alicante 169 D3
San Juan del Olmo 160 A2
San Juan del Puerto 171 C2
San Juano 157 C2
Sänkimäki 22 B2
Sanksnäs 15 D3
Sankt Aegyd am Neuwalde 94 A3
Sankt Andrä 94 A/B2
Sankt Andrä 127 C1
Sankt Andrä 96 A3
Sankt Andreasberg 69 C3
Sankt Anton am Arlberg 106 B1
Sankt Anton an der Jessnitz 94 A3
Sankt Augustin 80 A2
Sankt Blasien 90 B3
Sankt Donat 126 B1/2
Sankt Englmar 92 B1
Sankt Gallen 93 D3

Sankt Gallenkirch 106 A/B1
106 A/B1
Sankt Gangloff 82 A/B2
Sankt Georgen an der Stie-fing 127 C1
Sankt Georgen an der Gusen 93 D2
Sankt Georgen am Reith 93 D3
Sankt Georgen ob Juden-burg 126 B1
Sankt Georgen im Attergau 93 C3
Sankt Gilgen 93 C3
Sankt Goar 80 B3
Sankt Goarshausen 80 B3
Sankt Ibb 49 D3, 50 A3
Sankt Ingbert 89 D1, 90 A1
Sankt Jakob bei Mixnitz 94 A3, 127 C1
Sankt Johann in Pongau 93 C3, 126 A1
Sankt Johann in der Haide 127 D1
Sankt Johann in Tirol 92 B3
Sankt Johann am Tauern 93 D3, 126 B1
Sankt Johann im Walde 107 D1, 126 A1
Sankt Johann am Tauern 96 A3
Sankt Lambrecht 126 B1
Sankt Leonhard im Pitztal 106 B1
Sankt Leonhard am Forst 94 A2
Sankt Lorenzen am Wechsel 94 A3
Sankt Lorenzen im Lesachtal 107 D1/2, 126 A1/2
Sankt Marein am Pickelbach 127 C/D1
Sankt Marein im Mürztal 94 A3
Sankt Margarethen 52 B3
Sankt Margarethen an der Raab 127 C/D1
Sankt Margarethen im Bur-genland 94 B3
Sankt Märgen 90 B3
Sankt Martin am Grimming 93 C3
Sankt Michaelisdonn 52 A/B3
Sankt Michael in Obersteier-mark 93 D3, 127 C1
Sankt Michael im Burgen-land 127 D1
Sankt Michael im Lungau 126 B1
Sankt Michael in Obersteier-mark 96 A3
Sankt Münster-Sprakel 67 D2
Sankt Nikolai im Sölktal 126 B1
Sankt Olof 50 B3
Sankt Oswald in Freiland 127 C1
Sankt Oswald bei Freistadt 93 D2
Sankt Pankraz 93 D3
Sankt Paul 127 C1/2
Sankt Peter-Ording 52 A3
Sankt Peterburg (Leningrad) 74 B1
Sankt Pölten 94 A2
Sankt Pölten 96 A2/3
Sankt Ruprecht an der Raab 127 C1
Sankt Stefan an der Gail 126 A2
Sankt Stefan im Rosental 127 C/D1
Sankt Valentin 93 D2
Sankt Veit an der Glan 126 B1
Sankt Veit an der Gölsen 94 A2/3
Sankt Veit an der Glan 96 A3
Sankt Veit in Defereggen 107 D1
Sankt Veit im Mühlkreis 93 C/D2
Sankt Vith 79 D2
Sankt Wendel 80 A3, 90 A1
Sankt Willibald 93 C2

Sankt Wolfgang im Salz-kammergut 93 C3
Sankt Wolfgang 92 B2
San Lázzaro di Sávena 114 B1/2
San Leo 115 C2, 117 C1
San Leonardo in Passíria 107 C1
San Leonardo de Siete Fu-éntes 123 C2
San Leonardo de Yagüe 153 C3, 161 C1
San Leone 124 B3
San Lorenzo de Descardazar 157 C1/2
San Lorenzo Bellizzi 120 B3, 122 B1
San Lorenzo a Merse 114 B3, 116 B2
San Lorenzo in Campo 115 D3, 117 C2
San Lorenzo in Banale 106 B2
San Lorenzo al Mare 113 C2
San Lorenzo Nuovo 116 B3, 118 A1
San Lorenzo de Calatrava 167 C2/3
San Lorenzo de El Escorial 160 B2
San Lorenzo de la Parrilla 161 D3, 168 B1
Sanlúcar de Guadiana 170 B1
Sanlúcar de Barrameda 171 C/D2
Sanlúcar la Mayor 171 D1/2
San Lúcido 122 A2
San Lugano 107 C2
San Luis de Sabinillas 172 A3
Sanluri 123 C3
San Mamés de Campos 152 B2
San Marcello Pistoiese 114 B2, 116 A1
San Marcial 159 D1
San Marco 120 A3
San Marco Argentano 122 A1
San Marco dei Cavoti 119 D2/3, 120 A1/2
San Marco in Lámis 120 A/B1
San Marino 115 C/D2, 117 C1
San Marino 130 B1
San Martín de Pusa 160 A/B3, 166 B1
San Martín de la Vega del Alberche 160 A2
San Martín del Pedroso 151 C3, 159 C1
San Martín de la Vega 161 C3
San Martín de Maldá 155 D3, 163 D1
San Martín de Moncayo 154 A3, 162 A1
San Martín de Valdeiglesias 160 B2/3
San Martín de Montalbán 160 B3, 167 C1
San Martín 172 A3
San Martín 151 C3
San Martín de Boniches 162 A3, 168 B1
San Martín 159 C2
San Martín del Pimpollar 160 A2/3
San Martín del Río 163 C2
San Martín de Unx 154 A2
San Martín del Rey Aurelio 111 D3
San Martino di Castrozza 107 C2
San Martino Buon Albergo 107 B/C3
San Martino di Cellina 107 D2, 126 A2
San Martino 107 C2/3
San Martino in Rio 114 B1
San Martino in Pénsilis 119 D2, 120 A1
San Martino di Lota 113 D2

San Mateo 163 C2
San Mateo 169 D2
San Mateo de Gállego 154 B3, 162 B1
San Maurízio Canavese 105 C3, 113 B/C1
San Máuro Forte 120 B3
San Máuro Torinese 113 C1
San Menáio 120 B1
San Michele al Tagliamento 107 D3, 126 A2
San Michele all'Ádige 107 C2
San Michele di Ganzaría 125 C3
San Michele 107 D3, 126 A3
San Michele Salentino 121 C/D2
San Michele 115 D2/3, 117 C/D2
San Michele 118 B2
San Miguel 157 D3
San Miguel de Serrezuela 160 A2
San Miguel de Valero 159 D2
San Miguel del Arroyo 160 B1
San Miguel de Bernúy 160 B1
San Miguel de Aguayo 152 B1/2
San Miguel de Salinas 169 C3, 174 B1
San Millán de San Zadornil 153 C2
San Millán de la Cogolla 153 C3
San Millán de Lara 153 C3
San Muñoz 159 D2
Sannäs 44 B2
Sannazzaro de'Burgondi 113 D1
Sannicandro di Bari 121 C2
Sannicandro Gargánico 120 A1
San Nicola dell'Alto 122 B2
San Nicola da Crissa 122 A/B2
San Nicolás del Puerto 166 A3, 171 D1, 172 A1
San Nicolò Gerrei 123 D3
San Nicolò di Comélico 107 D2
San Nicolò Ferrarese 115 C1
San Nicolò d'Arcidano 123 C3
Sannidal 43 D2, 44 A2
Sännsjölandet 29 D3, 35 B/C1
Sanok 97 C/D2, 98 A2/3
San Pablo 167 C1
San Pancrázio/Sankt Pan-kraz 107 B/C2
San Pancrázio Salentino 121 D3
San Pantaleo 123 D1
San Pantaleón de Losa 153 C2
San Páolo di Civitate 120 A1
San Pedro 168 B2
San Pedro Alcántara 172 A3
San Pedro Bercianos 151 D2
San Pedro del Pinatar 169 C3, 174 B1
San Pedro de la Nave 151 D3, 159 D1
San Pedro de Latarce 152 A3, 159 D1, 160 A1
San Pedro de Mérida 165 D2, 166 A2
San Pedro de Palmiches 161 D2
San Pedro Manrique 153 D3
San Pelayo de Guareña 159 D2
San Pellegrino Terme 106 A3
San Piero in Bagno 115 C2, 116 B1

San Piero Patti 125 C/D2
San Pietro 125 C3
San Pietro in Casale 114 B1
San Pietro in Palazzi 114 A/B3, 116 A2
San Pietro in Valle 117 C3, 118 B1
San Pietro/Sankt Peter 107 C1
San Pietro Vara 113 D2, 114 A2
San Pietro Vernótico 121 D3
San Polo d'Enza 114 A/B1
San Polo di Piave 107 D3
Sanquhar 56 B2
San Quírico d'Órcia 115 C3, 116 B2
San Rafael 160 B2
San Rafael 169 D2
San Rafael del Río 163 C2
San Remo 113 C2
San Román 160 A3
San Román de la Cuba 152 A2/3
San Román de Cameros 153 D2/3
San Rómolo 113 B/C2
San Roque 172 A3
San Roque de Ríomiera 153 C1
San Rufo 120 A3
Sansa 156 A1/2
Sansac-de-Marmiesse 110 A1
San Sadurniño 150 B1
San Salvatore Monferrato 113 C1
San Salvo 119 D1/2
San Saturnino de Osormort 156 A/B2
San Savino 115 C3, 117 C2
San Sebastián de los Reyes 161 C2
San Sebastián de los Balle-steros 172 A/B1
San Sebastiano 106 B3
San Sebastiano Curone 113 D1
San Secondo Parmense 114 A1
Sansepolcro 115 C3, 117 C2
San Severino Lucano 120 B3, 122 A1
San Severino Marche 115 D3, 117 D2
San Severo 120 A1
San Silvestre de Guzmán 170 B1/2
Sanski Most 131 D1
Sansol 153 D2
San Sosti 122 A1
San Sperate 123 C/D3
Santa Amalia 165 D2, 166 A2
Santa Ana 165 D1, 166 A1/2
Santa Ana 164 B3
Santa Ana de Cambas 170 B1
Santa Ana do Campa 164 B2
Santa Ana la Real 165 D3, 171 C1
Santa Bárbara de Nexe 170 B2
Santa Bárbara de Padrões 170 B1
Santa Bàrbara 163 C2
Santa Bárbara de Casa 165 C3, 171 C1
Santa Calobra 157 C2
Santacara 154 A2
Santa Catarina da Fonte do Bispo 170 B2
Santa Caterina di Pittinuri 123 C2
Santa Caterina Valfurva 106 B2
Santa Caterina Villarmosa 125 B/C2
Santa Cesárea Terme 121 D3
Santa Cilia de Jaca 154 B2
Santa Clara de Louredo 164 B3, 170 B1

Santa Clara a Nova **170** A/B1
Santa Clara a Velha **170** A1
Santa Coloma de Gramanet **156** A3
Santa Coloma de Farnés **156** B2
Santa Coloma **153** D2
Santa Coloma de Queralt **155** C3, **163** C1
Santa Colomba de Somoza **151** D2
Santa Comba Dão **158** A/B2/3
Santa Comba **150** A1/2
Santa Comba de Rossas **151** C3, **159** C1
Santa Cristina de Valmadrigal **152** A2
Santa Croce Camerina **125** C3
Santa Croce sull'Arno **114** B2, **116** A1/2
Santa Croce del Sánnio **119** D2
Santa Croce di Magliano **119** D2, **120** A1
Santa Cruz **164** A/B3, **170** A1
Santa Cruz **164** A2
Santa Cruz **170** B1
Santa Cruz da Trapa **158** A/B2
Santa Cruz de Grío **162** A1
Santa Cruz de la Serós **154** B2
Santa Cruz de Mudela **167** D2
Santa Cruz del Retamar **160** B3
Santa Cruz de Moya **163** C3, **169** D1
Santa Cruz de Pinares **160** A/B2
Santa Cruz de Nogueras **162** A/B2
Santa Cruz de la Sierra **166** A1
Santa Cruz de los Cáñamos **167** D2, **168** A2
Santa Cruz de la Zarza **161** C3
Santadi **123** C3
Santa Doménica Talao **120** B3, **122** A1
Santa Doménica Vittória **125** C/D2
Santa Elena **167** D3
Santa Elena de Jamuz **151** D2/3
Santa Elisabetta **124** B2
Santaella **172** A/B1
Santa Eufémia Lamézia **122** A/B2
Santa Eufémia d'Aspromonte **122** A3
Santa Eufemia **166** B2
Santa Eugenia **157** C2
Santa Eulália **165** C2
Santa Eulalia de Oscos **151** C1
Santa Eulalia la Mayor **154** B2/3
Santa Eulalia **152** A1
Santa Eulalia **153** D2/3
Santa Eulalia **163** C2
Santa Eulalia del Río **157** D3
Santa Eulalia de Gállego **154** B2
Santa Fé **156** B3
Santafé **173** C2
Santa Fiora **116** B3
Santa Gadea del Cid **153** C2
Santa Galdana **157** C1
Sant'Ágata sul Santerno **115** C1/2, **116** B1
Sant'Ágata sui Due Golfi **119** D3
Sant'Ágata di Púglia **120** A2
Sant'Ágata di Ésaro **122** A1
Sant'Ágata Féltria **115** C2, **117** C1
Sant'Ágata di Militello **125** C2

Sant'Ágata del Bianco **122** A3
Sant'Ágata de'Goti **119** D3
Santa Gertrude/Sankt Gertraud **106** B2
Sant'Agostino **114** B1
Santahamina/Sandhamn **25** D3, **26** A3
Santa Inés **169** D2
Santa Iria **165** C3, **170** B1
Santa Justa **164** B2
Santa Lecina **155** C3, **163** C1
Santa Leocádia **158** B2
Santa Liestra y San Quílez **155** C2
Santa Linya **155** C/D3
Santa Luce **114** B3, **116** A2
Santa Lucia del Mela **125** D1/2
Santa Lucia **123** D2
Santa Luzia **170** A1
Santa Maddalena/Sankt Magdalena **107** D1
Santa Magdalena de Pulpis **163** C2/3
Santa Margalida **157** C2
Santa Margarida de Montbui **155** D3, **156** A3, **163** D1
Santa Margarida da Coutada **164** B1
Santa Margarida da Serra **164** B3
Santa Margarida do Sado **164** B3
Santa Margherita di Belice **124** A2
Santa Margherita Lígure **113** D2
Santa Margherita **123** C/D3
Santa Maria di Licodia **125** C2
Santa Maria della Strada **119** D2
Santa Maria di Neápolis **123** C3
Santa Maria di Merino **120** B1
Santa Maria del Cedro **122** A1
Santa Maria di Porto Novo **117** D2, **130** A3
Santa Maria degli Ángeli **115** D3, **117** C2
Santa Maria a Vico **119** D3
Santa Maria la Palma **123** C1/2
Santa Maria a Piè di Chienti **117** D2, **130** A3
Santa Maria della Versa **113** D1
Santa Maria Maggiore **105** C/D2
Santa Maria Rezzónico **105** D2, **106** A2
Santa Maria Navarrese **123** D2
Santa María del Campo **152** B3
Santa María de Campo Rus **168** A/B1
Santa María de Oló **156** A2
Santa María de Mercadillo **153** C3
Santa María de Melque **160** B3, **167** C1
Santa María del Páramo **151** D2
Santa María la Real de Nieva **160** B2
Santa María de las Hoyas **153** C3, **161** C1
Santa María de Huerta **161** D1
Santa Maria de Merlès **156** A2
Santa Maria del Taro **113** D2
Santa María del Val **161** D2
Santa Maria al Bagno **121** D3
Santa Maria di Siponto **120** B1
Santa Maria Cápua Vétere **119** C/D3

Santa Maria d'Anglona **120** B3
Santa Maria de Sando **159** D2
Santa María de Cayón **152** B1
Santa María de Naranco **151** D1
Santa Maria im Münstertal [Zernez] **106** B2
Santa María de Riaza **161** C1
Santa Maria de Meyà **155** D3
Santa María de los Caballeros **159** D2/3, **160** A2
Santa María **157** C2
Santa Marina del Rey **151** D2
Santa Marina de Valdeón **152** A1
Santa Marina **151** D1
Santa Marina Salina **125** C1
Santa Marinella **118** A2
Santa Marta **165** C3
Santa Marta **168** B2
Santa Marta de Magasca **165** D1, **166** A1
Santana **164** A2/3
Santana da Serra **170** A1
Sant'Anastasia **119** D3
Sant'Anatólia di Narco **117** C3, **118** B1
Santander **153** B/C1
Sant'Andrea Frius **123** D3
Sant'Andrea **123** D3
Sant'Andrea Bagni **114** A1
Sant'Andrea Bonagia **124** A2
Sant Andreu de Llavaneres **156** B3
Santandria **157** C1
Sant'Ángelo **119** C3
Sant'Ángelo in Vado **115** C2/3, **117** C2
Sant'Ángelo in Lízzola **115** D2, **117** C1
Sant'Ángelo Lodigiano **105** D3, **106** A3, **113** D1
Sant'Ángelo a Fasanella **120** A3
Sant'Ángelo di Brolo **125** C1/2
Sant'Ángelo **120** B2
Sant'Ángelo dei Lombardi **120** A2
Sant'Ángelo in Formis **119** C/D3
Sant'Ángelo **122** B1
Santa Ninfa **124** A2
Sant'Anna Arresi **123** C3
Sant'Anna d'Alfaedo **106** B3
Sant'Anna di Valdieri **112** B2
Sant'Ántimo **115** B/C3, **116** B2/3
Sant'Antíoco **123** C3
Sant'Antíoco di Bisárcio **123** C1/2
Sant'António Morignone **106** B2
Sant Antoni de Calonge **156** B2/3
Sant'António **123** D1
Sant'António di Santadi **123** C2/3
Santanyi **157** D2
Santa Olalla del Cala **165** D3, **166** A3, **171** D1
Santa Olalla **160** B3
Santa Pau **156** B2
Santa Pola **169** C/D3
Santa Pola del Este **169** D3
Sant'Apollinare in Classe **115** C1, **117** C1
Santa Ponça **157** C2
Santar **158** B2
Sant'Arcángelo **120** B3
Santarcángelo di Romagna **115** C/D2, **117** C1
Santarém **164** A/B1/2
Santa Severa **118** A2
Santa Severa **113** D2
Santa Severina **122** B2
Santas Martas **152** A2

Santa Sofia **115** C2, **116** B1
Santa Sofia d'Epiro **122** B1
Santa Sofia **164** B2
Santa Susana **165** C2
Santa Suzana **164** B2/3
Santa Tegra **150** A3
Santa Teresa di Riva **125** D2
Santa Teresa Gallura **123** D1
Santa Valburga/Sankt Walburg **107** B/C2
Santa Victoria do Ameixial **165** C2
Santa Vitoria **164** B3, **170** B1
Santa Vittória in Matenano **117** D2/3
Sant Bartomeu del Grau **156** A2
Sant Carles de la Ràpita **163** C2
Sant Celoni **156** B3
Sant Cugat de Vallés **156** A3
Santed **162** A2
Sant'Elia a Pianisi **119** D2, **120** A1
Sant'Elía Fiumerápido **119** C2
Sant Elm **157** C2
San Telmo **165** C3, **171** C1
Sant'Elpídio a Mare **117** D2, **130** A3
Sántena **113** C1
Santenay **103** C/D1
Santéramo in Colle **121** C2
Santesteban **108** A3, **154** A1
Sant'Eufémia a Maiella **119** C1
Sant'Eutízio **117** D3
Sant Feliu de Pallerols **156** B2
Sant Feliu de Llobregat **156** A3
Sant Feliu de Codines **156** A3
Sant Feliu de Guíxols **156** B3
Sant Feliu Sasserra **156** A2
Sant Genís de Vilasar **156** A/B3
Sant Gregori **156** B2
Santhià **105** C3
Sant Hilari Sacalm **156** B2
Santiago **150** A2
Santiago **158** B2
Santiago de Alcántara **165** C1
Santiago de la Ribera **169** C3, **174** B1
Santiago de la Puebla **160** A2
Santiago de Calatrava **172** B1
Santiago de la Espada **168** A3
Santiago del Campo **165** D1, **166** A1
Santiago do Escoural **164** B2
Santiago do Cacém **164** A/B3, **170** A1
Santiago Maior **165** C2
Santiago Millas **151** D2
Santibáñez de Tera **151** D3
Santibáñez de Ayllón **161** C1
Santibáñez de Béjar **159** D2
Santibáñez de la Peña **152** B2
Santibáñez de Vidriales **151** D3
Santibáñez Zarzaguda **153** B/C2
Santibañez el Alto **159** C3
Sant'Ilário d'Enza **114** A/B1
Santillana **152** B1
Santillana de Campos **152** B2
Santiponce **171** D1
San Tirso de Abres **151** C1
Santiso **150** B2

Santisteban del Puerto **167** D3, **168** A3
Santiuste de San Juan Bautista **160** B1/2
Santiz **159** D1/2
Sant Jaume dels Domenys **156** A3, **163** D1
Sant Joan de les Abadesses **156** A2
Sant Julià de Lória **155** D2
Sant Llorenç de Morunys **155** D2/3, **156** A2
Sant Llorenç Savall **156** A3
Sant Martí d'Empúries **156** B2
Sant Martí de Llémena **156** B2
Sant Martí Sarroca **156** A3, **163** D1
Sant Martí Sasgayolas **155** D3, **163** D1
Sant Martí de Maldà **155** D3, **163** D1
Sant Martí Sapresa **156** B2
Sant Michel **26** B1
Santo Aleixo **165** C3
Santo Aleixo **165** C3
Santo Amador **165** C3
Santo Amaro **165** C2
Santo André **164** A3, **170** A1
Santo Antão **164** A2
Santo António das Areias **165** C1
Santo Cruz del Comercio **172** B2
Santo Domingo de la Calzada **153** C2
Santo Domingo de Silos **153** C3
Santo Estêvão **164** A2
Santo Estêvão **170** B2
Santo Estêvão **159** B/C3
Santok **71** C2
Santolea **162** B2
Santomera **169** C3, **174** B1
Sant'Omobono Imagna **106** A3
Santoña **153** C1
Santo Pietro-di-Tenda **113** D2
Santoseso **151** D1
Santo Spírito **121** C2, **136** A3
Santo Stéfano Belbo **113** C1
Santo Stéfano di Camastra **125** C2
Santo Stéfano di Cadore **107** D2
Santo Stéfano d'Áveto **113** D1
Santo Stéfano di Magra **114** A2
Santo Stéfano Quisquina **124** B2
Santo Stino di Livenza **107** D3, **126** A3
Santo Tirso **158** A1
Santo Tomás **157** C1
Santo Tomé **167** D3, **168** A3, **173** C1
Santovenia **151** D3
Santovka **95** D2
Sant Pau de Segúries **156** A/B2
Santpedor **156** A3
Sant Pere de Ronda **156** B2
Sant Pere de Riubebitlles **155** D3, **156** A3, **163** D1
Sant Pere de Torelló **156** A2
Sant Pere de Ribes **156** A3, **163** D1
Sant Pere Pescador **156** B2
Sant Pol de Mar **156** B3
Sant Privat d'En Bas **156** A/B2
Sant Quintí de Mediona **155** D3, **156** A3, **163** D1
Sant Quirze de Besora **156** A2
Sant Sadurní de l'Heura **156** B2
Sant Sadurní d'Anoia **156** A3
Sant Salvador de Guardiola **156** A3, **163** D1

Sant Salvador de Toló 155 D3
Santuário d'Oropa 105 C3
Santuario de Aránzazu 153 D2
Santuário Hera Lacinia 122 B2
Santu Lussúrgiu 123 C2
Santurde 153 C2
Santurdejo 153 C2
Santurtzi 153 C1
Sant Vicenç 155 D2, 156 A2
Sant Vicenç de Castellet 156 A3
San Valentino in Abruzzo Citeriore 119 C1
San Valentino alla Muta/Sankt Valentin 106 B1
San Venanzo 117 C3
San Vicente de Toranzo 152 B1
San Vicente del Raspeig 169 D3
San Vicente de la Barquera 152 B1
San Vicente de Alcántara 165 C1
San Vigílio/Sankt Vigil 107 B/C2
San Vigílio/Sankt Vigil 107 C1/2
San Vincenzo 114 A/B3, 116 A2
San Vincenzo Valle Roveto 119 C2
San Vitero 151 D3, 159 C1
San Vito 123 D3
San Vito al Tagliamento 107 D2/3, 126 A2/3
San Vito Chietino 119 D1
San Vito dei Normanni 121 D2
San Vito di Cadore 107 D2
San Vito lo Capo 124 A1/2
San Vito Romano 118 B2
San Vittore delle Chiuse 115 D3, 117 C2
Sanxay 101 C2
Sanxenxo 150 A2
Sanza 120 A3
San Zeno Navíglio 106 B3
San Zenone degli Ezzelini 107 C3
Sanzoles 159 D1
São Barnabé 170 A/B1/2
São Bartolomeu dos Galegos 164 A1/2
São Bartolomeu de Messines 170 A2
São Bartolomeu da Serra 164 A/B3, 170 A1
São Bento 150 A3
São Brás de Alportel 170 B2
São Braz 165 C3, 170 B1
São Braz de Regedouro 164 B3
São Cristovão 164 B2/3
São Domingos 164 B3, 170 A1
São Felix 158 B2
São Félix da Marinha 158 A2
São Francisco da Serra 164 A/B3
São Gregorio 164 B2
São Gregorio 150 B3
São Jacinto 158 A2
São Joãn da Madeira 158 A2
São Joaninho 158 A/B2
São João da Ribeira 164 A1/2
São João da Serra 158 A2
São João do Monte 158 A2
São João das Lampas 164 A2
São João da Pesqueira 158 B1/2
São João dos Caldeireiros 170 B1
São Joâo da Venda 170 B2
São João de Tarouca 158 B2
São Leonardo 165 C3
São Lourenço de Mamporcão 165 C2
São Lourenço 164 A2
São Lourenço 151 B/C3, 158 B1
São Luis 170 A1
São Maméde de Riba Tua 158 B1
São Manços 165 B/C3
São Marcos da Ataboeira 170 B1
São Marcos do Campo 165 C3
São Marcos da Serra 170 A1/2
São Martinho 158 A/B3
São Martinho 164 B2
São Martinho 158 B1
São Martinho das Amoreiras 170 A1
São Martinho do Porto 164 A1
São Mateus 164 B2
São Matias 164 B2
São Matias 164 B3
São Miguel de Poiares 158 A3
São Miguel do Pinheiro 170 B1
São Miguel de Machede 165 B/C2
São Miguel de Acha 158 B3
São Pedro de Muel 164 A1
São Pedro da Torre 150 A3
São Pedro da Cadeira 164 A2
São Pedro de Solis 170 B1
São Pedro do Sul 158 B2
São Pedro 151 C3, 159 C1
São Quintino 164 A2
Saorge 112 B2
São Romão 165 C2
São Romão 158 B2/3
São Romão 164 B2
São Sebastião de Gommes Aires 170 A/B1
São Sebastião dos Carros 170 B1
São Simão 164 A2
São Teotónio 170 A1
São Tiago 159 C1
São Torcato 158 A1
Saou 111 C/D1
São Vicente 165 C2
São Vicente da Beira 158 B3
Sápai 145 D1
Sápai 149 C1
Saparevo banja 139 D2
Sapataria 164 A2
Sapiãos 150 B3, 158 B1
Sąpolno 71 D1
Sappada 107 D2, 126 A2
Sappee 25 C1/2
Sappee 25 C/D1, 26 A1
Sappen 4 B3
Sappetsele 15 D3
Sappisaasi 10 B3
Sapri 120 A3, 122 A1
Sapsalampi 21 C3
Saques 154 B2
Sara 20 B3
Saraby 5 C2, 6 A1
Sarajärvi 19 C1
Sarajärvi 27 C/D1
Sarajevo 132 B2
Sarakína 143 C2
Saramo 23 C1
Saramon 109 C3, 155 C1
Sarandë 142 A3
Sarandë 148 A1
Sarandinovo 138 B3, 143 C1
Saraorci 134 B2
Säräsiniemi 18 B3
Sarata 141 D1
Sarbia 71 D2
Sarbinowo 70 B2
Sárbogárd 129 B/C1
Sarche 106 B2
Sárdara 123 C3
Sardas 154 B2
Sardoal 164 B1
Sare 108 A3, 154 A1
Šarengrad 129 C3, 133 C1
Šarenik 133 D3, 134 A3
Sarentino/Sarntheim 107 C1/2
Sarezzo 106 B3
Sargans 105 D1, 106 A1
Sári 129 C1
Sariano 114 B1
Saricaali 145 D1, 145 D3
Sari-di-Porto-Vecchio 113 D3
Sari d'Orcino 113 D3
Sa Riera 156 B2
Sarigöl 149 D2
Sariñena 155 B/C3, 162 B1
Sárisáp 95 D3
Sarjankylä 21 C/D1, 22 A1
Sarjankylä 21 D2, 22 A2
Sårjåsjaurestugan 15 C1
Sarkamäki 23 B/C3
Särkelä 13 C2/3
Särkelä 19 C1
Sárkeresztes 128 B1
Sárkeresztúr 128 B1
Särkijärvi 11 C3, 12 A1
Särkijärvi 19 D3, 23 C1
Särkijärvi 19 B/C2
Särkijärvi 18 B1
Särkikylä 21 C2
Särkilahti 25 D1, 26 A1
Särkilahti 27 C/D1
Särkiluoma 19 D1
Särkimo 20 B2
Särkisalmi 27 D1
Särkisalo 21 D2, 22 A2
Särkisalo/Finby 24 B3
Särkivaara 23 C2
Sarkola 24 B1
Şarköy 149 D1
Sarlat-la-Canéda 108 B1
Sarleinsbach 93 C2
Sarliac-sur-l'Isle 101 D3
Sărmașu 97 D3, 140 B1
Sármellék 128 A2
Sarmijärvi 7 C3
Sarmingstein 93 D2
Särna 39 C1
Sarnadas 158 B3, 165 C1
Särnaheden 38 B1
Sarnano 115 D3, 117 D2
Sarnen 105 C1
Sárnico 106 A3
Sarno 119 D3
Sarnow 70 A1
Sarnowa 71 D3
Sarny 98 B2
Särö 49 D1, 50 A1
Sarone 107 D2
Saronís 147 D3
Saronno 105 D3
Sárosd 129 B/C1
Šarovce 95 D2
Sarpsborg 44 B1
Sarralbe 89 D1, 90 A1
Sarrance 108 B3, 154 B1
Sarras 103 D3
Sarratella 163 C3
Sarraz, La 104 B1/2
Sarreaus 150 B3
Sarrebourg 89 D1, 90 A2
Sarreguemines 89 D1, 90 A1
Sarre-Union 89 D1, 90 A1
Sarria 151 B/C2
Sarrión 162 B3
Sarroca de Bellera 155 D2
Sarroca de Segre 155 C3, 163 C1
Sarroch 123 C/D3
Sarron 108 B3, 154 B1
Sársina 115 C2, 117 C1
Sarstedt 68 B3
Sárszentlörinc 128 B2
Sárszentmiklós 129 B/C1
Sartaguda 153 D2
Sartène 113 D3
Sárti 144 B2
Sartilly 85 D1
Sartirana Lomellina 113 C1
Saruhanli 149 D2
Sarule 123 D2
Sárvár 128 A1
Sárvár 96 B3
Sarvaš 129 C3
Sarvela 20 B3
Sarvijoki 20 A/B2
Sarvikas 21 C3
Sarvikumpu 23 C3
Sarvinki 23 D2/3
Sarvisalo 27 D1
Sarvisvaara 16 B1
Sarvsalö 25 D3, 26 A3
Särvsjön 34 A2/3
Sarzana 114 A2
Sarzeau 85 C3
Sarzeda 158 B2
Sarzedas 158 B3, 165 C1
Sarzedo 158 B2
Šaš 128 A3, 131 D1
Sasa 139 C2
Sasamón 152 B2
Sasca-Română 135 C1
Sásd 128 B2
Sasi 24 B1
Sasina 131 D1
Šášov 95 D2
Sassali 12 B2
Sassano 120 A3
Sássari 123 C1
Sássari Argentiera 123 C1
Sássari La Corte 123 C1
Sássari Palmadula 123 C1
Sássari Stintino 123 C1
Sassello 113 C2
Sassenage 104 A3
Sassenberg 67 D3
Sassenburg-Neudorf-Platendorf 69 C2
Sassenburg-Westerbeck 69 C2
Sassetta 114 B3, 116 A2
Sassnitz 72 A2
Sassocorvaro 115 C/D2, 117 C1/2
Sassoferrato 115 D3, 117 C2
Sassoleone 115 B/C2, 116 B1
Sasso Marconi 114 B2, 116 B1
Sassuolo 114 B1
Sastago 162 B1
Šaštínske Stráže 94 B2
Sas van Gent 78 B1
Satanov 98 B3
Satão 158 B2
Säter 45 D2
Säter 39 D2/3, 40 A2
Sæter 32 A2
Saterland-Scharrel 67 D2
Saterland-Strücklingen 67 D1/2
Sätila 45 C3, 49 D1
Satillieu 103 C/D3
Satolas 103 D3
Sátoraljaújhely 97 C2
Šatornja 133 D2, 134 A/B2
Šatov 94 A2
Satow 53 D3
Säträbrunn 40 A3
Sátrai 145 C1
Sætran 9 C2
Sætran 9 C2
Satriano di Lucánia 120 A2/3
Satrup 52 B2
Šatry 75 C2
Såttåhaugvoll 33 C/D2
Sattajärvi 17 C/D1
Sattajärvi 17 D2, 18 A1
Sattanen 12 B2
Satteins 106 A1
Sattel [Sattel-Aegeri] 105 D1
Sattledt 93 C2/3
Sättna 35 D3
Satulung 97 D3, 140 B1
Satu Mare 97 D3, 98 A3
Sa Tuna 156 B2
Saubach 82 A1
Saubusse 108 B2/3
Saúca 161 D2
Saucats 108 B1
Saucedilla 159 D3, 166 A1
Saucelle 159 C2
Sauda 42 A/B1
Saudal 15 D2
Saudasjøen 42 A/B1
Saudron 89 C2
Sauerbrunn 94 B3
Sauerlach 92 A3
Saugon 100 B3
Saugues 110 B1
Saujon 100 B3
Saukkojärvi 18 B1
Saukkokoski 10 B2
Saukkola 21 D3, 22 A3
Saukkola 25 C3
Saukkola 17 D2, 18 A1
Saukkoperukka 23 C1
Saukkoriipi 12 A3, 17 D1
Saukonkylä 21 C2
Saukonperä 24 B1
Saukonsaari 27 C1
Sauland 43 C1
Saulce-sur-Rhône 111 C1
Sauldorf-Krumbach 91 C3
Saulgau 91 C3
Saulges 86 A2
Saulgrub 92 A3
Saulieu 88 B3, 103 C1
Saulkrasti 73 D1, 74 A2
Sault 111 D2
Sault-Brénaz 103 D2, 104 A3
Sault-de-Navailles 108 B3, 154 B1
Saulx 89 C/D3
Saulxures-sur-Moselotte 89 D2
Saulzet 102 B2
Saumur 86 A3, 101 C1
Saunajärvi 23 D1
Saunajoki 24 B1
Saunakylä 20 B3
Saunakylä 21 C2
Saunakylä 21 C/D2
Saunavaara 12 B2/3
Saundersfoot 62 B1
Sauøy 32 B1
Sauquillo de Paredes 161 C1
Saura 14 B1
Saura 14 A2
Saurat 155 D2, 156 A1
Saurier 102 B3
Sáuris 107 D2, 126 A2
Saussy 88 B3
Sausvatn 14 A3
Saut du Doubs 104 B1
Sauvagnat 102 B2/3
Sauve 110 B2
Sauveterre-de-Rouergue 110 A2
Sauveterre-de-Béarn 108 A3, 154 B1
Sauveterre-de-Guyenne 108 B1
Sauviat-sur-Vige 101 D2, 102 A2
Sauvo (Sagu) 24 B3
Sauxillanges 102 B3
Sauze d'Oulx 112 B1
Sauzet 108 B1/2
Sauzé-Vaussais 101 C2
Sauzon 84 B3
Sava 121 C/D3
Savalberget 33 C3, 37 D1
Savaloja 18 A/B3
Sävar 20 A1, 31 D2
Sävast 17 C3
Savaștepe 149 D1
Savci 127 D2
Säve 45 C3
Sävedalen 45 C3
Savelli 117 D3, 118 B1
Savelli 122 B1/2
Savenaho 25 D1, 26 A/B1
Savenay 85 C/D3
Säveni 98 B3
Saverdun 109 D3, 155 D1, 156 A1
Saverne 89 D1, 90 A2
Savero 26 B2
Sävi 24 B1
Säviä 22 B2
Saviaho 23 C1
Säviäntaipale 22 B2
Savigliano 113 B/C1
Savignac-les-Eglises 101 D3
Savignano di Rigo 115 C2, 117 C1
Savignano Irpino 120 A2
Savignano sul Rubicone 115 C2, 117 C1
Savigné-l'Évêque 86 B2
Savigno 114 B2, 116 B1
Savigny-sur-Braye 86 B2/3
Savijärvi 23 D1
Savijoki 25 D2, 26 A2
Savikylä 23 C1

Savilahti **27** C1/2
Saviñán **154** A3, **162** A1
Savina Voda **138** A1
Saviniemi **25** C2
Savino Selo **129** C3
Savio **21** D3, **22** A3
Sávio **115** C2, **117** C1
Saviore d'Adamello **106** B2
Saviselkä **21** D1, **22** A1
Savitaipale **27** C2
Sävja **40** B3
Sævlandsvik **42** A2
Šavnik **137** D1
Savo **25** C1
Savo **25** C1
Savognin [Tiefencastel] **106** A2
Sávoly **128** A2
Savona **113** C2
Savonkylä **21** C2
Savonlinna (Nyslot) **27** C1
Savonranta **23** C3
Sævråsvåg **36** A3
Sävsjö **51** C1
Sävsjö **72** A1
Sävsjön **31** C1
Sävsjön **39** C/D3
Sävsjöström **51** C1
Savudrija **126** A3
Savukoski **13** C2
Savulahti **22** B2
Sawley Abbey **59** D1, **60** B2
Sawston **65** C2
Sax **169** C2
Saxdalen **39** D3
Saxmundham **65** D2
Saxnäs **29** D1
Saxnäs **15** D3
Sayat **102** B2/3
Sayatón **161** C2/3
Sayda **83** C2
Säynäjä **19** D1
Säynätsalo **21** D3, **22** A3
Säyneinen **23** C2
Säynejärvi **23** D3
Säynelahti **23** C3
Säytsjärvi **6** B3
Sazes de Lorvão **158** A3
Sazonovo **75** D1
Sborino **145** D3
Scaër **84** B2
Scăiești **135** D2
Scalasaig **56** A1
Scalasaig **54** A2, **55** D1
Scalby **61** D2
Scalea **120** B3, **122** A1
Scaletta Zanclea **122** A3, **125** D2
Scálzeri **107** C2/3
Scampa **138** A3, **142** A1
Scandale **122** B2
Scandiano **114** B1
Scandicci **114** B2, **116** B1/2
Scandolara Ravara **114** A1
Scanno **119** C2
Scano di Montiferro **123** C2
Scansano **116** B3
Scanzano **121** C3
Scăpău **135** D2
Scarborough **61** D2
Scardovari **115** C/D1
Scarinish **54** A2, **55** D1
Scário **120** A3
Scarlino **116** A3
Scarmafigi **112** B1
Scarperia **114** B2, **116** B1
Scarva **58** A1
Scáuri **119** C3
Šćepan Polje **133** C3
Scey-sur-Saône **89** C3
Schaafheim **81** C3
Schaan **105** D1, **106** A1
Schachendorf **127** D1
Schackenborg **52** A2
Schadeleben **69** C3
Schaffhausen **90** B3
Schafstädt **82** A1
Schäftlarn **92** A3
Schagen **66** A/B2
Schalkau **81** D2, **82** A2
Schangnau [Wiggen] **105** C1
Schanz **91** D3
Schapbach **90** B2
Scharbeutz **53** C3

Scharbeutz-Gleschendorf **53** C3
Scharbeutz-Haffkrug **53** C3
Schärding **93** C2
Schärding **96** A2
Scharfling **93** C3
Scharnebeck **69** C1
Scharnitz **92** A3, **107** C1
Schartau **69** C/D2
Schattwald **91** D3
Schauenstein **82** A2
Schechingen **91** C1/2
Scheelenborg **49** C3, **53** C1
Scheemda **67** C1
Scheessel **68** B1/2
Schefflenz **91** C1
Schéggia **91** D3, **117** C2
Scheibbs **94** A3
Scheibenberg **82** B2
Scheidegg **91** C3
Scheifling **126** B1
Scheifling **96** A3
Scheinfeld **81** D3
Schelklingen **91** C2
Schellerten **68** B3
Schemmerhofen-Aufhofen **91** C2
Schenefeld **52** B3
Schenklengsfeld **81** C2
Schermbeck **67** C3, **80** A1
Schermen **69** D3
Schernsdorf **70** B3
Scherpenzeel **66** B3
Scherpenzeel **66** B2
Schesslitz **82** A3
Scheveningen **66** A3
Scheyern **92** A2
Schiedam **66** A3
Schieder-Schwalenberg **68** A3
Schierke **69** C3
Schierling **92** B2
Schierling-Eggmühl **92** B1/2
Schiermonnikoog **67** C1
Schiers **106** A1
Schiffdorf **68** A1
Schiffdorf-Wehdel **68** A1
Schifferstadt **90** B1
Schildau **82** B1
Schildow **70** A2
Schillingsfürst **91** D1
Schilpário **106** B2
Schiltach **90** B2
Schio **107** C3
Schirmeck **89** D2, **90** A2
Schirnding **82** B3
Schitu-Duca **141** C1
Schkeuditz **82** B1
Schkölen **82** A1/2
Schköna **69** D3, **82** B1
Schlabendorf **70** A/B3
Schladen **69** C3
Schladming **93** C3, **126** B1
Schladming **96** A3
Schlagsdorf **53** C3, **69** C1
Schlangen **68** A3
Schlangenbad **80** B3
Schleching **92** B3
Schleiden **79** D2
Schleiden-Gemünd **79** D2
Schleife **83** D1
Schleitheim [Schaffhausen] **90** B3
Schleiz **82** A2
Schleswig **52** B2
Schleusingen **81** D2
Schlieben **70** A3
Schliersee **92** A3
Schliersee-Valepp **92** A/B3
Schlitz **81** C2
Schlitz-Willofs **81** C2
Schlossvippach **82** A1
Schloss Wildegg **94** A/B2
Schlotheim **81** D1
Schluchsee **90** B3
Schlüchtern **81** C2
Schlüsselfeld **81** D3
Schmalkalden **81** D2
Schmallenberg-Dorlar **80** B1
Schmallenberg **80** B1
Schmallenberg-Fredeburg **80** B1
Schmelz **90** A1
Schmidmühlen **92** A/B1
Schmiedeberg **70** B1/2

Schmiedeberg **83** C2
Schmiedefeld **81** D2
Schmölln **82** B2
Schmölln **70** B1
Schnackenburg **69** C2
Schnaitsee **92** B2/3
Schnaittach **82** A3, **92** A1
Schnaittenbach-Kemnath **82** B3, **92** B1
Schnaittenbach **82** A/B3, **92** B1
Schneeberg **82** B2
Schnega **69** C2
Schneidlingen **69** C3
Schneizelreuth-Melleck **92** B3
Schnelldorf **91** D1
Schneverdingen **68** B2
Schneverdingen-Heber **68** B2
Schoenberg **79** D2
Schöffengrund **80** B2
Schöftland **105** C1
Schöfweg **93** C2
Scholen-Anstedt **68** A2
Schollene **69** D2
Schöllkrippen **81** C3
Schöllnach **93** C2
Schömberg **90** B2
Schöna **83** B/C1
Schonach **90** B2
Schönaich **91** C2
Schönau **93** B/C3
Schönau-Unterzeitlarn **92** B2
Schönbach **93** D2
Schönbeck **70** A1
Schönberg **83** D2
Schönberg **53** C2/3
Schönberg **53** C3, **69** C1
Schönberg-Schönberger-strand **53** C2/3
Schönbrunn **81** D2, **82** A2
Schönebeck **69** D3
Schönebeck **69** D2
Schöneben **93** C2
Schöneck **82** B2
Schönecken **79** D2/3
Schönefeld **70** A2/3
Schönenberg-Kübelberg **90** A1
Schöneuche **70** A/B2
Schönewalde **70** A3
Schönfeld **94** B2
Schönfeld **70** A/B2
Schongau **91** D3
Schöngleina **82** A2
Schönhausen **69** D2
Schönheide **68** B2
Schöningen **69** C3
Schönsee **82** B3, **92** B1
Schönthal **92** B1
Schonungen **81** D3
Schonungen-Löffelsterz **81** D3
Schönwald **90** B2/3
Schönwald (Rehau) **82** B2/3
Schönwalde am Bungsberg **53** C3
Schönwalde **70** A2
Schönwalde **70** A/B3
Schoonebeek **67** C2
Schoonhoven **66** A/B3
Schoonloo **67** C2
Schoonoord **67** C2
Schopfheim **90** A/B3
Schopfheim-Gersbach **90** B3
Schopfloch (Dinkelsbühl) **91** D1
Schopfloch **90** B2
Schöppenstedt **69** C3
Schöppingen **67** D3
Schora **69** D3
Schörfling am Attersee **93** C3
Schorndorf **91** C2
Schortens **67** D1
Schoten **78** B1
Schotten **81** C2
Schramberg **90** B2
Schrecksbach **81** C2
Schrems **93** D2
Schrick **94** B2
Schriesheim **80** B3, **90** B1
Schrobenhausen **92** A2

Schröcken **106** B1
Schrozberg **91** C/D1
Schrozberg-Leuzendorf **91** D1
Schruns **106** A1
Schuby **52** B2
Schulenburg (Leine) **68** B3
Schulzendorf **70** B2
Schulzhytta **28** B3, **33** D2
Schüpfheim **105** C1
Schuttertal **90** B2
Schuttertal-Schweighausen **90** B2
Schüttorf **67** D2/3
Schützen am Gebirge **94** B3
Schwaan **53** D3
Schwabach **91** D1, **92** A1
Schwabach-Grossschwar-zenlohe **91** D1, **92** A1
Schwabhausen bei Dachau **92** A2
Schwäbisch Hall **91** C1
Schwäbisch Gmünd **91** C2
Schwabmünchen **91** D2
Schwadorf **94** B2/3
Schwaförden **68** A2
Schwalmstad-Treysa **81** C2
Schwalmstadt-Ziegenhain **81** C2
Schwalmtal **81** C2
Schwanau-Ottenheim **90** A/B2
Schwanbeck **70** A1
Schwanberg **127** C1
Schwanden **105** D1, **106** A1
Schwandorf **92** B1
Schwanebeck **69** C3
Schwanenstadt **93** C2/3
Schwanewede **68** A1
Schwanewede-Meyenburg **68** A1
Schwanfeld **81** D3
Schwangau **91** D3
Schwanheide **69** C1
Schwanstetten-Schwand **92** A1
Schwante **70** A2
Schwarme **68** A2
Schwarmstedt **68** B2
Schwarza **81** D2
Schwarza **82** A2
Schwarzach **81** D3
Schwarzach **92** B1/2
Schwarzach im Pongau **107** D1, **126** A1
Schwarzau am Steinfelde **94** A/B3
Schwarzau im Gebirge **94** A3
Schwarzbach **81** D2
Schwärzelbach-Neuwirths-haus **81** C2/3
Schwarzenau **94** A2
Schwarzenbach **82** A2
Schwarzenbach **82** A/B2/3
Schwarzenbach (Neustadt) **82** A/B3
Schwarzenbek **69** B/C1
Schwarzenberg **82** B2
Schwarzenborn **81** C2
Schwarzenborn **79** D3, **80** A3
Schwarzenpung **104** B1
Schwarzenfeld **92** B1
Schwarzheide **83** C1
Schwarzhofen-Zangenstein **92** B1
Schwarzsee [Fribourg] **104** B2
Schwarzwaldalp [Meirin-gen] **105** C1/2
Schwaz **92** A3, **107** C1
Schwechat **82** B2
Schwechat **96** B2/3
Schwedt **72** A3
Schwedt **70** B2
Schwefelberg Bad [Fri-bourg] **105** B/C1/2
Schwegenheim **90** B1
Schweich **79** D3, **80** A3
Schweickershausen **81** D2/3
Schweinfurt **81** D3
Schweinitz **70** A3
Schweinitz **69** D3

Schweinrich **69** D1/2, **70** A1/2
Schweitenkirchen-Sünz-hausen **92** A2
Schwelm **80** A1
Schwemsal **69** D3, **82** B1
Schwendi **91** C/D2
Schwenningen (Stockach) **91** C2/3
Schwepnitz **83** C1
Schwerin **69** C1
Schwerte **80** A/B1
Schwetzingen **90** B1
Schweyen **89** D1, **90** A1
Schwiesau **69** C2
Schwinkendorf **53** D3, **69** D1, **70** A1
Schwülper **69** B/C2/3
Schwyz **105** D1
Sciacca **124** A2
Sciáves **107** C1
Scicli **125** C3
Sciez **104** A/B2
Scilla **122** A3, **125** D3
Šćit **132** A2/3
Šćitarjevo **127** D3
Scoarța **135** D1
Scoarța **140** B2
Scodra **137** D2
Scoglitti **125** C3
Scole **65** C2
Scone Palace **57** C1
Scopello **105** C3
Scorbé-Clairvaux **101** C1
Scordia **125** C3
Ščors **99** D2
Scorzè **107** C/D3
Scotch Corner **57** D3, **61** C1
Scotter **61** D3
Scourie **54** A1
Scrabster **54** B1
Ščučin **73** D2/3, **74** A3, **98** B1
Scunthorpe **61** D2/3
Scuol **106** B1
Seaca de Pădure **135** D2
Seaford **76** B1
Seaham **61** D1
Seamer **61** D1/2
Seascale **59** D1, **60** B1/2
Seaton **63** C2/3
Sebergham **57** C3, **60** B1
Sebersdorf **127** D1
Sebeș **140** B1
Šebestov **94** B1
Sebež **74** B2
Sebnitz **83** C/D1/2
Seč **83** C3, **93** C1
Sečanj **140** A2
Sečanj **140** A2
Secășeni **135** C1
Secastilla **155** C2/3
Secca Grande **124** B2
Séchault **88** B1
Seckach **91** C1
Seckau **127** C1
Seclin **78** A2
Secondigny **101** B/C1/2
Secorún **155** B/C2
Sečovce **97** C2
Secugnago **106** A3, **113** C1
Seda **165** B/C2
Seda **73** C1
Sedan **79** C3
Sedano **153** B/C2
Sedbergh **59** D1, **60** B2
Seddülbahir **149** C1
Sedella **172** B2
Sedemte Prestola **139** D1
Séderon **111** D2
Sedgefield **57** D3, **61** C1
Sédico **107** C/D2
Sédilo **123** C/D2
Sédini **123** C1
Sedlare **138** B2
Sedlčany **83** D3
Sedlec **83** C2
Sedlec-Prčice **83** D3, **93** D1
Sedlice **93** C1
Sedlitz **83** C1
Sedrina **106** A3
Sedrun **105** D1/2
Šeduva **73** D2

Sedzère 108 B3, 155 B/C1
See 83 D1
Seebach 126 B1
Seebeck 70 A2
Seebenstein 94 A/B3
Seeboden 126 A1
Seefeld 92 A3
Seefeld 94 A/B2
Seefeld in Tirol 92 A3, 107 C1
Seeg 91 D3
Seegrehna 69 D3
Seehaus 93 C3
Seehausen 69 C3
Seehausen 69 D2
Seeheim-Jugenheim 80 B3
Seelingstädt 82 B2
Seelow 70 B2
Seelscheid 80 A2
Seelze 68 B2/3
Seeon-Seebruck 92 B3
Seerhausen 83 C1
Sées 86 B2
Seesen 68 B3
Seesen-Grossrhuden 68 B3
Seeshaupt 92 A3
Seetal 126 B1
Seevetal 68 B1
Seewald-Besenfeld 90 B2
Seewiesen 94 A3
Séez 104 B3
Seferihisar 149 D2
Seffern 79 D3
Sefkerin 133 D1, 134 A1
Segalstad bru 37 D2, 38 A1
Segarcea 140 B2
Segart 162 B3, 169 D1
Seged 131 C3
Segeletz 69 D2
Segelnes 9 D2
Segelvik 4 B2
Segerstad 51 D2
Segesd 128 A2
Segesta 124 A2
Seggiano 115 C3, 116 B2/3
Seglinge 41 D3
Seglora 45 C3, 49 D1
Segmon 45 C1
Segni 118 B2
Segonzac 101 C3
Segorbe 162 B3, 169 D1
Segovia 160 B2
Segrate 105 D3, 106 A3
Segré 86 A3
Segrie 86 A/B2
Segura 159 C3, 165 C1
Segura de la Sierra 168 A3
Segura de León 165 D3
Segura de los Baños 162 B2
Sehnde 68 B3
Seia 158 B2/3
Seiches-sur-le-Loir 86 A3
Seida 7 C2
Seiersberg 127 C1
Seierstad 28 B1/2
Seignelay 88 A2/3
Seignosse 108 B2/3
Seikka 21 D1, 22 A1
Seilhac 102 A3
Seillans 112 A3
Seimsdal 37 C2
Seimsfoss 42 A1
Seinäjoki 20 B2
Seini 97 D3, 98 A3
Seinsheim 81 D3
Seipäjärvi 12 B2
Seira 155 C2
Seissan 109 C3, 155 C1
Seitajärvi 13 C2
Seitenoikea 19 C3
Seitenstetten Markt 93 D3
Seitlax 25 D3, 26 A3
Seivika 32 B2
Seixal 164 A2
Seixo 158 B2
Seixo de Gatães 158 A3
Sejerby 49 C3, 53 C1
Sejerslev 48 A2
Sejlflod 48 B1/2
Sekkemo 5 B/C2
Šekovići 133 C2
Sel 37 D1/2
Sel 30 B3
Selaño 152 A1
Selänsalmi 19 C1

Seläntaus 21 D2, 22 A2
Selb 82 B3
Selbu 28 B3, 33 D2
Selby 61 C2
Selca 131 D3, 132 A3, 136 A1
Selce 127 C3, 130 B1
Selcè 137 D2
Sel'co 99 D1
Selçuk 149 D2
Selde 48 A/B2
Selen 28 A/B2, 33 C1
Selendi 149 D2
Selenica 142 A2
Selent 53 C1
Sélestat 90 A2
Selet 30 A3, 35 C2
Selet 17 B/C3
Seleuš 134 B1
Selevac 134 B2
Selfjord 8 A2/3
Selgua 155 C3
Selí 143 C2
Selianítika 146 B2
Seligenstadt 81 C3
Seligenthal 81 D2
Selimiye 149 D2
Selinunte 124 A2
Selishte 138 A3
Selište 135 C2/3
Selizarovo 75 C2
Selja 39 C2
Seljänkulma 24 B2
Selje 36 A1
Seljelvnes 4 A3, 10 A1
Seljesåsen 21 C1
Seljestad 42 B1
Seljord 43 C1/2
Selkälä 13 C3
Selkentjakkstugan 29 D1
Selkirk 57 C2
Sella 107 C2
Sella 169 D2
Sella di Corno 117 D3, 118 B1
Sellafield 59 C1, 60 A1
Sellano 117 C3
Sellasía 147 C3
Sellerich 79 D2
Selles-sur-Cher 87 C3, 101 D1, 102 A1
Sellières 103 D1, 104 A1
Sellrain 107 C1
Sellye 128 B3
Selm 67 D3, 80 A1
Selm-Bork 67 D3, 80 A1
Selmes 165 B/C3
Selmsdorf 53 C3, 69 C1
Selnes 28 B2
Selnes 28 A2, 33 C1
Selnes 9 C2
Selnica 127 C2
Selommes 86 A/B3
Selongey 88 B3
Sélonnet 112 A2
Selseng 36 B2
Selsey 76 B1
Selsingen 68 A/B1
Selsjön 30 B3, 35 D2
Selters 80 B2
Selters-Niederselters 80 B2
Seltjärn 30 B2/3, 35 D1
Seltz 90 B1/2
Selva 113 D1
Selva 157 C2
Selva di Cadore 107 C2
Selva di Progno 107 C3
Selva di Val Gardena 107 C2
Selvåg 32 B1
Selvik 36 A2
Selvik 43 D1, 44 A/B1
Selvino 106 A3
Sembadel 103 C3
Sembrancher 104 B2
Semeljci 128 B3
Semenic 135 C1
Semenovka 99 D1
Semič 127 C3
Semily 83 D2
Seminara 122 A3
Semizovac 132 B2
Semlow 53 D3
Semmenstedt 69 C3
Šemoine 88 A/B1/2
Sem'onovka 99 D2/3
Semoutiers 88 B2

Šempeter 127 C2
Semproniano 116 B3, 118 A1
Semriach 127 C1
Sem (Semsbyen) 43 D2, 44 A/B1
Semur-en-Auxois 88 B3
Sena 155 C3, 163 C1
Sena 151 D2
Senáles/Schnals 106 B1
Sénarpont 77 D2/3
Senas 111 D2
Šenčur 126 B2
Senden 67 D3
Senden 91 D2
Sendenhorst 67 D3
Sendim 159 C1
Šenec 95 C2
Šenec 96 B2/3
Séneghe 123 C2
Senés 173 D2
Senftenberg 94 A2
Senftenberg 83 C1
Senftenberg 96 A1
Senhora da Atalaia 164 A2
Senhora da Graça dos Padrões 170 B1
Senhora das Neves 164 B3, 170 B1
Senica 95 C2
Senica 96 B2
Senigállia 115 D2, 117 D1/2
Sénis 123 C/D2
Senise 120 B3
Senj 130 B1
Senje 134 B2
Senjski Rudnik 135 B/C2
Senlis 87 D1
Sennecey-le-Grand 103 D1
Sennen 62 A3
Senno 74 B3
Sénnori 123 C1
Sennybridge 63 C1
Senohrad 95 D2
Senonches 86 B2
Senones 89 D2, 90 A2
Senorbì 123 D3
Senožeče 126 B3
Senrjošt 126 B2
Sens-de-Bretagne 85 D2
Sens-sur-Yonne 88 A2
Senta 129 D2/3
Senta 140 A1
Senterada 155 D2
Šentilj 127 C/D1/2
Šentjanž 127 C2
Šentjernej 127 C3
Šentjur 127 C2
Šentrupert 127 C2
Šentvid 126 B2
Šentvid na Slemenu 127 C2
Seoane 151 C2
Seoane Vello 150 B2
Seon 90 B3, 105 C1
Šepak 133 C2
Sepänkylä 27 C1
Šepetovka 98 B2
Sépey, Le 104 B2
Sępólno Krajeńskie 72 B3
Seppälä 25 C2
Seppois-le-Bas 89 D3, 90 A3
Septèmes-les-Vallons 111 D3
Septemvrijci 135 D2
Septeuil 87 C1
Septfonds 87 D3
Septfonds 109 D2
Sepulcro-Hilario 159 D2
Sepúlveda 160 B1
Sequals 107 D2, 126 A2
Sequeros 159 D2
Seraincourt 78 B3
Seraing 79 C2
Serapicos 151 B/C3, 158 B1
Seravezza 114 A2, 116 A1
Sercaia 141 B/C1
Sercoeur 89 D2
Sereď 95 C2
Sereď 96 B2/3
Seredina-Buda 99 D1
Seredka 74 B1
Seregélyes 128 B1
Seregno 105 D3, 106 A3
Sérent 85 C3

Serfaus 106 B1
Sergines 88 A2
Seriate 106 A3
Sérifontaine 77 D3, 87 C1
Sérigny 100 B2
Serina 106 A2/3
Serino 119 D3, 120 A2
Serinyà 156 B2
Sermaize-les-Bains 88 B1
Sérmide 114 B1
Sermoneta 118 B2
Sernache dos Alhos 158 A3
Sernancelhe 158 B2
Serón 173 D2
Serón de Nágima 153 D3, 161 D1
Seròs 155 C3, 163 C1
Serpa 165 C3, 170 B1
Serpins 158 A3
Serpuhov 75 D3
Serra 164 B1
Serra 162 B3, 169 D1
Serrabonne 156 B1/2
Serracapriola 119 D2, 120 A1
Serrada 107 C2/3
Serrada 160 A1
Serra da Boa Fé 164 B2
Serra de El-Rei 164 A1
Serradell 155 D2
Serradilla 159 D3, 165 D1, 166 A1
Serradilla del Arroyo 159 C2
Sérrai 144 A1
Serral 155 C3, 163 C1
Serramanna 123 C/D3
Serramazzoni 114 B2, 116 A1
Serranillos 160 B3
Serranillos 160 A2/3
Serra Nova 157 C2
Serrant 86 A3
Serra Orrios 123 D2
Serra San Bruno 122 B2/3
Serrastretta 122 B2
Serravalle 117 C/D3
Serravalle di Chienti 115 D3, 117 C2
Serravalle Scrívia 113 D1
Serre 120 A2
Serrejón 159 D3, 166 A1
Serrenti 123 C/D3
Serres 111 D1/2
Serres-sur-Arget 109 D3, 155 D1/2, 156 A1
Serri 123 D3
Serrières 103 D3
Sersale 122 B2
Sertã 158 A/B3, 164 B1
Sertig Dörfli [Davos Frauenkirch] 106 A1
Servance 89 D2
Serverette 110 B1
Sérvia 143 C2
Servian 110 B3
Serviana 142 B3
Servigliano 117 D2
Sesa 154 B3
Seščinskij 75 C3
Seseña 161 B/C3
Sesimbra 164 A3
Seskarö 17 D3
Sésklon 143 D3, 144 A3
Sesma 153 D2
Sessa Aurunca 119 C3
Sessa Cilento 120 A3
Ses Salines 157 D2
Sesslach 81 D2/3
Sesta Godano 113 D2, 114 A2
Šestanovac 131 D3, 132 A3
Sestao 153 C1
Sestino 115 C2/3, 117 C2
Sesto Calende 105 D3
Sesto Fiorentino 114 B2, 116 B1
Séstola 114 B2, 116 A1
Sesto San Giovanni 105 D3, 106 A3
Sestriere 112 B1
Sestri Levante 113 D2
Sestrunj 130 B2
Sestu 123 D3
Sesvete 127 D3

Séta 147 D1/2
Setcases 156 A2
Sète 110 B3
Setenil 172 C2
Seter 33 D3
Setermoen (Bardu) 9 D1
Seternes 32 A2
Setervik 28 A2
Setil 164 A2
Setiles 162 A2
Setså 15 C1
Setskog 38 B3
Séttima 113 D1, 114 A1
Séttimo Torinese 113 C1
Séttimo Vittone 105 C2
Settle 59 D1, 60 B2
Setúbal 164 A2
Seubersdorf 92 A1
Seui 123 D2
Seulingen 81 D1
Seurre 103 D1
Sevalla 40 A3
Sevaster 142 A2
Sevelen 105 D1, 106 A1
Sevenoaks 65 C3, 76 B1
Sevenum 79 D1
Sever 158 A2
Sévérac-le-Château 110 B2
Severin na Kupi 127 C3, 130 B1
Séveso 105 D3, 106 A3
Ševětín 93 D1
Sevettijärvi (Tševetjävri) 7 C2/3
Sévignacq 108 B3, 154 B1
Sevilla 171 D1/2
Sevilleja de la Jara 166 B1
Sevlievo 141 B/C3
Sevnica 127 C2
Sewekow 69 D1, 70 A1
Sewen 89 D3, 90 A3
Sexcles 102 A3, 109 D1
Seyches 109 C1
Seyda 70 A3
Seyne-les-Alpes 112 A2
Seyssel 104 A2
Seysses 108 B3, 155 C1
Sežana 126 B3
Sézanne 88 A1/2
Sezimovo Ústí 93 D1
Sezulfe 151 C3, 159 C1
Sezze 118 B2
Sfércia 115 D3, 117 D2
Sferro 125 C2
Sfîntu Gheorghe 141 D2
Sfîntu Gheorghe 141 C1
Sforzacosta 115 D3, 117 D2
's-Gravenhage 66 A3
Sgúrgola 118 B2
Shaftesbury 63 D2
Shaldon 63 C3
Shanklin 76 B2
Shannon Airport 55 C3
Shap 57 C3, 60 B1
's-Heerenberg 67 C3
Sheerness 65 C3
Sheffield 61 C2
Shefford 64 B2
Shëmri 138 A2
Shëngjergj 138 A3, 142 A1
Shëngjin 137 D2/3
Shëpaj 142 A1
Shepton Mallet 63 D2
Sherborne 63 D2
Sherburn 61 D2
Sherburn-in-Elmet 61 D2
Sheringham 61 D3, 65 C1
's-Hertogenbosch 66 B3, 79 C1
Shieldaig 54 A2
Shijak 137 D3, 142 A1
Shipdham 65 C1/2
Shipley 61 C2
Shipston on Stour 64 A2
Shiroka 137 D2
Shkodër 137 D2
Shoeburyness 65 C3
Shoreham-by-Sea 76 B1
Shorwell 76 B2
Shotley 65 C2
Shrewsbury 59 D3
Shupenze 138 A3
Siamanna-Siapiccia 123 C2
Siátista 143 C2
Siátista 148 B1
Šiauliai 73 D1/2

Síbari **122** B1
Sibbesse **68** B3
Sibbhult **50** B2
Sibbo/Sipoo **25** D3, **26** A3
Šibenik **131** C3
Sibinj **132** B1
Sibiu **140** B1/2
Sibnica **133** D2, **134** A2
Sibo **40** A1
Šibovska **132** A/B1
Sibratsgfäll **91** D3
Sičevo **135** C3
Siciny **71** D3
Siculiana **124** B3
Siculiana Marina **124** B3
Šid **133** C1
Sidárion **142** A3
Siddeburen **67** C1
Sideby/Siipyy **20** A3
Sidensjö **30** B3
Siderno **122** A/B3
Sidirókastron **139** D3, **144** A1
Sidirókastron **146** B3
Sidirón **145** D1, **145** D3
Sidmouth **63** C2/3
Sidskogen **39** D1, **40** A1
Siebe **11** C1/2
Siebeldingen **90** B1
Siebnen [Siebnen-Wangen] **105** D1
Siecq **101** C2/3
Siedenburg **68** A2
Siedenlangenbeck **69** C2
Siedlce **73** D3, **97** C1, **98** A1
Siedlice **71** C1
Siedlisko **71** C3
Siegbach **80** B2
Siegburg **80** A2
Siegen **80** B2
Siegenburg **92** A2
Siegen-Eiserfeld **80** B2
Siegen-Hüttental **80** B2
Sieghartskirchen **94** A2
Siegsdorf **92** B3
Siekierki **70** B2
Siekkinen **19** C1/2
Sielow **70** B3
Siemczyno **71** C/D1
Siemiatycze **73** D3, **98** A1
Sien **80** A3
Siena **114** B3, **116** B2
Sieniawa **71** C2/3
Sieppijärvi **12** A2, **17** D1
Sieradz **96** B1
Sieraków **71** C2
Sierck-les-Bains **79** D3
Sierndorf **94** A/B2
Sierning **93** D3
Siero **151** D1, **152** A1
Sierpc **73** C3
Sierra **168** B2
Sierra de Fuentes **165** D1, **166** A1
Sierra de Luna **154** B3
Sierra de Yeguas **172** A2
Sierra Engarcerán **163** C3
Sierre **105** C2
Sierro **173** D2
Siétamo **154** B3
Siete Iglesias de Trabancos **160** A1
Sieversdorf **69** D2
Sieverstedt **52** B2
Sievi **21** C1
Sievin asema **21** C1
Sifjord **9** C/D1
Sigdal **43** D1
Sigean **110** A/B3, **156** B1
Sigena **155** C3, **163** C1
Sigerfjord **9** C2
Sigersvoll **42** B3
Siggebohyttan **39** D3, **46** A1
Siggelkow **69** D1
Siggjarvåg **42** A1
Sighetu Marmației **97** D3, **98** A3
Sighișoara **97** D3, **140** B1
Sigillo **115** D3, **117** C2
Sigmaringen **91** C2/3
Sigmundsherberg **94** A2
Signa **114** B2, **116** B1/2
Signau **105** C1
Signes **111** D3, **112** A3
Signy-l'Abbaye **78** B3

Signy-le-Petit **78** B3
Sigogne **101** C3
Sigonce **111** D2, **112** A2
Sigridsbu **43** C/D1
Sigtuna **40** B3, **47** C1
Sigüeiro **113** D2
Sigüenza **161** D2
Sigüés **154** B2
Sigurdsristningen **47** B/C1
Sihtuuna **17** D2, **18** A1
Siikainen **24** A1
Siikajärvi **19** C2
Siikajoki **18** A2
Siika-Kämä **18** B1
Siikakoski **26** B2
Siikala **25** C2
Siikalainen **19** D1
Siikalampi **18** B1
Siikamäki **22** B3
Siikasaari **23** C3
Siikava **26** B2
Siikavaara **23** D2
Siilinjärvi **22** B2
Siimes **12** A2, **17** D1
Siitama **25** C1
Siivikko **19** C2
Sijarinska Banja **139** B/C1
Sikås **29** D3, **35** C1
Sikeå **31** D2
Sikéa **144** B2
Sikéa **143** C3
Sikfors **16** B3
Sikfors **39** D3
Sikí **144** A3
Sikiá **144** B2
Sikiá **146** A1/2
Sikidallseter **37** C/D2
Sikkerlia **38** A2
Sikkola **11** D3, **12** A1/2
Siklós **128** B3
Siknäs **17** C2/3
Sikory **71** D1
Sikoúrion **143** D3
Sikovuono **6** B3
Sikselberg **31** C1
Sikselet **15** D2
Siksjö **30** B1/2
Siksjö **30** B1
Siksjön **16** A3
Siksjönäs **30** A1
Sikyon **147** C2
Sil **30** A2, **35** C1
Sila **14** A/B2
Šilale **73** C/D2
Silandro/Schlanders **106** B2
Silánus **123** C2
Silba **130** B2
Silbaš **129** C3
Silberstedt **52** B2
Silberstedt-Esperstoft **52** B2
Silbertal **106** A/B1
Silenrieux **78** B2
Siles **168** A3
Silfiac **84** B2
Síligo **123** C2
Silió **152** B1
Silíqua **123** C3
Silistra **141** C2
Silivri **149** D1
Siljan **43** D2, **44** A1
Siljansfors **39** C2
Siljansnäs **39** D2
Siljeåsen **29** D2, **30** A2
Silkeborg **48** B3
Silken **39** D3
Silla **114** B2, **116** A/B1
Silla **169** D2
Sillamjaè **74** B1
Sillano **114** A2, **116** A1
Sillanpää **25** C2
Sillans-la-Cascade **112** A3
Silleda **150** B2
Sillé-le-Guillaume **86** A2
Sillerud **45** C1
Sillery **88** A/B1
Sílli **145** B/C1
Sillian **107** D1
Silloth **57** C3, **60** A1
Sillre **35** C/D2
Silmutjoki **21** D2/3, **22** A3
Šilo **130** B1
Šíls **162** B2/3
Silsand **9** D1
Silsjönäs **30** A2, **35** C1
Siltaharju **12** B1

Siltakylä/Broby **26** B2/3
Siltavaara **23** C1
Silute **73** C2
Silva **150** A1
Silvacane **111** D2
Silvakkajoki **17** D2, **18** A1
Silvåkra **50** B3
Silvalen **14** A2
Silvana Mánsio **122** B2
Silvaplana [St. Moritz] **106** A2
Silvares **158** B3
Silvberg **39** D2
Silverberg **15** C3
Silverdalen **46** B3
Silves **170** A2
Silvi **119** C1
Silyalde **158** A2
Silz **106** B1
Simanala **23** C3
Simancas **152** A3, **160** A1
Simandre **103** D1
Šimanovci **133** D1, **134** A1
Simaság **94** B3, **128** A1
Simat de Valldigna **169** D2
Simavik **5** C2
Simáxis **123** C2
Simbach **92** B2
Simbach **93** B/C2
Simbach-Haunersdorf **92** B2
Simbário **122** B2
Simeå **40** A1
Simeonovo **139** D1
Símeri-Crichi **122** B2
Sími **149** D3
Simiane-la-Rotonde **111** D2
Simin Han **133** B/C2
Simitli **139** D2
Simitli **140** B3
Simlångsdalen **72** A1
Simlångsdalen **50** A/B2
Simleu-Silvaniei **97** D3, **140** B1
Simlinge **50** B3
Simmelsdorf **82** A3
Simmerath **79** D2
Simmerath-Einruhr **79** D2
Simmerath-Steckenborn **79** D2
Simmern **80** A3
Simmertal **80** A3
Simo **18** A1
Simola **27** C2
Simonby **24** B3
Simonfa **128** B2
Simoniemi **17** D3, **18** A1
Simonkylä **17** D3, **18** A1
Simonneau **101** C3
Simonsberg **52** A2
Simonstorp **46** B2
Simonswald **90** B2/3
Simontornya **128** B1/2
Simópoulon **146** B2
Simorre **109** C3, **155** C1
Simpele **27** D1
Simpiänniemi **26** B1
Simplon [Brig] **105** C2
Simpnäs **41** C3
Simrishamn **50** B3
Simrishamn **72** A2
Šimsk **75** B/C1
Simskälä **41** C2
Simuni **130** B2
Sinabelkirchen **127** D1
Sinac **130** B1
Sinaia **141** C2
Sinalunga **115** C3, **116** B2
Sinarádes **142** A3
Sinarcas **163** C3, **169** D1
Sindal **48** B1
Sindelfingen **91** C2
Sindía **123** C2
Sindirgi **149** D1/2
Síndos **143** D2, **144** A2
Sines **164** A3, **170** A1
Sinetta **12** A3
Sineu **157** C2
Singen **90** B3
Singhofen **80** B2
Singistugorna **9** D3
Singö **41** C3
Singra **163** C2
Singsas **33** C2
Singusdal **43** C2
Siniscóla **123** D2

Sinj **131** D3
Sinlabajos **160** A2
Sinn **80** B2
Sinnai **123** D3
Sinnes **42** B2
Sinnes **32** B2
Sînnicolau Mare **129** D2
Sînnicolau Mare **140** A1
Sinntal **81** C2
Sinntal-Jossa **81** C2/3
Sinntal-Oberzell **81** C2
Sinntal-Sterbfritz **81** C2
Sinsheim **91** B/C1
Sint-Anthonis **67** B/C3, **79** D1
Šintava **95** C2
Sint-Eloois **78** A2
Sint-Joris-Winge **79** C2
Sint Nicolaasga **66** B2
Sint-Niklaas **78** B1
Sint-Oedenrode **79** C1
Sint-Pieters-Kapelle **78** A1
Sintra **164** A2
Sint-Truiden **79** C2
Sinzheim **90** B2
Sinzig **80** A2
Siófok **128** B1
Siófok **96** B3
Sion **104** B2
Sion-les-Mines **85** D3
Sion-sur-l'Océan **100** A1
Siorac-en-Périgord **109** C1
Sip **135** C1/2
Sipola **18** A3
Šipovo **131** D2, **132** A2
Sippola **26** B2
Šiprage **132** A2
Siracusa **125** D3
Siradan **109** C3, **155** C1/2
Siran **109** D1, **110** A1
Siresa **154** B2
Siret **98** B3
Sirevåg **42** A3
Sirig **129** D3
Sirijorda **14** A/B3
Sirkka **11** D3, **12** A2
Sirkkakoski **12** A3, **17** D1
Sirkkamäki **21** D3, **22** A3
Sirma fjellstue **6** B2
Sirmione **106** B3
Sirmium **133** C1, **134** A1
Sirnihtä **23** C2
Sirniö **19** C1
Široka Kula **131** B/C2
Široko Polje **128** B3
Sirolo **117** D2, **130** A3
Sirotino **74** B3
Siruela **166** B2
Širvintos **73** D2, **74** A3
Sisak **127** D3
Sisamón **161** D1/2
Šišan **130** A1
Sisante **168** B1
Sisatto **24** B1
Sisco **113** D2
Šišenci **135** C2
Šišicy **99** B/C1
Šišljavić **127** D3
Sissa **114** A1
Sissach **90** A/B3
Sissala **21** C2
Sissola **23** D2
Sissonne **78** B3
Sistelo **150** A/B3
Sisteron **111** D2, **112** A2
Sistiana **126** A/B3
Sistranda **32** B1
Sitasjaurestugorna **9** D3
Sitas kåte **9** D2/3
Sitges **156** A3
Sitía **149** C3
Sitneš **132** A1
Sitnica **131** D2, **132** A2
Sitno **131** C3
Sitno **71** D1
Sitojaurestugan **16** A1
Sitrama **151** D3
Sittard **79** D1/2
Sittensen **68** B1
Sitter **28** B2
Sittingbourne **65** C3, **77** C1
Sitzendorf **82** A2
Sitzendorf an der Schmida **94** A2
Sitzenroda **82** B1
Siuntio/Sjundeå **25** C3
Siuro **24** B1

Siurua **18** B1/2
Siurunmaa **12** B2
Siusi/Seis **107** C2
Sivac **129** C3
Sivakkajoki **17** D2, **18** A1
Sivakkavaara **23** C1
Sivakkavaara **23** C1
Siverskij **74** B1
Síviri **144** A2
Sívota **142** A/B3
Sívros **146** A1
Sivry **78** B2/3
Sixpenny Handley **63** D2
Sixt **104** B2
Siyilli **145** D3
Sizergh Castle **59** D1, **60** B2
Sizun **84** A/B2
Själevad **31** B/C3
Själlarim **16** B2
Sjenica **133** D3, **134** A3
Sjenica **140** A2/3
Sjeničak Lasinjski **127** D3
Sjoa **37** D2
Sjøåsen **28** B2
Sjöberg **30** A1
Sjöbo **50** B3
Sjöbo **72** A2
Sjöbotten **31** D1
Sjöbrånet **31** C1
Sjöfallsstugan **9** D3
Sjøholt **32** A3
Sjøli **38** A1
Sjömarken **45** C3
Sjonhagen **14** B2
Sjørring **48** A2
Sjørup **48** B2
Sjösanden **39** D1
Sjö Slott **40** B3
Sjötofta **50** B1
Sjötorp **45** D2
Sjoutnäs **29** D1/2
Sjøvegan **9** D1
Sjövik **45** C3
Sjulnäs **15** D3
Sjulsmark **30** A/B1
Sjuntorp **45** C3
Sjursheim **9** D2
Sjursvollen **33** D2
Sjusjøen **38** A1
Skå **47** C1
Skåbu **37** D2
Skåde **48** B3
Skademark **31** C3
Skafidiá **146** A3
Skafså **43** C2
Skaftet **46** B3
Skaftung **20** A3
Skag **41** C2/3
Skaga **14** A2
Skage **28** B2
Skagen **44** B3
Skagshamn **31** C3
Skagstad **8** B3
Skaidi **5** D2, **6** A1
Skaite **16** B1
Skaiti **15** C1
Skaitihytta **15** C1
Skála **147** C1
Skála **146** A2
Skála Kalliráchis **145** B/C2
Skála Leptokariás **143** D2
Skála Marión **145** B/C2
Skålan **34** B2/3
Skaland **9** C/D1
Skála Oropoú **147** D2
Skála Oropoú **148** B2
Skála Rachoníou **145** C1/2
Skalat **98** B3
Skålbygge **39** D1
Skälderviken **49** D2, **50** A2
Skåldö **25** B/C3
Skålevik **43** C3
Skalica **95** B/C1/2
Skalice **82** D2
Skalité **95** D1
Skallelv **7** D2
Skällinge **49** D1, **50** A1
Skallingen **48** A3, **52** A1
Skallsjön **30** A3, **35** C1
Skallskog **39** D2
Skalluvaara **6** B2
Skalmé **95** D1
Skalmodalen **14** B3
Skalmsjö **30** B3, **35** D1
Skalná **82** B3
Skålö **39** C2

Skalochórion 143 C2
Skalotí 144 B1
Skals 48 B2
Skålsjön 39 D1, 40 A1
Skælskør 53 C1
Skalstugan 28 B3, 33 D1, 34 A1
Skålvik 14 A3, 28 B1
Skamlingsbanke 52 B1
Skamsdalshytta 32 B3, 37 C1
Skån 35 C3
Skandáli 145 C3
Skanderborg 48 B3
Skånes Fagerhult 50 B2
Skånes Värsjö 50 B2
Skåne-Tranås 50 B3
Skåningsbukt 4 A2
Skänninge 46 A2
Skanör-Falsterbo 50 A3
Skansbacken 39 C/D2
Skansen 28 B3, 33 D1
Skansen 28 A2, 33 C1
Skansholm 30 A1
Skåpafors 45 C2
Skąpe 71 C3
Skar 9 C2
Skar 15 C1
Skara 45 D2
Skäran 31 D2
Skäråsen 34 A3
Skærbæk 52 A1/2
Skarberget 9 C2
Skærberget 38 B2
Skärblacka 46 B2
Škare 130 B1
Skåre 45 D1
Skare 42 B1
Skåren 14 A3
Skaret 4 B2
Skåret 38 B1
Skärhamn 44 B3
Skärkdalen 34 A2
Skärlöv 51 D2
Skarmunken 4 A3
Skarnes 38 B3
Skarpdalsvollen 28 B3, 33 D2
Skärplinge 40 B2
Skarpnåtö 41 C2
Skarp Salling 48 B2
Skärså 40 A/B1
Skärsnäs 50 B2
Skarstad 9 C2
Skarstein 9 C1
Skarsvåg 5 D1
Skarult 50 B3
Skärvagen 34 A3
Skarvfjordhamn 5 C1
Skarvsjöby 30 B1
Skarvvik 5 D1, 6 A1
Skarżysko-Kamienna 97 C1
Skattkärr 45 D1
Skattungbyn 39 D1
Skatval 28 A/B3, 33 C/D1
Skatvik 9 D1
Skau 28 A3, 33 C1
Skaugvoll 14 B1
Skaule 15 C2
Skaulo 10 B3
Skaun 28 A3, 33 C2
Skavdal 9 C1
Skævinge 49 D3, 50 A3
Skavnakk 4 B2
Skavvik 5 D1, 6 A1
Skeberg 39 D2
Skebobruk 41 B/C3
Skebokvarn 47 B/C1
Skeda udde 46 B2
Skedbrostugan 34 A3
Skede 46 A3, 51 C1
Skedevi 46 B2
Skedsmokorset 38 A3
Skee 44 B2
Skegness 61 D3, 65 C1
Skegrie 50 A3
Skei 36 B2
Skei 32 B2
Skei 14 A3, 28 B1
Skeie 42 B3
Skela 133 D1, 134 A1/2
Skelde 52 B2
Skellefteå 31 D1
Skelleftehamn 31 D1
Skelleftestrand 31 D1
Skelmorlie 56 B2
Skelund 48 B2
Skender Vakuf 131 D2, 132 A2
Skeppshamn 35 D3
Skeppshult 50 B1
Skeppshult 72 A1
Skeppsvik 20 A1, 31 D2
Skeppsvik 41 C3
Skerninge 53 C2
Skerries 58 A2
Sketaj 137 D3
Ski 38 A3, 44 B1
Skíathos 147 D1
Skíathos 148 B1/2
Skibbereen 55 C3
Skibby 49 D3, 53 D1
Skibotn 4 B3, 10 A1
Ski-Center 147 C1/2
Skídra 143 C/D1/2
Skidstuga 15 C3
Skien 43 D2, 44 A1
Skillefjordnes 5 C2
Skillingaryd 50 B1
Skillingaryd 72 A1
Skillinge 50 B3
Skillingmark 38 B3
Skinnarbu 43 C1
Skinnskatteberg 39 D3
Skipagurra 7 C2
Skiperón 142 A3
Skipmannvik 15 C1
Skipnes 8 B1/2
Skipness 56 A2
Skipsea 61 D2
Skipstadsand 44 B1/2
Skipton 59 D1, 61 B/C2
Skipton 54 B3
Skiptvet 44 B1
Skirö 51 C1
Skíros 149 C2
Skirva 43 C1
Skíti 143 D3, 144 A3
Skivarp 50 B3
Skive 48 A/B2
Skivjane 138 A2
Skivsjön 31 C2
Skjåholmen 5 C1, 6 A1
Skjåk 32 B3, 37 C1
Skjåmoen 14 B2/3
Skjånes 7 C1
Skjånes 14 B2
Skjårberger 9 C2
Skjærhalden 44 B2
Skjåvik 14 B3
Skjeberg 44 B1
Skjee 43 D2, 44 A/B1
Skjeggedal 43 C2
Skjelåvollen 33 D3
Skjeljavik 42 A1
Skjellelv 9 D1/2
Skjelnes 4 A3
Skjelten 32 A2/3
Skjern 48 A3
Skjersholmane 42 A1
Skjerstad 15 C1
Skjervøy 4 B2
Skjevik 28 B2
Skjold 42 A1/2
Skjoldehamn 9 C1
Skjolden 37 C2
Skjomen 9 D2
Skjøtningberg 6 B1
Sklabiňa 95 D1
Sklíthron 143 C2
Skoby 40 B3
Skočivir 143 C1
Škocjanska Jama 126 B3
Skodje 32 A3
Skodsborg 49 D3, 50 A3, 53 D1
Skødstrup 49 B/C2
Škofije 126 B3
Škofja Loka 126 B2
Škofljica 126 B2
Skog 40 A1
Skogaby 50 A/B2
Skogadalsbøen 37 C2
Skogalegerseter 37 D2
Skogalund 45 D1, 46 A1
Skoganvarre 5 D2, 6 A2
Skogboda 41 D3
Skoger 43 D1, 44 A1
Skogfoss 7 C3
Skoghall 45 D1
Skoghult 51 C/D1
Skogly 7 C3
Skogmo 14 A3
Skogn 28 B3, 33 D1
Skognes 4 A3
Skogså 17 C2
Skogsby 51 D2
Skogstad 37 C2
Skogstorp 49 D2, 50 A1
Skogstorp 46 B1
Skoki 71 D2
Skokloster 40 B3
Sköldinge 46 B1
Sköldvik 25 D3, 26 A3
Skole 97 D2, 98 A3
Skollenborg 43 D1, 44 A1
Sköllersta 46 A/B1
Skóllis 146 B2
Skóllis 148 A/B2
Skoltebyen 7 C2
Skölvene 45 D3
Skongseng 14 B2
Skópelos 147 D1
Skópelos 148 B2
Skopiá 147 C1
Skopje 138 B2
Skopje 140 A3
Skorenovac 134 B1
Skorica 135 B/C3
Skorild 33 C1/2
Skórka 71 D1
Skorovassgruver 29 C1/2
Skorovatn 29 C1/2
Skorped 30 B3, 35 D1/2
Skørping Stationsby 48 B2
Skorstad 28 B2
Skotfoss 43 D2, 44 A1
Skotoússa 139 D3, 144 A1
Skoträsk 15 D3
Skotselv 43 D1
Skotterud 38 B3
Skottevik 43 C3
Skottorp 50 A2
Skoulikariá 146 A1
Skoútari 144 A1
Skovballe 53 C2
Skovby 52 B2
Skovby 52 B1/2
Skovby 48 B3, 52 B1
Skövde 45 D2
Skovlund 48 A3, 52 A1
Skrá 139 C3, 143 D1
Skrad 127 C3
Skradin 131 C3
Skradinski buk 131 C3
Skråmestø 36 A3
Skrämträsk 31 D1
Skranstad 9 C3
Skrea 49 D2, 50 A1
Skredsvik 45 B/C2
Skreia 38 A2
Skreland 43 B/C2
Skridulaupbu 32 A3, 37 B/C1
Skrittskog 24 B3
Skriveri 73 D1, 74 A2
Skrolsvik 9 C1
Skromberga 50 A3
Skrova 8 B2
Skruv 51 C2
Skucku 34 B2
Skudeneshavn 42 A2
Skule 30 B3
Skulerud 38 A3, 44 B1
Skulgam 4 A2/3
Skulsfjord 4 A2
Skultorp 45 D2
Skultuna 40 A3
Skummeslövsstrand 50 A2
Skurdalen 37 C3
Skurträsk 31 C2
Skurup 50 B3
Skute 37 D3, 38 A2
Skutskär 40 B2
Skutvik 9 B/C3
Skutvik 4 A3, 9 D1
Skvira 99 C2/3
Skwierzyna 72 A/B3
Skwierzyna 71 C2
Skyarp 50 A/B1
Skyberg 37 D3, 38 A2
Skýcov 95 D2
Skyllberg 46 A1/2
Skyttmon 30 A3, 35 C1/2
Skyttorp 40 B3
Slabce 83 C3
Slabinja 127 D3, 131 D1
Sládečkovce 95 C2
Sládkovičovo 95 C2
Slagelse 53 C1
Slagnäs 15 D3
Slagstad 9 C1
Slaidburn 59 D1, 60 B2
Slanci 133 D1, 134 A/B1
Slancy 74 B1
Slane 58 A1/2
Slangenseter 37 D2
Slangerup 49 D3, 50 A3, 53 D1
Slănic 141 C2
Slano 136 B1
Slaný 83 C2/3
Slapany 82 B3
Slåstad 38 B3
Slatina 133 D2, 134 A2
Slatina 127 D2
Slatina 138 B2
Slatina 133 D2/3, 134 A3
Slatina 132 B1
Slatina 131 D1, 132 A1
Slatina 140 B2
Slatina-Timiş 135 C1
Slatine 131 C3
Slatinski Drenovac 128 B3
Slättåkra 49 D2, 50 A1/2
Slåttevik 42 A2
Slätthög 51 B/C1
Slåttholen 8 B2
Slättmon 35 D2
Slåttön 35 B/C2
Slattum 38 A3
Slåttvik 9 B/C3
Slavgorod 99 C/D1
Slavičín 95 C1
Slavina 133 C1/2, 134 A2
Slavinja 135 D3, 139 D1
Slavkov u Brna 94 B1
Slavonice 94 A1
Slavonska Požega 128 B3
Slavonske Bare 128 B3
Slavonski Brod 132 B1
Slavonski Kobaš 132 A/B1
Slavonski Šamac 132 B1
Slavotin 135 D3
Slavuta 98 B2
Sława 71 C1
Sława 71 C3
Sławno 72 B2
Sławoborze 71 C1
Sleaford 61 D3, 64 B1
Sleen 67 C2
Sleights 61 D1
Sleihage 78 A1
Slemmestad 38 A3, 43 D1
Sleneset 14 A2
Sleng 16 A2/3
Sletta 5 C2
Sletta 9 D1
Sletterstrand 48 B1
Sliač 95 D2
Sliač-kúpele 95 D2
Sliedrecht 66 A/B3
Sligo 55 C2
Slímnitsa 142 B2
Slinde 36 B2
Slindon 76 B1
Slipra 28 A/B3, 33 C/D1
Slipsikstugan 29 D1
Slipstensjön 31 C1
Slišane 139 B/C1
Slite 47 D2
Slite 73 B/C1
Sliven 141 C3
Slivnica 139 D1
Slivnica 127 C/D2
Šljivovica 133 C2/3
Slobodka 99 C3
Slobodzeja 141 D1
Slobozia 141 C2
Slochteren 67 C1
Slöinge 49 D2, 50 A1/2
Slonim 98 B1
Slonovice 71 C1
Słońsk 70 B2
Sloten 66 B2
Slotten 5 D1, 6 A1
Slottet 36 A3
Slottsbron 45 C/D1
Slough 64 B3
Sloup 94 B1
Slovac 133 D2, 134 A2
Sløvåg 36 A3
Slovenj-gradec 127 C2
Slovenj-gradec 96 A3
Slovenska Bistrica 96 A3
Slovenska Bistrica 127 C2
Slovenska L'upča 95 D2
Slovenské Ďarmoty 95 D2
Slovenske Konjice 127 C2
Słubice 70 B3
Sluck 99 B/C1
Sluderno/Schluderns 106 B1/2
Sluis 78 A/B1
Šluknov 83 D1/2
Slunj 131 C1
Słupsk (Stolp) 72 B2
Slušovice 95 C1
Slussen 45 B/C2/3
Smadalarö 47 D1
Smådalseter 37 C2/3
Smådalsseter 37 C2
Småge 32 A2
Smålandsstenar 50 B1
Smålandsstenar 72 A1
Smalfjord 7 C1
Smardzewo 71 C3
Šmarje 127 C2
Šmarješke Toplice 127 C2/3
Šmartno 126 B2
Šmartno ob Paki 127 C2
Šmartno ob Paki 127 C2
Småvatna 29 C1
Smečno 83 C2/3
Smedås 33 D3
Smedby 51 D2
Smedby 51 D2
Smědeč 93 C/D1
Smederevo 134 B2
Smederevo 140 A2
Smederevska Palanka 140 A2
Smederevska Palanka 134 B2
Smedjebacken 39 D3
Smedjeviken 29 C3, 34 A1
Smedjeviken 29 C3, 34 A1
Smedsbo 39 D2
Smedsbyn 17 C2/3
Smedstorp 50 B3
Smela 99 D3
Smeland 43 C2
Smelror 7 D1
Smessenbroek 78 B1/2
Smigádi 145 D1
Śmigiel 71 D3
Šmiklavž 127 C2
Smilčić 131 B/C2
Smilde 67 C2
Smiljan 130 B2
Smilovci 139 D1
Śmiłowo 71 D1/2
Smiltene 73 D1, 74 A2
Smines 8 B1/2
Smines 28 B1
Smínthi 145 C1
Smjadovo 141 C3
Smogasjøen 32 B1
Smögen 44 B2
Smøhamn 36 A1/2
Šmojlovo 74 B2
Smojmirovo 139 D3
Smokovliani 136 B1
Smokvica 136 A1
Smokvica 139 C3, 143 D1
Smolenice 95 C2
Smolensk 75 C3
Smolice 71 D3
Smoljan 140 B3
Smoljanovci 135 D3
Smolnica 70 B2
Smørfjord 5 D1/2, 6 A1
Smorgon' 74 A3
Smørliseter 37 C2
Smorten 8 B2
Smygehamn 50 B3
Snäckgärdsbaden 47 D2/3
Snaith 61 C2
Snappertuna 25 C3
Snaptun 48 B3, 52 B1
Snarby 4 A2/3
Snåre 20 B1
Snåsa 28 B2
Sn'atyn 98 B3
Snedsted 48 A2
Sneek 66 B2
Snejbjerg 48 A3
Snekkersten 49 D3, 50 A2/3
Snerta 38 B1
Snertinge 49 C3, 53 C1
Snesudden 16 B2
Snillfjord 28 A3, 33 C1/2

Snina 97 C/D2, 98 A3
Šnjegotina 132 A1
Snöberg 35 C3
Snøde 53 C2
Snøfjord 5 D1, 6 A1
Snogebæk 51 D3
Soave 107 C3
Sober 150 B2
Søberg 8 B2
Sobernheim 80 A/B3
Soběslav 93 D1
Soběslav 96 A2
Sobotište 95 C2
Sobotka 83 D2
Sobra 136 B1
Sobradillo 159 C2
Sobrado 150 B1/2
Sobral da Adiça 165 C3, 171 B/C1
Sobral de Abilheira 164 A2
Sobral de Monte Agraço 164 A2
Sobral do Campo 158 B3
Sobreira Formosa 158 B3, 164 B1
Sobrón 153 C2
Søby 53 B/C2
Soča 126 B2
Sočanica 138 B1
Soccia 113 D3
Sochaczew 73 C3, 97 C1
Sochaux 89 D3, 90 A3
Sochós 144 A1
Soci 115 C2, 116 B1/2
Socovos 168 B3
Socuéllamos 167 D1/2, 168 A1/2
Sodalen 35 D2/3
Sodankylä 12 B2
Söderåkra 51 D2
Söderala 40 A1
Söderarm 41 C3
Söderås 39 D2
Söderbärke 39 D3
Söderby Karl 41 C3
Söderfors 40 B2
Söderhamn 40 A/B1
Söderhamn-Stugsund 40 A/B1
Söderhögen 34 B3
Söderköping 46 B2
Söderlångvik 24 B3
Södertälje 47 C1
Söderudden 20 A2, 31 D3
Södervik 31 C/D2
Södra 31 D1
Södra Brännträsk 16 B3
Sodra Finnskoga 38 B2
Södra Harads 16 B2
Södra Leringen 35 C2/3
Södra Löten 38 B2
Södra Noret 30 B2
Södrany 45 C/D1
Södra Sandby 50 B3
Södra Sandby 51 D2
Södra Sandvik 35 C3
Södra Skärvången 29 D3, 34 B1
Södra Sunderbyn 17 C3
Södra Tannflo 30 A/B3, 35 D1/2
Södra Tresund 30 A1
Södra Unnaryd 50 B1
Södra Vallgrund 20 A2, 31 D3
Södra Vi 46 B3
Sodražica 127 B/C3
Sødring 49 B/C2
Sodupe 153 C1
Soest 66 B3
Soest 67 D3, 80 B1
Sofádes 143 C/D3
Sofadítikos 143 C/D3
Sofiero 49 D3, 50 A2
Sofija 139 D1
Sofija 140 B3
Sofikón 148 B2
Sofikón 147 C2/3
Søfteland 36 A3
Sofuentes 155 C2
Sögel 67 D2
Sogliano al Rubicone 115 C2, 117 C1
Sóglio [St. Moritz] 106 A2
Sogndal 36 B2
Sogndalstrand 42 A3
Søgne 43 B/C3
Sognefjellhytta 37 C2
Soham 65 C2
Sohland 83 D1
Söhlde-Hoheneggelsen 68 B3
Söhlde-Nettlingen 68 B3
Sohren 80 A3
Soidinvaara 19 C3, 23 C1
Soignies 78 B2
Soini 21 C2
Soinilansalmi 23 B/C3
Soinlahti 22 B2
Soinlahti 22 B1
Soissons 88 A1
Soivio 19 D1
Soizy-aux-Bois 88 A1
Söjtör 128 A2
Sokal' 97 D1, 98 A/B2
Söke 149 D2
Sokli 13 C2
Soklot 20 B1
Sokna 37 D3
Sokndal 42 A3
Soknedal 33 C2
Soko Banja 135 C3
Soko Banja 140 A2
Sokojärvi 23 D2
Sokolac 133 C2
Sokolac 131 D2, 132 A2
Sokółka 73 D3, 98 A1
Sokolov 82 B2/3
Sokołów Podlaski 73 D3, 98 A1
Sola 23 C2
Sola 42 A2
Solagna 107 C3
Solana de Béjar 159 D3
Solana de los Barros 165 D2
Solana del Pino 167 C2/3
Solana de Ríoalmar 160 A2
Solanillos del Extremo 161 C/D2
Solares 153 C1
Solarino 125 D3
Solarussa 123 C2
Solberg 30 B2, 35 D1
Solberg 15 D2
Solberga 46 A3
Solberget 16 B1
Solca 98 B3
Solčava 127 C2
Sol'ci 74 B1/2
Solda/Sulden 106 B2
Sölden 107 B/C1
Soldeu 155 D2, 156 A1/2
Soleggen 37 C1/2
Solem 28 A/B3, 33 C/D2
Solenzara 113 D3
Solera 173 C1
Solera de Gabaldón 161 D3, 168 B1
Solesmes 78 A/B2
Soleto 121 D3
Solferino 106 B3
Solfonn 42 B1
Solf/Sulva 20 A2, 31 D3
Solheim 36 A3
Solheimsstul 37 C3
Solheimsvik 42 B1
Solignac 101 C3
Soligorsk 99 B/C1
Solin 131 C/D3
Soline 130 B2
Solingen 80 A1
Solitude 91 C2
Solivella 155 C3, 163 C1
Solkan 126 B2
Solkei 27 C1/2
Söll 92 B3
Sollacaro 113 D3
Sollana 169 D1/2
Sollebrunn 45 C3
Sollefteå 30 B3, 35 D2
Sollenau 94 B3
Sollentuna 47 C1
Sóller 157 C2
Sollerön 39 D2
Sollia 37 D1/2, 38 A1
Söllichau 69 D3, 82 B1
Solliden 51 D1
Solliès-Pont 112 A3
Sollihøgda 38 A3, 43 D1
Solms 80 B2
Solms-Oberndorf 80 B2
Solmyra 39 D3, 40 A3
Solna 47 C1
Solnečnogorsk 75 D2
Solnes 7 C/D2
Solnje 138 B2
Solofra 119 D3, 120 A2
Solojärvi 6 B3
Sološnica 95 B/C2
Solothurn 105 C1
Solotvina 97 D3, 98 A3
Solpke 69 C2
Solre-le-Château 78 B2/3
Solre-sur-Sambre 78 B2
Solrød Strand 49 D3, 50 A3, 53 D1
Solsem 28 B1
Sølsnes 32 A2
Solsona 155 D3, 156 A2
Solstad 4 A3, 9 D1
Solstadström 46 B3
Solsvik 36 A3
Solt 129 C1
Solt 96 B3
Soltau 68 B2
Soltendieck 69 C2
Soltvadkert 129 C2
Solumshamn 35 D3
Solund 36 A2
Solunto 124 B2
Sölvesborg 51 B/C2/3
Sölvesborg 72 A1
Solvorn 36 B2
Solynieve 173 C2
Soma 149 D1/2
Sømådal 33 D3
Somberek 129 B/C2
Sombernon 88 B3
Sombor 129 C3
Sombreffe 79 B/C2
Someenjärvi 26 B1
Someren 79 C/D1
Somerleyton Hall 65 D2
Somerniemi 25 C2
Somero 25 B/C2
Someronkylä 18 A3
Somerovaara 18 B2
Somerton 63 D2
Somino 75 D1
Sommacampagna 106 B3
Somma Lombardo 105 D3
Sommariva del Bosco 113 C1
Sommarö 24 B3
Sommarset 9 C3
Sommatino 124 B3
Sommen 46 A3
Sommepy-Tahure 88 B1
Sömmerda 82 A1
Sommerland 48 A3
Sommersted 52 B1
Sommesous 88 B1/2
Somme-Tourbe 88 B1
Sommières 111 C2
Sommières-du-Clain 101 C2
Somo 153 C1
Somogyapáti 128 B2
Somogyszob 128 A2
Somogyvár 128 B2
Somolinos 161 C1
Somosierra 161 C1/2
Somozas 150 B1
Sompuis 88 B1/2
Sompujärvi 18 A1
Son 44 B1
Son 150 A2
Sonceboz [Sonceboz-Sombeval] 89 D3, 104 B1
Soncillo 153 B/C2
Soncino 106 A3
Sóndalo 106 B2
Sondby 25 D3, 26 A3
Søndeled 43 C2, 44 A2
Sønderborg 52 B2
Sønder Broby 53 B/C1
Sønderby 52 B2
Sønderby 53 C/D2
Sønder Dalby 50 A3, 53 D1
Sønder Felding 48 A3
Sønderhav 52 B2
Sønder-Havrvig 48 A3
Sønderho 52 A1
Sønder Kirkeby 53 D2
Sønder Kongerslev 48 B2
Sønder Omme 48 A3, 52 A/B1
Sønder Onsild 48 B2
Sondershausen 81 D1, 82 A1
Søndersø 49 B/C3, 53 B/C1
Sønderup 48 B3, 52 B1
Søndervig 48 A3
Sóndrio 106 A2
Sonega 164 A3, 170 A1
Soneja 162 B3, 169 D1
Songeons 77 D3
Sonka 12 A3
Sonkaja 23 D2/3
Sonkajärvi 22 B1
Sonkakoski 22 B1
Sonkamuotka 11 C2/3
Sönkkä 23 C3
Sonkovo 75 D1/2
Sonneberg 82 A2
Sonneborn 81 D1/2
Sonnefeld 82 A2/3
Sonnewalde 70 A3, 83 C1
Sonnino 119 B/C2
Sonntag 106 A/B1
Sonogno [Tenero] 105 D2
Son Parc 157 C1
Sonsbeck 67 C3, 79 D1
Sonseca 160 B3, 167 C1
Son Servera 157 C1
Sonstorp 46 B2
Sonta 129 C3
Sontheim 91 D2
Sontheim 91 D3
Sonthofen 91 D3
Sontra 81 C/D1
Sontra-Wichmannshausen 81 C/D1
Söörmarkku 24 A1
Sopeira 155 C2
Sopela 153 C1
Sopje 128 B3
Sopoćani 133 D3, 138 A1
Soponya 128 B1
Sopot 133 D2, 134 A/B2
Sopotnica 138 B3, 143 B/C1
Şopotu Nou 135 C1
Soppela 13 B/C3
Sopron 94 B3
Sopron 96 B3
Sopronhorpács 94 B3
Šor 133 C2
Sora 119 C2
Soragna 114 A1
Soråker 35 D3
Soraluze 153 D1
Sorano 116 B3, 118 A1
Sør-Arnøy 14 B1
Sør-Aukra 32 A2
Sorbara 114 B1
Sorbas 174 A2
Sørbø 42 A2
Sörböle 35 D3
Sorbollano 113 D3
Sórbolo 114 A/B1
Sörby 39 C3
Sörbygden 35 C2
Sörbyn 17 C2
Sore 108 B2
Söréd 95 C/D3, 128 B1
Søre Herefoss 43 C3
Søreidet 4 A2
Sør Eldøseter 37 D1/2
Sören 17 C2
Sörenberg [Schüpfheim] 105 C1
Søre Osen 38 B1
Soresina 106 A3
Sorèze 109 D3
Sörfjärden 35 D3
Sørfjorden 9 C2
Sørfjordmoen 9 C3
Sörflärke 30 B3, 35 D1
Sør-Flatanger 28 A2
Sørford 9 D1
Sörfors 31 C2
Sörfors 29 D1/2, 30 A1
Sörforsa 40 A/B1
Sør-Frøya 32 B1
Sorges 101 D3
Sørgjæslingan 28 A1
Sórgono 123 D2
Sorgues-sur-l'Ouvèze 111 C2
Sørgutvik 14 A3, 28 B1
Sori 113 D2
Soria 153 D3, 161 D1
Soriano Cálabro 122 A/B2
Soriano nel Cimino 117 C3, 118 A1
Sorihuela del Guadalimar 167 D3, 168 A3
Sorila 25 C1
Sørjær 28 A2
Sorjushytta 127 D1
Sorka 75 D1
Sørkedalen 38 A3
Sorken 33 D3
Sørkjosen 4 B2/3
Sør-Lenangen 4 A/B2
Sørli 9 D1
Sørli 29 C2
Sørli 9 C2
Sörliden 30 B1
Sörmark 38 B3
Sørmarka 28 A2
Sormás 128 A2
Sörmjöle 31 C2
Sørmo 14 B3
Sørmo 9 D2
Sornac 102 A3
Sørnesøy 14 A1/2
Sorno 83 C1
Sorø 49 C/D3, 53 C/D1
Sørodden 14 A3
Soroki 99 C3
Soroksár 95 D3, 129 C1
Sørreisa 9 D1
Sorrento 119 D3
Sørrollnes 9 C2
Sorsa 18 B3
Sorsakoski 22 B3
Sorsele 15 D3
Sörsidan 17 C3
Sörsjön 39 B/C1
Sørskjomen 9 D2
Sorso 123 C1
Sørstraumen 4 B2
Sort 155 C2
Sortelha 159 B/C3
Sortino 125 D3
Sörtjärn 34 B3
Sortland 9 C2
Sør-Tverrfjord 4 B2
Sørum 37 D3, 38 A2
Sørumsand 38 A3
Sorunda 47 C1/2
Sörup 52 B2
Sørvågen 8 A3
Sörvallen 34 A3
Sørvær 5 B/C1
Sørværøy 8 A3
Sörvattnet 34 A3
Sørvik 9 C/D1/2
Sørvika 33 D3
Sörviken 34 B3
Sörviken 30 A2/3, 35 C1
Sorzano 153 D2
Sos 109 B/C2
Sösdala 50 B2/3
Sos del Rey Católico 155 C2
Sosés 155 C3, 163 C1
Sošice 127 C3
Sösjö 35 C2
Sosnica 99 D2
Sosnowiec 97 B/C2
Soso 18 B2/3
Sospel 112 B2
Sospiro 114 A1
Sossoniemi 19 D1
Šoštanj 127 C2
Šostka 99 D1/2
Sot 133 C1
Sotaseter 37 C1/2
Sot de Chera 162 B3, 169 C1
Sotés 153 D2
Soteska 127 C3
Sotillo de las Palomas 160 A3
Sotillo del Rincón 153 D3
Sotillo de la Adrada 160 A/B3
Sotillo de la Ribera 153 B/C3, 160 B1
Sotin 129 C3, 133 C1
Sotka 18 B2/3
Sotkajärvi 18 B2/3
Sotkamo 19 C3, 23 C1
Sotkuma 23 C2/3
Sotobañado y Priorato 152 B2
Soto de la Vega 151 D2
Soto del Barco 151 D1
Soto de los Infantes 151 D1
Soto del Real 160 B2

Soto de Luiña **151** D1
Soto de Sajambre **152** A1
Soto de San Esteban **153** C3, **161** C1
Sotodosos **161** D2
Soto en Cameros **153** D2
Sotogrande Complejo Urbanístico **172** A3
Sótony **128** A1
Sotopalacios **153** C2
Sotos **161** D3
Sotoserrano **159** D2
Soto y Amío **151** D2
Sotres **111** C3
Sotresgudo **152** B2
Sotta **113** D3
Søttaren **14** A2
Sottens [Moudon] **104** B2
Sotteville-sur-Mer **77** C2/3
Sottomarina **107** D3
Sottrum **68** A/B2
Sottunga **41** D3
Sotuélamos **168** A2
Souain-Perthes-lès-Hurlus **88** B1
Soual **109** D3, **110** A3
Souchez **78** A2
Soúda **149** B/C3
Soudé **88** B1/2
Soueix **108** B3, **155** C2
Souesmes **87** C/D3
Souflíon **145** D1, **145** D3
Sougné-Remouchamps **79** C/D2
Souillac **109** D1
Souilly **89** C1
Soukainen **24** A2
Soulac-sur-Mer **100** B3
Soulaines-Dhuys **88** B2
Soulatge **156** B1
Soulaucourt-sur-Mouzon **89** C2
Soulgé-le-Bruant **86** A2
Soúlion **146** B2
Soulópoulon **142** B3
Soultz **89** D2/3, **90** A3
Soultz-sous-Forêts **90** B1
Soumoulou **108** B3, **155** B/C1
Soúnion **147** D3
Souppes-sur-Loing **87** D2
Souprosse **108** B2
Souquet **108** A2
Source de la Loue **104** A1
Source du Lison **104** A1
Sourdeval **85** D1, **86** A1
Sourdun **88** A2
Soure **158** A3
Sournia **156** B1
Soúrpi **147** C1
Sourton **63** C2/3
Sousceyrac **109** D1
Souselo **158** A2
Soustons **108** B2
Southam **65** C2
Southampton **76** B1
Southborough **65** C3, **77** B/C1
South Brent **63** C3
South Cave **61** D2
Southend **56** A2
Southend-on-Sea **65** C3
Southerness **57** C3, **60** A1
South Hayling **76** A1
Southminster **65** C3
South Molton **63** C2
Southport **59** C/D2, **60** B2
South Shields **57** D3, **61** C1
South Shields **54** B3
Southwell **61** C3, **64** B1
South Willingham **61** D3, **65** B/C1
Southwold **65** D2
Souto **164** B1
Souto da Carpalhosa **158** A3, **164** A1
Souto da Casa **158** B3
Souto Maior **158** B1
Soutomaior **150** A2
Souvála **147** D2/3
Souvigné **86** B3
Souvigny **102** B2
Souzel **165** C2
Souzelas **158** A3
Søvassli **28** A3, **33** C2
Sovata **141** B/C1
Sövdeborg **50** B3
Sover **107** C2
Soverato **122** B2
Sovereto **120** B2, **136** A3
Soveria Mannelli **122** B2
Sövestad **50** B3
Sovetsk (Tilsit) **73** C2
Søvik **32** A3, **36** B1
Sowia Góra **71** C2
Söyrinki **21** C2
Sozopol **141** C3
Spa **79** D2
Špačince **95** C2
Spadafora **125** D1
Spaichingen **90** B2/3
Špaj **135** C3, **139** C1
Spakenburg **66** B3
Spalding **61** D3, **65** C1
Spálené Poříčí **83** C3
Spalt **91** D1, **92** A1
Spången **50** A/B2/3
Spångenäs **46** B3
Spangenberg **81** C1
Spangeried **42** B3
Španovica **128** A3
Spantekow **70** A1
Sparanise **119** C3
Sparbu **28** B2/3, **33** D1
Sparreholm **47** C1
Spárta **147** C2
Spárti **147** C3
Spárti **148** B2/3
Spartílas **142** A3
Spas **138** B3, **143** C1
Spas-Demensk **75** C/D3
Spáta **147** D2
Speicher **79** D3, **80** A3
Speichersdorf **82** A3
Speke **38** B3, **45** C1
Spekedalssetra **33** D3
Spelle-Venhaus **67** D2
Spello **115** D3, **117** C2/3
Spenge **68** A3
Spennymoor **57** D3, **61** C1
Spenshult **50** A1
Spentrup **48** B2
Sperchiás **146** B1
Sperenberg **70** A3
Sperlinga **125** C2
Sperlonga **119** C3
Sperone **124** A2
Spétsai **147** C3
Speyer **90** B1
Spezzano Albanese **122** A/B1
Spezzano della Sila **122** B2
Spiegelau **93** C1/2
Spiegelberg **91** C1
Spiekeroog **67** D1
Spielfeld **127** C1/2
Spiez **105** C1/2
Spiggen **17** C3
Spigno Monferrato **113** C1/2
Spilamberto **114** B1
Spile **142** A2
Spíleon **143** C2/3
Spíleon **145** D2
Spiliá **143** D3
Spilimbergo **107** D2, **126** A2
Spílion **149** C3
Spillersboda **41** C3
Spilling **42** B3
Spillum **28** B2
Spilsby **61** D3, **65** C1
Spinazzola **120** B2
Spincourt **89** C1
Spinetta Marengo **113** C1
Spinoso **120** B3
Špionica **132** B1
Spira **15** D2
Špišić-Bukovica **128** A3
Spišská Belá **97** C2
Spišská Nová Ves **97** C2
Spital am Pyhrn **93** D3
Spital am Semmering **94** A3
Spiterstulen **37** C2
Spittal an der Drau **126** A1
Spitz **94** A2
Spjald **48** A3
Spjærøy **44** B1/2
Spjelkavik **32** A3
Spjutsbygd **51** C2
Spjutsund **25** D3, **26** A3
Spjutvik **9** C2
Split **131** C3
Splügen [Thusis] **105** D2, **106** A2
Spodnje Hoče **127** C/D2
Spodnji Brnik **126** B2
Spodsbjerg **53** C2
Špogi **74** A2
Špola **99** D3
Spoláïta **146** A1
Spoleto **117** C3, **118** B1
Spølrem **14** B3
Spondigna/Spondinig **106** B2
Sponvika **44** B1/2
Spornitz **69** C/D1
Spotorno **113** C2
Spøttrup **48** A2
Spraitbach **91** C1/2
Sprakensehl **69** B/C2
Spreenhagen **70** B2/3
Spreewitz **83** D1
Spremberg **83** D1
Spremberg **96** A1
Sprendlingen (Bingen) **80** B3
Spresiano **107** D3
Springe **68** B3
Springliden **16** A3
Spruga [Ponte Brolla] **105** D2
Spuhlija **127** D2
Spuž **137** D2
Spydeberg **38** A3, **44** B1
Squillace **122** B2
Squinzano **121** D3
Srbac **132** A1
Srbica **138** B1
Srbobran **129** D3
Srbobran **140** A1/2
Srbrenik **132** B1
Srebnoe **99** D2
Srebrenica **133** C2
Središče **127** D2
Središte **141** C2
Śrem **72** B3, **96** B1
Śrem **71** D3
Sremska Kamenica **129** D3, **133** D1, **134** A1
Sremska Mitrovica **133** C1
Sremska Rača **133** C1
Sremski Karlovci **129** D3, **133** D1, **134** A1
Sreser **136** B1
Srnetica **131** D2
Srní **93** C1
Srnice **132** B1
Sroczyn **71** D2
Środa Wielkopolska **71** D3
Srpska Crnja **129** D3
Srpske Moravice **127** C3
Srpski-Itebej **140** A1/2
Srpski Miletić **129** C3
Staatz **94** B2
Stabbestad **43** D2, **44** A2
Stabbforsmoen **14** B3
Staby **48** A2
Stachy **93** C1
Stackmora **39** D1/2
Staddajåkkstugorna **15** C/D1
Stade **68** B1
Stadecken-Elsheim **80** B3
Stadensen-Breitenhees **69** B/C2
Stadil **48** A2/3
Stadl an der Mur **126** B1
Stadsås **30** A1
Stadskanaal **67** C2
Stadtallendorf **81** C2
Stadtbergen **91** D2
Stadthagen **68** A3
Stadtilm **82** A2
Stadtkyll **79** D2
Stadtlauringen-Ballingshausen **81** D3
Stadtlauringen-Wettringen **81** D3
Stadtlauringen **81** D2/3
Stadtlengsfeld **81** D2
Stadtlohn **67** C3
Stadtoldendorf **68** B3
Stadtprozelten **81** C3
Stadtroda **82** A2
Stadtschlaining **94** B3, **127** D1
Stadtsteinach **82** A2/3
Stadum **52** A/B2
Stäfa **105** D1
Staffans **17** D2/3
Staffanstorp **50** A/B3
Staffelstein **81** D3, **82** A3
Stáffolo **115** D3, **117** D2
Stafford **59** D3, **60** B3, **64** A1
Staggträsk **15** D3
Stágira **144** B2
Stagno **114** A3, **116** A2
Stahovica **127** B/C2
Stai **38** A1
Stainach **93** C/D3
Staindrop **57** D3, **61** C1
Staines **64** B3
Stainville **89** B/C2
Stainz **127** C1
Staíti **122** A3
Staitz **82** B2
Stajićevo **129** D3, **133** D1, **134** A1
Stakevci **135** C3
Stakknes **32** B2
Stakkvik **4** A2
Stalać **134** B3
Stålboga **47** C1
Stalbridge **63** D2
Štalcerji **127** C3
Stalden [Stalden-Saas] **105** C2
Stalham **65** D1
Stalheim **36** B3
Stall **107** D1, **126** A1
Stallarholmen **47** C1
Ställberg **39** D3
Ställdalen **39** D3
Stallogargo **5** C1/2, **6** A1
Stalltjärnstugan **29** C3, **34** A1
Stallwang **92** B1
Stalmine **59** C/D1, **60** B2
Stalowa Wola **97** C1, **98** A2
Stamford **64** B1/2
Stamford Bridge **61** C3
Stammham **92** A1/2
Stamná **146** A2
Stamnes **36** A3
Stamora-Germană **134** B1
Stams **106** B1
Stamseter **32** B3, **37** C1
Stamsried **92** B1
Stamsund **8** B2
Stanari **132** B1
Standal **32** A3, **36** B1
Standnes **36** A2
Stånga **47** D3
Stånga **72** B1
Stange **38** A2
Stangerode **69** C3, **82** A1
Stanghella **107** C3, **115** C1
Stangnes **9** C/D1
Stangvik **32** B2
Stanhope **57** D3, **61** B/C1
Stanišić **129** C2/3
Stanisławów **73** C3, **97** C1, **98** A1
Štanjel **126** B3
Stanke Dimitrov **139** D2
Stanke Dimitrov **140** B3
Staňkov **83** B/C3, **93** B/C1
Stankovci **131** C2/3
Stanley **57** C1
Stanós **144** A/B2
Stanovice **82** B2/3
Stans **92** A3, **107** C1
Stans **105** C1
Stansted Airport **65** C2
Stansted Mountfitchet **65** C2
St. Antönien-Castels [Küblis] **106** A1
Stanzach **91** D3, **106** B1
Stapar **129** C3
Stapelburg **69** C3
Stapelford Park **64** B1
Staphorst **67** C2
Stappogiedde **7** B/C1
Stara Baška **130** B1
Stará Bystrica **95** D1
Stara Gradina **128** A3
Stara Gradiška **131** D1, **132** A1
Staraja Russa **75** C1/2
Staraja Toropa **75** C2
Staraja Ušica **98** B3
Starakonstantinov **98** B2/3
Stara Łubianka **71** D1
Stará L'ubovňa **97** C2
Stara Moravica **129** C3
Stara Novalja **130** B2
Stara Pazova **133** D1, **134** A1
Stará Role **82** B2
Stará Turá **95** C2
Staravina **139** C3, **143** C1
Stará Voda **82** B3
Stara Woda **71** C3
Stara Zagora **141** C3
Stare Czarnowo **70** B1
Stare Długie **71** D3
Stare Drawsko **71** C/D1
Staré Hory **95** D1/2
Staré Město u Uherské Hradiště **95** C1
Stare Osieczno **71** C2
Staré Sedlo **83** C/D3, **93** C/D1
Stargard Szczecinski **71** C1
Stargard Szczecinski **72** A3
Stårheim **36** A1
Stari Banovci **133** D1, **134** A1
Stari Bar **137** D2
Starica **75** D2
Stari-Dojran **139** D3, **143** D1, **144** A1
Stari Farkašić **127** D3
Starigrad **131** D3, **136** A1
Starigrad **130** B1
Stari Gradac **128** A2/3
Starigrad-Paklenica **130** B2
Stari Jankovci **129** C3, **133** C1
Stari Lec **134** B1
Stari Log **127** C3
Stari Majdan **131** D1
Stari Mikanovci **128** B3, **132** B1
Stari Trg **127** C3
Starnberg **92** A3
Stærnes **43** D1
Stärnö **51** C2
Starodub **99** D1
Starogard **71** C1
Starogard Gdański **72** B2
Starokazač'e **141** D1
Staro Nagoričane **139** C2
Staro Orjahovo **141** C/D3
Staro Petrovo Selo **128** A3, **131** D1, **132** A1
Starosiedle **70** B3
Starše **127** D2
Starsiedel **82** B1
Starup **48** A3, **52** A1
Stary Chwalim **71** D1
Starý Hrozenkov **95** C1
Staryje Dorogi **99** C1
Staryj Sambor **97** D2, **98** A3
Starý Plzenec **83** C3
Stary Tomyśl **71** C/D2/3
Stassfurt **69** C3
Staszów **97** C1
Stathelle **43** D2, **44** A1/2
Staträsk **16** B2
St-Aubin [Gorgier-St-Aubin] **104** B1
Staudach-Egerndach **92** B3
Staufen **90** A3
Staupåmoen **14** B1
Staurust **32** B3, **37** C1
Stavanger **42** A2
Stavarmon **30** B3, **35** D1
Stave **9** C1
Stavelot **79** D2
Staven **28** A2, **33** C1
Stavenisse **66** A3, **78** B1
Staveren **66** B2
Stavern **43** D2, **44** A2
Stavišče **99** C3
Stavkirke **37** C3
Stavn **48** B1/2
Stavnäs **45** C1
Stávoli Gnivizza **126** A2
Stavre **35** C2
Stavre **29** C/D3, **34** B1/2
Stavreviken **35** D3
Stavrodrómion **146** B3
Stavrós **144** B2
Stavrós **143** D3
Stavrós **146** A2
Stavrós **147** D2
Stavrós **148** B1
Stavroúpolis **145** C1

Stavsjø 38 A2
Stavsjö bruk 46 B2
Stavsnäs 47 D1
Stawiski 73 C/D3, 98 A1
St-Blaise 104 B1
St-Cergue 104 A2
Steane 43 C2
Steblevě 138 A3, 142 B1
Stechelberg [Lauterbrunnen] 105 C2
Štěchovice 83 D3
Steckborn 91 C3
Ste-Croix 104 B1
Steeg 106 B1
Steenbergen 66 A3, 78 B1
Steenbergen 67 C1/2
Steenderen 67 C3
Steenvoorde 78 A2
Steenwijk 67 C2
Ştefăneşti 98 B3
Ştefáni 146 A1
Steffenberg-Niedereisenhausen 80 B2
Stegaros 43 C1
Stegaurach 81 D3
Stege 53 D2
Stege 72 A2
Stegeborg 46 B2
Stegelitz 69 D3
Stegersbach 127 D1
Stehag 50 B2
Steige 89 D2, 90 A2
Steigen 8 B3
Steigertal 81 C2
Steigra 82 A1
Steikvassli 14 B2
Steimbke 68 B2
Steimbke-Lichtenhorst 68 B2
Stein 92 B3
Stein 91 D1, 92 A1
Stein 107 D1, 126 A1/2
Steinach 82 A2
Steinach am Brenner 107 C1
Steinakirchen am Forst 93 D2/3
Stein am Rhein 91 B/C3
Steinau 81 C2
Steinau 92 A3, 68 A1
Steinau-Ulmbach 81 C2
Steinbach 83 C2
Steinbach am Wald 82 A2
Steinbach (Giessen) 81 B/C2
Steinbach-Hallenberg 81 D2
Steinbergdalshytta 37 B/C3
Steinbergkirche 52 B2
Steinbueng 33 C2
Steinbukt 6 B1
Steine 28 B1
Steine 36 B3
Steinebrück 79 D2
Steinen 90 A3
Steinestø 36 A3
Steinfeld 67 D2, 68 A2
Steinfort 79 D3
Steinfurt-Borghorst 67 D3
Steingaden 91 D3
Steingaden-Wies 91 D3
Steinhagen 68 A3
Steinhausen-Rottum 91 C3
Steinhausen 80 B1
Steinheid 82 A2
Steinheim 4 A3, 9 D1
Steinheim 68 A3
Steinheim 91 C/D2
Steinhöfel 70 B2/3
Steinhorst 68 B2
Steinibach [Schwanden] 105 D1, 106 A1
Steinigtwolmsdorf 83 D1
Steinkjer 28 B2, 33 D1
Steinkjer 29 B/C2
Steinkyrkja 33 C3, 37 D1
Steinland 8 B1/2
Steinløysa 32 B2
Steinsåsen 33 D2/3
Steinsdorf 70 B3
Steinshamn 32 A2
Steinsland 36 A/B3
Steinsland 14 B2
Steinslandsseter 36 A/B2/3
Stein [Stein-Säckingen] 90 B3

Steinsvik 36 A1
Steinsvollen 4 A2
Steinvik 38 A1
Steinwiesen 82 A2
Steisslingen 91 B/C3
Stelle 68 B1
Stemshaug 32 B2
Stemwede 68 A2
Stemwede-Levern 68 A2/3
Stemwede-Twiehausen 68 A2/3
Stená Pétras 143 D2
Stenåsa 51 D2
Stenay 79 C3
Stenbacken 10 A2
Stenbjerg 48 A2
Stenbrohult 50 B2
Stendal 69 D2
Stenderup 48 B3, 52 B1
Stengårdshult 45 D3
Stenhammar 45 C/D2
Stenhamra 47 C1
Sténico 106 B2
Stení Dírfios 147 D1/2
Steninge strand 49 D2, 50 A2
Stenis 39 C2
Stenje 142 B1
Stenkullen 45 C3
Stenlille 49 C/D3, 53 C/D1
Stenløse 49 D3, 50 A3, 53 D1
Stennammar 46 B1
Stennäs 31 B/C2
Stenopós 145 C1
Stensdalsstugorna 34 A2
Stensjö 30 A3, 35 C2
Stensjön 46 A3
Stenstorp 45 D2/3
Stenstrand 15 C/D3
Stensträsk 16 A3
Stenstrup 53 C2
Stensund 16 A3
Stensund 31 C1
Stensund 15 D2
Stensund 15 D3
Stenträsk 16 A/B2
Stenudden 15 D2
Stenungsund 45 C3
Stenvadet 39 C1
Stepanci 139 B/C3
Stephanskirchen (Rosenheim) 92 B3
Stępień 71 D1
Stepnica 70 B1
Stepojevac 133 D2, 134 A2
Sterley 69 C1
Stérna 147 C3
Stérnai 149 B/C3
Sternberg 53 D3, 69 D1
Sternenfels 90 B1
Sterringi 32 B3, 37 C1
Sterup 52 B2
Stęszew 71 D3
Stęszew 72 B3, 96 B1
Štětí 83 D2
Stetten am kalten Markt 91 C2/3
Steutz 69 D3
Stevanovac 137 D1
Stevenage 65 B/C2
Stewarton 56 B2
Steyerberg 68 A2
Steyning 76 B1
Steyr 93 D2/3
Steyr 96 A3
Steyregg 93 D2
St. Gallen 91 C3
Stia 115 C2, 116 B1
Štiavnik 95 D1
Stichtse brug 66 B2/3
Stickney 61 D3, 65 C1
Stična 127 C2/3
Stiege 69 C3, 81 D1, 82 A1
Stiens 66 B1
Stift Göttweig 94 A2
Stigen 38 B1
Stigen 45 C2
Stigliano 120 B3
Stigsjö 35 D2/3
Stigtomta 47 C2
Stiklestad 28 B3, 33 D1
Stilís 147 C1
Stilís 148 B2
Stilla 5 C1
Stilling 48 B3
Stilo 122 B3

Stilton 64 B2
Stimánga 147 C2
St-Imier 89 D3, 104 B1
Štimlje 138 B2
Štimlje 140 A3
Stîna de Vale 97 D3, 140 B1
Ştinăpari 135 C1
Stio 120 A3
Štip 139 C3
Štip 140 A3
Stipshausen 80 A3
Stíra 149 C2
Stirling 54 B2
Stirling 56 B1
Štirovača 130 B1/2
Štit 145 D2
Štitar 133 C1
Štítary 94 A1
Štivan 130 A1
Štivica 132 A1
Stjärnhov 47 C1
Stjärnorp 46 B2
Stjärnsund 40 A2
Stjärnsund 46 A2
Stjern 28 A2
Stjerneobservatoriet 4 B3, 10 A/B1
Stjørdal 28 A/B3, 33 D1
Stjørdal 28 A3, 33 C1
St-Luc [Sierre] 105 C2
St. Margrethen 91 C3
St-Maurice 104 B2
St. Moritz 106 A2
St. Niklaus 105 C2
Stø 8 B1
Stobi 139 C3
Stobno 71 D2
Stobreč 131 C/D3
Stoby 50 B2
Stocka 35 D3
Stockach 91 C3
Stöckalp [Sarnen] 105 C1
Stockaryd 51 C1
Stockbäcken 16 B3
Stockbridge 64 A3, 76 A1
Stöcke 31 C/D2
Stockelsdorf 53 C3
Stocken 44 B3
Stockerau 94 B2
Stockerau 96 A/B2
Stockholm 47 C1
Stockport 59 D2, 60 B3
Stöcksjö 31 C/D2
Stockton-on-Tees 61 D1
Stod 28 B2
Stod 83 C3
Stöde 35 C/D3
Stödtlen 91 D1
Stoetze-Hohenzethen 69 C2
Stoholm 48 B2
Stokeasay Castle 59 D3
Stoke Ferry 65 C2
Stoke-on-Trent 59 D2, 60 B3, 64 A1
Stokesley 61 D1
Stokkasjøen 14 A3
Stokke 43 D2, 44 A/B1
Stokkebro 49 C2
Stokkemarke 53 C2
Stokkvågen 14 A2
Stokmarknes 8 B2
Štoky 94 A1
Stolac 132 B3, 137 B/C1
Stolbcy 98 B1
Stolberg 81 D1, 82 A1
Stolberg 79 D2
Stolberg-Gressenich 79 D2
Stolberg-Zeifall 79 D2
Stöle 43 D2, 44 A2
Stølen 33 C3
Stølen 32 B2
Stølensetra 33 C3
Stolin 98 B1/2
Stollberg 82 B2
Stolpe 70 B2
Stolpen 83 C1
Stolvizza 126 A2
Stolzenau 68 A2
Stolzenau-Nendorf 68 A2
Stolzenhain 70 A3
Stómion 143 D3
Stömne 45 C1
Stomorska 131 C3
Ston 136 B1
Stonařov 94 A1

Stone 59 D2/3, 60 B3, 64 A1
Stonehaven 54 B2
Stonehenge 64 A3, 76 A1
Stongfiorden 36 A2
Stonglandseidet 9 C/D1
Stønnesbotn 9 D1
Stony Stratford 64 B2
Stopanja 134 B3
Stöpen 45 D2
Storå 9 C2/3
Storå 39 D3
Storå 20 B3
Stora Anna 47 B/C2
Stora Blåsjön 29 C/D1
Storabränna 29 D2, 34 B1
Stora Dyrön 44 B3
Stora Laxemar 51 D1
Stora Mellby 45 C3
Stora Mellösa 46 B1
Storån 35 B/C3
Stora Olofsholm 47 D2
Stora Råda 45 D2, 46 A1
Storås 33 C2
Storåsen 30 A3, 35 C2
Störåsen 29 D3, 34 B1
Stora Skedvi 39 D2, 40 A2
Stora Stensjön 29 C2, 34 B1
Stora Sundby 46 B1
Stora Vika 47 C2
Storbacka 20 B2
Storbeck 69 D2, 70 A2
Storberg 16 A3
Storberget 17 C1
Storbergvika 29 C/D2
Storborgaren 30 B2, 35 D1
Storbränna 29 D3, 34 B1
Storbudalsetra 33 C2
Storbukt 5 C/D1, 6 A1
Storby 41 C3
Stordal 32 A3, 36 B1
Stordal 28 B3, 33 D1/2
Stordalselv 4 A3, 10 A1
Štore 127 C2
Storebro 46 B3
Storebru 36 A2
Store Darum 52 A1
Store Heddinge 50 A3, 53 D1
Store Heddinge 72 A2
Storekorsnes 5 C2
Storelv 5 C1
Stor-Elvdal 38 A1
Storelvvoll 33 D2
Store Merløse 49 D3, 53 D1
Store Molvik 7 C1
Støren 32 C2
Storeng 4 B2
Storenga 15 C1
Storerikvollen 33 D2
Store Skageseter 37 D2
Storeskarhotel 37 C3
Storestøen 37 C3
Storfinnträsk 16 B3
Storfjäten 34 A3
Storfjord 4 A3, 10 A1
Storfors 45 D1, 46 A1
Storforshei 14 B2
Storfosna 28 A3, 33 C1
Storfossen 9 D2
Storglomvassbrakka 14 B1
Storhögen 29 D3, 35 B/C1/2
Storhøliseter 37 D2
Storholmsjön 29 D3, 34 B1
Storholmsjön 29 D3, 34 B1
Storjord 15 B/C1
Storjorda 14 B1
Storjuktan 15 D3
Storjungfrun 40 B1
Storkläppvallen 34 A2
Storkow 70 B3
Storkowo 71 C1
Storkyro 20 B2
Storli 4 A3, 9 D1
Storli 32 B2
Storli 4 A3, 9 D1
Storlien 28 B3, 33 D1/2
Storlien 28 B3, 33 D1/2, 34 A2
Storlögda 30 B2
Stormark 31 D1
Stormoen 15 C1
Stormvloedkering 66 A3, 78 B1

Stormyren 15 D3
Stornarella 120 A/B2
Stornäs 29 D1
Stornes 9 C1/2
Stornorrfors 31 C2
Stornoway 54 A1
Storo 106 B3
Storoddan 32 B1/2
Storødegårdseter 38 A2
Storöhamn 17 C3
Storožinec 98 B3
Storrensjön 29 B/C3, 34 A1
Storrödtjärnstugan 34 A3
Storrøsta 33 D2
Storsand 38 A3, 44 B1
Storsand 16 B2
Storsandsjö 31 C1/2
Storsätern 34 A3
Storsävarträsk 31 C1
Storsele 30 A/B1
Storselsøy 14 A1/2
Storsjö 34 A2
Storsjön 30 B2
Storsjön 40 A1
Storskog 7 C/D2
Storslett 9 C2
Storslett (Nordreisa) 4 B2/3
Storsteinnes 4 A3, 10 A1
Storsteinnes 14 B3
Storsund 16 B3
Storträsk 16 A/B3
Storulvåns fjällstation 28 B3, 33 D2, 34 A2
Storulvsjön 35 C3
Storuman 15 D3
Storvedjan 17 C2
Storvik 5 C1, 6 A1
Storvik 5 C2
Storvik 4 B2
Storvik 40 A2
Storvist 20 B2
Storvollen 4 A2
Storvollseter 32 B3, 37 C1
Storvreta 40 B3
Stössen 82 A/B1
Stötten am Auerberg 91 D3
Stotternheim 81 D1, 82 A1
Stouby 48 B3, 52 B1
Stourbridge 59 D3, 64 A2
Stourhead House 63 D2, 64 A3
Stourport-on-Severn 59 D3, 64 A2
Støvring 48 B2
Stow 57 C2
Stowmarket 65 C/D2
Stow on the Wold 64 A2
Stožec 93 C1/2
Stra 107 C3
Straach 69 D3
Strabane 54 A3, 55 D2
Stracia 122 A3
Stracin 139 C2
Straczno 71 D1
Stradalovo 139 D2
Strada San Zeno 115 C2, 116 B1
Stradbroke 65 C2
Stradella 133 D1
Stradella 106 B3
Straden 127 D1
Straelen 79 D1
Stragari 133 D2, 134 B2
Straiton 56 B2
Strakonice 93 C1
Strakonice 96 A1
Strålsnäs 46 A2
Stralsund 72 A2
Strambino 105 C2
Strand 31 C2
Strand 14 B2
Strand 42 A2
Strand 9 C2/3
Stranda 32 A3, 36 B1
Strandåker 31 C2
Strandalshytta 42 B2
Strandby 49 C1
Strande 52 B2
Strandebarm 36 A/B3
Strandlinjer 5 D2, 6 A2
Strandlykkja 38 A2
Strandudden 45 D1, 46 A1
Strandval 28 B1
Strandvik 42 A1
Strangford 58 A1

Strangford 54 A3, 55 D2
Strängnäs 47 C1
Strängnäs 30 B1
Strangolagalli 119 C2
Strångsjö 46 B2
Strångsund 35 B/C2/3
Strání 95 C1
Stranice 127 C2
Stránoma 146 B1/2
Stranorlar 55 C/D2
Stranraer 54 A3, 55 D2
Stranraer 56 A/B3
Strasbourg 90 A/B2
Strasburg 70 A/B1
Strašice 83 C3
Strašín 93 C1
Straškov-Vodochody 83 C/D2
Stråssa 39 D3
Strassberg (Sigmaringen) 91 C2
Strassburg 126 B1
Strassenhaus 80 A2
Strass im Zillertal 92 A3, 107 C1
Strass in Steiermark 127 C1/2
Strasskirchen 92 B1/2
Strasswalchen 93 C3
Straszów 83 D1
Stratford Saint-Mary 65 C/D2
Stratford-upon-Avon 64 A2
Strathaven 56 B2
Strathblane 56 B1/2
Strathyre 56 B1
Stratoníki 144 B2
Stratónion 144 B2
Stratos 146 A1
Stratton 62 B2
Strau 126 B2
Straubenhardt-Conweiler 90 B2
Straubing 92 B1/2
Straum 14 B2
Straum 32 B1
Straumbu 33 C3, 37 D1
Straume 36 A/B3
Straume 43 C1
Straume 8 B2
Straume 43 C/D2, 44 A1/2
Straumen 28 B1
Straumen 32 B1/2
Straumen 9 C2
Straumen 4 A3, 9 D1
Straumen 14 B1
Straumfjordnes 4 B2
Straumsbotn 9 D1
Straumshamn 36 B1
Straumshella 4 A3
Straumsli 4 A3, 10 A1
Straumsnes 9 C/D1
Straumsnes 8 B2
Straupitz 70 B3
Strausberg 70 B2
Straussfurt 81 D1, 82 A1
Stráž 82 B3
Straža 134 B1
Straža 127 C3
Straže 127 D2
Strazeele 78 A2
Strážek 94 B1
Strazilovo 133 D1, 134 A1
Strážkovice 93 D1/2
Stráž nad Nežárkou 93 D1
Strážnice 95 C1
Strážný 93 C1/2
Strážný 96 A2
Strážov 93 C1
Stráž pod Ralskem 83 D2
Streatley 65 C3
Strečno 95 D1
Street 63 D2
Strehaia 135 D2
Strehaia 140 B2
Strehla 83 C1
Střekov 83 C2
Strekov 95 D3
Strem 127 D1
Strembo 106 B2
Strendene 14 B3
Strengberg 93 D2
Strengelvåg 8 B1
Strengen 43 C2, 44 A1
Strenggjerdet 14 A2
Strensall 61 C2
Stresa 105 D2/3
Stretford 59 D2, 60 B3
Streufdorf 81 D2
Strezimirovci 139 C1
Strezovce 138 B1
Strib 48 B3, 52 B1
Striberg 46 A1
Stříbrná Skalice 83 D3
Stříbro 82 B3
Stridbäck 16 B3
Strigno 107 C2
Štrigova 127 D2
Strijbeek 79 C1
Střílky 95 B/C1
Strimasund 15 C2
Strinda 94 A3
Strindmoen 28 B2
Strmac 128 A3, 131 D1
Strmen 128 A3, 131 D1
Strmica 131 C2
Strmilov 93 D1, 94 A1
Strobl 93 C3
Strøby 50 A3, 53 D1
Strofiliá 147 D1
Strofiliá 148 B2
Strojkovce 139 C1
Strøm 38 B3
Ström 31 C2
Strömbacka 35 C/D3
Stromberg 80 B3
Strómboli 125 D1
Stromeferry 54 A2, 55 D1
Strömfors 16 B3
Strömfors 16 A3
Strömfors 31 D1
Stromi 24 B1
Strömma 47 D1
Strömma 24 B3
Strömma 41 C2/3
Strömmen 34 A3
Strømmen 28 B2/3, 33 D1
Strømmen 33 C3
Strømmen 38 A3
Strømmen 5 D1, 6 A1
Strömnäs 30 A2, 35 C1
Stromness 54 B1
Strompdalen 29 C1
Strömsberg 40 B2
Strömsbro (Gävle) 40 B2
Strömsbruk 35 D3
Strömsholm 40 A3, 46 B1
Strömsnäs 30 A3, 35 C2
Strömsnäs 17 C2
Strömsnäsbruk 50 B2
Strømsoddbygda 37 D3
Strömstad 44 B2
Strömsund 29 D2/3, 30 A2, 35 C1
Strömsund 15 D3
Strömsund 17 C2
Strona 105 C2/3
Stronachlachar 56 B1
Strόngoli 122 B2
Stronsdorf 94 B2
Stroobrugge 78 B1
Stroppiana 105 C/D3, 113 C1
Strøsvik 14 B1
Stroud 63 D1, 64 A3
Štrpce 138 B2
Struer 48 A2
Struga 70 B1
Struga 138 A/B3, 142 B1
Strullendorf 81 D3, 82 A3
Strumica 139 D3
Strumica 140 A/B3
Strunjan 126 A/B3
Struppen 4 A3, 10 A1
Struth 81 D1
Strüth (Loreley) 80 B3
Strycksele 31 C1/2
Stryj 97 D2, 98 A3
Stryken 38 A3
Stryn 32 A3, 36 B1
Strzelce Krajeńskie 71 C2
Strzelce Opolskie 96 B1/2
Strzelno 72 B3
Strzmiele 71 C1
Stubbekøbing 53 D2
Stubbekøbing 72 A2
Stubberup 49 C3, 53 C1
Stubbuden 16 B1
Stuben 106 B1
Stubenberg 93 C2
Štubik 135 C2
Stubline 133 D2, 134 A2
Studená 94 A1
Studena 145 D2
Studena 139 C1
Studena 139 D1/2
Studenci 131 D3, 132 A3
Studenica 133 D3, 134 A/B3
Studenzen 127 C/D1
Studsvik 47 C2
Stuer 69 D1
Stugudal 33 D2
Stuguflaten 32 B3, 37 C1
Stuguliseter 33 C3, 37 D1
Stugun 30 A3, 35 C2
Stühlingen-Grimmelshofen 90 B3
Stühlingen 90 B3
Stuhr 68 A2
Stuhr-Brinkum 68 A2
Stuhr-Seckenhausen 68 A2
Stuibenfall 106 B1
Stulln 92 B1
Stülpe 70 A3
Stumiaga 106 B2
Stumlia 37 D2/3, 38 A2
Stumsnas 39 D2
Stuoraoaivve 5 C3, 11 C1
Stupari 132 B2
Stupava 94 B2
Stupinigi 112 B1
Stupnik 127 D3
St. Urban 105 C1
Sturefors 46 B2
Sturkö 51 C2
Sturno 119 D3, 120 A2
Štúrovo 95 D3
Štúrovo 96 B3
St-Ursanne 89 D3, 90 A3, 104 B1
Sturup 50 B3
Sturzelbronn 90 A1
Stutensee-Blankenloch 90 B1
Stuttgart 91 C2
Stuvland 14 A/B2
Stvolny 83 C3
Styggberget 35 C3
Styggdalen 14 B3, 29 C1
Styggedalen 4 A/B3, 10 A1
Stymphalos 147 C2
Stypułów 71 C3
Styri 38 A2/3
Styrkesnes 9 C3
Styrmannstø 4 A/B2
Styrnäs 30 B3, 35 D2
Styrsö 45 C3, 49 D1
Styrvoll 43 D2, 44 A1
Su 155 D3, 156 A2
Suances 152 B1
Suaningi 17 C1
Suaredda 123 D1
Suave Mar 150 A3, 158 A1
Subate 74 A2
Subbersta 30 B3, 35 D2
Subbiano 115 C3, 116 B2
Subiaco 118 B2
Subotica 129 C2
Subotica 140 A1
Subotište 133 D1, 134 A1
Sučany 95 D1
Suceava 141 C1
Sučevići 131 C2
Suchá Hora 97 C2
Suchań 71 C1
Suchdol nad Lužnicí 93 D1/2
Sucina 169 C3, 174 B1
Sückau 69 D1
Suckow 69 D1
Sućuraj 132 A3, 136 B1
Suda 75 D1
Sudanell 155 C3, 163 C1
Sudbø 43 C1
Südbrookmerland 67 D1
Südbrookmerland-Moordorf 67 D1
Sudbury 65 C2
Suddesjaur 16 A2
Süderbrarup 52 B2
Suderburg 69 B/C2
Süderlügum 52 A2
Südlohn 67 C3
Sudok 16 B2
Sudoměrice u Bechyně 93 D1
Sudovaja Višn'a 97 D2, 98 A2
Sudovec 127 D2
Süd-Rätansbyn 34 B3
Sueca 169 D2
Suellacabras 153 D3
Suelli 123 D3
Sueros de Cepeda 151 D2
Suèvres 87 C3
Şugag 140 B1/2
Sugenheim-Deutenheim 81 D3
Sugères 102 B3
Sugnet 39 C1
Suha 132 B2
Suha Punta 130 B1/2
Suhiniči 75 D3
Suhl 81 D2
Suhlendorf 69 C2
Suho Polje 133 C1
Suhopolje 128 A3
Suhostrel 139 D2
Suhr 90 B3, 105 C1
Šuica 131 D3, 132 A2/3
Suijavaara 11 C2
Suinula 25 C1
Suinula 25 C1, 26 A1
Suippes 88 B1
Sukarrieta 153 D1
Sukeva 22 B1
Sukobin 137 D2
Sukošan 130 B2
Sükösd 129 C2
Sukovo 139 C/D1
Suksela 24 B2
Sukth 137 D3, 142 A1
Sul 28 B3, 33 D1
Sula 32 B1
Šul'a 95 D2
Sulå 35 D3
Sulby 58 B1
Suldal 42 B1/2
Sulechów 71 C3
Sulęcin 71 C2
Sulejów 97 C1
Suleskar 42 B2
Sulesund 36 B1
Sulgen 91 C3
Sulibórz 71 C1
Sulików 83 D1
Sulina 141 D2
Sulingen 68 A2
Sulitjelma 15 C1
Sulkava 22 B2
Sulkava 27 C1
Sulkava 25 D2, 26 A2
Sulkavanjärvi 21 D2, 22 A2
Sulkavanjärvi 22 B1/2
Sulkavanperä 21 D1, 22 A1
Sully 103 C1
Sully-sur-Loire 87 D3
Sulmona 119 C1/2
Sulseter 37 D2
Sultaniçe 145 D2
Sulviken 29 C3, 34 A1
Sülysáp 129 C1
Sulz 90 B2
Sulzano 106 B3
Sulzbach 89 D1, 90 A1
Sulzbach 91 C1
Sulzbach am Main 81 C3
Sulzbach-Laufen 91 C1
Sulzbach-Rosenberg 82 A3, 92 A1
Sulzdorf-Oberessfeld 81 D2
Sulzemoos-Einsbach 92 A2
Sulzfeld am Main 81 D3
Sumacárcel 169 C2
Sumartin 131 D3, 132 A3, 136 A1
Sumbilla 108 A3, 154 A1
Šumburk 83 D2
Sümeg 128 A1
Sümeg 96 B3
Šumen 141 C3
Sumiainen 21 D3, 22 A3
Sumiswald [Sumiswald-Grünen] 105 C1
Šumjači 75 C3
Summa 26 B2
Sumony 128 B2/3
Šumperk 96 B2
Sumsa 19 D3
Sumstad 28 A2
Sünching 92 B1/2
Sund 8 A3
Sund 30 B3
Sund 35 C3
Sund 14 B1
Sund 41 D3
Sundborn 39 D2, 40 A2
Sundby 20 B1
Sunde 32 B1
Sunde 42 A1
Sunderland 61 D1
Sundern 80 B1
Sundern-Allendorf 80 B1
Sundern-Endorf 80 B1
Sundern-Hachen 80 B1
Sundet 29 C3, 34 A1
Sundklakk 8 B2
Sundlisetra 33 C2
Sundö 31 C2
Sundom 17 C3
Sundom 20 A2, 31 D3
Sunds 48 A/B2/3
Sundsbø 32 A2
Sundsfjord 14 B1
Sundsjö 35 B/C2
Sundsjöasen 35 B/C2
Sundskør 28 A2
Sundsli 43 C2
Sundsvall 35 D3
Sundsvall-Selånger 35 D3
Sundsvall-Stockvik 35 D3
Sundsvoll 14 A3
Sundvollen 38 A3, 43 D1
Suni 123 C2
Sunja 127 D3, 131 C/D1
Sunnan 28 B2
Sunnanhed 39 D1/2
Sunnansjö 15 C3
Sunnansjö 31 C2
Sunnansjö 39 D3
Sunndal 36 A2
Sunndalsøra 32 B2
Sunne 39 C3
Sunne 34 B2
Sunnemo 39 C3
Sunnersberg 45 C/D2
Sunnersta 30 B2, 35 D1
Suo-Anttila 27 C2
Suodenniemi 24 B1
Suojanperä 7 C3
Suojoki 20 A/B3
Suolahti 21 D3, 22 A3
Suolovuobme 5 C3
Suomasema 25 C1
Suomela 25 C2/3
Suomen keskipiste 18 B3
Suomenniemi 26 B1
Suomijärvi 20 B3
Suomusjärvi 25 C3
Suomussalmi 19 D2
Suonenjoki 22 B3
Suoniala 27 C2
Suoniemi 24 B1
Suonnankylä 19 C1
Suontaka 24 A2
Suontee 22 B3
Suonttajärvi 11 C2
Suopajärvi 12 A/B3
Suopelto 25 D1, 26 A1
Suopelto 21 D2, 22 A2
Suorajärvi 19 D1
Suorva 9 D3
Šuošjavrre 5 D3, 6 A3, 11 C1
Suostola 12 B2
Suotukylä 21 D1, 22 A1
Suovaaraa 23 C2
Suovanlahti 21 D2, 22 A2
Superbagnères 155 C2
Superbesse 102 B3
Super Nendaz [Sion] 104 B2
Supersano 121 D3
Supetar 131 C/D3
Supetarska Draga 130 B1
Supino 119 B/C2
Süplingen 69 C3
Šuplja Stijeno 133 C3
Süpplingen 69 C3
Supru 7 C3
Süptitz 82 B1
Supuru de Jos 97 D3, 140 B1
Surahammar 40 A3
Surany 95 C2/3
Suraž 75 B/C3
Suraž 99 D1
Surčin 133 D1, 134 A1
Surd 128 A2
Surdulica 139 C1
Surdulica 140 A3
Surgères 100 B2

Surhuisterveen 67 C1
Súria 156 A2/3
Surier 104 B3
Šurlan 138 B2
Surnadalsøra 32 B2
Surnuinmäki 22 B3
Sursee 105 C1
Surte 45 C3
Surwold 67 D2
Sury-ès-Bois 87 D3
Susa 112 B1
Susak 130 A2
Susch 106 B1
Suscinio 85 C3
Susegana 107 D2/3
Sušice 93 C1
Sušice 96 A2
Susikas 25 C2
Süssen 91 C2
Susten [Leuk] 105 C2
Susteren 79 D1
Sustrum 67 D2
Susurluk 149 D1
Šutesti 141 C2
Sutivan 131 C/D3
Sutjeska 134 B1
Sutjeska 132 B2
Sutkavankylä 21 C3
Sutme 29 D1
Sutomore 137 D2
Sutri 117 C3, 118 A1
Sútrio 107 D2, 126 A2
Sutterton 61 D3, 65 C1
Süttő 95 D3
Sutton 66 B2
Sutton Coldfld. 64 A2
Sutton in Ashfield 61 D3,
   65 C1
Sutton on Sea 61 D3,
   65 C1
Sutton Scotney 65 C3,
   76 B1
Suttrop 80 B1
Suurikylä 27 D1
Suurimäki 22 B2
Suurlahti 27 C1
Suur-Miehikkälä 27 B/C2
Suur-Saimaa 27 C1/2
Suutala 21 C2/3
Suutarinkylä 18 B3
Suvanto 12 B2
Suvantokumpu 11 D3,
   12 B2
Suva Reka 138 B2
Suvereto 114 B3, 116 A2
Suvodol 138 B3
Suvorov 75 D3
Suvorovo 75 D2
Suwałki 73 D2
Suze-la-Rousse 111 C2
Suzzara 114 B1
Svabensverk 39 D2,
   40 A1/2
Švajcernica 89 B/C3
Svaljava 97 D2, 98 A3
Svalöv 50 A3
Svanavattnet 30 A2
Svaneholm 50 B3
Svaneke 51 D3
Svaneke 72 A/B2
Svanesund 45 C3
Svängsta 51 C2
Svaningen 29 D2
Svannäs 16 A2
Svanninge 53 B/C2
Svansele 29 D2
Svansele 31 C1
Svanskog 45 C1
Svanstein 17 D1
Svanström 31 D1
Svanvik 7 C/D3
Svappavaara 10 B3
Svardnes 7 D1/2
Svärdsjö 39 D2, 40 A2
Svarstad 43 D2, 44 A1
Svartå 46 A1
Svärta 47 C2
Svartbäck 26 B2/3
Svartberg 17 C2
Svartbyn 17 C2
Svarthamarseter 37 D2
Svarthaugen 33 D3
Svärtinge 46 B2
Svartisdalen 14 B2
Svartliden 31 C1
Svartlöga 41 C3, 47 D1

Svartnäs 40 A2
Svartnes 14 B1
Svartnes 7 D1/2
Svartöstaden 17 C3
Svartvik 35 D3
Svarvar 20 A2
Sv'ataja Vol'a 98 B1
Svatsum 37 D2
Sved 29 C3, 34 B1
Sved 29 C3, 34 B1
Svedala 50 A/B3
Svedala 72 A2
Svedasai 73 D2, 74 A2/3
Svedja 40 A1
Svedjan 16 B3
Svedje 29 D2, 30 A1/2
Svedje 31 C3
Sveg 34 B3
Sveindal 42 B3
Sveio 42 A1
Svelgen 36 A1/2
Svelvik 38 A3, 43 D1,
   44 B1
Svenarum 46 A3, 50 B1
Švenčionys 74 A3
Svendborg 53 C2
Svene 43 D1
Svenes 43 C3
Svenljunga 50 A/B1
Svenljunga 72 A1
Svennevad 46 A/B1/2
Svenningvik 14 B3
Svensby 4 A3
Svensbygd 50 B1
Svensbyn 16 B3
Svenshögen 45 C3
Svenskby 24 B3
Svenstavik 34 B2
Svenstorp 50 A/B3
Svenstrup 48 B1/2
Sverdiá 145 C2/3
Sveta Marija 136 B1
Sveta Nedelja 127 D3
Sveta Petka 135 B/C2/3
Sveti Areh 127 C2
Sveti Arhandel 138 B2
Sveti Arhandel 131 C2
Sveti Bogorodica
   138 A/B3, 142 B1
Sveti Janez 126 B2
Sveti Jovan Bigorski
   138 A/B3
Sveti Jurij 127 D1
Svetilovići 99 D1
Sveti Martin 131 D3
Sveti Naum 142 B1
Sveti Naum 148 A1
Sveti Nikita 138 B2
Sveti Nikola 137 D2
Sveti Nikole 139 C2
Sveti Pantelejmon 138 B2
Sveti Rok 131 C2
Sveti Stefan 137 C2
Světlík 93 C2
Svetlogorsk 99 C1
Svetlovodsk 99 D3
Svetozarevo 140 A2
Svetozarevo 134 B2
Svetozar Miletić 129 C3
Svetvinčenat 130 A1
Švihov 83 C3, 93 C1
Svilajna 134 B2
Svilajnac 140 A2
Sviland 42 A2
Svilengrad 145 D2
Svilengrad 141 C3
Svindal 44 B1
Svindalen 9 C1
Svineng 5 D3, 6 A3, 11 D1
Svines 14 A2
Svinesund 44 B1/2
Svinevoll 43 D2, 44 A/B1
Svinhult 46 A/B3
Svinica 135 C2
Svinište 138 B3, 143 B/C1
Svinnegarn 40 A3, 47 C1
Svinninge 47 D1
Svinninge 49 C3, 53 C1
Svinvik 32 B2
Svištov 141 C2/3
Svitavy 96 B2
Svode 139 C1
Svodín 95 D3
Svoge 139 D1
Svoge 140 B3
Svolvær 8 B2
Svora 36 A/B1

Svorkmo 28 A3, 33 C2
Svortemyr 36 A2
Svrčinovec 95 D1
Svrljig 135 C3
Svrljig 140 A2/3
Svukuriset 33 D3
Svulrya 38 B2
Swadlincote 64 A1
Swaffham 65 C1/2
Swaffham Prior 65 C2
Swalmen 79 D1
Swanage 63 D3, 76 A2
Swansea 63 C1
Swarzędz 71 D2
Sweetheart Abbey 57 C3,
   60 A1
Świdnica 71 C3
Świdnica (Schweidnitz)
   96 B1
Świdwin 72 B2/3
Świdwin 71 C1
Świebodzin 71 C3
Świebodzin 72 A/B3,
   96 A1
Świecie 72 B3
Świętno 71 C3
Swindon 64 A3
Swineshead 61 D3,
   65 B/C1
Świnoujście (Swinemünde)
   72 A2
Swinton 57 D2
Swisttal-Essig 80 A2
Swobnica 70 B2
Swords 58 A2
Syčovka 75 C/D2/3
Sydänmaa 20 B3
Sydänmaa 24 A2
Sydänmaa 24 B1
Sydänmaankylä 21 D1,
   22 A1
Sydmo 24 B3
Sydnes 42 A1
Sygnesand 36 B2
Sykäräinen 21 C1
Syke 68 A2
Syke-Barrien 68 A2
Syke-Heiligenfelde 68 A2
Sykkylven 32 A3, 36 B1
Sylling 43 D1
Sylstationen 33 D2, 34 A2
Syltefjord 7 C1
Syltevikmyra 7 D1
Sylt-Ost-Keitum 52 A2
Sylvänä 25 B/C2
Sylvanès 110 A2
Synsiö 22 A/B3
Sypniewo 71 D1
Sypniewo 71 D1
Syrau 82 B2
Syri 21 C1
Syrjä 23 C3
Syrjäntaka 25 C2, 26 A2
Sysmä 25 D1, 26 A1
Sysslebäck 38 B2
Syston 64 B1
Syterstugan 15 C2
Syt'kovo 75 C2
Syväjärvi 12 B2
Syväjärvi 11 B/C2
Syvälahti 23 C3
Syvänniemi 22 B2
Syvänsi 22 B3
Syvde 36 A1
Syvdsnes 36 A1
Syvinki 21 C3
Syvsten 49 B/C1
Syyspohja 27 C1
Szabadbattyán 128 B1
Szabadhidvég 128 B1
Szabadszállás 129 C1
Szakály 128 B2
Szakcs 128 B2
Szakmár 129 C2
Szalánta 128 B2/3
Szalkszentmárton 129 C1
Szamocin 71 D2
Szamotuły 71 D2
Szántód 128 B1
Szany 95 C3
Szarvas 129 D1
Szarvas 97 C3, 140 A1
Százhalombatta 95 D3,
   129 C1
Szczecinek (Neustettin)
   71 D1

Szczecinek (Neustettin)
   72 B2/3
Szczecin (Stettin) 72 A3
Szczecin (Stettin) 70 B1
Szczekociny 97 C1
Szczerców 97 B/C1
Szczuczarz 71 C2
Szczuczyn 73 D3, 98 A1
Szczytno (Ortelsburg)
   73 C2
Szederkény 128 B2/3
Szeged 129 D2
Szeged 97 C3, 140 A1
Szeghalom 97 C3, 140 A1
Szegvár 129 D2
Székesfehérvár 128 B1
Székesfehérvár 96 B3
Székkutas 129 D2
Szekszárd 129 C2
Szekszárd 96 B3
Szemerecsörnye 127 D2,
   128 A2
Szend 95 C3
Szentendre 95 D3
Szentes 129 D2
Szentes 97 C3, 140 A1
Szentgotthárd 127 D1
Szentkút 95 C3
Szentlászló 128 B2
Szentlőrinc 128 B2
Szentmártonkáta 129 C1
Szenyér 128 A2
Szerencs 97 C2/3
Szigetszentmiklos 95 D3,
   129 C1
Szigetszentmiklós 95 D3,
   129 C1
Szigetújfalu 129 C1
Szigetvár 128 B2
Szigliget 128 A1
Szil 95 B/C3
Szilvágy 127 D1, 128 A1/2
Szlichtynogowa 71 D3
Szob 95 D3
Szolnok 129 D1
Szolnok 97 C3, 140 A1
Szőlősgyörök 128 B2
Szombathely 128 D1,
   128 A1
Szombathely 96 B3
Szomor 95 D3
Szőny 95 C3
Szprotawa (Sprottau)
   96 A1
Szulok 128 A2
Szwecja 71 D1
Szydłowo 71 D1/2

T

Tå 40 A1
Taalintehdas 24 B3
Taapajärvi 12 A2, 17 D1
Taasia 25 D2, 26 B2
Taatsijärvi 11 D2, 12 A/B1
Taaurainen 19 D1
Taavetti 27 B/C2
Tab 128 B1/2
Tabanera de Cerrato 152 B3
Tabanovce 139 C2
Tábara 151 D3, 159 D1
Taberg 45 D3
Tabernas 173 D2
Tabernas 154 B3
Tabernes de Valldigna
   169 D2
Taberno 174 A1
Tabiano Terme 114 A1
Taboada 150 B2
Taboadela 150 B2/3
Taboado 158 B1/2
Tábor 93 D1
Tábor 96 A2
Taborska Jama 127 B/C2/3
Tábua 158 B3
Tabuaço 158 B2
Tabuenca 154 A3, 162 A1
Täby 47 C1
Täby station (Vallentuna)
   47 C1
Tác 128 B1
Taceno 105 D2, 106 A2
T'ačev 97 D3, 98 A3

Tacherting 92 B2/3
Tacherting-Peterskirchen
   92 B2/3
Tachov 82 B3
Tackåsen 39 D1
Tacken 69 D1/2
Täcktom 24 B3
Tadcaster 61 D2
Tådene 45 C2
Taennilä 12 B3
Tafalla 154 A2
Tafjord 32 A3, 36 B1
Täfteå 31 C3
Täfteå 20 A1, 31 D2
Tåganes 42 A2
Tågarp 50 A3
Tåggia 113 C2
Tagliacozzo 119 B/C1/2
Táglio di Po 115 C1
Tagnon 78 B3
Tågsjöberg 30 A2, 35 C/D1
Tågsjöberg 30 A2, 35 C/D1
Tahkoranta 22 B3
Tähtelä 25 C3
Tähtelä 12 B3
Tahüll 155 D2
Tahús 155 C2
Tai di Cadore 107 D2
Taillebourg 100 B2/3
Taimoniemi 21 D2, 22 A2
Tain 54 B2
Tainijoki 18 B1
Taininiemi 18 B1
Tain-I'Hermitage 103 D3,
   111 C1
Taipale 12 B3
Taipale 24 B1
Taipale 18 A2
Taipale 22 B2
Taipaleenharju 18 B2
Taipaleenkylä 21 B/C3
Taipaleensuu 11 C3
Taipalsaari 27 C2
Taipana 126 A2
Taipas 158 A1
Taiskirchen im Innkreis
   93 C2
Taivalkoski 19 C1/2
Taivalmaa 20 B3
Taivassalo 24 A2
Tajmište 138 B3
Tajov 95 D2
Tajueco 153 C/D3, 161 C1
Takácsi 95 C3, 128 A1
Takelvdal 4 A3, 9 D1,
   10 A1
Takene 45 D1
Takkula 25 C3
Takkula 24 B2
Taklax 20 A2/3
Takovo 133 D2, 134 A2
Taksony 95 D3, 129 C1
Talamanca 157 C2
Talamantes 154 A3, 162 A1
Talamona 106 A2
Talamone 116 B3
Talana 123 D2
Talarn 155 D2/3
Talarrubias 166 B2
Talaván 159 C/D3, 165 D1,
   166 A1
Talavera 155 C3, 163 C1
Talavera de la Reina
   160 A3, 166 B1
Talavera la Real 165 D2
Talayuela 159 D3
Talayuelas 163 C3, 169 D1
Talcy 87 C3
Tales 162 B3, 169 D1
Talgarth 63 C1
Talhadas 158 A2
Táliga 165 C2
Talla 115 C3, 116 B3
Tallaght 58 A2
Tallard 112 A2
Tallås 15 C3
Tallåsen 38 B2
Tällberg 39 D2
Tallberg 31 C2
Tallberget 17 C2
Taller 108 A2
Tallhed 39 D1
Tallinn 74 A1
Talljärv 17 C2
Tallnäs 15 C2
Talloires 104 A3
Tallsjö 30 B2

Tallsund 16 A3
Tallträsk 30 B1
Tallträsk 31 C/D1
Tällträsk 16 B3
Talluskylä 22 B2
Talmont 100 A2
Talmont 100 B3
Tal'noe 99 C/D3
Talsi 73 D1
Tålsmark 20 A1, 31 D2
Talusperä 18 A3
Talvadas 6 B2
Talviainen 25 C1
Talvik 5 C2
Talvikstua 5 C2
Talybont 59 C3
Tamajón 161 C2
Tamame 159 D1
Tamames 159 D2
Tamanhos 158 B2
Támara 152 B3
Tamarinda 157 C1
Tamarite de Litera 155 C3
Tamási 128 B2
Tamási 96 B3
Tambach-Dietharz 81 D2
Tåme 31 D1
Tammela 25 C2
Tammela 19 D1
Tammerfors 25 C1
Tammijärvi 25 D1, 26 A1
Tammilahti 25 D1, 26 A/B1
Tammisilta 24 B2/3
Tamnay-en-Bazois 103 C1
Tamnes 33 D2
Tampere (Tammerfors) 25 C1
Tamsweg 126 B1
Tämta 45 C3
Tamurejo 166 B2
Tamworth 64 A1/2
Tana Bru 7 C2
Tanagård 7 C1
Tanágra 147 D2
Tanai/Thanai 106 B1
Tananger 42 A2
Tancarville 77 C3
Tăndărei 141 C2
Tanderagee 58 A1
Tandö 39 C2
Tandsbyn 34 B2
Tandsjöborg 39 D1
Tångaberg 49 D1, 50 A1
Tanganheira 164 A3, 170 A1
Tångböle 29 C3, 34 A1/2
Tangen 42 A/B1
Tangen 38 B3
Tangen 44 B1
Tangen 5 C2
Tangen 38 A2
Tänger 39 D2, 40 A2
Tangerhütte 69 D2
Tangermünde 69 D2
Tangleger 33 C3, 37 D1
Tangsjöstugan 38 B1
Tanhua 12 B2
Taninges 104 B2
Tankapirtti 12 B1
Tankavaaran kultakylä 12 B1
Tankolampi 21 D3, 22 A3
Tanlay 88 A/B3
Tann 81 D2
Tanna 82 A2
Tannåker 50 B1
Tännäs 34 A3
Tannay 88 A3
Tänndalen 34 A3
Tanne 69 C3, 81 D1
Tannenbergsthal 82 B2
Tännesberg 82 B3, 92 B1
Tannhausen (Aalen) 91 D1
Tannheim 91 D3
Tannheim (Biberach) 91 D3
Tannila 18 B2
Tann (Pfarrkirchen) 92 B2
Tannsjön 30 A2/3, 35 C1
Tannvik 33 B/C1/2
Tanowo 70 B1
Tantallon Castle 57 C1
Tantonville 89 C2
Tantow 70 B1
Tanttila 25 C/D2, 26 A2
Tanum 44 B2

Tanumshede 44 B2
Tanus 110 A2
Tanvald 83 D2
Taormina 125 D2
Tapa 74 A1
Tapale 24 B2
Tapaninkylä 19 D3
Tapfheim 91 D2
Tápia de Casariego 151 C1
Tápióbicske 129 C1
Tápiógyörgye 129 D1
Tapioles 151 D3, 152 A3, 159 D1
Tapionkylä 12 A3
Tapionniemi 12 B3
Tápiószele 129 D1
Tápiószentmárton 129 C/D1
Tápiószőlős 129 D1
Tapojärvi 11 C3
Tapojoki 11 C3
Tapolca 128 A1
Tapolca 96 B3
Tapolcafő 128 A1
Tapperskar 14 B2
Taps 52 B1
Tar 126 A/B3, 130 A1
Taracena 161 C2
Taradell 156 A2
Taraklija 141 D1
Taramundi 151 C1
Tarancón 161 C2
Tarancueña 161 C1
Táranto 121 C3
Táranto Talsano 121 C3
Tarare 103 C2
Taraš 129 D3
Tarašča 99 C3
Tarascon 111 C2
Tarascon-sur-Ariège 155 D2, 156 A1
Tarasp-Fontana [Scuol-Tarasp] 106 B1
Taravilla 161 D2
Tarazona 154 A3
Tarazona de Guareña 160 A1/2
Tarazona de la Mancha 168 B1/2
Tårbæk 49 D3, 50 A3, 53 D1
Tárbena 169 D2
Tarbert 56 A2
Tarbert 54 A2/3, 55 D1
Tarbert 54 A2
Tarbert 55 C3
Tarbes 108 B3, 155 C1
Tarbet 56 B1
Tarbet 54 A2, 55 D1
Tarcento 126 A2
Tarčin 132 B3
Tardajos 153 B/C2
Tardajos de Duero 153 D3, 161 D1
Tardelcuende 153 D3, 161 D1
Tardets-Sorholus 108 A/B3, 154 B1
Tardienta 154 B3
Tardobispo 159 D1
Tärendö 17 C1
Tarfalastugan 9 D3
Targon 108 B1
Tàrgoviște 141 C3
Tarhapää 21 C3
Tariego 152 B3
Tarifa 171 D3
Tarján 95 D3
Tarleton 59 D2, 60 B2
Tarm 48 A3
Tarmstedt 68 A1/2
Tärnaby 15 C3
Tärnala 27 D1
Tärnamo 15 C3
Tärnasjöstugan 15 C2
Tårnet 7 D2
Tarnobrzeg 97 C1, 98 A2
Tarnów 97 C2
Tarnów 71 B/C2
Tarnówka 71 D1
Tarnowo 71 D2
Tarnowo Podgórne 71 D2
Tärnsjö 40 A3
Tårnvik 6 B1
Tårnvik 8 B3
Taroda 161 D1
Tarouca 158 B2

Tarp 52 B2
Tarporley 59 D2, 60 B3
Tarquínia 116 B3, 118 A1
Tarraälvshyddan 15 D1
Tarragona 163 C2
Tårrajaur 16 A2
Tarraluoppalstugorna 15 D1
Tàrrega 155 C3, 163 C1
Tarrekaisestugan 15 D1
Tarrés 163 D1
Tarroja de Segarra 155 C3, 163 C1
Tårs 48 B1
Tårs 53 C2
Tarsele 30 A2, 35 C/D1
Társia 122 A/B1
Tartanedo 161 D2, 162 A2
Tártano 106 A2
Tartas 108 A/B2
Tărtăşeşti 141 C2
Tartu 74 A/B1
Tarutino 141 D1
Tarvaala 21 D2/3, 22 A2/3
Tarvainen 24 A/B2
Tarvasjoki 24 B2
Tarvin 59 D2, 60 B3
Tarvísio 126 A/B2
Tarvísio 96 A2
Tarvola 21 C2
Täsch 105 C2
Tåsjö 30 A2
Tåsnad 97 D3, 140 B1
Tasov 94 A/B1
Tasovčići 132 A/B3, 136 B1
Tasovice 94 A/B1/2
Tass 129 C1
Tassin-la-Demi-Lune 103 D2/3
Tåstrup 49 D3, 50 A3, 53 D1
Tát 95 D3
Tata 95 C/D3
Tataháza 129 C2
Tatarbunary 141 D1
Tatárszentgyörgy 129 C1
Tåtorp 45 D2, 46 A2
Tattershall 61 D3, 65 B/C1
Tatton Hall 59 D2, 60 B3
Tau 42 A2
Tauberbischofsheim 81 C3
Taucha 82 B1
Tauer 70 B3
Taufkirchen an der Pram 93 C2
Taufkirchen 92 B2
Taufkirchen 92 B2
Taulé 84 B2
Taulignan 111 C1/2
Taulu 25 D1, 26 A1
Taunton 63 C2
Taunusstein 80 B3
Tauragė 73 C/D2
Taurianova 122 A3
Taurisano 121 D3
Tauste 155 C3
Tauves 102 B3
Tauvo 18 A2/3
Tavankut 129 C2
Tavannes 89 D2, 104 B1
Tavarnelle Val di Pesa 114 B3, 116 B2
Tavasbarlang 128 A1
Tavascan 155 C2
Tavastehus 25 C2
Tavastila 26 B2
Tavastkenkä 18 B3, 22 A/B1
Tavastkyro 24 B1
Taveiro 158 A3
Tavela 19 C/D1
Tavelsjö 31 C2
Taverna 122 B2
Taverna Piccinini 117 D3
Tavernelle 115 C3, 117 C2/3
Tavernelle 114 A2, 116 A1
Tavernes 112 A3
Tavérnola Bergamasca 106 A/B3
Tavérnole sul Mella 106 B3
Taverny 87 C/D1
Taviano 121 D3
Tavíkovice 94 A/B1
Tavira 170 B2

Tavistock 63 B/C3
Tavoleto 115 D2, 117 C1
Täxan 30 A2, 35 C1
Taxenbach 107 D1, 126 A1
Tayinloan 56 A2
Taynuilt 56 A1
Tayport 57 C1
Tayvallich 56 A1
Tazones 152 A1
Tczew 73 B/C2
Tealby 61 D3
Teana 120 B3
Teano 119 C3
Teba 172 A2
Tébar 168 B1
Tebay 57 C3, 59 D1, 60 B1
Tebeljevo 127 C2
Tecklenburg 67 D3
Teckomatorp 50 A3
Tecuci 141 C1
Teeriranta 19 D2
Teerivaara 19 B/C1
Teersalo 24 A2/3
Teesside 61 D1
Tegea 147 C2
Tegelen 79 D1
Tegelsmora 40 B2/3
Tegelträsk 30 B2, 35 D1
Tegernau 90 A/B3
Tegernsee 92 A3
Teggiano 120 A3
Téglio 106 B2
Tegneby 44 B3
Tehi 25 D1, 26 A1
Teichel 82 A2
Teichwolframsdorf 82 B2
Teigen 4 A/B2
Teigen 32 B3, 37 C1
Teignmouth 63 C3
Teijo 24 B3
Teillet 110 A2
Teisendorf 92 B3
Teisko 25 C1
Teisnach 93 B/C1
Teistungen 81 D1
Teixeiro 150 B1/2
Teixoso 158 B3
Tejadillos 162 A3
Tejado 153 D3, 161 D1
Tejares 160 B1
Tejeda de Tiétar 159 D3
Tejn 51 D3
Tekeriš 133 C2
Tekija 135 C1/2
Tekija 133 C2
Tekirdağ 149 D1
Tekovské Lužany 95 D2
Teksdal 28 A2/3, 33 C1
Tekućica 132 B1
Telavåg 36 A3
Telč 94 A1
Telč 96 A2
Telenešty 141 D1
Telese 119 D3
Telford 59 D3, 64 A1
Telfs 107 B/C1
Telgte 67 D3
Telheira 170 A1
Teljo 23 D1
Telkkälä 18 B1
Tellancourt 79 C3
Tellingstedt 52 B3
Telnes 14 B1/2
Telnice 94 B1
Telões 158 B3
Telšiai 73 C/D1/2
Telti 123 D1
Teltow 70 A2/3
Telve 107 C2
Tembleque 161 C3, 167 D1
Temelín 93 D1
Temenica 127 C2/3
Temerin 129 D3
Temerin 140 A2
Temkino 75 D3
Temmes 18 A/B3
Tempelseter 37 D3
Témpio Pausánia 123 D1
Templeuve 78 A2
Templin 70 A2
Templin 72 A3
Temse 78 B1
Temska 135 C3, 139 C1
Tenala/Tenhola 24 B3
Tenay 103 D2, 104 A2/3
Ten Boer 67 C1
Tenbury Wells 59 D3

Tenby 62 B1
Tence 103 C3, 111 C1
Tende 112 B2
Tendilla 161 C2
Tenebrón 159 C2
Tengen 90 B3
Tengen-Watterdingen 90 B3
Tenhult 45 D3, 46 A3
Tenigerbad [Rabius-Surrein] 105 D1/2
Teningen 90 A/B2
Tenja 129 C3
Tennenbronn 90 B2
Tennevik 9 C2
Tennevoll 9 D2
Tennilä 25 D2, 26 A2
Tennilä 12 B3
Tenno 106 B2
Tennsjö 30 B2
Tennskjær 4 A3
Tennstrand 8 B2
Tennvalen 14 A2
Tensta 40 B3
Tenterden 77 C1
Tentúgal 158 A3
Teo 150 A2
Teora 120 A2
Teovo 138 B3
Tepasto 11 D3, 12 A1
Tepelenë 142 A2
Tepelenë 148 A1
Teplá 82 B3
Teplice 83 C2
Teplice 96 A1
Teplingan 28 B1
Tepsa 11 D3, 12 A/B2
Terälahti 25 C1
Téramo 117 D3, 119 C1
Ter Apel 67 C2
Terborg 67 C3
Terchová 95 D1
Terebovlja 99 D1
Teregova 135 C1
Terehovka 99 D1
Teremia Mare 129 D2/3
Terena 165 C2
Terento/Terenten 107 C1
Teresa 162 B3, 169 C1
Teresa de Cofrentes 169 C2
Terešov 83 C3
Terespol 73 D3, 97 D1, 98 A1
Terezín 83 C2
Terezino Polje 128 A2/3
Tergnier 78 A3
Terheijden 66 A/B3, 79 C1
Terjärv/Teerijärvi 21 C1
Terlet 67 B/C3
Terlizzi 120 B2, 136 A3
Termahovka 99 C2
Termas de Monfortinho 159 C3
Terme 122 A/B1
Terme di Brénnero/Brennerbad 107 C1
Terme di Casteldória 123 C1
Terme di Lurísia 113 B/C2
Terme di Miradolo 105 D3, 106 A3, 113 D1
Terme di Sárdara 123 C3
Terme di Valdieri 112 B2
Terme Luigiane 122 A1
Termeno/Tramin 107 C2
Térmens 155 D3, 163 C1
Termes 110 A3, 156 B1
Termes de Orion 156 B2/3
Termignon 104 B3
Terminiers 87 C2
Términi Imerese 124 B2
Terminón 153 C2
Térmoli 119 D2, 120 A1
Termunten 67 C1
Ternant 88 B3, 103 D1
Terndrup 48 B2
Ternell 79 D2
Terneuzen 78 B1
Terni 117 C3, 118 B1
Ternitz 94 A3
Ternopol' 98 B3
Terpani 142 A2
Térpillos 139 D3, 143 D1, 144 A1
Terpnás 143 C3
Terpnás 148 A1
Terpsithéa 146 B1/2
Terque 173 D2

Terracina 119 B/C2/3
Terrades 156 B2
Terradillos de Templarios 152 A2
Terråk 29 B/C1
Terralba 123 C2/3
Terranho 158 B2
Terranova da Sibari 122 B1
Terranova di Pollino 120 B3, 122 A/B1
Terranuova Bracciolini 115 C3, 116 B2
Terras do Bouro 150 B3, 158 A1
Terrasini 124 A1/2
Terrassa 156 A3
Terrasson-la-Villedieu 101 C3, 108 B1
Terrateig 169 D2
Terravécchia 122 B1
Terrer 162 A1
Terriente 162 A3
Terrinches 167 D2, 168 A2
Terrugem 164 A2
Tersløse 49 C3, 53 C/D1
Tertenía 123 D2/3
Teruel 162 A/B2/3
Tervahauta 24 B1
Tervajoki 20 B2
Tervakoski 25 C2
Tervala 21 D3, 22 A3
Tervavaara 19 C2
Tervel 141 C2
Tervo 22 B2
Tervola 17 D2, 18 A1
Tervolan asema 17 D2, 18 A1
Terz 94 A3
Terzone San Pietro 117 D3, 118 B1
Tésa 95 D2/3
Tešanj 132 B1/2
Teschendorf 70 A2
Tesijoki 25 D2, 26 B2/3
Teslić 132 B1/2
Tesserete [Lugano] 105 D2
Tessin 53 D3
Tessy-sur-Vire 85 D1
Testa del Gargano 120 B1, 136 A2/3
Testa dell'Acqua 125 C/D3
Tét 95 C3
Tetbury 63 D1, 64 A3
Teterow 53 D3, 69 D1, 70 A1
Teterow 72 A2
Teteven 140 B3
Teti 123 D2
Tetovo 138 B2
Tetovo 140 A3
Tetrálofon 143 C2
Tettau 82 A2
Tettnang 91 C3
Tettnang-Langnau 91 C3
Teublitz 92 B1
Teuchern 82 B1
Teufen 91 C3
Teufenbach 126 B1
Teulada 123 C3
Teulada 169 D2
Teupitz 70 A3
Teurajärvi 17 C1
Teurajärvi 12 A2
Teuro 25 C2
Teusajaurestugorna 9 D3
Teuschnitz 82 A2
Teutleben 81 D2
Teutschenthal 82 A1
Teuva (Östermark) 20 A3
Tevaniemi 24 B1
Tevansjö 35 C3
Teväntö 25 C2
Tevel 128 B2
Tewkesbury 63 D1, 64 A2
Thal 81 D2
Thale 69 C3
Thalfang 80 A3
Thalgau 93 C3
Thalheim 82 B2
Thalkirch [Versam-Safien] 105 D2, 106 A1/2
Thalmässing 92 A1
Thame 64 B3
Thann 89 D3, 90 A3
Thannhausen 91 D2
Thaon 76 B3, 86 A1
Thaon-les-Vosges 89 D2
Tharandt 83 C1/2
Thárros 123 C2
Tharsis 171 C1
Thásos 145 C1
Thásos 145 C1
Thásos 149 C1
Thaxted 65 C2
Thaya 94 A1/2
Thayngen 90 B3
Theddlethorpe Saint Helen 61 D3
Thedinghausen 68 A2
Theessen 69 D3
Theilenhofen-Dornhausen 91 D1
Theix 85 C3
Themar 81 D2
The Mumbles 63 C1
Thénezay 101 C1
Thenon 101 D3, 109 C1
Theodorákion 143 D1
Theodóriana 143 B/C3
Theológos 147 C1
Theológos 145 C2
Théoule-sur-Mer 112 B3
Thermes-d'Armagnac 108 B2/3
Thérmi 143 D2, 144 A2
Thermísia 147 D3
Thérmon (Kefalóvrison) 146 B1/2
Thermopylai 147 C1
Thérmos 146 B1/2
Thernberg 94 A/B3
Thérouanne 77 D2
Thespiaí 147 C2
Thesprotikón 142 B3
Thessaloníki 143 D2, 144 A2
Thessaloníki 148 B1
Thetford 65 C2
Theth 137 D2, 138 A2
The Trossachs 56 B1
Theux 79 D2
Thevet-Saint-Julien 102 A1
Thézan 110 A3, 156 B1
Thèze 108 B3, 154 B1
Thiaucourt-Regniéville 89 C1
Thiberville 86 B1
Thibie 88 B1
Thiéblemont-Farémont 88 B1/2
Thiendorf 83 C1
Thiene 107 C3
Thierhaupten 91 D2, 92 A2
Thierhaupten-Baar 91 D2, 92 A2
Thierhaupten-Unterbaar 91 D2
Thiers 103 B/C2
Thiersheim 82 B3
Thiesi 123 C2
Thiézac 110 A1
Thionville 89 C1
Thíra 149 C3
Thiron 86 B2
Thirsk 61 D2
Thisóa 146 B3
Thisted 48 A2
Thísvi 147 C2
Thívai 147 C/D2
Thívai 148 B2
Thiviers 101 D3
Thizy 103 C2
Thoirette 103 D2, 104 A2
Thoissey 103 D2
Thoisy-la-Berchère 88 B3, 103 C1
Tholen 78 B1
Tholey-Theley 80 A3, 90 A1
Tholón 146 B3
Thomatal 126 B1
Thonac 109 C1
Thônes 104 A/B2/3
Thonon-les-Bains 104 B2
Thorame-Basse 112 A2
Thorame-Haute 112 A2
Thorens-Glières 104 A2
Thorigné-sur-Dué 86 B2
Thorigny-sur-Oreuse 88 A2
Thorikón 147 D3
Thörl 94 A3
Thornaby-on-Tees 61 D1
Thornbury 63 D1
Thorne 61 C2
Thorney 65 C1/2
Thornhill 57 B/C2
Thornhill 54 B3
Thornton 59 C/D1, 60 B2
Thorsager 49 C2
Thorsø 48 B2
Thouarcé 86 A3, 100 B1
Thouars 101 C1
Thourie 85 D2/3
Thoúrion 145 D3
Thrapston 64 B2
Threave Castle 56 B3, 60 A1
Threshfield 59 D1, 61 B/C2
Thuès-les-Bains 156 A2
Thueyts 111 C1
Thuin 78 B2
Thuir 156 B1/2
Thun 105 C1
Thüngen 81 C3
Thurey 103 D1
Thurles 55 C/D3
Thurnau 82 A3
Thurøby 53 C2
Thursby 57 C3, 60 B1
Thurso 54 B1
Thury-Harcourt 86 A1
Thusis 105 D1, 106 A1
Thyborøn 48 A2
Thyregod 48 B3
Thyrnau 93 C2
Tiarp 45 D3
Ţibăneşti 141 C2
Tibble 47 C1
Tibro 45 D2, 46 A2
Tickhill 61 C3
Ţicleni 135 D1
Tidaholm 45 D3
Tidan 45 D2
Tidersrum 46 B3
Tidö 46 B1
Tiedra 152 A3, 160 A1
Tiefenbach 93 C2
Tiefenbach 92 B1
Tiefenbronn 90 B1/2
Tiefencastel 106 A1/2
Tiefensee 70 B2
Tiel 66 B3
Tielt 78 A1
Tiemassaari 23 B/C3
Tienen 79 C2
Tierga 154 A3, 162 A1
Tiermas 154 A/B2
Tierp 40 B2
Tierzo 161 D2, 162 A2
Tiffauges 100 B1
Ţigănaşi 135 C2
Ţigăneşti 141 C2
Tighnabruaich 56 A2
Tignes 104 B3
Tigy 87 C/D3
Tihany 128 B1
Tihilä 21 D1, 22 A/B1
Tihusniemi 22 B3
Tihvin 75 C1
Tiingvoll 32 B2
Tiistenjoki 20 B2
Tiitilankylä 22 A/B2
Tijesno 131 C3
Tijola 173 D2
Tikkakoski 21 D3, 22 A3
Tikkala 21 D3, 22 A3
Tikkala 23 D3
Tilburg 79 C1
Tilbury 65 C3
Til-Châtel 88 B3
Tilh 108 A/B3, 154 B1
Tilkainen 24 B2
Tillberga 40 A3, 46 B1
Tilleda 82 A1
Tillicoultry 57 B/C1
Tillières-sur-Avre 87 B/C1
Tillikkala 26 B1
Tilly 101 C2
Tilly-sur-Seulles 76 B3, 86 A1
Tiltrem 28 A2/3, 33 C1
Tim 48 A2/3
Timau 107 D2, 126 A2
Timbonäs 38 B3
Timelkam 93 C3
Timfristós 146 B1
Timişoara 140 A1
Timmele 45 D3
Timmendorfer Strand 53 C3
Timmernabben 51 D1
Timmersdala 45 D2
Timmervik 45 C2
Timoniemi 19 D3
Timrå 35 D3
Tinahely 58 A3
Tinajas 161 D2/3
Tinalhas 158 B3, 165 C1
Tinca 97 C3, 140 A1
Tinchebray 86 A1
Tineo 151 C/D1
Tinglev 52 B2
Tingsryd 51 C2
Tingsryd 72 A/B1
Tingstäde 47 D2
Tingvatyn 42 B3
Tinizong (Tinzen) [Tiefencastel] 106 A2
Tinjan 126 B3, 130 A1
Tinnoset 43 C1, 44 A1
Tinnye 95 D3
Tínos 149 C2
Tintagel 62 B3
Tînţăreni 135 D2
Tinténiac 85 C/D2
Tintern Abbey 63 D1
Tintern Parva 63 D1
Tintigny 79 C3
Tione di Trento 106 B2
Tipasjärvi 23 C1
Tipasjoki 23 C1
Tipasoja 23 C1
Tipperary 55 C3
Tiranë 137 D3, 138 A3, 142 A1
Tirano 106 B2
Tiraspol' 141 D1
Tire 149 D2
Tirgo 153 C2
Tîrgovişte 141 C2
Tîrgu Bujor 141 C/D1
Tîrgu Cărbuneşti 135 D1
Tîrgu-Frumos 141 C1
Tîrgu Jiu 140 B2
Tîrgu Jiu 135 D1
Tîrgu Lăpuş 97 D3, 140 B1
Tîrgu Mureş 97 D3, 140 B1
Tîrgu-Neamţ 141 C1
Tîrgu Ocna 141 C1
Tîrgu Secuiesc 141 C1
Tirig 163 C2
Tiriolo 122 B2
Tirli 116 A3
Tirmo 25 D3, 26 A3
Tîrnăveni 97 D3, 140 B1
Tírnavos 148 B1
Tírnavos 143 D3
Tirpersdorf 82 B2
Tirrénia 114 A3, 116 A2
Tirro 6 B3
Tirschenreuth-Wondreb 82 B3
Tirschenreuth 82 B3
Tirstrup 49 C2
Tirteafuera 167 C2
Tiryns 147 C3
Tiscar 167 D3, 168 A3, 173 C/D1
Tisleidalen 37 D3
Tismana 135 D1
Tišnov 94 B1
Tišnov 96 B2
Tisselskog 45 C2
Tistrup 48 A3, 52 A1
Tisvildeleje 49 D3, 50 A2/3
Tiszaalpár 129 D1
Tiszabecs 97 D3, 98 A3
Tiszabö 129 D1
Tiszaföldvár 129 D1
Tiszafüred 97 C3
Tiszakécske 129 D1
Tiszaroff 129 D1
Tiszasüly 129 D1
Tiszatenyö 129 D1
Tiszavárkony 129 D1
Tiszavasvári 97 C3
Titaguas 162 A/B3, 169 C1
Titane 147 C2
Titel 129 D3, 133 D1, 134 A1
Tithoréa 147 C1/2
Titisee-Neustadt 90 B3
Tito 120 A/B2
Titograd 137 D2
Titova Korenica 131 C1/2
Titova Mitrovica 138 B1
Titova Mitrovica 140 A3
Titova pećina 131 D2, 132 A2
Titov Drvar 131 C2
Titovo Užice 133 D2/3, 134 A2/3
Titovo Užice 140 A2
Titovo Velenje 96 A3
Titovo Velenje 127 C2
Titov Veles 139 C3
Titov Veles 140 A3
Titran 32 B1
Tittelsnes 42 A1
Titting 92 A1
Tittling 93 C2
Tittmoning 92 B3
Tittmoning-Wiesmühl 92 B3
Titu 141 C2
Titulcia 161 C3
Titz 79 D1
Titz-Rödingen 79 D1/2
Tiuccia 113 D3
Tiukurova 13 C3
Tiukuvaara 11 D3, 12 A2
Tiurajärvi 11 C3, 12 A2
Tiurana 155 C3
Tivat 137 C2
Tived 46 A2
Tivenys 163 C2
Tiverton 63 C2
Tivissa 163 C2
Tivoli 118 B2
Tivsjön 35 C2
Tizac-de-Courton 108 B1
Tizzano 113 D3
Tizzano Val Parma 114 A1
Tjåkkelestugan 14 B3, 29 D1
Tjälder 47 D2/3
Tjallingen 34 A2
Tjällmo 46 A/B2
Tjålme 10 A2
Tjåmotis 16 A1
Tjæreborg 48 A3, 52 A1
Tjärn 30 B2, 35 D1
Tjärnberg 16 A3
Tjärnkullen 29 D1
Tjärnmyrberget 29 D2, 30 A1
Tjarnö 44 B2
Tjärö 51 C2
Tjäruträsk 17 C2
Tjåurek 10 A3
Tjeldnes 9 C2
Tjeldstø 36 A3
Tjeldsund 9 C2
Tjele 48 B2
Tjelle 32 B2
Tjentište 133 B/C3
Tjernet 14 B3
Tjöck/Tiukka 20 A3
Tjolmen 14 B3
Tjolöholm 49 D1, 50 A1
Tjøme 43 D2, 44 B1
Tjøme 43 D2, 44 B1
Tjønnefoss 43 C2
Tjørholm 42 B2
Tjörnarp 50 B2/3
Tjøtta 14 A2/3
Tjourenstugan 29 C2, 34 A1
Tjuda 24 B3
Tjugum 36 B2
Tjuonajåkk 10 A3
Tjurkö 51 C2
Tkon 130 B2/3
Tlmače 95 D2
Tlumač 97 D2, 98 B3
Tlumačov 95 C1
Toano 114 B2, 116 A1
Toba 81 D1
Tobarra 168 B2
Tobed 163 C1
Tobelbad 127 C1
Tobermory 56 A1
Toberonochy 56 A1
Tobo 40 B2/3
Toboada 150 B2
Tobolić 130 B1
Tobru 38 A2
Toby 20 A/B2
Tocane-Saint-Apre 101 C3
Tocha 158 A3
Tocina 171 D1
Töcksfors 45 C1
Tocón 172 B2
Todal 32 B2

Todal 32 B2
Todi 117 C3
Todmorden 59 D1/2, 60 B2
Todolella 162 B2
Todorovo 131 C1
Todtmoos 90 B3
Todtnau 90 B3
Todtnau-Todtnauberg 90 B3
Toen 150 B2
Töffedal 45 C2
Tofta 47 D3
Toftaholm 50 B1
Tofte 43 D1, 44 B1
Toftlund 52 B1/2
Töging am Inn 92 B2
Tohmajärvi 23 D3
Tohmo 12 B3
Toholampi 21 C1
Toija 25 B/C3
Toijala 25 C2
Toikkala 26 B2
Toivakka 21 D3, 22 A3
Toivakka 18 B1
Toivala 22 B2
Toiviaiskylä 21 D1, 22 A/B1
Toivola 26 B1
Töjby 20 A2/3
Tojšići 133 B/C2
Tokačka 145 C/D1
Tokaj 97 C3
Tokod 95 D3
Tököl 95 D3, 129 C1
Tolbuhin 141 C/D2/3
Toledo 160 B3, 167 C1
Tolentino 115 D3, 117 D2
Tolfa 118 A1
Tolg 51 C1
Tolga 33 D3
Tolinas 151 D1
Tolja 18 B1
Tolkee 23 D1
Tolkkinen/Tolkis 25 D3, 26 A3
Tollarp 50 B3
Tollarp 72 A1/2
Tollered 45 C3
Tollesbury 65 C3
Tølløse 49 D3, 53 D1
Töllsjö 45 C3
Tolmačevo 74 B1
Tolmezzo 107 D2, 126 A2
Tolmin 126 B2
Tolmin 96 A3
Tolna 129 C2
Tolnanémedi 128 B2
Toločin 74 B3
Tolofón 146 B2
Tolón 147 C3
Tolón 148 B2
Tolonen 12 B1
Tolonen 12 A3
Tolosa 153 D1, 154 A1
Tolosa 165 C1
Tolosenmäki 23 D3
Tolox 172 A2
Tolpaniemi 19 D1
Tolsburgen 47 D3
Tolsby 45 C1
Tolskepp 46 B2
Tolstoe 98 B3
Tolva 19 C1
Tolva 155 C3
Tolvanniemi 19 C1
Tolve 120 B2
Tomar 164 B1
Tomaševac 129 D3, 133 D1, 134 A/B1
Tomaševo 137 D1
Tomašica 131 D1
Tomášikovo 95 C2/3
Tomašovka 97 D1, 98 A2
Tomašpol' 99 C3
Tomaszów Mazowiecki 97 C1
Tombeboeuf 109 C1
Tomelilla 50 B3
Tomelilla 72 A2
Tomelloso 167 D2, 168 A2
Tomiño 150 A3
Tommerdalen 28 A3, 33 C1
Tømmernes 9 C3
Tommerup 53 B/C1
Tommerup Stationsby 52 B1
Tømmervåg 32 B2
Tömörd 94 B3, 127 D1, 128 A1
Tompa 129 C2
Tomra 32 A2/3
Tomter 38 A3, 44 B1
Tôň 95 C3
Tona 156 A2/3
Tonara 123 D2
Tonbridge 65 C3, 77 B/C1
Tondela 158 B2
Tønder 52 A2
Tongeren 79 C2
Tongue 54 A/B1
Tönisvorst 79 D1
Tønjum 37 B/C2
Tonkopuro 13 C3
Tonnay-Boutonne 100 B2
Tonnay-Charente 100 B2
Tonneins 109 C2
Tonnerre 88 A3
Tönnersjö 50 A2
Tonnes 14 A/B2
Tönnet 39 C3
Tönning 52 A3
Tonquédec 84 B1/2
Tonsåsen 37 D3
Tønsberg 43 D2, 44 B1
Tonstad 42 B3
Toopanjoki 23 C2
Topares 168 B3, 173 D1, 174 A1
Topas 159 D1/2
Töpchin 70 A3
Töpen 82 A2
Topeno 25 C2
Toplanë 137 D2, 138 A2
Topleţ 135 C1
Topli Do 135 D3
Topliţa 141 C1
Topola 133 D2, 134 B2
Topolčani 138 B3, 143 C1
Topol'čany 95 C2
Topol'čany 96 B2
Topol'čianki 95 D2
Topolovac 127 D3
Topolovăţu Mare 140 A1
Topolovgrad 141 C3
Topolšica 127 C2
Toponár 128 B2
Toporów 71 C3
Töppeln 82 B2
Topsham 63 C2/3
Topusko 127 D3, 131 C1
Toques 150 B2
Torà de Riubregós 155 D3, 163 D1
Torajärvi 25 C2
Toral de los Guzmanes 151 D2/3, 152 A2/3
Toral de los Vados 151 C2
Torás 162 B3, 169 C1
Torasalo 23 C3
Torasjärvi 17 C1
Toras-Sieppi 11 C3, 12 A1
Toravaara 19 D2
Torbali 149 D2
Torbay 63 C3
Tórbole 106 B2/3
Törböle 17 C2
Torcello 107 D3
Torcy-le-Grand 76 B3
Torda 129 D3
Tordehumos 152 A3, 160 A1
Tordellego 162 A2
Tordera 156 B3
Tordesillas 152 A3, 160 A1
Tordesilos 162 A2
Tordillos 159 D2, 160 A2
Tordoia 150 A1
Tordómar 152 B3
Töre 17 C2
Töreboda 45 D2, 46 A2
Toreby 53 D2
Torekov 49 D2, 50 A2
Torekov 72 A1
Torella de'Lombardi 119 D3, 120 A2
Torella del Sánnio 119 D2
Torelló 156 A2
Toreno 151 C2
Torestorp 49 D1, 50 A1
Torfinnsbu 37 C2
Torfou 100 B1
Torgåsmon 39 C2
Torgau 82 B1
Torgau 96 A1
Torgelow 70 B1
Torhamn 51 C/D2
Torhamn 72 B1
Torhout 78 A1
Torhus 32 A2
Torigni-sur-Vire 85 D1, 86 A1
Torija 161 C2
Toril 162 A3
Torino 113 B/C1
Torino di Sangro Marina 119 D1
Toriseva 21 C3
Toritto 121 C2
Torittu 25 D1, 26 A1
Torjul 32 B2
Torla 155 C2
Torlengua 161 D1
Torljane 138 B1
Törmänen 12 B1
Törmänki 12 A3, 17 D1
Törmänmäki 19 C3
Tormantos 153 C2
Törmäsenvaara 19 D1
Törmäsjärvi 12 A3, 17 D2
Tórmini 106 B3
Tormua 19 D2
Tornada 164 A1
Tornadizos de Ávila 160 A/B2
Tornavacas 159 D3
Tørnby 38 B3, 45 C1
Torneå 17 D2, 18 A1
Tørnes 9 C3
Tornes 28 A2, 33 C1
Torneträsk 10 A2
Törnevik 46 B2/3
Torning 48 B2
Tornio (Torneå) 17 D2, 18 A1
Tornjoš 129 D3
Torno 105 D3, 106 A2/3
Tornos 162 A2
Toro 152 A3, 159 D1, 160 A1
Torö 47 C2
Törökkoppány 128 B2
Törökszentmiklós 129 D1
Törökszentmiklós 97 C3, 140 A1
Toróni 149 B/C1
Toróni 144 B2/3
Toropec 75 C2
Torp 51 D1
Torp 41 C3
Torp 41 C3
Torpa 50 B2
Torpa 46 A3
Torpa 45 D3
Torpa 37 D2/3
Torpè 123 D1/2
Torpo 37 C3
Torpoint 62 B3
Torppa 21 C1/2
Torpsbruk 51 C1
Torpshammar 35 C3
Torquemada 152 B3
Torraca 120 A3
Torralba 123 C2
Torralba 161 D3
Torralba de Aragón 154 B3
Torralba de los Sisones 162 A2
Torralba de Oropesa 160 A3, 166 B1
Torralba de Burgo 153 C3, 161 C1
Torralba de Calatrava 167 C2
Torralba del Río 153 D2
Torralbilla 163 C1
Torrão 164 B3
Torrböle 31 C2
Torre 150 A3, 158 A1
Torre Alháquime 172 A2
Torre a Ma 121 C2, 136 A/B3
Torre Annunziata 119 D3
Torrearévalo 153 D3
Torre Astura 118 B2
Torre Baja 163 C3
Torrebeleña 161 C2
Torre Beretti 113 C1
Torreblacos 153 C3, 161 C1
Torreblanca 163 C3
Torreblanca 172 B3
Torreblascopedro 167 D3, 173 C1
Torrebruna 119 D2
Torrecaballeros 160 B2
Torrecampo 166 B2/3
Torre Canne 121 C2
Torre-Cardela 173 C1
Torrechiva 162 B3
Torrecilla 161 D3
Torrecilla de la Orden 160 A1
Torrecilla del Rebollar 162 A/B2
Torrecilla del Monte 153 C3
Torrecilla de Alcañiz 163 B/C2
Torrecilla de Valmadrid 154 B3, 162 B1
Torrecilla de la Jara 160 A3, 166 B1
Torrecilla de los Ángeles 159 C3
Torrecilla en Cameros 153 D2/3
Torrecillas de la Tiesa 166 A1
Torrecuadrada de los Valles 161 D2
Torrecuadradilla 161 D2
Torre das Vargens 164 B1/2
Torre de Arcas 163 C2
Torre de Don Miguel 159 C3
Torre de Dona Chama 151 C3, 159 C1
Torre de Embesora 163 C3
Torre de Endoménech 163 C3
Torre de Hércules 150 A/B1
Torre de Juan Abad 167 D2, 168 A2
Torre de la Higuera 171 C2
Torre de las Arcas 162 B2
Torre del Bierzo 151 D2
Torre del Campo 167 C3, 173 B/C1
Torre del Compte 163 C2
Torre del Greco 119 D3
Torre del Lago Puccini 114 A2, 116 A1
Torre del Mar 172 B2
Torredembarra 163 C1/2
Torre de Miguel Sesmero 165 D2
Torre de Moncorvo 159 C1/2
Torre de'Pàsseri 119 C1
Torre di Bari 123 D2
Torredonjimeno 167 C3, 173 B/C1
Torrefarrera 155 C3, 163 C1
Torregáveta 119 C3
Torregrossa 155 C/D3, 163 C/D1
Torrehermosa 161 D1
Torre Horadada 169 C3, 174 B1
Torreiglesias 160 B2
Torreira 158 A2
Torrejoncillo 159 C3, 165 D1
Torrejoncillo del Rey 161 D3
Torrejón del Rey 161 C2
Torrejón de la Calzada 160 B3
Torrejón de Ardoz 161 C2
Torrejón el Rubio 159 D3, 165 D1, 166 A1
Torrelaguna 161 C2
Torrelameu 155 C3, 163 C1
Torrelapaja 153 D3, 154 A3, 161 D1, 162 A1
Torre la Ribera 155 C2
Torrelavega 152 B1
Torrellas 154 A3
Torrelobatón 152 A3, 160 A1
Torrelodones 160 B2
Torre los Negros 162 A/B2
Torremaggiore 120 A1
Torremanzanas 169 D2
Torremayor 165 D2
Torremegía 165 D2
Torre Melissa 122 B2
Torremezzo di Falconara 122 A2
Torre Mileto 120 A1
Torremocha 163 C2
Torremocha 165 D1, 166 A1
Torremocha del Pinar 161 D2
Torremolinos 172 B2/3
Torremontalbo 153 D2
Torremormojón 152 A/B3
Torrenieri 115 C3, 116 B2
Torrenostra 163 C3
Torrente 169 D1
Torrente de Cinca 155 C3, 163 C1
Torrenueva 167 D2
Torrenueva 173 C2
Torreorgaz 165 D1, 166 A1
Torre Orsáia 120 A3
Torre-Pacheco 174 B1
Torre Pedrera 115 C/D2, 117 C1
Torre Péllice 112 B1
Torre Pelosa 123 C1
Torreperogil 167 D3, 173 C1
Torrequebradilla 167 C/D3, 173 C1
Torrequemada 165 D1, 166 A1
Torres 167 D3, 173 C1
Torresandino 152 B3, 160 B1
Torre Santa Caterina 123 D3
Torre Santa Sabina 121 D2
Torre Santa Susanna 121 D3
Torres Cabrera 166 B3, 172 B1
Torrescárcela 160 B1
Torres de Albarracín 162 A2
Torres de Albánchez 168 A3
Torres de Berellén 154 B3, 162 A/B1
Torres de la Alameda 161 C2
Torres del Obispo 155 C3
Torres del Río 153 D2
Torres de Segre 155 C3, 163 C1
Torres Novas 164 B1
Torres Vedras 164 A2
Torretta 124 B1/2
Torretta 114 B1
Torretta Granítola 124 A2
Torrevelilla 163 B/C2
Torrevieja 169 C3, 174 B1
Torre Vignola 123 D1
Torrflonäs 35 B/C3
Torricella 121 C3
Torricella Peligna 119 C/D2
Torrico 160 A3, 166 B1
Torri del Benaco 106 B3
Torri di Quartesolo 107 C3
Torríglia 113 D1/2
Torrijas 162 B3
Torrijo de la Cañada 154 A3, 161 D1, 162 A1
Torrijo del Campo 163 C2
Torrijos 160 B3
Tørring 48 B3, 52 B1
Torrita 117 D3, 118 B1
Torrita di Siena 115 C3, 116 B2
Torrita Tiberina 117 C3, 118 B1
Torrivaara 17 C1
Torro 25 C2
Torroella de Fluvià 156 B2
Torroella de Montgrí 156 B2
Torrox 172 B2
Torrubia 161 D2, 162 A2
Torrubia de Soria 153 D3, 161 D1
Torrubia del Campo 161 C3, 167 D1, 168 A1
Torrubio del Castillo 161 D3, 168 B1
Torrvål 39 D2
Torsåker 30 B3, 35 D2
Torsåker 40 A2
Torsansalo 27 C/D1

Torsås 51 D2
Torsbo 45 D3
Torsborg 34 A2
Torsbua 32 B3, 37 C1
Torsby 39 C3
Torsby 39 B/C3
Torsenget 33 C2
Torsfjärden 29 D2
Torshälla 46 B1
Tórshavn 55 C1
Torsholma 24 A3, 41 D2
Torsken 9 C1
Torslanda 45 C3
Torsminde 48 A2
Torsmo 39 D1
Torsnes 44 B1
Torsö 45 D2
Torstrup 48 A3, 52 A1
Torsvåg 4 A2
Torsvid 45 D2, 46 A1/2
Törtel 129 D1
Tortellá 156 B2
Torteval 63 D3
Tortinmäki 24 B2
Tórtola 161 D3, 168 B1
Tórtola de Henares 161 C2
Tórtoles 160 A2
Tortolì 123 D2
Tortona 113 D1
Tórtora 120 B3, 122 A1
Tortorella 120 A3
Tortoreto Lido 117 D3
Tortorici 125 C2
Tortosa 163 C2
Tortosendo 158 B3
Tortuera 162 A2
Tortuna 40 A3, 47 B/C1
Toruń 73 B/C3
Torup 72 A1
Torup 50 A1
Torup 50 A/B3
Torup Strand 48 B1
Tor Vaiánica 118 B2
Torvastad 42 A2
Torvik 36 A1
Torvikbukt 32 B2
Tørvikbygd 36 B3
Torvinen 12 B2
Torviscón 173 C2
Torvoila 25 C1/2
Torvund 36 A2
Toržok 75 D2
Torzym 71 C3
Tosantos 153 C2
Tosas 156 A2
Tosbotn 14 A3, 29 C1
Toscana Nueva 168 A/B3, 173 D1
Toscolano-Maderno 106 B3
Tosen 14 A3, 29 C1
Tosno 75 C1
Tosos 162 A/B1
Tossa de Mar 156 B3
Tossåsen 34 A2
Tossåsen 34 B2
Tossavanlahti 21 D2, 22 A2
Tösse 45 C2
Tosse 108 B2/3
Tossignano 115 C2, 116 B1
Tost 155 C2
Tõstamaa 74 A1
Tostared 49 D1, 50 A1
Tostedt 68 B1
Tószeg 129 D1
Totalán 172 B2
Totana 169 B/C3, 174 A/B1
Totanés 160 B3, 167 C1
Tôtes 77 C3
Tótkomlós 129 D2
Tótkomlós 97 C3, 140 A1
Totland 76 A1/2
Totland 36 A1
Tøtlandsvik 42 A/B2
Totnes 63 C3
Totra 40 A/B2
Tøttdal 28 B2
Tottenham 65 C3
Tottijärvi 24 B1
Totton 76 A1
Tótvázsony 128 B1
Touça 159 B/C2
Toucy 88 A3
Touët-sur-Var 112 B2
Touffou 101 C1/2
Toul 89 C1/2
Toulon 111 D3, 112 A3
Toulon-sur-Allier 102 B2
Toulon-sur-Arroux 103 C1
Toulouse 109 D3, 155 D1
Tourcoing 78 A2
Tour de la Parata 113 D3
Tour Laffon 108 B3, 155 C1/2
Tourlaville 76 A3
Tournai 78 A/B2
Tournan-en-Bric 87 D1
Tournay 109 C3, 155 C1
Tournevite 101 C3
Tournoël 102 B2
Tournon 103 D3, 111 C1
Tournon-d'Agenais 109 C2
Tournon-Saint-Martin 101 D1
Tournus 103 D1/2
Touro 158 B2
Touro 150 B2
Tourouvre 86 B2
Tours 86 B3
Tours de Merle 102 A3, 109 D1, 110 A1
Tourtoirac 101 D3
Tourula 24 B2
Tourves 111 D3, 112 A3
Toury 87 C2
Tous 169 C2
Touvedo 150 A/B3, 158 A1
Touvois 100 A1
Toužim 82 B3
Tovačov 95 C1
Tovariševo 129 C3
Tovarnik 133 C1
Tovdal 43 C2
Tøvik 32 A2
Tovik 9 C2
Tövsala 24 A2
Towcester 64 B2
Tow Law 57 D3, 61 C1
Town Yetholm 57 D2
Toxótai 145 C1
Töyrenperä 21 D2, 22 A2
Töysä 21 C3
Töysänperä 21 D3, 22 A3
Tózar 173 C2
Tőzeggyźrmajor 94 B3
Trabada 151 C1
Trabanca 159 C1
Trabazos 151 C3, 159 C1
Traben-Trarbach 80 A3
Trabia 124 B2
Trabotivište 139 D2
Trachiá 147 C3
Tracy-le-Val 78 A3
Tradate 105 D3
Trädet 45 D3
Trafoi 106 B2
Tragacete 161 D2/3, 162 A2/3
Trahiá 147 C3
Traid 162 A2
Traiguera 163 C2
Traînel 88 A2
Traiskirchen 94 B3
Traismauer 94 A2
Traitsching 92 B1
Trakai 73 D2, 74 A3
Trakiszki 73 D2
Trakošćan 127 D2
Tralee 55 C3
Trælleborg 53 C1
Trælnes 14 A3
Tramacastiel 163 C3
Tramaríglio 123 C2
Tramayes 103 C/D2
Tramelan 89 D3, 104 B1
Tramnitz 69 D2
Tramonti di Sopra 107 D2, 126 A2
Tramonti di Sotto 107 D2, 126 A2
Tramore 55 D3
Tramútola 120 B3
Trân 139 C/D1
Trân 140 B3
Træna 14 A2
Tranås 46 A3
Tranby 43 D1
Trancoso 158 B2
Trandal 32 A3, 36 B1
Tranderup 53 C2
Tranebjerg 49 C3, 53 C1
Tranekær Slot 53 C2
Tranemo 50 B1
Tranemo 72 A1
Tranent 57 C2
Tranevåg 42 B3
Trangdalen 5 C2
Trångmon 29 D1/2
Trångsviken 29 C/D3, 34 B2
Tranhult 50 B1
Trani 120 B2, 136 A3
Tranøy 9 D1
Tranøy 9 C2
Trans 85 D2
Transtrand 39 C2
Tranum 48 B1
Tranvik 41 D3
Trapaga 153 C1
Trápani 124 A2
Trápani Fulgatore 124 A2
Trápani Marausa 124 A2
Trápani Rilievo 124 A2
Trappes 87 C1
Traryd 50 B2
Traryd 72 A1
Trasacco 119 C2
Träskvik 20 A3
Träslövsläge 49 D1, 50 A1
Trasmiras 150 B3
Trasobares 154 A3, 162 A1
Traspinedo 152 B3, 160 B1
Trassem 79 D3
Tråstølen 37 B/C3
Tratalías 123 C3
Traun 93 D2
Traunreut 92 B3
Traunstein 92 B3
Tråvad 45 C/D2/3
Travagliato 106 B3
Traversella 105 C3
Traversétolo 114 A1
Travnik 132 A2
Travnik 127 B/C3
Trawsfynydd 59 C3, 60 A3
Trazegnies 78 B2
Trazo 150 A1/2
Trbovlje 127 C2
Trbovlje 96 A3
Trbuk 132 B1/2
Trearddur Bay 58 B2
Trébago 153 D3
Trebaséleghe 107 C/D3
Trebatice 95 C2
Trebatsch 70 B3
Trebbin 70 A3
Trebel 69 C2
Třebenice 83 C2
Trèbes 110 A3, 156 A/B1
Trébeurden 84 B1
Třebíč 94 A1
Třebíč 96 A2
Trebinje 137 C1
Trebisacce 120 B3, 122 B1
Trebnje 127 C2/3
Třeboň 93 D1
Třeboň 83 C2/3
Třeboň 96 A2
Tréboul 84 A2
Trebsen 82 B1
Trebujena 171 D2
Trebur-Geinsheim 80 B3
Trecastagni 125 D2
Trecastle 63 C1
Trecate 105 D3
Trecenta 115 B/C1
Tredegar 63 C1
Tredózio 115 C2, 116 B1
Treffurt 81 D1
Trefnant 59 C2, 60 A3
Tregaron 59 C3, 63 C1
Trégastel-Plage 84 B1
Tregde 42 B3
Tregnano 107 C3
Tregony 62 B3
Tréguier 84 B1
Trégunc 84 B2/3
Trehörna 46 A2/3
Trehörningen 31 C2
Trehörningsjö 31 C2
Tréia 115 D3, 117 D2
Trei Ape 135 C1
Treib 105 D1
Treignac 102 A3
Treilles 110 A3, 156 B1
Treis 80 A2/3
Trekanten 51 D2
Trekilen 29 D3, 34 B1
Trekljano 139 C/D1/2
Trekljano 139 C/D1/2
Trelan 85 D3
Trélazé 86 A3
Trelech 62 B1
Trélechamp 104 B2
Trelleborg 50 A/B3
Trelleborg 72 A2
Trélon 78 B3
Tremelkovo 139 D1/2
Tremes 164 A1
Tremezzo 105 D2, 106 A2
Tremmen 69 D2, 70 A2
Trémorel 85 C2
Třemošná 83 C3
Tremp 155 D2/3
Trenčianska Turná 95 C1/2
Trenčianska Teplá 95 C1
Trenčianske Teplice 95 C1
Trenčín 95 C1
Trenčín 96 B2
Trendelburg 81 C1
Trendelburg-Deisel 81 C1
Trengereid 36 A3
Trenta 126 B2
Trento 107 C2
Treon 86 A/B1/2
Trepča 137 D1, 138 A1
Trepča 138 B1
Trepča 127 D3
Trepido 122 A2
Treponti 106 B3
Treppeln 70 B3
Trepuzzi 121 D3
Treriksröset 10 A/B1
Trescore Balneário 106 A3
Tresenda 106 B2
Tresfjord 32 A3
Tresjuncos 161 C/D3, 168 A1
Tresnurághes 123 C2
Trespaderne 153 C2
Tresparrett Posts 62 B2/3
Třešť 94 A1
Trets 111 D3
Tretten 37 D2, 38 A1
Tretten 4 B2/3
Treuchtlingen 91 D1, 92 A1
Treuen 82 B2
Treuenbrietzen 70 A3
Treuenbrietzen 72 A3, 96 A1
Treungen 43 C2
Trevélez 173 C2
Trevenzuolo 106 B3
Trèves 110 B2
Trevi 117 C3
Treviana 153 C2
Trévières 76 A/B3, 85 D1, 86 A1
Trevíglio 106 A3
Trevignano Romano 118 A/B1
Trevi nel Lázio 119 B/C2
Treviño 153 D2
Treviso 107 D3
Treviso Bresciano 106 B3
Trevol 102 B1/2
Trévoux 103 D2
Trézelles 103 B/C2
Trezzano san Naviglio 105 D3, 106 A3
Trezzo sull'Adda 106 A3
Trgovište 139 C2
Trhové Mýto 95 C3
Trhové Sviny 93 D1/2
Trhový Štěpánov 83 D3
Triacastela 151 C2
Triaize 101 C2
Triana 116 B3
Triánda 149 D3
Triaucourt-en-Argonne 88 B1
Tribaldos 161 C3
Tribanj Krušćica 130 B2
Tribano 107 C3
Triberg 90 B2
Tricárico 120 B2
Tricase 121 D3
Tricase Porto 121 D3
Tricerro 105 C3, 113 C1
Tricésimo 126 A2
Trichiana 107 C/D2
Tricot 78 A3
Triebel 82 B2
Trieben 93 D3
Trieben 96 A3
Triebes 82 B2
Triefenstein-Lengfurt 81 C3
Triel-sur-Seine 87 C1
Triengen [Triengen-Winikon] 105 C1
Trier 79 D3, 80 A3
Trier-Ehrang 79 D3, 80 A3
Trierweiler 79 D3
Trieste 126 B3
Trie-sur-Baïse 109 C3, 155 C1
Triftern 93 B/C2
Trigachos 164 B3
Triggiano 121 C2
Triglitz 69 D1/2
Trígonon 143 B/C1/2
Trigueros 171 C1/2
Trigueros del Valle 152 B3, 160 A/B1
Trijebine 133 D3, 134 A3, 138 A1
Trijueque 161 C2
Tríkala 147 C2
Tríkala 143 C3
Tríkala 148 B1
Trikérion 147 C1
Trilj 131 D3
Trillevallen 29 C3, 34 A2
Trillo 161 D2
Trindade 159 C1
Trindade 164 B3, 170 B1
Tring 64 B3
Trinità 113 C2
Trinità d'Agultu e Vignola 123 C1
Trinitápoli 120 B1/2
Trinité 113 D3
Trino 105 C3, 113 C1
Triollo 152 B2
Triora 113 C2
Trípi 147 B/C3
Trípolis 147 B/C3
Trípolis 148 B2
Triponzo 117 C3
Tripótama 146 B2
Tripótamon 146 B1
Tripótamos 144 B2
Tripoteau 108 B1
Trippstadt 90 A/B1
Triptis 82 A2
Triste 154 B2
Trittau 68 B1
Trittenheim 80 A3
Trivento 119 D2
Trivero 105 C3
Trivigno 120 B2
Trizac 102 A/B3
Trjavna 141 C3
Trnava 96 B2
Trnava 95 C2
Trnjani 132 B1
Trnovec nad Váhom 95 C2
Trnovo 132 B3
Trnovo 126 A/B2
Troarn 76 B3, 86 A1
Trobajo del Camino 151 D2, 152 A2
Tröbitz 83 C1
Trochtelfingen 91 C2
Trödje 40 B2
Troense 53 C2
Trofa 158 A1
Trofarello 113 C1
Trofors 14 B3
Trøgaset 37 D3
Trogen 82 A/B2
Trogen 91 C3
Trogir 131 C3
Trøgstad 38 A3, 44 B1
Trøgstad (Skjønhaug) 38 A3, 44 B1
Tróia 120 A1
Tróia 164 A2/3
Troia 149 C1
Troina 125 C2
Troisdorf 80 A2
Troisdorf-Sieglar 80 A2
Trois-Ponts 79 D2
Troissereux 77 D3
Troisvierges 79 D3
Trois-Villes 108 A3, 154 B1
Troizen 147 D3
Trojan 140 B3
Trojane 96 A3
Trojane 127 C2

Trojanova Tabla 135 C2
Troldhede 48 A3
Troldkirken 48 B1/2
Trolla 28 A3, 33 C1
Trollberget 16 A2
Trolleholm 50 A/B3
Trolle-Ljungby 50 B2/3
Trollerud 14 B3
Trollhättan 45 C2/3
Trollheimshytta 33 B/C2
Trollholmsundet 5 D2, 6 A2
Trollkirke 32 A2
Trollsved 35 D3
Tromello 105 D3, 113 D1
Tromsdalen 4 A3
Tromsnes 37 D2, 38 A1
Tromsø 4 A3
Tromvik 4 A2
Troncedo 155 C2
Tronchón 162 B2
Tronco 151 C3, 158 B1
Trondheim 28 A3, 33 C1
Trondjord 4 A2
Trones 29 C1
Tronhus 37 C/D2
Trönninge 50 A2
Tröno 40 A1
Tronoša 133 C2
Tronsjø 33 C/D3
Tronstad 43 D1
Trontveit 43 C2
Tronvik 28 A3, 33 C1
Tronvik 28 A/B3, 33 C1
Tronzano Vercellese 105 C3
Troo 86 B3
Troon 56 B2
Tropea 122 A2
Trópea 146 B3
Tropeoúchos 143 C1/2
Tropojë 138 A2
Trosa 47 C2
Trosky 83 D2
Trošmarija 127 C3, 130 B1
Trossingen 90 B2/3
Tröstau 82 A/B3
Trostberg 92 B3
Trosterud 38 B3, 45 C1
Trostjanec 99 C3
Trötvik 38 B3
Troubítsion 146 B3
Trou de Bozouls 110 A1/2
Trouville-sur-Mer 76 B3, 86 B1
Troviscal 158 B3, 164 B1
Trowbridge 63 D2, 64 A3
Troyes 88 A/B2
Trpanj 136 B1
Trpezi 138 A1
Trpinja 129 C3
Trsat 126 B3, 130 A/B1
Tršice 95 C1
Trstena 139 C1
Trstená 97 C2
Trstenik 136 B1
Trstenik 138 B1
Trstenik 134 B3
Trsteno 137 B/C1
Trstice 95 C3
Trstín 95 C2
Trubčevsk 99 D1
Trubia 151 D1
Trubjela 137 C1
Trubschachen 105 C1
Truchas 151 C/D2/3
Truébano 151 D2
Trujillanos 165 D2, 166 A2
Trujillo 166 A1
Trun 105 D1
Trun 86 A/B1
Truro 62 B3
Trușești 98 B3
Trustrup 49 C2
Trutnov 96 A/B1
Truvbacken 29 C3, 34 B1/2
Trvaala 21 D3, 22 A3
Tryggelev 53 C2
Trypití 144 B2
Tryserum 46 B3
Trysil (Innbygda) 38 B1
Tržac 131 C1
Trzcianka 71 D2
Trzcianka 72 B3
Trzciel 71 C2/3
Trzcińsko Zdrój 70 B2
Trzebicz 71 C2
Trzebiechów 71 C3
Trzebiel 70 B3, 83 D1
Trzebież 70 B1
Trzebnica 96 B1
Tržec 127 D2
Trzemeszno Lubuskie 71 C2
Tržič 126 B2
Tržič 96 A3
Trzin 126 B2
Tsa, Cabane de la 105 C2
Tsamandás 142 B3
Tsangaráda 144 A3
Tsangaráda 148 B1
Tsaritsáni 143 D3
Tsarkasiános 146 A2
Tschernitz 83 D1
Tševetjävri 7 C2/3
Tsielekjåkkstugan 15 D1
Tsotílion 143 C2
Tsoukalochóri 143 C2
Tua 28 B2, 33 D1
Tubba 37 C3
Tubbergen 67 C2
Tubilla del Agua 153 B/C2
Tübingen 91 C2
Tübingen-Unterjesingen 91 C2
Tubize 78 B2
Tubre/Taufers 106 B1/2
Tučapy 93 D1
Tučepi 131 D3, 132 A3, 136 B1
Tuchan 156 B1
Tucheim 69 D3
Tüchen 69 D2
Tuchola 72 B3
Tuckur 20 B2
Tuczno 71 C/D1/2
Tuddal 43 C1
Tuddal Høyjellshotell 43 C1
Tudela 154 A3
Tudela de Duero 152 B3, 160 B1
Tudelilla 153 D2
Tudweiliog 58 B3
Tuéjar 162 A/B3, 169 C1
Tuenno 107 B/C2
Tufjord 5 C1, 6 A1
Tufsingdalen 33 D3
Tuft 43 D1, 44 A/B1
Tufter 5 C1
Tuhaň 83 D2
Tuhkakylä 23 B/C1
Tui 150 A3
Tuiskula 20 B3
Tuixén 155 D2, 156 A2
Tuk 131 C2
Tukums 73 D1
Tula 123 C/D1
Tulare 138 B1
Tulce 71 D2/3
Tulcea 141 D2
Tul'čin 99 C3
Tulette 111 C2
Tullamore 55 D2/3
Tulle 102 A3
Tullebølle 53 C2
Tulleråsen 29 D3, 34 B1
Tüllgarn 47 C1/2
Tullins 103 D3, 104 A3
Tulln 94 A2
Tulln 96 A/B2
Tulppio 13 C2
Tumba 47 C1
Tumbo 46 B1
Tumleberg 45 C3
Tun 45 C2
Tuna 46 B3
Tunaberg 47 C2
Tunadal 35 D3
Tuna Hästberg 39 D2/3
Tunåsen 30 A2/3, 35 C1
Tune 49 D3, 50 A3, 53 D1
Tune 44 B1
Túnel de Lizarraga 153 D2, 154 A2
Tunes 158 B1
Tunes 170 A2
Tungaseter 32 B3, 37 C1
Tungastølen 36 B2
Tungenes 42 A2
Tunkkari 21 C1/2
Tunnhovd 37 C3
Tunnila 27 C1
Tunnsjø kapell 29 C1
Tunnsjø-Røyrvik 29 C1
Tunø 49 C3
Tunsjön 30 B3, 35 D2
Tunstall 59 D2, 60 B3, 64 A1
Tuntenhausen 92 B3
Tuntenhausen-Hohentann 92 A/B3
Tuohikotti 26 B2
Tuohikylä 13 C3
Tuohittu 24 B3
Tuomimäki 13 C3
Tuomioja 18 A3
Tuomiperä 21 D1, 22 A1
Tuorila 24 A1
Tuorlahti 24 A2, 41 D2
Tuoro sul Trasimeno 115 C3, 117 C2
Tuovilanlahti 22 B2
Tuplice 70 B3, 83 D1
Tupos 18 A/B2
Tuppuravaara 23 D1
Tuppurinmäki 22 B3
Turalići 133 C2
Tuřany 94 B1
Turany 95 C2/3
Turbe 132 A2
Turbenthal 90 B3
Turbigo 105 D3
Turburea 135 D1/2
Turčianske Teplice 95 D1/2
Turcifal 164 A2
Turda 97 D3, 140 B1
Turégano 160 B1/2
Turek 72 B3, 96 B1
Turenki 25 C2
Turenne 101 D3, 109 D1
Turgutlu 149 D2
Turhala 22 B1
Turi 121 C2
Türi 74 A1
Turija 129 D3
Turija 135 B/C2
Turís 169 C1
Turjak 127 B/C2/3
Türje 128 A1
Turka 97 D2, 98 A3
Túrkeve 129 D1
Turkhauta 25 C2, 26 A2
Turku/Åbo 24 B2/3
Turleque 167 D1
Turnau 94 A3
Turnberry 56 B2
Turnditch 61 C3, 64 A1
Turnhout 79 C1
Türnitz 94 A3
Turnov 83 D2
Turnov 96 A1
Turnu Măgurele 140 B2
Turón 173 C/D2
Turrach 126 B1
Turre 174 A2
Turri 123 C/D2/3
Turriers 112 A2
Turrillas 173 D2, 174 A2
Tursa 24 B2
Tursi 120 B3
Turtagrø 37 C2
Turtel 139 C2/3
Turtola 12 A3, 17 D1
Turzovka 95 D1
Tusa 125 C2
Tusby 25 D2/3, 26 A2/3
Tuscánia 116 B3, 118 A1
Tušilović 127 C3, 131 C1
Tussenhausen 91 D2/3
Tustervatn 14 B2/3
Tutaryd 50 B1/2
Tutin 138 A1
Tutin 140 A3
Tutjunniemi 23 C/D3
Tutrakan 141 C2
Tuttlingen 90 B3
Tuttlingen-Möhringen 90 B3
Tutzing 92 A3
Tuuhonen 21 C3
Tuukkala 26 B1
Tuulenkylä 20 B3
Tuulimäki 19 C3
Tuulos 25 C2, 26 A2
Tuunajärvi 24 B1
Tuupovaara 23 D3
Tuurala 20 B2
Tuusjärvi 23 C2
Tuuski 26 B3
Tuusmäki 23 B/C3
Tuusniemi 23 C2
Tuusula (Tusby) 25 D2/3, 26 A2/3
Tuv 37 C3
Tuv 14 B1
Tuvås 20 A3
Tuve 45 C3
Tuven 14 B2/3
Tuvträsk 31 B/C1
Tuxford 61 C3, 64 B1
Tuzi 137 D2
Tuzla 132 B2
Tuzla 149 C1
Tuzly 141 D1
Tvååker 49 D1, 50 A1
Tvaråbäck 31 C2
Tvärålund 31 C2
Tväråmark 20 A1, 31 D2
Tväråträsk 15 D3
Tvårdica 141 C3
Tvärminne 24 B3
Tved 49 C2/3
Tvedestrand 43 C3
Tveit 43 C3
Tveit 36 B3
Tveita 36 A3
Tverrå 14 B2
Tverråmo 15 C1
Tverrelvdalen 5 C2
Tverrvik 14 B1
Tversted 44 A3, 48 B1
Tving 51 C2
Tvrdošovce 95 C2/3
Tweede Exloërmond 67 C2
Tweedmouth 57 D2
Twello 67 C3
Tweng 126 A/B1
Twimberg 127 C1
Twimberg 96 A3
Twist 67 C2
Twistetal-Berndorf 81 C1
Twistringen 68 A2
Twistringen-Heiligenloh 68 A2
Twist-Schöninghsdorf 67 C2
Two Bridges 63 C3
Tychy 96 B2
Tydal 33 D2
Tyfjord 7 C1
Tyfors 39 C3
Tygelsjö 50 A3
Tyin 37 C2
Tyinholmen 37 C2
Tykarp 50 B2
Tykölä 25 C1/2
Tyldum 28 B1/2
Tylldal 33 C/D3
Tylösand 49 D2, 50 A2
Tylösand 72 A1
Tylstrup 48 B1
Týn 93 D1
Tyndaris 125 D1/2
Tynderö 35 D3
Tyndrum 56 B1
Tyndrum 54 A2, 55 D1
Tynemouth 54 B3
Tynemouth 57 D3, 61 C1
Tyngsjö kapell 39 C3
Tynnelsö 47 C1
Tynnerås 30 A3, 35 C1
Tynset 33 C/D3
Typpö 18 A3, 21 C1
Typpyrä 12 A3, 17 D1
Tyrämäki 19 C2
Tyrävaara 19 C2
Tyrella 58 A1
Tyresö 47 D1
Tyringe 50 B2
Tyristrand 43 D1
Tyrjänsaari 23 D2
Tyrnävä 18 B3
Tyrväntö 25 C2
Tyry 25 D1, 26 A1
Tysres 9 C2
Tysse 36 A3
Tyssebotn 36 A3
Tyssedal 42 B1
Tystberga 47 C2
Tysvær 42 A2
Tyttbo 40 A3
Tyvelä 19 C1
Tywyn 59 C3
Tyykiluoto 18 A2
Tyynismaa 21 B/C2
Tzummarum 66 B1

U

Ub 133 D2, 134 A2
Übach-Palenberg 79 D2
Ubbergen 66 B3
Ubeda 167 D3, 173 C1
Übelbach-Markt 127 C1
Überlingen 91 C3
Ubide 153 D1/2
Ubli 137 C1
Ubli 137 D2
Ubli 136 A1
Ubli 137 D2
Ubrique 172 A2
Ubstadt-Weiher 90 B1
Uceda 161 C2
Ucero 153 C3, 161 C1
Uchacq 108 B2
Uchaud 111 C2
Uchte 68 A2
Uchte-Woltringhausen 68 A2
Uchtspringe 69 C/D2
Uckange 89 C1
Uckfield 76 B1
Uckro 70 A3
Ucria 125 C2
Udalla 153 C1
Udbina 131 C2
Udby 53 D2
Udby 49 B/C2
Uddebo 50 B1
Uddeholm 39 C3
Uddevalla 45 C2
Uden 66 B3, 79 C1
Uder 81 D1
Udestedt 82 A1
Údine 126 A2
Údine Paparotti 126 A2
Udovo 139 C3, 143 D1
Udvar 129 B/C3
Uebigau 83 C1
Ueckermünde 70 B1
Ueckermünde 72 A2/3
Uedem 67 C3, 79 D1
Uehlfeld 81 D3
Uelsen 67 C2
Uelzen 69 C2
Uelzen-Holdenstedt 69 C2
Uetendorf 105 C1
Uetersen 52 B3, 68 B1
Uettingen 81 C3
Uetze 68 B2
Uetze-Dollbergen 68 B2/3
Uetze-Hänigsen 68 B2
Uffenheim 81 D3, 91 D1
Uffenheim-Langensteinach 81 D3, 91 D1
Ugāle 73 C1
Ugao 138 A1
Ugao 153 C1
Ugento 121 D3
Ugerløse 49 C/D3, 53 D1
Uggiano la Chiesa 121 D3
Ugglarp 49 D2, 50 A1/2
Uggleheden 38 B2
Ugílar 173 C/D2
Ugine 104 A/B3
Ugljan 130 B2
Ugljane 131 D3
Ugljarevo 134 B3
Ugljevik 133 C1/2
Ugra 75 D3
Ugulvik 36 B2
Uharte 154 A2
Uherské Hradiště 95 C1
Uherské Hradiště 96 B2
Uherský Brod 96 B2
Uherský Brod 95 C1
Uherský Ostroh 95 C1
Uhingen 91 C2
Ühlingen-Birkendorf 90 B3
Uhlířské Janovice 83 D3
Uhlstädt 82 A2
Uhříněves 83 D3
Uhrovec 95 C/D2
Uhyst 83 D1
Uig 54 A2
Uimaharju 23 D2
Uimaniemi 12 A/B2
Uimila 25 D2, 26 B2
Uithoorn 66 A/B3
Uithuizen 67 C1
Ujhartyán 129 C1
Uji i ftohët 142 A2

Újpetre 128 B2/3
Ujście 71 D2
Ujsoły 95 D1
Újszász 129 D1
Ujué 154 A2
Ukkola 23 D2
Ukmergė 73 D2, 74 A3
Ukna 46 B3
Ukonvaara 23 C2
Ula 43 D2, 44 A1/2
Uland 35 D2
Ul'anka 95 D2
Ulbjerg 48 B2
Ulceby 61 D2
Ulcinj 137 D2
Uldum 48 B3, 52 B1
Ulea 169 D3
Uleåborg 18 A/B2
Ulebergshamn 44 B2
Ulefoss 43 D2, 44 A1
Uleila del Campo 173 D2, 174 A2
Ulëzë 138 A3
Ulfborg 48 A2
Úlice 83 C3
Uljanik 128 A3
Uljanovka 99 C3
Ul'janovo 75 D3
Uljma 140 A2
Uljma 134 B1
Ulkuvaara 11 C3, 12 A1/2
Ullånger 30 B3, 35 D2
Ullapool 54 A2
Ullared 72 A1
Ullared 49 D1, 50 A1
Ullatti 17 C1
Ullava 21 C1
Ullbergsträsk 16 A3
Ulldecona 163 C2
Ulldemolins 163 C/D1
Ullensvang 36 B3
Ulleren 38 A/B3
Ullerslev 53 C1
Ullerup 52 B2
Ullervad 45 D2
Üllés 129 D2
Ullfors 40 B2/3
Ullisjaur 15 C3
Üllő 95 D3, 129 C1
Ullsfjord 4 A3
Ulm 91 C/D2
Ulme 164 B1
Ulmen 80 A2/3
Ulmtal 80 B2
Ulog 132 B3
Uløybukt 4 B2
Ulricehamn 45 D3
Ulricehamn 72 A1
Ulrichen 105 C2
Ulrichsberg 93 C2
Ulrichstein 81 C2
Ulrika 46 B3
Ulriksfors 29 D2/3, 30 A2, 35 C1
Ulsberg 33 C2
Ulsnes 37 D2/3
Ulsta 54 A1
Ulsted 49 B/C1
Ulsteinvik 36 A1
Ulstrup 48 B2
Ultrasniemi 27 D1
Ulvan 32 B1
Ulvangen 14 A2
Ulvåsa 46 A2
Ulverston 59 C1, 60 B2
Ulvestad 36 B2
Ulvik 36 B3
Ulvila (Ulvsby) 24 A1
Ulvinsalon Luonnonpuisto 23 D1
Ulvkälla (Sveg) 34 B3
Ulvoberg 30 B1
Ulvöhamn 31 B/C3
Ulvsås 29 D3, 34 B1
Ulvsby 24 A1
Ulvshyttan 39 D2/3
Ulvsjön 35 C3
Ulvsvåg 9 C2
Umag 126 A3
Uman' 99 C3
Umasjö 15 C2
Umbértide 115 C3, 117 C2
Umbriático 122 B1/2
Umbukta fjellstue 14 B2
Umčari 134 B2
Umeå 31 C/D2
Ume-Ersmark 20 A1, 31 D2
Umetić 127 D3, 131 C1
Umfors 15 C2
Umhausen 106 B1
Umin Dol 139 B/C2
Umka 133 D1, 134 A1/2
Ummeljoki 26 B2
Ummendorf 69 C3
Ummerstadt 81 D2
Umnäs 15 C3
Umpferstedt 82 A1/2
Uña 161 D3
Uña de Quintana 151 D3
Unaja 24 A2
Unari 12 A/B2
Unbyn 17 C3
Uncastillo 155 C2
Unciti 154 A2
Undenäs 45 D2, 46 A2
Undersåker 29 C3, 34 A2
Undersåker 29 C3, 34 A2
Undersvik 40 A1
Undheim 42 A2/3
Undredal 36 B3
Undués de Lerda 155 C2
Uneča 99 D1
Unelanperä 18 B3
Úněšov 83 C3
Ungeny 141 C1
Ungerdorf 127 C/D1
Unhais da Serra 158 B3
Unhošť 83 C3
Unije 130 A2
Unimäki 23 B/C3
Unirea 135 D2
Unna 80 B1
Unna Allakasstugorna 9 D2
Unquera 152 B1
Unstad 8 B2
Untamala 20 B2
Untamala 24 A2
Unterach 93 C3
Unterägeri [Baar] 105 D1
Unterdietfurt 92 B2
Untergriesbach 93 C2
Unterhaching 92 A2/3
Unterhochsteg 91 C3
Unterloibl 126 B2
Unterlüss 68 B2
Untermeitingen 95 D2
Untermünkheim 91 C1
Unterneukirchen 92 B2
Unterpinswang 91 D3
Unterpremstätten 127 C1
Unterreichenbach (Calw) 90 B2
Unterreit 92 B2/3
Unterschächen [Altdorf] 105 D1
Unterschleissheim 92 A2
Unterschneidheim-Zöbingen 91 D1
Unterschwaningen 91 D1
Untersiemau 81 D2/3, 82 A2/3
Untersteinach 82 A3
Untertauern 126 A1
Unterwasser [Nesslau-Neu St. Johann] 105 D1, 106 A1
Unterweid 81 D2
Unterweissenbach 93 D2
Unterwössen 92 B3
Untorp 39 C1
Upavon 64 A3, 76 A1
Úpega 113 B/C2
Upinniemi/Obbnäs 25 C3
Uplengen 67 D1
Uplengen-Remels 67 D1
Upper Tean 59 D2/3, 61 B/C3, 64 A1
Uppgränna 46 A3
Upphärad 45 C3
Uppingham 64 B2
Upplands-Väsby 47 C1
Uppsala 40 B3
Uppsala-Gamla Uppsala 40 B3
Uppsala-Sunnersta 40 B3
Uppsälje 39 C2
Uppsete 36 B3
Upton upon Severn 63 D1, 64 A2
Ur 156 A2
Uraiújfalu 94 B3, 128 A1
Uramonkylä 23 C1
Úras 123 C2/3
Urbach 91 C2
Urbánia 115 C/D2/3, 117 C2
Urbeis 89 D2, 90 A2
Urbino 115 D2, 117 C2
Urbiola 153 D2
Urbise 103 C2
Urçay 102 B1
Urda 167 C1
Urdari 135 D1
Urdiáin 153 D2
Urdiales del Páramo 151 D2
Urdos 154 B2
Urduliz 153 C1
Urduña 153 C2
Ure 8 B2/3
Urepel 108 A3, 154 A1
Ureterp 67 C1/2
Urheiluopisto 27 D1
Urheiluopisto 21 C2
Urheiluopisto 25 D2, 26 A2
Urheiluopisto 25 D2, 26 A2
Uriage-les-Bains 104 A3, 112 A1
Uricani 135 D1
Urizaharra 153 D2
Urjala 25 B/C2
Urjalan asema 25 C2
Urk 66 B2
Urla 149 D2
Urmatt 89 D2, 90 A2
Urmenor 174 B1
Urmince 95 C2
Urnäsch 105 D1, 106 A1
Urnes 36 B2
Urnieta 153 D1, 154 A1
Uroševac 138 B2
Uroševac 140 A3
Urovica 135 C2
Urrácal 173 D1/2
Urraca-Miguel 160 B2
Urrea de Gaén 162 B1/2
Urrea de Jalón 155 C3, 163 C1
Urretxu 153 D1
Urroz 154 A2
Urrugne 108 A3, 154 A1
Ursberg 91 D2
Ursensollen 82 A3, 92 A1
Urshult 51 C2
Urshult 72 A1
Urspringen (Marktheidenfeld) 81 C3
Ursviken 31 D1
Urtimjaur 16 B1
Urtoče 131 C2
Urtuella 153 C1
Urtx 156 A2
Urueñas 160 B1
Uruñuela 153 D2
Ururi 119 D2, 120 A1
Urville-Nacqueville 76 A3
Urzainqui 154 B2
Urziceni 141 C2
Urzicuța 135 D2
Urzulei 123 D2
Usagre 165 D3, 166 A3
Usanos 161 C2
Ušće 133 D3, 134 A/B3
Ušće 140 A2
Úscio 113 D2
Used 162 A2
Usedom 70 B1
Useldange 79 D3
Uséllus 123 C2
Useras 163 B/C3
Usingen 80 B2
Úsini 123 C1/2
Usk 63 D1
Uskali 23 D3
Uskedal 42 A1
Uskoplje 137 C2
Üsküdar 149 D1
Uslar 68 B3, 81 C1
Uslar-Schönhagen 68 B3, 81 C1
Usmate Velate 105 D3, 106 A3
Ussássai 123 D2
Ussat-les-Bains 155 D2, 156 A1
Ussé 86 B3, 101 C1
Usseau 100 B2
Usséglio 104 B3, 112 B1
Ussel 102 A3
Ussel 102 B3, 110 A1
Usson-du-Poitou 101 C2
Usson-en-Forez 103 C3
Usson-les-Bains 156 A1
Ustaoset 37 C3
Ustaritz 108 A3, 154 A1
Ust'-Čorna 97 D2, 98 A3
Ust'-Dunajsk 141 D2
Úštěk 83 D2
Uster 90 B3, 105 D1
Ustibar 133 C3
Uštica 128 A3, 131 D1, 132 A1
Ústica 124 B1
Ustikolina 133 C3
Ústí nad Labem 83 C2
Ústí nad Labem 96 A1
Ústí nad Orlicí 96 B2
Ustiprača 133 C3
Ustjužna 75 D1
Ustka 72 B2
Ust'-Luga 74 B1
Ustrzyki Górne 97 D2, 98 A3
Usurbil 153 D1, 154 A1
Uszód 129 C2
Uta 123 C/D3
Utajärvi 18 B3
Utåker 42 A1
Utakleiv 8 B2
Utande 161 C2
Utanen 18 B3
Utanlandsjö 31 C3
Utansjö 35 D2
Utbjoa 42 A1
Utebo 154 B3, 162 B1
Utelle 112 B2
Utena 73 D2, 74 A3
Utersum 52 A2
Úterý 82 B3
Uthaug 28 A3, 33 C1
Utiel 169 D1
Utifällan 31 C2
Utlångan 51 C/D2/3
Utne 36 B3
Utö 47 D1/2
Utöhus 47 C1
Utomälven 40 A/B2/3
Utorgoš 74 B1
Utrecht 66 B3
Utrera 171 D2
Utrilla 161 D1
Utrillas 162 B2
Utsikten 42 B1
Utsjoki (Ohtsejohka) 6 B2
Utskor 8 B1/2
Utstein Kloster 42 A2
Uttendorf 93 C2
Uttendorf 107 D1, 126 A1
Uttenweiler 91 C2
Uttenweiler-Ahlen 91 C2
Utterliden 16 A3
Uttermossa 20 A3
Uttersberg 39 D3
Uttersjöbäcken 31 D1
Utterslev 53 C2
Utti 26 B2
Uttoxeter 59 D2/3, 61 C3, 64 A1
Utula 27 C1
Utvalnäs 40 B2
Utvik 36 B1/2
Utvorda 28 B2
Uuao 23 D2/3
Uukuniemi 27 D1
Uura 19 C3
Uurainen 21 D3, 22 A3
Uuro 20 B3
Uusikaupunki (Nystad) 24 A2, 41 D2
Uusikylä 19 C3
Uusikylä 25 D2, 26 A2
Uusi-Lavola 27 C2
Uusi-Värtsilä 23 D3
Uva 19 C3
Uvac 133 C3
Uvåg 8 B2
Úvaly 83 D3
Uvdal 37 C3
Üxheim 79 D2, 80 A2
Uza 108 B2
Uzdin 129 D3, 133 D1, 134 A/B1
Uzerche 101 D3
Uzès 111 C2
Uzeste 108 B1/2
Užgorod 97 C/D2, 98 A3
Uzin 99 C2
Uznach 105 D1, 106 A1
Uztárroz 154 B2
Uzunköprü 145 D3

Vå 43 B/C1
Vä 50 B3
Vaaiasalmi 22 B2/3
Vaajakoski 21 D3, 22 A3
Vaajasalmi 22 B2/3
Vääkiö 19 C2
Vääksy 25 D2, 26 A2
Vaala 18 B3
Vaalajärvi 12 B2
Vaalijala 22 B3
Vaalimaa 27 C2
Vaals 79 D2
Väänälänranta 22 B2
Vaania 25 D2, 26 A2
Vääräkoski 21 C3
Vaarakylä 19 C1
Vaarankylä 19 C1
Vaaranniva 19 C2
Vaaraperä 19 D1
Vaaraslahti 22 B2
Vaasa/Vasa 20 A2, 31 D3
Vaassen 67 B/C3
Väätäiskylä 21 C3
Vaattojärvi 12 A2, 17 D1
Vabalninkas 73 D1, 74 A2
Vabre 110 A2
Vabres-l'Abbaye 110 A2
Vác 95 D3
Vác 97 B/C3
Vacha 81 D2
Váchartyán 95 D3
Väckelsång 51 C2
Väcklax 24 A3
Vacov 93 C1
Vacqueyras 111 C2
Vad 39 C3
Vada 114 A/B3, 116 A2
Vada 139 D2
Väddö 41 C3
Väderstad 46 A2
Vadheim 36 A2
Vadillo de la Guareña 159 D1, 160 A1
Vadillo de la Sierra 160 A2
Vadla 42 B2
Vado 114 B2, 116 B1
Vadocondes 153 C3, 161 C1
Vado Lígure 113 C2
Vadsbro 46 B1/2
Vadskinn 9 C1
Vadsø 7 C2
Vadstena 46 A2
Vaduz [Schaan] 105 D1, 106 A1
Vaektarstua 33 D2
Vaféika 145 C1
Vafiochórion 143 D1
Våg 43 D2, 44 A2
Vág 95 B/C3, 128 A1
Våga 42 A2
Vågaholmen 14 B1
Vågåmo 33 B/C3, 37 D1
Vågan 33 B/C1
Vågan 9 D1
Vaganac 131 C1
Vågen 29 C1/2
Vägersjön 30 A3, 35 C2
Vagge 7 C2
Væggerløse 53 D2
Vaggeryd 46 A3, 50 B1
Vaggeryd 72 A1
Vágia 147 C2
Vågland 32 B2
Váglia 114 B2, 116 B1
Vågnes 4 A2/3
Vagnhärad 47 C2
Vagos 158 A2
Vägsele 30 B1
Vägsjöfors 39 B/C3
Vågslid 42 B1
Vågsodden 14 A3
Vågstranda 32 A2/3
Vagueira 158 A2
Vágur 55 C1
Vähäjoki 18 A1
Vähäkangas 18 A3, 21 C1
Vähäkyrö 20 B2
Vahalahti 23 D3

Vähäniva 11 C2
Vahanka 21 C2
Vähä-Vuoto 18 B2
Vaheri 25 D1, 26 A1
Vähikkälä 25 C2
Vahterpää 26 B3
Vahto 24 B2
Vaiamonte 165 C2
Vaiano 114 B2, 116 B1
Vaiges 86 A2
Vaihingen 91 B/C1
Vailly-sur-Aisne 78 A/B3
Vailly-sur-Sauldre 87 D3
Vaimosuo 19 D1
Vainikkala 27 C2
Vairano Scalo 119 C2
Väisälä 22 B3
Vaisaluoktastugan 9 D3
Vaison-la-Romaine 111 C/D2
Vaîte 89 C3
Vaivo 23 C3
Väjern 44 B2
Vajkijaur 16 A/B1
Vajmat 16 A2
Vajska 129 C3
Vajszló 128 B3
Vajta 129 B/C2
Vajza 142 A2
Vakern 39 C2/3
Vakerskogen 39 C2/3
Vække 5 D2, 6 A2
Vakkerstølen 32 B3, 37 C1
Vakkola 25 D2, 26 A2
Vakkotavarestugan 9 D3
Vakkuri 20 B2
Vaksdal 36 A3
Vaksliden 16 A3
Vál 95 D3, 129 B/C1
Valada 164 A2
Vålådalen 29 C3, 34 A2
Valadouro 151 B/C1
Valajanaapa 18 B1
Valajaskoski 12 A3
Valalta 130 A1
Valandovo 139 C/D3, 143 D1
Valanhamn 4 B2
Valanída 143 C2/3
Valareña 155 C3
Valaská Belá 95 D1/2
Vålåskaret 33 C2
Valašské Klobouky 95 C1
Valašské Meziříčí 95 C1
Valašské Meziříčí 96 B2
Vålåstugan 34 A2
Valay 89 C3, 104 A1
Valberg 112 B2
Vålberg 45 C/D1
Valberg 8 B2
Valbom 159 C2
Valbona 162 B3
Valbondione 106 A/B2
Valbone 137 D2, 138 A2
Valbonnais 111 D1, 112 A1
Valbo-Ryr 45 C2
Valbuena de Duero 152 B3, 160 B1
Valburg 66 B3
Vălcani 129 D2
Valcarlos 108 B3, 155 C1
Vâlčedrâm 135 D3
Vâlčedrâm 140 B2
Valchiusella 105 C3
Valdagno 107 C3
Valdahon 89 D3, 104 A/B1
Valdaj 75 C1/2
Val-d'Ajol 89 D2/3
Valdalen 33 D3
Valdanzo 153 C3, 161 C1
Valdaracete 161 C3
Valdealgorfa 163 C2
Valdeande 153 C3, 161 C1
Valdearenas 161 C2
Valdeavellano de Tera 153 D3
Valdeaveruelo 161 C2
Valdecaballeros 166 B1/2
Valdecabras 161 D3
Valdecañas de Tajo 159 D3, 166 A1
Valdecastillo 152 A2
Valdeconcha 161 C2
Valdefinjas 159 D1, 160 A1
Valdeflores 171 C/D1
Valdefuentes 165 D1/2, 166 A1/2
Valdeganga 168 B2
Valdeganga de Cuenca 161 D3, 168 B1
Valdehúncar 159 D3, 166 A/B1
Valdelacasa 160 A3, 166 B1
Valdelacasa 159 D2
Valdelageve 159 D2/3
Valdelarco 165 D3, 171 C1
Valdelateja 153 B/C2
Valdelinares 162 B2/3
Valdelosa 159 D1/2
Valdeltormo 163 C2
Valdemadera 153 D3
Valdemaluque 153 C3, 161 C1
Valdemanco del Esteras 166 B2
Valdemārpils 73 C/D1
Valdemars Slot 53 C2
Valdemarsvik 46 B2/3
Valdemeca 162 A3
Valdemorillo 160 B2
Valdemorillo de la Sierra 162 A3
Valdemoro 161 B/C3
Valdemoro-Sierra 162 A3
Valdenarros 153 C3, 161 C1
Valdenebro 153 C3, 161 C1
Valdenebro de los Valles 152 A3
Valdenoceda 153 C2
Valdenuño Fernández 161 C2
Valdeolivas 161 D2
Valdeolmillos 152 B3
Valdepeñas 167 D2
Valdepeñas de Jaén 173 C1
Valdepolo 152 A2
Valderas 152 A3
Valdérice 124 A2
Valderiès 110 A2
Valderrobres 163 C2
Valderrodrigo 159 C2
Val de Santo Domingo 160 B3
Valdesaz 161 C2
Valdesimonte 160 B1
Valdespina 152 B3
Valdestillas 160 A1
Valdeteja 152 A2
Valdetorres 165 D2, 166 A2
Valdeverdeja 160 A3, 166 B1
Valdevimbre 151 D2, 152 A2
Valdezcaray 153 C2/3
Valdieri 112 B2
Valdilecha 161 C3
Val d'Isère 104 B3
Val-d'Izé 86 A2
Valdobbiádene 107 C2/3
Val do Dubra 150 A1/2
Val Dorizzo 106 B2/3
Valdoviño 150 B1
Valdresflya 37 C2
Valdunquillo 152 A3
Valdurna/Durnholz 107 C1
Vale 63 D3
Valea Marcului 135 D2
Valebø 43 D2, 44 A1
Valebru 37 D2
Vale de Cambra 158 A2
Vale de Cavalos 164 B1/2
Vale de Figueira 164 B1
Vale de Guiso 164 B3
Vale de Prazeres 158 B3
Vale de Salgueiro 151 C3, 159 B/C1
Vale de Santiago 164 B3, 170 A1
Vale de Santarém 164 A2
Vale de Vargo 165 C3, 170 B1
Vale do Peso 165 C1
Vale Frechoso 159 C1
Válega 158 A2
Valéggio sul Míncio 106 B3
Valen 42 A1
Valen 5 C/D1, 6 A1
Valença 158 B1/2
Valença do Minho 150 A3
Valençay 87 C3, 101 D1, 102 A1
Valence 111 C1
Valence-d'Agen 109 C2
Valence-d'Albigeois 110 A2
Valence-en-Brie 87 D2
Valence-sur-Baïse 109 C2
Valencia 169 D1
Valencia de Alcántara 165 C1
Valencia de Don Juan 151 D2, 152 A2
Valencia de las Torres 165 D3, 166 A3
Valencia de Mombuey 165 C3
Valencia del Ventoso 165 D3
Valenciennes 78 B2
Vălenii de Munte 141 C2
Valensole 111 D2, 112 A2
Valentano 116 B3, 118 A1
Valenza 113 C1
Valenzuela 167 C3, 172 B1
Valenzuela de Calatrava 167 C2
Våler 38 B2
Våler 44 B1
Valera de Abajo 161 D3, 168 B1
Valera de Arriba 161 D3, 168 B1
Valérien 87 D2
Valer'jany 99 B/C1
Valevåg 42 A1
Valevatn 42 B2
Vale Verde 159 C2
Valeyrac 100 B3
Valezim 158 B3
Valfábbrica 115 D3, 117 C2
Valfarta 155 B/C3, 163 B/C1
Valfermoso de Tajuña 161 C2
Valflaunès 110 B2
Valga 150 A2
Valga 74 A2
Valgañón 153 C2
Valgorge 111 C1
Valgrisanche 104 B3
Valguarnera Caropepe 125 C2
Valhelhas 158 B2/3
Valhermoso 161 D2
Välijoki 27 B/C2
Välijoki 18 B1
Välikangas 12 B3
Väli-Kannus 21 C1
Välikoski 17 D2
Välikylä 21 C1
Valimítika 146 B2
Välitalo 12 B2
Valittula 25 D1, 26 A1
Väliug 135 C1
Väli-Viirre 21 C1
Valjevo 133 D2, 134 A2
Valjevo 140 A2
Valjok fjellstue 6 B2
Valjunquera 163 C2
Valkeajärvi 21 C3
Valkeakoski 25 C1/2
Valkeala 26 B2
Valkealahti 21 C3
Valkeamäki 27 C1
Valkeavaara 27 D1
Valkeiskylä 22 B1
Valkeiskylä 23 B/C2
Valkenburg-Houthem 79 D2
Valkenswaard 79 C1
Valkininkai 73 D2, 74 A3
Valko/Valkom 25 D2/3, 26 B3
Vall 47 D3
Valla 46 B1
Valla 29 D3, 34 B2
Vallada 169 C2
Valladolid 152 A/B3, 160 A1
Vallåkra 49 D3, 50 A3
Vallamediana 153 D2
Vallanca 163 C3
Vallarsa 107 C3
Vallarvatnet 29 C1
Vallata 120 A2
Vallavik 36 B3
Vallbo 29 C3, 34 A2
Vallbona d'Anoia 155 D3, 156 A3, 163 D1
Vallda 49 D1, 50 A1
Valldal 32 A3, 36 B1
Vall d'Alba 163 C3
Valldemosa 157 C2
Vall de Uxó 162 B3, 169 D1
Valle 14 B1
Valle 42 B2
Valle 42 B3
Vallecas 161 C2/3
Valle Castellana 117 D3, 119 C1
Valle Cerrina 113 C1
Vallecorsa 119 C2
Vallecrósia 112 B2/3
Valle d'Alesani 113 D3
Valle de Abdalagís 172 B2
Valle de Cerrato 152 B3
Valle de la Serena 166 A2
Valle de los Caídos 160 B2
Valle de Matamoros 165 D3
Valle de Mena 153 C1
Valle de Santa Ana 165 D3
Valledolmo 124 B2
Valledória 123 C1
Valleiry 104 A2
Valle Lomellina 105 D3, 113 C1
Vallelunga Pratameno 124 B2
Vallen 17 C3
Vallen 31 D1
Vallen 30 A2, 35 C/D1
Vallendar 80 A/B2
Vallentuna 47 C/D1
Vallepietra 119 B/C2
Vallerås 39 C2
Valleraugue 110 B2
Vallermosa 123 C3
Vallespinosa 155 C3, 163 C1
Válles/Vals 107 C1
Vallet 86 A3, 101 C1
Valleviken 47 D2
Valley 58 B2
Vallfogona de Ripollès 156 A2
Vallfogona de Riucorb 155 C3, 163 C1
Vallgorguina 156 B3
Vallibona 163 C2
Valli del Pasúbio 107 C3
Vallières 102 A2
Vallières 104 A2/3
Vallières-les-Grandes 86 A/B3
Valli Mocenighe 107 C3, 115 C1
Vallioniemi 13 C3
Vallmoll 163 C1
Vallø 50 A3, 53 D1
Valløby 50 A3, 53 D1
Vallo della Lucánia 120 A3
Valloire 104 A/B3, 112 A1
Vallombrosa 115 C2, 116 B1/2
Vallon-en-Sully 102 B2
Vallon-Pont-d'Arc 111 C2
Vallorbe 104 A/B1/2
Vallorcine 104 B2
Vallouise 112 A1
Valløy 43 D2, 44 B1
Vallrun 29 D3, 34 B1
Valls 163 C1
Vallset 38 A2
Vallsjärv 17 C1
Vallsta 40 A1
Vallter 156 A2
Valluhn 69 C1
Vallvik 40 B1
Valmaña 155 C3, 163 C1
Valmanya 156 B2
Valmiera 73 D1, 74 A2
Valmojado 160 B3
Valmont 77 C3
Valmontone 118 B2
Valne 29 D3, 34 B2
Valö 40 B2/3
Valognes 76 A3
Valongo 158 A1/2
Válor 173 C2
Valoría la Buena 152 B3, 160 B1
Valøy 28 A/B1
Valpaços 151 C3, 158 B1
Valpalmas 154 B2/3
Valpelline 104 B3
Valperga 105 C3
Valpiana 114 B3, 116 A2
Valpovo 128 B3
Valpperi 24 B2
Valprato Soana 105 C3
Valpromaro 114 A2, 116 A1
Valpuesta 153 C2
Valras-Plage 110 B3, 156 B1
Valréas 111 C2
Valsavaranche 104 B3
Valseca 160 B2
Valsemé 76 B3, 86 B1
Valsequillo 166 B3
Valset 28 A3, 33 C1
Valsinni 120 B3
Valsjöbyn 29 C/D2, 34 B1
Valsjön 35 C3
Valskog 46 B1
Valskrå 28 B2
Vals-les-Bain 111 C1
Valsneset 28 A2/3, 33 C1
Valsøybotn 32 B2
Valsøyfjord 32 B2
Vals-Platz [Ilanz] 105 D2, 106 A2
Valstad 45 D3
Valstagna 107 C3
Val-Suzon 88 B3
Valtesiníkon 146 B3
Válti 143 D1, 144 A1
Valtice 94 B2
Valtierra 154 A2/3
Valtimo 23 C1
Valtola 26 B1/2
Valtopina 115 D3, 117 C2
Valtorta 106 A2
Váltos 145 D3
Valtournanche 105 C2/3
Valtueña 161 D1
Valtura 130 A1
Valun 130 A1
Valverde 153 D3, 154 A3
Valverde 167 C2
Valverde de Leganés 165 C2
Valverde de Llerena 166 A3
Valverde de Júcar 161 D3, 168 B1
Valverde de la Vera 161 C3
Valverde de Burguillos 165 D3
Valverde de Majano 160 B2
Valverde del Fresno 159 C3
Valverde del Camino 171 C1
Valverdejo 161 D3, 168 B1
Valvträsk 17 C2
Våmartveit 43 C1
Vamdrup 52 B1
Våmhus 39 C1/2
Vamlingbo 47 D3
Vamlingbo 72 B1
Vammala/Tyrvää 24 B1
Vámosmikola 95 D3
Vámosszabadi 95 C3
Vampula 24 B2
Vamvakoú 143 D3
Vamvakoú 147 C3
Vanaja 25 C2
Vanaja 22 B3
Vanås 50 B2
Vanault-les-Dames 88 B1
Vandans 106 A1
Vändburg 47 D3
Vandel 48 B3, 52 B1
Vandellòs 163 C/D2
Vandenesse 103 C1
Vandóies/Vintl 107 C1
Vandoma 158 A1/2
Vändträsk 16 B3
Väne-Åsaka 45 C3
Vänersborg 45 C2
Vänersnäs 45 C2
Väng 45 C1
Vang 37 C2
Vang 51 D3
Vånga 50 B2
Vängel 30 A2, 35 C1
Vangshylla 28 B2/3, 33 D1
Vangsnes 36 B2
Vangsvik 9 D1

Vanhakirkko **21** C3
Vanhakylä **27** C1/2
Vanhakylä **20** A/B3
Vanhala **26** B1
Vanhamäki **26** B1
Vanha-Pihlajavesi **21** C3
Vänjaurbäck **31** B/C1/2
Vänjaurfräsk **31** C2
Vännacka **45** C1
Vannakammen **4** A2
Vannareid **4** A2
Vännäs **31** C2
Vännäsberget **17** C2
Vännäsby **31** C2
Vannavalen **4** A/B2
Vannes **85** C3
Vannes-le-Châtel **89** C2
Vannes-sur-Cosson **87** C/D3
Vännfors **31** C2
Vannvåg **4** A/B2
Våno **24** B3
Vanonen **26** B2
Vanovelles **156** A3
Vansäter **40** A1
Vansbro **39** C2
Vanse **42** B3
Vänsjö **34** B3
Vantaa/Vanda **25** C3, **26** A3
Väntholm **47** C1
Vanttaja **19** D1
Vanttausjärvi **12** B3
Vanttauskoski **12** B3
Vanttila **24** B2
Vanvik **8** B3
Vanvik **42** A/B1
Vanvikan **28** A3, **33** C1
Vanylven **36** A1
Vaour **109** D2
Vapavaara **19** D1
Vaplan **29** D3, **34** B2
Vàprio d'Adda **106** A3
Vaqueiros **170** B1/2
Vara **45** C2/3
Varades **85** D3
Varages **111** D3, **112** A3
Varajärvi **12** A3, **17** D2
Varajoki **19** D3
Varaklani **74** A2
Värälä **26** B2
Varaldsøy **42** A1
Varallo **105** C3
Varamobaden **46** A2
Varangerbotn **7** C2
Varano de'Melegari **114** A1
Varaždin **127** D2
Varaždin **96** A/B3
Varaždinske Toplice **127** D2
Varazze **113** C2
Varberg **49** D1, **50** A1
Varberg **72** A1
Vârbica **141** C3
Vårby **47** C1
Varchentin **69** D1, **70** A1
Várda **146** A2
Varde **48** A3, **52** A1
Vardište **133** C3
Vardø **7** D1/2
Vårdö **41** D3
Vårdomb **129** B/C2
Vårdsberg **46** B2
Varejoki **17** D2, **18** A1
Varel **67** D1, **68** A1
Varel-Conneforde **67** D1
Varel-Dangast **67** D1, **68** A1
Varen **109** D2
Varengeville-sur-Mer **77** C2/3
Varenna **105** D2, **106** A2
Varennes-en-Argonne **88** B1
Varennes-Saint-Sauveur **103** D2
Varennes-sur-Amance **89** C2/3
Varennes-sur-Allier **102** B2
Varennes-sur-Usson **102** B3
Varennes sur Saine **87** D2
Vareš **132** B2
Varese **105** D3
Varese Lígure **113** D2, **114** A2
Varetz **101** D3
Vårgårda **45** C3
Vargas **152** B1
Vargeneset **9** C2
Vargfjord **9** C2
Vargön **45** C2
Varhaug **42** A3
Varigotti **113** C2
Varilhes **109** D3, **155** D1, **156** A1
Varín **95** D1
Väring **45** D2
Váris **143** C2
Variskylä **19** C3
Varislahti **23** C2
Varistaipale **23** C3
Varize **87** C2
Varjakka **18** A2
Varkaus **22** B3
Várkiza **147** D2
Varland **43** C1
Vårli **4** A3, **10** A1
Värmbol **46** B1/2
Värmdö **47** D1
Värmlands Bro **45** C1
Varmo **27** D1
Varmo **107** D2/3, **126** A2/3
Värmskog **45** C1
Varna **141** C/D3
Värnamo **72** A1
Värnamo **50** B1
Varnæs **52** B2
Varnhem **45** D2
Varnsdorf **83** D2
Varntresk **14** B2/3
Varnum **45** D3
Väröbacka **49** D1, **50** A1
Varois-et-Chaignot **88** B3
Városlöd **128** A/B1
Varpa **23** D2
Varpaisjärvi **22** B2
Várpalota **128** B1
Várpalota **96** B3
Varpanen **26** B1
Varparanta **23** C3
Varpasalo **23** C3
Varpnes **28** B2
Varpsjö **30** A2
Varpula **20** B2
Varpuselkä **13** C3
Varpuvaara **13** C3
Varrel **68** A2
Värriö **13** C2
Värriönpirtti **13** C2
Varsád **128** B2
Värsås **45** D2, **46** A2
Vâršec **135** D3, **139** D1
Varsi **114** A1
Varsseveld **67** C3
Vårsta **40** B3, **47** C1
Vartdal **36** B1
Varteig **44** B1
Vartiala **23** B/C2
Vartiala **23** C2
Vartius **19** D3
Vartofta **45** D3
Vartsala **24** B3
Värtsilä **23** D3
Varuträsk **31** D1
Varvára **144** B2
Varvaria **131** C2/3
Varvarin **134** B3
Varvekstugan **15** C/D1
Vårvik **28** A3, **33** C1
Varvikko **13** C3
Varzi **113** D1
Varzo **105** C2
Varzy **88** A3
Vås **35** C3
Vasad **129** C1
Vasaniemi **12** B2
Vasara **19** C/D2
Vasarainen **24** A2
Vasaraperä **19** C1
Vasarás **147** C3
Vásárosnamény **97** D2/3, **98** A3
Vascœuil **76** B3
Väse **45** D1
Väse **45** D1
Vaset **37** C/D2/3
Vasilákion **146** B3
Vasiliká **144** A2
Vasiliká **147** D1
Vasilikí **146** A1
Vasilikí **148** A2
Vasilikón **142** B2
Vasilikón **147** D2
Vasilikós **146** A3
Vasil'kov **99** C2
Vaski **18** A2
Vaskijärvi **25** C2
Vaskio **24** B2/3
Vaskivesi **21** C3
Vaskuu **21** C3
Vasles **101** C1/2
Vaslui **141** C1
Vassbø **42** A/B2/3
Vassbotn **9** C/D2
Vassbotnfjell **15** C1
Vassbotten **44** B2
Vassdal **9** D2
Vassdal **43** D2, **44** A1
Vassdalsvik **14** B1
Vassenden **37** D2
Vassenden **36** B2
Vassendvik **42** A2
Vassmoen **28** B2
Vassmolösa **51** D2
Vassnäs **35** C3
Vasstrand **4** A3
Vassy **86** A1
Vassy-sous-Pisy **88** A/B3
Vasszentmihály **127** D1
Västanå **30** A3, **35** C2
Västanå **31** C3
Västanbäck **30** A1
Västanbäck **35** C2
Västanfjärd **24** B3
Västanhede **40** A2
Västannäs **17** C2
Västansjö **15** C3
Västansjö **30** B1
Västansjö **35** D3
Västbyn **29** D3, **34** B1
Västeränga **41** D3
Väster Ärnäs **39** C2
Västerås **31** C2
Västerås **40** A3, **46** B1
Västerasen **30** A3, **35** C2
Västerby **39** D2/3, **40** A2
Väster Fågelvik **45** C1
Västerfärnebo **40** A3
Västerfjäll **15** D1
Västergarn **47** D3
Västergissjö **31** C2/3
Västerhaninge **47** C/D1
Västerhaninge-Tungelsta **47** C1
Väster Husby **46** B2
Västerlandsjö **31** C3
Västerlandsjö **31** C3
Västermyckeläng **39** C1
Västernyliden **31** C2
Väster Ritjemjåkk **9** D3
Västerrottna **38** B3
Västerstråsjö **35** C3
Västervåla **40** A3
Västervik **46** B3
Västervik **72** B1
Västilä **25** C1, **26** A1
Vastila **26** B2
Västinki **21** C/D2
Västinniemi **23** C2
Västland **40** B2
Vasto **119** D1
Vastogirardi **119** C/D2
Västra Ämtervik **39** C3, **45** C/D1
Västra Bodarna **45** C3
Västra Hjoggböle **31** D1
Västra Lainijaur **16** A3
Västra Ormsjö **30** A1
Västra Sjulsmark **31** D2
Västra Skedvi **39** D3, **46** B1
Västra Stugusjö **35** C2
Västra Tunhem **45** C2
Västsjön **29** C3, **34** B1
Västvattnet **30** A3, **35** C1
Vasvár **128** A1
Vasvár **96** B3
Vát **128** A1
Vataala **23** D3
Vatan **102** A1
Väte **47** D3
Vaterholm **28** B3, **33** D1
Váthi **139** D3, **143** D1, **144** A1
Vathí **146** A1
Vathí **147** D2
Vathílakkos **143** D1/2
Vathítopos **144** B1
Vatin **134** B1
Vatjusjärvi **18** A3, **21** D1, **22** A1
Vatland **42** B3
Vatnås **43** D1
Vatne **43** C3
Vatne **32** A2/3
Vatne **43** C3
Vatne **36** B1
Vatnet **14** A/B2
Vatnhamn **5** C1/2
Vatnstraum **43** C3
Vätö **41** C3
Vatochórion **143** B/C2
Vatólakkos **143** C2
Vatopédi **144** B2
Vatra Dornei **141** C1
Vatry **88** B1
Vats **42** A1/2
Vattholma **40** B3
Vättilä **24** B2
Vättis [Bad Ragaz] **105** D1, **106** A1
Vattnäs **39** D2
Vattrång **35** D3
Vattukylä **18** A3, **21** D1, **22** A1
Vau **164** A1
Vauchamps **88** A1
Vauclaix **88** A3, **103** C1
Vaucouleurs **89** C2
Vaud **104** B3
Vaugneray **103** C/D3
Vau i Dejës **137** D2
Vauldalen **33** D2
Vaulruz **104** B2
Vaumoise **87** D1
Vausseroux **101** C2
Vautorte **86** A2
Vauvenargues **111** D3
Vauvert **111** C2
Vaux **88** A3
Vaux-en-Beaujolais **103** C/D2
Vaux-le-Vicomte **87** D2
Vávdos **144** A2
Väversunda **46** A2
Vaxholm **47** D1
Växjö **51** C1
Växjö **72** A1
Våxtorp **50** A2
Väylä **6** B3
Väylänpää **17** D1
Vayrac **109** D1
Väyrylä **19** C3
Väystäjä **12** A3, **17** D2
Vazzola **107** D3
Vean **32** B2
Veberöd **50** B3
Veblungsnes **32** A/B3
Vebomark **31** D1
Vebron **110** B2
Vechelde **69** B/C3
Vechta **67** D2, **68** A2
Vechta-Langförden **67** D2, **68** A2
Vecinos **159** D2
Veckholm **47** C1
Vecsés **95** D3, **129** C1
Vedavågen **42** A2
Vedbæk **49** D3, **50** A3, **53** D1
Vedde **49** C3, **53** C/D1
Veddige **49** D1, **50** A1
Vedelago **107** C3
Vederslöv **51** C2
Vedeseta **106** A2/3
Vedevåg **46** A/B1
Vedra **150** A2
Vedum **45** C3
Veendam **67** C1/2
Veenhuizen **67** C2
Veere **78** B1
Vegacervera **151** D2, **152** A2
Vega de Espinareda **151** C2
Vega de Infanzones **151** D2, **152** A2
Vegadeo **151** C1
Vega de Pas **153** B/C1
Vega de Tera **151** D3
Vega de Valcarce **151** C2
Vega de Valdetronco **152** A3, **160** A1
Veganzones **160** B1/2
Vegaquemada **152** A2
Vegarienza **151** D2
Vegårshei **43** C2
Vegas de Matute **160** B2
Vegasetra **33** B/C3
Vegby **45** D3
Vegger **48** B2
Veggli **43** C1
Veghel **66** B3, **79** C1
Véglie **121** D3
Veguillas **161** C2
Vegusdal **43** C3
Vehanen **24** A2
Vehkajärvi **25** C1, **26** A1
Vehkalahti **25** D1, **26** B1
Vehkaperä **21** C2
Vehkasalo **25** D1, **26** A1
Vehkataipale **27** C2
Vehlow **69** D2
Vehmaa **24** A2
Vehmalainen **24** B2
Vehmasjärvi **22** B1
Vehmasmäki **22** B2/3
Vehmersalmi **23** B/C2
Vehniä **21** D3, **22** A3
Vehu **21** C2/3
Vehuvarpe **24** B1
Veidholmen **32** B1
Veidnesklubben **6** B1
Veigy-Foncenex **104** A2
Veihtivaara **19** D3
Veikars **20** A/B2
Veikkola **25** C3
Veimo **28** B2, **33** D1
Veines **7** C1
Veinge **50** A2
Veio **118** B2
Veiros **165** C2
Veitsch **94** A3
Veitservasa **11** D3, **12** A1/2
Veitshöchheim **81** C/D3
Veitsiluoto **17** D3, **18** A1
Veitsivuoma **12** A2, **17** D1
Vejano **118** A1
Vejbystrand **49** D2, **50** A2
Vejen **48** B3, **52** B1
Vejer de la Frontera **171** D3
Vejers Strand **48** A3, **52** A1
Vejle **48** B3, **52** B1
Vejprty **83** B/C2
Vejrup **48** A3, **52** A1
Vejstrup **53** C2
Vejti **128** B3
Vekara **27** C1
Vekšino **75** C2
Veksø **49** D3, **50** A3, **53** D1
Velaatta **25** C1
Velada **160** A3
Velagici **131** D2
Velaine **79** B/C2
Vela Luka **136** A1
Velanda **45** C3
Velanidiá **146** A1
Velaóra **146** A/B1
Velayos **160** A/B2
Velbert **80** A1
Velbert-Langenberg **80** A1
Velburg **92** A1
Velburg-Prönsdorf **92** A1
Veldemelen **28** B2
Velden **79** D1
Velden **92** B2
Velden **82** A3
Velden am Wörthersee **126** B2
Veldwezelt **79** C2
Veldzigt **78** B1
Velefique **173** D2
Velemér **127** D1
Velen **67** C3
Velence **129** B/C1
Velen-Ramsdorf **67** C3
Velešin **93** D2
Velešta **138** A/B3, **142** B1
Velestínon **143** D3
Vélez Blanco **174** A1
Vélez de Benaudalla **173** C2
Vélez Málaga **172** B2
Vélez Rubio **174** A1
Vélia **120** A3
Veličani **137** B/C1
Velika **128** A/B3
Velika Gorica **127** D3
Velika Greda **134** B1
Velika Ilova **132** A1
Velika Ivanča **133** D2, **134** A/B2
Velika Kladuša **127** D3, **131** C1
Velika Kopanica **132** B1
Velika Kopašnica **139** C1
Velika Kruša **138** A/B2
Velika Mučna **128** A2

Velika Pisanica **128** A3
Velika Plana **134** B2
Velika Sablanica **138** A1
Velike Bonjince **139** C1
Velike Lašče **127** B/C3
Veliki Bastaji **128** A3
Velikie Luki **75** B/C2
Veliki Gaj **134** B1
Veliki Grđevac **128** A3
Veliki Izvor **135** C2/3
Veliki Popović **134** B2
Veliki Prolog **131** D3, **132** A3, **136** B1
Veliki Radić **131** C1
Veliki Radinci **133** C1, **134** A1
Veliki Zaton **137** C1
Veliki Zdenci **128** A3
Veliko Crniće **134** B2
Veliko Gradište **134** B1
Veliko Gradište **140** A2
Veliko Orašje **134** B2
Velikoploskoe **141** D1
Veliko Selo **134** B2
Veliko Središte **134** B1
Veliko Târnovo **141** C3
Veliko Trgovišće **127** D2
Velilla de Cinca **155** C3, **163** C1
Velilla de Ebro **162** B1
Velilla de Guardo **152** A2
Velilla de los Ajos **161** D1
Velilla de Medinaceli **161** D1/2
Velilla de San Esteban **153** C3, **161** C1
Veli Lošinj **130** A/B2
Velingrad **140** B3
Velіž **75** C3
Veljun **127** C3, **131** C1
Velká Bíteš **94** B1
Velká Černoc **83** C2/3
Velká Dobrá **83** C3
Velká Hleďsebe **82** B3
Vel'ká Mača **95** C2
Vel'ká Maňa **95** C2
Velká nad Veličkou **95** C1/2
Velké Bílovice **94** B1/2
Vel'ké Bošany **95** C2
Velké Březno **83** C2
Velké-Hleďsebe **82** B3
Vel'ké Kapušany **97** C/D2, **98** A3
Velké Karlovice **95** C1
Vel'ké Kostol'any **95** C2
Vel'ké Leváre **94** B2
Vel'ké Ludince **95** D3
Velké Meziříčí **94** A1
Velké Meziříčí **96** A/B2
Velké Němčice **96** B2
Velké Němčice **94** B1
Velké Pavlovice **94** B1
Vel'ké Pole **95** D2
Velké Přílepy **83** D3
Vel'ké Ripňany **95** C2
Vel'ké Rovné **95** D1
Vel'ké Zálužie **95** C2
Velké Žernoseky **83** C2
Velkua **24** A2/3
Velkuanmaa **24** A2/3
Velký Bor **93** C1
Vel'ký Krtíš **95** D2
Vellahn **69** C1
Vellberg **91** C1
Velleia **114** A1
Velles **101** D1, **102** A1
Velletri **118** B2
Vellevans **89** D3, **104** B1
Vellinge **50** A3
Vellinge **72** A2
Vellisca **161** C3
Velliza **152** A3, **160** A1
Velo Veronese **107** C3
Velpke **69** C2/3
Velsen **66** A2
Velsvik **36** A1
Velta **38** B2
Velten **70** A2
Veltrusy **83** C/D2
Velvary **83** C/D2
Velvendós **143** C2
Vemb **48** A2
Vemdalen **34** B3
Vemdalsskalet **34** B3
Véménd **128** B2
Vemhån **34** B3
Vemmenæs **53** C2
Vemundvik **28** B2
Vena **46** B3
Venabygd **37** D2
Venaco **113** D3
Venafro **119** C2
Venäjä **24** B2
Venarey-les-Laumes **88** B3
Venaría **112** B1
Venarotta **117** D3
Venasca **112** B1/2
Venas di Cadore **107** D2
Venåsen **37** D2
Venasque **111** D2
Venåsseter **37** D2
Venčane **133** D2, **134** A2
Vence **112** B3
Venda Nova **150** B3, **158** B1
Vendargues **110** B2/3
Vendas Novas **164** B2
Vendays **100** B3
Vendel **40** B3
Vendesund **14** A3, **28** B1
Vendeuvre-du-Poitou **101** C1
Vendeuvre-sur-Barse **88** B2
Vendôme **87** B/C3
Veneheitto **18** B3
Venejärvi **12** A2
Venejärvi **12** B3
Venejoki **23** C/D2
Venekoski **21** D3, **22** A3
Vénès **110** A2
Venesjärvi **24** B1
Veneskoski **24** B1
Veneskoski **20** B2
Venetmäki **22** B3
Venetpalo **21** D1, **22** A1
Venetti **12** A2, **17** D1
Venézia **107** D3
Venézia-Alberoni **107** D3
Venézia-Burano **107** D3
Venézia-Cavallino **107** D3
Venézia Fusina **107** D3
Venézia-Lido **107** D3
Venézia-Malamocco **107** D3
Venézia-Mestre **107** D3
Venézia-Murano **107** D3
Venézia-Pellestrina **107** D3
Venézia-Punta Sabbioni **107** D3
Venézia-San Pietro in Volta **107** D3
Vengsøy **4** A2
Venialbo **159** D1
Venjan **39** C2
Venlo **79** D1
Venna **145** C/D1
Vennesla **43** C3
Venngarn **40** B3, **47** C1
Venosa **120** B2
Venraij **79** D1
Vent **106** B1
Venta de Arraco **108** A3, **154** B1/2
Venta de Baños **152** B3
Venta del Baúl **173** D1/2
Venta del Charco **167** C3
Venta del Moro **169** D1
Venta de Zuriza **154** B2
Ventälä **20** B2
Ventanilla **152** B2
Ventanueva **151** C1/2
Ventas de Huelma **173** C2
Ventas de Zafarraya **172** B2
Ventimíglia **112** B2/3
Ventnor **76** B2
Ventosa **164** A2
Ventosa de la Sierra **153** D3
Ventosa del Río Almar **159** D2, **160** A2
Ventosa de Pisuerga **152** B2
Ventoténe **119** C3
Ventrosa **153** C/D3
Ventry **55** C3
Ventspils **73** C1
Venturina **114** B3, **116** A2
Venzone **126** A2
Veolia **37** C/D2
Vép **127** D1, **128** A1
Veprovac **129** C3
Vepsä **18** B2
Vepsä **23** C1
Vera **28** B3, **33** D1, **34** A1
Vera **129** C3
Vera **174** A2
Vera Cruz de Marmelar **165** C3
Vera de Bidasoa **108** A3, **154** A1
Vera de Moncayo **154** A3, **162** A1
Verbánia **105** D2/3
Verbas **142** A2
Verberie **87** D1
Verbicaro **122** A1
Verbier [Le Châble] **104** B2
Vercelli **105** C/D3
Vercel-Villedieu **89** D3, **104** A/B1
Verchen **70** A1
Verdaches **112** A2
Verdalsøra **28** B3, **33** D1
Verdello **106** A3
Verden **68** A/B2
Verden-Dauelsen **68** A/B2
Verdens Ende **43** D2, **44** B1/2
Verdikoússa **143** C3
Verdonnet **88** B3
Verdú **155** C3, **163** C1
Verdun-sur-Garonne **108** B2
Verdun-sur-le-Doubs **103** D1
Verdun-sur-Meuse **89** C1
Verea **150** B3
Vereja **75** D3
Veresegyház **95** D3
Verfeil **109** D2/3
Vergato **114** B2, **116** B1
Vergel **169** D2
Vergeletto [Ponte Brolla] **105** D2
Verges **156** B2
Vergiate **105** D3
Vergína **143** D2
Vergons **112** A2
Vergt **109** C1
Verhnedvinsk **74** B2/3
Verhovina **97** D2, **98** B3
Vería **148** B1
Vería **143** D2
Verín **151** B/C3
Veringenstadt **91** C2
Verkenseter **33** C3, **37** D1
Verket **38** A3, **43** D1, **44** B1
Verl **68** A3
Verla **26** B2
Verma **32** B3, **37** C1
Vermala (Montana) [Montana-Vermala] **105** C2
Vermand **78** A3
Vermenton **88** A3
Vermíglio **106** B2
Vermiosa **159** C2
Vermoil **158** A3, **164** A/B1
Vermoim **158** A1
Vermosh **137** D1/2
Vermuntila **24** A2
Vernantes **86** A/B3
Vernasca **114** A1
Vernazza **114** A2
Vern-d'Anjou **86** A3
Verneřice **83** D2
Vernet **109** D3, **155** D1
Vernet-les-Bains **156** A/B2
Verneuil **88** A1
Verneuil-sur-Avre **86** B1/2
Vérnio **114** B2, **116** B1
Verniolle **109** D3, **155** D1, **156** A1
Vérnole **121** D3
Vernon **87** C1
Vernou-en-Sologne **87** C3
Vernoux-en-Vivarais **111** C1
Verny **89** C1
Verőcemaros **95** D3
Verolanuova **106** B3
Verolengo **105** C3, **113** C1
Véroli **119** C2
Verona **107** B/C3
Verrabotn **28** A3, **33** C1
Verran **28** B2/3, **33** D1
Verrastrand **28** A/B2/3, **33** C/D1
Verrès **105** C3
Verrey-sous-Salmaise **88** B3
Verride **158** A3
Verrière **109** C1
Verrières **101** C2
Verrières, Les **104** B1
Verrone **105** C3
Vers **109** D1
Versailles **87** C1
Versam [Versam-Safien] **105** D1, **106** A1
Versmold **67** D3
Versmold-Peckeloh **67** D3
Versoix **104** A2
Ver-sur-Mer **76** B3, **86** A1
Verteillac **101** C3
Vértesacsa **95** D3, **128** B1
Vértesboglár **95** D3, **128** B1
Verteuil-d'Agenais **109** C1/2
Vertheuil **100** B3
Vertijevka **99** D2
Vertus **88** A1
Verúcchio **115** C2, **117** C1
Verum **50** B2
Verveln **46** B3
Verviers **79** D2
Vervins **78** B3
Verwood **63** D2, **76** A1
Veržej **127** D2
Verzino **122** B1/2
Verzuolo **112** B1
Vesajärvi **24** B1
Vesala **18** B2
Vešala **138** B2
Vesamäki **22** A/B2
Vesanka **21** D3, **22** A3
Vesanto **21** D2, **22** A2
Vescovato **106** B3
Vése **128** A2
Ves'egonsk **75** D1
Veselí nad Lužnicí **93** D1
Veselí nad Moravou **95** C1
Vésenaz [Genève] **104** A2
Vesijärvi **20** A3
Vesilahti **25** C1
Vésio **106** B3
Vesivehmaa **25** D2, **26** A2
Veskoniemi **6** B3
Vesmajärvi **11** D3, **12** A/B2
Vesoul **89** C3
Vespolate **105** D3
Vessigebro **49** D1/2, **50** A1
Vestby **38** A3, **44** B1
Vestby **38** A3
Vestbygd **9** C2
Vestenanova **107** C3
Vesterby **48** B1
Vester Egesborg **53** D2
Vester Hassing **48** B1
Vesterø Havn **49** C1
Vestertana **6** B1
Vester Torup **48** B1
Vester Vedsted **52** A1
Vestervig **48** A2
Vestfossen **43** D1, **44** A1
Vestmanna **55** C1
Vestmarka **38** B3
Vestnes **9** C1
Vestnes (Helland) **32** A2/3
Vestola **24** B1
Vestone **106** B3
Vestra Harg **46** A/B2
Vestra Malmagen **33** D2
Vestra Torsås **51** B/C2
Vestra Torup **50** B2
Vestre Gausdal **37** D2
Vestre Jakobselv **7** C2
Vestvågen **14** A2
Veszprém **128** B1
Veszprém **96** B3
Veszprémvarsány **95** C3, **128** B1
Veteli-Kainu **21** C1/2
Veteren **37** D3
Vétheuil **87** C1
Vetlanda **46** A3, **51** C1
Vetlanda **72** A/B1
Vetlefjord **36** B2
Vetovo **141** C2
Vetralla **117** B/C3, **118** A1
Vetrino **141** C3
Větrný Jeníkov **94** A1
Vetschau **70** B3
Vetsikko **6** B2
Vette **44** B2
Vettelschoss **80** A2
Vetti **37** C2
Vetto **114** A1/2
Vettweiss **79** D2, **80** A2
Veules-les-Roses **77** C2/3
Veulettes-sur-Mer **77** C3
Veum **43** C2
Veurne **78** A1
Veuves **87** B/C3
Vevelstad **14** A3
Vevey **104** B2
Vévi **143** C1/2
Vevring **36** A2
Vexala **20** B1/2
Veynes **111** D1, **112** A1/2
Veyre-Monton **102** B3
Vez **87** D1
Vezdemarbán **152** A3, **159** D1, **160** A1
Vézelay **88** A3
Vézelise **89** C2
Vézenobres **111** C2
Vezins **100** B1
Vezins-de-Levezou **110** A2
Vezza d'Óglio **106** B2
Vezzani **113** D3
Vezzano **107** B/C2
Vezzano sul Cróstolo **114** B1
Vi **35** D3
Viadana **114** B1
Viade de Baixo **150** B3, **158** B1
Viadotto Itália **120** B3, **122** A1
Viaduc de Garabit **110** B1
Viaduc des Fades **102** B2
Viaduc du Viaur **110** A2
Viais **100** A1
Viana de Cega **152** A/B3, **160** A1
Viana do Alentejo **164** B3
Viana do Bolo **151** C3
Viana do Castelo **150** A3, **158** A1
Viandar de la Vera **159** D3
Vianden **79** D3
Viane **110** A2
Vianen **66** B3
Vianta **22** B2
Viantie **17** D3, **18** A1
Viaréggio **114** A2, **116** A1
Viarouge **110** A2
Vias **110** B3
Viasvesi **24** A1
Viator **173** D2
Vibo Marina **122** A2
Viborg **48** B2
Vibo Valéntia **122** A2
Vibraye **86** B2
Viby **49** D3, **50** A3, **53** D1
Viby **48** B3
Vic **156** A2
Vič **127** C2
Vicar **173** D2
Vicarello **114** A/B3, **116** A2
Vícari **124** B2
Vicchio **115** B/C2, **116** B1
Vicdessos **155** D2, **156** A1
Vicedo **150** B1
Vic-en-Bigorre **108** B3, **155** C1
Vicenza **107** C3
Vic-Fézensac **109** C2
Vichtenstein **93** C2
Vichy **102** B2
Vickan **49** D1, **50** A1
Vickleby **51** D2
Vic-le-Comte **102** B3
Vic-le-Fesq **111** C2
Vico **113** D3
Vico del Gargano **120** B1
Vico Equense **119** D3
Vicovaro **118** B2
Vic-sur-Cère **110** A1
Victoria **140** B1/2
Vidago **150** B3, **158** B1
Vidais **164** A1
Vidángoz **154** B2
Vidauban **112** A3
Vida Vättern **46** A2/3
Viddal **32** A3, **36** B1
Vide **158** B3
Videbæk **48** A3
Videferre **150** B3, **158** B1
Videle **141** C2
Videm **127** C3
Videm **127** D2
Vidigueira **164** B3
Vidin **135** D2
Vidin **140** B2

Vidomja **73** D3, **98** A1
Vidor **107** C2/3
Vidrá **156** A2
Vidra **141** C1
Vidra **141** C2
Vidreres **156** B3
Vidsel **16** B2/3
Vidstrup **48** B1
Viduševac **127** D3, **131** C1
Vidzy **74** A3
Viechtach **92** B1
Vieillevigne **100** A/B1
Vieira **158** A3, **164** A1
Vieira **150** B3, **158** A/B1
Viejenäs **15** D2
Vieki **23** C1/2
Vielank **69** C1
Viella **108** B3, **155** B/C1
Viella **155** C/D2
Vielle-Brioude **102** B3
Vielmesmakke **29** D1
Vielmur-sur-Agout **109** D2/3, **110** A2/3
Vielsalm **79** D2
Viels-Maisons **88** A1
Viemerö **20** B2
Vienand **28** B3, **33** D1
Vienenburg **69** C3
Vienne **103** D3
Viereck **70** B1
Vieremä **22** B1
Viereth-Trunstadt **81** D3
Vierhouten **66** B2/3
Vierlingsbeek **67** B/C3, **79** D1
Viernheim **80** B3, **90** B1
Vierraden **70** B2
Viersen **79** D1
Vierville-sur-Mer **76** A/B3, **86** A1
Vierzon **87** C3, **102** A1
Vieselbach **82** A1/2
Viesimo **23** D3
Viesīte **74** A2
Vieste **120** B1, **136** A2
Vietas turistanläggning **9** D3
Vietgest **53** D3, **69** D1
Vietri di Potenza **120** A2
Vietri sul Mare **119** D3
Vieux-Boucau-les-Bains **108** B2
Vieux-Genappe **78** B2
Vievis **73** D2, **74** A3
Vif **111** D1
Vig **49** C/D3, **53** C/D1
Viganj **136** B1
Vigarano Mainarda **115** B/C1
Vigásio **106** B3
Vigeland **42** B3
Vigeois **101** D3
Vigévano **105** D3
Vigge **34** B2
Vigge **35** C/D3
Viggiano **120** B3
Viggiù **105** D2/3
Viglesdalshytta **42** A/B2
Vigmostad **42** B3
Vignale Monferrato **113** C1
Vignanello **117** C3, **118** A/B1
Vigneulles-les-Hattonchâtel **89** C1
Vignola **114** B1/2
Vignole **107** C/D2
Vignory **88** B2
Vigny **87** C1
Vigo **150** A2/3
Vigo di Cadore **107** D2
Vigo di Fassa **107** C2
Vígolo Vattaro **107** C2
Vigone **112** B1
Vigonza **107** C3
Vigo Rendena **106** B2
Vigrestad **42** A3
Vigsnæs **53** D2
Viguera **153** D2
Vigy **89** C/D1
Vihals **32** B1/2
Vihanninkylä **21** C2/3
Vihantasalmi **26** B1
Vihanti **18** A3
Vihiers **86** A3, **100** B1
Vihren **139** D2/3
Vihtajärvi **22** B2
Vihtalahti **21** D3, **22** A3
Vihtamo **19** C3
Vihtari **23** C3
Vihtasuo **23** C2
Vihtavuori **21** D3, **22** A3
Vihteljärvi **24** B1
Vihti **25** C3
Vihtijärvi **25** C2
Vii **22** B2
Viiala **25** C1/2
Viinamäki **23** B/C1
Viiniemi **23** D1
Viinijärvi **23** C3
Viinikka **20** B2
Viinikoski **18** B2
Viiperi **21** C1
Viirinkylä **12** B3
Viisarimäki **21** D3, **22** A3
Viitaila **25** D2, **26** A2
Viitajärvi **21** D2, **22** A2
Viitala **20** B2/3
Viitamäki **21** D1, **22** A/B1
Viitaniemi **23** C2
Viitapohja **25** C1
Viitaranta **19** C1
Viitasaari **21** D2, **22** A2
Viitavaara **19** C/D3
Viitavaara **19** D3
Vik **9** B/C2
Vik **14** A3, **28** B1
Vik **50** B3
Vik **40** B3
Vika **39** D2, **40** A2
Vika **28** B3, **33** D1
Vika **38** B1
Vika **33** D2
Vika **12** B3
Vikajärvi **12** B3
Vikan **32** B1/2
Vikane **44** B1
Vikanes **36** A3
Vikarbodarna **35** D3
Vikarbyn **39** D2
Vike **35** C2
Vike **36** A3
Vikebukt **32** A2/3
Vikebygd **42** A1
Vikedal **42** A1/2
Viken **49** D3, **50** A2
Viken **29** C1/2
Viken **35** C3
Viken (Ramsjö) **35** C3
Viker **46** A1
Viker **37** D3
Vikersund **43** D1
Vikeså **42** A3
Vikestad **14** A3, **28** B1
Vikevag **42** A1
Vikevåg **42** A2
Vikholmen **14** A2
Vikingstad **46** B2
Vikjo **42** A2
Vikmanshyttan **39** D2/3, **40** A2/3
Vikna **28** B1
Viknel **15** C2
Vikran **9** C1
Vikran **4** A3
Viksdalen **36** A/B2
Viksjö **35** D2
Viksjöfors **39** D1, **40** A1
Viksmon **30** A/B3, **35** D2
Viksøyri **36** B2
Viksta **40** B3
Viktoriakyrkan **15** C3
Vila Alva **164** B3
Vilaboa **150** A2
Vila Boim **165** C2
Vilac **155** C/D2
Vila Chã **158** B1
Vila Cortez **158** B2
Vila Cova de Lixa **158** A/B1
Vilada **156** A2
Viladamat **156** B2
Viladecáns **156** A3
Vila de Estrela **158** B2
Vila de Frades **164** B3
Vila de Rei **158** A/B3, **164** B1
Vila do Bispo **170** A2
Vila do Conde **158** A1
Viladrau **156** A/B2/3
Vila Fernando **159** C2
Vila Fernando **165** C2
Vila Flôr **159** C1
Vila Franca das Naves **158** B2
Vila Franca de Xira **164** A2
Vilafranca del Penedès **156** A3, **163** D1
Vilagarcia de Arousa **150** A2
Vilaka **74** B2
Vila kapell **15** B/C2
Vilalba dels Arcs **163** C2
Vilaller **155** C2
Vilalonga de Ter **156** A2
Vilamaior **150** B1
Vilamarín **150** B2
Vilameá **151** C1
Vila Meã **158** A/B1
Vilamitjana **155** D2/3
Vilamós **155** C2
Vilamur **155** C2
Viļāni **74** A/B2
Vilank **19** D2/3
Vilanova d'Apicat **155** C3, **163** C1
Vila Nova da Baronia **164** B3
Vila Nova da Rainha **164** A2
Vila Nova de Paiva **158** B2
Vilanova de Bellpuig **155** D3, **163** D1
Vila Nova de Cerveira **150** A3
Vila Nova de Famalicão **158** A1
Vila Nova de Gaia **158** A1/2
Vila Nova de Ourém **158** A3, **164** B1
Vila Nova de Milfontes **170** A1
Vila Nova de Foz Côa **159** C2
Vilanova de la Barca **155** C3, **163** C1
Vilanova de Sau **156** A/B2
Vilanova de les Avellanes **155** C/D3
Vilanova de Meià **155** D3
Vilanova de L'Aguda **155** C3
Vilanova de Arousa **150** A2
Vilanova i la Geltrú **156** A3, **163** D1
Vilaodriz **151** C1
Vilapouca **150** A/B2
Vila Pouca de Aguiar **158** B1
Vila Praia de Ancora **150** A3, **158** A1
Vilar **164** A2
Vilarandelo **151** C3, **158** B1
Vilar de Amargo **159** C2
Vilar de Barrio **150** B3
Vilar de Maçada **158** B1
Vilar de Santos **150** B3
Vilardevós **151** C3
Vilar do Paraiso **158** A2
Vilar d'Ossos **151** C3, **159** C1
Vila Real **158** B1
Vila Real de Santo António **170** B2
Vilares **158** B1
Vilar Formoso **159** C2
Vilarinho **158** A3
Vilarinho da Castanheira **159** B/C1/2
Vilarinho das Axenhas **159** B/C1
Vilarinho de Galegos **159** C1
Vilarinho de Samardã **158** B1
Vilariño de Conso **151** C3
Vilarouco **158** B2
Vila Ruiva **164** B3
Vila-sacra **156** B2
Vilasantar **150** B1/2
Vila Sêca **158** A1
Vila Sêca **158** A3
Vilassar de Mar **156** A/B3
Vila Velha de Ródão **158** B3, **165** C1
Vilaverd **163** C1
Vila Verde **151** B/C3, **158** B1
Vila Verde **150** A3, **158** A1
Vila Verde de Ficalho **165** C3, **170** B1
Vila Viçosa **165** C2
Vilches **167** D3
Vildbjerg **48** A2/3
Vilejka **74** A3
Vilgertshofen-Stadl **91** D3
Vilhelmina **30** A1
Vília **147** D2
Vilikkala **24** B3
Viljakkala **24** B1
Vil'jandi **74** A1
Viljaniemi **25** D2, **26** A2
Viljevo **128** B3
Viljolahti **23** C3
Vilkija **73** D2
Vilkjärvi **27** C2
Villa Adriana **118** B2
Villabáñez **152** B3, **160** B1
Villa Bartolomea **107** C3, **114** B1
Villabate **124** B2
Villablanca **170** B2
Villablino **151** D2
Villabrázaro **151** D3
Villacadima **161** C1
Villacañas **161** C3, **167** D1
Villa Carlotta **105** D2, **106** A2
Villacarriedo **153** B/C1
Villacarrillo **167** D3, **168** A3
Villa Castelli **121** C2
Villacastín **160** B2
Villach **126** B2
Villach **96** A3
Villacid de Campos **152** A3
Villacidro **123** C3
Villaciervos **153** D3, **161** D1
Villaconancio **152** B3
Villaconejos **161** C3
Villaconejos de Trabaque **161** D2/3
Villada **152** A2/3
Villadangos del Páramo **151** D2
Villa del Prado **160** B3
Villa del Rey **159** C3, **165** C/D1
Villa del Río **167** C3, **172** B1
Villadepera **151** D3, **159** D1
Villa de Ves **169** D2
Villadiego **152** B2
Villadose **115** C1
Villadóssola **105** C2
Villaeles de Valdavia **152** B2
Villaescusa la Sombría **153** C2
Villaescusa **159** D1, **160** A1
Villaescusa de Haro **168** A1
Villa Estense **107** C3, **115** C1
Villaester **152** A3
Villafáfila **151** D3, **152** A3, **159** D1
Villafamés **163** C3
Villafeliche **162** A1
Villafer **151** D3, **152** A3
Villaferrueña **151** D3
Villaflor **160** A2
Villaflores **160** A2
Villafrades de Campos **152** A3
Villafranca del Cid **162** B2
Villafranca de los Barros **165** D2, **166** A2
Villafranca del Bierzo **151** C2
Villafranca del Campo **163** C2
Villafranca de Ebro **154** B3, **162** B1
Villafranca de Bon Any **157** C2
Villafranca de Duero **160** A1
Villafranca-Montes de Oca **153** C2
Villafranca de Córdoba **167** C3, **172** B1
Villafranca in Lunigiana **114** A2
Villafranca Piemonte **112** B1
Villafranca de los Caballeros **167** D1
Villafranca di Verona **106** B3
Villafranca **154** A2
Villafranca Tirrena **125** D1
Villafrati **124** B2
Villafrechos **152** A3
Villafruela **152** B3
Villafuerte **152** B3, **160** B1
Villafuertes **153** B/C3
Villagalijo **153** C2
Villagarcía de Campos **152** A3, **160** A1
Villagarcía de la Torre **165** D3, **166** A3
Villagarcía del Llano **168** B1
Villagatón **151** D2
Villággio Améndola **120** A/B1
Villággio di Capo Ferrato **123** D3
Villággio Moschella **120** B2
Villággio Mancuso **122** B2
Villággio Turístico Ostuni Marina **121** D2
Villággio Turístico Capo Rizzuto **122** B2
Villagómez la Nueva **152** A3
Villagonzalo **165** D2, **166** A2
Villagrains **108** B1
Villagrande Strisáili **123** D2
Villagrande **117** D3, **119** B/C1
Villaharta **166** B3
Villähde **25** D2, **26** A2
Villahermosa **167** D2, **168** A2
Villahermosa del Río **162** B3
Villahizán de Treviño **152** B2
Villahoz **152** B3
Villaines-en-Duesmois **88** B3
Villaines-la-Juhel **86** A2
Villaines-les-Rochers **86** B3, **101** C1
Villajoyosa **169** D2/3
Villala **23** C/D3
Villala **27** C2
Villalar de los Comuneros **152** A3, **160** A1
Villalba **124** B2
Villalba **150** B1
Villalba Baja **162** A/B2
Villalba de los Barros **165** D2
Villalba de la Lampreana **151** D3, **152** A3, **159** D1
Villalba de la Sierra **161** D3
Villalba de los Alcores **152** A3
Villalba de Guardo **152** A2
Villalba de los Llanos **159** D2
Villalba de los Morales **162** A2
Villalba del Alcor **171** C1/2
Villalba del Rey **161** D2/3
Villalcázar de Sirga **152** B2
Villalcón **152** A2
Villaldemiro **152** B2/3
Villalengua **154** A3, **161** D1, **162** A1
Villalgordo del Jucar **168** B1/2
Villalgordo del Marquesado **161** D3, **168** A1
Villa Literno **119** C3
Villalobos **152** A3
Villalón de Campos **152** A3
Villalonga **169** D2
Villalpando **152** A3
Villalpardo **168** B1
Villalube **151** D3, **152** A3, **159** D1, **160** A1
Villaluenga del Rosario **172** A2
Villalumbroso **152** A/B3
Villálvaro **153** C3, **161** C1
Villalvérnia **113** D1
Villamalea **168** B1
Villamañán **151** D2, **152** A2
Villamanín **151** D2, **152** A2
Villamanrique **167** D2, **168** A2
Villamanrique de la Condesa **171** D2
Villamanrique de Tajo **161** C3

Villamanta **160** B3
Villamar **123** C/D3
Villamarchante **169** C/D1
Villamartín **171** D2
Villamartín de Campos **152** B3
Villamartín de Don Sancho **152** A2
Villamartín de Valdeorras **151** C2
Villamassárgia **123** C3
Villamayor **159** D2
Villamayor de Santiago **161** C3, **167** D1, **168** A1
Villamayor de Calatrava **167** C2
Villamayor de Gállego **154** B3, **162** B1
Villambistia **153** C2
Villamblard **109** C1
Villamediana **153** D2
Villamejil **151** D2
Villameriel **152** B2
Villamesías **166** A1/2
Villamiel de la Sierra **153** C3
Villamiel de Toledo **160** B3, **167** C1
Villaminaya **160** B3, **167** C1
Villa Minozzo **114** A/B2, **116** A1
Villamizar **152** A2
Villamor de Cadozos **159** D1
Villamoronta **152** B2
Villamuelas **160** B3, **167** C1
Villamuriel de Campos **152** A3
Villamuriel de Cerrato **152** B3
Villa Napoleone **116** A3
Villandraut **108** B1/2
Villandry **86** B3
Villanova **121** C/D2
Villanova **112** B1
Villanova d'Asti **113** C1
Villanovafranca **123** C/D3
Villanova Monteleone **123** C2
Villanova Mondovì **113** C2
Villanova Strisáili **123** D2
Villanova Truschedu **123** C2
Villanova Tulo **123** D2
Villantério **105** D3, **106** A3, **113** D1
Villanúa **154** B2
Villanubla **152** A3, **160** A1
Villanueva **153** D2, **154** A2
Villanueva del Campo **152** A3
Villanueva de San Juan **172** A2
Villanueva de Gumiel **153** C3, **161** C1
Villanueva de Duero **152** A3, **160** A1
Villanueva de Gormaz **161** C1
Villanueva de Alcolea **163** C3
Villanueva de la Cañada **160** B2
Villanueva de Oscos **151** C1
Villanueva de Alcardete **161** C3, **167** D1, **168** A1
Villanueva de Castellón **169** D2
Villanueva de Cameros **153** D3
Villanueva del Arzobispo **167** D3, **168** A3
Villanueva de la Concepción **172** B2
Villanueva de San Carlos **167** C2
Villanueva de la Sierra **159** C3
Villanueva de Córdoba **167** B/C3
Villanueva del Duque **166** B3
Villanueva de Argaño **152** B2
Villanueva de los Infantes **167** D2, **168** A2
Villanueva de Viver **162** B3

Villanueva de los Castillejos **171** B/C1
Villanueva de Henares **152** B2
Villanueva de Gállego **154** B3, **162** B1
Villanueva de Guadamajud **161** D3
Villanueva de San Mancio **152** A3
Villanueva de la Fuente **168** A2
Villanueva del Río Segura **169** D3
Villanueva de Algaidas **172** B2
Villanueva de las Manzanas **151** D2, **152** A2
Villanueva de la Jara **168** B1
Villanueva de la Serena **166** A2
Villanueva de la Reina **167** C3, **173** B/C1
Villanueva de Bogas **161** B/C3, **167** C/D1
Villanueva de Alcorón **161** D2
Villanueva del Trabuco **172** B2
Villanueva de las Cruces **171** C1
Villanueva de Sigena **155** C3, **163** C1
Villanueva del Fresno **165** C3
Villanueva del Rey **166** B3
Villanueva del Río **171** D1
Villanueva de Tapia **172** B2
Villanueva del Aceral **160** A2
Villanueva de las Minas **171** D1
Villanueva del Huerva **162** A/B1
Villanueva de las Torres **173** C1
Villanueva del Pardillo **160** B2
Villanueva del Rosario **172** B2
Villa Nuova **115** C2, **117** C1
Villány **128** B3
Villa Opicina **126** B3
Villapalacios **168** A2
Villapiana Lido **120** B3, **122** B1
Villa Potenza **115** D3, **117** D2
Villaputzu **123** D3
Villaquejida **151** D3, **152** A3
Villaquilambre **151** D2, **152** A2
Villaralto **166** B3
Villarcayo **153** C2
Villard-Bonnot **104** A3, **112** A1
Villard-de-Lans **103** D3, **111** D1
Villardebelle **110** A3, **156** A/B1
Villar de Canes **163** C2/3
Villar de Cañas **161** D3, **168** A1
Villar de Chinchilla **169** B/C2
Villar de Ciervo **159** C2
Villardeciervos **151** D3
Villar de Cobeta **161** D2
Villar de Domingo García **161** D3
Villardefrades **152** A3, **160** A1
Villar de Gallimazo **160** A2
Villar de Horno **161** D3
Villar de la Encina **161** D3, **168** A1
Villar del Águila **161** D3
Villar del Arzobispo **162** B3, **169** C1
Villar de la Yegua **159** C2
Villar del Buey **159** D1
Villar del Cobo **162** A2/3
Villar del Humo **162** A3, **168** B1

Villar del Infantado **161** D2
Villar de los Navarros **162** A/B1/2
Villar del Olmo **161** C3
Villar del Pedroso **160** A3, **166** B1
Villar del Rey **165** C/D2
Villar del Río **153** D3
Villar del Salz **162** A2
Villar del Saz de Navalón **161** D3
Villar de Maya **153** D3
Villar de Peralonso **159** C/D2
Villar de Rena **166** A2
Villárdiga **152** A3, **159** D1, **160** A1
Villardompardo **167** C3, **172** B2
Villarejo de Fuentes **161** D3, **168** A1
Villarejo de Medina **161** D2
Villarejo de Salvanés **161** C3
Villarejo de Montalbán **160** A/B3, **167** B/C1
Villa Rendena **106** B2
Villarente **152** A2
Villares de Yeltes **159** C2
Villares del Saz **161** D3, **168** A1
Villaretto **112** B1
Villargordo del Cabriel **169** C1
Villargordo **167** C3, **173** C1
Villarino **159** C1
Villarluengo **162** B2
Villarmayor **159** D2
Villarmuerto **159** C2
Villa Romana del Casale **125** C2/3
Villarosa **125** C2
Villar Perosa **112** B1
Villarquemado **163** C2
Villarramiel **152** A3
Villarrasa **171** C1/2
Villarreal **165** C2
Villarreal de San Carlos **159** D3, **165** D1, **166** A1
Villarreal de los Infantes **163** B/C3, **169** D1
Villarreal de la Canal **154** B2
Villarrín de Campos **151** D3, **152** A3, **159** D1
Villarrobledo **168** A1/2
Villarroga de los Pinares **162** B2
Villarroya **153** D3
Villarroya de la Sierra **154** A3, **162** A1
Villarrubia de los Ojos **167** D2
Villarrubia de Santiago **161** C3
Villarrubio **161** C3
Villars-lès-Blamont **89** D3, **90** A3, **104** B1
Villars-les-Dombes **103** D2
Villars-sur-Ollon **104** B2
Villarta **168** B1
Villarta de los Montes **166** B2
Villarta de San Juan **167** D2
Villasalto **123** D3
Villasana de Mena **153** C1
Villasandino **152** B2
Villa San Giovanni **122** A3, **125** D1
Villa Santa Maria **119** D2
Villa Sant'António **117** D3
Villasante **153** C1/2
Villa Santina **107** D2, **126** A2
Villasayas **161** D1
Villasbuenas de Gata **159** C3
Villaseca de la Sagra **160** B3, **167** C1
Villaseca de Arciel **153** D3, **161** D1
Villaseco de los Gamitos **159** D2
Villaseco de los Reyes **159** D1/2
Villasequilla de Yepes **160** B3, **167** C1
Villasilos **152** B2

Villasimíus **123** D3
Villasmundo **125** D3
Villasor **123** C/D3
Villasrubias **159** C3
Villastar **163** C3
Villastellone **113** B/C1
Villa Superiore **114** B1
Villasur de Herreros **153** C2
Villatobas **161** C3, **167** D1
Villatoro **160** A2
Villatoya **169** D1
Villatuerta **153** D2, **154** A2
Villaurbana **123** C2
Villava **154** A2
Villavaliente **169** B/C2
Villavallelonga **119** C2
Villavelayo **153** C3
Villavendimio **152** A3, **159** D1, **160** A1
Villaverde **161** B/C2/3
Villaverde de Iscar **160** B1
Villaverde de Guadalimar **168** A2/3
Villaverde del Río **171** D1
Villaverde del Ducado **161** D2
Villaverde de Arcayos **152** A2
Villaverde de Trucíos **153** C1
Villaverde de Medina **160** A1
Villaverde y Pasaconsol **161** D3, **168** B1
Villaviciencio de los Caballeros **152** A3
Villaviciosa de Córdoba **166** B3, **172** A1
Villaviciosa **152** A1
Villaviciosa de la Ribera **151** D2
Villaviciosa de Odón **160** B2/3
Villavieja **162** B3, **169** D1
Villavieja del Lozoya **161** B/C2
Villavieja de Yeltes **159** C2
Villaviudas **152** B3
Villa Vomano **117** D3, **119** C1
Villayón **151** C1
Villdalsseter **38** A/B1
Villé **89** D2, **90** A2
Villebaudon **86** A1
Villebois-Lavalette **101** C3
Villebret **102** B2
Villechenève **103** C2/3
Villecomtal-sur-Arros **109** B/C3, **155** C1
Villecomtal **110** A1
Villedaigne **110** A3, **156** B1
Villedieu-les-Poêles **86** A/B1
Villedieu-sur-Indre **101** D1, **102** A1
Villedômain **101** C1
Villedoux **100** B2
Ville-en-Tardenois **88** A1
Villefagnan **101** C2
Villefort **110** B1/2
Villefranche-de-Lauragais **109** D3, **155** D1
Villefranche de Longchat **108** B1
Villefranche-de-Rouergue **109** D2
Villefranche-du-Périgord **109** C1
Villefranche-de-Conflent **156** A/B1/2
Villefranche-Saint-Phal **87** D2, **88** A2
Villefranche **109** C3, **155** C1
Villefranche **102** B2
Villefranche-de-Panat **110** A2
Villefranche-d'Albigeois **110** A2
Villefranche-sur-Cher **87** C3
Villefranche-sur-Saône **103** D2
Villegas **152** B2
Villegly **110** A3, **156** B1
Villel **163** C3
Villel de Mesa **161** D1/2

Villemaur-sur-Vanne **88** A2
Villemontais **103** C2
Villemorien **88** B2
Villemur-sur-Tarn **109** D2
Villena **169** C2
Villenauxe la Grande **88** A2
Villenave **108** A/B2
Villeneuve **109** D1/2
Villeneuve **104** B3
Villeneuve **104** B2
Villeneuve-de-Berg **111** C1
Villeneuve-de-Marsan **108** B2
Villeneuve-lès-Avignon **111** C2
Villeneuve-la-Guyard **87** D2
Villeneuve-l'Archevêque **88** A2
Villeneuve-les-Bordes **87** D2
Villeneuve-sur-Lot **109** C2
Villeneuve-Saint-Georges **87** D1
Villeneuve-sur-Tarn **110** A2
Villeneuve-Saint-Martin **87** C1
Villeneuve-sur-Yonne **88** A2
Villeneuve-sur-Allier **102** B1
Villeneuve-sur-Vère **109** D2
Villentrois **87** C3, **101** D1
Villepinte **109** D3, **156** A1
Villequier-Aumont **78** A3
Villeréal **109** C2
Villerías **152** A3
Villeromain **86** A/B3
Villerouge-Termenès **110** A3, **156** B1
Villers-Bocage **86** A1
Villers-Bocage **77** D2
Villers-Bretonneux **78** A3
Villers-Carbonnel **78** A3
Villers-Cotterêts **87** D1, **88** A1
Villers-devant-Orval **79** C3
Villersexel **89** D3
Villers-la-Montagne **79** D3
Villers-la-Ville **79** B/C2
Villers-sur-Mer **76** B3, **86** A/B1
Villers-sur-Meuse **89** C1
Villerville **76** B3, **86** B1
Villesèque **108** B2
Villes-sur-Auzon **111** D2
Ville-sur-Illon **89** C2
Ville-sur-Tourbe **88** B1
Villevalier **88** A2
Villeveyrac **110** B3
Ville-Vieille **112** B1
Villiers-Charlemagne **86** A2/3
Villiers-Saint-Georges **88** A2
Villiers-Saint-Benoît **87** D3, **88** A3
Villikkala **26** B2
Villimpenta **107** B/C3, **114** B1
Villingen-Schwenningen **90** B3
Villingsberg **46** A1
Villmanstrand **27** C2
Villmar-Aumenau **80** B2
Villmergen **90** B3, **105** C1
Villoldo **152** B2
Villora **162** A3, **168** B1
Villores **162** B2
Villoría **159** D2, **160** A2
Villoslada de Cameros **153** D3
Villotta **107** D2/3, **126** A2/3
Villovela de Pirón **160** B1/2
Villshärad **49** D2, **50** A2
Vilmikkala **21** D2, **22** A2
Vilnius **73** D2, **74** A3
Vilpiano/Vilpian **107** C2
Vilppula **21** C3
Vils **48** A2
Vils **91** D3
Vilsbiburg **92** B2
Vilsbiburg-Wolferding **92** B2
Vilseck **82** A3
Vilshofen **93** C2

Vilshult 51 B/C2
Vilslev 52 A1
Vilsund 48 A2
Vilusi 137 C1
Vilvoorde 78 B1/2
Vimbodí 163 D1
Vimianzo 150 A1
Vimieiro 164 B2
Vimioso 151 C3, 159 C1
Vimmerby 46 B3
Vimmerby 72 B1
Vimoutiers 86 B1
Vimpeli (Vindala) 21 C2
Vimperk 93 C1
Vimperk 96 A2
Vinac 131 D2, 132 A2
Vinaceite 162 B1
Vinádio 112 B2
Vinadi [Scuol-Tarasp]
  106 B1
Vinaixa 155 D3, 163 D1
Vinaroz 163 C2
Vinäs 39 C/D2
Vinay 103 D3
Vinca 156 B1/2
Vinča 133 D1, 134 A/B1
Vincelles 88 A3
Vinchiaturo 119 D2
Vinci 114 B2, 116 A1/2
Vinciarello 122 B3
Vindala 21 C2
Vindelkroken 15 C2
Vindeln 31 C2
Vinderup 48 A2
Vindsvik 42 A/B2
Vinebre 163 C1/2
Viñegra de Moraña 160 A2
Vines 36 B3
Vinga 44 B3, 49 C1
Vingåker 46 B1
Vingelen 33 C/D3
Vingen 36 A1
Vingrau 156 B1
Vingstad 4 A3, 10 A1
Vinhais 151 C3, 159 C1
Vinica 95 D2
Vinica 139 C2
Vinica 127 C3
Viniegra de Arriba
  153 C/D3
Viniegra de Abajo 153 C3
Vinišce 131 C3
Vinište 135 D3
Vinje 43 B/C1
Vinje 36 B3
Vinje 8 B2
Vinje 9 D1
Vinjeøra 32 B2
Vinju Mare 135 D2
Vinju Mare 140 B2
Vinkià 25 C1, 26 A1
Vinkkilä 24 A2
Vinkovci 129 C3, 133 C1
Vinliden 30 B1
Vinnäset 17 C2
Vinne 28 B3, 33 D1
Vinni 21 C2
Vinnica 99 C3
Vinogradov 97 D2/3,
  98 A3
Vinon 47 D2
Vinon-sur-Verdon 111 D2,
  112 A2/3
Vinovo 113 B/C1
Vinsa 17 C1
Vinslöv 50 B2
Vinsternes 32 B2
Vinstra 37 D2
Vintervollen 7 D2
Vintjärn 40 A2
Vintrosa 46 A1
Viñuela 172 B2
Viñuela 167 C2
Viñuela de Sayago 159 D1
Viñuelas 161 C2
Vinuesa 153 D3
Vipava 126 B3
Vipiteno/Sterzing 107 C1
Vir 130 B2
Vira 131 C3, 136 A1
Virdois 21 C3
Vire 85 D1, 86 A1
Vireda 46 A3
Virenoja 25 D2, 26 A2
Vireši 74 A2
Virestad 50 B2
Vireux-Molhain 79 C3

Vîrfurile 97 D3, 140 B1
Virginia 54 A3, 55 D2
Virieu-le-Grand 104 A3
Virieu-sur-Bourbre 103 D3,
  104 A3
Virine 134 B2
Virisen 15 C3
Virje 128 A2
Virkkala/Virkby 25 C3
Virkkula 19 D1
Virkkunen 19 C1
Virklund 48 B3
Virksund 48 B3, 52 B1
Virmaanpää 22 B2
Virmaila 25 D1, 26 A1
Virmutjoki 27 C1
Virojoki 27 C2
Virolahti 27 C2
Virovitica 128 A3
Virpazar 137 D2
Virpiniemi 18 A2
Virrat (Virdois) 21 C3
Virsbo 40 A3
Virserum 51 C1
Virtaa 25 D1, 26 A1
Virtala 21 C2
Virtaniemi 7 C3
Virton 79 C3
Vîrtopu 135 D2
Virtsu 74 A1
Virttaa 24 B2
Vis 136 A1
Vişagu 97 D3, 140 B1
Visala 19 C1
Visan 111 C2
Visbek 67 D2, 68 A2
Visby 47 D2/3
Visby 72 B1
Visé 79 C/D2
Visegrád 95 D3
Višegrad 133 C3
Višegradska Banja
  133 C2/3
Viseu 158 B2
Vişeul de Sus 97 D3,
  98 A/B3
Višići 136 B1
Visiedo 162 A/B2
Visingsö 45 D3, 46 A3
Viskafors 45 C3, 49 D1
Viskan 35 C3
Viskinge 49 C3, 53 C1
Vislanda 51 B/C2
Vislanda 72 A1
Visnes 42 A2
Višnja Gora 127 C2/3
Višnjan 126 B3, 130 A1
Višnjica 127 D2
Višňové 94 A/B1
Visnums-Kil 45 D1, 46 A1
Viso del Marqués 167 D2/3
Visoka 133 D3, 134 A3
Visoki Dečani 138 A1/2
Visoko 132 B2
Visone 113 C1
Visp 105 C2
Viš Revúca 95 D1
Vissefjärda 51 C2
Vissefjärda 72 B1
Visselhövede-Wittorf 68 B2
Visselhövede 68 B2
Vissinéa 143 C2
Vissiniá 143 C2
Visso 115 D3, 117 D2/3
Vissoie [Sierre] 105 C2
Vistabella 163 C1
Vistabella del Maestrazgo
  162 B3
Vistasstugan 9 D2/3
Vistdal 32 B2
Vistheden 16 B3
Visthus 14 A1
Vistnes 14 A3
Vistoft 49 C2/3
Visuvesi 21 C3
Visz 128 B1/2
Vita 124 A2
Vitåfors 17 C2
Vitakylä 21 D2, 22 A2
Vitanen 18 B3
Vitanje 127 C2
Vitanovac 134 B3
Vitebsk 74 B3
Viteml'a 99 D1
Vitemölla 50 B3
Viterbo 117 C3, 118 A1

Vitez 132 B2
Vithkuqi 142 B2
Vitigudino 159 C2
Vitina 138 B2
Vitina 146 B3
Vitina 132 A3, 136 B1
Vitis 93 D2, 94 A2
Vitis 96 A2
Vitlycke 44 B2
Vitna 74 A1
Vitolište 139 C3, 143 C1
Vitomirica 138 A1
Vitoševac 135 B/C3
Vitovlje 131 D2, 132 A2
Vitré 86 A/B2
Vitrey-sur-Mance 89 C3
Vitry-aux-Loges 87 D2/3
Vitry-en-Artois 78 A2
Vitry-en-Perthois 88 B1
Vitry-la-Ville 88 B1
Vitry-le-François 88 B1/2
Vítsa 142 B3
Vitsai 27 C2
Vitsakumpu 11 D3, 12 A2
Vitsand 39 B/C2/3
Vitsikkovuoma 12 A2/3,
  17 D1
Vitskøl Kloster 48 B2
Vittangi 10 B3
Vittaryd 50 B1
Vitteaux 88 B3
Vittel 89 C2
Vittiko 13 C3
Vittinge 40 A/B3
Vittjärn 38 B3
Vittjärv 17 C2
Vittória 125 C3
Vittório Véneto 107 D2
Vitträsk (Pålkem) 16 B2
Vittsjö 50 B2
Vittskövle 50 B3
Vitulázio 119 C/D3
Vitvattnet 17 C2
Vitvattnet 34 B3
Viù 104 B3, 112 B1
Viuf 88 B3
Viuhkola 26 B2
Viuruniemi 23 C3
Vivario 113 D3
Viveiro 150 B1
Vivel del Río Martín 162 B2
Viveli 36 B3
Viver 162 B3, 169 C/D1
Viver 156 A2
Viverols 103 C3
Viveros 168 A2
Viviere 112 B2
Viviers 111 C1
Viviers-les-Montagnes
  110 A3
Vivonne 101 C2
Vivungi 10 B3
Vizcaínos 153 C3
Vize 141 C3
Vizić 133 C1
Vizille 111 D1, 112 A1
Vižinada 126 B3, 130 A1
Vižnica 98 B3
Vizovice 95 C1
Vizvár 128 A2
Vizzavona 113 D3
Vizzini 125 C3
Vjaz'ma 75 D3
Vjetrenica 137 B/C1
Vlaardingen 66 A3
Vlachokeraséa 146 A1
Vlachokeraséa 148 A2
Vlachokerasiá 147 B/C3
Vlachovice 95 C1
Vlachovo Březí 93 C1
Vlǎdeni 141 C1
Vladičin Han 139 C1
Vladimirci 133 C/D1/2,
  134 A2
Vladimirovac 134 B1
Vladimirskij Tupik 75 C3
Vladimir-Volynskij 97 D1,
  98 A/B2
Vlagtwedde 67 C2
Vlajkovac 134 B1
Vlaole 135 C2
Vlasenica 133 C2
Vlasiá 146 B2
Vlašići 130 B2
Vlašim 83 D3
Vlasina Okruglica 139 C1
Vlasotince 139 C1

Vlasotince 140 A3
Vlásti 143 C2
Vlčany 95 C2/3
Vlichón 146 A1
Vlieland 66 B1
Vlissingen 78 B1
Vlkava 83 D2
Vlochós 143 C/D3
Vlönkylä 24 B3
Vlorë 142 A2
Vlorë 148 A1
Vlotho 68 A3
Vlotho-Valdorf 68 A3
Vnà [Scuol-Tarasp] 106 B1
Vo 106 B3
Vobarno 106 B3
Voćin 138 A3
Vöcklabruck 93 C3
Vöcklabruck 96 A3
Vöcklamarkt 93 C3
Vodice 131 C2
Vodice 126 B3
Vodňany 93 C/D1
Vodňany 96 A2
Vodnjan 130 A1
Vodo Cadore 107 D2
Vodskov 48 B1
Voer 49 B/C2
Voerde 67 C3, 79 D1,
  80 A1
Voergård 49 B/C1
Voerså 49 C1
Vogatsikón 143 C2
Vogelsang 70 A2
Voghera 113 D1
Vognill 33 C2/3
Vogogna 105 C2
Vogošca 132 B2
Vogt 91 C3
Vogtareuth 92 B3
Vogtsburg-Burkheim
  90 A2/3
Vogué 111 C1
Vohburg 92 A2
Vohdensaari 24 A2, 41 D2
Vohenstrauss 82 B3
Vöhl-Herzhausen 81 C1
Vohonjoki 19 B/C1
Vöhrenbach 90 B3
Vöhringen 91 D2
Vöhringen (Horb) 90 B2
Void 89 C1/2
Voikkaa 26 B2
Voikoski 26 B1/2
Voineasa 140 B2
Voiron 103 D3, 104 A3
Voise 87 C2
Voiteur 103 D1, 104 A1
Voitsberg 127 C1
Voitsdorf 93 C3
Vojakkala 25 C2
Vojakkala 17 D2, 18 A1
Vojens 52 B1
Vojka 133 D1, 134 A1
Vojnić 127 C/D3, 131 C1
Vojnice 95 D3
Vojnik 127 C2
Vojtjajaure kapell 15 C3
Volary 93 C1/2
Vólax 144 B1
Volda 36 B1
Volden 37 C/D2
Volden 33 C/D2
Volders 107 C1
Volendam 66 B2
Volenice 93 C1
Volhov 75 C1
Volímai 148 A2
Volímai 146 A2
Volissós 149 C2
Volkach 81 D3
Volkenschwand 92 A/B2
Völkermarkt 127 B/C2
Völkermarkt 96 A3
Völklingen 89 D1, 90 A1
Volkmarsen 81 C1
Volkmarsen-Ehringen
  81 C1
Volkovija 138 A/B3
Volkovysk 73 D3, 98 B1
Vollan 4 A3, 10 A1
Vollen 33 B/C1/2
Vollen 38 A3, 43 D1
Vollenhove 67 B/C2
Vollersode 68 A1
Vollerwiek 52 A3
Vollmoen 29 C1/2

Vollore-Montagne
  103 C2/3
Vollrathsruhe 53 D3, 69 D1
Vollseter 32 A3, 36 B1
Vollsjö 50 B3
Volmadonna 113 C1
Volmsjö 30 B2
Volnes 14 A2
Volokolamsk 75 D2
Vólos 148 B1
Vólos 143 D3, 144 A3
Volosovo 74 B1
Volot 75 B/C2
Volovec 97 D2, 98 A3
Voložin 74 A3
Volpago del Montello
  107 C/D3
Volpiano 105 C3, 113 C1
Völpke 69 C3
Volpriehausen 68 B3,
  81 C1
Voltággio 113 D1
Volta Mantovana 106 B3
Volterra 114 B3, 116 A2
Voltlage-Hosckel 67 D2
Voltti 20 B2
Volturara Áppula 119 D2,
  120 A1
Volturara Irpina 119 D3,
  120 A2
Volvic 102 B2
Volx 111 D2, 112 A2
Volyně 93 C1
Vónitsa 146 A1
Vonnas 103 D2
Vönöck 94 B3, 128 A1
Voorthuizen 66 B3
Vorau 94 A3, 127 D1
Vörå/Vöyri 20 B2
Vorbasse 48 A/B3, 52 B1
Vorchdorf 93 C3
Vorde 48 B2
Vorden 67 C3
Vordernberg 93 D3
Vordingborg 53 D2
Vorë 137 D3, 142 A1
Voreppe 104 A3
Vorey 103 C3
Vormsi 74 A1
Vormträsk 31 C1
Vorna 18 B3
Vorn'any 74 A3
Vorpbukt 28 A2, 33 C1
Voskopoje 142 B2
Voskresenskoe 75 C1
Voskresenskoe 75 D1
Vosne-Romanée 88 B3,
  103 D1
Vosočka Ržana 135 D3,
  139 D1
Voss 36 B3
Votice 83 D3
Votice 96 A2
Votonósion 143 B/C3
Voué 88 A/B2
Vouillé 101 C1/2
Voúla 147 D2
Vouliagméni 147 D2
Voulx 87 D2
Voúnargon 146 A3
Vouneuil-sur-Vienne
  101 C1
Vourvourou 144 B2
Voutenay-sur-Cure 88 A3
Vouvant 100 B2
Vouvray 86 B3
Vouvry 104 B2
Vouzela 158 A/B2
Vouzeron 87 D3, 102 A1
Vouziers 88 B1
Voúzion 147 B/C1
Vouzon 87 C3
Voves 87 C2
Voxna 39 D1
Voxna 39 D1
Voz 126 B3, 130 B1
Vozmediano 154 A3,
  161 D1, 162 A1
Vrå 50 B2
Vrå 48 B1
Vrabča 139 D1
Vráble 95 C/D2
Vraca 135 D3, 139 D1
Vraca 140 B3
Vračev Gaj 134 B1
Vračevšnica 133 D2,
  134 A/B2

Vracov 95 B/C1
Vrådal 43 C2
Vråliosen 43 C2
Vrana 131 C2
Vrana 130 A1
Vranduk 132 B2
Vrångö 45 C3, 49 D1
Vranić 133 D1/2, 134 A2
Vranishti 142 A2
Vranja Stena 139 D2
Vranje 139 C1/2
Vranje 126 B3, 130 A1
Vranje 140 A3
Vranjina 137 D2
Vranjska Banja 139 C1/2
Vranov 94 A1
Vranovice 94 B1
Vransko 127 C2
Vrapče Polje 137 D1, 138 A1
Vrata 135 D2
Vratarnica 135 C3
Vratěnín 94 A1
Vrátna 95 D1
Vratna 135 C2
Vratnica 138 B2
Vratnjanske Kapike 135 C2
Vratno 127 D2
Vrâv 135 D2
Vražogrnac 135 C2
Vrba 134 B3
Vrbanja 133 C1
Vrbanja 131 D1, 132 A1
Vŗbas 129 C3
Vrbljani 131 D2, 132 A2
Vrbnica 138 A2
Vrbnik 130 B1
Vrboska 131 D3, 136 A1
Vrbovce 95 C2
Vrbové 95 C2
Vrbovec 127 D2/3
Vrbovsko 127 C3, 130 B1
Vrchlabí 96 A1
Vrčin 133 D1, 134 A/B1/2
Vrdnik 133 C/D1, 134 A1
Vreden 67 C3
Vreden-Ammeloe 67 C3
Vreeland 66 B3
Vrees 67 D2
Vrejlev Kirke 48 B1
Vrela 138 A1
Vrelo 135 C3
Vrelo 131 C1
Vrena 47 B/C2
Vreoci 133 D2, 134 A2
Vřesovice 95 B/C1
Vrésthena 147 C3
Vreta 24 B3
Vreta Kloster 46 B2
Vretstorp 46 A1
Vrginmost 127 D3, 131 C1
Vrgorac 131 D3, 132 A3, 136 B1
Vrhnika 126 B2
Vrhovine 130 B1
Vrhpolje 131 D2
Vries 67 C2
Vriezenveen 67 C2
Vriezenveensewijk 67 C2
Vrigstad 51 B/C1
Vrigstad 72 A1
Vrin [Ilanz] 105 D2, 106 A1/2
Vrlika 131 C2/3
Vrmdža 135 C3
Vrnjačka Banja 134 B3
Vrnjačka Banja 140 A2
Vrnograč 127 D3, 131 C1
Vronderón 142 B1/2
Vrosína 142 B3
Vrosína 148 A1
Vroutek 83 C2/3
Vrpolje 131 C3
Vrpolje 128 B3, 132 B1
Vršac 134 B1
Vršac 140 A2
Vrsar 130 A1
Vrsi 130 B2
Vrška-Čuka 135 C3
Vrtoče 131 C2
Vrútky 95 D1
Vrutok 138 B2/3
Všeruby 93 B/C1
Všetaty 83 D2
Vsetín 95 C1
Vsetín 96 B2
Vuarrens [Yverdon] 104 B1/2
Vučedol 129 C3, 133 C1
Vučijak 132 A/B1
Vučitrn 138 B1
Vučje 139 C1
Vučje Luka 132 B2
Vučkovec 127 D2
Vučkovica 134 B2
Vufflens-le-Château 104 B2
Vught 66 B3, 79 C1
Vuka 128 B3
Vukovar 129 C3
Vukovina 127 D3
Vuku 28 B3, 33 D1
Vulaines 88 A2
Vulcan 135 D1
Vulkaneşty 141 D1/2
Vulpera [Scuol-Tarasp] 106 B1
Vultureşti 141 C1
Vuno 142 A2
Vuoggatjålme 15 C1/2
Vuohijärvi 26 B2
Vuohiniemi 25 C2
Vuohtomäki 21 D1, 22 A1
Vuojärvi 12 B2
Vuojelahti 22 B3
Vuokatti 19 C3, 23 C1
Vuokko 23 C2
Vuolenkoski 25 D2, 26 A/B2
Vuolijoki 18 B3
Vuolijoki 25 C1/2
Vuolle 21 C1
Vuollerim 16 B2
Vuomahytta 10 A2
Vuomajärvi 17 D2
Vuonajåkk 10 A3
Vuonatjviken 15 D2
Vuonislahti 23 D2
Vuontisjärvi 11 C2, 12 A1
Vuontisjoki 11 C2, 12 A1
Vuorenkylä 25 D1, 26 A1
Vuorenmaa 24 B2
Vuorenmaa 22 B3
Vuoreslahti 19 C3
Vuorijärvi 20 B3
Vuorilahti 21 D2, 22 A2
Vuorimäki 22 B1
Vuoriniemi 27 D1
Vuosalmi 27 C1
Vuoskojaure 10 A2
Vuostimo 13 B/C3
Vuostimojärvi 12 B3
Vuotinainen 25 C2
Vuotner 16 A3
Vuotso 12 B1
Vuottas 17 C2
Vuottolahti 19 C3, 22 B1
Vuotunki 19 D1
Výčapy 94 A1
Vydor 74 B2
Vydropužsk 75 D2
Vy-lès-Lure 89 D3
Vyöni 17 D1/2
Vyra 74 B1
Vyrica 74 B1
Vyškov 96 B2
Vyškov 94 B1
Vyskytná 94 A1
Vyšnij Voloček 75 D2
Vyšný Kubín 95 D1
Vysoká Libyně 83 C3
Vysoká pri Morave 94 B2
Vysokoje 73 D3, 98 A1
Vysokovsk 75 D2
Vyšší Brod 93 D2
Vystupoviči 99 C2

W

Waabs 52 B2
Waakirchen 92 A3
Waal (Kaufbeuren) 91 D3
Waalwijk 66 B3
Waben 77 D2
Wabern 81 C1
Wąbrzeźno 73 C3
Wachau 82 B1
Wachtendonk 79 D1
Wächtersbach 81 C2
Wackersdorf 92 B1
Wackersleben 69 C3
Waddesdon 64 B2/3
Waddeweitz-Dommatzen 69 C2
Wadebridge 62 B3
Wädenswil 105 D1
Wadern 80 A3, 90 A1
Wadern-Nunkirchen 80 A3, 90 A1
Wadersloh 67 D3, 68 A3
Wadersloh-Liesborn 67 D3, 68 A3, 80 B1
Wadowice 97 C2
Wagenfeld 68 A2
Wagenfeld-Förlingen 68 A2
Wagenfeld-Ströhen 68 A2
Wageningen 66 B3
Waghäusel-Kirrlach 90 B1
Waghäusel-Wiesental 90 B1
Waging am See 92 B3
Wagrain 93 C3, 126 A1
Wągrowiec 71 D2
Wągrowiec 72 B3
Wahlsdorf 70 A3
Wahlstedt 52 B3
Waiblingen 91 C2
Waidhaus 82 B3
Waidhofen an der Thaya 94 A1/2
Waidhofen an der Ybbs 93 D3
Waidhofen an der Thaya 96 A2
Waidhofen an der Ybbs 96 A3
Waidring 92 B3
Waimes 79 D2
Wainfleet All Saints 61 D3, 65 C1
Wainhouse Corner 62 B2/3
Waischenfeld 82 A3
Waizenkirchen 93 C2
Wakefield 61 C2
Wałbrzych (Waldenburg) 96 B1
Walchsee 92 B3
Wałcz (Deutsch Krone) 71 D1
Wałcz (Deutsch Krone) 72 B3
Wald 92 B1
Wald 105 D1
Waldachtal-Lützenhardt 90 B2
Waldböckelheim 80 A/B3
Waldbreitbach 80 A2
Waldbröl 80 A/B2
Waldbrunn 80 B2
Waldeck 81 C1
Waldeck-Höringhausen 81 C1
Waldeck-Sachsenhausen 81 C1
Waldems-Esch 80 B2/3
Waldenbuch 91 C2
Waldenburg 90 A3, 105 C1
Waldenburg 82 B2
Waldenburg-Obersteinbach 91 C1
Waldershof 82 B3
Waldfischbach-Burgalben 90 A1
Waldheim 82 B1
Waldighoffen 89 D3, 90 A3
Wald im Pinzgau 107 D1
Waldkappel 81 C1
Waldkappel-Gehau 81 C1
Waldkirch 90 B2/3
Waldkirchen 93 C2
Waldkirchen-Böhmzwiesel 93 C2
Waldkraiburg 92 B2
Wald-Michelbach-Unter-Schönmattenwag 81 C3, 91 B/C1
Wald Michelbach 81 B/C3, 90 B1
Waldmohr 89 D1, 90 A1
Waldmünchen 92 B1
Wałdowice 71 C2
Waldsassen 82 B3
Waldshut-Tiengen 90 B3
Wald (Sigmaringen) 91 C3
Waldsolms 80 B2
Waldthurn 82 B3
Waldwisse 79 D3
Walenstadt 105 D1, 106 A1
Walferdange 79 D3
Walkendorf 53 D3
Walkenried 81 D1
Walkersdorf 127 D1
Wall 57 D3, 60 B1
Wall 70 A2
Wallasey 59 C2, 60 B3
Walldorf 90 B1
Walldorf 81 D2
Walldorf (Gross-Gerau) 80 B3
Walldürn 81 C3, 91 C1
Walldürn-Altheim 81 C3, 91 C1
Wallendorf 82 B1
Wallenfels 82 A2
Wallenhorst 67 D2/3
Wallerfangen 89 D1
Wallersdorf 92 B2
Wallerstein 91 D1/2
Wallers-Trélon 78 B3
Wallertheim 80 B3
Wallingford 65 C3
Wallington Hall 57 D3
Wallsbüll 52 B2
Walmer 65 C3, 76 B1
Walsall 59 D3, 64 A1/2
Walsrode 68 B2
Walsrode-Ebbingen 68 B2
Walsrode-Kirchboitzen 68 B2
Walsrode-Westenholz 68 B2
Waltenhofen 91 D3
Waltenhofen-Martinszell 91 D3
Waltershausen 81 D2
Waltham Abbey 65 C3
Walting-Pfünz 92 A1/2
Walton on the Naze 65 C2/3
Waltrop 67 D3, 80 A1
Wambeek 79 B/C2
Wamel 66 B3
Wamin 77 D2
Wanderup 52 B2
Wandlitz 70 A2
Wanfried 81 D1
Wangels 53 C3
Wangenheim 81 D1/2
Wangen im Allgäu-Neuravensburg 91 C3
Wangen im Allgäu 91 C3
Wangerland 67 D1
Wangerland-Hohenkirchen 67 D1
Wangerland-Hooksiel 52 A3, 67 D1
Wangerland-Minsen 52 A3, 67 D1
Wangerooge 67 D1
Wankendorf 52 B3
Wanna 52 A3, 68 A1
Wanroij 66 B3, 79 D1
Wansford 64 B2
Wanssum 79 D1
Wantage 64 A3
Wanzleben 69 C3
Wapenveld 67 C2
Wapnica 71 C1
Warboys 65 C2
Warburg 81 C1
Warburg-Bonenburg 81 C1
Warburg-Ossendorf 81 C1
Warburg-Scherfede 68 A2
Wardenburg 67 D2, 68 A2
Ware 65 C2/3
Waregem 78 A/B2
Wareham 63 D2/3
Waremme 79 C2
Waren 69 D1, 70 A1
Waren 72 A3
Warendorf 67 D3
Warendorf-Freckenhorst 67 D3
Warendorf-Milte 67 D3
Warffum 67 C1
Warfusée-Abancourt 78 A3
Warin 53 D3, 69 C/D1
Wark 57 D3
Warkworth 57 D2
Warmenhuizen 66 A/B2
Warmensteinach 82 A3
Warminster 63 D2, 64 A3
Warmsen-Bohnhorst 68 A2
Warneton 78 A2
Warnice 70 B2
Warnow 53 D3, 69 D1
Warrenpoint 58 A1
Warrington 59 D2, 60 B3
Warsow 69 C1
Warstein 80 B1
Warstein-Allagen 80 B1
Warstein-Belecke 80 B1
Warstein-Suttrop 80 B1
Warszawa 73 C3, 97 C1
Wartberg im Mürztal 94 A3
Wartburg 81 D2
Wartenberg 92 A/B2
Wartenberg-Berglern 92 A/B2
Warth 106 B1
Warthe 70 A1
Wartin 70 B1
Warwick 64 A2
Wasbek 52 B3
Wasen im Emmental 105 C1
Washington 57 D3, 61 C1
Waspik 66 B3
Wasselonne 90 A2
Wassen 105 D1/2
Wassenaar 66 A3
Wasserauen 105 D1, 106 A1
Wasserbillig 79 D3
Wasserburg 92 B2/3
Wasserburg (Bodensee) 91 C3
Wasserburg-Attel 92 B3
Wasserleben 69 C3
Wasserlosen-Schwemmelsbach 81 D3
Wassertrüdingen 91 D1
Wassigny 78 B3
Wassy-sur-Blaise 88 B2
Wasungen 81 D2
Watchet 63 C2
Waterford (Port Lairge) 55 D3
Waterloo 78 B2
Waterville 55 C3
Watervliet 78 B1
Watford 64 B3
Watlington 64 B3
Watten 77 D1
Wattendorf 82 A3
Wattens 107 C1
Watton 65 C2
Wattwil 105 D1, 106 A1
Waulsort 79 C2
Wavignies 77 D3
Wavre 79 B/C2
Waxweiler 79 D3
Wechingen 91 D1/2
Wechingen-Fessenheim 91 D1/2
Wechmar 81 D2
Wechselburg 82 B1/2
Weckersdorf 82 A/B2
Wedde 67 C2
Weddingstedt 52 A/B3
Wedel 68 B1
Wedellsborg 52 B1
Wedemark 68 B2
Wedemark-Bissendorf 68 B2
Wedemark-Elze 68 B2
Weedon 64 B2
Weelde-Statie 79 C1
Weener 67 D1
Weerselo 67 C2/3
Weert 79 C/D1
Weesen 105 D1, 106 A1
Weesp 66 B2/3
Weeze 67 C3, 79 D1
Weferlingen 69 C3
Wegberg 79 D1
Wegberg-Arsbeck 79 D1
Wegeleben 69 C3
Węgliniec 83 D1
Węgorzewo (Angerburg) 73 C2
Węgorzyno 71 C1
Węgrzynice 71 C3
Wegscheid 93 C2
Wegscheid 94 A3
Wehingen 90 B2
Wehr 90 B3
Wehretal 81 D1

Wehrheim 80 B2
Wehr (Mayen) 80 A2
Weichensdorf 70 B3
Weichselboden 94 A3
Weida 82 B2
Weiden 82 B3
Weidenbach (Feuchtwangen) 91 D1
Weidenberg 82 A3
Weiden-Rothenstadt 82 B3
Weidenstetten 91 C/D2
Weidenthal 90 B1
Weikendorf 94 B2
Weikersdorf am Steinfelde 94 A/B3
Weikersheim 81 C/D3, 91 C1
Weil am Rhein 90 A3
Weilburg 80 B2
Weil der Stadt 91 B/C2
Weiler-Simmerberg 91 C3
Weilerswist 79 D2, 80 A2
Weilerswist-Lommersum 79 D2, 80 A2
Weilheim 91 C2
Weilheim in Oberbayern 92 A3
Weilmünster-Laubuseschbach 80 B2
Weilmünster 80 B2
Weilrod-Altweilnau 80 B2
Weilstetten 91 B/C2
Weimar 82 A1/2
Weinböhla 83 C1
Weinfelden 91 C3
Weingarten 90 B1
Weinheim 80 B3, 90 B1
Weinsberg 91 C1
Weischlitz 82 B2
Weisen 69 D2
Weisenbach 90 B2
Weisendorf 81 D3
Weiskirchen 79 D3, 80 A3, 90 A1
Weismain 82 A3
Weissach 91 B/C2
Weissagk 70 B3
Weissandt-Gölzau 69 D3, 82 B1
Weissbach bei Lofer 92 B3
Weissbriach 126 A1/2
Weissenbach am Attersee 93 C3
Weissenbach am Lech 91 D3
Weissenberg 83 D1
Weissenborn-Lüderode 81 D1
Weissenborn 81 D1
Weissenbrunn 82 A2/3
Weissenburg in Bayern 91 D1, 92 A1
Weissenburg-Rothenstein 91 D1, 92 A1
Weissenburg 105 C2
Weissenfels 82 A/B1
Weissenhorn 91 D2
Weissenkirchen in der Wachau 94 A2
Weissensee 81 D1, 82 A1
Weissenstadt 82 A3
Weissenthurm 80 A2
Weissewarthe 69 D2
Weissig 83 C1
Weissig 83 C1
Weisskirchen in Steiermark 127 C1
Weisstannen [Mels] 105 D1, 106 A1
Weisswasser 83 D1
Weitendorf 53 D3
Weitersfeld 94 A2
Weitersfelden 93 D2
Weiterstadt 80 B3
Weitin 70 A1
Weitnau 91 D3
Weitnau-Siebratshofen 91 D3
Weitnau-Wengen 91 D3
Weitra 93 D2
Weitramsdorf-Weidach 81 D2, 82 A2
Weiz 127 C1
Weiz 96 A3
Wejherowo 72 B2
Welbourn 61 D3, 64 B1
Wellaune 82 B1
Welle 68 B1
Wellendingen (Rottweil) 90 B2
Wellerlooij 79 D1
Wellheim 92 A1/2
Wellheim-Biesenhard 92 A2
Wellingborough 64 B2
Wellington 63 C2
Wellington 59 D3, 64 A1
Wells 63 D2
Wells next-the-Sea 65 C1
Wels 93 C2
Wels 96 A2/3
Welschbillig 79 D3
Welschenrohr [Gänsbrunnen] 105 C1
Welshpool 59 C3
Welsleben 69 C/D3
Weltenburg 92 A1/2
Welver 67 D3, 80 B1
Welwyn Garden City 65 B/C3
Welzheim 91 C1/2
Welzow 83 C1
Wem 59 D3, 60 B3
Wembach 90 B3
Wemding 91 D1/2
Wemperhardt 79 D2/3
Wemyss Bay 56 B2
Wemyss Bay 54 A2/3, 55 D1
Wendelsheim (Alzey) 80 B3
Wenden 80 B2
Wendlingen am Neckar 91 C2
Wendover 64 B3
Wenduine 78 A1
Weng bei Admont 93 D3
Wengen 105 C2
Wenigzell 94 A3
Wennigsen 68 B3
Wenningstedt 52 A2
Wennington 59 D1, 60 B2
Wenns 106 B1
Wentorf bei Hamburg 68 B1
Wenzenbach 92 B1
Weobley 63 D1
Wépion 79 C2
Werbach 81 C3
Werben 70 B3
Werben 69 D2
Werbig 70 A3
Werbomont 79 C2
Werdau 82 B2
Werder 70 A2/3
Werdohl 80 B1
Werfen 93 C3
Werl 80 B1
Werlte 67 D2
Wermelskirchen 80 A1
Wermsdorf 82 B1
Wernau 91 C2
Wernberg-Köblitz 82 B3, 92 B1
Werne 67 D3, 80 A/B1
Werneck 81 D3
Werneuchen 70 A/B2
Wernhout 79 C1
Wernigerode 69 C3
Wernshausen 81 D2
Wertach 91 D3
Wertheim 81 C3
Wertheim-Nassig 81 C3
Wertheim-Reichholzheim 81 C3
Werther 68 A3
Wertingen 91 D2
Wesel 67 C3, 79 D1, 80 A1
Weselberg 90 A1
Wesel-Bislich 67 C3
Wesel-Büderich 67 C3, 79 D1, 80 A1
Wesenberg 70 A1
Wesendorf 69 C2
Wesendorf-Wahrenholz 69 C2
Wesenufer 93 C2
Wesepe 67 C2/3
Wesselburen 52 A3
Wesseling 80 A2
Wessem 79 D1
Wessling 92 A2/3
Wessobrunn 91 D3, 92 A3
West-Auckland 57 D3, 61 C1
West Bay 63 D2/3
West Bromwich 59 D3, 64 A2
West Burton 59 D1, 61 B/C2
Westbury 63 D2, 64 A3
West-Calder 57 C2
Westende-Bad 78 A1
Westerbork 67 C2
Westerburg 80 B2
Westerham 65 C3, 76 B1
Westerhausen 69 C3
Westerheim (Münsingen) 91 C2
Westerhever 52 A2/3
Westerholt 67 D1
Westerkappeln 67 D2/3
Westerland 52 A2
Westerstede-Ihausen 67 D1
Westerstede 67 D1
Westerstede-Tarbarg 67 D1
Westerstetten 91 C2
Westerwalsede 68 A/B2
Westerwalsede-Süderwalsede 68 B2
Westfehmarn-Petersdorf 53 C2
Westgate on Sea 65 C3, 76 B1
West Hartlepool 61 D1
Westhausen 91 D1/2
Westheim-Ostheim 91 D1
Westhofen 80 B3
Westkapelle 78 A1
West Kilbride 56 B2
West Linton 57 C2
West-Looe 62 B3
West Lulworth 63 D3
West Mersea 65 C3
Weston-super-Mare 63 C/D2
Westoverledingen 67 D1/2
Westport 55 C2
West Tanfield 61 C2
West Tarbert 56 A2
West-Terschelling 66 B1
West Town 76 A1
West Wycombe 64 B3
Wetherby 61 D2
Wetter 80 B2
Wetteren 78 B1
Wetterzeube 82 B1/2
Wettin 82 A1
Wettingen 90 B3
Wettringen 67 D3
Wetwang 61 D2
Wetzikon 105 D1
Wetzlar 80 B2
Wetzleinsdorf 94 B2
Wevelgem 78 A2
Wewelsfleth 52 B3, 68 B1
Wexford 58 A3
Wexford 55 D3
Weybridge 64 B3, 76 B1
Weyerbusch 80 A2
Weyer Markt 93 D3
Weyer Markt 96 A3
Weyersheim 90 A/B2
Weyhausen (Gifhorn) 69 C2
Weyhe 68 A2
Weyhe-Leeste 68 A2
Weyhill 64 A3, 76 A1
Weymouth 63 D3
Weyregg am Attersee 93 C3
Wezep 67 B/C2
Whalley 59 D1, 60 B2
Whalton 57 D3
Wharram le-Street 61 D2
Wheddon Cross 63 C2
Whipsnade Zoo 64 B2/3
Whitburn 57 B/C2
Whitburn 54 B2/3
Whitby 61 D1
Whitchurch 59 D2/3, 60 B3
Whitchurch 65 C3, 76 B1
Whitebeck 54 B3
Whitehall 54 B1
Whitehaven 54 B3
Whitehaven 57 C3, 60 A1
Whitehead 56 A3
Whitehouse 56 A2
Whithorn 56 B3, 60 A1
Whiting Bay 56 A2
Whitley Bay 57 D3, 61 C1
Whitstable 65 C/D3, 77 C1
Whitstone 62 B2/3
Whittingham 57 D2
Whittington 59 C/D3, 60 B3
Whittlesey 65 C2
Wichmannshausen 81 C/D1
Wichów 71 C3
Wick 54 B1
Wickede 80 B1
Wickford 65 C3
Wickham 76 B1
Wickham Market 65 C2
Wicklow 58 A2
Wicklow 55 D3
Wickwar 63 D1, 64 A3
Widecombe-in-the-Moor 63 C3
Widnes 59 D2, 60 B3
Widuchowa (Fiddichow) 70 B2
Wiechowo 71 C1
Wiedenbrück 68 A3
Wiefelstede 67 D1, 68 A1
Wiehe 82 A1
Wiehl 80 A2
Wieleń 71 C/D2
Wielenbach 92 A3
Wieleń Polny 71 C/D2
Wielichowo 71 D3
Wieluń 96 B1
Wien 96 B2/3
Wien 94 B2
Wiener Neustadt 94 B3
Wiener Neustadt 96 A/B3
Wienhausen 68 B2
Wiepke 69 C2
Wierden 67 C2/3
Wieren 69 C2
Wiernsheim 90 B1/2
Wierzbięcin 71 C1
Wierzbno 71 B/C1
Wierzchowo 71 D1
Wies 127 C1/2
Wiesau-Schönhaid 82 B3
Wiesbaden 80 B3
Wiesbaden-Naurod 80 B3
Wieselburg 93 D2
Wiesen 81 C3
Wiesenburg 69 D3
Wiesenfelden-Hötzelsdorf 92 B1
Wiesenfelden 92 B1
Wiesensteig 91 C2
Wiesenthal 81 D2
Wiesenttal-Streitberg 82 A3
Wieslautern 90 A/B1
Wiesloch 90 B1
Wiesmath 94 B3
Wiesmoor 67 D1
Wietmarschen 67 C/D2
Wietmarschen-Lohne 67 C/D2
Wietze 68 B2
Wietze-Jeversen 68 B2
Wietzen 68 A2
Wietzendorf 68 B2
Wiewierz 71 D3
Wigan 59 D2, 60 B2/3
Wiggen 105 C1
Wiggensbach 91 D3
Wigton 57 C3, 60 B1
Wigtown 56 B3, 60 A1
Wijchen 66 B3
Wijhe 67 C2
Wil 91 C3
Wilburgstetten 91 D1
Wilczkowice 69 D3
Wildalpen 93 D3
Wildbad-Calmbach 90 B2
Wildbad im Schwarzwald 90 B2
Wildberg 90 B2
Wildberg 70 A1
Wildberg 69 D2, 70 A2
Wildeck 81 C1/2
Wildeck-Hönebach 81 C/D2
Wildeck-Richelsdorf 81 D1/2
Wildenberg 92 A/B2
Wildenbruch 70 A3
Wildendürnbach 94 B2
Wildenhain 83 C1
Wildenthal 82 B2
Wildervank 67 C2
Wildeshausen-Kleinenkneten 68 A2
Wildeshausen 68 A2
Wildetaube 82 B2
Wildflecken-Neuwildflecken 81 C/D2
Wildflecken-Oberbach 81 C2
Wildon 127 C1
Wildpoldsried 91 D3
Wilfersdorf 94 B2
Wilhamstead 64 B2
Wilhelm-Pieck-Stadt Guben 70 B3
Wilhelm-Pieck-Stadt Guben 72 A3, 96 A1
Wilhelmsburg 96 A3
Wilhelmsburg 94 A2
Wilhelmsdorf 91 C3
Wilhelmshaven 67 D1, 68 A1
Wilhelmshaven-Sengwarden 52 A3, 67 D1
Wilhelmsthal 82 A2
Wilhermsdorf 81 D3, 91 D1
Wilkau-Hasslau 82 B2
Wilkowo Polskie 71 D3
Willebadessen 68 A3, 81 C1
Willebadessen-Peckelsheim 81 C1
Willebroek 78 B1
Willemstad 66 A3
Willenhall 59 D3, 64 A2
Willgottheim 90 A2
Willingen 80 B1
Willingen-Usseln 80 B1
Willingshausen 81 C2
Willisau 105 C1
Williton 63 C2
Willofs (Lauterbach) 81 C2
Willstätt 90 B2
Wilmslow 59 D2, 60 B3, 64 A1
Wilnsdorf 80 B2
Wilnsdorf-Rudersdorf 80 B2
Wilsickow 70 B1
Wilstedt 68 A1/2
Wilster 52 B3
Wilsum 67 C2
Wilthen 83 D1
Wiltingen 79 D3
Wilton 63 D2, 64 A3, 76 A1
Wilton House 63 D2, 64 A3, 76 A1
Wiltz 79 D3
Wimbledon 65 B/C3
Wimborne Minster 63 D2
Wimereux 77 D1
Wimmenau 90 A1
Wimpassing an der Leitha 94 B3
Wincanton 63 D2
Winchcombe 63 D1, 64 A2
Winchelsea 77 C1
Wincheringen 79 D3
Winchester 76 B1
Windach 91 D2/3, 92 A2/3
Windeck-Herchen 80 A2
Windeck-Rosbach 80 A/B2
Windermere 59 C/D1, 60 B1/2
Windermere 54 B3
Windesheim 80 B3
Windischeschenbach 82 B3
Windischgarsten 93 D3
Windischgarsten 96 A3
Windorf 93 C2
Windorf 93 C2
Windsbach 91 D1
Windsor 64 B3
Wingham 65 C3, 76 B1
Wingst 52 A/B3, 68 A1
Winhöring 92 B2
Winkel 89 D3, 90 A3
Winklarn 92 B1
Winklern 107 D1, 126 A1
Winnenden 91 C1/2
Winschoten 67 C1/2
Winsen 68 B2
Winsen (Luhe) 68 B1

Winsen-Meissendorf 68 B2
Winsen-Pattensen 68 B1
Winsford 59 D2, 60 B3, 64 A1
Winslow 64 B2
Winster 61 C3, 64 A1
Winsum 66 B1/2
Winsum 67 C1
Winterberg 80 B1
Winterberg-Altastenberg 80 B1
Winterberg-Niedersfeld 80 B1
Winterberg-Siedlinghausen 80 B1
Winterfeld 69 C2
Winterswijk 67 C3
Winterthur 90 B3
Winterton 61 D2
Wintrich 80 A3
Wintzenheim 89 D2, 90 A2/3
Wipperdorf 81 D1
Wipperfürth 80 A1
Wipperfürth-Klüppelberg 80 A1
Wippingen 67 D2
Wippra 82 A1
Wirdum 67 C/D1
Wirges 80 B2
Wirksworth 61 C3, 64 A1
Wirsberg 82 A3
Wisbech 65 C1/2
Wischhafen 52 B3, 68 B1
Wismar 53 C3
Wissant 77 D1
Wissembourg 90 B1
Wissen 80 B2
Wistedt 68 B1
Witankowo 71 D1
Witham 65 C2/3
Witheridge 63 C2
Withern 61 D3, 65 C1
Withernsea 61 D2
Witney 64 A3
Witnica 70 B2
Witnica 71 B/C2
Witry-lès-Reims 88 A/B1
Wittdün 52 A2
Wittelshofen 91 D1
Witten 80 A1
Wittenberge 69 D2
Wittenburg 69 C1
Witterda 81 D1/2, 82 A1
Wittibreut 93 B/C2
Wittichenau 83 C/D1
Wittighausen-Unterwittighausen 81 C3
Wittingen 69 C2
Wittingen-Knesebeck 69 C2
Wittingen-Ohrdorf 69 C2
Wittislingen 91 D2
Wittlich 80 A3
Wittmund 67 D1
Wittmund-Ardorf 67 D1
Wittmund-Burhafe 67 D1
Wittmund-Carolinensiel 67 D1
Wittmund-Harlesiel 67 D1
Wittorf 68 B2
Wittstock 69 D1/2
Wittstock 72 A3
Witzenhausen 81 C1
Witzin 53 D3, 69 D1
Witzke 69 D2
Wiveliscombe 63 C2
Wivenhoe 65 C/D2/3
Wizernes 77 D1
Włocławek 73 C3
Włodawa 97 D1, 98 A2
Włoszakowice 71 D3
Włoszczowa 97 C1
Wöbbelin 69 C1
Woburn 64 B2
Woerden 66 B3
Woerth-sur-Sauer 90 A/B1
Wohlen 90 B3, 105 C1
Wohratal-Wohra 81 C2
Wöhrden 52 A/B3
Wojtaszyce 71 C1
Woking 64 B3, 76 B1
Wokingham 64 B3
Woldegk 70 A1
Wolfach 90 B2
Wolfegg 91 C3
Wolfen 69 D3, 82 B1
Wolfenbüttel 69 C3
Wölfersheim-Berstadt 81 C2
Wölfersheim 81 B/C2
Woifhagen 81 C1
Wolfhagen-Istha 81 C1
Wolframs-Eschenbach 91 D1
Wolfrathshausen 92 A3
Wolfsberg 127 C1
Wolfsberg 96 A3
Wolfsburg 69 C2/3
Wolfsburg-Hehlingen 69 C2/3
Wolfsfeld 79 D3
Wolfshagen 70 A1
Wolfstein 80 A3
Wolgast 72 A2
Wolhusen 105 C1
Wolin 70 B1
Wolkenstein 83 B/C2
Wolkersdorf 94 B2
Wölkisch 83 C1
Wolkramshausen 81 D1
Wollaston 64 B2
Wollin 69 D3
Wöllstadt 81 B/C2
Wöllstein 80 B3
Wolmirstedt 69 C/D3
Wolnzach 92 A2
Wolnzach-Geroldshausen 92 A2
Wołowe Lasy 71 D2
Wolpertshausen 91 C1
Wolpertswende 91 C3
Wolsfeld 79 D3
Wolsingham 57 D3, 61 C1
Wolsztyn 71 C/D3
Wolsztyn 72 B3, 96 B1
Woltersdorf 70 A/B2
Woltersdorf 69 C2
Wolvega 67 B/C2
Wolverhampton 59 D3, 64 A1/2
Wolvertem 78 B1/2
Wolverton 64 B2
Wolviston 61 D1
Wombwell 61 D2/3
Wommels 66 B1/2
Woodbridge 65 C2
Woodenbridge 58 A3
Woodhall Spa 61 D3, 65 B/C1
Woodstock 65 C2/3
Woofferton 59 D3
Wooler 57 D2
Woore 59 D2, 60 B3, 64 A1
Wootton Bassett 63 D1, 64 A3
Wootz 69 C2
Worb 105 C1
Worbis 81 D1
Worcester 59 D3, 63 D1, 64 A2
Wörgl 92 B3
Workington 57 C3, 60 A1
Worksop 61 D3, 65 C1
Workum 66 B2
Wörlitz 69 D3
Wormhoudt 77 D1, 78 A1/2
Worms 80 B3
Worms-Pfeddersheim 80 B3
Worpswede 68 A1/2
Wörrstadt 80 B3
Wörschach 93 C/D3
Wört 91 D1
Wörth 81 C3
Wörth 92 B1
Wörth 107 D1, 126 A1
Wörth am Rhein 90 B1
Wörth-Büchelberg 90 B1
Worthing 76 B1
Wotton under Edge 63 D1, 64 A3
Woudenberg 66 B3
Wragby 61 D3, 64 B1
Wredenhagen 69 D1
Wremen 52 A3, 68 A1
Wrentham 65 D2
Wrestedt 69 C2
Wrexham 59 C/D2, 60 B3
Wriedel-Lintzel 68 B2
Wriezen 70 B2
Wróblewo 71 D2
Wrocław (Breslau) 96 B1
Wrohm 52 B3
Wroniawy 71 C/D3
Wronki 71 D2
Wronki 72 B3
Wroughton 64 A3
Wroxham 65 C1
Września 72 B3, 96 B1
Wschowa 71 D3
Wulfen 69 D3
Wulfersdorf 69 D1
Wülfershausen 81 D2
Wülfrath 80 A1
Wulften 68 B3, 81 D1
Wullersdorf 94 A/B2
Wünnenberg 80 B1
Wünnenberg-Haaren 80 B1
Wünnenberg-Fürstenberg 81 B/C1
Wünschendorf 82 B2
Wünsdorf 70 A3
Wunsiedel 82 B3
Wunstorf 68 B2
Wunstorf-Steinhude 68 B2
Wuppertal 80 A1
Würenlingen 90 B3
Wurmannsquick 92 B2
Würselen 79 D2
Wurzbach 82 A2
Würzburg 81 C/D3
Wurzen 82 B1
Wust 69 D2
Wüstenrot-Neuhütten 91 C1
Wusterhausen 69 D2
Wustermark 70 A2
Wüstermarke 70 A3
Wusterwitz 69 D2/3
Wustrau 70 A2
Wustrow 70 A1
Wustrow 69 C2
Wuustwezel 79 C1
Wybelsum 67 C1
Wyhl 90 A2
Wyk auf Föhr 52 A2
Wymondham 65 D2
Wymondham 64 B1
Wyrzysk 71 D1/2
Wysoka 71 D1/2
Wysoka 71 C3
Wyszków 73 C3, 98 A1
Wyszogród 73 C3
Wyszyna 97 C1

X

Xanten 67 C3, 79 D1
Xanten-Marienbaum 67 C3
Xánthi 145 C1
Xánthi 149 C1
Xermade 150 B1
Xermaménil 89 D2
Xerta 163 C2
Xertigny 89 D2
Xesteda 150 A1
Xeve 150 A2
Xidéika 147 C3
Xilaganí 145 C1
Xilókastron 147 C2
Xilókastron 148 B2
Xinón Nerón 143 C2
Xinzo de Limia 150 B3
Xironda 150 B3
Xove 150 B1
Xunqueira de Ambía 150 B3
Xunqueira de Espadañedo 150 B2

Y

Yablŭnka 95 C1
Yanci 108 A3, 154 A1
Yanguas 153 D3
Yarmouth 76 A1/2
Yatağan 149 D2
Yate 63 D1/2, 64 A3
Yátova 169 C1
Ybbs an der Donau 93 D2
Ybbsitz 93 D3
Ychoux 108 A2
Ydrefors 46 B3
Yebes 161 C2
Yebra 161 C2/3
Yebra de Basa 154 B2
Yecla 169 C2
Yecla de Yeltes 159 C2
Yélamos de Arriba 161 C2
Yelo 161 D1
Yelverton 63 C3
Yémeda 162 A3, 168 B1
Yeniköy 149 D1
Yenne 104 A3
Yeovil 63 D2
Yepes 161 B/C3, 167 C/D1
Yerville 77 C3
Yesa 155 C2
Yeste 168 B3
Yetminster 63 D2
Ygos-Saint-Saturnin 108 B2
Ygrande 102 B2
Ykspihlaja 20 B1
Ylä-Kintaus 21 D3, 22 A3
Ylä-Kolkki 21 C3
Yläköngäs 6 B2
Ylä-Kuolna 5 D3, 6 A3, 11 D1
Ylä Kuona 23 C3
Ylä-Luosta 23 C2
Ylämaa 27 C2
Ylämylly 23 C3
Yläne 24 B2
Ylä-Uura 19 C3
Ylä-Valtimo 23 C1
Ylihärmä 20 B2
Yli-Ii 18 B2
Ylijärvi 27 C2
Yli-Kärppä 18 B1
Ylikiiminki 18 B2
Yli-Körkkö 12 B3
Ylikulma 25 B/C3
Yli-Kurki 19 C2
Ylikylä 23 C1
Ylikylä 20 A3
Ylikylä 20 B2
Ylikylä 21 C2
Ylikylä 20 B3
Yli-Lesti 21 C1/2
Yli-Livo 19 B/C1/2
Ylimarkku 20 A3
Yli-Muonio 11 C3
Yli-Nampa 12 B3
Ylinenoja 18 A3
Yli-Olhava 18 A/B2
Ylipää 18 B3
Ylipää 21 C2
Ylipää 18 B3
Ylipää 18 A2/3
Ylipää 21 D1, 22 A1
Ylipää 18 A3
Yli-Paakkola 17 D2, 18 A1
Ylisevä 20 B3
Yli-Siurua 18 B1/2
Ylistaro 20 B2
Ylistaron 20 B2
Yli-Tannila 18 B2
Ylitornio (Övertorneå) 17 D2
Yli-Utos 18 B2/3
Ylivesi 27 C1
Ylivieska 18 A3, 21 C1
Yli-Viirre 21 C1
Yli-Vuotto 18 B2
Ylläsjärvi 11 C/D3, 12 A2
Yllivalli 20 B3
Ylöjärvi 25 C1
Ylträ 21 C3
Ylvingen 14 A3
Ymonville 87 C2
Yngsjö 50 B3
Ynnesdal 36 A2/3
Yonne 104 B2
York 61 C2
York 54 B3
Yoxford 65 D2
Ypäjä 24 B2
Ypäjän asema 24 B2
Yport 77 C3
Yppäri 18 A3
Ypyä 21 C1
Ypykkävaara 19 D3
Yrbovski 133 D1, 134 A1
Yrittaperä 19 C2
Yrkje 42 A2
Yrouerre 88 A3
Yrttivaara 17 C1
Yset 33 C2/3
Ysgubor-y-coed 59 C3
Ysjö 30 A2, 35 C1
Yssingeaux 103 C3, 111 C1
Ystad 50 B3
Ystad 72 A2
Ystebrød 42 A3
Ysterbø 36 A2
Ystrad-Rhondda 63 C1
Ytre Arna 36 A3
Ytre Årnes 9 D1
Ytre Billefjord 5 D2, 6 A1/2
Ytre Brenna 5 D1, 6 B1
Ytre Enebakk 38 A3, 44 B1
Ytre Flåbygd 43 C2
Ytre Fræna 32 A2
Ytre Kårvik 4 A2
Ytre Kjæs 5 D1, 6 B1
Ytre Korsnes 6 B1
Ytre Laksvatn 4 A3, 10 A1
Ytre Mannskarvik 5 D1, 6 A/B1
Ytre Oppedal 36 A2
Ytre Snillfjord 33 B/C1/2
Ytre Veines 5 D2, 6 A1
Ytterån 29 D3, 34 B2
Ytterberg 34 B3
Ytter Bodane 45 C2
Ytterby 47 D1
Ytterby (Kungälv) 45 C3
Ytterbyn 17 C2/3
Ytteresse 20 B1
Ytterfors 30 B1
Ytterhogdal 34 B3
Ytterjeppo 20 B2
Yttermalung 39 C2
Yttermark 20 A3
Ytterocke 29 C3, 34 B2
Ytterøy 28 B3, 33 D1
Yttersjö 31 C2
Ytterstmark 31 C/D2
Yttertällmo 30 B2, 35 D1
Yttertällmo 30 B2, 35 D1
Ytterturingen 34 B3
Yttervik 15 C3
Yttilä 24 B2
Yuncos 160 B3
Yunquera 172 A2
Yunquera de Henares 161 C2
Yverdon-les-Bains 104 B1
Yvetot 77 C3
Yvoire 104 A/B2
Yvonand 104 B1
Yvré-l'Évêque 86 B2
Yxnerum 46 B2
Yxsjö 30 B2
Yxskaftkälen 29 D3, 35 C1
Yyteri 24 A1
Yzeron 103 C/D3

Z

Zaanstad 66 A/B2
Zaatzke 69 D1/2
Žabalj 129 D3, 134 A1
Žabalj 140 A2
Žabari 134 B2
Žabin 71 C1
Ząbkowice Śląskie 96 B1
Zablaće 131 C3
Záblatí 93 C1
Zableće 131 D2, 132 A2
Žabljak 137 D2
Žabljak 133 C3, 137 D1
Žabno 71 D3
Žabno 127 D2
Zabok 127 D2
Zabór 71 C3
Zaborowice 71 D3
Žabowo 71 C1
Zabrežje 133 D1, 134 A1/2
Zabrze (Hindenburg) 96 B2
Zacháro 146 B3
Zacharzyn 71 D2
Zachow 69 D2, 70 A2
Zadar 130 B2
Zadvarje 131 D3, 132 A3
Zafarraya 172 B2
Zafferana Étnea 125 D2

Zafra 165 D3
Żaga 126 A2
Żagań (Sagan) 83 D1
Żagań (Sagan) 96 A1
Zagarise 122 B2
Zagarolo 118 B2
Zagorá 144 A3
Zagorá 148 B1
Zagorje 127 C2
Zagra 172 B2
Zagreb 127 D3
Zagrilla 172 B1
Žagubica 135 C2
Žagubica 140 A2
Zagvozd 131 D3, 132 A3
Zahara 172 A2
Zahara de los Atunes 171 D3
Zahinos 165 C3
Zahna 69 D3, 70 A3
Záhoří 93 D1
Záhorská Ves 94 B2
Zahrádka 83 D3
Zahrádka 83 C3
Zaidín 155 C3, 163 C1
Zajača 133 C2
Zajas 138 B3
Zajcevo 75 D2/3
Zaječar 140 A/B2
Zaječar 135 C2/3
Zaječov 83 C3
Zajezda 127 D2
Zajezierze 71 C1
Zákamenné 95 D1
Zákas 143 C2
Zákinthos 146 A2/3
Zákinthos 148 A2
Zakopane 97 C2
Zákros 149 C3
Zakrzewo 71 D1
Zákupy 83 D2
Zalaapáti 128 A1/2
Zalabaksa 127 D1/2
Zalabér 128 A1
Zalaegerszeg 128 A1
Zalaegerszeg 96 B3
Zalahaláp 128 A1
Zalakaros 128 A2
Zalakomár 128 A2
Zalalövő 127 D1
Zalamea de la Serena 166 A2
Zalamea la Real 171 C1
Zalaszabar 128 A2
Zalaszántó 128 A1
Zalaszentbalázs 128 A2
Zalaszentgrót 128 A1
Zalaszentiván 128 A1
Zalaszentmihály 128 A1/2
Zaláta 128 B3
Zalatárnok 128 A2
Zalău 97 D3, 140 B1
Zalavár 128 A2
Zalduendo 153 C2
Zalduondo 153 D2
Žalec 127 C2
Zaleščiki 98 B3
Zalese 75 D1
Zalla 153 C1
Zall Reç 138 A2
Zaltbommel 66 B3
Zalužnica 130 B1
Zamárdi 128 B1
Zamarra 159 C2
Zambra 172 B1/2
Zambrana 153 C2
Zambrów 73 D3, 98 A1
Zambujeira do Mar 170 A1
Zamęcin 71 C2
Zámoly 95 D3, 128 B1
Zamora 159 D1
Zamość 97 D1, 98 A2
Žandov 83 D2
Zandvoort 66 A2
Zanglivérion 144 A2
Zaniemyśl 71 D3
Zánka 128 B1
Zaorejas 161 D2
Zaostrog 132 A3, 136 B1
Zapfendorf 82 A/B3
Záppion 143 D3
Zapponeta 120 B1
Zaprešić 127 D3
Zaragoza 154 B3, 162 B1
Zarasai 74 A2/3
Zaratán 152 A/B3, 160 A1
Zarautz 153 D1
Zarcilla de Ramos 168 B3, 174 A1
Żarki Wielki 83 D1
Zárkos 143 C/D3
Žarkovskij 75 C2/3
Zărnești 141 C2
Žarnovica 95 D2
Żarnowo 70 B1
Zaroúchla 146 B2
Zarratón 153 C2
Zarrentin 69 C1
Żary (Sorau) 71 C3, 83 D1
Żary (Sorau) 96 A1
Zarza Capilla 166 B2
Zarza de Alange 165 D2, 166 A2
Zarza de Montánchez 165 D1/2, 166 A1/2
Zarza de Tajo 161 C3
Zarzadilla de Totana 168 B3, 174 A1
Zarza la Mayor 159 C3, 165 C/D1
Zarzuela 161 D3
Zarzuela del Monte 160 B2
Zarzuela del Pinar 160 B1
Zás 150 A1
Zasavica 133 C1
Zasieki 70 B3
Žaškov 99 C3
Zásmuky 83 D3
Zastavna 98 B3
Žatec 96 A1/2
Žatec 83 C2
Zatom 71 C2
Zaton 130 B2
Zaton 136 B1
Zaton 131 C3
Zatonie 71 C3
Zátouna 146 B3
Zavala 137 B/C1
Zavala 136 A1
Zavalje 131 C1
Zavattarello 113 D1
Zavidov 83 C3
Zavidovići 132 B2
Zavlaka 133 C2
Zavrč 127 D2
Zawada 71 C3
Zawidów 83 D1
Zawiercie 97 C1/2
Žažina 127 D3
Zázrivá 95 D1
Zbaraž 98 B2/3
Zbarzewo 71 D3
Zbąszyń 71 C3
Zbehy 95 C2
Zbiroh 83 C3
Zborov 97 D2, 98 B2/3
Zbraslav 83 D3
Zbraslavice 83 D3
Ždala 128 A2
Ždánice 94 B1
Žďár 83 C3
Žďár 83 C2
Žďárec 94 B1
Žďár nad Sázavou 96 A/B2
Zdenac 127 C3, 130 B1
Zdenčina 127 D3
Zdiby 83 D2/3
Zdice 83 C3
Zdounky 95 C1
Ždrelac 130 B2
Ždrelo 134 B2
Zdunje 138 B2/3
Zeanuri 153 C/D1
Žebrák 83 C3
Zechin 70 B2
Zechlinerhütte 70 A1/2
Zeddam 67 C3
Zeddiani 123 C2
Žednik 129 C2/3
Zeebrugge 78 A1
Zeeland 66 B3
Zegama 153 D2
Žegar 131 C2
Žegra 138 B2
Žegulja 137 C1
Zehdenick 70 A2
Zehlendorf 70 A2
Zehren 83 C1
Zeil am Main 81 D3
Zeilfeld 81 D2
Zeist 66 B3
Zeitlarn 92 B1
Zeitz 82 B1
Zele 78 B1
Zelenika 137 C2
Zelenograd 75 D2
Zelenogradsk (Cranz) 73 C2
Želetava 94 A1
Železná Ruda 93 C1
Železnica 139 D1/2
Železnik 133 D1, 134 A1/2
Železniki 126 B2
Železnodorožnyj (Gerdauen) 73 C2
Železný Brod 83 D2
Zelhem 67 C3
Želiezovce 95 D2/3
Želin 126 B2
Zelina 127 D2
Zélion 147 C1
Želiv 83 D3, 94 A1
Željuša 132 B3
Zell 80 A3
Zella-Mehlis 81 D2
Zell am Harmersbach 90 B2
Zell am Moos 93 C3
Zell am See 107 D1, 126 A1
Zell am Ziller 107 C1
Zell im Wiesental 90 A/B3
Zellingen 81 C3
Želnava 93 C2
Zeltingen-Rachtig 80 A3
Zeltweg 127 C1
Zelzate 78 B1
Zemblaku 142 B2
Zeme 105 D3, 113 C1
Zemen 139 D2
Zemendorf 94 B3
Zemné 95 C3
Zemun 133 D1, 134 A1
Zemun 140 A2
Zenica 132 B2
Zennor 62 A3
Zenting 93 C2
Žepče 132 B2
Zepernick 70 A2
Zerbst 69 D3
Zerf 79 D3, 80 A3
Zeri 114 A2
Zermatt 105 C2
Zernez 106 B1/2
Zero Branco 107 D3
Zerpenschleuse 70 A2
Zerqan 138 A3
Zervaskë 142 B1
Zestoa 153 D1
Zetel 67 D1
Zetel-Neuenburg 67 D1
Zeulenroda 82 A/B2
Zeuthen 70 A2/3
Zeven 68 A/B1
Zevenaar 67 C3
Zevenbergen 66 A3, 79 C1
Zevenbergschen Hoek 66 A3
Zévio 107 C3
Zgierz 73 C3, 97 C1
Zgornja Kungota 127 C2
Zgornji Duplek 127 C/D2
Zgorzelec 83 D1
Zgorzelec 96 A1
Zgurovka 99 D2
Zgurovo 139 D2
Žiar nad Hronom 95 D2
Zibello 114 A1
Zibreira 159 C3, 165 C1
Žiča 133 D3, 134 A/B3
Zicavo 113 D3
Zidani Most 127 C2
Židlochovice 94 B1
Ziegendorf 69 D1
Ziegenrück 82 A2
Zieleniewo 71 C2
Zielona Góra (Grünberg) 71 C3
Zielona Góra (Grünberg) 72 A/B3, 96 A1
Ziemendorf 69 C2
Ziemetshausen 91 D2
Zierau 69 C2
Zierikzee 66 A3, 78 B1
Ziersdorf 94 A2
Zierzow 69 C/D1
Ziesar 69 D3
Žihle 83 C3
Žilina 95 D1
Žilina 96 B2
Zilly 69 C3
Zilotí 145 C1
Ziltendorf 70 B3
Zilupe 74 B2
Zimnicea 141 C2
Zinal 105 C2
Zinkgruvan 46 A2
Ziortza 153 D1
Zirc 128 B1
Zirchow 70 B1
Žiri 126 B2
Zirl 107 C1
Zirndorf 81 D3, 82 A3, 91 D1, 92 A1
Žirovnica 126 B2
Žirovnice 93 D1, 94 A1
Zislow 69 D1
Zistersdorf 94 B2
Zistersdorf 96 B2
Zisterzienserstift 127 C1
Žitište 129 D3
Žitkovac 135 C3
Žitkoviči 99 C1
Žitni Potok 139 B/C1
Žitomir 99 C2
Žitorađa 135 C3, 139 C1
Zítsa 142 B3
Zittau 83 D2
Zittau 96 A1
Živinice 132 B2
Živogošće 131 D3, 132 A3, 136 B1
Žizdra 75 D3
Zizenhausen-Mahlspüren 91 C3
Zlatá Koruna 93 D1/2
Zlatar 127 D2
Zlatar Bistrica 127 D2
Zlatarevo 139 D3, 143 D1, 144 A1
Zlaté Moravce 95 D2
Zlatica 140 B3
Zlatná na Ostrove 95 C3
Zlatna Panega 140 B3
Zlatograd 145 C1
Zlatokop 139 C2
Zlatorog 126 B2
Zletovo 139 C2
Zliechov 95 D1
Žlne 135 C3
Žlobin 99 C1
Złocieniec 72 B3
Złocieniec 71 C1
Zlokućane 138 A1
Zlonice 83 C2
Zlot 135 C2
Złotów 71 D1
Žlutice 83 C3
Zmajevac 129 C3
Zmajevo 129 C3
Žman 130 B2
Žminj 130 A1
Znamenka 99 D3
Żnin 72 B3
Znojmo 96 A/B2
Znojmo 94 A1/2
Zoagli 113 D2
Zöbern 94 A/B3
Zöblitz 83 C2
Zocca 114 B2, 116 A/B1
Žodino 74 B3
Zoetermeer 66 A3
Zofingen 105 C1
Zogno 106 A3
Zohor 94 B2
Zola Predosa 114 B1/2
Zölkow 69 D1
Zollikofen 105 C1
Zolling 92 A2
Zoločev 97 D2, 98 B2/3
Zoloutoša 99 D2/3
Żółwino 71 C1
Zóni 145 D3
Zonza 113 D3
Zörbig 69 D3, 82 B1
Zorita 166 A1/2
Zorita de la Frontera 160 A2
Zorita del Maestrazgo 162 B2
Zorneding 92 A2/3
Zornotza 153 D1
Zossen 70 A3
Zotes del Páramo 151 D2/3
Zoutkamp 67 C1
Zrenjanin 129 D3, 134 A1
Zrenjanin 140 A2
Zrin 127 D3, 131 C1
Zrínyivár 128 B2
Zrmanja Vrelo 131 C2
Zrnovci 139 C2
Zruč nad Sázavou 83 D3
Zrze 138 A/B2
Zsámbék 95 D3
Zschopau 83 B/C2
Zschorlau 82 B2
Zschornewitz 69 D3
Zschortau 82 B1
Zubia 173 C2
Zubieta 154 A1
Zubiri 108 A3, 154 A1/2
Zubki Białostockie 73 D3, 98 A1
Žuč 134 B3, 138 B1
Zucaina 162 B3
Zudaire 153 D2
Zuera 154 B3
Zufre 165 D3, 171 C/D1
Zug 105 C/D1
Zugarramurdi 108 A3, 154 A1
Zuheros 172 B1
Zuidhorn 67 C1
Zuidlaren 67 C1/2
Zuidwolde 67 C2
Zújar 173 D1
Żukowice 71 C3
Žuljana 136 B1
Zülpich 79 D2, 80 A2
Zumaia 153 D1
Zumarraga 153 D1
Žumerinka 99 C3
Zundert 79 C1
Zungri 122 A2
Zúñiga 153 D2
Zuoz 106 A/B2
Županja 133 B/C1
Zupčići 133 C3
Žur 138 A/B2
Zurgena 174 A1/2
Zürich 90 B3, 105 D1
Zurich 66 B1/2
Zurow 53 D3, 69 C1
Zürs 106 B1
Zurzach 90 B3
Zusmarshausen 91 D2
Zusmarshausen-Horgau 91 D2
Züsow 53 D3
Žuta Lokva 130 B1
Zutphen 67 C3
Žužemberk 127 C3
Zvečan 138 B1
Zvíkov 93 D1
Zvikovec 83 C3
Zvikovské Podhradí 93 D1
Žvirče 127 C3
Zvole 94 B1
Zvolen 95 D2
Zvolen 97 B/C2
Zvolenská Slatina 95 D2
Zvonce 139 C/D1
Zvornik 133 C2
Zwardoń 95 D1
Zwardoń 96 B2
Zwartenbroek 78 B2
Zwartsluis 67 C2
Zweedorf 53 D3
Zweibrücken 89 D1, 90 A1
Zweibrücken-Mörsbach 89 D1, 90 A1
Zweilütschinen 105 C2
Zweisimmen 104 B2
Zwenkau 82 B1
Zwesten 81 C1/2
Zwettl an der Rodl 93 D2
Zwettl / Niederösterreich 93 D2, 94 A2
Zwettl / Niederösterreich 96 A2
Zwevezele 78 A1
Zwickau 82 B2
Zwiefalten 91 C2
Zwiesel 93 C1
Zwingen 90 A3
Zwingendorf 94 B2
Zwochau 82 B1
Zwoleń 97 C1, 98 A2
Zwolle 67 C2
Zwönitz 82 B2
Żyrardów 73 C3, 97 C1
Żytowań 70 B3